The British
BOXING
Board of Control
YEARBOOK
1997

Edited and compiled by
Barry J. Hugman

Queen Anne Press

First published in 1996

© Barry J. Hugman

Barry J. Hugman has asserted his right under
the Copyright, Designs and Patent Act, 1988
to be identified as the author of this work

First published in Great Britain in 1996 by
Queen Anne Press
a division of Lennard Associates
Mackerye End, Harpenden
Hertfordshire, AL5 5DR

A CIP catalogue record for this book
is available from the British Library

ISBN 1 85291 576 5

Typeset and designed by Typecast (Artwork and Design)
West Country Marketing, 8 Mudford Road
Yeovil, Somerset, BA21 4AA

Printed and bound in Great Britain by
Butler & Tanner, London and Frome

Front cover: Steve Collins and Neville Brown (Stephen Munday/Allsport)
Back cover (top): Naseem Hamed and Said Lawal (Clive Mason/Allsport)
Back cover (bottom): Joe Calzaghe (Mark Thompson/Allsport)

Contents

TARA PROMOTIONS & MANAGEMENT

headquarters:
TARA SPORTS & LEISURE CENTRE,
Grains Road, Shaw, Oldham, Lancs.
Tel: (01706) 841460   Fax: (01706) 882810
STAGING REGULAR SHOWS THROUGHOUT THE NORTH-WEST

Our gymnasium includes:-
2 Rings, Spacious Weights Room, Showers, Sauna and Sunbeds

Other facilities include:-
Toning Salon, Badminton Courts, Snooker Hall, 3 Bars, Restaurant, Function Rooms, Cabaret Lounge and Large Enclosed Car Park

BOXERS

Ady Lewis (Bury) Flyweight
Marcus Duncan (Morecambe) Bantamweight
Charles Shepherd (Carlisle) Super-Featherweight
Dave Clavering (Bury) Super-Featherweight
Gary Hibbert (Oldham) Super-Featherweight
Wayne Rigby (Manchester) Lightweight
Scott Walker (Oldham) Light-Welterweight
Bobbie Vanzie (Bradford) Light-Welterweight
Wayne Shepherd (Carlisle) Welterweight
Jeff Finlayson (Manchester) Light-Middleweight
Mike Whittaker (Rochdale) Light-Middleweight
Derek Wormald (Rochdale) Middleweight
Lee Blundell (Wigan) Middleweight
Darren Swords (Manchester) Middleweight
Warren Stowe (Burnley) Middleweight
Johnny Whiteside (Preston) Middleweight
Glenn Campbell (Bury) Super-Middleweight
Craig Joseph (Bradford) Super-Middleweight

Manager/Coach: Jack Doughty
Trainers: Roy Tindall, Tony Ogden, Kenny Daniels, Bob Shannon,
Godfrey Brown, Frank Harrington and John Bradshaw
Matchmaker: Graham Lockwood

Acknowledgements

In introducing the 13th edition of the *British Boxing Yearbook*, I would like to welcome on board, a new publisher, Adrian Stephenson, of Lennard, Queen Anne Press, and a specialist in the marketing and publishing of sporting yearbooks, whose list includes my own PFA Footballers' Factfile, The Cricketers' Who's Who, and Rugby World. Boxing publications, despite much public interestfor the big occasion, have always lagged behind those for other sports and it is time to redress that situation.

I would also like to thank John Morris, the General Secretary of the BBBoC, for his continued support, not only in spreading the gospel, but in allowing me every access to the Board's good offices. As in the case of Ray Clarke, OBE, John's predecessor, our relationship goes far beyond that of authorship; it is one of real friendship and trust. Boxing, a subject that abounds the sensational with rumours often rife, does not need to shoot itself in the foot and it is on that basis that the *British Boxing Yearbook* tries to present all that is good within the sport. With more and more details requiring extra analysis, I am afraid I burdened Karyn Locke more than usual, but to her credit she responded superbly. Other information and help was forthcoming, as in previous years, from Simon Block (Assistant Secretary), Joanne Landers and, more recently, Robert Smith, the new Southern Area Secretary. Their efforts were much appreciated.

Again, Ron Olver, despite health problems which he continues to waive aside in the cause of duty, gave great support. A former Assistant Editor of both *Boxing News* and *Boxing World*, Ron is also well-known for being the British correspondent of *The Ring*; the author of *The Professionals*: producing the boxing section within *Encyclopedia Britannica*; his work on *Boxing*, Foyle's library service; and as the former co-editor of the *Boxing News Annual*. His honorary work, which includes being the Chairman of the BBBoC Benevolent Fund Grants Committee; the Vice President of many ex-boxers' associations; the Public Relations Officer of the London Ex-Boxers' Association; and membership of the Commonwealth Boxing Council and the International Hall of Fame Committee, has recently, and deservedly so, seen him honoured by both the Boxing Writers' Club and the BBBoC. If nothing else, he can be identified as the man behind the "Old Timers" feature in *Boxing News* for close on 30 years. It is also common knowledge, and if not should be, that he was the man who, more than anyone else, inspired the formation of the many ex-boxers' associations, where former fighters attend and are often cared for.

Once again, Bob Lonkhurst and Ralph Oates gave excellent support. Bob, who is in the process of finally publishing *Man of Courage: The Life and Career of Tommy Farr* (for further details see page 27), and who is a BBBoC Southern Area Inspector, has produced In The Corner, an insider view of some of the men who, not only keep boxing alive, but keep some of the country's leading fighters on top of the pile. Ralph, well-known for his boxing quiz books, *Boxing Clever* can still be purchased from any good bookstore, has given an insight into the career of Jim Watt, our former WBC lightweight champion and current TV pundit. Especially pleasing was the fact that he found time to produce a 50 question quiz. With Les Clark, the Yearbook's resident photographer, having also put together a quiz, we are spoilt for choice and there is no reason why boxing quizzes should not become a regular feature of the Yearbook.

I would also like to acknowledge the good works of John Jarrett – Home and Away with British Boxers During 1995-96 – the BBBoC's Northern Area Secretary; Eric Armit – A-Z of Current World Champions – an authority on boxers' records world-wide and who is responsible for *Boxing News'* World Scene; David Prior – Highlights From the 1995-96 Amateur Season – who covers amateur boxing for the *Amateur Boxing Scene* and *Boxing News*; Bob Yalen – World Title Bouts During 1995-96; Robert Soderman – One of Our Champions is Missing; and Neil Blackburn – Welcome to the International Boxing Hall of Fame – who also researches world-wide obituaries for the Yearbook.

Just as in previous years, the largest chunk of research has been in the World Title Bouts Since Gloves' section and I would like to thank Harold Alderman, George D. Blair, Joseph Brower, Professor Luckett Davis, Herb Goldman, Bill Matthews, Gary Phillips, Robert Soderman, and Paul Zabala, for their continued contributions. Listed alphabetically, and not in any order of merit, all of these men somehow find the time to research newspapers of a dim and distant age in their quest to add to the knowledge of historians. Work will continue in this section and right now, even on going to press, I have 300 more fights to hand, which would have involved world title claims, plus 400 more to analyse before the exercise can be deemed anyway complete.

Other editorial help was gratefully received from Mrs Enza Jacoponi (EBU data); Patrick Myler (Irish amateur boxing); Brian McAllister, Dai Corp, John Jarrett, Harry Warner, Robert Smith, and Paul Thomas (Area title data); Ray Allen (Welsh amateur boxing); Donald Campbell, Donald McNaughton, and Frank Hendrie (Scottish amateur boxing).

Regarding photographs, as in previous years, the majority were produced by Les Clark, who has built up a large library of both action and poses from British rings. If anyone requires a photo that has appeared in the Yearbook, or requires a list, Les can be reached at 352 Trelawney Avenue, Langley, Bucks SL3 7TS. Other photographs were supplied by my good friends, Harry Goodwin, Pennie Bracey, Steve Parkin, Derek Rowe, and Chris Bevan.

Others who need to be mentioned are: Bernard Hart, the Managing Director of Lonsdale Sports Equipment Ltd, who sponsors the BBBoC Awards which coincide with the launch of the Yearbook; Jean Bastin, who sets such high standards with the typesetting and design; my wife, Jennifer, who looks after the proof-reading; and the sponsor, Jonathan Ticehurst, Managing Director of the Sports Division of Windsor Insurance Brokers, whose generous support and enthusiasm has helped the *British Boxing Yearbook* to, hopefully, maintain the high standards it has set over the years.

Barry J. Hugman (Editor)

Introduction

by Barry J. Hugman

Hopefully, not unlucky, this is the 13th edition of the *British Boxing Yearbook,* which continues to expand both in size and content, mirroring the last 12 months activity along with reflections on the past.

Because this is the only yearbook of its kind to be found, and since the closure of the *Ring Record Book* in the late 1980s, it is important that research into the history of the sport continues and has a platform that it can be expressed upon. In America, men like Herb Goldman, the editor of the RRB on its demise and now the editor of the *International Boxing Digest* magazine, and Professor Luckett Davis, record compiler extraordinaire, continue their researches, while, aided by fellow-countrymen, Bob Soderman, Paul Zabala and Gary Phillips and others, and Harold Alderman from this side of the Atlantic, I move closer to completing what will ultimately be the complete history of world championship boxing since gloves. In the meantime, however, the *British Boxing Yearbook* is the perfect vehicle to introduce the information as it is uncovered.

This year, in an attempt to "spice" the book up, two boxing quizzes have been introduced, one by Ralph Oates, the other by Les Clark, the Yearbook's resident photographer. Ralph Oates, of course, is well known for his quiz books, the most recent being *Boxing Clever.* As the material for the quizzes has been culled from past Yearbooks, it should not present too many problems for regular readers and those interested in the history of the sport. If nothing else, it should prove a reasonable yardstick as to how much one knows about the history of the noble art.

Once again, apart from the accepted reference work, there are excellent articles in keeping with previous editions, such as Jim Watt: The Fighting Scot (the story of the much-liked and respected former world champion), In The Corner (an insight on some of Britain's top cornermen), Home and Away with British Boxers During 1995-96 (a regular feature covering last season, month by month), A-Z of Current World Champions (the synopsis and seasonal record for all of the current non-British IBF, WBA, WBC and WBO champions, including those who won and lost titles in 1995-96), One of Our Champions is Missing (the mystery surrounding the bantamweight championship in 1923-24 finally uncovered), Welcome to the International Hall of Fame (a contributor's personal experiences from this year's event), Highlights From the 1995-96 Amateur Season (another regular feature that reports on the season's leading events and stories), and Obituaries (a brief synopsis of the leading amateur and pros who passed away between July 1995 and going to press).

Although the obituary of Dickie Gunn is ably reported within Ron Olver's section, I would still like to add a few words of my own, having first met Dickie in unusual circumstances. That meeting, I think, summed up what Dickie was all about. Entered by Finchley ABC for the 1961-62 ABAs (London North-West Division, which, incidentally, in those days, took in an area reaching up to the Wash and across several counties, certainly as far as Oxford) at bantamweight, I somehow failed to make the requisite 118 lbs at the mid-day weigh-in. With several ounces to remove inside the alloted half hour or so, and my trainer, Les Kirk, not due to arrive until the evening, it was Dickie, the then Hayes ABC trainer, who tried tooth and nail to help me get the weight off and argued with officials for more time. Unfortunately, it was all to no avail and, considerably weakened, I turned down the offer of competing at featherweight, especially with the likes of Brian and Jimmy Anderson, Johnny Head and Billy Schwer (senior) on the programme. Other fine men from the list of obituaries whom I got to know rather well, and who will be sorely missed, include Al Aldridge, Stan Baker, Reg Hoblyn, Gilbert Odd, Jack Powell, and Harry Griver. The last named also epitomised all that is good in boxing. Only small of stature, but with a huge heart, Harry battled away against a serious disease for several years before finally succumbing, still putting others first. It was a privilege to have known him.

Abbreviations and Definitions used in the record sections of the Yearbook: PTS (Points), CO (Count Out), RSC (Referee Stopped Contest), RTD (Retired), DIS (Disqualified), NC (No Contest), ND (No Decision).

British Boxing Board of Control Ltd: Structure

(Members of the World Boxing Council, World Boxing Association, International Boxing Federation, World Boxing Organisation, Commonwealth Boxing Council and European Boxing Union)

PRESIDENT	Sir David Hopkin
VICE PRESIDENT	Leonard E. Read, QPM
CHAIRMAN	Sir David Hopkin
VICE CHAIRMAN	Leonard E. Read, QPM
GENERAL SECRETARY	John Morris
ADMINISTRATIVE STEWARDS	Sir David Hopkin Leonard E. Read QPM Dr Adrian Whiteson, OBE Dr Oswald Ross William Sheeran Dennis Lockton Lincoln Crawford Frank Butler, OBE Tom Pendry, MP Cliff Curvis Bill Martin Lord Brooks of Tremorfa Gerald Woolard Charles Giles Sebastian Coe, OBE, MP Judge Alan Simpson John Clifford
HONORARY STEWARD*	Dr James Shea
STEWARDS OF APPEAL*	Robin Simpson, QC John Mathew, QC Nicholas Valios, QC Robert Harman, QC William Tudor John Geoffrey Finn Judge Brian Capstick, QC Colin Ross Munro, QC Peter Richards Lord Meston
HONORARY CONSULTANT*	Ray Clarke, OBE
HEAD OFFICE	Jack Petersen House 52a Borough High Street London SE1 1XW Tel. 0171 403 5879 Fax. 0171 378 6670 Telegrams: BRITBOX, LONDON

* Not directors of the company

AREA COUNCILS - AREA SECRETARIES

AREA NO 1 (SCOTLAND)
Brian McAllister
11 Woodside Crescent, Glasgow G3 7UL
Telephone 0141 332 0392

AREA NO 2 (NORTHERN IRELAND)
Stanley Anderson
5 Ardenlee Avenue, Ravenhill Road, Belfast,
Northern Ireland BT6 0AA
Telephone 01232 453829

AREA NO 3 (WALES)
Dai Corp
113 Hill Crest, Brynna, Llanharan, Mid Glamorgan
CF7 9SN
Telephone 01443 226465

AREA NO 4 (NORTHERN)
(Northumberland, Cumbria, Durham, Cleveland, Tyne and Wear, North Yorkshire [north of a line drawn from Whitby to Northallerton to Richmond, including these towns].)
John Jarrett
5 Beechwood Avenue, Gosforth, Newcastle NE3 5DM
Telephone 0191 2856556

AREA NO 5 (CENTRAL)
(North Yorkshire [with the exception of the part included in the Northern Area - see above], Lancashire, West and South Yorkshire, Greater Manchester, Merseyside and Cheshire, Isle of Man, North Humberside.)
Ron Hackett
38 Grangethorpe Road,
Urmston, Manchester,
Lancashire M31 1HT
Telephone 0161 748 3545

AREA NO 6 (SOUTHERN)
(Bedfordshire, Berkshire, Buckinghamshire, Cambridgeshire, Channel Islands, Isle of Wight, Essex, Hampshire, Kent, Hertfordshire, Greater London, Norfolk, Suffolk, Oxfordshire, East and West Sussex.)
Robert W. Smith
British Boxing Board of Control
Jack Petersen House, 52a Borough High Street, London
SE1 1XW
Telephone 0171 403 5879

AREA NO 7 (WESTERN)
(Cornwall, Devon, Somerset, Dorset, Wiltshire, Avon, Gloucestershire.)
Dai Corp
113 Hill Crest, Brynna, Llanharan, Mid Glamorgan
CF7 9SN
Telephone 01443 226465

AREA NO 8 (MIDLANDS)
(Derbyshire, Nottinghamshire, Lincolnshire, Salop, Staffordshire, Herefordshire and Worcestershire, Warwickshire, West Midlands, Leicestershire, South Humberside, Northamptonshire.)
Alec Kirby
105 Upper Meadow Road, Quinton, Birmingham B32
Telephone 0121 421 1194

Foreword

by John Morris *(General Secretary, British Boxing Board of Control)*

These are crucial times for boxing in Britain, a period of change when the sport has to take the right steps to move it successfully into the 21st century. It would be wrong to talk of crisis yet, but, if lessons are not being learned, then it is inevitable that the sport will be under intense pressure. We need to make those in authority in Britain aware of who we are, what we do to move towards greater safety and medical care, what the sport of boxing is all about, and what it means to the young people who come into it.

Into the present climate comes Barry Hugman's latest edition of the British Boxing Yearbook, now firmly established as one of the world's top reference books for the sport. Once again it is packed with information, including an update on the boxing record of every British Champion of modern times. Barry's evaluation of all world championship fights has been spread over the past two volumes and has created great interest. Now it has been updated yet again and the special features include articles on Scotland's pride, Jim Watt, former world champion and now star ringside pundit, and Britain's leading trainers. While I am the last person to spread gloom and doom, I am convinced that the pattern set throughout the world of boxing over the next few years will determine the long-term future, possibly even the survival or otherwise of the sport. We have to find a unity that currently does not exist, both on the amateur and professional sides, and if boxing stays in the Olympic Games for Sydney in the year 2000 it may not be there much longer if the nonsensical scoring system is not changed. The computerised stupidity we watched from Atlanta worked against any kind of skilful boxing, eradicating body punches, and even combination punching, in favour of the single shot.

We are learning to live with the ever-spreading rash of so-called world championships, but so far the National Federations and Commissions around the globe have not rallied to the call we sent out in 1995 for the standardisation of all boxing, including medical and safety rules within the professional sport. Encouragingly, there is genuine interest and we might yet achieve this aim.

The tragedy of the year under review was the death of James Murray after collapsing in the final round of his British bantamweight challenge to fellow Scot, Drew Docherty, in Glasgow on 13 October, 1995. Murray had played his full part in a superb contest of courage and skill and is a terrible loss. I would like to repeat the tribute I have given many times since to his family for their steadfast support for boxing, despite their cruel loss.

Murray's death came while an independent neurological panel was at work, studying the Board's Medical Procedures and their recommendations have already been put into operation. When the new Regulations were first mooted there was a groundswell of opposition within British boxing. However, once a period of explanation and debate had been completed our license holders showed their unity by passing every suggested Regulation, virtually on a unanimous vote.

The Olympic seeding system may have contributed to Britain's sorry showing in Atlanta, with only two boxers able to compete and both beaten by fancied opponents in their opening contests, but what concerns me more is the state of amateur boxing generally in Britain. The ABA Championships, once graced by Scotland and Wales, as well as England, are no more. We are left with a purely English competition. Numbers drop and rebel groups have broken from the national bodies of both Scotland and Wales. More recently, the London ABA has moved to sever itself from the ABA of England.

The amateurs call for more help from the professionals and closer liaison. Personally, nothing would please me more because it is the future, but who do we work with without becoming embroiled in the fray? Such schism is dangerous and the sooner we can talk with those who speak for a united amateur organisation the more chance we have of progress.

Enough, I will stop before I start to get too political, although something needs to be done and quickly. Enjoy the book – it is a great read.

Sporting Club
LONSDALE
INTERNATIONAL

THE LONSDALE INTERNATIONAL SPORTING CLUB

President: The Earl Grey
Vice-President: Lord Addington
Patrons: Reg Gutteridge, OBE (UK); Tom Pendry, MP (UK);
                 Angelo Dundee (USA); Thomas Hauser (USA);
                 Kepler Wessels (SA); Joe Koizumi (Japan)

The Club is now accepting applications for membership for the new season. If you are interested in becoming a member of the World's No. 1 Boxing Fan Club please contact the Club Administrator.

1997 will see the celebration of a momentous date in British Boxing history; the Centenary of Bob Fitzsimmons' capture of the undisputed World Heavyweight Title from James J. Corbett in Carson City. The Club will honour the memory of one of the greatest fighters of all time on Sunday 16th March 1997 at the London Marriott Hotel.

Office address: 21 Beak Street, London W1R 3LB.
                 Tel: 0171 434 1290   Fax: 0171 734 2094

British Boxing Board of Control Awards

The Awards, inaugurated in 1984, in the form of statuettes of boxers, and designed by Morton T. Colver, the manufacturer of the Lonsdale Belt, are supplied by Len Fowler Trophies of Holborn. Len was an early post-war light-heavyweight favourite. Right from the start, the winners have been selected by an Award's Committee, which currently comprises John Morris, Simon Block, Frank Butler OBE, Bill Martin, Doctor Adrian Whiteson OBE, Ray Clarke OBE, and Barry J. Hugman, the editor of the *British Boxing Yearbook*. As in 1995, the Awards Ceremony, which has reverted back to a luncheon format, is due to be held this coming Autumn in London and will again be hosted by the Lonsdale International Sporting Club's Bernard Hart, the Managing Director of Lonsdale Sports Equipment Ltd, and sponsor of the Awards.

British Boxer of the Year: The outstanding British Boxer at any weight. 1984: Barrry McGuigan. 1985: Barry McGuigan. 1986: Dennis Andries. 1987: Lloyd Honeyghan. 1988: Lloyd Honeyghan. 1989: Dennis Andries. 1990: Dennis Andries. 1991: Dave McAuley. 1992: Colin McMillan. 1993: Lennox Lewis. 1994: Steve Robinson. 1995: Nigel Benn.

British Contest of the Year: Although a fight that took place in Europe won the 1984 Award, since that date, the Award, presented to both participants, has applied to the best all-action contest featuring a British boxer in a British ring. 1984: Jimmy Cable v Said Skouma. 1985: Barry McGuigan v Eusebio Pedroza. 1986: Mark Kaylor v Errol Christie. 1987: Dave McAuley v Fidel Bassa. 1988: Tom Collins v Mark Kaylor. 1989: Michael Watson v Nigel Benn. 1990: Orlando Canizales v Billy Hardy. 1991: Chris Eubank v Nigel Benn. 1992: Dennis Andries v Jeff Harding. 1993: Andy Till v Wally Swift Jnr. 1994: Steve Robinson v Paul Hodkinson. 1995: Steve Collins v Chris Eubank.

Overseas Boxer of the Year: For the best performance by an overseas boxer in a British ring. 1984: Buster Drayton. 1985: Don Curry. 1986: Azumah Nelson. 1987: Maurice Blocker. 1988: Fidel Bassa. 1989: Brian Mitchell. 1990: Mike McCallum. 1991: Donovan Boucher. 1992: Jeff Harding. 1993: Crisanto Espana. 1994: Juan Molina. 1995: Mike McCallum.

Special Award: Covers a wide spectrum, and is an appreciation for services to boxing. 1984: Doctor Adrian Whiteson. 1985: Harry Gibbs. 1986: Ray Clarke. 1987: Hon. Colin Moynihan. 1988: Tom Powell. 1989: Winston Burnett. 1990: Frank Bruno. 1991: Muhammad Ali. 1992: Doctor Oswald Ross. 1983: Phil Martin. 1994: Ron Olver. 1995: Gary Davidson.

Sportsmanship Award: This Award recognises boxers who set a fine example, both in-and-out of the ring. 1986: Frank Bruno. 1987: Terry Marsh. 1988: Pat Cowdell. 1989: Horace Notice. 1990: Rocky Kelly. 1991: Wally Swift Jnr. 1992: Duke McKenzie. 1993: Nicky Piper. 1994: Francis Ampofo. 1995: Paul Wesley.

Mike McCallum, the winner of the 1996 "Overseas Boxer of the Year" award, seen here with the BBBoC's John Morris

Les Clark

Insure You Keep Your Guard Up

Insurance Brokers and Insurance Consultants to the:-
British Boxing Board of Control, Football Association,
F.A. Premier League, Football League, British Olympic Association,
Professional Board Sailors Association, Cricketer's Association,
Spanish Basketball Association, St Moritz Tobogganing Club.

Windsor is one of the world's largest specialist sports, leisure and entertainment brokers, servicing national sports associations, leagues, clubs and players throughout the U.K., Europe, and North America.

While Personal Accident forms the major part of our sports related business, the group can also offer many other types of insurance cover, including Stadium Risks, Commercial Fire, High-Risk Liability, Professional Indemnity, Marine and Aviation - at highly competitive rates.

For sponsors and event organisers we offer wide experience of contingency risks such as Event Cancellation/Abandonment, Prize Indemnity, Death and Disgrace, Bonus Protection, and other insurance-protected sponsorship enhancements and marketing initiatives.

A separate group company provides consultancy on Life Assurance, Group Pensions and Personal Financial Planning.

Boxing and the Need for Insurance

by Jonathan Ticehurst (Managing Director, Sports Division of Windsor Insurance Brokers Ltd)

To all of us in the insurance industry, our clients are of paramount importance. But, in our case, not only are they important, they are also in the public eye – because our speciality is professional sports and, in particular, boxing.

Boxing is, of course, a national sport, enjoyed at amateur level through schools and clubs by thousands of people and watched at top professional level by millions worldwide through the eyes of television.

How many of us see claims, or potential claims, occurring on television, or read about them in the papers before we get to the office? Millions have seen both promising, mature and lucrative careers ended in a matter of seconds as we have watched late night title fights and supporting bouts from our sitting room chairs.

Many people might wonder how such a direct contact sport can possibly qualify for Accident and Injury insurance cover. The answer lies in the definition of "injury" and the definition of "disablement". For many years, the British Boxing Board of Control has provided and paid for a Personal Accident Policy for every one of its licensed boxers. This includes overseas boxers who have acquired a temporary licence for the purposes of fighting in this country in specific bouts. Traditionally, that policy provided cover for death, blindness, deafness and loss of limbs or parts of limbs whilst the licensed boxer was in the ring or climbing into or out of the ring.

Windsor have been managing the insurance affairs of the world of professional football and cricket for 20 years or more. During this time, various policies have paid out millions of pounds against claims by the national associations, the leagues, the clubs and counties, in respect of players who have gone out of the game early through injury. Some names you will only remember, others you may well have seen or, in early days, even played with, like Ian Storey-Moore, Steve Coppell, Gary Bailey, Alan Brazil, John O'Neill, Norman Whiteside, Gary Stevens, Siggi Jonsson, Mick McCarthy, Paul Elliott, John Fashanu, "Syd" Lawrence, Paul Downton, Nigel Felton, Rodney Ontong and many others.

It was, perhaps, no surprise, therefore, that the Board should turn to Windsor in the course of its review of the insurance cover which has been available historically for boxers. The London insurance market is nothing if not imaginative and when brokers who are experts in their field put their heads together with underwriters who have made it their business to specialise in a particular class of insurance worldwide, then almost anything is possible at an affordable premium. The result was that the Board has now been able to include within their policy the all-important additional cover of Permanent & Total Disablement.

Experience has taught us that where an association, a federation, or affinity body takes out insurance for the benefit of its membership, then any individual member who needs additional or more wide-ranging cover for his own particular needs, should be able to buy his or her own cover as an extension to the group cover. That is what happens in football, cricket and many other sports. The Board's policy provides basic benefits for its licensed members and, although the benefits could not be, and, as is generally known, was never intended to be, regarded as a "retirement fund", the policy is a very important starting point.

The Professional Boxers' Association recognised the hard work and imagination that the Board put into their new policy and were quick to endorse its value to all their members. Perhaps, more importantly, the PBA then worked closely with Windsor in designing tailor-made additional insurance cover which could be purchased, through their association, by members individually.

It is an ideal arrangement. The British Boxing Board of Control, through their own funds, are providing a general benefit for all their licensed boxers which can act as a platform for individual members to buy top-up cover, at their own expense, to suit their own particular requirements and financial obligations. The insurance wraps itself around the actual business of boxing and those in it and responds directly to the risks associated with it. It may be marginally more expensive than "off the shelf" Accident & Injury policies, but then "off the shelf" policies will not respond to the peculiarities and the particular risks associated with a sport having such pugnacious characteristics.

Between them, the Board and the PBA have taken a giant leap forward for the benefit of all professional boxers. We, at Windsor, are happy that another high profile professional sport has the protection from the insurance market that it needs and deserves.

Jim Watt: The Fighting Scot

by Ralph Oates

Every now and then a boxer emerges who progresses a great deal further in his career than anyone could ever have anticipated. Such a boxer was Jim Watt from Scotland. A talented southpaw who appeared to have all the necessary skills to eventually become a British lightweight champion and, if the right breaks came along, even a European title holder, but a world crown – the odds had to be very much against it.

The 135 lbs division was a tough poundage to compete in, it was a hot-bed of talent and, to reach the pinnacle, one had to be blessed not only with their share of talent but a little luck also.

Watt, born in Glasgow on 18 July 1948, first came to notice when he won the ABA lightweight title by outpointing Bobby Fisher in the 1968 championships. In the semi-finals Jim had knocked out his opponent Johnny Stracey in the first round. (Stracey later went on in the pro ranks to win the WBC world welterweight title by stopping the great Jose Napoles in six rounds in Mexico). Thus the news that Watt was to depart from the amateur ranks to punch for pay came as something of a shock to the fans, since Jim had looked a fair bet to win a medal of some description at the 1968 Olympic games, which were to be held in Mexico City.

However, the decision had been made and Jim, under the guidance of manager, James Murray, made his pro debut at Hamilton on 30 October 1968, knocking out his opponent, Santos Martins of Ghana, in round four. Having his second bout on 11 December at the same venue against Alex Gibson of Belfast, another victory was assured when the referee moved in and stopped the contest in the Scot's favour in round two. Once again, he had shown punching power to compliment his impressive boxing ability.

At the time, the British champion was Ken Buchanan, another Scot from Edinburgh, and a man who would go on in time to become one of Britain's best post-war boxers. The world champion was Carlos Teo Cruz and the world's top ten was filled with quality names like Ismael Laguna, Pedro Carrasco, Carlos Ortiz, Mando Ramos, Frankie Narvaez, Jaguar Kakizawa, Carlos Hernandez, Chango Carmona, Lloyd Marshall, and, of course, Buchanan. These were boxers who had class with a capital C and one needed to have a good solid fistic education to survive, let alone win against any one of them. True, many of these fighters would not be around when Watt was ready to make his move, but could he ever hope to mix with similar formidable opposition in the future with any realistic chance of success? It was, of course, early days, but it was a question which would have to be answered in due course.

The learning process continued the following year, with Jim defeating Victor Paul on points over eight rounds at Govan on 10 April. Next came Winston Thomas, who was stopped in the eighth round at the World Sporting Club in London on 15 September, followed by his debut at the National Sporting Club in London on 24 November, Tommy Tiger being outscored over eight rounds.

In each of the three bouts the Scot had continued to look good and confirmed that he was every inch championship material. However, a return with Victor Paul at the National Sporting Club on 16 February 1970 provided Watt with his first setback, when he was stopped in round six, a cut over the Scot's right eye prompting referee, Sid Nathan, to halt the bout, when he appeared to be on course for yet another victory.

A third meeting between the two took place at the National Sporting Club on 1 June and the Scot was fully aware that he could not slip up a second time against Paul, since to do so would put a serious question mark against his future prospects in the game. In spite of that, another defeat looked more than imminent when he returned to his corner at the end of round one with a cut over his left eye. Yet Jim showed no outward sign of panic or concern when the bell sounded to start round two. Instead, he remained calm and really turned it on with a confident display of boxing and handed out so much punishment that referee Harry Gibbs eventually stepped in to save the brave Paul in round five. Jim had reversed his sole defeat in style and was once again on the upward climb towards the British title. There would be four more bouts during 1970 and all of them would be won inside the distance.

However, the really big news of the year for the lightweight division, and British boxing, was Ken Buchanan's magnificent upset victory over Ismael Laguna in San Juan, Puerto Rico, on 26 September. After 15 hard and difficult rounds, Ken was given the points decision and with it the WBA crown. Buchanan thus became the first Briton to hold the world lightweight title since Freddie Welsh from Wales, who outpointed defending king, Willie Ritchie, over 20 rounds on 7 July 1914. Welsh eventually lost the crown to Benny Leonard on 28 May 1917, a stoppage in round nine deciding it.

On 11 January 1971, Jim scored another victory when he outpointed David Pesenti over eight rounds. Next up on 22 March came Henri Nesi, who was stopped in round six, prior to Jim being matched with fellow Scot, Willie Reilly, in the most important fight of his career to-date, a final eliminator for the British lightweight title.

The bout was to take place on 27 September at Wembley and Reilly was quite a talented boxer who would not be easy to overcome. Going into the contest against Watt, Willie's record stood at 11 wins, three draws, and six defeats, which on the surface appeared rather ordinary. Yet a close look at the record revealed top names like Kokkie Olivier, Borge Krogh and Al Ford. He had also boxed abroad in South Africa. Australia (twice), Denmark and Canada, so it was clear that Watt held no fears for him. Watt won when the contest was brought to a close in round seven after referee Harry Gibbs decided that the cut over Reilly's right eye was far too bad for him to continue. So he was now the official challenger for the British crown held by Ken Buchanan.

While waiting for his championship chance, Jim kept

busy with a contest against Frenchman, Leonard Taverez, a very experienced ring-man who had, in past bouts, lost twice to Buchanan on points over the eight and ten round distance. The contest, which took place on 1 November, gave Watt the chance to see if he could better Buchanan's efforts and stop Taverez and thus gain a slight psychological edge over his Edinburgh rival. Taverez, however, turned out to be more dangerous than expected and almost provided Watt with his second professional defeat. In round two, the Scot suffered a cut over his left eye which Harry Gibbs inspected a couple of times during the course of the fight. Jim had to dig deep for victory, something that was achieved in round nine when the referee intervened to save Taverez from taking further punishment.

It had been a difficult bout and one had to ponder about the cut eye-brows which he seemed to be receiving, would they prove to be a problem in his future bouts and hinder his progress? At this time the situation looked a little bleak.

Buchanan, as expected, later relinquished the British crown to concentrate on world title defences, so Watt was once again matched with Willie Reilly, this time for the vacant British championship. The bout was to take place at the Nottingham Ice Rink on 1 February 1972 and to all extent and purposes, the Lonsdale belt was poised to be strapped around Watt's waist. It is a known fact that in boxing shocks can be commonplace and dreams can often turn into nightmares, bringing ambitious plans to a sharp and cruel end.

An example of this was seen on the night of the fight when, in round ten, referee Roland Dakin stopped the bout in Reilly's favour, due to a bad cut over Watt's right-eye. The contest had been close and Reilly boxed well, presenting Jim with various problems, but, in truth, the ending was inconclusive. The loss was not catastrophic, due to the circumstances, and it was clearly obvious that the blond southpaw more than deserved a return bout for the championship, but he faced a long and lengthy wait as Reilly was committed to make the first defence of the title against Midlands Area champion, Tony Riley, who had stopped Herbie McLean in round 11 of a final eliminator on 12 January 1972. Yet fate can be very strange, a fact which was highlighted when Willie Reilly caused something of a shock by announcing his retirement from boxing due to a dispute over the purse he would be paid to meet his challenger. With the door wide open, Watt jumped at the chance to meet the Midlands Area champion for the vacant British title. This time the Scot made no mistakes. On 3 May, at the Midlands Sporting Club in Solihull, he stopped Tony Riley in the 12th round. Riley gave his all, but Watt was superb, giving a first class display of boxing. So Jim was now the British lightweight champion, back on the winning track, and ready to tackle the men at the top.

The following month, a result took place in America which would have an important bearing on Watt's future plans. Ken Buchanan lost his world title on 26 June to Panama's thunderous punching Roberto Duran when stopped in round 13 under controversial circumstances. It seemed logical that Buchanan would consider challenging for the domestic crown, since a victory would further boost his chances of gaining another world title fight.

Jim next boxed on 11 December against Noel McIvor and won in three rounds on a cut eye stoppage. His next contest would be a British title defence on 29 January 1973 against Buchanan at the St Andrew's Sporting Club in Glasgow. This was without a shadow of a doubt Jim's baptism of fire.

Buchanan had an impressive record of 47 bouts against some of the best lightweights in the world, with only two defeats. The champion had a total of just 17 contests with two defeats against good solid opponents, none of whom were world ranked. Jim clearly had a difficult task against a much more experienced fighter and would be hard pressed to retain his crown. A win for Buchanan would see him make the Lonsdale Belt his own property, since he had first won the championship with an 11 round knockout over the then holder, Maurice Cullen, in 1968, before a five round knockout over challenger, Brian Hudson, in 1970, put a second notch on the belt. At the end of the 15 round contest, Ken's arm was raised in victory by referee George Smith, with a scoreline of $74^1/_4$ points to $72^1/_2$ points. Jim had lost the fight and the championship, but was not disgraced in anyway whatsoever, since he won the respect of the boxing world and fans alike with his magnificent performance. Ken had to fight hard for every point in each round and Watt, so full of confidence and pride, gave him plenty to think about during the hard fought encounter. Going the full distance of 15 rounds for the first time in his career against a man of Buchanan's class, also spoke volumes for his ability.

That year, Jim had three more bouts, an eight round points victory over Johnny Cheshire, a return with Noel McIvor which resulted in a four round cut eye victory, then an eight round points decision win over Angus McMillan.

On 16 February 1974, Watt had his first professional bout abroad when he met Andries Steyn in Johannesburg, South Africa. This was not an easy assignment. Steyn, who had retired in three rounds against Ken Buchanan in 1972 was world ranked in some quarters and fighting on home turf would not be easy to defeat. Jim was clearly the underdog, with Steyn being the favourite to put another win on his record. Yet Jim produced something of an upset when he stopped the South African in seven rounds due to a cut eye. However, even without the eye damage, Steyn seemed booked for defeat, since Jim looked both in control and ahead on points. This was a fine win, in fact the best of his career at that time, one which would move him up the world rankings.

He stayed in South Africa for his next bout and this time met another highly-rated opponent in the shape of Kokkie Oliver. Once again, Jim pulled off a victory when he outpointed his man over the ten round distance in Johannesburg on 2 March. Watt's performance was first class and one that further enchanced his reputation. His next contest was in Caerphilly on 19 June against the talented Welshman, Billy Waith. The match was a final eliminator for the British lightweight title, made over the duration of 12 rounds, and at the end of the bout the former champion was given the decision on points. Jim had once again given a commanding performance.

Around this time, the British champion, Ken Buchanan, was now also the king of Europe, having knocked out holder, Antonio Puddu, in six rounds in Italy. Ken was still after another world title fight and it seemed that he would relinquish the British crown and go after bigger targets, rather than defend against his old rival.

Jim went back to South Africa for his next contest against the well regarded Anthony Morodi. The bout, which took place in Johannesburg on 26 October, provided the Scot with a slight setback. After ten good rounds, he was declared a loser on points.

Watt's next date in the ring was on 27 January 1975. Buchanan had relinquished the British title and Jim was matched with former opponent, Johnny Cheshire, for the vacant crown. Cheshire, who had won the ABA featherweight title in 1968, had lost an eight round points decision to Watt in 1973 and was a good puncher who was capable of giving anyone trouble. However, Watt looked a good bet to repeat his victory over Johnny and regain his title. The form book ran true when referee Wally Thom stopped the contest in round seven and proclaimed Watt the winner and new British champion.

His next outing was a non-title ten round contest against another former opponent, Billy Waith, on 19 March, and again he defeated the Welshman on points.

Given the chance to win another title, when he was paired with Jonathan Dele for the vacant Commonwealth championship on 3 May, Jim had to travel to Lagos in Nigeria in his bid to win the title. After 15 rounds of hard endeavour, Dele was given the decison on points. The result was a disappointment to Watt and manager, James Murray, but there was a light at the end of the tunnel.

After stopping the Italian, Giancarlo Usai, in round 12, in defence of his European title on 25 July, Ken Buchanan announced his retirement from boxing, leaving the EBU championship vacant. The Scot was thus matched with Frenchman, Andre Holyk, in a 12 round eliminator. Holyk was a good fighter, but Watt had the class to defeat him. However, the British champion had to pack his bags and travel once more, this time to Lyons in France. Fighting in the other man's backyard can be a big disadvantage, since very few favours are given if the decision is close and, true to form, at the end of the contest which took place on 31 October, Holyk was declared the victor on points by way of a split decision. Watt's route to Europe was now blocked and it was going to be a most difficult task to get back amongst the contenders.

In the early part of 1976, Jim left the management of James Murray to join the Terry Lawless stable in London. At the time, Lawless was one of the most successful managers in British boxing, turning out champion after champion. Watt would now join the company of former amateur rival, John H. Stracey, who was the reigning WBC world welterweight champion, with Maurice Hope, Kirkland Laing, Jimmy Batten, Charlie Magri and many others, who would go on and win titles at various levels and weights. In fact, Terry's gym, based at the Royal Oak Pub in the East End of London, was the personification of the best in British boxing talent. The Scot, with manager, Lawless, and promoters, Mickey Duff and Mike Barrett

behind him, now had every chance of going beyond domestic honours.

His first contest under Lawless took place at the Albert Hall on 2 March, against George Turpin from Liverpool. Turpin, who had won the ABA bantamweight title in 1971 and 1972, along with a bronze medal at the 1972 Munich Olympic games, was no match for the Scot and was duly knocked out in four rounds. Watt's next bout came against former British featherweight king, Jimmy Revie, on 30 March. The Scot once again put up a good performance and won with a cut eye stoppage in round seven. Next to cross gloves with the British champion was Hector Diaz from the Dominican Republic, and the visitor was stopped in round four of a match which took place on 10 May. Then, on 22 June, Watt suffered an unexpected setback when Johnny Claydon stopped him with a cut eye in round three. This was without doubt an upset and the winner was in a good position to challenge for the British crown. On the same night Stracey lost his world welterweight title to Carlos Palomino when stopped in round 12, making it an occasion that the Lawless camp would not forget in a hurry.

Jim next entered the fray on 12 October against Italian, Franco Diana, getting back on the victory trail when referee, Paddy Sower, stopped the bout in round six. On 21 February 1977, he was then given the opportunity to gain revenge for a previous defeat, and also make the Lonsdale Belt his own property, when he defended his British crown against Johnny Claydon. The Scot put the record straight when he stopped Claydon in round ten.

Jim was next due to defend his British title against Irishman Charlie Nash, but, rather than go to Northern Ireland, he relinquished the championship. On 5 August, Jim had the chance to gain revenge, yet again, for a previous defeat when he was matched with Andre Holyk for the vacant European lightweight title. There was a great deal of excitement about the contest, which was to take place in Scotland, as a victory for Watt would greatly enhance his chances of a world title challenge. When the bell rang out to start the contest the fans were full of anticipation, expecting a real battle for the supremacy of Europe, but the fight was over before it had hardly begun, Watt stopping his man in the first round when Holyk sustained a cut right-eyebrow. "They say revenge is sweet", if that is so then Watt must have had a very large jar of honey on this occasion. By his victory, Jim became the first Scot to win a European title in Glasgow since Peter Keenan outpointed the Frenchman, Maurice Sandeyron, over 15 rounds on 16 June 1953 to regain the bantamweight title.

Jim's first defence of the European title took place on 16 November at Solihull against Jeronimo Lucas of Spain, the Scot retaining his laurels when referee Angelo Poletti of Italy stopped the bout in round ten, due to the Spaniard being too badly cut over the left-eye to continue.

Defence number two took place on 17 February 1978 against another Spanish fighter, Perico Fernandez, the former WBC light-welterweight titleholder. This was without doubt a most difficult contest for Watt, since Fernandez was a dangerous puncher who had mixed with and beaten some of best fighters in both the 135 lb and 140 lb weight divisions. To make matters worse, he had to travel to Madrid to meet his challenger. At that time, not one British boxer had won a European title fight in Spain. Bantamweight Alan Rudkin (twice), heavyweight Jack Bodell, and lightweight Ken Buchanan, had all tasted defeat in that country. Thus, the critics were not all that enthusiastic about Jim's chances of success. Yet, once again, the Scot put on an excellent display of boxing, after being floored in the first round, to retain his title on a 15 round points decision. Fernandez had really been taken to school by Watt and this victory moved the winner that much closer to a world title shot, with the dubious pleasure of meeting the undisputed champion, Roberto Duran.

Watt kept punch sharp in his next contest on 12 June, by outpointing Billy Vivian of Wales over eight rounds, before, on 18 October, making the third defence of his European title against yet another Spanish fighter, Antonio Guinaldo, at the Kelvin Hall, Glasgow. Jim stayed king of the continent when the Spaniard retired in round five. At this moment in time, he looked every inch a world class fighter, and clearly there was no-one in Europe capable of defeating him.

In January 1979, the world lightweight champion, Roberto Duran, relinquished his title due to problems in making the weight. This meant that both the World Boxing Council and the World Boxing Association's titles were vacant and the Scot was in a fine position to contest one of them. And, on 17 April 1979, Watt was matched with Alfredo Pitalua of Columbia for the vacant WBC version of the world lightweight title at the Kelvin Hall, Glasgow. The pressure on him was enormous, Scotland, and indeed the whole of Britain, was looking for him to win. Yet Pitalua was far from being an easy touch, he was a

competent, hard-punching boxer, fully expecting to take the championship home with him. The Scottish fans were being treated to their first world title fight on home-ground since 10 July 1946, when Jackie Paterson successfully retained his flyweight crown with a 15 round points decision over challenger, Joe Curran. A victory for Watt would also give the Lawless camp their second world title holder, for on 4 March, Maurice Hope had travelled to San Remo in Italy to win the WBC light-middleweight crown, the championship changing hands when Rocky Mattioli retired in round eight. On that particular occasion, Watt assisted in Hope's corner.

The atmosphere on the night of the fight was highly charged, at nearly 31 years of age, Watt knew there would be no second chance if he were to lose. As it was, the fight lived up to all expectations once the bell sounded to start the proceeding's, with both men demonstrating their desire for the championship, taking and giving solid blows. Often Watt was driven back, only to reverse the process and thus get the upper-hand by outpunching his opponent. The intensity of the action seemed to increase with each round. Then in round seven, Pitalua was sent to the canvas for a count. Although getting to his feet and fighting back with the heart of a lion, the end finally came in dramatic fashion in round 12 when the American referee, Arthur Mercante, stopped the contest with Pitalua taking punishment on the ropes. Watt's arm was raised in victory. He was the new WBC lightweight champion of the world. At long last his dream had come true and it was indeed a magical moment.

Jim made his first defence of the WBC title on 3 November and once again the venue was the Kelvin Hall in Glasgow, the challenger being Mexican-American, Roberto Vasquez. Watt was favoured to win, but often in world title

Jim (right), seen here making the first defence of his WBC title against Roberto Vasquez

fights the underdog can be inspired to new heights by the nothing to lose philosophy, tear in and thus cause an upset. However, Jim dominated from the first and retained his championship when he stopped his challenger in round nine. Once again the fighting Scot put on a fine display of boxing to keep the title in Britain.

Watt made the second defence of the title against Ireland's Charlie Nash on 14 March. Nash, an accomplished boxer, had won the vacant British title which Jim had relinquished, by stopping Johnny Claydon in 12 rounds in Derry on 28 February 1978. He had also picked up the vacant European championship (which Watt had relinquished upon winning the world crown) on 27 June 1979, by outpointing Andre Holyk of France over 12 rounds. The Irishman had also made a dangerous, but successful defence of the EBU title on 6 December in Copenhagen when outpointing Ken Buchanan. A win by Buchanan would have projected the former world champion into the challenger's role against Watt, but it was Nash who confirmed his position with this victory.

In the first round of the Watt-Nash confrontation, the fans at the Kelvin Hall were given a few moments of anguish when Jim was floored without a count, yet this was not going to be a night of glory for Nash, his challenge being over in round four when the bout was stopped in Watt's favour. The Irishman gave of his very best, but Jim proved to be too strong for him.

At this time, British boxing was on a crest of a wave, Alan Minter having won the undisputed world middleweight title by outpointing holder, Vito Antuofermo, over 15 rounds in Las Vegas on 16 March (interesting to note that the then three British-world champions, Minter, Watt and Maurice Hope all boxed in the southpaw stance).

The acid test came in his next defence of the WBC crown against the American, Howard Davis, on 7 June, in the open air at the Ibrox Park in Glasgow. Davis had an impressive pedigree, having won the gold medal in the lightweight division at the 1976 Montreal Olympic Games, and was coming into the championship contest with an undefeated professional record of 13 bouts. His whole persona was that of a champion-in-waiting, a man born to be king, and many experts were of the opinion that the very talented American would take the title back home to the States with him. Even with homeground advantage, Jim was not favoured to win. But, at the end of 15 rounds, the well conditioned Watt proved his right to the championship by taking a clear points decision, much to the great joy of his many fans, who joined him in song with a rendering of "Flower of Scotland", during the after fight celebrations. This was a magnificent victory and if there had been any doubts at all about Jim's ability to deal with the top American contenders, the win over Davis completely dispelled them. The following week, Watt was given a further honour when he was awarded the MBE in the Queen's Birthday List.

After a well deserved rest it was time to don the gloves and go back to work. This meant another defence of the title, the challenger being Sean O'Grady of America and the venue being the Kelvin Hall, Glasgow, on 1 November.

O'Grady, from Oklahoma, proved to be a dangerous

Another victory for Jim Watt   Derek Rowe Photos Ltd

opponent. Statistically, he had a most impressive record, having taken part in 74 bouts with just one defeat, that being a four round retirement to Danny Lopez in 1976 (Lopez went on to win the WBC world featherweight title three bouts later). Sixty-five of Sean's victories had been achieved inside the scheduled distance, with 23 wins scored in the first round. True, many of his opponents were not ranked fighters, but his record was really quite incredible, especially when one considered that he was only 21 years of age.

The kid from Oklahoma had come to fight and his challenge to Watt was an exciting one, the Scot having to come through some bad patches to retain his title for the fourth time. The champions's fans were filled with feelings of consternation when, during the course of the fight, his right-eye was badly cut and thus examined by the ringside doctor, who indicated that any further damage to the wound would result in the fight being stopped in the American's favour. However, just when it appeared that the crown seemed set to change hands, O'Grady sustained a bad cut on his forehead, the referee, Raymond Baldeyrou of France, eventually calling a halt to the bout in round 12. Paradoxically, this may have been one of the Scot's best wins for, on 12 April 1981, O'Grady challenged Hilmer Kenty for the WBA title in Atlantic City and won the championship with a 15 round points decision, thus giving Watt's claim to being the best lightweight in the world even more credence.

Jim's next challenger was Alexis Arguello of Nicaragua. To say that Arguello was a little special would be an under-statement. In fact, he was a magnificent fighting machine who appeared to be on his way to greatness. Alexis was a former double world champion, having held the WBA featherweight title and the WBC super-featherweight crown, relinquishing both to move up in weight.

In facing Arguello at Wembley on 20 June 1981, the Scot was a clear underdog, but there was just a slight hope that he might be able to pull off a shock victory. However, the man from Nicaragua proved to be one mountain too high for Jim to climb and at the end of the 15 round contest Arguello was declared the winner and new WBC lightweight champion of the world. Alexis had won his third world crown in as many divisions, following in the illustrious footsteps of Bob Fitzsimmons (middleweight, heavyweight and light-heavyweight), Tony Canzoneri (featherweight, lightweight and light-welterweight), Barney Ross (lightweight, light-welterweight and welterweight), Henry Armstrong (featherweight, welterweight and lightweight), and Wilfred Benitez (light-welterweight, welterweight and light-middleweight).

Watt may have lost his crown, but he did so with pride, dignity, and courage. The man was a champion in victory and a champion in defeat. Indeed, going the full 15 round route with a man like Arguello was in itself an accomplishment worthy of high praise.

The Arguello encounter proved to be Jim's last professional bout, and at the age of nearly 33, he retired from the ring with a record of 46 bouts - 38 wins, and eight defeats. At this moment in time, Jim has the distinction of taking part in more world lightweight title fights than any other British boxer to-date, the total being six in all. It is also interesting to note that everytime Jim challenged for a championship it was vacant.

After hanging up his gloves, he did not disappear altogether from the fistic scene, but became involved in a great deal of television work, giving his opinions about various fights shown. Later, he joined Reg Gutteridge at ringside, once again giving his views on the bouts in progress. The team of Gutteridge and Watt, has proven most successful, with both men having a vast knowledge of the game and thus give the fans an excellent commentary on each big fight which is televised on ITV. On top of this, Jim is an excellent after-dinner speaker, whose services in this capacity are much sought after. He also has various business interests and when time allows he plays a few rounds of golf. Music too figures very much in his life, since he enjoys playing the guitar.

Sadly, Jim suffered a terrible tragedy when he lost his young son, James, 17, in a car accident in October 1995. Jim is striving, along with his wife, Margaret, and their other children, Andrew and Michelle, to put their lives back together again, but their grief is heavy and will only lighten with the passing of time.

On behalf of the Yearbook, I spoke to Jim about his career and other aspect of the sport. I was curious to know why he did not continue to box after the Arguello defeat, since he was still a high profile fighter and after a couple of warm up bouts could have challenged for, and won, the WBA version of the lightweight title. At that particular time, the champion was Claude Noel (the crown had been taken away from Sean O'Grady by the WBA and Noel outpointed Rodolfo Gonzalez over 15 rounds for the vacant championship on 12 September 1981). Noel was a good fighter, but Jim had the tools to defeat him.

"Yes, explained Jim, I think I could have beaten Noel, but I had been in boxing for a long time and at 33 years of age I did not relish the thought of going over old ground by perhaps winning the European crown to secure my chance at Noel. I had done well during my career and felt it was time to retire."

How did Jim feel about old rival Ken Buchanan? "I have a great deal of admiration for Kenny. When we fought for the British crown he was at his peak, while I was inexperienced, but his style suited me since he would lead and I would counter. I was hopeful that one day we would meet again, this time with me defending my world crown against him. The fight would have been big in Scotland and it would have given me the chance to gain revenge". But it was not to be, for Charlie Nash defeated Ken in a European title fight.

These days, many fans of the sport are most critical about the vast amount of world titles on offer and I asked Jim his view on this subject.

"When I fought in world title fights – they were exactly that, world title fights, but these days the situation is a little ridiculous with there being so many championship bouts. However, it does give the respective boxers a chance to get a good pay day and that can't be a bad thing."

What was Jim's most difficult contest?

"Without a doubt my losing title defence against Alexis Arguello. The man was a terrific boxer."

Did Jim have a favourite boxer?

"Sugar Ray Leonard. This man was around in an era which produced so many greats like Thomas Hearns, Roberto Duran, Marvin Hagler, Wilfred Benitez, etc., and he traded punches with them all. His record is confirmation of his ability."

After saying goodbye to Jim, I thought for a moment on how lucky the sport had been in having a man like him to represent it. He has proven to be a fine ambassador for boxing, both inside and outside of the ropes. Watt's name is synonymous with all that is good in the sport and it is hoped that in the years to follow these home shores will produce more fighters of the calibre of Jim Watt – The Fighting Scot.

Now a TV commentator, this picture was taken recently by Les Clark

In The Corner

by Bob Lonkhurst

Before, during, and after a fight, there is nobody closer to a boxer than his trainer. He is the man who spends countless hours on the road and in the gymnasium developing the skill and fitness of his charge. Generally full of ambition and enthusiasm, his job will sometimes become frustrating when the training does not go according to plan.

To understand the position of the trainer, it is worth recalling a remark once made by that great American teacher of the noble art, Ray Arcel. In an interview, he said "You're only as good as the fighter you work with. I don't care how much you know, if your fighter can't fight you're just another bum in the park." The man who trained such great champions as Benny Leonard, Barney Ross, Kid Gavilan, Tony Zale, Ezzard Charles, and, in later years, Roberto Duran and Larry Holmes, certainly knew his stuff, but he had plenty of losers as well.

Boxing trainers are men whose patience, determination and understanding have, over the years, taken thousands of youngsters from the streets and saved them from lives of crime. By giving encouragement and guidance in the skills of the noble art, they have handed kids with no future, pride, discipline and self respect. And, in doing so, they have done a public service.

I will always remember a remark made to me a few years ago by Matchroom trainer, Freddie King, when he said, "If we in the boxing game keep several hundred violent youngsters off the streets and channel their aggression, we have done society a favour." It was a realistic comment which the opponents of boxing would do well to digest.

A man well known for getting kids off the street is Brendan Ingle, who runs the St Thomas' club in the Wincobank district of Sheffield. All kinds of problem people have turned up at his gym, and many have been helped. Thieves, glue sniffers, alcoholics, homeless, and unemployed. Nobody is turned away, provided they behave and respect the club rules.

Born in June 1940 at Ringsend, a tough dockside area of Dublin, Ingle comes from a big boxing family. There were 15 kids, and all 11 boys boxed at some stage, The most successful was elder brother Jimmy, who won the European amateur flyweight title in 1939. As a schoolboy, Brendan had a good record, but he was not in the class of Jimmy.

Brendan moved to Sheffield in 1957, due to the success achieved by another brother, Eddie, who had gone there just after the war. Whenever Eddie went home, he had plenty of money and this attracted Brendan. So as soon as a job was found for him he too moved to the north of England. He had a host of jobs on building sites and in the steelworks, and even did chores such as hair-cutting and shoe-mending in his lunch breaks.

As an amateur, Brendan boxed for the Croft House Club in Sheffield, where he was trained by former British welterweight champion, Henry Hall. Even in those days,

Ingle had his own training manual written out in a large exercise book. All aspects of training were covered, including running, punchbag work, relaxation and diet, the book being founded on information picked up from his brothers and in the Dublin gyms.

In 1965, Ingle turned professional at middleweight with Liverpool manager, Johnny Campbell, and joined a good stable of fighters, which included Les and Gordon McAteer, and Johnny Cooke. In a career which lasted until 1973, he had 19 wins and 14 defeats, but, unfortunately, suffered a lot from cut eyes. Such an injury forcing him to retire after eight rounds against Chris Finnegan In 1969. A cut right-eye sustained in the first round against Joe Gregory in 1973 required 14 stitches, but, in that fight, Brendan showed tremendous courage and aggression. By throwing caution to the wind, he knocked Gregory out in the third.

After retiring from the ring, Ingle turned his hand to training and became involved with the St Thomas' club. It was there that he joined forces with Herol Graham who, at that stage, was still an amateur. Brendan was quite happy training amateurs, but became involved in a political row with the ABA, who accused him of assisting a professional. His license was suspended and although the allegations levelled at him were never proven, he'd had enough of the amateur game. Graham had turned professional, being unbeaten after eight fights, and Ingle applied for a professional license so that he could continue to train him. It developed into a tremendous partnership, and after winning the British light-middleweight title in 1981, Graham went on to become one of the most skilful British boxers of modern times.

Brendan has remained at St Thomas', which nowadays is his second home, and the club has gone from strength to strength over the years due largely to his efforts and the love of what he does. There are few men in boxing as energetic and enthusiastic as Brendan Ingle, and writer Tim Mo once described him as "a golden-hearted, rough-mannered, grey-haired ex-pug. A Dubliner with piercing blue eyes and an unstoppable tongue." His constant chat and instruction from the corner during contests has often got him into trouble with referees' and Board of Control officials. While there have been occasions when he has been ordered from the corner, his "offences" have been brought about by nothing more than over-enthusiasm.

The St Thomas' club has been visited by politicians, Lord Mayors, and top businessmen, as well as TV crews and countless numbers of pressmen. Ingle himself has risen in statute from a young Irish labourer to a man who, in 1980, was invited to attend a Cutlers Civic Hall function which was graced by the Prince of Wales. There have been plenty of other prestigious invitations as well.

Although Brendan is best known at present for his handling of Prince Nassem Hamed, who he took over as a small boy, he also has a current crop of fine prospects, and among other champions he has trained are Brian Anderson and Johnny Nelson. Amongst his hobbies is jazz music, and it was at a jazz club where he met his wife, Alma. Married in 1961, they have five grown up children, and Dominic and John assist their father with the training of the boxers and work in the corner.

Another man always prepared to help street kids who go into his gym is Nobby Nobbs, a Birmingham based trainer and manager. Many of the lads have no amateur experience, but Nobby never turns them away. If they show any talent and are prepared to work and learn, he will get them fights. With a stable of about 20 journeymen fighters, Nobbs is a promoters dream. He is trusted, and will provide opponents for any promoter. If a boxer drops out of a contest at short notice, Nobby is often the first man a matchmaker will contact. Good pro Pete Buckley, a former Midlands Area super-bantam and super-featherweight champion, has had more than 80 fights, whilst light-welterweight, Brian Coleman, has amassed more than 50 in just five years. It is commonplace for Nobbs' managed boxers to travel many miles to take a substitute job at a few hours notice.

Nobby has not been without his successes, with 15 Midland Area champions coming from his camp over the years. His lone British champion was Lloyd Hibbert who, in March 1987, won the title and that of the Commonwealth by outpointing Nick Wilshire at the Royal Albert Hall.

Although he never boxed, Nobbs joined forces with Dick Gwilliam in 1968 and they formed their own amateur club which they named "Rum Runner". Within three years they had produced three England internationals in Glen and Garfield McEwan, and Dick's son, Des. Garfield and Des represented England at the 1975 European Championships in Poland, with McEwan winning a bronze medal at heavyweight. When the McEwans moved into the professional ranks, Nobby took out a seconds' license and in 1977 he took out a manager's license to look after the affairs of Des Gwilliam, who went on to win the Midland Area light-welterweight title the following year.

Born in Birmingham, Nobby worked as a bouncer for many years, but now is devoted to boxing and handles the affairs of his fighters from home. He encourages all his stable to get what they can out of the sport, but to put plenty back as well. Consequently, a number of his lads currently hold seconds' licenses.

Wally Swift from Nottingham was a top class professional in his day. Between 1957 and 1969 he had 88 fights, winning 68, drawing three, and losing 17. He won the Midlands Area welterweight title by beating Ray Corbett at Birmingham in September 1959, but really sprang to notice three months later when he outpointed the brilliant South African, Willie Toweel.

In February 1960, Wally won the British welterweight title by outpointing Tommy Molloy and followed that victory with dazzling displays of boxing to beat former world champion, Virgil Akins, Emile Vlaemynck, Larry Baker, Assane Fakyh and Henri Cabelduc, all on points. In November of the same year, Wally lost his title to Brian Curvis, but, after beating Tony Smith in an eliminator, he met Curvis again in May 1961 for the British and Empire titles. Again the Welshman's skill won the day.

Wally was also a skilful boxer and most of his successes were on points. After a run of 11 consecutive wins he again outpointed Tony Smith in a final eliminator for the British welterweight title in October 1962 and just two weeks later he won the Midlands Area Middleweight title by beating Maxie Smith. Realising that his future lay at middleweight, Swift met Irishman, Mick Leahy, in December 1962 in a final eliminator for the British title. The result was a 12 rounds draw, but when they met again two months later, Leahy got the decision. Worse was to follow when, in his next fight, Wally lost his Midlands Area title to Teddy Haynes.

Determination got Wally back into championship contention and in May 1964 he beat Harry Scott in a final eliminator for the British middleweight title. His reward was a fight against old foe, Mick Leahy, in December . In front of his home crowd, Wally turned in his finest performance. His immaculate left hand, backed by a succession of solid rights to the body, taking him to victory against the aggressive champion. At the end he was a clear winner.

Wally held the title for only a year, and in November 1965 was stopped by the undefeated Johnny Pritchett, a badly cut left-eye partly contributed to his downfall. However, at the age of 29, he felt he still had plenty left.

After seven consecutive victories in 1966, including one over Al Sharpe in Belfast in a final eliminator for his old title, Wally met Pritchett again in February 1967. At the end of 15 gruelling, blood splattered rounds, although Pritchett got the decision by a narrow margin, thousands in the capacity crowd strongly disagreed with referee Wally Thom's decision and, for some minutes, the place was in uproar. Items including bottles were thrown towards the ring and only strong action from a posse of police prevented the ring from being invaded. Wally was convinced he had done enough to win, and let it be known that he had plenty left. He carried on for another couple of years, but lost most of the big ones. European title defeats by Sandro Mazzinghi in Milan (RSF 6), and Carlos Duran at Birmingham (Disq 10), were followed by a fifth round stoppage by Tom Bogs in Denmark.

In 1969, at the age of 33, Wally showed signs of coming again with wins over Bunny Sterling and Les McAteer. When he met McAteer in July 1969, the vacant British middleweight title was at stake, but, sadly, it was youth against age. At the end of 11 bitterly contested rounds, Wally was retired by his corner with a badly cut left-eye. Yet it had been a gallant effort by the veteran, and at the end it was very close. It was his last fight, but as his manager George Biddles said, "Wally has been a great pro and he went out fighting."

Wally was a rich man when he retired from the ring and set himself up in business with a chain of betting shops. Despite his business activities, he never lost interest in boxing, and for some years has put his skill to good use by training and managing Midlands based boxers.

Although many of his lads are good journeymen, he has produced three British champions, Roy Smith winning the cruiserweight title in 1987, son Wally, won the light-middleweight title in March 1991, and Del Bryan, the welterweight title after outpointing Kirkland Laing at the Royal Albert Hall the previous January.

Most of Wally's coaching these days is done at the Woollaton Grange Community Centre in Nottingham, although some of his lads come from as far afield as Stoke and Leicester. His boxers are in demand, not only in Britain, but in many other parts of the world, and this year alone, Wally has taken fighters to South Africa (twice), Finland (twice) and Denmark (twice). His only regret is the difficulty he has experienced in getting regular fights for his sons, Tony and Wally, both of whom are good professionals.

Bristol-based Chris Sanigar was one of the most exciting fighters in Britain during the late 1970s and early 1980s. When he retired from the ring in 1984, he had a record of 18 wins, 11 defeats and two draws, yet his sheer bravery and love of a fight surely cost him a more impressive record and a major title.

The height of Chris's career was on the night of 30 November 1981 when, in front of a capacity crowd at the Elephant & Castle, he battered the Southern Area light-welterweight title away from Sid Smith. They had previously met at the Albert Hall five months earlier, when Smith had won the vacant title on a third round stoppage. The return lived up to all expectations and was ranked as one of the most exciting domestic fights seen for years. Sanigar took a real belting in the second round, was floored for a count of six, and then pounded on the ropes looking destined for defeat. Somehow he survived and showed amazing reserves of courage and strength to fight back in the third. Sheer brute force swung the fight back his way as he smashed away remorselessly at Smith, completing the job with a knock-out in the fourth.

In April 1982, Chris was involved in another war when he defended his Area title against Sylvester Mittee. Again, he gave a gallant, blood spattered display, but the punch power of Mittee was the deciding factor and he was stopped in round nine.

Chris retired from the ring following a half point defeat by Rocky Kelly, after a tremendous fight at the Royal Albert Hall in February 1984 for the vacant Southern Area welterweight title. Fortunes swung back and forth in a fight that was among the best of the year.

In recent years, he has become highly respected as a trainer and manager, and has been responsible for bringing professional boxing back to the West Country. Amongst his fine stable of fighters are Western Area champions, Darren Dorrington, Dean Cooper, and Greg Upton, middleweight prospect, Glenn Catley, and former British and Commonwealth light-welterweight champion, Ross Hale.

One of the most talented boxers of the last few years to become a trainer must be Pat Cowdell. He began boxing when he was just nine years old and, as a member of the Warley Amateur Boxing Club in the West Midlands, he

had almost 300 contests. Pat was a tremendous amateur boxer and his honours list makes absorbing reading.

In the 1976 Olympics at Montreal, points victories over representatives from Poland, Puerto Rico, and the Philippines, took him into the bantamweight semi final, where he lost a questionable decision to the eventual gold medalist, Yong-Jo Gu of North Korea, his bronze medal being the only honour won by the British team.

Turning professional in 1977 under Ron Gray, Pat boxed in a final eliminator for the British featherweight title in only his tenth contest. He beat Les Pickett on points over 12 rounds and then met Dave Needham in September 1979 at Wolverhampton for the British title, losing a highly questionable decision which so outraged the fans that demonstrations raged for 15 minutes, despite promoter Ron Gray's appeals for calm. A rematch was ordered and this took place at the Royal Albert Hall and Pat won on points after a terrific fight. He was British champion in his 13th contest.

Successful defenses against Jimmy Flint and Needham won him a Lonsdale Belt in a then record time of 203 days . They were part of an unbeaten run of eight fights which led to a WBC featherweight title challenge against Salvatore Sanchez at Houston, Texas, in December 1981. Sanchez was regarded as the best pound for pound fighter of his time, but, in a wonderful fight, Pat came mighty close to beating him. His skill silenced the thousands of Mexican fans who expected Sanchez to win easily. Going into the last round there was nothing in it, but Pat was badly cut above both eyes and the injuries later required 20 stitches. His face was a mass of blood and he was floored in that final session. Sanchez got a majority verdict, but had the contest been over the present day distance of 12 rounds, Pat would have been champion of the world.

After such a gruelling battle, Cowdell could have been expected to go down hill from that point, but just three months later he won the European featherweight title by stopping Salvatore Melluzzi of Italy in ten rounds at Wembley. It turned out to be the first of a sequence of 11 winning contests, which included a European title defence against Sepp Iten in Switzerland (RSF 12), a victory over Jean-Marc Renard (PTS) to take the European super-

The former British champion, Pat Cowdell, looks to pass on his great experience   Pennie Bracey

featherweight title, Robert Castanon (RSF 5), in defence of that title, and Carlos Hernandez (PTS) also in defence of the European super-featherweight title.

Pat's next defeat was in October 1985, a shocking first round knockout at the hands of the great Azumah Nelson of Ghana. However, in April 1986, he won the British super-featherweight title by stopping John Doherty, but lost it the following month, following a devastating first round kayo by Najib Daho. Although Cowdell regained the title by stopping Daho in October 1987, the following May he came to the end of the road when he was stopped by Floyd Havard. Commonsense prevailed and one of Britain's most respected boxers hung up his gloves with a creditable professional record of 36 wins and just six defeats.

Since retirement, Pat has been involved in training and promoting and, together with Ron Gray, he has kept boxing alive in the Midlands for the last two years. He currently trains 15 boxers at his gym at Great Tindall Street in the centre of Birmingham, among them Malcolm Melvin, the All-Ireland and Midland Area light-welterweight champion, who, in 1995 pushed Ross Hale to a points decision in a challenge for the British and Commonwealth titles.

Although boxing takes up most of his time, Pat plays a lot of golf, is married with two sons aged 20 and 18, the eldest being at university studying to become a teacher, whilst the youngest is studying pharmacy.

In the north of England there are a number of good ex-fighters currently involved in training. The extremely popular George Bowes from West Hartlepool was a pro for 11 years, commencing in 1957. He retired with a record of 61 contests (44 wins, two draws and 15 defeats), but, amazingly, failed to win a British title. Three times he fought in final eliminators for the bantam and featherweight titles, and each time he was beaten. Yet he still had the ability to defeat men such as Jake Tuli, Frankie Jones, Young Martin, John Morrissey and Frankie Taylor. Now aged 60, George is still very enthusiastic about his training.

Howard Hayes currently trains fighters at The Prince of Wales pub at Doncaster, along with another ex-pro, Mick O'Neill, formerly of Collier Wood. Boxing for the Plant

George Bowes in the corner with one of his fighters
Pennie Bracey

Works Club, Hayes was a brilliant amateur. North East Counties Junior Champion in 1966, North-East Counties lightweight champion in 1967 and 1968, ABA lightweight champion in 1969, and Northern Counties lightweight champion in 1970. He was also an England international.

Howard turned professional in November 1970, going undefeated in his first 16 fights, before being stopped by Evan Armstrong when he challenged for the British featherweight title in April 1972. In his next contest, Howard beat Billy Waith in an eliminator for the title. Armstrong, who had meanwhile lost his title to Tommy Glencross, met Hayes in a final eliminator in November 1972. Again, Howard was stopped in the sixth round. He had just two more fights and retired from boxing with the respectable record of 18 wins, two defeats and a draw.

John Rushton, from Balby in Yorkshire, runs gyms at the Tom Hill Community Centre at Denaby and The Plough at Balby. The Plough, in fact, holds a place in the boxing history of the north of England because it was the regular training gym of Bruce Woodcock back in the late 1940s and early '50s. Empty for many years, surviving demolition because it was a listed building, Rushton re-opened it to train his fighters including Jonjo Irwin, the former British featherweight champion.

In his boxing days, John was an amateur with Elmfield House, Tom Hill Youth, and Plant Works Clubs, winning the Northern Counties light-heavyweight title in 1970. He boxed as a professional from 1970 until 1977, with a record of eight wins, 14 defeats and a draw, meeting good men like Les Avoth, Pat Brogan and Pat McCann. With a team of five, Rushton runs fitness programmes for men and women three nights a week at the Tom Hill Centre, and amongst his current stable of boxers are Area champions Chris Jickells and Trevor Meikle. He also holds a promoters' license.

The man largely responsible for the healthy state of boxing in Wales is Dai Gardiner, who boxed as an amateur with the Bargoed Club, before turning professional with Eddie Thomas in 1963. Sadly, after only four fights (three wins and a draw), Dai was forced to retire from the sport with a detached retina. He quickly turned to training and has been doing it ever since.

Dai gradually built up his stable and the late Johnny Owen was the first British champion he trained and managed. A number of Welsh champions have also been guided by him and he now has about 25 boxers training at his gym at Cwmcarn, including such talented men as Robbie Regan, Steve Robinson, Neil Swain, and young flyweight prospect, Harry Wood.

Boxing is Dai Gardiner's life and he is at the gym seven days a week. He holds manager, second, and promoter's licenses, and first started promoting local shows in the Welsh valleys back in 1976. Married with four daughters, and having four grandchildren, Dai likes football, supports local valley rugby, and closely follows the Welsh national side.

Considering that he has never boxed at any level, Dean Powell has achieved considerable success within the sport. In just 15 years he has graduated from being a labourer and boxing fan to a respected trainer and matchmaker.

Born at Tipton, Dean became interested in boxing when he was about 15 years old. Three years later he became involved with the Merryhill Amateur Club at Brierley Hill in the West Midlands, but strictly as a trainer, going to the club most evenings after work. Anxious to learn whatever he could, he also made frequent trips to the famous Royal Oak Gym at Canning Town in east London, where he closely watched Jimmy Tibbs working with the Terry Lawless stable, at the time the most successful in the country.

One day, the junior trainer at the Royal Oak was taken ill and a number of youngsters were left without anyone to assist them. Dean offered to help out and having carefully watched Tibbs working with the pads, copied his style. It was the start of a close relationship he has formed with the former West Ham professional fighter.

Dean worked with three amateur clubs in the Midlands before moving to London in 1988, and taking up lodgings at the Thomas A'Beckett pub in the Old Kent Road, which at the time was run by Gary Davidson. Dean was put in charge of the gym on the first floor, where he spent a lot of time with Joe Devitt an experienced trainer. In his career, Joe had worked with George Francis at the Wellington Gym at Highgate, training great fighters such as John Conteh, Bunny Sterling and Bunny Johnson. Dean learned a great deal from Joe, and is also grateful for the help he was given by Davidson.

As he got involved in the London fight scene, he got to know Jimmy Tibbs extremely well and in September 1989 was invited to work with Jimmy in the corner of Tony Wilson, who was fighting Steve McCarthy at Southampton in an eliminator for the British light-heavyweight title. The fight is best remembered for the invasion of the ring by Wilson's mother, who attacked McCarthy with her shoe. Dean continued to work with Tibbs until Jimmy re-joined the Frank Warren stable.

Powell remained close to Jimmy Tibbs, and when he suffered from serious personal problems it was Jimmy and his wife who helped him through it. Dean openly admits that it was the latter who brought him through the crisis and has been very involved in his success professionally.

Dean currently trains seven boxers, including Commonwealth cruiserweight champion, Chris Okoh, whom he also manages. He works five days a week at the Fitzroy Lodge and Peacock gyms and is also matchmaker for Frank Maloney and Panix Promotions.

Since becoming involved in professional boxing, Powell has worked with many good fighters, such as Lloyd Honeygan, Mark Kaylor, Mickey Hughes, Joe Kelly, Mickey Cantwell, Johnny Graham, Derek Angol and Chris Pyatt and, contrary to many peoples belief, he regards Lloyd Honeygan as the most disciplined of fighters, having run with him at 5 am in Regents Park. As a boxing fan, he watched Lloyd beat Don Curry in Atlantic City to become world champion in September 1986, before training him for his Commonwealth title defence against Kevin Adamson, which he won in six rounds.

Powell makes no secret of his respect for men like Terry Lawless and Dennie Mancini, for what they have put

into boxing, and for Tommy Gilmour for keeping the sport alive in Scotland.

Away from boxing, his interests include running and, in October this year, he intends competing in a full marathon at Manchester to raise funds for Robert Hay, a 22-year-old Scottish boxer who is suffering from Leukemia.

Music also forms a big part of Dean's relaxation and he has a large collection from the 1960s. And, as a big fan of The Small Faces, he is currently involved in organising a Small Faces convention due to take place in London by the end of 1996.

A devout christian, who regularly attends East Street Baptist Church at Walworth, he became involved in the Church in 1995 when he went through what he describes as the most difficult period of his life. Since then, things have got considerably better, both in his personal and professional life.

Jimmy Tibbs was ten years old when one rainy day at St Bonaventures Roman Catholic School at West Ham, his schoolmaster got out the boxing gloves and started matching the boys against each other. Now, 40 years later, Jimmy is recognised and respected as one of the finest trainers in boxing. Even as a boy, Jimmy was quite useful, and his Dad took him along to the West Ham Amateur Boxing Club where he began training under the watchful eye of Jackie Gubbins. Born at West Ham in 1946, Tibbs had his first contest at the age of 11, and in 1960 won the Schoolboy Junior "A" seven stone title. The following year, he was Junior "B" 8-10 champion and, in 1962, was losing finalist in the ABA Junior 9-7 "A" Class. Jimmy

Jimmy Tibbs (left), seen here in his ring days sparring with the one and only Muhammad Ali

British boxing could ill-afford to lose the late Phil Martin (right), seen here with one of his champions, Paul Burke

Harry Goodwin

also won Boys Club titles before moving to senior level where, in 1965, he won the London North-East divisional light-middleweight title. The same year he was outpointed by Mark Rowe in the London ABA semi-final. It was one of the best amateur contests seen in Britain for years and had the crowd on their feet throughout the three rounds. Brilliant boxing by both boys in the first two rounds was followed by a tremendous toe-to-toe punch up in the third. Tibbs and Rowe had met a few weeks earlier at a West Ham Club show, where the latter had been given a highly disputed decision in another contest which had the crowd on their feet. Jimmy's performance that night prompted *Boxing News* to comment. "Tibbs has put himself up amongst the best in the country at his weight."

In October, the same year, Jimmy was the only winner in the West Ham Club's 5-1 defeat in Paris, a brilliant display of vicious body punching bringing him victory over 22-years-old Michel Petit. Two weeks later, Jimmy triumphed over another Frenchman, as West Ham won the return match 4-3 on home ground, before being chosen to represent London against Helsinki, where he was a points winner in the 5-5 draw.

At the age of 19, Tibbs looked to have a promising ring career ahead of him, and it was no surprise when he turned professional under Terry Lawless early in 1966. Starting at light-heavyweight, he won all of his nine fights that year, six inside the distance. Amongst his high spots was a sparring session with Muhammad Ali, when the world champion was training at Shepherds Bush to meet Henry Cooper. Jimmy also worked with Johnny Pritchett as he trained for his British title defence against Wally Swift the following year.

Tibbs was a tremendous hitter, but suffered from a series of hand injuries, and during the next four years he had just 11 more fights, the last being in 1970. He left boxing with a professional record of 17 victories, (13 inside the distance), two defeats and a draw, Guinea Roger being the only man to stop him. As an amateur he had more than 70 fights, losing only six. Unfortunately, it was problems away from boxing which cut Jimmy's promising career short.

For much of his early life, Jimmy worked in the successful family scrap business in the East End of London, but in 1981 that too was taken away. After the Greater London Council decided to put a road right through the business premises, even though they were prepared to pay a large amount of compensation, Jimmy decided that he'd had enough of the scrap business and wanted another way of life. At the time he was working out at the Royal Oak, where Terry Lawless eventually gave him the opportunity to turn his hand to training. The first move was to assist Frank Black while Terry was away. It was just the beginning, and from 1981 until 1986, Jimmy worked at the Royal Oak with a stable which produced a steady stream of good champions.

In 1986, Tibbs made a successful move to the Frank Warren camp. At the time, ITV were running a series of Fight Night programmes made up entirely of Warren managed, Tibbs trained, fighters. Jimmy's partnership with Warren has been a good one because Frank has put many good boxers Jimmy's way, but never interfered with the training.

It is well known within boxing circles that Jimmy is a born-again Christian and it is a situation he will discuss openly without trying to force his beliefs upon others. Brought up as a Catholic, he admits to having wondered about religion without pursuing it. Then, in 1990, while sitting at home, he started thinking about his life. He pondered over his boxing career, the troubles in his younger days, and tried to justify everything he had done. Gradually he began to think about religion and became sufficiently curious to look for some answers.

Later in the year, Jimmy got to know a Christian who trained at an East End gym, although they did not discuss religion. Then, one day when Jimmy was being very heavy and vocal with one of his fighters, the man, who was passing by, put a hand on his shoulder and said, "Jimmy, you want the peace of Jesus." It was the start of Jimmy Tibbs becoming a bornagain Christian.

Six years later, the Christian beliefs of Tibbs are widely known. Interest is so great that he is frequently invited to talk about his life at business lunches and churches all over the country, being in such demand that he now uses the services of an agent to arrange his bookings. Public fascination has reached such levels that he has spoken in front of audiences as large as 1,000 and the *News of the World* ran a feature about his beliefs.

Married to Claudette, Jimmy is the proud father of Mark, himself a successful boxer until he retired in 1994, and Jimmy junior, a semi-professional footballer who currently plays for Dagenham & Redbridge. Jimmy and Claudette also have three grandchildren. Amongst his hobbies is freshwater fishing, but he also has a promising career as an actor. Having featured in leading roles in the boxing documentary "Fighters" (1993) and the drama, "Real Money" (1996), his natural ability and confidence will surely guarantee him more work in films.

Boxing, however, remains a very big part of Jimmy's life, and working with Frank Warren, he trains fighters most days of the week at the Peacock Gym at Canning Town and the Fitzroy Lodge at Walworth. Recognised in Britain as probably the best man at his job, his record supports it. At various stages of his career as a trainer he has worked with 20 British boxers who have won championships at all levels, Charlie Magri, Jim McDonnell, Ray Cattouse, Mark Kaylor, Lloyd Honeygan, Nick Wilshire, Horace Notice, Frank Bruno, Nigel Benn, Mo Hussain, Chris Pyatt, Gary Stretch, Pat Clinton, Terry Marsh, Tony Sibson, Glenn McCrory, Maurice Core, and Barry McGuigan. There are few trainers who could match the record of Jimmy Tibbs.

There are of course many other good men up and down the country who devote their time to training boxers. In paying tribute to the work done by the boxing trainers, one must never forget the contribution to the game by the late Phil Martin. After turning two derelict houses in the deprived area of Moss Side in Manchester into a fine gymnasium, Phil got many wild kids off the streets. His patience, skill and dedication producing champions, such as Paul Burke, Frank Grant, Carl Thompson and Maurice Core. He will always be remembered.

The future of boxing in Britain depends very much on men with the dedication of Phil Martin, Brendan Ingle, Jimmy Tibbs, and the others. Experienced professionals must be encouraged to stay in the game after they retire, for, without the knowledge that has been passed down through generations, the sport will not survive.

NOBLE ART PROMOTIONS LTD
GREG STEENE & BRUCE BAKER
INTERNATIONAL PROMOTERS, MANAGERS,
MATCHMAKERS AND AGENTS

LICENCED BY B.B.B. OF C.

BOXERS MANAGED BY GREG STEENE:

ANDY WRIGHT...................FORMER UNDEFEATED SOUTHERN AREA
SUPER-MIDDLEWEIGHT CHAMPION

HORACE FLEARY ....FORMER GERMAN INTERNATIONAL
SUPER-MIDDLEWEIGHT CHAMPION

R. F. MCKENZIE ....FORMER SOUTHERN AREA HEAVYWEIGHT
CHAMPION

BRIAN GENTRY ....LIGHTWEIGHT

DAVID BAPTISTE ...............WELTERWEIGHT

DARREN BLACKFORD .........MIDDLEWEIGHT

TRAINERS

CASEY MCCULLUM, TREVOR CATTOUSE, LLOYD WALFORD AND GERRY CONTEH (USA)

ANY UNATTACHED PROFESSIONALS OR SERIOUS AMATEURS SEEKING FIRST CLASS
TRAINING AND MANAGEMENT, PLEASE CONTACT THE NUMBER BELOW

Casey's Gym, The Park Tavern, Mitcham Lane, Streatham, London SW16
Telephone: 0181 769 4626   Fax: 0171 377 1769

Company Reg. No. 02840916

Home and Away with British Boxers During 1995-96

by John Jarrett

JULY

The major players in the super-middleweight division were in action this month with Nigel Benn and Henry Wharton taking centre stage and Chris Eubank and Sugar Boy Malinga filling minor roles down the bill. At the London Arena, WBC champion Benn stuck his title on the line for the eighth time and once again came home a winner, Italian Vincenzo Nardiello giving up in round eight. On the deck five times, only twice officially, the challenger complained about everything, but his only real beef was with Benn who was hitting him too hard!

In front of the hometown folks at York, big puncher Wharton faced another Italian in Mauro Galvano for the vacant European title. Out of the ring for six months, since he was comprehensively outboxed in an attempt on Eubank's WBO championship, Henry did what he does best, punch! In the fourth round, a cracking left hook ended Signor Galvano's interest in the proceedings, leaving King Henry the champion of Europe to the delight of the capacity crowd.

Bournemouth's Trevor Ambrose made Sugar Boy Malinga look very ordinary over eight rounds on the London Arena undercard, and the South African, who still claimed he was robbed against Benn in 1992, did nothing to justify his number one ranking in taking a points decision.

The Chris Eubank roadshow drew a 5,000 capacity crowd to the Whitley Bay Ice Rink and they enjoyed everything, right up to the first bell. After that there wasn't much to see as the outclassed and mismatched Spaniard, Jose Ignacio Barruetabena, folded in 55 seconds of round one!

At the Royal Albert Hall, Prince Nassem Hamed, another star performer who prefers to come into the ring over the ropes rather than through them, strutted his stuff and drew another stack of superlatives from an ever-growing army of admirers as he disposed of veteran Colombian, Juan Polo Perez, in two rounds. The former IBF super-flyweight champion never knew what hit him as he became Hamed's 19th straight victim, 17 inside the scheduled distance. "I'm blessed from God," announced the Yemeni from Yorkshire afterwards. "I'm the best and everyone knows that." If they don't they are gradually getting the message!

Down in Cardiff, however, they thought the Prince was all style and no substance. They had Steve Robinson, WBO featherweight champion of the world! He proved it once again when he stopped the Spanish challenger, Pedro Ferradas, in nine rounds to retain his title for the seventh time with a competent but unspectacular performance that did not impress ringsider Hamed, who told reporters, "He's the champ and he'll stay champ until I beat him!"

Staying with the little men, Belfast's Wayne McCullough travelled from his Las Vegas base all the way to Nagoya in Japan to snatch the WBC bantamweight crown from the head of Yasuei Yakushiji in a tremendous battle that saw the "Pocket Rocket" clinch a split decision, his 17th straight victory since taking a silver medal at the Barcelona Olympics. Trained to perfection by veteran Eddie Futch, the 25-year-old Irishman outboxed and out-punched the tough Japanese warrior to become champion.

Boxing history tells us that becoming a champion makes a man a better fighter overnight. Neil Swain certainly looked the part in defending his newly-won Commonwealth super-bantamweight title against Tony Falcone at Bristol, dumping the Chippenham challenger three times before John Coyle stopped it in the fifth to give the Welshman victory.

Paul "Scrap Iron" Ryan became the latest fighter to benefit from the proliferation of boxing titles when he won the inaugural WBO Inter-continental light-welterweight championship at the Royal Albert Hall by beating Oscar Palomino in a hectic scrap that saw the unbeaten Hackney lad climb off the canvas twice to stop the Spaniard in round eight.

Lennox Lewis is one of the best heavyweights in the world, but he may never get the chance to prove he is the very best, boxing politics being what they are. The former WBC champion marked time, toying with game but out-classed Australian, Justin Fortune, before turning up the heat to bring the referee's intervention in round four of their Dublin bout.

Commonwealth heavyweight champion, Henry Akinwande, kept his name in the frame with an easy stoppage of American import, Stanley Wright. Big Henry stands six-foot-seven in his socks but he started the fight looking up at his taller opponent. By the second round, however, Akinwande was looking down as Wright took his third count. When he got up this time the referee called it off.

A big punch brought victory for heavyweight Scott Welch, who rallied to floor Julius Francis four times for a tenth round stoppage at the Royal Albert Hall to win the Southern Area title and earn a crack at former conqueror, James Oyebola, for his British championship.

AUGUST

The mythical title of world's best fighter, pound-for-pound, was in dispute between Roy Jones and Pernell Whitaker, but at the Convention Centre in Atlantic City, it was Whitaker's WBC welterweight title that was in dispute with Glasgow's Gary Jacobs hoping to hit the jackpot. On paper his chances looked better with the roulette wheels and blackjack dealers in the casinos just along the Boardwalk. Whitaker was virtually undefeated in 37 professional contests since winning Olympic gold at Los Angeles in 1984, the single official defeat being a scandalous decision in favour of defending WBC lightweight champion, Jose Luis Ramirez, in Paris. Then there was the draw they fobbed him off with when it looked as though he had ended the long winning run of Julio Cesar Chavez. But if the odds were stacked against Jacobs as he faced Whitaker in this all-southpaw meeting you would not have known it from his performance. Bringing a 41-5 pro record to the ring, and the experience logged in winning Scottish, British, Commonwealth, European, and WBC International titles, the Scot mounted a stubborn if eventually losing battle against the slick skills of the American. The world champion sealed victory in the last round with two knockdowns and Gary was still on the deck when the final bell rang, beaten but unbowed.

With no boxing scheduled for mainland Britain this month, attention focused on Belfast where Ballymena favourite, Eamonn Loughran, put his WBO welterweight title on the line for the fourth time, against American Tony Ganarelli at the Ulster Hall. The man from Arizona was not expected to win this one, having had only three weeks notice of the fight and still on his honeymoon! Loughran did what he had to do and referee Roy Francis halted the one-sided affair in the sixth round, after Ganarelli had taken a count. It was another "so what!" fight for the champion.

On his previous visit to Belfast, Paul "Silky" Jones blasted out Damien Denny inside a round to win the WBO Inter-Continental light-middleweight title, but this time he had to go all the way to retain his crown against Danny Juma, as the tough Belfast-based Ghanaian gallantly contested the issue right down to the final bell. After compiling a 4-1-1 record as a heavyweight, Darren Corbett left about 30 pounds of puppy fat on the gym floor and made a successful debut as a cruiserweight, taking a six rounds decision from Midlands champion, Nigel Rafferty.

The luck of the Irish was certainly not with John Lowey as the Belfast exile came a cropper against classy American, Kennedy McKinney, in Chicago. The boys were contesting the vacant WBU super-bantamweight title and the former IBF champion had too much of everything for Lowey, who was fighting in his adopted hometown. Unbeaten in 21 bouts, the Irishman got away to a good start, but once the American turned up the heat there was only one man in it. Sadly, it was not John Lowey.

Yet another of the "Second Division" titles was on the line when WBF heavyweight champion, Johnny Nelson, made the long haul to Sao Paulo, Brazil, to fight local hot-shot, Adilson Rodriguez. The Sheffield enigma outboxed his man most of the way, but, at the final bell, surprise, surprise, the winner, and new champion, was Adilson Rodriguez!

Pat Barrett, former undefeated British and European light-welterweight champion, retired with a 37-4-1 record, aged 28.

SEPTEMBER

He had always been big enough, always been fit enough, always hit hard enough, and on a chilly Saturday night at long last he was good enough. At Wembley Stadium, 30,000 people jumped up and down, yelled, sang, cheered, and cried unashamedly as big Frank Bruno became the new WBC heavyweight champion of the world.

Jonjo Irwin displaying the featherweight Lonsdale Belt following his victory over Mike Deveney   Les Clark

He only just made it, hanging on grimly through the final round as defending champion, Oliver McCall, suddenly realised that his precious title was slipping from his grasp. The American hurled tremendous blows at Bruno in a desperate bid to cancel out Frank's points lead and the crowd willed the big fellow to hang on. And this time he did.

Against Bonecrusher Smith, against Tim Witherspoon, against Mike Tyson, and against Lennox Lewis, Bruno had come apart when stunned by a big shot, but not this night. Frank wrapped those big arms around McCall, held him, stopped him working, stopped him punching, hung on to the champion, and hung on to his lead until the final bell triggered off a night of emotional celebration, such as has rarely been seen in a British fight stadium. The place was awash with tears, some of them mingling with the sweat on the cheeks of the new champion. At the age of 33, after 13 years and 44 professional fights, Frank Bruno knew it had all been worth while!

One of the first into the ring to congratulate Bruno was his pal, fellow WBC world champion, Nigel Benn, who had defended his super-middleweight title for the ninth time earlier in the evening, knocking out Danny Ray Perez in seven rounds. The man from Albuquerque should have brought his six-guns with him, because that was what it would have taken to relieve Benn of his beloved title.

The Cinderella story of Steve Robinson ended with the entry of the handsome Prince Nassem Hamed into the Cardiff kingdom to a storm of booing and hissing from the assembled citizens. For the next half hour, poor Steve was bewitched, bothered, and bewildered by the wizardry of Prince Naz,who brought the curtain down in round eight and rode off with the glittering WB0 featherweight crown perched firmly on his dusky head, looking for new conquests. It was a virtuoso performance by Hamed and Steve Robinson may take some consolation from the fact that he lost his title to a fighter whose trainer, Brendan Ingle, said afterwards, "This guy's going to be as good, if not better, than Muhammad Ali. He's got something special . . . I've never seen anything like him!" And most everyone agrees that this is more than just some more blarney from a biased Irishman.

In Cork City, some 25,000 biased Irishmen gathered to cheer Steve Collins as he prepared to defend the WBO super-middleweight title he had taken from Chris Eubank six months previously. In handing Eubank his first defeat in 44 fights, Collins had upset the odds, yet he was still second choice with the experts for the rematch. But once again he rose to the occasion to confound Chris and the critics, hammering his way to victory and Eubank into retirement.

Mansfield Leisure Centre was the scene of an upset British title victory as Barnsley's Chris Saunders knocked defending welterweight champion, Del Bryan, to his knees in the final round to seal a dramatic points win. It was Bryan's fourth trip to the canvas in this all-southpaw battle and the knockdowns made the difference in a tremendous fight. The Yorkshireman, cut over both eyes, simply refused to be beaten again. He had already lost 16 fights. Enough, already!

Doncaster's Jonjo Irwin abandoned his fancy boxing to bring another British championship to Yorkshire, powering his way to victory over defending Scot, Mike Deveney, in a one-sided win to take the featherweight title.

In Cardiff in the rain, Nicky Piper made it third time lucky as he won the Commonwealth and WBO Inter-Continental light-heavyweight titles with a stunning ninth round knockout over Belfast's Noel Magee. The Irishman had upset Garry Delaney to become a champion and he looked on the way to victory over Piper until the bomb dropped.

Scot Dave Anderson had won 18 fights in a row, but he was found wanting as Michael Ayers retained his British lightweight crown with an emphatic victory at Basildon, Anderson retiring after seven rounds. His right hand was gone, but so was everything else as Ayers turned in a champion performance.

On paper, Croydon cruiserweight, Chris Okoh,was in over his head going against Francis Wanyama for the Commonwealth title at Bethnal Green's York Hall, but on canvas it was Okoh who looked like the champ, and in round eight he was, the referee stopping the fight. Another new Commonwealth champion was crowned when Justin Juuko, the Millwall-based Ugandan, punched out a decisive victory over the Canadian, Tony Pep, for the featherweight title in Cardiff.

A couple of those Inter-Continental titles were on the line with the vacant IBF light-middleweight crown being placed on the head of Yugoslav, Bahri Ahmeti, when a badly-cut left eye ended the challenge of Steve Foster in round four of their Wembley clash, while Mark Delaney outpunched Andy Flute to take the decision and the vacant WBO super-middleweight title in the West Hammer's 18th straight victory at Basildon.

OCTOBER

James Murray became a footnote in the annals of British championship boxing on Sunday 15 October when he was pronounced dead at Glasgow's Southern General Hospital. The little Scottish bantamweight deserved more than that. Two days earlier he had mounted a tremendous challenge on Drew Docherty's British title at the Hospitality Inn, putting the champion on the deck three times, with many at ringside thinking he only had to get through the final round to realise his dream.

Sadly, it was not to be. The 18th line on Drew Docherty's professional record reads . . . James Murray w rsc 12. When the gallant little warrior fell to the canvas in that 12th round, it was the first time he had been knocked down in his amateur and pro career. He never got up again! And the memory of James Murray's last heroic night inside the ring was stained forever by disgraceful scenes outside the ring as mindless thugs rampaged through the hall.

Two excellent results in foreign rings saw heavyweight Lennox Lewis and featherweight Billy Hardy bring home the bacon. Former WBC champion, Lewis, still chasing his old title, kept his place at the sharp end of the division with a fine display against Tommy Morrison in Atlantic City, taking Tommy apart in six rounds and decking him four times en-route to the winning post.

Battle-hardened veteran Hardy was up against it, challenging Mehdi Labdouni for the European title in France, but the Sunderland man had done his work in the gym and on the roads and he outfought the champion to hand him his first defeat in four-and-a-half years. Already Commonwealth champion, the 31-year-old Hardy is still hungry for a world title.

British super-bantamweight champion, Richie Wenton, was not so fortunate when he went after Vincenzo Belcastro's European title at San Benedetto Del Tronto, losing a unanimous decision over 12 gruelling rounds. The lad from Liverpool got away to a fine start and after six rounds Belcastro looked the worse for wear. But the champion finished like a train over the second half of the fight to hang on to his title.

Biggest is not always best, especially in boxing. British heavyweight champion, James Oyebola, tipped the scales at 16st 10lbs and stood 6ft 8½ins in his socks, but hometown boy, Scott Welch, cut him down to size in ten rounds to take the title, along with the vacant Commonwealth and WBO Inter-Continental championships, in a savage fight at Brighton.

Defending his WBO welterweight title for the fifth time, Eamonn Loughran failed to set Belfast's Ulster Hall alight as he took a lop-sided decision from Angel Beltre of the Dominican Republic. On the undercard, a more impressive winner was Adrian Dodson, who collected the vacant WBO Inter-Continental light-middleweight title with a fourth round stoppage of Canadian, Hughes Daigneault, to take his pro log to 13-0.

They both came to the ring in Telford with identical unbeaten 19-0 records so something had to go, barring a draw of course. At the final bell, local favourite Richie Woodhall still had his perfect record and, more importantly, still had his European middleweight title and his number one ranking for the WBC championship. Slovenian challenger, Zdravko Kostic, had provided a stubborn challenge over 12 rounds, but he was going home a loser, for the first time.

Scot Charlie Kane had won a Commonwealth gold

medal and boxed in the Olympics, but his nine pro wins did not warrant a British light-welterweight title shot and champion Ross Hale dismissed him in two rounds at Bristol.

Title action at the Royal Albert Hall saw Billy Schwer retain his Commonwealth lightweight title for the fourth time against Ditau Molefyane, the South African failing to beat the count in round eight after being knocked through the ropes. Billy's stablemate, Joe Calzaghe, also favoured the eighth round as he fulfilled his early promise when beating Stephen Wilson for the vacant British super-middleweight championship, but in winning his 14th fight (13 inside) the London-born Calzaghe needs more work before stepping up with the big lads.

WBO Inter-Continental light-middleweight champion, Paul "Silky" Jones, had an easy night out in Mayfair as he retained his title inside two rounds against ill-matched South African, Eric Spalding. Another fighter in over his head was Basingstoke's Dean Francis, who was found out against WBC International super-middleweight champion, Zafarou Ballogou, at Ipswich. With a mere nine fights behind him, Francis was no match for a tough champion and was pulled out by the referee in round ten.

At Cardiff, young Gareth Jordan brought a record of 12-0 (8 inside) to the ring and his supporters fully expected him to relieve Mervyn Bennett of his Welsh lightweight title. But they, and young Mr Jordan, received a shock as the 35-year-old veteran hammered his way to victory over ten gruelling rounds.

At home in Hove, Chris Eubank announced he was finished with boxing at the age of 29 after suffering back-to-back defeats to Irishman, Steve Collins, who relieved the Brighton enigma of his WBO super-middleweight title. The figures were good, 43-2-2, and so was the money, but now it was all over.

NOVEMBER

Baby Jake Matlala, the world's smallest professional fighter, was walking tall when he boarded the plane in Glasgow on his way home to South Africa after taking the WBO light-flyweight title from Paul Weir at the Kelvin Hall. The fight had ended amid confusion, with Weir cut over the right eye in the fifth round, the doctor saying he could go on, and the referee stopping it. Then followed an interminable delay before it was announced that Matlala, ahead on the scorecards, was the winner and new champion. Then the referee confessed that he had mis-understood the doctor, thinking he wanted the fight stopped. He said the cut was caused by an accidental head clash, although it appeared to most observers to have been caused by a right hand. At the time of the stoppage, Jake looked to be winning the fight, although that was an opinion to be voiced quietly as one cleared the city limits.

Dreams do come true! Salford's Steve Foster, pushing 35, and 15 years a pro, finally heard the man with the mike announce him as, "the winner, and new champion!" Steve's Viking army of supporters nearly took the roof off the Bowlers Arena at Manchester's Trafford Park at the end of

Despite fighting gamely, Billy Schwer lost his Commonwealth lightweight title to Ghana's David Tetteh (left)   Les Clark

his fight with tough German-based Yugoslav, Bahri Ahmeti, who lost for the first time in 25 fights. Foster had retired after four rounds with a cut eye in their previous fight, but this night he did not put a glove wrong.

Boxer turned slugger as British middleweight champion, Neville Brown, retained his title with a stunning fifth round knockout over Shaun Cummins at Derby, just down the road from his Burton hometown. Cut by the right eye after a clash of heads, Brown turned on the heat and it was the man they called " The Guvnor" who wilted first.

European and Commonwealth super-middleweight champion, Henry Wharton, has always had the power to dispense with the arithmetic as he demonstrated to the discomfort of Belfast southpaw, Sam Storey, when retaining his titles at Halifax. The end came in round four, courtesy of a left hook. After world title defeats against Eubank and Benn, the York favourite is hoping that one day it will be third time lucky.

It happened for Paul "Silky" Jones in another Yorkshire ring, as the Sheffield stylist climbed off the canvas in the first round to outbox Verno Phillips and take a majority verdict, along with the American's WB0 light-middleweight title, in a fine performance.

The pro career of Steve Collins peaked when he twice beat Chris Eubank to become WB0 super-middleweight champion, and he couldn't mount the same drive and motivation for his title defence against Cornelius Carr at the Point Depot. Collins took the decision, but there were times when Carr looked capable of winning with just a little more self-belief in his ability.

Frenchman, Redha Abbas, with a modest 10-2-1 pro log, and no punch to speak of, didn't figure to trouble Johnny Armour as the Chatham southpaw made the first defence of his European bantamweight title at the York Hall. Nor did he, as Johnny took his record to 20-0 with a fifth round knockout.

Ghana's tough David Tetteh ruined Billy Schwer's evening at the Goresbrook Leisure Centre, forcing the referee's intervention in the final round to grab Billy's Commonwealth lightweight crown and knock him out of a mandatory European title shot. Schwer was cut over and under his right eye, bruised, and under pressure when it was stopped 64 seconds into round 12, much to the disgust of the Luton man's supporters and manager, Mickey Duff.

Win some, lose some. Three weeks before the Schwer fight, Mr Duff saw his former British light-middleweight champion, Robert McCracken, take the vacant Commonwealth middleweight title with a decision over Canada's Fitzgerald Bruney at Dudley. It was the Brummie's 25th straight victory, but many observers thought it should have been his first defeat.

Former British and Commonwealth light-welterweight champion, Andy Holligan, exploded in the second round to demolish Darlington's Allan Hall in their final eliminator at Liverpool, and was looking forward to a rematch with Ross Hale for his old titles.

The fireworks display came to York Hall three days after Guy Fawkes Day and lasted only two minutes, 22 seconds. That was all it took for newly-crowned Common-

wealth cruiserweight champion, Chris Okoh, to dismiss the challenge of Paul Lawson. Four knockdowns convinced the referee it was time to call it a night.

In faraway Cape Town it wasn't fireworks, it was the real thing, as gun shots rang out during the eighth round of a contest between Warren Stowe and Simon Maseko. The Burnley middleweight took a dive, literally, out of the ring, seeking cover as a hold-up gang fired more shots, fatally wounding a box office cashier. "I thought they were shooting at me," said Warren, who now has a No-Contest decision on his record for the fight he will never forget.

In April 1987 I saw a coloured middleweight calling himself Slugger O'Toole beat Ian Bayliss at Newcastle. It was his pro debut and he told me his real name was Fidel Castro Smith. His father was a communist and his manager was an Irishman, Brendan Ingle, which explained the name business. Fighting under his own name, he put it in the book as British super-middleweight champion, winning 22 of his 30 fights. He retired this month.

DECEMBER

The crowd at York Hall in the east end of London expected fireworks and they were not too disappointed. WBO Inter-Continental welterweight champion, Paul "Scrap Iron" Ryan, had won 19 of his 21 fights inside the distance, while Bristol's defending British and Commonwealth champ, Ross Hale, had sent 18 of his 26 victims home early. It lasted just two minutes, 12 seconds, but it was the favourite Hale who finished on the floor as the Londoner powered to a stunning upset to become a triple champ!

Four months after winning the WBC bantamweight championship in Japan, Wayne McCullough made a triumphant return to Belfast where a packed King's Hall gave him a hero's welcome as he made his first title defence against Danish challenger, Johnny Bredahl. The former WBO super-flyweight champ made a bright start, using the ring well, and his light punches troubled the local favourite, but McCullough moved up a gear and gradually wore his man down for a stoppage in round eight. The "Pocket Rocket" returned to his Las Vegas home with his perfect record still intact... fights 18, won 18.

Paul Ingle (left) retained his unbeaten record with a comprehensive win over Bulgarian, Damir Nanev

Les Clark

Robbie Regan is no Jimmy Wilde, but in his seven year pro career he has reigned as champion of Wales, Britain, and Europe, falling painfully short of world class when beaten by WBO champ, Alberto Jiminez, last time out. Back after six months rest, Regan was in devastating form as he demolished limited Tunisian, Ferid Ben Jeddou, inside two rounds at Cardiff to win the IBF interim flyweight title. However, a few weeks later, champion Danny Romero, who had been on the shelf through injury, announced he was giving up the title, whereupon the IBF stated that Regan had in fact won only a final eliminator and would be considered in the shake-up to determine a new champion. Born in Denaby, but based in Doncaster, Jojo Irwin ruled as featherweight champion of Britain after beating Mike Deveney. He was still the champion after bringing his title to London and crushing the challenge of Elvis Parsley inside eight rounds. The man from Bloxwich gave it a brave try but he was outboxed and eventually outpunched by the confident Irwin.

Mixed fortunes for a couple of our big men in foreign rings. London's giant Henry Akinwande punched out a decision over Tony Tucker on the Tyson-Mathis card in Philadelphia, the 6' 7" former Commonwealth and European heavyweight champion turning in the finest victory of his unbeaten career against the one-time IBF titleholder.

Johnny Nelson knew he was on a hiding to nothing when he returned to Sao Paulo to fight Adilson Rodriguez again for the spurious WBF heavyweight title, but he did not think it would be as bad as it turned out. Nelson outboxed Rodriguez, rocked him in rounds eight and nine, and smashed him to the floor in the tenth. At the final bell, the local hero had a busted face with his nose swollen and one eye shut. He also had the decision! "What do you expect?" a ringsider told Johnny: "This is Brazil!"

Australian Kevin Kelly could sympathise with Nelson as he returned home minus his Commonwealth light-middleweight title, having being adjudged a points loser to former champion, Chris Pyatt, at Cardiff. Pyatt finished the fight bleeding from facial injuries and had been on the deck, but he came out with the decision and the title much to the disgust of Kevin Kelly.

Two months after winning the WBO Inter-Continental light-middleweight title in Belfast, Islington's Adrian Dodson returned to the King's Hall to put the crown on the line against moderate American, Craig Snyder. Dodson stopped his man inside eight rounds to keep his title and take his unbeaten record to 14-0.

North-east lads on the winning trail were former amateur stars, Allan Hall, Paul Ingle, and Peter Richardson. Hall, twice ABA champion from Darlington, kept his light-welterweight hopes alive with a sixth round stoppage of substitute Peter Till at Glasgow, while featherweight Ingle, Scarborough's former ABA flyweight champ, had a one-sided fifth round victory over Bulgarian, Damir Nanev, at York Hall to take his pro log to 10-0. Karl Taylor is a tough nut for anyone and Richardson did well to finish a clear winner over eight rounds against the man from the

Midlands at York Hall. Richardson, the Commonwealth Games champion from Middlesbrough, made it six out of six.

Winston Rupert Walters from Birmingham, was not a bad fighter really, put 20 pro fights in the book and won 14 of them, boxed fellows like Eubank and Benn, and was WBC International middleweight champion for a while. Using his stage name, Kid Milo, he pulled the gloves on again at Cardiff, after four-and-a-half years on the shelf, but found it hard going against Dean Francis and the referee pulled him out in round three after Francis had decked him for nine. It's a tough racket when you're a Kid and pushing 32.

Of course there was Shamus Casey, a month shy of his 36th birthday and celebrating already by winning two of his last three fights! Yes, WINNING! The Alfreton middleweight passed Dean Bramhald's 141-fight record by taking a decision from Wayne Shepherd at Morecambe just a couple of months after stopping Andy Neri. A popular pug, Shamus deserved a win now and then and he celebrated Christmas with a 28-109-5 record in the book. Just like Ol' Man River.

In another successful defence of the EBU middles title, Richie Woodhall (left) stopped fellow Brit, Derek Wormald

Les Clark

JANUARY

Ensley Bingham was 32 and had lost six of his 19 fights as a pro. He hadn't fought at all in 1994, and only twice in 1995, and now he was going to fight Gilbert Jackson for the vacant British light-middleweight championship and you figured maybe it was too late for the Manchester veteran. After losing his debut, Jackson had won 15 straight and he was bigger and he was younger, but was he better? In the ring at Bowlers, Trafford Park, the local favourite answered the question the best way possible – with his fists. One thing the old guy always had was his left hook. It was enough, and in the third round Jackson had enough, the referee stopping it to crown a new champ.

The left hook is also the favourite weapon of Henry Wharton, York's European super-middleweight champion. It had brought him victory in his last two title bouts and it looked to be enough to account for cagey Italian challenger, Vincenzo Nardiello, at Halifax. But in round three it was Wharton on the deck and it was round five before the Yorkshireman started to look like the champion. The scrappy Italian was cut on the right eyelid in the sixth, which brought the referee's intervention, but all talk of Henry having another go at a world title was put on the back burner.

European middleweight champion Richie Woodhall, already accepted as the number one challenger for the WBC title, marked time with a defence of his Continental crown against Derek Wormald at Birmingham, and the Rochdale southpaw gave him a stubborn argument before being stopped in the tenth round after his fifth trip to the canvas. The fight was overshadowed by the tragic death of Wormald's chief second, Peter McElhinney, who collapsed at the ringside and was pronounced dead at hospital. In his last fight, British bantamweight champion, Drew Docherty, had seen challenger James Murray carried from the ring to a hospital where he died two days later. Now, three months afterwards, Docherty was going back into the ring and you had to wonder, as did Tommy Gilmour, his manager. Gilmour did the right thing, putting Drew into a WBO title fight with the champion, Daniel Jimenez, rather than an easy tune-up bout, and the fight was in Mansfield, away from home turf. Jimenez had taken the title from Alfred Kotey, who had stopped Docherty inside four rounds, so the Scot had to keep his mind on the job in hand and he did so admirably, even if he didn't win the fight. It was a points victory for the Puerto Rican, but in a way it was also a victory for Drew Docherty.

After winning his 12 fights as a lightweight, P. J. Gallagher dropped down to super-featherweight to win the Southern Area title and put himself in line for a crack at the vacant British championship against Dave McHale. But when the Scot pulled out through injury, P. J. found himself in with unknown Ukranian, Rakhim Mingaleev, for the vacant WBC International bauble. At the final bell of a torrid 12 rounds at Bracknell, the London-based Irishman looked like the loser, face all busted up, and had been floored in the ninth, but he fought well enough to impress all three judges to come out a winner.

Born in Uganda, Justin Juuko turned pro in America before settling in London and winning the Commonwealth super-featherweight title. On a freezing cold night in Brighton he proved too hot for Jackie Gunguluza, stopping the South African in seven rounds to keep his title. After 12 rounds at the York Hall, Mark Delaney still had his WBO Inter-Continental super-middleweight title intact, along with his unbeaten 21-fight record, but his bout with Darron Griffiths would be best forgotten.

There was a time when Colin McMillan's silky skills evoked comparisons with those of Sugar Ray Leonard. He dazzled his way to a Lonsdale Belt as British featherweight champion, before assuming the Commonwealth mantle and then the WBO title, only a cut eye defeat spoiling his 24-fight record. Then it all went wrong as he lost the WBO crown to Ruben Palacio, albeit on a shoulder injury. That was in September 1992, and when he came back a year later, new WBO champ, Steve Robinson, shut him out over 12 rounds. Another long lay-off, then four wins followed by a further six months inactivity before he was again ready for the roped square. So anxious to please this time, he agreed to box for nothing, his purse going to the PBA and the King George Hospital. At the Broadway Theatre in Barking, Colin turned it on to stop Justin Murphy inside four rounds. He was back again, but on the eve of his 30th birthday his future seemed all behind him.

Reading heavyweight Keith Fletcher had his limitations cruelly exposed as he pitched his 8-3 pro log against the southpaw fists of South African Corrie Sanders at Brighton. The IBF's number four contender hardly broke a sweat as he knocked out Fletcher in the fourth round.

Sheffield cruiserweight, John Keeton, is known as Buster in the fight business, and little wonder. He had busted up 12 of his 13 victims in compiling a 13-7 record, but when he crossed gloves with Cesar Kazadi at the Grand Palace in Lille, it was Buster who was on the deck and looking booked for an early shower. However, he kept taking the fight to his man and in round three it paid off as Kazadi came apart.

FEBRUARY

It is not often we have a British champion who has lost as many fights as he has won, but Chris Saunders was a better fighter than his 16-16-1 record indicated and had already beaten his challenger inside four rounds, In fact, that was the only defeat on Kevin Lueshing's 17-fight record, so when he climbed into the ring at the York Hall he had two things on his mind, revenge and the championship. Kevin achieved both his goals inside three sensational rounds that saw Saunders on the deck five times and Lueshing himself floored twice before referee, Mickey Vann, called a halt. The new champ is charismatic and a kayo puncher, a combination guaranteed to bring a smile to the face of his promoter, Frank Warren.

In another sensational fight on the bill, Paul "Scrap Iron" Ryan, a one-round winner when smashing Ross Hale loose from his British and Commonwealth light-welterweight titles a couple of months previously, was himself blasted out in 2.18 of round one by substitute, Jonathan Thaxton. A tremendous left hand knocked Ryan

It was out with the old and in with the new, as Kevin Lueshing (left) lifted the British welterweight title from the head of the gutsy Chris Saunders   Les Clark

spark out and gave him his first defeat in 23 fights. As it was a non-title bout, Paul's three championships (he is also the WBO Inter-Continental champion) were safe, but for how long?

It was St Valentine's Day in Sunderland, but there was no love lost between veteran European featherweight champion, Billy Hardy, and his challenger, Michael Alldis, when they clashed at the Crowtree Leisure Centre. Billy's Commonwealth title was not on the line, but defeat would see him stripped of the bauble. As it turned out, however, neither title was in danger as the Crawley boy boxed a mainly negative fight, refusing to be drawn into a punch-up with the local hero, who pressed the action all the way and closed the range over the last few rounds to take the decision.

The Board of Control had to order up another Lonsdale Belt for the super-bantamweight division after the champion, Richie Wenton, retained his title for the second time to take the coveted trophy home for keeps. The Devon-based Liverpudlian boxed well to take the measure of brave Scot, Wilson Docherty, over 12 rounds at the Basildon Festival Hall.

Chris Okoh continued to improve by leaps and bounds as he added the vacant WBO Inter-Continental cruiserweight title to his Commonwealth championship with a crushing two rounds victory over previously undefeated Darren Westover at Bexleyheath. It was the Croydon man's

tenth straight win (6 inside) and afterwards, when he said, "I'm the premier cruiserweight in Britain," nobody laughed.

Welshman Neil Swain was laughing after he regained the Commonwealth super-bantamweight title, stripped from him following a non-title bout loss to Anton Gilmore in South Africa, with a comprehensive points decision over Australian, Nathan Sting, at Cardiff. Sting brought his 13-0 record all the way from Tasmania to contest the vacant title, but it proved a fruitless journey.

Yes, Dennis Andries was still fighting, aged 42, having another shot at Terry Dunstan, the fellow who relieved him of his British cruiserweight title with a somewhat controversial decision at Glasgow. This time, fighting in London at the York Hall, the younger man spelled out that it was time to go for the veteran former triple WBC champ.

Scunthorpe welterweight, Trevor Meikle, had only fought once in his hometown in 57 fights and nearly seven years. Now he was back to contest the vacant Central Area title against Hull rival, Kevin Toomey, and a sell-out crowd jammed the local Baths Hall to cheer Trevor to a well-earned victory after a gruelling scrap. Welcome home, champ!

The longest losing streak in British boxing ended at Weston super Mare, as Ernie Loveridge pinched a points decision over the Welshman, Carl Winstone, to notch his first win in four years, after 29 defeats! Hey, maybe God does pop into the Heavenly Gym now and then just to see how things are going.

At 31, Manchester heavyweight, Michael Murray, was still looking for another title shot, three years after being stopped in five forgettable rounds when meeting Herbie Hide for the vacant British championship. Murray took his record to 15-9 following a tight decision over Julius Francis at Bexleyheath. Francis thought he had won, but the other Francis in the ring, referee Roy, pointed to Murray. Another bout on the card saw Scarborough's former amateur star, Paul Ingle, notch his 11th victory with a tenth round stoppage over featherweight, Greg Upton. In a four-rounder, the "Cockney Kid", featherweight Benny May of Peckham, won his pro debut in good style as he outpointed Battersea rival, Abdul Mannon.

A knockout punch is a handy thing to have. At Liverpool, local favourite Shea Neary's unbeaten record looked in danger when he received a bad cut on his left eye in round two. However, he roared out for the third and flattened American import, Terry Southerland, with a terrific right hand to save the day, and that record! And, at Sunderland, middleweight hopeful, David Johnson, was on his way to victory when he walked on to a blasting left hook from Dave Radford and it was all over in round five. At Batley, it was a stunning left hook thrown by unbeaten Lincoln cruiserweight, Martin Langtry, that separated 60-fight veteran, Nigel Rafferty, from his Midlands Area title in round four.

In what was to say the least controversial, Mickey Cantwell (left) won both the decision and the vacant British flyweight title when outpointing Keith Knox

Les Clark

MARCH

This was definitely not a good month for promoter Frank Warren. Within a fortnight, Frank sent his top three box-office stars into action and two of them came home badly mauled. Frank Bruno limped back from Las Vegas after a dismal showing against Mike Tyson, who relieved the Briton of his WBC championship, and Nigel Benn, hoping to enjoy a black-and-white Saturday night at the Newcastle Arena, was beaten black-and-blue by South African veteran, Sugar Boy Malinga. Only Prince Naz saved the Warren team from a whitewash as he annihilated the abject Said Lawal with just three punches in Glasgow.

Big Frank Bruno landed in Las Vegas hoping to avenge a five rounds defeat by Iron Mike back in 1989. This time he was the champ, although Tyson was still taking all the money, reckoned to be between £15-20,000,000 with Bruno picking up £4,000,000. But, for Bruno, this was not about money, it was about beating THE MAN, finally getting the credibility he craved, and showing the Yanks he really was THE CHAMP! Sadly, it was not to be. Bruno came into the arena like a Christian being fed to hungry lions and was devoured with just two rounds and 50 seconds on the clock. Tyson was terrific, terrifying, and triumphant, as he reclaimed one of his old world titles, and all Bruno could do to try and escape Mike's savage fists was to hold blatantly until he was beaten down by the ropes in round three. The dream was ended.

The dream of Sugar Boy Malinga came true on Tyneside as he outboxed and outpunched Nigel Benn throughout 12 rounds to become WBC super-middleweight champion at the age of 36. The South African thought he was robbed against Benn in 1992, this time he made sure.

The 10,000 Geordies, who welcomed big-time boxing to their brand-new arena, gave Benn a tremendous reception as he entered the ring and stayed to cheer Malinga to victory. He had to come off the floor to do it, a right cross dumping him in round five, but he was rarely in trouble again and Benn looked a sorry sight at the final bell when, after announcing his retirement, he dropped to one knee and asked his fiancee to marry him. She said yes, so the night wasn't a total loss for Nigel. And a couple of days later he was talking of fighting again. Surprise, surprise!

Said Lawal, a small African gentleman living in Austria, was mugged on a Saturday night in Glasgow. He was hit with just three punches and finished up with a broken nose, but it was no more than he expected. Lawal is a featherweight boxer and he came to the Scottish Exhibition Centre to try and take the WBO championship from Prince Nassem Hamed. A tall order for a little man. As he makes his regal entrance these days, Hamed takes longer to get from the dressing room to the ring than he spends in actual combat. On this night he needed just three punches and 35 seconds to dispose of his hopelessly-outmatched challenger, almost a world record. The 8,000 crowd enjoyed the starter, but weren't impressed with the main course, which left a sour taste in the mouth.

The Irish had plenty to sing about as their two world champions came through successful defences. At Millstreet in Cork, WBO super-middleweight champion, Steve Collins, proved too strong for British middleweight title-holder, Neville Brown, whose brave challenge ended in round 11. Brown fought out of his skin, but found the Irishman just too powerful for him and was on the deck three times before the referee saw fit to end hostilities in the penultimate round.

In Dublin, Wayne McCullough had to pull out all the stops to hang on to his WBC bantamweight title against the fierce challenge of Jose Luis Bueno. The Mexican, a former WBC super-flyweight champ, was adjudged to have lost a split decision, but the champion looked the loser coming out of the ring, with his face bruised and swollen and his left eardrum perforated.

The decision of the British Boxing Board not to licence Joe Bugner for his fight with Scott Welch was fully vindicated as the 46-year-old former British, Commonwealth, and European heavyweight champion showed himself a washed-up veteran with nothing left to offer. The fight went on in Berlin, with Scott's WBO Inter-Continental title on the line, not his British and Commonwealth titles. In round six, Bugner was smashed to the canvas and when he got up the referee brought the fight to an end.

At the age of 32, Mickey Cantwell won the vacant British flyweight title with a disputed decision over Keith Knox in London. It was a cracking contest with Knox forcing the action all the way, while the London man stuck to his boxing, which ultimately paid off.

At Brent Town Hall, Glasgow's Gary Jacobs kept his welterweight title hopes alive with an easy five rounds knockout over Edwin Murillo, which gave him the IBF Inter-Continental title, British super-middleweight champ, Joe Calzaghe, warmed up for his title defence against Mark Delaney with a second round stoppage of American, Anthony Brooks, and British light-heavy champion, Crawford Ashley, poleaxed Dublin's Ray Kane inside two rounds.

Veteran Walworth featherweight, Joe Donohoe, spent more time on the canvas than he did standing up in his eight rounder with Gary Marston at Stoke. Would you believe 25 trips to the floor? It's true! Just for the record, Marston won on points.

APRIL

Seven months after Steve Robinson lost his WBO featherweight title to Prince Naz, little Robbie Regan put Wales back on the gold standard when he hammered the WBO bantamweight crown loose from the swarthy brow of Puerto Rican, Daniel Jimenez, on a crazy night in Cardiff. The fiery Welshman had reigned as Welsh, British, European, and IBF Interim flyweight champion, but had been forced to retire after nine painful rounds against Alberto Jimenez for the WBO title.

With no form at bantamweight, Regan was lucky to be given a crack at the title, but he grabbed it with both fists, coming out with a unanimous decision after 12 gruelling rounds, sealing his victory with a knockdown in round eight. Jimenez, no relation to Alberto, had beaten Duke McKenzie, Alfred Kotey, and Drew Docherty, on previous visits to the UK and must have viewed Regan as a safe defence. He knows better now!

Scotland's mighty mite, Paul Weir, found it tough going at Liverpool when he tried to reclaim the WBO light-flyweight title from Baby Jake Matlala, who had beaten him on a technical decision following a cut eye in Glasgow. This time there was no room for argument as the South African ignored Weir's best punches to grind him down inside ten rounds. Whoever coined the phrase, "There's good stuff in little bundles" must have been thinking of Baby Jake, truly a pocket dynamo!

The battle of unbeaten super-middles saw Joe Calzaghe stop Mark Delaney in defence of his British title

Les Clark

It was a bad night for Ireland, as well as Scotland, as Eamonn Loughran crashed to a shock defeat against Jose Luis Lopez. It was all over in 51 seconds and when the smoke cleared the Mexican was the new WBO welterweight champion. Making the sixth defence of his title, Loughran never got started and was down three times from hard, accurate punches for an automatic kayo.

In a tremendous action thriller at the Crystal Palace, P. J. Gallagher outlasted the brave Scot, Dave McHale, to add the vacant British super-featherweight championship to his WBC International title. The Glasgow fighter was stopped in round ten when challenging Floyd Havard for the same title in December 1994 and when the Welshman relinquished the title, Dave had hoped to go one better against the Manchester-born Gallagher. He gave it a helluva try but it just was not enough. Promoter-manager, Frank Maloney, called P. J. "the most exciting fighter in Britain," and on this night nobody argued.

At Wythenshawe, Ensley Bingham retained his British light-middleweight championship against Gary Logan and told reporters that, at 32, "I'm getting better every time I step into the ring." The challenger from Croydon had won 28 of 32 fights, half inside the distance, but he could not take the champion's punches and had been down twice when it was stopped in the sixth.

At the York Hall in Bethnal Green, Robert McCracken took his unbeaten run to 26 and retained his newly-won Commonwealth middleweight title when Paul Busby was retired by his corner after seven painful rounds. British super-middleweight champion, Joe Calzaghe, had no trouble hanging on to his title when stopping Mark Delaney inside five rounds at Brentwood for his 17th pro win, 16 inside. The West Hammer was no mean puncher himself, with 17 of his 21 wins via the short route, but the 24-year-old Welsh southpaw had him bloodied and on the deck four times before it was called off.

Boxing returned to the Glasgow hotel where James Murray fought his last tragic fight and a minute's silence was observed in his memory. Top of the bill was a belter of a scrap, with the skill of Brian Carr overcoming the experience of former British champion, Mike Deveney, to take the decision and the Scottish featherweight title.

The Northern Area featherweight title was on the line for the first time since 1951 as the local favourite, Colin Innes, clashed with Sunderland rival, Chip O'Neill, at Newcastle. Previously, the lads had fought a draw and the latter had taken the points, but this time Innes would not be denied and O'Neill's courageous effort ended in the ninth round with the referee stopping the fight.

On the comeback trail were former champions, Ross Hale, Daren Fifield, Carl Thompson, and Paul Burke. Hale, the former British and Commonwealth light-welterweight champion, was out of luck as a fourth round clash of heads brought a summary end to his fight with Paul Denton at Cardiff just when it looked like he was getting on top. However, former British and European cruiserweight champ, Thompson, was fully recovered from the shoulder injury that ended his WBO title challenge against Ralf Rocchigiani as he showed when beating Albert Call in four rounds at Wythenshawe, while Burke, the former British and Commonwealth lightweight champion now boxing at light-welter, took a points decision over Peter Till, and Fifield had a few rough moments with Shaun Norman before taking a six rounds verdict at Crystal Palace.

Woolwich heavyweight, Julius Francis, had more trouble getting to the Arts and Leisure Centre in Stevenage than he did with Damien Caesar in their clash for the vacant Southern Area title. Julius missed his turn-off on the M25, but he did not miss Caesar when he finally climbed into the ring, a big right hand poleaxing the Stepney man in just 46 seconds!

After 30 years, the Midlands Sporting Club at Solihull closed its doors with a six-twos featherweight bout that saw Steve Conway outpoint Ervine Blake in the final contest. In the main event Gary Marston scored a stirring victory over Welsh veteran, Miguel Matthews. It was the end of an era.

MAY

Lennox Lewis won two decisions in America in four days to stay on track for a summit meeting with Mike Tyson. In the ring at Madison Square Garden, Britain's former WBC champion won a majority decision after ten gruelling rounds with Ray Mercer, and four days later the New Jersey Supreme Court voted unanimously to uphold

Colin McMillan (right) and Jonjo Irwin gave it everything in a fight where the latter lost his British feathers title

Les Clark

an earlier decision that Tyson's next fight must be against Lewis. The court ruling delighted manager Frank Maloney and the fight in the Garden pleased Lewis' trainer, Emanuel Steward. "I always said Ray Mercer would be tougher than Tyson," Steward told reporters. "Tyson would get knocked out in two rounds, but Mercer could take that punishment." Mercer not only took it, he handed it out in sufficient quantities to make it a close call on the scorecards and convince a lot of people he had won the fight. He raised lumps and bumps on the Briton's handsome face, but Lewis was sharper, punched harder, and deserved his 29th win in 30 professional contests. But regardless of the court ruling, Lennox Lewis knows that he will fight Tyson only when Mr Tyson and Mr King are ready.

Colin McMillan regained the British featherweight championship when he outpointed Jonjo Irwin in a cracking contest at Dagenham, but the fight took so much out of him he had to be taken to hospital afterwards where he was found to be suffering from exhaustion and dehydration. With all due respect to Irwin, and the splendid defence he made in the ring, albeit a losing one, the 30-year-old McMillan's dream of challenging Prince Nassem Hamed for his old WBO championship must be regarded as nothing more than a dream.

Fight number 13 on Terry Dunstan's pro record proved unlucky for his challenger, John "Buster" Keeton. Making the second defence of his British cruiserweight title, Dunstan smashed aside the Sheffield man in just 44 seconds of round one at York Hall to take the Lonsdale Belt home to keep. It was almost the quickest victory in British championship annals, only Dave Charnley's 40-second slaughter of Darkie Hughes in 1961 beating it to the punch.

Another British champion who doesn't waste time is super-middleweight, Joe Calzaghe, who racked up another two wins inside 11 days to take his score to 19-0, 18 inside schedule. Just a couple of weeks after retaining his title against Mark Delaney, the Welsh southpaw forced Warren Stowe to retire after two rounds at Dagenham, then moved on to Cardiff where American Pat Lawlor lost interest in the proceedings halfway through the second round. It is obviously time for Joe to step out in better company.

Billy Schwer, the former British and Commonwealth lightweight champion and IBF title challenger, took another step back to the top as he outboxed and outpunched the tough Welshman, Gareth Jordan, at Dunstable. Billy didn't put a glove wrong, forcing a third round stoppage over a game but overmatched opponent, to take his record to 31-3 with 26 inside the distance.

Former Olympian, Adrian Dodson, failed to impress in stopping substitute John Bosco in seven rounds to retain his WBO Inter-Continental light-middleweight title at Dagenham, although he claimed to have damaged his left hand in the third round. Dodson took his unbeaten run to 15, 12 coming early.

Three Midlands Area titles went on the block inside ten days. At Cleethorpes, Alfreton's Richard O'Brien took the vacant welterweight crown after a tough ten rounds with Rick North of Grimsby, who did well to come back from a first round knockdown. Having failed at British title level against Ross Hale, light-welterweight, Malcolm Melvin, dropped down a class to retain his Area championship with a decision over tough guy, Karl Taylor, at Edgbaston, while, at Lincoln, local favourite, Martin Langtry, took another step towards national honours and sent his fans home happy as he retained his cruiserweight title with a sixth round stoppage over Chris Woollas, who was down twice from Langtry's right hand. It was Martin's 12th straight win in the money ranks.

Former British welterweight champion, Del Bryan, travelled to Cape Town for a WBO light-middleweight title eliminator with Nika Kumalo, but was always playing second fiddle to the local, losing a unanimous decision. A trip to Copenhagen for Peter Harris, saw the former British featherweight champion concede half-a-stone and a points verdict to Jimmy Bredahl, the former WBO super-featherweight titleholder and there were mixed fortunes for a couple of Welsh wanderers who landed in St Petersburg, Russia. Contesting the WBC International welterweight championship, Michael Smyth smashed Maxim Nesterenko to the canvas in the fifth, but the Russian got up and promptly dropped Smyth and the referee stopped the fight as the bell rang. However, featherweight Gareth Lawrence salvaged something when he outboxed Rusian Smolenkov in a six-rounder to make the score Russia 1-Wales 1.

Denied a licence by the British Board and out of the ring three years, former British and Commonwealth cruiserweight champion, Derek Angol, turned up in France with an Austrian licence to hammer Cesar Kazadi to a three rounds stoppage at Epernay. Promoter Barry Hearn set up his stall in Belfast with a five-fight card topped by former Commonwealth Games champion, Neil Sinclair, who took his pro log to 7-1 with a second round stoppage of Prince Kasi Kaihau at the Ulster Hall.

JUNE

There was a shock for Naz in Newcastle when the Yorkshire Yemeni faced the mandatory challenger, Daniel Alicea, at the Arena. The Puerto Rican hoped to use his height and reach advantages to prise the WBO feather-

P. J. Gallagher (right) successfully defended his British super-featherweight title against Charles Shepherd, but it was mighty close　　　　　　　　　　Les Clark

weight crown loose from Hamed's grasp and almost succeeded in a sensational opening round. Alicea landed three rights to Nassem's head and the third one sent him tumbling backwards to the canvas for the first time in his 22-fight professional career. Naz was back on his feet almost immediately, more embarrassed than hurt, and finished it in the second. A heavy right to the head slammed Alicea to the canvas and he did well to get up. He tried to fight back, but was caught again with a thudding right-left hook combination and it was all over. Another win for the Prince and, hopefully, a lesson learned.

Definitely the fight of the month, and a hot candidate for fight of the year, was P. J. Gallagher's first defence of his British super-featherweight title against chunky challenger, Charles Shepherd, at Erith in Kent. The champion claimed his 17th straight victory by half a point, but referee John Coyle's arithmetic was almost rendered academic in the final round, when the Carlisle man sent Gallagher crashing to the canvas with a screaming right to the head. P. J. was up at eight to scramble through to the bell, and victory. But as he said afterwards, "I can't keep having fights like this!"

Henry Akinwande has always been big. At 6' 7" in his socks, and hitting the scales around 16½ stones, they do not come much bigger, even in this day and age. But Henry was never big where it counted, at the box office and with the sultans of the satellite. So he took the age-old advice, go west young man! And you cannot get much further west than Indio in California where, at the Fantasy Springs Casino, big Henry hit the jackpot. Facing Jeremy Williams for the vacant WBO title, Akinwande knocked the American out in round three to keep his unbeaten record (30-0-1) and put himself among the heavyweight hierarchy.

Unsung hero, Billy Hardy, did it again when he journeyed to San Remo to confirm his position as featherweight champion of Europe, turning back the mandatory challenge of the awkward Italian, Stefano Zoff, with a unanimous decision and keeping alive his dream of fighting Nassem

Hamed in front of his Sunderland supporters for the world title. The defeat of Alicea by Hamed moved Hardy up into the number one spot, so the dream may come true.

The dream became a nightmare for Gary Jacobs in the French town of Gravelines, where the Glasgow southpaw was trying to regain the European welterweight title he held two years previously. After six rounds, Gary was ahead and champion Patrick Charpentier was bleeding heavily from a cut left eyebrow. But, in the seventh, Jacobs was caught with a big right to the head and Charpentier crashed in blows in a desperate bid to turn the fight his way. The Scot suddenly came apart and after two knockdowns the referee called it off.

Liverpool was always a good fight town and with talented youngsters like Peter Culshaw emerging, it continues the tradition. The 23-year-old flyweight, with only ten pro fights behind him, zoomed into the fistic firmament with a stunning three rounds demolition job on South African veteran, Danny Ward, at Stevenage to become Commonwealth champion.

It all came right for Olympic gold medallist, Michael Carruth, as the Dublin southpaw outpunched former British welterweight champion, Chris Saunders, for a tenth round stoppage at Mansfield. Top of the bill that night saw Jonathan Thaxton confirm his reputation as a devastating puncher, when he took out Mark Elliot in the fifth to win the vacant IBF Inter-Continental light-welterweight title. But the Norwich southpaw had to get off the deck to win this one against the Walsall man, a third-choice opponent who came in on 24 hours notice

Commonwealth super-middleweight champion, Henry Wharton, had a good workout in front of the hometown folks at York, when he took a ten rounds decision from tough Frenchman, Stephane Nizard and, in Glasgow, local favourite, Paul Weir, got back on the winning trail with an easy win over Louis Veitch, a crippling left to the body knocking the fight out of the Blackpool man after just 1.47 of round one.

On the big Newcastle show, British champions, Scott Welch and Kevin Lueshing, made short work of their respective opponents. Heavyweight Welch needed a mere 80 seconds to send the American, Mike Sedillo, off to an early shower, while welterweight boss, Lueshing, sunk his Northern Area counterpart, Paul King, in round two with a wicked body shot.

Out for 15 months, former triple champ, Duke McKenzie, did not get a chance to work the kinks out in preparation for a non-title crack at WBC bantamweight champ, Wayne McCullough, in Denver. At Mansfield, Duke sent Elvis Parsley into retirement after just 2.41 of the opening round, but will have his hands full against the unbeaten Irishman.

Have gloves, will travel. Alfreton's veteran campaigner, Shamus Casey, did not win his 150th professional contest against Joe Townsley at Glasgow's St Andrews Sporting Club, the latter taking the six rounds decision, but Casey took home an engraved silver salver, presented by club members as a token of appreciation for his contribution to boxing. Nice one lads!

Facts and Figures, 1995-96

There were 685 British-based boxers who were active between 1 July 1995 and 30 June 1996, spread over 223 promotions held in Britain (not including Eire) during the same period. The above figure comprised 538 boxers already holding licenses or having been licensed previously, four foreign-born boxers who started their careers elsewhere, and 143 new professionals, an increase of 16 on the previous season.

Unbeaten during season (minimum qualification: 6 contests): 11: Jason Matthews. 9: Alan Bosworth (1 draw). 8: Joe Calzaghe. 7: Glenn Catley, Robin Reid, Peter Richardson, Harry Woods (2 draws). 6: Michael Brodie, Scott Dixon, Colin Dunne, P. J. Gallagher, Paul Griffin, Dean Pithie (1 draw), Ryan Rhodes, Steve Roberts, Neil Sinclair, Clinton Woods.

Longest unbeaten sequence (minimum qualification: 10 Contests): 31: Henry Akinwande. 27: Robert McCracken. 22: Prince Nassem Hamed. 21: Justin Juuko (1 draw), Robin Reid (1 draw), Richie Woodhall. 20: John Armour. 19: Joe Calzaghe, Colin Dunne, Willie Quinn. 17: P. J. Gallagher, Kevin McBride (1 draw), Bruce Scott. 16: Shea Neary. 15: Michael Brodie, Adrian Dodson. 14: Barry Jones, Nicky Thurbin. 13: Tanveer Ahmed (1 draw), Terry Dunstan, Wayne Llewelyn, Robert Norton (1 draw), Mark Prince, Gary Thornhill (1 draw). 12: Glenn Catley, Howard Eastman, Paul Ingle, Martin Langtry, Clinton Woods. 11: Steve Collins, Peter Culshaw (1 draw), Chris Okoh, Jason Matthews, Derek Roche. 10: Mark Baker, Fran Harding (1 draw), Peter Richardson, David Starie.

Most wins during season (minimum qualification: 6 contests): 11: Jason Matthews. 8: Alan Bosworth, Joe Calzaghe. 7: Anthony Campbell, Glenn Catley, Robin Reid, Peter Richardson. 6: Jason Blanche, Michael Brodie, Garry Burrell, Scott Dixon, Colin Dunne, P. J. Gallagher, Paul Griffin, Lee Murtagh, Ryan Rhodes, George Richards, Steve Roberts, Neil Sinclair, Clinton Woods.

Most contests during season (minimum qualification: 10): 20: Graham McGrath. 18: Ernie Loveridge. 17: Brian Coleman. 14: Mark Dawson. 13: Kid McAuley, Michael Pinnock, John Smith. 12: Pete Buckley, Shamus Casey, Miguel Matthews. 11: Tony Booth, Anthony Campbell, John T. Kelly, Chris Lyons, Jason Matthews. 10: John Duckworth, Robert Grubb, Chris Jickells, Martin Jolley, Ram Singh, Gary Williams.

Most contests during career (minimum qualification: 50): 150: Shamus Casey. 112: Des Gargano. 109: Paul Murray. 92: Miguel Matthews. 84: Pete Buckley. 83: John Smith. 66: Steve Pollard. 65: Graham McGrath. 64: Dennis Andries. 62: Nigel Rafferty. 61: Ernie Loveridge. 60: Tony Booth. 59: Tony Foster, Trevor Meikle. 55: Steve Osborne. 54: Brian Coleman. 52: Ray Newby, Peter Till. 51: Chris Clarkson, Phil Lashley. 50: Spencer Alton, Gary Jacobs, Rick North, Paul Wesley.

Diary of British Boxing Tournaments, 1995-96

Tournaments are listed by date, town, venue, and promoter, and cover the period 1 July 1995 - 30 June 1996

Code: SC = Sporting Club

Date	Town	Venue	Promoters
01.07.95	Kensington	Albert Hall	Warren
06.07.95	Hull	Ennerdale Leisure Centre	Gray
07.07.95	Cardiff	Ice Rink	Warren
08.07.95	York	Barbican Centre	National Promotions
17.07.95	Mayfair	Grosvenor House	Matchroom
22.07.95	Millwall	London Arena	Warren
28.07.95	Bristol	Whitchurch Leisure Centre	Warren
28.07.95	Epworth	Leisure Centre	Rushton
29.07.95	Whitley Bay	Ice Rink	Matchroom
26.08.95	Belfast	Ulster Hall	Matchroom
01.09.95	Wolverhampton	Civic Hall	National Promotions
02.09.95	Wembley	The Stadium	Warren
06.09.95	Stoke	Moat House Hotel	Brogan
08.09.95	Liverpool	Everton Park Sports Centre	Hyland
14.09.95	Battersea	Town Hall	Panix
15.09.95	Mansfield	Leisure Centre	Warren
15.09.95	Glasgow	Hospitality Inn	Morrison
15.09.95	Darlington	Dolphin Centre	Sportsman Promotions
18.09.95	Glasgow	Forte Crest Hotel	St Andrew's SC
20.09.95	Ystrad	Leisure Centre	Gardiner
20.09.95	Potters Bar	Furzefield Leisure Centre	Matchroom
20.09.95	Plymouth	New Continental Hotel	Adair
21.09.95	Sheffield	Hillsborough Leisure Centre	Hobson
21.09.95	Battersea	Town Hall	Panix
22.09.95	Hull	City Hall	Billany
25.09.95	Bradford	Norfolk Gardens Hotel	Yorkshire Executive SC
25.09.95	Cleethorpes	Winter Gardens	Dalton
27.09.95	Bethnal Green	York Hall	National Promotions
28.09.95	Sunderland	Crowtree Leisure Centre	Winning Combination
29.09.95	Liverpool	Everton Park Sports Centre	Vaughan
29.09.95	Bethnal Green	York Hall	Panix
29.09.95	Hartlepool	Borough Hall	Robinson
29.09.95	Bloomsbury	Royal National Hotel	Matthews
30.09.95	Basildon	Festival Hall	Matchroom
30.09.95	Cardiff	Rugby Club	Warren
02.10.95	Birmingham	Albany Hotel	Cowdell
02.10.95	Mayfair	Grosvenor House	Matchroom
05.10.95	Glasgow	Forte Crest Hotel	St Andrew's SC
05.10.95	Hull	Royal Hotel	Hull & District SC
05.10.95	Queensferry	Styles Night Club	Davies
07.10.95	Belfast	Ulster Hall	Matchroom
09.10.95	Manchester	Piccadilly Hotel	Trickett
11.10.95	Stoke	Trentham Gardens	North Staffs SC
11.10.95	Solihull	Conference Centre	Midland SC
13.10.95	Glasgow	Hospitality Inn	Morrison/Warren
16.10.95	Mayfair	Marriott Hotel	National Promotions
17.10.95	Wolverhampton	Park Hall Hotel	Wolverhampton SC
18.10.95	Batley	Frontier Club	UK Pro Box Promotions
20.10.95	Mansfield	Leisure Centre	Ashton
20.10.95	Ipswich	Corn Exchange	Panix
21.10.95	Bethnal Green	York Hall	Warren
23.10.95	Glasgow	Forte Crest Hotel	St Andrew's SC

DIARY OF BRITISH BOXING TOURNAMENTS, 1995-96

Date	Town	Venue	Promoters
23.10.95	Leicester	Leicester City FC	Griffin
24.10.95	Southwark	Elephant & Castle Leisure Centre	Panix
25.10.95	Telford	Ice Rink	National Promotions
25.10.95	Cardiff	Star Leisure Centre	Gardiner
25.10.95	Stoke	Moat House Hotel	Brogan
26.10.95	Birmingham	Albany Hotel	Cowdell
27.10.95	Brighton	Metropole Hotel	Warren
28.10.95	Kensington	Albert Hall	National Promotions
28.10.95	Bristol	Whitchurch Leisure Centre	Warren
29.10.95	Shaw	Tara Sports & Leisure Centre	Tara Promotions
30.10.95	Bradford	Norfolk Gardens Hotel	Yorkshire Executive SC
30.10.95	Heathrow	Park Hotel	Holland
02.11.95	Houghton le Spring	McEwans' Indoor Centre	Winning Combination
02.11.95	Mayfair	Hilton Hotel	Nordoff Robbins Charity
03.11.95	Dudley	Town Hall	National Promotions
04.11.95	Liverpool	Everton Park Sports Centre	Vaughan
08.11.95	Walsall	Saddlers' Club	Gray
08.11.95	Scunthorpe	Baths Hall	Rushton
08.11.95	Bethnal Green	York Hall	Panix
10.11.95	Derby	Moorways Leisure Centre	Warren
10.11.95	Bristol	Marriott Hotel	Sanigar
11.11.95	Halifax	North Bridge Sports Centre	National Promotions
13.11.95	Barnstaple	Barnstaple Hotel	Adair
14.11.95	Yarm	Tall Trees Hotel	Spensley
14.11.95	Bury	Castle Leisure Centre	Tara Promotions
16.11.95	Evesham	Public Hall	Evesham SC
17.11.95	Bethnal Green	York Hall	Peacock Promotions
18.11.95	Glasgow	Kelvin Hall	Matchroom/St Andrew's SC
20.11.95	Glasgow	Forte Crest Hotel	St Andrew's SC
21.11.95	Edgbaston	Tower Ballroom	Cowdell
22.11.95	Sheffield	Hillsborough Leisure Centre	St Andrew's SC
22.11.95	Mayfair	Cafe Royal	Panix
23.11.95	Tynemouth	Park Hotel	St Andrew's SC
23.11.95	Marton	Country Club	Robinson
24.11.95	Manchester	Bowlers Arena	Warren
24.11.95	Chester	Northgate Arena	Hyland
25.11.95	Dagenham	Goresbrook Leisure Centre	Matchroom
28.11.95	Cardiff	Star Leisure Centre	Gardiner
28.11.95	Wolverhampton	Park Hall Hotel	Wolverhampton SC
29.11.95	Solihull	Conference Centre	Midland SC
29.11.95	Southwark	Elephant & Castle Leisure Centre	Panix
29.11.95	Bethnal Green	York Hall	National Promotions
02.12.95	Belfast	King's Hall	Matchroom
03.12.95	Southwark	Elephant & Castle Leisure Centre	Gee
04.12.95	Birmingham	Albany Hotel	Cowdell
04.12.95	Manchester	Piccadilly Hotel	Trickett
06.12.95	Stoke	Moat House Hotel	Brogan
06.12.95	Stoke	Trentham Gardens	North Staffs SC
07.12.95	Hull	Royal Hotel	Hull & District SC
07.12.95	Sunderland	Crowtree Leisure Centre	Winning Combination
08.12.95	Bethnal Green	York Hall	National Promotions
08.12.95	Leeds	Hilton Hotel	Sportsman Promotions
08.12.95	Liverpool	Adelphi Hotel	Vaughan
09.12.95	Bethnal Green	York Hall	Warren
11.12.95	Bradford	Norfolk Gardens Hotel	Yorkshire Executive SC
11.12.95	Morecambe	Carlton Club	Tara Promotions
11.12.95	Cleethorpes	Winter Gardens	Dalton
15.12.95	Bethnal Green	York Hall	Panix

Date	Town	Venue	Promoters
16.12.95	Cardiff	Welsh Institute of Sport	Warren
17.12.95	Glasgow	Moat House Hotel	Morrison
18.12.95	Mayfair	Grosvenor House	Matchroom
20.12.95	Usk	Helmaen Country Club	Gardiner
13.01.96	Manchester	Bowlers Arena	Warren
13.01.96	Halifax	North Bridge Leisure Centre	National Promotions
17.01.96	Solihull	Conference Centre	Midland SC
19.01.96	Bracknell	Leisure Centre	Panix
20.01.96	Mansfield	Leisure Centre	Warren
22.01.96	Glasgow	Forte Crest Hotel	St Andrew's SC
23.01.96	Bethnal Green	York Hall	Matchroom
24.01.96	Stoke	Trentham Gardens	North Staffs SC
26.01.96	Brighton	Metropole Hotel	Warren
26.01.96	Doncaster	Brodsworth Miners Welfare Hall	Rushton
29.01.96	Piccadilly	Cafe Royal	Panix
30.01.96	Barking	Broadway Theatre	Panix
31.01.96	Birmingham	Aston Villa Leisure Centre	National Promotions
31.01.96	Stoke	Moat House Hotel	Brogan
03.02.96	Liverpool	Everton Park Sports Centre	Hyland
05.02.96	Bexleyheath	Crook Log Leisure Centre	Panix
05.02.96	Bradford	Norfolk Gardens Hotel	Yorkshire Executive SC
06.02.96	Basildon	Festival Hall	Matchroom
12.02.96	Glasgow	Moat House Hotel	Morrison
12.02.96	Heathrow	Park Hotel	Holland
13.02.96	Bethnal Green	York Hall	Warren
13.02.96	Cardiff	Welsh Institute of Sport	National Promotions/Gardiner
13.02.96	Wolverhampton	Park Hall Hotel	Wolverhampton SC
14.02.96	Sunderland	Crowtree Leisure Centre	St Andrew's SC
15.02.96	Sheffield	Grosvenor House Hotel	M & M Promotions
16.02.96	Irvine	Volunteer Rooms	St Andrew's SC
19.02.96	Glasgow	Forte Crest Hotel	St Andrew's SC
21.02.96	Batley	Frontier Club	UK Pro Box Promotions
21.02.96	Piccadilly	Cafe Royal	Panix
22.02.96	Walsall	Town Hall	Gray
22.02.96	Sunderland	Swallow Hotel	Winning Combination
23.02.96	Weston super Mare	Winter Gardens	Queensberry Yeo Ltd
26.02.96	Hull	Royal Hotel	Ulyatt
26.02.96	Manchester	Piccadilly Hotel	Trickett
29.02.96	Scunthorpe	Baths Hall	Rushton
02.03.96	Newcastle	The Arena	Warren
05.03.96	Bethnal Green	York Hall	National Promotions
05.03.96	Barrow	Forum 28 Club	Vaughan
06.03.96	Solihull	Conference Centre	Midland SC
07.03.96	Bradford	Norfolk Gardens Hotel	Yorkshire Executive SC
13.03.96	Wembley	Brent Town Hall	National Promotions
15.03.96	Dunstable	Queensway Hall	National Promotions
15.03.96	Hull	Hessle Country Park Inn	Hull & District SC
16.03.96	Sheffield	Pinegrove Country Club	Hobson
16.03.96	Glasgow	Scottish Exhibition Centre	Warren
16.03.96	Barnstaple	Barnstaple Hotel	Adair
18.03.96	Glasgow	Forte Crest Hotel	St Andrew's SC
19.03.96	Leeds	Irish Centre	Sportsman Promotions
20.03.96	Cardiff	City Hall	Gardiner
20.03.96	Stoke	Moat House Hotel	Brogan
21.03.96	Southwark	Elephant & Castle Leisure Centre	Panix
22.03.96	Mansfield	Leisure Centre	Ashton
24.03.96	Shaw	Tara Sports & Leisure Centre	Tara Promotions
25.03.96	Birmingham	Centennial Centre	Cowdell

Date	Town	Venue	Promoters
26.03.96	Wolverhampton	Park Hall Hotel	Wolverhampton SC
27.03.96	Whitwick	Hermitage Leisure Centre	Griffin
27.03.96	Stoke	Trentham Gardens	North Staffs SC
29.03.96	Doncaster	Brodsworth Miners Welfare Hall	Rushton
01.04.96	Bradford	Norfolk Gardens Hotel	Yorkshire Executive SC
02.04.96	Southwark	Elephant & Castle Leisure Centre	Panix
03.04.96	Bethnal Green	York Hall	National Promotions
04.04.96	Plymouth	Continental Hotel	Christian
09.04.96	Stevenage	Arts & Leisure Centre	Matchroom
09.04.96	Salford	The Willows	Wood
13.04.96	Wythenshawe	The Forum	Warren
13.04.96	Liverpool	Everton Park Sports Centre	Matchroom/St Andrew's SC
20.04.96	Brentwood	International Centre	Matchroom
22.04.96	Manchester	Piccadilly Hotel	Trickett
22.04.96	Glasgow	Forte Crest Hotel	St Andrew's SC
22.04.96	Crystal Palace	National Sports Centre	Panix
22.04.96	Cleethorpes	Beachcomber Club	Frater
24.04.96	Stoke	Moat House Hotel	Brogan
24.04.96	Solihull	Conference Centre	Midland SC
25.04.96	Mayfair	Hilton Hotel	National Promotions
25.04.96	Newcastle	Mayfair Ballroom	Fawcett
26.04.96	Glasgow	Hospitality Inn	Morrison
26.04.96	Cardiff	Welsh Institute of Sport	Warren
29.04.96	Mayfair	Marriott Hotel	National Promotions
03.05.96	Sheffield	Hillsborough Leisure Centre	M & M Promotions
04.05.96	Dagenham	Goresbrook Leisure Centre	Matchroom
07.05.96	Mayfair	Marriott Hotel	Matchroom
09.05.96	Hull	Royal Hotel	Ulyatt
09.05.96	Glasgow	Forte Crest Hotel	St Andrew's SC
09.05.96	Sunderland	Swallow Hotel	Winning Combination
10.05.96	Wembley	Brent Town Hall	National Promotions
10.05.96	Liverpool	Everton Park Sports Centre	Vaughan
11.05.96	Bethnal Green	York Hall	Warren
14.05.96	Dagenham	Goresbrook Leisure Centre	Panix
15.05.96	Cardiff	Star Leisure Centre	National Promotions
16.05.96	Dunstable	Queensway Hall	National Promotions
17.05.96	Hull	Royal Hotel	Hull & District SC
20.05.96	Cleethorpes	Winter Gardens	Dalton
20.05.96	Bradford	Norfolk Gardens Hotel	Yorkshire Executive SC
21.05.96	Edgbaston	Tower Ballroom	Cowdell
23.05.96	Queensferry	Styles Night Club	Davies
24.05.96	Glasgow	Hospitality Inn	Morrison
28.05.96	Belfast	Ulster Hall	Matchroom
29.05.96	Ebbw Vale	Leisure Centre	Gardiner
30.05.96	Lincoln	Drill Hall	UK Pro Box Promotions
02.06.96	Shaw	Tara Sports & Leisure Centre	Tara Promotions
03.06.96	Birmingham	Albany Hotel	Cowdell
03.06.96	Glasgow	Forte Crest Hotel	St Andrew's SC
04.06.96	York	Barbican Centre	National Promotions
08.06.96	Newcastle	The Arena	Warren
13.06.96	Sheffield	Pinegrove Country Club	Hobson
24.06.96	Bradford	Norfolk Gardens Hotel	Yorkshire Executive SC
25.06.96	Stevenage	Arts & Leisure Centre	Matchroom
25.06.96	Mansfield	Leisure Centre	Warren
29.06.96	Erith	Leisure Centre	Panix

Current British-Based Champions: Career Records

Shows the complete record of all British champions, or British boxers holding Commonwealth, European, IBF, WBA, WBC and WBO titles, who have been active between 1 July 1995 and 30 June 1996. Names in brackets are real names, where they differ from ring names, and the first place name given is the boxer's domicile. Boxers are either shown as self managed, or with a named manager, the information being supplied by the BBBoC shortly before going to press. Included this year is the record for the Ugandan, Justin Juuko, the Commonwealth super-featherweight champion, who has had his last nine fights in Britain and currently holds a BBBoC licence.

Henry Akinwande

Lewisham. *Born* London, 12 October, 1965
WBO Heavyweight Champion. Former
Undefeated European & Commonwealth
Heavyweight Champion. Ht. 6'7"
Manager Self

04.10.89 Carlton Headley W CO 1 Kensington
08.11.89 Dennis Bailey W RSC 2 Wembley
06.12.89 Paul Neilson W RSC 1 Wembley
10.01.90 John Fairbairn W RSC 1 Kensington
14.03.90 Warren Thompson W PTS 6 Kensington
09.05.90 Mike Robinson W CO 1 Wembley
10.10.90 Tracy Thomas W PTS 6 Kensington
12.12.90 Francois Yrius W RSC 1 Kensington
06.03.91 J. B. Williamson W RSC 2 Wembley
06.06.91 Ramon Voorn W PTS 8 Barking
28.06.91 Marshall Tillman W PTS 8 Nice, France
09.10.91 Gypsy John Fury W CO 3 Manchester
 (Elim. British Heavyweight Title)
06.12.91 Tim Bullock W CO 3 Dussledorf, Germany
28.02.92 Young Joe Louis W RSC 3 Issy les Moulineaux, France
26.03.92 Tucker Richards W RSC 2 Telford
10.04.92 Lumbala Tshimba W PTS 8 Carquefou, France
05.06.92 Kimmuel Odum W DIS 6 Marseille, France
18.07.92 Steve Garber W RTD 2 Manchester
19.12.92 Axel Schulz DREW 12 Berlin, Germany
 (Vacant European Heavyweight Title)
18.03.93 Jimmy Thunder W PTS 12 Lewisham
 (Vacant Commonwealth Heavyweight Title)
01.05.93 Axel Schulz W PTS 12 Berlin, Germany
 (Vacant European Heavyweight Title)
06.11.93 Frankie Swindell W PTS 10 Sun City, South Africa
01.12.93 Biagio Chianese W RSC 4 Kensington
 (European Heavyweight Title Defence)
05.04.94 Johnny Nelson W PTS 10 Bethnal Green
23.07.94 Mario Schiesser W CO 7 Berlin, Germany
 (European Heavyweight Title Defence)
08.04.95 Calvin Jones W CO 2 Las Vegas, USA
22.07.95 Stanley Wright W RSC 2 Millwall
16.12.95 Tony Tucker W PTS 10 Philadelphia, USA
27.01.96 Brian Sergeant W RSC 1 Phoenix, USA
23.03.96 Gerard Jones W DIS 7 Miami, USA
29.06.96 Jeremy Williams W CO 3 Indio, USA
 (Vacant WBO Heavyweight Title)
Career: 31 contests, won 30, drew 1.

Henry Akinwande Tony Fitch

(Gary) Crawford Ashley (Crawford)

Leeds. *Born* Leeds, 20 May, 1964
British L. Heavyweight Champion. Former
Undefeated Central Area L. Heavyweight
Champion. Ht. 6'3"
Manager Self

26.03.87 Steve Ward W RSC 2 Merton
29.04.87 Lee Woolis W RSC 3 Stoke
14.09.87 Glazz Campbell L PTS 8 Bloomsbury
07.10.87 Joe Frater W RSC 4 Burnley
28.10.87 Ray Thomas W RSC 1 Stoke
03.12.87 Jonjo Greene W RSC 7 Leeds
04.05.88 Johnny Nelson L PTS 8 Solihull
15.11.88 Richard Bustin W CO 3 Norwich
22.11.88 Cordwell Hylton W CO 3 Basildon
24.01.89 John Foreman W RSC 4 Kings Heath
08.02.89 Lavell Stanley W CO 1 Kensington
28.03.89 Blaine Logsdon L RSC 2 Glasgow
10.05.89 Serg Fame W RTD 7 Solihull
31.10.89 Carl Thompson W RSC 6 Manchester
 (Vacant Central Area L. Heavyweight Title)
24.01.90 Brian Schumacher W RSC 3 Preston
 (Central Area L. Heavyweight Title Defence)
25.04.90 Dwain Muniz W RSC 1 Brighton
26.11.90 John Williams W RSC 1 Mayfair
12.02.91 Melvin Ricks W CO 1 Belfast
01.03.91 Graciano Rocchigiani L PTS 12 Dusseldorf, Germany
 (Vacant European L. Heavyweight Title)
25.07.91 Roy Skeldon W RSC 7 Dudley
 (Vacant British L. Heavyweight Title)

30.01.92 Jim Peters W RSC 1 Southampton
 (British L. Heavyweight Title Defence)
25.04.92 Glazz Campbell W RSC 8 Belfast
 (British L. Heavyweight Title Defence)
23.09.92 Yawe Davis DREW 12 Campione d'Italia, Italy
 (Vacant European L. Heavyweight Title)
23.04.93 Michael Nunn L RSC 6 Memphis, USA
 (WBA S. Middleweight Title Challenge)
29.01.94 Dennis Andries L RTD 4 Cardiff
19.11.94 Nicky Piper W PTS 12 Cardiff
 (Vacant British L. Heavyweight Title)
25.02.95 Hunter Clay W RTD 3 Millwall
01.04.95 Virgil Hill L PTS 12 Stateline, USA
 (WBA L. Heavyweight Title Challenge)
01.07.95 Lenzie Morgan W PTS 8 Kensington
24.11.95 Jesus Castaneda W RSC 3 Manchester
10.02.96 Frank Minton W RSC 1 Cottbus, Germany
02.03.96 Ray Kane W CO 2 Newcastle
Career: 32 contests, won 24, drew 1, lost 7.

Crawford Ashley Les Clark

Michael Ayers

Tooting. *Born* London, 26 January, 1965
British Lightweight Champion. Former
Undefeated WBC International & Southern
Area Lightweight Champion. Ht. 5'8"
Manager B. Hearn

16.05.89 Young Joe Rafiu W RSC 5 Wandsworth

47

27.06.89 Greg Egbuniwe W CO 1 Kensington
15.11.89 Mille Markovic W RSC 2 Lewisham
05.12.89 Darren Mount W RSC 2 Catford
26.04.90 Nick Hall W CO 3 Wandsworth
04.06.91 Stuart Rimmer W CO 1 Bethnal Green
22.06.91 Wayne Weekes W RSC 6 Earls Court
(Vacant Southern Area Lightweight Title)
21.09.91 Peter Till W RSC 5 Tottenham
(Elim. British Lightweight Title)
28.01.92 Jorge Pompey W PTS 8 Hamburg, Germany
19.02.92 Rudy Valentino W RSC 7 Muswell Hill
(Southern Area Lightweight Title Defence. Elim. British Lightweight Title)
27.06.92 Sugar Gibiliru W RSC 6 Quinta do Lago, Portugal
13.10.92 Scott Brouwer W RSC 4 Mayfair
(Vacant WBC International Lightweight Title)
20.02.93 Danny Myburgh W RSC 5 Earls Court
(WBC International Lightweight Title Defence)
16.04.93 Giovanni Parisi L PTS 12 Rome, Italy
(WBO Lightweight Title Challenge)
24.05.94 Karl Taylor DREW 8 Sunderland
30.09.94 John O. Johnson W RSC 3 Bethnal Green
07.11.94 Bamana Dibateza W PTS 6 Bethnal Green
17.02.95 Paul Burke W RSC 6 Crawley
(Vacant British Lightweight Title)
31.03.95 Karl Taylor W RSC 8 Crystal Palace
(British Lightweight Title Defence)
23.05.95 Charles Shepherd W RSC 3 Potters Bar
(British Lightweight Title Defence)
30.09.95 Dave Anderson W RTD 7 Basildon
(British Lightweight Title Defence)

Career: 21 contests, won 19, drew 1, lost 1.

Michael Ayers   Les Clark

Ensley Bingham

Manchester. *Born* Manchester, 27 May, 1963
British L. Middleweight Champion.
Ht. 5'8½"
Manager F. Warren

20.11.86 Steve Ward W CO 5 Bredbury

16.12.87 Tony Britland W CO 1 Manchester
23.02.88 Frankι Moro W PTS 6 Oldham
01.03.88 Kelvin Mortimer W PTS 8 Manchester
26.04.88 Clinton McKenzie L PTS 8 Bethnal Green
18.10.88 Kostas Petrou L RSC 7 Oldham
22.03.89 Gary Cooper L PTS 8 Reading
26.09.89 Wally Swift Jnr W PTS 10 Oldham
(Elim. British L. Middleweight Title)
28.03.90 Fernando Alanis L RSC 3 Manchester
06.06.90 Andy Till W DIS 3 Battersea
(Final Elim. British L. Middleweight Title)
19.03.91 Wally Swift Jnr L RSC 4 Birmingham
(Vacant British L. Middleweight Title)
29.11.91 Russell Washer W RSC 4 Manchester
29.05.92 Graham Jenner W CO 5 Manchester
18.07.92 Gordon Blair W CO 2 Manchester
02.11.92 Robert McCracken L RSC 10 Wolverhampton
(Elim. British L. Middleweight Title)
28.05.93 Mark Kelly W RSC 5 Middleton
14.08.93 Robert Peel W RTD 3 Hammersmith
25.02.95 Kevin Adamson W CO 5 Millwall
28.07.95 Mark McCreath W RSC 2 Bristol
13.01.96 Gilbert Jackson W RSC 3 Manchester
(Vacant British L. Middleweight Title)
13.04.96 Garry Logan W RSC 6 Wythenshawe
(British L. Middleweight Title Defence)

Career: 21 contests, won 15, lost 6.

Ensley Bingham   Harry Goodwin

Neville Brown

Burton. *Born* Burton, 26 February, 1966
British Middleweight Champion. Ht. 5'10"
Manager F. Warren

08.11.89 Spencer Alton W RSC 4 Wembley
10.01.90 Colin Ford W RTD 3 Kensington
27.03.90 Jimmy McDonagh W RSC 2 Mayfair
09.05.90 William Pronzola W RSC 3 Wembley
13.09.90 Anthony Campbell W RSC 2 Watford
10.10.90 Nigel Moore W CO 1 Kensington
13.12.90 Chris Richards W RSC 2 Dewsbury
17.01.91 Shamus Casey W RSC 4 Alfreton
13.02.91 Jimmy Thornton W RSC 1 Wembley
28.03.91 Tony Booth W PTS 6 Alfreton

12.04.91 Winston Wray W RSC 1 Willenhall
04.07.91 Paul Wesley L RSC 1 Alfreton
29.08.91 Paul Smith W RSC 3 Oakengates
03.10.91 Paul Wesley W PTS 8 Burton
21.11.91 Colin Pitters W RSC 3 Burton
26.03.92 Paul Murray W CO 3 Telford
01.10.92 Ernie Loveridge W CO 4 Telford
02.11.92 Horace Fleary W PTS 8 Wolverhampton
04.12.92 Karl Barwise W RSC 6 Telford
20.01.93 Graham Burton W CO 4 Wolverhampton
16.03.93 Paul Busby W PTS 10 Wolverhampton
(Elim. British Middleweight Title)
10.11.93 Frank Grant W RSC 7 Bethnal Green
(British Middleweight Title Challenge)
26.01.94 Andrew Flute W RTD 7 Birmingham
(British Middleweight Title Defence)
16.03.94 Wallid Underwood W PTS 10 Birmingham
20.07.94 Agostino Cardamone L RSC 7 Solofra, Italy
(European Middleweight Title Challenge)
29.10.94 Colin Pitters W CO 2 Cannock
29.11.94 Antonio Fernandez W RSC 9 Cannock
(British Middleweight Title Defence)
10.02.95 Steve Goodwin W RSC 3 Birmingham
03.03.95 Carlo Colarusso W RSC 7 Bethnal Green
(British Middleweight Title Defence)
22.07.95 Anthony Ivory L PTS 8 Millwall
02.09.95 Trevor Ambrose W PTS 8 Wembley
10.11.95 Shaun Cummins W CO 5 Derby
(British Middleweight Title Defence)
09.03.96 Steve Collins L RSC 11 Millstreet
(WBO S. Middleweight Title Challenge)

Career: 33 contests, won 29, lost 4.

Neville Brown   Les Clark

Joe Calzaghe   Les Clark

Joe Calzaghe

Newbridge. *Born* Hammersmith, 23 March, 1972
British S. Middleweight Champion.
Ht. 5'11"
Manager M. Duff/T. Lawless

01.10.93	Paul Hanlon W RSC 1 Cardiff	
10.11.93	Stinger Mason W RSC 1 Watford	
16.12.93	Spencer Alton W RSC 2 Newport	
22.01.94	Martin Rosamond W RSC 1 Cardiff	
01.03.94	Darren Littlewood W RSC 1 Dudley	
04.06.94	Karl Barwise W RSC 1 Cardiff	
01.10.94	Mark Dawson W RSC 1 Cardiff	
30.11.94	Trevor Ambrose W RSC 2 Wolverhampton	
14.02.95	Frank Minton W CO 1 Bethnal Green	
22.02.95	Bobbi Joe Edwards W PTS 8 Telford	
19.05.95	Robert Curry W RSC 1 Southwark	
08.07.95	Tyrone Jackson W RSC 4 York	
30.09.95	Nick Manners W RSC 8 Kensington	
28.10.95	Stephen Wilson W RSC 8 Kensington	
	(Vacant British S. Middleweight Title)	
13.02.96	Guy Stanford W RSC 1 Cardiff	
13.03.96	Anthony Brooks W RSC 2 Wembley	
20.04.96	Mark Delaney W RSC 5 Brentwood	
	(British S. Middleweight Title Defence)	
04.05.96	Warren Stowe W RTD 2 Dagenham	
15.05.96	Pat Lawlor W RSC 2 Cardiff	

Career: 19 contests, won 19.

Mickey Cantwell

Eltham. *Born* London, 23 November, 1964
British Flyweight Champion. Former Undefeated Southern Area Flyweight Champion. Ht. 5'2½"
Manager Self

21.01.91	Eduardo Vallejo W RSC 4 Crystal Palace	
26.03.91	Mario Alberto Cruz W PTS 6 Bethnal Green	
30.09.91	Ricky Beard W PTS 8 Kensington	
23.10.91	Carlos Manrigues W RSC 5 Bethnal Green	
14.12.91	Shaun Norman W PTS 8 Bexleyheath	
16.05.92	Louis Veitch W PTS 6 Muswell Hill	

10.02.93	Louis Veitch DREW 8 Lewisham	
14.04.93	Daren Fifield W PTS 10 Kensington	
	(Vacant Southern Area Flyweight Title)	
15.09.93	Pablo Tiznado L PTS 12 Bethnal Green	
	(Vacant WBC International L. Flyweight Title)	
03.11.93	Anthony Hanna W PTS 8 Bristol	
27.04.94	Luigi Camputaro L PTS 12 Bethnal Green	
	(European Flyweight Title Challenge)	
15.06.94	Lyndon Kershaw L PTS 8 Southwark	
27.04.95	Anthony Hanna W PTS 6 Bethnal Green	
02.07.95	Anthony Hanna W PTS 6 Dublin	
21.03.96	Keith Knox W PTS 12 Southwark	
	(Vacant British Flyweight Title)	
29.06.96	Krasimir Tcholakov W PTS 6 Erith	

Career: 16 contests, won 12, drew 1, lost 3.

Mickey Cantwell   Les Clark

Steve Collins

Dublin. *Born* Dublin, 21 July, 1964
WBO S. Middleweight Champion. Former Undefeated WBO, USBA, WBO, Penta-Continental & All-Ireland Middleweight Champion. Ht. 5'11"
Manager Self

24.10.86	Julio Mercado W RSC 3 Lowell, USA	
26.11.86	Mike Bonislawski W PTS 4 Dorchester, USA	
20.12.86	Richard Holloway W RSC 2 Dorchester, USA	
10.10.87	Jim Holmes W CO 1 Attleboro, USA	
20.10.87	Harold Souther W PTS 8 Lowell, USA	
20.11.87	Mike Williams W PTS 6 Atlantic City, USA	
09.12.87	Benny Sims W PTS 8 Atlantic City, USA	
18.03.88	Sammy Storey W PTS 10 Boston, USA	
	(Vacant All-Ireland Middleweight Title)	
26.05.88	Lester Yarborough W PTS 10 Boston, USA	
30.07.88	Mike Dale W PTS 8 Brockton, USA	

22.10.88	Muhammad Shabbaz W RSC 4 Salem, USA	
10.12.88	Jesse Lanton W PTS 10 Salem, USA	
07.02.89	Paul McPeek W RSC 9 Atlantic City, USA	
09.05.89	Kevin Watts W PTS 12 Atlantic City, USA	
	(USBA Middleweight Title Challenge)	
26.07.89	Tony Thornton W PTS 12 Atlantic City, USA	
	(USBA Middleweight Title Defence)	
21.11.89	Roberto Rosiles W RSC 9 Las Vegas, USA	
03.02.90	Mike McCallum L PTS 12 Boston, USA	
	(WBA Middleweight Title Challenge)	
16.08.90	Fermin Chirino W RSC 6 Boston, USA	
24.11.90	Eddie Hall W PTS 10 Boston, USA	
11.05.91	Kenny Snow W RSC 3 Belfast	
25.05.91	Jean-Noel Camara W CO 3 Brest, France	
11.12.91	Danny Morgan W RSC 3 Dublin	
22.04.92	Reggie Johnson L PTS 12 East Rutherford, USA	
	(Vacant WBA Middleweight Title)	
22.10.92	Sumbu Kalambay L PTS 12 Verbania, Italy	
	(European Middleweight Title Challenge)	
06.02.93	Johnny Melfah W RSC 3 Cardiff	
20.02.93	Ian Strudwick W RSC 7 Kensington	
26.06.93	Gerhard Botes W RSC 7 Kensington	
	(Vacant WBO Penta-Continental Middleweight Title)	
30.11.93	Wayne Ellis W RSC 9 Cardiff	
	(WBO Penta-Continental Middleweight Title Defence)	
22.01.94	Johnny Melfah W RSC 4 Belfast	
09.02.94	Paul Wesley W PTS 8 Brentwood	
11.05.94	Chris Pyatt W RSC 5 Sheffield	
	(WBO Middleweight Title Challenge)	
18.03.95	Chris Eubank W PTS 12 Millstreet	
	(WBO S. Middleweight Title Challenge)	
09.09.95	Chris Eubank W PTS 12 Cork	
	(WBO S. Middleweight Title Defence)	
25.11.95	Cornelius Carr W PTS 12 Dublin	
	(WBO S. Middleweight Title Defence)	
09.03.96	Neville Brown W RSC 11 Millstreet	
	(WBO S. Middleweight Title Defence)	

Career: 35 contests, won 32, lost 3.

Steve Collins   Les Clark

Peter Culshaw   Les Clark

Drew Docherty   George Ashton, Sportapics Ltd

Peter Culshaw

Liverpool. *Born* Liverpool, 15 May, 1973
Commonwealth Flyweight Champion.
Former Undefeated Central Area Flyweight
Champion. Ht. 5'6"
Manager S. Vaughan

02.07.93	Graham McGrath W PTS 6 Liverpool
28.09.93	Vince Feeney W PTS 6 Liverpool
11.12.93	Nick Tooley W RSC 1 Liverpool
25.02.94	Des Gargano W PTS 6 Chester
06.05.94	Neil Swain W PTS 6 Liverpool
26.09.94	Daryl McKenzie W PTS 6 Liverpool
20.04.95	Rowan Williams W CO 6 Liverpool
29.09.95	Maxim Pougatchev DREW 8 Liverpool
05.03.96	Louis Veitch W RSC 3 Barrow
	(Central Area Flyweight Title Challenge)
13.04.96	Lyndon Kershaw W RSC 3 Liverpool
25.06.96	Danny Ward W RSC 3 Stevenage
	(Commonwealth Flyweight Title Challenge)

Career: 11 contests, won 10, drew 1.

(Andrew) Drew Docherty

Croy. *Born* Glasgow, 29 November, 1965
British Bantamweight Champion. Ht. 5'6"
Manager T. Gilmour

14.09.89	Gordon Shaw W PTS 6 Motherwell
23.11.89	Chris Clarkson W PTS 6 Motherwell
09.05.90	Rocky Lawlor DREW 8 Solihull
03.10.90	Steve Robinson W PTS 8 Solihull
21.11.90	Pete Buckley W PTS 8 Solihull
14.11.91	Stevie Woods W RSC 1 Edinburgh
27.01.92	Neil Parry W RSC 4 Glasgow
27.04.92	Pete Buckley W PTS 8 Glasgow
01.06.92	Joe Kelly W RSC 5 Glasgow
	(British Bantamweight Title Challenge)
25.01.93	Donnie Hood W PTS 12 Glasgow
	(British Bantamweight Title Defence)
26.04.93	Russell Davison W PTS 8 Glasgow
25.10.93	Pete Buckley W PTS 8 Glasgow
02.02.94	Vincenzo Belcastro L PTS 12 Glasgow
	(European Bantamweight Title Challenge)
09.07.94	Conn McMullen W PTS 8 Earls Court

20.09.94	Miguel Matthews W PTS 8 Musselburgh
23.11.94	Ady Benton W PTS 12 Irvine
	(British Bantamweight Title Defence)
17.02.95	Alfred Kotey L RSC 4 Cumbernauld
	(WBO Bantamweight Title Challenge)
13.10.95	James Murray W CO 12 Glasgow
	(British Bantamweight Title Defence)
20.01.96	Daniel Jimenez L PTS 12 Mansfield
	(WBO Bantamweight Title Challenge)

Career: 19 contests, won 15, drew 1, lost 3.

Terry Dunstan   Les Clark

Terry Dunstan

Hackney. *Born* London, 21 October, 1968
British Cruiserweight Champion. Ht. 6'3"
Manager F. Warren

12.11.92	Steve Osborne W PTS 6 Bayswater

25.11.92	Steve Yorath W PTS 8 Mayfair
31.03.93	Lee Prudden W PTS 6 Barking
15.09.93	Paul McCarthy W RSC 3 Ashford
02.12.93	Devon Rhooms W CO 2 Sheffield
30.09.94	Michael Murray W PTS 8 Bethnal Green
20.12.94	Trevor Small W RTD 4 Bethnal Green
04.03.95	Art Stacey W CO 1 Livingston
13.05.95	Dennis Andries W PTS 12 Glasgow
	(British Cruiserweight Title Challenge)
09.09.95	Dave Robinson W RSC 5 Cork
25.11.95	Jimmy Bills W RSC 7 Dublin
13.02.96	Dennis Andries W PTS 12 Bethnal Green
	(British Cruiserweight Title Defence)
11.05.96	John Keeton W RSC 1 Bethnal Green
	(British Cruiserweight Title Defence)

Career: 13 contests, won 13.

(Patrick) P. J. Gallagher

Wood Green. *Born* Manchester, 14
February, 1973
British & WBC International S.
Featherweight Champion. Former
Undefeated Southern Area S. Featherweight
Champion. Ht. 5'7"
Manager F. Maloney

15.09.93	John T. Kelly W RSC 2 Bethnal Green
13.10.93	Mike Morrison W PTS 4 Bethnal Green
01.12.93	Mark Antony W PTS 4 Bethnal Green
09.02.94	Simon Hamblett W RSC 1 Bethnal Green
29.03.94	Brian Coleman W PTS 6 Bethnal Green
15.06.94	Mark O'Callaghan W RSC 4 Southwark
29.09.94	Anthony Campbell W PTS 6 Bethnal Green
12.11.94	Karl Taylor W PTS 6 Dublin
23.01.95	David Thompson W RSC 1 Bethnal Green
30.03.95	Phil Found W PTS 6 Bethnal Green
25.05.95	Marco Fattore W RSC 5 Reading

02.07.95 Chris Clarkson W RSC 3 Dublin
29.09.95 Marc Smith W RSC 3 Bethnal Green
08.11.95 Justin Murphy W RSC 6 Bethnal
Green
*(Vacant Southern Area
S. Featherweight Title & Elim. British
S. Featherweight Title)*
19.01.96 Rakhim Mingaleev W PTS 12
Bracknell
*(Vacant WBC International
S. Featherweight Title)*
22.04.96 Dave McHale W RSC 10 Crystal
Palace
(Vacant British S. Featherweight Title)
29.06.96 Charles Shepherd W PTS 12 Erith
*(British S. Featherweight Title
Defence)*
Career: 17 contests, won 17.

P. J. Gallagher   Les Clark

Prince Nassem Hamed
Sheffield. *Born* Sheffield, 12 February,
1974
WBO Featherweight Champion. Former
Undefeated WBC International S.
Bantamweight Champion. Former
Undefeated European Bantamweight
Champion. Ht. 5'3"
Manager B. Ingle

14.04.92 Ricky Beard W CO 2 Mansfield
25.04.92 Shaun Norman W RSC 2 Manchester
23.05.92 Andrew Bloomer W RSC 2
Birmingham
14.07.92 Miguel Matthews W RSC 3 Mayfair
07.10.92 Des Gargano W RSC 4 Sunderland
12.11.92 Pete Buckley W PTS 6 Liverpool
24.02.93 Alan Ley W CO 2 Wembley
26.05.93 Kevin Jenkins W RSC 3 Mansfield
24.09.93 Chris Clarkson W CO 2 Dublin
29.01.94 Pete Buckley W RSC 4 Cardiff
09.04.94 John Miceli W CO 1 Mansfield
11.05.94 Vincenzo Belcastro W PTS 12
Sheffield
*(European Bantamweight Title
Challenge)*

Prince Nassem Hamed   Les Clark

17.08.94 Antonio Picardi W RSC 3 Sheffield
*(European Bantamweight Title
Defence)*
12.10.94 Freddy Cruz W RSC 6 Sheffield
*(Vacant WBC International S.
Bantamweight Title)*
19.11.94 Laureano Ramirez W RTD 3 Cardiff
*(WBC International S. Bantamweight
Title Defence)*
21.01.95 Armando Castro W RSC 4 Glasgow
*(WBC International S. Bantamweight
Title Defence)*
04.03.95 Sergio Liendo W RSC 2 Livingston
*(WBC International S. Bantamweight
Title Defence)*

06.05.95 Enrique Angeles W CO 2 Shepton
Mallet
*(WBC International S. Bantamweight
Title Defence)*
01.07.95 Juan Polo Perez W CO 2 Kensington
*(WBC International S. Bantamweight
Title Defence)*
30.09.95 Steve Robinson W RSC 8 Cardiff
(WBO Featherweight Title Challenge)
16.03.96 Said Lawal W RSC 1 Glasgow
(WBO Featherweight Title Defence)
08.06.96 Daniel Alicea W RSC 2 Newcastle
(WBO Featherweight Title Defence)
Career: 22 contests, won 22.

Billy Hardy   Les Clark

Billy Hardy

Sunderland. *Born* Sunderland, 5 September, 1964
European & Commonwealth Featherweight Champion. Former Undefeated British Featherweight & Bantamweight Champion. Ht. 5'6"
Manager T. Gilmour

21.11.83	Kevin Downer W PTS 6 Eltham
03.12.83	Brett Styles W PTS 6 Marylebone
27.01.84	Keith Ward W PTS 6 Longford
13.02.84	Johnny Mack W RSC 5 Eltham
01.03.84	Graham Kid Clarke W PTS 8 Queensway
27.03.84	Glen McLaggon W PTS 6 Battersea
06.04.84	Graham Kid Clarke W RSC 7 Watford
25.04.84	Anthony Brown W RSC 5 Muswell Hill
04.06.84	Roy Webb L PTS 6 Mayfair
06.09.84	Les Walsh W PTS 8 Gateshead
10.10.84	Jorge Prentas L RSC 5 Shoreditch
12.02.85	Ivor Jones W PTS 8 Kensington
17.04.85	Ivor Jones W PTS 10 Bethnal Green
08.06.85	Valerio Nati L RSC 4 Florence, Italy
10.10.85	Keith Wallace W RSC 7 Alfreton *(Final Elim. British Bantamweight Title)*
02.06.86	Rocky Lawlor W PTS 8 Mayfair
19.02.87	Ray Gilbody W RSC 3 St Helens *(British Bantamweight Title Challenge)*
23.04.87	Rocky Lawlor W RSC 7 Newcastle
04.06.87	Brian Holmes W PTS 10 Sunderland
17.03.88	John Hyland W CO 2 Sunderland *(British Bantamweight Title Defence)*
11.05.88	Luis Ramos W RSC 2 Wembley
29.09.88	Jose Gallegos W RSC 4 Sunderland
02.11.88	Vincenzo Belcastro L PTS 12 Paolo, Italy *(European Bantamweight Title Challenge)*
14.02.89	Ronnie Carroll W PTS 12 Sunderland *(British Bantamweight Title Defence)*
29.03.89	Jose Soto W PTS 8 Wembley
28.06.89	Vincenzo Belcastro DREW 12 Pavia, Italy *(European Bantamweight Title Challenge)*
10.10.89	Brian Holmes W CO 1 Sunderland *(British Bantamweight Title Defence)*
24.01.90	Orlando Canizales L PTS 12 Sunderland *(IBF Bantamweight Title Challenge)*
22.05.90	Miguel Pequeno W RSC 4 Stockton
29.11.90	Ronnie Carroll W RSC 8 Sunderland *(British Bantamweight Title Defence)*
28.02.91	Francisco Ortiz W RSC 7 Sunderland
04.05.91	Orlando Canizales L RSC 8 Laredo, USA *(IBF Bantamweight Title Challenge)*
03.03.92	Chris Clarkson W RSC 5 Houghton le Spring
07.10.92	Ricky Raynor W RSC 10 Sunderland *(Vacant Commonwealth Featherweight Title)*
19.05.93	Barrington Francis W PTS 12 Sunderland *(Commonwealth Featherweight Title Defence)*
15.06.93	Angel Fernandez W PTS 10 Hemel Hempstead
30.11.93	Mustapha Hame L PTS 8 Marseilles, France
24.05.94	Alan McKay W RSC 8 Sunderland *(Vacant British Featherweight Title. Commonwealth Featherweight Title Defence)*
15.10.94	Stanford Ngcebeshe W PTS 12 Sun City, South Africa *(Commonwealth Featherweight Title Defence)*
21.02.95	Percy Commey W RSC 11 Sunderland *(Commonwealth Featherweight Title Defence)*
04.03.95	Fabrice Benichou DREW 10 St Quentin, France
28.10.95	Mehdi Labdouni W PTS 12 Fontenay sous Bois, France *(European Featherweight Title Challenge)*
14.02.96	Michael Alldis W PTS 12 Sunderland *(Commonwealth Featherweight Title Defence)*
20.06.96	Stefano Zoff W PTS 12 San Remo, Italy *(European Featherweight Title Defence)*

Career: 44 contests, won 35, drew 2, lost 7.

Justin Juuko

London. *Born* Musaka, Uganda, 21 September, 1972
Commonwealth S. Featherweight Champion. Ht. 5'7"
Manager P. De Freitas

Justin Juuko   Les Clark

18.03.91 Gilbert Diaz W RSC 3 Las Vegas, USA
26.03.91 Jorge Lopez W PTS 4 Las Vegas, USA
02.06.91 Kevin Childrey W RSC 2 Las Vegas, USA
12.06.91 Juan Carlos Lopez W CO 4 Irvine, USA
06.07.91 Norberto Bravo L RSC 2 Las Vegas, USA
29.10.91 Danny Gonzalez W RSC 1 Phoenix, USA
30.11.91 Ruben Rivera W RSC 5 Las Vegas, USA
14.02.92 Chris Crespin W RSC 3 Las Vegas, USA
28.03.92 Amador Martinez W RSC 2 Las Vegas, USA
24.05.92 Mario Lozano W CO 2 Las Vegas, USA
26.06.92 Victor Miranda T DREW 2 Las Vegas, USA
21.08.92 Jose Manjarez W RSC 6 Las Vegas, USA
21.10.92 Roberto Torres W RSC 2 Las Vegas, USA
26.12.92 Roberto Torres W RSC 1 Las Vegas, USA
24.01.93 Cesar Guzman W CO 3 Lynwood, USA
24.02.93 Abe Gomez W PTS 8 Las Vegas, USA
17.04.93 Russell Mosley W CO 4 Sacramento, USA
28.11.93 Derek Amory W RSC 1 Southwark
09.02.94 Charles Shepherd W RSC 5 Bethnal Green
09.04.94 Bamana Dibateza W RSC 5 Mansfield
12.10.94 Juan Amando Reyes W PTS 8 Sheffield
18.02.95 Alberto Lopez W RTD 3 Shepton Mallet
13.05.95 Peter Till W RTD 4 Glasgow
07.07.95 Mark Smith W RSC 4 Cardiff
30.09.95 Tony Pep W PTS 12 Cardiff
(Commonwealth S. Featherweight Title Challenge)
26.01.96 Jackie Gunguluza W RSC 7 Brighton
(Commonwealth S. Featherweight Title Defence)
Career: 26 contests, won 24, drew 1, lost 1.

Kevin Lueshing

Beckenham. *Born* Beckenham, 17 April, 1968
British Welterweight Champion. Former Undefeated Southern Area L. Middleweight Champion. Ht. 5'11"
Manager F. Warren

30.09.91 John McGlynn W RSC 2 Kensington
23.10.91 Julian Eavis W RSC 2 Bethnal Green
14.12.91 Trevor Meikle W CO 3 Bexleyheath
18.01.92 Simon Eubank W CO 4 Kensington
25.03.92 Tracy Jocelyn W RSC 3 Dagenham
30.04.92 Newton Barnett W PTS 6 Kensington
03.02.93 Ian Chantler W RSC 2 Earls Court
17.02.93 Leigh Wicks W PTS 6 Bethnal Green
31.03.93 Ernie Loveridge W RSC 5 Bethnal Green
14.04.93 Marty Duke W RSC 2 Kensington

23.06.93 Kirkland Laing W RSC 5 Edmonton
(Vacant Southern Area L. Middleweight Title)
03.03.94 Chris Saunders L RSC 4 Ebbw Vale
30.07.94 Dennis Berry W CO 2 Bethnal Green
25.10.94 Peter Waudby W RSC 2 Middlesbrough
17.06.95 Michael Smyth W RSC 3 Cardiff
(Final Elim. British Welterweight Title)
30.09.95 Danny Quacoe W PTS 8 Cardiff
09.12.95 Steve Goodwin W RTD 2 Bethnal Green
13.02.96 Chris Saunders W RSC 3 Bethnal Green
(British Welterweight Title Challenge)
08.06.96 Paul King W RSC 2 Newcastle
Career: 19 contests, won 18, lost 1.

Kevin Lueshing   Les Clark

Robert McCracken

Birmingham. *Born* Birmingham, 31 May, 1968
Commonwealth Middleweight Champion. Former Undefeated British L. Middleweight Champion. Ht. 6'0"
Manager M. Duff

24.01.91 Mick Mulcahy W RSC 1 Brierley Hill
13.02.91 Gary Barron W RTD 2 Wembley
06.03.91 Tony Britland W RSC 2 Wembley
12.04.91 Dave Andrews W RSC 4 Willenhall
08.05.91 Tony Gibbs W CO 1 Kensington
30.05.91 Paul Murray W RSC 2 Birmingham
04.07.91 Marty Duke W RSC 1 Alfreton
25.07.91 John Smith W RTD 1 Dudley
31.10.91 Newton Barnett W DIS 2 Oakengates
28.11.91 Michael Oliver W RSC 3 Liverpool
12.02.92 Paul Lynch W RSC 4 Wembley
01.10.92 Horace Fleary W PTS 8 Telford
02.11.92 Ensley Bingham W RSC 10 Wolverhampton
(Elim. British L. Middleweight Title)
20.01.93 Leigh Wicks W PTS 8 Wolverhampton
17.02.93 Ernie Loveridge W CO 4 Bethnal Green
24.04.93 Martin Smith W RSC 10 Birmingham
(Final Elim. British L. Middleweight Title)
29.06.93 Steve Langley W RSC 4 Edgbaston
01.12.93 Chris Peters W PTS 8 Kensington
23.02.94 Andy Till W PTS 12 Watford
(British L. Middleweight Title Challenge)
10.09.94 Steve Foster W PTS 12 Birmingham
(British L. Middleweight Title Defence)
11.10.94 Dean Cooper W RSC 4 Bethnal Green
10.02.95 Paul Wesley W PTS 12 Birmingham
(British L. Middleweight Title Defence)
21.04.95 Sergio Medina W RSC 7 Dudley
01.09.95 Jorge Sclarandi W PTS 10 Wolverhampton
03.11.95 Fitzgerald Bruney W PTS 12 Dudley
(Vacant Commonwealth Middleweight Title)
03.04.96 Paul Busby W RTD 7 Bethnal Green
(Commonwealth Middleweight Title Defence)
15.05.96 Humberto Aranda W RSC 5 Cardiff
Career: 27 contests, won 27.

Robert McCracken   Les Clark

Colin McMillan   Les Clark

Colin McMillan

Barking. *Born* London, 12 February, 1966
British Featherweight Champion. Former
WBO Featherweight Champion. Former
Undefeated Commonwealth Featherweight
Champion. Ht. 5'5¼"
Manager Self

29.11.88	Mike Chapman W PTS 6 Battersea
10.12.88	Aldrich Johnson W PTS 6 Crystal Palace
31.01.89	Alan McKay L RSC 3 Bethnal Green
12.06.89	Miguel Matthews W RSC 3 Battersea
19.09.89	Graham O'Malley W PTS 8 Millwall
11.10.89	Marcel Herbert W PTS 6 Millwall
30.11.89	Sylvester Osuji W RSC 4 Barking
14.02.90	Vidal Tellez W RSC 2 Millwall
17.04.90	Jesus Muniz W PTS 8 Millwall
03.05.90	Steve Walker W PTS 6 Kensington
05.07.90	Tyrone Miller W CO 2 Greensville, USA
17.07.90	Malcolm Rougeaux W CO 1 Lake Charles, USA
25.09.90	Darren Weller W RSC 2 Millwall
10.10.90	Graham O'Malley W PTS 6 Millwall
12.11.90	Mark Holt W PTS 8 Norwich
05.03.91	Russell Davison W PTS 6 Millwall
26.04.91	Willie Richardson W PTS 8 Crystal Palace
22.05.91	Gary de Roux W RSC 7 Millwall
	(British Featherweight Title Challenge)
03.07.91	Herbie Bivalacqua W RSC 3 Reading
04.09.91	Kevin Pritchard W RSC 7 Bethnal Green
	(British Featherweight Title Defence)
29.10.91	Sean Murphy W PTS 12 Kensington
	(British Featherweight Title Defence)
18.01.92	Percy Commey W PTS 12 Kensington
	(Vacant Commonwealth Featherweight Title)
25.03.92	Tommy Valdez W CO 6 Dagenham
16.05.92	Maurizio Stecca W PTS 12 Muswell Hill
	(WBO Featherweight Title Challenge)
26.09.92	Ruben Palacio L RSC 8 Earls Court
	(WBO Featherweight Title Defence)
23.10.93	Steve Robinson L PTS 12 Cardiff
	(WBO Featherweight Title Challenge)

04.02.95	Harry Escott W PTS 8 Cardiff
25.02.95	Mark Hargreaves W RSC 4 Millwall
06.05.95	Peter Judson W PTS 8 Shepton Mallet
22.07.95	Dean Phillips W PTS 8 Millwall
30.01.96	Justin Murphy W RSC 4 Barking
21.03.96	Pete Buckley W RSC 3 Southwark
14.05.96	Jonjo Irwin W PTS 12 Dagenham
	(British Featherweight Title Challenge)

Career: 33 contests, won 30, lost 3.

Chris Okoh

Camberwell. *Born* Carshalton, 18 April, 1969
Commonwealth & WBO Inter-Continental
Cruiserweight Champion. Former
Undefeated Southern Area Cruiserweight
Champion. Ht. 6'2"
Manager D. Powell

16.03.93	Lee Prudden W PTS 6 Mayfair
10.07.93	Steve Yorath W PTS 6 Cardiff
28.09.93	Steve Osborne W RSC 5 Bethnal Green
06.11.93	Chris Henry W RSC 2 Bethnal Green
09.04.94	Art Stacey W PTS 6 Bethnal Green
17.09.94	Art Stacey W PTS 6 Crawley
23.02.95	Paul Lawson W RSC 5 Southwark
	(Vacant Southern Area Cruiserweight Title)
29.09.95	Francis Wanyama W RSC 8 Bethnal Green
	(Commonwealth Cruiserweight Title Challenge)
08.11.95	Paul Lawson W RSC 1 Bethnal Green
	(Commonwealth Cruiserweight Title Defence)
05.02.96	Darren Westover W RSC 2 Bexleyheath
	(Vacant WBO Inter-Continental Cruiserweight Title)
22.04.96	Gypsy Carman W RSC 6 Crystal Palace
	(WBO Inter-Continental Cruiserweight Title Defence)

Career: 11 contests, won 11.

Chris Okoh   Les Clark

Nicky Piper   Chris Bevan

Nicky Piper

Cardiff. *Born* Cardiff, 5 May, 1966
Commonwealth & WBO Inter-Continental
L. Heavyweight Champion. Former
Undefeated WBA Penta-Continental S.
Middleweight Champion. Ht. 6'3"
Manager Self

06.09.89	Kevin Roper W CO 2 Aberavon
17.10.89	Gus Mendes W RSC 3 Cardiff
19.12.89	Dave Owens W CO 1 Gorleston
17.04.90	Darren McKenna W RTD 4 Millwall
22.05.90	Maurice Core DREW 6 St Albans
23.10.90	Paul McCarthy W RSC 3 Leicester
12.11.90	John Ellis W CO 1 Norwich
05.03.91	Johnny Held W RSC 3 Millwall
08.05.91	Serge Bolivard W RSC 1 Millwall
22.05.91	Martin Lopez W CO 1 Millwall
03.07.91	Simon Harris W RSC 1 Reading
04.09.91	Carl Thompson L RSC 3 Bethnal Green
29.10.91	Franki Moro W RSC 4 Kensington
20.11.91	Carlos Christie W CO 6 Cardiff
22.01.92	Frank Eubanks W PTS 10 Cardiff
	(Elim. British S. Middleweight Title)
11.03.92	Ron Amundsen W PTS 10 Cardiff
16.05.92	Larry Prather W PTS 8 Muswell Hill
25.07.92	Johnny Melfah W RSC 5 Manchester
	(Elim. British S. Middleweight Title)
12.12.92	Nigel Benn L RSC 11 Muswell Hill
	(WBC S. Middleweight Title Challenge)
13.02.93	Miguel Maldonado W PTS 12 Manchester
	(Vacant WBA Penta-Continental S. Middleweight Title)
10.04.93	Chris Sande W RSC 9 Swansea
	(WBA Penta-Continental S. Middleweight Title Defence)
10.07.93	Trevor Ambrose W RSC 5 Cardiff
23.10.93	Frank Rhodes DREW 8 Cardiff
29.01.94	Leonzer Barber L RSC 9 Cardiff
	(WBO L. Heavyweight Title Challenge)
21.09.94	Charles Oliver W RSC 5 Cardiff

19.11.94 Crawford Ashley L PTS 12 Cardiff
(Vacant British L. Heavyweight Title)
17.06.95 Tim Bryan W RSC 1 Cardiff
07.07.95 John Keeton W RTD 2 Cardiff
30.09.95 Noel Magee W CO 9 Cardiff
*(Commonwealth L. Heavyweight Title
Challenge. Vacant WBO Inter-
Continental L. Heavyweight Title)*
26.04.96 Danny Juma W RTD 2 Cardiff
Career: 30 contests, won 24, drew 2, lost 4.

Chris Pyatt

Leicester. *Born* Islington, 3 July, 1963
Commonwealth L. Middleweight
Champion. Former WBO Middleweight
Champion. Former Undefeated WBC
International Middleweight Champion.
Former European L. Middleweight
Champion. Former Undefeated British L.
Middleweight Champion. Ht. 5'8½"
Manager Self

Chris Pyatt   Les Clark

01.03.83 Paul Murray W RTD 2 Kensington
05.04.83 Billy Waith W RSC 8 Kensington
28.04.83 Lee Hartshorn W RSC 3 Leicester
27.09.83 Darwin Brewster W PTS 8 Wembley
08.10.83 Tyrone Demby W RSC 2 Atlantic City,
USA
22.11.83 Tony Britton W RSC 4 Wembley
22.02.84 Judas Clottey W PTS 8 Kensington
15.03.84 Pat Thomas W PTS 10 Leicester
09.05.84 Franki Moro W CO 4 Leicester
23.05.84 Alfonso Redondo W RSC 3 Mayfair
16.10.84 John Ridgman W RSC 1 Kensington
16.11.84 Brian Anderson W PTS 12 Leicester
*(Final Elim. British L. Middleweight
Title)*
12.02.85 Helier Custos W RSC 5 Kensington
05.06.85 Graeme Ahmed W RSC 3 Kensington
01.07.85 Mosimo Maeleke W RSC 6 Mayfair
23.09.85 Sabiyala Diavilia L RSC 4 Mayfair
19.02.86 Prince Rodney W CO 9 Kensington
*(British L. Middleweight Title
Challenge)*

20.05.86 Thomas Smith W RSC 1 Wembley
17.09.86 John van Elteren W RSC 1 Kensington
*(Vacant European L. Middleweight
Title)*
25.10.86 Renaldo Hernandez W RSC 3 Paris,
France
28.01.87 Gianfranco Rosi L PTS 12 Perugia,
Italy
*(European L. Middleweight Title
Defence)*
18.04.87 Dennis Johnson W CO 2 Kensington
26.05.87 Sammy Floyd W RSC 2 Wembley
28.10.87 Gilbert Josamu W PTS 8 Wembley
28.05.88 Jose Duarte W RSC 4 Kensington
23.11.88 Eddie Hall W RSC 2 Bethnal Green
01.12.88 Knox Brown W RSC 2 Edmonton
14.12.88 Tyrone Moore W CO 1 Bethnal Green
15.02.89 Russell Mitchell W RSC 4 Bethnal
Green
17.05.89 Daniel Dominguez W RSC 10 Millwall
11.10.89 Wayne Harris W RSC 3 Millwall
25.04.90 Daniel Sclarandi W RSC 2 Millwall
23.10.90 John David Jackson L PTS 12
Leicester
*(WBO L. Middleweight Title
Challenge)*
05.11.91 Craig Trotter W PTS 12 Leicester
*(Vacant Commonwealth L.
Middleweight Title)*
01.02.92 Ambrose Mlilo W RSC 3 Birmingham
*Commonwealth L. Middleweight Title
Defence)*
31.03.92 Melvyn Wynn W CO 3 Norwich
28.04.92 James Tapisha W RSC 1
Wolverhampton
*(Commonwealth L. Middleweight Title
Defence)*
23.05.92 Ian Strudwick W PTS 10 Birmingham
27.10.92 Adolfo Caballero W CO 5 Leicester
*(Vacant WBC International
Middleweight Title)*
26.01.93 Danny Garcia W PTS 12 Leicester
*(WBC International Middleweight Title
Defence)*
23.02.93 Colin Manners W CO 3 Doncaster
16.03.93 Paul Wesley W PTS 10 Mayfair
10.05.93 Sumbu Kalambay W PTS 12 Leicester
(Vacant WBO Middleweight Title)
18.09.93 Hugo Corti W CO 6 Leicester
(WBO Middleweight Title Defence)
09.02.94 Mark Cameron W CO 1 Brentwood
(WBO Middleweight Title Defence)
11.05.94 Steve Collins L RSC 5 Sheffield
(WBO Middleweight Title Defence)
13.05.95 Anthony Ivory W PTS 8 Glasgow
02.09.95 James Mason W RSC 5 Wembley
16.12.95 Kevin Kelly W PTS 12 Cardiff
*(Commonwealth L. Middleweight Title
Challenge)*
Career: 49 contests, won 45, lost 4.

Robbie Regan

Cefn Forest. *Born* Caerphilly, 30 August,
1968
WBO Bantamweight Champion. Former
Undefeated British, European & Welsh
Flyweight Champion. Ht. 5'4"
Manager Self

19.08.89 Eric George DREW 6 Cardiff
06.03.90 Francis Ampofo W PTS 6 Bethnal
Green
26.04.90 Kevin Downer W RSC 4 Merthyr

20.06.90 Dave McNally DREW 6 Basildon
19.11.90 Ricky Beard W RSC 6 Cardiff
21.12.90 Michele Poddighe DREW 6 Sassari,
Italy
12.02.91 Kevin Jenkins W PTS 10 Cardiff
(*Vacant Welsh Flyweight Title*)
28.05.91 Joe Kelly W PTS 12 Cardiff
(*Vacant British Flyweight Title*)
03.09.91 Francis Ampofo L RSC 11 Cardiff
(*British Flyweight Title Defence*)
17.12.91 Francis Ampofo W PTS 12 Cardiff
(*British Flyweight Title Challenge*)
11.02.92 Juan Bautista W CO 1 Cardiff
19.05.92 James Drummond W RSC 9 Cardiff
(*British Flyweight Title Defence*)
14.11.92 Salvatore Fanni W PTS 12 Cardiff
(*European Flyweight Title Challenge*)
30.03.93 Danny Porter W RSC 3 Cardiff
(*European Flyweight Title Defence*)
26.06.93 Adrian Ochoa W PTS 10 Earls Court
29.01.94 Michele Poddighe W PTS 10 Cardiff
12.03.94 Mauricio Bernal W PTS 8 Cardiff
01.10.94 Shaun Norman W RSC 2 Cardiff
19.11.94 Luigi Camputaro W PTS 12 Cardiff
(*European Flyweight Title Challenge*)
17.06.95 Alberto Jimenez L RTD 9 Cardiff
(*WBO Flyweight Title Challenge*)
16.12.95 Ferid Ben Jeddou W RSC 2 Cardiff
(*Vacant Interim IBF Flyweight Title*)
26.04.96 Daniel Jimenez W PTS 12 Cardiff
(*WBO Bantamweight Title Challenge*)
Career: 22 contests, won 17, drew 3, lost 2.

Robbie Regan   Les Clark

Paul Ryan

Hackney. *Born* South Ockenham, 2
February, 1965
British, Commonwealth & WBO Inter-
Continental L. Welterweight Champion.
Ht. 5'8"
Manager F. Warren

26.09.91 Chris Mylan W PTS 6 Dunstable
18.01.92 Alex Sterling W RSC 4 Kensington
25.03.92 Michael Clynch W RSC 4 Dagenham

Paul Ryan   Les Clark

16.05.92 Greg Egbuniwe W RSC 4 Muswell Hill
26.09.92 Korso Aleain W CO 4 Earls Court
17.12.92 Rick Bushell W RSC 1 Barking
03.02.93 Neil Smith W RSC 1 Earls Court
27.02.93 Mike Morrison W PTS 6 Dagenham
15.09.93 Shaun Cogan W RSC 3 Ashford
10.11.93 Steve Phillips W RSC 3 Bethnal Green
17.02.94 Rob Stewart W RSC 4 Dagenham
09.04.94 Carl Wright W RSC 8 Mansfield
17.08.94 John Smith W RTD 2 Sheffield
10.09.94 Dave Lovell W RSC 3 Birmingham
09.11.94 Massimo Bertozzi W RSC 2 San
Remo, Italy
04.02.95 George Wilson W RSC 4 Cardiff
25.02.95 Paul Denton W RSC 4 Millwall
13.05.95 Jorge Aquino W RSC 4 Glasgow

01.07.95 Oscar Palomino W RSC 8 Kensington
(*Vacant WBO Inter-Continental
L. Welterweight Title*)
02.09.95 Karl Taylor W RSC 3 Wembley
21.10.95 Eric Jakubowski W RSC 3 Bethnal
Green
(*WBO Inter-Continental L.
Welterweight Title Defence*)
09.12.95 Ross Hale W CO 1 Bethnal Green
(*British & Commonwealth L.
Welterweight Title Challenge. WBO
Inter-Continental L. Welterweight Title
Defence*)
13.02.96 Jonathan Thaxton L RSC 1 Bethnal
Green

Career: 23 contests, won 22, lost 1.

Neil Swain

Neil Swain

Gilfach Goch. *Born* Pontypridd, 4
September, 1971
Commonwealth S. Bantamweight
Champion. Ht. 5'5"
Manager D. Gardiner

29.04.93 Vince Feeney W PTS 6 Mayfair
27.05.93 Marcus Duncan W PTS 6 Burnley
01.10.93 Rowan Williams W PTS 6 Cardiff
16.10.93 Philippe Desavoye W PTS 6 Levallois,
France
10.11.93 Barry Jones L PTS 6 Ystrad
29.01.94 Alan Ley W RSC 3 Cardiff
12.03.94 Ceri Farrell W CO 1 Cardiff
09.04.94 Vince Feeney L PTS 6 Mansfield
06.05.94 Peter Culshaw L PTS 6 Liverpool
25.05.94 Paul Ingle L CO 4 Bristol
30.07.94 Jose Lopez L RTD 4 Bethnal Green
21.09.94 Yusuf Vorajee W RTD 1 Cardiff
01.10.94 Richie Wenton W RTD 5 Cardiff
19.11.94 Dave Hardie W RSC 2 Cardiff
29.11.94 Pete Buckley W PTS 6 Cardiff
25.01.95 Rowan Williams W PTS 6 Cardiff
04.02.95 Chris Jickells W PTS 6 Cardiff
12.04.95 Mike Parris W RSC 20 Llanelli
(*Vacant Commonwealth
S. Bantamweight Title*)
28.07.95 Tony Falcone W RSC 5 Bristol
(*Commonwealth S. Bantamweight Title
Defence*)
20.09.95 Graham McGrath W RSC 1 Ystrad
04.11.95 Anton Gilmore L PTS 10 Sun City,
South Africa
13.02.96 Nathan Sting W PTS 12 Cardiff
(*Vacant Commonwealth
S. Bantamweight Title*)
Career: 22 contests, won 16, lost 6.

Scott Welch

Brighton. *Born* Yarmouth, 21 April, 1968
British, Commonwealth & WBO Inter-
Continental Heavyweight Champion.
Former Undefeated Southern Area
Heavyweight Champion. Ht. 6'2"
Manager F. Warren

08.09.92 John Williams W RSC 5 Norwich

06.10.92 Gary Williams W PTS 4 Antwerp,
Belgium
23.02.93 Gary Charlton L RSC 3 Doncaster
11.05.93 Denroy Bryan W RSC 4 Norwich
29.06.93 John Harewood W RSC 5 Mayfair
18.09.93 Des Vaughan W RSC 2 Leicester
28.09.93 Gypsy Carman W RSC 3 Bethnal
Green
05.10.93 Cordwell Hylton W RSC 1 Mayfair
06.11.93 Joey Paladino W RSC 3 Bethnal Green
30.11.93 Chris Coughlan W CO 1 Cardiff
21.12.93 Carl Gaffney W RSC 3 Mayfair
15.03.94 Steve Garber W RSC 4 Mayfair
06.05.94 James Oyebola L CO 5 Atlantic City,
USA
(*Vacant WBC International
Heavyweight Title*)

17.09.94 R. F. McKenzie W RSC 1 Crawley
10.12.94 Michael Murray W PTS 8 Manchester
13.05.95 Eduardo Carranza W CO 1 Glasgow
01.07.95 Julius Francis W RSC 10 Kensington
(*Southern Area Heavyweight Title
Challenge. Final Elim. British
Heavyweight Title*)
27.10.95 James Oyebola W RSC 10 Brighton
(*British Heavyweight Title Challenge.
Vacant Commonwealth & WBO Inter-
Continental Heavyweight Titles*)
16.03.96 Joe Bugner W RSC 6 Berlin, Germany
(*WBO Inter-Continental Heavyweight
Title Defence*)
08.06.96 Mike Sedillo W RSC 1 Newcastle
Career: 20 contests, won 18, lost 2.

Scott Welch　　　　　　　　　　　　　　　　Les Clark

57

Richie Wenton   Les Clark

Richie Wenton

Liverpool. *Born* Liverpool, 28 October, 1967
British & WBO Inter-Continental S. Bantamweight Champion. Ht. 5'8"
Manager F. Warren

14.12.88	Miguel Matthews W CO 2 Kirkby
25.01.89	Sean Casey W PTS 4 Belfast
10.04.89	Stuart Carmichael W RSC 2 Mayfair
13.12.89	Joe Mullen W RSC 5 Kirkby
21.02.90	Ariel Cordova W PTS 6 Belfast
17.03.90	Mark Johnson W PTS 4 Belfast
28.03.90	Jose Luis Vasquez W PTS 6 Manchester
23.05.90	Graham O'Malley W PTS 6 Belfast

09.07.90	Eugene Pratt W CO 1 Miami Beach, USA
15.09.90	Graham O'Malley W PTS 6 Belfast
30.10.90	Alejandro Armenta W RSC 2 Belfast
12.02.91	Sean Casey W PTS 4 Belfast
31.03.92	Graham O'Malley W PTS 6 Stockport
25.07.92	Ramos Agare W RSC 3 Manchester
26.09.92	Floyd Churchill L RSC 2 Earls Court
28.04.93	Kelton McKenzie W PTS 8 Dublin
13.11.93	Des Gargano W PTS 8 Cullompton
26.04.94	Bradley Stone W RSC 10 Bethnal Green
	(Vacant British S. Bantamweight Title)
01.10.94	Neil Swain L RTD 5 Cardiff
25.03.95	Paul Lloyd W RSC 5 Chester
	(British S. Bantamweight Title Defence)
30.06.95	Mike Parris W PTS 12 Liverpool
	(Vacant WBO Inter-Continental S. Bantamweight Title)
09.10.95	Vincenzo Belcastro L PTS 12 San Benedetto, Italy
	(European S. Bantamweight Title Challenge)
06.02.96	Wilson Docherty W PTS 12 Basildon
	(British S. Bantamweight Title Defence)

Career: 23 contests, won 20, lost 3.

Henry Wharton

York. *Born* Leeds, 23 November, 1967
Commonwealth S. Middleweight Champion. Former Undefeated British & European S. Middleweight Champion. Ht. 5'10½"
Manager M. Duff

21.09.89	Dean Murray W RSC 1 Harrogate
25.10.89	Mike Aubrey W PTS 6 Wembley
05.12.89	Ron Malek W RSC 1 Dewsbury
11.01.90	Guillermo Chavez W CO 1 Dewsbury
03.03.90	Joe Potts W CO 4 Wembley

11.04.90	Juan Elizondo W RSC 3 Dewsbury
18.10.90	Chuck Edwards W RSC 1 Dewsbury
31.10.90	Dino Stewart W PTS 8 Wembley
21.03.91	Francisco Lara W CO 1 Dewsbury
09.05.91	Frankie Minton W CO 7 Leeds
27.06.91	Rod Carr W PTS 12 Leeds
	(Vacant Commonwealth S. Middleweight Title)
30.10.91	Lou Gent DREW 12 Leeds
	(Commonwealth S. Middleweight Title Defence)
23.01.92	Nicky Walker W PTS 10 York
19.03.92	Kenny Schaefer W CO 1 York
08.04.92	Rod Carr W RSC 8 Leeds
	(Commonwealth S. Middleweight Title Defence)
23.09.92	Fidel Castro W PTS 12 Leeds
	(Commonwealth S. Middleweight Title Defence. British S. Middleweight Title Challenge)
07.04.93	Ray Domenge W RSC 3 Leeds
01.07.93	Royan Hammond W RSC 3 York
07.10.93	Ron Amundsen W RSC 8 York
26.02.94	Nigel Benn L PTS 12 Earls Court
	(WBC S. Middleweight Title Challenge)
10.09.94	Guy Stanford W RTD 3 Birmingham
26.10.94	Sipho Moyo W CO 1 Leeds
	(Commonwealth S. Middleweight Title Defence)
10.12.94	Chris Eubank L PTS 12 Manchester
	(WBO S. Middleweight Title Challenge)
08.07.95	Mauro Galvano W CO 4 York
	(Vacant European S. Middleweight Title)
11.11.95	Sammy Storey W CO 4 Halifax
	(European & Commonwealth S. Middleweight Title Defence)
13.01.96	Vincenzo Nardiello W RSC 6 Halifax
	(European S. Middleweight Title Defence)
04.06.96	Stephane Nizard W PTS 10 York

Career: 27 contests, won 24, drew 1, lost 2.

Henry Wharton   Les Clark

Active British-Based Boxers: Career Records

Shows the complete record for all British-based boxers, excluding those currently holding British, Commonwealth, European, IBF, WBA, WBC and WBO titles, who have been active between 1 July 1995 and 30 June 1996. Names in brackets are real names, where they differ from ring names, and the first place name given is the boxer's domicile. Boxers are either shown as self-managed or with a named manager, the information being supplied by the BBBoC shortly before going to press. Also included are foreign-born fighters who made their pro debuts in Britain, along with others like Bamana Dibateza (Zaire), John McAlpine (Australia), and Yifru Retta (Ethiopia), who, although starting their careers elsewhere, now hold BBBoC licenses and had three or more fights in this country last season in order to qualify for this section.

Ojay Abrahams

Watford. *Born* Lambeth, 17 December, 1964
Welterweight. Ht. 5'8½"
Manager Self

21.09.91 Gordon Webster W RSC 3 Tottenham
26.10.91 Mick Reid W RSC 5 Brentwood
26.11.91 John Corcoran W PTS 6 Bethnal Green
21.01.92 Dave Andrews DREW 6 Norwich
31.03.92 Marty Duke W RSC 2 Norwich
19.05.92 Michael Smyth L PTS 6 Cardiff
16.06.92 Ricky Mabbett W PTS 6 Dagenham
13.10.92 Vince Rose L RSC 3 Mayfair
30.01.93 Vince Rose DREW 6 Brentwood
19.05.93 Ricky Mabbett L RSC 4 Leicester
18.09.93 Ricky Mabbett L PTS 6 Leicester
09.12.93 Nick Appiah W PTS 6 Watford
24.01.94 Errol McDonald W RSC 2 Glasgow
09.02.94 Vince Rose W PTS 6 Brentwood
23.05.94 Spencer McCracken L PTS 6 Walsall
11.06.94 Darren Dyer W RSC 1 Bethnal Green
29.09.94 Gary Logan L PTS 10 Bethnal Green
(Southern Area Welterweight Title Challenge)
13.12.94 Geoff McCreesh L PTS 6 Potters Bar
11.02.95 Gary Murray L PTS 8 Hamanskraal, South Africa
17.07.95 Andreas Panayi L PTS 8 Mayfair
02.10.95 Larbi Mohammed L RTD 5 Mayfair
08.12.95 Jason Beard W CO 2 Bethnal Green
09.04.96 Kevin Thompson W RSC 3 Stevenage
07.05.96 Harry Dhami L RSC 5 Mayfair
(Vacant Southern Area Welterweight Title)
Career: 24 contests, won 11, drew 2, lost 11.

Kevin Adamson

Walthamstow. *Born* Hackney, 29 February, 1968
Middleweight. Ht. 6'0½"
Manager F. Warren

17.07.89 Carlton Myers W RSC 1 Stanmore
04.12.90 Darron Griffiths L RSC 4 Southend
12.11.91 Danny Shinkwin W RSC 4 Milton Keynes
30.04.92 Wayne Appleton W RSC 2 Bayswater
03.02.93 Joel Ani W RSC 6 Earls Court
27.02.93 Robert Whitehouse W RSC 1 Dagenham
31.03.93 Russell Washer W PTS 6 Barking
07.09.93 Bullit Andrews W PTS 6 Stoke
22.09.93 Russell Washer W PTS 6 Bethnal Green
27.10.93 Mick Duncan W RSC 3 Stoke
10.11.93 Clayon Stewart W RSC 1 Bethnal Green
01.12.93 Dave Maj W RSC 2 Stoke
19.01.94 Spencer Alton W RSC 1 Stoke

26.02.94 Lloyd Honeyghan L RSC 6 Earls Court
(Commonwealth L. Middleweight Title Challenge)
25.05.94 Chris Richards W RSC 2 Stoke
17.08.94 Ernie Loveridge W RSC 2 Sheffield
25.02.95 Ensley Bingham L CO 5 Millwall
28.07.95 Glenn Catley L CO 1 Bristol
Career: 18 contests, won 14, lost 4.

Tanveer Ahmed (Niazi)

Glasgow. *Born* Glasgow, 25 October, 1968
Lightweight. Ht. 5'10"
Manager A. Morrison

22.10.92 John T. Kelly W PTS 6 Glasgow
01.12.92 Shaun Armstrong L PTS 6 Hartlepool
26.03.93 David Thompson W PTS 6 Glasgow
14.05.93 Dean Bramhald W PTS 6 Kilmarnock
09.09.93 Brian Wright W RTD 5 Glasgow
21.10.93 Martin Campbell W PTS 6 Glasgow
21.03.94 Chris Aston W CO 5 Glasgow
06.06.94 Chris Aston W CO 4 Glasgow
28.09.94 Norman Dhalie W CO 5 Glasgow
10.12.94 Kevin McKillan W PTS 6 Manchester
16.01.95 Micky Hall W RSC 4 Musselburgh
13.05.95 John O. Johnson W CO 3 Glasgow
01.07.95 Cham Joof W PTS 6 Kensington
16.03.96 Kevin McKillan W PTS 4 Glasgow
24.05.96 Kevin McKillan DREW 8 Glasgow
Career: 15 contests, won 13, drew 1, lost 1.

Rob Albon

Hayes. *Born* Hayes, 21 April, 1964
Heavyweight. Ht. 6'1½"
Manager Self

10.05.89 Massimo Mighaccio L RSC 3 Tallin, Estonia
15.09.89 L. A. Williams DREW 6 High Wycombe
20.02.90 Steve Osborne W PTS 6 Brentford
03.04.90 Dennis Bailey L RSC 4 Canvey Island
08.05.90 Steve Yorath W PTS 6 Brentford
12.09.90 Phil Soundy L RSC 1 Bethnal Green
18.02.91 Des Vaughan W PTS 6 Windsor
25.01.95 Darren Fearn L PTS 6 Cardiff
03.03.95 Keith Fletcher L RSC 3 Bracknell
09.05.95 Darren Westover L RSC 2 Basildon
28.07.95 Shane Woollas L RTD 4 Epworth
Career: 11 contests, won 3, drew 1, lost 7.

Michael Alexander

Doncaster. *Born* Doncaster, 31 August, 1971
Welterweight. Ht. 5'9"
Manager Self

25.01.93 Tim Hill W PTS 6 Bradford
09.03.93 J. T. Kelly L PTS 6 Hartlepool

29.04.93 Pete Roberts W RSC 2 Hull
06.05.93 Ian Noble W PTS 6 Hartlepool
28.06.93 Mick Hoban W PTS 6 Morecambe
04.10.93 Micky Hall L CO 1 Bradford
28.11.93 Everald Williams L PTS 6 Southwark
28.02.94 Paul Hughes W PTS 6 Manchester
28.03.94 Laurence Roche W PTS 6 Cleethorpes
20.05.94 Andrew Morgan W PTS 6 Neath
13.06.94 Laurence Roche L PTS 6 Bradford
26.09.94 Derek Roche L RSC 6 Bradford
21.11.94 Alan Peacock L RSC 1 Glasgow
06.03.95 Brian Dunn L CO 3 Bradford
26.02.96 Charlie Paine W PTS 6 Manchester
05.03.96 John Jones L PTS 6 Barrow
29.03.96 Cam Raeside L PTS 6 Doncaster
22.04.96 Peter Reid L PTS 6 Cleethorpes
03.05.96 Andy Davidson W RTD 2 Sheffield
10.05.96 Tony Mock L PTS 6 Liverpool
03.06.96 Tommy Quinn L PTS 6 Glasgow
24.06.96 Lee Murtagh L PTS 6 Bradford
Career: 22 contests, won 10, lost 12.

Wayne Alexander

Croydon. *Born* Tooting, 17 July, 1973
L. Middleweight. Ht. 5'8¾"
Manager F. Warren

10.11.95 Andrew Jervis W RTD 3 Derby
13.02.96 Paul Murray W PTS 4 Bethnal Green
11.05.96 Jim Webb W RSC 2 Bethnal Green
Career: 3 contests, won 3.

Wayne Alexander   Les Clark

Michael Alldis

Crawley. *Born* London, 25 May, 1968
S. Bantamweight. Ht. 5'6"
Manager Self

15.09.92 Ceri Farrell W RSC 3 Crystal Palace
10.11.92 Kid McAuley W PTS 6 Dagenham
12.12.92 Kid McAuley W CO 1 Muswell Hill
16.02.93 Ceri Farrell W CO 1 Tooting
29.06.93 Ady Benton L DIS 3 Mayfair
28.09.93 Alan Ley W PTS 6 Bethnal Green
06.11.93 Pete Buckley W PTS 8 Bethnal Green
09.04.94 Fernando Lugo W CO 1 Bethnal Green
11.06.94 Conn McMullen W PTS 8 Bethnal Green
20.12.94 Pete Buckley W PTS 6 Bethnal Green
17.02.95 Miguel Matthews W PTS 8 Crawley
25.03.95 Chip O'Neill W RSC 2 Chester
13.06.95 Laureano Ramirez L PTS 12 Basildon
(*Vacant WBO Inter-Continental S. Bantamweight Title*)
25.11.95 Conn McMullen W CO 4 Dagenham
13.01.96 Garry Burrell W RSC 7 Halifax
14.02.96 Billy Hardy L PTS 12 Sunderland
(*Commonwealth Featherweight Title Challenge*)
Career: 16 contests, won 12, lost 4.

Carl Allen

Wolverhampton. *Born* Wolverhampton, 20 November, 1969
Featherweight. Ht. 5'7'/4"
Manager R. Gray/P. Cowdell

26.11.95 Gary Jenkinson W PTS 6 Birmingham
29.11.95 Jason Squire L PTS 6 Solihull
17.01.96 Andrew Robinson L PTS 6 Solihull
13.02.96 Ervine Blake W RSC 5 Wolverhampton
21.02.96 Ady Benton L PTS 6 Batley
29.02.96 Chris Jickells W PTS 6 Scunthorpe
27.03.96 Jason Squire DREW 6 Whitwick
26.04.96 Paul Griffin L RSC 3 Cardiff
30.05.96 Roger Brotherhood W RSC 5 Lincoln
Career: 9 contests, won 4, drew 1, lost 4.

Mark Allen (Hodgson)

Denaby. *Born* Mexborough, 11 January, 1970
L. Welterweight. Ht. 5'11"
Manager Self

24.03.92 Jamie Morris L PTS 6 Wolverhampton
04.06.92 Blue Butterworth L RSC 5 Burnley
10.11.92 Bobby Guynan L RSC 2 Dagenham
09.12.92 Simon Hamblett DREW 6 Stoke
09.02.93 Simon Hamblett W PTS 6 Wolverhampton
23.02.93 Simon Hamblett L PTS 6 Doncaster
11.03.93 Jamie Morris DREW 6 Walsall
20.04.93 Paul Knights L PTS 6 Brentwood
06.05.93 Brian Coleman L PTS 6 Walsall
28.05.93 Nick Boyd L CO 2 Middleton
29.06.93 Robbie Sivyer W PTS 6 Edgbaston
14.08.93 Cham Joof L RSC 3 Hammersmith
28.10.93 Paul Bowen L RSC 2 Walsall
09.02.94 Paul Knights L RSC 2 Brentwood
18.04.94 Patrick Parton L PTS 6 Walsall
23.05.94 Patrick Parton L PTS 6 Walsall
13.06.94 James Jiora L PTS 6 Bradford
21.07.94 Bradley Welsh L PTS 6 Edinburgh
11.10.94 Marc Smith L PTS 6 Wolverhampton
20.10.94 Marc Smith W PTS 6 Walsall
02.11.94 Mark Breslin L PTS 6 Solihull

29.11.94 Simon Hamblett L PTS 6 Wolverhampton
18.12.94 Gordon Blair L RSC 3 Glasgow
09.03.95 Patrick Parton L PTS 6 Walsall
16.03.95 Tim Hill L PTS 6 Sunderland
11.05.95 Shaun O'Neill L PTS 6 Sunderland
18.05.95 Scott Walker L RSC 2 Middleton
06.07.95 Shaun Stokes L PTS 6 Hull
29.07.95 Paul Scott L RSC 5 Whitley Bay
22.01.96 John Stovin L PTS 6 Glasgow
26.02.96 Shaun Gledhill L RSC 3 Manchester
24.04.96 Kid McAuley L PTS 6 Stoke
Career: 32 contests, won 3, drew 2, lost 27.

Spencer Alton

Derby. *Born* Derby, 4 October, 1966
S. Middleweight. Ht. 5'11"
Manager Self

13.06.88 Ian Midwood-Tate W PTS 6 Manchester
10.07.88 Lou Ayres L PTS 6 Eastbourne
31.08.88 Ian Midwood-Tate L PTS 6 Stoke
13.09.88 Steve West L CO 3 Battersea
19.10.88 Wil Halliday W CO 6 Evesham
31.10.88 Michael Oliver W RSC 2 Leicester
14.11.88 G. L. Booth L RSC 7 Manchester
13.12.88 Paul Dolan W RTD 4 Glasgow
20.12.88 Wayne Ellis L RTD 4 Swansea
27.01.89 Neil Patterson W CO 1 Durham
31.01.89 Brian Robinson L PTS 6 Reading
15.02.89 Mark Holden DREW 6 Stoke
06.03.89 Mark Howell L PTS 8 Manchester
21.03.89 Ricky Nelson L PTS 6 Cottingham
04.04.89 Graham Burton L RSC 3 Sheffield
09.05.89 Wayne Ellis L RSC 3 St Albans
20.06.89 Peter Vosper L PTS 6 Plymouth
06.07.89 Ian Strudwick L PTS 8 Chigwell
26.09.89 Frank Eubanks W PTS 6 Oldham
10.10.89 Terry Morrill L PTS 6 Hull
17.10.89 Peter Vosper DREW 8 Plymouth
08.11.89 Neville Brown L RSC 4 Wembley
20.12.89 Mickey Morgan W RSC 5 Swansea
15.01.90 Andy Marlow DREW 6 Northampton
30.01.90 Darren Pilling L PTS 6 Manchester
13.02.90 Colin Pitters W PTS 6 Wolverhampton
26.02.90 Antoine Tarver L PTS 4 Crystal Palace
22.03.90 Richard Carter L PTS 6 Wolverhampton
24.05.90 Andrew Flute W RSC 1 Dudley
21.06.90 Paul Murray W PTS 6 Alfreton
10.09.92 Dave Johnson L PTS 6 Sunderland
23.10.92 Terry French L PTS 6 Gateshead
07.12.92 Jimmy Alston L PTS 6 Manchester
02.02.93 Chris Mulcahy W RSC 3 Derby
09.03.93 Mark Jay L RSC 4 Hartlepool
08.06.93 Eddie Collins W PTS 6 Derby
20.09.93 Sean Byrne L PTS 6 Northampton
03.11.93 Paul Busby L RTD 4 Worcester
16.12.93 Joe Calzaghe L RSC 2 Newport
19.01.94 Kevin Adamson L RSC 1 Stoke
28.03.94 Willie Quinn L RTD 3 Musselburgh
13.06.94 Craig Joseph L PTS 6 Bradford
02.07.94 Danny Peters L PTS 6 Liverpool
03.08.94 Dean Cooper L RSC 6 Bristol
06.10.94 Mark Jay L PTS 6 Cramlington
09.11.94 Andy McVeigh L RTD 3 Stafford
02.03.95 Mark Jay L PTS 6 Cramlington
18.03.95 Packie Collins L PTS 4 Millstreet
20.04.95 Steve McNess L RSC 2 Mayfair
19.09.95 Peter Vosper L RTD 3 Plymouth
Career: 50 contests, won 12, drew 3, lost 35.

Trevor Ambrose

Leicester. *Born* Leicester, 8 September, 1963
S. Middleweight. Ht. 5'11"
Manager Self

19.02.90 Ian Thomas L RSC 3 Kettering
06.04.90 Colin Pitters W PTS 6 Telford
24.04.90 Barry Messam W RSC 4 Stoke
14.05.90 Gordon Blair L CO 5 Northampton
12.09.90 Dave Fallon W CO 3 Battersea
23.10.90 David Lake W PTS 6 Leicester
14.11.90 Eddie King W RSC 3 Doncaster
21.11.90 Andreas Panayi W RSC 5 Solihull
14.02.91 Adrian Riley W CO 6 Southampton
28.03.91 Richard O'Brien W RSC 1 Alfreton
25.04.91 Gary Logan L PTS 8 Mayfair
03.07.91 Darren Dyer L PTS 6 Brentwood
24.09.91 Willie Beattie L PTS 8 Glasgow
11.03.92 John Davies L RSC 5 Cardiff
19.05.92 Paul Jones L PTS 6 Cardiff
19.03.93 Errol Christie W CO 2 Manchester
10.07.93 Nicky Piper L RSC 5 Cardiff
30.09.93 Simon Harris L PTS 6 Hayes
27.11.93 Cesar Kazadi L CO 4 Echirolles, France
23.02.94 W. O. Wilson W RSC 5 Watford
06.03.94 Ray Webb L RSC 6 Southwark
14.05.94 Bernard Bonzon L PTS 8 Sierre, Switzerland
04.06.94 Zdravco Kostic L RSC 4 Paris, France
30.11.94 Joe Calzaghe L RSC 2 Wolverhampton
31.03.95 Mark Delaney L RSC 1 Crystal Palace
22.07.95 Thulani Malinga L PTS 8 Millwall
02.09.95 Neville Brown L PTS 8 Wembley
15.09.95 Robin Reid L CO 5 Mansfield
11.05.96 Mads Larsen L RSC 2 Bethnal Green
Career: 29 contests, won 11, lost 18.

Dean Amory

Birmingham. *Born* Marston Green, 2 July, 1969
Lightweight. Ht. 5'7"
Manager Self

21.10.92 Brian Hickey W PTS 6 Stoke
20.01.93 Dean Bramhald W PTS 6 Solihull
28.04.93 Elvis Parsley W PTS 6 Solihull
19.05.93 Neil Smith W PTS 6 Leicester
19.12.93 Alan McDowall L PTS 8 Glasgow
26.01.94 Kevin McKillan L PTS 8 Stoke
26.04.95 Joe Donohoe W PTS 6 Stoke
17.06.95 Gareth Lawrence L RSC 2 Cardiff
13.02.96 Miguel Matthews W PTS 8 Wolverhampton
Career: 9 contests, won 6, lost 3.

Dave Anderson

Bellahouston. *Born* Glasgow, 23 December, 1965
Lightweight. Ht. 5'8"
Manager A. Morrison/F. Warren

25.09.90 Junaido Musah W RSC 3 Glasgow
09.10.90 Alan Peacock W RSC 3 Glasgow
10.12.90 Chris Bennett W RSC 7 Glasgow
11.02.91 Steve Pollard W PTS 6 Glasgow
15.04.91 Tony Foster W PTS 8 Glasgow
24.09.91 Ian Honeywood W PTS 8 Glasgow
28.11.91 Pete Roberts W RSC 3 Glasgow
11.09.92 Kevin Toomey W PTS 6 Glasgow
22.10.92 Kevin McKenzie W RSC 3 Glasgow
10.06.94 Peter Till W PTS 6 Glasgow

21.07.94 John Stovin W CO 4 Edinburgh
01.10.94 Wayne Windle W RSC 2 Cardiff
21.10.94 Peter Till W PTS 8 Glasgow
19.11.94 Nigel Haddock W PTS 6 Cardiff
18.12.94 Peter Till W PTS 10 Glasgow
 (*Elim. British Lightweight Title*)
21.01.95 Carlos Javier Pena Lopez W PTS 8
 Glasgow
04.03.95 Michael Hermon W PTS 8 Livingston
08.06.95 Floyd Churchill W PTS 8 Glasgow
30.09.95 Michael Ayers L RTD 7 Basildon
 (*British Lightweight Title Challenge*)
Career: 19 contests, won 18, lost 1.

Larry Anderson
Edinburgh. *Born* London, 1 January, 1968
L. Welterweight. Ht. 5'8"
Manager A. Morrison

15.09.95 James Clamp L RSC 5 Glasgow
Career: 1 contest, lost 1.

Shaun Anderson   Les Clark

Shaun Anderson
Maybole. *Born* Girvan, 20 September, 1969
Bantamweight. Ht. 5'5"
Manager A. Melrose

29.05.92 Tucker Thomas W RSC 1 Glasgow
11.09.92 Mark Hargreaves W PTS 6 Glasgow
10.12.92 Graham McGrath W PTS 6 Glasgow
29.01.93 Graham McGrath W PTS 6 Glasgow
26.03.93 Dave Campbell W RSC 5 Glasgow
30.04.93 Paul Kelly W RSC 5 Glasgow
14.05.93 Kid McAuley W PTS 8 Kilmarnock
29.05.93 Ronnie Stephenson W PTS 6 Paisley
09.09.93 Graham McGrath W PTS 8 Glasgow
19.12.93 Pete Buckley W PTS 6 Glasgow
13.04.94 Paul Wynn DREW 6 Glasgow
13.05.94 Paul Wynn L PTS 8 Kilmarnock
08.09.94 Graham McGrath W PTS 8 Glasgow
23.09.94 Johnny Armour L RSC 11 Bethnal
 Green
 (*Commonwealth Bantamweight Title
 Challenge*)

18.11.94 James Murray L PTS 10 Glasgow
 (*Vacant Scottish Bantamweight Title*)
21.01.95 Brian Carr L PTS 6 Glasgow
04.03.95 Shaun Norman W PTS 6 Livingston
21.04.95 Donnie Hood W PTS 8 Glasgow
12.05.95 Warren Bowers L RSC 7 Bethnal
 Green
25.11.95 Spencer Oliver L RSC 3 Dagenham
16.03.96 Colin Innes W PTS 4 Glasgow
24.04.96 Ady Benton L PTS 6 Solihull
Career: 22 contests, won 14, drew 1, lost 7.

Dave Andrews
Merthyr. *Born* Merthyr, 22 July, 1968
Middleweight. Ht. 5'11"
Manager Self

12.09.88 Ian Midwood-Tate L RTD 4
 Northampton
05.12.88 Robert Dugdale W PTS 6 Northampton
16.01.89 Graham Burton L PTS 6 Northampton
06.03.89 Jimmy Thornton W PTS 6
 Northampton
28.03.89 Jim Beckett L PTS 6 Chigwell
08.06.89 John Davies L RSC 3 Cardiff
26.02.90 Rocky Bryan L RSC 2 Crystal Palace
17.09.90 Julian Eavis W PTS 6 Cardiff
19.11.90 Andy Williams W RSC 1 Cardiff
05.03.91 Brian Cullen W RSC 1 Cardiff
12.04.91 Robert McCracken L RSC 4 Willenhall
19.11.91 Paul Dyer L PTS 6 Norwich
17.12.91 Mark Atkins W RSC 3 Cardiff
21.01.92 Ojay Abrahams DREW 6 Norwich
09.02.92 Paul Burke L PTS 6 Bradford
03.03.92 Howard Clarke L RSC 3 Cradley Heath
22.04.96 Anthony McFadden L RSC 2 Crystal
 Palace
Career: 17 contests, won 6, drew 1, lost 10.

Dave Andrews   Les Clark

Simon Andrews
Plymouth. *Born* Birmingham, 24 April,
1970
Middleweight. Ht. 5'9¹/₂"
Manager G. Mitchell

19.09.95 J. P. Matthews L RSC 3 Plymouth
13.11.95 Carl Winstone L PTS 6 Barnstaple
03.12.95 Jason Hart L PTS 6 Southwark
12.02.96 Neville Smith L RSC 3 Heathrow
04.04.96 Jetty Williams W PTS 6 Plymouth
10.05.96 Graham Townsend L RSC 5 Wembley
Career: 6 contests, won 1, lost 5.

Simon Andrews   Les Clark

Dennis Andries
Hackney. *Born* Guyana, 5 November, 1953
Former British Cruiserweight Champion.
Former WBC L. Heavyweight Champion.
Former Undefeated WBC International L.
Heavyweight Champion. Former
Undefeated British & Southern Area L.
Heavyweight Champion. Ht. 5'11"
Manager Self

16.05.78 Ray Pearce W CO 2 Newport
01.06.78 Mark Seabrook W RSC 1 Heathrow
20.06.78 Bonny McKenzie L PTS 8 Southend
18.09.78 Ken Jones W PTS 6 Mayfair
31.10.78 Neville Estaban W PTS 6 Barnsley
14.11.78 Les McAteer DREW 8 Birkenhead
22.11.78 Glen McEwan W RSC 7 Stoke
04.12.78 Tom Collins W PTS 8 Southend
22.01.79 Bunny Johnson L PTS 10
 Wolverhampton
30.01.79 Tom Collins W CO 6 Southend
05.04.79 Francis Hand W RSC 8 Liverpool
06.06.79 Bonny McKenzie W PTS 8 Burslem
17.09.79 Johnny Waldron W RTD 10 Mayfair
 (*Southern Area L. Heavyweight Title
 Challenge*)
27.02.80 Bunny Johnson L PTS 15 Burslem
 (*British L. Heavyweight Title
 Challenge*)
17.04.80 Mustafa Wasajja L PTS 8 Copenhagen,
 Denmark
18.06.80 Chris Lawson W RSC 8 Burslem
23.03.81 Shaun Chalcraft W PTS 10 Mayfair
 (*Southern Area L. Heavyweight Title
 Challenge*)
16.09.81 Liam Coleman W RSC 6 Burslem

12.10.81 David Pearce L RSC 7 Bloomsbury
23.11.81 Alek Penarski W PTS 10 Chesterfield
15.03.82 Tom Collins L PTS 15 Bloomsbury
(Vacant British L. Heavyweight Title)
10.08.82 Keith Bristol W PTS 10 Strand
*(Southern Area L. Heavyweight Title
Defence)*
28.02.83 Karl Canwell W CO 4 Strand
*(Southern Area L. Heavyweight Title
Defence & Elim. British L.
Heavyweight Title)*
19.05.83 Chris Lawson W CO 4 Queensway
22.09.83 Keith Bristol W CO 4 Strand
*(Southern Area L. Heavyweight Title
Defence & Elim. British L.
Heavyweight Title)*
26.01.84 Tom Collins W PTS 12 Strand
*(British L. Heavyweight Title
Challenge)*
06.04.84 Tom Collins W PTS 12 Watford
(British L. Heavyweight Title Defence)
10.10.84 Devon Bailey W CO 12 Shoreditch
(British L. Heavyweight Title Defence)
23.03.85 Jose Seys W RSC 3 Strand
07.05.85 Jeff Meacham W CO 4 New Orleans,
USA
25.05.85 Tim Broady W RSC 5 Atlantic City,
USA
06.06.85 Marcus Dorsey W CO 3 Lafayette,
USA
11.12.85 Alex Blanchard DREW 12 Fulham
*(European L. Heavyweight Title
Challenge)*
13.02.86 Keith Bristol W RSC 6 Longford
(British L. Heavyweight Title Defence)
30.04.86 J. B. Williamson W PTS 12 Edmonton
(WBC L. Heavyweight Title Challenge)
10.09.86 Tony Sibson W RSC 9 Muswell Hill
*(WBC & British L. Heavyweight Title
Defence)*
07.03.87 Thomas Hearns L RSC 10 Detroit,
USA
(WBC L. Heavyweight Title Defence)
06.10.87 Robert Folley W PTS 10 Phoenix, USA
20.02.88 Jamie Howe W PTS 10 Detroit, USA
22.05.88 Bobby Czyz W PTS 10 Atlantic City,
USA
10.09.88 Tony Harrison W RTD 7 Detroit, USA
17.10.88 Paul Maddison W RSC 4 Tucson, USA
21.02.89 Tony Willis W RSC 5 Tucson, USA
(Vacant WBC L. Heavyweight Title)
24.06.89 Jeff Harding L RSC 12 Atlantic City,
USA
(WBC L. Heavyweight Title Defence)
26.10.89 Art Jimmerson W PTS 10 Atlantic
City, USA
20.01.90 Clarismundo Silva W RSC 7 Auburn
Hills, USA
*(Vacant WBC International L.
Heavyweight Title)*
28.07.90 Jeff Harding W CO 7 Melbourne,
Australia
(WBC L. Heavyweight Title Challenge)
10.10.90 Sergio Merani W RTD 4 Kensington
(WBC L. Heavyweight Title Defence)
19.01.91 Guy Waters W PTS 12 Adelaide,
Australia
(WBC L. Heavyweight Title Defence)
11.09.91 Jeff Harding L PTS 12 Hammersmith
(WBC L. Heavyweight Title Defence)
15.11.91 Ed Neblett W RSC 4 Tampa, USA
11.12.91 Paul Maddison W RTD 8 Duluth, USA
27.02.92 Akim Tafer L PTS 12 Beausoleil,
France
(Vacant European Cruiserweight Title)

27.02.93 David Sewell W PTS 10 Dagenham
31.03.93 Willie Jake W RTD 6 Barking
29.01.94 Crawford Ashley W RTD 4 Cardiff
26.02.94 Mike Peak W PTS 4 Earls Court
23.03.94 Chemek Saleta L PTS 12 Cardiff
*(Vacant WBC International
Cruiserweight Title)*
01.10.94 Sylvester White W RSC 5 Carpentras,
France
21.01.95 Denzil Browne W RSC 11 Glasgow
(Vacant British Cruiserweight Title)
04.03.95 Mike Peak W PTS 10 Livingston
13.05.95 Terry Dunstan L PTS 12 Glasgow
(British Cruiserweight Title Defence)
28.10.95 Artis Pendergrass W PTS 8 Bristol
13.02.96 Terry Dunstan L PTS 12 Bethnal Green
(British Cruiserweight Title Challenge)
Career: 64 contests, won 49, drew 2, lost 13.

(Mohammed) Naveed Anwar

Rochdale. *Born* Pakistan, 14 August, 1970
Cruiserweight. Ht. 5'11¼"
Manager A. Talbot

08.06.96 Peter Mason L RSC 4 Newcastle
Career: 1 contest, lost 1.

Wayne Appleton

Pontefract. *Born* Hemsworth, 9 November,
1967
L. Middleweight. Ht. 5'10"
Manager T. Callighan

13.11.90 Bullit Andrews W RSC 5 Edgbaston
26.11.90 Stuart Good W CO 4 Lewisham
10.12.90 Wayne Timmins W CO 4 Birmingham
15.03.91 Andre Wharton L RSC 7 Willenhall
14.11.91 Dave Hindmarsh W RSC 8 Edinburgh
30.04.92 Kevin Adamson L RSC 2 Bayswater
01.03.93 Hughie Davey W PTS 6 Bradford
12.05.93 Richard O'Brien W RTD 2 Sheffield
25.10.93 Errol McDonald W PTS 8 Glasgow
04.12.93 Gary Murray L RTD 7 Sun City, South
Africa
18.01.95 Delroy Waul L PTS 6 Solihull
10.06.95 Joni Nyman L PTS 6 Pori, Finland
26.01.96 Leigh Wicks W PTS 6 Brighton
Career: 13 contests, won 8, lost 5.

Wayne Appleton   Les Clark

John Armour   Les Clark

John Armour

Chatham. *Born* Chatham, 26 October, 1968
Former Undefeated European &
Commonwealth Bantamweight Champion.
Ht. 5'4¾"
Manager M. Duff

24.09.90 Lupe Castro W PTS 6 Lewisham
31.10.90 Juan Camero W RSC 4 Crystal Palace
21.01.91 Elijro Mejia W RSC 1 Crystal Palace
30.09.91 Pat Maher W CO 1 Kensington
29.10.91 Pete Buckley W PTS 6 Kensington
14.12.91 Gary Hickman W RSC 6 Bexleyheath
25.03.92 Miguel Matthews W PTS 6 Dagenham
30.04.92 Ndabe Dube W RSC 12 Kensington
*(Vacant Commonwealth Bantamweight
Title)*
17.10.92 Mauricio Bernal W PTS 8 Wembley
03.12.92 Albert Musankabala W RSC 5
Lewisham
*(Commonwealth Bantamweight Title
Defence)*
28.01.93 Ricky Romero W CO 1 Southwark
10.02.93 Morgan Mpande W PTS 12 Lewisham
*(Commonwealth Bantamweight Title
Defence)*
09.06.93 Boualem Belkif W PTS 10 Lewisham
01.12.93 Karl Morling W CO 3 Kensington
14.01.94 Rufus Adebayo W RSC 7 Bethnal
Green
*(Commonwealth Bantamweight Title
Defence)*
23.09.94 Shaun Anderson W RSC 11 Bethnal
Green
*(Commonwealth Bantamweight Title
Defence)*
14.02.95 Tsitsi Sokutu W RSC 7 Bethnal Green
*(Commonwealth Bantamweight Title
Defence)*
19.04.95 Antonio Picardi W RSC 8 Bethnal
Green
(Vacant European Bantamweight Title)
19.05.95 Matthew Harris W RSC 3 Southwark
29.11.95 Redha Abbas W CO 5 Bethnal Green
*(European Bantamweight Title
Defence)*
Career: 20 contests, won 20.

(Shaun) Lee Armstrong

Huddersfield. *Born* Hartlepool, 18 October, 1972
Featherweight. Ht. 5'8"
Manager C. Aston

26.04.96 Daryl McKenzie L RSC 4 Glasgow
10.05.96 Charlie Rumbol W PTS 6 Wembley
23.05.96 Ian Richardson W PTS 6 Queensferry
Career: 3 contests, won 2, lost 1.

Darren Ashton

Stoke. *Born* Stoke, 26 February, 1969
L. Heavyweight. Ht. 6'1"
Manager W. Swift

13.10.93 Tony Colclough W RSC 1 Stoke
08.12.93 Nigel Rafferty W PTS 6 Stoke
23.03.94 L. A. Williams W PTS 6 Stoke
23.05.94 Nigel Rafferty W PTS 4 Walsall
30.11.94 Carlos Christie L PTS 6 Solihull
04.03.95 John Wilson NC 3 Livingston
06.05.95 Dale Nixon W RSC 4 Shepton Mallet
13.05.95 Stefan Wright W PTS 6 Glasgow
11.10.95 Neil Simpson L RSC 3 Solihull
17.11.95 Mark Baker L RSC 1 Bethnal Green
12.01.96 Frederic Alvarez L PTS 6 Copenhagen, Denmark
27.05.96 Harri Hakulinen L PTS 4 Helsinki, Finland
Career: 12 contests, won 6, lost 5, no contest 1.

Chris Aston

Leeds. *Born* Huddersfield, 7 August, 1961
L. Welterweight. Ht. 5'7"
Manager Self

07.10.91 Mick Holmes W RSC 2 Bradford
28.10.91 Charles Shepherd L PTS 6 Leicester
21.11.91 Dean Hiscox W PTS 6 Stafford
09.12.91 David Thompson W PTS 6 Bradford
21.01.92 Rob Stewart L RSC 4 Stockport
28.02.92 Mark Legg L RSC 5 Irvine
29.04.92 Richard Swallow L RSC 3 Solihull
02.11.93 Jason Beard L RSC 3 Southwark
08.12.93 Kevin Toomey L PTS 6 Hull
26.01.94 Paul Hughes L PTS 6 Stoke
17.02.94 Nick Boyd L CO 3 Bury
21.03.94 Tanveer Ahmed L CO 5 Glasgow
20.05.94 Keith Marner L PTS 8 Acton
06.06.94 Tanveer Ahmed L CO 4 Glasgow
06.10.94 John T. Kelly DREW 6 Hull
17.11.94 Tim Hill W PTS 6 Sheffield
20.01.95 Colin Dunne L RSC 4 Bethnal Green
21.04.95 James Montgomerie L PTS 6 Glasgow
12.05.95 Colin Dunne L RSC 4 Bethnal Green
14.06.95 Robert Grubb W CO 1 Batley
25.09.95 James Jiora DREW 6 Bradford
05.10.95 John Docherty L PTS 6 Glasgow
23.10.95 Dave McHale L RTD 3 Glasgow
Career: 23 contests, won 5, drew 2, lost 16.

David Bain

Walsall. *Born* Peterborough, 2 October, 1966
L. Middleweight. Ht. 5'8"
Manager C. Flute

29.03.94 Warren Stephens W PTS 6 Wolverhampton
23.05.94 Andy Peach W RSC 6 Walsall
11.10.94 Warren Stephens W PTS 6 Wolverhampton
07.02.95 Peter Reid L PTS 6 Wolverhampton

28.03.95 Prince Kasi Kaihau W PTS 6 Wolverhampton
11.05.95 Howard Clarke L RSC 1 Dudley
03.11.95 Rob Stevenson W PTS 6 Dudley
28.11.95 Nick Ingram L PTS 8 Wolverhampton
Career: 8 contests, won 5, lost 3.

David Bain   Les Clark

Mark Baker

Sidcup. *Born* Farnborough, 14 July, 1969
Southern Area Middleweight Champion. Ht. 5'9½"
Manager M. Duff/T. Lawless

07.09.92 Jason McNeill W RSC 2 Bethnal Green
15.10.92 Graham Jenner W RTD 4 Lewisham
03.12.92 Adrian Wright W RSC 1 Lewisham
10.02.93 Paul Hanlon W RSC 2 Lewisham
26.04.93 Karl Mumford W CO 1 Lewisham
15.06.93 Alan Baptiste W PTS 6 Hemel Hempstead
14.01.94 Karl Barwise L PTS 6 Bethnal Green
11.03.94 Graham Jenner W RSC 2 Bethnal Green
26.04.94 Jerry Mortimer W PTS 6 Bethnal Green
23.09.94 Alan Baptiste W RSC 1 Bethnal Green
17.10.94 Steve Thomas W RSC 5 Mayfair
27.10.94 Chris Richards W PTS 6 Milwall
13.12.94 Stinger Mason W RSC 4 Ilford
20.01.95 Mark Dawson W RSC 3 Bethnal Green
17.11.95 Darren Ashton W RSC 1 Bethnal Green
13.01.96 Mark Dawson W RSC 3 Halifax
05.03.96 Sven Hamer W PTS 10 Bethnal Green
(Vacant Southern Area Middleweight Title)
Career: 17 contests, won 16, lost 1.

Sean Baker

Bristol. *Born* Bristol, 21 February, 1969
Welterweight. Ht. 5'10"
Manager Self

08.09.92 Delwyn Panayiotiou W RSC 2 Southend
05.10.92 Raziq Ali W PTS 6 Bristol
01.12.92 Wayne Panayiotiou W RSC 3 Bristol
27.01.93 Danny Harper W PTS 4 Cardiff
09.03.93 Rick North W PTS 8 Bristol
24.03.93 Steve Levene DREW 6 Belfast
27.05.93 Gavin Lane W PTS 8 Bristol
26.06.93 David Lake W PTS 4 Keynsham
13.09.93 Mark Pearce W PTS 4 Bristol
03.11.93 George Wilson W RSC 2 Bristol
13.12.93 Hughie Davey W PTS 4 Bristol
10.03.94 Paul Quarrie W RTD 3 Bristol
31.03.94 Paul Lynch L RSC 3 Bristol
25.05.94 Andrew Jervis DREW 4 Bristol
03.08.94 Colin Petters L PTS 6 Bristol
22.11.94 Julian Eavis W PTS 6 Bristol
18.02.95 Dave Lovell W PTS 6 Shepton Mallet
06.05.95 John Janes W PTS 4 Shepton Mallet
28.07.95 George Wilson W PTS 6 Bristol
Career: 19 contests, won 15, drew 2, lost 2.

Adam Baldwin

Nuneaton. *Born* Nuneaton, 20 March, 1976
Welterweight. Ht. 5'7"
Manager Self

08.03.95 Mike Watson L PTS 6 Bloomsbury
03.04.95 Jamie Gallagher W PTS 6 Northampton
02.06.95 Martin Holgate L RSC 3 Bethnal Green
15.09.95 Craig Lynch L PTS 6 Glasgow
08.11.95 Paul Miles L RSC 2 Bethnal Green
17.01.96 George Richards L PTS 6 Solihull
24.01.96 Andy Peach W PTS 6 Stoke
Career: 7 contests, won 2, lost 5.

Phil Ball

Doncaster. *Born* Doncaster, 23 May, 1968
S. Middleweight. Ht. 6'0½"
Manager H. Hayes

24.11.92 Martin Jolley DREW 6 Doncaster
23.02.93 Martin Jolley L RSC 5 Doncaster
01.04.93 Chris Nurse DREW 6 Evesham
29.05.93 Alan Smiles L PTS 6 Paisley
07.06.93 Justin Clements L PTS 6 Walsall
17.06.93 Mark Smallwood L RSC 1 Bedworth
13.10.93 Dean Ashton L PTS 6 Stoke
25.10.93 Peter Flint W RSC 3 Liverpool
30.11.93 Chris Nurse L PTS 6 Wolverhampton
10.02.94 Tim Robinson W PTS 6 Hull
07.03.94 Tim Robinson W PTS 6 Doncaster
10.05.94 Dave Proctor W PTS 6 Doncaster
26.08.94 Dave Battey L PTS 6 Barnsley
12.09.94 Shamus Casey W PTS 6 Doncaster
12.10.94 Mark Hale L RSC 3 Stoke
09.02.95 Pat Durkin W PTS 6 Doncaster
07.04.95 Dave Battey L RSC 5 Sheffield
20.10.95 Clinton Woods L RSC 4 Mansfield
04.12.95 Lee Whitehead L PTS 6 Manchester
16.03.96 Scott Beasley L PTS 6 Sheffield
14.05.96 David Starie L RSC 1 Dagenham
Career: 21 contests, won 6, drew 2, lost 13.

Dean Barclay

Enfield. *Born* Ponders End, 12 April, 1964
L. Middleweight. Ht. 6'0"
Manager Self

30.10.85 Nick Harty W RSC 3 Basildon
16.01.86 Karl Ince W PTS 6 Preston
21.04.86 Gary Flear W RSC 1 Birmingham
29.09.86 Dean Murray W RSC 3 Mayfair

13.10.86 Wally Swift Jnr DREW 8 Dulwich
11.03.87 Ian Chantler L PTS 8 Kensington
21.03.88 Kesem Clayton DREW 8 Bethnal Green
25.04.88 Kevin Hayde W PTS 6 Bethnal Green
29.06.88 Ken Foreman W PTS 6 Basildon
02.05.89 Jason Rowe W PTS 8 Chigwell
17.11.95 Ernie Loveridge W PTS 4 Bethnal Green

Career: 11 contests, won 8, drew 2, lost 1.

Nicky Bardle

Ealing. *Born* Ware, 30 January, 1972
Welterweight. Ht. 5'9½"
Manager H. Holland

07.11.91 Michael Clynch W RSC 4 Peterborough
12.02.92 Steve Hearn W RSC 1 Watford
30.04.92 James Campbell L CO 1 Watford
17.09.92 Brian Coleman W RSC 4 Watford
19.11.94 Anthony Campbell W PTS 6 Heathrow
21.09.95 Andy Davidson W CO 1 Battersea
30.10.95 Paul Salmon W CO 1 Heathrow
03.12.95 Vince Burns W RSC 1 Southwark
12.02.96 Richard Swallow L RSC 4 Heathrow
25.06.96 John Smith W PTS 4 Stevenage

Career: 10 contests, won 8, lost 2.

Nicky Bardle   Les Clark

Gavin Barker

Great Yarmouth. *Born* Nottingham, 11 May, 1969
Welterweight. Ht. 5'9"
Manager G. Holmes

17.05.95 Seth Jones W PTS 4 Ipswich
14.09.95 Darren Covill L CO 1 Battersea

Career: 2 contests, won 1, lost 1.

Jason Barker

Sheffield. *Born* Chesterfield, 1 June, 1973
Welterweight. Ht. 6'0"
Manager G. Rhodes

30.01.92 Nicky Lucas W PTS 6 Southampton
12.02.92 Roger Hunte L RTD 4 Wembley

29.04.92 Dave Lovell L PTS 6 Stoke
03.06.92 John O. Johnson L PTS 6 Newcastle under Lyne
07.07.92 Patrick Loughran L PTS 6 Bristol
21.10.92 Brian Coleman L PTS 6 Stoke
02.11.92 Shea Neary L RSC 3 Liverpool
09.12.92 John O. Johnson L PTS 8 Stoke
28.01.93 Jason Beard L RSC 3 Southwark
22.04.93 Marco Fattore L PTS 6 Mayfair
12.05.93 Shaba Edwards W PTS 6 Stoke
14.06.93 Delroy Leslie L RTD 3 Bayswater
21.09.95 Jamie Gallagher W RSC 2 Sheffield
20.10.95 Wesley Jones W RSC 2 Mansfield
22.11.95 Darren Covill W PTS 4 Sheffield
08.12.95 James Donoghue L PTS 6 Leeds
05.02.96 Darren Covill L RSC 1 Bexleyheath
03.05.96 Shamus Casey W RSC 1 Sheffield
09.05.96 Hughie Davey L PTS 6 Sunderland

Career: 19 contests, won 6, lost 13.

Jason Barker   Les Clark

Chris Barnett

Wolverhampton. *Born* Coventry, 15 July, 1973
Welterweight. Ht. 5.5½"
Manager F. Warren

18.02.95 Wayne Jones W RSC 5 Shepton Mallet
24.11.95 Brian Coleman W PTS 6 Manchester
09.04.96 Charlie Paine W RSC 2 Salford

Career: 3 contests, won 3.

(Martin) Wee Barry (Moore)

Staines. *Born* Limavaay, Ireland, 5 April, 1971
Featherweight. Ht. 5'6½"
Manager H. Holland

30.10.95 Martin Evans L PTS 6 Heathrow
12.02.96 Martin Evans W RSC 4 Heathrow

Career: 2 contests, won 1, lost 1.

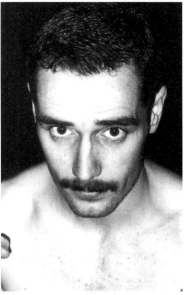

Wee Barry   Les Clark

Dave Battey

Worksop. *Born* Gainsborough, 14 December, 1972
L. Heavyweight. Ht. 6'1¼"
Manager Self

24.05.94 Johnny Hooks L PTS 6 Leicester
28.06.94 Justin Clements L RSC 2 Edgbaston
26.08.94 Phil Ball W PTS 6 Barnsley
26.09.94 Greg Scott-Briggs L RSC 4 Cleethorpes
25.10.94 Darren Sweeney L CO 1 Edgbaston
05.12.94 Dave Owens W PTS 6 Cleethorpes
15.12.94 Andy McVeigh LRSF 3 Walsall
09.02.95 Kevin Burton W PTS 6 Doncaster
07.04.95 Phil Ball W RSC 5 Sheffield
05.05.95 Kevin Burton W PTS 6 Doncaster
15.05.95 Mark Hale W PTS 6 Bradford
21.09.95 David Radford L PTS 6 Sheffield
20.10.95 David Radford L CO 1 Mansfield

Career: 13 contests, won 6, lost 7.

Jason Beard

Beckton. *Born* Whitechapel, 24 April, 1967
Welterweight. Ht. 5'8½"
Manager Self

03.12.92 Robert Whitehouse W RSC 3 Lewisham
28.01.93 Jason Barker W RSC 3 Southwark
24.02.93 Michael Dick W RSC 6 Wembley
26.04.93 Brian Coleman W PTS 6 Lewisham
09.06.93 Phil Found W PTS 6 Lewisham
16.09.93 David Lake W PTS 6 Southwark
02.11.93 Chris Aston W RSC 3 Southwark
07.12.93 Jason Campbell W RSC 2 Bethnal Green
14.01.94 Steve Phillips W RTD 3 Bethnal Green
11.03.94 Dave Maj W PTS 6 Bethnal Green
23.09.94 Mark McCreath L PTS 6 Bethnal Green
09.09.94 Dewi Roberts W RSC 4 Millwall
09.12.94 Marty Duke W PTS 6 Bethnal Green

14.02.95 Richard Swallow W PTS 6 Bethnal Green
19.04.95 Steve McGovern W PTS 6 Bethnal Green
27.09.95 George Wilson W PTS 6 Bethnal Green
08.12.95 Ojay Abrahams L CO 2 Bethnal Green
Career: 17 contests, won 15, lost 2.

Ricky Beard
Dagenham. *Born* Hackney, 1 March, 1963
Former Southern Area Flyweight Champion. Ht. 5'7½"
Manager Self

02.05.89 Ged Goodwin W RSC 1 Chigwell
06.06.89 Ged Goodwin W RTD 1 Chigwell
19.09.89 Eric George L PTS 6 Bethnal Green
04.10.89 Gordon Shaw L PTS 6 Basildon
03.10.90 Neil Johnston DREW 6 Basildon
19.11.90 Robbie Regan L RSC 6 Cardiff
26.03.91 Francis Ampofo L PTS 8 Bethnal Green
30.09.91 Mickey Cantwell L PTS 8 Kensington
25.02.92 Francis Ampofo L PTS 8 Crystal Palace
14.04.92 Prince Nassem Hamed L CO 2 Mansfield
20.04.93 Tim Yeates L PTS 6 Brentwood
11.05.93 Mickey Bell W RSC 2 Norwich
29.06.93 James Drummond W PTS 8 Mayfair
05.09.94 Shaun Norman L PTS 8 Brentwood
16.09.94 Jesper D. Jensen L RTD 2 Aalborg, Denmark
23.11.94 James Drummond W RSC 2 Irvine
30.03.95 Daren Fifield W RSC 8 Bethnal Green
(Vacant Southern Area Flyweight Title)
20.10.95 Mark Reynolds L PTS 10 Ipswich
(Southern Area Flyweight Title Defence)
18.11.95 Lehlohonolo Ledwaba L RSC 3 Glasgow
23.01.96 Spencer Oliver L RSC 3 Bethnal Green
04.05.96 Graham McGrath L PTS 6 Dagenham
Career: 21 contests, won 6, drew 1, lost 14.

Gary Beardsley   Les Clark

Gary Beardsley
Belper. *Born* Belper, 18 July, 1968
Welterweight. Ht. 5'10"
Manager J. Ashton

09.02.95 Shaun Stokes W RSC 3 Doncaster
01.03.95 Eddie Haley W RSC 1 Glasgow
06.03.95 Stefan Scriggins L PTS 6 Leicester
15.03.95 Jamie Gallagher W PTS 6 Stoke
20.10.95 Dewi Roberts W PTS 6 Mansfield
22.11.95 Richard Swallow DREW 6 Sheffield
06.12.95 John Smith W PTS 8 Stoke
06.02.96 Georgie Smith L RSC 1 Basildon
22.03.96 Mark Legg W PTS 6 Mansfield
Career: 9 contests, won 6, drew 1, lost 2.

Scott Beasley
Northampton. *Born* Northampton, 14 March, 1974
L. Heavyweight. Ht. 5'9"
Manager M. Shinfield

07.12.95 Jamie Warters L PTS 6 Hull
31.01.96 Lee Simpkin W RSC 3 Stoke
15.02.96 P. R. Mason L PTS 6 Sheffield
16.03.96 Phil Ball W PTS 6 Sheffield
24.03.96 David Larkin L RTD 3 Shaw
Career: 5 contests, won 2, lost 3.

Gordon Behan
Leamington. *Born* Dublin, 13 February, 1976
Middleweight. Ht. 5'10¾"
Manager R. Gray/P. Cowdell

24.04.96 Michael Pinnock W PTS 6 Solihull
03.06.96 Peter Mitchell DREW 6 Birmingham
Career: 2 contests, won 1, drew 1.

Robbie Bell
Sunderland. *Born* Sunderland, 11 February, 1977
L. Middleweight. Ht. 5'10"
Manager T. Conroy

11.05.95 Paul Webb W PTS 6 Sunderland
22.06.95 Nick Ingram W PTS 6 Houghton le Spring
15.09.95 Phil Epton W PTS 6 Darlington
28.09.95 Jetty Williams W PTS 6 Sunderland
02.11.95 Prince Kasi Kaihau W PTS 6 Houghton le Spring
18.03.96 Joe Townsley L PTS 6 Glasgow
Career: 6 contests, won 5, lost 1.

Nigel Benn
Ilford. *Born* Ilford, 22 January, 1964
Former WBC S. Middleweight Champion.
Former WBO & Commonwealth Middleweight Champion. Ht. 5'9½"
Manager P. De Freitas

28.01.87 Graeme Ahmed W RSC 2 Croydon
04.03.87 Kevin Roper W RSC 1 Basildon
22.04.87 Bob Niewenhuizen W RSC 1 Kensington
09.05.87 Winston Burnett W RSC 4 Wandsworth
17.06.87 Reggie Marks W RSC 1 Kensington
01.07.87 Leon Morris W CO 1 Kensington
09.08.87 Eddie Smith W CO 1 Windsor
16.09.87 Winston Burnett W RSC 3 Kensington

13.10.87 Russell Barker W RSC 1 Windsor
03.11.87 Ronnie Yeo W RSC 1 Bethnal Green
24.11.87 Ian Chantler W CO 1 Wisbech
02.12.87 Reggie Miller W CO 7 Kensington
27.01.88 Fermin Chirinos W CO 2 Bethnal Green
07.02.88 Byron Prince W RSC 2 Stafford
24.02.88 Greg Taylor W RSC 2 Aberavon
14.03.88 Darren Hobson W CO 1 Norwich
20.04.88 Abdul Amoru Sanda W RSC 2 Muswell Hill
(Vacant Commonwealth Middleweight Title)
28.05.88 Tim Williams W RSC 2 Kensington
26.10.88 Anthony Logan W CO 2 Kensington
(Commonwealth Middleweight Title Defence)
10.12.88 David Noel W RSC 1 Crystal Palace
(Commonwealth Middleweight Title Defence)
08.02.89 Mike Chilambe W CO 1 Kensington
(Commonwealth Middleweight Title Defence)
28.03.89 Mbayo Wa Mbayo W CO 2 Glasgow
21.05.89 Michael Watson L CO 6 Finsbury Park
(Commonwealth Middleweight Title Defence)
20.10.89 Jorge Amparo W PTS 10 Atlantic City, USA
01.12.89 Jose Quinones W RSC 1 Las Vegas, USA
14.01.90 Sanderline Williams W PTS 10 Atlantic City, USA
29.04.90 Doug de Witt W RSC 8 Atlantic City, USA
(WBO Middleweight Title Challenge)
18.08.90 Iran Barkley W RSC 1 Las Vegas, USA
(WBO Middleweight Title Defence)
18.11.90 Chris Eubank L RSC 9 Birmingham
(WBO Middleweight Title Defence)
03.04.91 Robbie Sims W RSC 7 Bethnal Green
03.07.91 Kid Milo W RSC 4 Brentwood
26.10.91 Lenzie Morgan W PTS 10 Brentwood
07.12.91 Hector Lescano W CO 3 Manchester
19.02.92 Dan Sherry W RSC 3 Muswell Hill
23.05.92 Thulani Malinga W PTS 10 Birmingham
03.10.92 Mauro Galvano W RTD 3 Marino, Italy
(WBC S. Middleweight Title Challenge)
12.12.92 Nicky Piper W RSC 11 Muswell Hill
(WBC S. Middleweight Title Defence)
06.03.93 Mauro Galvano W PTS 12 Glasgow
(WBC S. Middleweight Title Defence)
26.06.93 Lou Gent W RSC 4 Earls Court
(WBC S. Middleweight Title Defence)
09.10.93 Chris Eubank DREW 12 Manchester
*(WBC S. Middleweight Title Defence.
WBO S. Middleweight Title Challenge)*
26.02.94 Henry Wharton W PTS 12 Earls Court
(WBC S. Middleweight Title Defence)
10.09.94 Juan Carlos Gimenez W PTS 12 Birmingham
(WBC S. Middleweight Title Defence)
25.02.95 Gerald McClellan W CO 10 Millwall
(WBC S. Middleweight Title Defence)
22.07.95 Vincenzo Nardiello W RTD 8 Millwall
(WBC S. Middleweight Title Defence)
02.09.95 Danny Ray Perez W CO 7 Wembley
(WBC S. Middleweight Title Defence)
02.03.96 Thulani Malinga L PTS 12 Newcastle
(WBC S. Middleweight Title Defence)
Career: 46 contests, won 42, drew 1, lost 3.

Mervyn Bennett

Cardiff. *Born* Cardiff, 20 February, 1960
Former Undefeated Welsh Lightweight
Champion. Ht. 5'6½"
Manager D. Gardiner

06.01.81	Geoff Smart W RSC 6 Bethnal Green
26.01.81	Paddy McGuire W RSC 2 Edgbaston
07.04.81	Philip Morris W PTS 6 Newport
25.09.81	Alec Irvine W PTS 6 Nottingham
12.10.81	Richie Foster W PTS 8 Bloomsbury
19.11.81	Don George L PTS 10 Ebbw Vale
	(Vacant Welsh Featherweight Title)
26.10.82	Mike Rowley L PTS 8 Newport
24.11.82	Jimmy Duncan L PTS 8 Stoke
17.02.83	Kevin Pritchard L RSC 5 Coventry
18.04.83	Keith Foreman L RSC 6 Bradford
17.02.86	Dave Smith W PTS 8 Mayfair
10.04.86	Dave Pratt W CO 6 Leicester
29.10.86	Keith Parry L RSC 3 Ebbw Vale
19.01.87	John Mullen W CO 1 Glasgow
16.02.87	Ray Newby L CO 8 Glasgow
19.05.92	Edward Lloyd L RSC 5 Cardiff
28.10.92	Mike Morrison W PTS 6 Cardiff
14.12.92	Mike Morrison W PTS 6 Cardiff
27.01.93	Carl Hook W PTS 10 Cardiff
	(Vacant Welsh Lightweight Title)
17.06.95	Vince Burns W CO 4 Cardiff
20.09.95	Dean Phillips L PTS 6 Ystrad
25.10.95	Gareth Jordan W PTS 10 Cardiff
	(Welsh Lightweight Title Defence)
20.03.96	Karl Taylor L PTS 8 Cardiff

Career: 23 contests, won 13, lost 10.

Andrew Benson

Mile End. *Born* Islington, 8 May, 1969
Cruiserweight. Ht. 6'0"
Manager F. Warren

02.09.94	Trevor Small W PTS 6 Spitalfields
18.11.94	Gypsy Carman W PTS 6 Bracknell
26.04.95	Martin Langtry L PTS 6 Solihull
17.05.95	Paul Lawson L RSC 2 Ipswich
13.04.96	Kelly Oliver L PTS 4 Wythenshawe

Career: 5 contests, won 2, lost 3.

(Adrian) Ady Benton

Bradford. *Born* Dewsbury, 26 August, 1973
S. Bantamweight. Ht. 5'6"
Manager K. Tate

27.04.92	Mark Hargreaves W PTS 6 Bradford
29.10.92	Vince Feeney DREW 6 Bayswater
09.11.92	Stevie Woods W PTS 6 Bradford
25.01.93	Neil Parry W RSC 6 Bradford
26.02.93	James Drummond DREW 6 Irvine
08.03.93	Dave Campbell W PTS 6 Leeds
29.06.93	Michael Alldis W DIS 3 Mayfair
20.09.93	Mike Deveney L PTS 8 Glasgow
08.11.93	Chip O'Neill W RSC 5 Bradford
24.01.94	Mike Deveney W PTS 6 Glasgow
25.02.94	Paul Lloyd L RSC 5 Chester
	(Vacant Central Area S. Bantamweight Title)
25.04.94	Pat Clinton W RSC 1 Glasgow
16.09.94	Johnny Bredahl L PTS 8 Aalborg, Denmark
23.11.94	Drew Docherty L PTS 12 Irvine
	(British Bantamweight Title Challenge)
21.04.95	James Murray L RSC 7 Glasgow
14.06.95	Louis Veitch L RSC 2 Batley
11.10.95	Lyndon Kershaw W RTD 6 Solihull
18.10.95	Graham McGrath W PTS 6 Batley
29.11.95	Greg Upton L PTS 6 Solihull
21.02.96	Carl Allen W PTS 6 Batley
24.04.96	Shaun Anderson W PTS 6 Solihull

Career: 21 contests, won 12, drew 2, lost 7.

Dennis Berry

Alfreton. *Born* Birmingham, 4 April, 1967
Welterweight. Ht. 5'8"
Manager Self

01.04.93	Lee Renshaw W RSC 3 Evesham
08.06.93	David Sumner W PTS 6 Derby
04.11.93	Andy Peach W PTS 6 Stafford
17.03.94	Rick North L PTS 6 Lincoln
16.05.94	Rick North W RSC 6 Cleethorpes
24.05.94	Norman Hutcheon W RSC 2 Leicester
28.06.94	Howard Clarke W RSC 3 Edgbaston
30.07.94	Kevin Lueshing L CO 2 Bethnal Green
07.11.94	Vince Rose L PTS 6 Bethnal Green
15.12.94	Warren Stephens W PTS 6 Evesham
25.01.95	Howard Clarke W PTS 8 Stoke
03.03.95	Geoff McCreesh W RTD 5 Bracknell
01.09.95	Gordon Blair W RSC 3 Wolverhampton
25.10.95	Rick North W PTS 6 Telford
18.03.96	Brian Dunn W RSC 2 Glasgow

Career: 15 contests, won 12, lost 3.

Barrie Bessant

Plymouth. *Born* Bournemouth, 29 June, 1973
Middleweight. Ht. 6'2¼"
Manager N. Christian

28.10.95	Andy Edge L PTS 6 Bristol
13.11.95	Peter Mitchell L RSC 2 Barnstaple
17.12.95	John Wilson L RSC 1 Glasgow

Career: 3 contests, lost 3.

Lee Bird

Doncaster. *Born* Doncaster, 17 June, 1971
Middleweight. Ht. 5'6"
Manager T. Petersen

13.02.96	Paul Bowen L RSC 2 Bethnal Green

Career: 1 contest, lost 1.

Gordon Blair

Glasgow. *Born* Glasgow, 26 February, 1969
Welterweight. Ht. 5'10"
Manager A. Melrose/A. Morrison

21.11.89	Gavin Fitzpatrick W RSC 3 Glasgow
18.12.89	John Ritchie W PTS 4 Glasgow
19.02.90	Trevor Meikle W PTS 6 Glasgow
26.02.90	Jim Conley W RSC 3 Bradford
26.04.90	Kid Sylvester L PTS 6 Halifax
14.05.90	Trevor Ambrose W CO 5 Northampton
25.09.90	Calum Rattray W RSC 3 Glasgow
22.10.90	Shamus Casey W RSC 3 Glasgow
06.11.90	Leigh Wicks L PTS 8 Mayfair
10.12.90	Quinn Paynter W PTS 6 Glasgow
25.01.91	Danny Quigg W PTS 6 Shotts
18.02.91	Gary Logan L CO 1 Mayfair
15.04.91	Rob Pitters L PTS 6 Glasgow
31.05.91	Paul King W PTS 8 Glasgow
20.06.91	Delroy Waul W CO 2 Liverpool
24.09.91	Bozon Haule W RSC 8 Glasgow
19.11.91	Tony McKenzie L RSC 5 Norwich
31.01.92	Willie Beattie L RSC 3 Glasgow
	(Vacant Scottish Welterweight Title)
12.03.92	Mark Jay DREW 8 Glasgow
29.05.92	Ossie Maddix L PTS 6 Manchester
18.07.92	Ensley Bingham L CO 2 Manchester
27.10.92	Howard Clarke W RSC 4 Cradley Heath
24.11.92	Errol McDonald L RSC 5 Doncaster
29.01.93	Mark Cichocki L PTS 8 Glasgow
15.02.93	Lindon Scarlett L CO 4 Mayfair
25.06.93	Gary Logan L RSC 6 Battersea
12.03.94	Michael Smyth L RSC 4 Cardiff
13.04.94	Gilbert Jackson L RTD 1 Glasgow
21.07.94	Mark Antony L PTS 6 Edinburgh
08.09.94	Lee Blundell DREW 6 Glasgow
18.12.94	Mark Allen W RSC 3 Glasgow
21.01.95	Michael Carruth W PTS 6 Glasgow
13.05.95	Kevin McKenzie W RTD 5 Glasgow
02.06.95	Maurice Forbes L RSC 4 Bethnal Green
01.09.95	Dennis Berry L RSC 3 Wolverhampton
09.03.96	Michael Carruth L RTD 3 Millstreet

Career: 36 contests, won 17, drew 2, lost 17.

Ervine Blake

Worcester. *Born* Belfast, 17 February, 1966
S. Featherweight. Ht. 5'7½"
Manager Self

08.10.90	Colin Innes W PTS 6 Bradford
16.10.90	Barrie Kelley L PTS 6 Evesham
07.10.91	Derek Amory W PTS 6 Birmingham
13.02.96	Carl Allen L RSC 5 Wolverhampton
27.03.96	Michael Edwards W RSC 2 Stoke
24.04.96	Steve Conway L PTS 6 Solihull
10.05.96	Mark Bowers W RSC 3 Wembley
03.06.96	Wayne Jones W RSC 1 Birmingham
29.06.96	Paul Ingle L RSC 2 Erith

Career: 9 contests, won 5, lost 4.

Jason Blanche

Leeds. *Born* New Ross, 29 April, 1972
Lightweight. Ht. 5'4"
Manager J. Celebanski

25.09.95	T. J. Smith W PTS 6 Bradford
30.10.95	Muhammad Shaffique W CO 2 Bradford
11.11.95	Brian Robb W RSC 4 Halifax
11.12.95	Colin Innes W PTS 6 Bradford
13.01.96	Alan Bosworth L PTS 6 Halifax
07.03.96	John T. Kelly DREW 6 Bradford
01.04.96	John T. Kelly DREW 6 Bradford
20.05.96	G. G. Goddard W RSC 4 Bradford
24.06.96	Kid McAuley W PTS 6 Bradford

Career: 9 contests, won 6, drew 2, lost 1.

Jason Blanche   Les Clark

Lee Blundell

Wigan. *Born* Wigan, 11 August, 1971
Middleweight. Ht. 6'2"
Manager Self

25.04.94	Robert Harper W RSC 2 Bury	
20.05.94	Freddie Yemofio W RSC 6 Acton	
08.09.94	Gordon Blair DREW 6 Glasgow	
07.12.94	Kesem Clayton W RTD 2 Stoke	
18.02.95	Glenn Catley L RSC 6 Shepton Mallet	
11.12.95	Martin Jolley W PTS 6 Morecambe	

Career: 6 contests, won 4, drew 1, lost 1.

Jason Booth

Radford. *Born* Nottingham, 7 November, 1977
Flyweight. Ht. 5'4"
Manager M. Shinfield

13.06.96 Darren Noble W RSC 3 Sheffield
Career: 1 contest, won 1.

Tony Booth

Sheffield. *Born* Hull, 30 January, 1970
Former Undefeated Central Area
Cruiserweight Champion. Ht. 5'11¾"
Manager Self

08.03.90 Paul Lynch L PTS 6 Watford
11.04.90 Mick Duncan W PTS 6 Dewsbury
26.04.90 Colin Manners W PTS 6 Halifax
16.05.90 Tommy Warde W PTS 6 Hull
05.06.90 Gary Dyson W PTS 6 Liverpool
05.09.90 Shaun McCrory L PTS 6 Stoke
08.10.90 Bullit Andrews W RSC 3 Cleethorpes
23.01.91 Darron Griffiths DREW 6 Stoke
06.02.91 Shaun McCrory L PTS 6 Liverpool
06.03.91 Billy Brough L PTS 6 Glasgow
18.03.91 Billy Brough W PTS 6 Glasgow
28.03.91 Neville Brown L PTS 6 Alfreton
17.05.91 Glenn Campbell L RSC 2 Bury
(*Central Area S. Middleweight Title Challenge*)
25.07.91 Paul Murray W PTS 6 Dudley
01.08.91 Nick Manners DREW 8 Dewsbury
11.09.91 Jim Peters L PTS 8 Hammersmith
28.10.91 Eddie Smulders L RSC 6 Arnhem, Holland
09.12.91 Steve Lewsam L PTS 8 Cleethorpes
30.01.92 Serg Fame W PTS 6 Southampton
12.02.92 Tenko Ernie W RSC 4 Wembley
05.03.92 John Beckles W RSC 6 Battersea
26.03.92 Dave Owens W PTS 6 Hull
08.04.92 Michael Gale L PTS 8 Leeds
13.05.92 Phil Soundy W PTS 6 Kensington
02.06.92 Eddie Smulders L RSC 1 Rotterdam, Holland
18.07.92 Maurice Core L PTS 6 Manchester
07.09.92 James Cook L PTS 8 Bethnal Green
30.10.92 Roy Richie DREW 6 Istrees, France
18.11.92 Tony Wilson DREW 8 Solihull
25.12.92 Francis Wanyama L PTS 6 Izegem, Belgium
09.02.93 Tony Wilson W PTS 8 Wolverhampton
01.05.93 Ralf Rocchigiani DREW 8 Berlin, Germany
03.06.93 Victor Cordoba L PTS 8 Marseille, France
23.06.93 Tony Behan W PTS 6 Gorleston
01.07.93 Michael Gale L PTS 8 York
17.09.93 Ole Klemetsen L PTS 8 Copenhagen, Denmark
07.10.93 Denzil Browne DREW 8 York

02.11.93 James Cook L PTS 8 Southwark
12.11.93 Carlos Christie W PTS 6 Hull
28.01.94 Francis Wanyama L RSC 2 Waregem, Belgium
(*Vacant Commonwealth Cruiserweight Title*)
26.03.94 Torsten May L PTS 6 Dortmund, Germany
21.07.94 Mark Prince L RSC 3 Battersea
24.09.94 Johnny Held L PTS 8 Rotterdam, Holland
07.10.94 Dirk Wallyn L PTS 6 Waregem, Belgium
27.10.94 Dean Francis L CO 1 Bayswater
23.01.95 Jan Lefeber L PTS 8 Rotterdam, Holland
07.03.95 John Foreman L PTS 6 Edgbaston
27.04.95 Art Stacey W PTS 10 Hull
(*Vacant Central Area Cruiserweight Title*)
04.06.95 Montell Griffin L RSC 2 Bethnal Green
06.07.95 Nigel Rafferty W RSC 7 Hull
22.07.95 Mark Prince L RSC 2 Millwall
06.09.95 Leif Keiski L PTS 8 Helsinki, Finland
25.09.95 Neil Simpson W PTS 8 Cleethorpes
06.10.95 Don Diego Poeder L RSC 2 Waregem, Belgium
11.11.95 Bruce Scott L RSC 3 Halifax
16.12.95 John Marceta L RSC 2 Cardiff
20.01.96 Johnny Nelson L RSC 2 Mansfield
15.03.96 Slick Miller W PTS 6 Hull
27.03.96 Neil Simpson L PTS 6 Whitwick
17.05.96 Mark Richardson W RSC 2 Hull
Career: 60 contests, won 20, drew 6, lost 34.

John Bosco (Waigo)

Mitcham. *Born* Uganda, 16 July, 1967
L. Middleweight. Ht. 5'8½"
Manager M. Duff

05.12.91 Tony Kosova W CO 2 Peterborough
17.02.92 Gilbert Jackson W PTS 6 Mayfair
03.09.92 Russell Washer W RSC 2 Dunstable
19.10.92 Steve Goodwin W RSC 2 Mayfair
07.12.92 Griff Jones W RSC 1 Mayfair
28.01.93 Jerry Mortimer W RSC 4 Southwark
15.02.93 Mark Dawson W PTS 6 Mayfair
29.03.93 Winston May W RSC 3 Mayfair
10.11.93 Mark Dawson W RTD 4 Watford
26.01.94 Julian Eavis W RSC 1 Birmingham
14.03.94 Carlo Colarusso W PTS 6 Mayfair
28.04.94 Chris Peters W PTS 8 Mayfair
05.10.94 Robert Wright L RSC 7 Wolverhampton
16.10.95 J. P. Matthews DREW 6 Mayfair
17.11.95 Harry Dhami W PTS 6 Bethnal Green
04.05.96 Adrian Dodson L RSC 7 Dagenham
(*WBO Inter-Continental L. Middleweight Title Challenge*)
Career: 16 contests, won 13, drew 1, lost 2.

Alan Bosworth

Northampton. *Born* Northampton, 31 December, 1967
L. Welterweight. Ht. 5'7"
Manager M. Shinfield

17.10.95 Simon Hamblett W RSC 2 Wolverhampton
29.10.95 Shaun Gledhill W PTS 6 Shaw
16.11.95 Brian Coleman W PTS 6 Evesham
23.11.95 David Thompson W RSC 4 Tynemouth

13.01.96 Jason Blanche W PTS 6 Halifax
31.01.96 Arv Mittoo W PTS 6 Stoke
16.02.96 John Docherty W PTS 6 Irvine
24.03.96 Scott Walker DREW 6 Shaw
16.05.96 Yifru Retta W PTS 6 Dunstable
Career: 9 contests, won 8, drew 1.

Alan Bosworth   Les Clark

Michael Bowen

West Ham. *Born* Forest Gate, 14 November, 1974
Middleweight. Ht. 6'1½"
Manager P. De Freitas

02.06.95 Robert Harper W PTS 6 Bethnal Green
09.12.95 Peter Varnavas W CO 3 Bethnal Green
13.02.96 Henry Price W RSC 1 Bethnal Green
13.04.96 Danny Ryan W RSC 2 Wythenshawe
11.05.96 Mark Dawson W PTS 4 Bethnal Green
Career: 5 contests, won 5.

Paul Bowen

West Ham. *Born* Barking, 14 May, 1973
Middleweight. Ht. 6'0"
Manager P. De Freitas

13.02.96 Lee Bird W RSC 2 Bethnal Green
13.04.96 Pat Durkin W RSC 3 Wythenshawe
Career: 2 contests, won 2.

Mark Bowers

Lock Heath. *Born* Fareham, 19 October, 1970
Featherweight. Ht. 5'5"
Manager M. Duff/T. Lawless

13.05.92 Hamid Moulay W CO 1 Kensington
17.10.92 Miguel Matthews W PTS 6 Wembley
17.12.92 Chris Lyons W CO 2 Wembley
26.04.93 Andrew Bloomer W PTS 6 Lewisham
09.06.93 Kurt Griffiths W RSC 1 Lewisham
02.11.93 Chris Jickells W RSC 3 Southwark
07.12.93 Thomas Bernard W RSC 1 Bethnal Green

05.04.94 Pete Buckley W PTS 6 Bethnal Green
11.05.94 Dean Lynch W RSC 2 Stevenage
09.12.94 Ian Reid W PTS 6 Bethnal Green
14.02.95 Graham McGrath W PTS 6 Bethnal Green
03.03.95 Des Gargano W RTD 2 Bracknell
12.05.95 Shaun Anderson W RSC 7 Bethnal Green
15.03.96 Graham McGrath W PTS 6 Dunstable
10.05.96 Ervine Blake L RSC 3 Wembley
Career: 15 contests, won 14, lost 1.

Nigel Bradley

Sheffield. *Born* Sheffield, 24 February, 1968
L. Welterweight. Ht. 5'8"
Manager Self

14.12.87 Lee Amass L RSC 4 Piccadilly
29.01.88 John Townsley L PTS 6 Durham
23.03.88 Darren Darby W RSC 1 Sheffield
28.03.88 Adam Muir NC 4 Glasgow
18.04.88 Mark Kelly L PTS 6 Manchester
08.06.88 Mike Russell W PTS 6 Sheffield
09.09.88 David Bacon W RSC 5 Doncaster
26.10.88 Dean Dickinson W PTS 6 Sheffield
23.02.89 Chris Mulcahy W RSC 2 Stockport
09.03.89 Michael McDermott W RSC 5 Glasgow
04.04.89 John Mullen W RSC 6 Sheffield
08.10.90 John Townsley DREW 8 Glasgow
14.11.90 B. F. Williams W CO 2 Sheffield
29.01.91 Sugar Gibiliru L PTS 8 Stockport
11.02.92 Dean Hollington L PTS 6 Barking
18.03.92 Kris McAdam W CO 2 Glasgow
14.04.92 Dave Whittle W CO 3 Mansfield
29.09.92 Tony Swift L PTS 8 Stoke
08.02.94 Howard Clarke L RTD 6 Wolverhampton
17.11.94 John Smith W PTS 6 Sheffield
03.03.95 Jason Rowland L RSC 3 Bethnal Green
13.04.95 Allan Hall L RSC 2 Bloomsbury
08.09.95 Shea Neary L RSC 2 Liverpool
(*Vacant Central L. Welterweight Title*)
25.10.95 Michael Smyth L RSC 4 Cardiff
Career: 24 contests, won 11, drew 1, lost 11, no contest 1.

Nigel Bradley   Les Clark

Thomas Bradley

Sheffield. *Born* Sheffield, 29 August, 1972
Lightweight. Ht. 5'7"
Manager B. Ingle

15.05.95 Simon Hamblett W PTS 6 Cleethorpes
15.09.95 Mark Haslam L CO 4 Mansfield
14.11.95 Ian Richardson W PTS 6 Yarm
06.12.95 Scott Marshall W RSC 5 Stoke
13.06.96 Ram Singh W RSC 1 Sheffield
Career: 5 contests, won 4, lost 1.

Mark Breslin

Barrhead. *Born* Paisley, 5 January, 1972
L. Welterweight. Ht. 5'9½"
Manager T. Gilmour

19.09.94 Brian Coleman W CO 1 Glasgow
02.11.94 Mark Allen W PTS 6 Solihull
23.11.94 Kevin McKenzie W PTS 6 Irvine
05.04.95 T. J. Smith W PTS 6 Irvine
01.06.95 T. J. Smith W RSC 3 Musselburgh
18.09.95 Mike Watson W PTS 6 Glasgow
18.11.95 Paul Scott W PTS 6 Glasgow
22.04.96 Mark Legg W PTS 8 Glasgow
Career: 8 contests, won 8.

Henry Brewer

Shipley. *Born* Bradford, 18 September, 1969
Cruiserweight. Ht. 6'0"
Manager Self

16.05.89 Steve Osborne L PTS 6 Halifax
14.06.95 Cliff Elden W PTS 6 Batley
18.10.95 Nigel Williams W RSC 2 Batley
Career: 3 contests, won 2, lost 1.

Steve Bristow

Liverpool. *Born* Northwich, 27 February, 1970
Cruiserweight. Ht. 6'0"
Manager S. Vaughan

10.05.96 David Jules W RSC 2 Liverpool
Career: 1 contest, won 1.

Michael Brodie

Manchester. *Born* Manchester, 10 May, 1974
Featherweight. Ht. 5'6"
Manager J. Trickett

03.10.94 Graham McGrath W RSC 5 Manchester
20.10.94 Chip O'Neill W CO 3 Middleton
28.11.94 Muhammad Shaffique W CO 2 Manchester
13.12.94 Pete Buckley W PTS 6 Potters Bar
16.02.95 G. G. Goddard W PTS 6 Bury
03.04.95 Garry Burrell W RSC 4 Manchester
05.05.95 G. G. Goddard W PTS 6 Swansea
17.05.95 Ian Reid W RSC 3 Ipswich
10.06.95 Chris Clarkson W PTS 6 Manchester
14.11.95 Niel Leggett W CO 1 Bury
25.11.95 Karl Morling W RSC 1 Dagenham
18.12.95 Marty Chestnut W RTD 3 Mayfair
26.02.96 Bamana Dibateza W PTS 6 Manchester
13.04.96 John Sillo W CO 1 Liverpool
07.05.96 Elvis Parsley W RSC 1 Mayfair
Career: 15 contests, won 15.

Eamonn Brolly

Dungiven. *Born* Gavanagh, 18 November, 1972
S. Featherweight. Ht. 5'7"
Manager B. Hearn

26.08.95 Chris Lyons W PTS 4 Belfast
07.10.95 Mark O'Callaghan W PTS 4 Belfast
02.12.95 Mark O'Callaghan W RTD 3 Belfast
Career: 3 contests, won 3.

Elwen Brooks

Doncaster. *Born* Doncaster, 7 March, 1970
S. Middleweight. Ht. 6'0"
Manager T. Petersen

13.01.96 Lee Whitehead L PTS 6 Manchester
09.03.96 Paschal Collins L CO 1 Millstreet
Career: 2 contests, lost 2.

Vic Broomhead

Buxton. *Born* Buxton, 20 March, 1974
Lightweight. Ht. 5'5"
Manager J. Ashton

24.04.96 Dave Madden W RSC 3 Stoke
13.06.96 Chris Lyons L PTS 6 Sheffield
Career: 2 contests, won 1, lost 1.

Roger Brotherhood

Mansfield. *Born* Mansfield, 10 June, 1971
S. Featherweight. Ht. 5'7½"
Manager J. Ashton

07.04.94 Robert Grubb W PTS 6 Walsall
05.12.94 Garry Burrell W PTS 6 Bradford
09.02.95 Kid McAuley L PTS 6 Doncaster
07.04.95 Paul Wynn W RSC 5 Sheffield
22.03.96 Marty Chestnut W PTS 6 Mansfield
30.05.96 Carl Allen L RSC 5 Lincoln
Career: 6 contests, won 4, lost 2.

Colin Brown

Glasgow. *Born* Glasgow, 14 March, 1969
Cruiserweight. Ht. 5'11¼"
Manager T. Gilmour

18.09.95 Declan Faherty W RSC 4 Cleethorpes
18.11.95 David Flowers W DIS 3 Glasgow
19.02.96 Sean Daly W RTD 4 Glasgow
18.03.96 Albert Call W PTS 6 Glasgow
22.04.96 John Pierre W PTS 6 Glasgow
Career: 5 contests, won 5.

Matt Brown

Walworth. *Born* Camberwell, 17 February, 1971
S. Featherweight. Ht. 5'6"
Manager F. Maloney

15.06.94 Chris Lyons W CO 3 Southwark
25.10.94 Jason Hutson W PTS 4 Southwark
23.01.95 Andrew Reed W PTS 4 Bethnal Green
21.09.95 Niel Leggett W PTS 4 Battersea
24.10.95 Jason Hutson W RSC 3 Southwark
05.02.96 Des Gargano W RSC 4 Bexleyheath
02.04.96 Marco Fattore W PTS 4 Southwark
29.06.96 Pete Buckley L RSC 1 Erith
Career: 8 contests, won 7, lost 1.

Matt Brown (right) lands to the jaw of Simon Frailing   Les Clark

Mike Anthony Brown

Brixton. *Born* Jamaica, 8 February, 1970
Lightweight. Ht. 5'8"
Manager Self

23.05.93	Norman Dhalie L PTS 4 Brockley	
25.06.93	G.G. Goddard W CO 2 Battersea	
14.08.93	Simon Frailing W RSC 4 Hammersmith	
14.04.94	Norman Dhalie W PTS 6 Battersea	
22.05.94	Miguel Matthews L RSC 5 Crystal Palace	
21.07.94	Miguel Matthews W PTS 6 Battersea	
31.03.95	Barrie Kellie W RSC 2 Crystal Palace	
28.10.95	Michael Hermon L PTS 6 Bristol	
16.03.96	Dean Phillips L RSC 6 Glasgow	

Career: 9 contests, won 5, lost 4.

Denzil Browne

Leeds. *Born* Leeds, 21 January, 1969
Central Area Cruiserweight Champion.
Ht. 6'2½"
Manager M. Duff

18.10.90	Mark Bowen W PTS 6 Dewsbury	
29.11.90	R. F. McKenzie L PTS 6 Sunderland	
13.12.90	Gary Railton W RSC 2 Dewsbury	
21.02.91	Mark Bowen W PTS 6 Walsall	
21.03.91	R. F. McKenzie W PTS 6 Dewsbury	
09.05.91	Darren McKenna W PTS 6 Leeds	
27.06.91	Steve Yorath W PTS 6 Leeds	
01.08.91	Tony Colclough W RSC 1 Dewsbury	
09.10.91	R. F. McKenzie L PTS 6 Manchester	
30.10.91	Gus Mendes W RSC 6 Leeds	
23.01.92	Darren McKenna W PTS 6 York	
19.03.92	Ian Bulloch W PTS 8 York	
23.09.92	Steve Yorath W PTS 8 Leeds	
29.10.92	Sean O'Phoenix W RSC 4 Leeds	
25.02.93	Cordwell Hylton W PTS 8 Bradford	
22.04.93	Dave Muhammed W PTS 8 Mayfair	
01.07.93	Steve Osborne W RSC 1 York	
07.10.93	Tony Booth DREW 8 York	
01.12.93	Lennie Howard W RSC 6 Kensington	
26.10.94	Steve Lewsam W CO 2 Leeds	
21.01.95	Dennis Andries L RSC 11 Glasgow	
	(Vacant British Cruiserweight Title)	
08.07.95	Bobbi Joe Edwards L PTS 8 York	
11.11.95	John Keeton L RSC 4 Halifax	
13.01.96	Albert Call W PTS 6 Halifax	
04.06.96	Bobbi Joe Edwards W PTS 10 York	
	(Vacant Central Area Cruiserweight Title)	

Career: 25 contests, won 19, drew 1, lost 5.

Frank Bruno

Wandsworth. *Born* Hammersmith, 16
November, 1961
Former WBC Heavyweight Champion.
Former Undefeated European Heavyweight
Champion. Ht. 6'3½"
Manager Self

17.03.82	Lupe Guerra W CO 1 Kensington	
30.03.82	Harvey Steichen W RSC 2 Wembley	
20.04.82	Tom Stevenson W CO 1 Kensington	
04.05.82	Ron Gibbs W RSC 4 Wembley	
01.06.82	Tony Moore W RSC 2 Kensington	
14.09.82	George Scott W RSC 1 Wembley	
23.10.82	Ali Lukasa W CO 2 Berlin, Germany	
09.11.82	Rudi Gauwe W CO 2 Kensington	
23.11.82	George Butzbach W RTD 1 Wembley	
07.12.82	Gilberto Acuna W RSC 1 Kensington	
18.01.83	Stewart Lithgo W RTD 4 Kensington	
08.02.83	Peter Mulendwa W CO 3 Kensington	
01.03.83	Winston Allen W RSC 2 Kensington	
05.04.83	Eddie Neilson W RSC 3 Kensington	
03.05.83	Scott Ledoux W RSC 3 Wembley	
31.05.83	Barry Funches W RSC 5 Kensington	
09.07.83	Mike Jameson W CO 2 Chicago, USA	
27.09.83	Bill Sharkey W CO 1 Wembley	
11.10.83	Floyd Cummings W RSC 7 Kensington	
06.12.83	Walter Santemore W CO 4 Kensington	
13.03.84	Juan Figueroa W CO 1 Wembley	
13.05.84	James Smith L CO 10 Wembley	
25.09.84	Ken Lakusta W CO 2 Wembley	
	(Elim. Commonwealth Heavyweight Title)	
06.11.84	Jeff Jordan W RSC 3 Kensington	
27.11.84	Phil Brown W PTS 10 Wembley	
26.03.85	Lucien Rodriguez W RSC 1 Wembley	
01.10.85	Anders Eklund W CO 4 Wembley	
	(European Heavyweight Title Challenge)	
04.12.85	Larry Frazier W CO 2 Kensington	
04.03.86	Gerrie Coetzee W CO 1 Wembley	
	(Final Elim. WBA Heavyweight Title)	
19.07.86	Tim Witherspoon L RSC 11 Wembley	
	(WBA Heavyweight Title Challenge)	
24.03.87	James Tillis W RSC 5 Wembley	
27.06.87	Chuck Gardner W CO 1 Cannes, France	
30.08.87	Reggie Gross W RSC 8 Marbella, Spain	
24.10.87	Joe Bugner W RSC 8 Tottenham	
25.02.89	Mike Tyson L RSC 5 Las Vegas, USA	
	(WBC Heavyweight Title Challenge)	
20.11.91	John Emmen W CO 1 Kensington	
22.04.92	Jose Ribalta W CO 2 Wembley	

17.10.92 Pierre Coetzer W RSC 8 Wembley
(Elim. IBF Heavyweight Title)
24.04.93 Carl Williams W RSC 10 Birmingham
01.10.93 Lennox Lewis L RSC 7 Cardiff
(WBC Heavyweight Title Challenge)
16.03.94 Jesse Ferguson W RSC 1 Birmingham
18.02.95 Rodolfo Marin W RSC 1 Shepton Mallet
13.05.95 Mike Evans W CO 2 Glasgow
02.09.95 Oliver McCall W PTS 12 Wembley
(WBC Heavyweight Title Challenge)
16.03.96 Mike Tyson L RSC 3 Las Vegas, USA
(WBC Hevyweight Title Defence)
Career: 45 contests, won 40, lost 5.

(Delroy) Del Bryan

Birmingham. *Born* Nottingham, 16 April, 1967
Former British Welterweight Champion. Former Undefeated Midlands Area Welterweight Champion. Ht. 5'8"
Manager W. Swift

21.04.86 Wil Halliday W PTS 6 Birmingham
15.05.86 Gary Sommerville L PTS 6 Dudley
28.05.86 Trevor Hopson W RTD 4 Lewisham
26.06.86 Gary Sommerville L PTS 8 Edgbaston
26.09.86 Gary Cass W PTS 6 Swindon
06.10.86 Gary Sommerville W PTS 8 Birmingham
14.10.86 Mickey Lerwill W PTS 8 Wolverhampton
04.11.86 George Collins L RSC 4 Oldham
16.12.86 Ray Golding W PTS 6 Alfreton
08.01.87 Darren Dyer W PTS 6 Bethnal Green
17.02.87 Tommy Shiels L RSC 2 Alfreton
30.09.87 Peter Ashcroft W PTS 8 Solihull
26.10.87 Gary Sommerville W RSC 7 Birmingham
(Vacant Midlands Area Welterweight Title)
03.12.87 Mickey Hughes W PTS 8 Southend
15.12.87 Lloyd Christie W PTS 8 Bradford
24.02.88 Gary Jacobs L PTS 10 Glasgow
(Final Elim. British Welterweight Title)
09.03.88 Michael Justin DREW 8 Wembley
20.04.88 Kelvin Mortimer W RSC 4 Stoke
04.05.88 Gary Sommerville W PTS 8 Solihull
09.08.88 Jimmy Thornton W PTS 6 St Helier
28.09.88 Ossie Maddix W PTS 8 Solihull
12.12.88 Michael Justin W RSC 8 Nottingham
(Midlands Area Welterweight Title Defence)
22.03.89 Lenny Gloster W PTS 8 Solihull
10.05.89 Crisanto Espana L PTS 8 Kensington
19.08.89 Javier Castillejos W PTS 8 Benidorm, Spain
04.09.89 Joni Nyman L PTS 8 Helsinki, Finland
30.01.90 Simon Eubank W PTS 6 Battersea
16.02.90 Arvey Castro W RSC 1 Bilbao, Spain
17.04.90 Damien Denny W PTS 10 Millwall
(Final Elim. British Welterweight Title)
30.09.90 Phumzile Madikane L RSC 6 Capetown, South Africa
16.01.91 Kirkland Laing W PTS 12 Kensington
(British Welterweight Title Challenge)
16.04.91 Anthony Ivory W PTS 10 Nottingham
26.11.91 Mickey Hughes W RSC 3 Bethnal Green
(British Welterweight Title Defence)
20.02.92 Gary Jacobs L PTS 12 Glasgow
(British Welterweight Title Defence)
12.05.92 Darren Dyer L RSC 10 Crystal Palace

29.09.92 Chris Peters W PTS 10 Stoke
02.01.93 Godfrey Nyakana L PTS 8 Differdange, Luxembourg
05.05.93 Oscar Checca W CO 2 Belfast
11.08.93 Sidney Msutu W PTS 10 Durban, South Africa
22.09.93 Pat Barrett W PTS 12 Bethnal Green
(Vacant British Welterweight Title)
17.02.94 Derek Grainger W CO 7 Dagenham
(British Welterweight Title Defence)
11.05.94 Paul Lynch W PTS 8 Sheffield
10.09.94 Lindon Scarlett W PTS 12 Birmingham
(British Welterweight Title Defence)
17.12.94 Jose Luis Navarro L RSC 10 Cordoba, Spain
(Vacant European Welterweight Title)
02.06.95 Gary Logan W RSC 11 Bethnal Green
(British Welterweight Title Defence)
15.09.95 Chris Saunders L PTS 12 Mansfield
(British Welterweight Title Defence)
12.05.96 Nika Kumalo L PTS 10 Cape Town, South Africa
Career: 47 contests, won 32, drew 1, lost 14.

Brendan Bryce

Birmingham. *Born* Berwick on Tweed, 18 October, 1973
Bantamweight. Ht. 5'6"
Manager N. Nobbs

06.09.95 Shaun Norman L PTS 6 Stoke
02.10.95 Darren Greaves W PTS 6 Birmingham
26.10.95 Graham McGrath W PTS 6 Birmingham
03.12.95 Dave Martin L PTS 6 Southwark
20.12.95 Henry Jones L PTS 6 Usk
27.03.96 Chris Lyons W PTS 6 Whitwick
02.04.96 Dharmendra Singh Yadav L PTS 4 Southwark
14.05.96 Vince Feeney L PTS 6 Dagenham
Career: 8 contests, won 3, lost 5.

Brendan Bryce   Les Clark

Alston Buchanan

Glasgow. *Born* Glasgow, 25 December, 1972
S. Bantamweight. Ht. 5'5"
Manager A. Morrison

26.04.96 Amjed Mamond W RTD 1 Glasgow
24.05.96 Marty Chestnut W PTS 6 Glasgow
Career: 2 contests, won 2.

Pete Buckley

Birmingham. *Born* Birmingham, 9 March, 1969
Former Undefeated Midlands Area S. Featherweight Champion. Former Midlands Area S. Bantamweight Champion. Ht. 5'8"
Manager Self

04.10.89 Alan Baldwin DREW 6 Stafford
10.10.89 Ronnie Stephenson L PTS 6 Wolverhampton
30.10.89 Robert Braddock W PTS 6 Birmingham
14.11.89 Neil Leitch W PTS 6 Evesham
22.11.89 Peter Judson W PTS 6 Stafford
11.12.89 Stevie Woods W PTS 6 Bradford
21.12.89 Wayne Taylor W PTS 6 Kings Heath
10.01.90 John O'Meara W PTS 6 Kensington
19.02.90 Ian McGirr L PTS 6 Birmingham
27.02.90 Miguel Matthews DREW 6 Evesham
14.03.90 Ronnie Stephenson DREW 6 Stoke
04.04.90 Ronnie Stephenson L PTS 8 Stafford
23.04.90 Ronnie Stephenson W PTS 6 Birmingham
30.04.90 Chris Clarkson L PTS 8 Mayfair
17.05.90 Johnny Bredahl L PTS 6 Aars, Denmark
04.06.90 Ronnie Stephenson W PTS 8 Birmingham
28.06.90 Robert Braddock W RSC 5 Birmingham
01.10.90 Miguel Matthews W PTS 8 Cleethorpes
09.10.90 Miguel Matthews L PTS 8 Wolverhampton
17.10.90 Tony Smith W PTS 6 Stoke
29.10.90 Miguel Matthews W PTS 8 Birmingham
21.11.90 Drew Docherty L PTS 8 Solihull
10.12.90 Neil Leitch W PTS 8 Birmingham
10.01.91 Duke McKenzie L RSC 5 Wandsworth
18.02.91 Jamie McBride L PTS 8 Glasgow
04.03.91 Brian Robb W RSC 7 Birmingham
26.03.91 Neil Leitch DREW 8 Wolverhampton
01.05.91 Mark Geraghty W PTS 8 Solihull
05.06.91 Brian Robb W PTS 10 Wolverhampton
(Vacant Midlands Area S. Featherweight Title)
09.09.91 Mike Deveney L PTS 8 Glasgow
24.09.91 Mark Bates W RTD 5 Basildon
29.10.91 John Armour L PTS 6 Kensington
14.11.91 Mike Deveney L PTS 6 Edinburgh
28.11.91 Craig Dermody L PTS 6 Liverpool
19.12.91 Craig Dermody L PTS 6 Oldham
18.01.92 Alan McKay DREW 8 Kensington
20.02.92 Brian Robb W RSC 10 Oakengates
(Midlands Area S. Featherweight Title Defence)
27.04.92 Drew Docherty L PTS 8 Glasgow
15.05.92 Ruben Condori L PTS 10 Augsburg, Germany
29.05.92 Donnie Hood L PTS 8 Glasgow
07.09.92 Duke McKenzie L RTD 3 Bethnal Green

12.11.92 Prince Nassem Hamed L PTS 6 Liverpool
19.02.93 Harald Geier L PTS 12 Vienna, Austria
(Vacant WBA Penta-Continental S. Bantamweight Title)
26.04.93 Bradley Stone L PTS 8 Lewisham
18.06.93 Eamonn McAuley L PTS 6 Belfast
01.07.93 Tony Silkstone L PTS 8 York
06.10.93 Jonjo Irwin L PTS 8 Solihull
25.10.93 Drew Docherty L PTS 8 Glasgow
06.11.93 Michael Alldis L PTS 8 Bethnal Green
30.11.93 Barry Jones L PTS 4 Cardiff
19.12.93 Shaun Anderson L PTS 6 Glasgow
22.01.94 Barry Jones L PTS 6 Cardiff
29.01.94 Prince Nassem Hamed L RSC 4 Cardiff
10.03.94 Tony Falcone L PTS 4 Bristol
29.03.94 Conn McMullen W PTS 6 Bethnal Green
05.04.94 Mark Bowers L PTS 6 Bethnal Green
13.04.94 James Murray L PTS 6 Glasgow
06.05.94 Paul Lloyd L RTD 4 Liverpool
03.08.94 Greg Upton L PTS 6 Bristol
26.09.94 John Sillo L PTS 6 Liverpool
05.10.94 Matthew Harris L PTS 6 Wolverhampton
07.11.94 Marlon Ward L PTS 4 Piccadilly
23.11.94 Justin Murphy L PTS 4 Piccadilly
29.11.94 Neil Swain L PTS Cardiff
13.12.94 Michael Brodie L PTS 6 Potters Bar
20.12.94 Michael Alldis L PTS 6 Bethnal Green
10.02.95 Matthew Harris W RSC 6 Birmingham
(Midlands Area S. Bantamweight Title Challenge)
23.02.95 Paul Ingle L PTS 8 Southwark
20.04.95 John Sillo L PTS 6 Liverpool
27.04.95 Paul Ingle L PTS 8 Bethnal Green
09.05.95 Adey Lewis L PTS 4 Basildon
23.05.95 Spencer Oliver L PTS 4 Potters Bar
01.07.95 Dean Pithie L PTS 4 Kensington
21.09.95 Patrick Mullings L PTS 6 Battersea
29.09.95 Marlon Ward L PTS 4 Bethnal Green
25.10.95 Matthew Harris L PTS 10 Telford
(Midlands Area S. Bantamweight Title Defence)
08.11.95 Vince Feeney L PTS 8 Bethnal Green
28.11.95 Barry Jones L PTS 6 Cardiff
15.12.95 Patrick Mullings L PTS 4 Bethnal Green
05.02.96 Patrick Mullings L PTS 8 Bexleyheath
09.03.96 Paul Griffin L PTS 4 Millstreet
21.03.96 Colin McMillan L RSC 3 Southwark
14.05.96 Venkatesan Deverajan L PTS 4 Dagenham
29.06.96 Matt Brown W RSC 1 Erith
Career: 84 contests, won 21, drew 5, lost 58.

(Andrew) Stefy Bull (Bullcroft)

Denaby. *Born* Doncaster, 10 May, 1977
Featherweight. Ht. 5'10"
Manager J. Rushton

30.06.95 Andy Roberts W PTS 4 Doncaster
11.10.95 Michael Edwards W PTS 6 Stoke
18.10.95 Alan Hagan W RSC 1 Batley
28.11.95 Kevin Sheil W PTS 6 Wolverhampton
26.01.96 Robert Grubb W PTS 6 Doncaster
Career: 5 contests, won 5.

Paul Burke

Preston. *Born* Preston, 25 July, 1966
Former British & Commonwealth
Lightweight Champion. Ht. 5'10"
Manager Self

Paul Burke   Harry Goodwin

21.01.87 Steve Brown W CO 4 Stoke
30.01.87 Paul Marriott L PTS 6 Kirkby
02.03.87 Brian Murphy W CO 2 Marton
06.04.87 Paul Marriott W PTS 6 Newcastle
30.04.87 Paul Gadney W PTS 6 Bethnal Green
01.06.87 Pat Barrett W PTS 6 Bradford
15.09.87 Marvin P. Gray L RSC 6 Batley
18.11.87 Rudy Valentino W PTS 6 Bethnal Green
15.12.87 James Jiora L PTS 4 Bradford
11.02.88 Paul Gadney DREW 8 Gravesend
25.01.89 Paul Charters W PTS 6 Bethnal Green
23.02.89 Mark Kelly L DIS 5 Stockport
07.03.89 Tony Connellan W RSC 5 Manchester
11.04.89 Billy Buchanan W RSC 4 Oldham
21.10.89 Aaron Kabi DREW 8 Middlesbrough
09.12.89 Angel Mona L RSC 3 Toulouse, France
23.04.90 Tony Richards L PTS 10 Glasgow
(Elim. British Lightweight Title)
25.09.90 Robert Harkin W PTS 8 Glasgow
21.01.91 Peter Bradley W PTS 10 Glasgow
(Elim. British Lightweight Title)
31.05.91 Art Blackmore W RSC 3 Manchester
20.09.91 Tony Richards W PTS 8 Manchester
09.02.92 Dave Andrews W PTS 6 Bradford
28.04.92 Paul Charters W RSC 7 Houghton le Spring
(Final Elim. British Lightweight Title)
28.09.92 Marcel Herbert W PTS 6 Manchester
17.11.92 Jean-Baptiste Mendy L PTS 12 Paris, France
(European Lightweight Title Challenge)
24.02.93 Billy Schwer W RSC 7 Wembley
(British & Commonwealth Lightweight Title Challenge)
25.07.93 Lyndon Paul Walker W PTS 8 Oldham
10.11.93 Billy Schwer L PTS 12 Watford
(British & Commonwealth Lightweight Title Defence)
22.04.94 Racheed Lawal L RSC 4 Aalborg, Denmark
(European Lightweight Title Challenge)
04.10.94 Rudy Valentino W PTS 6 Mayfair
17.02.95 Michael Ayers L RSC 6 Crawley
(Vacant British Lightweight Title)
27.05.95 Patrick Gallagher W PTS 8 Belfast
13.01.96 Cham Joof W RSC 2 Manchester
13.04.96 Peter Till W PTS 8 Wythenshawe
Career: 34 contests, won 22, drew 2, lost 10.

Paul Burns   Les Clark

Paul Burns

Liverpool. *Born* Liverpool, 15 July, 1971
Welterweight. Ht. 5'9½"
Manager J. Hyland

16.06.95	Mick Mulcahy W RSC 3 Liverpool
08.09.95	Peter Varnavas W RSC 3 Liverpool
24.11.95	Donovan Davey W PTS 6 Chester
03.02.96	Rick North W PTS 4 Liverpool

Career: 4 contests, won 4.

Vince Burns   Les Clark

Vince Burns

Battersea. *Born* Paddington, 27 July, 1970
Lightweight. Ht. 5'7"
Manager B. Dawson

29.04.93	Jason Hutson W RSC 1 Hayes
04.10.93	Yifru Retta L PTS 6 Mayfair
17.10.94	Danny Lutaaya L RSC 6 Mayfair
25.03.95	Lewis Reynolds L RSC 4 Millwall
17.06.95	Mervyn Bennett L CO 4 Cardiff
03.12.95	Nicky Bardle L RSC 1 Southwark

Career: 6 contests, won 1, lost 5.

Garry Burrell   Les Clark

Garry Burrell

Kirkcaldy. *Born* Musselburgh, 9 July, 1965
Lightweight. Ht. 5'7½"
Manager Self

21.09.92	Alan Graham W PTS 6 Glasgow
09.11.92	Alan Graham L PTS 6 Bradford
22.02.93	Tim Hill L PTS 6 Glasgow
23.03.93	Yusuf Vorajee L PTS 6 Wolverhampton
26.04.93	Robbie Sivyer W PTS 6 Glasgow
20.09.93	Phil Found L RSC 4 Glasgow
25.11.93	Colin Innes L PTS 6 Newcastle
24.05.94	Alan Graham L PTS 6 Sunderland
29.09.94	Tim Hill L PTS 6 Tynemouth
07.10.94	Dennis Holbaek Pedersen L PTS 6 Copenhagen, Denmark
05.12.94	Roger Brotherhood L PTS 6 Bradford
23.01.95	Trevor George L PTS 6 Glasgow
24.02.95	Colin Innes W PTS 6 Irving
16.03.95	Liam Dineen L PTS 6 Sunderland
25.03.95	John Sillo L PTS 6 Chester
03.04.95	Michael Brodie L RSC 4 Manchester
15.05.95	Paul Goode W RSC 1 Bradford
22.05.95	Trevor Sumner L PTS 6 Morecambe
01.06.95	Marty Chestnut W RTD 3 Musselburgh
05.06.95	Robert Hay L PTS 6 Glasgow
16.06.95	Paul Lloyd L RSC 2 Liverpool
05.10.95	Ram Singh W PTS 8 Glasgow
23.10.95	Ian Richardson W PTS 6 Glasgow
20.11.95	Glen Hopkins W PTS 6 Glasgow
13.01.96	Michael Alldis L RSC 7 Halifax
16.02.96	Ian Richardson W PTS 8 Irvine
19.03.96	Shaun Hall W PTS 6 Leeds
02.04.96	Venkatesan Deverajan L RSC 1 Southwark
09.05.96	Richard Vowles W PTS 8 Glasgow
28.05.96	Paul Ireland L PTS 6 Belfast

Career: 30 contests, won 11, lost 19.

Kevin Burton

Doncaster. *Born* Doncaster, 20 February, 1965
L. Heavyweight. Ht. 5'10½"
Manager J. Rushton

10.05.93	Pat McNamara W RSC 2 Cleethorpes
07.06.93	Tony Colclough W PTS 6 Walsall
20.09.93	Bullit Andrews W PTS 6 Cleethorpes
30.09.93	Tony Colclough W DIS 5 Walsall
13.12.93	Tony Colclough W RSC 3 Doncaster
07.03.94	Bullit Andrews W RSC 1 Doncaster
07.04.94	Johnny Hooks L PTS 6 Walsall
10.05.94	Declan Faherty L RSC 4 Doncaster
12.10.94	Tony Colclough W PTS 6 Stoke
25.10.94	Chris Nurse W RSC 1 Edgbaston
12.12.94	Jem Jackson W RSC 4 Doncaster
09.02.95	Dave Battey L PTS 6 Doncaster
05.05.95	Dave Battey L PTS 6 Doncaster
16.05.95	Clinton Woods L PTS 6 Cleethorpes
14.06.95	Clinton Woods L RSC 6 Batley
28.07.95	Paul Murray W PTS 6 Epworth
25.09.95	Robert Harper W DIS 4 Cleethorpes
11.10.95	John Kaighin L CO 1 Stoke
26.01.96	Paul Murray W PTS 6 Doncaster
26.02.96	Lee Whitehead L PTS 6 Manchester
24.04.96	David Jules L PTS 6 Stoke
11.05.96	Frederik Alvarez L RSC 1 Bethnal Green

Career: 22 contests, won 12, lost 10.

Paul Busby

Worcester. *Born* Worcester, 20 April, 1966
Former WBO Inter-Continental
Middleweight Champion. Former
Undefeated WBO Penta-Continental
Middleweight Champion. Ht. 5'11½"
Manager B. Hearn

18.11.90	Carlos Christie W PTS 6 Birmingham
04.12.90	Marty Duke W PTS 6 Bury St Edmunds
23.01.91	Tony Wellington W RSC 2 Brentwood
27.02.91	Paul Murray W PTS 6 Wolverhampton
19.03.91	Paul Smith W PTS 6 Leicester
10.09.91	Nigel Rafferty W RSC 2 Wolverhampton
12.11.91	Graham Burton W RSC 3 Wolverhampton
17.12.91	Paul Murray W CO 3 Cardiff
01.02.92	John Kaighin W PTS 4 Birmingham
23.05.92	Stinger Mason W RSC 2 Birmingham
06.10.92	Chris Richards W PTS 6 Antwerp, Belgium
14.11.92	Paul Wesley W PTS 8 Cardiff
19.01.93	Stan King W PTS 8 Cardiff
16.03.93	Neville Brown L PTS 10 Wolverhampton *(Elim. British Middleweight Title)*
10.07.93	Wayne Ellis L RSC 5 Cardiff
03.11.93	Spencer Alton W RTD 4 Worcester
19.01.94	Colin Manners DREW 8 Solihull
15.03.94	Colin Manners W PTS 8 Mayfair
28.06.94	Wayne Ellis L TD 4 Mayfair *(Vacant WBO Penta-Continental Middleweight Title)*
29.10.94	Wayne Ellis W PTS 12 Cannock *(WBO Penta-Continental Middleweight Title Challenge)*
17.01.95	Warren Stowe W PTS 12 Worcester *(WBO Penta-Continental Middleweight Title)*
01.06.95	Willie Quinn L RTD 8 Musselburgh *(Vacant WBO Inter-Continental Middleweight Title)*

28.11.95 Barry Thorogood W PTS 8 Cardiff
03.04.96 Robert McCracken L RTD 7 Bethnal Green
(Commonwealth Middleweight Title Challenge)
Career: 24 contests, won 18, drew 1, lost 5.

Richard Bustin
Norwich. *Born* Norwich, 9 October, 1964
S. Middleweight. Ht. 5'9"
Manager Self

15.02.88 Roger Silsby L PTS 6 Copthorne
14.03.88 Tony Behan W RSC 3 Norwich
05.04.88 Steve Conway W RSC 4 Basildon
28.05.88 Winston Burnett W PTS 6 Kensington
17.10.88 Dennis Banton W RSC 5 Mayfair
15.11.88 Crawford Ashley L CO 3 Norwich
07.02.89 Alan Baptiste W PTS 6 Southend
15.05.89 Alex Romeo L RSC 2 Northampton
03.10.89 Alan Baptiste W PTS 6 Southend
17.10.89 Mick Maw W CO 2 Cardiff
14.03.90 Paul McCarthy L RSC 7 Battersea
(Vacant Southern Area S. Middleweight Title)
12.11.90 Alan Baptiste W RSC 1 Norwich
29.01.91 Simon Harris L RSC 3 Wisbech
18.04.91 John Foreman W PTS 8 Earls Court
11.06.91 Gary Ballard L PTS 8 Leicester
19.11.91 Glazz Campbell L CO 7 Norwich
(Vacant Southern Area L. Heavyweight Title)
31.01.92 Bobbi Joe Edwards L PTS 6 Manchester
31.03.92 Gypsy Carman L PTS 6 Norwich
27.06.92 Dariusz Michalczewski L RSC 4 Quinta do Lago, Portugal
08.09.92 Karl Barwise W PTS 6 Norwich
17.04.93 Paul Hitch W PTS 6 Washington
06.03.94 Ali Forbes L PTS 10 Southwark
(Vacant Southern Area S. Middleweight Title)
20.10.95 Carlos Christie L PTS 6 Ipswich
Career: 23 contests, won 11, lost 12.

Damien Caesar
Stepney. *Born* Stepney, 2 October, 1965
Heavyweight. Ht. 6'5"
Manager Self

22.04.91 Larry Peart W RSC 2 Mayfair
30.05.91 Tony Colclough W RSC 1 Mayfair
17.02.92 Steve Stewart W RSC 5 Mayfair
27.04.92 Gary Williams W RSC 4 Mayfair
05.10.92 Denroy Bryan W RSC 5 Bristol
07.12.93 Joey Paladino W RSC 3 Bethnal Green
14.03.94 Vance Idiens W RSC 4 Mayfair
13.12.94 Gary Williams W RSC 2 Ilford
23.02.95 Julius Francis L RSC 8 Southwark
(Vacant Southern Area Heavyweight Title)
09.04.96 Julius Francis L CO 1 Stevenage
(Vacant Southern Area Heavyweight Title)
Career: 10 contests, won 8, lost 2.

Albert Call
Grimsby. *Born* Grimsby, 17 April, 1967
Cruiserweight. Ht. 6'2"
Manager Self

21.09.92 John Pierre W PTS 6 Cleethorpes
14.12.92 Art Stacey W PTS 6 Cleethorpes

22.02.93 Kenny Sandison W PTS 6 Liverpool
25.08.93 Peter Smith L PTS 6 Hammanskrall, South Africa
20.09.93 Trevor Small DREW 6 Cleethorpes
28.09.93 Dennis Bailey DREW 6 Liverpool
30.10.93 Kenley Price DREW 6 Chester
13.12.93 Trevor Small W RSC 5 Cleethorpes
17.03.94 Art Stacey W PTS 6 Lincoln
15.04.94 Cordwell Hylton L RSC 4 Hull
(Vacant Midlands Area Cruiserweight Title)
11.12.95 Art Stacey W RSC 3 Cleethorpes
13.01.96 Denzil Browne L PTS 6 Halifax
18.03.96 Colin Brown L PTS 6 Glasgow
13.04.96 Carl Thompson L RTD 4 Wythenshawe
20.05.96 Nigel Rafferty DREW 6 Cleethorpes
Career: 15 contests, won 6, drew 4, lost 5.

Albert Call   Les Clark

Anthony Campbell
Battersea. *Born* Kensington, 20 January, 1967
L. Welterweight. Ht. 5'6"
Manager D. Currivan

05.04.94 Andrew Reed W PTS 6 Bethnal Green
20.05.94 Malcolm Thomas W PTS 6 Acton
29.09.94 P. J. Gallagher L PTS 6 Bethnal Green
19.11.94 Nicky Bardle L PTS 6 Heathrow
25.01.95 Gareth Lawrence L PTS 6 Cardiff
07.02.95 Anthony Maynard L PTS 8 Wolverhampton
26.05.95 M. T. Atkin DREW 6 Norwich
09.09.95 Mark Winters L PTS 4 Cork
30.09.95 Bobby Guynan W RSC 5 Basildon
21.10.95 Dean Pithie L PTS 4 Bethnal Green
30.10.95 Wayne Jones W RSC 1 Heathrow
02.11.95 Marc Smith W PTS 6 Mayfair
24.11.95 Mark Haslam W PTS 4 Manchester
19.01.96 Tommy Lawler W PTS 4 Bracknell
15.03.96 Roger Hunte DREW 4 Dunstable
24.04.96 Neil Smith W PTS 8 Solihull
04.05.96 Bobby Guynan W RSC 4 Dagenham
02.06.96 Bobby Vanzie L PTS 6 Shaw
Career: 18 contests, won 9, drew 2, lost 7.

Jason Campbell
Brighton. *Born* Northampton, 12 November, 1970
L. Welterweight. Ht. 5'8"
Manager D. Currivan

06.05.93 Adrian Chase L CO 2 Bayswater
07.12.93 Jason Beard L RSC 2 Bethnal Green
15.03.94 M. T. Atkin L RSC 5 Mayfair
22.04.96 Craig Stanley L RSC 2 Crystal Palace
Career: 4 contests, lost 4.

Gypsy Carman   Les Clark

(George) Gypsy Carman
Ipswich. *Born* Wisbech, 23 November, 1964
Cruiserweight. Ht. 6'0"
Manager Self

30.01.84 Dave Mowbray W PTS 6 Manchester
16.02.84 Lennie Howard L RTD 1 Basildon
03.04.84 Gordon Stacey W PTS 6 Lewisham
07.06.84 Deka Williams L PTS 6 Dudley
29.10.84 Wes Taylor W PTS 6 Streatham
04.02.85 Lee White W PTS 6 Lewisham
20.02.85 Charlie Hostetter L PTS 6 Muswell Hill
27.03.85 Glenn McCrory L PTS 8 Gateshead
09.05.85 Barry Ellis L PTS 8 Acton
10.06.85 Chris Jacobs DREW 6 Cardiff
02.09.85 Barry Ellis L PTS 8 Coventry
31.08.85 Tee Jay L PTS 6 Wandsworth
15.03.86 Mick Cordon W PTS 8 Norwich
24.03.86 Chris Harbourne W PTS 6 Mayfair
13.09.86 Tee Jay L RSC 4 Norwich
(Vacant Southern Area Cruiserweight Title)
20.11.86 Lou Gent L CO 1 Merton
12.01.87 Patrick Collins W PTS 8 Glasgow
19.01.87 Johnny Nelson L PTS 6 Mayfair
19.02.87 Danny Lawford L PTS 6 Peterborough
04.03.87 Tommy Taylor L PTS 8 Dudley
24.11.87 Tommy Taylor W PTS 8 Wisbech
14.03.88 Blaine Logsdon L RSC 8 Norwich
25.04.88 Gerry Storey L PTS 6 Bethnal Green
15.09.89 Carlton Headley W PTS 6 High Wycombe
22.02.90 Lou Gent L PTS 10 Wandsworth
(Southern Area Cruiserweight Title Challenge)

07.05.90 Eddie Smulders L RSC 4 Arnhem, Holland
26.11.90 Everton Blake L PTS 6 Bethnal Green
22.10.91 Tenko Ernie W PTS 6 Wandsworth
21.01.92 Dave Lawrence W PTS 6 Norwich
31.03.92 Richard Bustin W PTS 6 Norwich
29.10.92 Everton Blake L RSC 4 Hayes
(*Southern Area Cruiserweight Title Challenge*)
29.04.93 Paul McCarthy W PTS 6 Hayes
28.09.93 Scott Welch L RSC 3 Bethnal Green
18.11.94 Andrew Benson L PTS 6 Bracknell
03.03.95 Steve Osborne W PTS 6 Bracknell
26.05.95 Art Stacey W PTS 6 Norwich
16.11.95 Tim Redman W PTS 6 Evesham
12.02.96 Art Stacey W RSC 3 Heathrow
22.04.96 Chris Okoh L RSC 6 Crystal Palace
(*WBO Inter-Continental Cruiserweight Title Challenge*)
Career: 39 contests, won 17, drew 1, lost 21.

Brian Carr

Auchengeich. *Born* Glasgow, 20 June, 1969
Scottish Featherweight Champion. Ht. 5'6"
Manager A. Morrison

18.12.94 Fred Reeve W CO 2 Glasgow
21.01.95 Shaun Anderson W PTS 6 Glasgow
04.03.95 G. G. Goddard W PTS 8 Livingston
13.05.95 Paul Wynn W RTD 2 Glasgow
08.06.95 Abdul Manna W PTS 6 Glasgow
13.10.95 Muhammad Shaffique W PTS 6 Glasgow
17.12.95 Abdul Mannon W PTS 8 Glasgow
16.03.96 Chip O'Neill W PTS 4 Glasgow
26.04.96 Mike Deveney W PTS 10 Glasgow
(*Vacant Scottish Featherweight Title*)
Career: 9 contests, won 9.

(John) Cornelius Carr

Middlesbrough. *Born* Middlesbrough, 9 April, 1969
Former Undefeated British S. Middleweight Champion. Ht. 5'9½"
Manager M. Duff

22.09.87 Paul Burton W RSC 5 Bethnal Green
28.11.87 Dave Heaver W RSC 2 Windsor
12.01.88 Shamus Casey W RSC 6 Cardiff
27.01.88 Kesem Clayton W PTS 6 Bethnal Green
29.03.88 Darren Parker W RSC 1 Bethnal Green
12.04.88 Franki Moro W PTS 6 Cardiff
10.05.88 Andy Catesby W RSC 5 Tottenham
15.11.88 Skip Jackson W CO 1 Norwich
20.12.88 Kevin Hayde W PTS 6 Swansea
22.03.89 Bocco George L RSC 3 Reading
24.10.89 Carlo Colarusso W RTD 4 Watford
20.02.90 Peter Gorny W RSC 4 Millwall
21.04.90 Franki Moro W PTS 8 Sunderland
26.09.90 John Maltreaux W CO 1 Metairie, USA
27.10.90 Jerry Nestor W CO 1 Greenville, USA
16.02.91 Frank Eubanks W RSC 5 Thornaby
02.03.91 Carlo Colarusso W PTS 8 Darlington
18.05.91 Paul Burton W RSC 3 Verbania, Italy
06.09.91 Marvin O'Brien W RSC 7 Salemi, Italy
29.10.92 Alan Richards W PTS 8 Bayswater
24.04.93 Graham Burton W PTS 6 Birmingham
19.05.93 Stan King W PTS 8 Sunderland
22.09.93 Horace Fleary W PTS 8 Wembley
11.03.94 James Cook W PTS 12 Bethnal Green
(*British S. Middleweight Title Challenge*)

04.02.95 Colin Manners W PTS 8 Cardiff
13.05.95 Chris Richards W RTD 3 Glasgow
07.07.95 Barry Thorogood W RSC 6 Cardiff
25.11.95 Steve Collins L PTS 12 Dublin
(*WBO S. Middleweight Title Challenge*)
02.03.96 Danny Juma W PTS 8 Newcastle
Career: 29 contests, won 27, lost 2.

Cornelius Carr   Les Clark

Paul Carr

Sidcup. *Born* Basildon, 16 April, 1973
L. Middleweight. Ht. 5'10"
Manager F. Warren

02.06.95 Dave Curtis W PTS 6 Bethnal Green
01.07.95 Rob Stevenson W PTS 6 Kensington
22.07.95 Wesley Jones W RSC 3 Millwall
21.10.95 Andrew Jervis L RSC 3 Bethnal Green
13.02.96 Ernie Loveridge W PTS 4 Bethnal Green
Career: 5 contests, won 4, lost 1.

Michael Carruth

Dublin. *Born* Dublin, 9 July, 1967
Welterweight. Ht. 5'8"
Manager F. Warren

26.02.94 George Wilson W PTS 6 Earls Court
21.05.94 Ricky Mabbett W CO 3 Belfast
17.08.94 Mark Antony W RSC 3 Sheffield
17.09.94 Kim-Ken Jackson W RSC 4 Las Vegas, USA
12.10.94 Rick North W PTS 6 Sheffield
19.11.94 Dave Lovell W RSC 2 Cardiff
21.01.95 Gordon Blair L PTS 6 Glasgow
17.03.95 Vernice Harvard W RSC 3 Worcester, USA
17.06.95 Steve McGovern W RSC 4 Cardiff
09.09.95 John Smith W PTS 8 Cork
25.11.95 Paul Denton W PTS 8 Dublin
09.03.96 Gordon Blair W RTD 3 Millstreet
25.06.96 Chris Saunders W RSC 10 Mansfield
Career: 13 contests, won 12, lost 1.

Michael Carruth   Les Clark

Shamus Casey (West)

Alfreton. *Born* Pinxton, 13 January, 1960
Middleweight. Ht. 5'11"
Manager Self

25.01.84 Tony Burke L CO 1 Solihull
16.04.84 Ronnie Fraser L RSC 3 Nottingham
05.07.84 Craig Edwards L PTS 6 Prestatyn
21.09.84 Dave Foley W PTS 6 Alfreton
28.09.84 Dennis Boy O'Brien L PTS 6 Longford
11.10.84 Terry Gilbey L PTS 6 Barnsley
22.10.84 Dave King W PTS 6 South Shields
09.11.84 Reuben Thurley W CO 4 Alfreton
16.11.84 Tucker Watts L PTS 6 Leicester
26.11.84 Terry Gilbey L RSC 1 Liverpool
14.01.85 Mark Walker L PTS 6 Manchester
24.01.85 Tommy Campbell L PTS 8 Manchester
11.02.85 Paul Smith W PTS 6 Manchester
18.02.85 John Graham L PTS 6 Mayfair
01.03.85 Dennis Sheehan W PTS 6 Mansfield
11.03.85 Sean O'Phoenix L PTS 6 Manchester
20.03.85 Sean O'Phoenix L PTS 6 Stoke
15.04.85 Ronnie Tucker L PTS 6 Manchester
14.05.85 Dennis Sheehan L PTS 10 Mansfield
(*Midlands Area L. Middleweight Title Challenge*)
05.06.85 Gary Stretch L RSC 2 Kensington
02.09.85 Newton Barnett DREW 8 Coventry
12.09.85 Cliff Curtis W RSC 7 Swindon
23.09.85 Danny Quigg L PTS 8 Glasgow
10.10.85 Davey Cox W PTS 6 Alfreton
22.10.85 Mick Mills L RSC 3 Hull
02.12.85 Newton Barnett DREW 8 Dulwich
09.12.85 Steve Ward L PTS 6 Nottingham
16.12.85 Robert Armstrong W PTS 6 Bradford
20.01.86 Billy Ahearne L PTS 8 Leicester
06.02.86 Denys Cronin L RSC 6 Doncaster
10.03.86 Neil Munn L PTS 8 Cardiff
20.03.86 Andy Wright L RSC 4 Merton
22.04.86 Franki Moro L PTS 8 Carlisle
29.04.86 John Graham L PTS 8 Piccadilly
08.05.86 Randy Henderson L PTS 8 Bayswater
19.05.86 Joe Lynch W RSC 3 Plymouth
28.05.86 Andy Wright L PTS 6 Lewisham
15.09.86 Gerry Sloof L PTS 6 Scheidam, Holland

23.09.86	Derek Wormald L PTS 8 Batley	
06.10.86	David Scere L PTS 6 Leicester	
21.10.86	David Scere W PTS 8 Hull	
29.10.86	Peter Elliott W PTS 6 Stoke	
25.11.86	Steve Foster L PTS 8 Manchester	
15.12.86	Tucker Watts DREW 6 Loughborough	
13.01.87	Robert Armstrong L PTS 6 Oldham	
26.01.87	Richard Wagstaff W PTS 8 Bradford	
05.02.87	Neil Patterson L PTS 6 Newcastle	
20.02.87	Dennis Boy O'Brien L PTS 8 Maidenhead	
02.03.87	Roddy Maxwell L PTS 6 Glasgow	
24.03.87	Ian Chantler L PTS 8 Nottingham	
07.04.87	Richard Wagstaff L PTS 8 Batley	
28.04.87	Sean Leighton DREW 8 Manchester	
05.05.87	Dave Owens L PTS 6 Leeds	
12.05.87	Jason Baxter L PTS 6 Alfreton	
23.06.87	Terry Magee L CO 6 Swansea	

(Vacant All-Ireland L. Middleweight Title)

31.07.87	Cyril Jackson L RSC 5 Wrexham	
22.09.87	Brian Robinson L PTS 6 Bethnal Green	
28.09.87	Sean Leighton L PTS 8 Bradford	
19.10.87	Sammy Storey L PTS 6 Belfast	
10.11.87	Peter Brown L PTS 8 Batley	
19.11.87	Kid Murray W PTS 6 Ilkeston	
26.11.87	Trevor Smith L CO 4 Fulham	
12.01.88	Cornelius Carr L RSC 6 Cardiff	
15.02.88	Leigh Wicks L PTS 6 Copthorne	
25.02.88	R. W. Smith L RSC 3 Bethnal Green	
28.03.88	Tony Britton L PTS 8 Birmingham	
13.06.88	Jim Kelly L PTS 6 Glasgow	
25.06.88	Wayne Ellis L PTS 6 Luton	
12.09.88	Shaun Cummins L CO 3 Northampton	
17.10.88	Jim Kelly L PTS 6 Glasgow	
01.11.88	Brian Robinson L PTS 6 Reading	
17.11.88	Mark Howell L CO 1 Ilkeston	
16.12.88	Conrad Oscar L PTS 6 Brentwood	
25.01.89	Tony Velinor L RTD 3 Basildon	
22.02.89	Mickey Murray DREW 6 Doncaster	
01.03.89	Nigel Fairbairn L PTS 6 Stoke	
21.03.89	Dave Thomas L PTS 6 Cottingham	
29.03.89	W. O. Wilson L RSC 5 Wembley	
08.05.89	Antonio Fernandez L PTS 6 Edgbaston	
31.05.89	Ossie Maddix L CO 3 Manchester	
11.09.89	Terry French W PTS 6 Nottingham	
18.09.89	Skip Jackson W PTS 6 Northampton	
26.09.89	Theo Marius L PTS 8 Chigwell	
05.10.89	Val Golding L PTS 6 Stevenage	
17.10.89	Carl Harney L PTS 4 Oldham	
13.11.89	Ian Vokes W RSC 5 Bradford	
29.11.89	Ray Close L CO 2 Belfast	
21.06.90	Skip Jackson W PTS 6 Alfreton	
04.09.90	Pete Bowman W PTS 6 Southend	
14.09.90	Chris Richards L PTS 6 Telford	
08.10.90	Billy Brough W PTS 6 Leicester	
22.10.90	Gordon Blair L RSC 3 Glasgow	
22.11.90	Jimmy Thornton W PTS 6 Ilkeston	
14.12.90	Stefan Wright L PTS 6 Peterborough	
17.01.91	Neville Brown L RSC 4 Alfreton	
21.02.91	Richie Woodhall L RSC 3 Walsall	
28.03.91	Pete Bowman L PTS 4 Oldham	
12.04.91	Martin Rosamond W PTS 6 Willenhall	
13.05.91	Paul King W PTS 6 Northampton	
04.07.91	Dave Hall W PTS 6 Alfreton	
11.09.91	Clay O'Shea L PTS 6 Hammersmith	
10.10.91	Dave Johnson L PTS 6 Gateshead	
17.10.91	Tyrone Eastmond L PTS 6 Mossley	
14.11.91	Dave Johnson L PTS 6 Gateshead	
28.11.91	Ian Vokes W PTS 6 Hull	
07.12.91	Steve Foster L PTS 8 Manchester	
17.03.92	Gary Osborne L RSC 5 Wolverhampton	

(Vacant Midlands Area L. Middleweight Title)

28.05.92	Mark Jay L PTS 8 Gosforth	
25.07.92	Warren Stowe L CO 2 Manchester	
16.10.92	Terry Morrill L PTS 6 Hull	
23.10.92	Fran Harding L PTS 6 Liverpool	
12.11.92	Gypsy Johnny Price L PTS 6 Burnley	
14.12.92	Peter Waudby L PTS 6 Cleethorpes	
22.02.93	Lee Ferrie L CO 3 Bedworth	
07.06.93	Stephen Wilson L PTS 6 Glasgow	
16.09.93	Peter Waudby L PTS 6 Hull	
03.11.93	Warren Stephens W PTS 6 Worcester	
13.11.93	Terry Morrill L PTS 8 Hull	
30.11.93	Stuart Dunn L PTS 6 Leicester	
13.12.93	Glenn Catley L PTS 4 Bristol	
20.01.94	Darren Dorrington L PTS 6 Battersea	
26.02.94	Adrian Dodson L CO 1 Earls Court	
21.04.94	Mark Jay L PTS 6 Gateshead	
16.05.94	Peter Waudby L PTS 6 Cleethorpes	
02.06.94	Eric Noi L PTS 6 Middleton	
02.07.94	Paul Wright L RSC 1 Liverpool	
12.09.94	Phil Ball L PTS 6 Doncaster	
20.09.94	Willie Quinn RSC 3 Musselburgh	
24.10.94	John Stronach L PTS 6 Bradford	
31.10.94	Jon Stocks L PTS 6 Liverpool	
07.11.94	Sven Hamer L PTS 4 Piccadilly	
24.11.94	Peter Waudby L PTS 6 Hull	
05.12.94	Derek Roche L PTS 6 Bradford	
15.12.94	Ray Golding L PTS 6 Evesham	
16.01.95	Billy Collins L PTS 6 Musselburgh	
30.01.95	Shaun Hendry L PTS 6 Bradford	
16.02.95	Darren Swords L PTS 6 Bury	
04.03.95	Ryan Rhodes L CO 1 Livingston	
19.09.95	Justin Simmons L PTS 6 Plymouth	
05.10.95	Andy Neri W RSC 4 Queensferry	
29.10.95	Darren Swords L PTS 6 Shaw	
11.12.95	Wayne Shepherd W PTS 6 Morecambe	
13.01.96	Derek Roche L PTS 6 Halifax	
05.02.96	Lee Murtagh L PTS 6 Bradford	
14.02.96	Joe Townsley L PTS 6 Sunderland	
26.02.96	Rob Stevenson L PTS 6 Hull	
16.03.96	Tommy Quinn L PTS 4 Glasgow	
24.03.96	Jeff Finlayson L PTS 6 Shaw	
03.05.96	Jason Barker L RSC 1 Sheffield	
03.06.96	Joe Townsley L PTS 6 Glasgow	

Career: 150 contests, won 28, drew 5, lost 117.

Glenn Catley

Bristol. *Born* Sodbury, 15 March, 1972
Middleweight. Ht. 5'8"
Manager Self

27.05.93	Rick North W PTS 4 Bristol	
26.06.93	Chris Vassiliou W CO 2 Keynsham	
31.08.93	Marty Duke W RSC 2 Croydon	
13.09.93	Barry Thorogood W PTS 4 Bristol	
03.11.93	Marty Duke W RSC 1 Bristol	
13.12.93	Shamus Casey W PTS 4 Bristol	
10.03.94	Mark Cichocki W PTS 6 Bristol	
23.03.94	Carlo Colarusso L RSC 5 Cardiff	
25.05.94	Chris Davies W RSC 1 Bristol	
02.07.94	Martin Jolley W RSC 1 Keynsham	
22.11.94	Kirkland Laing W RSC 5 Bristol	
18.02.95	Lee Blundell W RSC 6 Shepton Mallet	
06.05.95	Mark Dawson W RSC 5 Shepton Mallet	
28.07.95	Kevin Adamson W CO 1 Bristol	
02.09.95	Quinn Paynter W RSC 1 Wembley	
30.09.95	John Duckworth W RSC 3 Cardiff	
28.10.95	Carlos Christie W PTS 8 Bristol	
10.11.95	Carlos Christie W CO 3 Bristol	
16.12.95	Peter Vosper W RSC 2 Cardiff	
26.04.96	Lee Crocker W RSC 2 Cardiff	

Career: 20 contests, won 19, lost 1.

Adrian Chase   Les Clark

Adrian Chase

Watford. *Born* St Albans, 18 October, 1968
L. Welterweight. Ht. 5'9"
Manager H. Holland

06.05.93	Jason Campbell W CO 2 Bayswater	
24.06.93	Delwyn Panayiotiou W CO 1 Watford	
23.02.94	Dennis Griffin W PTS 6 Watford	
16.05.94	Tony Gibbs W PTS 6 Heathrow	
21.07.94	Steve Burton W PTS 6 Battersea	
19.11.94	Wayne Jones W PTS 6 Heathrow	
21.04.95	Juha Temonen L PTS 4 Pori, Finland	
28.10.95	Tom Welsh L RSC 2 Bristol	
03.12.95	Delroy Leslie L RSC 4 Southwark	
12.02.96	Marc Smith W CO 1 Heathrow	
21.03.96	Peter Richardson L RSC 2 Southwark	

Career: 11 contests, won 7, lost 4.

(Martin) Marty Chestnut (Concannon)

Birmingham. *Born* Birmingham, 8 March, 1968
S. Bantamweight. Ht. 5'8"
Manager Self

29.04.93	Fred Reeve L PTS 6 Hull	
07.06.93	Ian McGirr L PTS 6 Glasgow	
30.10.93	Paul Lloyd L RSC 1 Chester	
11.12.93	John Sillo L PTS 6 Liverpool	
25.01.94	Anthony Hanna L PTS 4 Piccadilly	
10.02.94	James Murray L PTS 6 Glasgow	
01.03.94	Chris Lyons W PTS 6 Dudley	
27.04.94	Chris Lyons L RSC 3 Bethnal Green	
02.06.94	Des Gargano L PTS 6 Middleton	
02.09.94	Tiger Ray W PTS 4 Spitalfields	
17.09.94	Stephen Smith L RSC 5 Leverkusen, Germany	
27.10.94	Abdul Mannon W DIS 2 Millwall	
30.11.94	Matthew Harris L RSC 3 Wolverhampton	
23.01.95	Paul Webster L RSC 3 Bethnal Green	
20.02.95	Paul Hamilton W PTS 6 Manchester	
09.03.95	Graham McGrath W PTS 6 Walsall	
20.03.95	Graham McGrath L PTS 6 Birmingham	
13.04.95	Spencer Oliver L RSC 4 Bloomsbury	

75

01.06.95 Garry Burrell L RTD 3 Musselburgh
08.09.95 Alex Moon L RSC 3 Liverpool
07.10.95 Paul Ireland L RSC 6 Belfast
21.11.95 Graham McGrath W PTS 6 Edgbaston
02.12.95 Frankie Slane L PTS 4 Belfast
18.12.95 Michael Brodie L RTD 3 Mayfair
31.01.96 Anthony Hanna DREW 6 Stoke
22.03.96 Roger Brotherhood L PTS 6 Mansfield
24.05.96 Alston Buchanan L PTS 6 Glasgow
Career: 27 contests, won 6, drew 1, lost 20.

Roy Chipperfield

Bury. *Born* Radcliffe, 29 April, 1965
Middleweight. Ht. 5'10¾"
Manager B. Myers

22.09.94 Darren Swords L PTS 6 Bury
30.11.94 Eddie Haley L RSC 3 Solihull
27.02.95 Jon Stocks L RSC 3 Barrow
09.10.95 Lee Whitehead L RSC 2 Manchester
23.11.95 Mark Owens W RSC 6 Marton
07.12.95 Mark Cichocki L RSC 5 Sunderland
14.02.96 David Maw L PTS 6 Sunderland
25.03.96 Darren Sweeney L CO 1 Birmingham
29.04.96 Steve McNess L RSC 3 Mayfair
25.06.96 Ryan Rhodes L RSC 1 Mansfield
Career: 10 contests, won 1, lost 9.

(Peter) Carlos Christie

Birmingham. *Born* Birmingham, 17
August, 1966
Midlands Area S. Middleweight Champion.
Ht. 6'0"
Manager C. Sanigar

04.06.90 Roger Wilson L PTS 6 Birmingham
17.09.90 John Kaighin W PTS 6 Cardiff
27.09.90 Colin Manners W PTS 6 Birmingham
29.10.90 Paul Murray W PTS 6 Birmingham
18.11.90 Paul Busby L PTS 6 Birmingham
27.11.90 Nigel Rafferty W PTS 8
Wolverhampton
06.12.90 Nigel Rafferty W PTS 6
Wolverhampton
10.01.91 Ray Webb L PTS 6 Wandsworth
28.01.91 Gil Lewis W PTS 8 Birmingham
04.03.91 Nigel Rafferty W PTS 8 Birmingham
14.03.91 Michael Gale L PTS 8 Middleton
01.05.91 Peter Elliott W RSC 9 Solihull
*(Vacant Midlands Area S.
Middleweight Title)*
11.05.91 Ray Close L PTS 6 Belfast
07.09.91 Ray Close L PTS 6 Belfast
20.11.91 Nicky Piper L CO 6 Cardiff
10.03.92 Glenn Campbell DREW 8 Bury
15.09.92 Roland Ericsson W RSC 4 Crystal
Palace
28.01.93 James Cook L PTS 8 Southwark
28.04.93 Sammy Storey L RSC 8 Dublin
31.08.93 Simon Harris L CO 3 Croydon
12.11.93 Tony Booth L PTS 6 Hull
28.11.93 Ali Forbes L CO 4 Southwark
22.01.94 Darron Griffiths L PTS 8 Cardiff
21.02.94 Stephen Wilson L RSC 2 Glasgow
15.06.94 William Joppy L PTS 6 Southwark
27.08.94 Antonio Fernandez L PTS 8 Cardiff
26.09.94 Paul Wright L PTS 6 Liverpool
29.10.94 Andrew Flute W PTS 8 Cannock
30.11.94 Darren Ashton W PTS 6 Solihull
23.01.95 Robert Allen L CO 2 Bethnal Green
16.03.95 Mark Delaney L CO 1 Basildon
20.10.95 Richard Bustin W PTS 6 Ipswich
28.10.95 Glenn Catley L PTS 8 Bristol
10.11.95 Glenn Catley L PTS 6 Bristol
15.12.95 David Starie L CO 4 Bethnal Green
Career: 35 contests, won 12, drew 1, lost 22.

Floyd Churchill

Kirkby. *Born* Liverpool, 19 January, 1969
L. Welterweight. Former Undefeated
Central Area S. Featherweight Champion.
Ht. 5'4"
Manager T. Miller

29.04.92 T. J. Smith W RSC 2 Liverpool
14.05.92 Jamie Davidson W RSC 4 Liverpool
12.06.92 Kevin McKillan L PTS 6 Liverpool
26.09.92 Richie Wenton W RSC 2 Earls Court
12.11.92 Brian Hickey W CO 1 Liverpool
04.05.93 Jimmy Owens W CO 1 Liverpool
*(Vacant Central Area S. Featherweight
Title)*
02.07.94 Mark Antony L RSC 1 Liverpool
09.11.94 Jason Rowland L RSC 2 Millwall
25.03.95 Tony Mock L PTS 6 Chester
08.06.95 Dave Anderson L PTS 8 Glasgow
15.09.95 Alan McDowall L RSC 5 Glasgow
Career: 11 contests, won 5, lost 6.

Mark Cichocki (Weatherill)

Hartlepool. *Born* Hartlepool, 18 October,
1967
Former Northern Area L. Middleweight
Champion. Ht. 5'7"
Manager T. Conroy

01.12.92 Tony Trimble W PTS 6 Hartlepool
29.01.93 Gordon Blair W PTS 8 Glasgow
09.03.93 Rob Pitters W RSC 10 Hartlepool
*(Vacant Northern Area L.
Middleweight Title)*
06.05.93 Mick Duncan W RSC 7 Hartlepool
*(Northern Area L. Middleweight Title
Defence)*
12.05.93 Glyn Rhodes L PTS 6 Sheffield
02.12.93 Mark Jay W RSC 4 Hartlepool
*(Northern Area L. Middleweight Title
Defence)*
22.01.94 Anibal Acevedo L RTD 3 Cardiff
10.03.94 Glenn Catley L PTS 6 Bristol
07.12.95 Roy Chipperfield W RSC 5 Sunderland
14.02.96 Craig Winter L PTS 6 Sunderland
Career: 10 contests, won 6, lost 4.

James Clamp

Selkirk. *Born* Hawick, 17 May, 1972
Welterweight. Ht. 5'9½"
Manager J. Murray

25.03.91 Jason Brattley L RSC 3 Bradford
13.05.95 Craig Lynch DREW 6 Glasgow
15.09.95 Larry Anderson W RSC 5 Glasgow
02.11.95 Shaun O'Neill L PTS 6 Houghton le
Spring
Career: 4 contests, won 1, drew 1, lost 2.

Howard Clarke

Warley. *Born* London, 23 September, 1967
Welterweight. Ht. 5'10"
Manager Self

15.10.91 Chris Mylan W PTS 4 Dudley
09.12.91 Claude Rossi W RSC 3 Brierley Hill
04.02.92 Julian Eavis W PTS 4 Alfreton
03.03.92 Dave Andrews W RSC 3 Cradley Heath
21.05.92 Richard O'Brien W CO 1 Cradley
Heath
29.09.92 Paul King W PTS 6 Stoke
27.10.92 Gordon Blair L RSC 4 Cradley Heath
16.03.93 Paul King W PTS 6 Edgbaston

07.06.93 Dean Bramhald W RTD 2 Walsall
29.06.93 Paul King W PTS 6 Edgbaston
06.10.93 Julian Eavis L PTS 8 Solihull
30.11.93 Julian Eavis W PTS 8 Wolverhampton
08.02.94 Nigel Bradley W RTD 6
Wolverhampton
18.04.94 Andy Peach W PTS 6 Walsall
28.06.94 Dennis Berry L RSC 3 Edgbaston
12.10.94 Julian Eavis W PTS 8 Stoke
25.10.94 Andy Peach W RSC 3 Edgbaston
02.11.94 Julian Eavis W PTS 8 Birmingham
29.11.94 Julian Eavis W PTS 6 Cannock
07.12.94 Peter Reid W PTS 8 Stoke
25.01.95 Dennis Berry L PTS 8 Stoke
08.03.95 Andrew Jervis W PTS 6 Solihull
11.05.95 David Bain W RSC 1 Dudley
20.09.95 Michael Smyth DREW 6 Ystrad
02.10.95 Nigel Wenton L PTS 6 Mayfair
Career: 25 contests, won 19, drew 1, lost 5.

Chris Clarkson

Hull. *Born* Hull, 15 December, 1967
Lightweight. Former Undefeated Central
Area Bantamweight & Featherweight
Champion. Ht. 5'4"
Manager Self

18.03.85 Gypsy Johnny L PTS 4 Bradford
09.04.85 Terry Allen W PTS 4 South Shields
30.04.85 Terry Allen W PTS 4 Chorley
30.05.85 Gypsy Johnny L PTS 4 Blackburn
17.10.85 Tony Heath W PTS 4 Leicester
13.02.86 Glen Dainty L RSC 4 Longford
17.03.86 Jamie McBride L PTS 4 Glasgow
03.11.86 Gerry McBride DREW 6 Manchester
13.11.86 Gordon Stobie W RSC 4 Huddersfield
01.12.86 Nigel Crook L RSC 6 Nottingham
27.01.87 Donnie Hood L PTS 6 Glasgow
23.02.87 Dave Boy Mallaby W PTS 4 Bradford
02.03.87 Dave Boy Mallaby W CO 3
Nottingham
16.03.87 Pepe Webber W PTS 6 Glasgow
24.03.87 Nigel Crook W PTS 6 Hull
06.04.87 Joe Kelly L PTS 8 Glasgow
14.04.87 Jamie McBride L RSC 6 Cumbernauld
28.04.87 John Green L RSC 6 Manchester
13.06.87 Ronnie Stephenson W PTS 8 Great
Yarmouth
23.09.87 Mitchell King L PTS 6 Loughborough
15.11.88 Gordon Shaw W PTS 6 Hull
29.11.88 Des Gargano L PTS 6 Manchester
14.12.88 Dave George L PTS 6 Evesham
16.02.89 Johnny Bredahl L PTS 6 Copenhagen,
Denmark
09.03.89 Mark Geraghty L PTS 6 Glasgow
20.03.89 George Bailey W PTS 6 Bradford
11.07.89 Des Gargano W PTS 6 Batley
10.10.89 Gerry McBride W PTS 10 Hull
*(Vacant Central Area Bantamweight
Title)*
23.11.89 Drew Docherty L PTS 6 Motherwell
15.03.90 Noel Carroll W PTS 6 Manchester
19.04.90 Gerry McBride W DIS 5 Oldham
*(Vacant Central Area Featherweight
Title)*
30.04.90 Pete Buckley W PTS 8 Mayfair
19.11.90 James Drummond W PTS 8 Glasgow
02.03.91 Francesco Arroyo L RSC 4 Darlington
*(Vacant IBF Inter-Continental
Bantamweight Title)*
04.04.91 Duke McKenzie L RSC 5 Watford
09.10.91 Mark Geraghty L PTS 6 Glasgow
21.10.91 Ian McGirr DREW 6 Glasgow

16.12.91 Noel Carroll L PTS 6 Manchester
03.03.92 Billy Hardy L RSC 5 Houghton le Spring
14.12.92 David Ramsden W PTS 4 Bradford
24.02.93 Bradley Stone L PTS 8 Wembley
24.09.93 Prince Nassem Hamed L CO 2 Dublin
03.03.94 Alfred Kotey L PTS 8 Ebbw Vale
15.04.94 Mike Deveney L RSC 3 Hull
13.06.94 Wayne Rigby L PTS 6 Liverpool
26.09.94 Paul Lloyd W RSC 4 Liverpool
28.04.95 Julian Lorcy L RSC 1 Randers, Denmark
10.06.95 Michael Brodie L PTS 6 Manchester
02.07.95 P. J. Gallagher L RSC 3 Dublin
22.09.95 Trevor Sumner NC 1 Hull
28.10.95 Colin Dunne L RSC 4 Kensington
Career: 51 contests, won 19, drew 2, lost 29, no contest 1.

Dave Clavering

Bury. *Born* Bury, 21 October, 1973
Lightweight. Ht. 5'6"
Manager J. Doughty

16.05.94 Al Garrett W RTD 4 Morecambe
22.09.94 Ian Richardson W RSC 1 Bury
26.09.94 Chris Jickells W PTS 6 Morecambe
16.02.95 Trevor George W PTS 6 Bury
18.05.95 Kid McAuley W PTS 6 Middleton
29.10.95 John T. Kelly W PTS 6 Shaw
14.11.95 Dave Madden W RSC 1 Bury
24.03.96 Frankie Foster W RSC 4 Shaw
Career: 8 contests, won 8.

Shaun Cogan

Birmingham. *Born* Birmingham, 7 August, 1967
L. Welterweight. Ht. 5'8"
Manager Self

25.09.89 Peter Bowen W RSC 1 Birmingham
24.10.89 Gary Quigley W RSC 2 Wolverhampton
06.12.89 George Jones W PTS 6 Stoke
14.03.90 Dean Bramhald W PTS 6 Stoke
27.03.90 Mark Antony W CO 1 Wolverhampton
23.04.90 Mike Morrison W PTS 8 Birmingham
21.02.91 Tony Britland W PTS 6 Walsall
19.03.91 Rocky Lawlor W RSC 2 Birmingham
25.07.91 David Thompson W CO 1 Dudley
05.12.91 Steve Pollard W PTS 6 Oakengates
27.11.92 Soren Sondergaard L PTS 6 Randers, Denmark
16.03.93 Malcolm Melvin L PTS 10 Edgbaston
(Vacant All-Ireland L. Welterweight Title & Midlands Area L. Welterweight Title Challenge)
18.05.93 Seth Jones W RSC 2 Edgbaston
15.09.93 Paul Ryan L RSC 3 Ashford
06.11.93 Bernard Paul DREW 6 Bethnal Green
02.12.93 Kane White W RSC 1 Evesham
11.01.94 Bernard Paul W PTS 6 Bethnal Green
01.03.94 Karl Taylor W PTS 6 Dudley
10.05.94 Andreas Panayi L RSC 7 Doncaster
28.09.94 John Smith W RSC 3 Glasgow
24.10.94 Charlie Kane L PTS 10 Glasgow
(Elim. British L. Welterweight Title)
29.11.94 John Smith W RSC 4 Cannock
06.03.95 Delroy Leslie L RSC 1 Mayfair
06.05.95 Ross Hale L RSC 4 Shepton Mallet
(Commonwealth L. Welterweight Title Challenge)
21.11.95 Shaun Stokes W PTS 8 Edgbaston
Career: 25 contests, won 17, drew 1, lost 7.

Mark Cokely

Port Talbot. *Born* Neath, 31 October, 1970
Flyweight. Ht. 5'3"
Manager Self

27.04.94 Lyndon Kershaw L PTS 6 Solihull
20.05.94 Graham McGrath L PTS 6 Neath
06.03.95 Adey Lewis L RSC 5 Mayfair
05.05.95 Anthony Hanna L RSC 4 Swansea
22.11.95 Dave Martin L RTD 2 Mayfair
Career: 5 contests, lost 5.

Carlo Colarusso

Llanelli. *Born* Swansea, 11 February, 1970
Welsh L. Middleweight Champion. Ht. 5'7"
Manager Self

14.09.89 Paul Burton W RSC 5 Basildon
11.10.89 Lindon Scarlett L PTS 8 Stoke
24.10.89 Cornelius Carr L RTD 4 Watford
22.11.89 Lindon Scarlett L PTS 8 Solihull
01.03.90 Kevin Hayde W RTD 3 Cardiff
14.03.90 Kevin Plant W PTS 8 Stoke
21.03.90 Sammy Sampson W RSC 3 Preston
06.04.90 Ray Webb W PTS 6 Telford
19.11.90 Gary Pemberton W RSC 3 Cardiff
29.11.90 Nigel Moore L PTS 6 Bayswater
24.01.91 Gary Pemberton W RSC 8 Gorseinon
(Vacant Welsh L. Middleweight Title)
02.03.91 Cornelius Carr L PTS 8 Darlington
11.05.92 Russell Washer W RSC 5 Llanelli
(Welsh L. Middleweight Title Defence)
27.06.92 Newton Barnett W RTD 5 Quinta do Lago, Portugal
28.10.92 Lloyd Honeyghan L RSC 6 Kensington
16.03.93 Richie Woodhall L PTS 8 Wolverhampton
30.03.93 Tony Velinor W RSC 3 Cardiff
14.03.94 John Bosco L PTS 6 Mayfair
23.03.94 Glenn Catley W RSC 5 Cardiff
03.03.95 Neville Brown L RSC 7 Bethnal Green
(British Middleweight Title Challenge)
29.09.95 Danny Peters L PTS 6 Liverpool
16.10.95 Howard Eastman L RSC 1 Mayfair
Career: 22 contests, won 11, lost 11.

Carlo Colarusso   Les Clark

Brian Coleman

Birmingham. *Born* Birmingham, 27 July, 1969
L. Welterweight. Ht. 5'11"
Manager Self

21.11.91 Jamie Morris DREW 6 Stafford
11.12.91 Craig Hartwell DREW 6 Leicester
22.01.92 John O. Johnson L PTS 6 Stoke
20.02.92 Davy Robb L PTS 6 Oakengates
31.03.92 Blue Butterworth L PTS 6 Stockport
17.05.92 Korso Aleain L RSC 1 Harringay
17.09.92 Nicky Bardle L RSC 4 Watford
21.10.92 Jason Barker W PTS 6 Stoke
10.12.92 A. M. Milton DREW 6 Bethnal Green
31.03.93 A. M. Milton L PTS 4 Bethnal Green
26.04.93 Jason Beard L PTS 6 Lewisham
06.05.93 Mark Allen W PTS 6 Walsall
18.05.93 Sean Metherell DREW 6 Kettering
27.05.93 Blue Butterworth L PTS 6 Burnley
23.06.93 Jonathan Thaxton L PTS 8 Gorleston
11.08.93 Steve Howden L RSC 4 Mansfield
13.09.93 Mick Hoban L PTS 6 Middleton
01.12.93 A. M. Milton L PTS 4 Bethnal Green
08.12.93 Chris Pollock W PTS 6 Stoke
16.12.93 Mark Newton L RSC 4 Bethnal Green
11.01.94 Paul Knights L RSC 4 Bethnal Green
08.02.94 Andy Peach W PTS 6 Wolverhampton
18.02.94 Cam Raeside L PTS 6 Leicester
08.03.94 Chris Pollock L PTS 6 Edgbaston
29.03.94 P. J. Gallagher L PTS 6 Bethnal Green
14.04.94 Cham Joof L CO 3 Battersea
02.06.94 Scott Walker L CO 1 Middleton
12.09.94 Shabba Edwards L PTS 6 Mayfair
19.09.94 Mark Breslin L CO 1 Glasgow
09.11.94 Kenny Scott L PTS 6 Stafford
23.11.94 Billy McDougall W PTS 4 Piccadilly
29.11.94 Warren Stephens W PTS 6 Wolverhampton
09.12.94 Danny Stevens L RTD 2 Bethnal Green
24.01.95 Wayne Jones L PTS 6 Piccadilly
07.02.95 Alan Temple L PTS 6 Ipswich
23.02.95 Darren Covill L PTS 4 Southwark
16.03.95 Paul Knights L RSC 2 Basildon
02.07.95 Tommy Lawler L PTS 4 Dublin
08.09.95 George Naylor L PTS 6 Liverpool
27.09.95 Allan Gray L PTS 6 Bethnal Green
20.10.95 Mikael Nilsson L PTS 6 Ipswich
02.11.95 Marco Fattore W PTS 6 Mayfair
16.11.95 Alan Bosworth L PTS 6 Evesham
24.11.95 Chris Barnett L PTS 6 Manchester
02.12.95 Neil Sinclair L RTD 1 Belfast
20.01.96 James Hare L PTS 6 Mansfield
29.01.96 Dave Fallon L PTS 6 Piccadilly
13.02.96 Martin Holgate L PTS 4 Bethnal Green
21.02.96 Marco Fattore W PTS 6 Piccadilly
13.03.96 Paul Samuels L PTS 6 Wembley
03.04.96 Ian Honeywood L PTS 6 Bethnal Green
20.04.96 Ray Robinson L PTS 6 Brentwood
24.05.96 Scott Dixon L PTS 8 Glasgow
08.06.96 Mark Winters L PTS 4 Newcastle
Career: 54 contests, won 8, drew 4, lost 42.

Billy Collins

Stirling. *Born* Stirling, 20 May, 1968
L. Middleweight. Ht. 5'9"
Manager T. Gilmour

25.04.94 Raziq Ali W PTS 6 Glasgow
16.01.95 Shamus Casey W PTS 6 Musselburgh
23.01.95 Eddie Haley W RSC 4 Glasgow
24.02.95 Rob Stevenson W PTS 6 Irvine
24.04.95 Phil Epton W RSC 3 Glasgow
05.06.95 Ernie Loveridge W PTS 8 Glasgow
20.11.95 Brian Dunn L PTS 8 Glasgow
Career: 7 contests, won 6, lost 1.

Hugh Collins

Stirling. *Born* Stirling, 17 August, 1969
Lightweight. Ht. 5'6"
Manager T. Gilmour

29.03.93	Tim Hill W PTS 6 Glasgow
20.09.93	Robert Braddock W PTS 8 Glasgow
24.11.93	Paul Bowen W PTS 6 Solihull
24.01.94	Colin Innes W PTS 6 Glasgow
21.02.94	Norman Dhalie W RTD 4 Glasgow
28.03.94	Trevor Royal W RSC 2 Musselburgh
25.04.94	Miguel Matthews W PTS 8 Glasgow
20.09.94	Russell Davison W RTD 4 Musselburgh
02.11.94	Michael Hermon L RSC 3 Solihull
16.01.95	John T. Kelly W PTS 6 Musselburgh
17.02.95	Paul Wynn W RSC 3 Cumbernauld
05.04.95	Kid McAuley W PTS 6 Irvine
05.06.95	Wayne Rigby L RSC 4 Glasgow
18.11.95	John T. Kelly W PTS 8 Glasgow
18.03.96	Kid McAuley W PTS 8 Glasgow

Career: 15 contests, won 13, lost 2.

Steve Conway

Dewsbury. *Born* Hartlepool, 6 October, 1977
S. Featherweight. Ht. 5'8"
Manager K. Tate

21.02.96	Robert Grubb W PTS 6 Batley
24.04.96	Ervine Blake W PTS 6 Solihull
20.05.96	Chris Lyons W PTS 6 Cleethorpes
30.05.96	Ram Singh W PTS 6 Lincoln

Career: 4 contests, won 4.

Darren Corbett

Belfast. *Born* Belfast, 8 July, 1972
Cruiserweight. Ht. 5'11"
Manager B. Hearn

10.12.94	David Jules W RSC 1 Manchester
13.12.94	Carl Gaffney W RSC 1 Potters Bar
21.02.95	Steve Garber W PTS 6 Sunderland
18.03.95	Gary Williams DREW 6 Millstreet
14.04.95	Dennis Bailey W RSC 2 Belfast
27.05.95	R. F. McKenzie L PTS 6 Belfast
26.08.95	Nigel Rafferty W PTS 6 Belfast
07.10.95	Nigel Rafferty W PTS 6 Belfast
02.12.95	Bobbi Joe Edwards W PTS 6 Belfast
07.05.96	Cliff Elden W RSC 1 Mayfair
28.05.96	Darren Fearn W RSC 1 Belfast

Career: 11 contests, won 9, drew 1, lost 1.

Maurice Core (Coore)

Manchester. *Born* Manchester, 22 June, 1965
Former Undefeated British L. Heavyweight Champion. Ht. 6'5"
Manager F. Warren

15.01.90	Dennis Banton W PTS 6 Mayfair
03.05.90	Everton Blake W PTS 8 Kensington
22.05.90	Nicky Piper DREW 6 St Albans
22.02.91	Everton Blake W RSC 8 Manchester
12.04.91	Glazz Campbell W CO 2 Manchester
31.05.91	Rodney Brown W RSC 6 Manchester

Maurice Core

Harry Goodwin

29.11.91	Steve Osborne W PTS 6 Manchester	
31.01.92	Denroy Bryan W RSC 1 Manchester	
05.04.92	Willie Ball W RSC 3 Bradford	
18.07.92	Tony Booth W PTS 6 Manchester	
28.09.92	Noel Magee W RSC 9 Manchester	
	(Vacant British L. Heavyweight Title)	
05.02.93	Larry Prather W PTS 10 Manchester	
25.07.93	John Kaighin W PTS 6 Oldham	
01.12.93	Simon Harris W RSC 11 Bethnal Green	
	(British L. Heavyweight Title Defence)	
25.10.94	Fabrice Tiozzo L RSC 4 Besancon, France	
	(European Light-Heavyweight Title Challenge)	
10.06.95	Eric French W RSC 2 Manchester	
21.10.95	Frank Minton W RSC 5 Ronse, Belgium	

Career: 17 contests, won 15, drew 1, lost 1.

Darren Covill

Welling. *Born* Welling, 11 April, 1970
Welterweight. Ht. 5'8"
Manager D. Powell

23.02.95	Brian Coleman W PTS 4 Southwark	
19.05.95	Allan Gray L PTS 6 Southwark	
04.06.95	Dick Hanns-Kat W RSC 3 Bethnal Green	
14.09.95	Gavin Barker W CO 1 Battersea	
21.09.95	Shaun Stokes L PTS 6 Sheffield	
22.11.95	Jason Barker L PTS 4 Sheffield	
05.02.96	Jason Barker W RSC 1 Bexleyheath	
21.03.96	Paul Miles L PTS 4 Southwark	

Career: 8 contests, won 4, lost 4.

Lee Crocker

Swansea. *Born* Swansea, 9 May, 1969
L. Middleweight. Ht. 6'0"
Manager Self

31.01.91	Colin Manners L PTS 6 Bredbury	
12.02.91	Paul Evans W RSC 2 Cardiff	
04.04.91	Johnny Pinnock W RSC 5 Watford	
30.06.91	Andrew Furlong DREW 6 Southwark	
30.09.91	Fran Harding L RSC 3 Kensington	
11.03.92	Russell Washer W PTS 6 Cardiff	
30.04.92	Winston May W RSC 2 Bayswater	
23.09.92	Nick Manners L CO 1 Leeds	
17.12.92	Jamie Robinson L RTD 2 Barking	
20.01.93	Ernie Loveridge W PTS 6 Wolverhampton	
28.01.93	Clay O'Shea L RSC 1 Southwark	
14.06.93	Gilbert Jackson L RSC 2 Bayswater	
07.10.93	David Larkin L RSC 5 York	
23.04.94	Leif Keiski L CO 2 Cardiff	
04.06.94	Derek Grainger L RSC 3 Cardiff	
04.02.95	Ryan Rhodes L RSC 2 Cardiff	
24.03.95	Darren Dorrington W PTS 6 Swansea	
05.05.95	Carl Harney W CO 4 Swansea	
16.06.95	Andy Ewen W RSC 3 Southwark	
26.04.96	Glenn Catley L RSC 2 Cardiff	
31.05.96	Mads Larsen L RSC 1 Copenhagen, Denmark	

Career: 21 contests, won 8, drew 1, lost 12.

Ryan Cummings

London. *Born* Lancaster, 17 November, 1973
L. Heavyweight. Ht. 5'11"
Manager F. Warren

10.03.94	Terry Duffus W PTS 6 Watford	
07.11.94	Mark Hale W RSC 6 Bethnal Green	
10.06.95	Mark Dawson L PTS 6 Manchester	
11.05.96	Nicky Wadman W RSC 2 Bethnal Green	

Career: 4 contests, won 3, lost 1.

Shaun Cummins

Leicester. *Born* Leicester, 8 February, 1968
Middleweight. Former Undefeated WBA
Penta-Continental L. Middleweight
Champion. Ht. 6'1"
Manager P. De Freitas

29.09.86	Michael Justin W PTS 6 Loughborough	
24.11.86	Gary Pemberton W RSC 6 Cardiff	
09.02.87	Rob Thomas W PTS 8 Cardiff	
23.09.87	Chris Richards W PTS 6 Loughborough	
07.03.88	Antonio Fernandez W PTS 6 Northampton	
12.09.88	Shamus Casey W CO 3 Northampton	
24.10.88	Frank Grant L RTD 7 Northampton	
01.03.89	Gary Pemberton W CO 2 Cardiff	
05.04.89	Efren Olivo W RSC 1 Kensington	
04.10.89	Kesem Clayton L RSC 6 Solihull	
31.01.90	Tony Velinor W PTS 8 Bethnal Green	
20.02.90	Brian Robinson W RSC 5 Millwall	
26.04.90	Wally Swift Jnr L PTS 10 Merthyr	
	(Vacant Midlands Area L. Middleweight Title & Elim. British L. Middleweight Title)	
18.09.90	Paul Wesley W RSC 1 Wolverhampton	
31.10.90	Terry Morrill W RSC 1 Crystal Palace	
23.01.91	Ian Chantler W PTS 10 Brentwood	
19.03.91	Martin Smith DREW 8 Leicester	
07.11.91	Jason Rowe W RSC 2 Peterborough	
05.12.91	Winston May W RSC 2 Peterborough	
18.06.92	Leroy Owens W RSC 2 Peterborough	
26.09.92	John Kaighin W RTD 4 Earls Court	
28.11.92	Steve Foster W PTS 12 Manchester	
	(Vacant WBA Penta-Continental L. Middleweight Title)	
20.04.93	Mickey Hughes W CO 11 Brentwood	
	(WBA Penta-Continental L. Middleweight Title Defence)	
16.02.94	John Kaighin W RSC 3 Stevenage	
11.05.94	Colin Manners L RSC 6 Sheffield	
09.11.94	Agostino Cardamone L PTS 12 San Remo, Italy	
	(European Middleweight Title Challenge)	
06.05.95	Val Golding W RSC 7 Shepton Mallet	
01.07.95	Mark Dawson W PTS 8 Kensington	
10.11.95	Neville Brown L CO 5 Derby	
	(British Middleweight Title Challenge)	

Career: 29 contests, won 22, drew 1, lost 6.

Dave Curtis

Hull. *Born* Hull, 19 January, 1967
Middleweight. Ht. 5'9"
Manager L. Billany

15.04.94	Brian Hickey W PTS 6 Hull	
09.05.94	Laurence Roche L RSC 8 Bradford	
20.09.94	Steve McLevy L RTD 3 Musselburgh	
24.11.94	Steve Pollard L RTD 4 Hull	
02.06.95	Paul Carr L PTS 6 Bethnal Green	
12.06.95	Lee Murtagh L PTS 6 Bradford	
22.09.95	Steve Pollard L RSC 6 Hull	

Career: 7 contests, won 1, lost 6.

Sean Daly

Leigh. *Born* Leigh, 1 May, 1966
Heavyweight. Ht. 6'1"
Manager R. Jones

22.04.86	Gary Fairclough W PTS 4 Carlisle	
08.05.86	Tony Hallett DREW 6 Newcastle	
22.05.86	Steve Garber L PTS 6 Horwich	
17.06.86	Tony Hallett W PTS 6 Blackpool	
25.09.86	Mick Cordon W PTS 6 Preston	
20.10.86	Ramon Voorn L PTS 4 Eindhoven, Holland	
18.11.86	Dave Madden W RSC 1 Doncaster	
01.12.86	Mick Cordon W PTS 6 Nottingham	
27.01.87	John Williams W RSC 2 Manchester	
10.03.87	Johnny Nelson L RSC 1 Manchester	
06.10.87	Ian Bulloch L RSC 4 Manchester	
24.03.88	Lennie Howard L RSC 6 Bethnal Green	
05.10.95	Paul Thompson W RSC 5 Hull	
17.11.95	Mika Kihlstrom L PTS 4 Helsinki, Finland	
07.12.95	John Pierre DREW 6 Hull	
19.02.96	Colin Brown L RTD 4 Glasgow	
23.05.96	Declan Faherty L RSC 5 Queensferry	

Career: 17 contests, won 7, drew 2, lost 8.

Shaune Danskin

Peterborough. *Born* Spalding, 28
December, 1975
Lightweight. Ht. 5'5"
Manager K. Whitney

08.12.95	Gary Jenkinson L PTS 6 Leeds	
19.02.96	Paul Hamilton L CO 2 Glasgow	

Career: 2 contests, lost 2.

Richard Darkes

Huddersfield. *Born* Huddersfield, 5
October, 1968
Cruiserweight. Ht. 6'0"
Manager C. Aston

20.05.96	Phil Reid W RSC 2 Bradford	

Career: 1 contest, won 1.

Donovan Davey

Bradford. *Born* Shipley, 20 July, 1967
Welterweight. Ht. 5'7"
Manager B. Myers

14.11.95	Shaun Marsh W PTS 6 Yarm	
24.11.95	Paul Burns L PTS 6 Chester	
11.12.95	Lee Murtagh L PTS 6 Bradford	
13.02.96	George Richards L PTS 6 Wolverhampton	
06.03.96	George Richards L PTS 6 Solihull	

Career: 5 contests, won 1, lost 4.

Donovan Davey   Les Clark

Hughie Davey

Newcastle. *Born* Wallsend, 27 January, 1966
Welterweight. Ht. 5'8"
Manager Self

30.03.92	Wayne Shepherd W PTS 6 Bradford
28.04.92	Benji Joseph W RSC 4 Houghton le Spring
10.09.92	Darren McInulty W PTS 6 Southwark
21.09.92	Rick North DREW 6 Cleethorpes
23.10.92	Richard O'Brien W PTS 6 Gateshead
01.03.93	Wayne Appleton L PTS 6 Bradford
29.04.93	Paul King L PTS 6 Newcastle
11.06.93	Wayne Shepherd W PTS 6 Gateshead
04.10.93	Steve Scott W PTS 6 Bradford
08.11.93	Warren Bowers W RSC 2 Bradford
13.12.93	Sean Baker L PTS 4 Bristol
03.03.94	Paul King L PTS 10 Newcastle
	(Vacant Northern Area Welterweight Title)
06.10.94	Mick Hoban W PTS 6 Cramlington
24.11.94	John Stronach W PTS 6 Newcastle
10.12.94	Craig Winter L PTS 6 Manchester
21.02.95	David Maw W RSC 3 Sunderland
20.03.95	Joe Townsley W PTS 6 Glasgow
22.06.95	David Maw W PTS 6 Houghton le Spring
29.07.95	Kevin McKenzie W RSC 5 Whitley Bay
25.09.95	Derek Roche L PTS 6 Bradford
22.10.95	Peter Malinga L PTS 10 Durban, South Africa
02.03.96	Craig Lynch W PTS 4 Newcastle
13.04.96	Neil Sinclair L PTS 6 Liverpool
09.05.96	Jason Barker W PTS 6 Sunderland
08.06.96	Craig Lynch W PTS 4 Newcastle

Career: 25 contests, won 16, drew 1, lost 8.

Andy Davidson

Salford. *Born* Salford, 11 March, 1972
L. Welterweight. Ht. 5'9"
Manager J. Trickett

18.04.94	Kevin McKenzie W RSC 1 Manchester
28.06.94	M. T. Atkin W RSC 1 Mayfair
03.10.94	Wahid Fats L RSC 4 Manchester
03.04.95	Andrew Jervis L CO 3 Manchester
21.09.95	Nicky Bardle L CO 1 Battersea
03.02.96	Gary Ryder L RSC 1 Liverpool
03.05.96	Michael Alexander L RTD 2 Sheffield

Career: 7 contests, won 2, lost 5.

Andy Davidson   Les Clark

Chris Davies

Blaencldrach. *Born* Pontypridd, 24 August, 1974
L. Heavyweight. Ht. 5'9"
Manager D. Gardiner

27.04.94	Craig Joseph L PTS 6 Solihull
25.05.94	Glenn Catley L RSC 1 Bristol
29.05.96	Mark Hickey W RSC 1 Ebbw Vale

Career: 3 contests, won 1, lost 2.

Jason Davies

Doncaster. *Born* Doncaster, 4 February, 1970
L. Heavyweight. Ht. 6'2"
Manager T. Petersen

23.11.95	Mark Richardson L RSC 2 Marton
26.01.96	Nicky Wadman L RSC 2 Brighton

Career: 2 contests, lost 2.

Jason Davies   Les Clark

Mark Dawson (Lee)

Burton. *Born* Burton, 26 February, 1971
Middleweight. Ht. 5'8"
Manager Self

03.06.92	Rick North W PTS 6 Newcastle under Lyme
09.09.92	Jimmy Vincent W PTS 6 Stoke
29.09.92	Steve Goodwin L RSC 1 Stoke
28.10.92	Steve McNess W RSC 2 Kensington
07.12.92	Steve Goodwin W PTS 6 Mayfair
27.01.93	Rick North W PTS 8 Stoke
15.02.93	John Bosco L PTS 6 Mayfair
27.02.93	Robin Reid L RSC 1 Dagenham
30.03.93	Matthew Turner L PTS 6 Cardiff
12.05.93	Steve Goodwin L PTS 10 Stoke
	(Vacant Midlands Area L. Middleweight Title)
27.05.93	Derek Wormald L RTD 5 Burnley
10.11.93	John Bosco L RTD 4 Watford
15.03.94	Stinger Mason W RSC 6 Stoke
22.03.94	Geoff McCreesh L PTS 6 Bethnal Green

Chris Davies (continued)

05.09.94	Tony Griffiths W PTS 6 Brentwood
17.09.94	Mark Delaney L PTS 6 Crawley
01.10.94	Joe Calzaghe L RSC 1 Cardiff
29.11.94	Andrew Flute L PTS 8 Cannock
07.12.94	John Duckworth W PTS 6 Stoke
20.01.95	Mark Baker L RSC 3 Bethnal Green
08.03.95	Lester Jacobs L PTS 6 Bloomsbury
30.03.95	David Starie L RSC 1 Bethnal Green
06.05.95	Glenn Catley L RSC 5 Shepton Mallet
10.06.95	Ryan Cummings W PTS 6 Manchester
01.07.95	Shaun Cummins L PTS 8 Kensington
22.07.95	Lester Jacobs L PTS 4 Millwall
06.09.95	Robert Harper W PTS 6 Stoke
15.09.95	Jason Matthews L RSC 3 Mansfield
25.10.95	Jetty Williams W PTS 6 Telford
10.11.95	Ryan Rhodes L PTS 6 Derby
25.11.95	Danny Ryan L PTS 4 Dublin
02.12.95	Frederik Alvarez L RTD 6 Belfast
13.01.96	Mark Baker L RSC 3 Halifax
04.03.96	Harri Hakulinen L PTS 4 Helsinki, Finland
13.04.96	Paul Wright L PTS 6 Liverpool
11.05.96	Michael Bowen L PTS 4 Bethnal Green
31.05.96	Peter H. Madsen L PTS 4 Copenhagen, Denmark
08.06.96	Robin Reid L RSC 5 Newcastle

Career: 38 contests, won 11, lost 27.

Phill Day

Swindon. *Born* Swindon, 5 November, 1974
Cruiserweight. Ht. 5'11½"
Manager C. Sanigar

07.07.95	Tim Redman L RSC 2 Cardiff
21.09.95	John Pettersson L RSC 4 Battersea
10.11.95	L. A. Williams W PTS 6 Bristol
21.02.96	Carl Heath L PTS 6 Piccadilly

Career: 4 contests, won 1, lost 3.

Garry Delaney

West Ham. *Born* Newham, 12 August, 1970
Cruiserweight. Former Commonwealth L. Heavyweight Champion. Former Undefeated WBO Penta-Continental, WBO Inter-Continental & Southern Area L. Heavyweight Champion. Ht. 6'3"
Manager Self

02.10.91	Gus Mendes W RSC 1 Barking
23.10.91	Joe Frater W RSC 1 Bethnal Green
13.11.91	John Kaighin W PTS 6 Bethnal Green
11.12.91	Randy B. Powell W RSC 1 Basildon
11.02.92	Simon Harris DREW 8 Barking
12.05.92	John Williams W PTS 6 Crystal Palace
16.06.92	Nigel Rafferty W CO 5 Dagenham
15.09.92	Gil Lewis W CO 2 Crystal Palace
06.10.92	Simon McDougall W PTS 8 Antwerp, Belgium
10.11.92	John Oxenham W CO 5 Dagenham
12.12.92	Simon McDougall W PTS 8 Muswell Hill
30.01.93	Simon Collins W PTS 8 Brentwood
28.09.93	Glazz Campbell W CO 6 Bethnal Green
	(Southern Area L. Heavyweight Title Challenge)
06.11.93	John Kaighin W CO 1 Bethnal Green
21.12.93	Ray Albert W RSC 3 Mayfair
	(Vacant WBO Penta-Continental L. Heavyweight Title)

11.01.94 Jim Murray W RSC 7 Bethnal Green
*(WBO Penta-Continental L.
Heavyweight Title Defence)*
09.04.94 Simon Harris W CO 6 Bethnal Green
*(WBO Penta-Continental & Southern
Area L. Heavyweight Title Defence)*
09.07.94 Sergio Merani W PTS 12 Earls Court
*(WBO Penta-Continental
L. Heavyweight Title)*
30.09.94 Arigoma Chiponda W CO 2 Bethnal
Green
*(Vacant Commonwealth
L. Heavyweight Title)*
18.03.95 Ernest Mateen W RTD 7 Millstreet
*(Vacant WBO Inter-Continental
L. Heavyweight Title)*
09.05.95 Noel Magee L RTD 7 Basildon
*(Commonwealth L. Heavyweight Title
Defence)*
06.02.96 Francis Wanyama W PTS 6 Basildon
09.04.96 Joey Paladino W RSC 1 Stevenage
Career: 23 contests, won 21, drew 1, lost 1.

Mark Delaney

West Ham. *Born* London, 1 December,
1971
WBO Inter-Continental S. Middleweight
Champion. Ht. 5'11"
Manager B. Hearn

05.10.93 Lee Sara W RTD 5 Mayfair
11.01.94 Jason McNeill W RSC 2 Bethnal Green
22.01.94 Graham Jenner W RTD 3 Belfast
09.02.94 Tony Colclough W RSC 4 Brentwood
19.03.94 Paul Murray W CO 3 Millwall
09.04.94 Tim Robinson W RSC 2 Bethnal Green
11.06.94 Ernie Loveridge W RSC 5 Bethnal
Green
09.07.94 Eddie Knight W CO 4 Earls Court
17.09.94 Mark Dawson W PTS 6 Crawley
30.09.94 Jerry Mortimer W RSC 3 Bethnal
Green
07.11.94 Martin Jolley W RSC 3 Bethnal Green
23.11.94 Marvin O'Brien W RTD 1 Irvine
20.12.94 Martin Jolley W RSC 4 Bethnal Green
17.02.95 Peter Vosper W RSC 1 Crawley
16.03.95 Carlos Christie W CO 1 Basildon
31.03.95 Trevor Ambrose W RSC 1 Crystal
Palace
09.05.95 Eddie Knight W RSC 2 Basildon
30.09.95 Andrew Flute W PTS 12 Basildon
*(Vacant WBO Inter-Continental S.
Middleweight Title)*
28.10.95 Hunter Clay W RTD 2 Kensington
14.11.95 Armando Rodriguez W PTS 12 Bury
*(WBO Inter-Continental S.
Middleweight Title Defence)*
23.01.96 Darron Griffiths W PTS 12 Bethnal
Green
*(WBO Inter-Continental S.
Middleweight Title Defence)*
20.04.96 Joe Calzaghe L RSC 5 Brentwood
*(British S. Middleweight Title
Challenge)*
Career: 22 contests, won 21, lost 1.

Paul Denton (Ramsey)

Walthamstow. *Born* Birmingham, 12 April,
1970
L. Welterweight. Ht. 5'10"
Manager B. Ingle

Mark Delaney (left) exchanges blows with Darron Griffiths   Les Clark

18.03.93 Mark O'Callaghan W RSC 4 Lewisham
29.04.93 Dave Maj DREW 6 Mayfair
11.08.93 Billy McDougall W PTS 6 Mansfield
01.10.93 Ferid Bennecer W CO 3 Waregem,
Belgium
01.12.93 Brian Hickey W CO 1 Kensington
28.01.94 Youssef Bakhouche L PTS 6 Waregem,
Belgium
07.05.94 Viktor Fesechko L PTS 6
Dnepropetrousk, Ukraine
23.09.94 Roy Rowland W RSC 5 Bethnal Green
03.01.95 Patrick Charpentier L RSC 4 Epernay,
France
25.02.95 Paul Ryan L RSC 4 Millwall
25.11.95 Michael Carruth L PTS 8 Dublin
03.02.96 George Naylor W RSC 3 Liverpool
26.04.96 Ross Hale W RSC 4 Cardiff
Career: 13 contests, won 7, drew 1, lost 5.

Mike Deveney

Paisley. *Born* Elderslie, 14 December, 1965
Former British Featherweight Champion.
Ht. 5'5"
Manager N. Sweeney

18.02.91 John George W PTS 6 Glasgow
18.03.91 Frankie Ventura W PTS 6 Piccadilly
22.04.91 Neil Leitch W PTS 6 Glasgow
09.09.91 Pete Buckley W PTS 8 Glasgow
19.09.91 Noel Carroll L PTS 6 Stockport
14.11.91 Pete Buckley W PTS 6 Edinburgh
28.01.92 Graham O'Malley L RSC 1 Piccadilly
28.02.92 Gary Hickman W PTS 6 Irvine
14.09.92 David Ramsden L PTS 6 Bradford
07.10.92 Mark Hargreaves L RSC 7 Glasgow
07.12.92 Carl Roberts W PTS 6 Manchester
27.01.93 Barry Jones L PTS 6 Cardiff
26.02.93 Alan Graham W PTS 6 Irvine
23.03.93 Colin Lynch W PTS 6 Wolverhampton
29.05.93 Dave Buxton W PTS 6 Paisley
20.09.93 Ady Benton W PTS 8 Glasgow
30.11.93 Elvis Parsley L PTS 6 Wolverhampton
24.01.94 Ady Benton L PTS 6 Glasgow
02.03.94 Yusuf Vorajee W PTS 6 Solihull
21.03.94 Chris Jickells W RSC 5 Glasgow
15.04.94 Chris Clarkson W RSC 3 Hull
06.06.94 Mark Hargreaves W PTS 6 Manchester

15.06.94 Justin Murphy L PTS 6 Southwark
29.09.94 Henry Armstrong W PTS 8 Tynemouth
24.10.94 Henry Armstrong W PTS 10 Glasgow
(Elim. British Featherweight Title)
23.01.95 Wilson Docherty W PTS 12 Glasgow
(Vacant British Featherweight Title)
04.03.95 Dean Phillips L PTS 8 Livingston
20.09.95 Jonjo Irwin L PTS 12 Potters Bar
(British Featherweight Title Defence)
16.03.96 Abdul Mannon W RSC 2 Glasgow
26.04.96 Brian Carr L PTS 10 Glasgow
(Vacant Scottish Featherweight Title)
Career: 30 contests, won 19, lost 11.

Venkatesan Deverajan

Plaistow. *Born* India, 22 July, 1973
S. Featherweight. Ht. 5'9"
Manager F. Maloney

02.04.96 Garry Burrell W RSC 1 Southwark
14.05.96 Pete Buckley W PTS 4 Dagenham
Career: 2 contests, won 2.

Norman Dhalie

Birmingham. *Born* Birmingham, 24 March,
1971
Lightweight. Ht. 5'7"
Manager Self

06.04.92 Karl Morling L PTS 6 Northampton
27.04.92 Wilson Docherty L RSC 2 Glasgow
02.07.92 John White L RSC 6 Middleton
29.09.92 Gary Marston DREW 6 Stoke
07.10.92 Jacob Smith W PTS 6 Sunderland
03.12.92 Bradley Stone L CO 4 Lewisham
26.01.93 Neil Smith L PTS 4 Leicester
13.02.93 John White L CO 2 Manchester
20.04.93 Bobby Guynan L PTS 6 Brentwood
29.04.93 Kevin Toomey L PTS 6 Hull
23.05.93 Mike Anthony Brown W PTS 4
Brockley
09.06.93 Joey Moffat L RTD 4 Liverpool
30.09.93 Simon Frailing W PTS 6 Hayes
06.10.93 Kevin McKillan L RSC 1 Solihull
06.12.93 Colin Innes W PTS 6 Bradford
16.12.93 Peter Till L PTS 8 Walsall

81

19.01.94 John Naylor L RSC 3 Stoke
21.02.94 Hugh Collins L RTD 4 Glasgow
14.04.94 Mike Anthony Brown L PTS 6 Battersea
28.04.94 John Stovin DREW 6 Hull
06.05.94 Sugar Gibiliru L RTD 5 Liverpool
02.09.94 Dave Fallon L DIS 4 Spitalfields
28.09.94 Tanveer Ahmed L CO 5 Glasgow
24.11.94 Tony Foster L RTD 7 Hull
17.02.95 Paul Knights L RTD 5 Crawley
16.06.95 George Naylor L PTS 6 Liverpool
25.10.95 Joe Donohoe W PTS 6 Stoke
20.12.95 J. T. Williams L CO 2 Usk
16.03.96 Robbie Sivyer L CO 4 Barnstaple
Career: 29 contests, won 5, drew 2, lost 22.

(Hardip) Harry Dhami

Gravesend. *Born* Gravesend, 17 April, 1972
Southern Area Welterweight Champion.
Ht. 5'10"
Manager T. Toole

29.10.92 Johnny Pinnock W PTS 6 Hayes
20.05.94 Nick Appiah W RSC 4 Acton
27.05.94 Chris Vassiliou W RSC 5 Ashford
11.10.94 Steve McNess DREW 6 Bethnal Green
09.11.94 Clay O'Shea L PTS 6 Millwall
30.11.94 Robert Wright L PTS 8 Wolverhampton
17.11.95 John Bosco L PTS 6 Bethnal Green
08.12.95 Nicky Thurbin L PTS 8 Bethnal Green
25.04.96 Chris Pollock W PTS 6 Mayfair
07.05.96 Ojay Abrahams W RSC 5 Mayfair
(Vacant Southern Area Welterweight Title)
Career: 10 contests, won 5, drew 1, lost 4.

(Guillaume) Bamana Dibateza

Dagenham. *Born* Kinshasha, Zaire, 27 June, 1968
S. Featherweight. Ht. 5'5"
Manager R. Colson

13.12.88 Nicola Cara L PTS 6 San Pellegrino
27.12.88 Massimo Spinelli W PTS 6 San Pellegrino
21.01.89 Nicola Cara L PTS 6 Vasto
10.03.90 Djamel Ayed W PTS 6 Brest, France
20.04.90 Abdelac Lahmeri L PTS 6 Istres
10.05.90 Zahir Nemer W PTS 6 Vaulk
30.09.90 Boualem Belkif L PTS 8 Calais, France
02.03.91 Pascal Ragaut W PTS 6 Salon
12.04.91 Didier Schaeffer W PTS 6 Elbeuf
25.05.91 Santiago Galan L PTS 8 Mondragon
07.06.91 Frederic Malesa W PTS 6 La Seyne, France
23.11.91 Mustapha Hame W PTS 6 Beziers
09.04.94 Justin Juuko L RSC 5 Mansfield
11.05.94 Yifru Retta W PTS 6 Stevenage
04.10.94 Michael Armstrong W RSC 3 Mayfair
07.11.94 Michael Ayers L PTS 6 Bethnal Green
13.12.94 Jonjo Irwin L PTS 12 Potters Bar
(WBO Penta-Continental S. Featherweight Title Challenge)
08.03.95 Charles Shepherd L PTS 8 Solihull
24.03.95 Dean Phillips L PTS 6 Swansea
02.07.95 Julien Lorcy L PTS 8 Dublin
03.11.95 Yifru Retta L PTS 6 Dudley
13.02.96 Gareth Jordan L PTS 8 Cardiff
26.02.96 Michael Brodie L PTS 6 Manchester
26.04.96 Dean Phillips L PTS 6 Cardiff
Career: 24 contests, won 8, lost 16.

Bamana Dibateza   Les Clark

Liam Dineen

Peterlee. *Born* Horden, 17 October, 1972
Lightweight. Ht. 5'10"
Manager T. Conroy

24.05.94 Carl Roberts W PTS 6 Sunderland
05.12.94 Ram Singh W PTS 6 Houghton le Spring
21.02.95 T. J. Smith W PTS 6 Sunderland
16.03.95 Garry Burrell W PTS 6 Sunderland
09.05.96 Ram Singh W PTS 6 Sunderland
02.06.96 Scott Walker L RSC 1 Shaw
Career: 6 contests, won 5, lost 1.

Scott Dixon

Glasgow. *Born* Hamilton, 28 September, 1976
Featherweight. Ht. 5'9"
Manager A. Morrison

13.10.95 Andrew Smith W PTS 4 Glasgow
17.12.95 Martin Evans W RSC 4 Glasgow
12.02.96 Colin Innes W PTS 6 Glasgow
16.03.96 Ian Richardson W PTS 4 Glasgow
26.04.96 Andy Green W RSC 5 Glasgow
24.05.96 Brian Coleman W PTS 8 Glasgow
Career: 6 contests, won 6.

John Docherty

Edinburgh, *Born* Edinburgh, 10 December, 1974
L. Welterweight. Ht. 5'11"
Manager T. Gilmour

05.10.95 Chris Aston W PTS 6 Glasgow
22.01.96 Wahid Fats DREW 6 Glasgow
16.02.96 Alan Bosworth L PTS 6 Irvine
09.05.96 Dean Nicholas W PTS 6 Glasgow
Career: 4 contests, won 2, drew 1, lost 1.

Wilson Docherty

Croy. *Born* Glasgow, 15 April, 1968
Former Undefeated WBO Penta-Continental Featherweight Champion.
Ht. 5'6"
Manager Self

27.04.92 Norman Dhalie W RSC 2 Glasgow
09.07.92 Graham McGrath W RSC 4 Glasgow
26.04.93 Des Gargano W PTS 6 Glasgow
07.06.93 Chris Jickells W RSC 5 Glasgow
14.07.93 Anton Gilmore L PTS 8 Marula, South Africa
07.11.93 Robert Braddock W RSC 3 Glasgow
24.01.94 Paul Harvey W PTS 12 Glasgow
(Vacant WBO Penta-Continental Featherweight Title)
27.08.94 Peter Harris W PTS 12 Cardiff
(WBO Penta-Continental Featherweight Title Defence)
23.01.95 Mike Deveney L PTS 12 Glasgow
(Vacant British Featherweight Title)
24.04.95 Peter Harris L PTS 10 Glasgow
(Final Elim. British Featherweight Title)
06.02.96 Richie Wenton L PTS 12 Basildon
(British S. Bantamweight Title Challenge)
09.05.96 John T. Kelly W PTS 8 Glasgow
Career: 12 contests, won 8, lost 4.

Wilson Docherty   Les Clark

Adrian Dodson

St Pancras. *Born* Georgetown, Guyana, 20 September, 1970
WBO Inter-Continental L. Middleweight Champion. Ht. 5'10"
Manager Self

31.03.93 Chris Mulcahy W RSC 1 Bethnal Green
14.04.93 Rick North W RTD 1 Kensington
06.05.93 Greg Wallace W RSC 3 Las Vegas, USA
23.06.93 Russell Washer W PTS 6 Edmonton
22.09.93 Robert Peel W CO 1 Bethnal Green
23.10.93 Julian Eavis W RSC 4 Cardiff

26.02.94	Shamus Casey W CO 1 Earls Court
12.03.94	Danny Juma W PTS 6 Cardiff
09.04.94	Stuart Dunn W RSC 1 Mansfield
04.06.94	Andrew Jervis W RSC 2 Cardiff
10.09.94	Colin Pitters W PTS 6 Birmingham
25.05.95	Lloyd Honeyghan W RSC 3 Millwall
07.10.95	Hughes Daigneault W RSC 4 Belfast

(Vacant WBO Inter-Continental L. Middleweight Title)

02.12.95	Craig Snyder W RSC 8 Belfast

(WBO Inter-Continental L. Middleweight Title Defence)

04.05.96	John Bosco W RSC 7 Dagenham

(WBO Inter-Continental L. Middleweight Title Defence)

Career: 15 contests, won 15.

James Donoghue

Middlesbrough. *Born* Middlesbrough, 12 January, 1973
Welterweight. Ht. 5'9"
Manager T. O'Neill

15.09.95	George Wilson W PTS 6 Darlington
08.12.95	Jason Barker W PTS 6 Leeds
19.03.96	Ernie Loveridge W PTS 6 Leeds

Career: 3 contests, won 3.

Joe Donohoe

Walworth. *Born* London, 2 March, 1962
S. Featherweight. Ht. 5'4¼"
Manager Self

13.10.82	Shaun Shinkwin W PTS 6 Walthamstow
09.05.85	Gary King DREW 6 Acton
02.09.85	Billy Joe Dee W PTS 6 Coventry
07.10.85	Gary King W PTS 6 Dulwich
24.03.86	Nigel Senior W PTS 6 Mayfair
12.02.88	Lars Lund Jensen L PTS 6 Elsinore, Denmark
08.03.88	Kid Sumali W PTS 6 Holborn
18.03.88	Kid Sumali W PTS 6 Wandsworth
15.11.88	Derek Amory W PTS 8 Piccadilly
07.12.88	Roy Webb L CO 2 Belfast
25.11.89	Herve Jacob L DIS 6 Gravelines, France
19.03.90	Mark Geraghty W RSC 3 Glasgow
18.03.91	Derek Amory W PTS 8 Piccadilly
26.04.95	Dean Amory L PTS 6 Stoke
25.10.95	Norman Dhalie L PTS 6 Stoke
06.02.96	Richard Evatt L RSC 2 Basildon
27.03.96	Gary Marston L PTS 8 Stoke

Career: 17 contests, won 9, drew 1, lost 7.

Tony Dowling

Lincoln. *Born* Lincoln, 5 January, 1976
Cruiserweight. Ht. 6'2"
Manager J. Ashton

22.03.96	Slick Miller W RSC 4 Mansfield
30.05.96	Nigel Rafferty W PTS 6 Lincoln

Career: 2 contests, won 2.

John Duckworth

Burnley. *Born* Burnley, 25 May, 1971
L. Middleweight. Ht. 6'2"
Manager B. Myers

04.04.92	Warren Stephens W RSC 5 Cleethorpes
13.04.92	Steve Goodwin L PTS 6 Manchester
04.06.92	Phil Foxon W RSC 4 Burnley
05.10.92	Dave Maj DREW 6 Manchester
29.10.92	Tony Massey W RTD 4 Leeds
20.01.93	James McGee W PTS 6 Solihull
25.02.93	Tony Trimble W PTS 6 Burnley
31.03.93	Jamie Robinson L RSC 3 Barking
27.05.93	Warren Stephens W RSC 5 Burnley
15.09.93	Mark Jay W RSC 4 Newcastle
11.11.93	Darren Pilling W PTS 6 Burnley
02.03.94	Dave Johnson L PTS 8 Solihull
15.03.94	Andrew Jervis W PTS 6 Stoke
18.04.94	Craig Winter L RSC 5 Manchester
26.09.94	Danny Peters L PTS 6 Liverpool
26.10.94	Darren Littlewood L PTS 6 Stoke
07.11.94	Paolo Roberto W RSC 6 Piccadilly
28.11.94	Carl Harney L PTS 6 Manchester
07.12.94	Mark Dawson L PTS 6 Stoke
27.02.95	Paul Wright DREW 6 Barrow
05.04.95	Willie Quinn L PTS 8 Irvine
12.06.95	Carl Smith W PTS 6 Manchester
20.06.95	Andy McVeigh DREW 6 Birmingham
22.07.95	Robin Reid L PTS 8 Millwall
02.09.95	Jason Matthews L PTS 4 Wembley
14.09.95	David Starie L PTS 6 Battersea
30.09.95	Glenn Catley L RSC 3 Cardiff
24.11.95	Eric Noi L PTS 4 Manchester
06.12.95	Stinger Mason L PTS 6 Stoke
17.12.95	John McAlpine DREW 6 Glasgow
20.01.96	Ryan Rhodes L RSC 2 Mansfield
16.03.96	Clinton Woods L PTS 8 Sheffield
29.04.96	Howard Eastman L RSC 5 Mayfair

Career: 33 contests, won 10, drew 5, lost 18.

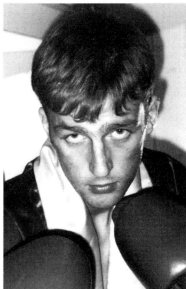

John Duckworth   Les Clark

Marty Duke

Yarmouth. *Born* Yarmouth, 19 June, 1967
L. Middleweight. Ht. 5'9"
Manager T. Toole

16.05.88	Wayne Timmins L PTS 6 Wolverhampton
06.09.88	Tony Cloak W PTS 6 Southend
26.09.88	Tony Cloak L RSC 2 Bedford
27.10.88	Matthew Jones L PTS 6 Birmingham
06.12.88	Peter Mundy W PTS 6 Southend
25.01.89	Tony Hodge W RSC 2 Basildon
07.02.89	Dennis White L PTS 6 Southend
04.04.89	Tony Cloak W RSC 5 Southend
27.04.89	Steve West L RSC 1 Southwark
03.10.89	Colin Ford L PTS 6 Southend
23.10.89	Andy Catesby W PTS 6 Mayfair
19.12.89	Mike Jay DREW 6 Gorleston
08.02.90	Dean Lake L RSC 4 Southwark
14.03.90	Ahmet Canbakis L RSC 6 Battersea
12.11.90	Chris Haydon W PTS 6 Norwich
04.12.90	Paul Busby L PTS 6 Bury St Edmunds
29.01.91	Paul Smith L PTS 6 Wisbech
15.04.91	James McGee W PTS 6 Leicester
08.05.91	Martin Rosamond DREW 8 Millwall
16.05.91	Danny Shinkwin L PTS 6 Battersea
30.05.91	Richie Woodhall L RSC 4 Birmingham
04.07.91	Robert McCracken L RSC 1 Alfreton
03.09.91	Eamonn Loughran L PTS 6 Cardiff
26.09.91	Adrian Riley L PTS 6 Dunstable
05.11.91	Tony McKenzie L RSC 7 Leicester
31.03.92	Ojay Abrahams L RSC 2 Norwich
08.09.92	Ricky Mabbett DREW 6 Norwich
14.11.92	Vince Rose L PTS 6 Cardiff
26.01.93	Ricky Mabbett W CO 1 Leicester
14.04.93	Kevin Lueshing L RSC 2 Kensington
23.06.93	Billy McDougall W PTS 6 Gorleston
31.08.93	Glenn Catley L RSC 2 Croydon
03.11.93	Glenn Catley L RSC 1 Bristol
28.03.94	Spencer McCracken L RSC 2 Birmingham
27.11.94	Maurice Forbes L PTS 6 Southwark
09.12.94	Jason Beard L PTS 6 Bethnal Green
20.01.95	Nicky Thurbin L PTS 6 Bethnal Green
06.03.95	Howard Eastman L RSC 1 Mayfair
14.04.95	Neil Sinclair L RSC 2 Belfast
12.05.95	Nicky Thurbin L RSC 3 Bethnal Green
29.04.96	Paul Webb W PTS 6 Mayfair
16.05.96	Paul Webb W PTS 6 Dunstable

Career: 42 contests, won 11, drew 3, lost 28.

Marcus Duncan

Morecambe. *Born* Blackpool, 9 January, 1971
Bantamweight. Ht. 5'6"
Manager Self

12.11.92	Andrew Bloomer W PTS 6 Burnley
22.04.93	Chris Lyons W RSC 2 Bury
27.05.93	Neil Swain L PTS 6 Burnley
28.06.93	Neil Parry L RSC 2 Morecambe
13.09.93	Neil Parry W PTS 6 Middleton
11.11.93	Dave Campbell W PTS 6 Burnley
17.02.94	Jason Morris W RSC 6 Bury
21.03.94	Graham McGrath W PTS 6 Bradford
16.05.94	Daryl McKenzie W PTS 6 Morecambe
13.06.94	Matthew Harris L RSC 1 Bradford
26.09.94	Dave Campbell W PTS 6 Morecambe
22.05.95	Robert Hay L RSC 3 Morecambe
30.06.95	Luigi Mancini L RSC 4 Vigneux, France
11.12.95	Lyndon Kershaw W RSC 6 Morecambe

(Vacant Central Area Bantamweight Title)

Career: 14 contests, won 9, lost 5.

Brian Dunn

Hull. *Born* Cleethorpes, 16 July, 1969
L. Middleweight. Ht. 5'10"
Manager L. Billany

15.04.94	Warren Stephens W PTS 6 Hull
16.05.94	Peter Reid W RSC 4 Cleethorpes
06.06.94	Eddie Haley L PTS 6 Glasgow
26.09.94	Japhet Hans L PTS 6 Cleethorpes
26.10.94	Ron Hopley W PTS 6 Leeds

12.12.94 Japhet Hans W PTS 6 Cleethorpes
06.03.95 Michael Alexander W CO 5 Bradford
05.04.95 Joe Townsley L RSC 3 Irvine
16.05.95 Andy Peach L RSC 1 Cleethorpes
22.09.95 Rob Stevenson W PTS 6 Hull
02.11.95 Mickey Johnson W RSC 3 Houghton le
Spring
20.11.95 Billy Collins W PTS 8 Glasgow
11.12.95 Carlton Williams W RSC 4
Cleethorpes
18.03.96 Dennis Berry L RSC 2 Glasgow
22.04.96 Paul Webb W PTS 6 Cleethorpes
27.05.96 Joni Nyman L PTS 8 Helsinki, Finland
Career: 16 contests, won 10, lost 6.

Robbie Dunn

Plymouth. *Born* Mexborough, 29 May,
1969
L. Middleweight. Ht. 5'10½"
Manager N. Christian

24.01.95 Chris Vassiliou L PTS 6 Piccadilly
03.03.95 Dennis Gardner L RSC 4 Bracknell
13.06.95 Steve Roberts L RSC 3 Basildon
28.07.95 Andy Edge L RSC 2 Bristol
25.06.96 Pat Wright L RSC 2 Stevenage
Career: 5 contests, lost 5.

Robbie Dunn   Les Clark

Stuart Dunn

Leicester. *Born* Leicester, 19 January, 1970
Middleweight. Ht. 5'10½"
Manager J. Griffin

15.10.91 Spencer McCracken DREW 6 Dudley
09.12.91 Wayne Panayiotiou W CO 4 Brierley
Hill
23.01.92 Charlie Moore L RSC 3 York
27.10.92 Andy Peach W RSC 3 Leicester
26.01.93 Wayne Panayiotiou W RSC 2 Leicester
28.04.93 Barry Thorogood W RSC 2 Solihull
19.05.93 Matthew Turner W RSC 3 Leicester
18.09.93 Lee Ferrie L RSC 1 Leicester
10.11.93 Jamie Robinson L PTS 6 Bethnal
Green

30.11.93 Shamus Casey W PTS 6 Leicester
18.02.94 Jimmy Alston W RSC 1 Leicester
09.04.94 Adrian Dodson L RSC 1 Mansfield
18.02.95 Dean Cooper L RSC 1 Shepton Mallet
20.04.95 Howard Eastman L RSC 2 Mayfair
22.07.95 Jason Matthews L CO 1 Millwall
Career: 15 contests, won 7, drew 1, lost 7.

Colin Dunne

Holloway. *Born* Liverpool, 19 September,
1970
Southern Area Lightweight Champion.
Ht. 5'6"
Manager T. Toole

07.12.93 Mark O'Callaghan W RSC 1 Bethnal
Green
14.01.94 Wayne Jones W RSC 3 Bethnal Green
04.03.94 Malcolm Thomas W CO 1 Bethnal
Green
26.04.94 Steve Burton W CO 2 Bethnal Green
17.05.94 Phil Found W PTS 6 Kettering
23.09.94 Steve Howden W CO 1 Bethnal Green
11.10.94 Jimmy Phelan W PTS 6 Bethnal Green
09.11.94 Mark O'Callaghan W RSC 2 Millwall
09.12.94 David Thompson W RSC 3 Bethnal
Green
20.01.95 Chris Aston W RSC 4 Bethnal Green
03.03.95 Marco Fattore W RSC 3 Bethnal Green
19.04.95 Rudy Valentino W PTS 6 Bethnal
Green
12.05.95 Chris Aston W RSC 4 Bethnal Green
27.09.95 Steve Howden W RSC 4 Bethnal
Green
28.10.95 Chris Clarkson W RSC 4 Kensington
08.12.95 Jonathan Thaxton W RSC 5 Bethnal
Green
*(Vacant Southern Area Lightweight
Title)*
05.03.96 Rudy Valentino W RSC 4 Bethnal
Green
03.04.96 Kino Rodriguez W RSC 2 Bethnal
Green
10.05.96 Lajos Nagy W RSC 5 Wembley
Career: 19 contests, won 19.

Colin Dunne (right) catches Rudy Valentino with a right to the head   Les Clark

Pat Durkin

Southport. *Born* Southport, 15 February,
1969
L. Heavyweight. Ht. 6'2"
Manager N. Basso

28.10.87 Paul Jones L PTS 4 Sheffield
09.11.87 Michael Justin L PTS 4 Leicester
16.11.87 Michael McDermott L PTS 4 Glasgow
30.11.87 Mike Snagg W RSC 6 Manchester
14.12.87 Dave Kettlewell L PTS 4 Bradford
18.01.88 Frank Harrington L PTS 4 Bradford
29.01.88 Dave Kettlewell L PTS 4 Durham
08.02.88 Adrian Din L CO 2 Nottingham
11.03.88 Frank Mobbs L RSC 3 Cottingham
03.11.88 Chris Mulcahy L RSC 2 Manchester
09.10.90 Trevor Meikle L DIS 3 Liverpool
07.02.91 Phil Epton L PTS 6 Watford
25.02.91 Willie Yeardsley L PTS 6 Bradford
05.03.91 Chris Mulcahy L PTS 6 Leicester
06.06.94 Laurence Rowe L PTS 6 Manchester
15.12.94 Chris Nurse L PTS 6 Walsall
09.02.95 Phil Ball L PTS 6 Doncaster
15.03.95 Steve Loftus L PTS 6 Stoke
13.04.96 Paul Bowen L RSC 3 Wythenshawe
Career: 19 contests, won 1, lost 18.

Paul Dyer

Portsmouth. *Born* Portsmouth, 11 July,
1970
Welterweight. Ht. 5'11½"
Manager C. Sanigar

24.09.91 Mick Reid W PTS 6 Basildon
19.11.91 Dave Andrews W PTS 6 Norwich
23.02.93 Kevin Mabbutt L PTS 6 Kettering
17.06.94 Dewi Roberts W PTS 6 Plymouth
27.10.94 George Wilson W PTS 4 Bayswater
25.01.95 John Janes W PTS 6 Cardiff
08.03.95 Anthony Huw Williams W PTS 6
Cardiff
06.05.95 Wahid Fats W PTS 4 Shepton Mallet
15.09.95 Mark Ramsey W PTS 6 Mansfield
16.12.95 Dennis Gardner W RSC 1 Cardiff
26.01.96 Danny Quacoe W PTS 6 Brighton
Career: 11 contests, won 10, lost 1.

Gilbert Eastman

Battersea. *Born* Guyana, 16 November, 1972
Welterweight. Ht. 5'10"
Manager F. Maloney

22.04.96 Wayne Shepherd W PTS 4 Crystal
Palace
Career: 1 contest, won 1.

Howard Eastman

Battersea. *Born* New Amsterdam, Guyana,
8 December, 1970
L. Middleweight. Ht. 5'11"
Manager D. Mancini/M. Duff

06.03.94 John Rice W RSC 1 Southwark
14.03.94 Andy Peach W PTS 6 Mayfair
22.03.94 Steve Phillips W RSC 5 Bethnal Green
17.10.94 Barry Thorogood W RSC 6 Mayfair
06.03.95 Marty Duke W RSC 1 Mayfair
20.04.95 Stuart Dunn W RSC 2 Mayfair
23.06.95 Peter Vosper W RSC 1 Bethnal Green
16.10.95 Carlo Colarusso W RSC 1 Mayfair
29.11.95 Brendan Ryan W RSC 2 Bethnal Green
31.01.96 Paul Wesley W RSC 1 Birmingham
13.03.96 Steve Goodwin W RSC 5 Wembley
29.04.96 John Duckworth W RSC 5 Mayfair
Career: 12 contests, won 12.

Andy Edge   Les Clark

Andy Edge

Reading. *Born* Manchester, 8 April, 1971
Middleweight. Ht. 5'11"
Manager C. Sanigar

28.07.95 Robbie Dunn W RSC 2 Bristol
14.09.95 Andy Ewen L PTS 4 Battersea
20.10.95 Andy Ewen L PTS 4 Ipswich
28.10.95 Barrie Bessant W PTS 6 Bristol
05.02.96 Steve Ford L CO 1 Bexleyheath
Career: 5 contests, won 2, lost 3.

(Clive) Bobbi Joe Edwards

Manchester. *Born* Jamaica, 25 December,
1957
Cruiserweight. Ht. 5'10"
Manager F. Turner

09.10.90 Doug McKay W RSC 1 Glasgow
26.11.90 Keith Inglis W RSC 1 Mayfair
22.02.91 Cordwell Hylton L RTD 6 Manchester
29.11.91 David Brown W RSC 4 Manchester
31.01.92 Richard Bustin W PTS 6 Manchester
29.05.92 John Foreman L RSC 4 Manchester
29.10.92 Michael Gale L PTS 10 Leeds
(*Vacant Central Area L. Heavyweight
Title*)
30.03.93 Simon Collins W PTS 6 Cardiff
16.10.93 Ginger Tshabala L RSC 5 Belfast
25.12.93 Francis Wanyama L PTS 8 Izegem,
Belgium
14.05.94 Dirk Walleyn L RSC 5 Bredene,
Belgium
17.10.94 Bruce Scott L PTS 8 Mayfair
26.10.94 Michael Gale L PTS 8 Leeds
11.12.94 Eddy Smulders L PTS 8 Amsterdam,
Holland
22.02.95 Joe Calzaghe L PTS 8 Telford
14.05.95 Ray Kane L PTS 6 Belfast
27.05.95 Ray Kane L PTS 6 Belfast
08.07.95 Denzil Browne W PTS 8 York
02.12.95 Darren Corbett L PTS 6 Belfast
29.01.96 Torsten May L PTS 8 Piccadilly
16.03.96 Juan Carlos Gomez L RSC 5 Berlin,
Germany
04.06.96 Denzil Browne L PTS 10 York
(*Vacant Central Area Cruiserweight
Title*)
Career: 22 contests, won 6, lost 16.

Michael Edwards

Dudley. *Born* Swindon, 21 February, 1971
Featherweight. Ht. 5'6"
Manager C. Flute

29.09.94 Jon Peg L RSC 5 Walsall
07.02.95 Chris Lyons L PTS 6 Wolverhampton
22.03.95 Andy Roberts W PTS 6 Stoke
06.06.95 Jason Squire L RSC 1 Leicester
11.10.95 Stefy Bull L PTS 6 Stoke
08.11.95 Jon Pegg W PTS 6 Walsall
24.01.96 Graham McGrath W PTS 6 Stoke
22.02.96 Graham McGrath W PTS 6 Walsall
06.03.96 Graham McGrath L PTS 6 Solihull
27.03.96 Ervine Blake L RSC 2 Stoke
Career: 10 contests, won 4, lost 6.

Richie Edwards   Les Clark

Richie Edwards

Greenford. *Born* Ealing, 25 March, 1969
L. Welterweight. Ht. 5'8"
Manager F. Maloney

30.03.95 John O. Johnson W PTS 4 Bethnal
Green
04.06.95 Seth Jones W RSC 4 Bethnal Green
16.06.95 Mikael Nilsson W PTS 4 Southwark
24.10.95 John Smith W PTS 4 Southwark
02.04.96 Delroy Leslie W RSC 3 Southwark
Career: 5 contests, won 5.

Shaba Edwards

Clapham. *Born* Clapham, 29 April, 1966
L. Welterweight. Ht. 5'7½"
Manager B. Padget

12.05.93 Jason Barker L PTS 6 Stoke
23.06.93 Steve Howden L RSC 1 Gorleston
12.09.94 Brian Coleman W PTS 6 Mayfair
29.09.94 Everald Williams L CO 1 Bethnal Green
30.11.94 Clayton Hollingsworth L PTS 6
Wolverhampton
22.02.95 Clayton Hollingsworth L PTS 6 Telford
16.03.95 Georgie Smith L CO 2 Basildon
29.11.95 Chris Francis DREW 6 Bethnal Green
12.01.96 Lars Myrberg L RSC 3 Copenhagen,
Denmark
Career: 9 contests, won 1, drew 1, lost 7.

Cliff Elden

Norwich. *Born* Norwich, 6 September, 1967
Cruiserweight. Ht. 6'2"
Manager Self

25.01.95 Johnny Moth L PTS 6 Stoke
26.05.95 Newby Stevens W RSC 3 Norwich
14.06.95 Henry Brewer L PTS 6 Batley
25.09.95 Chris Woollas DREW 6 Cleethorpes
30.10.95 Declan Faherty L PTS 6 Bradford
08.11.95 Dean Wray W RSC 3 Scunthorpe
23.11.95 Declan Faherty W RSC 3 Tynemouth
11.12.95 Chris Woollas DREW 6 Cleethorpes
29.01.96 Rudiger May L PTS 6 Piccadilly
07.05.96 Darren Corbett L RSC 1 Mayfair
Career: 10 contests, won 3, drew 2, lost 5.

Mark Elliot

Telford. *Born* Telford, 2 February, 1966
L. Welterweight. Ht. 5'9"
Manager C. Sanigar

10.09.91 Dean Bramhald W CO 5
Wolverhampton
12.11.91 John Smith W PTS 6 Wolverhampton
05.12.91 Mick Mulcahy W RSC 2 Cannock
17.03.92 Andrew Morgan W PTS 6
Wolverhampton
20.01.93 Wayne Windle W CO 3
Wolverhampton
16.03.93 Chris Saunders W PTS 6
Wolverhampton
27.10.93 Rob Stewart W PTS 6 West Bromwich
26.01.94 Dave Lovell W PTS 6 Birmingham
16.03.94 Phil Found W PTS 6 Birmingham
05.10.94 Tony Swift W PTS 8 Wolverhampton
30.11.94 Mark Ramsey L RSC 10
Wolverhampton
(*Elim. British L. Welterweight Title*)
01.09.95 Phil Found W RSC 6 Wolverhampton
25.06.96 Jonathan Thaxton L CO 5 Mansfield
(*Vacant IBF Inter-Continental
L. Welterweight Title*)
Career: 13 contests, won 11, lost 2.

85

Matthew Ellis   Les Clark

Matthew Ellis
Blackpool. *Born* Oldham, 12 April, 1974
Heavyweight. Ht. 5'11¾"
Manager J. Hyland

03.02.96 Laurent Rouze W CO 1 Liverpool
01.04.96 Ladislav Husarik W RTD 4 Den Bosch, Holland
Career: 2 contests, won 2.

Phil Epton (Hampton)
Doncaster. *Born* Doncaster, 14 June, 1968
Welterweight. Ht. 5'8"
Manager T. Petersen

18.10.90 Mark Jay W PTS 6 Dewsbury
15.11.90 Paul King L PTS 6 Oldham
07.02.91 Pat Durkin W PTS 6 Watford
21.03.91 Paul King L PTS 6 Dewsbury
13.06.91 Willie Yeardsley W RSC 3 Hull
23.01.92 Carl Hook W PTS 6 York
19.03.92 Ricky Mabbett L RSC 3 York
23.09.92 Jimmy Vincent L RSC 6 Leeds
08.12.94 David Maw L PTS 6 Hull
24.04.95 Billy Collins L RSC 3 Glasgow
24.06.95 Warren Bowers W PTS 6 Cleethorpes
08.07.95 Ron Hopley W RSC 4 York
15.09.95 Robbie Bell L PTS 6 Darlington
11.12.95 John Stronach L PTS 6 Bradford
09.03.96 Jim Webb L PTS 4 Millstreet
Career: 15 contests, won 6, lost 9.

Harry Escott
Sunderland. *Born* West Germany, 17 October, 1969
S. Featherweight. Ht. 5'8"
Manager N. Fawcett

26.02.87 Kenny Walsh W RSC 4 Hartlepool
06.04.87 Gypsy Finch W PTS 4 Newcastle
23.04.87 Gypsy Finch W PTS 4 Newcastle
30.04.87 Craig Windsor W RSC 3 Washington
22.05.87 Ginger Staples W RSC 1 Peterlee
04.06.87 Barry Bacon W RSC 2 Sunderland

04.09.87 Kevin Plant L RSC 2 Gateshead
26.01.88 Michael Howell W RSC 4 Hartlepool
17.03.88 Ian Honeywood W RSC 4 Sunderland
25.04.88 Les Walsh W PTS 8 Bradford
23.05.88 Tony Foster L RSC 6 Bradford
22.09.88 Dave Kettlewell W PTS 6 Newcastle
14.11.88 John Townsley W PTS 8 Glasgow
30.01.89 Tony Dore DREW 8 Glasgow
14.02.89 Kevin Pritchard W RSC 3 Sunderland
13.03.89 Young Joe Rafiu W PTS 8 Glasgow
11.04.89 Muhammad Lovelock W PTS 6 Oldham
05.06.89 Gary Maxwell W PTS 8 Glasgow
11.09.89 Gary Maxwell W PTS 8 Nottingham
19.10.89 Rudy Valentino W RTD 4 Manchester
07.12.89 Joey Jacobs W PTS 6 Manchester
24.01.90 Tomas Arguelles W PTS 6 Sunderland
15.05.90 Kevin Pritchard L PTS 8 South Shields
13.11.90 Brian Roche L RSC 3 Hartlepool
02.03.91 Steve Walker DREW 6 Darlington
06.04.91 Darren Elsdon L RSC 2 Darlington
06.07.91 Jackie Gunguluza L CO 6 Imperia, Italy
20.09.91 Steve Walker DREW 6 Manchester
04.02.92 Neil Smith W PTS 8 Alfreton
17.03.92 Floyd Havard L RSC 7 Mayfair
27.05.92 Wilson Rodriguez L PTS 10 Cologne, Germany
07.10.92 Dominic McGuigan W RTD 5 Sunderland
30.10.92 Eugene Speed L PTS 8 Istres, France
01.12.92 Neil Haddock L PTS 10 Liverpool
18.06.93 Medhi Labdouni L PTS 8 Fontenay Sous Bois, France
21.07.93 Phillip Holiday L PTS 8 Marula, South Africa
01.12.93 Floyd Havard L PTS 8 Bethnal Green
27.04.94 Kid McAuley W RTD 6 Solihull
10.05.94 Kelton McKenzie W PTS 6 Doncaster
04.10.94 Jonjo Irwin L PTS 12 Mayfair
(WBO Penta-Continental S. Featherweight Title Challenge)
04.02.95 Colin McMillan L PTS 8 Cardiff
01.04.95 Julien Lorcy L RSC 1 Levallois Perret, France
20.10.95 Jimmy Bredahl L PTS 8 Copenhagen, Denmark
Career: 43 contests, won 23, drew 3, lost 17.

Chris Eubank
Brighton. *Born* Dulwich, 8 August, 1966
Former WBO S. Middleweight Champion.
Former Undefeated WBO Middleweight
Champion. Former Undefeated WBC
International Middleweight Champion.
Ht. 5'10"
Manager Self

03.10.85 Tim Brown W PTS 4 Atlantic City, USA
07.11.85 Kenny Cannida W PTS 4 Atlantic City, USA
08.01.86 Mike Bragwell W PTS 4 Atlantic City, USA
25.02.86 Eric Holland W PTS 4 Atlantic City, USA
25.03.87 James Canty W PTS 4 Atlantic City, USA
15.02.88 Darren Parker W RSC 1 Copthorne
07.03.88 Winston Burnett W PTS 6 Hove
26.04.88 Michael Justin W RSC 5 Hove
04.05.88 Greg George W RSC 5 Wembley
18.05.88 Steve Aquilina W RSC 4 Portsmouth
31.01.89 Simon Collins W RSC 4 Bethnal Green
08.02.89 Anthony Logan W PTS 8 Kensington

01.03.89 Franki Moro W PTS 8 Bethnal Green
26.05.89 Randy Smith W PTS 10 Bethnal Green
28.06.89 Les Wisniewski W RSC 2 Brentwood
04.10.89 Ron Malek W RSC 5 Basildon
24.10.89 Jean-Noel Camara W RSC 2 Bethnal Green
05.11.89 Johnny Melfah W CO 4 Kensington
20.12.89 Jose da Silva W RTD 6 Kirkby
16.01.90 Denys Cronin W RSC 3 Cardiff
06.03.90 Hugo Corti W RSC 8 Bethnal Green
(WBC International Middleweight Title Challenge)
25.04.90 Eduardo Contreras W PTS 12 Brighton
(WBC International Middleweight Title Defence)
05.09.90 Kid Milo W RSC 8 Brighton
(WBC International Middleweight Title Defence)
22.09.90 Reginaldo Santos W CO 1 Kensington
18.11.90 Nigel Benn W RSC 9 Birmingham
(WBO Middleweight Title Challenge)
23.02.91 Dan Sherry W TD 10 Brighton
(WBO Middleweight Title Defence)
18.04.91 Gary Stretch W RSC 6 Earls Court
(WBO Middleweight Title Defence)
22.06.91 Michael Watson W PTS 12 Earls Court
(WBO Middleweight Title Defence)
21.09.91 Michael Watson W RSC 12 Tottenham
(Vacant WBO S. Middleweight Title)
01.02.92 Thulani Malinga W PTS 12 Birmingham
(WBO S. Middleweight Title Defence)
25.04.92 John Jarvis W CO 3 Manchester
(WBO S. Middleweight Title Defence)
27.06.92 Ronnie Essett W PTS 12 Quinta do Lago, Portugal
(WBO S. Middleweight Title Defence)
19.09.92 Tony Thornton W PTS 12 Glasgow
(WBO S. Middleweight Title Defence)
28.11.92 Juan Carlos Giminez W PTS 12 Manchester
(WBO S. Middleweight Title Defence)
20.02.93 Lindell Holmes W PTS 12 Earls Court
(WBO S. Middleweight Title Defence)
15.05.93 Ray Close DREW 12 Glasgow
(WBO S. Middleweight Title Defence)
09.10.93 Nigel Benn DREW 12 Manchester
(WBO S. Middleweight Title Defence, WBC S. Middleweight Title Challenge)
05.02.94 Graciano Rocchigiani W PTS 12 Berlin, Germany
(WBO S. Middleweight Title Defence)
21.05.94 Ray Close W PTS 12 Belfast
(WBO S. Middleweight Title Defence)
09.07.94 Mauricio Amaral W PTS 12 Earls Court
(WBO S. Middleweight Title Defence)
27.08.94 Sammy Storey W RSC 7 Cardiff
(WBO S. Middleweight Title Defence)
15.10.94 Dan Schommer W PTS 12 Sun City, South Africa
(WBO S. Middleweight Title Defence)
10.12.94 Henry Wharton W PTS 12 Manchester
(WBO S. Middleweight Title Defence)
18.03.95 Steve Collins L PTS 12 Millstreet, Eire
(WBO S. Middleweight Title Defence)
27.05.95 Bruno Godoy W RSC 1 Belfast
29.07.95 Jose Barruetabena W CO 1 Whitley Bay
09.09.95 Steve Collins L PTS 12 Cork
(WBO S. Middleweight Title Challenge)
Career: 47 contests, won 43, drew 2, lost 2.

Martin Evans   Les Clark

Martin Evans

Ellesmere Port. *Born* Liverpool, 3 August, 1967
S. Featherweight. Ht. 5'7¹/₂"
Manager N. Christian

27.03.90	Tony Doyle L RSC 3 Leicester	
04.05.90	Jimmy Owens L RSC 2 Liverpool	
05.06.90	Tony Ward L RSC 3 Liverpool	
09.10.90	Neil Berry W RSC 2 Liverpool	
10.11.90	Jimmy Owens L RSC 3 Liverpool	
24.01.91	Barrie Kelley L PTS 6 Gorseinon	
06.06.91	Nicky Lucas L PTS 6 Barking	
20.06.91	Charlie Coke L RTD 3 Liverpool	
19.09.95	Dave Hinds L RSC 5 Plymouth	
30.10.95	Wee Barry W PTS 6 Heathrow	
29.11.95	Eddie Sica W RSC 2 Southwark	
17.12.95	Scott Dixon L RSC 4 Glasgow	
12.02.96	Wee Barry L RSC 4 Heathrow	
04.06.96	Michael Gibbons L RSC 2 York	

Career: 14 contests, won 3, lost 11.

Richard Evatt   Les Clark

Richard Evatt

Coventry. *Born* Coventry, 26 August, 1973
Featherweight. Ht. 5'6"
Manager B. Hearn

18.12.95	Kevin Sheil W RSC 1 Mayfair	
06.02.96	Joe Donohoe W RSC 2 Basildon	
09.04.96	Fred Reeve W RSC 1 Stevenage	
20.04.96	Wayne Jones W RSC 2 Brentwood	
04.05.96	Miguel Matthews W PTS 6 Dagenham	

Career: 5 contests, won 5.

Andy Ewen

Ipswich. *Born* Ipswich, 12 January, 1966
Middleweight. Ht. 5'9"
Manager Self

12.10.94	Peter Mitchell W PTS 6 Sheffield	
23.11.94	Sven Hamer L RSC 1 Piccadilly	
07.02.95	Russell Washer W PTS 4 Ipswich	
31.03.95	Jason Hart L PTS 6 Crystal Palace	
17.05.95	Robert Peel W RSC 4 Ipswich	
16.06.95	Lee Crocker L RSC 3 Southwark	
14.09.95	Andy Edge W PTS 4 Battersea	
20.10.95	Andy Edge W PTS 4 Ipswich	
08.11.95	Panayiotis Panayiotiou L PTS 4 Bethnal Green	
22.11.95	Clinton Woods L RSC 3 Sheffield	

Career: 10 contests, won 5, lost 5.

Andy Ewen   Les Clark

Barry Exton

Lincoln. *Born* Lincoln, 27 December, 1970
S. Middleweight. Ht. 6'0"
Manager J. Gaynor

20.06.95	Robert Harper W PTS 6 Birmingham	
21.09.95	P. R. Mason DREW 6 Sheffield	
26.10.95	Carlton Williams DREW 6 Birmingham	
23.02.96	Peter Vosper W PTS 6 Weston super Mare	

Career: 4 contests, won 2, drew 2.

Declan Faherty

Huddersfield. *Born* Leeds, 23 August, 1969
Cruiserweight. Ht. 6'4"
Manager P. Coleman

24.02.94	Lee Avery W RSC 2 Hull	
28.02.94	Shane Meadows W CO 3 Marton	
28.03.94	Jem Jackson W RTD 5 Birmingham	
28.04.94	Slick Miller W RSC 2 Hull	
10.05.94	Kevin Burton W RSC 4 Doncaster	
08.12.94	Art Stacey L PTS 6 Hull	
15.05.95	John Pierre W PTS 6 Bradford	
18.09.95	Colin Brown L RSC 4 Glasgow	
30.10.95	Cliff Elden W PTS 6 Bradford	
23.11.95	Cliff Elden L RSC 3 Tynemouth	
12.02.96	John Wilson L PTS 6 Glasgow	
19.03.96	Jamie Warters L PTS 6 Leeds	
23.05.96	Sean Daly W RSC 5 Queensferry	

Career: 13 contests, won 8, lost 5.

(Antonio) Tony Falcone

Chippenham. *Born* Chippenham, 15 October, 1966
Western Area S. Bantamweight Champion. Ht. 5'6"
Manager C. Sanigar

22.10.90	Karl Morling L PTS 6 Mayfair	
21.11.90	Barrie Kelley L PTS 6 Chippenham	
18.02.91	Barrie Kelley W PTS 6 Mayfair	
28.02.91	Paul Wynn W PTS 6 Sunderland	
21.03.91	Tony Silkstone L PTS 6 Dewsbury	
22.04.91	Alan Smith L RSC 5 Mayfair	
30.05.91	Alan Smith W PTS 6 Mayfair	
11.12.91	Dennis Adams W RTD 4 Basildon	
30.04.92	Andrew Bloomer W PTS 6 Mayfair	
07.07.92	Miguel Matthews W PTS 6 Bristol	
05.10.92	Andrew Bloomer W PTS 8 Bristol	
13.12.93	Des Gargano W PTS 4 Bristol	
23.02.94	Conn McMullen DREW 4 Watford	
10.03.94	Pete Buckley W PTS 4 Bristol	
29.03.94	Justin Murphy L RSC 2 Bethnal Green	
22.11.94	Fred Reeve W PTS 6 Bristol	
18.02.95	Danny Ruegg W PTS 10 Shepton Mallet *(Vacant Western Area S. Bantamweight Title)*	
06.05.95	Danny Lawson W RSC 2 Shepton Mallet	
28.07.95	Neil Swain L RSC 5 Bristol *(Commonwealth S. Bantamweight Title Challenge)*	

Career: 19 contests, won 12, drew 1, lost 6.

Dave Fallon

Watford. *Born* Watford, 22 June, 1967
Welterweight. Ht. 6'0"
Manager Self

12.09.90	Trevor Ambrose L CO 3 Battersea	
14.02.91	Richard Swallow L RSC 4 Southampton	
12.11.91	Tim Harmey W PTS 6 Milton Keynes	
05.12.91	Sean Cave W PTS 6 Peterborough	
06.05.93	Noel Henry W PTS 6 Bayswater	
24.06.93	Erwin Edwards L RSC 3 Watford	
10.03.94	Dave Madden L PTS 6 Watford	
02.09.94	Norman Dhalie W DIS 4 Spitalfields	
26.05.95	Dennis Gardner L RSC 2 Norwich	
22.11.95	Dewi Roberts DREW 6 Mayfair	
29.01.96	Brian Coleman W PTS 6 Piccadilly	
21.02.96	Ram Singh W PTS 6 Piccadilly	
16.05.96	John Harrison L RSC 4 Dunstable	

Career: 13 contests, won 6, drew 1, lost 6.

(Noor Alam) Wahid Fats

Manchester. *Born* Manchester, 22
September, 1971
L. Welterweight. Ht. 5'8"
Manager N. Basso

06.06.94 Ram Singh W RSC 3 Manchester
03.10.94 Andy Davidson W RSC 4 Manchester
20.10.94 Blue Butterworth DREW 6 Middleton
28.11.94 Scott Walker W RSC 4 Manchester
06.05.95 Paul Dyer L PTS 4 Shepton Mallet
12.06.95 John Smith L CO 3 Manchester
21.09.95 Tommy Lawler L PTS 4 Battersea
04.12.95 Shaun O'Neill W RSC 5 Manchester
22.01.96 John Docherty DREW 6 Glasgow
22.04.96 Brandon Woodhouse W RSC 3
Manchester
03.06.96 Steve McLevy L RSC 3 Glasgow
Career: 11 contests, won 5, drew 2, lost 4.

Marco Fattore

Watford. *Born* Italy, 17 October, 1968
Lightweight. Ht. 5'8"
Manager Self

03.09.92 Jason White W RSC 1 Dunstable
19.10.92 Carlos Domonkos W RTD 4 Mayfair
07.12.92 Steve Patton W RSC 6 Mayfair
15.02.93 Jason Hutson W PTS 6 Mayfair
29.03.93 T. J. Smith DREW 6 Mayfair
22.04.93 Jason Barker W PTS 6 Mayfair
04.10.93 Andrew Bloomer W PTS 6 Mayfair
10.11.93 Lee Fox W PTS 6 Watford
09.12.93 Jason Hutson W PTS 6 Watford
10.03.94 Simon Frailing DREW 6 Watford
28.04.94 Andrew Reed DREW 6 Mayfair
12.09.94 Keith Jones W PTS 6 Mayfair
30.11.94 Kid McAuley L PTS 6 Solihull
03.05.95 Colin Dunne L RSC 3 Bethnal Green
25.05.95 P. J. Gallagher L RSC 5 Reading
02.11.95 Brian Coleman L PTS 6 Mayfair
22.11.95 Marc Smith L PTS 6 Mayfair
29.01.96 Ram Singh DREW 6 Piccadilly
21.02.96 Brian Coleman L PTS 6 Piccadilly
02.04.96 Matt Brown L PTS 4 Southwark
Career: 20 contests, won 8, drew 5, lost 7.

Darren Fearn

Carmarthen. *Born* Carmarthen, 21
February, 1969
Heavyweight. Ht. 6'2"
Manager D. Gardiner

25.06.94 Keith Fletcher W PTS 6 Cullompton
25.01.95 Rob Albon W PTS 6 Cardiff
12.04.95 L. A. Williams W PTS 6 Llanelli
19.01.96 Mika Kihlstrom L PTS 4 Bracknell
07.05.96 Julius Francis L PTS 8 Mayfair
28.05.96 Darren Corbett L RSC 1 Belfast
Career: 6 contests, won 3, lost 3.

Vince Feeney

Sligo. *Born* Sligo, 12 May, 1973
Bantamweight. Ht. 5'4"
Manager Self

29.10.92 Ady Benton DREW 6 Bayswater
06.02.93 Kevin Jenkins W PTS 6 Cardiff
29.03.93 Andrew Bloomer W PTS 6 Mayfair
29.04.93 Neil Swain L PTS 6 Mayfair
28.09.93 Peter Culshaw L PTS 6 Liverpool
30.11.93 Tiger Singh W PTS 6 Leicester
18.02.94 Shaun Norman W RSC 2 Leicester
09.04.94 Neil Swain W PTS 6 Mansfield
24.05.94 Louis Veitch W PTS 6 Leicester
07.10.94 Jesper D. Jensen L PTS 6 Copenhagen,
Denmark
12.11.94 Mark Reynolds W PTS 6 Dublin
02.07.95 Louis Veitch W PTS 4 Dublin
08.11.95 Pete Buckley W PTS 8 Bethnal Green
15.12.95 Willy Perdomo L RSC 6 Bethnal Green
*(WBC International Bantamweight
Title Challenge)*
30.03.96 Rowan Williams W RSC 6 Dublin
14.05.96 Brendan Bryce W PTS 6 Dagenham
Career: 16 contests, won 11, drew 1, lost 4.

Antonio Fernandez (Golding)

Birmingham. *Born* Birmingham, 3 January,
1965
Midlands Area Middleweight Champion.
Ht. 5'11¼"
Manager Self

10.03.87 David Heath W RSC 5 Manchester
29.04.87 Darren Hobson L PTS 6 Stoke
18.11.87 Tony White W PTS 6 Solihull
19.01.88 Malcolm Melvin W RSC 4 Kings
Heath
07.03.88 Shaun Cummins L PTS 6 Northampton
10.10.88 Chris Richards W PTS 6 Edgbaston
23.11.88 Chris Richards W PTS 8 Solihull
24.01.89 Paul Murray W PTS 6 Kings Heath
08.05.89 Shamus Casey W PTS 6 Edgbaston
13.11.89 Cyril Jackson W PTS 8 Brierley Hill
03.12.89 Steve Foster L PTS 8 Birmingham
06.03.90 Paul Jones L PTS 8 Stoke
30.04.90 Alan Baptiste W PTS 6 Brierley Hill
04.06.90 Chris Richards W PTS 8 Edgbaston
13.11.90 Chris Walker W PTS 6 Edgbaston
24.01.91 Franki Moro W PTS 6 Brierley Hill
07.10.91 Paul Murray W RSC 7 Birmingham
09.12.91 Paul McCarthy W PTS 8 Brierley Hill
03.03.92 Paul Wesley W PTS 10 Cradley Heath
*(Vacant Midlands Area Middleweight
Title)*
28.10.92 Darron Griffiths L PTS 10 Cardiff
(Elim. British Middleweight Title)
18.05.93 Ernie Loveridge W PTS 8 Edgbaston
28.07.93 Paul Wesley W RSC 3 Brixton
*(Midlands Area Middleweight Title
Defence)*
27.08.94 Carlos Christie W PTS 8 Cardiff
29.11.94 Neville Brown L RSC 9 Cannock
(British Middleweight Title Challenge)
17.01.95 Colin Manners W PTS 8 Worcester
30.06.95 Derek Wormald L PTS 10 Doncaster
(Final Elim. British Middleweight Title)
17.02.96 Giovanni Pretorius L CO 7
Hammanskraal, South Africa
Career: 27 contests, won 19, lost 8.

Daren Fifield

Henley. *Born* Wantage, 9 October, 1969
Former Commonwealth Flyweight
Champion. Ht. 5'2"
Manager Self

22.10.92 Glyn Shepherd DREW 4 Bethnal
Green
10.12.92 Anthony Hanna W RSC 6 Bethnal
Green
14.01.93 Graham McGrath W PTS 4 Mayfair
17.02.93 Kevin Jenkins DREW 6 Bethnal Green
14.04.93 Mickey Cantwell L PTS 10 Kensington
(Vacant Southern Area Flyweight Title)
28.08.93 Eric Burton W CO 1 Bismark, USA

13.10.93 Danny Porter W RSC 9 Bethnal Green
*(Vacant Commonwealth Flyweight
Title)*
09.02.94 Danny Porter W RSC 6 Bethnal Green
*(Commonwealth Flyweight Title
Defence)*
15.06.94 Ladislao Vazquez W RSC 4 Southwark
03.08.94 Luigi Camputaro L PTS 12 Bristol
(European Flyweight Title Challenge)
20.12.94 Francis Ampofo L RSC 2 Bethnal
Green
*(British Flyweight Title Challenge.
Commonwealth Flyweight Title
Defence)*
30.03.95 Ricky Beard L RSC 8 Bethnal Green
(Vacant Southern Area Flyweight Title)
22.04.96 Shaun Norman W PTS 6 Crystal Palace
Career: 13 contests, won 7, drew 2, lost 4.

Jeff Finlayson

Manchester. *Born* Manchester, 12 March,
1968
Middleweight. Ht.5'7¼"
Manager J. Doughty

04.12.95 Earl Ling W PTS 6 Manchester
24.03.96 Shamus Casey W PTS 6 Shaw
02.06.96 Carlton Williams L PTS 6 Shaw
Career: 3 contests, won 2, lost 1.

Stuart Fleet

Grimsby. *Born* Grimsby, 15 January, 1963
Cruiserweight. Ht. 6'0"
Manager Self

09.12.91 Rocky Shelly L RSC 1 Cleethorpes
16.09.93 Lee Avery W RSC 1 Hull
30.09.93 Robert Norton L CO 2 Walsall
12.11.93 Richard Atkinson W CO 1 Hull
10.02.94 Eddie Pyott W RSC 2 Hull
26.02.96 Nigel Williams W RSC 1 Hull
22.04.96 Mark Hale W PTS 6 Cleethorpes
Career: 7 contests, won 5, lost 2.

Andy Fletcher

Leigh. *Born* Leigh, 20 February, 1965
L. Heavyweight. Ht. 5'8"
Manager F. Britton

02.06.96 Lee Whitehead L RSC 2 Shaw
Career: 1 contest, lost 1.

Keith Fletcher

Reading. *Born* Reading, 20 July, 1967
Heavyweight. Ht. 6'0"
Manager C. Sanigar

25.06.94 Darren Fearn L PTS 6 Cullompton
24.09.94 John Pettersson W RSC 1 Wembley
12.10.94 Dermot Gascoyne W PTS 6 Sheffield
18.11.94 Art Stacey W PTS 6 Bracknell
04.02.95 Richard Fenton W CO 1 Cardiff
03.03.95 Rob Albon W RSC 3 Bracknell
30.03.95 Pat Passley W RSC 6 Bethnal Green
27.04.95 Julius Francis L PTS 10 Bethnal Green
*(Southern Area Heavyweight Title
Challenge)*
25.05.95 John Williams W RSC 2 Reading
16.06.95 Derek Williams W RSC 5 Southwark
16.12.95 Michael Murray L DIS 3 Cardiff
26.01.96 Corrie Sanders L CO 4 Brighton
02.04.96 Cedric Boswell L RSC 3 Southwark
11.05.96 Pele Reid L CO 1 Bethnal Green
Career: 14 contests, won 8, lost 6.

David Flowers

Leeds. *Born* Leeds, 29 December, 1974
L. Heavyweight. Ht. 5'10½"
Manager G. Lockwood

25.03.95 Laurence Rowe W PTS 6 Rothwell
19.05.95 Michael Pinnock W PTS 6 Leeds
15.09.95 Greg Scott-Briggs W PTS 6 Darlington
18.11.95 Colin Brown L DIS 3 Glasgow
Career: 4 contests, won 3, lost 1.

Andrew Flute   Les Clark

Andrew Flute

Tipton. Born Wolverhampton, 5 March, 1970
Middleweight. Ht. 6'1"
Manager Self

24.05.89 Stinger Mason W PTS 6 Hanley
24.10.89 Paul Murray W RSC 3 Wolverhampton
22.03.90 Dave Maxwell W RSC 5 Wolverhampton
24.05.90 Spencer Alton L RSC 1 Dudley
18.09.90 Tony Hodge W CO 2 Wolverhampton
24.10.90 Nigel Rafferty W CO 6 Dudley
27.11.90 Paul Burton L PTS 6 Stoke
13.03.91 Robert Peel W PTS 6 Stoke
10.04.91 Russell Washer W PTS 6 Wolverhampton
14.05.91 Alan Richards W PTS 8 Dudley
16.10.91 Karl Barwise L RSC 8 Stoke
05.12.91 Richard Okumu DREW 8 Cannock
17.03.92 Graham Burton W PTS 8 Wolverhampton
28.04.92 Paul Smith W RSC 5 Wolverhampton
20.01.93 Glen Payton W RSC 4 Wolverhampton
16.03.93 Mark Hale W RSC 2 Wolverhampton
24.04.93 Steve Thomas W RSC 1 Birmingham
21.10.93 Terry Magee W RSC 6 Bayswater
26.01.94 Neville Brown L RTD 7 Birmingham
         (British Middleweight Title Challenge)
16.03.94 Graham Burton W PTS 6 Birmingham
29.10.94 Carlos Christie L PTS 8 Cannock
29.11.94 Mark Dawson W PTS 8 Cannock

17.01.95 Chris Richards W PTS 6 Worcester
11.05.95 Paul Murray W PTS 6 Dudley
30.09.95 Mark Delaney L PTS 12 Basildon
         (Vacant WBO Inter-Continental S. Middleweight Title)
16.03.96 Robin Reid L RSC 7 Glasgow
25.05.96 Norbert Nieroba L RTD 4 Leipzig, Germany
Career: 27 contests, won 18, drew 1, lost 8.

Simon Ford

Shrewsbury. *Born* Wolverhampton, 8 February, 1971
L. Welterweight. Ht. 5'4"
Manager D. Nelson

03.09.92 Shea Neary L RSC 1 Liverpool
25.10.95 Clayton Hollingsworth L PTS 6 Telford
17.11.95 Lewis Reynolds L RSC 3 Bethnal Green
Career: 3 contests, lost 3.

Steve Ford

Cirencester. *Born* Swindon, 9 March, 1971
L. Middleweight. Ht. 5'8"
Manager W. Ball

05.02.96 Andy Edge W CO 1 Bexleyheath
Career: 1 contest, won 1.

Steve Ford   Les Clark

Frankie Foster

Newcastle. *Born* Newcastle, 25 May, 1968
Former Northern Area S. Featherweight Champion. Ht. 5'6"
Manager B. Hardy

22.09.88 Mick Mulcahy W PTS 6 Newcastle
29.09.88 Paul Chedgzoy W PTS 6 Sunderland
07.11.88 Pete Roberts W PTS 4 Bradford
01.12.88 Peter English L PTS 8 Manchester
26.01.89 James Jiora W PTS 6 Newcastle
09.03.89 John Townsley W PTS 8 Glasgow
03.04.89 Jose Tuominen L PTS 4 Helsinki, Finland

24.04.89 Jim Moffat L PTS 8 Glasgow
21.06.89 Paul Gadney L PTS 6 Eltham
02.10.89 Shaun White DREW 6 Bradford
11.10.89 Lester James W PTS 6 Stoke
21.10.89 Chad Broussard L PTS 6 Middlesbrough
13.11.89 Steve Winstanley L PTS 6 Bradford
24.01.90 Kid Sumali W PTS 6 Sunderland
05.02.90 Muhammad Shaffique L PTS 6 Brierley Hill
20.03.90 Dominic McGuigan DREW 4 Hartlepool
26.04.90 Les Walsh W PTS 8 Manchester
04.06.90 Stuart Rimmer W PTS 6 Glasgow
18.10.90 Nigel Senior W CO 2 Hartlepool
         (Vacant Northern Area S. Featherweight Title)
19.11.90 Sugar Gibiliru DREW 8 Manchester
22.04.91 John Doherty L PTS 10 Glasgow
         (Elim. British S. Featherweight Title)
14.08.91 Gianni di Napoli L PTS 8 Alcamo, Italy
22.10.91 Darren Elsdon L RSC 7 Hartlepool
         (Northern Area S. Featherweight Title Defence)
31.03.92 Sugar Gibiliru L PTS 8 Stockport
10.09.92 Darren Elsdon W PTS 10 Sunderland
         (Northern Area S. Featherweight Title Challenge)
04.07.93 Stanford Ngcebeshe L PTS 10 Eldorado, South Africa
21.03.94 Dave McHale L PTS 8 Glasgow
29.09.94 Charles Shepherd L RSC 3 Tynemouth
02.03.95 Dominic McGuigan L RSC 6 Cramlington
         (Northern Area S. Featherweight Title Defence)
24.03.96 Dave Clavering L RSC 4 Shaw
Career: 30 contests, won 11, drew 3, lost 16.

Steve Foster

Manchester. *Born* Salford, 28 December, 1960
IBF Inter-Continental L. Middleweight Champion. Ht. 5'8½"
Manager F. Warren

09.02.81 Pat McCarthy W RSC 3 Manchester
16.03.81 Dave Dunn L PTS 6 Manchester
26.03.81 John Lindo L RSC 1 Newcastle
28.11.85 Malcolm Melvin DREW 6 Ilkeston
06.03.86 Taffy Morris L PTS 6 Manchester
17.04.86 Martin Kielty W RSC 3 Wolverhampton
25.11.86 Shamus Casey W PTS 8 Manchester
28.04.87 Cyril Jackson W RSC 7 Manchester
11.05.87 Fidel Castro L PTS 8 Manchester
19.10.87 Cyril Jackson W RTD 3 Manchester
14.12.87 Sean Leighton L PTS 8 Bradford
27.01.88 Sammy Storey L RSC 4 Belfast
20.04.88 Tony Collins L PTS 6 Muswell Hill
19.10.88 Ray Close L RSC 2 Belfast
14.12.88 Fran Harding L PTS 6 Kirkby
01.03.89 Dario Deabreu W RSC 2 Cardiff
06.03.89 Steve Aquilina W PTS 6 Manchester
03.12.89 Antonio Fernandez W PTS 8 Birmingham
06.02.90 Sean O'Phoenix W RSC 4 Oldham
14.03.90 Andy Till L RTD 5 Battersea
02.06.90 Ian Chantler DREW 4 Manchester
22.02.91 Kesem Clayton W CO 6 Manchester
20.09.91 Colin Pitters W RTD 5 Manchester
07.12.91 Shamus Casey W PTS 8 Manchester

Steve Foster

Harry Goodwin

10.03.92 Mike Phillips W RSC 4 Bury
25.04.92 Mark Jay W RSC 7 Manchester
28.11.92 Shaun Cummins L PTS 12 Manchester
(*Vacant WBA Penta-Continental L. Middleweight Title*)
25.07.93 Russell Washer W PTS 6 Oldham
18.12.93 Kevin Sheeran W RSC 3 Manchester
10.09.94 Robert McCracken L PTS 12 Birmingham
(*British L. Middleweight Title Challenge*)
10.06.95 Tony Enna W RSC 6 Manchester
02.09.95 Bahri Ahmeti W RSC 4 Wembley
(*Vacant IBF Inter-Continental L. Middleweight Title*)
24.11.95 Bahri Ahmeti W PTS 12 Manchester
(*IBF Inter-Continental L. Middleweight Title Challenge*)
Career: 33 contests, won 18, drew 2, lost 13.

Tony Foster

Hull. *Born* Hull, 9 July, 1964
L. Welterweight. Former Central Area Lightweight Champion. Ht. 5'7"
Manager S. Pollard

04.09.87 Paul Kennedy L PTS 6 Gateshead
17.09.87 Ian Hosten L PTS 6 Gravesend
28.09.87 Steve Winstanley L PTS 6 Bradford
06.10.87 Roy Doyle L PTS 6 Manchester
03.11.87 Darren Darby L PTS 6 Cottingham
25.11.87 Kevin McCoy W RSC 4 Cottingham
02.12.87 Alan Roberts W RSC 5 Piccadilly
11.12.87 Mitchell King DREW 8 Coalville
11.01.88 Paul Chedgzoy W PTS 6 Manchester
25.01.88 Johnny Walker L PTS 6 Glasgow
01.02.88 Sean Hogg W PTS 6 Manchester
11.02.88 Lee Amass L RSC 6 Gravesend
28.03.88 Darryl Pettit W PTS 6 Bradford

22.04.88 Paul Charters L PTS 6 Gateshead
09.05.88 Gary Maxwell L PTS 6 Nottingham
17.05.88 Warren Slaney W PTS 6 Leicester
23.05.88 Harry Escott W RSC 6 Bradford
26.09.88 Peter Bradley L PTS 8 Piccadilly
17.10.88 John Townsley L PTS 8 Glasgow
15.11.88 Steve Pollard W RSC 3 Hull
12.12.88 Mark Kelly W PTS 6 Nottingham
08.02.89 Paul Gadney W PTS 6 Kensington
03.04.89 Jari Gronroos W PTS 4 Helsinki, Finland
15.04.89 Paul Moylett W PTS 6 Salisbury
27.06.89 Ian Honeywood L PTS 6 Kensington
10.10.89 Steve Pollard W RSC 3 Hull
16.11.89 Sugar Gibiliru W PTS 8 Manchester
30.11.89 Joey Jacobs L CO 4 Oldham
30.01.90 Sugar Gibiliru L PTS 10 Manchester
(*Vacant Central Area Lightweight Title*)
21.04.90 Marvin P. Gray DREW 6 Sunderland
22.05.90 Marvin P. Gray L PTS 6 Stockton
15.06.90 Marcel Herbert L RSC 4 Telford
15.02.91 Jimmy Bredahl L PTS 6 Randers, Denmark
05.03.91 Floyd Havard L PTS 8 Millwall
15.04.91 Dave Anderson L PTS 8 Glasgow
12.05.91 Alain Simoes W PTS 8 Voiron, France
11.09.91 Billy Schwer L PTS 8 Hammersmith
21.11.91 Giovanni Parisi L RSC 6 Perugia, Italy
31.01.92 Angel Mona L PTS 8 Esch, Luxembourg
30.03.92 Ian Honeywood L RSC 4 Eltham
13.06.92 Pierre Lorcy L PTS 8 Levallois Perret, France
16.10.92 Tony Doyle W PTS 8 Hull
31.10.92 Dingaan Thobela L PTS 8 Earls Court
14.01.93 Allan Hall L PTS 6 Mayfair
27.02.93 Steve Foran DREW 6 Ellesmere Port
09.07.93 Giorgio Campanella L PTS 8 Barisardo, Italy

12.11.93 Micky Hall W PTS 8 Hull
10.02.94 Kid McAuley W RTD 4 Hull
18.02.94 Racheed Lawal L PTS 8 Randers, Denmark
21.04.94 Charles Shepherd W PTS 10 Hull
(*Vacant Central Area Lightweight Title*)
24.11.94 Norman Dhalie W RTD 7 Hull
07.12.94 Shea Neary L RSC 2 Stoke
25.02.95 Cham Joof L PTS 8 Millwall
11.05.95 Spencer McCracken L PTS 6 Dudley
30.06.95 Andy Holligan L CO 2 Liverpool
22.09.95 Jimmy Phelan L PTS 10 Hull
(*Central Area Lightweight Title Defence*)
29.09.95 Peter Richardson L RSC 1 Bethnal Green
02.03.96 Alan Temple L PTS 6 Newcastle
13.03.96 Yifru Retta L RSC 3 Wembley
Career: 59 contests, won 20, drew 3, lost 36.

Phil Found

Hereford. *Born* Hereford, 9 June, 1967
L. Welterweight. Ht. 5'9"
Manager Self

30.03.93 Paul Davies W PTS 6 Cardiff
29.04.93 Delroy Leslie L PTS 6 Mayfair
09.06.93 Jason Beard L PTS 6 Lewisham
26.06.93 Paul Knights L PTS 4 Earls Court
14.08.93 Maurice Forbes L PTS 4 Hammersmith
20.09.93 Garry Burrell W RSC 4 Glasgow
16.10.93 Julien Lorcy L PTS 6 Paris, France
10.11.93 Robert Dickie W RTD 2 Ystrad
16.12.93 Gareth Jordan L PTS 6 Newport
20.01.94 Cham Joof L RSC 1 Battersea
02.03.94 Mark Legg W RTD 4 Solihull
16.03.94 Mark Elliot L PTS 6 Birmingham
27.04.94 Micky Hall W RSC 5 Solihull
17.05.94 Colin Dunne L PTS 6 Kettering
13.06.94 Tony Brown W RSC 4 Liverpool
11.10.94 Jason Rowland L RSC 4 Bethnal Green
22.11.94 Alan Temple L PTS 6 Bristol
08.03.95 Gareth Lawrence L PTS 6 Cardiff
30.03.95 P. J. Gallagher L PTS 6 Bethnal Green
01.09.95 Mark Elliot L RSC 6 Wolverhampton
20.12.95 Mark McGowan L PTS 6 Usk
Career: 21 contests, won 6, lost 15.

Simon Frailing

Hayes. *Born* London, 13 June, 1966
Lightweight. Ht. 5'7"
Manager D. Currivan

29.04.93 Bruce Ruegg DREW 6 Hayes
15.06.93 Bruce Ruegg L PTS 6 Hemel Hempstead
14.08.93 Mike Anthony Brown L RSC 4 Hammersmith
30.09.93 Norman Dhalie L PTS 6 Hayes
09.12.93 Andrew Reed W PTS 6 Watford
25.01.94 Craig Kelley L PTS 4 Piccadilly
10.03.94 Marco Fattore DREW 6 Watford
17.05.94 T. J. Smith L RSC 1 Kettering
03.03.95 Jason Lepre W PTS 6 Bracknell
25.05.95 Lewis Reynolds L CO 1 Reading
06.02.96 David Kehoe L CO 1 Basildon
Career: 11 contests, won 2, drew 2, lost 7.

Chris Francis

Stepney. *Born* London, 23 October, 1968
Lightweight. Ht. 5'6"
Manager Self

02.10.91 Rick Dimmock W PTS 6 Barking
11.02.92 Paul Donaghey L CO 2 Barking
17.02.93 Jason Lepre W RSC 2 Bethnal Green
31.03.93 Steve Patton W CO 4 Bethnal Green
13.10.93 Anthony Wanza W RSC 2 Bethnal Green
27.05.94 Andrew Reed W PTS 6 Ashford
23.06.95 Brian Robb W RSC 1 Bethnal Green
29.11.95 Shaba Edwards DREW 6 Bethnal Green
30.01.96 Andrew Robinson W PTS 6 Barking
Career: 9 contests, won 7, drew 1, lost 1.

Dean Francis

Basingstoke. *Born* Basingstoke, 23 January, 1974
S. Middleweight. Ht. 5'10½"
Manager C. Sanigar

28.05.94 Darren Littlewood W PTS 4 Queensway
17.06.94 Martin Jolley W PTS 6 Plymouth
21.07.94 Horace Fleary W RSC 4 Tooting
02.09.94 Steve Osborne W RTD 4 Spitalfields
27.10.94 Tony Booth W CO 1 Bayswater
22.11.94 Darron Griffiths W RTD 1 Bristol
30.03.95 Paul Murray W RSC 2 Bethnal Green
25.05.95 Hunter Clay W RSC 8 Reading
16.06.95 Paul Murray W RTD 3 Southwark
20.10.95 Zafarou Ballogou L RSC 10 Ipswich
        (WBC International S. Middleweight Title Challenge)
16.12.95 Kid Milo W RSC 3 Cardiff
13.02.96 Mike Bonislawski W RSC 2 Bethnal Green
26.04.96 Neil Simpson W RSC 3 Cardiff
08.06.96 John Marceta W RSC 8 Newcastle
Career: 14 contests, won 13, lost 1.

Julius Francis

Woolwich. *Born* Peckham, 8 December, 1964
Southern Area Heavyweight Champion. Ht. 6'2"
Manager F. Maloney

23.05.93 Graham Arnold W RSC 5 Brockley
23.06.93 Joey Paladino W CO 4 Edmonton
24.07.93 Andre Tisdale W PTS 4 Atlantic City, USA
28.08.93 Don Sargent W RSC 2 Bismark, USA
01.12.93 John Keeton W PTS 4 Bethnal Green
27.04.94 Manny Burgo W PTS 4 Bethnal Green
25.05.94 John Ruiz L CO 4 Bristol
12.11.94 Conroy Nelson W RSC 4 Dublin
23.11.94 Gary Charlton W RSC 1 Piccadilly
23.02.05 Damien Caesar W RSC 8 Southwark
        (Vacant Southern Area Heavyweight Title)
27.04.95 Keith Fletcher W PTS 10 Bethnal Green
        (Southern Area Heavyweight Title Defence)
25.05.95 Steve Garber W PTS 8 Reading
01.07.95 Scott Welch L RSC 10 Kensington
        (Southern Area Heavyweight Title Defence. Final Elim. British Heavyweight Title)
24.10.95 Neil Kirkwood W RSC 7 Southwark
30.11.95 Nikolai Kulpin L PTS 10 Saratov, Russia
05.02.96 Michael Murray L PTS 10 Bexleyheath
        (Elim. British Heavyweight Title)

09.04.96 Damien Caesar W CO 1 Stevenage
        (Vacant Southern Area Heavyweight Title)
07.05.96 Darren Fearn W PTS 8 Mayfair
Career: 18 contests, won 14, lost 4.

Dave Fulton

Cardiff. *Born* Cardiff, 7 May 1973
S. Middleweight. Ht. 5'11½"
Manager D. Gardiner

08.11.95 Toks Owoh L RSC 1 Bethnal Green
Career: 1 contest, lost 1.

Michael Gale

Leeds. *Born* Cardiff, 28 October, 1967
Central Area L. Heavyweight Champion. Ht. 5'11"
Manager T. Callighan/T. Gilmour

21.09.89 Dave Lawrence W RTD 4 Harrogate
13.11.89 Coco Collins W CO 1 Manchester
05.12.89 Randy B. Powell W RSC 1 Dewsbury
11.01.90 Cliff Curtis W RSC 2 Dewsbury
24.01.90 Andy Marlow W RSC 2 Sunderland
03.03.90 Peter Vosper W RSC 2 Wembley
11.04.90 Teo Arvizu W PTS 6 Dewsbury
18.10.90 Mick Queally W RSC 5 Dewsbury
15.11.90 Steve Osborne W PTS 6 Oldham
14.03.91 Carlos Christie W PTS 8 Middleton
21.03.91 David Haycock W RSC 2 Dewsbury
09.05.91 Steve Osborne W RSC 2 Leeds
13.06.91 Graham Burton W CO 4 Hull
27.06.91 Mark Bowen W PTS 8 Leeds
30.10.91 Denys Cronin DREW 8 Leeds
23.01.92 John Kaighin W PTS 8 York
08.04.92 Tony Booth W PTS 8 Leeds
29.10.92 Bobbi Joe Edwards W PTS 10 Leeds
        (Vacant Central Area L. Heavyweight Title)
07.04.93 Brent Kosolofski L RSC 9 Leeds
        (Vacant Commonwealth L. Heavyweight Title)
01.07.93 Tony Booth W PTS 8 York
07.10.93 John Kaighin W PTS 8 York
26.10.94 Bobbi Joe Edwards W PTS 8 Leeds
22.11.95 Simon McDougall W PTS 10 Sheffield
        (Central Area L. Heavyweight Title Defence)
Career: 23 contests, won 21, drew 1, lost 1.

Jamie Gallagher

Northampton. *Born* Northampton, 16 June, 1970
Welterweight. Ht. 5'8"
Manager J. Cox

28.11.94 Steve Lynch W RSC 3 Northampton
15.03.95 Gary Beardsley L PTS 6 Stoke
03.04.95 Adam Baldwin L PTS 6 Northampton
22.06.95 Shaun O'Neill L PTS 6 Houghton le Spring
21.09.95 Jason Barker L RSC 2 Sheffield
Career: 5 contests, won 1, lost 4.

Brian Galloway

Sheffield. *Born* West Germany, 4 June, 1964
L. Middleweight. Ht. 6'0"
Manager G. Rhodes

02.11.95 Ernie Loveridge W PTS 6 Mayfair
08.12.95 Shaun Hendry L RSC 3 Leeds
Career: 2 contests, won 1, lost 1.

Steve Garber

Bradford. *Born* Bradford, 20 June, 1962
Heavyweight. Ht. 6'6"
Manager Self

22.04.85 Mick Cordon DREW 6 Bradford
30.05.85 Mick Cordon L PTS 6 Blackburn
02.07.85 Joe Threlfall W RSC 2 Preston
03.10.85 Dave Shelton W PTS 4 Bradford
27.11.85 Mick Cordon W PTS 6 Bradford
06.02.86 Mick Cordon L PTS 6 Doncaster
27.04.86 Mick Cordon L PTS 6 Doncaster
22.05.86 Sean Daly W PTS 6 Horwich
18.09.86 Gary McConnell L PTS 6 Weston super Mare
25.09.86 Carl Timbrell W PTS 6 Wolverhampton
20.10.86 Dave Madden W PTS 4 Bradford
01.12.86 Tony Hallett W PTS 6 Nottingham
24.02.87 Gary McConnell L CO 1 Ilford
07.10.87 Gypsy John Fury L PTS 6 Burnley
18.01.88 Mick Cordon W PTS 6 Bradford
11.02.88 John Love L CO 1 Gravesend
21.03.88 Ted Shaw W CO 4 Leicester
22.04.88 Manny Burgo L PTS 6 Gateshead
23.05.88 Ted Shaw W CO 3 Bradford
26.09.88 Gifford Shillingford W RSC 4 Bradford
25.10.88 Paul Lister L PTS 6 Hartlepool
17.11.88 Michael Murray L PTS 6 Stockport
18.01.89 Peter Nyman W PTS 6 Kensington
19.05.89 Joe Threlfall W RSC 3 Gateshead
10.10.89 Lennox Lewis L CO 1 Hull
20.03.90 Chris Hubbert W RSC 1 Hartlepool
05.05.90 Knut Blin L PTS 6 Hamburg, Germany
12.11.90 David Jules W RSC 6 Bradford
30.11.90 Steve Gee W PTS 6 Birmingham
19.03.91 Al Malcolm W RSC 5 Birmingham
30.04.91 Michael Murray L CO 1 Stockport
31.05.91 Axel Schulz L CO 5 Berlin, Germany
10.10.91 Paul Lister L PTS 8 Gateshead
09.02.92 Carl Gaffney L PTS 6 Bradford
05.04.92 David Jules W PTS 6 Bradford
08.05.92 Alexandr Miroshnichenko L RSC 1 Waregem, Belgium
18.07.92 Henry Akinwande L RTD 2 Manchester
24.02.93 J. A. Bugner W RSC 6 Wembley
15.03.94 Scott Welch L RSC 4 Mayfair
21.05.94 Clifton Mitchell L CO 1 Belfast
30.07.94 Richard Bango L CO 1 Bethnal Green
21.02.95 Darren Corbett L PTS 5 Sunderland
25.05.95 Julius Francis L PTS 8 Reading
10.06.95 Gypsy John Fury W CO 4 Manchester
02.07.95 Kevin McBride L RSC 7 Dublin
26.04.96 Wayne Llewelyn L CO 1 Cardiff
Career: 46 contests, won 20, drew 1, lost 25.

Dennis Gardner

Slough. *Born* Slough, 29 March, 1970
Welterweight. Ht. 5'10"
Manager W. Ball

18.11.94 Paul Simon W RSC 1 Bracknell
20.01.95 Charlie Paine W RSC 1 Bethnal Green
03.03.95 Robbie Dunn W RSC 4 Bracknell
26.05.95 Dave Fallon W RSC 2 Norwich
16.12.95 Paul Dyer L RSC 1 Cardiff
19.01.96 Steve McGovern W PTS 6 Bracknell
12.02.96 Justin Simmons L RSC 3 Heathrow
Career: 7 contests, won 5, lost 2.

Des Gargano (Southern)

Manchester. *Born* Brighton, 20 December, 1960
S. Bantamweight. Ht. 5'5"
Manager Self

25.01.85	Sugar Gibiliru L PTS 4 Liverpool
18.03.85	Sugar Gibiliru L PTS 6 Liverpool
24.04.85	Glen McLaggon L PTS 6 Stoke
03.06.85	Anthony Wakefield DREW 6 Manchester
17.06.85	Anthony Wakefield W PTS 6 Manchester
03.10.85	Anthony Brown L PTS 6 Liverpool
13.10.85	Gary Maxwell L PTS 6 Sheffield
09.12.85	Robert Newbiggin W PTS 6 Nottingham
16.12.85	Gypsy Johnny W PTS 6 Bradford
24.02.86	Kevin Taylor W PTS 6 Bradford
01.04.86	Carl Cleasby L PTS 6 Leeds
07.04.86	Gerry McBride W PTS 6 Manchester
29.04.86	Pat Clinton L PTS 6 Manchester
23.09.86	David Ingram L PTS 6 Batley
24.11.86	Andrew Steadman L PTS 6 Leicester
03.12.86	Sean Murphy L PTS 6 Muswell Hill
15.12.86	Tony Heath L PTS 8 Loughborough
30.01.87	Nigel Crook L PTS 6 Kirkby
16.02.87	Pat Clinton L PTS 6 Glasgow
13.04.87	Jimmy Lee W PTS 6 Manchester
26.05.87	John Green L PTS 6 Oldham
19.10.87	John Green L PTS 6 Manchester
28.10.87	Paul Thornton W RSC 6 Stoke
09.11.87	Tony Heath L PTS 6 Leicester
26.01.88	Graham O'Malley L PTS 6 Hartlepool
23.03.88	Lambsy Kayani L PTS 6 Sheffield
29.03.88	Graham O'Malley L PTS 8 Marton
25.04.88	Ronnie Stephenson W PTS 8 Bradford
06.06.88	Darryl Pettit W PTS 6 Manchester
13.06.88	Joe Mullen L PTS 6 Glasgow
05.09.88	Wull Strike DREW 6 Glasgow
22.09.88	John Davison L PTS 8 Newcastle
29.09.88	John Davison L PTS 8 Sunderland
10.10.88	Shane Silvester L PTS 8 Edgbaston
18.10.88	Peter English L PTS 4 Oldham
28.10.88	Eyub Can L PTS 6 Copenhagen, Denmark
21.11.88	Ronnie Stephenson W PTS 6 Leicester
29.11.88	Chris Clarkson W PTS 6 Manchester
07.12.88	Renny Edwards L PTS 6 Aberavon
16.12.88	Jimmy Clark L PTS 6 Brentwood
14.02.89	Nigel Crook L PTS 10 Manchester
17.03.89	Jimmy Bredahl L PTS 6 Braedstrup, Denmark
17.04.89	Mark Priestley W PTS 8 Middleton
10.05.89	Mark Goult L PTS 8 Solihull
17.05.89	Mark Geraghty L PTS 8 Glasgow
12.06.89	Neil Parry W PTS 6 Manchester
11.07.89	Chris Clarkson L PTS 6 Batley
04.09.89	Ronnie Stephenson W PTS 6 Hull
11.09.89	Paul Dever W RSC 1 Manchester
20.09.89	Miguel Matthews W PTS 6 Stoke
05.10.89	Wayne Windle W PTS 6 Middleton
16.10.89	Wayne Windle L PTS 6 Manchester
31.10.89	Dave McNally L PTS 6 Manchester
10.11.89	Kruga Hydes L PTS 6 Liverpool
20.11.89	Dave Buxton L PTS 6 Leicester
30.11.89	Noel Carroll L PTS 6 Oldham
11.12.89	Joe Kelly L PTS 6 Bayswater
14.02.90	Danny Porter L PTS 6 Brentwood
06.03.90	Bradley Stone L PTS 6 Bethnal Green
17.03.90	John Lowey L RSC 6 Belfast
24.04.90	Jamie Morris W PTS 4 Stoke
09.05.90	Terry Collins L PTS 6 Kensington
16.05.90	Tony Doyle W PTS 6 Hull
11.06.90	Steve Armstrong W PTS 6 Manchester
05.09.90	John George L PTS 6 Stoke
01.10.90	Tony Smith W PTS 6 Cleethorpes
09.10.90	Brian Robb L PTS 6 Wolverhampton
22.10.90	John George L PTS 6 Cleethorpes
26.11.90	Tony Smith W PTS 8 Bury
03.12.90	Tony Smith W PTS 6 Cleethorpes
11.12.90	Stewart Fishermac W PTS 8 Evesham
16.01.91	Tony Smith W PTS 6 Stoke
06.02.91	Tim Driscoll L PTS 6 Bethnal Green
28.02.91	Carl Roberts W PTS 6 Bury
07.05.91	James Drummond L PTS 8 Glasgow
16.05.91	Jimmy Owens L RSC 2 Liverpool
19.08.91	Petteri Rissanen L PTS 4 Helsinki, Finland
02.10.91	Eric George L PTS 6 Solihull
24.10.91	Edward Cook L RSC 5 Glasgow
29.11.91	Harald Geier L DIS 8 Frohsdorf, Austria
31.01.92	Edward Cook L PTS 6 Glasgow
24.02.92	Colin Lynch L PTS 6 Coventry
04.03.92	Neil Armstrong L PTS 6 Glasgow
11.03.92	Dennis Oakes L PTS 6 Stoke
27.04.92	David Ramsden L PTS 6 Bradford
01.06.92	Mark Hargreaves L PTS 6 Manchester
08.06.92	David Ramsden L PTS 6 Bradford
07.10.92	Prince Nassem Hamed L RSC 4 Sunderland
20.11.92	Paul Lloyd L PTS 4 Liverpool
26.02.93	Alex Docherty W RSC 4 Irvine
04.04.93	Rowan Williams L PTS 4 Brockley
26.04.93	Wilson Docherty L PTS 6 Glasgow
01.06.93	Neil Parry W PTS 6 Manchester
09.09.93	James Murray L PTS 6 Glasgow
13.11.93	Richie Wenton L PTS 8 Cullompton
13.12.93	Tony Falcone L PTS 4 Bristol
17.02.94	Daryl McKenzie DREW 6 Bury
25.02.94	Peter Culshaw L PTS 6 Chester
15.03.94	Gary Marston L PTS 6 Stoke
02.06.94	Marty Chestnut W PTS 6 Middleton
20.10.94	Paul Quarmby W PTS 6 Middleton
05.12.94	Chip O'Neill L PTS 6 Houghton le Spring
23.01.95	Patrick Mullings L PTS 4 Bethnal Green
17.02.95	Spencer Oliver L PTS 4 Cumbernauld
03.03.95	Mark Bowers L RTD 2 Bracknell
18.05.95	Paul Quarmby W PTS 6 Middleton
04.06.95	Patrick Mullings L PTS 6 Bethnal Green
16.06.95	Paul Ingle L RSC 2 Southwark
22.11.95	Abdul Mannon W PTS 6 Mayfair
29.11.95	Brian Gentry L PTS 4 Southwark
08.12.95	Gary Thornhill L RTD 2 Liverpool *(Vacant Central Area S. Featherweight Title)*
05.02.96	Matt Brown L RSC 4 Bexleyheath

Career: 112 contests, won 32, drew 3, lost 77.

Dermot Gascoyne

Bexleyheath. *Born* Alfreton, 23 April, 1967
Heavyweight. Ht. 6'5"
Manager Self

17.12.92	John Harewood W RSC 5 Barking
03.02.93	Steve Stewart W RSC 4 Earls Court
10.04.93	Denroy Bryan W PTS 6 Swansea
23.10.93	Vance Idiens W RSC 4 Cardiff
17.02.94	John Keeton W RSC 1 Dagenham
09.04.94	Steve Yorath W CO 3 Mansfield
12.10.94	Keith Fletcher L PTS 6 Sheffield
08.06.96	Wayne Llewelyn L RSC 4 Newcastle

Career: 8 contests, won 6, lost 2.

(Terrance) Terry Gaskin

Doncaster. *Born* Doncaster, 20 October, 1974
Flyweight. Ht. 5'4"
Manager H. Hayes

28.03.94	Keith Knox L PTS 6 Musselburgh
09.05.94	Tiger Singh L RSC 2 Bradford
26.09.94	Ian Baillie W RSC 3 Bradford
29.10.94	Neil Parry L PTS 6 Cannock
28.11.94	Tiger Singh L PTS 6 Manchester
08.12.94	Ian Baillie W RTD 3 Hull
11.03.95	Neil Parry DREW 6 Barnsley
22.03.95	Neil Parry L PTS 8 Stoke
19.05.95	Shaun Hall L RSC 3 Leeds
21.09.95	Darren Noble DREW 6 Sheffield
20.10.95	Steve Williams L PTS 6 Mansfield

Career: 11 contests, won 2, drew 2, lost 7.

Roy Gbasai

Leicester. *Born* Manchester, 16 April, 1966
L. Middleweight. Ht. 5'7"
Manager Self

25.09.95	Lee Murtagh L PTS 6 Bradford
18.10.95	Shaun Marsh L CO 4 Batley
21.11.95	Steve Levene L CO 2 Edgbaston

Career: 3 contests, lost 3.

Brian Gentry

Morden. *Born* Balham, 2 January, 1975
Featherweight. Ht. 5'6"
Manager G. Steene

29.11.95	Des Gargano W PTS 4 Southwark

Career: 1 contest, won 1.

Michael Gibbons

Middlesbrough. *Born* Middlesbrough, 24 December, 1970
S. Featherweight. Ht. 5'4"
Manager T. Callighan

04.06.96	Martin Evans W RSC 2 York

Career: 1 contest, won 1.

Enzo Giordano

Islington. *Born* London, 15 April, 1971
L. Middleweight. Ht. 5'11"
Manager C. Magri

29.09.95	John Janes W RSC 4 Bloomsbury

Career: 1 contest, won 1.

Shaun Gledhill

Manchester. *Born* Oldham, 22 April, 1976
L. Welterweight. Ht. 5'8"
Manager N. Basso

12.06.95	Tom Welsh L RSC 4 Manchester
06.09.95	Chris Price W PTS 6 Stoke
29.10.95	Alan Bosworth L PTS 6 Shaw
20.11.95	Dean Nicholas L RSC 4 Glasgow
26.02.96	Mark Allen W RSC 3 Manchester

Career: 5 contests, won 2, lost 3.

(Godfrey) G. G. Goddard

Alfreton. *Born* Swaziland, 6 April, 1966
Lightweight. Ht. 5'7"
Manager Self

22.11.90	Shaun Hickey W RTD 4 Ilkeston
17.01.91	Paul Chedgzoy W RSC 3 Alfreton

13.05.91	Finn McCool L PTS 6 Northampton
20.05.91	Finn McCool W PTS 6 Bradford
23.10.91	Chubby Martin L PTS 8 Stoke
04.02.92	Kevin Toomey L PTS 6 Alfreton
11.03.92	Micky Hall DREW 6 Solihull
28.04.92	Michael Clynch L RTD 4 Corby
09.07.92	Dave McHale L RTD 4 Glasgow
18.11.92	Ian McGirr L PTS 6 Solihull
23.02.93	Jonjo Irwin L RSC 6 Doncaster
25.06.93	Mike Anthony Brown L CO 2 Battersea
13.06.94	Keith Jones W PTS 6 Liverpool
21.07.94	Keith Jones W RSC 1 Battersea
17.10.94	Michael Hermon L PTS 6 Birmingham
07.12.94	Trevor Royal W RSC 6 Stoke
18.01.95	Muhammad Shaffique W RSC 2 Solihull
16.02.95	Michael Brodie L PTS 6 Bury
04.03.95	Brian Carr L PTS 8 Livingston
05.05.95	Michael Brodie L PTS 6 Swansea
22.07.95	Dean Pithie L PTS 4 Millwall
09.09.95	Paul Griffin L PTS 4 Cork
20.10.95	Fred Reeve W PTS 6 Mansfield
16.11.95	Greg Upton DREW 6 Evesham
24.11.95	Alex Moon W RTD 2 Chester
22.02.96	John T. Kelly L PTS 6 Sunderland
06.03.96	Anthony Maynard L RSC 3 Solihull
20.05.96	Jason Blanche L RSC 4 Bradford

Career: 28 contests, won 9, drew 2, lost 17.

Michael Gomez (Armstrong)

Manchester. *Born* Dublin, 21 June, 1977
S. Bantamweight. Ht. 5'5"
Manager F. Warren

10.06.95	Danny Ruegg W PTS 6 Manchester
15.09.95	Greg Upton L PTS 4 Mansfield
24.11.95	Danny Ruegg L PTS 4 Manchester

Career: 3 contests, won 1, lost 2.

Paul Goode

Halifax. *Born* Northampton, 8 September, 1962
S. Featherweight. Ht. 5'6"
Manager T. Callighan

19.04.93	Tony Smith DREW 6 Manchester
01.06.93	Tony Smith L PTS 6 Manchester
07.02.94	Leo Turner L RSC 3 Bradford
13.10.94	Paul Quarmby L RSC 3 Houghton le Spring
24.11.94	Colin Innes L PTS 6 Newcastle
05.12.94	Paul Quarmby L PTS 6 Houghton le Spring
12.01.95	Paul Hamilton L RTD 1 Leeds
20.02.95	Paul Watson L RSC 1 Glasgow
15.05.95	Garry Burrell L RSC 1 Bradford
06.07.95	Fred Reeve L RSC 2 Hull

Career: 10 contests, drew 1, lost 9.

Steve Goodwin

Sheffield. *Born* Derby, 17 February, 1966
Midlands Area L. Middleweight Champion.
Ht. 5'11"
Manager Self

13.04.92	John Duckworth W PTS 6 Manchester
29.04.92	John Corcoran W PTS 8 Stoke
03.09.92	Steve McNess L PTS 6 Dunstable
29.09.92	Mark Dawson W RSC 1 Stoke
19.10.92	John Bosco L PTS 6 Mayfair
07.12.92	Mark Dawson L PTS 6 Mayfair
12.02.93	Said Bennajem L PTS 6 Aubervilliers, France

12.05.93	Mark Dawson W PTS 10 Stoke *(Vacant Midlands Area L. Middleweight Title)*
28.07.93	Gary Stretch L PTS 6 Brixton
07.09.93	Wally Swift Jnr W RSC 7 Stoke *(Midlands Area L. Middleweight Title Defence)*
02.11.93	Lloyd Honeyghan L RSC 6 Southwark
25.05.94	Wally Swift Jnr L PTS 8 Stoke
10.02.95	Neville Brown L RSC 3 Birmingham
06.05.95	Robin Reid L CO 1 Shepton Mallet
27.09.95	Nicky Thurbin L PTS 8 Bethnal Green
25.10.95	Ernie Loveridge W PTS 4 Stoke
10.11.95	Brendan Ryan L RSC 4 Derby
09.12.95	Kevin Lueshing L RTD 2 Bethnal Green
19.01.96	Geoff McCreesh W DIS 5 Bracknell
13.03.96	Howard Eastman L RSC 5 Wembley

Career: 20 contests, won 7, lost 13.

Steve Goodwin　　　　　　Les Clark

Allan Gray

Putney. *Born* Roehampton, 4 August, 1971
Welterweight. Ht. 5'9"
Manager D. Mancini/M. Duff

19.05.95	Darren Covill W PTS 6 Southwark
23.06.95	Wayne Jones W PTS 6 Bethnal Green
27.09.95	Brian Coleman W PTS 6 Bethnal Green
28.10.95	John O. Johnson W PTS 6 Kensington
29.11.95	Justin Simmons L PTS 6 Bethnal Green
08.12.95	Mike Watson W PTS 8 Bethnal Green
15.03.96	Mike Watson DREW 6 Dunstable
29.04.96	Mike Watson W PTS 6 Mayfair

Career: 8 contests, won 6, drew 1, lost 1.

Andy Gray

Great Yarmouth. *Born* Great Yarmouth, 19 February, 1966
S. Middleweight. Ht. 5'10"
Manager T. Toole

15.03.96	Robert Harper W DIS 6 Dunstable
25.04.96	Jimmy Steel L PTS 6 Mayfair

Career: 2 contests, won 1, lost 1.

Carl Greaves

Newark. *Born* Nottingham, 12 June, 1976
S. Featherweight. Ht. 5'7"
Manager J. Ashton

22.03.96	Paul Hamilton W PTS 6 Mansfield
30.05.96	Kevin Sheil W PTS 6 Lincoln

Career: 2 contests, won 2.

Darren Greaves

Alfreton. *Born* Chesterfield, 21 May, 1971
S. Bantamweight. Ht. 5'5"
Manager J. Gaynor

06.12.93	Graham McGrath DREW 6 Birmingham
16.12.93	Graham McGrath L PTS 6 Walsall
04.03.94	Danny Ruegg W PTS 6 Weston super Mare
25.04.94	Adey Lewis L RSC 1 Bury
02.11.94	Graham McGrath L RSC 4 Birmingham
05.12.94	Graham McGrath L PTS 6 Birmingham
24.02.95	Anthony Hanna L RSC 5 Weston super Mare
02.10.95	Brendan Bryce L PTS 6 Birmingham
26.01.96	Andy Roberts L RSC 5 Doncaster

Career: 9 contests, won 1, drew 1, lost 7.

Andy Green

Middlesbrough. *Born* Middlesbrough, 31 December, 1970
Lightweight. Ht. 5'8"
Manager Self

22.02.96	Wayne Pardoe W RSC 3 Walsall
19.03.96	Ram Singh W PTS 6 Leeds
27.03.96	Neil Smith L RSC 3 Whitwick
26.04.96	Scott Dixon L RSC 5 Glasgow

Career: 4 contests, won 2, lost 2.

Paul Griffin　　　　　　Les Clark

Paul Griffin

Dublin. *Born* Dublin, 3 June, 1971
Featherweight. Ht. 5'7"
Manager F. Warren

04.03.95 Chris Jickells W RSC 5 Livingston
10.06.95 Andrew Reed W RSC 5 Manchester
09.09.95 G. G. Goddard W PTS 4 Cork
25.11.95 Michael Hermon W PTS 4 Dublin
13.01.96 Jason Thomas W RSC 2 Manchester
09.03.96 Pete Buckley W PTS 4 Millstreet
26.04.96 Carl Allen W RSC 3 Cardiff
25.06.96 Miguel Matthews W PTS 6 Mansfield
Career: 8 contests, won 8.

Darron Griffiths

Cardiff. *Born* Pontypridd, 11 February, 1972
Welsh S. Middleweight Champion. Ht. 6'0"
Manager Self

26.11.90 Colin Ford DREW 6 Mayfair
04.12.90 Kevin Adamson W RSC 4 Southend
23.01.91 Tony Booth DREW 6 Stoke
06.03.91 Barry Messam W PTS 6 Croydon
10.04.91 John Kaighin W PTS 6 Newport
25.04.91 Michael Graham W RSC 2 Mayfair
02.05.91 Carlton Myers W RTD 5 Kensington
21.10.91 John Ogiste W PTS 6 Mayfair
11.12.91 Adrian Wright W PTS 6 Stoke
22.01.92 Richard Okumu W PTS 8 Solihull
17.02.92 John Ogiste W RSC 5 Mayfair
29.04.92 Colin Manners DREW 8 Solihull
30.09.92 Colin Manners W PTS 10 Solihull
    (Elim. British Middleweight Title)
28.10.92 Antonio Fernandez W PTS 10 Cardiff
    (Elim. British Middleweight Title)
24.03.93 John Kaighin W RSC 6 Cardiff
    (Vacant Welsh S. Middleweight Title)
22.01.94 Carlos Christie W PTS 8 Cardiff
09.02.94 Paul Hitch W PTS 6 Bethnal Green
23.03.94 Karl Barwise W PTS 8 Cardiff
27.04.94 Ray Webb W RSC 6 Bethnal Green
    (Elim. British S. Middleweight Title)
15.06.94 Nigel Rafferty W RSC 4 Southwark
29.09.94 Ali Forbes L PTS 12 Bethnal Green
    (Final Elim. British S. Middleweight Title)
22.11.94 Dean Francis L RTD 1 Bristol
05.05.95 Wayne Ellis W PTS 10 Swansea
    (Welsh S. Middleweight Title Defence)
29.09.95 Andy Till W RSC 3 Bethnal Green
23.01.96 Mark Delaney L PTS 12 Bethnal Green
    (WBO Inter-Continental S. Middleweight Title Challenge)
02.04.96 Chris Johnson L RTD 3 Southwark
Career: 26 contests, won 19, lost 4, drew 3.

Robert Grubb

Tipton. *Born* Stourbridge, 18 April, 1972
Lightweight. Ht. 5'4"
Manager Self

17.02.94 Paul Wynn L PTS 6 Walsall
07.04.94 Roger Brotherhood L PTS 6 Walsall
11.10.94 Chris Lyons L PTS 6 Wolverhampton
20.10.94 Andy Roberts DREW 6 Walsall
07.12.94 Fred Reeve L RSC 3 Stoke
09.02.95 Andy Roberts DREW 6 Doncaster
09.03.95 Andrew Smith DREW 6 Walsall
28.03.95 Andrew Smith L PTS 6 Wolverhampton
14.06.95 Chris Aston L CO 1 Batley
17.10.95 Andy Roberts W PTS 6 Wolverhampton
25.10.95 Brian Robb L PTS 6 Telford

08.11.95 Paul Hamilton L PTS 6 Walsall
04.12.95 Robbie Sivyer L PTS 6 Birmingham
26.01.96 Stefy Bull L PTS 6 Doncaster
21.02.96 Steve Conway L PTS 6 Batley
27.03.96 Phil Lashley W PTS 6 Stoke
03.04.96 Charlie Rumbol L PTS 6 Bethnal Green
24.04.96 Johnny Miller L PTS 6 Stoke
15.05.96 David Jay L RSC 4 Cardiff
Career: 19 contests, won 2, drew 3, lost 14.

Robert Grubb   Les Clark

Bobby Guynan

East Ham. *Born* Plaistow, 4 July, 1967
Lightweight. Ht. 5'9"
Manager Self

17.10.90 John O'Meara W RTD 2 Bethnal Green
26.11.90 Lee Fox L PTS 6 Bethnal Green
06.02.91 Lee Fox W PTS 6 Bethnal Green
26.03.91 Lee Fox L RTD 3 Bethnal Green
10.11.92 Mark Allen W RSC 2 Dagenham
30.01.93 Shaun Shinkwin W PTS 6 Brentwood
20.04.93 Norman Dhalie W PTS 6 Brentwood
26.06.93 Mike Morrison L PTS 4 Earls Court
29.11.93 Mike Morrison W PTS 6 Ingatestone
09.02.94 Mark Antony W DIS 5 Brentwood
09.07.94 Wayne Jones W PTS 6 Earls Court
05.09.94 Steve Burton L RTD 1 Brentwood
16.03.95 Jimmy Phelan L RSC 5 Basildon
30.09.95 Anthony Campbell L RSC 5 Basildon
06.02.96 Mark O'Callaghan W RSC 3 Basildon
04.05.96 Anthony Campbell L RSC 4 Dagenham
Career: 16 contests, won 9, lost 7.

Alan Hagan

Liverpool. *Born* Andover, 13 January, 1967
Bantamweight. Ht. 5'4"
Manager D. Isamaan

18.10.95 Stefy Bull L RSC 1 Batley
Career: 1 contest, lost 1.

Mark Hale

Nuneaton. *Born* Nuneaton, 13 October, 1969
L. Heavyweight. Ht. 5'11"
Manager Self

07.10.91 Andy Manning L PTS 6 Liverpool
07.11.91 Marc Rowley W PTS 6 Peterborough
15.01.92 Paul Murray W PTS 6 Stoke
25.03.92 Marc Rowley W PTS 6 Hinckley
11.05.92 Martin Jolley L PTS 6 Coventry
21.05.92 Tony Colclough DREW 6 Cradley Heath
01.06.92 Tony Colclough L PTS 6 Solihull
05.10.92 Martin Jolley L RSC 4 Bardon
16.03.93 Andrew Flute L RSC 2 Wolverhampton
11.05.93 Earl Ling W RSC 2 Norwich
08.12.93 Dean Ashton L RSC 1 Stoke
25.05.94 Steve Loftus L PTS 6 Stoke
06.09.94 Steve Loftus L PTS 6 Stoke
17.09.94 Eddie Knight L PTS 6 Crawley
12.10.94 Phil Ball W RSC 3 Stoke
07.11.94 Ryan Cummings L RSC 6 Bethnal Green
15.12.94 Darren Sweeney L PTS 6 Walsall
17.03.95 Frederik Alvarez L CO 1 Copenhagen, Denmark
26.04.95 Steve Loftus L PTS 6 Stoke
15.05.95 Dave Battey L PTS 6 Bradford
29.09.95 Kenley Price L RSC 1 Liverpool
22.04.96 Stuart Fleet L PTS 6 Cleethorpes
21.05.96 Darren Sweeney L RSC 8 Edgbaston
Career: 23 contests, won 5, drew 1, lost 17.

Ross Hale

Bristol. *Born* Bristol, 28 February, 1967
Former British & Commonwealth L. Welterweight Champion. Former Undefeated Western Area Welterweight Champion. Ht. 5'9"
Manager C. Sanigar

16.11.89 Dave Jenkins W PTS 6 Weston super Mare
30.11.89 Tony Gibbs W PTS 6 Mayfair
12.12.89 Chris McReedy W RSC 4 Brentford
13.03.90 Davey Hughes W RSC 3 Bristol
30.04.90 Andy Robins W RSC 4 Bristol
12.09.90 Derrick Daniel W PTS 6 Bethnal Green
21.11.90 Mark Kelly W PTS 8 Chippenham
29.11.90 Chris Saunders W PTS 6 Bayswater
24.10.91 Greg Egbuniwe W RSC 4 Bayswater
22.01.92 Tony Borg W PTS 6 Cardiff
30.04.92 J. P. Matthews W RSC 3 Bayswater
12.05.92 John Smith W CO 1 Crystal Palace
07.07.92 Julian Eavis W RSC 8 Bristol
    (Vacant Western Area Welterweight Title)
05.10.92 Malcolm Melvin W PTS 10 Bristol
    (Elim. British L. Welterweight Title)
01.12.92 Sugar Gibiliru W RSC 1 Bristol
27.01.93 Andreas Panayi L RSC 3 Cardiff
26.06.93 Mark Antony W RSC 1 Keynsham
28.07.93 Gary Barron W CO 2 Brixton
01.10.93 Carlos Chase W RTD 8 Cardiff
    (Elim. British L. Welterweight Title)
03.11.93 Regino Caceres W CO 2 Bristol
11.12.93 Stephen Schramm W RSC 4 Dusseldorf, Germany
22.01.94 Michael Driscoll W RSC 7 Cardiff
    (Elim. British L. Welterweight Title)
25.05.94 Andy Holligan W RSC 3 Bristol
    (British & Commonwealth L. Welterweight Title Challenge)

03.08.94 Hugh Forde W RSC 7 Bristol
(*British L. Welterweight Title Defence*)
18.02.95 Malcolm Melvin W PTS 12 Shepton Mallet
(*British & Commonwealth L. Welterweight Title Defence*)
06.05.95 Shaun Cogan W RSC 4 Shepton Mallet
(*Commonwealth L. Welterweight Title Defence*)
28.10.95 Charlie Kane W CO 2 Bristol
(*British & Commonwealth L. Welterweight Title Defence*)
09.12.95 Paul Ryan L CO 1 Bethnal Green
(*British & Commonwealth L. Welterweight Title Defence. WBO Inter-Continental L. Welterweight Title Challenge*)
26.04.96 Paul Denton L RSC 4 Cardiff
Career: 29 contests, won 26, lost 3.

Allan Hall

Darlington. *Born* Darlington, 16 November, 1969
L. Welterweight. Ht. 5'8"
Manager Self

10.10.89 Saturnin Cabanas W RSC 2 Hull
08.12.89 John Smith W RSC 2 Doncaster
22.02.90 Muhammad Lovelock W RSC 1 Hull
21.04.90 Darren Mount W PTS 6 Sunderland
09.05.90 George Jones W RSC 1 Kensington
22.05.90 Mohamed Ouhmad W PTS 6 Stockton
15.10.90 Marvin P. Gray W RSC 2 Lewisham
31.10.90 Gino de Leon W RSC 1 Crystal Palace
02.03.91 Steve Pollard W RSC 4 Darlington
06.04.91 Alan Peacock W PTS 6 Darlington
11.06.91 Abram Gumede W PTS 8 Leicester
25.04.92 Michael Driscoll W PTS 6 Manchester
27.06.92 Russell Mosley W PTS 6 San Diego, USA
11.07.92 Steve Barreras L RSC 5 Las Vegas, USA
11.09.92 Dave Pierre W PTS 10 Watford
(*Elim. British L. Welterweight Title*)
14.01.93 Tony Foster W PTS 6 Mayfair
13.04.95 Nigel Bradley W RSC 2 Bloomsbury
04.11.95 Andy Holligan L RSC 2 Liverpool
(*Final Elim. British L. Welterweight Title*)
17.12.95 Peter Till W RSC 6 Glasgow
Career: 19 contests, won 17, lost 2.

Micky Hall

Ludworth. *Born* Ludworth, 23 April, 1967
Lightweight. Ht. 5'8"
Manager T. Conroy

03.03.92 Mick Holmes W RSC 2 Houghton le Spring
11.03.92 G. G. Goddard DREW 6 Solihull
28.04.92 Jamie Davidson L PTS 6 Houghton le Spring
19.09.92 Mark Geraghty L PTS 6 Glasgow
12.10.92 Leo Turner W RSC 5 Bradford
18.11.92 Alan Ingle W RSC 3 Solihull
09.03.93 Kevin McKenzie L PTS 6 Hartlepool
17.04.93 John T. Kelly DREW 4 Washington
06.05.93 Brian Wright W PTS 6 Hartlepool
01.06.93 Kevin McKillan L PTS 6 Manchester
27.09.93 Paul Hughes W PTS 6 Manchester
04.10.93 Michael Alexander W CO 1 Bradford
12.11.93 Tony Foster L PTS 8 Hull
02.12.93 Kevin McKenzie W PTS 4 Hartlepool

10.02.94 Jimmy Phelan W PTS 6 Hull
02.03.94 Charlie Kane L RSC 2 Glasgow
27.04.94 Phil Found L RSC 5 Solihull
06.06.94 Kevin McKillan L PTS 6 Manchester
13.10.94 Charlie Paine W PTS 6 Houghton le Spring
05.12.94 T. J. Smith W RTD 3 Houghton le Spring
16.01.95 Tanveer Ahmed L RSC 4 Musselburgh
01.03.95 Alan Peacock L RSC 6 Glasgow
19.05.95 Steve Tuckett W RSC 2 Leeds
01.06.95 Steve McLevy W RSC 1 Musselburgh
17.11.95 Jyrkki Vierela L RSC 8 Helsinki, Finland
20.04.96 Bernard Paul L RSC 3 Brentwood
08.06.96 Alan Temple L RSC 2 Newcastle
Career: 27 contests, won 12, drew 2, lost 13.

Shaun Hall

Leeds. *Born* Leeds, 13 February, 1974
Bantamweight. Ht. 5'4"
Manager G. Lockwood

06.03.95 Steve Williams DREW 6 Bradford
19.05.95 Terry Gaskin W RSC 3 Leeds
05.10.95 Neil Parry L PTS 6 Glasgow
08.12.95 Tiger Singh L PTS 6 Leeds
19.03.96 Garry Burrell L PTS 6 Leeds
Career: 5 contests, won 1, drew 1, lost 3.

Simon Hamblett

Walsall. *Born* Walsall, 10 October, 1966
L. Welterweight. Ht. 5'8"
Manager Self

24.02.92 Jamie Morris DREW 6 Coventry
11.03.92 Mark Antony L CO 1 Stoke
09.12.92 Mark Allen DREW 6 Stoke
09.02.93 Mark Allen L PTS 6 Wolverhampton
23.02.93 Mark Allen W PTS 6 Doncaster
19.04.93 Kevin McKillan L CO 2 Manchester
07.06.93 Robbie Sivyer L PTS 6 Walsall
13.10.93 Shaun Shinkwin L PTS 6 Watford
02.12.93 Paul Robinson L RSC 2 Walsall
09.02.94 P. J. Gallagher L RSC 1 Bethnal Green
07.04.94 Paul Bowen L PTS 6 Walsall
29.09.94 Peter Hickenbottom L RSC 5 Walsall
29.11.94 Mark Allen W PTS 6 Wolverhampton
09.03.95 Marc Smith W PTS 6 Walsall
18.03.95 Bernard McComiskey L RSC 1 Millstreet
15.05.95 Thomas Bradley L PTS 6 Cleethorpes
17.10.95 Alan Bosworth L RSC 2 Wolverhampton
28.11.95 Wayne Pardoe L RTD 2 Wolverhampton
Career: 18 contests, won 3, drew 2, lost 13.

Sven Hamer

Margate. *Born* Margate, 6 June, 1973
Middleweight. Ht. 5'11"
Manager C. Sanigar

25.10.94 Eddie Haley W RSC 4 Southwark
07.11.94 Shamus Casey W PTS 4 Piccadilly
23.11.94 Andy Ewen W RSC 1 Piccadilly
20.12.94 Tony Velinor W RSC 4 Bethnal Green
24.01.95 Delroy Matthews L PTS 6 Piccadilly
28.07.95 Russell Washer W PTS 6 Bristol
09.12.95 Jason Matthews L RSC 4 Bethnal Green
05.03.96 Mark Baker L PTS 10 Bethnal Green
(*Vacant Southern Area Middleweight Title*)
Career: 8 contests, won 5, lost 3.

Paul Hamilton

Darlington. *Born* Darlington, 10 January, 1969
S. Featherweight. Ht. 5'7½"
Manager G. Lockwood

12.01.95 Paul Goode W RTD 1 Leeds
20.02.95 Marty Chestnut L PTS 6 Manchester
25.03.95 Colin Innes L PTS 6 Rothwell
27.04.95 Ram Singh L RSC 2 Hull
15.09.95 Colin Innes L PTS 6 Darlington
05.10.95 Ian Richardson W PTS 6 Hull
08.11.95 Robert Grubb W PTS 6 Walsall
19.02.96 Shaune Danskin W CO 2 Glasgow
22.03.96 Carl Greaves L PTS 6 Mansfield
25.04.96 Ian Richardson L PTS 6 Newcastle
Career: 10 contests, won 4, lost 6.

Anthony Hanna

Birmingham. *Born* Birmingham, 22 September, 1974
Midlands Area Flyweight Champion. Ht. 5'6"
Manager Self

19.11.92 Nick Tooley L PTS 6 Evesham
10.12.92 Daren Fifield L RSC 6 Bethnal Green
11.05.93 Tiger Singh W PTS 6 Norwich
24.05.93 Lyndon Kershaw L PTS 6 Bradford
16.09.93 Chris Lyons W PTS 6 Southwark
06.10.93 Tiger Singh W PTS 6 Solihull
03.11.93 Mickey Cantwell L PTS 8 Bristol
25.01.94 Marty Chestnut W PTS 6 Piccadilly
10.02.94 Allan Mooney W RTD 1 Glasgow
13.04.94 Allan Mooney L PTS 6 Glasgow
22.04.94 Jesper D. Jenson L PTS 6 Aalborg, Denmark
03.08.94 Paul Ingle L PTS 6 Bristol
01.10.94 Mark Hughes L PTS 4 Cardiff
30.11.94 Shaun Norman W PTS 10 Solihull
(*Vacant Midlands Area Flyweight Title*)
24.02.95 Darren Greaves W RSC 5 Weston super Mare
06.03.95 Mark Hughes L PTS 6 Mayfair
27.04.95 Mickey Cantwell L PTS 6 Bethnal Green
05.05.95 Mark Cokely W RSC 4 Swansea
04.06.95 Mark Reynolds L PTS 10 Bethnal Green
(*Elim. British Flyweight Title*)
02.07.95 Mickey Cantwell L PTS 6 Dublin
02.11.95 Shaun Norman DREW 10 Mayfair
(*Midlands Area Flyweight Title Defence*)
31.01.96 Marty Chestnut DREW 6 Stoke
20.03.96 Harry Woods L PTS 6 Cardiff
22.04.96 Neil Parry W PTS 6 Manchester
14.05.96 Dharmendra Singh Yadav L PTS 4 Dagenham
Career: 25 contests, won 9, drew 2, lost 14.

Dick Hanns-Kat (Katende-Kigula)

Stratford. *Born* Kampala, Uganda, 10 February, 1969
Welterweight. Ht. 5'10"
Manager B. Lynch

04.06.95 Darren Covill L RSC 3 Bethnal Green
30.09.95 Steve Roberts L CO 1 Basildon
Career: 2 contests, lost 2.

Fran Harding

Liverpool. *Born* Liverpool, 5 September, 1966
S. Middleweight. Ht. 6'0½"
Manager S. Foster

27.07.87	Johnny Taupau W PTS 6 Sydney, Australia
04.05.88	B. K. Bennett W RSC 1 Wembley
14.12.88	Steve Foster W PTS 6 Kirkby
04.05.90	Quinn Paynter W PTS 6 Liverpool
30.09.91	Lee Crocker W RSC 3 Kensington
25.09.92	Terry Magee W PTS 6 Liverpool
23.10.92	Shamus Casey W PTS 6 Liverpool
20.11.92	Marvin O'Brien W RSC 4 Liverpool
18.12.93	John Kaighin W PTS 6 Manchester
09.04.96	Craig Joseph DREW 6 Salford

Career: 10 contests, won 9, drew 1.

James Hare

Robertown. *Born* Dewsbury, 16 July, 1976
Welterweight. Ht. 5'6"
Manager B. Ingle

20.01.96	Brian Coleman W PTS 6 Mansfield
25.06.96	Mike Watson W PTS 4 Mansfield

Career: 2 contests, won 2.

Robert Harper   Les Clark

Robert Harper

Doncaster. *Born* Doncaster, 1 April, 1969
S. Middleweight. Ht. 5'8"
Manager Self

16.09.93	Smokey Enison L RSC 1 Hull
02.12.93	Kevin Bailey L PTS 6 Sheffield
24.02.94	Dave Proctor L PTS 6 Hull
08.03.94	Chris Nurse L PTS 6 Edgbaston
25.04.94	Lee Blundell L RSC 2 Bury
25.01.95	Steve Loftus L PTS 6 Stoke
07.03.95	Andy McVeigh L RSC 5 Edgbaston
13.04.95	Russell Washer L PTS 6 Bloomsbury
	Freddie Yemofio L PTS 6 Norwich
02.06.95	Michael Bowen L PTS 6 Bethnal Green

20.06.95	Barry Exton L PTS 6 Birmingham
06.09.95	Mark Dawson L PTS 6 Stoke
25.09.95	Kevin Burton L DIS 4 Cleethorpes
06.12.95	Steve Loftus L PTS 6 Stoke
26.01.96	Mark Snipe L PTS 6 Brighton
12.02.96	John McAlpine L PTS 6 Glasgow
15.03.96	Andy Gray L DIS 6 Dunstable

Career: 17 contests, lost 17.

Matthew Harris

Aldridge. *Born* Brownhills, 2 May, 1971
Midlands Area S. Bantamweight
Champion. Ht. 5'7"
Manager M. Shinfield

23.03.94	Yusuf Vorajee W PTS 6 Stoke
13.06.94	Marcus Duncan W RSC 1 Bradford
02.09.94	Karl Morling W CO 5 Spitalfields
	(Vacant Midlands Area S. Bantamweight Title)
05.10.94	Pete Buckley W PTS 6 Wolverhampton
30.11.94	Marty Chestnut W RSC 3 Wolverhampton
15.12.94	Kid McAuley W PTS 6 Evesham
10.02.95	Pete Buckley L RSC 6 Birmingham
	(Midlands Area S. Bantamweight Title Defence)
21.04.95	Chris Lyons W PTS 6 Dudley
19.05.95	John Armour L RSC 3 Southwark
26.08.95	Lehlohomolo Ledwaba L CO 2 Durban, South Africa
25.10.95	Pete Buckley W PTS 10 Telford
	(Midlands Area S. Bantamweight Title Challenge)
19.02.96	Robert Hay L RTD 5 Glasgow

Career: 12 contests, won 8, lost 4.

Peter Harris

Swansea. *Born* Swansea, 23 August, 1962
Welsh Featherweight Champion. Former
British Featherweight Champion. Ht. 5'6½"
Manager Self

28.02.83	Dave Pratt L PTS 6 Birmingham
25.04.83	Jim Harvey DREW 6 Aberdeen
27.05.83	Brett Styles W PTS 8 Swansea
20.06.83	Danny Knaggs W PTS 6 Piccadilly
19.12.83	Kevin Howard W PTS 8 Swansea
06.02.84	Ivor Jones DREW 8 Bethnal Green
27.03.84	Johnny Dorey W RSC 6 Bethnal Green
13.06.84	Keith Wallace W PTS 10 Aberavon
28.09.84	Ray Minus L PTS 10 Nassau, Bahamas
21.11.84	John Farrell L PTS 8 Solihull
20.03.85	Kid Sumali W PTS 8 Solihull
09.05.85	John Feeney L PTS 10 Warrington
09.11.85	Antoine Montero L PTS 8 Grenoble, France
26.03.86	Steve Pollard W RSC 3 Swansea
22.04.86	Roy Webb W RTD 8 Belfast
18.11.86	Kelvin Smart W PTS 10 Swansea
	(Vacant Welsh Featherweight Title)
30.04.87	Albert Parr W RSC 3 Newport
30.09.87	John Farrell W PTS 12 Solihull
	(Final Elim. British Featherweight Title)
15.12.87	Roy Williams W RSC 2 Cardiff
24.02.88	Kevin Taylor W PTS 12 Aberavon
	(Vacant British Featherweight Title)
18.05.88	Paul Hodkinson L RSC 12 Aberavon
	(British Featherweight Title Defence)
06.09.89	Paul Hodkinson L RSC 9 Aberavon
	(British & European Featherweight Title Challenge)

24.04.91	Colin Lynch W PTS 8 Aberavon
18.07.91	Steve Robinson L PTS 10 Cardiff
	(Welsh Featherweight Title Defence)
05.06.92	Stephane Haccoun L PTS 8 Marseille, France
22.12.92	Paul Harvey L PTS 8 Mayfair
21.12.93	Jonjo Irwin L PTS 8 Mayfair
20.05.94	Nigel Haddock W PTS 10 Neath
	(Vacant Welsh Featherweight Title)
27.08.94	Wilson Docherty L PTS 12 Cardiff
	(WBO Penta-Continental Featherweight Title Challenge)
24.04.95	Wilson Docherty W PTS 10 Glasgow
	(Final Elim. British Featherweight Title)
26.09.95	Welcome Ncita L RSC 3 Hammanskraal, South Africa
31.05.96	Jimmy Bredahl L PTS 8 Copenhagen, Denmark

Career: 32 contests, won 16, drew 2, lost 14.

John Harrison

Devonport. *Born* Scunthorpe, 18 March, 1977
Welterweight. Ht. 5'11½"
Manager G. Mitchell

13.01.96	Mark Haslam L PTS 6 Manchester
13.02.96	Paul Samuels L CO 1 Cardiff
16.05.96	Dave Fallon W RSC 4 Dunstable

Career: 3 contests, won 1, lost 2.

Jason Hart

Bromley. *Born* Beckenham, 23 January, 1970
Middleweight. Ht. 5'9½"
Manager T. Toole

02.06.94	Paul Matthews L RSC 3 Tooting
28.07.94	Julian Eavis W PTS 6 Tooting
30.09.94	Freddie Yemofio W PTS 6 Bethnal Green
31.03.95	Andy Ewen W PTS 6 Crystal Palace
20.09.95	Steve Roberts L RSC 5 Potters Bar
03.12.95	Simon Andrews W PTS 6 Southwark
30.01.96	Ernie Loveridge W PTS 6 Barking
05.03.96	Martin Jolley W PTS 6 Bethnal Green
03.04.96	Michael Pinnock W PTS 6 Bethnal Green

Career: 9 contests, won 7, lost 2.

Mark Haslam

Manchester. *Born* Bury, 20 October, 1969
L. Welterweight. Ht. 5'8"
Manager N. Basso/F. Warren

12.06.95	Steve Burton W PTS 6 Manchester
15.09.95	Thomas Bradley W CO 4 Mansfield
24.11.95	Anthony Campbell L PTS 4 Manchester
13.01.96	John Harrison W PTS 6 Manchester
09.04.96	Pete Roberts W CO 2 Salford

Career: 5 contests, won 4, lost 1.

Floyd Havard

Swansea. *Born* Swansea, 16 October, 1965
Featherweight. Former Undefeated British
S. Featherweight Champion. Ht. 5'8"
Manager Self

30.11.85	Dean Brahmald W RSC 3 Cardiff
22.01.86	Sugar Gibiliru W PTS 6 Muswell Hill

20.02.86	Dean Brahmald W PTS 6 Halifax
10.03.86	Russell Jones W PTS 8 Cardiff
28.04.86	Tony McLaggon W CO 2 Cardiff
24.05.86	Sugar Gibiliru W PTS 8 Manchester
20.09.86	George Jones W RSC 4 Hemel Hempstead
25.10.86	Joe Duffy W RSC 3 Stevenage
29.11.86	Marvin P. Gray W RSC 2 Wandsworth
14.03.87	Nigel Senior W RSC 5 Southwark
14.04.87	Ray Newby W RSC 7 Cumbernauld
28.04.87	Hector Clottey W RSC 5 Halifax
19.05.87	Kid Sumali W RTD 2 Cumbernauld
22.09.87	Frank Loukil W RSC 4 Bethnal Green
11.11.87	Cedric Powell W PTS 8 Usk
12.01.88	Mario Salazar W RSC 2 Cardiff
24.02.88	Richard Fowler W RSC 1 Aberavon
20.04.88	Benji Marquez W PTS 8 Muswell Hill
18.05.88	Pat Cowdell W RSC 8 Aberavon (British S. Featherweight Title Challenge)
15.11.88	John Kalbhenn W PTS 10 Norwich
11.04.89	Idabeth Rojas W PTS 10 Aberavon
06.09.89	John Doherty L RTD 11 Aberavon (British S. Featherweight Title Defence)
05.03.91	Tony Foster W PTS 8 Millwall
29.10.91	Thunder Aryeh W RTD 6 Cardiff
17.12.91	Patrick Kamy W DIS 5 Cardiff
17.03.92	Harry Escott W RSC 7 Mayfair
01.12.93	Harry Escott W PTS 8 Bethnal Green
22.01.94	Juan Molina L RTD 6 Cardiff (IBF S. Featherweight Title Challenge)
23.03.94	Neil Haddock W RSC 10 Cardiff (British S. Featherweight Title Challenge)
29.09.94	Edward Lloyd W RSC 4 Bethnal Green
13.12.94	Dave McHale W PTS 10 Ilford (British S. Featherweight Title Defence)
24.03.95	Elvis Parsley W RSC 6 Swansea
05.05.95	Michael Armstrong W CO 9 Swansea (British S. Featherweight Title Defence)
16.03.96	Sergio Pena W PTS 8 Glasgow

Career: 34 contests, won 32, lost 2.

Robert Hay

Coatbridge. *Born* Coatbridge, 6 November 1974
Featherweight. Ht. 5'7"
Manager T. Gilmour

20.02.95	Muhammad Shaffique W RSC 2 Glasgow
24.04.95	Paul Quarmby W PTS 6 Glasgow
22.05.95	Marcus Duncan W RSC 3 Morecambe
05.06.95	Garry Burrell W PTS 6 Glasgow
19.02.96	Matthew Harris W RTD 5 Glasgow
30.03.96	Jose Enciso Vincento L RSC 3 Dublin

Career: 6 contests, won 5, lost 1.

Carl Heath

Hull. *Born* Hull, 7 June, 1968
Cruiserweight. Ht. 6'2"
Manager S. Pollard

21.02.96	Phill Day W PTS 6 Piccadilly

Career: 1 contest, won 1.

Shaun Hendry

Leeds. *Born* Leeds, 30 March 1971
Middleweight. Ht. 6'0"
Manager G. Lockwood

12.01.95	Jason Brown W CO 1 Leeds

30.01.95	Shamus Casey W PTS 6 Bradford
25.03.95	Mark Jay W RSC 2 Rothwell
06.06.95	Lawrence Ryan W RSC 1 Leicester
17.10.95	Darren Sweeney W RSC 1 Wolverhampton
08.12.95	Brian Galloway W RSC 3 Leeds

Career: 6 contests, won 6.

Tony Henry

Telford. *Born* Birmingham, 6 August, 1962
Heavyweight. Ht. 6'2"
Manager Self

03.11.95	Gary Williams L PTS 6 Dudley

Career: 1 contest, lost 1.

Tony Henry   Les Clark

Lee Herman

North Shields. *Born* Tynemouth, 12 March, 1971
L. Middleweight. Ht. 5'9"
Manager N. Fawcett

25.04.96	Mark Owens W PTS 6 Newcastle

Career: 1 contest, won 1.

Michael Hermon

Birmingham. *Born* Birmingham, 29 April, 1968
S. Featherweight. Ht. 5'6"
Manager C. Sanigar

04.03.94	Trevor Royal W PTS 6 Weston super Mare
17.10.94	G. G. Goddard W PTS 6 Birminghan
02.11.94	Hugh Collins W RSC 3 Solihull
04.03.95	Dave Anderson L PTS 8 Livingston
20.04.95	Gary Thornhill L RSC 6 Liverpool
28.10.95	Mike Anthony Brown W PTS 6 Bristol
10.11.95	Barrie Kelley DREW 8 Bristol
25.11.95	Paul Griffin L PTS 4 Dublin

Career: 8 contests, won 4, drew 1, lost 3.

Gary Hibbert

Oldham. *Born* Oldham, 5 February, 1975
Lightweight. Ht. 5'8½"
Manager J. Doughty

02.06.96	John T. Kelly W PTS 6 Shaw

Career: 1 contest, won 1.

Mark Hickey

Barnstaple. *Born* Barnstaple, 20 May, 1972
Middleweight. Ht. 6'2¾"
Manager J. Gaynor

16.03.96	Michael Pinnock W PTS 6 Barnstaple
29.05.96	Chris Davies L RSC 1 Ebbw Vale

Career: 2 contests, won 1, lost 1.

Gary Hickman

Sunderland. *Born* Easington, 9 April, 1970
Featherweight. Ht. 5'6"
Manager Self

06.06.88	Darren Weller L PTS 4 Northampton
17.10.88	Brian Connal W RSC 2 Glasgow
28.10.88	Jimmy Clark L PTS 6 Brentwood
13.12.88	Joe Mullen L PTS 4 Glasgow
14.02.89	Mark Geraghty W PTS 6 Sunderland
30.10.89	Phil Lashley W RSC 4 Piccadilly
30.11.89	Jimmy Clark L PTS 6 Barking
18.12.89	Tommy Graham W RTD 3 Glasgow
26.02.90	Marvin Stone L RSC 5 Crystal Palace
03.05.90	Alan McKay L PTS 8 Kensington
29.05.90	Bradley Stone DREW 6 Bethnal Green
20.06.91	Craig Dermody L RSC 2 Liverpool
14.12.91	John Armour L RSC 6 Bexleyheath
28.02.92	Mike Deveney L PTS 6 Irvine
02.03.96	Colin Innes L PTS 4 Newcastle
09.04.96	Spencer Oliver L PTS 6 Stevenage
08.06.96	Colin Innes L PTS 4 Newcastle

Career: 17 contests, won 4, drew 1, lost 12.

Dave Hinds

Birmingham. *Born* Leicester, 5 January, 1971
S. Featherweight. Ht. 5'5"
Manager E. Cashmore

19.09.95	Martin Evans W RSC 5 Plymouth
08.11.95	Wayne Pardoe L CO 4 Walsall
04.04.96	Paul Salmon L RTD 5 Plymouth

Career: 3 contests, won 1, lost 2.

Gary Hiscox

Dudley. *Born* Dudley, 25 May, 1970
L. Welterweight. Ht. 5'7¾"
Manager Self

14.10.92	Alan Ingle L PTS 6 Stoke
12.11.92	Shane Sheridan W PTS 6 Stafford
27.01.93	Dave Madden W PTS 6 Stoke
03.03.93	Erwin Edwards W PTS 6 Solihull
26.06.93	Mark Tibbs L RSC 4 Earls Court
28.10.93	Dean Bramhald W RSC 5 Walsall
04.11.93	Paul Hughes W PTS 6 Stafford
25.11.93	Mark Legg L RSC 3 Tynemouth
01.03.94	Gary Cogan W PTS 6 Dudley
29.09.94	Patrick Parton W PTS 6 Walsall
26.10.94	Steve Howden W RSC 4 Stoke
09.02.95	Cam Raeside W RSC 5 Doncaster
06.03.95	Neil Smith W PTS 6 Leicester

11.05.95 Anthony Maynard L RSC 4 Dudley
03.11.95 Mike Watson W PTS 6 Dudley
11.12.95 Rick North W PTS 6 Cleethorpes
15.05.96 Paul Samuels L RSC 3 Cardiff
Career: 17 contests, won 12, lost 5.

Gary Hiscox   Les Clark

Mike Holden

Manchester. *Born* Ashton under Lyme, 13 March, 1968
Heavyweight. Ht. 6'4"
Manager B. Hearn

04.10.94 Gary Williams W RSC 4 Mayfair
20.12.94 Pat Passley L RTD 3 Bethnal Green
07.10.95 R. F. McKenzie W RSC 2 Belfast
14.11.95 Michael Murray L PTS 6 Bury
Career: 4 contests, won 2, lost 2.

Martin Holgate

Walthamstow. *Born* Waltham Forest, 24 November, 1968
L. Welterweight. Ht. 5'6½"
Manager F. Warren

02.06.95 Adam Baldwin W PTS 6 Bethnal Green
22.07.95 Mike Watson W PTS 6 Millwall
02.09.95 Trevor Smith W RSC 2 Wembley
21.10.95 John O. Johnson W PTS 4 Bethnal Green
09.12.95 Andrew Reed W RSC 1 Bethnal Green
13.02.96 Brian Coleman W PTS 4 Bethnal Green
Career: 6 contests, won 6.

Andy Holligan

Liverpool. *Born* Liverpool, 6 June, 1967
Former British & Commonwealth L. Welterweight Champion. Ht. 5'5¾"
Manager S. Vaughan

19.10.87 Glyn Rhodes W PTS 6 Belfast
03.12.87 Jimmy Thornton W RTD 2 Belfast
27.01.88 Andrew Morgan W RSC 5 Belfast
26.03.88 Tony Richards W RSC 2 Belfast

08.06.88 David Maw W RSC 1 Sheffield
19.10.88 Lenny Gloster W PTS 8 Belfast
14.12.88 Sugar Gibiliru W PTS 8 Kirkby
16.03.89 Jeff Connors W RSC 5 Southwark
19.09.89 Billy Buchanan W RSC 4 Belfast
25.10.89 Tony Adams W RSC 5 Wembley
26.09.90 Mike Durvan W CO 1 Mayfair
31.10.90 Eric Carroyez W RTD 2 Wembley
17.04.91 Pat Ireland W RSC 1 Kensington
16.05.91 Simon Eubank W RSC 2 Liverpool
20.06.91 Tony Ekubia W PTS 12 Liverpool
(British & Commonwealth L. Welterweight Title Challenge)
28.11.91 Steve Larrimore W RSC 8 Liverpool
(Commonwealth L. Welterweight Title Defence)
27.02.92 Tony McKenzie W RSC 3 Liverpool
(British & Commonwealth L. Welterweight Title Defence)
15.09.92 Tony Ekubia W CO 7 Liverpool
(British & Commonwealth L. Welterweight Title Defence)
07.10.92 Dwayne Swift W PTS 10 Sunderland
12.11.92 Mark Smith W PTS 10 Liverpool
26.05.93 Lorenzo Garcia W RSC 2 Mansfield
18.12.93 Julio Cesar Chavez L RTD 5 Puebla, Mexico
(WBC L. Welterweight Title Challenge)
26.02.94 Massimo Bertozzi W CO 5 Earls Court
25.05.94 Ross Hale L RSC 3 Bristol
(British & Commonwealth L. Welterweight Title Defence)
30.06.95 Tony Foster W CO 2 Liverpool
04.11.95 Allan Hall W RSC 2 Liverpool
(Final Elim. British L. Welterweight Title)
05.03.96 Karl Taylor W PTS 6 Barrow
Career: 27 contests, won 25, lost 2.

Clayton Hollingsworth

Telford. *Born* Wolverhampton, 5 April, 1974
L. Welterweight. Ht. 5'7"
Manager D. Bradley

30.11.94 Shabba Edwards W PTS 6 Wolverhampton
10.02.95 Steve Howden W PTS 6 Birmingham
22.02.95 Shaba Edwards W PTS 6 Telford
20.04.95 Delroy Leslie L PTS 6 Mayfair
01.09.95 Mike Watson L PTS 6 Wolverhampton
25.10.95 Simon Ford W PTS 6 Telford
Career: 6 contests, won 4, lost 2.

Ian Honeywood

Bexley. *Born* Newmarket, 20 July, 1964
L. Welterweight. Former Undefeated Southern Area Lightweight Champion.
Ht. 5'7"
Manager Self

22.10.86 Wayne Weekes W PTS 6 Greenwich
10.11.86 Andrew Pybus W RTD 2 Birmingham
17.11.86 Lee West L PTS 6 Dulwich
28.11.86 Nigel Senior L RSC 5 Peterborough
01.05.87 Bill Smith W PTS 6 Peterborough
26.05.87 Jess Rundan W RTD 3 Plymouth
10.09.87 Gary Maxwell DREW 6 Peterborough
25.09.87 Doug Munro L RSC 5 Southend
18.01.88 Andrew Furlong W PTS 8 Mayfair
17.03.88 Harry Escott L RSC 4 Sunderland
19.04.88 Jim Moffat L PTS 8 Glasgow
09.05.88 Ray Newby L RSC 1 Nottingham
30.08.88 Tony Borg W PTS 6 Kensington

31.10.88 Brian Nickels L PTS 6 Bedford
01.12.88 Kid Sumali W PTS 4 Gravesend
18.01.89 Nigel Wenton L RSC 3 Kensington
18.02.89 Sonny Long W PTS 8 Budapest, Hungary
28.03.89 Willie Beattie L PTS 4 Glasgow
24.04.89 Nigel Senior W PTS 4 Nottingham
21.05.89 Wayne Weekes W RSC 4 Finsbury Park
(Vacant Southern Area Lightweight Title)
27.06.89 Tony Foster W PTS 6 Kensington
25.09.89 Dean Bramhald W RTD 4 Crystal Palace
18.12.89 John Kalbhenn L PTS 8 Kitchener, Canada
23.04.90 Paul Gadney W PTS 10 Crystal Palace
(Southern Area Lightweight Title Defence)
22.06.90 Martin Cruz W RSC 3 Gillingham
24.09.90 Marvin P. Gray W PTS 8 Lewisham
19.12.90 Carl Crook L RSC 4 Preston
(British & Commonwealth Lightweight Title Challenge)
10.03.91 Pierre Lorcy L CO 5 Paris, France
24.09.91 Dave Anderson L PTS 8 Glasgow
13.11.91 Steve Walker W PTS 6 Bethnal Green
18.01.92 Steve Pollard W PTS 6 Kensington
30.03.92 Tony Foster W RSC 4 Eltham
30.04.92 Sean Murphy L RSC 1 Kensington
14.04.93 Carlos Chase L RSC 1 Kensington
03.04.96 Brian Coleman W PTS 6 Bethnal Green
Career: 35 contests, won 19, drew 1, lost 15.

Glen Hopkins

Hetton. *Born* Easington, 8 November, 1974
Lightweight. Ht. 5'7"
Manager T. Conroy

05.12.94 John T. Kelly L PTS 6 Houghton le Spring
21.02.95 Ram Singh W RSC 1 Sunderland
11.05.95 Kid McAuley DREW 6 Sunderland
22.06.95 Niel Leggett L PTS 6 Houghton le Spring
28.09.95 Kid McAuley W PTS 6 Sunderland
20.11.95 Garry Burrell L PTS 6 Glasgow
Career: 6 contests, won 2, drew 1, lost 3.

Mark Hopkins

Derby. *Born* Holbrook, 4 October, 1967
L. Heavyweight. Ht. 6'3"
Manager M. Shinfield

16.11.95 P. R. Mason L PTS 6 Evesham
Career: 1 contest, lost 1.

Ron Hopley

Ripon. *Born* Ripon, 3 April, 1969
L. Middleweight. Ht. 5'8½"
Manager D. Mancini

27.11.91 William Beaton W RSC 2 Marton
23.01.92 Rick North W PTS 6 York
08.04.92 Steve Howden L PTS 6 Leeds
25.02.93 Rob Stevenson DREW 6 Bradford
07.04.93 Warren Stephens W PTS 6 Leeds
01.07.93 Rob Stevenson L PTS 6 York
07.10.93 Warren Bowers W PTS 6 York
28.02.94 Warren Bowers W RSC 1 Marton
26.10.94 Brian Dunn L PTS 6 Leeds
08.07.95 Phil Epton L RSC 4 York
04.06.96 Paul Webb W PTS 6 York
Career: 11 contests, won 6, drew 1, lost 4.

Steve Howden
Sheffield. *Born* Sheffield, 4 June, 1969
L. Welterweight. Ht. 5'8¾"
Manager Self

08.04.92	Ron Hopley W PTS 6 Leeds
01.06.92	Kevin McKillan L RSC 2 Manchester
07.07.92	Mike Morrison L CO 3 Bristol
01.10.92	Jimmy Reynolds L RTD 2 Telford
23.06.93	Shaba Edwards W RSC 1 Gorleston
11.08.93	Brian Coleman W RSC 4 Mansfield
30.11.93	Colin Anderson W PTS 6 Leicester
17.08.94	Rick North L PTS 6 Sheffield
23.09.94	Colin Dunne L CO 1 Bethnal Green
26.10.94	Gary Hiscox L RSC 4 Stoke
25.01.95	Mike Watson W RSC 2 Stoke
10.02.95	Clayton Hollingsworth L PTS 6 Birmingham
03.03.95	Danny Stevens L RSC 2 Bethnal Green
26.04.95	Mark Legg L RTD 2 Stoke
01.09.95	Patrick Parton L PTS 6 Wolverhampton
27.09.95	Colin Dunne L RSC 4 Bethnal Green
25.10.95	Dave Madden W PTS 6 Stoke

Career: 17 contests, won 6, lost 11.

(Michael) Hurricane Hughes (Unsworth)
Warrington. *Born* St Helens, 16 January, 1968
Lightweight. Ht. 5'8½"
Manager R. Jones

15.02.96	Sean Morrison L PTS 6 Sheffield
01.04.96	Ram Singh L PTS 6 Bradford

Career: 2 contests, lost 2.

Mark Hughes
Swansea. *Born* Swansea, 8 July, 1971
Flyweight. Ht. 5'2"
Manager M. Duff

21.09.94	Graham McGrath W PTS 4 Cardiff
01.10.94	Anthony Hanna W PTS 4 Cardiff
06.03.95	Anthony Hanna W PTS 6 Mayfair
19.05.95	Shaun Norman W PTS 6 Southwark
25.10.95	Harry Woods DREW 8 Cardiff

Career: 5 contests, won 4, drew 1.

Roger Hunte　　　　Les Clark

Roger Hunte
Leyton. *Born* London, 28 October, 1971
L. Welterweight. Ht. 5'6"
Manager M. Duff

12.02.92	Jason Barker W RTD 4 Wembley
25.03.92	Phil Cullen W RSC 3 Kensington
15.03.96	Anthony Campbell DREW 4 Dunstable
16.05.96	Paul Salmon W RSC 5 Dunstable

Career: 4 contests, won 3, drew 1.

Geoff Hunter
Manchester. *Born* Runcorn, 28 October, 1969
Heavyweight. Ht. 6'0¾"
Manager T. Miller

13.01.96	Slick Miller DREW 6 Halifax

Career: 1 contest, drew 1.

Geoff Hunter　　　　Les Clark

Jason Hutson
Thame. *Born* London, 11 March, 1972
S. Featherweight. Ht. 5'6"
Manager Self

15.02.93	Marco Fattore L PTS 6 Mayfair
29.04.93	Vince Burns L RSC 1 Hayes
31.08.93	Ian Reid L RSC 6 Croydon
09.12.93	Marco Fattore DREW 6 Watford
07.10.94	Greg Upton W RSC 1 Taunton
25.10.94	Matt Brown L PTS 4 Southwark
19.11.94	Lewis Reynolds W RSC 3 Bracknell
20.01.95	Craig Kelley L RSC 2 Bethnal Green
17.03.95	Dennis H. Pedersen L RSC 4 Copenhagen, Denmark
14.09.95	Danny Lutaaya W RSC 2 Battersea
24.10.95	Matt Brown L RSC 3 Southwark

Career: 11 contests, won 3, drew 1, lost 7.

Nelson Ide
Leytonstone. *Born* Worthing, 24 July, 1969
Lightweight. Ht. 5'7"
Manager B. Lynch

16.03.95	Marc Smith W RSC 4 Basildon
04.06.95	Jimmy Singh W CO 1 Bethnal Green
08.11.95	Gareth Lawrence L RSC 5 Bethnal Green

Career: 3 contests, won 2, lost 1.

Vance Idiens
Cannock. *Born* Walsall, 9 June, 1962
Heavyweight. Ht. 6'4"
Manager Self

24.10.89	Mick Cordon W PTS 6 Wolverhampton
28.11.89	Ted Shaw W CO 1 Wolverhampton
06.12.89	Mick Cordon W PTS 6 Stoke
19.02.90	David Jules W PTS 6 Birmingham
22.03.90	Mick Cordon W PTS 6 Wolverhampton
24.05.90	Tucker Richards L RSC 5 Dudley
28.06.90	Paul Neilson W PTS 8 Birmingham
27.09.90	Paul Neilson W PTS 8 Birmingham
14.11.90	Paul Neilson L RSC 2 Doncaster
05.12.91	David Jules W RSC 4 Cannock
06.03.92	Mario Scheisser L RSC 1 Berlin, Germany
09.12.92	David Jules W PTS 8 Stoke
11.03.93	Wayne Buck L PTS 8 Walsall
06.05.93	Joey Paladino W PTS 8 Walsall
19.05.93	John Harewood L CO 3 Sunderland
26.06.93	Justin Fortune L RSC 1 Keynsham
23.10.93	Dermot Gascoyne L RSC 4 Cardiff
14.03.94	Damien Caesar L RSC 4 Mayfair
14.04.94	Wayne Llewelyn L RSC 1 Battersea
05.12.94	Wayane Buck L PTS 6 Cleethorpes
07.05.95	Wayne Llewelyn L RSC 1 Cardiff
21.10.95	Danny Williams L CO 2 Bethnal Green
26.01.96	Pele Reid L RSC 1 Brighton

Career: 23 contests, won 10, lost 13.

Paul Ingle
Scarborough. *Born* Scarborough, 22 June, 1972
Featherweight. Ht. 5'5"
Manager F. Maloney

23.03.94	Darren Noble W RSC 3 Cardiff
27.04.94	Graham McGrath W PTS 4 Bethnal Green
25.05.94	Neil Swain W CO 4 Bristol
03.08.94	Anthony Hanna W PTS 6 Bristol
24.11.94	Graham McGrath W PTS 6 Hull
23.02.95	Pete Buckley W PTS 8 Southwark
27.04.95	Pete Buckley W PTS 8 Bethnal Green
16.06.95	Des Gargano W RSC 2 Southwark
29.09.95	Miguel Matthews W RSC 4 Bethnal Green
15.12.95	Damir Nanev W RSC 5 Bethnal Green
05.02.96	Greg Upton W RSC 10 Bexleyheath
29.06.96	Ervine Blake W RSC 2 Erith

Career: 12 contests, won 12.

Paul Ingle　　　　Les Clark

99

Nick Ingram

Northampton. *Born* Chester, 3 October, 1972
L. Middleweight. Ht. 5'11"
Manager Self

20.09.93	Mark Brogan W RSC 4 Northampton
04.11.93	Peter Reid L RSC 5 Stafford
08.03.94	Warren Stephens W PTS 6 Kettering
16.05.94	Roger Dean W RSC 3 Heathrow
27.05.94	Roy Dehara W PTS 6 Ashford
28.11.94	Peter Reid W PTS 6 Northampton
03.04.95	Stefan Scriggins L PTS 6 Northampton
12.06.95	John Stronach W PTS 6 Bradford
22.06.95	Robbie Bell L PTS 6 Houghton le Spring
30.06.95	Danny Peters L RSC 6 Liverpool
28.11.95	David Bain W PTS 8 Wolverhampton

Career: 11 contests, won 7, lost 4.

Colin Innes

Newcastle. *Born* Newcastle, 24 July, 1964
Northern Area Featherweight Champion.
Ht. 5'6"
Manager N. Fawcett

10.09.90	Lee Christian W RSC 5 Northampton
24.09.90	Steve Armstrong W PTS 6 Manchester
08.10.90	Ervine Blake L PTS 6 Bradford
22.10.90	Steve Armstrong W RSC 6 Manchester
26.11.90	Carl Roberts L RSC 3 Bury
11.02.91	Steve Armstrong W PTS 6 Manchester
18.02.91	Ian McGirr L PTS 6 Glasgow
02.03.91	Tommy Smith W PTS 6 Darlington
28.03.91	Darryl Pettit W RTD 3 Alfreton
30.04.91	Noel Carroll L PTS 4 Stockport
19.09.91	Carl Roberts L PTS 4 Stockport
12.12.91	Tommy Smith L PTS 6 Hartlepool
24.02.92	Mark Geraghty L PTS 8 Glasgow
30.03.92	Chris Jickells L RSC 3 Bradford
28.05.92	Tommy Smith L PTS 6 Gosforth
05.10.92	Wayne Rigby L PTS 6 Manchester
18.11.92	Al Garrett DREW 6 Solihull
15.09.93	Chris Bennett DREW 6 Newcastle
25.11.93	Garry Burrell W PTS 6 Newcastle
06.12.93	Norman Dhalie L PTS 6 Bradford
24.01.94	Hugh Collins L PTS 6 Glasgow
03.03.94	Leo Turner DREW 6 Newcastle
21.04.94	Leo Turner W PTS 6 Gateshead
13.05.94	Rocky Ferrari L PTS 6 Kilmarnock
13.06.94	Leo Turner L PTS 6 Bradford
12.09.94	Kid McAuley L PTS 6 Doncaster
06.10.94	Chip O'Neill DREW 6 Cramlington
24.11.94	Paul Goode W PTS 6 Newcastle
24.02.95	Garry Burrell L PTS 6 Irvine
11.03.95	Trevor Sumner L PTS 6 Barnsley
25.03.95	Paul Hamilton W PTS 6 Rothwell
05.04.95	Ian McLeod L RSC 5 Irvine
11.05.95	Chip O'Neill L PTS 6 Sunderland
05.06.95	Paul Watson L RSC 4 Glasgow
15.09.95	Paul Hamilton W PTS 6 Darlington
05.10.95	Fred Reeve L PTS 6 Hull
14.11.95	Chris Price L PTS 6 Yarm
11.12.95	Jason Blanche L PTS 6 Bradford
12.02.96	Scott Dixon L PTS 6 Glasgow
02.03.96	Gary Hickman W PTS 4 Newcastle
16.03.96	Shaun Anderson L PTS 4 Glasgow
25.04.96	Chip O'Neill W RSC 9 Newcastle
	(Vacant Northern Area Featherweight Title)
08.06.96	Gary Hickman W PTS 4 Newcastle

Career: 43 contests, won 14, drew 4, lost 25.

Paul Ireland

Belfast. *Born* Belfast, 22 April, 1970
S. Bantamweight. Ht. 5'7"
Manager B. Hearn

26.08.95	Graham McGrath W PTS 4 Belfast
07.10.95	Marty Chestnut W RSC 6 Belfast
20.04.96	Graham McGrath W PTS 6 Brentwood
28.05.96	Garry Burrell W PTS 6 Belfast

Career: 4 contests, won 4.

(John) Jonjo Irwin

Doncaster. *Born* Denaby, 31 May, 1969
Former British Featherweight Champion.
Former Undefeated WBO Inter-Continental
Featherweight Champion. Former
Undefeated WBO Penta-Continental S.
Featherweight Champion. Former
Undefeated All-Ireland Featherweight
Champion. Ht. 5'8"
Manager J. Rushton/B. Hearn

08.09.92	Kid McAuley W PTS 6 Doncaster
30.09.92	Miguel Matthews W PTS 6 Solihull
24.11.92	Colin Lynch W RSC 4 Doncaster
20.01.93	Mark Hargreaves W RSC 4 Solihull
23.02.93	G. G. Goddard W RSC 8 Doncaster
16.03.93	Kid McAuley W PTS 10 Mayfair
	(Vacant All-Ireland Featherweight Title)
28.04.93	Kevin Middleton L RSC 6 Solihull
06.10.93	Pete Buckley W PTS 8 Solihull
21.12.93	Peter Harris W PTS 8 Mayfair
22.01.94	Derek Amory L RSC 2 Belfast
10.05.94	Michael Armstrong W PTS 12 Doncaster
	(Vacant WBO Penta-Continental S. Featherweight Title)
04.10.94	Harry Escott W PTS 12 Mayfair
	(WBO Penta-Continental S. Featherweight Title Defence)
13.12.94	Bamana Dibateza W PTS 12 Potters Bar
	(WBO Penta-Continental S. Featherweight Title Defence)
30.06.95	Manuel Calvo W PTS 12 Doncaster
	(Vacant WBO Inter-Continental Featherweight Title)
17.07.95	Learie Bruce W RSC 8 Mayfair
	(WBO Inter-Continental Featherweight Title Defence)
20.09.95	Mike Deveney W PTS 12 Potters Bar
	(British Featherweight Title Challenge)
18.12.95	Elvis Parsley W RSC 8 Mayfair
	(British Featherweight Title Defence)
14.05.96	Colin McMillan L PTS 12 Dagenham
	(British Featherweight Title Defence)

Career: 18 contests, won 15, lost 3.

Gilbert Jackson (Amponsan)

Battersea. *Born* Ghana, 21 August, 1970
L. Middleweight. Ht. 5'10"
Manager Self

17.02.92	John Bosco L PTS 6 Mayfair
05.03.92	Tony Wellington W CO 2 Battersea
22.04.92	Russell Washer W PTS 6 Wembley
08.09.92	Paul Gamble W RSC 1 Norwich
05.02.93	Carl Harney W CO 3 Manchester
14.06.93	Lee Crocker W RSC 2 Bayswater
16.09.93	Alan Baptiste W RSC 5 Southwark
02.11.93	Ernie Loveridge W RTD 3 Southwark

Paul Ireland

01.12.93	Jerry Mortimer W RSC 3 Kensington
16.02.94	Chris Richards W RSC 2 Stevenage
14.03.94	Mark Atkins W PTS 6 Mayfair
13.04.94	Gordon Blair W RTD 1 Glasgow
23.09.94	Martin Jolley W CO 3 Bethnal Green
09.11.94	Chris Peters W RSC 3 Millwall
14.02.95	Chris Richards W RTD 2 Bethnal Green
21.04.95	Paul Wesley W RSC 6 Dudley
	(Elim. British L. Middleweight Title)
13.01.96	Ensley Bingham L RSC 3 Manchester
	(Vacant British L. Middleweight Title)

Career: 17 contests, won 15, lost 2.

Gary Jacobs

Glasgow. *Born* Glasgow, 10 December, 1965
Former European & Commonwealth
Welterweight Champion. Former
Undefeated British, WBC International &
Scottish Welterweight Champion. Ht. 5'7½"
Manager M. Duff

20.05.85	John Conlan W PTS 6 Glasgow
03.06.85	Nigel Burke W PTS 6 Glasgow
12.08.85	Mike McKenzie W PTS 6 Glasgow
07.10.85	Albert Buchanan W PTS 6 Cambuslang
11.11.85	Tyrell Wilson W CO 5 Glasgow
02.12.85	Dave Heaver W PTS 6 Glasgow
10.02.86	Courtney Phillips W RSC 5 Glasgow
10.03.86	Alistair Laurie W PTS 8 Glasgow
14.04.86	Billy Cairns W PTS 8 Glasgow
24.06.86	Dave Douglas L PTS 10 Glasgow
	(Vacant Scottish Welterweight Title)
15.09.86	Jeff Connors W RSC 3 Glasgow
20.10.86	Kelvin Mortimer W RSC 5 Glasgow
27.01.87	Dave Douglas W PTS 10 Glasgow
	(Scottish Welterweight Title Challenge)
24.02.87	Gary Williams W CO 7 Glasgow
06.04.87	Robert Armstrong W RTD 5 Glasgow
19.05.87	Gary Williams W RSC 3 Cumbernauld
08.06.87	Tommy McCallum W RSC 5 Glasgow
	(Scottish Welterweight Title Defence)
26.11.87	Jeff Connors W PTS 8 Fulham
24.02.88	Del Bryan W PTS 10 Glasgow
	(Final Elim. British Welterweight Title)
19.04.88	Wilf Gentzen W PTS 12 Glasgow
	(Commonwealth Welterweight Title Challenge)
06.06.88	Juan Alonzo Villa W RSC 5 Mayfair
16.09.88	Javier Suazo W CO 10 Las Vegas, USA
	(Vacant WBC International Welterweight Title)
29.11.88	Richard Rova W CO 4 Kensington
	(Commonwealth Welterweight Title Defence)
14.02.89	Rocky Kelly W RTD 7 Wandsworth
	(Commonwealth & WBC International Welterweight Title Defence)
05.04.89	George Collins W PTS 12 Kensington
	(Commonwealth & WBC International Welterweight Title Defence)
27.06.89	Rollin Williams W RSC 1 Kensington
27.08.89	James McGirt L PTS 10 New York, USA
23.11.89	Donovan Boucher L PTS 12 Motherwell
	(Commonwealth Welterweight Title Defence)
26.04.90	Pascal Lorcy W RSC 2 Wandsworth
09.05.90	Mike Durvan W CO 1 Kensington
17.10.90	Mickey Hughes L CO 8 Bethnal Green

05.03.91	Kenny Louis W CO 2 Glasgow	
20.11.91	Peter Eubank W PTS 8 Kensington	
20.02.92	Del Bryan W PTS 12 Glasgow	
	(British Welterweight Title Challenge)	
25.03.92	Tommy Small W RSC 2 Kensington	
22.04.92	Cirillo Nino W PTS 10 Wembley	
09.07.92	Robert Wright W RSC 6 Glasgow	
	(British Welterweight Title Defence)	
16.10.92	Ludovic Proto L PTS 12 Paris, France	
	(Vacant European Welterweight Title)	
06.02.93	Ludovic Proto W RTD 9 Paris, France	
	(European Welterweight Title Challenge)	
19.05.93	Horace Fleary W RTD 4 Sunderland	
22.09.93	Daniel Bicchieray W RSC 5 Wembley	
	(European Welterweight Title Defence)	
01.02.94	Tek Nkalankete W PTS 12 Paris, France	
	(European Welterweight Title Defence)	
13.04.94	Alessandro Duran W CO 8 Glasgow	
	(European Welterweight Title Defence)	
05.10.94	Rusty deRouen W RSC 6 Wolverhampton	
09.11.94	Marcelo di Croce W PTS 10 Millwall	
04.03.95	Jose Miguel Fernandez W PTS 10 Atlantic City, USA	
26.08.95	Pernell Whitaker L PTS 12 Atlantic City, USA	
	(WBC Welterweight Title Challenge)	
18.11.95	Leigh Wicks W RTD 3 Glasgow	
13.03.96	Edwin Murillo W CO 5 Wembley	
	(IBF Inter-Continental Welterweight Title Challenge)	
14.06.96	Patrick Charpentier L RSC 7 Gravelines, France	
	(European Welterweight Title Challenge)	

Career: 50 contests, won 43, lost 7.

Jacklord Jacobs

London. *Born* Nigeria, 1 January, 1970
Cruiserweight. Ht. 6'1"
Manager Self

03.03.94	Cordwell Hylton W RSC 3 Ebbw Vale	
30.07.94	Cordwell Hylton W RSC 4 Bethnal Green	
01.11.94	Bobby Anderson DREW 4 Las Vegas, USA	
14.11.95	John Pierre W PTS 6 Yarm	
05.02.96	Tim Redman DREW 6 Bexleyheath	
22.04.96	Chris Woollas DREW 4 Crystal Palace	

Career: 6 contests, won 3, drew 3.

Lester Jacobs

Peckham. *Born* London, 29 January, 1962
S. Middleweight. Ht. 5'7"
Manager Self

01.03.89	Peter Vosper W PTS 6 Bethnal Green	
29.03.89	Reuben Thurley W RSC 4 Bethnal Green	
30.01.90	David Brown W PTS 6 Battersea	
12.09.90	Peter Gorny W RSC 2 Battersea	
18.10.90	Alan Pennington W RSC 2 Wandsworth	
20.03.91	Karl Barwise W PTS 6 Battersea	
16.05.91	Paul McCarthy W PTS 6 Battersea	
11.09.91	John Kaighin W RSC 2 Hammersmith	
05.03.92	John Kaighin W RSC 1 Battersea	
17.05.92	Marvin O'Brien W PTS 6 Harringay	
16.11.94	Stinger Mason W PTS 6 Bloomsbury	
23.02.95	Paul Murray W RSC 2 Southwark	

08.03.95	Mark Dawson W PTS 6 Bloomsbury	
22.07.95	Mark Dawson W PTS 4 Millwall	
02.09.95	Butch Lesley W PTS 4 Wembley	

Career: 15 contests, won 15.

John Janes

Cardiff. *Born* Worcester, 3 March, 1974
Lightweight. Ht. 5'7"
Manager D. Gardiner

29.11.94	Steve Burton W PTS 6 Cardiff	
25.01.95	Paul Dyer L PTS 6 Cardiff	
06.05.95	Sean Baker L PTS 4 Shepton Mallet	
20.09.95	Gavin Lane W PTS 6 Ystrad	
29.09.95	Enzo Giordano L RSC 4 Bloomsbury	
13.11.95	Justin Simmons L PTS 6 Barnstaple	
28.11.95	Mark McGowan W PTS 6 Cardiff	
19.01.96	Paul Miles W PTS 4 Bracknell	
29.05.96	Gavin Lane W PTS 6 Ebbw Vale	

Career: 9 contests, won 5, lost 4.

Tommy Janes

Cardiff. *Born* Cardiff, 28 November, 1976
Lightweight. Ht. 5'10"
Manager D. Gardiner

20.12.95	Craig Kelley W PTS 6 Usk	
13.02.96	Arv Mittoo W PTS 6 Cardiff	
20.03.96	Marc Smith L RSC 6 Cardiff	
15.05.96	Chris Price W RSC 4 Cardiff	

Career: 4 contests, won 3, lost 1.

David Jay

Cefn Hengoed. *Born* Merthyr Tydfil, 4 May, 1971
S. Featherweight. Ht. 5'10"
Manager D. Gardiner

15.05.96	Robert Grubb W RSC 4 Cardiff	
29.05.96	Gary Jenkinson DREW 6 Ebbw Vale	

Career: 2 contests, won 1, drew 1.

Gary Jenkinson

Lincoln. *Born* Lincoln, 16 January, 1969
S. Featherweight. Ht. 5'5½"
Manager J. Gaynor

26.10.95	Carl Allen L PTS 6 Birmingham	
02.11.95	Paul Quarmby W PTS 6 Houghton le Spring	
08.12.95	Shaune Danskin W PTS 6 Leeds	
23.02.96	Wayne Jones DREW 6 Weston super Mare	
16.03.96	Chris Lyons W PTS 6 Barnstaple	
29.05.96	David Jay DREW 6 Ebbw Vale	

Career: 6 contests, won 3, drew 2, lost 1.

Andrew Jervis

Liverpool. *Born* Liverpool, 28 June, 1969
L. Middleweight. Ht. 5'11"
Manager Self

05.10.92	Rick North W PTS 6 Liverpool	
02.11.92	Shaun Martin W CO 2 Liverpool	
01.12.92	Cliff Churchward W PTS 6 Liverpool	
27.01.93	Mark Ramsey L PTS 6 Stoke	
22.02.93	Alan Williams W PTS 6 Liverpool	
29.03.93	Bullit Andrews W PTS 6 Liverpool	
09.06.93	Chris Mulcahy W PTS 6 Liverpool	
15.03.94	John Duckworth L PTS 6 Stoke	
25.05.94	Sean Baker DREW 4 Bristol	
04.06.94	Adrian Dodson L RSC 2 Cardiff	
17.08.94	Robin Reid L RSC 1 Sheffield	

26.10.94	David Larkin L CO 5 Leeds	
08.03.95	Howard Clarke L PTS 6 Solihull	
22.03.95	Andy Peach W PTS 6 Stoke	
03.04.95	Andy Davidson W CO 3 Manchester	
27.05.95	Neil Sinclair W RSC 3 Belfast	
22.09.95	Peter Waudby L PTS 10 Hull	
	(Vacant Central Area L. Middleweight Title)	
21.10.95	Paul Carr W RSC 3 Bethnal Green	
10.11.95	Wayne Alexander L RTD 3 Derby	
23.01.96	Steve Roberts L PTS 6 Bethnal Green	

Career: 20 contests, won 10, drew 1, lost 9.

Andrew Jervis   Les Clark

Chris Jickells

Brigg. *Born* Scunthorpe, 26 March, 1971
Central Area Featherweight Champion.
Ht. 5'5"
Manager J. Rushton

18.11.91	Tony Smith W RSC 4 Manchester	
09.12.91	Al Garrett W RSC 2 Bradford	
15.01.92	Ronnie Stephenson L PTS 6 Stoke	
30.03.92	Colin Innes W RSC 3 Bradford	
29.04.92	Kevin Middleton W RSC 6 Solihull	
01.06.92	Dave McHale L RSC 4 Glasgow	
12.10.92	Ian McGirr W RSC 3 Bradford	
10.02.93	Kevin Middleton L CO 1 Lewisham	
07.06.93	Wilson Docherty L RSC 5 Glasgow	
02.11.93	Mark Bowers L RSC 3 Southwark	
21.03.94	Mike Deveney L RSC 5 Glasgow	
26.09.94	Dave Clavering L PTS 6 Morecambe	
11.10.94	Yifru Retta L PTS 6 Bethnal Green	
11.11.94	Dennis Holback Pedersen L PTS 6 Randers, Denmark	
23.11.94	Ian McLeod L PTS 6 Irvine	
04.02.95	Neil Swain L PTS 6 Cardiff	
04.03.95	Paul Griffin L RSC 5 Livingston	
30.06.95	Graham McGrath W PTS 4 Doncaster	
28.07.95	Graham McGrath W PTS 6 Epworth	
11.10.95	Gary Marston L PTS 8 Stoke	
25.10.95	Barry Jones L PTS 6 Cardiff	
29.11.95	Miguel Matthews L PTS 6 Solihull	
22.01.96	Ian McLeod L PTS 8 Glasgow	
29.02.96	Carl Allen L PTS 6 Scunthorpe	

101

01.04.96 Kid McAuley W PTS 6 Bradford
03.05.96 Trevor Sumner W RSC 5 Sheffield
*(Vacant Central Area Featherweight
Title)*
25.05.96 Stephen Smith L RSC 3 Leipzig,
Germany
25.06.96 Gary Thornhill L PTS 6 Stevenage
Career: 28 contests, won 9, lost 19.

James Jiora (Iwenjiora)

Otley. *Born* Nigeria, 6 April, 1968
L. Welterweight. Ht. 5'5"
Manager J. Celebanski

07.06.87 Paul Kennedy W RSC 6 Bradford
15.09.87 Ian Murray W RSC 2 Batley
02.11.87 Michael Howell W RSC 3 Bradford
10.11.87 Marvin P. Gray L PTS 8 Batley
30.11.87 John Townsley W PTS 8 Nottingham
15.12.87 Paul Burke W PTS 4 Bradford
08.03.88 Rudy Valentino L PTS 6 Batley
26.01.89 Frankie Foster L PTS 6 Newcastle
20.02.89 Paul Bowen L PTS 6 Birmingham
20.03.89 Dean Dickinson W PTS 6 Bradford
31.03.89 Chris Bennett L PTS 6 Scarborough
11.07.89 Craig Walsh L PTS 8 Batley
05.12.89 Paul Charters L RSC 4 Dewsbury
11.01.90 Kid Sumali W PTS 4 Dewsbury
26.02.90 Brendan Ryan W PTS 6 Bradford
11.04.90 Rick Bushell L PTS 6 Dewsbury
29.11.90 Marvin P. Gray L PTS 8 Marton
13.06.91 David Thompson DREW 6 Hull
01.08.91 Chris Saunders L PTS 6 Dewsbury
09.10.91 John O. Johnson L PTS 6 Manchester
21.10.91 Charlie Kane L PTS 6 Glasgow
02.03.92 Carl Tilley L PTS 6 Marton
12.03.92 Alan McDowall L CO 2 Glasgow
13.06.94 Mark Allen W PTS 6 Bradford
24.10.94 Paul Scott W PTS 6 Bradford
05.12.94 Alan Peacock W PTS 6 Bradford
25.09.95 Chris Aston DREW 6 Bradford
05.02.96 John Stovin L PTS 6 Bradford
Career: 28 contests, won 11, drew 2, lost 15.

Dave Johnson

Sunderland. *Born* Boldon, 10 August, 1972
Middleweight. Ht. 5'10"
Manager T. Conroy

13.05.91 Rocky Tyrell W PTS 6 Manchester
20.05.91 Griff Jones W PTS 6 Bradford
10.06.91 Tyrone Eastmond W PTS 6 Manchester
10.10.91 Shamus Casey W PTS 6 Gateshead
14.11.91 Shamus Casey W PTS 6 Gateshead
25.11.91 Mike Phillips L PTS 6 Liverpool
12.12.91 Mick Duncan W PTS 6 Hartlepool
03.03.92 Mark Jay W PTS 6 Houghton le Spring
28.04.92 Shaun McCrory DREW 6 Houghton le
Spring
10.09.92 Spencer Alton W PTS 6 Sunderland
23.10.92 Griff Jones W PTS 6 Gateshead
17.04.93 Mike Phillips W PTS 6 Washington
11.06.93 Robert Riley W PTS 8 Gateshead
15.09.93 Darren Pilling W PTS 6 Newcastle
25.11.93 Dave Owens W PTS 8 Tynemouth
02.03.94 John Duckworth W PTS 8 Solihull
17.03.94 Peter Waudby L PTS 6 Lincoln
27.04.94 Barry Thorogood DREW 8 Solihull
24.05.94 Martin Jolley W PTS 6 Sunderland
13.10.94 Japhet Hans W RSC 2 Houghton le
Spring
10.12.94 Derek Wormald DREW 8 Manchester
21.02.95 Vince Rose W PTS 8 Sunderland

01.03.95 Ernie Loveridge W PTS 6 Glasgow
23.11.95 Martin Jolley W PTS 6 Tynemouth
14.02.96 David Radford L RSC 5 Sunderland
Career: 25 contests, won 19, drew 3, lost 3.

(Paul) John O. Johnson (Johnson)

Nottingham. *Born* Nottingham, 2
November, 1969
L. Welterweight. Ht. 5'5"
Manager W. Swift

29.08.91 Seth Jones W DIS 1 Oakengates
09.10.91 James Jiora W PTS 6 Manchester
24.10.91 Carl Hook L PTS 6 Dunstable
31.10.91 Darren Morris W PTS 6 Oakengates
26.11.91 Bernard Paul L PTS 6 Bethnal Green
22.01.92 Brian Coleman W PTS 6 Stoke
30.01.92 Chris Saunders W PTS 6 Southampton
20.02.92 Alan Peacock W PTS 6 Glasgow
09.03.92 Ricky Sackfield W PTS 6 Manchester
26.03.92 Davy Robb L PTS 6 Telford
03.06.92 Jason Barker W PTS 6 Newcastle
under Lyme
09.09.92 Chris Saunders DREW 6 Stoke
05.10.92 Andreas Panayi L RTD 1 Liverpool
09.12.92 Jason Barker W PTS 8 Stoke
10.02.93 Dean Hollington L PTS 6 Lewisham
17.03.93 Jonathan Thaxton L PTS 6 Stoke
19.01.94 Billy McDougall L RSC 3 Stoke
10.03.94 Keith Marner L RSC 5 Watford
10.05.94 Mark Legg W RSC 6 Doncaster
11.06.94 Paul Knights W PTS 6 Bethnal Green
28.06.94 Andreas Panayi L RSC 5 Mayfair
30.09.94 Michael Ayers L RSC 3 Bethnal Green
23.02.95 Peter Richardson L RSC 5 Southwark
30.03.95 Richie Edwards L PTS 4 Bethnal Green
20.04.95 Carl Wright L PTS 6 Liverpool
13.05.95 Tanveer Ahmed L CO 3 Glasgow
21.09.95 Paul Miles L PTS 4 Battersea
21.10.95 Martin Holgate L PTS 4 Bethnal Green
28.10.95 Allan Gray L PTS 6 Kensington
25.11.95 Mark Winters L RSC 2 Dublin
13.01.96 Ricky Sackfield L PTS 6 Manchester
20.01.96 Jonathan Thaxton L RSC 4 Mansfield
Career: 32 contests, won 11, drew 1, lost 20.

Mickey Johnson

Newcastle. *Born* Newcastle, 28 July, 1970
Middleweight. Ht. 5'11"
Manager T. Conroy

28.09.95 David Larkin W PTS 6 Sunderland
02.11.95 Brian Dunn L RSC 3 Houghton le
Spring
Career: 2 contests, won 1, lost 1.

Martin Jolley

Alfreton. *Born* Chesterfield, 22 November,
1967
Middleweight. Ht. 5'11½"
Manager M. Shinfield

10.03.92 Gypsy Johnny Price W RSC 3 Bury
06.04.92 Sean Byrne L RSC 6 Northampton
11.05.92 Mark Hale W PTS 6 Coventry
08.09.92 Brian McGloin W PTS 6 Doncaster
05.10.92 Mark Hale W RSC 4 Bardon
14.10.92 Carl Smallwood W PTS 6 Stoke
02.11.92 Bobby Mack L PTS 6 Wolverhampton
24.11.92 Phil Ball DREW 6 Doncaster
02.02.93 Mark McBiane W RSC 5 Derby
23.02.93 Phil Ball W RSC 5 Doncaster
12.05.93 Marvin O'Brien W PTS 6 Sheffield

08.06.93 Paul Hanlon W PTS 6 Derby
22.09.93 Nigel Rafferty L PTS 6 Chesterfield
29.10.93 Mads Larsen L CO 2 Korsoer,
Denmark
02.12.93 Darren Littlewood L PTS 6 Evesham
17.03.94 Paul Hitch W RSC 2 Lincoln
25.04.94 Derek Wormald L RSC 4 Bury
24.05.94 Dave Johnson L PTS 6 Sunderland
17.06.94 Dean Francis L PTS 6 Plymouth
02.07.94 Glenn Catley L RSC 1 Keynsham
23.09.94 Gilbert Jackson L CO 3 Bethnal Green
24.10.94 Craig Joseph L PTS 6 Bradford
07.11.94 Mark Delaney L RSC 3 Bethnal Green
12.12.94 Darren Littlewood L PTS 6
Cleethorpes
20.12.94 Mark Delaney L RSC 4 Bethnal Green
17.02.95 Willie Quinn L CO 5 Cumbernauld
11.05.95 Darren Sweeney L PTS 6 Dudley
19.05.95 Steve McNess L PTS 6 Southwark
10.06.95 Robin Reid L CO 1 Manchester
27.09.95 Steve McNess W RTD 4 Bethnal Green
29.10.95 Warren Stowe L PTS 6 Shaw
13.11.95 Peter Vosper W PTS 6 Barnstaple
23.11.95 Dave Johnson L PTS 6 Tynemouth
11.12.95 Lee Blundell L PTS 6 Morecambe
26.01.96 Ryan Rhodes L CO 3 Brighton
05.03.96 Jason Hart L PTS 6 Bethnal Green
16.03.96 Willie Quinn L RSC 4 Glasgow
11.05.96 Ryan Rhodes L RSC 2 Bethnal Green
25.06.96 Jason Matthews L RSC 3 Mansfield
Career: 39 contests, won 13, drew 1, lost 25.

Martin Jolley   Les Clark

Barry Jones

Cardiff. *Born* Cardiff, 3 May, 1974
Featherweight. Ht. 5'7"
Manager Self

28.10.92 Conn McMullen W PTS 6 Cardiff
14.12.92 Miguel Matthews W PTS 6 Cardiff
27.01.93 Mike Deveney W PTS 6 Cardiff
24.03.93 Greg Upton W RSC 2 Cardiff
28.04.93 Kid McAuley W PTS 8 Solihull
09.10.93 John White W PTS 4 Manchester
10.11.93 Neil Swain W PTS 6 Ystrad
30.11.93 Pete Buckley W PTS 4 Cardiff

16.12.93 Elvis Parsley W PTS 6 Newport
22.01.94 Pete Buckley W PTS 6 Cardiff
27.08.94 Kelton McKenzie W PTS 6 Cardiff
25.05.95 Justin Murphy W PTS 10 Reading
(Elim. British Featherweight Title)
25.10.95 Chris Jickells W PTS 6 Cardiff
28.11.95 Pete Buckley W PTS 6 Cardiff
Career: 14 contests, won 14.

Craig Jones

Stoke on Trent. *Born* Stoke on Trent, 17
November, 1970
Cruiserweight. Ht. 6'1½"
Manager D. Powell

06.12.95 Nigel Williams L RSC 1 Stoke
22.02.96 Stevie Pettit L RSC 1 Walsall
Career: 2 contests, lost 2.

Henry Jones

Pembroke. *Born* Haverfordwest, 23
December, 1975
Bantamweight. Ht. 5'0"
Manager G. Davies

17.06.95 Abdul Mannon W PTS 6 Cardiff
07.07.95 Harry Woods L PTS 4 Cardiff
07.10.95 Frankie Slane L PTS 4 Belfast
28.11.95 Jason Thomas L PTS 4 Cardiff
20.12.95 Brendan Bryce W PTS 6 Usk
20.03.96 Danny Lawson W CO 1 Cardiff
29.05.96 Ian Turner L PTS 6 Ebbw Vale
Career: 7 contests, won 3, lost 4.

John Jones

Liverpool. *Born* Liverpool, 13 July, 1968
Welterweight. Ht. 5'9"
Manager S. Vaughan

29.09.95 John Smith W PTS 6 Liverpool
05.03.96 Michael Alexander W PTS 6 Barrow
10.05.96 Charlie Paine W PTS 6 Liverpool
Career: 3 contests, won 3.

Paul Jones

Sheffield. *Born* Sheffield, 19 November,
1966
Former Undefeated WBO, WBO Inter-
Continental & Central Area L.
Middleweight Champion. Ht. 6'0"
Manager B. Hearn

08.12.86 Paul Gillings W PTS 6 Liverpool
28.10.87 Pat Durkin W PTS 4 Sheffield
10.11.87 David Binns L PTS 6 Batley
11.01.88 Humphrey Harrison L PTS 8
Manchester
27.09.88 George Sponagle DREW 8 Halifax,
Canada
07.12.88 Jimmy Thornton W PTS 6 Stoke
23.01.89 Donovan Boucher L DIS 6 Toronto,
Canada
13.03.89 Dale Moreland W PTS 6 Toronto,
Canada
30.03.89 Benoit Boudreau W PTS 10 Moncton,
Canada
19.04.89 Tony Collier W CO 3 Toronto, Canada
06.06.89 George Sponagle L PTS 8 Halifax,
Canada
06.09.89 Kid Ford W PTS 6 Mississouga,
Canada
13.11.89 Ian Midwood-Tate W RSC 4
Manchester

08.12.89 Antoine Tarver L PTS 4 Doncaster
06.03.90 Antonio Fernandez W PTS 8 Stoke
22.03.90 Darren Pilling W RTD 7 Gateshead
26.04.90 Newton Barnett W PTS 8 Mayfair
20.05.90 Jim Beckett W CO 1 Sheffield
22.05.90 Wayne Ellis L PTS 6 St Albans
14.11.90 Jason Rowe W PTS 10 Sheffield
(Central Area L. Middleweight Title
Challenge)
12.03.91 Tony Velinor W PTS 8 Mansfield
16.08.91 Hugo Marinangelli L CO 2 Marbella,
Spain
01.10.91 Simon Eubank W CO 6 Sheffield
14.04.92 Paul Lynch W RSC 3 Mansfield
19.05.92 Trevor Ambrose W PTS 6 Cardiff
02.06.92 Patrick Vungbo W PTS 10 Rotterdam,
Holland
19.09.92 Ernie Loveridge W PTS 6 Glasgow
24.11.92 Paul Wesley L RSC 2 Doncaster
17.01.95 Julian Eavis W RSC 4 Worcester
06.03.95 Peter Waudby W PTS 6 Mayfair
14.04.95 Damien Denny W CO 1 Belfast
(Vacant WBO Inter-Continental
L. Middleweight Title)
26.08.95 Danny Juma W PTS 12 Belfast
(WBO Inter-Continental L.
Middleweight Title Defence)
02.10.95 Eric Spalding W RSC 2 Mayfair
(WBO Inter-Continental L.
Middleweight Title Defence)
22.11.95 Verno Phillips W PTS 12 Sheffield
(WBO L. Middleweight Title
Challenge)
Career: 34 contests, won 25, drew 1, lost 8.

Paul Jones   Les Clark

Wayne Jones

Saltash. *Born* Halifax, 6 October, 1968
Lightweight. Ht. 5'8"
Manager N. Christian

13.11.93 Robbie Sivyer W PTS 6 Cullompton
14.01.94 Colin Dunne L RSC 3 Bethnal Green
04.03.94 Robbie Sivyer W PTS 6 Weston super
Mare
17.06.94 Trevor Royal W PTS 6 Plymouth
09.07.94 Bobby Guynan L PTS 6 Earls Court

30.07.94 Sean Knight L RSC 2 Bethnal Green
01.10.94 Gareth Jordan L RSC 2 Cardiff
19.11.94 Adrian Chase L PTS 6 Heathrow
27.11.94 Everald Williams L RSC 2 Southwark
24.01.95 Brian Coleman W PTS 6 Piccadilly
18.02.95 Chris Barnett L RSC 5 Shepton Mallet
25.03.95 Danny Lutaaya L RSC 3 Millwall
09.05.95 Georgie Smith L RSC 3 Basildon
16.06.95 Lewis Reynolds L PTS 4 Southwark
23.06.95 Allan Gray L PTS 6 Bethnal Green
02.09.95 A. M. Milton L RSC 1 Wembley
30.10.95 Anthony Campbell L RSC 1 Heathrow
06.02.96 Michael Wright L PTS 4 Basildon
23.02.96 Gary Jenkinson DREW 6 Weston super
Mare
16.03.96 Phil Lashley W PTS 6 Barnstaple
20.04.96 Richard Evatt L RSC 2 Brentwood
03.06.96 Ervine Blake L RSC 1 Birmingham
Career: 22 contests, won 5, drew 1, lost 16.

Wesley Jones

Colwyn Bay. *Born* Rhuddlan, 13
November, 1974
L. Middleweight. Ht. 5'10¾"
Manager D. Davies

12.06.95 Lee Power L PTS 6 Manchester
22.07.95 Paul Carr L RSC 3 Millwall
20.10.95 Jason Barker L RSC 2 Mansfield
Career: 3 contests, lost 3.

Cham Joof

Brixton. *Born* London, 19 November, 1968
Former Undefeated Southern Area
Lightweight Champion. Ht. 5'8"
Manager F. Warren/C. Carew

22.02.93 Chris Saunders W PTS 4 Eltham
04.04.93 Anthony Wanza W RSC 2 Brockley
14.04.93 Mike Morrison W PTS 4 Kensington
23.05.93 Charles Shepherd L PTS 4 Brockley
25.06.93 Scott Smith W RTD 2 Battersea
14.08.93 Mark Allen W RSC 3 Hammersmith
20.01.94 Phil Found W RSC 1 Battersea
14.04.94 Brian Coleman W CO 3 Battersea
22.05.94 Felix Kelly W RSC 5 Crystal Palace
(Southern Area Lightweight Title
Challenge)
25.02.95 Tony Foster W PTS 8 Millwall
06.05.95 Karl Taylor L PTS 8 Shepton Mallet
01.07.95 Tanveer Ahmed L PTS 6 Kensington
13.01.96 Paul Burke L RSC 2 Manchester
Career: 13 contests, won 9, lost 4.

Gareth Jordan

Monmouth. *Born* Usk, 19 December, 1971
Lightweight. Ht. 5'6¾"
Manager M. Duff

02.11.92 Con Cronin W RSC 2 Wolverhampton
04.12.92 Jason White W RSC 2 Telford
16.03.93 Lee Fox W RSC 3 Wolverhampton
26.05.93 Mark O'Callaghan W RSC 3 Mansfield
27.10.93 Dave Madden W RSC 5 West
Bromwich
16.12.93 Phil Found W PTS 6 Newport
04.06.94 T. J. Smith W RSC 1 Cardiff
01.10.94 Wayne Jones W RSC 2 Cardiff
30.11.94 Kevin McKenzie W PTS 6
Wolverhampton
04.02.95 Mark O'Callaghan W RSC 2 Cardiff
21.04.95 Peter Till W PTS 6 Dudley
07.07.95 Kelton McKenzie W PTS 4 Cardiff

25.10.95 Mervyn Bennett L PTS 10 Cardiff
(Welsh Lightweight Title Challenge)
13.02.96 Bamana Dibateza W PTS 8 Cardiff
16.05.96 Billy Schwer L RSC 3 Dunstable
Career: 15 contests, won 13, lost 2.

Craig Joseph
Bradford. *Born* Bradford, 15 December, 1968
L. Heavyweight. Ht. 6'0"
Manager J. Doughty

04.10.93 Pat McNamara W RSC 2 Bradford
07.02.94 Jimmy Tyers W PTS 6 Bradford
27.04.94 Chris Davies W PTS 6 Solihull
13.06.94 Spencer Alton W PTS 6 Bradford
24.10.94 Martin Jolley W PTS 6 Bradford
20.02.95 Ray Webb L PTS 6 Glasgow
26.04.95 Neil Simpson W PTS 6 Solihull
20.10.95 Thomas Hansvoll L PTS 4 Copenhagen, Denmark
07.03.96 P. R. Mason W PTS 6 Bradford
09.04.96 Fran Harding DREW 6 Salford
Career: 10 contests, won 7, drew 1, lost 2.

Michael Joyce
Huddersfield. *Born* Huddersfield, 4 February, 1967
Cruiserweight. Ht. 5'10½"
Manager C. Aston

05.02.96 P. R. Mason L RSC 4 Bradford
Career: 1 contest, lost 1.

Peter Judson
Keighley. *Born* Keighley, 14 January, 1970
S. Featherweight. Ht. 5'7"
Manager N. Basso/F. Warren

24.04.89 Darryl Pettit DREW 6 Bradford
11.07.89 Neil Leitch W PTS 6 Batley
18.09.89 Phil Lashley W PTS 6 Mayfair
02.10.89 Stevie Woods L PTS 6 Bradford
22.11.89 Pete Buckley L PTS 6 Stafford
19.02.90 Phil Lashley W CO 6 Nottingham
08.03.90 Wayne Goult L PTS 6 Peterborough
19.03.90 Andrew Robinson W PTS 6 Grimsby
26.03.90 Wayne Marston W PTS 6 Nottingham
30.04.90 Derek Amory L PTS 6 Brierley Hill
09.05.90 Brian Robb W PTS 6 Solihull
04.06.90 Jamie McBride L PTS 8 Glasgow
17.09.90 Mark Geraghty W PTS 8 Glasgow
26.09.90 Carl Roberts W PTS 6 Manchester
08.10.90 Mark Geraghty L PTS 8 Glasgow
19.11.90 Russell Davison L PTS 8 Manchester
27.11.90 Rocky Lawlor W PTS 8 Wolverhampton
29.01.91 Russell Davison L PTS 10 Stockport
(Vacant Central Area Featherweight Title)
21.02.91 Noel Carroll W PTS 8 Leeds
20.03.91 Colin Lynch W RTD 5 Solihull
01.05.91 Jimmy Owens L PTS 6 Liverpool
28.05.91 Scott Durham L PTS 6 Cardiff
24.09.91 Ian McGirr L PTS 6 Glasgow
11.11.91 Miguel Matthews W PTS 6 Stratford upon Avon
18.11.91 Jamie McBride DREW 6 Glasgow
09.02.92 Ceri Farrell W PTS 6 Bradford
05.04.92 Barrie Kelley W PTS 6 Bradford
14.11.92 J. T. Williams DREW 6 Cardiff
25.02.93 Dominic McGuigan DREW 6 Bradford
16.05.94 Carlos Chase W PTS 4 Heathrow

25.03.95 Sugar Gibiliru W PTS 6 Chester
06.05.95 Colin McMillan L PTS 8 Shepton Mallet
30.09.95 Daniel Alicea L PTS 6 Cardiff
16.03.96 Cassius Baloyi L PTS 6 Glasgow
Career: 34 contests, won 17, drew 4, lost 13.

Peter Judson   Harry Goodwin

David Jules
Doncaster. *Born* Doncaster, 11 July, 1965
Heavyweight. Ht. 6'2"
Manager J. Rushton

12.06.87 Carl Timbrell W CO 5 Leamington
07.10.87 Carl Timbrell L RSC 3 Stoke
17.03.88 Peter Fury W RTD 2 Sunderland
21.03.88 Jess Harding L RSC 2 Bethnal Green
29.09.88 Gary McCrory L PTS 6 Sunderland
22.11.88 Gary McCrory L PTS 6 Marton
05.12.88 Denroy Bryan DREW 6 Dudley
18.01.89 Denroy Bryan W RSC 2 Stoke
22.02.89 Tony Hallett W RSC 1 Doncaster
19.04.89 Rocky Burton L RSC 3 Doncaster
11.11.89 Jimmy di Stolfo W RSC 1 Rimini, Italy
30.11.89 Biagio Chianese L RSC 2 Milan, Italy
19.02.90 Vance Idiens L PTS 6 Birmingham
07.05.90 Ramon Voorn L RSC 3 Arnhem, Holland
12.11.90 Steve Garber L RSC 6 Bradford
09.04.91 Herbie Hide L RSC 1 Mayfair
05.12.91 Vance Idiens L RSC 4 Cannock
24.02.92 Rocky Burton W CO 1 Coventry
05.04.92 Steve Garber L RSC 4 Bradford
08.09.92 Wayne Buck L RSC 3 Doncaster
09.12.92 Vance Idiens L PTS 8 Stoke
10.05.93 Steve Lewsam L CO 6 Cleethorpes
28.10.93 Joey Paladino L PTS 2 Walsall
10.12.94 Darren Corbett L RSC 1 Manchester
14.06.95 Martin Langtry L RSC 3 Batley
08.11.95 Shane Woollas L PTS 6 Scunthorpe
15.12.95 Mika Kihlstrom L RSC 2 Bethnal Green
31.01.96 Shane Woollas W PTS 6 Stoke
16.03.96 Chris Woollas L PTS 6 Sheffield

25.03.96 Andy Lambert L RSC 1 Birmingham
24.04.96 Kevin Burton W PTS 6 Stoke
10.05.96 Steve Bristow L RSC 2 Liverpool
Career: 32 contests, won 8, drew 1, lost 23.

John Kaighin
Swansea. *Born* Brecknock, 26 August, 1967
L. Heavyweight. Ht. 5'11¾"
Manager M. Copp

17.09.90 Carlos Christie L PTS 6 Cardiff
24.09.90 James F. Woolley L PTS 6 Lewisham
15.10.90 Max McCracken L PTS 6 Brierley Hill
22.10.90 Stefan Wright L PTS 6 Peterborough
15.11.90 Tony Wellington W PTS 6 Oldham
13.12.90 Nick Manners L CO 3 Dewsbury
24.01.91 Robert Peel L PTS 6 Gorseinon
12.02.91 Robert Peel W PTS 6 Cardiff
15.03.91 Max McCracken DREW 6 Willenhall
10.04.91 Darron Griffiths L PTS 6 Newport
24.04.91 Paul Murray W PTS 6 Aberavon
08.05.91 Benji Good W RSC 3 Kensington
15.05.91 Robert Peel L PTS 8 Swansea
06.06.91 Peter Vosper DREW 6 Barking
30.06.91 John Ogistie L PTS 6 Southwark
29.08.91 Adrian Wright W PTS 6 Oakengates
09.09.91 Terry Johnson W RTD 2 Liverpool
11.09.91 Lester Jacobs L RSC 2 Hammersmith
22.10.91 Andy Wright DREW 6 Wandsworth
13.11.91 Garry Delaney L PTS 6 Bethnal Green
20.11.91 Keith Inglis W RSC 1 Kensington
23.01.92 Michael Gale L PTS 8 York
01.02.92 Paul Busby L PTS 4 Birmingham
25.02.92 Andy Wright L PTS 6 Crystal Palace
05.03.92 Lester Jacobs L RSC 1 Battersea
27.04.92 Bruce Scott L CO 4 Mayfair
18.07.92 Carl Harney L PTS 6 Manchester
15.09.92 Paul Wright L DIS 5 Liverpool
26.09.92 Shaun Cummins L RTD 4 Earls Court
28.10.92 Joey Peters DREW 4 Kensington
12.11.92 Graham Jenner L RSC 5 Baywater
01.12.92 Peter Vosper W RSC 4 Bristol
22.12.92 Darrit Douglas W PTS 6 Mayfair
14.01.93 Ole Klemetsen L RTD 3 Mayfair
24.03.93 Darron Griffiths L RSC 6 Cardiff
(Vacant Welsh S. Middleweight Title)
28.04.93 Ray Kane L PTS 6 Dublin
23.05.93 Mark Prince L RSC 3 Brockley
25.07.93 Maurice Core L PTS 6 Oldham
22.09.93 Sammy Storey L PTS 6 Bethnal Green
07.10.93 Michael Gale L PTS 8 York
16.10.93 Noel Magee L PTS 6 Belfast
08.11.93 Garry Delaney L CO 1 Bethnal Green
18.12.93 Fran Harding L PTS 6 Manchester
16.02.94 Shaun Cummins L RSC 3 Stevenage
11.10.95 Kevin Burton W CO 1 Stoke
Career: 45 contests, won 11, drew 4, lost 30.

Prince Kasi Kaihau
Doncaster. *Born* Doncaster, 3 October, 1967
L. Middleweight. Ht. 5'11"
Manager J. Rushton

12.10.93 Prince Louis W PTS 6 Wolverhampton
24.11.93 Steve Levene W PTS 6 Solihull
13.12.93 Rob Stevenson W RSC 5 Doncaster
07.03.94 Steve Levene W RSC 3 Doncaster
10.05.94 Billy McDougall W RTD 4 Doncaster
12.09.94 Rick North W PTS 6 Doncaster
12.10.94 Andy Peach W PTS 6 Stoke
30.11.94 Billy McDougall W PTS 6 Solihull

12.12.94	Andy Peach W PTS 6 Doncaster	
28.03.95	David Bain L PTS 6 Wolverhampton	
05.05.95	Andy Peach W PTS 6 Doncaster	
02.11.95	Robbie Bell L PTS 6 Houghton le Spring	
26.01.96	Ozzy Orrock W RSC 5 Doncaster	
29.03.96	Chris Pollock L RSC 2 Doncaster	
10.05.96	Jon Stocks L PTS 6 Liverpool	
28.05.96	Neil Sinclair L RSC 2 Belfast	

Career: 16 contests, won 11, lost 5.

Charlie Kane

Clydebank. *Born* Glasgow, 2 July, 1968
L. Welterweight. Ht. 5'10½"
Manager T. Gilmour

05.03.91	Dean Bramhald W RSC 6 Glasgow
21.10.91	James Jiora W PTS 6 Glasgow
24.02.92	Karl Taylor W PTS 8 Glasgow
10.12.92	Mick Mulcahy W RSC 2 Glasgow
07.11.93	Mick Mulcahy W RSC 2 Glasgow
25.11.93	John Smith W PTS 6 Tynemouth
02.03.94	Micky Hall W RSC 2 Glasgow
28.03.94	John Smith W PTS 6 Musselburgh
24.10.94	Shaun Cogan W PTS 10 Glasgow
	(Elim. British L. Welterweight Title)
28.10.95	Ross Hale L CO 2 Bristol
	(British & Commonwealth L. Welterweight Title Challenge)
22.04.96	Paul King W PTS 8 Glasgow

Career: 11 contests, won 10, lost 1.

Ray Kane

Belfast. *Born* Dublin, 4 June, 1968
Cruiserweight. Ht. 6'0"
Manager B. Eastwood

07.09.91	R. F. McKenzie W PTS 4 Belfast
11.12.91	Chris Coughlan W PTS 6 Dublin
28.04.93	John Kaighin W PTS 6 Dublin
05.05.93	Johnny Uphill W CO 2 Belfast
16.10.93	Jason McNeill W PTS 6 Belfast
12.03.94	Kent Davis W PTS 6 Cardiff
21.05.94	Nicky Wadman W PTS 6 Belfast
12.11.94	Steve Osborne W PTS 6 Dublin
14.04.95	Bobbi Joe Edwards W PTS 6 Belfast
27.05.95	Bobbi Joe Edwards W PTS 6 Belfast
02.03.96	Crawford Ashley L CO 2 Newcastle

Career: 11 contests, won 10, lost 1.

(Sunday) Sandy Katerega

Canning Town. *Born* Uganda, 6 July, 1969
L. Middleweight. Ht. 5'6"
Manager Self

25.03.95	Julian Eavis W PTS 6 Millwall
02.09.95	J. P. Matthews L PTS 4 Wembley

Career: 2 contests, won 1, lost 1.

John Keeton

Sheffield. *Born* Sheffield, 19 May, 1972
Cruiserweight. Ht. 6'0"
Manager Self

11.08.93	Tony Colclough W RSC 1 Mansfield
15.09.93	Val Golding L PTS 6 Ashford
27.10.93	Darren McKenna W RSC 3 Stoke
01.12.93	Julius Francis L PTS 4 Bethnal Green
19.01.94	Dennis Bailey W RTD 2 Stoke
17.02.94	Dermot Gascoyne L RSC 1 Dagenham
09.04.94	Eddie Knight W RTD 5 Mansfield
11.05.94	John Rice W RSC 5 Sheffield
02.06.94	Devon Rhooms W RSC 2 Tooting

06.09.94	Mark Walker W RSC 5 Stoke
24.09.94	Dirk Wallyn L CO 3 Middlekerke, Belgium
26.10.94	Lee Archer W PTS 6 Stoke
09.12.94	Bruce Scott L CO 2 Bethnal Green
11.02.95	Rudiger May L PTS 6 Frankfurt, Germany
06.03.95	Simon McDougall W RSC 5 Mayfair
07.07.95	Nicky Piper L RTD 2 Cardiff
15.09.95	Steve Osborne W RSC 4 Mansfield
27.10.95	Nicky Wadman W RSC 1 Brighton
03.11.95	Monty Wright W RSC 4 Dudley
11.11.95	Denzil Browne W RSC 4 Halifax
30.01.96	Cesar Kazadi W RSC 3 Lille, France
11.05.96	Terry Dunstan L RSC 1 Bethnal Green
	(British Cruiserweight Title Challenge)

Career: 22 contests, won 14, lost 8.

David Kehoe

Witham. *Born* Northampton, 24 December, 1972
Lightweight. Ht. 5'10½"
Manager F. King

06.02.96	Simon Frailing W CO 1 Basildon
20.04.96	Paul Salmon W PTS 6 Brentwood

Career: 2 contests, won 2.

David Kehoe   Les Clark

Barrie Kelley

Llanelli. *Born* Llanelli, 14 February, 1972
Former Welsh S. Featherweight Champion.
Ht. 5'6"
Manager Self

16.10.90	Ervine Blake W PTS 6 Evesham
21.11.90	Tony Falcone W PTS 6 Chippenham
29.11.90	John O'Meara W RSC 5 Bayswater
24.01.91	Martin Evans W PTS 6 Gorseinon
18.02.91	Tony Falcone L RSC 6 Mayfair
26.03.91	Dennis Adams W PTS 6 Bethnal Green
18.07.91	Robert Smyth DREW 6 Cardiff
16.09.91	Dominic McGuigan DREW 6 Mayfair
14.10.91	Michael Armstrong L CO 4 Manchester
20.11.91	Neil Haddock L PTS 6 Cardiff

03.02.92	Noel Carroll L PTS 8 Manchester
18.03.92	Mark Geraghty L PTS 8 Glasgow
05.04.92	Peter Judson L PTS 6 Bradford
30.09.92	Dean Bramhald W PTS 6 Solihull
28.10.92	Derek Amory W PTS 6 Cardiff
19.01.93	Edward Lloyd W PTS 10 Cardiff
	(Vacant Welsh S. Featherweight Title)
10.11.93	J. T. Williams L RTD 3 Ystrad
	(Welsh S. Featherweight Title Defence)
24.02.94	Peter Till L PTS 6 Walsall
19.11.94	Marcus McCrae W PTS 6 Cardiff
31.03.95	Mike Anthony Brown L RSC 2 Crystal Palace
04.06.95	Paul Webster L RTD 1 Bethnal Green
10.11.95	Michael Hermon DREW 8 Bristol
12.01.96	Dennis Pedersen L RSC 4 Copenhagen, Denmark

Career: 23 contests, won 9, drew 3, lost 11.

Craig Kelley

Dyfed. *Born* Swansea, 6 November, 1975
S. Featherweight. Ht. 5'8"
Manager B. Aird

25.01.94	Simon Frailing W PTS 4 Piccadilly
25.02.94	John Sillo L PTS 6 Cardiff
27.08.94	Dean Phillips L RSC 4 Cardiff
20.01.95	Jason Hutson W RSC 2 Bethnal Green
25.03.95	Gary Thornhill L PTS 6 Chester
20.09.95	Marc Smith L RSC 1 Ystrad
20.12.95	Tommy Janes L PTS 6 Usk

Career: 7 contests, won 2, lost 5.

John T. Kelly

Hartlepool. *Born* Hartlepool, 12 June, 1970
Lightweight. Ht. 5'7"
Manager T. Conroy

22.10.92	Tanveer Ahmed L PTS 6 Glasgow
02.11.92	Kevin Lowe W PTS 6 Liverpool
01.12.92	Wayne Rigby W PTS 6 Hartlepool
15.02.93	Kevin McKillan L PTS 6 Manchester
09.03.93	Michael Alexander W PTS 6 Hartlepool
17.04.93	Micky Hall DREW 4 Washington
06.05.93	Alan Graham W PTS 6 Hartlepool
15.09.93	P. J. Gallagher L RSC 2 Bethnal Green
02.12.93	Brian Wright W PTS 6 Hartlepool
02.02.94	Dave McHale L CO 1 Glasgow
13.04.94	Bradley Welsh L PTS 6 Glasgow
06.10.94	Chris Aston DREW 6 Hull
13.10.94	Tim Hill W PTS 6 Houghton le Spring
24.11.94	Dominic McGuigan L PTS 6 Newcastle
05.12.94	Glen Hopkins W PTS 6 Houghton le Spring
16.01.95	Hugh Collins L PTS 6 Musselburgh
16.02.95	Scott Walker L PTS 6 Bury
06.03.95	Steve Tuckett L RSC 3 Bradford
18.05.95	Wayne Rigby L PTS 6 Middleton
22.06.95	Dave Madden W PTS 6 Houghton le Spring
28.09.95	Ram Singh W PTS 6 Sunderland
09.10.95	T. J. Smith DREW 6 Manchester
29.10.95	Dave Clavering L PTS 6 Shaw
18.11.95	Hugh Collins L PTS 8 Glasgow
07.12.95	Kid McAuley W PTS 6 Sunderland
22.02.96	G. G. Goddard W PTS 6 Sunderland
07.03.96	Jason Blanche DREW 6 Bradford
01.04.96	Jason Blanche DREW 6 Bradford
22.04.96	Ram Singh W PTS 6 Manchester
09.05.96	Wilson Docherty L PTS 8 Glasgow
02.06.96	Gary Hibbert L PTS 6 Shaw

Career: 31 contests, won 12, drew 5, lost 14.

Lyndon Kershaw

Halifax. *Born* Halifax, 17 September, 1972
Bantamweight. Ht. 5'6"
Manager T. Callighan

19.10.92	Stevie Woods W PTS 6 Glasgow
14.12.92	Louis Veitch DREW 6 Bradford
26.04.93	Golfraz Ahmed W PTS 6 Bradford
24.05.93	Anthony Hanna W PTS 6 Bradford
07.10.93	Louis Veitch L PTS 10 Hull
	(*Vacant Central Area Flyweight Title*)
06.12.93	Ian Baillie W PTS 6 Bradford
02.03.94	Tiger Singh W PTS 6 Solihull
27.04.94	Mark Cokely W PTS 6 Solihull
09.05.94	Ian Baillie W PTS 6 Bradford
15.06.94	Mickey Cantwell W PTS 8 Southwark
02.11.94	Louis Veitch L PTS 10 Solihull
	(*Central Area Flyweight Title Challenge*)
13.01.95	Jesper D. Jensen L PTS 6 Aalborg, Denmark
20.02.95	Keith Knox DREW 6 Glasgow
08.03.95	Tiger Singh W PTS 6 Solihull
21.05.95	Jaji Sibali L RTD 8 Cape Town, South Africa
11.10.95	Ady Benton L RTD 6 Solihull
11.12.95	Marcus Duncan L RSC 6 Morecambe
	(*Vacant Central Area Bantamweight Title*)
22.02.96	Chip O'Neill W PTS 6 Sunderland
13.04.96	Peter Culshaw L RSC 3 Liverpool
25.06.96	Spencer Oliver L RSC 3 Stevenage

Career: 20 contests, won 10, drew 2, lost 8.

Paul King

Newcastle. *Born* Newcastle, 3 June, 1965
Northern Area Welterweight Champion. Ht. 5'8½"
Manager Self

04.09.87	Willie MacDonald W PTS 6 Gateshead
03.11.87	Mick Mason L PTS 6 Sunderland
24.11.87	Mick Mason L PTS 6 Marton
31.01.89	Jim Larmour W RTD 4 Glasgow
27.02.90	Ian Thomas W PTS 6 Marton
06.03.90	Mick Duncan W PTS 6 Newcastle
15.11.90	Phil Epton W PTS 6 Oldham
28.02.91	Dave Kettlewell W RSC 1 Sunderland
21.03.91	Phil Epton W PTS 6 Dewsbury
13.05.91	Shamus Casey L PTS 6 Northampton
31.05.91	Gordon Blair L PTS 8 Glasgow
09.10.91	Delroy Waul L RSC 6 Manchester
29.09.92	Howard Clarke L PTS 6 Stoke
16.03.93	Howard Clarke L PTS 6 Edgbaston
29.04.93	Hughie Davey W PTS 6 Newcastle
29.06.93	Howard Clarke L PTS 6 Edgbaston
14.08.93	Gary Logan L CO 2 Hammersmith
28.11.93	Gary Logan L CO 4 Southwark
03.03.94	Hughie Davey W PTS 10 Newcastle
	(*Vacant Northern Area Welterweight Title*)
02.03.95	Peter Reid W RSC 3 Cramlington
20.04.95	Craig Winter L RSC 4 Liverpool
12.06.95	Derek Roche L PTS 6 Bradford
23.11.95	Kevin McKenzie L PTS 6 Marton
	(*Northern Area Welterweight Title Defence*)
12.01.96	Frank Olsen L RTD 4 Copenhagen, Denmark
02.03.96	Kevin McKenzie W RSC 2 Newcastle
	(*Northern Area Welterweight Title Challenge*)
22.04.96	Charlie Kane L PTS 8 Glasgow
08.06.96	Kevin Lueshing L RSC 2 Newcastle

Career: 27 contests, won 11, lost 16.

Neil Kirkwood　　　　　Les Clark

Neil Kirkwood

Barnsley. *Born* Barnsley, 30 November, 1969
Central Area Heavyweight Champion. Ht. 6'4"
Manager S. Doyle

17.03.94	Gary Williams W RSC 1 Lincoln
16.05.94	Joey Paladino W RSC 2 Cleethorpes
26.08.94	Shane Woollas W RSC 6 Barnsley
11.03.95	Carl Gaffney W RSC 2 Barnsley
	(*Vacant Central Area Heavyweight Title*)
24.10.95	Julius Francis L RSC 7 Southwark

Career: 5 contests, won 4, lost 1.

Adrian Kneeshaw

Leeds. *Born* Wakefield, 19 June, 1968
Heavyweight. Ht. 6'2"
Manager B. Ingle

15.09.95	Gary Williams L RSC 6 Mansfield

Career: 1 contest, lost 1.

Eddie Knight

Ashford. *Born* Ashford, 4 October, 1966
L. Heavyweight. Ht. 5'11"
Manager Self

05.10.92	Shaun McCrory L PTS 6 Bristol
29.10.92	Adrian Wright L PTS 6 Bayswater
25.11.92	Julian Johnson L RSC 2 Mayfair
15.09.93	Terry Duffus W PTS 6 Ashford
09.04.94	John Keeton L RTD 5 Mansfield
27.05.94	Lee Sara W CO 2 Ashford
09.07.94	Mark Delaney L CO 4 Earls Court
17.09.94	Mark Hale W PTS 6 Crawley
13.12.94	Tim Robinson W RTD 2 Potters Bar
09.05.95	Mark Delaney L RSC 2 Basildon
30.01.96	Graham Townsend W PTS 4 Barking
04.03.96	Marko Salminen W RSC 2 Helsinki, Finland

Career: 12 contests, won 6, lost 6.

Paul Knights

Redhill. *Born* Redhill, 5 February, 1971
L. Welterweight. Ht. 5'10"
Manager B. Hearn

26.11.91	Steve Hearn W RSC 4 Bethnal Green
19.02.92	Seth Jones W RSC 5 Muswell Hill
16.06.92	Seth Jones W PTS 6 Dagenham
10.11.92	Alex Moffatt W CO 3 Dagenham
30.01.93	Dave Lovell W PTS 6 Brentwood
20.04.93	Mark Allen W PTS 6 Brentwood
26.06.93	Phil Found W PTS 4 Earls Court
28.09.93	Pat Delargy W RSC 3 Bethnal Green
11.01.94	Brian Coleman W RSC 4 Bethnal Green
09.02.94	Mark Allen W RSC 2 Brentwood
19.03.94	Alan Peacock W PTS 6 Millwall
11.06.94	John O. Johnson L PTS 6 Bethnal Green
17.09.94	Dewi Roberts W PTS 6 Crawley
17.02.95	Norman Dhalie W RTD 5 Crawley
16.03.95	Brian Coleman W RSC 2 Basildon
09.05.95	Alan Peacock W PTS 6 Basildon
28.10.95	Tony Swift W PTS 6 Kensington
23.01.96	Karl Taylor DREW 6 Bethnal Green

Career: 18 contests, won 16, drew 1, lost 1.

Keith Knox

Bonnyrigg. *Born* Edinburgh, 20 June, 1967
Scottish Flyweight Champion. Ht. 5'3"
Manager T. Gilmour

04.03.94	Ian Bailie W CO 3 Irvine
28.03.94	Terry Gaskin W PTS 6 Musselburgh
20.09.94	Tiger Singh W PTS 6 Musselburgh
21.11.94	Neil Parry W PTS 6 Glasgow
16.01.95	Neil Parry W PTS 6 Musselburgh
20.02.95	Lyndon Kershaw DREW 6 Glasgow
05.04.95	Louis Veitch DREW 6 Irvine
18.09.95	Shaun Norman W PTS 8 Glasgow
20.11.95	Louis Veitch W RSC 6 Glasgow
	(*Vacant Scottish Flyweight Title. Elim. British Flyweight Title*)
21.03.96	Mickey Cantwell L PTS 12 Southwark
	(*Vacant British Flyweight Title*)

Career: 10 contests, won 7, drew 2, lost 1.

Andy Lambert

Birmingham. *Born* Selly Oak, 22 July, 1962
Heavyweight. Ht. 6'4"
Manager E. Cashmore

25.03.96	David Jules W RSC 1 Birmingham
21.05.96	Jim Pallatt W RSC 1 Edgbaston
25.06.96	Pele Reid L CO 1 Mansfield

Career: 3 contests, won 2, lost 1.

Gavin Lane (Keeble)

Paignton. *Born* Rainham, 14 July, 1971
L. Middleweight. Ht. 5'11¼"
Manager G. Bousted

28.11.91	Dewi Roberts W PTS 6 Evesham
30.03.92	Razza Campbell L PTS 6 Coventry
27.05.93	Sean Baker L PTS 8 Bristol
28.10.93	Kevin Mabbutt L PTS 6 Torquay
20.09.95	John Janes L PTS 6 Ystrad
26.03.96	James McGee W PTS 6 Wolverhampton
29.05.96	John Janes L PTS 6 Ebbw Vale

Career: 7 contests, won 2, lost 5.

Martin Langtry

Lincon. *Born* Hampstead, 22 May, 1964
Midlands Area Cruiserweight Champion.
Ht. 5'10"
Manager Self

29.04.93	Stevie R. Davies W RSC 2 Newcastle
12.05.93	Simon McDougall W PTS 6 Sheffield
20.09.93	John Pierre W PTS 6 Cleethorpes
13.12.93	Steve Osborne W PTS 6 Cleethorpes
17.03.94	Lee Archer W CO 4 Lincoln
26.08.94	Steve Osborne W PTS 8 Barnsley
26.04.95	Andrew Benson W PTS 6 Solihull
16.05.95	L. A. Williams W CO 2 Cleethorpes
14.06.95	David Jules W RSC 3 Batley
18.10.95	Steve Osborne W RSC 6 Batley
21.02.96	Nigel Rafferty W CO 4 Batley
	(Midlands Area Cruiserweight Title Challenge)
30.05.96	Chris Woollas W RSC 6 Lincoln
	(Midlands Area Cruiserweight Title Defence)

Career: 12 contests, won 12.

David Larkin

Leeds. *Born* Pontefract, 26 April, 1972
Middleweight. Ht. 5'10½"
Manager H. Hayes

29.10.92	Rick North W PTS 6 Leeds
07.04.93	Cliff Churchward W RSC 4 Leeds
19.05.93	Ray Golding W PTS 6 Sunderland
01.07.93	David Sumner W CO 5 York
07.10.93	Lee Crocker W RSC 5 York
26.10.94	Andrew Jervis W CO 5 Leeds
03.03.95	Robert Peel L PTS 6 Bethnal Green
08.07.95	Carl Winstone W RSC 2 York
28.09.95	Mickey Johnson L PTS 6 Sunderland
16.10.95	Butch Lesley W RSC 4 Mayfair
06.03.96	Darren Sweeney L PTS 6 Solihull
24.03.96	Scott Beasley W RTD 3 Shaw
03.05.96	Michael Pinnock DREW 6 Sheffield

Career: 13 contests, won 9, drew 1, lost 3.

Phil Lashley

Birmingham. *Born* Birmingham, 1 May, 1965
S. Featherweight. Ht. 5'5"
Manager Self

27.04.86	Ronnie Stephenson L PTS 4 Doncaster
30.05.86	David Beech L PTS 6 Stoke
10.09.86	Gypsy Johnny W RSC 1 Stoke
17.09.86	Paul Hodkinson L RSC 2 Kensington
10.11.86	Roy Williams W CO 1 Birmingham
18.11.86	Dean Lynch L PTS 6 Swansea
08.12.86	Frank Monkhouse L RSC 4 Birmingham
28.01.87	Shane Porter L RSC 1 Dudley
03.03.87	John Carlin L PTS 6 Livingston
24.03.87	John Carlin W RSC 1 Wolverhampton
08.04.87	Gary King L CO 1 Evesham
13.10.87	Mick Greenwood L PTS 6 Wolverhampton
09.11.87	Ronnie Stephenson DREW 4 Birmingham
24.11.87	Mark Goult L CO 1 Wisbech
14.02.88	Steve Pike L CO 1 Peterborough
21.03.88	Dean Lynch L PTS 6 Bethnal Green
13.04.88	Paul Bowen W RSC 1 Wolverhampton
20.04.88	Chris Cooper W PTS 6 Torquay
23.05.88	Roy Williams W RSC 2 Mayfair
09.09.88	Ronnie Stephenson W PTS 6 Doncaster
29.09.88	Peter Gabbitus L CO 2 Stafford
14.11.88	Mark Antony L RSC 2 Stratford upon Avon
02.02.89	Lester James L PTS 4 Wolverhampton
28.02.89	Lester James L PTS 6 Dudley
15.03.89	Andrew Robinson L PTS 6 Stoke
17.04.89	Lester James L RSC 5 Birmingham
28.06.89	Jamie Morris L RSC 1 Kenilworth
18.09.89	Peter Judson L PTS 6 Mayfair
04.10.89	Craig Garbutt L PTS 6 Stafford
16.10.89	Neil Leitch L PTS 6 Manchester
30.10.89	Gary Hickman L RSC 4 Piccadilly
28.11.89	Neil Leitch L PTS 6 Wolverhampton
04.12.89	Neil Leitch L PTS 6 Grimsby
12.12.89	John O'Meara L CO 3 Brentford
08.02.90	Jason Primera L PTS 6 Southwark
19.02.90	Peter Judson L CO 6 Nottingham
19.03.90	Neil Leitch L PTS 6 Grimsby
27.03.90	Ronnie Stephenson W PTS 6 Wolverhampton
21.05.90	Ronnie Stephenson L PTS 6 Grimsby
04.06.90	Elvis Parsley L RSC 3 Birmingham
23.01.91	Mark Bates L RTD 3 Brentwood
04.03.91	Dave Annis W CO 2 Birmingham
01.05.91	Mark Bates L PTS 6 Bethnal Green
04.06.91	Paul Donaghey L CO 1 Bethnal Green
21.10.91	Ronnie Stephenson L PTS 6 Cleethorpes
21.11.91	Ronnie Stephenson L PTS 6 Stafford
30.03.92	Jamie McBride L RSC 1 Glasgow
05.10.92	Chip O'Neill L PTS 6 Manchester
12.05.93	Gary Marston L RSC 2 Stoke
16.03.96	Wayne Jones L PTS 6 Barnstaple
27.03.96	Robert Grubb L PTS 6 Stoke

Career: 51 contests, won 9, drew 1, lost 41.

Tommy Lawler

Kilcullen. *Born* Kilcullen, 24 May, 1973
Welterweight. Ht. 5'6½"
Manager Self

02.07.95	Brian Coleman W PTS 4 Dublin
21.09.95	Wahid Fats W PTS 4 Battersea
19.01.96	Anthony Campbell L PTS 4 Bracknell

Career: 3 contests, won 2, lost 1.

Tommy Lawler   Les Clark

Gareth Lawrence

Gilfach Goch. *Born* Pontypridd, 1 February, 1975
Lightweight. Ht. 5'6½"
Manager D. Gardiner

25.01.95	Anthony Campbell W PTS 6 Cardiff
08.03.95	Phil Found W PTS 6 Cardiff
17.06.95	Dean Amory W RSC 2 Cardiff
08.11.95	Nelson Ide W RSC 5 Bethnal Green
20.12.95	Kid McAuley W PTS 6 Usk
25.05.96	Ruslan Smolenkov W PTS 6 St Petersburg, Russia

Career: 6 contests, won 6.

(Ian) Pele Lawrence

Sheffield. *Born* Sheffield, 20 November, 1968
S. Middleweight. Ht. 6'0"
Manager Self

06.04.90	P. D. Taylor W PTS 6 Telford
24.04.90	Mark Bowen L CO 5 Eltham
18.09.90	Adrian Wright L CO 2 Stoke
15.02.96	Chris Woollas L RSC 6 Sheffield

Career: 4 contests, won 1, lost 3.

Danny Lawson

Plymouth. *Born* Plymouth, 27 May, 1971
Bantamweight. Ht. 5'5¾"
Manager D. Sullivan

17.06.94	Danny Ruegg W PTS 6 Plymouth
07.10.94	Jobie Tyers L PTS 6 Taunton
07.02.95	Mark Reynolds L PTS 4 Ipswich
06.05.95	Tony Falcone L RSC 2 Shepton Mallet
20.03.96	Henry Jones L CO 1 Cardiff

Career: 5 contests, won 1, lost 4.

Paul Lawson

Bethnal Green. *Born* Dundee, 2 December, 1966
Cruiserweight. Ht. 6'3"
Manager F. Maloney

15.09.93	Bobby Mack W PTS 4 Bethnal Green
13.10.93	Art Stacey W RSC 2 Bethnal Green
01.12.93	Des Vaughan W RSC 3 Bethnal Green
09.02.94	Nicky Wadman W RSC 1 Bethnal Green
29.03.94	Terry Duffus W RSC 1 Bethnal Green
15.06.94	Art Stacey W RSC 2 Southwark
24.09.94	Lennie Howard W RSC 2 Wembley
25.10.94	Newby Stevens W RSC 2 Southwark
13.12.94	Nigel Rafferty W RSC 4 Ilford
23.02.95	Chris Okoh L RSC 5 Southwark
	(Vacant Southern Area Cruiserweight Title)
17.05.95	Andrew Benson W RSC 2 Ipswich
02.07.95	Newby Stevens W RSC 6 Dublin
29.09.95	Nigel Rafferty W PTS 6 Bethnal Green
08.11.95	Chris Okoh L RSC 1 Bethnal Green
	(Commonwealth Cruiserweight Title Challenge)

Career: 14 contests, won 12, lost 2.

Mark Legg

Newcastle. *Born* South Shields, 25 March, 1970
L. Welterweight. Ht. 5'9½"
Manager T. Callighan

28.02.92	Chris Aston W RSC 5 Irvine

17.03.92 Dean Hiscox W PTS 6 Wolverhampton
18.05.92 Charles Shepherd L PTS 6 Marton
24.09.92 Ricky Sackfield W PTS 6 Stockport
25.11.93 Gary Hiscox W RSC 3 Tynemouth
07.02.94 Erwin Edwards W RSC 6 Bradford
02.03.94 Phil Found L RTD 4 Solihull
10.05.94 John O. Johnson L RSC 6 Doncaster
02.11.94 Alan Peacock W PTS 6 Solihull
21.11.94 Steve McLevy L RSC 5 Glasgow
21.02.95 Bernard Paul L RSC 4 Sunderland
26.04.95 Steve Howden W RTD 2 Stoke
10.06.95 Juha Temonen L PTS 4 Pori, Finland
15.09.95 Steve Tuckett L PTS 6 Darlington
22.03.96 Gary Beardsley L PTS 6 Mansfield
22.04.96 Mark Breslin L PTS 8 Glasgow
Career: 16 contests, won 7, lost 9.

Niel Leggett

Peterborough. *Born* Boreham, 10
December, 1966
Lightweight. Ht. 5'6"
Manager J. Cox

14.02.88 Jimmy Vincent W PTS 6 Peterborough
29.02.88 Steve Winstanley L PTS 6 Bradford
09.04.88 Paul Moylett L PTS 6 Bristol
17.04.88 Steve Winstanley DREW 6
          Peterborough
05.09.88 Tony Dore L PTS 6 Glasgow
02.10.88 Mick Mulcahy DREW 6 Peterborough
10.10.88 Tony Dore L PTS 6 Glasgow
19.10.88 Nigel Wenton L RTD 2 Belfast
03.04.95 Andrew Smith W PTS 6 Northampton
22.06.95 Glen Hopkins W PTS 6 Houghton le
          Spring
21.09.95 Matt Brown L PTS 4 Battersea
14.11.95 Michael Brodie L CO 1 Bury
Career: 12 contests, won 3, drew 2, lost 7.

(Herbert) Butch Lesley

Islington. *Born* Chelmsford, 21 April, 1973
S. Middleweight. Ht. 6'2½"
Manager J. Harding

02.09.95 Lester Jacobs L PTS 4 Wembley
16.10.95 David Larkin L RSC 4 Mayfair
23.01.96 Michael Pinnock W PTS 4 Bethnal
          Green
09.04.96 Jerry Mortimer W RSC 3 Stevenage
25.06.96 Graham Townsend L PTS 6 Stevenage
Career: 5 contests, won 2, lost 3.

Delroy Leslie

Wallington, *Born* Jamaica, 22 February,
1970
L. Welterweight. Ht. 5'11½"
Manager Self

29.04.93 Phil Found W PTS 6 Mayfair
14.06.93 Jason Barker W RTD 3 Bayswater
16.09.93 Jamie Davidson W PTS 6 Southwark
06.03.95 Shaun Cogan W RSC 1 Mayfair
20.04.95 Clayton Hollingsworth W PTS 6
          Mayfair
23.06.95 Jonathan Thaxton L PTS 6 Bethnal
          Green
03.12.95 Adrian Chase W RSC 4 Southwark
02.04.96 Richie Edwards L RSC 3 Southwark
Career: 8 contests, won 6, lost 2.

Steve Levene

Birmingham. *Born* Birmingham, 23
September, 1969
L. Middleweight. Ht. 5'8½"
Manager Self

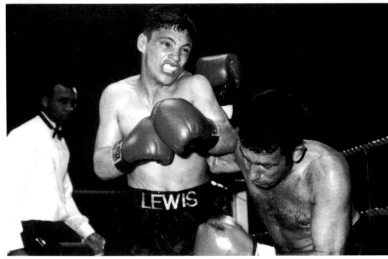

Adey Lewis (left) blasts into Graham McGrath   Les Clark

27.10.92 Steve Scott L RSC 1 Cradley Heath
07.12.92 Warren Stephens W CO 2 Birmingham
16.03.93 Alan Williams W RSC 1 Edgbaston
24.03.93 Sean Baker DREW 6 Belfast
19.04.93 Bullit Andrews W PTS 6 Northampton
18.05.93 Mark Antony L RSC 1 Edgbaston
06.09.93 Danny Peters L RSC 4 Liverpool
24.11.93 Prince Kasi Kaihau L PTS 6 Solihull
06.12.93 Bullit Andrews W RSC 6 Birmingham
17.02.94 Bullit Andrews W PTS 6 Walsall
07.03.94 Prince Kasi Kaihau L RSC 3 Doncaster
20.06.95 Paul Webb W PTS 6 Birmingham
17.10.95 Ozzy Orrock W RSC 1
          Wolverhampton
21.11.95 Roy Gbasai W CO 2 Edgbaston
22.02.96 Andy Peach W PTS 6 Walsall
21.05.96 James McGee L PTS 6 Edgbaston
Career: 16 contests, won 9, drew 1, lost 6.

Steve Levene   Les Clark

(Jason) Jay Levy

Bromley. *Born* Bromley, 1 January, 1970
Lightweight. Ht. 5'6½"
Managers M. Duff/T. Lawless

05.03.96 Brian Robb L RTD 3 Bethnal Green
Career: 1 contest, lost 1.

(Adrian) Adey Lewis

Bury. *Born* Bury, 31 May, 1975
Bantamweight. Ht. 5'0"
Manager J. Doughty/B. Hearn

25.04.94 Darren Greaves W RSC 1 Bury
02.06.94 Dave Campbell W RSC 1 Middleton
22.09.94 Neil Parry W RSC 3 Bury
21.11.94 Daryl McKenzie W RSC 4 Glasgow
17.01.95 Yusuf Vorajee W RSC 2 Worcester
16.02.95 Chip O'Neill W RSC 1 Bury
06.03.95 Mark Cokely W RSC 5 Mayfair
09.05.95 Pete Buckley W PTS 4 Basildon
25.06.96 Graham McGrath W RSC 1 Stevenage
Career: 9 contests, won 9.

Lennox Lewis

Crayford. *Born* London, 2 September, 1965
Former WBC Heavyweight Champion.
Former Undefeated British, European &
Commonwealth Heavyweight Champion.
Ht. 6'4¾"
Manager F. Maloney

27.06.89 Al Malcolm W CO 2 Kensington
21.07.89 Bruce Johnson W RSC 2 Atlantic City,
          USA
25.09.89 Andrew Gerrard W RSC 4 Crystal
          Palace
10.10.89 Steve Garber W CO 1 Hull
05.11.89 Melvin Epps W DIS 2 Kensington
18.12.89 Greg Gorrell W RSC 5 Kitchener,
          Canada
31.01.90 Noel Quarless W RSC 2 Bethnal Green
22.03.90 Calvin Jones W CO 1 Gateshead
14.04.90 Mike Simwelu W CO 1 Kensington
09.05.90 Jorge Dascola W CO 1 Kensington
20.05.90 Dan Murphy W RSC 6 Sheffield

Lennox Lewis

Les Clark

27.06.90	Ossie Ocasio W PTS 8 Kensington
11.07.90	Mike Acey W RSC 2 Mississuaga, Canada
31.10.90	Jean Chanet W RSC 6 Crystal Palace *(European Heavyweight Title Challenge)*
06.03.91	Gary Mason W RSC 7 Wembley *(British Heavyweight Title Challenge. European Heavyweight Title Defence)*
12.07.91	Mike Weaver W CO 6 Lake Tahoe, USA
30.09.91	Glenn McCrory W CO 2 Kensington *(British & European Heavyweight Title Defence)*
21.11.91	Tyrell Biggs W RSC 3 Atlanta, USA
01.02.92	Levi Billups W PTS 10 Las Vegas, USA
30.04.92	Derek Williams W RSC 3 Kensington *(British & European Heavyweight Title Defence. Commonwealth Heavyweight Title Challenge)*
11.08.92	Mike Dixon W RSC 4 Atlantic City, USA
31.10.92	Razor Ruddock W RSC 2 Earls Court *(Final Elim. WBC Heavyweight Title & Commonwealth Heavyweight Title Defence)*

08.05.93	Tony Tucker W PTS 12 Las Vegas, USA *(WBC Heavyweight Title Defence)*
01.10.93	Frank Bruno W RSC 7 Cardiff *(WBC Heavyweight Title Defence)*
06.05.94	Phil Jackson W RSC 8 Atlantic City *(WBC Heavyweight Title Defence)*
24.09.94	Oliver McCall L RSC 2 Wembley *(WBC Heavyweight Title Defence)*
13.05.95	Lionel Butler W RSC 5 Sacramento, USA *(Elim. WBC Heavyweight Title)*
02.07.95	Justin Fortune W RSC 4 Dublin
07.10.95	Tommy Morrison W RSC 6 Atlantic City, USA
10.05.96	Ray Mercer W PTS 10 New York City, USA

Career: 30 contests, won 29, lost 1.

Earl Ling

Norwich. *Born* Kings Lynn, 9 March, 1972
S. Middleweight. Ht. 5'10"
Manager Self

08.09.92	Eddie Collins W PTS 6 Norwich
11.05.93	Mark Hale L RSC 2 Norwich
12.12.94	Clinton Woods L RSC 5 Cleethorpes

04.12.95	Jeff Finlayson L PTS 6 Manchester
26.02.96	Peter Waudby L PTS 6 Hull
19.03.96	James Lowther L RSC 4 Leeds

Career: 6 contests, won 1, lost 5.

Darren Littlewood

Sheffield. *Born* Sheffield, 6 November, 1974
S. Middleweight. Ht. 6'0"
Manager B. Ingle

24.11.93	Mark Smallwood L PTS 8 Solihull
02.12.93	Martin Jolley W PTS 6 Evesham
01.03.94	Joe Calzaghe L RSC 1 Dudley
28.05.94	Dean Francis L PTS 4 Queensway
17.08.94	Chris Woollas L RSC 4 Sheffield
26.10.94	John Duckworth W PTS 6 Stoke
24.11.94	Tim Robinson W PTS 6 Hull
12.12.94	Martin Jolley W PTS 6 Cleethorpes
23.01.95	Roland Ericsson W RSC 4 Bethnal Green
11.11.95	Jetty Williams L PTS 6 Halifax

Career: 10 contests, won 5, lost 5.

Wayne Llewelyn

Deptford. *Born* Greenwich, 20 April, 1970
Heavyweight. Ht. 6'3½"
Manager F. Warren

18.01.92	Chris Coughlan W RSC 3 Kensington
30.03.92	Steve Stewart W RSC 4 Eltham
23.04.92	Gary Charlton W RSC 6 Eltham
10.12.92	Gary McCrory W RSC 2 Glasgow
23.05.93	Cordwell Hylton W PTS 6 Brockley
01.12.93	Manny Burgo W PTS 6 Bethnal Green
14.04.94	Vance Idiens W RSC 1 Battersea
22.05.94	Cordwell Hylton W CO 2 Crystal Palace
03.05.95	Mitch Rose W PTS 4 New York City, USA
07.07.95	Vance Idiens W RSC 1 Cardiff
11.08.95	Carlos Monroe W RSC 3 Louisiana, USA
26.04.96	Steve Garber W CO 1 Cardiff
08.06.96	Dermot Gascoyne W RSC 4 Newcastle

Career: 13 contests, won 13.

Edward Lloyd

Rhyl. *Born* St Asaph, 23 April, 1963
Lightweight. Ht. 5'7½"
Manager Self

07.02.83	Stan Atherton W PTS 6 Liverpool
14.02.83	Sammy Rodgers W RSC 4 Manchester
21.02.83	Paul Cook L RSC 1 Mayfair
27.04.83	Bobby Welburn W PTS 6 Rhyl
09.05.83	Jimmy Thornton L RSC 1 Manchester
16.09.83	Jim Paton L PTS 6 Rhyl
28.11.83	John Murphy L PTS 8 Rhyl
06.02.84	Paul Keers W PTS 6 Liverpool
06.03.84	Gary Felvus L PTS 8 Stoke
12.06.84	Mickey Brooks L RSC 6 St Helens
06.08.84	Henry Arnold W RSC 6 Aintree
15.10.84	Steve Griffith L RTD 4 Liverpool
05.12.84	Jaswant Singh Ark W RSC 2 Stoke
01.02.85	Andy Williams DREW 6 Warrington
29.03.85	Billy Laidman W RSC 2 Liverpool
10.04.85	Brian Roche L RSC 7 Leeds
20.05.85	Gary Flear L PTS 8 Nottingham
19.07.85	Stanley Jones DREW 10 Colwyn Bay *(Vacant Welsh Lightweight Title)*
10.02.86	Peter Bradley L PTS 8 Glasgow
06.03.86	Najib Daho L PTS 8 Manchester

24.11.86 Keith Parry L PTS 8 Cardiff
13.01.87 Sugar Gibiliru W PTS 8 Oldham
09.02.87 Craig Windsor W RSC 1 Cardiff
24.02.87 Alonzo Lopez W RTD 1 Marbella, Spain
31.10.87 Abdeselan Azowogue W PTS 6 Marbella, Spain
30.11.87 Gary Maxwell L PTS 8 Nottingham
01.02.88 Colin Lynch L RTD 4 Northampton
11.02.92 Dewi Roberts W RSC 1 Cardiff
19.05.92 Mervyn Bennett W RSC 5 Cardiff
07.10.92 Steve Robinson L RTD 8 Barry
14.11.92 Carl Hook W PTS 6 Cardiff
19.01.93 Barrie Kelley L PTS 10 Cardiff
(Vacant Welsh S. Featherweight Title)
30.03.93 Nigel Haddock L RTD 4 Cardiff
05.05.93 Francisco Arroyo L RTD 3 Belfast
18.12.93 Jyrki Vierela L PTS 8 Turku, Finland
25.02.94 Gary Thornhill DREW 6 Chester
14.04.94 Felix Kelly W RSC 6 Battersea
29.09.94 Floyd Havard L RSC 4 Bethnal Green
08.03.95 J. T. Williams DREW 10 Cardiff
(Welsh S. Featherweight Title Challenge)
15.03.96 Billy Schwer L RTD 5 Dunstable
Career: 40 contests, won 15, drew 4, lost 21.

Paul Lloyd　　　　　　　　Les Clark

Paul Lloyd

Ellesmere Port. *Born* Bebington, 7 December, 1968
Central Area S. Bantamweight Champion. Ht. 5'7"
Manager J. Hyland

25.09.92 Graham McGrath W RSC 3 Liverpool
23.10.92 Kid McAuley W PTS 4 Liverpool
20.11.92 Des Gargano W PTS 4 Liverpool
15.12.92 Glyn Shepherd W RSC 1 Liverpool
27.02.93 Miguel Matthews W PTS 6 Ellesmere Port
04.05.93 Andrew Bloomer W PTS 6 Liverpool
02.07.93 Ronnie Stephenson W RTD 1 Liverpool

30.10.93 Marty Chestnut W RSC 1 Chester
11.12.93 Gerald Shelton W RSC 3 Liverpool
25.02.94 Ady Benton W RSC 5 Chester
(Vacant Central Area S. Bantamweight Title)
06.05.94 Pete Buckley W RTD 4 Liverpool
26.09.94 Chris Clarkson L RSC 4 Liverpool
25.03.95 Richie Wenton L RSC 5 Chester
(British S. Bantamweight Title Challenge)
16.06.95 Garry Burrell W RSC 2 Liverpool
24.11.95 Michael Parris L RSC 4 Chester
03.02.96 Julian Gomez W CO 2 Liverpool
Career: 16 contests, won 13, lost 3.

Steve Loftus

Stoke. *Born* Stoke, 10 October, 1971
L. Heavyweight. Ht. 6'2½"
Manager Self

29.09.92 Bobby Mack L PTS 6 Stoke
21.10.92 Paul Murray W PTS 6 Stoke
09.12.92 Lee Prudden L PTS 6 Stoke
17.03.93 Chris Nurse L PTS 6 Stoke
12.05.93 Zak Goldman W PTS 6 Stoke
07.09.93 Greg Scott-Briggs L RSC 2 Stoke
01.12.93 Tony Colclough W PTS 6 Stoke
15.03.94 Tim Robinson W PTS 6 Stoke
25.05.94 Mark Hale W PTS 6 Stoke
06.09.94 Mark Hale W PTS 6 Stoke
16.11.94 Paul Murray L PTS 6 Bloomsbury
07.12.94 Paul Murray L PTS 6 Stoke
25.01.95 Robert Harper W PTS 6 Stoke
15.03.95 Pat Durkin W PTS 6 Stoke
26.04.95 Mark Hale W PTS 6 Stoke
06.09.95 Michael Pinnock W PTS 6 Stoke
06.12.95 Robert Harper W PTS 6 Stoke
Career: 17 contests, won 11, lost 6.

Gary Logan

Brixton. *Born* Lambeth, 10 October, 1968
Former Undefeated Southern Area
Welterweight Champion. Ht. 5'8¾"
Manager F. Maloney

05.10.88 Peppy Muire W RTD 3 Wembley
02.11.88 Tony Gibbs W PTS 6 Southwark
07.12.88 Pat Dunne W PTS 6 Piccadilly
12.01.89 Mike Russell W CO 1 Southwark
20.02.89 Dave Griffiths W RSC 5 Mayfair
29.03.89 Ronnie Campbell W PTS 6 Wembley
10.05.89 Tony Britland W CO 1 Kensington
07.06.89 Davey Hughes W CO 1 Wembley
24.08.89 Mike English W CO 2 Tampa, USA
04.10.89 Simon Eubank W PTS 6 Kensington
12.10.89 Jimmy Thornton W PTS 6 Southwark
08.11.89 Chris Blake L PTS 8 Wembley
10.01.90 Julian Eavis W PTS 8 Kensington
03.03.90 Anthony Joe Travis W CO 5 Wembley
09.05.90 Joseph Alexander W PTS 8 Wembley
13.09.90 Manuel Rojas W PTS 8 Watford
16.01.91 Julian Eavis W RSC 5 Kensington
18.02.91 Gordon Blair W CO 1 Mayfair
25.04.91 Trevor Ambrose W PTS 8 Mayfair
17.10.91 Des Robinson W PTS 8 Southwark
15.10.92 Mick Duncan W PTS 8 Lewisham
17.12.92 Roy Rowland W RSC 4 Wembley
(Vacant Southern Area Welterweight Title)
23.05.93 Glyn Rhodes W CO 3 Brockley
25.06.93 Gordon Blair W RSC 6 Battersea
14.08.93 Paul King W CO 2 Hammersmith
28.11.93 Paul King W CO 4 Southwark
11.12.93 Horace Fleary W PTS 8 Dusseldorf, Germany

09.02.94 Graham Cheney L RSC 10 Bethnal Green
(WBC International Welterweight Title Challenge)
29.09.94 Ojay Abrahams W PTS 10 Bethnal Green
(Southern Area Welterweight Title Defence)
25.10.94 Nick Hall DREW 8 Southwark
02.06.95 Del Bryan L RSC 11 Bethnal Green
(British Welterweight Title Challenge)
21.03.96 Paul Wesley W PTS 6 Southwark
13.04.96 Ensley Bingham L RSC 6 Wythenshawe
(British L. Middleweight Title Challenge)
Career: 33 contests, won 28, drew 1, lost 4.

Eamonn Loughran

Ballymena. *Born* Ballymena, 5 June, 1970
Former WBO Welterweight Champion.
Former Undefeated Commonwealth
Welterweight Champion. Ht. 5'9"
Manager B. Hearn

03.12.87 Adam Muir W DIS 4 Belfast
08.06.88 Tony Britland W RSC 1 Sheffield
25.06.88 Antonio Campbell DREW 4 Panama City, Panama
19.10.88 Stan King W PTS 6 Belfast
19.09.89 Ricky Nelson W RSC 3 Belfast
31.10.89 Mark Pearce W PTS 6 Belfast
29.11.89 Ronnie Campbell W RSC 1 Belfast
24.11.90 Parrish Johnson W RSC 2 Benalmadena, Spain
12.12.90 Mike Morrison W PTS 6 Basildon
12.02.91 Nick Meloscia W CO 1 Cardiff
05.03.91 Julian Eavis W PTS 6 Cardiff
26.03.91 Stan Cunningham W RSC 2 Bethnal Green
24.04.91 Kevin Plant W RTD 1 Preston
28.05.91 Terry Morrill W CO 1 Cardiff
03.09.91 Marty Duke W PTS 6 Cardiff
21.09.91 Glyn Rhodes W PTS 8 Tottenham
15.10.91 Juan Carlos Ortiz W PTS 8 Hamburg, Germany
10.03.92 Tony Ekubia L DIS 5 Bury
(Elim. British Welterweight Title)
19.05.92 Kelvin Mortimer W RSC 1 Cardiff
29.09.92 Judas Clottey W PTS 8 Hamburg, Germany
24.11.92 Donovan Boucher W RSC 3 Doncaster
(Commonwealth Welterweight Title Challenge)
18.12.92 Desbon Seaton W RSC 2 Hamburg, Germany
06.02.93 Michael Benjamin W RSC 6 Cardiff
(Commonwealth Welterweight Title Defence)
16.10.93 Lorenzo Smith W PTS 12 Belfast
(Vacant WBO Welterweight Title)
22.01.94 Alessandro Duran W PTS 12 Belfast
(WBO Welterweight Title Defence)
10.12.94 Manning Galloway W TD 4 Manchester
(WBO Welterweight Title Defence)
27.05.95 Angel Beltre ND 3 Belfast
(WBO Welterweight Title Defence)
26.08.95 Tony Ganarelli W RSC 6 Belfast
(WBO Welterweight Title Defence)
07.10.95 Angel Beltre W PTS 12 Belfast
(WBO Welterweight Title Defence)
13.04.96 Jose Luis Lopez L RSC 1 Liverpool
(WBO Welterweight Title Defence)
Career: 30 contests, won 26, drew 1, lost 2, no contest 1.

Patrick Loughran

Ballymena. *Born* Ballymena, 15 September, 1972
L. Welterweight. Ht. 5'6"
Manager Self

11.09.91	Kevin Lowe W PTS 6 Stoke	
11.12.91	Keith Hardman W PTS 6 Stoke	
11.03.92	Rick North W PTS 6 Stoke	
07.07.92	Jason Barker W PTS 6 Bristol	
24.03.93	Felix Kelly W PTS 6 Bristol	
22.06.95	Dave Clark L PTS 6 Atlantic City, USA	
13.07.95	Arnoldo Franco W RSC 1 Atlantic City, USA	
17.08.95	Frank Duarte W RSC 1 Atlantic City, USA	

Career: 8 contests, won 7, lost 1.

Ernie Loveridge

Wolverhampton. *Born* Bromsgrove, 7 July, 1970
S. Middleweight. Former Undefeated Midlands Area Welterweight Champion. Ht. 5'10"
Manager Self

06.02.89	Ricky Nelson L RSC 6 Nottingham
17.04.89	Martin Robinson L PTS 4 Birmingham
08.05.89	Bullit Andrews W PTS 6 Edgbaston
05.06.89	Alan Richards L PTS 6 Birmingham
19.06.89	Ian Thomas DREW 6 Manchester
28.06.89	Barry Messam L PTS 6 Kenilworth
10.10.89	Matt Sturgess W RSC 1 Wolverhampton
25.10.89	Darren Mount L PTS 6 Stoke
11.12.89	Cliff Churchward W PTS 6 Birmingham
27.02.90	Julian Eavis W PTS 6 Evesham
14.03.90	Mickey Lerwill W PTS 6 Stoke
27.03.90	Eddie King W PTS 6 Wolverhampton
24.04.90	Mark Jay W PTS 6 Stoke
24.05.90	Mickey Lerwill DREW 6 Dudley
18.09.90	Ronnie Campbell W PTS 6 Wolverhampton
24.10.90	Trevor Meikle W PTS 6 Dudley
23.01.91	Cliff Churchward W PTS 6 Solihull
27.02.91	Ronnie Campbell W PTS 8 Wolverhampton
13.03.91	John Corcoran W RSC 4 Stoke
10.04.91	Julian Eavis DREW 8 Wolverhampton
14.05.91	Paul Murray W PTS 8 Dudley
05.06.91	Cliff Churchward W PTS 8 Wolverhampton
10.09.91	Gary Osborne W RSC 1 Wolverhampton *(Midlands Area Welterweight Title Challenge)*
12.11.91	Mickey Lerwill W PTS 6 Wolverhampton
05.12.91	Jim Lawlor W PTS 8 Cannack
01.02.92	Michael Oliver W PTS 8 Birmingham
19.09.92	Paul Jones L PTS 6 Glasgow
01.10.92	Neville Brown L CO 4 Telford
20.01.93	Lee Crocker L PTS 6 Wolverhampton
17.02.93	Robert McCracken L CO 4 Bethnal Green
31.03.93	Kevin Lueshing L RSC 5 Bethnal Green
18.05.93	Antonio Fernandez L PTS 8 Edgbaston
10.07.93	Michael Smyth L RSC 6 Cardiff
09.10.93	Robin Reid L PTS 4 Manchester
02.11.93	Gilbert Jackson L RTD 3 Southwark
11.06.94	Mark Delaney L RSC 5 Bethnal Green
28.07.94	Dave Cranston L PTS 6 Tooting
17.08.94	Kevin Adamson L RSC 2 Sheffield
01.03.95	Dave Johnson L PTS 6 Glasgow
17.03.95	Mads Larsen L RSC 3 Copenhagen, Denmark
20.04.95	Danny Peters L PTS 6 Liverpool
05.06.95	Billy Collins L PTS 8 Glasgow
16.06.95	Craig Winter L PTS 6 Liverpool
08.09.95	Craig Winter L PTS 6 Liverpool
21.09.95	Paolo Roberto L PTS 4 Battersea
29.09.95	Panayiotis Panayiotiou L PTS 4 Bethnal Green
16.10.95	Vince Rose L PTS 4 Heybridge
25.10.95	Steve Goodwin L PTS 4 Stoke
02.11.95	Brian Galloway L PTS 6 Mayfair
17.11.95	Dean Barclay L PTS 4 Bethnal Green
25.11.95	Steve Roberts L PTS 4 Dagenham
15.12.95	Luan Morena L PTS 4 Bethnal Green
19.01.96	Toks Owoh L PTS 4 Bracknell
30.01.96	Jason Hart L PTS 6 Barking
13.02.96	Paul Carr L PTS 4 Bethnal Green
23.02.96	Carl Winstone W PTS 8 Weston super Mare
05.03.96	Paul Wright L PTS 6 Barrow
19.03.96	James Donoghue L PTS 6 Leeds
30.03.96	Anthony McFadden L PTS 4 Dublin
14.05.96	Panayiotis Panayiotiou L PTS 4 Dagenham
13.06.96	Clinton Woods L PTS 6 Sheffield

Career: 61 contests, won 19, drew 3, lost 39.

James Lowther

Leeds. *Born* Leeds, 28 June, 1976
Welterweight. Ht. 5'11"
Manager G. Lockwood

12.01.95	Warren Stephens W CO 4 Leeds
25.03.95	Scott Doyle W PTS 6 Rothwell
19.05.95	Eddie Haley W RSC 5 Leeds
19.03.96	Earl Ling W RSC 4 Leeds

Career: 4 contests, won 4.

Danny Lutaaya

Canning Town. *Born* Uganda, 23 December, 1971
S. Featherweight. Ht. 5'5½"
Manager D. Powell

17.10.94	Vince Burns W RSC 6 Mayfair
27.11.94	Keith Jones W CO 1 Southwark
23.01.95	Elvis Parsley L RSC 3 Bethnal Green
25.03.95	Wayne Jones W RSC 3 Millwall
16.06.95	Dean Phillips L RSC 2 Southwark
14.09.95	Jason Hutson L RSC 2 Battersea
21.02.96	Arv Mittoo W PTS 6 Piccadilly

Career: 7 contests, won 4, lost 3.

Craig Lynch

Edinburgh. *Born* Edinburgh, 22 July, 1974
Welterweight. Ht. 6'1"
Manager T. Miller

13.05.95	James Clamp DREW 6 Glasgow
08.06.95	Gary Silvester W RSC 3 Glasgow
15.09.95	Adam Baldwin W PTS 6 Glasgow
25.11.95	Jim Rock L PTS 4 Dublin
02.03.96	Hughie Davey L PTS 4 Newcastle
08.06.96	Hughie Davey L PTS 4 Newcastle

Career: 6 contests, won 2, drew 1, lost 3.

Chris Lyons

Birmingham. *Born* Birmingham, 2 September, 1972
Featherweight. Ht. 5'9"
Manager Self

02.12.91	Ronnie Sephenson L PTS 6 Birmingham
09.12.91	Ronnie Stephenson L PTS 6 Cleethorpes
22.01.92	Dennis Oakes L RSC 3 Stoke
17.05.92	Dave Martin DREW 6 Harringay
08.09.92	Robert Braddock L CO 5 Doncaster
13.10.92	Paul Kelly W PTS 6 Wolverhampton
30.10.92	Paul Kelly W CO 1 Birmingham
17.12.92	Mark Bowers L CO 2 Wembley
08.03.93	Chip O'Neill L PTS 6 Leeds
22.04.93	Marcus Duncan L RSC 2 Bury
26.06.93	Tim Yeates L PTS 4 Earls Court
16.09.93	Anthony Hanna L PTS 6 Southwark
30.11.93	Kid McAuley L RSC 5 Wolverhampton
01.03.94	Marty Chestnut L PTS 6 Dudley
27.04.94	Marty Chestnut W RSC 3 Bethnal Green

Chris Lyons (left) on the receiving end of an Eddie Sica right hand   Les Clark

06.05.94 John Sillo L RSC 3 Liverpool
15.06.94 Matt Brown L CO 3 Southwark
19.09.94 Daryl McKenzie L PTS 6 Glasgow
11.10.94 Robert Grubb W PTS 6 Wolverhampton
02.11.94 Daryl McKenzie L PTS 6 Solihull
16.11.94 Danny Ruegg L PTS 6 Bloomsbury
28.11.94 Andrew Bloomer W PTS 6 Northampton
24.01.95 Abdul Mannon L PTS 6 Piccadilly
07.02.95 Michael Edwards W PTS 6 Wolverhampton
21.04.95 Matthew Harris L PTS 6 Dudley
26.08.95 Eamonn Brolly L PTS 4 Belfast
11.10.95 Jason Squire L PTS 6 Solihull
24.10.95 Eddie Sica L PTS 4 Southwark
21.11.95 Andrew Smith L PTS 6 Edgbaston
07.12.95 Fred Reeve L PTS 6 Hull
31.01.96 Brian Robb L PTS 6 Birmingham
16.03.96 Gary Jenkinson L PTS 6 Barnstaple
27.03.96 Brendan Bryce L PTS 6 Whitwick
03.05.96 Sean Morrison L PTS 6 Sheffield
20.05.96 Steve Conway L PTS 6 Cleethorpes
13.06.96 Vic Broomhead W PTS 6 Sheffield
Career: 36 contests, won 7, drew 1, lost 28.

John McAlpine

Glasgow. *Born* Melbourne, Australia, 28 November, 1970
Middleweight. Ht. 6'0"
Manager A. Morrison

08.12.89 Mark Glover L PTS 6 Melbourne, Australia
14.07.90 Les Davis W PTS 8 Melbourne, Australia
27.04.91 Chris Schaefer W PTS 6 Sydney, Australia
19.06.91 Jason Hall L PTS 10 Melbourne, Australia
23.08.91 Patrick Axisa L RTD 7 Sydney, Australia
17.12.95 John Duckworth DREW 6 Glasgow
12.02.96 Robert Harper W PTS 6 Glasgow
16.03.96 Jason Matthews L RSC 1 Glasgow
Career: 8 contests, won 3, drew 1, lost 4.

(Colin) Kid McAuley

Liverpool. *Born* Liverpool, 6 June, 1968
Lightweight. Ht. 5'6"
Manager J. Rushton

08.09.92 Jonjo Irwin L PTS 6 Doncaster
19.09.92 Alex Docherty L PTS 6 Glasgow
30.09.92 Yusuf Vorajee W PTS 6 Solihull
13.10.92 John White L PTS 4 Bury
23.10.92 Paul Lloyd L PTS 4 Liverpool
10.11.92 Michael Alldis L PTS 6 Dagenham
24.11.92 Miguel Matthews W PTS 6 Doncaster
12.12.92 Michael Alldis L CO 1 Muswell Hill
27.01.93 Yusuf Vorajee L RSC 5 Stoke
03.03.93 Kevin Middleton L PTS 8 Solihull
16.03.93 Jonjo Irwin L PTS 10 Mayfair
(Vacant All-Ireland Featherweight Title)
28.04.93 Barry Jones L PTS 8 Solihull
14.05.93 Shaun Anderson L PTS 8 Kilmarnock
29.05.93 James Murray L PTS 6 Paisley
28.06.93 Carl Roberts W PTS 6 Morecambe
25.07.93 Mario Culpeper L PTS 6 Oldham
12.10.93 Elvis Parsley L PTS 6 Wolverhampton
30.11.93 Chris Lyons W RSC 5 Wolverhampton
22.01.94 Eamonn McAuley L PTS 6 Belfast

10.02.94 Tony Foster L RTD 4 Hull
11.03.94 Donnie Hood L PTS 8 Glasgow
27.04.94 Harry Escott L RTD 6 Solihull
02.06.94 Wayne Rigby L PTS 6 Middleton
10.06.94 Bradley Welsh L RTD 1 Glasgow
12.09.94 Colin Innes W PTS 6 Doncaster
30.11.94 Marco Fattore W PTS 6 Solihull
15.12.94 Martin Harris L PTS 6 Evesham
09.02.95 Roger Brotherhood W PTS 6 Doncaster
17.02.95 Dean Pithie L RSC 3 Cumbernauld
28.03.95 Anthony Maynard L PTS 8 Wolverhampton
05.04.95 Hugh Collins L PTS 6 Irvine
13.04.95 Dean Pithie L RSC 1 Bloomsbury
11.05.95 Glen Hopkins DREW 6 Sunderland
18.05.95 Dave Clavering L PTS 6 Middleton
06.06.95 Neil Smith L RTD 1 Leicester
28.09.95 Glen Hopkins L PTS 6 Sunderland
18.10.95 Terry Whittaker L PTS 6 Batley
04.11.95 Gary Thornhill L PTS 6 Liverpool
29.11.95 Terry Whittaker DREW 6 Solihull
07.12.95 John T. Kelly L PTS 6 Sunderland
20.12.95 Gareth Lawrence L PTS 6 Usk
17.01.96 Wayne Rigby L PTS 6 Solihull
18.03.96 Hugh Collins L PTS 8 Glasgow
01.04.96 Chris Jickells L PTS 6 Bradford
24.04.96 Mark Allen W PTS 6 Stoke
30.05.96 Terry Whittaker L PTS 6 Lincoln
13.06.96 Robbie Sivyer L PTS 6 Sheffield
24.06.96 Jason Blanche L PTS 6 Bradford
Career: 48 contests, won 8, drew 2, lost 38.

Kevin McBride

Clones. *Born* Monaghan, 10 May, 1973
Heavyweight. Ht. 6'5"
Manager F. Maloney

17.12.92 Gary Charlton DREW 6 Barking
13.02.93 Gary Williams W PTS 4 Manchester
15.09.93 Joey Paladino W CO 2 Bethnal Green
13.10.93 Chris Coughlan W PTS 4 Bethnal Green
01.12.93 John Harewood W RSC 3 Bethnal Green
06.05.94 Edgar Turpin W RSC 1 Atlantic City, USA
04.06.94 Roger Bryant W CO 1 Reno, USA
17.06.94 Stanley Wright W PTS 6 Atlantic City, USA
26.08.94 James Truesdale W RSC 3 Upper Marlboro, USA
24.09.94 Graham Arnold W RSC 2 Wembley
12.11.94 Dean Storey W RSC 3 Dublin
10.12.94 John Lamphrey W RSC 1 Portland, USA
07.02.95 Carl Gaffney W RSC 1 Ipswich
03.03.95 Carl McGrew W RSC 5 Boston, USA
22.04.95 Jimmy Harrison W RSC 1 Boston, USA
13.05.95 Atelea Kalhea W CO 1 Sacramento, USA
02.07.95 Steve Garber W RSC 7 Dublin
Carrer: 17 contests, won 16, drew 1.

Marcus McCrae

Hackney. *Born* London, 13 November, 1969
S. Featherweight. Ht. 5'7"
Manager Self

22.09.93 Miguel Matthews W PTS 6 Bethnal Green
10.11.93 Ian Reid W PTS 6 Bethnal Green

17.02.94 Thomas Bernard W RSC 1 Dagenham
04.06.94 Andrew Reed W PTS 6 Cardiff
01.10.94 Ceri Farrell W RTD 1 Cardiff
19.11.94 Barrie Kelley L PTS 6 Cardiff
25.02.95 Andrew Reed W RSC 4 Millwall
07.07.95 Daniel Alicea L RSC 3 Cardiff
Career: 8 contests, won 6, lost 2.

Mark McCreath

Lincoln. *Born* Bradford, 30 May, 1964
Welterweight. Former Undefeated Benelux Welterweight Champion. Ht. 5'8½"
Manager Self

11.05.89 Tom Heiskonen W RSC 6 Tallin, Estonia
01.11.89 Bianto Baekelandt W CO 2 Izegem, Belgium
29.11.89 Abdel Lahjar W RTD 4 Paris, France
09.12.89 Pierre Conan W RSC 4 Toul, France
10.02.90 Josef Rajic W PTS 6 Roulers, France
26.03.90 Eric Capoen W RSC 1 Nogent sur Marne, France
19.05.90 Mohammed Berrabah W RSC 6 Montpelier, France
11.08.90 Mohamed Oumad W RTD 5 Le Cap d'Agde, France
05.09.90 Mehmet Demir W RSC 5 Belgrade, Yugoslavia
05.10.90 Patrick Vungbo L PTS 10 Waregem, Belgium
(Vacant Belgium Welterweight Title)
17.04.91 Pat Barrett L RSC 6 Kensington
(European L. Welterweight Title Challenge)
21.06.91 Freddy Demeulenaere W RSC 5 Waregem, Belgium
(Vacant Benelux Welterweight Title)
30.04.92 Gary Barron W RSC 5 Mayfair
01.10.92 Chris Saunders W RSC 4 Telford
07.12.92 Gary Barron W RSC 5 Mayfair
06.03.93 Valery Kayumba L RSC 11 Levallois-Perret, France
(European L. Welterweight Title Challenge)
26.05.93 Peter Till W PTS 8 Mansfield
27.10.93 John Smith W RSC 7 West Bromwich
01.03.94 Dave Lovell L RSC 5 Dudley
23.07.94 Ahmed Katejev L RSC 6 Berlin, Germany
23.09.94 Jason Beard W PTS 6 Bethnal Green
10.02.95 Robert Wright W PTS 8 Birmingham
28.07.95 Ensley Bingham L RSC 2 Bristol
25.11.95 Dingaan Thobela L RSC 9 East London, South Africa
Career: 24 contests, won 17, lost 7.

Geoff McCreesh

Bracknell. *Born* Stockton, 12 June, 1970
Former Undefeated Southern Area L. Middleweight Champion. Ht. 5'10"
Manager J. Evans

16.02.94 Tony Walton W PTS 6 Stevenage
12.03.94 Barry Thorogood W PTS 6 Cardiff
22.03.94 Mark Dawson W PTS 6 Bethnal Green
20.05.94 Robert Peel W RSC 2 Acton
02.07.94 Julian Eavis W PTS 4 Keynsham
18.11.94 Andrew Furlong W PTS 6 Bracknell
13.12.94 Ojay Abrahams W PTS 6 Potters Bar
20.01.95 Clay O'Shea W RSC 1 Bethnal Green
(Vacant Southern Area L. Middleweight Title)

03.03.95 Dennis Berry L RTD 5 Bracknell
16.12.95 Michael Smyth L DIS 4 Cardiff
19.01.96 Steve Goodwin L DIS 5 Bracknell
02.03.96 Peter Varnavas W PTS 4 Newcastle
13.03.96 Kevin Thompson W PTS 6 Wembley
09.04.96 Vince Rose W RSC 4 Stevenage
10.05.96 George Wilson W PTS 6 Wembley
25.06.96 Wayne Shepherd W PTS 4 Stevenage
Career: 16 contests, won 13, lost 3.

Errol McDonald

Nottingham. *Born* Nottingham, 11 March, 1964
Welterweight. Ht. 5'10"
Manager Self

21.10.85 Dave Heaver W CO 1 Mayfair
05.11.85 Robert Armstrong W RSC 4 Wembley
20.01.86 Lenny Gloster W PTS 8 Mayfair
17.02.86 Kid Milo DREW 6 Mayfair
27.02.86 Gary Flear W RSC 4 Bethnal Green
09.04.86 Lenny Gloster W PTS 6 Kensington
29.10.86 Gerry Beard W RSC 4 Piccadilly
19.01.87 Mark Simpson W CO 5 Mayfair
30.08.87 Jose Maria Castillo W RSC 3 Marbella, Spain
30.09.87 Roy Callaghan W RSC 4 Mayfair
18.11.87 Billy Cairns W RTD 3 Bethnal Green
03.02.88 Mike English W RSC 2 Wembley
29.03.88 Ramon Nunez W RSC 3 Wembley
21.04.88 Nick Meloscia W PTS 8 Bethnal Green
26.09.88 Jimmy Thornton W RTD 2 Piccadilly
05.10.88 Alfredo Reyes W CO 2 Wembley
30.11.88 Sammy Floyd W RSC 3 Southwark
18.01.89 Nick Meloscia W RSC 1 Kensington
19.12.89 Mick Mulcahy W RSC 3 Bethnal Green
27.01.90 Joe Hernandez W PTS 8 Sheffield
28.03.90 Robert Lewis W RSC 4 Bethnal Green
25.04.90 Mario Lopez W CO 1 Brighton
05.06.90 Steve Larrimore W PTS 9 Nottingham
18.11.90 Ray Taylor W RTD 3 Birmingham
23.02.91 Juan Rondon W RSC 7 Brighton
08.06.91 Patrizio Oliva L DIS 12 La Spezia, Italy
(*European Welterweight Title Challenge*)
10.12.91 Jose Luis Saldivia W PTS 8 Sheffield
10.03.92 Robert Wright L CO 3 Bury
24.11.92 Gordon Blair W RSC 5 Doncaster
12.01.93 Orlando Otero W RSC 4 Aachen, Germany
16.02.93 Peter Till W PTS 8 Tooting
16.03.93 Michael Driscoll L PTS 10 Mayfair
(*Elim. British L. Welterweight Title*)
25.10.93 Wayne Appleton L PTS 8 Glasgow
24.01.94 Ojay Abrahams L RSC 2 Glasgow
07.05.96 Nick Odore L RSC 4 Mayfair
Career: 35 contests, won 28, drew 1, lost 6.

Simon McDougall

Blackpool. *Born* Manchester, 11 July, 1968
L. Heavyweight. Ht. 5'10½"
Manager Self

14.11.88 Andrew Bravardo W CO 4 Manchester
16.01.89 Steve Osborne L PTS 6 Bradford
25.01.89 Steve Osborne L PTS 6 Stoke
20.02.89 Willie Connell W RSC 4 Bradford
04.04.89 Lee Woolis L PTS 6 Manchester
12.10.89 George Ferrie W PTS 6 Glasgow
30.11.89 Jimmy Cropper W PTS 6 Oldham
07.12.89 Sean O'Phoenix L PTS 6 Manchester
07.04.90 Eddy Smulders L PTS 6 Eindhoven, Holland

15.05.90 Terry French W PTS 4 South Shields
12.10.90 Ray Alberts L PTS 6 Cayenne, France
22.10.90 Glenn Campbell L RSC 4 Manchester
10.12.90 Morris Thomas W RSC 2 Bradford
28.01.91 Ian Henry W PTS 8 Bradford
28.02.91 Glenn Campbell L PTS 10 Bury
(*Central Area S. Middleweight Title Challenge*)
23.04.91 Paul Burton L PTS 8 Evesham
10.05.91 Ian Henry L PTS 6 Gateshead
30.09.91 Doug Calderwood W RSC 4 Liverpool
10.10.91 Terry French L PTS 8 Gateshead
19.10.91 Andrea Magi L RSC 5 Terni, Italy
03.03.92 Paul Hitch L PTS 6 Houghton le Spring
11.03.92 Ian Henry L PTS 8 Solihull
30.03.92 Nigel Rafferty L PTS 8 Coventry
08.06.92 Mark McBiane L PTS 6 Bradford
06.10.92 Garry Delaney L PTS 8 Antwerp, Belgium
12.12.92 Garry Delaney L PTS 8 Muswell Hill
04.03.93 Alan Smiles L PTS 6 Glasgow
26.03.93 Roland Ericsson W RSC 5 Copenhagen, Denmark
17.04.93 Terry French L PTS 6 Washington
12.05.93 Martin Langtry L PTS 8 Sheffield
14.08.93 Mark Prince L PTS 6 Hammersmith
04.10.93 Bruce Scott L PTS 6 Mayfair
15.10.93 Christophe Girard L PTS 8 Romorantin, France
08.12.93 Stevie R. Davies W RSC 5 Hull
29.01.94 Ole Klemetsen L RTD 5 Cardiff
08.03.94 John Foreman W PTS 6 Edgbaston
11.05.94 Monty Wright W PTS 6 Stevenage
19.09.94 Stephen Wilson L RTD 3 Glasgow
21.01.95 Sean Heron L PTS 4 Glasgow
16.02.95 Glenn Campbell L PTS 6 Bury
06.03.95 John Keeton L RSC 5 Mayfair
17.04.95 Stefan Angehrn W RSC 5 Berne, Switzerland
22.11.95 Michael Gale L PTS 10 Sheffield
(*Central Area L. Heavyweight Title Challenge*)
Career: 43 contests, won 14, lost 29.

Alan McDowall

Renfrew. *Born* Renfrew, 29 September, 1967
Lightweight. Ht. 5'10"
Manager A. Morrison

24.09.91 Johnny Patterson W PTS 4 Glasgow
28.11.91 Johnny Patterson W PTS 6 Glasgow
31.01.92 Charles Shepherd W RSC 3 Glasgow
20.02.92 Mark O'Callaghan W PTS 6 Glasgow
12.03.92 James Jiora W CO 2 Glasgow
29.05.92 Karl Taylor W PTS 6 Glasgow
22.10.92 Robert Lloyd W RTD 4 Glasgow
30.04.93 Dean Bramhald W PTS 6 Glasgow
29.05.93 Rob Stewart DREW 6 Paisley
19.12.93 Dean Amory W PTS 8 Glasgow
10.06.94 Mark Antony W PTS 8 Glasgow
08.09.94 Peter Till L PTS 6 Glasgow
15.09.95 Floyd Churchill W RSC 5 Glasgow
13.10.95 Peter Till W RSC 5 Glasgow
12.02.96 Mark Ramsey W PTS 8 Glasgow
16.03.96 Mark Ramsey W PTS 6 Glasgow
Career: 16 contests, won 14, drew 1, lost 1.

Anthony McFadden

Donegal. *Born* Leeds, 21 December, 1971
Middleweight. Ht. 5'10"
Manager F. Maloney

30.03.96 Ernie Loveridge W PTS 4 Dublin
22.04.96 Dave Andrews W RSC 2 Crystal Palace
29.06.96 Peter Vosper W PTS 4 Erith
Career: 3 contests, won 3.

James McGee

Bedworth. *Born* Nuneaton, 9 May, 1968
L. Middleweight. Ht. 6'1"
Manager Self

19.03.91 Adrian Din W PTS 6 Leicester
15.04.91 Marty Duke L PTS 6 Leicester
20.05.91 Cliff Churchward W PTS 6 Leicester
11.06.91 Julian Eavis W PTS 6 Leicester
01.10.91 Trevor Meikle L PTS 8 Bedworth
21.10.91 Crain Fisher L RSC 4 Bury
11.12.91 Julian Eavis DREW 6 Leicester
11.02.92 Chris Mulcahy W PTS 6 Wolverhampton
25.03.92 Darren Morris DREW 6 Hinckley
11.05.92 Julian Eavis W RSC 3 Coventry
05.10.92 Julian Eavis L PTS 6 Bardon
23.11.92 James Campbell DREW 6 Coventry
20.01.93 John Duckworth L PTS 6 Solihull
22.02.93 Julian Eavis W PTS 6 Bedworth
24.03.93 Damien Denny L CO 2 Belfast
(*Final Elim. All-Ireland L. Middleweight Title*)
16.12.93 Anthony Lawrence DREW 6 Walsall
26.01.94 Wayne Shepherd L PTS 6 Stoke
26.03.96 Gavin Lane L PTS 6 Wolverhampton
21.05.96 Steve Levene L PTS 6 Edgbaston
Career: 19 contests, won 7, drew 4, lost 8.

Steve McGovern

Bembridge. *Born* Newport, IOW, 17 April, 1969
Welterweight. Ht. 5'9"
Manager J. Bishop

21.09.89 Mike Morrison W PTS 6 Southampton
17.04.90 Justin Graham W PTS 6 Millwall
21.01.91 Mark Dinnadge W PTS 6 Crystal Palace
23.02.91 Tim Harmey W PTS 6 Brighton
23.04.91 Frank Harrington L PTS 6 Evesham
08.05.91 A.M.Milton W PTS 6 Millwall
16.12.91 Chris Mylan W PTS 8 Southampton
03.03.92 Tony Swift L RSC 4 Cradley Heath
27.10.92 Ricky Mabbett DREW 6 Leicester
29.04.93 Michael Dick W PTS 6 Hayes
23.06.93 Joel Ani W PTS 6 Edmonton
23.02.94 David Lake W PTS 6 Watford
17.12.94 Ahmet Katejev L RSC 4 Berlin, Germany
31.03.95 Maurice Forbes L PTS 6 Crystal Palace
19.04.95 Jason Beard L PTS 6 Bethnal Green
17.06.95 Michael Carruth L RSC 4 Cardiff
19.01.96 Dennis Gardner L PTS 6 Bracknell
09.03.96 Eamonn Magee L PTS 4 Millstreet
04.04.96 Justin Simmons DREW 6 Plymouth
Career: 19 contests, won 10, drew 2, lost 7.

Mark McGowan

Plymouth. *Born* Plymouth, 5 February, 1972
L. Welterweight. Ht. 5'7½"
Manager D. Sullivan

10.06.95 Mark Winters L PTS 6 Manchester
28.11.95 John Janes L PTS 6 Cardiff
20.12.95 Phil Found W PTS 6 Usk
Career: 3 contests, won 1, lost 2.

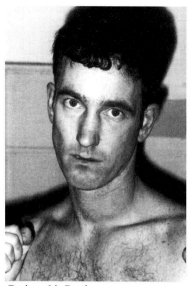

Graham McGrath   Les Clark

Graham McGrath

Warley. *Born* West Bromwich, 31 July, 1962
S. Bantamweight. Ht. 5'4"
Manager Self

21.05.92	Paul Kelly W RSC 2 Cradley Heath
01.06.92	Greg Upton L PTS 6 Solihull
09.07.92	Wilson Docherty L RSC 4 Glasgow
25.09.92	Paul Lloyd L RSC 3 Liverpool
02.11.92	Dennis Oakes L PTS 4 Liverpool
01.12.92	Leo Beirne L PTS 6 Liverpool
10.12.92	Shaun Anderson L PTS 6 Glasgow
14.01.93	Daren Fifield L PTS 4 Mayfair
29.01.93	Shaun Anderson L PTS 6 Glasgow
23.02.93	Ian Baillie W PTS 6 Kettering
29.03.93	Ian McLeod L PTS 6 Glasgow
19.04.93	Karl Morling L RSC 6 Northampton
23.06.93	Rowan Williams L PTS 4 Edmonton
02.07.93	Peter Culshaw L PTS 6 Liverpool
09.09.93	Shaun Anderson L PTS 8 Glasgow
28.09.93	John Sillo L PTS 6 Liverpool
06.10.93	Neil Parry DREW 6 Glasgow
21.10.93	James Murray L PTS 6 Glasgow
28.10.93	Greg Upton L PTS 8 Torquay
07.11.93	Alex Docherty L RSC 3 Glasgow
06.12.93	Darren Greaves DREW 6 Birmingham
16.12.93	Darren Greaves W PTS 6 Walsall
19.01.94	Gary White L PTS 6 Solihull
21.02.94	Ian McLeod L CO 6 Glasgow
21.03.94	Marcus Duncan L PTS 6 Bradford
28.03.94	Jason Morris W PTS 6 Birmingham
27.04.94	Paul Ingle L PTS 4 Bethnal Green
20.05.94	Mark Cokely W PTS 6 Neath
10.06.94	James Murray L PTS 8 Glasgow
08.09.94	Shaun Anderson L PTS 8 Glasgow
21.09.94	Mark Hughes L PTS 4 Cardiff
03.10.94	Michael Brodie L RSC 5 Manchester
02.11.94	Darren Greaves W RSC 4 Birmingham
24.11.94	Paul Ingle L PTS 6 Hull
05.12.94	Darren Greaves W PTS 6 Birmingham
13.12.94	Patrick Mullings L PTS 4 Ilford
18.01.95	Rowan Williams L CO 6 Solihull
	(Vacant Midlands Area Bantamweight Title)

14.02.95	Mark Bowers L PTS 6 Bethnal Green
09.03.95	Marty Chestnut L PTS 6 Walsall
20.03.95	Marty Chestnut W PTS 6 Birmingham
30.03.95	Patrick Mullings L RSC 3 Bethnal Green
11.05.95	Jon Pegg W PTS 6 Dudley
05.06.95	Jon Pegg W PTS 6 Birmingham
20.06.95	Jon Pegg W PTS 6 Birmingham
30.06.95	Chris Jickells L PTS 4 Doncaster
28.07.95	Chris Jickells L PTS 6 Epworth
26.08.95	Paul Ireland L PTS 4 Belfast
20.09.95	Neil Swain L RSC 1 Ystrad
18.10.95	Ady Benton L PTS 6 Batley
26.10.95	Brendan Bryce L PTS 6 Birmingham
08.11.95	Andy Roberts L PTS 6 Scunthorpe
21.11.95	Marty Chestnut L PTS 6 Edgbaston
28.11.95	Andy Roberts W PTS 6 Wolverhampton
04.12.95	Andrew Robinson L PTS 6 Birmingham
18.12.95	Miguel Matthews L PTS 8 Mayfair
24.01.96	Michael Edwards L PTS 6 Stoke
22.02.96	Michael Edwards L PTS 6 Walsall
06.03.96	Michael Edwards W PTS 6 Solihull
15.03.96	Mark Bowers L PTS 6 Dunstable
29.03.96	Andy Roberts W PTS 6 Doncaster
20.04.96	Paul Ireland L PTS 6 Brentwood
04.05.96	Ricky Beard W PTS 6 Dagenham
28.05.96	Tommy Waite L PTS 4 Belfast
04.06.96	Noel Wilders L PTS 6 York
25.06.96	Ady Lewis L RSC 1 Stevenage

Career: 65 contests, won 16, drew 2, lost 47.

Dominic McGuigan

Newcastle. *Born* Hexham, 13 June, 1963
Northern Area S. Featherweight Champion.
Ht. 5'6"
Manager B. Hardy

10.10.89	Dave Buxton W PTS 6 Sunderland
24.01.90	John Milne DREW 6 Sunderland
20.03.90	Frankie Foster DREW 4 Hartlepool
21.04.90	Chris Bennett W PTS 6 Sunderland
22.05.90	Lester James L PTS 6 Stockton
16.09.91	Barrie Kelley DREW 6 Mayfair
28.11.91	John Milne W RTD 3 Glasgow
30.04.92	Kevin Lowe W RSC 6 Mayfair
15.05.92	Rene Weller L PTS 8 Augsburg, Germany
07.10.92	Harry Escott L RTD 5 Sunderland
12.11.92	Kevin Lowe W RSC 2 Liverpool
25.02.93	Peter Judson DREW 6 Bradford
27.03.93	Giorgio Campanella L RSC 3 Evian, France
19.05.93	J.T.Williams W PTS 6 Sunderland
03.06.93	Eugene Speed L CO 1 Marseille, France
21.10.93	John Stovin L PTS 6 Bayswater
02.12.93	Peter Till L RSC 2 Walsall
24.11.94	John T. Kelly W PTS 6 Newcastle
13.01.95	Dennis Holbaek Pedersen L PTS 6 Aalborg, Denmark
02.03.95	Frankie Foster W RSC 6 Cramlington
	(Northern Area S. Featherweight Title Challenge)
29.07.95	Kelton McKenzie DREW 6 Whitley Bay
13.04.96	Gary Thornhill L RSC 3 Liverpool

Career: 22 contests, won 8, drew 5, lost 9.

Dave McHale

Glasgow. *Born* Glasgow, 29 April, 1967
S. Featherweight. Ht. 5'7"
Manager T. Gilmour

08.10.90	Sol Francis W RSC 2 Glasgow
25.11.91	Eddie Garbutt W RSC 1 Liverpool
30.03.92	Kevin Lowe W RSC 5 Glasgow
01.06.92	Chris Jickells W RSC 4 Glasgow
09.07.92	G. G. Goddard W RTD 4 Glasgow
19.10.92	Lee Fox W RSC 3 Glasgow
23.11.92	Karl Taylor W PTS 8 Glasgow
15.05.93	Miguel Matthews W RSC 4 Glasgow
02.02.94	John T. Kelly W CO 1 Glasgow
21.03.94	Frankie Foster W PTS 8 Glasgow
13.12.94	Floyd Havard L RSC 10 Ilford
	(British S. Featherweight Title Challenge)
23.10.95	Chris Aston W RTD 3 Glasgow
22.04.96	P. J. Gallagher L RSC 10 Crystal Palace
	(Vacant British S. Featherweight Title)

Career: 13 contests, won 11, lost 2.

(Anthony) Daryl McKenzie

Paisley. *Born* Johnstone, 20 August, 1965
S. Bantamweight. Ht. 5'4"
Manager N. Sweeney

17.02.94	Des Gargano DREW 6 Bury
02.03.94	Al Garrett W PTS 6 Glasgow
25.04.94	Al Garrett L PTS 6 Glasgow
16.05.94	Marcus Duncan L PTS 6 Morecambe
19.09.94	Chris Lyons W PTS 6 Glasgow
26.09.94	Peter Culshaw L PTS 6 Liverpool
24.10.94	Jobie Tyers L PTS 6 Glasgow
02.11.94	Chris Lyons W PTS 6 Solihull
21.11.94	Adey Lewis L RSC 4 Glasgow
26.04.96	Lee Armstrong W RSC 4 Glasgow

Career: 10 contests, won 4, drew 1, lost 5.

Duke McKenzie

Croydon. *Born* Croydon, 5 May, 1963
Former Undefeated British Featherweight
Champion. Former WBO S. Bantamweight
& Bantamweight Champion. Former IBF
Flyweight Champion. Former Undefeated
British & European Flyweight Champion.
Ht. 5'7"
Manager Self

23.11.82	Charlie Brown W RSC 1 Wembley
24.01.83	Andy King W RSC 2 Mayfair
27.02.83	Dave Pearson W RSC 1 Las Vegas, USA
03.03.83	Gregorio Hernandez W RSC 3 Los Angeles, USA
19.03.83	Lupe Sanchez W CO 2 Reno, USA
18.10.83	Jerry Davis W RSC 2 Atlantic City, USA
22.11.83	Alain Limarola W PTS 6 Wembley
15.01.84	David Capo W PTS 4 Atlantic City, USA
23.05.84	Gary Roberts W CO 1 Mayfair
06.03.85	Julio Guerrero W PTS 8 Kensington
05.06.85	Danny Flynn W RSC 4 Kensington
	(Vacant British Flyweight Title)
16.10.85	Orlando Maestre W PTS 8 Kensington
19.02.86	Sonny Long W PTS 10 Kensington
20.05.86	Charlie Magri W RTD 5 Wembley
	(British Flyweight Title Defence & European Flyweight Title Challenge)
19.11.86	Lee Cargle W PTS 10 Atlantic City, USA
17.12.86	Piero Pinna W PTS 12 Acqui Terme, Italy
	(European Flyweight Title Defence)
24.03.87	Jose Manuel Diaz W PTS 8 Wembley

02.12.87   Juan Herrera W PTS 10 Wembley
09.03.88   Agapito Gomez W CO 2 Wembley
           (European Flyweight Title Defence)
04.05.88   Jose Gallegos W PTS 10 Wembley
05.10.88   Rolando Bohol W CO 11 Wembley
           (IBF Flyweight Title Challenge)
30.11.88   Artemio Ruiz W PTS 10 Southwark
08.03.89   Tony de Luca W RSC 4 Kensington
           (IBF Flyweight Title Defence)
07.06.89   Dave Boy McAuley L PTS 12
           Wembley
           (IBF Flyweight Title Defence)
12.10.89   Dave Moreno W PTS 10 Southwark
08.11.89   Memo Flores W PTS 8 Wembley
30.09.90   Thierry Jacob L PTS 12 Calais, France
           (Vacant European Bantamweight Title)
10.01.91   Pete Buckley W RSC 5 Wandsworth
07.02.91   Julio Blanco W RSC 7 Watford
04.04.91   Chris Clarkson W RSC 5 Watford
30.06.91   Gaby Canizales W PTS 12 Southwark
           (WBO Bantamweight Title Challenge)
12.09.91   Cesar Soto W PTS 12 Wandsworth
           (WBO Bantamweight Title Defence)
25.03.92   Wilfredo Vargas W RSC 8 Kensington
           (WBO Bantamweight Title Defence)
13.05.92   Rafael del Valle L CO 1 Kensington
           (WBO Bantamweight Title Defence)
07.09.92   Pete Buckley W RTD 3 Bethnal Green
15.10.92   Jesse Benavides W PTS 12 Lewisham
           *(WBO S. Bantamweight Title
           Challenge)*
09.06.93   Daniel Jimenez L PTS 12 Lewisham
           (WBO S. Bantamweight Title Defence)
18.12.93   John Davison W RSC 4 Manchester
           (Vacant British Featherweight Title)
29.01.94   Marcelo Rodriguez W PTS 8 Cardiff
17.08.94   Mark Hargreaves W RSC 3 Sheffield
01.10.94   Steve Robinson L CO 9 Cardiff
           (WBO Featherweight Title Challenge)
28.04.95   Mehdi Labdouni L PTS 12 Fontenay
           sous Bois
           *(European Featherweight Title
           Challenge)*
25.06.96   Elvis Parsley W RSC 1 Mansfield
Career: 43 contests, won 37, lost 6.

Kelton McKenzie

Nottingham. *Born* Leicester, 18 September,
1968
S. Featherweight. Midlands Area
Featherweight Champion. Ht. 5'7"
Manager J. Griffin

18.10.90   Tony Silkstone L PTS 6 Dewsbury
29.11.90   Neil Leitch DREW 6 Marton
11.12.90   Sylvester Osuji W PTS 6 Evesham
21.01.91   J. T. Williams DREW 6 Crystal Palace
14.03.91   Craig Dermody L RSC 3 Middleton
01.05.91   Tim Yeates W PTS 6 Bethnal Green
17.06.91   Derek Amory W RSC 6 Edgbaston
05.11.91   Richard Woolgar W RSC 5 Leicester
22.01.92   Colin Lynch W RSC 5 Solihull
26.03.92   Brian Robb W RSC 4 Telford
29.04.92   Elvis Parsley W RSC 5 Solihull
           *(Vacant Midlands Area Featherweight
           Title)*
18.07.92   Steve Walker W CO 2 Manchester
27.10.92   Alan McKay L PTS 10 Cradley Heath
           (Elim. British Featherweight Title)
28.04.93   Richie Wenton L PTS 8 Dublin
19.05.93   Paul Harvey L RSC 7 Leicester
04.10.93   Mehdi Labdouni L PTS 8 Paris, France
10.05.94   Harry Escott L PTS 6 Doncaster
27.08.94   Barry Jones L PTS 6 Cardiff

31.10.94   Sugar Gibiliru L PTS 6 Liverpool
09.12.94   Yifru Retta L PTS 4 Bethnal Green
06.03.95   Wayne Rigby W PTS 8 Leicester
26.04.95   Charles Shepherd L RSC 7 Solihull
07.07.95   Gareth Jordan L PTS 4 Cardiff
29.07.95   Dominic McGuigan DREW 6 Whitley
           Bay
08.09.95   Dennis Holbaek Pedersen L RSC 5
           Aalborg, Denmark
10.11.95   Dean Pithie DREW 6 Derby
01.12.95   Arlindo de Abreu L PTS 8 Gien,
           France
26.04.96   Dean Pithie L PTS 6 Cardiff
Career: 28 contests, won 9, drew 4, lost 15.

Kevin McKenzie

Hartlepool. *Born* Hartlepool, 18 October,
1968
Former Northern Area Welterweight
Champion. Ht. 5'7½"
Manager Self

08.06.92   Jason Brattley W RTD 3 Bradford
21.09.92   Alan Ingle W PTS 6 Glasgow
22.10.92   Dave Anderson L RSC 3 Glasgow
01.12.92   Seth Jones L RSC 3 Hartlepool

09.03.93   Micky Hall W PTS 6 Hartlepool
17.04.93   Paul Charters L RSC 4 Washington
           *(Vacant Northern Area L.Welterweight
           Title)*
13.09.93   Blue Butterworth W PTS 6 Middleton
02.12.93   Micky Hall L PTS 4 Hartlepool
02.02.94   Steve McLevy L PTS 6 Glasgow
28.02.94   Rocky Ferrari W PTS 6 Marton
18.04.94   Andy Davidson L RSC 1 Manchester
22.09.94   Kevin McKillan L PTS 6 Bury
25.10.94   A. M. Milton W PTS 4 Middlesbrough
23.11.94   Mark Breslin L PTS 6 Irvine
30.11.94   Gareth Jordan L PTS 6 Wolverhampton
17.02.95   Alan Peacock W PTS 6 Cumbernauld
02.03.95   Rocky Ferrari DREW 6 Glasgow
20.03.95   Alan Peacock W RSC 6 Glasgow
13.05.95   Gordon Blair L RTD 5 Glasgow
30.06.95   Tony Mock L PTS 6 Liverpool
29.07.95   Hughie Davey L RSC 5 Whitley Bay
29.09.95   Kevin Toomey DREW 6 Hartlepool
23.11.95   Paul King W PTS 10 Marton
           *(Northern Area Welterweight Title
           Challenge)*
11.12.95   Derek Roche L RSC 3 Bradford
02.03.96   Paul King L RSC 2 Newcastle
           *(Northern Area Welterweight Title
           Defence)*
Career: 25 contests, won 9, drew 2, lost 14.

Kevin McKenzie

(Roger) R. F. McKenzie

Croydon. *Born* Croydon, 3 October, 1965
Former Southern Area Heavyweight
Champion. Ht. 6'2"
Manager Self

31.01.89	Gerry Storey W PTS 6 Bethnal Green
24.09.90	Mark Bowen L RSC 1 Mayfair
29.11.90	Denzil Browne W PTS 6 Sunderland
12.02.91	Noel Magee L PTS 6 Belfast
21.03.91	Denzil Browne L PTS 6 Dewsbury
28.05.91	Steve Yorath L PTS 6 Cardiff
07.09.91	Ray Kane L PTS 4 Belfast
09.10.91	Denzil Browne W PTS 6 Manchester
28.10.91	Pedro van Raamsdonk W CO 7 Arnhem, Holland
12.12.91	Norbert Ekassi L RSC 3 Massy, France
14.03.92	Neils H. Madsen L PTS 6 Copenhagen, Denmark
25.04.92	Noel Magee L PTS 8 Belfast
31.10.92	Warren Richards DREW 6 Earls Court
13.02.93	Magne Havnaa W RTD 5 Randers, Denmark
31.03.93	Warren Richards W RSC 8 Bethnal Green
	(Vacant Southern Area Heavyweight Title)
17.09.93	Brian Neilsen L PTS 6 Copenhagen, Denmark
13.10.93	James Oyebola L RSC 1 Bethnal Green
	(Southern Area Heavyweight Title Defence)
11.12.93	Bernd Friedrich W RSC 2 Dusseldorf, Germany
25.03.94	Mark Hulstrom L PTS 6 Bernholme, Denmark
17.09.94	Scott Welch L RSC 1 Crawley
27.05.95	Darren Corbett W PTS 6 Belfast
07.10.95	Mike Holden L RSC 2 Belfast

Career: 22 contests, won 8, drew 1, lost 13.

Kevin McKillan

Manchester. *Born* Belfast, 1 March, 1969
L. Welterweight. Ht. 5'8"
Manager T. Miller

28.10.91	Michael Byrne W PTS 6 Leicester
13.11.91	Barry Glanister W PTS 6 Liverpool
22.01.92	Sugar Boy Wright W PTS 6 Solihull
10.02.92	Jamie Davidson L PTS 6 Liverpool
11.03.92	Jamie Davidson DREW 6 Liverpool
01.06.92	Steve Howden W RSC 2 Manchester
12.06.92	Floyd Churchill W PTS 6 Liverpool
25.09.92	John Smith W PTS 6 Liverpool
07.10.92	J. T. Williams L PTS 6 Barry
20.11.92	Steve Foran L PTS 6 Liverpool
15.02.93	John T. Kelly W PTS 6 Manchester
19.04.93	Simon Hamblett W CO 2 Manchester
26.04.93	Steve Walker DREW 6 Manchester
01.06.93	Micky Hall W PTS 6 Manchester
06.10.93	Norman Dhalie W RSC 1 Solihull
29.10.93	Soren Sondergaard L CO 2 Korsoer, Denmark
26.01.94	Dean Amory W PTS 8 Stoke
06.06.94	Micky Hall W PTS 6 Manchester
22.09.94	Kevin McKenzie W PTS 6 Bury
10.12.94	Tanveer Ahmed L PTS 6 Manchester
18.05.95	Shaun Stokes DREW 8 Middleton
29.09.95	Alan Temple L PTS 6 Hartlepool
28.10.95	Georgie Smith L CO 2 Kensington
16.03.96	Tanveer Ahmed L PTS 4 Glasgow
10.05.96	Carl Wright L PTS 8 Liverpool
24.05.96	Tanveer Ahmed DREW 8 Glasgow
29.06.96	Peter Richardson L CO 2 Erith

Career: 27 contests, won 13, drew 4, lost 10.

Ian McLeod

Kilmarnock. *Born* Edinburgh, 11 June, 1969
S. Featherweight. Ht. 5'9"
Manager Self

23.11.92	Robert Braddock DREW 6 Glasgow
29.03.93	Graham McGrath W PTS 6 Glasgow
21.02.94	Graham McGrath W CO 6 Glasgow
04.03.94	Chip O'Neill W RSC 2 Irvine
23.11.94	Chris Jickells W PTS 6 Irvine
05.04.95	Colin Innes W RSC 5 Irvine
22.01.96	Chris Jickells W PTS 8 Glasgow

Career: 7 contests, won 6, drew 1.

Steve McLevy

Glasgow. *Born* Glasgow, 23 September, 1972
Scottish L. Welterweight Champion. Ht. 5'8"
Manager Self

22.11.93	Dewi Roberts W RSC 1 Glasgow
02.02.94	Kevin McKenzie W PTS 6 Glasgow
28.03.94	Mark Antony W CO 1 Musselburgh
20.09.94	Dave Curtis W RTD 3 Musselburgh
21.11.94	Mark Legg W RSC 3 Glasgow
24.02.95	John Smith W PTS 6 Irvine
01.06.95	Micky Hall L RSC 1 Musselburgh
23.10.95	Alan Peacock W RSC 6 Glasgow
	(Vacant Scottish L. Welterweight Title)
22.01.96	Tony Swift L PTS 8 Glasgow
03.06.96	Wahid Fats W RSC 3 Glasgow

Career: 10 contests, won 8, lost 2.

Conn McMullen

Acton. *Born* Larne, 21 June, 1967
S. Bantamweight. Ht. 5'6"
Manager Self

06.06.90	Ceri Farrell W RSC 5 Battersea
04.12.90	Neil Parry W RSC 2 Southend
12.11.91	Mark Loftus W PTS 6 Milton Keynes
28.10.92	Barry Jones L PTS 6 Cardiff
26.03.93	Neil Armstrong W RSC 5 Glasgow
05.05.93	Miguel Matthews DREW 6 Belfast
18.06.93	Wayne McCullough L RSC 3 Belfast
25.08.93	Anton Gilmore L PTS 8 Hammanskraal, South Africa
23.10.93	John Green W PTS 6 Cardiff
23.02.94	Tony Falcone DREW 4 Watford
29.03.94	Pete Buckley L PTS 6 Bethnal Green
11.06.94	Michael Alldis L PTS 8 Bethnal Green
09.07.94	Drew Docherty L PTS 8 Earls Court
07.10.94	Johnny Bredahl L PTS 8 Copenhagen, Denmark
04.11.94	Salim Medjkoune L PTS 8 Aubiere, France
25.11.95	Michael Alldis L CO 4 Dagenham

Career: 16 contests, won 5, drew 2, lost 9.

Steve McNess

Bethnal Green. *Born* Bow, 17 November, 1969
Middleweight. Ht. 5'10½"
Manager Self

22.04.92	Rick North W PTS 6 Wembley
13.05.92	Mark Verikios L RSC 5 Kensington
03.09.92	Steve Goodwin W PTS 6 Dunstable
28.10.92	Mark Dawson L RSC 2 Kensington
28.01.93	Steve Scott W PTS 6 Southwark
26.04.93	Bullit Andrews W RSC 3 Lewisham

(continued)

15.06.93	Martin Rosamond L RSC 5 Hemel Hempstead
07.12.93	Robert Whitehouse W RSC 3 Bethnal Green
16.02.94	Billy McDougall W PTS 4 Stevenage
11.03.94	Tony Walton W PTS 4 Bethnal Green
11.10.94	Harry Dhami DREW 6 Bethnal Green
23.02.95	Julian Eavis W PTS 6 Southwark
25.03.95	Peter Vosper W RSC 5 Millwall
20.04.95	Spencer Alton W RSC 2 Mayfair
19.05.95	Martin Jolley W PTS 6 Southwark
27.09.95	Martin Jolley L RTD 4 Bethnal Green
29.04.96	Roy Chipperfield W RSC 3 Mayfair

Career: 17 contests, won 12, drew 1, lost 4.

Dave Madden

Birmingham. *Born* Birmingham, 18 June, 1967
Welterweight. Ht. 5'10"
Manager J. Cox

12.11.92	Blue Butterworth L RSC 2 Burnley
27.01.93	Gary Hiscox L PTS 6 Stoke
22.02.93	Kris McAdam L PTS 8 Glasgow
20.09.93	Lee Heggs W PTS 6 Northampton
27.10.93	Gareth Jordan L RSC 5 West Bromwich
19.12.93	Dennis Griffin L RSC 1 Northampton
10.03.94	Dave Fallon W PTS 6 Watford
16.05.94	Danny Quacoe L RSC 4 Heathrow
03.04.95	Ram Singh W PTS 6 Northampton
22.06.95	John T. Kelly L PTS 6 Houghton le Spring
25.10.95	Steve Howden L PTS 6 Stoke
14.11.95	Dave Clavering L RSC 1 Bury
24.04.96	Vic Broomhead L RSC 3 Stoke

Career: 13 contests, won 3, lost 10.

Eamonn Magee

Belfast. *Born* Belfast, 13 July, 1971
Welterweight. Ht. 5'9"
Manager M. O'Callaghan

25.11.95	Pete Roberts W CO 4 Dublin
09.03.96	Steve McGovern W PTS 4 Millstreet
28.05.96	John Stovin W RSC 2 Belfast

Career: 3 contests, won 3.

Noel Magee

Belfast. *Born* Belfast, 16 December, 1965
Former Commonwealth L. Heavyweight
Champion. Ht. 6'1"
Manager Self

22.05.85	Nigel Prickett W CO 1 Stoke
12.09.85	Dave Furneaux W RSC 3 Swindon
28.10.85	Eddie Chatterton W RSC 1 Stoke
06.11.85	Winston Burnett W PTS 8 Nantwich
11.12.85	Winston Burnett W PTS 8 Stoke
22.01.86	Blaine Logsdon W PTS 8 Stoke
20.02.86	Barry Ahmed W PTS 8 Newcastle
05.03.86	Winston Burnett W PTS 8 Stoke
23.04.86	Barry Ahmed W RSC 7 Stoke
30.05.86	Geoff Rymer W CO 1 Stoke
13.10.86	Jimmy Ellis W PTS 8 Dulwich
17.11.86	Serg Fame W PTS 8 Dulwich
24.02.87	Lennie Howard W RSC 1 Ilford
03.08.87	Jimmy Ellis W RSC 6 Stoke
20.10.87	Johnny Held L PTS 8 Stoke
13.02.88	Rufino Angulo DREW 8 Paris, France
03.05.88	Mike Brothers W CO 6 Stoke
15.11.88	Ian Bulloch DREW 10 Hull
15.02.89	Yves Monsieur L RSC 5 Stoke
02.10.89	Paul McCarthy W CO 2 Hanley

29.11.89 Sammy Storey L RSC 9 Belfast
(British S. Middleweight Title Challenge)
15.09.90 Glazz Campbell W PTS 8 Belfast
30.10.90 Johnny Melfah W PTS 6 Belfast
12.02.91 R. F. McKenzie W PTS 6 Belfast
11.05.91 Simon Collins W PTS 8 Belfast
13.11.91 Frank Minton W RSC 3 Belfast
11.12.91 Tony Wilson W RSC 3 Dublin
25.04.92 R. F. McKenzie W PTS 8 Belfast
28.09.92 Maurice Core L RSC 9 Manchester
(Vacant British L. Heavyweight Title)
22.05.93 Dariusz Michalczewski L RSC 8 Aachen, Germany
(Vacant IBF Inter-Continental L. Heavyweight Title)
16.10.93 John Kaighin W PTS 6 Belfast
21.05.94 John J. Cooke W PTS 6 Belfast
05.03.95 Fabrice Tiozzo L RSC 4 Vitrolles, France
(European L. Heavyweight Title Challenge)
09.05.95 Garry Delaney W RTD 7 Basildon
(Commonwealth L. Heavyweight Title Challenge)
30.09.95 Nicky Piper L CO 9 Cardiff
(Commonwealth L. Heavyweight Title Defence. Vacant WBO Inter-Continental L. Heavyweight Title)
Career: 35 contests, won 26, drew 2, lost 7.

Jay Mahoney

Peterborough. *Born* Peterborough, 21 September, 1971
L. Welterweight. Ht 5'8"
Manager Self

05.12.94 Shaun O'Neill W PTS 6 Houghton le Spring
20.02.95 David Thompson W RSC 4 Manchester
08.03.95 Peter Hickenbottom W PTS 6 Solihull
03.04.95 Blue Butterworth W PTS 6 Manchester
02.10.95 Anthony Maynard L PTS 8 Birmingham
Career: 5 contests, won 4, lost 1.

Amjed Mamond

Rochdale. *Born* Pakistan, 7 February, 1972
Featherweight. Ht. 5'7"
Manager A. Talbot

26.04.96 Alston Buchanan L RSC 1 Glasgow
Career: 1 contest, lost 1.

Nick Manners

Leeds. *Born* Leeds, 23 November, 1966
S. Middleweight. Ht. 6'2"
Manager M. Duff

18.10.90 Paul Murray W PTS 6 Dewsbury
13.12.90 John Kaighin W CO 3 Dewsbury
31.01.91 Terry Duffus W RSC 1 Bredbury
21.03.91 Marvin O'Brien W CO 2 Dewsbury
09.05.91 Peter Gorny W RSC 1 Leeds
27.06.91 Peter Vosper W RSC 1 Leeds
01.08.91 Tony Booth DREW 8 Dewsbury
30.10.91 Kevin Morton L PTS 8 Leeds
23.09.92 Lee Crocker W CO 1 Leeds
29.10.92 Ali Forbes L RSC 3 Leeds
25.02.93 Jason Fores W RSC 2 Bradford
07.04.93 Joe McKenzie W RSC 2 Leeds
21.10.94 Sean Heron L PTS 6 Glasgow
30.09.95 Joe Calzaghe L RSC 4 Basildon
05.03.96 Bruce Scott L RSC 5 Bethnal Green
Career: 15 contests, won 9, drew 1, lost 5.

Abdul Mannon

Battersea. *Born* Bangladesh, India, 5 April, 1972
Featherweight. Ht. 5'3"
Manager T. Toole

08.03.94 Brian Eccles W RSC 2 Kettering
17.05.94 Keith Jones W PTS 6 Kettering
27.10.94 Marty Chestnut L DIS 2 Millwall
24.01.95 Chris Lyons W PTS 6 Piccadilly
08.06.95 Brian Carr L PTS 6 Glasgow
17.06.95 Henry Jones L PTS 6 Cardiff
14.10.95 Stephen Smith L RSC 3 Munich, Germany
22.11.95 Des Gargano L PTS 6 Mayfair
17.12.95 Brian Carr L PTS 8 Glasgow
05.02.96 Benny May L PTS 4 Bexleyheath
16.03.96 Mike Deveney L RSC 2 Glasgow
Career: 11 contests, won 3, lost 8.

Abdul Mannon   Les Clark

Shaun Marsh

Barnsley. *Born* Barnsley, 1 February, 1972
L. Middleweight. Ht. 6'0"
Manager K. Tate

18.10.95 Roy Gbasai W CO 4 Batley
14.11.95 Donovan Davey L PTS 6 Yarm
Career: 2 contests, won 1, lost 1.

Scott Marshall (Calow)

Nottingham. *Born* Mansfield, 6 July, 1973
L. Welterweight. Ht. 5'9"
Manager J. Ashton

02.03.95 James Montgomerie L PTS 6 Glasgow
16.03.95 Shaun O'Neill L RSC 3 Sunderland
06.12.95 Thomas Bradley L RSC 5 Stoke
Career: 3 contests, lost 3.

Gary Marston

Stoke. *Born* Taunton, 11 December, 1966
Featherweight. Ht. 5'4"
Manager Self

29.09.92 Norman Dhalie DREW 6 Stoke
17.03.93 Jason Morris W PTS 6 Stoke
12.05.93 Phil Lashley L RSC 2 Stoke
07.09.93 Joe Fannin W RSC 2 Stoke
27.10.93 Jobie Tyers W PTS 6 Stoke
01.12.93 Dougie Fox W RSC 1 Stoke
15.03.94 Des Gargano W PTS 8 Stoke
11.10.95 Chris Jickells W PTS 8 Stoke
06.12.95 Miguel Matthews W PTS 8 Stoke
24.01.96 Miguel Matthews L PTS 8 Stoke
27.03.96 Joe Donohoe W PTS 8 Stoke
24.04.96 Miguel Matthews W PTS 8 Solihull
Career: 12 contests, won 10, drew 1, lost 1.

Dave Martin

Pimlico. *Born* Cardiff, 11 May, 1967
Bantamweight. Ht. 5'9"
Manager C. Magri

23.10.91 Mark Hargreaves L PTS 6 Stoke
14.11.91 Dave Campbell L PTS 6 Marble Arch
17.05.92 Chris Lyons DREW 6 Harringay
29.09.95 Harry Woods DREW 4 Bloomsbury
22.11.95 Mark Cokely W RTD 2 Mayfair
03.12.95 Brendan Bryce W PTS 6 Southwark
20.12.95 Harry Woods L CO 2 Usk
Career: 7 contests, won 2, drew 2, lost 3.

Dave Martin   Les Clark

(Paul) P. R. Mason

Sheffield. *Born* Sheffield, 18 October, 1965
S. Middleweight. Ht. 6'0"
Manager G. Rhodes

21.09.95 Barry Exton DREW 6 Sheffield
29.09.95 Mark Owens W RSC 3 Hartlepool
16.11.95 Mark Hopkins W PTS 6 Evesham
05.02.96 Michael Joyce W RSC 4 Bradford
15.02.96 Scott Beasley W PTS 6 Sheffield
07.03.96 Craig Joseph L PTS 6 Bradford
Career: 6 contests, won 4, drew 1, lost 1.

P. R. Mason   Les Clark

Peter Mason

Hartlepool. *Born* Hartlepool, 19 March, 1971
L. Heavyweight. Ht. 6'1"
Manager G. Robinson

08.06.96 Naveed Anwar W RSC 4 Newcastle
Career: 1 contest, won 1.

(Paul) Stinger Mason

Sheffield. *Born* Sheffield, 27 February, 1964
L. Heavyweight. Ht. 5'8"
Manager Self

19.04.89 Sean Stringfellow W PTS 6 Stoke
24.05.89 Andrew Flute L PTS 6 Hanley
16.11.89 Tony Lawrence DREW 4 Ilkeston
27.01.90 Ian Vokes W PTS 6 Sheffield
28.03.90 Cliff Curtis W PTS 6 Bethnal Green
20.05.90 Tony Hodge W CO 2 Sheffield
11.06.90 Glenn Campbell L RTD 5 Manchester
12.11.90 Adrian Wright L RSC 4 Stratford upon Avon
13.03.91 Mike Phillips DREW 6 Stoke
13.05.91 Doug Calderwood L CO 3 Manchester
23.10.91 Roger Wilson DREW 6 Stoke
11.11.91 Russell Washer W PTS 4 Stratford upon Avon
23.05.92 Paul Busby L RSC 2 Birmingham
28.09.92 Quinn Paynter L CO 1 Manchester
20.09.93 Stephen Wilson L RSC 6 Glasgow
10.11.93 Joe Calzaghe L RSC 1 Watford
15.03.94 Mark Dawson L RSC 6 Stoke
02.06.94 Luan Morena L PTS 6 Tooting
05.10.94 Lee Archer L PTS 6 Wolverhampton
16.11.94 Lester Jacobs L PTS 6 Bloomsbury
05.12.94 Jason Brown W RSC 2 Cleethorpes
13.12.94 Mark Baker L RSC 4 Ilford
23.01.95 Naveed Mirza L RSC 3 Bethnal Green
07.03.95 Justin Clements L RSC 4 Edgbaston
02.07.95 Paschal Collins L PTS 4 Dublin
09.09.95 Danny Ryan L PTS 6 Cork

27.10.95 Mark Snipe DREW 6 Brighton
06.12.95 John Duckworth W PTS 6 Stoke
26.01.96 Robin Reid L RSC 2 Brighton
20.03.96 Greg Scott-Briggs L PTS 6 Stoke
Career: 30 contests, won 8, drew 4, lost 18.

(Jason) J. P. Matthews

Bargoed. *Born* Caerphilly, 26 June, 1969
L. Middleweight. Ht. 5'9"
Manager D. Gardiner

18.07.91 Carl Hook W PTS 6 Cardiff
29.10.91 Robert Peel W RSC 6 Cardiff
21.11.91 Chris Saunders W RSC 4 Burton
11.02.92 Carl Hook W PTS 6 Cardiff
30.04.92 Ross Hale L RSC 3 Bayswater
02.09.95 Sandy Katerega W PTS 4 Wembley
09.09.95 Jim Webb L PTS 6 Cork
19.09.95 Simon Andrews W RSC 3 Plymouth
16.10.95 John Bosco DREW 6 Mayfair
Career: 9 contests, won 6, drew 1, lost 2.

Jason Matthews

Hackney. *Born* London, 20 July, 1970
Middleweight. Ht. 5'10½"
Manager F. Warren

01.07.95 Chris Richards W CO 4 Kensington
22.07.95 Stuart Dunn W CO 1 Millwall
02.09.95 John Duckworth W PTS 4 Wembley
15.09.95 Mark Dawson W RSC 3 Mansfield
30.09.95 Marvin O'Brien W PTS 6 Cardiff
09.10.95 Salah Eddine Kobba W RSC 1 San Benedetto, Italy
27.10.95 Russell Washer W RSC 5 Brighton
09.12.95 Sven Hamer W RSC 6 Bethnal Green
16.03.96 John McAlpine W RSC 1 Glasgow
11.05.96 Peter Vosper W RSC 1 Bethnal Green
25.06.96 Martin Jolley W RSC 3 Mansfield
Career: 11 contests, won 11.

(Nicholas) Miguel Matthews

Ystalfera. *Born* Glanamman, 22 December, 1965
S. Featherweight. Ht. 5'7"
Manager R. Gray

21.09.88 Terry Collins L PTS 6 Basildon
28.09.88 Eugene Maloney DREW 6 Edmonton
25.10.88 Hugh Ruse L PTS 6 Pontadawe
15.11.88 Tommy Bernard W RSC 2 Chigwell
14.12.88 Richie Wenton L CO 2 Kirkby
14.02.89 Brian Robb W RSC 2 Wolverhampton
06.03.89 Mickey Markie L PTS 8 Northampton
21.03.89 Ronnie Stephenson DREW 6 Wolverhampton
11.04.89 Hugh Ruse W PTS 6 Aberavon
05.06.89 Lester James DREW 6 Birmingham
12.06.89 Colin McMillan L RSC 3 Battersea
06.09.89 Marcel Herbert L PTS 6 Aberavon
20.09.89 Des Gargano L PTS 6 Stoke
28.09.89 Steve Walker L PTS 6 Cardiff
17.10.89 Alan Roberts W PTS 6 Cardiff
24.10.89 Jimmy Clark L PTS 6 Watford
06.11.89 Mickey Markie DREW 8 Northampton
03.12.89 Johnny Bredahl L PTS 6 Copenhagen, Denmark
19.02.90 Mickey Markie L PTS 8 Kettering
27.02.90 Pete Buckley DREW 6 Evesham
21.03.90 Rocky Lawlor L PTS 8 Solihull
03.09.90 Derek Amory L PTS 6 Dudley
01.10.90 Pete Buckley L PTS 8 Cleethorpes
09.10.90 Pete Buckley W PTS 6 Wolverhampton
29.10.90 Pete Buckley L PTS 8 Birmingham
21.11.90 Jason Primera L PTS 8 Solihull

12.12.90 Paul Harvey L PTS 6 Basildon
19.12.90 Paul Forrest L PTS 6 Preston
07.03.91 Bradley Stone L RSC 4 Basildon
04.04.91 Mark Tierney L PTS 6 Watford
16.04.91 Craig Dermody L PTS 6 Nottingham
25.04.91 Bradley Stone L PTS 6 Basildon
23.05.91 Jason Lepre L PTS 6 Southampton
31.05.91 Danny Connelly L PTS 8 Glasgow
13.06.91 Tony Silkstone L PTS 6 Hull
24.06.91 Jimmy Owens L PTS 6 Liverpool
09.09.91 Moussa Sangare L RSC 5 Forges les Eux, France
09.10.91 Mark Loftus DREW 6 Manchester
24.10.91 Kevin Middleton L PTS 6 Dunstable
31.10.91 Brian Robb DREW 6 Oakengates
11.11.91 Peter Judson L PTS 6 Stratford on Avon
21.11.91 Craig Dermody L PTS 6 Burton
28.11.91 Dave Hardie L PTS 6 Glasgow
11.12.91 Jimmy Clark L PTS 6 Basildon
08.01.92 Ceri Farrell W PTS 6 Burton
31.01.92 John Green DREW 6 Manchester
20.02.92 Edward Cook L PTS 6 Glasgow
27.02.92 Craig Dermody L PTS 6 Liverpool
25.03.92 John Armour L PTS 6 Dagenham
01.06.92 Danny Porter L PTS 6 Glasgow
07.07.92 Tony Falcone L PTS 6 Bristol
14.07.92 Prince Nassem Hamed L RSC 3 Mayfair
30.09.92 Jonjo Irwin L PTS 6 Solihull
17.10.92 Mark Bowers L PTS 6 Wembley
24.11.92 Kid McAuley L PTS 6 Doncaster
14.12.92 Barry Jones L PTS 6 Cardiff
30.01.93 Tim Yeates L PTS 6 Brentwood
27.02.93 Paul Lloyd L PTS 6 Ellesmere Port
18.03.93 Kevin Middleton L PTS 6 Lewisham
17.04.93 Fabian Zavattini L PTS 6 Lausanne, Switzerland
05.05.93 Conn McMullen DREW 6 Belfast
15.05.93 Dave McHale L RSC 4 Glasgow
10.07.93 Russell Rees L PTS 6 Cardiff
22.09.93 Marcus McCrae L PTS 6 Bethnal Green
06.10.93 Mark Geraghty L PTS 6 Glasgow
30.10.93 Gary Thornhill L PTS 6 Chester
22.11.93 Ian McGirr L PTS 6 Glasgow
29.11.93 Tim Yeates DREW 6 Ingatestone
18.12.93 John White L PTS 6 Manchester
14.01.94 Kevin Middleton L PTS 6 Bethnal Green
28.01.94 Frederic Perez L PTS 8 Sete, France
10.04.94 Mark Geraghty L PTS 8 Glasgow
25.04.94 Hugh Collins L PTS 8 Glasgow
22.05.94 Mike Anthony Brown W RSC 5 Crystal Palace
06.06.94 Russell Davison W PTS 6 Glasgow
21.07.94 Mike Anthony Brown L PTS 6 Battersea
20.09.94 Drew Docherty L PTS 8 Musselburgh
17.02.95 Michael Alldis L PTS 8 Crawley
06.03.95 Michael Armstrong L PTS 6 Mayfair
09.06.95 Moussa Sangare L CO 2 Grande Synthe, France
29.09.95 Paul Ingle L RSC 4 Bethnal Green
29.11.95 Chris Jickells W PTS 6 Solihull
06.12.95 Gary Marston L PTS 8 Stoke
18.12.95 Graham McGrath W PTS 8 Mayfair
24.01.96 Gary Marston W PTS 8 Stoke
13.02.96 Dean Amory L PTS 8 Wolverhampton
21.02.96 Terry Whittaker L PTS 6 Batley
06.03.96 Fred Reeve W PTS 6 Solihull
24.04.96 Gary Marston L PTS 8 Solihull
04.05.96 Richard Evatt L PTS 6 Dagenham
14.05.96 Patrick Mullings L PTS 6 Dagenham
25.06.96 Paul Griffin L PTS 6 Mansfield
Career: 92 contests, won 12, drew 10, lost 70.

Paul Matthews

Llanelli. *Born* Gorseinon, 26 September, 1968
Middleweight. Ht. 5'8"
Manager Self

23.03.94	Steve Thomas W PTS 6 Cardiff
02.06.94	Jason Hart W RSC 3 Tooting
21.09.94	Peter Mitchell L PTS 6 Cardiff
12.11.94	Mads Larsen L RTD 4 Randers, Denmark
08.03.95	Barry Thorogood L PTS 4 Cardiff
12.04.95	Carl Winstone L PTS 6 Llanelli
06.05.95	Danny Ryan L PTS 6 Shepton Mallet
29.05.96	Carl Winstone W PTS 6 Ebbw Vale

Career: 8 contests, won 3, lost 5.

David Maw

Sunderland. *Born* Sunderland, 14 January, 1967
L. Middleweight. Ht. 5'9½"
Manager B. Hardy

22.05.87	Kevin Plant W PTS 6 Peterlee
04.06.87	Dean Bramhald W PTS 6 Sunderland
04.09.87	Dean Bramhald W PTS 6 Gateshead
22.09.87	John Reid DREW 4 Oldham
16.10.87	Kevin Spratt L PTS 8 Gateshead
03.11.87	Jeff Connors W PTS 6 Sunderland
08.06.88	Andy Holligan L RSC 1 Sheffield
26.09.89	Steve Foran L PTS 8 Chigwell
10.09.89	Delroy Waul L PTS 4 Sunderland
14.10.91	Dave Maj W PTS 6 Manchester
08.12.94	Phil Epton W PTS 6 Hull
21.02.95	Hughie Davey L RSC 3 Sunderland
25.03.95	Craig Winter L RSC 3 Rothwell
22.06.95	Hughie Davey L PTS 6 Houghton le Spring
14.02.96	Roy Chipperfield W PTS 6 Sunderland

Career: 15 contests, won 7, drew 1, lost 7.

Benny May

Peckham. *Born* Dulwich, 19 August, 1976
S. Featherweight. Ht. 5'6"
Manager F. Maloney

05.02.96	Abdul Mannon W PTS 4 Bexleyheath
02.04.96	Eddie Sica L RSC 1 Southwark

Career: 2 contests, won 1, lost 1.

Benny May   Les Clark

Anthony Maynard

Birmingham. *Born* Birmingham, 12 January, 1972
L. Welterweight. Ht. 5'8"
Manager Self

17.10.94	Malcolm Thomas W PTS 6 Birmingham
02.11.94	Dean Phillips W PTS 6 Birmingham
25.01.95	Neil Smith L PTS 6 Stoke
07.02.95	Anthony Campbell W PTS 8 Wolverhampton
08.03.95	Scott Walker W PTS 6 Solihull
28.03.95	Kid McAuley W PTS 8 Wolverhampton
11.05.95	Gary Hiscox W RSC 4 Dudley
06.06.95	Richard Swallow L RSC 2 Leicester
02.10.95	Jay Mahoney W PTS 8 Birmingham
26.10.95	Ray Newby W PTS 8 Birmingham
17.01.96	Tom Welsh W RSC 8 Solihull
06.03.96	G. G. Goddard W RSC 3 Solihull

Career: 12 contests, won 10, lost 2.

Trevor Meikle

Scunthorpe. *Born* Scunthorpe, 29 January, 1967
Central Area Welterweight Champion. Ht. 5'9"
Manager J. Rushton

16.05.89	Lewis Welch DREW 6 Halifax
12.06.89	Chris Mulcahy L PTS 6 Manchester
19.06.89	Anthony Lawrence L PTS 6 Manchester
11.07.89	Chris Mulcahy L PTS 6 Batley
16.10.89	Steve Hardman DREW 6 Manchester
23.10.89	Mick Mulcahy W PTS 6 Cleethorpes
06.11.89	Ian Thomas W PTS 6 Northampton
14.11.89	Cliff Churchward W PTS 6 Evesham
22.11.89	Cliff Churchward W PTS 6 Stafford
11.12.89	Barry Messam L CO 5 Nottingham
05.02.90	Malcolm Melvin L PTS 6 Brierley Hill
19.02.90	Gordon Blair L PTS 6 Glasgow
27.02.90	Dave Whittle DREW 8 Marton
14.03.90	Carlos Chase L PTS 6 Battersea
27.03.90	Barry Messam W PTS 6 Leicester
30.04.90	Young Gully L PTS 6 Brierley Hill
21.05.90	Frank Harrington W RSC 5 Hanley
30.05.90	Mark Jay DREW 6 Stoke
15.06.90	Mark Jay W RSC 5 Telford
14.09.90	Mickey Lerwill DREW 8 Telford
03.10.90	Jim Lawlor L PTS 6 Solihull
09.10.90	Pat Durkin W DIS 3 Liverpool
24.10.90	Ernie Loveridge L PTS 6 Dudley
06.11.90	Stuart Good L PTS 6 Southend
21.11.90	Jim Lawlor L PTS 6 Solihull
29.11.90	Dave Whittle L PTS 6 Marton
10.12.90	Kevin Spratt L PTS 6 Bradford
11.02.91	Steve Hardman L PTS 6 Manchester
21.02.91	Colin Sinnott W PTS 6 Leeds
27.02.91	Andreas Panayi W PTS 6 Wolverhampton
03.04.91	Mick Mulcahy W PTS 6 Manchester
10.04.91	Wayne Timmins L PTS 6 Wolverhampton
22.04.91	Nick Cope W RSC 2 Glasgow
01.05.91	Tommy Milligan L PTS 6 Liverpool
09.05.91	Tod Riggs L PTS 6 Leeds
03.06.91	Tommy Milligan L PTS 6 Glasgow
10.06.91	Chris Mulcahy DREW 6 Manchester
14.08.91	Efren Calamati L RSC 4 Alcamo, Italy
23.09.91	Alan Peacock W PTS 6 Glasgow
01.10.91	James McGee W PTS 6 Bedworth
05.11.91	Lee Ferrie L PTS 6 Leicester
25.11.91	Mark Kelly W PTS 8 Cleethorpes
05.12.91	Mickey Lerwill L PTS 6 Oakengates
14.12.91	Kevin Lueshing L CO 3 Bexleyheath
28.01.92	Alan Peacock L PTS 8 Piccadilly
29.02.92	Andre Kimbu L RTD 5 Gravelines, France
13.04.92	Crain Fisher L PTS 6 Manchester
30.04.92	B. F. Williams L PTS 6 Watford
14.09.92	Kevin Spratt W RSC 4 Bradford
23.10.92	Andreas Panayi L PTS 6 Liverpool
26.11.92	Willie Yeardsley W PTS 6 Hull
03.02.93	Derek Grainger L RSC 6 Earls Court
13.12.93	Rick North L PTS 6 Cleethorpes
22.05.94	Maurice Forbes L RTD 3 Crystal Palace
23.09.94	Clay O'Shea L RSC 1 Bethnal Green
08.11.95	Andy Peach W PTS 6 Scunthorpe
06.12.95	Andy Peach W RSC 3 Stoke
29.02.96	Kevin Toomey W PTS 10 Scunthorpe *(Vacant Central Area Welterweight Title)*
14.05.96	Peter Richardson L RSC 2 Dagenham

Career: 59 contests, won 20, drew 6, lost 33.

Malcolm Melvin

Birmingham. *Born* Birmingham, 5 February, 1967
All-Ireland & Midlands Area L. Welterweight Champion. Ht. 5'7"
Manager Self

28.11.85	Steve Foster DREW 6 Ilkeston
04.12.85	Simon Collins L PTS 6 Stoke
24.03.86	Rocky McGran L PTS 6 Mayfair
10.04.86	Lincoln Pennant W PTS 6 Leicester
21.04.86	Malcolm Davies W PTS 6 Birmingham
07.05.86	Julian Monville W PTS 6 Solihull
19.01.88	Antonio Fernandez L RSC 4 Kings Heath
07.03.88	John Ellis L PTS 6 Piccadilly
03.12.89	Dave Jenkins W PTS 6 Birmingham
05.02.90	Trevor Meikle W PTS 6 Brierley Hill
22.02.90	Chris Saunders L PTS 4 Hull
19.03.90	Barry North W PTS 6 Brierley Hill
30.04.90	Andy Kent W RSC 5 Brierley Hill
04.06.90	Brendan Ryan L RSC 7 Edgbaston
03.09.90	Dave Jenkins W PTS 8 Dudley
13.11.90	Brendan Ryan W PTS 8 Edgbaston *(Vacant Midlands Area L. Welterweight Title)*
18.03.91	Carl Brasier W PTS 6 Piccadilly
17.06.91	Dean Bramhald W PTS 6 Edgbaston
21.05.92	Mark Kelly W PTS 8 Cradley Heath
05.10.92	Ross Hale L PTS 10 Bristol *(Elim. British L. Welterweight Title)*
17.11.92	Tusikoleta Nkalankete DREW 8 Paris, France
16.03.93	Shaun Cogan W PTS 10 Edgbaston *(Vacant All-Ireland L. Welterweight Title & Midlands Area L. Welterweight Title Defence)*
29.06.93	Mark Kelly W PTS 6 Edgbaston
24.11.93	Alan Peacock W PTS 8 Solihull
08.03.94	Julian Eavis W PTS 6 Edgbaston
28.06.94	John Smith W PTS 6 Edgbaston
18.02.95	Ross Hale L PTS 12 Shepton Mallet *(British & Commonwealth L. Welterweight Title Challenge)*
21.05.96	Karl Taylor W PTS 10 Edgbaston *(Midlands Area L. Welterweight Title Defence)*
03.06.96	Jamie Morris W RSC 2 Birmingham

Career: 29 contests, won 19, drew 2, lost 8.

Paul Miles   Les Clark

Paul Miles

Walton on Thames. *Born* Coventry, 6
February, 1974
Welterweight. Ht. 5'9¼"
Manager F. Maloney

21.09.95	John O. Johnson W PTS 4 Battersea
08.11.95	Adam Baldwin W RSC 2 Bethnal Green
29.11.95	John Smith W PTS 4 Southwark
19.01.96	John Janes L PTS 4 Bracknell
21.03.96	Darren Covill W PTS 4 Southwark
14.06.96	Jyri Kjall L RSC 4 Gravelines, France

Career: 6 contests, won 4, lost 2.

Johnny Miller

Northampton. *Born* Northampton, 15
January, 1971
Lightweight. Ht. 5'9"
Manager J. Cox

20.03.96 Chris Price W PTS 6 Stoke
24.04.96 Robert Grubb W PTS 6 Stoke
Career: 2 contests, won 2.

(Alvin) Slick Miller

Doncaster. *Born* Doncaster, 12 May, 1968
Cruiserweight. Ht. 6'2"
Manager T. Petersen

28.04.94 Declan Faherty L RSC 2 Hull
06.10.94 Kent Davis L PTS 6 Hull
17.11.94 Graham Wassell L RSC 1 Sheffield
29.09.95 Mark Richardson L PTS 6 Hartlepool
13.01.96 Geoff Hunter DREW 6 Halifax
13.02.96 Danny Williams L RSC 1 Bethnal Green
15.03.96 Tony Booth L PTS 6 Hull
22.03.96 Tony Dowling L RSC 4 Mansfield
Career: 8 contests, drew 1, lost 7.

Slick Miller   Les Clark

(Winston) Kid Milo (Walters)

Birmingham. *Born* Birmingham, 15
February, 1964
L. Heavyweight. Former Undefeated WBC
International Middleweight Champion.
Ht. 5'9"
Manager A. Urry

22.04.85 Darren Bowen W RSC 3 Birmingham
21.05.85 Tony Stevens W PTS 6 Birmingham
16.06.85 Julian Monville W PTS 6 Bethnal Green
09.10.85 Paul Boyce W RSC 3 Evesham
15.10.85 Mickey Lerwill W PTS 6 Wolverhampton
27.11.85 Charlie Watson L PTS 6 Bradford
17.02.86 Errol McDonald DREW 6 Mayfair
10.11.86 Darwin Brewster W RTD 4 Birmingham
18.02.87 Jimmy Cable W PTS 8 Fulham
15.12.87 Steve Davies W RSC 2 Cardiff
07.02.88 John Ashton L PTS 10 Stafford
(*Vacant Midlands Area
L. Middleweight Title*)
09.03.88 Tommy Shiels L RSC 2 Bethnal Green
06.10.88 Kesem Clayton W RSC 4 Dudley
24.05.89 Bocco George W RSC 1 Sheppey
27.06.89 Johnny Melfah W CO 7 Kensington
05.10.89 Simon Collins W PTS 8 Stevenage
21.03.91 Frank Grant W PTS 10 Solihull
(*Elim. British S. Middleweight Title*)
05.09.90 Chris Eubank L RSC 8 Brighton
(*WBC International Middleweight Title
Challenge*)
23.01.91 Lou Cafaro W CO 10 Solihull
(*Vacant WBC International
Middleweight Title*)
03.07.91 Nigel Benn L RSC 4 Brentwood
16.12.95 Dean Francis L RSC 3 Cardiff
Career: 21 contests, won 14, drew 1, lost 6.

(Alkis) A. M. Milton (Alkiviadov)

Streatham. *Born* London, 5 May, 1965
L. Welterweight. Ht. 5'3¾"
Manager Self

24.10.84 Kenny Watson L PTS 6 Mayfair
24.01.85 John Wilder W RTD 3 Streatham
04.02.85 John Faulkner L PTS 6 Lewisham
30.04.85 Kenny Watson W PTS 6 Merton
28.11.85 Brian Nickels L CO 4 Bethnal Green
04.09.86 Kevin Spratt DREW 6 Merton
19.11.87 Lee West L PTS 6 Wandsworth
10.05.88 Peter Hart L RSC 1 Tottenham
06.12.88 Shane Tonks W PTS 6 Southend
03.04.90 Dave Jenkins L PTS 6 Southend
25.09.90 Ray Newby W PTS 6 Millwall
12.11.90 Darren Morris W PTS 6 Norwich
08.05.91 Steve McGovern L PTS 6 Millwall
08.01.92 Darren Morris L PTS 6 Burton
31.10.92 Rick Bushell DREW 4 Earls Court
10.12.92 Brian Coleman DREW 4 Bethnal Green
17.02.93 Rick Bushell W RSC 1 Bethnal Green
31.03.93 Brian Coleman W PTS 4 Bethnal Green
23.06.93 Felix Kelly L CO 8 Edmonton
(*Vacant Southern Area Lightweight Title*)
01.12.93 Brian Coleman W PTS 4 Bethnal Green
30.07.94 Tony Gibbs W CO 1 Bethnal Green
25.10.94 Kevin McKenzie L PTS 4 Middlesbrough
01.07.95 Jimmy Phelan L PTS 6 Kensington
22.07.95 Tom Welsh L RSC 2 Millwall
02.09.95 Wayne Jones W RSC 1 Wembley
Career: 25 contests, won 10, drew 3, lost 12.

Clifton Mitchell

Sheffield. *Born* Derby, 29 October, 1965
Heavyweight. Ht. 6'2½"
Manager F. Warren

06.04.91 John Harewood W RSC 2 Darlington
01.08.91 John Harewood W CO 1 Dewsbury
03.10.91 Tucker Richards W PTS 6 Burton
21.11.91 Tucker Richards W RSC 6 Burton
14.04.92 Michael Murray W RSC 8 Mansfield
16.03.93 Vivian Schwalger W CO 1 Wolverhampton
26.05.93 John Harewood W RSC 4 Mansfield
18.12.93 Jim Huffman W CO 3 Manchester
29.01.94 Cordwell Hylton W RSC 1 Cardiff
26.02.94 Jean Chanet W RSC 2 Earls Court
11.05.94 Emanuel Brites Camargo W RSC 1 Sheffield
21.05.94 Steve Garber W CO 1 Belfast
17.08.94 Carl Gaffney W CO 1 Sheffield
10.09.94 Jeff Williams W CO 1 Birmingham
19.11.94 James Oyebola L CO 4 Cardiff
(*WBC International Heavyweight Title
Challenge & Vacant British
Heavyweight Title*)
10.11.95 Brian Sargent W CO 2 Derby
20.01.96 Jimmy Bills W CO 1 Mansfield
09.03.96 Rick Sullivan W RSC 3 Millstreet
08.06.96 Levi Billups W PTS 8 Newcastle
Career: 19 contests; won 18, lost 1.

Kevin Mitchell (George)

Brockley. *Born* Greenwich, 13 March, 1970
Cruiserweight. Ht. 6'2"
Manager T. Toole

25.04.96 Carl Nicholson W RSC 4 Mayfair
Career: 1 contest, won 1.

Norman Mitchell

Alfreton. *Born* Rotherham, 7 November, 1965
L. Middleweight. Ht. 5'11"
Manager Self

22.09.93 Warren Stephens W PTS 6 Chesterfield
22.02.96 Mark Owens L PTS 6 Sunderland
Career: 2 contests, won 1, lost 1.

Peter Mitchell

Southampton. *Born* Southampton, 26 May, 1967
Middleweight. Ht. 5'10½"
Manager J. Bishop

21.09.94 Paul Matthews W PTS 6 Cardiff
12.10.94 Andy Ewen L PTS 6 Sheffield
08.03.95 Paul Webb W RSC 1 Bloomsbury
19.04.95 Nicky Thurbin L PTS 6 Bethnal Green
02.06.95 Danny Ryan L PTS 6 Bethnal Green
13.11.95 Barrie Bessant W RSC 2 Barnstaple
04.12.95 Darren Sweeney L PTS 8 Birmingham
09.03.96 Jim Rock L PTS 6 Millstreet
03.06.96 Gordon Behan DREW 6 Birmingham
Career: 9 contests, won 3, drew 1, lost 5.

(Arvill) Arv Mittoo

Birmingham. *Born* Birmingham, 8 July, 1971
L. Welterweight. Ht. 5'8"
Manager N. Nobbs

31.01.96 Alan Bosworth L PTS 6 Stoke
13.02.96 Tommy Janes L PTS 6 Cardiff
21.02.96 Danny Lutaaya L PTS 6 Piccadilly
20.05.96 Terry Whittaker L CO 5 Cleethorpes
29.06.96 Craig Stanley L PTS 4 Erith
Career: 5 contests, lost 5.

Tony Mock

Liverpool. *Born* Liverpool, 3 May, 1969
Welterweight. Ht. 5'8"
Manager S. Vaughan

30.10.93 Tony Britland W PTS 6 Chester
11.12.93 Mark Antony W RSC 4 Liverpool
25.02.94 Mike Morrison W PTS 6 Chester
06.05.94 Scott Doyle W PTS 6 Liverpool
31.10.94 Charlie Paine W PTS 6 Liverpool
25.03.95 Floyd Churchill W PTS 6 Chester
30.06.95 Kevin McKenzie W PTS 6 Liverpool
10.05.96 Michael Alexander L PTS 6 Liverpool
Career: 8 contests, won 7, lost 1.

Alex Moon

Liverpool. *Born* Fazackerley, 17 November, 1971
Featherweight. Ht. 5'7½"
Manager J. Hyland

08.09.95 Marty Chestnut W RSC 3 Liverpool
24.11.95 G. G. Goddard L RTD 2 Chester
03.02.96 Chris Price W RSC 2 Liverpool
Career: 3 contests, won 2, lost 1.

Alex Moon   Les Clark

Karl Morling   Les Clark

Karl Morling

Northampton. *Born* Douglas, IOM, 26 December, 1970
Featherweight. Ht. 5'4"
Manager Self

15.10.90 Lee Christian W RSC 2 Kettering
22.10.90 Tony Falcone W PTS 6 Mayfair
31.01.91 Craig Dermody L RSC 5 Bredbury
02.05.91 Sol Francis W RSC 3 Northampton
13.05.91 Paul Wynn W PTS 2 Northampton
06.04.92 Norman Dhalie W PTS 6 Northampton
05.10.92 Robert Braddock W PTS 6 Northampton

14.12.92 Dean Lynch L RSC 4 Northampton
19.04.93 Graham McGrath W RSC 6 Northampton
01.12.93 John Armour L CO 3 Kensington
02.09.94 Matthew Harris L CO 5 Spitalfields
(Vacant Midlands Area S. Bantamweight Title)
20.09.95 Spencer Oliver L RSC 5 Potters Bar
25.11.95 Michael Brodie L RSC 1 Dagenham
Career: 13 contests, won 7, lost 6.

Terry Morrill

Hull. *Born* Hull, 2 February, 1965
Former Central Area L. Middleweight Champion. Ht. 5'10¼"
Manager S. Pollard

10.12.88 Chris Richards W PTS 6 Crystal Palace
08.02.89 Newton Barnett W PTS 6 Kensington
28.03.89 Skip Jackson L RSC 5 Glasgow
27.06.89 Mark Howell W PTS 6 Kensington
10.10.89 Spencer Alton W PTS 6 Hull
15.11.89 Davey Hughes DREW 4 Lewisham
08.12.89 Tony Baker W PTS 6 Doncaster
22.02.90 Mark Holden W RSC 7 Hull
(Central Area L. Middleweight Title Challenge)
10.04.90 Ernie Noble W RSC 7 Doncaster
20.05.90 Jason Rowe L CO 6 Sheffield
(Central Area L. Middleweight Title Defence)
31.10.90 Shaun Cummins L RSC 1 Crystal Palace
14.03.91 Delroy Waul DREW 8 Middleton
28.05.91 Eamonn Loughran L CO 1 Cardiff
16.10.92 Shamus Casey W PTS 6 Hull
16.09.93 Des Robinson W PTS 8 Hull
12.11.93 Shamus Casey W PTS 8 Hull
09.05.96 Lee Simpkin W RSC 5 Hull
Career: 17 contests, won 11, drew 2, lost 4.

Jamie Morris

Nuneaton. *Born* Nuneaton, 15 February, 1970
L. Welterweight. Ht. 5'9"
Manager Self

28.06.89 Phil Lashley W RSC 1 Kenilworth
05.09.89 Carl Brasier L RSC 3 Southend
10.10.89 Andrew Robinson L PTS 6 Wolverhampton
06.12.89 Wayne Taylor L RSC 5 Leicester
17.01.90 Lee Ahmed L PTS 6 Stoke
05.02.90 Lee Ahmed W PTS 6 Leicester
27.02.90 Lee Ahmed W PTS 6 Evesham
26.03.90 George Bailey W PTS 6 Bradford
06.04.90 Rick Dimmock L PTS 6 Stevenage
24.04.90 Des Gargano L PTS 4 Stoke
30.04.90 Neil Leitch L PTS 6 Nottingham
14.05.90 Tony Heath L PTS 6 Leicester
01.10.91 Michael Byrne DREW 4 Bedworth
16.10.91 Michael Byrne W PTS 6 Stoke
11.11.91 Mitchell Barney DREW 6 Stratford upon Avon
21.11.91 Brian Coleman DREW 6 Stafford
04.12.91 Sugar Boy Wright L PTS 6 Stoke
20.01.92 Mark Antony L RSC 5 Coventry
24.02.92 Simon Hamblett DREW 6 Coventry
11.03.92 Razza Campbell L PTS 6 Stoke
24.03.92 Mark Allen W PTS 6 Wolverhampton
27.01.93 Billy McDougall L PTS 6 Stoke
11.03.93 Mark Allen DREW 6 Walsall

17.06.93 Chris Pollock L RSC 2 Bedworth
13.12.93 Dean Bramhald L RSC 3 Doncaster
26.03.96 Patrick Parton L PTS 6 Wolverhampton
03.06.96 Malcolm Melvin L RSC 2 Birmingham
Career: 27 contests, won 6, drew 5, lost 16.

Sean Morrison

Sheffield. *Born* Sheffield, 6 November, 1972
Lightweight. Ht. 5'7"
Manager G. Rhodes

15.02.96 Hurricane Hughes W PTS 6 Sheffield
03.05.96 Chris Lyons W PTS 6 Sheffield
Career: 2 contests, won 2.

Jerry Mortimer

Clapham. *Born* Mauritius, 22 June, 1962
S. Middleweight. Ht. 5'9"
Manager B. Aird

21.10.91 Steve Thomas L PTS 6 Mayfair
12.02.92 Darren Murphy W PTS 6 Watford
02.03.92 Lee Farrell W PTS 6 Merthyr
28.04.92 Stefan Wright L RSC 4 Corby
08.09.92 Robert Whitehouse W RSC 3 Southend
15.10.92 Russell Washer W RSC 5 Lewisham
14.12.92 Gareth Boddy W PTS 6 Cardiff
28.01.93 John Bosco L RSC 4 Southwark
09.03.93 Paul Smith W PTS 6 Bristol
01.12.93 Gilbert Jackson L RSC 3 Kensington
20.01.94 Dean Cooper L PTS 8 Battersea
24.02.94 Mark Smallwood L PTS 6 Walsall
10.03.94 Dale Nixon DREW 4 Bristol
26.04.94 Mark Baker L PTS 6 Bethnal Green
27.05.94 Val Golding L PTS 6 Ashford
30.09.94 Mark Delaney L RSC 3 Bethnal Green
31.03.95 Andy Wright L RSC 1 Crystal Palace
27.09.95 Monty Wright L RTD 3 Bethnal Green
09.04.96 Butch Lesley L RSC 3 Stevenage
Career: 19 contests, won 6, drew 1, lost 12.

Patrick Mullings　　　　　Les Clark

Patrick Mullings

Harrow. *Born* Harlesden, 19 October, 1970
S. Bantamweight. Ht. 5'4½"
Manager F. Maloney

13.12.94 Graham McGrath W PTS 4 Ilford
23.01.95 Des Gargano W PTS 4 Bethnal Green
30.03.95 Graham McGrath W RSC 3 Bethnal Green
04.06.95 Des Gargano W PTS 6 Bethnal Green
21.09.95 Pete Buckley W PTS 6 Battersea
15.12.95 Pete Buckley W PTS 4 Bethnal Green
05.02.96 Pete Buckley W PTS 8 Bexleyheath
21.03.96 Danny Ruegg W RSC 3 Southwark
14.05.96 Miguel Matthews W PTS 6 Dagenham
Career: 9 contests, won 9.

Justin Murphy

Brighton. *Born* Brighton, 21 February, 1974
Featherweight. Ht. 5'7"
Manager Self

15.09.93 Andrew Bloomer W PTS 4 Bethnal Green
13.10.93 Thomas Bernard W RSC 1 Bethnal Green
01.12.93 Mark Hargreaves W PTS 4 Bethnal Green
25.01.94 Jobie Tyers W RSC 3 Piccadilly
29.03.94 Tony Falcone W RSC 2 Bethnal Green
15.06.94 Mike Deveney W PTS 6 Southwark
23.11.94 Pete Buckley W PTS 4 Piccadilly
25.05.95 Barry Jones L PTS 10 Reading
(*Elim. British Featherweight Title*)
16.06.95 Paul Webster L PTS 6 Southwark
08.11.95 P. J. Gallagher L RSC 6 Bethnal Green
(*Vacant Southern Area S. Featherweight Title & Elim. British S. Featherweight Title*)
30.01.96 Colin McMillan L RSC 4 Barking
Career: 11 contests, won 7, lost 4.

James Murray

Newmains. *Born* Lanark, 7 December, 1969
Former Scottish Bantamweight Champion.
Ht. 5'4"
Manager Self

26.03.93 L. C. Wilson W RSC 4 Glasgow
30.04.93 Dave Campbell W PTS 6 Glasgow
29.05.93 Kid McAuley W PTS 6 Paisley
09.09.93 Des Gargano W PTS 6 Glasgow
21.10.93 Graham McGrath W PTS 6 Glasgow
10.11.93 Paul Webster L PTS 4 Bethnal Green
10.02.94 Marty Chestnut W PTS 6 Glasgow
11.03.94 Paul Wynn W PTS 6 Glasgow
13.04.94 Pete Buckley W PTS 6 Glasgow
10.06.94 Graham McGrath W PTS 8 Glasgow
21.07.94 Dave Campbell W RSC 3 Edinburgh
21.10.94 Keith Jones W CO 3 Glasgow
18.11.94 Shaun Anderson W PTS 10 Glasgow
(*Vacant Scottish Bantamweight Title*)
21.01.95 Louis Veitch W RSC 3 Glasgow
(*Scottish Bantamweight Title Defence*)
21.04.95 Ady Benton W RSC 7 Glasgow
13.05.95 Danny Ruegg W PTS 6 Glasgow
13.10.95 Drew Docherty L CO 12 Glasgow
(*British Bantamweight Title Challenge*)
Career: 17 contests, won 15, lost 2.

Michael Murray

Manchester. *Born* Preston, 3 September, 1964
Former Undefeated Central Area Heavyweight Champion. Ht. 6'1"
Manager J. Trickett

23.02.88 Gypsy John Fury L PTS 6 Oldham
28.04.88 Ian Nelson W RSC 6 Manchester
17.11.88 Steve Garber W PTS 6 Stockport
07.02.89 Rocky Burton W PTS 6 Manchester
10.05.89 Barry Ellis W RSC 3 Solihull
08.09.89 Noel Quarless L PTS 8 Liverpool
17.10.89 John Westgarth W RTD 4 Oldham
06.02.90 Al Malcolm W RSC 5 Oldham
02.06.90 Gypsy John Fury L RTD 6 Manchester
30.04.91 Steve Garber W CO 1 Stockport
19.09.91 Carl Gaffney W RSC 8 Stockport
(*Vacant Central Area Heavyweight Title*)
22.10.91 Markus Bott W RSC 7 Hamburg, Germany
07.12.91 Steve Gee W RSC 7 Manchester
14.04.92 Clifton Mitchell L RSC 8 Mansfield
28.11.92 Ricky Sekorski W PTS 8 Manchester
27.02.93 Herbie Hide L RSC 5 Dagenham
(*Vacant British Heavyweight Title*)
30.09.94 Terry Dunstan L PTS 8 Bethnal Green
10.12.94 Scott Welch L PTS 8 Manchester
23.02.95 Derek Williams W PTS 8 Southwark
17.05.95 John Ruiz L RSC 4 Ipswich
14.10.95 Zeljko Mavrovic L RSC 4 Munich, Germany
14.11.95 Mike Holden W PTS 6 Bury
16.12.95 Keith Fletcher W DIS 3 Cardiff
05.02.96 Julius Francis L PTS 10 Bexleyheath
(*Elim. British Heavyweight Title*)
31.05.96 Mark Hulstrom L RSC 2 Copenhagen, Denmark
Career: 25 contests, won 15, lost 10.

Paul Murray

Birmingham. *Born* Birmingham, 8 January, 1961
Middleweight. Ht. 5'9"
Manager Self

04.09.80 Gerry White W PTS 6 Morecambe
11.09.80 Graeme Ahmed L PTS 6 Hartlepool
29.09.80 Richard Wilson L PTS 6 Bedworth
08.10.80 Carl North W CO 2 Stoke
14.10.80 Steve McLeod W PTS 6 Wolverhampton
20.10.80 Steve Davies DREW 6 Birmingham
30.10.80 John Wiggins W PTS 6 Wolverhampton
07.11.80 Archie Salmon L PTS 6 Cambuslang
18.11.80 John Wiggins L PTS 6 Shrewsbury
26.11.80 Mike Clemow L PTS 8 Stoke
08.12.80 John Wiggins L PTS 6 Nottingham
26.01.81 Errol Dennis W PTS 6 Edgbaston
16.03.81 Dennis Sheehan DREW 6 Nottingham
15.04.81 Nigel Thomas DREW 8 Evesham
28.05.81 Martin McGough L PTS 6 Edgbaston
09.07.81 Roger Guest L CO 8 Dudley
21.09.81 Gary Buckle DREW 6 Wolverhampton
07.10.81 Kostas Petrou W RSC 5 Solihull
13.10.81 Gary Buckle L PTS 6 Wolverhampton
24.11.81 Nick Riozzi W PTS 6 Wolverhampton
25.01.82 Martin McGough L RSC 4 Wolverhampton
21.02.82 Gary Buckle W PTS 8 Nottingham
10.03.82 Ron Pearce L PTS 8 Solihull

23.03.82	Errol Dennis L PTS 6 Wolverhampton	
29.03.82	Tony Brown L PTS 6 Liverpool	
07.04.82	Dennis Sheehan W PTS 6 Evesham	
28.04.82	Lee Roy W CO 3 Burslem	
17.05.82	Paul Costigan L PTS 8 Manchester	
24.05.82	Dennis Sheehan DREW 6 Nottingham	
07.06.82	Kostas Petrou L PTS 6 Edgbaston	
13.09.82	Paul Costigan W PTS 6 Manchester	
18.10.82	Kostas Petrou L RSC 5 Edgbaston	
15.02.83	Bert Myrie L PTS 6 Wolverhampton	
21.02.83	Steve Tempro L DIS 3 Edgbaston	
01.03.83	Chris Pyatt L RTD 2 Kensington	
17.05.83	T. P. Jenkins L PTS 6 Bethnal Green	
23.06.83	Wayne Hawkins L PTS 6 Wolverhampton	
19.09.83	Bert Myrie W PTS 8 Nottingham	
26.10.83	Steve Henty L PTS 6 Stoke	
14.11.83	Kid Sadler L PTS 8 Manchester	
14.12.83	John Andrews L PTS 6 Stoke	
19.03.84	Wayne Barker L PTS 8 Manchester	
27.03.84	Rocky Kelly L RTD 5 Battersea	
08.10.84	Gavin Stirrup L PTS 6 Manchester	
22.01.87	Chris Walker L PTS 4 Bethnal Green	
10.02.87	Chris Walker W PTS 4 Wolverhampton	
16.02.87	Chris Galloway W PTS 6 Mayfair	
24.02.87	Nicky Thorne L PTS 6 Wandsworth	
03.08.87	Peter Elliott L PTS 6 Stoke	
07.09.87	Dusty Miller L RTD 4 Mayfair	
25.01.88	Paul Wesley L PTS 8 Birmingham	
29.02.88	Paul Wesley DREW 8 Birmingham	
14.03.88	Mickey Hughes L RSC 4 Mayfair	
19.10.88	Geoff Calder NC 5 Evesham	
26.10.88	Franki Moro L PTS 6 Stoke	
05.12.88	Richard Carter L PTS 6 Dudley	
24.01.89	Antonio Fernandez L PTS 6 Kings Heath	
24.10.89	Andrew Flute L RSC 3 Wolverhampton	
21.06.90	Spencer Alton L PTS 6 Alfreton	
13.09.90	Nigel Rafferty L PTS 6 Watford	
27.09.90	Nigel Rafferty DREW 6 Birmingham	
09.10.90	Nigel Rafferty L PTS 6 Wolverhampton	
18.10.90	Nick Manners L PTS 6 Dewsbury	
29.10.90	Carlos Christie L PTS 6 Birmingham	
06.12.90	Wayne Hawkins L PTS 6 Wolverhampton	
28.01.91	Lee Prudden L PTS 6 Birmingham	
06.02.91	Paul Walters DREW 6 Liverpool	
27.02.91	Paul Busby L PTS 6 Wolverhampton	
13.03.91	Lee Prudden DREW 6 Stoke	
24.04.91	John Kaighin L PTS 6 Aberavon	
14.05.91	Ernie Loveridge L PTS 8 Dudley	
30.05.91	Robert McCracken L RSC 2 Birmingham	
25.07.91	Tony Booth L PTS 6 Dudley	
07.10.91	Antonio Fernandez L RSC 7 Birmingham	
12.11.91	Lee Archer L PTS 6 Wolverhampton	
05.12.91	Richard Carter L PTS 8 Cannock	
17.12.91	Paul Busby L CO 3 Cardiff	
15.01.92	Mark Hale L PTS 6 Stoke	
06.02.92	John McKenzie L PTS 6 Peterborough	
19.02.92	James F. Woolley W CO 4 Muswell Hill	
26.03.92	Neville Brown L CO 3 Telford	
05.10.92	Lee Archer L PTS 6 Bardon	
13.10.92	Lee Archer L PTS 6 Wolverhampton	
21.10.92	Steve Loftus L PTS 6 Stoke	
23.11.92	John J. Cooke L CO 1 Coventry	
17.06.93	Carl Smallwood L PTS 6 Bedworth	

18.09.93	Zak Chelli W RSC 2 Leicester	
02.12.93	Justin Clements W PTS 6 Walsall	
19.03.94	Mark Delaney L CO 3 Millwall	
17.06.94	Peter Vosper L PTS 8 Plymouth	
02.07.94	Darren Dorrington L RSC 3 Keynsham	
24.09.94	David Starie L RSC 2 Wembley	
16.11.94	Steve Loftus W PTS 6 Bloomsbury	
29.11.94	Mark Smallwood L PTS 8 Wolverhampton	
07.12.94	Steve Loftus W PTS 6 Stoke	
15.12.94	Neil Simpson L PTS 6 Walsall	
17.01.95	Andy McVeigh L PTS 6 Worcester	
23.02.95	Lester Jacobs L RSC 2 Southwark	
30.03.95	Dean Francis L RSC 2 Bethnal Green	
11.05.95	Andrew Flute L PTS 6 Dudley	
16.06.95	Dean Francis L RTD 3 Southwark	
28.07.95	Kevin Burton L PTS 6 Epworth	
21.09.95	Clinton Woods L PTS 6 Sheffield	
29.09.95	Paul Wright L RSC 5 Liverpool	
04.11.95	Jon Stocks L PTS 6 Liverpool	
26.01.96	Kevin Burton L PTS 6 Doncaster	
13.02.96	Wayne Alexander L PTS 4 Bethnal Green	
22.02.96	George Richards L PTS 6 Walsall	
21.03.96	David Starie L RSC 1 Southwark	

Career: 109 contests, won 19, drew 9, lost 80, no contest 1.

Lee Murtagh

Leeds. *Born* Leeds, 30 September, 1973
L. Middleweight. Ht. 5'9¼"
Manager J. Celebanski

12.06.95	Dave Curtis W PTS 6 Bradford	
25.09.95	Roy Gbasai W PTS 6 Bradford	
30.10.95	Cam Raeside L PTS 6 Bradford	
11.12.95	Donovan Davey W PTS 6 Bradford	
13.01.96	Peter Varnavas W PTS 6 Halifax	
05.02.96	Shamus Casey W PTS 6 Bradford	
20.05.96	Shaun O'Neill W PTS 6 Bradford	
24.06.96	Michael Alexander W PTS 6 Bradford	

Career: 8 contests, won 7, lost 1.

Lee Murtagh Les Clark

George Naylor

Liverpool. *Born* Liverpool, 4 September, 1968
L. Welterweight. Ht. 5'7"
Manager S. Vaughan

25.09.92	Charles Shepherd L RSC 4 Liverpool	
30.10.92	Dean Martin W PTS 6 Birmingham	
20.11.92	Emlyn Rees W PTS 6 Liverpool	
15.12.92	Renny Edwards L RSC 5 Liverpool	
02.07.93	Bruce Ruegg W PTS 6 Liverpool	
30.10.93	Paul Wynn W RSC 3 Chester	
25.02.94	Steve Edwards W RTD 3 Chester	
31.10.94	Jimmy Phelan W PTS 6 Liverpool	
16.06.95	Norman Dhalie W PTS 6 Liverpool	
08.09.95	Brian Coleman W PTS 6 Liverpool	
03.02.96	Paul Denton L RSC 3 Liverpool	

Career: 11 contests, won 8, lost 3.

George Naylor Les Clark

(Jimmy) Shea Neary

Liverpool. *Born* Liverpool, 18 May, 1968
Central Area L. Welterweight Champion.
Ht. 5'7½"
Manager B. Devine/J. Hyland

03.09.92	Simon Ford W RSC 1 Liverpool	
05.10.92	Shaun Armstrong W RSC 6 Liverpool	
02.11.92	Jason Barker W RSC 3 Liverpool	
01.12.92	Chris Saunders W PTS 6 Liverpool	
22.02.93	Vaughan Carnegie W RSC 1 Liverpool	
29.03.93	John Smith W PTS 6 Liverpool	
06.09.93	Wayne Shepherd W RTD 2 Liverpool	
25.10.93	Mark Antony W RSC 1 Liverpool	
13.06.94	Mark Pearce W RSC 4 Liverpool	
07.12.94	Tony Foster W RSC 2 Stoke	
25.01.95	John Smith W RSC 5 Stoke	
15.03.95	Tony Swift W RSC 3 Stoke	
16.06.95	Hugh Forde W RTD 6 Liverpool	
08.09.95	Nigel Bradley W RSC 2 Liverpool *(Vacant Central Area L. Welterweight Title)*	
24.11.95	Mark Richardson W CO 1 Chester	
03.02.96	Terry Sutherland W CO 2 Liverpool	

Career: 16 contests, won 16.

123

Shea Neary   Les Clark

Johnny Nelson

Sheffield. *Born* Sheffield, 4 January, 1967
Former WBF Heavyweight Champion.
Former WBF Cruiserweight Champion.
Former Undefeated British, European &
Central Area Cruiserweight Champion.
Ht. 6'2"
Manager G. Steene

18.03.86	Peter Brown L PTS 6 Hull
15.05.86	Tommy Taylor L PTS 6 Dudley
03.10.86	Magne Havnaa L PTS 4 Copenhagen, Denmark
20.11.86	Chris Little W PTS 6 Bredbury
19.01.87	Gypsy Carman W PTS 6 Mayfair
02.03.87	Doug Young W PTS 6 Huddersfield
10.03.87	Sean Daly W RSC 1 Manchester
28.04.87	Brian Schumacher L PTS 8 Halifax
03.06.87	Byron Pullen W RSC 3 Southwark
14.12.87	Jon McBean W RSC 6 Edgbaston
01.02.88	Dennis Bailey L PTS 8 Northampton
24.02.88	Cordwell Hylton W RSC 1 Sheffield
25.04.88	Kenny Jones W CO 1 Liverpool
04.05.88	Crawford Ashley W PTS 8 Solihull
06.06.88	Lennie Howard W CO 2 Mayfair
31.08.88	Andrew Gerrard W PTS 8 Stoke
26.10.88	Danny Lawford W RSC 2 Sheffield
	(Vacant Central Area Cruiserweight Title)
04.04.89	Steve Mormino W RSC 2 Sheffield
21.05.89	Andy Straughn W CO 8 Finsbury Park
	(British Cruiserweight Title Challenge)
02.10.89	Ian Bulloch W CO 2 Hanley
	(British Cruiserweight Title Defence)
27.01.90	Carlos de Leon DREW 12 Sheffield
	(WBC Cruiserweight Title Challenge)
14.02.90	Dino Homsey W RSC 7 Brentwood
28.03.90	Lou Gent W CO 4 Bethnal Green
	(British Cruiserweight Title Defence)
27.06.90	Arthur Weathers W RSC 2 Kensington
05.09.90	Andre Smith W PTS 8 Brighton

14.12.90	Markus Bott W RSC 12 Karlsruhe, Germany
	(Vacant European Cruiserweight Title)
12.03.91	Yves Monsieur W RTD 8 Mansfield
	(European Cruiserweight Title Defence)
16.05.92	James Warring L PTS 12 Fredericksburg, USA
	(IBF Cruiserweight Title Challenge)
15.08.92	Norbert Ekassi L RSC 3 Ajaccio, France
29.10.92	Corrie Sanders L PTS 10 Morula, South Africa
30.04.93	Dave Russell W RSC 11 Melbourne, Australia
	(WBF Cruiserweight Title Challenge)
11.08.93	Tom Collins W RSC 1 Mansfield
	(WBF Cruiserweight Title Defence)
01.10.93	Francis Wanyama L DIS 10 Waregem, Belgium
	(WBF Cruiserweight Title Defence)
20.11.93	Jimmy Thunder W PTS 12 Auckland, New Zealand
	(WBF Heavyweight Title Challenge)
05.04.94	Henry Akinwande L PTS 10 Bethnal Green
05.11.94	Nikolai Kulpin W PTS 12 Bangkok, Thailand
	(WBF Heavyweight Title Defence)
22.08.95	Adilson Rodrigues L PTS 12 Sao Paulo, Brazil
	(WBF Heavyweight Title Defence)
03.12.95	Adilson Rodrigues L PTS 12 Sao Paulo, Brazil
	(WBF Heavyweight Title Challenge)
20.01.96	Tony Booth W RSC 2 Mansfield

Career: 39 contests, won 26, drew 1, lost 12.

Andy Neri

Plymouth. *Born* Ilford, 5 November, 1972
Middleweight. Ht. 5'10"
Manager G. Mitchell

05.10.95	Shamus Casey L RSC 4 Queensferry

Career: 1 contest, lost 1.

Ray Newby

Nottingham. *Born* Sunderland, 16
December, 1963
Welterweight. Former Midlands Area
Lightweight Champion. Ht. 5'7"
Manager J. Griffin

20.09.84	Rocky Lawlor DREW 6 Dudley
10.10.84	Jeff Rumdan W RSC 3 Evesham
29.10.84	Dean Bramhald W PTS 6 Nottingham
07.11.84	Gary Flear L PTS 6 Evesham
21.11.84	Glenn Tweedie W PTS 6 Solihull
10.12.84	Wayne Trigg W RSC 6 Nottingham
04.02.85	Peter Bowen W PTS 8 Nottingham
07.03.85	Steve Cooke L PTS 8 Nottingham
25.09.85	Billy Laidman W RSC 2 Stoke
03.10.85	John Faulkner W PTS 8 Nottingham
21.11.85	Michael Marsden L PTS 6 Huddersfield
20.01.86	Steve Griffith L RSC 3 Mayfair
24.02.86	Ian Harrison W PTS 6 Coventry
05.03.86	Mark Pearce DREW 6 Stoke
24.03.86	Paul Dawson W RSC 3 Wandsworth
07.04.86	Wayne Cooper W RSC 2 Nottingham
14.04.86	Les Remikie L PTS 6 Mayfair

03.06.86	Peter Till W PTS 10 Wolverhampton
	(Vacant Midlands Area Lightweight Title)
15.09.86	George Baigrie W PTS 8 Coventry
06.10.86	Muhammad Lovelock W PTS 8 Leicester
29.10.86	Andrew Williams L PTS 8 Ebbw Vale
01.12.86	George Baigrie W DIS 1 Nottingham
11.12.86	Ian McLeod L PTS 8 Livingston
16.02.87	Mervyn Bennett W CO 8 Glasgow
24.03.87	Joey Joynson L PTS 8 Wembley
07.04.87	Mark Pearce L PTS 8 West Bromwich
14.04.87	Floyd Havard L RSC 7 Cumbernauld
12.10.87	Brian Nickels L PTS 8 Mayfair
19.10.87	Tony Borg L PTS 8 Nottingham
11.12.87	Joey Dee W PTS 8 Coalville
17.02.88	Wayne Weekes W PTS 8 Bethnal Green
08.03.88	Darren Connellan W RSC 7 Batley
10.04.88	Aladin Stevens L RSC 8 Eldorado Park, South Africa
09.05.88	Ian Honeywood W RSC 1 Nottingham
14.06.88	Peter Till L PTS 10 Dudley
	(Midlands Area Lightweight Title Defence)
31.10.88	Les Remikie W PTS 8 Leicester
11.11.88	Mahjid Mahdjoub L PTS 8 Vennissieux, France
25.09.90	Rocky Milton L PTS 6 Millwall
12.11.90	Brian Cullen W PTS 6 Stratford on Avon
30.11.90	Peter Till L PTS 8 Birmingham
12.04.91	Henry Armstrong L PTS 8 Manchester
22.01.92	Dean Bramhald W PTS 8 Solihull
11.02.92	Dean Bramhald W RSC 7 Wolverhampton
24.03.92	Ronnie Shinkwin W PTS 8 Wolverhampton
18.05.92	Ronnie Shinkwin W RSC 5 Bardon
02.07.92	Richard Burton L PTS 6 Middleton
10.11.92	Bernard Paul DREW 6 Dagenham
20.01.93	Richard Swallow L PTS 8 Solihull
03.03.93	Richard Swallow W PTS 8 Solihull
20.04.93	Bernard Paul DREW 6 Brentwood
19.05.93	Michael Driscoll L RTD 2 Leicester
26.10.95	Anthony Maynard L PTS 8 Birmingham

Career: 52 contests, won 26, drew 4, lost 22.

Dean Nicholas

South Shields. *Born* South Shields, 9 May,
1973
Welterweight. Ht. 5'9"
Manager T. Callighan

22.09.95	David Thompson W PTS 6 Hull
02.11.95	Paul Scott W PTS 6 Houghton le Spring
20.11.95	Shaun Gledhill W RSC 4 Glasgow
14.02.96	Shaun O'Neill W PTS 6 Sunderland
22.04.96	John Smith W PTS 6 Glasgow
09.05.96	John Docherty L PTS 6 Glasgow

Career: 6 contests, won 5, lost 1.

Carl Nicholson

Wakefield. *Born* Dewsbury, 19 May, 1974
Cruiserweight. Ht. 6'1"
Manager T. Callighan

22.03.96	Rocky Shelly W RTD 3 Mansfield
25.04.96	Kevin Mitchell L RSC 4 Mayfair

Career: 2 contests, won 1, lost 1.

Darren Noble

Newcastle. *Born* Newcastle, 2 October, 1969
Flyweight. Ht. 5'3"
Manager T. Callighan

21.10.93	Allan Mooney W PTS 6 Glasgow
23.03.94	Paul Ingle L RSC 3 Cardiff
26.04.95	Tiger Singh L PTS 6 Solihull
21.09.95	Terry Gaskin DREW 6 Sheffield
22.03.96	Steve Williams L PTS 6 Mansfield
13.06.96	Jason Booth L RSC 3 Sheffield

Career: 6 contests, won 1, drew 1, lost 4.

Eric Noi

Manchester. *Born* Manchester, 12 May, 1967
S. Middleweight. Ht. 5'11"
Manager F. Warren

05.02.93	Tim Robinson W RSC 4 Manchester
19.03.93	Smokey Enison W RSC 5 Manchester
26.04.93	Karl Barwise W PTS 6 Manchester
28.05.93	Karl Barwise W RSC 4 Middleton
25.07.93	Horace Fleary W PTS 6 Oldham
18.12.93	Graham Jenner W CO 1 Manchester
02.06.94	Shamus Casey W PTS 6 Middleton
10.09.94	Tim Robinson W RSC 1 Birmingham
12.10.94	Val Golding L PTS 6 Sheffield
24.11.95	John Duckworth W PTS 4 Manchester

Career: 10 contests, won 9, lost 1.

Shaun Norman

Leicester. *Born* Leicester, 1 April, 1970
Flyweight. Ht. 5'3"
Manager Self

11.11.91	Louis Veitch W RSC 5 Bradford
27.11.91	Dave Campbell L PTS 6 Marton
14.12.91	Mickey Cantwell L PTS 8 Bexleyheath
20.02.92	Dave Hardie L PTS 6 Glasgow
10.04.92	Neil Armstrong DREW 8 Glasgow
25.04.92	Prince Nassem Hamed L RSC 2 Manchester
16.06.92	Francis Ampofo L RSC 4 Dagenham
19.10.92	Alan Ley L PTS 6 Mayfair
23.11.92	Paul Weir L PTS 8 Glasgow
04.03.93	Neil Armstrong L RSC 8 Glasgow
21.10.93	Neil Armstrong L RSC 7 Glasgow
18.02.94	Vince Feeney L RSC 2 Leicester
24.05.94	Ian Baillie W RSC 2 Leicester
05.09.94	Ricky Beard W PTS 8 Brentwood
24.09.94	Mark Reynolds L PTS 4 Wembley
01.10.94	Robbie Regan L RSC 2 Cardiff
30.11.94	Anthony Hanna L PTS 10 Solihull *(Vacant Midlands Area Flyweight Title)*
04.03.95	Shaun Anderson L PTS 6 Livingston
15.03.95	Chris Thomas W RSC 2 Stoke
06.04.95	Adam Tate W RSC 6 Sheffield
26.04.95	Neil Parry DREW 6 Stoke
19.05.95	Mark Hughes L PTS 6 Southwark
06.09.95	Brendan Bryce W PTS 6 Stoke
18.09.95	Keith Knox L PTS 8 Glasgow
02.11.95	Anthony Hanna DREW 10 Mayfair *(Midlands Area Flyweight Title Challenge)*
29.11.95	Dharmendra Singh Yadav L PTS 4 Southwark
22.04.96	Daren Fifield L PTS 6 Crystal Palace
29.05.96	Harry Woods L RSC 5 Ebbw Vale

Career: 28 contests, won 6, drew 3, lost 19.

Rick North   Les Clark

Rick North

Grimsby. *Born* Grimsby, 2 February, 1968
Welterweight. Ht. 5'8½"
Manager B. Ingle

28.05.91	Michael Smyth L RSC 1 Cardiff
16.09.91	Eddie King W RSC 5 Cleethorpes
21.10.91	Steve Bricknell W PTS 6 Cleethorpes
11.11.91	Darren McInulty L PTS 6 Stratford upon Avon
09.12.91	Michael Byrne W RSC 2 Cleethorpes
23.01.92	Ron Hopley L PTS 6 York
19.02.92	Bernard Paul L PTS 6 Muswell Hill
11.03.92	Patrick Loughran L PTS 6 Stoke
22.04.92	Steve McNess L PTS 6 Wembley
03.06.92	Mark Dawson L PTS 6 Newcastle under Lyme
03.09.92	Andreas Panayi DREW 6 Liverpool
21.09.92	Hughie Davey DREW 6 Cleethorpes
05.10.92	Andrew Jervis L PTS 6 Liverpool
21.10.92	Jim Lawlor W PTS 6 Stoke
29.10.92	David Larkin L PTS 6 Leeds
20.11.92	Andreas Panayi L PTS 6 Liverpool
14.12.92	Lee Soar W PTS 6 Cleethorpes
27.01.93	Mark Dawson L PTS 8 Stoke
22.02.93	Spencer McCracken L PTS 8 Birmingham
09.03.93	Sean Baker L PTS 8 Bristol
14.04.93	Adrian Dodson L RTD 1 Kensington
27.05.93	Glenn Catley L PTS 4 Brisol
20.09.93	Dean Bramhald W PTS 6 Cleethorpes
30.09.93	Gary Osborne L PTS 6 Walsall
19.10.93	Chris Mulcahy DREW 6 Cleethorpes
27.10.93	Chris Mulcahy W PTS 6 Stoke
13.12.93	Trevor Meikle W PTS 6 Cleethorpes
26.01.94	Lindon Scarlett L RSC 6 Birmingham *(Vacant Midlands Area Welterweight Title)*
08.03.94	Kevin Mabbutt L PTS 6 Kettering
17.03.94	Dennis Berry W PTS 6 Lincoln
21.04.94	Dave Whittle L PTS 6 Gateshead
16.05.94	Dennis Berry L RSC 6 Cleethorpes
17.08.94	Steve Howden W PTS 6 Sheffield
06.09.94	Tony Brown DREW 8 Stoke

12.09.94	Prince Kasi Kaihau L PTS 6 Doncaster
12.10.94	Michael Carruth L PTS 6 Sheffield
26.10.94	Carl Smith DREW 6 Stoke
12.11.94	Damien Denny L PTS 6 Dublin
12.12.94	Richard O'Brien W PTS 6 Cleethorpes
25.01.95	Michael Smyth L DIS 4 Cardiff
22.02.95	Anthony Lawrence L PTS 6 Telford
02.06.95	Jim Webb L PTS 6 Bethnal Green
06.07.95	Andy Peach L RSC 4 Hull
08.09.95	Frank Olsen L PTS 6 Aalborg, Denmark
25.10.95	Dennis Berry L PTS 6 Telford
11.11.95	Derek Roche L RSC 2 Halifax
11.12.95	Gary Hiscox L PTS 6 Cleethorpes
13.01.96	Mark Winters L PTS 4 Manchester
03.02.96	Paul Burns L PTS 4 Liverpool
20.05.96	Richard O'Brien L PTS 10 Cleethorpes *(Vacant Midlands Area Welterweight Title)*

Career: 50 contests, won 11, drew 5, lost 34.

Robert Norton

Stourbridge. *Born* Dudley, 20 January, 1972
Cruiserweight. Ht. 6'2"
Manager D. Bradley

30.09.93	Stuart Fleet W CO 2 Walsall
27.10.93	Kent Davis W PTS 6 West Bromwich
02.12.93	Eddie Pyatt W RSC 2 Walsall
26.01.94	Lennie Howard W PTS 6 Birmingham
17.05.94	Steve Osborne W PTS 6 Kettering
05.10.94	Chris Woollas DREW 6 Wolverhampton
30.11.94	L. A. Williams W RSC 2 Wolverhampton
10.02.95	Newby Stevens W RSC 3 Birmingham
22.02.95	Steve Osborne W PTS 6 Telford
21.04.95	Cordwell Hylton W PTS 6 Dudley
25.10.95	Nigel Rafferty W RSC 6 Telford
31.01.96	Gary Williams W RSC 2 Birmingham
25.04.96	Steve Osborne W RSC 5 Mayfair

Career: 13 contests, won 12, drew 1.

Robert Norton   Les Clark

125

(David) Marvin O'Brien (Powell)

Leeds. *Born* Leeds, 3 September, 1966
L. Heavyweight. Ht. 5'11"
Manager Self

31.01.90	Tony Hodge L RSC 3 Bethnal Green
04.04.90	Gary Osborne L CO 2 Stafford
07.09.90	Mike Phillips L RSC 1 Liverpool
12.11.90	Mike Phillips W PTS 6 Liverpool
17.01.91	Barry Messam L PTS 6 Alfreton
21.02.91	Russell Washer DREW 6 Walsall
02.03.91	Quinn Paynter DREW 6 Irvine
21.03.91	Nick Manners L CO 2 Dewsbury
31.05.91	Carl Harney W RSC 5 Manchester
24.06.91	Frank Eubanks L PTS 6 Liverpool
06.09.91	Cornelius Carr L RSC 7 Salemi, Italy
02.03.92	John Oxenham L PTS 6 Marton
26.03.92	John Ashton L PTS 8 Telford
05.04.92	Quinn Paynter L PTS 6 Bradford
17.05.92	Lester Jacobs L PTS 6 Harringay
20.11.92	Fran Harding L RSC 4 Liverpool
16.02.93	Andy Wright L PTS 6 Tooting
12.05.93	Martin Jolley L PTS 6 Sheffield
15.09.93	Paul Hitch L PTS 4 Newcastle
15.10.93	Bruno Girard L PTS 6 Romorantin, France
03.12.93	Mads Larsen L PTS 6 Randers, Denmark
02.02.94	Willie Quinn L PTS 6 Glasgow
06.06.94	Willie Quinn L RSC 4 Glasgow
20.10.94	Derek Wormald L PTS 6 Middleton
23.11.94	Mark Delaney L RTD 1 Irvine
18.01.95	Mark Smallwood L PTS 6 Solihull
07.02.95	David Starie L PTS 6 Ipswich
04.03.95	Robin Reid L RSC 6 Livingston
17.05.95	David Starie L RSC 5 Ipswich
01.09.95	John Wilson L PTS 6 Wolverhampton
15.09.95	John Wilson L PTS 6 Glasgow
30.09.95	Jason Matthews L PTS 6 Cardiff
24.10.95	Toks Owoh L RSC 2 Southwark
25.11.95	Paschal Collins L PTS 4 Dublin
09.03.96	Danny Ryan L PTS 4 Millstreet
16.03.96	Kelly Oliver L RSC 2 Glasgow

Career: 36 contests, won 2, drew 2, lost 32.

Richard O'Brien

Alfreton. *Born* Chesterfield, 29 October, 1971

Midlands Area Welterweight Champion. Ht. 5'10"
Manager Self

14.05.90	Finn McCool W RSC 3 Northampton
21.05.90	Andy Rowbotham W RSC 5 Bradford
21.06.90	Jim Lawlor DREW 6 Alfreton
15.10.90	Richard Swallow W RTD 1 Kettering
22.10.90	Crain Fisher L CO 3 Manchester
13.12.90	Mick Duncan L PTS 6 Hartlepool
17.01.91	Steve Hardman L PTS 6 Alfreton
11.02.91	Neil Porter W RSC 4 Manchester
21.02.91	Darren Morris W PTS 6 Walsall
28.03.91	Trevor Ambrose L RSC 1 Alfreton
21.10.91	Tony Connellan L PTS 8 Bury
21.11.91	Chris Mulcahy W RSC 2 Ilkeston
02.12.91	Tony Britland W RSC 2 Birmingham
04.02.92	Darren McInulty W PTS 4 Alfreton
03.03.92	Scott Doyle L PTS 4 Cradley Heath
21.05.92	Howard Clarke L CO 1 Cradley Heath
23.10.92	Hughie Davey L PTS 6 Gateshead
11.03.93	Andy Peach W PTS 6 Walsall
01.04.93	Dave Lovell W PTS 6 Evesham
12.05.93	Wayne Appleton L RTD 2 Sheffield
20.09.93	Kevin Mabbutt L PTS 6 Northampton
09.11.94	Mark Antony DREW 6 Stafford
12.12.94	Rick North L PTS 6 Cleethorpes
16.02.96	Tommy Quinn L CO 4 Irvine
20.05.96	Rick North W PTS 10 Cleethorpes *(Vacant Midlands Area Welterweight Title)*

Career: 25 contests, won 11, drew 2, lost 12.

Mark O'Callaghan

Tunbridge Wells. *Born* Tunbridge Wells, 17 January, 1969
Lightweight. Ht. 5'7"
Manager F. Turner

03.10.91	Chris Mylan DREW 6 Burton
24.10.91	Nicky Lucas W PTS 6 Dunstable
11.12.91	Richard Joyce L RSC 3 Stoke
20.02.92	Alan McDowall L PTS 6 Glasgow
12.11.92	Erwin Edwards L RSC 6 Bayswater
20.01.93	Sugar Boy Wright W CO 1 Wolverhampton
05.02.93	Nick Boyd L PTS 6 Manchester
18.03.93	Paul Denton L RSC 4 Lewisham
22.04.93	Trevor Royal W PTS 6 Mayfair
26.05.93	Gareth Jordan L RSC 3 Mansfield
22.09.93	Dean Hollington L CO 1 Wembley
07.12.93	Gareth Jordan L RSC 1 Bethnal Green
15.06.94	P. J. Gallagher L RSC 4 Southwark
09.11.94	Colin Dunne L RSC 2 Millwall
04.02.95	Gareth Jordan L RSC 2 Cardiff
23.05.95	Andrew Reed L PTS 4 Potters Bar
30.09.95	Michael Wright W RSC 1 Basildon
07.10.95	Eamonn Brolly L PTS 4 Belfast
25.11.95	Michael Wright L PTS 4 Dagenham
02.12.95	Eamonn Brolly L RTD 3 Belfast
06.02.96	Bobby Guynan L RSC 3 Basildon

Career: 21 contests, won 4, drew 1, lost 16.

Spencer Oliver (left) in attacking mode against Lyndon Kershaw

Les Clark

Nick Odore

Hayes. *Born* Nairobi, Kenya, 24 February, 1965
L. Middleweight. Ht. 5'11"
Manager G. Taylor/H. Holland

07.05.96 Errol McDonald W RSC 4 Mayfair
Career: 1 contest, won 1.

Kelly Oliver

Bristol. *Born* Lincoln, 11 November, 1973
Cruiserweight. Ht. 6'3"
Manager C. Sanigar

20.01.96 Steve Osborne W RSC 4 Mansfield
16.03.96 Marvin O'Brien W RSC 2 Glasgow
13.04.96 Andrew Benson W PTS 4 Wythenshawe
Career: 3 contests, won 3.

Spencer Oliver

Finchley, *Born* Barnet, 27 March 1975
S. Bantamweight. Ht. 5'4½"
Manager J. Harding

17.02.95 Des Gargano W PTS 4 Cumbernauld
13.04.95 Marty Chestnut W RSC 4 Bloomsbury
23.05.95 Pete Buckley W PTS 4 Potters Bar
20.09.95 Karl Morling W RSC 5 Potters Bar
25.11.95 Shaun Anderson W RSC 3 Dagenham
23.01.96 Ricky Beard W RSC 3 Bethnal Green
09.04.96 Gary Hickman W PTS 6 Stevenage
25.06.96 Lyndon Kershaw W RSC 3 Stevenage
Career: 8 contests, won 8.

(Mike) Chip O'Neill

Sunderland. *Born* Sunderland, 10 December, 1963
Featherweight. Ht. 5'6½"
Manager T. Conroy

28.06.82 Charlie Brown L PTS 6 Bradford
20.09.82 Danny Flynn L RSC 2 Glasgow
07.03.83 Charlie Brown L RSC 3 Glasgow
28.04.92 Robert Braddock W PTS 6 Houghton le Spring
10.09.92 Vince Wilson W RSC 1 Sunderland
21.09.92 Ian McGirr L PTS 6 Glasgow
05.10.92 Phil Lashley W PTS 6 Manchester
09.11.92 Robert Braddock L RSC 3 Bradford
19.01.93 Russell Rees L RSC 1 Cardiff
08.03.93 Chris Lyons W PTS 6 Leeds
29.04.93 Paul Wynn L PTS 6 Newcastle
07.10.93 Fred Reeve W RSC 2 Hull
08.11.93 Ady Benton L RSC 5 Bradford
13.12.93 Paul Richards L PTS 6 Bristol
04.03.94 Ian McLeod L RSC 2 Irvine
24.05.94 Paul Wynn W PTS 6 Sunderland
06.10.94 Colin Innes DREW 6 Cramlington
20.10.94 Michael Brodie L CO 3 Middleton
05.12.94 Des Gargano W PTS 6 Houghton le Spring
16.02.95 Adey Lewis L RSC 1 Bury
25.03.95 Michael Alldis L RSC 2 Chester
11.05.95 Colin Innes W PTS 6 Sunderland
30.06.95 Gary Thornhill L RTD 3 Liverpool
22.02.96 Lyndon Kershaw L PTS 6 Sunderland
16.03.96 Brian Carr L PTS 4 Glasgow
25.04.96 Colin Innes L RSC 9 Newcastle
 (Vacant Northern Area Featherweight Title)
Career: 26 contests, won 8, drew 1, lost 17.

Shaun O'Neill

Sunderland. *Born* Sunderland, 21 December, 1968
L. Welterweight. Ht. 5'9"
Manager T. Conroy

13.10.94 Trevor George W RSC 6 Houghton le Spring
05.12.94 Jay Mahoney L PTS 6 Houghton le Spring
16.03.95 Scott Marshall W RSC 3 Sunderland
11.05.95 Mark Allen W PTS 6 Sunderland
22.06.95 Jamie Gallagher W PTS 6 Houghton le Spring
29.07.95 Wayne Shepherd W PTS 4 Whitley Bay
18.09.95 Tommy Quinn L PTS 6 Glasgow
02.11.95 James Clamp W PTS 6 Houghton le Spring
04.12.95 Wahid Fats L RSC 5 Manchester
14.02.96 Dean Nicholas L PTS 6 Sunderland
09.05.96 Mark Owens W RTD 2 Sunderland
20.05.96 Lee Murtagh L PTS 6 Bradford
Career: 12 contests, won 7, lost 5.

(Brendan) Ozzy Orrock

Nottingham. *Born* Barnsley, 4 June, 1971
L. Middleweight. Ht. 5'8¾"
Manager K. Richardson

17.10.95 Steve Levene L RSC 1 Wolverhampton
06.12.95 George Richards L RSC 3 Stoke
26.01.96 Prince Kasi Kaihau L RSC 5 Doncaster
26.03.96 Andy Peach L RSC 2 Wolverhampton
Career: 4 contests, lost 4.

Steve Osborne

Nottingham. *Born* Nottingham, 27 June, 1965
Cruiserweight. Ht. 5'9"
Manager Self

28.05.87 Gary Railton L PTS 6 Jarrow
09.06.87 Ian Bulloch L PTS 6 Manchester
24.09.87 Bobby Frankham L RSC 6 Glasgow
05.10.87 Ray Thomas L RSC 8 Piccadilly
14.12.87 Branko Pavlovic L RSC 3 Bedford
16.01.89 Simon McDougall W PTS 6 Bradford
25.01.89 Simon McDougall W PTS 6 Halifax
02.02.89 Dave Furneaux W CO 4 Southwark
13.02.89 Carl Thompson L RSC 6 Manchester
06.03.89 Jimmy Cropper W PTS 6 Manchester
05.04.89 Jimmy Cropper L PTS 6 Halifax
16.05.89 Henry Brewer W PTS 6 Halifax
12.06.89 Carl Thompson L PTS 8 Manchester
16.11.89 Dave Lawrence W PTS 6 Ilkeston
19.12.89 Herbie Hide L RSC 6 Bethnal Green
05.02.90 Dave Lawrence W PTS 8 Piccadilly
20.02.90 Rob Albon L PTS 6 Brentford
03.03.90 Darren Westover L RSC 6 Wembley
15.11.90 Michael Gale L PTS 6 Oldham
08.12.90 Neils H. Madsen L RSC 5 Aalborg, Denmark
16.04.91 Art Stacey DREW 6 Nottingham
09.05.91 Michael Gale L RSC 2 Leeds
11.11.91 Art Stacey L PTS 6 Bradford
21.11.91 Bruce Scott L PTS 5 Burton
29.11.91 Maurice Core L PTS 6 Manchester
12.02.92 Phil Soundy L PTS 6 Wembley
12.11.92 Terry Dunstan L PTS 6 Bayswater
10.12.92 Ole Klemetsen L RSC 1 Bethnal Green
27.01.93 Darren McKenna L PTS 6 Stoke
22.02.93 Nicky Wadman L PTS 6 Eltham
26.04.93 Joe Frater W PTS 6 Cleethorpes

01.07.93 Denzil Browne L RSC 1 York
28.09.93 Chris Okoh L RSC 5 Bethnal Green
10.11.93 Monty Wright L RSC 3 Watford
13.12.93 Martin Langtry L PTS 6 Cleethorpes
28.03.94 Joe Frater W RSC 5 Cleethorpes
05.04.94 Bruce Scott L RSC 5 Bethnal Green
17.05.94 Robert Norton L PTS 6 Kettering
28.07.94 Devon Rhooms W PTS 6 Tooting
26.08.94 Martin Langtry L PTS 8 Barnsley
02.09.94 Dean Francis L RTD 4 Spitalfields
27.10.94 Phil Soundy L PTS 6 Millwall
12.11.94 Ray Kane L PTS 6 Dublin
26.11.94 Rudiger May L PTS 6 Wuppertal, Germany
05.12.94 Justin Clements L PTS 6 Birmingham
22.02.95 Robert Norton L PTS 6 Telford
03.03.95 Gypsy Carman L PTS 6 Bracknell
30.03.95 John Pettersson L PTS 4 Bethnal Green
02.06.95 Mark Prince L RSC 3 Bethnal Green
17.07.95 Darren Westover L RSC 5 Mayfair
15.09.95 John Keeton L RSC 4 Mansfield
18.10.95 Martin Langtry L RSC 6 Batley
29.11.95 Luan Morena L PTS 4 Southwark
20.01.96 Kelly Oliver L RSC 4 Mansfield
25.04.96 Robert Norton L RSC 5 Mayfair
Career: 55 contests, won 10, drew 1, lost 44.

Mark Owens

Billingham. *Born* Stockton, 25 January, 1973
S. Middleweight. Ht. 5'8"
Manager G. Robinson

29.09.95 P. R. Mason L RSC 3 Hartlepool
23.11.95 Roy Chipperfield L RSC 6 Marton
22.02.96 Norman Mitchell W PTS 6 Sunderland
25.04.96 Lee Herman L PTS 6 Newcastle
09.05.96 Shaun O'Neill L RTD 2 Sunderland
Career: 5 contests, won 1, lost 4.

Mark Owens

127

Toks Owoh   Les Clark

(Tokunbo) Toks Owoh (Owomoyela)

Belsize Park. *Born* Newham, 21 July, 1972
S. Middleweight. Ht. 5'10½"
Manager I. Akay

24.10.95	Marvin O'Brien W RSC 2 Southwark
08.11.95	Dave Fulton W RSC 1 Bethnal Green
29.11.95	Nicky Wadman W PTS 6 Southwark
19.01.96	Ernie Loveridge W PTS 4 Bracknell

Career: 4 contests, won 4.

James Oyebola

Paddington. *Born* Nigeria, 10 June, 1961
Former British & WBC International
Heavyweight Champion. Former
Undefeated Southern Area Heavyweight
Champion. Ht. 6'9"
Manager I. Akay

01.07.87	Andrew Gerrard W PTS 6 Kensington
16.09.87	Ian Priest W RSC 2 Kensington
03.11.87	Carl Timbrell W CO 2 Bethnal Green
24.11.87	Mike Jones L RSC 2 Wisbech
09.02.88	Denroy Bryan W RSC 6 Bethnal Green
10.05.88	Andrew Gerrard DREW 6 Tottenham
07.09.88	Tee Lewis W CO 1 Reading
01.11.88	Dorcey Gayman W RSC 1 Reading
23.11.88	Everton Christian W CO 1 Bethnal Green
31.01.89	John Westgarth W CO 3 Reading
15.02.89	Art Terry W CO 5 Bethnal Green
07.03.89	John Westgarth L RSC 5 Wisbech
12.04.91	Stan Campbell W CO 1 Greenville, USA
18.05.91	Bonyongo Destroyer W CO 1 Harare, Zimbabwe
	(Final Elim. African Heavyweight Title)
15.09.93	Denroy Bryan W RSC 5 Bethnal Green
13.10.93	R. F. McKenzie W RSC 1 Bethnal Green
	(Southern Area Heavyweight Title Challenge)
01.12.93	Jimmy Bills W PTS 8 Bethnal Green

09.02.94	Ladislao Mijangos W RSC 2 Bethnal Green
06.05.94	Scott Welch W CO 5 Atlantic City, USA
	(Vacant WBC International Heavyweight Title)
19.11.94	Clifton Mitchell W CO 4 Cardiff
	(WBC International Heavyweight Title Defence & Vacant British Heavyweight Title)
07.02.95	Keith McMurray W RSC 7 Ipswich
27.10.95	Scott Welch L RSC 10 Brighton
	(British Heavyweight Title Defence. Vacant Commonwealth & WBO Inter-Continental Heavyweight Titles)

Career: 22 contests, won 18, drew 1, lost 3.

Thomas Padgett

Bradford. *Born* Bradford, 19 February, 1978
Lightweight. Ht. 5'7"
Manager K. Tate

21.02.96	Andrew Robinson L PTS 6 Batley

Career: 1 contest, lost 1.

Charlie Paine (Bird)

Liverpool. *Born* Liverpool, 27 August, 1970
Welterweight. Ht. 5'7"
Manager Self

09.06.93	Delwyn Panayiotiou W PTS 6 Liverpool
13.10.94	Micky Hall L PTS 6 Houghton le Spring
31.10.94	Tony Mock L PTS 6 Liverpool
20.01.95	Dennis Gardner L RSC 1 Bethnal Green
23.02.95	Derek Roche L CO 1 Hull
30.06.95	Andreas Panayi L CO 1 Liverpool
26.02.96	Michael Alexander L PTS 6 Manchester
09.04.96	Chris Barnett L RSC 2 Salford
10.05.96	John Jones L PTS 6 Liverpool

Career: 9 contests, won 1, lost 8.

Joey Paladino

St Helens. *Born* Whiston, 29 August, 1965
Heavyweight. Ht. 6'6"
Manager N. Basso

06.05.93	Vance Idiens L PTS 8 Walsall
23.06.93	Julius Francis L CO 4 Edmonton
15.09.93	Kevin McBride L CO 2 Bethnal Green
28.10.93	David Jules W RSC 2 Walsall
06.11.93	Scott Welch L RSC 3 Bethnal Green
07.12.93	Damien Caesar L RSC 3 Bethnal Green
29.03.94	Graham Arnold W RSC 5 Wolverhampton
16.05.94	Neil Kirkwood L RSC 2 Cleethorpes
10.06.95	Gary Williams W PTS 6 Manchester
14.10.95	Willy Fischer L CO 2 Munich, Germany
09.12.95	Danny Williams L RSC 1 Bethnal Green
20.01.96	Pele Reid L RSC 1 Mansfield
09.04.96	Garry Delaney L RSC 1 Stevenage

Career: 13 contests, won 3, lost 10.

Jim Pallatt

Leicester. *Born* Leicester, 8 September, 1969
Cruiserweight. Ht. 6'0"
Manager J. Gill

18.02.94	Johnny Hooks L RSC 1 Leicester
21.05.96	Andy Lambert L RSC 1 Edgbaston

Career: 2 contests, lost 2.

Andreas Panayi

St Helens. *Born* Cyprus, 14 July, 1969
L. Welterweight. Ht. 5'6"
Manager B. Hearn

21.11.90	Trevor Ambrose L RSC 5 Solihull
04.02.91	Cliff Churchward W PTS 6 Leicester
12.02.91	Eddie King W CO 2 Wolverhampton
27.02.91	Trevor Meikle L PTS 6 Wolverhampton
15.04.91	Mick Mulcahy W RSC 2 Leicester
24.04.91	Darren Morris DREW 6 Stoke
11.09.91	Robert Riley W PTS 6 Stoke
30.09.91	Steve Hardman W RSC 5 Liverpool
23.10.91	Darren Morris W PTS 6 Stoke
25.11.91	Marvin P. Gray W PTS 8 Liverpool
11.12.91	Mark Kelly DREW 8 Stoke
11.03.92	Dean Bramhald L PTS 8 Stoke
14.05.92	Dave Maj W CO 6 Liverpool
03.09.92	Rick North DREW 6 Liverpool
05.10.92	John O. Johnson W RTD 1 Liverpool
23.10.92	Trevor Meikle W PTS 6 Liverpool
20.11.92	Rick North W PTS 6 Liverpool
15.12.92	Mark Kelly W PTS 6 Liverpool
27.01.93	Ross Hale W RSC 3 Cardiff
27.02.93	Darren McInulty W PTS 6 Ellesmere Port
04.05.93	Jimmy Thornton W CO 2 Liverpool
02.07.93	Mark Ramsey DREW 6 Liverpool
28.09.93	Hugh Forde W PTS 8 Liverpool
11.12.93	Bobby Butters W CO 3 Liverpool
09.04.94	Tony Swift L PTS 8 Bethnal Green
10.05.94	Shaun Cogan W RSC 7 Doncaster
11.06.94	Tony Swift W PTS 8 Bethnal Green
28.06.94	John O. Johnson W RSC 5 Mayfair
17.09.94	Sammy Fuentes L RSC 4 Crawley
	(Vacant WBC Penta-Continental L. Welterweight Title)
11.02.95	Dingaan Thobela L CO 1 Hammanskraal, South Africa
20.04.95	John Smith W RSC 4 Liverpool
30.06.95	Charlie Paine W CO 1 Liverpool
17.07.95	Ojay Abrahams W PTS 8 Mayfair

Career: 33 contests, won 23, drew 4, lost 6.

Panayiotis Panayiotiou   Les Clark

Panayiotis Panayiotiou

Stratford. *Born* Limassol, Cyprus, 18 September, 1973
Middleweight. Ht. 5'11"
Manager B. Lynch

29.09.95 Ernie Loveridge W PTS 4 Bethnal Green
08.11.95 Andy Ewen W PTS 4 Bethnal Green
05.03.96 Michael Pinnock W PTS 4 Bethnal Green
03.04.96 Peter Varnavas W PTS 4 Bethnal Green
14.05.96 Ernie Loveridge W PTS 4 Dagenham
Career: 5 contests, won 5.

Wayne Pardoe

Wolverhampton. *Born* Walsall, 25 April, 1970
Lightweight. Ht. 5'8"
Manager C. Flute

08.11.95 Dave Hinds W CO 4 Walsall
28.11.95 Simon Hamblett W RTD 2 Wolverhampton
22.02.96 Andy Green L RSC 3 Walsall
27.03.96 Stuart Rimmer W RSC 3 Stoke
Career: 4 contests, won 3, lost 1.

Neil Parry

Middlesbrough. *Born* Middlesbrough, 21 June, 1969
Bantamweight. Ht. 5'5"
Manager T. Callighan

12.06.89 Des Gargano L PTS 6 Manchester
21.12.89 Kevin Jenkins L PTS 6 Kings Heath
31.01.90 Francis Ampofo L PTS 6 Bethnal Green
12.03.90 Paul Dever W PTS 6 Hull
19.03.90 James Drummond L RSC 4 Glasgow
27.11.90 Stevie Woods W PTS 6 Glasgow
04.12.90 Conn McMullen L RSC 2 Southend
21.01.91 Stevie Woods L PTS 8 Glasgow
06.02.91 Paul Dever W PTS 6 Liverpool
05.03.91 Tony Smith DREW 6 Leicester
24.04.91 Paul Dever DREW 6 Stoke
17.05.91 Gary White L PTS 6 Bury
03.06.91 Stevie Woods W RSC 2 Glasgow
20.06.91 Tony Smith W PTS 6 Liverpool
12.09.91 Mark Tierney L PTS 6 Wandsworth
21.10.91 Neil Johnston L PTS 8 Glasgow
27.01.92 Drew Docherty L RSC 4 Glasgow
28.02.92 Stevie Woods W PTS 6 Irvine
11.05.92 Tim Yeates L PTS 6 Piccadilly
21.09.92 Paul Weir L RSC 4 Glasgow
27.11.92 Eyup Can L PTS 6 Randers, Denmark
25.01.93 Ady Benton L RSC 6 Bradford
29.03.93 Louis Veitch L PTS 6 Bury
01.06.93 Des Gargano L PTS 6 Manchester
28.06.93 Marcus Duncan W RSC 2 Morecambe
13.09.93 Marcus Duncan L PTS 6 Middleton
06.10.93 Graham McGrath DREW 6 Glasgow
25.10.93 James Drummond L RSC 2 Glasgow
19.02.94 Harald Geier L CO 3 Hamburg, Germany
22.09.94 Adey Lewis L RSC 3 Bury
29.10.94 Terry Gaskin W PTS 6 Cannock
21.11.94 Keith Knox L PTS 6 Glasgow
16.01.95 Keith Knox L PTS 6 Musselburgh
23.01.95 Ian Baillie W RTD 3 Glasgow
11.03.95 Terry Gaskin DREW 6 Barnsley
22.03.95 Terry Gaskin W PTS 8 Stoke
26.04.95 Shaun Norman DREW 6 Stoke

17.05.95 Mark Reynolds L PTS 6 Ipswich
01.06.95 Rowan Williams L PTS 8 Musselburgh
05.10.95 Shaun Hall W PTS 6 Glasgow
23.10.95 Richard Vowles L PTS 6 Glasgow
22.11.95 Steve Williams L PTS 6 Sheffield
07.12.95 Paul Quarmby W PTS 6 Sunderland
02.02.96 Philippe Desavoye L PTS 8 Dieppe, France
16.03.96 Noel Wilders L RTD 4 Sheffield
22.04.96 Anthony Hanna L PTS 6 Manchester
20.05.96 Andy Roberts W PTS 6 Bradford
24.06.96 Andy Roberts W PTS 6 Bradford
Career: 48 contests, won 14, drew 5, lost 29.

Elvis Parsley

Bloxwich. *Born* Walsall, 6 December, 1962
Featherweight. Ht. 5'7½"
Manager P. Cowdell/R. Gray

04.06.90 Phil Lashley W RSC 3 Birmingham
20.06.90 Mark Bates L CO 1 Basildon
27.09.90 Andrew Robinson W RTD 3 Birmingham
10.12.90 Karl Taylor W PTS 6 Birmingham
18.02.91 Peter Campbell W RSC 3 Derby
01.05.91 Neil Leitch W CO 2 Solihull
20.05.91 Neil Smith L RSC 5 Leicester
02.10.91 Muhammad Shaffique W CO 1 Solihull
29.04.92 Kelton McKenzie L RSC 5 Solihull
(Vacant Midlands Area Featherweight Title)
28.04.93 Dean Amory L PTS 6 Solihull
12.10.93 Kid McAuley W PTS 6 Wolverhampton
30.11.93 Mike Deveney W PTS 6 Wolverhampton
16.12.93 Barry Jones L PTS 6 Newport
05.04.94 Kevin Middleton W RSC 4 Bethnal Green
23.01.95 Danny Lutaaya W RSC 3 Bethnal Green
24.03.95 Floyd Havard L RSC 6 Swansea
29.09.95 Paul Webster W RSC 5 Bethnal Green
18.12.95 Jonjo Irwin L RSC 8 Mayfair
(British Featherweight Title Challenge)
07.05.96 Michael Brodie L RSC 1 Mayfair
25.06.96 Duke McKenzie L RSC 1 Mansfield
Career: 20 contests, won 11, lost 9.

Bernard Paul (left) temporarily on the receiving end from Micky Hall   Les Clark

Patrick Parton

Telford. *Born* Shifnal, 5 September, 1964
L. Welterweight. Ht. 5'11"
Manager Self

23.02.93 T. J. Smith L PTS 6 Kettering
24.06.93 Shaun Shinkwin DREW 6 Watford
17.02.94 Tim Hill W PTS 6 Walsall
24.02.94 Malcolm Thomas W PTS 6 Walsall
18.04.94 Mark Allen W PTS 6 Walsall
23.05.94 Mark Allen W PTS 6 Walsall
29.09.94 Gary Hiscox L PTS 6 Walsall
09.03.95 Mark Allen W PTS 6 Walsall
28.03.95 Shaun Stokes L CO 1 Wolverhampton
01.09.95 Steve Howden W PTS 6 Wolverhampton
26.03.96 Jamie Morris W PTS 6 Wolverhampton
Career: 11 contests, won 7, drew 1, lost 3.

Bernard Paul

Tottenham. *Born* Mauritius, 22 October, 1965
Southern Area L. Welterweight Champion. Ht. 5'7½"
Manager Self

01.05.91 Trevor Royal W CO 1 Bethnal Green
04.06.91 Dave Jenkins W RSC 1 Bethnal Green
24.09.91 Pat Delargy W RSC 5 Basildon
26.10.91 Gordon Webster W RSC 4 Brentwood
26.11.91 John O. Johnson W PTS 6 Bethnal Green
19.02.92 Rick North W PTS 6 Muswell Hill
17.03.92 Mick Mulcahy W PTS 6 Mayfair
16.06.92 Brendan Ryan W CO 6 Dagenham
13.10.92 Dean Bramhald DREW 6 Mayfair
10.11.92 Ray Newby DREW 6 Dagenham
12.12.92 Michael Driscoll L RSC 2 Muswell Hill
20.04.93 Ray Newby DREW 6 Brentwood
28.09.93 Dean Bramhald W PTS 8 Bethnal Green
06.11.93 Shaun Cogan DREW 6 Bethnal Green
11.01.94 Shaun Cogan L PTS 6 Bethnal Green
09.07.94 Carlos Chase W RSC 2 Earls Court
30.09.94 Richard Swallow L PTS 8 Bethnal Green
13.12.94 Steve Burton W PTS 6 Potters Bar
21.02.95 Mark Legg W RSC 4 Sunderland

18.03.95	Jean Chiarelli W RTD 4 Millstreet
23.05.95	Keith Marner W PTS 10 Potters Bar *(Southern Area L. Welterweight Title Challenge)*
20.09.95	John Smith W PTS 6 Potters Bar
29.11.95	Jason Rowland W CO 1 Bethnal Green *(Southern Area L. Welterweight Title Defence. Elim. British L. Welterweight Title)*
20.04.96	Micky Hall W RSC 3 Brentwood

Career: 24 contests, won 17, drew 4, lost 3.

Quinn Paynter

Manchester. *Born* Bermuda, 19 August, 1965
S. Middleweight. Ht. 5'9"
Manager Self

12.10.89	Willie Beattie L PTS 8 Glasgow
19.10.89	Paul Hendrick W RSC 5 Manchester
11.01.90	Tommy McCallum W RSC 2 Dewsbury
15.01.90	Benji Good W PTS 6 Mayfair
23.02.90	Mike Paul W RTD 4 Irvine
08.03.90	Graeme Watson W PTS 6 Glasgow
26.03.90	George Ferrie W RSC 6 Glasgow

Quinn Paynter   Harry Goodwin

04.05.90	Fran Harding L PTS 6 Liverpool
17.08.90	Hector Rosario L PTS 8 Hamilton, Bermuda
10.12.90	Gordon Blair L PTS 6 Glasgow
21.01.91	W. O. Wilson W PTS 8 Crystal Palace
02.03.91	Marvin O'Brien DREW 6 Irvine
16.05.91	Ali Forbes DREW 6 Battersea
14.11.91	Terry French W CO 6 Gateshead
18.01.92	Val Golding W RSC 7 Kensington
05.04.92	Marvin O'Brien W PTS 6 Bradford
18.07.92	Chris Richards W RSC 6 Manchester
15.09.92	John Ogiste W PTS 6 Liverpool
28.09.92	Stinger Mason W CO 1 Manchester
14.08.93	Russell Washer W RSC 4 Hammersmith
15.09.93	Hussain Shah W PTS 8 Bethnal Green
03.12.93	Abdul Amidou L RSC 7 Randers, Denmark
02.09.95	Glenn Catley L RSC 1 Wembley

Career: 23 contests, won 15, drew 2, lost 6.

Andy Peach

Bloxwich. *Born* Bloxwich, 1 August, 1971
L. Middleweight. Ht. 5'8"
Manager Self

27.10.92	Stuart Dunn L RSC 3 Leicester
09.12.92	Jason Fores W PTS 6 Stoke
09.02.93	Ray Golding L PTS 6 Wolverhampton
11.03.93	Richard O'Brien L PTS 6 Walsall
06.05.93	Billy McDougall L PTS 6 Walsall
30.09.93	Ernie Locke L PTS 6 Walsall
04.11.93	Dennis Berry L PTS 6 Stafford
02.12.93	Ernie Locke L RTD 3 Walsall
08.02.94	Brian Coleman L PTS 6 Wolverhampton
04.03.94	Nicky Thurbin L PTS 6 Bethnal Green
14.03.94	Howard Eastman L PTS 6 Mayfair
18.04.94	Howard Clarke L PTS 6 Walsall
28.04.94	Scott Doyle L PTS 6 Mayfair
23.05.94	David Bain L RSC 6 Walsall
26.08.94	Cam Raeside L PTS 6 Barnsley
12.10.94	Prince Kasi Kaihau L PTS 6 Stoke
25.10.94	Howard Clarke L RSC 3 Edgbaston
29.11.94	Mark Antony W PTS 6 Wolverhampton
12.12.94	Prince Kasi Kaihau L PTS 6 Doncaster
18.01.95	John Stronach L RSC 5 Solihull
06.03.95	Norman Hutcheon W RSC 2 Leicester
22.03.95	Andrew Jervis L PTS 6 Stoke
05.05.95	Prince Kasi Kaihau L PTS 6 Doncaster
16.05.95	Brian Dunn W RSC 1 Cleethorpes
23.05.95	Steve Roberts L RSC 3 Potters Bar
06.07.95	Rick North W RSC 4 Hull
17.07.95	Neil Sinclair L RSC 1 Mayfair
08.11.95	Trevor Meikle L PTS 6 Scunthorpe
06.12.95	Trevor Meikle L RSC 3 Stoke
24.01.96	Adam Baldwin L PTS 6 Stoke
13.02.96	Paul Webb W PTS 6 Wolverhampton
22.02.96	Steve Levene L PTS 6 Walsall
26.03.96	Ozzy Orrock W RSC 2 Wolverhampton
29.03.96	Shaun Stokes L RSC 3 Doncaster

Career: 34 contests, won 7, lost 27.

Alan Peacock

Cumbernauld. *Born* Glasgow, 17 February, 1969
L. Welterweight. Ht. 5'7"
Manager T. Gilmour

23.02.90	Gary Quigley W PTS 6 Irvine
08.03.90	Gary Quigley W PTS 6 Glasgow
29.05.90	John Ritchie W PTS 6 Glasgow
11.06.90	Chris Mulcahy W RSC 3 Manchester
17.09.90	John Ritchie W PTS 6 Glasgow
09.10.90	Dave Anderson L RSC 3 Glasgow
27.11.90	Stuart Rimmer W RSC 4 Glasgow
11.02.91	Oliver Harrison L RSC 6 Glasgow
18.03.91	Darren Mount W PTS 8 Glasgow
27.03.91	Giovanni Parisi L PTS 6 Mestre, Italy
06.04.91	Allan Hall L PTS 6 Darlington
23.05.91	Giorgio Campanella L CO 1 Trezzano, Italy
23.09.91	Trevor Meikle L PTS 6 Glasgow
27.11.91	Dave Whittle L PTS 6 Marton
28.01.92	Trevor Meikle W PTS 8 Piccadilly
20.02.92	John O. Johnson L PTS 6 Glasgow
04.03.92	Rob Stewart DREW 8 Glasgow
12.03.92	Dave Whittle DREW 8 Glasgow
30.03.92	Peter Bradley L PTS 8 Glasgow
07.10.92	John Smith DREW 6 Glasgow
18.11.92	Dave Lovell W PTS 6 Solihull
22.02.93	Dave Lovell W PTS 8 Glasgow
23.03.93	Dean Bramhald L PTS 6 Wolverhampton
24.11.93	Malcolm Melvin L PTS 8 Solihull
21.02.94	John Smith W RSC 4 Glasgow
19.03.94	Paul Knights L PTS 6 Millwall
19.09.94	John Smith W PTS 8 Glasgow

02.11.94   Mark Legg L PTS 6 Solihull
21.11.94   Michael Alexander W RSC 1 Glasgow
05.12.94   James Jiora L PTS 6 Bradford
17.02.95   Kevin McKenzie L PTS 6
           Cumbernauld
01.03.95   Micky Hall L RSC 6 Glasgow
20.03.95   Kevin McKenzie L RSC 6 Glasgow
09.05.95   Paul Knights L PTS 6 Basildon
22.05.95   Bobby Vanzie L RSC 1 Morecambe
23.10.95   Steve McLevy L RSC 6 Glasgow
           (Vacant Scottish L. Welterweight Title)
Career: 36 contests, won 14, drew 3, lost 19.

Jon Pegg

Birmingham. *Born* Marston Green, 10 June
1974
Featherweight. Ht. 5'6"
Manager E. Cashmore

29.09.94   Michael Edwards W RSC 5 Walsall
25.10.94   Danny Ruegg L PTS 6 Edgbaston
07.12.94   Andrew Smith DREW 6 Stoke
07.02.95   Andrew Smith L PTS 6
           Wolverhampton
11.05.95   Graham McGrath L PTS 6 Dudley
05.06.95   Graham McGrath L PTS 6 Birmingham
20.06.95   Graham McGrath L PTS 6 Birmingham
08.11.95   Michael Edwards L PTS 6 Walsall
Career: 8 contests, won 1, drew 1, lost 6.

Danny Peters

Liverpool. *Born* Liverpool, 19 July, 1973
Middleweight. Ht. 5'10"
Manager B. Devine

06.09.93   Steve Levene W RSC 4 Liverpool
25.10.93   Russell Washer W PTS 6 Liverpool
02.07.94   Spencer Alton W PTS 6 Liverpool
26.09.94   John Duckworth W PTS 6 Liverpool
20.04.95   Ernie Loveridge W PTS 6 Liverpool
30.06.95   Nick Ingram W RSC 6 Liverpool
29.09.95   Carlo Colarusso W PTS 6 Liverpool
04.11.95   Carl Smith W CO 3 Liverpool
Career: 8 contests, won 8.

Stevie Pettit

Walsall. *Born* Birmingham, 28 April, 1969
Cruiserweight. Ht. 6'2"
Manager E. Cashmore

08.11.95   Chris Woollas L PTS 6 Walsall
22.02.96   Craig Jones W RSC 1 Walsall
21.05.96   Nigel Williams W RTD 3 Edgbaston
Career: 3 contests, won 2, lost 1.

Jimmy Phelan

Hull. *Born* London, 18 June, 1971
Central Area Lightweight Champion.
Ht. 5'9"
Manager M. Brooks

23.11.93   T. J. Smith L PTS 6 Kettering
16.12.93   Paul Bowen W PTS 6 Walsall
10.02.94   Micky Hall L PTS 6 Hull
11.10.94   Colin Dunne L PTS 6 Bethnal Green
31.10.94   George Naylor L PTS 6 Liverpool
16.03.95   Bobby Guynan W RSC 5 Basildon
01.07.95   A. M. Milton W PTS 6 Kensington
22.09.95   Tony Foster W PTS 10 Hull
           (Central Area Lightweight Title
           Challenge)
08.12.95   Yifru Retta L RSC 5 Bethnal Green
15.03.96   Carl Tilley L PTS 6 Hull
Career: 10 contests, won 4, lost 6.

Dean Phillips

Swansea. *Born* Swansea, 1 February, 1976
Featherweight. Ht. 5'6"
Manager Self

10.03.94   Paul Richards L PTS 6 Bristol
23.03.94   Phil Janes W RSC 1 Cardiff
27.08.94   Craig Kelley W RSC 4 Cardiff
21.09.94   Steve Edwards W RTD 4 Cardiff
02.11.94   Anthony Maynard L PTS 6
           Birmingham
04.02.95   Greg Upton W PTS 6 Cardiff
04.03.95   Mike Deveney W PTS 8 Livingston
24.03.95   Bamana Dibateza W PTS 6 Swansea
16.06.95   Danny Luutaya W RSC 2 Southwark
22.07.95   Colin McMillan L PTS 8 Millwall
20.09.95   Mervyn Bennett W PTS 6 Ystrad
16.03.96   Mike Anthony Brown W RSC 6
           Glasgow
26.04.96   Bamana Dibateza W PTS 6 Cardiff
Career: 13 contests, won 10, lost 3.

(Warren) John Pierre

Newcastle. *Born* Newcastle, 22 April, 1966
Cruiserweight. Ht. 6'0"
Manager N. Fawcett

10.10.91   Gary Charlton W PTS 6 Gateshead
20.01.92   Art Stacey L PTS 6 Bradford
21.09.92   Albert Call L PTS 6 Cleethorpes
20.09.93   Martin Langtry L PTS 6 Cleethorpes
12.10.93   Richard Atkinson W PTS 6
           Wolverhampton
21.10.93   Alan Smiles L PTS 6 Glasgow
08.12.93   Art Stacey L PTS 6 Hull
19.12.93   Alan Smiles DREW 6 Glasgow
25.10.94   Richard Bango L RSC 3
           Middlesbrough
27.02.95   Kenley Price L PTS 6 Barrow
15.05.95   Declan Faherty L PTS 6 Bradford
12.06.95   Brian McDermott L PTS 6 Bradford
14.11.95   Jacklord Jacobs L PTS 6 Yarm
07.12.95   Sean Daly DREW 6 Hull
29.02.96   Chris Woollas DREW 6 Scunthorpe
16.03.96   Mark Prince L PTS 6 Glasgow
22.04.96   Colin Brown L PTS 6 Glasgow
23.05.96   Tim Redman W PTS 6 Queensferry
Career: 18 contests, won 3, drew 3, lost 12.

Michael Pinnock

Birmingham. *Born* Birmingham, 6 June,
1965
L. Heavyweight. Ht. 6'0"
Manager Self

19.05.95   David Flowers L PTS 6 Leeds
13.06.95   Mark Snipe L PTS 6 Basildon
20.06.95   Darren Sweeney W PTS 8 Birmingham
06.09.95   Steve Loftus L PTS 6 Stoke
21.09.95   Luan Morena L PTS 4 Battersea
24.10.95   Graham Townsend L PTS 4 Southwark
17.11.95   Graham Townsend L PTS 4 Bethnal
           Green
03.12.95   Neville Smith L RSC 5 Southwark
23.01.96   Butch Lesley L PTS 4 Bethnal Green
05.03.96   Panayiotis Panayiotiou L PTS 4
           Bethnal Green
16.03.96   Mark Hickey L PTS 6 Barnstaple
25.03.96   Lee Simpkin L PTS 6 Birmingham
03.04.96   Jason Hart L PTS 6 Bethnal Green
24.04.96   Gordon Behan L PTS 6 Solihull
03.05.96   David Larkin DREW 6 Sheffield
14.05.96   Mervyn Penniston L RSC 2 Dagenham
Career: 16 contests, won 1, drew 1, lost 14.

Dean Pithie   Les Clark

Dean Pithie

Coventry. *Born* Coventry, 18 January 1974
S. Featherweight. Ht. 5'5"
Manager F. Warren

17.02.95   Kid McAuley W RSC 3 Cumbernauld
13.04.95   Kid McAuley W RSC 1 Bloomsbury
01.07.95   Pete Buckley W PTS 4 Kensington
22.07.95   G. G. Goddard W PTS 4 Millwall
21.10.95   Anthony Campbell W PTS 4 Bethnal
           Green
10.11.95   Kelton McKenzie DREW 6 Derby
26.04.96   Kelton McKenzie W PTS 6 Cardiff
25.06.96   Lewis Reynolds W RSC 2 Mansfield
Career: 8 contests, won 7, drew 1.

Steve Pollard

Hull. *Born* Hull, 18 December, 1957
Welterweight. Former Central Area
Featherweight Champion. Ht. 5'7"
Manager Self

28.04.80   Bryn Jones W PTS 6 Piccadilly
27.05.80   Pat Mallon W PTS 6 Glasgow
02.06.80   Andy Thomas W PTS 6 Piccadilly
02.10.80   Eddie Glass W PTS 6 Hull
03.11.80   Rocky Bantleman W CO 2 Piccadilly
01.12.80   Chris McCallum W PTS 6 Hull
17.02.81   Billy Laidman W PTS 6 Leeds
02.03.81   Bryn Jones W RSC 5 Piccadilly
30.03.81   John Sharkey L RSC 5 Glasgow
27.04.81   Ian McLeod L PTS 8 Piccadilly
01.06.81   Gary Lucas L PTS 8 Piccadilly
11.06.81   John Sharkey W PTS 8 Hull
08.03.82   Brian Hyslop DREW 8 Hamilton
22.04.82   Rocky Bantleman W RSC 8 Piccadilly
10.05.82   Lee Graham DREW 8 Piccadilly
26.05.82   Alan Tombs DREW 8 Piccadilly
23.09.82   Pat Doherty L PTS 8 Merton
26.10.82   Lee Halford L PTS 8 Hull
25.11.82   Kevin Howard L PTS 6 Sunderland
10.02.83   Keith Foreman L PTS 8 Sunderland
29.03.83   Steve Farnsworth W RSC 2 Hull
           (Central Area Featherweight Title
           Challenge)
18.06.83   Andre Blanco W PTS 8 Izegem,
           Belgium

131

04.10.83 Jim McDonnell L RSC 5 Bethnal Green
22.11.83 Joey Joynson L PTS 8 Wembley
22.01.84 Jean-Marc Renard L PTS 8 Izegem, Belgium
13.11.84 Jim McDonnell L RSC 6 Bethnal Green
17.12.84 John Doherty L PTS 10 Bradford *(Central Area Featherweight Title Defence)*
12.03.85 Mike Whalley L RSC 8 Manchester
20.01.86 Alex Dickson L RSC 7 Glasgow
10.03.86 Dave Savage L PTS 8 Glasgow
26.03.86 Peter Harris L RSC 3 Swansea
13.11.86 Dean Marsden L CO 7 Huddersfield
07.04.87 Darren Connellan W PTS 8 Batley
15.04.87 Paul Gadney L PTS 8 Lewisham
30.04.87 Gary Nickels L RSC 1 Wandsworth
22.09.87 Kevin Taylor L PTS 8 Oldham
18.11.87 Gary de Roux DREW 8 Peterborough
11.12.87 Gary Maxwell L PTS 8 Coalville
28.01.88 John Bennie L PTS 6 Bethnal Green
24.02.88 Craig Windsor L PTS 8 Glasgow
09.03.88 Peter Bradley L PTS 8 Wembley
30.03.88 Scott Durham W PTS 8 Bethnal Green
25.04.88 Colin Lynch W PTS 8 Birmingham
18.05.88 John Bennie W PTS 8 Lewisham
30.08.88 Mike Chapman W PTS 8 Kensington
15.11.88 Tony Foster L RSC 3 Hull
17.01.89 Peter Bradley L PTS 8 Chigwell
31.05.89 Carl Crook L RSC 4 Manchester
04.09.89 Michael Armstrong L PTS 8 Hull
10.10.89 Tony Foster L RSC 3 Hull
22.03.90 Chris Bennett W PTS 4 Gateshead
07.04.90 Frankie Dewinter L PTS 6 St Elois Vyve, Belgium
20.05.90 Mark Ramsey L PTS 6 Sheffield
30.11.90 Shaun Cooper L PTS 6 Birmingham
11.02.91 Dave Anderson L PTS 6 Glasgow
02.03.91 Allan Hall L PTS 6 Darlington
05.12.91 Shaun Cogan L PTS 6 Oakengates

18.01.92 Ian Honeywood L PTS 6 Kensington
30.03.92 J. T. Williams W PTS 6 Eltham
30.04.92 Jason Rowland L RSC 2 Kensington
10.09.92 Paul Charters L RTD 5 Sunderland
16.10.92 Kevin Toomey L RSC 7 Hull
12.11.93 Kevin Toomey W PTS 8 Hull
24.11.94 Dave Curtis W RTD 4 Hull
22.09.95 Dave Curtis W RSC 6 Hull
19.01.96 Peter Richardson L PTS 8 Bracknell
Career: 66 contests, won 22, drew 4, lost 40.

Chris Pollock
Bedworth. *Born* Coventry, 2 October, 1972
Welterweight. Ht. 5'10½"
Manager P. Byrne

17.06.93 Jamie Morris W RSC 2 Bedworth
03.11.93 Kenny Scott W PTS 6 Worcester
08.12.93 Brian Coleman L PTS 6 Stoke
08.03.94 Brian Coleman W PTS 6 Edgbaston
29.03.94 Gary Cogan L PTS 6 Wolverhampton
29.03.96 Prince Kasi Kaihau W RSC 2 Doncaster
25.04.96 Harry Dhami L PTS 6 Mayfair
Career: 7 contests, won 4, lost 3.

Lee Power
Manchester. *Born* Manchester, 11 March, 1967
L. Middleweight. Ht. 5'11½"
Manager N. Basso

12.06.95 Wesley Jones W PTS 6 Manchester
09.10.95 Peter Varnavas W PTS 6 Manchester
Career: 2 contests, won 2.

Chris Price
Sheffield. *Born* Rotherham, 4 March, 1977
Lightweight. Ht. 5'9"
Manager B. Ingle

06.09.95 Shaun Gledhill L PTS 6 Stoke
23.10.95 Jason Squire L PTS 6 Leicester
14.11.95 Colin Innes W PTS 6 Yarm
03.02.96 Alex Moon L RSC 2 Liverpool
20.03.96 Johnny Miller L PTS 6 Stoke
15.05.96 Tommy Janes L RSC 4 Cardiff
Career: 6 contests, won 1, lost 5.

Henry Price
Cardiff. *Born* Cardiff, 20 April, 1973
S. Middleweight. Ht. 5'7"
Manager W. Burnett

13.02.96 Michael Bowen L RSC 1 Bethnal Green
Career: 1 contest, lost 1.

Kenley Price
Liverpool. *Born* Liverpool, 30 December, 1965
Cruiserweight. Ht. 6'1½"
Manager S. Vaughan

15.12.92 Zak Goldman W RTD 2 Liverpool
27.02.93 Tony Colclough W RSC 5 Ellesmere Port
02.07.93 Paul McCarthy W PTS 6 Liverpool
30.10.93 Albert Call DREW 6 Chester
27.02.95 John Pierre W PTS 6 Barrow
29.09.95 Mark Hale W RSC 1 Liverpool
Career: 6 contests, won 5, drew 1.

Mark Prince
Tottenham. *Born* London, 10 March, 1969
L. Heavyweight. Ht. 6'1"
Manager F. Warren/C. Carew

04.04.93 Bobby Mack W RSC 2 Brockley

Mark Prince (right) on his way to victory over the American, Lenzie Morgan

Les Clark

23.05.93	John Kaighin W RSC 3 Brockley
25.06.93	Art Stacey W CO 2 Battersea
14.08.93	Simon McDougall W PTS 6 Hammersmith
20.01.94	Zak Chelli W CO 1 Battersea
14.04.94	John Foreman W CO 3 Battersea
21.07.94	Tony Booth W RSC 3 Battersea
25.02.95	Kofi Quaye W RSC 7 Millwall
02.06.95	Steve Osborne W RSC 3 Bethnal Green
22.07.95	Tony Booth W RSC 2 Millwall
09.09.95	Scott Lindecker W RSC 2 Cork
27.10.95	Lenzie Morgan W PTS 8 Brighton
16.03.96	John Pierre W PTS 6 Glasgow

Career: 13 contests, won 13.

Danny Quacoe

Horsham. *Born* Hammersmith, 30 December, 1965
Welterweight. Ht. 5'10"
Manager Self

22.10.92	Joel Ani L CO 1 Bethnal Green
28.11.93	Roger Dean W RSC 3 Southwark
06.03.94	Prince Louis W RSC 2 Southwark
16.05.94	Dave Madden W RSC 4 Heathrow
19.11.94	Dennis Griffin W RSC 5 Heathrow
30.09.95	Kevin Lueshing L PTS 8 Cardiff
27.10.95	Leigh Wicks L RSC 4 Brighton
26.01.96	Paul Dyer L PTS 6 Brighton
09.03.96	Mark Winters L RSC 2 Millstreet
20.04.96	Georgie Smith L PTS 6 Brentwood
31.05.96	Frank Olsen L RSC 2 Copenhagen, Denmark

Career: 11 contests, won 4, lost 7.

Paul Quarmby

Hetton. *Born* Easington, 2 June, 1973
Featherweight. Ht. 5'6"
Manager T. Conroy

13.10.94	Paul Goode W RSC 3 Houghton le Spring
20.10.94	Des Gargano L PTS 6 Middleton
05.12.94	Paul Goode W PTS 6 Houghton le Spring
16.03.95	Paul Watson L RSC 3 Sunderland
24.04.95	Robert Hay L PTS 6 Glasgow
18.05.95	Des Gargano L PTS 6 Middleton
22.06.95	Andy Roberts W PTS 6 Houghton le Spring
02.11.95	Gary Jenkinson L PTS 6 Houghton le Spring
07.12.95	Neil Parry L PTS 6 Sunderland

Career: 9 contests, won 3, lost 6.

Tommy Quinn

Tranent. *Born* Edinburgh, 2 November, 1975
Welterweight. Ht. 5'11"
Manager T. Gilmour

16.01.95	Billy McDougall W CO 5 Musselburgh
20.03.95	Paul Scott W RSC 4 Glasgow
24.04.95	Billy McDougall W RSC 3 Glasgow
01.06.95	Wayne Shepherd W PTS 6 Musselburgh
18.09.95	Shaun O'Neill W PTS 6 Glasgow
16.02.96	Richard O'Brien W CO 4 Irvine
16.03.96	Shamus Casey W PTS 4 Glasgow
03.06.96	Michael Alexander W PTS 6 Glasgow

Career: 8 contests, won 8.

Willie Quinn

Haddington. *Born* Edinburgh, 17 February, 1972
WBO Inter-Continental Middleweight Champion. Ht. 5'11½"
Manager T. Gilmour

09.10.91	Mark Jay L PTS 6 Glasgow
27.01.92	Hugh Fury W RSC 3 Glasgow
18.03.92	Andy Manning W PTS 6 Glasgow
30.03.92	John McKenzie W RSC 4 Glasgow
19.09.92	Martin Rosamond W RSC 4 Glasgow
25.01.93	Mike Phillips W PTS 6 Glasgow
06.03.93	Steve Thomas W RSC 4 Glasgow
15.05.93	Dave Owens W PTS 6 Glasgow
30.11.93	Russell Washer W PTS 6 Cardiff
02.02.94	Marvin O'Brien W PTS 6 Glasgow
28.03.94	Spencer Alton W RTD 3 Musselburgh
06.04.94	Marvin O'Brien W RSC 4 Glasgow
20.09.94	Shamus Casey RSC 3 Musselburgh
23.11.94	Mark Jay W RSC 1 Irvine
16.01.95	Mark Jay W RSC 2 Musselburgh
17.02.95	Martin Jolley W CO 5 Cumbernauld
05.04.95	John Duckworth W PTS 8 Irvine
01.06.95	Paul Busby W RTD 8 Musselburgh *(Vacant WBO Inter-Continental Middleweight Title)*
18.11.95	Peter Waudby W RTD 6 Glasgow *(WBO Inter-Continental Middleweight Title Defence)*
16.03.96	Martin Jolley W RSC 4 Glasgow

Career: 20 contests, won 19, lost 1.

David Radford

Hemsworth. *Born* Hemsworth, 30 May, 1969
Middleweight. Ht. 6'0"
Manager T. Callighan

27.03.90	Tommy Warde L CO 3 Leicester
09.05.90	Chris Micolazczyk W PTS 6 Solihull
21.05.90	Brian Keating W PTS 6 Bradford
28.06.90	Paul Hanlon W RSC 2 Birmingham
03.09.90	Andre Wharton L RSC 5 Dudley
16.01.91	Tony Kosova W PTS 6 Stoke
21.02.91	Griff Jones L PTS 6 Leeds
15.04.91	Paul Burton L RTD 1 Wolverhampton
13.05.91	Pete Bowman W CO 2 Manchester
02.12.91	Dave Binsteed W RSC 6 Liverpool
14.12.91	Delroy Matthews L CO 1 Bexleyheath
24.02.92	Mark Jay L PTS 6 Bradford
09.03.92	Tyrone Eastmond DREW 6 Manchester
25.04.92	Warren Stowe L RSC 3 Manchester
11.03.95	Richard Munro W RSC 5 Barnsley
28.04.95	Thomas Hansvoll L PTS 6 Randers, Denmark
21.09.95	Dave Battey W PTS 6 Sheffield
20.10.95	Dave Battey W CO 1 Mansfield
22.11.95	Darren Swords W PTS 6 Sheffield
04.12.95	Rob Stevenson W CO 2 Manchester
14.02.96	Dave Johnson W RSC 5 Sunderland
04.06.96	Kevin Thompson L PTS 6 York

Career: 22 contests, won 12, drew 1, lost 9.

Cam Raeside

Ilkeston. *Born* Toronto, Canada, 7 May, 1968
Welterweight. Ht. 5'8"
Manager Self

02.12.93	Billy McDougall W RSC 5 Evesham
18.02.94	Brian Coleman W PTS 6 Leicester

26.08.94	Andy Peach W PTS 6 Barnsley
09.02.95	Gary Hiscox L RSC 5 Doncaster
30.10.95	Lee Murtagh W PTS 6 Bradford
29.02.96	Paul Webb W PTS 6 Scunthorpe
29.03.96	Michael Alexander W PTS 6 Doncaster

Career: 7 contests, won 6, lost 1.

Nigel Rafferty

Wolverhampton. *Born* Wolverhampton, 29 December, 1967
Former Midlands Area Cruiserweight Champion. Ht. 5'11"
Manager R. Gray

05.06.89	Carl Watson L PTS 6 Birmingham
28.06.89	Tony Hodge L PTS 6 Brentwood
06.07.89	Tony Hodge W PTS 6 Chigwell
04.09.89	Joe Frater L PTS 6 Grimsby
24.10.89	Paul Wesley W PTS 6 Wolverhampton
22.11.89	Paul Wesley W PTS 8 Stafford
28.11.89	Paul Wesley W PTS 6 Wolverhampton
04.12.89	Dean Murray W PTS 6 Grimsby
20.12.89	Paul Wright DREW 6 Kirkby
17.01.90	Gil Lewis L PTS 6 Stoke
31.01.90	Antoine Tarver L PTS 4 Bethnal Green
19.02.90	Paul Wright W PTS 8 Birmingham
19.03.90	Terry Gilbey W PTS 6 Grimsby
01.05.90	Sean Heron L RSC 2 Oldham
13.09.90	Paul Murray W PTS 6 Watford
27.09.90	Paul Murray DREW 6 Birmingham
09.10.90	Paul Murray W PTS 6 Wolverhampton
24.10.90	Andrew Flute L CO 6 Dudley
27.11.90	Carlos Christie L PTS 8 Wolverhampton
06.12.90	Carlos Christie L PTS 6 Wolverhampton
28.01.91	Alan Richards DREW 8 Birmingham
04.03.91	Carlos Christie L PTS 8 Birmingham
26.03.91	Lee Prudden W PTS 6 Wolverhampton
13.05.91	Tony Behan W DIS 7 Birmingham
05.06.91	Lee Prudden W PTS 6 Wolverhampton
10.09.91	Paul Busby L RSC 2 Wolverhampton
20.11.91	Julian Johnson DREW 6 Cardiff
02.12.91	Kesem Clayton W PTS 8 Birmingham
21.01.92	Glenn Campbell L RSC 6 Stockport
30.03.92	Simon McDougall W PTS 8 Coventry
25.04.92	Sammy Storey L RSC 3 Belfast
16.06.92	Garry Delaney L CO 5 Dagenham
24.11.92	Graham Burton W PTS 8 Wolverhampton
02.12.92	John J. Cooke L PTS 6 Bardon
23.03.93	Stephen Wilson W RSC 3 Wolverhampton
14.04.93	Ole Klemetsen L RSC 2 Kensington
19.05.93	Zak Chelli L RSC 3 Leicester
22.09.93	Martin Jolley W PTS 6 Chesterfield
12.10.93	Carl Smallwood DREW 8 Wolverhampton
28.10.93	Lee Archer L PTS 8 Walsall
08.12.93	Darren Ashton L PTS 6 Stoke
26.01.94	Monty Wright L PTS 6 Birmingham
08.02.94	Greg Scott-Briggs W PTS 6 Wolverhampton
17.02.94	Glenn Campbell L RSC 7 Bury
18.04.94	Graham Burton W PTS 8 Walsall
23.05.94	Darren Ashton L PTS 6 Walsall
15.06.94	Darron Griffiths L RSC 4 Southwark
03.08.94	Leif Keiski L RSC 5 Bristol
20.10.94	John J. Cooke L RSC 7 Walsall *(Midlands Area L. Heavyweight Title Challenge)*
13.12.94	Paul Lawson L RSC 4 Ilford

133

20.03.95 John Foreman W PTS 10 Birmingham
(Midlands Area Cruiserweight Title Challenge)
19.04.95 Bruce Scott L RSC 2 Bethnal Green
17.05.95 Ole Klemetsen L RSC 4 Ipswich
06.07.95 Tony Booth L RSC 7 Hull
26.08.95 Darren Corbett L PTS 6 Belfast
20.09.95 Darren Westover L PTS 6 Potters Bar
29.09.95 Paul Lawson L PTS 6 Bethnal Green
07.10.95 Darren Corbett L PTS 6 Belfast
25.10.95 Robert Norton L RSC 6 Telford
21.02.96 Martin Langtry L CO 4 Batley
(Midlands Area Cruiserweight Title Defence)
20.05.96 Albert Call DREW 6 Cleethorpes
30.05.96 Tony Dowling L PTS 6 Lincoln
Career: 62 contests, won 20, drew 6, lost 36.

Mark Ramsey

Small Heath. *Born* Birmingham, 24 January, 1968
L. Welterweight. Ht. 5'7½"
Manager B. Ingle

15.11.89 Mick O'Donnell W RSC 1 Lewisham
08.12.89 Dave Pierre L RSC 2 Doncaster
22.02.90 Karl Taylor W RSC 4 Hull
10.04.90 George Jones W RSC 6 Doncaster
20.05.90 Steve Pollard W PTS 6 Sheffield
18.10.90 Neil Haddock L RSC 5 Birmingham
30.05.91 Colin Sinnott W PTS 6 Birmingham
05.12.91 Carl Hook W RSC 5 Oakengates
27.01.93 Andrew Jervis W PTS 6 Stoke
12.02.93 Reymond Deva W PTS 6 Aubervilliers, France
04.03.93 Dave Pierre L PTS 8 Peterborough
01.05.93 Vyacheslav Ianowski L PTS 8 Berlin, Germany
02.07.93 Andreas Panayi DREW 6 Liverpool
05.08.93 Jean Chiarelli W RSC 4 Ascona, Italy
01.10.93 Freddy Demeulenaere W RSC 3 Waregem, Belgium
26.03.94 James Osunsedo W RSC 4 Dortmund, Germany
07.05.94 Andrei Sinepupov L PTS 12 Dnepropetrousk, Ukraine
(Vacant WBO Penta-Continental Lightweight Title)
30.11.94 Mark Elliot W RSC 10 Wolverhampton
(Elim. British L. Welterweight Title)
20.05.95 Ahmet Katejev L RTD 5 Hamburg, Germany
(WBC International Welterweight Title Challenge)
15.09.95 Paul Dyer L PTS 6 Mansfield
23.10.95 Stefan Scriggins L PTS 8 Leicester
12.02.96 Alan McDowall L PTS 8 Glasgow
16.03.96 Alan McDowall L PTS 6 Glasgow
28.06.96 Poli Diaz W RSC 4 Madrid, Spain
Career: 24 contests, won 13, drew 1, lost 10.

Tim Redman

Dolgellau. *Born* Dolgellau, 1 May, 1970
Cruiserweight. Ht. 6'2"
Manager D. Davies

07.07.95 Phill Day W RSC 2 Cardiff
16.10.95 Peter Oboh L RTD 2 Mayfair
16.11.95 Gypsy Carman L PTS 6 Evesham
05.02.96 Jacklord Jacobs DREW 6 Bexleyheath
23.05.96 John Pierre L PTS 6 Queensferry
Career: 5 contests, won 1, drew 1, lost 3.

Tim Redman   Les Clark

(Peter) Andrew Reed

Potters Bar. *Born* Egham, 22 November, 1962
Lightweight. Ht. 5'7"
Manager Self

09.12.93 Simon Frailing L PTS 6 Watford
29.01.94 Russell Rees L PTS 6 Cardiff
08.03.94 T. J. Smith L PTS 6 Kettering
05.04.94 Anthony Campbell L PTS 6 Bethnal Green
28.04.94 Marco Fattore DREW 6 Mayfair
27.05.94 Chris Francis L PTS 6 Ashford
04.06.94 Marcus McCrae L PTS 6 Cardiff
29.09.94 Lewis Reynolds L PTS 4 Bethnal Green
16.11.94 Greg Upton L PTS 6 Bloomsbury
23.01.95 Matt Brown L PTS 4 Bethnal Green
25.02.95 Marcus McCrae L RSC 4 Millwall
23.05.95 Mark O'Callaghan W PTS 4 Potters Bar
10.06.95 Paul Griffin L RSC 5 Manchester
09.12.95 Martin Holgate L RSC 1 Bethnal Green
Career: 14 contests, won 1, drew 1, lost 12.

Fred Reeve

Hull. *Born* Hull, 14 April, 1969
S. Featherweight. Ht. 5'5½"
Manager Self

09.11.92 Tim Hill L CO 4 Bradford
14.12.92 Leo Turner L RSC 2 Bradford
19.03.93 Kevin Haidarah W RSC 2 Manchester
29.04.93 Marty Chestnut W PTS 6 Hull
07.10.93 Chip O'Neill L RSC 2 Hull
03.03.94 Ian Richardson L PTS 6 Newcastle
28.03.94 Dougie Fox W RSC 2 Cleethorpes
28.04.94 Ian Richardson L RSC 2 Hull
26.09.94 Jobie Tyers L PTS 6 Bradford
22.11.94 Tony Falcone L PTS 6 Bristol
07.12.94 Robert Grubb W RSC 3 Stoke
18.12.94 Brian Carr L CO 2 Glasgow
11.02.95 Stephen Smith L CO 1 Frankfurt, Germany

06.07.95 Paul Goode W RSC 2 Hull
05.10.95 Colin Innes W PTS 6 Hull
20.10.95 G. G. Goddard L PTS 6 Mansfield
07.12.95 Chris Lyons W PTS 6 Hull
06.03.96 Miguel Matthews L PTS 6 Solihull
09.04.96 Richard Evatt L RSC 1 Stevenage
17.05.96 Jason Squire DREW 6 Hull
Career: 20 contests, won 7, drew 1, lost 12.

Pele Reid

Birmingham. *Born* Birmingham, 11 January, 1973
Heavyweight. Ht. 6'3"
Manager B. Ingle

24.11.95 Gary Williams W RSC 1 Manchester
20.01.96 Joey Paladino W RSC 1 Mansfield
26.01.96 Vance Idiens W RSC 1 Brighton
11.05.96 Keith Fletcher W CO 1 Bethnal Green
25.06.96 Andy Lambert W CO 1 Mansfield
Career: 5 contests, won 5.

Pele Reid   Les Clark

Peter Reid

Alfreton. *Born* Derby, 19 February, 1966
L. Middleweight. Ht. 5'10½"
Manager Self

01.09.86 Andy Till L RSC 6 Ealing
10.10.86 John Davies L RSC 2 Gloucester
12.12.88 Mark Holden L RSC 4 Manchester
16.01.89 Steve Kiernan W PTS 6 Bradford
27.01.89 Frank Mobbs W PTS 4 Durham
20.02.89 Frank Mobbs W PTS 4 Bradford
01.03.89 Bullit Andrews W RSC 2 Stoke
08.05.89 Gary Osborne L CO 5 Edgbaston
26.09.89 Jim Beckett L PTS 8 Chigwell
13.11.89 Martin Robinson L PTS 6 Brierley Hill
20.12.89 Paul Lynch L RSC 4 Swansea
10.03.90 Martin Rosamond W RSC 6 Bristol
22.03.90 Gary Osborne L CO 1 Wolverhampton
18.10.90 Andrew Tucker L PTS 6 Hartlepool
29.10.90 Dean Cooper L RSC 1 Nottingham
21.11.91 Robert Riley W PTS 6 Ilkeston

04.12.91 Julian Eavis L PTS 6 Stoke
20.02.92 James Campbell L PTS 6 Oakengates
06.04.92 Kevin Mabbutt W PTS 6 Northampton
13.04.92 Dave Maj L CO 1 Manchester
04.06.92 Warren Bowers W RSC 2 Cleethorpes
12.11.92 Dean Hiscox W PTS 6 Stafford
19.10.93 Adey Allen W PTS 6 Cleethorpes
04.11.93 Nick Ingram W RSC 5 Stafford
08.12.93 Julian Eavis W PTS 6 Stoke
23.03.94 Julian Eavis W PTS 8 Stoke
16.05.94 Brian Dunn L RSC 4 Cleethorpes
09.11.94 Billy McDougall W PTS 6 Stafford
28.11.94 Nick Ingram L PTS 6 Northampton
07.12.94 Howard Clarke L PTS 8 Stoke
30.01.95 John Stronach W PTS 6 Bradford
07.02.95 David Bain W PTS 6 Wolverhampton
02.03.95 Paul King L RSC 3 Cramlington
22.04.96 Michael Alexander W PTS 6
Cleethorpes
Career: 34 contests, won 17, lost 17.

Phil Reid

Newcastle. *Born* Newcastle, 31 March, 1973
L. Heavyweight. Ht. 6'3"
Manager N. Fawcett

15.09.95 Jamie Warters L RSC 5 Darlington
25.04.96 Mark Richardson W PTS 6 Newcastle
20.05.96 Richard Darkes L RSC 2 Bradford
Career: 3 contests, won 1, lost 2.

Robin Reid

Warrington. Liverpool, 19 February, 1971
Middleweight. Ht. 5'9"
Manager F. Warren

27.02.93 Mark Dawson W RSC 1 Dagenham
06.03.93 Julian Eavis W RSC 2 Glasgow
10.04.93 Andrew Furlong W PTS 6 Swansea
10.09.93 Juan Garcia W PTS 6 San Antonio, USA
09.10.93 Ernie Loveridge W PTS 4 Manchester
18.12.93 Danny Juma DREW 6 Manchester
09.04.94 Kesem Clayton W RSC 1 Mansfield
04.06.94 Andrew Furlong W RSC 2 Cardiff
17.08.94 Andrew Jervis W RSC 1 Sheffield
19.11.94 Chris Richards W RSC 3 Cardiff
04.02.95 Bruno Westenberghs W RSC 1 Cardiff
04.03.95 Marvin O'Brien W RSC 6 Livingston
06.05.95 Steve Goodwin W CO 1 Shepton Mallet
10.06.95 Martin Jolley W CO 1 Manchester
22.07.95 John Duckworth W PTS 8 Millwall
15.09.95 Trevor Ambrose W CO 5 Mansfield
10.11.95 Danny Juma W PTS 8 Derby
26.01.96 Stinger Mason W RSC 2 Brighton
16.03.96 Andrew Flute W RSC 7 Glasgow
26.04.96 Hunter Clay W RSC 1 Cardiff
08.06.96 Mark Dawson W RSC 5 Newcastle
Career: 21 contests, won 20, drew 1.

Yifru Retta

Canning Town. *Born* Ethiopia, 24 September, 1971
S. Featherweight. Ht. 5'8½"
Manager T. Lawless/M. Duff

10.11.90 Paul Kaoma L RSC 4 Monsano
15.02.91 Branco Kuslakovic W PTS 4 Wiener Neustadt, Germany
01.03.91 Esteban Perez W PTS 6 Wiener Neustadt, Germany

05.07.91 Mauro Corrente L CO 4 Civitavecchia
14.06.93 Lee Fox W RTD 3 Bayswater
04.10.93 Vince Burns W PTS 6 Mayfair
07.12.93 Robert Braddock W RSC 2 Bethnal Green
04.03.94 Derek Amory W RSC 1 Bethnal Green
22.03.94 John Stovin W RSC 3 Bethnal Green
11.05.94 Bamana Dibateza W PTS 6 Stevenage
11.10.94 Chris Jickells W PTS 6 Bethnal Green
09.12.94 Kelton McKenzie W PTS 4 Bethnal Green
03.03.95 Alan McKay W PTS 6 Bethnal Green
20.04.95 Carl Tilley W PTS 6 Mayfair
03.11.95 Bamana Dibateza W PTS 6 Dudley
08.12.95 Jimmy Phelan W RSC 5 Bethnal Green
13.03.96 Tony Foster W RSC 3 Wembley
16.05.96 Alan Bosworth L PTS 6 Dunstable
Career: 18 contests, won 15, lost 3.

Lewis Reynolds

Lambeth. *Born* Hatfield, 25 February, 1970
Lightweight. Ht. 5'8"
Manager D. Powell/F. Maloney

29.09.94 Andrew Reed W PTS 4 Bethnal Green
18.11.94 Jason Hutson L RSC 3 Bracknell
25.03.95 Vince Burns W RSC 4 Millwall
25.05.95 Simon Frailing W CO 1 Reading
16.06.95 Wayne Jones W PTS 4 Southwark
17.11.95 Simon Ford W RSC 3 Bethnal Green
25.06.96 Dean Pithie L RSC 2 Mansfield
Career: 7 contests, won 5, lost 2.

Lewis Reynolds   Les Clark

Mark Reynolds

Sudbury. *Born* Sudbury, 27 July, 1969
Southern Area Flyweight Champion.
Ht. 5'5½"
Manager F. Maloney

24.09.94 Shaun Norman W PTS 4 Wembley
12.11.94 Vince Feeney L PTS 6 Dublin
07.02.95 Danny Lawson W PTS 4 Ipswich
17.05.95 Neil Parry W PTS 6 Ipswich

04.06.95 Anthony Hanna W PTS 10 Bethnal Green
(Elim. British Flyweight Title)
14.09.95 Tiger Singh W RSC 3 Battersea
20.10.95 Ricky Beard W PTS 10 Ipswich
(Southern Area Flyweight Title Challenge)
15.12.95 Mzukisi Skali L RSC 2 Bethnal Green
(WBC International L. Flyweight Title Challenge)
21.03.96 Rowan Williams DREW 6 Southwark
Career: 9 contests, won 6, drew 1, lost 2.

Mark Reynolds   Les Clark

Ryan Rhodes

Sheffield. *Born* Sheffield, 20 November, 1976
Middleweight. Ht. 5'8½"
Manager B. Ingle

04.02.95 Lee Crocker W RSC 2 Cardiff
04.03.95 Shamus Casey W CO 1 Livingston
06.05.95 Chris Richards W PTS 6 Shepton Mallet
15.09.95 John Rice W RSC 2 Mansfield
10.11.95 Mark Dawson W PTS 6 Derby
20.01.96 John Duckworth W RSC 2 Mansfield
26.01.96 Martin Jolley W CO 3 Brighton
11.05.96 Martin Jolley W RSC 2 Bethnal Green
25.06.96 Roy Chipperfield W RSC 1 Mansfield
Career: 9 contests, won 9.

John Rice

Brighton. *Born* Johnstone, 25 June, 1965
S. Middleweight. Ht. 5'9"
Manager Self

23.11.93 Sean Byrne L PTS 6 Kettering
07.12.93 Nicky Thurbin L PTS 6 Bethnal Green
06.03.94 Howard Eastman L RSC 1 Southwark
11.05.94 John Keeton L RSC 5 Sheffield
15.09.95 Ryan Rhodes L RSC 2 Mansfield
Career: 5 contests, lost 5.

Chris Richards

Nottingham. *Born* Nottingham, 4 April, 1964
Middleweight. Ht. 5'5¼"
Manager Self

07.09.87	Darren Bowen W RSC 1 Mayfair
23.09.87	Shaun Cummins L PTS 6 Loughborough
13.10.87	Damien Denny L PTS 6 Windsor
03.11.87	Brian Robinson L PTS 6 Bethnal Green
18.01.88	Stan King W CO 5 Mayfair
29.01.88	Lou Ayres W RSC 3 Holborn
26.03.88	Terry Magee L PTS 8 Belfast
26.05.88	Tony Collins L RSC 3 Kensington
10.10.88	Antonio Fernandez L PTS 6 Edgbaston
23.11.88	Antonio Fernandez L PTS 8 Solihull
10.12.88	Terry Morrill L PTS 6 Crystal Palace
16.01.89	Mark Holden L DIS 3 Northampton
24.01.89	Ian Strudwick L PTS 6 Wandsworth
13.02.89	G. L. Booth W RSC 8 Manchester
10.03.89	Theo Marius L RSC 2 Brentwood
08.05.89	G. L. Booth W RSC 2 Manchester
22.05.89	B. K. Bennett L PTS 8 Mayfair
16.05.90	Mick Duncan L PTS 6 Hull
04.06.90	Antonio Fernandez L PTS 8 Edgbaston
15.06.90	Gary Pemberton W RTD 1 Telford
14.09.90	Shamus Casey W PTS 6 Telford
17.10.90	Gary Osborne L PTS 8 Stoke
13.11.90	Andrew Tucker W RSC 2 Hartlepool
13.12.90	Neville Brown L RSC 2 Dewsbury
13.02.91	Delroy Waul L PTS 6 Wembley
16.04.91	Paul Smith DREW 6 Nottingham
24.04.91	Colin Pitters L RSC 6 Stoke
26.11.91	Adrian Strachan L PTS 6 Bethnal Green
26.03.92	Glen Payton W PTS 6 Telford
18.06.92	Stefan Wright L PTS 6 Peterborough
18.07.92	Quinn Paynter L RSC 6 Manchester
06.10.92	Paul Busby L PTS 6 Antwerp, Belgium
13.12.93	Peter Waudby L PTS 6 Cleethorpes
16.02.94	Gilbert Jackson L RSC 2 Stevenage
25.04.94	Warren Stowe L PTS 6 Bury
25.05.94	Kevin Adamson L RSC 2 Stoke
27.10.94	Mark Baker L PTS 6 Millwall
19.11.94	Robin Reid L RSC 3 Cardiff
17.01.95	Andrew Flute L PTS 6 Worcester
14.02.95	Gilbert Jackson L RTD 2 Bethnal Green
20.04.95	Paul Wright L PTS 6 Liverpool
06.05.95	Ryan Rhodes L PTS 6 Shepton Mallet
13.05.95	Cornelius Carr L RTD 3 Glasgow
01.07.95	Jason Matthews L CO 4 Kensington

Career: 44 contests, won 9, drew 1, lost 34.

George Richards

Birmingham. *Born* Birmingham, 19 December, 1967
Welterweight. Ht. 5'9"
Manager P. Cowdell/R. Gray

06.12.95	Ozzy Orrocks W RSC 3 Stoke
17.01.96	Adam Baldwin W PTS 6 Solihull
13.02.96	Donovan Davey W PTS 6 Wolverhampton
22.02.96	Paul Murray W PTS 6 Walsall
06.03.96	Donovan Davey W PTS 6 Solihull
26.03.96	George Wilson W PTS 8 Wolverhampton
04.05.96	Steve Roberts L PTS 6 Dagenham

Career: 7 contests, won 6, lost 1.

Mark Richardson

Ian Richardson

Newcastle. *Born* Newcastle, 26 March, 1971
S. Featherweight. Ht. 5'6"
Manager N. Fawcett

06.12.93	Dean James W RSC 4 Bradford
03.03.94	Fred Reeve W PTS 6 Newcastle
28.04.94	Fred Reeve W RSC 2 Hull
09.05.94	Leo Turner DREW 6 Bradford
22.09.94	Dave Clavering L RSC 1 Bury
24.11.94	Leo Turner L RSC 6 Newcastle
05.10.95	Paul Hamilton L PTS 6 Hull
23.10.95	Garry Burrell L PTS 6 Glasgow
14.11.95	Thomas Bradley L PTS 6 Yarm
16.02.96	Garry Burrell L PTS 8 Irvine
16.03.96	Scott Dixon L PTS 4 Glasgow
25.04.96	Paul Hamilton W PTS 6 Newcastle
23.05.96	Lee Armstrong L PTS 6 Queensferry

Career: 13 contests, won 4, drew 1, lost 8.

Mark Richardson

Middlesbrough. *Born* West Ham, 19 August, 1969
L. Heavyweight. Ht. 6'0"
Manager G. Robinson

29.09.95	Slick Miller W PTS 6 Hartlepool
23.11.95	Jason Davies W RSC 2 Marton
25.04.96	Phil Reid L PTS 6 Newcastle
17.05.96	Tony Booth L RSC 2 Hull

Career: 4 contests, won 2, lost 2.

Peter Richardson

Middlesbrough. *Born* Middlesbrough, 24 June, 1970
Welterweight. Ht. 5'9¼"
Manager F. Maloney

23.02.95	John O. Johnson W RSC 5 Southwark
27.04.95	Carl Roberts W RSC 1 Bethnal Green
25.05.95	Everald Williams W RSC 6 Reading
02.07.95	John Smith W PTS 6 Dublin
29.09.95	Tony Foster W RSC 1 Bethnal Green
15.12.95	Karl Taylor W PTS 8 Bethnal Green
19.01.96	Steve Pollard W PTS 8 Bracknell
21.03.96	Adrian Chase W RSC 2 Southwark
14.05.96	Trevor Meikle W RSC 2 Dagenham
29.06.96	Kevin McKillan W CO 2 Erith

Career: 10 contests, won 10.

Peter Richardson stands over Adrian Chase   Les Clark

13.02.90 Dave Croft W PTS 6 Wolverhampton
07.03.90 Mark Antony L RSC 1 Doncaster
23.04.90 Dave Croft W CO 2 Birmingham
01.05.90 Neil Foran L RSC 2 Oldham
04.06.90 Frankie Foster L PTS 6 Glasgow
27.06.90 Bernard McComiskey L PTS 6 Kensington
12.09.90 Steve Griffith W RSC 2 Bethnal Green
27.09.90 Andrew Morgan W PTS 6 Birmingham
09.10.90 Jim Lawler W CO 2 Wolverhampton
29.10.90 Tony Feliciello L RSC 5 Birmingham
27.11.90 Alan Peacock L RSC 4 Glasgow
12.02.91 Andrew Morgan L PTS 8 Wolverhampton
24.04.91 Steve Winstanley L PTS 6 Preston
04.06.91 Michael Ayers L CO 1 Bethnal Green
10.09.91 Shaun Cooper L RSC 2 Wolverhampton
27.03.96 Wayne Pardoe L RSC 3 Stoke

Career: 16 contests, won 5, lost 11.

Brian Robb   Les Clark

Brian Robb

Telford. *Born* Liverpool, 5 April, 1967
Lightweight. Ht. 5'6"
Manager Self

14.02.89 Miguel Matthews L RSC 2 Wolverhampton
27.03.90 Neil Leitch W PTS 6 Wolverhampton
09.05.90 Peter Judson L PTS 6 Solihull
22.05.90 Nicky Lucas W PTS 6 Canvey Island
20.06.90 Paul Harvey L PTS 6 Basildon
09.10.90 Des Gargano W PTS 6 Wolverhampton
24.10.90 Paul Harvey L RSC 2 Dudley
23.01.91 Jason Primera L RSC 7 Solihull
04.03.91 Pete Buckley L RSC 7 Birmingham
05.06.91 Pete Buckley L PTS 10 Wolverhampton
(Vacant Midlands Area S. Featherweight Title)
29.08.91 Renny Edwards W PTS 6 Oakengates
31.10.91 Miguel Matthews DREW 6 Oakengates
05.12.91 Neil Leitch W CO 2 Oakengates

Wayne Rigby

Manchester. *Born* Manchester, 19 July, 1973
S. Featherweight. Ht. 5'6"
Manager J. Doughty

27.02.92 Lee Fox L PTS 6 Liverpool
08.06.92 Leo Turner W PTS 6 Bradford
02.07.92 Leo Turner W CO 5 Middleton
05.10.92 Colin Innes W PTS 6 Manchester
01.12.92 John T. Kelly L PTS 6 Hartlepool
02.06.94 Kid McAuley W PTS 6 Middleton
13.06.94 Chris Clarkson W PTS 6 Liverpool
22.09.94 Mark Hargreaves W PTS 6 Bury
06.03.95 Kelton McKenzie L PTS 8 Leicester
18.05.95 John T. Kelly W PTS 6 Middleton
05.06.95 Hugh Collins W RSC 4 Glasgow
17.01.96 Kid McAuley W PTS 6 Solihull
24.03.96 Steve Tuckett W PTS 6 Shaw

Career: 13 contests, won 10, lost 3.

Stuart Rimmer

St Helens. *Born* St Helens, 22 April, 1971
Lightweight. Ht. 5'6"
Manager Self

20.02.92 Pete Buckley L RSC 10 Oakengates
(Midlands Area S. Featherweight Title Challenge)
26.03.92 Kelton McKenzie L RSC 4 Telford
13.10.92 Paul Harvey L RSC 2 Mayfair
04.12.92 Kevin Middleton L RSC 1 Telford
22.02.95 Andrew Smith W PTS 6 Telford
21.04.95 Andrew Smith DREW 6 Dudley
23.06.95 Chris Francis L RSC 1 Bethnal Green
25.10.95 Robert Grubb W PTS 6 Telford
11.11.95 Jason Blanche L RSC 4 Halifax
31.01.96 Chris Lyons W PTS 6 Birmingham
05.03.96 Jay Levy W RTD 3 Bethnal Green
22.06.96 Stephen Smith L RSC 4 Dortmund, Germany
Career: 25 contests, won 9, drew 2, lost 14.

Andy Roberts

Doncaster. *Born* Doncaster, 4 March, 1976
S. Bantamweight. Ht. 5'3"
Manager J. Rushton

20.10.94 Robert Grubb DREW 6 Walsall
12.12.94 Jason Morris W PTS 6 Doncaster
09.02.95 Robert Grubb DREW 6 Doncaster
22.03.95 Michael Edwards L PTS 6 Stoke
06.04.95 Steve Williams L PTS 6 Sheffield
05.05.95 Jason Morris W PTS 6 Doncaster
22.06.95 Paul Quarmby L PTS 6 Houghton le Spring
30.06.95 Stefy Bull L PTS 4 Doncaster
17.10.95 Robert Grubb L PTS 6 Wolverhampton
08.11.95 Graham McGrath W PTS 6 Scunthorpe
28.11.95 Graham McGrath L PTS 6 Wolverhampton
26.01.96 Darren Greaves W RSC 5 Doncaster
29.03.96 Graham McGrath L PTS 6 Doncaster
20.05.96 Neil Parry L PTS 6 Bradford
24.06.96 Neil Parry L PTS 6 Bradford
Career: 15 contests, won 4, drew 2, lost 9.

Dewi Roberts

Dolgellau. *Born* Bangor, 11 September, 1968
L. Welterweight. Ht. 5'10"
Manager Self

28.11.91 Gavin Lane L PTS 6 Evesham
11.02.92 Edward Lloyd L RSC 1 Cardiff
11.05.92 Nigel Burder W CO 3 Llanelli
22.11.93 Steve McLevy L RSC 1 Glasgow
24.02.94 Paul Robinson W RSC 6 Walsall
04.03.94 Jason Rowland L RSC 1 Bethnal Green
17.06.94 Paul Dyer L PTS 6 Plymouth
25.06.94 Carl van Bailey W RSC 2 Cullompton
02.09.94 Keith Marner L PTS 6 Spitalfields
17.09.94 Paul Knights L PTS 6 Crawley
25.10.94 Everald Williams L PTS 6 Southwark
09.11.94 Jason Beard L RSC 4 Millwall
17.02.95 Georgie Smith L RSC 2 Crawley
05.10.95 Paul Salmon W PTS 6 Queensferry
20.10.95 Gary Beardsley L PTS 6 Mansfield
22.11.95 Dave Fallon DREW 6 Mayfair
Career: 16 contests, won 4, drew 1, lost 11.

Pete Roberts

Hull. *Born* Liverpool, 15 July, 1967
L. Welterweight. Ht. 5'4"
Manager Self

25.10.88 Mark Jackson W CO 2 Hartlepool
07.11.88 Frankie Foster L PTS 4 Bradford

17.11.88 Tony Banks L PTS 6 Stockport
20.03.89 Brendan Ryan L PTS 6 Nottingham
05.04.90 Mike Close W CO 1 Liverpool
23.04.90 Brendan Ryan L PTS 6 Bradford
04.05.90 John Smith W PTS 6 Liverpool
09.10.90 John Smith L PTS 8 Liverpool
25.02.91 Peter Crook W RSC 6 Bradford
13.06.91 Wayne Windle L RSC 7 Hull
(Vacant Central Area Lightweight Title)
07.10.91 John Smith W PTS 8 Liverpool
28.11.91 Dave Anderson L RSC 3 Glasgow
27.01.92 Kris McAdam L CO 2 Glasgow
29.04.92 Joey Moffat L RSC 3 Liverpool
29.04.93 Michael Alexander L RSC 2 Hull
29.11.93 Mick Hoban L RSC 4 Manchester
25.11.95 Eamonn Magee L CO 4 Dublin
09.04.96 Mark Haslam L CO 2 Salford
Career: 18 contests, won 5, lost 13.

Steve Roberts

West Ham. *Born* Newham, 3 December, 1972
L. Middleweight. Ht. 5'11"
Manager B. Hearn

16.03.95 Julian Eavis W PTS 6 Basildon
23.05.95 Andy Peach W RSC 3 Potters Bar
13.06.95 Robbie Dunn W RSC 3 Basildon
20.09.95 Jason Hart W RSC 5 Potters Bar
30.09.95 Dick Hanns-Kat W CO 1 Basildon
25.11.95 Ernie Loveridge W PTS 4 Dagenham
23.01.96 Andrew Jervis W PTS 6 Bethnal Green
20.04.96 Peter Vosper W PTS 6 Brentwood
04.05.96 George Richards W PTS 6 Dagenham
Career: 9 contests, won 9.

Andrew Robinson

Birmingham. *Born* Birmingham, 6 November, 1965
S. Featherweight. Ht. 5'6"
Manager Self

14.06.88 Darryl Pettit DREW 6 Birmingham
29.09.88 Darryl Pettit W PTS 6 Stafford
17.10.88 Sean Hogg L PTS 6 Birmingham
01.12.88 Mark Antony L PTS 6 Stafford
12.12.88 Peter Bowen L CO 4 Birmingham
15.03.89 Phil Lashley W PTS 6 Stoke
10.10.89 Jamie Morris W PTS 6 Wolverhampton
07.03.90 Dean Bramhald W PTS 6 Doncaster
19.03.90 Peter Judson L PTS 6 Cleethorpes
11.04.90 Tony Silkstone L PTS 6 Dewsbury
26.04.90 Tony Silkstone L PTS 6 Halifax
30.05.90 Kruga Hydes L PTS 6 Stoke
21.06.90 Mark Antony L PTS 6 Alfreton
10.07.90 Bradley Stone L PTS 6 Canvey Island
27.09.90 Elvis Parsley L RTD 3 Birmingham
24.10.90 Richard Woolgar L RSC 3 Dudley
26.11.90 Sugar Free Somerville W PTS 6 Bethnal Green
15.04.91 Finn McCool DREW 6 Leicester
13.05.91 Dean Bramhald W RTD 1 Birmingham
16.05.91 Craig Dermody L PTS 6 Liverpool
29.04.92 Lee Fox L PTS 6 Stoke
04.12.95 Graham McGrath W PTS 6 Birmingham
17.01.96 Carl Allen W PTS 6 Solihull
30.01.96 Chris Francis L PTS 6 Barking
21.02.96 Thomas Padgett W PTS 6 Batley
Career: 25 contests, won 9, drew 2, lost 14.

Ed Robinson   Les Clark

(Edwin) Ed Robinson

Islington. *Born* Taplow, 21 October, 1971
L. Middleweight. Ht. 5'11"
Manager F. Maloney

02.04.96 Lee Simpkin W PTS 4 Southwark
Career: 1 contest, won 1.

(Andrew) Ray Robinson

Pembroke. *Born* Pembroke, 28 May, 1971
L. Welterweight. Ht. 5'9"
Manager B. Hearn

20.04.96 Brian Coleman W PTS 6 Brentwood
Career: 1 contest, won 1.

Steve Robinson

Cardiff. *Born* Cardiff, 13 December, 1968
Former WBO Featherweight Champion.
Former Undefeated WBA Penta-Continental & Welsh Featherweight Champion. Ht. 5'8"
Manager D. Gardiner

01.03.89 Alan Roberts W PTS 6 Cardiff
13.03.89 Terry Smith W RTD 4 Piccadilly
06.04.89 Nicky Lucas L PTS 8 Cardiff
04.05.89 John Devine W PTS 6 Mayfair
19.08.89 Marcel Herbert L PTS 6 Cardiff
13.11.89 Shane Silvester W RSC 2 Brierley Hill
10.07.90 Mark Bates L PTS 6 Canvey Island
12.09.90 Tim Driscoll L PTS 8 Bethnal Green
26.09.90 Russell Davison W PTS 8 Manchester
03.10.90 Drew Docherty L PTS 8 Solihull
22.10.90 Alan McKay L PTS 6 Mayfair
19.11.90 Neil Haddock W RSC 9 Cardiff
19.12.90 Brian Roche DREW 6 Preston
24.04.91 Russell Davison W RTD 6 Preston
28.05.91 Colin Lynch W RSC 6 Cardiff
18.07.91 Peter Harris W PTS 10 Cardiff
(Welsh Featherweight Title Challenge)
31.01.92 Henry Armstrong L PTS 6 Manchester

11.05.92	Neil Haddock L PTS 10 Llanelli
	(Vacant Welsh S. Featherweight Title)
07.10.92	Edward Lloyd W RTD 8 Barry
30.10.92	Stephane Haccoun W PTS 8 Istres, France
01.12.92	Dennis Oakes W RTD 2 Liverpool
19.01.93	Paul Harvey W PTS 12 Cardiff
	(Vacant WBA Penta-Continental Featherweight Title)
13.02.93	Medhi Labdouni L PTS 8 Paris, France
17.04.93	John Davison W PTS 12 Washington
	(Vacant WBO Featherweight Title)
10.07.93	Sean Murphy W CO 9 Cardiff
	(WBO Featherweight Title Defence)
23.10.93	Colin McMillan W PTS 12 Cardiff
	(WBO Featherweight Title Defence)
12.03.94	Paul Hodkinson W CO 12 Cardiff
	(WBO Featherweight Title Defence)
04.06.94	Freddy Cruz W PTS 12 Cardiff
	(WBO Featherweight Title Defence)
01.10.94	Duke McKenzie W CO 9 Cardiff
	(WBO Featherweight Title Defence)
04.02.95	Domingo Damigella W PTS 12 Cardiff
	(WBO Featherweight Title Defence)
07.07.95	Pedro Ferradas W RSC 9 Cardiff
	(WBO Featherweight Title Defence)
30.09.95	Prince Nassem Hamed L RSC 8 Cardiff
	(WBO Featherweight Title Defence)

Career: 32 contests, won 21, drew 1, lost 10.

Derek Roche   Les Clark

Derek Roche

Leeds. *Born* New Ross, 19 July 1972
L. Middleweight. Ht. 5'9"
Manager J. Celebanski

26.09.94	Michael Alexander W RSC 6 Bradford
05.12.94	Shamus Casey W PTS 6 Bradford
30.01.95	Carl Smith W RSC 3 Bradford
23.02.95	Charlie Paine W CO 1 Hull
25.03.95	Rob Stevenson W PTS 6 Rothwell
12.06.95	Paul King W PTS 6 Bradford
25.09.95	Hughie Davey W PTS 6 Bradford
11.11.95	Rick North W RSC 2 Halifax

11.12.95	Kevin McKenzie W RSC 3 Bradford
13.01.96	Shamus Casey W PTS 6 Halifax
07.03.96	Wayne Shepherd W RSC 3 Bradford

Career: 11 contests, won 11.

Jim Rock

Dublin. *Born* Dublin, 12 March, 1972
L. Middleweight. Ht. 5'11"
Manager M. O'Callaghan

25.11.95	Craig Lynch W PTS 4 Dublin
09.03.96	Peter Mitchell W PTS 6 Millstreet

Career: 2 contests, won 2.

Vince Rose

Tottenham. *Born* London, 9 July, 1968
L. Middleweight. Ht. 5'8"
Manager Self

13.10.92	Ojay Abrahams W RSC 3 Mayfair
14.11.92	Marty Duke W PTS 6 Cardiff
30.01.93	Ojay Abrahams DREW 6 Brentwood
11.05.93	Gary Pemberton W PTS 6 Norwich
11.01.94	Warren Stephens W PTS 6 Bethnal Green
09.02.94	Ojay Abrahams L PTS 6 Brentwood
28.06.94	Said Bennajem L PTS 6 Mayfair
27.08.94	Matthew Turner L RSC 4 Cardiff
07.11.94	Dennis Berry W PTS 6 Bethnal Green
21.02.95	Dave Johnson L PTS 8 Sunderland
14.04.95	Danny Juma L RSC 3 Belfast
23.06.95	Nicky Thurbin L PTS 10 Bethnal Green
	(Vacant Southern Area L. Middleweight Title)
16.10.95	Ernie Loveridge W PTS 4 Heybridge
17.11.95	Joni Nyman DREW 8 Helsinki, Finland
09.04.96	Geoff McCreesh L RSC 4 Stevenage

Career: 15 contests, won 7, drew 2, lost 6.

Jason Rowland

West Ham. *Born* London, 6 August, 1970
L. Welterweight. Ht. 5'9¾"
Manager F. Warren

19.09.89	Terry Smith W RSC 1 Millwall
15.11.89	Mike Morrison W PTS 6 Reading
14.02.90	Eamonn Payne W PTS 6 Millwall
17.04.90	Dave Jenkins W CO 1 Millwall
22.05.90	Mike Morrison W PTS 6 St Albans
12.02.91	Vaughan Carnegie W PTS 6 Basildon
07.03.91	Vaughan Carnegie W CO 2 Basildon
11.12.91	Brian Cullen W RSC 4 Basildon
30.04.92	Steve Pollard W RSC 2 Kensington
17.12.92	Jimmy Vincent W PTS 6 Wembley
10.02.93	Seth Jones W RSC 2 Lewisham
18.03.93	John Smith W PTS 6 Lewisham
04.03.94	Dewi Roberts W RSC 1 Bethnal Green
26.04.94	Ray Hood W CO 1 Bethnal Green
12.09.94	Steve Burton W RSC 1 Mayfair
11.10.94	Phil Found W RSC 4 Bethnal Green
09.11.94	Floyd Churchill W RSC 2 Millwall
09.12.94	Richard Swallow W RSC 2 Bethnal Green
03.03.95	Nigel Bradley W RSC 3 Bethnal Green
29.11.95	Bernard Paul L CO 1 Bethnal Green
	(Southern Area L. Welterweight Title Challenge. Elim. British L. Welterweight Title)

Career: 20 contests, won 19, lost 1.

Danny Ruegg

Bournemouth. *Born* Poole, 28 November, 1974
Featherweight. Ht. 5'5"
Manager J. Bishop

30.09.93	Johnny Simpson L PTS 6 Hayes
17.02.94	Paul Webster L PTS 4 Dagenham
04.03.94	Darren Greaves L PTS 6 Weston super Mare
17.06.94	Danny Lawson L PTS 6 Plymouth
25.10.94	Jon Pegg W PTS 6 Edgbaston
16.11.94	Chris Lyons W PTS 6 Bloomsbury
18.02.95	Tony Falcone L PTS 10 Shepton Mallet
	(Vacant Western Area S. Bantamweight Title)
13.05.95	James Murray L PTS 6 Glasgow
10.06.95	Michael Gomez L PTS 4 Manchester
02.10.95	Richard Vowles L PTS 4 Mayfair
24.11.95	Michael Gomez W PTS 4 Manchester
21.03.96	Patrick Mullings L RSC 3 Southwark

Career: 12 contests, won 3, lost 9.

Charlie Rumbol

Camberwell. *Born* Lambeth, 24 November, 1977
Featherweight. Ht. 5'6½"
Manager M. Duff

03.04.96	Robert Grubb W PTS 6 Bethnal Green
10.05.96	Lee Armstrong L PTS 6 Wembley

Career: 2 contests, won 1, lost 1.

Charlie Rumbol   Les Clark

Brendan Ryan

Nottingham. *Born* Nottingham, 2 November, 1970
L. Middleweight. Ht. 5'9¼"
Manager Self

06.03.89	Andy Rowbotham W RSC 2 Leicester
20.03.89	Pete Roberts W PTS 6 Nottingham
08.05.89	Andy Sweeney W PTS 6 Leicester
15.05.89	Andy Kent W PTS 6 Northampton

22.05.89 Andy Kent W PTS 6 Peterborough
05.06.89 John Ritchie L PTS 6 Glasgow
25.09.89 Lyn Davies L RSC 2 Leicester
20.11.89 Mick Mulcahy W PTS 6 Leicester
04.12.89 Wayne Windle DREW 6 Manchester
11.12.89 Paul Bowen W PTS 6 Nottingham
24.01.90 Brian Cullen L PTS 8 Stoke
05.02.90 Oliver Henry DREW 6 Leicester
19.02.90 Brian Cullen W PTS 8 Nottingham
26.02.90 James Jiora L PTS 6 Bradford
19.03.90 John Smith W PTS 6 Leicester
10.04.90 Mark Kelly L PTS 6 Doncaster
23.04.90 Pete Roberts W PTS 6 Bradford
14.05.90 Vaughan Carnegie L PTS 6 Leicester
21.05.90 Dean Bramhald DREW 6 Cleethorpes
04.06.90 Malcolm Melvin W RSC 7 Edgbaston
17.09.90 John Townsley DREW 8 Glasgow
13.11.90 Malcolm Melvin L PTS 10 Edgbaston
(Vacant Midlands Area
L. Welterweight Title)
24.04.91 Richard Joyce L PTS 8 Stoke
14.05.92 Carl Wright L PTS 4 Liverpool
16.06.92 Bernard Paul L CO 6 Dagenham
10.11.95 Steve Goodwin W RSC 4 Derby
29.11.95 Howard Eastman L RSC 2 Bethnal
Green
Career: 27 contests, won 12, drew 4, lost 11.

Brendan Ryan Les Clark

Danny Ryan

Donegal. *Born* Glasgow, 6 March, 1973
Middleweight. Ht. 5'10"
Manager F. Warren

06.05.95 Paul Matthews W PTS 6 Shepton
Mallet
02.06.95 Peter Mitchell W PTS 6 Bethnal Green
09.09.95 Stinger Mason W PTS 6 Cork
25.11.95 Mark Dawson W PTS 4 Dublin
09.03.96 Marvin O'Brien W PTS 4 Millstreet
13.04.96 Michael Bowen L RSC 2
Wythenshawe
Career: 6 contests, won 5, lost 1.

Gary Ryder Les Clark

Gary Ryder

Liverpool. *Born* Fazackerley, 17 December,
1971
L. Welterweight. Ht. 5'7"
Manager J. Hyland

03.02.96 Andy Davidson W RSC 1 Liverpool
Career: 1 contest, won 1.

Ricky Sackfield

Salford. *Born* Birmingham, 11 April, 1967
Welterweight. Ht. 5'7"
Managers F. Warren/N. Basso

30.04.91 Willie Yeardsley W PTS 4 Stockport
19.09.91 Seth Jones W RSC 1 Stockport
21.10.91 Rob Stewart L PTS 6 Bury
21.01.92 David Thompson W CO 1 Stockport
03.02.92 Scott Doyle W PTS 6 Manchester
09.03.92 John O. Johnson L PTS 6 Manchester
31.03.92 Carl Wright L RSC 1 Stockport
24.09.92 Mark Legg L PTS 6 Stockport
15.02.93 Robert Lloyd W RSC 4 Manchester
26.03.93 Soren Sondergaard L RSC 2
Copenhagen, Denmark
12.06.95 Wayne Windle W PTS 6 Manchester
13.01.96 John O. Johnson W PTS 6 Manchester
13.04.96 John Smith W PTS 4 Wythenshawe
Career: 13 contests, won 8, lost 5.

Paul Salmon

Plymouth. *Born* Plymouth, 27 March, 1971
Welterweight. Ht. 5'9½"
Manager Self

12.10.94 Anthony Huw Williams L RSC 4
Sheffield
18.11.94 Dennis Gardner L RSC 1 Bracknell
24.02.95 Billy McDougall W PTS 6 Weston
super Mare
28.04.95 Frank Olsen L RSC 2 Randers,
Denmark
05.10.95 Dewi Roberts L PTS 6 Queensferry

30.10.95 Nicky Bardle L CO 1 Heathrow
04.04.96 Dave Hinds W RTD 5 Plymouth
20.04.96 David Kehoe L PTS 6 Brentwood
16.05.96 Roger Hunte L RSC 5 Dunstable
Career: 9 contests, won 2, lost 7.

Paul Samuels

Newport. *Born* Newport, 23 March, 1973
L. Welterweight. Ht. 6'0"
Manager M. Duff

11.11.95 Wayne Windle W RSC 2 Halifax
13.02.96 John Harrison W CO 1 Cardiff
05.03.96 Tom Welsh W RSC 3 Bethnal Green
13.03.96 Brian Coleman W PTS 6 Wembley
15.05.96 Gary Hiscox W RSC 3 Cardiff
Career: 5 contests, won 5.

Paul Samuels Les Clark

Chris Saunders

Barnsley. *Born* Barnsley, 15 August, 1969
Former British Welterweight Champion.
Ht. 5'8"
Manager B. Ingle

22.02.90 Malcolm Melvin W PTS 4 Hull
10.04.90 Mike Morrison W PTS 6 Doncaster
20.05.90 Justin Graham W RSC 3 Sheffield
29.11.90 Ross Hale L PTS 6 Bayswater
05.03.91 Rocky Ferrari W PTS 4 Glasgow
19.03.91 Richard Woolgar W RSC 3 Leicester
26.03.91 Felix Kelly L PTS 6 Bethnal Green
17.04.91 Billy Schwer L RSC 1 Kensington
16.05.91 Richard Burton L PTS 6 Liverpool
06.06.91 Mark Tibbs W RSC 6 Barking
30.06.91 Billy Schwer L RSC 3 Southwark
01.08.91 James Jiora W PTS 6 Dewsbury
03.10.91 Gary Flear L PTS 6 Burton
24.10.91 Ron Shinkwin W PTS 6 Dunstable
21.11.91 J. P. Matthews L RSC 4 Burton
30.01.92 John O. Johnson L PTS 6 Southampton
11.02.92 Eddie King W RSC 4 Wolverhampton
27.02.92 Richard Burton L PTS 10 Liverpool
(Vacant Central Area L. Welterweight
Title)

09.09.92 John O. Johnson DREW 6 Stoke
01.10.92 Mark McCreath L RSC 4 Telford
01.12.92 Shea Neary L PTS 6 Liverpool
22.02.93 Cham Joof L PTS 4 Eltham
16.03.93 Mark Elliot L PTS 6 Wolverhampton
26.04.93 Dean Hollington W RSC 5 Lewisham
23.10.93 Michael Smyth L PTS 6 Cardiff
02.12.93 Rob Stewart L PTS 4 Sheffield
03.03.94 Kevin Lueshing W RSC 4 Ebbw Vale
04.06.94 Jose Varela W CO 2 Dortmund, Germany
26.08.94 Julian Eavis W PTS 6 Barnsley
26.09.94 Julian Eavis W PTS 6 Cleethorpes
26.10.94 Lindon Scarlett W PTS 8 Leeds
17.12.94 Roberto Welin W RSC 7 Cagliari, Italy
15.09.95 Del Bryan W PTS 12 Mansfield
 (British Welterweight Title Challenge)
13.02.96 Kevin Lueshing L RSC 3 Bethnal Green
 (British Welterweight Title Defence)
25.06.96 Michael Carruth L RSC 10 Mansfield
Career: 35 contests, won 16, drew 1, lost 18.

Billy Schwer

Luton. *Born* Luton, 12 April, 1969
Former Commonwealth Lightweight Champion. Former Undefeated British Lightweight Champion. Ht. 5'8½"
Manager M. Duff

04.10.90 Pierre Conan W RSC 1 Bethnal Green
31.10.90 Mark Antony W RSC 2 Wembley
12.12.90 Sean Casey W RSC 1 Kensington
16.01.91 Dave Jenkins W PTS 6 Kensington
07.02.91 John Smith W RSC 2 Watford
06.03.91 Chubby Martin W RSC 3 Wembley
04.04.91 Andy Robins W RSC 2 Watford
17.04.91 Chris Saunders W RSC 1 Kensington
02.05.91 Karl Taylor W RSC 2 Northampton
30.06.91 Chris Saunders W RSC 3 Southwark
11.09.91 Tony Foster W PTS 8 Hammersmith
26.09.91 Felix Kelly W RSC 2 Dunstable
24.10.91 Patrick Kamy W CO 1 Dunstable
20.11.91 Marcel Herbert W PTS 8 Kensington
12.02.92 Tomas Quinones W CO 8 Wembley
25.03.92 Bobby Brewer W RSC 4 Kensington
03.09.92 Wayne Windle W CO 1 Dunstable
28.10.92 Carl Crook W RTD 9 Kensington
 (British & Commonwealth Lightweight Title Challenge)
17.12.92 Mauricio Aceves W RSC 3 Wembley
24.02.93 Paul Burke L RSC 7 Wembley
 (British & Commonwealth Lightweight Title Defence)
15.06.93 Farid Benredjeb W PTS 8 Hemel Hempstead
10.11.93 Paul Burke W PTS 12 Watford
 (British & Commonwealth Lightweight Title Challenge)
16.02.94 Sean Murphy W RSC 3 Stevenage
 (British & Commonwealth Lightweight Title Defence)
04.03.94 John Roby W RSC 2 Bethnal Green
22.03.94 Edgar Castro W CO 5 Bethnal Green
11.05.94 Howard Grant W RSC 9 Stevenage
 (Commonwealth Lightweight Title Defence)
09.11.94 Manuel Hernandez W CO 6 Millwall
28.01.95 Rafael Ruelas L RSC 8 Las Vegas, USA
 (IBF Lightweight Title Challenge)
12.05.95 Stephen Chungu W RSC 11 Bethnal Green
 (Commonwealth Lightweight Title Defence)

23.06.95 Bruno Rabanales W DIS 6 Bethnal Green
28.10.95 Ditau Molefyane W CO 8 Kensington
 (Commonwealth Lightweight Title Defence)
25.11.95 David Tetteh L RSC 12 Dagenham
 (Commonwealth Lightweight Title Defence)
15.03.96 Edward Lloyd W RTD 5 Dunstable
16.05.96 Gareth Jordan W RSC 3 Dunstable
Career: 34 contests, won 31, lost 3.

Bruce Scott

Hackney. *Born* Jamaica, 16 August, 1969
L. Heavyweight. Ht. 5'9½"
Manager M. Duff

25.04.91 Mark Bowen L PTS 6 Mayfair
16.09.91 Randy B. Powell W RSC 5 Mayfair
21.11.91 Steve Osborne W PTS 6 Burton
27.04.92 John Kaighin W CO 4 Mayfair
07.09.92 Lee Prudden W PTS 6 Bethnal Green
03.12.92 Mark Pain W RSC 5 Lewisham
15.02.93 Paul McCarthy W PTS 6 Mayfair
22.04.93 Sean O'Phoenix W RSC 3 Mayfair
14.06.93 John Oxenham W RSC 1 Bayswater
04.10.93 Simon McDougall W PTS 6 Mayfair
16.12.93 Bobby Mack W RSC 4 Newport
05.04.94 Steve Osborne W RSC 5 Bethnal Green
17.10.94 Bobbi Joe Edwards W PTS 8 Mayfair
09.12.94 John Keeton W CO 2 Bethnal Green
19.04.95 Nigel Rafferty W RSC 2 Bethnal Green
19.05.95 Cordwell Hylton W RSC 1 Southwark
11.11.95 Tony Booth W RSC 3 Halifax
05.03.96 Nick Manners W RSC 5 Bethnal Green
Career: 18 contests, won 17, lost 1.

Paul Scott

Newbiggin. *Born* Ashington, 27 November, 1969
L. Welterweight. Ht. 5'7"
Manager T. Conroy

06.10.94 Trevor George W PTS 6 Cramlington
24.10.94 James Jiora L PTS 6 Bradford
24.11.94 Ram Singh W PTS 6 Newcastle
20.03.95 Tommy Quinn L RSC 4 Glasgow
12.06.95 Lambsy Kayani L PTS 6 Bradford
29.07.95 Mark Allen W RSC 5 Whitley Bay
02.11.95 Dean Nicholas L PTS 6 Houghton le Spring
18.11.95 Mark Breslin L PTS 6 Glasgow
Career: 8 contests, won 3, lost 5.

Greg Scott-Briggs

Chesterfield. *Born* Swaziland, 6 February, 1966
L. Heavyweight. Ht. 6'1"
Manager Self

04.02.92 Mark McBiane W PTS 6 Alfreton
03.03.92 Tony Colclough W RSC 2 Cradley Heath
30.03.92 Carl Smallwood L PTS 6 Coventry
27.04.92 Richard Atkinson L PTS 6 Bradford
28.05.92 Steve Walton W PTS 6 Gosforth
04.06.92 Joe Frater L PTS 6 Cleethorpes
30.09.92 Carl Smallwood L PTS 6 Solihull
17.03.93 Carl Smallwood L PTS 8 Stoke
26.04.93 Tony Colclough W RSC 4 Glasgow
08.06.93 Peter Flint W RSC 1 Derby
07.09.93 Steve Loftus W PTS 2 Stoke
22.09.93 Paul Hanlon W PTS 6 Chesterfield
04.11.93 Lee Archer L PTS 8 Stafford

24.11.93 Tony Colclough W PTS 6 Solihull
08.12.93 Lee Archer W RTD 6 Stoke
08.02.94 Nigel Rafferty L PTS 6 Wolverhampton
17.02.94 Lee Archer L PTS 8 Walsall
11.03.94 Monty Wright L CO 1 Bethnal Green
26.09.94 Dave Battey W RSC 4 Cleethorpes
11.10.94 Mark Smallwood L PTS 8 Wolverhampton
29.10.94 Mark Smallwood L PTS 6 Cannock
12.11.94 Thomas Hansvold L PTS 4 Randers, Denmark
30.11.94 Monty Wright L PTS 6 Wolverhampton
06.03.95 Neil Simpson L RTD 5 Leicester
15.09.95 David Flowers L PTS 6 Darlington
29.11.95 Neil Simpson L DIS 7 Solihull
 (Vacant Midlands Area L. Heavyweight Title)
20.03.96 Stinger Mason W PTS 6 Stoke
Career: 27 contests, won 11, lost 16.

Stefan Scriggins

Leicester. *Born* Leicester, 17 April, 1970
Welterweight. Ht. 6'2¾"
Manager C. Gunns

30.10.92 Bradley Mayo W PTS 10 Melbourne, Australia
05.12.92 Don Demezen W PTS 10 Lawnton, Australia
16.04.93 Danny Bellert W RSC 3 Strathpine, Australia
22.05.93 Danny Wilkinson W CO 1 Strathpine, Australia
10.07.93 Graham Cheney L PTS 10 Gold Coast, Australia
 (Australian Welterweight Title Challenge)
17.12.93 Bradley Mayo W DIS 6 Carrara, Australia
13.03.94 Sean Sullivan W PTS 8 Brighton, Australia
19.03.94 Paula Tuilau W PTS 10 Suva, Fiji
20.05.94 Luvtho Kakaza L RSC 4 Cape Town, South Africa
06.03.95 Gary Beardsley W PTS 6 Leicester
03.04.95 Nick Ingram W PTS 6 Northampton
05.06.95 Spencer McCracken W PTS 8 Birmingham
23.10.95 Mark Ramsey W PTS 8 Leicester
29.11.95 Andrej Pestraev L RSC 4 Southwark
Career: 14 contests, won 11, lost 3.

Muhammad Shaffique

Huddersfield. *Born* Huddersfield, 19 February, 1969
S. Featherweight. Ht. 5'9"
Manager T. Miller

07.02.89 Erwin Edwards W PTS 6 Southend
12.06.89 Mick Mulcahy W RSC 2 Manchester
12.12.89 Mick Moran L PTS 6 Brentford
05.02.90 Frankie Foster W PTS 6 Brierley Hill
12.11.90 Steve Walker L PTS 6 Stratford on Avon
27.11.90 Mark Geraghty W PTS 8 Glasgow
02.10.91 Elvis Parsley L CO 1 Solihull
28.11.94 Michael Brodie L RSC 2 Manchester
18.01.95 G. G. Goddard L RSC 2 Solihull
20.02.95 Robert Hay L PTS 6 Brentford
13.10.95 Brian Carr L PTS 6 Glasgow
30.10.95 Jason Blanche L CO 2 Bradford
Career: 12 contests, won 4, lost 8.

Kevin Sheil   Les Clark

Kevin Sheil

Cardiff. *Born* Wexford, 8 May, 1972
Featherweight. Ht. 5'6"
Manager K. Hayde

28.11.95 Stefy Bull L PTS 6 Wolverhampton
18.12.95 Richard Evatt L RSC 1 Mayfair
30.05.96 Carl Greaves L PTS 6 Lincoln
Career: 3 contests, lost 3.

(Rufus) Rocky Shelly (Davies)

Mansfield. *Born* Oldham, 18 August, 1970
Cruiserweight. Ht. 5'10½"
Manager B. Ingle

09.12.91 Stuart Fleet W RSC 1 Cleethorpes
26.12.91 Issa Moluh L RSC 2 Berne, Switzerland
05.03.92 Des Vaughan L RSC 5 Battersea
22.03.96 Carl Nicholson L RTD 3 Mansfield
Career: 4 contests, won 1, lost 3.

Charles Shepherd

Carlisle. *Born* Burnley, 28 June, 1970
Lightweight. Ht. 5'4"
Manager J. Doughty

28.10.91 Chris Aston W PTS 6 Leicester
31.01.92 Alan McDowall L RSC 3 Glasgow
18.05.92 Mark Legg W PTS 6 Marton
25.09.92 George Naylor W RSC 4 Liverpool
22.10.92 Didier Hughes L PTS 4 Bethnal Green
13.02.93 Nigel Wenton W PTS 8 Manchester
23.05.93 Cham Joof W PTS 4 Brockley
21.10.93 Karl Taylor W RTD 5 Bayswater
09.02.94 Justin Juuko L RSC 5 Bethnal Green
21.04.94 Tony Foster L PTS 10 Hull
          (Vacant Central Area Lightweight Title)
29.09.94 Frankie Foster W RSC 3 Tynemouth
08.03.95 Bamana Dibateza W PTS 8 Solihull
26.04.95 Kelton McKenzie W RSC 7 Solihull
23.05.95 Michael Ayers L RSC 3 Potters Bar
          (British Lightweight Title Challenge)

14.11.95 John Stovin W RSC 4 Bury
22.04.96 Marc Smith W RSC 2 Crystal Palace
29.06.96 P. J. Gallagher L PTS 12 Erith
          (British S. Featherweight Title Challenge)
Career: 17 contests, won 11, lost 6.

Wayne Shepherd

Carlisle. *Born* Whiston, 3 June, 1959
Welterweight. Ht. 5'6"
Manager J. Doughty

07.10.91 Benji Joseph W PTS 6 Bradford
28.10.91 Noel Henry W PTS 6 Leicester
16.12.91 Dave Maj DREW 6 Manchester
03.02.92 Dave Maj L PTS 6 Manchester
30.03.92 Hughie Davey L PTS 6 Bradford
18.05.92 Dave Whittle W PTS 6 Marton
14.10.92 Richard Swallow L PTS 8 Stoke
31.10.92 George Scott L RSC 6 Earls Court
13.02.93 Delroy Waul L RSC 5 Manchester
31.03.93 Derek Grainger L RSC 4 Barking
11.06.93 Hughie Davey L PTS 6 Gateshead
06.09.93 Shea Neary L RTD 2 Liverpool
26.01.94 James McGee W PTS 6 Stoke
28.02.94 Craig Winter L PTS 6 Manchester
02.03.95 Denny Johnson L PTS 6 Cramlington
06.04.95 Shaun Stokes L PTS 6 Sheffield
22.05.95 Peter Varnavas W PTS 6 Morecambe
01.06.95 Tommy Quinn L PTS 6 Musselburgh
29.07.95 Shaun O'Neill L PTS 4 Whitley Bay
07.10.95 Neil Sinclair L PTS 6 Belfast
30.10.95 John Stronach L PTS 6 Bradford
11.12.95 Shamus Casey L PTS 6 Morecambe
07.03.96 Derek Roche L RSC 3 Bradford
22.04.96 Gilbert Eastman L PTS 4 Crystal Palace
25.06.96 Geoff McCreesh L PTS 4 Stevenage
Career: 25 contests, won 5, drew 1, lost 19.

Eddie Sica   Les Clark

Eddie Sica

Highbury. *Born* Islington, 5 September, 1968
Featherweight. Ht. 5'4½"
Manager F. Maloney

24.10.95 Chris Lyons W PTS 4 Southwark
29.11.95 Martin Evans L RSC 2 Southwark
02.04.96 Benny May W RSC 1 Southwark
Career: 3 contests, won 2, lost 1.

John Sillo   Les Clark

John Sillo (Sillitoe)

Liverpool. *Born* Oxford, 10 February, 1965
Featherweight. Ht. 5'5"
Manager S. Vaughan

28.09.93 Graham McGrath W PTS 6 Liverpool
11.12.93 Marty Chestnut W PTS 6 Liverpool
25.02.94 Craig Kelley W PTS 6 Chester
06.05.94 Chris Lyons W RSC 3 Liverpool
26.09.94 Pete Buckley W PTS 6 Liverpool
25.03.95 Garry Burrell W PTS 6 Chester
20.04.95 Pete Buckley W PTS 6 Liverpool
29.09.95 Alexander Tiranov L RTD 3 Liverpool
08.12.95 Jason Thomas W PTS 6 Liverpool
13.04.96 Michael Brodie L CO 1 Liverpool
Career: 10 contests, won 8, lost 2.

Justin Simmons

Plymouth. *Born* Plymouth, 3 November, 1974
L. Middleweight. Ht. 5'11½"
Manager Self

19.09.95 Shamus Casey W PTS 6 Plymouth
13.11.95 John Janes W PTS 6 Barnstaple
29.11.95 Allan Gray W PTS 6 Bethnal Green
12.02.96 Dennis Gardner W RSC 3 Heathrow
04.04.96 Steve McGovern DREW 6 Plymouth
Career: 5 contests, won 4, drew 1.

Justin Simmons   Les Clark

Lee Simpkin

Swadlincote. *Born* Ashby, 26 September, 1974
L. Heavyweight. Ht. 6'1"
Manager N. Nobbs

31.01.96	Scott Beasley L RSC 3 Stoke
25.03.96	Michael Pinnock L PTS 6 Birmingham
02.04.96	Ed Robinson L PTS 4 Southwark
09.05.96	Terry Morrill L RSC 5 Hull

Career: 4 contests, lost 4.

Neil Simpson

Coventry. *Born* London, 5 July, 1970
Midlands Area L. Heavyweight Champion.
Ht. 6'2"
Manager J. Griffin

04.10.94	Kenny Nevers W PTS 4 Mayfair
20.10.94	Johnny Hooks W RSC 2 Walsall
05.12.94	Chris Woollas L PTS 6 Cleethorpes
15.12.94	Paul Murray W PTS 6 Walsall
06.03.95	Greg Scott-Briggs W RTD 5 Leicester
17.03.95	Thomas Hansvold L PTS 4 Copenhagen, Denmark
26.04.95	Craig Joseph L PTS 6 Solihull
11.05.95	Andy McVeigh L CO 2 Dudley
24.06.95	Dave Owens W RSC 1 Cleethorpes
25.09.95	Tony Booth L PTS 8 Cleethorpes
11.10.95	Darren Ashton W RSC 3 Solihull
29.11.95	Greg Scott-Briggs W DIS 7 Solihull
	(Vacant Midlands Area L. Heavyweight Title)
19.02.96	Stephen Wilson L PTS 6 Glasgow
27.03.96	Tony Booth W PTS 6 Whitwick
26.04.96	Dean Francis L RSC 3 Cardiff

Career: 15 contests, won 8, lost 7.

Neil Sinclair

Belfast. *Born* Belfast, 23 February, 1974
Welterweight. Ht. 5'10½"
Manager B. Hearn

14.04.95	Marty Duke W RSC 2 Belfast
27.05.95	Andrew Jervis L RSC 3 Belfast
17.07.95	Andy Peach W RSC 1 Mayfair
26.08.95	George Wilson W PTS 4 Belfast
07.10.95	Wayne Shepherd W PTS 6 Belfast
02.12.95	Brian Coleman W RTD 1 Belfast
13.04.96	Hughie Davey W PTS 6 Liverpool
28.05.96	Prince Kasi Kaihau W RSC 2 Belfast

Career: 8 contests, won 7, lost 1.

Neil Sinclair   Les Clark

(Raminderbir) Ram Singh

Wisbech. *Born* Crewe, 13 August, 1969
Lightweight. Ht. 5'11"
Manager B. Lee

06.06.94	Wahid Fats L RSC 3 Manchester
26.09.94	Robert Howard W PTS 6 Morecambe
17.11.94	Terry Whittaker L PTS 6 Sheffield
24.11.94	Paul Scott L PTS 6 Newcastle
05.12.94	Liam Dineen L PTS 6 Houghton le Spring
12.01.95	Steve Tuckett L RSC 6 Leeds
21.02.95	Glen Hopkins L RSC 1 Sunderland
03.04.95	Dave Madden L PTS 6 Northampton
27.04.95	Paul Hamilton W RSC 2 Hull
14.06.95	Terry Whittaker L PTS 6 Batley
28.09.95	John T. Kelly L PTS 6 Sunderland
05.10.95	Garry Burrell L PTS 8 Glasgow
29.01.96	Marco Fattore DREW 6 Piccadilly
21.02.96	Dave Fallon L PTS 6 Piccadilly
19.03.96	Andy Green L PTS 6 Leeds
01.04.96	Hurricane Hughes W PTS 6 Bradford
22.04.96	John T. Kelly L PTS 6 Manchester
09.05.96	Liam Dineen L PTS 6 Sunderland
30.05.96	Steve Conway L PTS 6 Lincoln
13.06.96	Thomas Bradley L RSC 1 Sheffield

Career: 20 contests, won 3, drew 1, lost 16.

(Sukhdarshan) Tiger Singh (Mahal)

Peterborough. *Born* India, 28 October, 1970
Flyweight. Ht. 5'8"
Manager Self

| 10.12.92 | Ian Baillie W PTS 6 Corby |

11.05.93	Anthony Hanna L PTS 6 Norwich
06.10.93	Anthony Hanna L PTS 6 Solihull
28.10.93	Nick Tooley L PTS 6 Torquay
30.11.93	Vince Feeney L PTS 6 Leicester
02.03.94	Lyndon Kershaw L PTS 6 Solihull
09.05.94	Terry Gaskin W RSC 2 Bradford
20.09.94	Keith Knox L PTS 6 Musselburgh
28.11.94	Terry Gaskin W PTS 6 Manchester
08.03.95	Lyndon Kershaw L PTS 6 Solihull
26.04.95	Darren Noble W PTS 6 Solihull
14.09.95	Mark Reynolds L RSC 3 Battersea
08.12.95	Shaun Hall W PTS 6 Leeds

Career: 13 contests, won 5, lost 8.

Robbie Sivyer

Alfreton. *Born* Chesterfield, 22 September, 1973
Lightweight. Ht. 5'9"
Manager M. Shinfield

26.04.93	Garry Burrell L PTS 6 Glasgow
07.06.93	Simon Hamblett W PTS 6 Walsall
29.06.93	Mark Allen L PTS 6 Edgbaston
22.09.93	John Stovin L PTS 6 Chesterfield
13.11.93	Wayne Jones L PTS 6 Cullompton
04.03.94	Wayne Jones L PTS 6 Weston super Mare
05.06.95	Trevor Royal W CO 5 Birmingham
02.10.95	T. J. Smith L RSC 4 Birmingham
04.12.95	Robert Grubb W PTS 6 Birmingham
16.03.96	Norman Dhalie W CO 4 Barnstaple
13.06.96	Kid McAuley W PTS 6 Sheffield

Career: 11 contests, won 5, lost 6.

Frankie Slane

Belfast. *Born* Belfast, 2 July, 1974
Bantamweight. Ht. 5'4"
Manager B. Hearn

| 07.10.95 | Henry Jones W PTS 4 Belfast |
| 02.12.95 | Marty Chestnut W PTS 4 Belfast |

Career: 2 contests, won 2.

Andrew Smith

Bedworth. *Born* Nuneaton, 15 February, 1975
S. Featherweight. Ht. 5'5"
Manager Self

20.05.94	Marc Smith DREW 6 Neath
16.09.94	Dennis Holbaek Pedersen L RSC 6 Aalborg, Denmark
07.12.94	Jon Pegg DREW 6 Stoke
07.02.95	Jon Pegg W PTS 6 Wolverhampton
22.02.95	Brian Robb L PTS 6 Telford
09.03.95	Robert Grubb DREW 6 Walsall
28.03.95	Robert Grubb W PTS 6 Wolverhampton
03.04.95	Niel Leggett L PTS 6 Northampton
21.04.95	Brian Robb DREW 6 Dudley
13.10.95	Scott Dixon L PTS 6 Glasgow
21.11.95	Chris Lyons W PTS 6 Edgbaston

Career: 11 contests, won 3, drew 4, lost 4.

Carl Smith

Manchester. *Born* Hereford, 31 March, 1968
L. Middleweight. Ht. 5'9"
Manager N. Basso

29.11.93	Chris Mulcahy W CO 1 Manchester
26.01.94	Anthony Lawrence L RSC 4 Stoke
28.02.94	Japhet Hans W RSC 4 Manchester

18.04.94	Jimmy Alston L PTS 6 Manchester
06.06.94	Jimmy Alston DREW 6 Manchester
03.10.94	Peter Varnavas W RSC 2 Manchester
26.10.94	Rick North DREW 6 Stoke
30.01.95	Derek Roche L RSC 3 Bradford
25.03.95	Jon Stocks W PTS 6 Chester
12.06.95	John Duckworth L PTS 6 Manchester
04.11.95	Danny Peters L CO 3 Liverpool
08.12.95	Paul Wright L RSC 2 Liverpool

Career: 12 contests, won 4, drew 2, lost 6.

Georgie Smith

Basildon. *Born* Basildon, 29 August, 1971
L. Welterweight. Ht. 5'10"
Manager B. Hearn

07.11.94	Malcolm Thomas W PTS 6 Bethnal Green
20.12.94	Stevie Bolt W RSC 2 Bethnal Green
17.02.95	Dewi Roberts W RSC 2 Crawley
16.03.95	Shaba Edwards W CO 2 Basildon
09.05.95	Wayne Jones W RSC 3 Basildon
13.06.95	Rudy Valentino W PTS 6 Basildon
28.10.95	Kevin McKillan W CO 2 Kensington
06.02.96	Gary Beardsley W RSC 1 Basildon
20.04.96	Danny Quacoe W PTS 6 Brentwood

Career: 9 contests, won 9.

John Smith

Liverpool. *Born* Liverpool, 13 October, 1959
Welterweight. Ht. 5'9"
Manager Self

26.06.86	Ray Golding W PTS 6 Edgbaston
22.09.86	John Townsley W PTS 6 Edgbaston
06.11.86	Robert Harkin L PTS 8 Glasgow
20.11.86	John Best L PTS 6 Bredbury
08.12.86	Gary Sommerville DREW 8 Edgbaston
18.03.87	John Best L RSC 2 Solihull
24.04.87	Brian Wareing L PTS 8 Liverpool
24.09.87	John Dickson L PTS 6 Glasgow
01.02.88	Peter Crook L PTS 6 Manchester
17.03.88	Mick Mason DREW 8 Sunderland
29.03.88	Paul Seddon W RSC 4 Marton
17.06.88	Gary Sommerville W RSC 5 Edgbaston
28.11.88	Gary Sommerville L PTS 8 Edgbaston
24.01.89	Mark Kelly L PTS 8 Kings Heath
22.03.89	John Davies L PTS 8 Solihull
17.07.89	Richard Adams W RSC 3 Stanmore
08.09.89	Muhammad Lovelock W PTS 6 Liverpool
14.09.89	Roy Rowland L RSC 3 Basildon
17.10.89	Jim Talbot L PTS 6 Oldham
25.10.89	Kevin Plant L PTS 6 Doncaster
10.11.89	Seamus O'Sullivan L PTS 6 Battersea
30.11.89	Dave Pierre L PTS 6 Mayfair
08.12.89	Allan Hall L RSC 2 Doncaster
29.01.90	Darren Mount L PTS 8 Liverpool
08.03.90	Dave Pierre L PTS 6 Peterborough
19.03.90	Brendan Ryan L PTS 6 Leicester
05.04.90	Darren Mount L PTS 8 Liverpool
04.05.90	Pete Roberts L PTS 6 Liverpool
24.09.90	Mark Dinnadge W RTD 2 Lewisham
09.10.90	Pete Roberts W PTS 8 Liverpool
13.11.90	Paul Charters L RSC 4 Hartlepool
21.01.91	Kris McAdam L PTS 6 Glasgow
07.02.91	Billy Schwer L RSC 2 Watford
26.03.91	Andrew Morgan L RSC 4 Wolverhampton
24.04.91	Andrew Morgan L PTS 6 Aberavon
16.05.91	Kevin Toomey L PTS 6 Liverpool

13.06.91	Kevin Toomey L PTS 6 Hull
25.07.91	Robert McCracken L RTD 1 Dudley
07.10.91	Pete Roberts L PTS 8 Liverpool
23.10.91	Dean Hollington L PTS 6 Bethnal Green
12.11.91	Mark Elliot L PTS 6 Wolverhampton
21.11.91	Richard Burton L PTS 6 Burton
02.12.91	Mike Calderwood DREW 8 Liverpool
19.12.91	Richard Burton L PTS 6 Oldham
01.02.92	George Scott L RSC 3 Birmingham
03.03.92	Paul Charters L PTS 8 Houghton le Spring
12.05.92	Ross Hale L CO 1 Crystal Palace
03.09.92	Chris Mulcahy DREW 6 Liverpool
25.09.92	Kevin McKillan L PTS 6 Liverpool
07.10.92	Alan Peacock DREW 6 Glasgow
12.11.92	Mark Tibbs L RSC 6 Bayswater
18.03.93	Jason Rowland L PTS 6 Lewisham
29.03.93	Shea Neary L PTS 6 Liverpool
13.09.93	Rob Stewart DREW 6 Middleton
22.09.93	Jonathan Thaxton L PTS 6 Wembley
27.10.93	Mark McCreath L RSC 7 West Bromwich
25.11.93	Charlie Kane L PTS 6 Tynemouth
21.02.94	Alan Peacock L RSC 4 Glasgow
28.03.94	Charlie Kane L PTS 6 Musselburgh
10.04.94	Kris McAdam W PTS 8 Glasgow
28.06.94	Malcolm Melvin L PTS 6 Edgbaston
17.08.94	Paul Ryan L RTD 2 Sheffield
19.09.94	Alan Peacock L PTS 8 Glasgow
28.09.94	Shaun Cogan L RSC 3 Glasgow
17.11.94	Nigel Bradley L PTS 6 Sheffield
29.11.94	Shaun Cogan L RSC 4 Cannock
25.01.95	Shea Neary L RSC 5 Stoke
24.02.95	Steve McLevy L PTS 6 Irvine
20.04.95	Andreas Panayi L RSC 4 Liverpool
12.06.95	Wahid Fats W CO 3 Manchester
02.07.95	Peter Richardson L PTS 6 Dublin
09.09.95	Michael Carruth L PTS 8 Cork
20.09.95	Bernard Paul L PTS 6 Potters Bar
29.09.95	John Jones L PTS 6 Liverpool
24.10.95	Richie Edwards L PTS 4 Southwark
14.11.95	Bobby Vanzie L PTS 6 Bury
29.11.95	Paul Miles L PTS 4 Southwark
06.12.95	Gary Beardsley L PTS 8 Stoke
07.03.96	Bobby Vanzie L PTS 6 Bradford
15.03.96	John Stovin DREW 6 Hull
13.04.96	Ricky Sackfield L PTS 4 Wythenshawe
22.04.96	Dean Nicholas L PTS 6 Glasgow
25.06.96	Nicky Bardle L PTS 4 Stevenage

Career: 83 contests, won 10, drew 7, lost 66.

Marc Smith

Swansea. *Born* Kingston, 31 August, 1974
Lightweight. Ht. 5'9"
Manager P. Boyce

20.05.94	Andrew Smith DREW 6 Neath
11.10.94	Mark Allen W PTS 6 Wolverhampton
20.10.94	Mark Allen L PTS 6 Walsall
09.03.95	Simon Hamblett L PTS 6 Walsall
16.03.95	Nelson Ide L RSC 4 Basildon
20.09.95	Craig Kelley W RSC 1 Ystrad
29.09.95	P. J. Gallagher L RSC 3 Bethnal Green
02.11.95	Anthony Campbell L PTS 6 Mayfair
22.11.95	Marco Fattore W PTS 6 Mayfair
12.02.96	Adrian Chase L CO 1 Heathrow
20.03.96	Tommy Janes W RSC 6 Cardiff
22.04.96	Charles Shepherd L RSC 2 Crystal Palace

Career: 12 contests, won 4, drew 1, lost 7.

Neil Smith

Leicester. *Born* Leicester, 15 January, 1972
Lightweight. Ht. 6'1½"
Manager J. Griffin

13.12.90	Tony Silkstone L PTS 6 Dewsbury
06.02.91	Dennis Adams L PTS 6 Bethnal Green
14.03.91	John Naylor W RSC 6 Middleton
20.05.91	Elvis Parsley W RSC 5 Leicester
11.06.91	Lee Fox W PTS 6 Leicester
05.11.91	Neil Leitch W RSC 1 Leicester
04.02.92	Harry Escott L PTS 8 Alfreton
26.01.93	Norman Dhalie W PTS 4 Leicester
03.02.93	Paul Ryan L RSC 1 Earls Court
19.05.93	Dean Amory L PTS 6 Leicester
25.01.95	Anthony Maynard W PTS 6 Stoke
06.03.95	Gary Hiscox L PTS 6 Leicester
06.06.95	Kid McAuley W RTD 1 Leicester
27.03.96	Andy Green W RSC 3 Whitwick
24.04.96	Anthony Campbell L PTS 8 Solihull

Career: 15 contests, won 8, lost 7.

Neville Smith

Cranford. *Born* Isleworth, 7 January, 1976
S. Middleweight. Ht. 6'2"
Manager H. Holland

03.12.95	Michael Pinnock W RSC 5 Southwark
12.02.96	Simon Andrews W RSC 3 Heathrow

Career: 2 contests, won 2.

Neville Smith　　　　　　　　Les Clark

(Terry) T. J. Smith

Kettering. *Born* Kettering 17 October, 1967
Lightweight. Ht. 5'7½"
Manager C. Hogben

29.04.92	Floyd Churchill L RSC 2 Liverpool
10.12.92	Alan Graham L PTS 6 Corby
23.02.93	Patrick Parton W PTS 6 Kettering
29.03.93	Marco Fattore DREW 6 Mayfair
19.04.93	Lee Ryan W RSC 2 Northampton
18.05.93	Dean Martin W RSC 3 Kettering
23.11.93	Jimmy Phelan W PTS 6 Kettering
08.03.94	Andrew Reed W PTS 6 Kettering
17.05.94	Simon Frailing W RSC 1 Kettering
04.06.94	Gareth Jordan L RSC 1 Cardiff
05.12.94	Micky Hall L RTD 3 Houghton le Spring

21.02.95 Liam Dineen L PTS 6 Sunderland
05.04.95 Mark Breslin L PTS 6 Irvine
01.06.95 Mark Breslin L RSC 3 Musselburgh
25.09.95 Jason Blanche L PTS 6 Bradford
02.10.95 Robbie Sivyer W RSC 4 Birmingham
09.10.95 John T. Kelly DREW 6 Manchester
29.10.95 Scott Walker L PTS 6 Shaw
Career: 18 contests, won 7, drew 2, lost 9.

Trevor Smith

Birmingham. *Born* Birmingham, 24 October, 1965
L. Welterweight. Ht. 5'8"
Manager E. Cashmore

04.02.95 Steve Burton W RSC 6 Cardiff
04.03.95 Mark Winters L PTS 6 Livingston
05.05.95 Shaun Stokes DREW 6 Doncaster
02.09.95 Martin Holgate L RSC 2 Wembley
Career: 4 contests, won 1, drew 1, lost 2.

Michael Smyth

Barry. *Born* Caerphilly, 22 February, 1970
Welterweight. Ht. 5'9¾"
Manager D. Gardiner

02.05.91 Carl Brasier W RSC 2 Kensington
28.05.91 Rick North W RSC 1 Cardiff
18.07.91 Mike Morrison W RSC 2 Cardiff
03.09.91 Julian Eavis W PTS 6 Cardiff
20.11.91 Mike Russell W RSC 3 Cardiff
17.12.91 Julian Eavis W PTS 6 Cardiff
19.05.92 Ojay Abrahams W PTS 6 Cardiff
07.10.92 David Lake W CO 2 Barry
14.11.92 Des Robinson W PTS 6 Cardiff
10.07.93 Ernie Loveridge W RSC 6 Cardiff
23.10.93 Chris Saunders W PTS 6 Cardiff
12.03.94 Gordon Blair W RSC 4 Cardiff
21.07.94 Maurice Forbes W RSC 3 Battersea
24.09.94 Mike DeMoss W RSC 1 Wembley
25.10.94 Scott Doyle W CO 1 Southwark
25.01.95 Rick North W DIS 4 Cardiff
17.06.95 Kevin Lueshing L RSC 3 Cardiff
         (Final Elim. British Welterweight Title)
20.09.95 Howard Clarke DREW 6 Ystrad
25.10.95 Nigel Bradley W RSC 4 Cardiff
16.12.95 Geoff McCreesh W DIS 4 Cardiff
25.05.96 Maxim Nesterenko L RSC 5 St Petersburg, Russia
         (Vacant WBC International Welterweight Title)
Career: 21 contests, won 18, drew 1, lost 2.

Mark Snipe   Les Clark

Mark Snipe

Brighton. *Born* Brighton, 9 March, 1972
L. Heavyweight. Ht. 6'1"
Manager P. Byrne

13.06.95 Michael Pinnock W PTS 6 Basildon
27.10.95 Stinger Mason DREW 6 Brighton
26.01.96 Robert Harper W PTS 6 Brighton
13.04.96 Lee Whitehead W PTS 4 Wythenshawe
Career: 4 contests, won 3, drew 1.

Jason Squire

Leicester. *Born* Leicester, 18 June, 1975
Featherweight. Ht. 5'4½"
Manager J. Griffin

06.06.95 Michael Edwards W RSC 1 Leicester
11.10.95 Chris Lyons W PTS 6 Solihull
23.10.95 Chris Price W PTS 6 Leicester
29.11.95 Carl Allen W PTS 6 Solihull
27.03.96 Carl Allen DREW 6 Whitwick
17.05.96 Fred Reeve DREW 6 Hull
Career: 6 contests, won 4, drew 2.

(Mick) Art Stacey

Leeds. *Born* Leeds, 26 September, 1964
Cruiserweight. Ht. 6'0½"
Manager K. Tate

09.10.90 Trevor Barry DREW 6 Liverpool
06.11.90 Chris Coughlan W RSC 4 Southend
27.11.90 Allan Millett W PTS 6 Liverpool
21.02.91 Tony Lawrence W PTS 6 Leeds
18.03.91 Paul Gearon W RSC 1 Derby
16.04.91 Steve Osborne DREW 6 Nottingham
03.06.91 Dennis Afflick W PTS 6 Glasgow
11.11.91 Steve Osborne W PTS 6 Bradford
21.11.91 Gil Lewis L RSC 4 Stafford
20.01.92 John Pierre W PTS 8 Bradford
26.10.92 Ian Bulloch L PTS 6 Cleethorpes
27.11.92 Neils H. Madsen L PTS 8 Randers, Denmark
14.12.92 Albert Call L PTS 6 Cleethorpes
20.01.93 Trevor Small L PTS 6 Solihull
08.03.93 Lee Prudden DREW 6 Leeds
11.06.93 Ian Henry L PTS 6 Gateshead
25.06.93 Mark Prince L CO 2 Battersea
22.09.93 Phil Soundy L PTS 6 Wembley
06.10.93 Trevor Small L PTS 6 Solihull
13.10.93 Paul Lawson L RSC 2 Bethnal Green
25.11.93 Stevie R. Davies W PTS 6 Newcastle
08.12.93 John Pierre W PTS 6 Hull
17.03.94 Albert Call L PTS 6 Lincoln
09.04.94 Chris Okoh L PTS 6 Bethnal Green
21.04.94 Darren McKenna W PTS 6 Hull
11.05.94 Darren Westover L PTS 6 Stevenage
22.05.94 Owen Bartley L PTS 6 Crystal Palace
15.06.94 Paul Lawson L RSC 2 Southwark
17.09.94 Chris Okoh L PTS 6 Crawley
08.10.94 Rudiger May L PTS 6 Halle, Germany
17.10.94 John Foreman L PTS 8 Birmingham
18.11.94 Keith Fletcher L PTS 6 Bracknell
08.12.94 Declan Faherty W PTS 6 Hull
04.03.95 Terry Dunstan L CO 1 Livingston
27.04.95 Tony Booth L PTS 10 Hull
         (Vacant Central Area Cruiserweight Title)
26.05.95 Gypsy Carman L PTS 6 Norwich
08.06.95 John Wilson L PTS 6 Glasgow
23.06.95 Monty Wright L RSC 2 Bethnal Green
11.12.95 Albert Call L RSC 3 Cleethorpes
12.02.96 Gypsy Carman L RSC 3 Heathrow
Career: 40 contests, won 11, drew 3, lost 26.

Craig Stanley

Croydon. *Born* Croydon, 16 March, 1974
L. Welterweight. Ht. 5'6"
Manager F. Maloney

22.04.96 Jason Campbell W RSC 2 Crystal Palace
29.06.96 Arv Mittoo W PTS 4 Erith
Career: 2 contests, won 2.

David Starie

Bury St Edmunds. *Born* Bury St Edmunds, 11 June, 1974
S. Middleweight. Ht. 6'0"
Manager G. Holmes

24.09.94 Paul Murray W RSC 2 Wembley
25.10.94 Dave Owens W PTS 6 Southwark
07.02.95 Marvin O'Brien W PTS 6 Ipswich
30.03.95 Mark Dawson W RSC 1 Bethnal Green
17.05.95 Marvin O'Brien W RSC 5 Ipswich
14.09.95 John Duckworth W PTS 6 Battersea
20.10.95 Hunter Clay W PTS 8 Ipswich
15.12.95 Carlos Christie W CO 4 Bethnal Green
21.03.96 Paul Murray W RSC 1 Southwark
14.05.96 Phil Ball W RSC 1 Dagenham
Career: 10 contests, won 10.

Jimmy Steel

Stoke. *Born* Stoke, 22 June, 1970
Middleweight. Ht. 5'7"
Manager W. Swift

25.04.96 Andy Gray W PTS 6 Mayfair
Career: 1 contest, won 1.

Rob Stevenson   Les Clark

Rob Stevenson

Hull. *Born* Hull, 16 March, 1971
L. Middleweight. Ht. 5'9"
Manager M. Brooks

28.11.91 Matt Mowatt L PTS 6 Hull
26.03.92 Steve Scott W PTS 6 Hull

04.04.92 Chris Mulcahy L PTS 8 Cleethorpes
29.04.92 Alan Williams W PTS 6 Liverpool
01.06.92 Chris Mulcahy L PTS 6 Manchester
13.10.92 Dean Hiscox L PTS 6 Wolverhampton
26.11.92 Steve Scott L PTS 6 Hull
18.02.93 Warren Stephens W PTS 6 Hull
25.02.93 Ron Hopley DREW 6 Bradford
29.04.93 Billy McDougall DREW 6 Hull
01.07.93 Ron Hopley W PTS 6 York
02.12.93 Ian Noble W PTS 6 Hartlepool
13.12.93 Prince Kasi Kaihau L RSC 5 Doncaster
24.02.94 David Sumner W PTS 6 Hull
24.02.95 Billy Collins L PTS 6 Irvine
25.03.95 Derek Roche L RSC 6 Rothwell
01.07.95 Paul Carr L PTS 6 Kensington
22.09.95 Brian Dunn L PTS 6 Hull
03.11.95 David Bain L PTS 6 Dudley
25.11.95 Jim Webb L PTS 6 Dublin
04.12.95 David Radford L CO 2 Manchester
26.02.96 Shamus Casey W PTS 6 Hull
09.05.96 Carlton Williams L PTS 6 Hull
Career: 23 contests, won 7, drew 2, lost 14.

Jon Stocks

Liverpool. *Born* Liverpool, 22 January, 1969
Middleweight. Ht. 6'0½"
Manager S. Vaughan

14.02.91 Benji Good W PTS 6 Southampton
28.02.91 Griff Jones W PTS 6 Sunderland
02.07.94 John Hughes W RSC 1 Liverpool
31.10.94 Shamus Casey W PTS 6 Liverpool
27.02.95 Roy Chipperfield W RSC 3 Barrow
25.03.95 Carl Smith L PTS 6 Chester
04.11.95 Paul Murray W PTS 6 Liverpool
08.12.95 Carl Winstone W RSC 3 Liverpool
10.05.96 Prince Kasi Kaihau W PTS 6 Liverpool
Career: 9 contests, won 8, lost 1.

Shaun Stokes

Sheffield. *Born* Sheffield, 19 November, 1969
Welterweight. Ht. 5'7"
Manager J. Rushton

09.02.95 Gary Beardsley L RSC 3 Doncaster
22.03.95 Kenny Scott W RSC 1 Stoke
28.03.95 Patrick Parton W CO 1 Wolverhampton
06.04.95 Wayne Shepherd W PTS 6 Sheffield
05.05.95 Trevor Smith DREW 6 Doncaster
18.05.95 Kevin McKillan DREW 8 Middleton
06.07.95 Mark Allen W PTS 6 Hull
21.09.95 Darren Covill W PTS 6 Sheffield
11.10.95 Tony Swift L PTS 6 Solihull
23.10.95 Richard Swallow W PTS 6 Leicester
21.11.95 Shaun Cogan L PTS 8 Edgbaston
17.01.96 Richard Swallow L PTS 6 Solihull
04.03.96 Jyrki Vierela W RSC 4 Helsinki, Finland
29.03.96 Andy Peach W RSC 3 Doncaster
Career: 14 contests, won 8, drew 2, lost 4.

Sammy Storey

Belfast. *Born* Belfast, 9 August, 1963
Former Undefeated British S. Middleweight Champion. Former All-Ireland Middleweight Champion. Ht. 6'0"
Manager Self

03.12.85 Nigel Shingles W RSC 6 Belfast
05.02.86 Sean O'Phoenix W PTS 6 Sheffield
22.04.86 Karl Barwise W PTS 6 Belfast

29.10.86 Jimmy Ellis W RSC 5 Belfast
25.04.87 Rocky McGran W PTS 10 Belfast
(Vacant All-Ireland Middleweight Title)
19.10.87 Shamus Casey W PTS 6 Belfast
05.12.87 Paul Mitchell W PTS 6 Doncaster
27.01.88 Steve Foster W RSC 4 Belfast
18.03.88 Steve Collins L PTS 10 Boston, USA
(All-Ireland Middleweight Title Defence)
19.10.88 Tony Lawrence W RSC 3 Belfast
07.12.88 Darren Hobson W RSC 6 Belfast
25.01.89 Abdul Amoru Sanda W RSC 8 Belfast
08.03.89 Kevin Roper W RSC 3 Belfast
19.09.89 Tony Burke W PTS 12 Belfast
(Vacant British S. Middleweight Title)
29.11.89 Noel Magee W RSC 9 Belfast
(British S. Middleweight Title Defence)
17.03.90 Simon Collins W CO 7 Belfast
30.10.90 James Cook L RSC 10 Belfast
(British S. Middleweight Title Defence)
31.05.91 Saldi Ali L PTS 8 Berlin, Germany
07.09.91 Johnny Melfah W PTS 8 Belfast
13.11.91 Karl Barwise W PTS 6 Belfast
25.04.92 Nigel Rafferty W RSC 3 Belfast
03.02.93 Graham Jenner W RSC 4 Earls Court
28.04.93 Carlos Christie W RSC 8 Dublin
22.09.93 John Kaighin W PTS 6 Bethnal Green
21.05.94 Fidel Castro W PTS 6 Belfast
27.08.94 Chris Eubank L RSC 7 Cardiff
(WBO S. Middleweight Title Challenge)
18.03.95 Colin Manners W PTS 8 Millstreet
27.04.95 Ali Forbes W PTS 12 Bethnal Green
(British S. Middleweight Title Challenge)
11.11.95 Henry Wharton L CO 4 Halifax
(European & Commonwealth S. Middleweight Title Challenge)
Career: 29 contests, won 24, lost 5.

John Stovin

Hull. *Born* Hull, 20 April, 1972
Lightweight. Ht. 6'0"
Manager Self

22.09.93 Robbie Sivyer W PTS 6 Chesterfield
07.10.93 Alan Graham W PTS 6 Hull
21.10.93 Dominic McGuigan W PTS 6 Bayswater
22.03.94 Yifru Retta L RSC 3 Bethnal Green
28.04.94 Norman Dhalie DREW 6 Hull
02.06.94 Nick Boyd L RSC 5 Middleton
21.07.94 Dave Anderson L CO 4 Edinburgh
14.11.95 Charles Shepherd L RSC 4 Bury
22.01.96 Mark Allen W PTS 6 Glasgow
05.02.96 James Jiora W PTS 6 Bradford
15.03.96 John Smith DREW 6 Hull
28.05.96 Eamonn Magee L RSC 2 Belfast
Career: 12 contests, won 5, drew 2, lost 5.

Warren Stowe

Burnley. *Born* Burnley, 30 January, 1965
Middleweight. Former Undefeated Central Area L. Middleweight Champion. Ht. 5'8"
Manager J. Doughty/T. Gilmour

21.10.91 Matt Mowatt W RSC 3 Bury
07.12.91 Griff Jones W RSC 6 Manchester
03.02.92 Robert Peel W PTS 6 Manchester
10.03.92 B. K. Bennett W PTS 6 Hull
25.04.92 David Radford W RSC 3 Manchester
04.06.92 Rob Pitters W PTS 8 Burnley

25.07.92 Shamus Casey W CO 2 Manchester
24.09.92 Mike Phillips W RSC 1 Stockport
12.11.92 Steve Thomas W RSC 1 Burnley
28.11.92 Julian Eavis W RSC 6 Manchester
25.02.93 Robert Riley W DIS 4 Burnley
(Vacant Central Area L. Middleweight Title)
22.04.93 Leigh Wicks W PTS 6 Bury
27.05.93 Peter Waudby W PTS 6 Burnley
09.10.93 Paul Wesley L PTS 10 Manchester
(Elim. British L. Middleweight Title)
17.02.94 Rob Pitters W RSC 1 Bury
25.04.94 Chris Richards W PTS 6 Bury
22.09.94 Jimmy Alston W CO 4 Bury
17.01.95 Paul Busby L PTS 12 Worcester
(WBO Penta-Continental Middleweight Title Challenge)
29.10.95 Martin Jolley W PTS 6 Shaw
26.11.95 Simon Maseko NC 8 Cape Town, South Africa
04.05.96 Joe Calzaghe L RTD 2 Dagenham
Career: 21 contests, won 17, lost 3, no contest 1.

John Stronach

Keighley. *Born* Middlesbrough, 14 October, 1969
L. Middleweight. Ht. 5'10"
Manager Self

26.04.93 Steve Scott W PTS 6 Bradford
24.10.94 Shamus Casey W PTS 6 Bradford
24.11.94 Hughie Davey L PTS 6 Newcastle
18.01.95 Andy Peach W RSC 5 Solihull
30.01.95 Peter Reid L PTS 6 Bradford
15.05.95 Denny Johnson W PTS 6 Bradford
12.06.95 Nick Ingram L PTS 6 Bradford
30.10.95 Wayne Shepherd W PTS 6 Bradford
11.11.95 Phil Epton W PTS 6 Bradford
Career: 9 contests, won 6, lost 3.

Trevor Sumner

Sheffield. *Born* Sheffield, 26 August, 1963
Featherweight. Ht. 5'4"
Manager Self

09.11.83 Ian Murray W RSC 5 Sheffield
14.11.83 Les Walsh L PTS 6 Manchester
05.12.83 Mike Whalley L CO 4 Manchester
29.02.84 Steve Enright W PTS 6 Sheffield
19.03.84 Les Walsh L PTS 8 Manchester
16.10.84 Dave Adam L PTS 6 Wolverhampton
11.03.95 Colin Innes W PTS 6 Barnsley
03.04.95 Russell Davison W PTS 6 Manchester
22.05.95 Garry Burrell W PTS 6 Morecambe
22.09.95 Chris Clarkson NC 1 Hull
15.02.96 Richard Vowles W PTS 6 Sheffield
03.05.96 Chris Jickells L RSC 5 Sheffield
(Vacant Central Area Featherweight Title)
Career: 12 contests, won 6, lost 5, no contest 1.

Richard Swallow

Northampton. *Born* Northampton, 10 February, 1970
Welterweight. Ht. 5'8"
Manager J. Griffin

15.10.90 Richard O'Brien L RTD 1 Kettering
14.02.91 Dave Fallon W RSC 4 Southampton
06.03.91 Carl Brasier W PTS 6 Croydon
02.05.91 Mike Morrison W PTS 6 Northampton
24.03.92 Dean Bramhald W PTS 8 Wolverhampton

06.04.92	Dean Bramhald W PTS 6 Northampton	
29.04.92	Chris Aston W RSC 3 Solihull	
14.10.92	Wayne Shepherd W PTS 8 Stoke	
24.11.92	Chris Mulcahy W PTS 6 Wolverhampton	
20.01.93	Ray Newby W PTS 8 Solihull	
03.03.93	Ray Newby L PTS 8 Solihull	
11.06.93	Soren Sondergaard L RTD 3 Randers, Denmark	
08.02.94	Billy McDougall W PTS 6 Wolverhampton	
30.09.94	Bernard Paul W PTS 8 Bethnal Green	
31.10.94	Carl Wright L PTS 6 Liverpool	
09.12.94	Jason Rowland L RSC 2 Bethnal Green	
14.02.95	Jason Beard L PTS 6 Bethnal Green	
17.03.95	Frank Olsen L RSC 1 Copenhagen, Denmark	
06.06.95	Anthony Maynard W RSC 2 Leicester	
23.10.95	Shaun Stokes L PTS 6 Leicester	
22.11.95	Gary Beardsley DREW 6 Sheffield	
17.01.96	Shaun Stokes W PTS 6 Solihull	
12.02.96	Nicky Bardle W RSC 4 Heathrow	

Career: 23 contests, won 14, drew 1, lost 8.

Darren Sweeney

Birmingham. *Born* London, 3 March, 1971
Middleweight. Ht. 5'11"
Manager Self

28.06.94	Japhet Hans W PTS 6 Edgbaston
25.10.94	Dave Battey W CO 1 Edgbaston
15.12.94	Mark Hale W PTS 6 Walsall
07.03.95	Colin Pitters W PTS 6 Edgbaston
20.03.95	Carl Winstone W PTS 6 Birmingham
11.05.95	Martin Jolley W PTS 6 Dudley
20.06.95	Michael Pinnock W PTS 8 Birmingham
17.10.95	Shaun Hendry L RSC 1 Wolverhampton
21.11.95	Carl Winstone W PTS 6 Edgbaston
04.12.95	Peter Mitchell W PTS 8 Birmingham
06.03.96	David Larkin W PTS 6 Solihull
25.03.96	Roy Chipperfield W CO 1 Birmingham
21.05.96	Mark Hale W RSC 8 Edgbaston

Career: 13 contests, won 12, lost 1.

Darren Sweeney   Les Clark

Karl Taylor (left) clashes heads with Paul Knights   Les Clark

Tony Swift

Birmingham. *Born* Solihull, 29 June, 1968
L. Welterweight. Ht. 5'10"
Manager Self

25.09.86	Barry Bacon W PTS 6 Wolverhampton
06.10.86	Wil Halliday W PTS 6 Birmingham
23.10.86	Patrick Loftus W PTS 6 Birmingham
26.11.86	Adam Muir W PTS 6 Wolverhampton
08.12.86	George Baigrie W PTS 6 Birmingham
26.01.87	Dean Bramhald W PTS 8 Birmingham
04.03.87	Dean Bramhald W RSC 5 Dudley
25.03.87	Peter Bowen W PTS 8 Stafford
22.06.87	Peter Bowen W PTS 8 Stafford
07.10.87	Dean Bramhald W PTS 8 Stoke
19.10.87	Kevin Plant W PTS 8 Birmingham
02.12.87	Dean Bramhald W PTS 8 Stoke
16.03.88	Ron Shinkwin W PTS 8 Solihull
04.05.88	Kevin Plant DREW 8 Solihull
28.09.88	Kevin Plant DREW 8 Solihull
23.11.88	Lenny Gloster L PTS 8 Solihull
12.06.89	Humphrey Harrison W PTS 8 Manchester
28.11.89	Seamus O'Sullivan W RSC 1 Battersea
16.02.90	Ramses Evilio W PTS 6 Bilbao, Spain
30.05.90	Darren Mount W PTS 8 Stoke
05.09.90	Glyn Rhodes L RSC 7 Stoke
25.10.90	Jimmy Harrison L PTS 6 Battersea
19.04.91	Gary Barron DREW 8 Peterborough
12.11.91	Carlos Chase W PTS 6 Milton Keynes
03.03.92	Steve McGovern W RSC 4 Cradley Heath
10.04.92	Willie Beattie W PTS 10 Glasgow *(Elim. British Welterweight Title)*
29.09.92	Nigel Bradley W PTS 8 Stoke
05.10.93	Andrew Murray L RSC 6 Mayfair *(Vacant Commonwealth Welterweight Title)*
09.04.94	Andreas Panayi W PTS 8 Bethnal Green
11.06.94	Andreas Panayi L PTS 8 Bethnal Green
05.10.94	Mark Elliot L PTS 8 Wolverhampton
15.03.95	Shea Neary L RSC 3 Stoke
11.10.95	Shaun Stokes W PTS 6 Solihull
28.10.95	Paul Knights L PTS 6 Kensington
22.01.96	Steve McLevy W PTS 8 Glasgow
04.02.96	Naas Scheepers L PTS 8 Johannesburg, South Africa

Career: 36 contests, won 24, drew 3, lost 9.

(Danny) Darren Swords (Muir)

Manchester. *Born* Manchester, 7 July, 1968
S. Middleweight. Ht. 5'9½"
Manager J. Doughty

22.09.94	Roy Chipperfield W PTS 6 Bury
05.12.94	Paul Clarkson W RSC 3 Bradford
16.02.95	Shamus Casey W PTS 6 Bury
29.10.95	Shamus Casey W PTS 6 Shaw
22.11.95	David Radford L PTS 6 Sheffield

Career: 5 contests, won 4, lost 1.

Karl Taylor

Birmingham. *Born* Birmingham, 5 January, 1966
Midlands Area Lightweight Champion.
Ht. 5'5"
Manager Self

18.03.87	Steve Brown W PTS 6 Stoke
06.04.87	Paul Taylor L PTS 6 Southampton
12.06.87	Mark Begley W RSC 1 Leamington
18.11.87	Colin Lynch W RSC 4 Solihull
29.02.88	Peter Bradley L PTS 8 Birmingham
04.10.89	Mark Antony W CO 2 Stafford
30.10.89	Tony Feliciello L PTS 8 Birmingham
06.12.89	John Davison L PTS 8 Leicester
23.12.89	Regilio Tuur L RTD 1 Hoogvliet, Holland
22.02.90	Mark Ramsey L RSC 4 Hull
29.10.90	Steve Walker DREW 6 Birmingham
10.12.90	Elvis Parsley L PTS 6 Birmingham
16.01.91	Wayne Windle W PTS 8 Stoke
02.05.91	Billy Schwer L RSC 2 Northampton
25.07.91	Peter Till L RSC 4 Dudley *(Midlands Area Lightweight Title Challenge)*
24.02.92	Charlie Kane L PTS 8 Glasgow
28.04.92	Richard Woolgar W PTS 6 Wolverhampton
29.05.92	Alan McDowall L PTS 6 Glasgow
25.07.92	Michael Armstrong L RSC 3 Manchester
02.11.92	Hugh Forde L PTS 6 Wolverhampton
23.11.92	Dave McHale L PTS 8 Glasgow
22.12.92	Patrick Gallagher L RSC 3 Mayfair

13.02.93	Craig Dermody L RSC 5 Manchester	
31.03.93	Craig Dermody W PTS 6 Barking	
07.06.93	Mark Geraghty W PTS 8 Glasgow	
13.08.93	Giorgio Campanella L CO 6 Arezzo, Italy	
05.10.93	Paul Harvey W PTS 6 Mayfair	
21.10.93	Charles Shepherd L RTD 5 Bayswater	
21.12.93	Patrick Gallagher L PTS 6 Mayfair	
09.02.94	Alan Levene W RSC 2 Brentwood	
01.03.94	Shaun Cogan L PTS 6 Dudley	
15.03.94	Patrick Gallagher L PTS 6 Mayfair	
18.04.94	Peter Till W PTS 10 Walsall	
	(Midlands Area Lightweight Title Challenge)	
24.05.94	Michael Ayers DREW 8 Sunderland	
12.11.94	P. J. Gallagher L PTS 6 Dublin	
29.11.94	Dingaan Thobela W PTS 8 Cannock	
31.03.95	Michael Ayers L RSC 8 Crystal Palace	
	(British Lightweight Title Challenge)	
06.05.95	Cham Joof W PTS 8 Shepton Mallet	
23.06.95	Poli Diaz L PTS 8 Madrid, Spain	
02.09.95	Paul Ryan L RSC 3 Wembley	
04.11.95	Carl Wright L PTS 6 Liverpool	
15.12.95	Peter Richardson L PTS 8 Bethnal Green	
23.01.96	Paul Knights DREW 6 Bethnal Green	
05.03.96	Andy Holligan L PTS 6 Barrow	
20.03.96	Mervyn Bennett W PTS 8 Cardiff	
21.05.96	Malcolm Melvin L PTS 10 Edgbaston	
	(Midlands Area L. Welterweight Title Challenge)	

Career: 46 contests, won 14, drew 3, lost 29.

Alan Temple

Hartlepool. *Born* Hartlepool, 21 October, 1972
L. Welterweight. Ht. 5'8"
Manager G. Robinson

29.09.94	Stevie Bolt W CO 2 Bethnal Green
22.11.94	Phil Found W PTS 6 Bristol
07.02.95	Brian Coleman W PTS 6 Ipswich
27.04.95	Everald Williams L PTS 6 Bethnal Green
29.09.95	Kevin McKillan W PTS 6 Hartlepool
23.11.95	Rudy Valentino L RSC 3 Marton
02.03.96	Tony Foster W PTS 6 Newcastle
08.06.96	Micky Hall W RSC 2 Newcastle

Career: 8 contests, won 6, lost 2.

Jonathan Thaxton

Norwich. *Born* Norwich, 10 September, 1974
IBF Inter-Continental L. Welterweight Champion. Former Southern Area L. Welterweight Champion. Ht. 5'6"
Manager Self

09.12.92	Scott Smith W PTS 6 Stoke
03.03.93	Dean Hiscox W PTS 6 Solihull
17.03.93	John O. Johnson W PTS 6 Stoke
23.06.93	Brian Coleman W PTS 8 Gorleston
22.09.93	John Smith W PTS 6 Wembley
07.12.93	Dean Hollington W RSC 3 Bethnal Green
10.03.94	B. F. Williams W RSC 4 Watford
	(Vacant Southern Area L. Welterweight Title)
18.11.94	Keith Marner L PTS 10 Bracknell
	(Southern Area L. Welterweight Title Defence)

26.05.95	David Thompson W RSC 6 Norwich
23.06.95	Delroy Leslie W PTS 6 Bethnal Green
12.08.95	Rene Prins L PTS 8 Zaandam, Holland
08.12.95	Colin Dunne L RSC 5 Bethnal Green
	(Vacant Southern Area Lightweight Title)
20.01.96	John O. Johnson W RSC 4 Mansfield
13.02.96	Paul Ryan W RSC 1 Bethnal Green
25.06.96	Mark Elliot W CO 5 Mansfield
	(Vacant IBF Inter-Continental L. Welterweight Title)

Career: 15 contests, won 12, lost 3.

Chris Thomas

Sheffield. *Born* Merthyr Tydfil, 13 December, 1971
Flyweight. Ht. 5'3½"
Manager B. Ingle

15.03.95	Shaun Norman L RSC 2 Stoke
28.11.95	Harry Woods L RSC 1 Cardiff

Career: 2 contests, lost 2.

Jason Thomas

Merthyr Tydfill. *Born* Pontypridd, 7 October, 1976
Bantamweight. Ht. 5'6"
Manager B. Ingle

28.11.95	Henry Jones W PTS 4 Cardiff
08.12.95	John Sillo L PTS 6 Liverpool
13.01.96	Paul Griffin L RSC 2 Manchester

Career: 3 contests, won 1, lost 2.

(Adrian) Carl Thompson

Manchester. *Born* Manchester, 26 May, 1964
Former European Cruiserweight Champion. Former Undefeated British & WBC International Cruiserweight Champion. Ht. 6'0"
Manager N. Basso/F. Warren

06.06.88	Darren McKenna W RSC 2 Manchester
11.10.88	Paul Sheldon W PTS 6 Wolverhampton
13.02.89	Steve Osborne W PTS 6 Manchester
07.03.89	Sean O'Phoenix W RSC 4 Manchester
04.04.89	Keith Halliwell W RSC 1 Manchester
04.05.89	Tenko Ernie W CO 4 Mayfair
12.06.89	Steve Osborne W PTS 8 Manchester
11.07.89	Peter Brown W RSC 5 Batley
31.10.89	Crawford Ashley L RSC 6 Manchester
	(Vacant Central Area L. Heavyweight Title)
21.04.90	Francis Wanyama L PTS 6 St Amandsberg, Belgium
07.03.91	Terry Dixon W PTS 8 Basildon
01.04.91	Yawe Davis L RSC 2 Monaco, Monte Carlo
04.09.91	Nicky Piper W RSC 3 Bethnal Green
04.06.92	Steve Lewsam W RSC 8 Cleethorpes
	(Vacant British Cruiserweight Title)
17.02.93	Arthur Weathers W CO 2 Bethnal Green
	(Vacant WBC International Cruiserweight Title)
31.03.93	Steve Harvey W CO 1 Bethnal Green
25.07.93	Willie Jake W CO 3 Oldham
02.02.94	Massimiliano Duran W CO 8 Ferrara, Italy
	(European Cruiserweight Title Challenge)

14.06.94	Akim Tafer W RSC 6 Epernay, France
	(European Cruiserweight Title Defence)
10.09.94	Dionisio Lazario W RSC 1 Birmingham
13.10.94	Tim Knight W RSC 5 Paris, France
10.06.95	Ralf Rocchigiani L RSC 11 Manchester
	(Vacant WBO Cruiserweight Title)
13.04.96	Albert Call W RTD 4 Wythenshawe

Career: 23 contests, won 19, lost 4.

David Thompson

Hull. *Born* Hull, 14 March, 1969
L. Welterweight. Ht. 5'8"
Manager M. Brooks

26.03.90	Mark Conley W PTS 4 Bradford
09.04.90	Andy Rowbotham W PTS 6 Manchester
26.04.90	Andy Rowbotham DREW 6 Manchester
21.05.90	Johnny Walker L CO 1 Bradford
01.11.90	Colin Sinnott L PTS 6 Hull
16.11.90	Carl Tilley L CO 1 Telford
17.12.90	Eddie King W PTS 6 Manchester
18.02.91	Barry North W PTS 6 Birmingham
25.02.91	Steve Winstanley W RTD 4 Bradford
28.03.91	Shane Sheridan L CO 5 Alfreton
17.05.91	Jason Brattley DREW 6 Bury
13.06.91	James Jiora DREW 6 Hull
30.06.91	Nicky Lucas W PTS 6 Southwark
25.07.91	Shaun Cogan L CO 1 Dudley
13.11.91	Mark Tibbs L PTS 6 Bethnal Green
28.11.91	Kevin Toomey L PTS 6 Hull
09.12.91	Chris Aston L PTS 6 Bradford
21.01.92	Ricky Sackfield L CO 1 Stockport
30.03.92	Jason Brattley L PTS 6 Bradford
26.03.92	Tanveer Ahmed L PTS 6 Glasgow
09.12.94	Colin Dunne L RSC 3 Bethnal Green
23.01.95	P. J. Gallagher L RSC 1 Bethnal Green
20.02.95	Jay Mahoney L RSC 4 Manchester
26.05.95	Jonathan Thaxton L RSC 6 Norwich
22.09.95	Dean Nicholas L PTS 6 Hull
29.09.95	Rudy Valentino L RSC 1 Bloomsbury
23.11.95	Alan Bosworth L RSC 4 Tynemouth

Career: 27 contests, won 6, drew 3, lost 18.

Kevin Thompson

Birmingham. *Born* Wolverhampton, 11 February, 1967
Welterweight. Ht. 6'0"
Manager D. Bradley

09.04.87	Roy Horn W PTS 6 Piccadilly
13.10.87	Eddie Collins W CO 1 Wolverhampton
26.10.87	Dusty Miller W PTS 4 Piccadilly
11.11.87	Danny Shinkwin W CO 4 Stafford
09.12.87	Wil Halliday W PTS 6 Evesham
12.01.88	Frank McCord W RSC 6 Cardiff
09.03.88	Robert Armstrong W RSC 6 Stoke
15.09.89	Mickey Lloyd L CO 7 High Wycombe
02.12.89	Patrick Vungbo L PTS 8 Brussels, Belgium
13.02.90	Julian Eavis W PTS 8 Wolverhampton
14.02.91	Leigh Wicks L PTS 8 Southampton
04.12.92	Mickey Lerwill W PTS 6 Telford
05.03.96	Leigh Wicks W PTS 6 Bethnal Green
13.03.96	Geoff McCreesh L PTS 6 Wembley
09.04.96	Ojay Abrahams L RSC 3 Stevenage
04.06.96	David Radford W PTS 6 York

Career: 16 contests, won 11, lost 5.

Paul Thompson

Doncaster. *Born* Dunscroft, 29 December, 1967
Heavyweight. Ht. 6'1"
Manager T. Petersen

05.10.95 Sean Daly L RSC 5 Hull
Career: 1 contest, lost 1.

Gary Thornhill

Liverpool. *Born* Liverpool, 11 February, 1968
Central Area S. Featherweight Champion. Ht. 5'6½"
Manager S. Vaughan

27.02.93 Brian Hickey W CO 4 Ellesmere Port
02.07.93 Dougie Fox W CO 1 Liverpool
30.10.93 Miguel Matthews W PTS 6 Chester
01.12.93 Wayne Windle W PTS 6 Stoke
25.02.94 Edward Lloyd DREW 6 Chester
06.05.94 Derek Amory W RSC 1 Liverpool
25.03.95 Craig Kelley W PTS 6 Chester
20.04.95 Michael Hermon W RSC 6 Liverpool
30.06.95 Chip O'Neill W RTD 3 Liverpool
04.11.95 Kid McAuley W PTS 6 Liverpool
08.12.95 Des Gargano W RTD 2 Liverpool
  (Vacant Central Area S. Featherweight Title)
13.04.96 Dominic McGuigan W RSC 3 Liverpool
25.06.96 Chris Jickells W PTS 6 Stevenage
Career: 13 contests, won 12, drew 1.

Gary Thornhill   Les Clark

Barry Thorogood

Cardiff. *Born* Cardiff, 1 December, 1972
Welsh Middleweight Champion. Ht. 6'0"
Manager D. Gardiner

28.10.92 Robert Peel W PTS 6 Cardiff
14.12.92 James Campbell W RSC 4 Cardiff
27.01.93 Russell Washer W PTS 6 Cardiff

24.03.93 Darren McInulty W PTS 6 Cardiff
28.04.93 Stuart Dunn L RSC 2 Solihull
13.09.93 Glenn Catley L PTS 4 Bristol
23.10.93 Mark Atkins W PTS 4 Cardiff
10.11.93 Robert Peel W PTS 6 Ystrad
29.01.94 Darren Dorrington DREW 6 Cardiff
02.03.94 Darren Pilling W PTS 6 Solihull
12.03.94 Geoff McCreesh L PTS 6 Cardiff
27.04.94 Dave Johnson DREW 8 Solihull
20.05.94 Andrew Furlong L RSC 4 Acton
17.10.94 Howard Eastman L RSC 6 Mayfair
29.11.94 Robert Peel W PTS 10 Cardiff
  (Vacant Welsh Middleweight Title)
08.03.95 Paul Matthews W PTS 4 Cardiff
12.04.95 Robert Peel W RSC 8 Llanelli
  (Welsh Middleweight Title Defence)
07.07.95 Cornelius Carr L RSC 6 Cardiff
28.11.95 Paul Busby L PTS 8 Cardiff
Career: 19 contests, won 10, drew 2, lost 7.

Nicky Thurbin

Ilford. *Born* Ilford, 26 October, 1971
Southern Area L. Middleweight Champion. Ht. 5'10"
Manager M. Duff

07.12.93 John Rice W PTS 6 Bethnal Green
14.01.94 Delwyn Panayiotiou W RTD 3 Bethnal Green
16.02.94 Warren Stephens W PTS 6 Stevenage
04.03.94 Andy Peach W PTS 6 Bethnal Green
22.03.94 Carl Winstone W PTS 6 Bethnal Green
11.10.94 Billy McDougall W RSC 6 Bethnal Green
09.12.94 Julian Eavis W PTS 6 Bethnal Green
20.01.95 Marty Duke W PTS 6 Bethnal Green

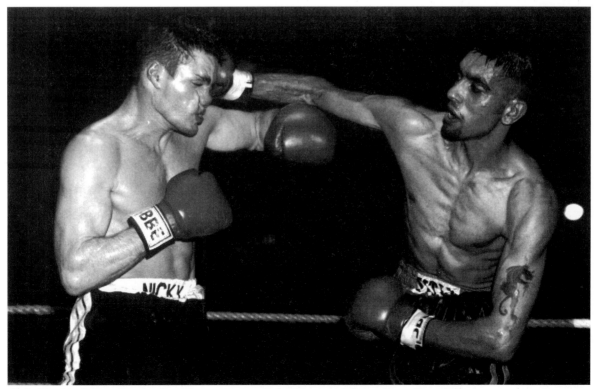

Nicky Thurbin (left) well and truly on the receiving end of a thumping right hand from Harry Dhami   Les Clark

19.04.95	Peter Mitchell W PTS 6 Bethnal Green
12.05.95	Marty Duke W RSC 3 Bethnal Green
19.05.95	Anthony Lawrence W PTS 6 Southwark
23.06.95	Vince Rose W PTS 10 Bethnal Green
	(Vacant Southern Area L. Middleweight Title)
27.09.95	Steve Goodwin W PTS 8 Bethnal Green
08.12.95	Harry Dhami W PTS 8 Bethnal Green

Career: 14 contests, won 14.

Andy Till

Northolt. *Born* Perivale, 22 August, 1963
Former British L. Middleweight Champion.
Former Undefeated WBC International &
Southern Area L. Middleweight Champion.
Ht. 5'9"
Manager Self

01.09.86	Peter Reid W RSC 6 Ealing
25.09.86	Graham Jenner W PTS 6 Crystal Palace
10.11.86	Randy Henderson W PTS 6 Longford
12.01.87	Tony Lawrence W RSC 4 Ealing
18.02.87	Ian Bayliss W PTS 6 Fulham
30.04.87	Dean Scarfe L PTS 8 Wandsworth
24.09.87	Andy Wright W RSC 2 Crystal Palace
19.02.88	Geoff Sharp W RSC 5 Longford
29.11.88	W. O. Wilson W PTS 10 Battersea
01.03.89	Wally Swift Jnr W PTS 8 Bethnal Green
12.06.89	Tony Britton W RTD 8 Battersea
	(Vacant Southern Area L. Middleweight Title)
10.11.89	Nigel Fairbairn W RSC 8 Battersea
14.03.90	Steve Foster W RTD 5 Battersea
06.06.90	Ensley Bingham L DIS 3 Battersea
	(Final Elim. British L. Middleweight Title)
12.09.90	Alan Richards W PTS 8 Battersea
06.02.91	Alan Richards W PTS 8 Battersea
01.06.91	Terry Magee W RSC 4 Bethnal Green
15.10.91	John Davies W PTS 12 Dudley
	(Vacant WBC International L. Middleweight Title)
17.09.92	Wally Swift Jnr W PTS 12 Watford
	(British L. Middleweight Title Challenge)
10.12.92	Tony Collins W RSC 3 Bethnal Green
	(British L. Middleweight Title Defence)
14.04.93	Wally Swift Jnr W RSC 4 Kensington
	(British L. Middleweight Title Defence)
23.06.93	Laurent Boudouani L RTD 4 Edmonton
	(European L. Middleweight Title Challenge)
23.02.94	Robert McCracken L PTS 12 Watford
	(British L. Middleweight Title Defence)
29.09.95	Darron Griffiths L RSC 3 Bethnal Green

Career: 24 contests, won 19, lost 5.

Peter Till

Walsall. *Born* Walsall, 19 August, 1963
Former Midlands Area Lightweight
Champion. Ht. 5'6"
Manager Self

25.04.85	Clinton Campbell W CO 1 Wolverhampton
23.05.85	J. J. Mudd W PTS 6 Dudley
17.10.85	Patrick Loftus W PTS 6 Leicester
14.11.85	Paul Wetter W RSC 3 Dudley

27.01.86	George Jones W PTS 8 Dudley
17.04.86	Tyrell Wilson W CO 5 Wolverhampton
15.05.86	Les Remikie W PTS 6 Dudley
03.06.86	Ray Newby L PTS 10 Wolverhampton
	(Vacant Midlands Area Lightweight Title)
25.09.86	Gerry Beard DREW 8 Wolverhampton
26.11.86	Gerry Beard W CO 4 Wolverhampton
28.01.87	George Baigrie W PTS 8 Dudley
04.03.87	Carl Merrett W PTS 8 Dudley
30.03.87	Tony Richards L PTS 8 Birmingham
19.07.87	Aladin Stevens L CO 4 Johannesburg, South Africa
19.10.87	Dean Bramhald W PTS 8 Birmingham
24.11.87	Dean Bramhald W PTS 8 Wolverhampton
07.02.88	Michael Marsden W CO 1 Stafford
24.02.88	Neil Haddock W PTS 8 Aberavon
13.04.88	Sugar Gibiliru W PTS 8 Wolverhampton
14.06.88	Ray Newby W PTS 10 Dudley
	(Midlands Area Lightweight Title Challenge)
22.09.88	Jim Moffat W RSC 4 Wolverhampton
10.11.88	George Jones W RSC 8 Wolverhampton
	(Midlands Area Lightweight Title Defence)
02.02.89	Camel Touati W RSC 3 Wolverhampton
13.04.89	Phillipe Binante W RSC 3 Wolverhampton
21.12.89	Tony Richards L CO 8 Kings Heath
18.10.90	Nick Hall W PTS 6 Birmingham
30.11.90	Ray Newby W PTS 8 Birmingham
21.02.91	Paul Charters L RSC 6 Walsall
	(Elim. British Lightweight Title)
31.05.91	Valery Kayumba L RSC 3 Grenoble, France
25.07.91	Karl Taylor W RSC 4 Dudley
	(Midlands Area Lightweight Title Defence)
21.09.91	Michael Ayers L RSC 5 Tottenham
	(Elim. British Lightweight Title)
09.12.91	Scott Doyle W CO 3 Brierley Hill
01.02.92	Michael Driscoll L RSC 3 Birmingham
17.03.92	Mark Reefer W RSC 3 Mayfair
04.06.92	Racheed Lawal L RSC 1 Randers, Denmark
15.08.92	Dingaan Thobela L RSC 9 Springs, South Africa
16.02.93	Errol McDonald L PTS 8 Tooting
26.05.93	Mark McCreath L PTS 8 Mansfield
02.12.93	Dominic McGuigan W RSC 2 Walsall
16.12.93	Norman Dhalie W PTS 8 Walsall
24.02.94	Barrie Kelley W PTS 6 Walsall
18.04.94	Karl Taylor L PTS 10 Walsall
	(Midlands Area Lightweight Title Challenge)
10.06.94	Dave Anderson L PTS 6 Glasgow
08.09.94	Alan McDowall W PTS 6 Glasgow
21.10.94	Dave Anderson L PTS 8 Glasgow
18.12.94	Dave Anderson L PTS 10 Glasgow
	(Elim. British Lightweight Title)
02.03.95	Carl Roberts W RSC 6 Glasgow
21.04.95	Gareth Jordan L PTS 6 Dudley
13.05.95	Justin Juuko L RTD 4 Glasgow
13.10.95	Alan McDowall L RSC 5 Glasgow
17.12.95	Allan Hall L RSC 6 Glasgow
13.04.96	Paul Burke L PTS 8 Wythenshawe

Career: 52 contests, won 30, drew 1, lost 21.

Carl Tilley

Doncaster. *Born* Doncaster, 4 October, 1967
Lightweight. Ht. 5'6½"
Manager T. Petersen

04.09.90	Stuart Good W RSC 5 Southend
16.11.90	David Thompson W CO 1 Telford
13.05.91	Steve Winstanley W RTD 4 Marton
09.10.91	Bobby Beckles W RSC 4 Marton
02.03.92	James Jiora W PTS 6 Marton
30.04.92	Greg Egbuniwe L PTS 6 Kensington
15.09.92	Joey Moffat L PTS 6 Liverpool
26.09.94	Scott Walker L PTS 6 Morecambe
20.04.95	Yifru Retta L PTS 6 Mayfair
15.03.96	Jimmy Phelan W PTS 6 Hull

Career: 10 contests, won 6, lost 4.

Kevin Toomey

Hull. *Born* Hull, 19 September, 1967
Former Undefeated Central Area
Lightweight Champion. Ht. 5'9"
Manager Self

24.04.89	Chris Mulcahy L PTS 6 Bradford
04.09.89	Andy Rowbotham W RSC 1 Grimsby
03.10.89	Mick Mulcahy L CO 5 Cottingham
01.11.90	Joel Forbes W PTS 6 Hull
12.12.90	Andy Kent DREW 6 Leicester
24.01.91	Barry North W PTS 6 Brierley Hill
18.02.91	Andy Kent L RSC 5 Derby
22.04.91	Trevor Royal W PTS 6 Bradford
16.05.91	John Smith W PTS 6 Liverpool
13.06.91	John Smith W PTS 6 Hull
30.09.91	Mike Calderwood L RSC 2 Liverpool
28.11.91	David Thompson W PTS 6 Hull
10.12.91	Wayne Windle L PTS 6 Sheffield
04.02.92	G. G. Goddard W PTS 6 Alfreton
26.03.92	Wayne Windle W DIS 8 Hull
	(Central Area Lightweight Title Challenge)
11.09.92	Dave Anderson L PTS 8 Glasgow
16.10.92	Steve Pollard W RSC 7 Hull
26.11.92	Dean Bramhald L PTS 10 Hull
	(Central Area Lightweight Title Defence)
18.02.93	Dean Bramhald W PTS 10 Hull
	(Central Area Lightweight Title Challenge)
29.04.93	Norman Dhalie W PTS 6 Hull
28.05.93	Phillip Holiday L RSC 2 Johannesburg, South Africa
12.11.93	Steve Pollard L PTS 8 Hull
08.12.93	Chris Aston W PTS 6 Hull
09.02.94	Mark Tibbs L RSC 4 Bethnal Green
08.12.94	Tony Brown W PTS 6 Hull
23.02.95	Tony Brown L RSC 10 Hull
	(Vacant Central Area Welterweight Title)
29.09.95	Kevin McKenzie DREW 6 Hartlepool
18.11.95	Joe Townsley L RSC 6 Glasgow
29.02.96	Trevor Meikle L PTS 10 Scunthorpe
	(Vacant Central Area Welterweight Title)

Career: 29 contests, won 14, drew 2, lost 13.

Graham Townsend

Hailsham. *Born* Eastbourne, 9 March, 1971
L. Heavyweight. Ht. 6'0½"
Manager D. Smith

24.10.95	Michael Pinnock W PTS 4 Southwark

17.11.95 Michael Pinnock W PTS 4 Bethnal Green
30.01.96 Eddie Knight L PTS 4 Barking
10.05.96 Simon Andrews W RSC 5 Wembley
25.06.96 Butch Lesley W PTS 6 Stevenage
Career: 5 contests, won 4, lost 1.

Graham Townsend   Les Clark

Joe Townsley
Cleland. *Born* Bellshill, 13 January, 1972
Welterweight. Ht. 5'9¼"
Manager T. Gilmour

20.03.95 Hughie Davey L PTS 6 Glasgow
05.04.95 Brian Dunn W RSC 3 Irvine
18.11.95 Kevin Toomey W RSC 6 Glasgow
14.02.96 Shamus Casey W PTS 6 Sunderland
18.03.96 Robbie Bell W PTS 6 Glasgow
03.06.96 Shamus Casey W PTS 6 Glasgow
Career: 6 contests, won 5, lost 1.

Steve Tuckett
Wakefield. *Born* Leeds, 27 January, 1973
L. Welterweight. Ht. 5'9"
Manager G. Lockwood

12.01.95 Ram Singh W RSC 6 Leeds
20.02.95 Paul Hughes W PTS 6 Manchester
06.03.95 John T. Kelly W RSC 3 Bradford
26.04.95 George Wilson W RSC 6 Solihull
19.05.95 Micky Hall L RSC 2 Leeds
15.09.95 Mark Legg W PTS 6 Darlington
29.10.95 Bobby Vanzie L RSC 2 Shaw
24.03.96 Wayne Rigby L PTS 6 Shaw
Career: 8 contests, won 5, lost 3.

Ian Turner
Ebbw Vale. *Born* Abergavenny, 6 November, 1975
Bantamweight. Ht. 5'8"
Manager D. Gardiner

29.05.96 Henry Jones W PTS 6 Ebbw Vale
Career: 1 contest, won 1.

Greg Upton
Teignmouth. *Born* Canada, 11 June, 1971
Lightweight. Western Area S. Featherweight Champion. Ht. 5'5½"
Manager G. Bousted

28.11.91 Eunan Devenney W PTS 6 Evesham
29.04.92 Chris Morris W RSC 2 Liverpool
01.06.92 Graham McGrath W PTS 6 Solihull
19.11.92 Mark Hargreaves L RSC 3 Evesham
24.03.93 Barry Jones L RSC 2 Cardiff
27.05.93 Trevor Royal W CO 2 Bristol
(*Vacant Western Area S. Featherweight Title*)
28.10.93 Graham McGrath W PTS 8 Torquay
03.03.94 Sean Knight L RSC 6 Ebbw Vale
25.06.94 Steve Edwards DREW 6 Cullompton
03.08.94 Pete Buckley W PTS 6 Bristol
07.10.94 Jason Hutson L RSC 1 Taunton
16.11.94 Andrew Reed W PTS 6 Bloomsbury
04.02.95 Dean Phillips L PTS 6 Cardiff
27.04.95 Paul Webster L RSC 1 Bethnal Green
15.09.95 Michael Gomez W PTS 4 Mansfield
16.11.95 G. G. Goddard DREW 6 Evesham
29.11.95 Ady Benton W PTS 6 Solihull
05.02.96 Paul Ingle L RSC 10 Bexleyheath
Career: 18 contests, won 9, drew 2, lost 7.

Rudy Valentino (Isaacs)
Plumstead. *Born* London, 6 July, 1964
L. Welterweight. Ht. 5'6"
Manager Self

22.10.86 Mike Russell W PTS 6 Greenwich
26.11.86 Tim O'Keefe W PTS 6 Lewisham
19.03.87 Neil Haddock W PTS 6 Bethnal Green
30.04.87 Marvin P. Gray W PTS 6 Washington
15.09.87 Peter Crook L PTS 6 Kensington
18.11.87 Paul Burke L PTS 6 Bethnal Green
02.12.87 Mark Pearce W PTS 6 Piccadilly
18.01.88 John Dickson W PTS 6 Mayfair
08.03.88 James Jiora W PTS 6 Batley
05.04.88 Hugh Forde L RSC 2 Birmingham
18.05.88 Chubby Martin L RSC 5 Lewisham
02.08.89 Paul Moylett W RSC 2 Kensington
15.02.89 Richard Joyce L PTS 6 Stoke
24.04.89 Steve Topliss W PTS 6 Nottingham
21.06.89 Sugar Gibiliru W PTS 6 Eltham
04.09.89 Jose Tuominen L RSC 2 Helsinki, Finland
19.10.89 Harry Escott L RTD 4 Manchester
27.03.90 Peter Bradley L PTS 8 Mayfair
23.04.90 Lee Amass W RSC 6 Crystal Palace
28.05.90 Pierre Lorcy L PTS 8 Paris, France
20.10.90 Gianni di Napoli DREW 8 Leon, France
15.12.90 Angel Mona L PTS 8 Vichy, France
10.04.91 Marcel Herbert W RSC 3 Newport
(*Elim. British Lightweight Title*)
17.07.91 Giovanni Parisi L PTS 8 Abbiategrasso, Italy
13.09.91 Giorgio Campanella L PTS 8 Gaggiano, Italy
19.02.92 Michael Ayers L RSC 7 Muswell Hill
(*Southern Area Lightweight Title Challenge & Elim. British Lightweight Title*)
17.09.93 Soren Sondergaard L PTS 6 Copenhagen, Denmark
29.10.93 Racheed Lawal L CO 1 Korsoer, Denmark
04.10.94 Paul Burke L PTS 6 Mayfair
07.11.94 Patrick Gallagher L PTS 6 Bethnal Green

19.04.95 Colin Dunne L PTS 6 Bethnal Green
13.06.95 Georgie Smith L PTS 6 Basildon
29.09.95 David Thompson W RSC 1 Bloomsbury
23.11.95 Alan Temple W RSC 3 Marton
05.03.96 Colin Dunne L RSC 4 Bethnal Green
Career: 35 contests, won 14, drew 1, lost 20.

Bobby Vanzie
Bradford. *Born* Bradford, 11 January, 1974
L. Welterweight. Ht. 5'5"
Manager J. Doughty

22.05.95 Alan Peacock W RSC 1 Morecambe
29.10.95 Steve Tuckett W RSC 2 Shaw
14.11.95 John Smith W PTS 6 Bury
07.03.96 John Smith W PTS 6 Bradford
02.06.96 Anthony Campbell W PTS 6 Shaw
Career: 5 contests, won 5.

Peter Varnavas
Burnley. *Born* Burnley, 27 March, 1974
Middleweight. Ht. 5'6"
Manager B. Myers

03.10.94 Carl Smith L RSC 2 Manchester
02.11.94 Andy McVeigh L RSC 3 Birmingham
22.05.95 Wayne Shepherd L PTS 6 Morecambe
08.09.95 Paul Burns L RSC 3 Liverpool
09.10.95 Lee Power L PTS 6 Manchester
09.12.95 Michael Bowen L CO 3 Bethnal Green
13.01.96 Lee Murtagh L PTS 6 Halifax
02.03.96 Geoff McCreesh L PTS 4 Newcastle
15.03.96 Pat Wright L PTS 6 Dunstable
03.04.96 Panayiotis Panayiotiou L PTS 4 Bethnal Green
Career: 10 contests, lost 10.

Peter Varnavas   Les Clark

Louis Veitch
Glasgow. *Born* Glasgow, 9 March, 1963
Former Central Area Flyweight Champion. Ht. 5'2"
Manager J. McMillan

09.10.91 Tucker Thomas W RSC 4 Marton
11.11.91 Shaun Norman L RSC 5 Bradford
12.03.92 Neil Armstrong L PTS 6 Glasgow
10.04.92 Mark Robertson L PTS 6 Glasgow
16.05.92 Mickey Cantwell L PTS 6 Muswell Hill
09.07.92 Paul Weir L PTS 6 Glasgow
11.09.92 Neil Armstrong L PTS 6 Glasgow
26.10.92 Nick Tooley L PTS 6 Cleethorpes
14.12.92 Lyndon Kershaw DREW 6 Bradford
29.01.93 Neil Armstrong L PTS 6 Glasgow
10.02.93 Mickey Cantwell DREW 8 Lewisham
29.03.93 Neil Parry W PTS 6 Glasgow
29.05.93 Neil Armstrong L PTS 10 Paisley
07.10.93 Lyndon Kershaw W PTS 10 Hull
        (Vacant Central Area Flyweight Title)
22.11.93 James Drummond L PTS 8 Glasgow
02.02.94 Ian Baillie W RSC 1 Glasgow
25.03.94 Jesper D. Jensen L PTS 6 Bornholme, Denmark
24.05.94 Vince Feeney L PTS 6 Leicester
02.11.94 Lyndon Kershaw W PTS 6 Solihull
        (Central Area Flyweight Title Defence)
21.01.95 James Murray L RSC 3 Glasgow
        (Scottish Bantamweight Title Challenge)
05.04.95 Keith Knox DREW 6 Irvine
14.06.95 Ady Benton W RSC 2 Batley
02.07.95 Vince Feeney L PTS 4 Dublin
20.11.95 Keith Knox L RSC 6 Glasgow
        (Vacant Scottish Flyweight Title. Elim. British Flyweight Title)
05.03.96 Peter Culshaw L RSC 3 Barrow
        (Central Area Flyweight Title Defence)
03.06.96 Paul Weir L CO 1 Glasgow
Career: 26 contests, won 6, drew 3, lost 17.

Peter Vosper

Plymouth. *Born* Plymouth, 6 October, 1966
S. Middleweight. Ht. 5'10"
Manager N. Christian

15.02.89 Mark White W PTS 6 Bethnal Green
01.03.89 Lester Jacobs L PTS 6 Bethnal Green
29.03.89 George Moody L PTS 6 Bethnal Green
09.05.89 Tony Cloak W RSC 2 Plymouth
20.06.89 Spencer Alton W PTS 6 Plymouth
17.10.89 Spencer Alton DREW 8 Plymouth
30.11.89 Ray Webb L PTS 6 Southwark
03.03.90 Michael Gale L RSC 2 Wembley
26.04.90 Michael Clarke L PTS 6 Wandsworth
21.05.90 Chris Walker W RSC 2 Mayfair
26.09.90 Ali Forbes L PTS 6 Mayfair
12.04.91 Frank Eubanks L RSC 1 Manchester
30.05.91 Russell Washer W PTS 6 Mayfair
06.06.91 John Kaighin DREW 6 Barking
27.06.91 Nick Manners L RSC 1 Leeds
16.12.91 Paul McCarthy L PTS 6 Southampton
25.02.92 Roland Ericsson L RSC 6 Crystal Palace
01.12.92 John Kaighin L RSC 4 Bristol
13.11.93 Martin Rosamond W PTS 6 Cullompton
04.03.94 Cliff Churchward W PTS 8 Weston super Mare
17.06.94 Paul Murray W PTS 8 Plymouth
07.10.94 Darren Dorrington L RSC 6 Taunton
        (Vacant Western Area S. Middleweight Title)
13.01.95 Thomas Hansvold L PTS 6 Aalborg, Denmark
17.02.95 Mark Delaney L RSC 1 Crawley
25.03.95 Steve McNess L RSC 5 Millwall

23.05.95 Howard Eastman L RSC 1 Bethnal Green
19.09.95 Spencer Alton W RTD 3 Plymouth
13.11.95 Martin Jolley L PTS 6 Barnstaple
16.12.95 Glenn Catley L RSC 2 Cardiff
23.02.96 Barry Exton L PTS 6 Weston super Mare
04.04.96 Carl Winstone W PTS 6 Plymouth
20.04.96 Steve Roberts L PTS 6 Brentwood
11.05.96 Jason Matthews L RSC 1 Bethnal Green
29.06.96 Anthony McFadden L PTS 4 Erith
Career: 34 contests, won 10, drew 2, lost 22.

Richard Vowles

Llanharan. *Born* Bridgend, 30 August, 1973
S. Bantamweight. Ht. 5'6"
Managers T. Gilmour/B. Hearn

02.10.95 Danny Ruegg W PTS 4 Mayfair
23.10.95 Neil Parry W PTS 6 Glasgow
15.02.96 Trevor Sumner L PTS 6 Sheffield
09.05.96 Garry Burrell L PTS 8 Glasgow
Career: 4 contests, won 2, lost 2.

Nicky Wadman   Les Clark

Nicky Wadman

Brighton. *Born* Brighton, 8 August, 1965
Cruiserweight. Ht. 6'1"
Manager Self

11.03.92 Julian Johnson W PTS 6 Cardiff
23.04.92 Mark McBiane W RSC 1 Eltham
26.09.92 Hussain Shah L RSC 4 Earls Court
29.01.93 Alan Smiles L PTS 6 Glasgow
22.02.93 Steve Osborne W PTS 6 Eltham
21.10.93 Bobby Mack L PTS 6 Bayswater
09.02.94 Paul Lawson L RSC 1 Bethnal Green
21.05.94 Ray Kane L PTS 6 Belfast
17.09.94 Rudiger May L PTS 4 Leverkusen, Germany
23.02.95 John Pettersson L RSC 3 Southwark
12.05.95 Monty Wright L CO 2 Bethnal Green
13.06.95 Darren Westover L RSC 1 Basildon
27.10.95 John Keeton L RSC 1 Brighton

29.11.95 Toks Owoh L PTS 6 Southwark
26.01.96 Jason Davies W RSC 2 Brighton
22.04.96 Luan Morena DREW 4 Crystal Palace
11.05.96 Ryan Cummings L RSC 2 Bethnal Green
Career: 17 contests, won 4, drew 1, lost 12.

Tommy Waite

Belfast. *Born* Belfast, 11 March, 1972
Bantamweight. Ht. 5'4"
Manager B. Hearn

28.05.96 Graham McGrath W PTS 4 Belfast
Career: 1 contest, won 1.

Chris Walker (Bonnick)

Nottingham. *Born* Trowbridge, 25 December, 1961
S. Middleweight. Ht. 5'8"
Manager J. Gill

22.01.87 Paul Murray W PTS 4 Bethnal Green
10.02.87 Paul Murray L PTS 4 Wolverhampton
23.10.89 Terry French L PTS 6 Nottingham
24.01.90 Darren Parker L PTS 6 Stoke
05.02.90 Willy James W CO 1 Leicester
19.02.90 Anthony Lawrence L PTS 6 Nottingham
10.03.90 Louis Johnson W RTD 3 Bristol
26.03.90 Tony Lawrence W PTS 6 Nottingham
09.04.90 Tony Lawrence W RSC 5 Manchester
30.04.90 Andy Marlow W PTS 6 Nottingham
14.05.90 Alan Baptiste W PTS 6 Leicester
21.05.90 Peter Vosper L RSC 2 Mayfair
29.10.90 Russell Washer W RSC 2 Nottingham
13.11.90 Antonio Fernandez L PTS 6 Edgbaston
10.12.90 Paul Burton W RSC 4 Nottingham
13.03.91 Adrian Wright W PTS 4 Stoke
10.10.91 Ian Henry L PTS 6 Gateshead
22.10.91 Paul Hitch L PTS 6 Hartlepool
11.03.92 Doug Calderwood W PTS 6 Solihull
28.04.92 Paul Hitch W RSC 2 Houghton le Spring
14.05.92 Paul Wright L PTS 6 Liverpool
05.02.96 Clinton Woods L RSC 6 Bradford
Career: 22 contests, won 12, lost 10.

Scott Walker

Shaw. *Born* Oldham, 5 December, 1970
L. Welterweight. Ht. 5'5"
Manager J. Doughty

18.04.94 Paul Bowen W PTS 6 Manchester
02.06.94 Brian Coleman W CO 1 Middleton
26.09.94 Carl Tilley W PTS 6 Morecambe
28.11.94 Wahid Fats L RSC 4 Manchester
16.02.95 John T. Kelly W PTS 6 Bury
08.03.95 Anthony Maynard L PTS 6 Solihull
18.05.95 Mark Allen W RSC 2 Middleton
29.10.95 T. J. Smith W PTS 6 Shaw
24.03.96 Alan Bosworth DREW 6 Shaw
02.06.96 Liam Dineen W RSC 1 Shaw
Career: 10 contests, won 7, drew 1, lost 2.

Marlon Ward

Bethnal Green. *Born* Newham, 23 March, 1968
Featherweight. Ht. 5'5"
Manager F. Maloney

29.09.94 Keith Jones W PTS 4 Bethnal Green
07.11.94 Pete Buckley W PTS 4 Piccadilly
29.09.95 Pete Buckley W PTS 4 Bethnal Green
Career: 3 contests, won 3.

Jamie Warters

York. *Born* York, 16 December, 1973
L. Heavyweight. Ht. 6'1"
Manager T. O'Neill

15.09.95 Phil Reid W RSC 5 Darlington
07.12.95 Scott Beasley W PTS 6 Hull
19.03.96 Declan Faherty W PTS 6 Leeds
Career: 3 contests, won 3.

Russell Washer

Swansea. *Born* Swansea, 21 January, 1962
Middleweight. Ht. 5'10"
Manager Self

15.09.90 Dean Cooper L PTS 6 Bristol
02.10.90 Nick Gyaamie W RSC 4 Eltham
16.10.90 Wayne Panayiotiou W RSC 2 Evesham
29.10.90 Chris Walker L RSC 2 Nottingham
11.12.90 Matt Mowatt W RSC 6 Evesham
24.01.91 Wayne Panayiotiou W RSC 4 Gorseinon
21.02.91 Marvin O'Brien DREW 6 Walsall
19.03.91 Tony Meszaros L PTS 6 Birmingham
10.04.91 Andrew Flute L PTS 6 Wolverhampton
30.05.91 Peter Vosper L PTS 6 Mayfair
04.09.91 Val Golding L RTD 5 Bethnal Green
11.11.91 Stinger Mason L PTS 4 Stratford on Avon
20.11.91 Alan Richards L PTS 6 Cardiff
29.11.91 Ensley Bingham L RSC 4 Manchester
11.03.92 Lee Crocker L PTS 6 Cardiff
22.04.92 Gilbert Jackson L PTS 6 Wembley
11.05.92 Carlo Colarusso L RSC 5 Llanelli
(Welsh L. Middleweight Title Challenge)
18.06.92 Tony Collins L RSC 2 Peterborough
03.09.92 John Bosco L RSC 2 Dunstable
05.10.92 Sean Byrne L PTS 6 Northampton
15.10.92 Jerry Mortimer L RSC 5 Lewisham
28.11.92 Paul Wright L PTS 8 Manchester
10.12.92 Abel Asinamali W PTS 6 Bethnal Green
27.01.93 Barry Thorogood L PTS 6 Cardiff
03.02.93 Kevin Sheeran L PTS 6 Earls Court
27.02.93 Jamie Robinson L PTS 6 Dagenham
24.03.93 Robert Peel L PTS 6 Cardiff
31.03.93 Kevin Adamson L PTS 6 Barking
10.04.93 Ray Price W RSC 4 Swansea
23.05.93 Darren Blackford W PTS 6 Brockley
23.06.93 Adrian Dodson L PTS 6 Edmonton
25.07.93 Steve Foster L PTS 6 Oldham
14.08.93 Quinn Paynter L RSC 4 Hammersmith
22.09.93 Kevin Adamson L PTS 6 Bethnal Green
25.10.93 Danny Peters L PTS 6 Liverpool
03.11.93 Darren Dorrington L PTS 4 Bristol
10.11.93 Kevin Sheeran L PTS 6 Bethnal Green
30.11.93 Willie Quinn L PTS 6 Cardiff
23.02.94 Robert Allen L RSC 4 Watford
21.09.94 Jamie Robinson W PTS 6 Cardiff
27.10.94 Darren Dorrington L PTS 8 Bayswater
18.11.94 Sean Heron L PTS 6 Glasgow
07.02.95 Andy Ewen L PTS 4 Ipswich
13.04.95 Robert Harper W PTS 6 Bloomsbury
28.07.95 Sven Hamer L PTS 6 Bristol
27.10.95 Jason Matthews L RSC 5 Brighton
Career: 46 contests, won 9, drew 1, lost 36.

Mike Watson

Nottingham. *Born* Nottingham, 17 December, 1973
L. Welterweight. Ht. 5'9"
Manager W. Swift

25.01.95 Steve Howden L RSC 2 Stoke
08.03.95 Adam Baldwin W PTS 6 Bloomsbury
22.07.95 Martin Holgate L PTS 6 Millwall
01.09.95 Clayton Hollingsworth W PTS 6 Wolverhampton
18.09.95 Mark Breslin L PTS 6 Glasgow
05.10.95 Tom Welsh L CO 3 Queensferry
03.11.95 Gary Hiscox L PTS 6 Dudley
08.12.95 Allan Gray L PTS 6 Bethnal Green
15.03.96 Allan Gray DREW 6 Dunstable
29.04.96 Allan Gray L PTS 6 Mayfair
25.06.96 James Hare L PTS 4 Mansfield
Career: 11 contests, won 2, drew 1, lost 8.

Peter Waudby

Hull. *Born* Hull, 18 November, 1970
Central Area L. Middleweight Champion.
Ht. 5'10½"
Manager L. Billany

21.09.92 Simon Fisher W RSC 2 Cleethorpes
16.10.92 Chris Mulcahy W RSC 4 Hull
14.12.92 Shamus Casey W PTS 6 Cleethorpes
10.05.93 Julian Eavis W PTS 6 Cleethorpes
27.05.93 Warren Stowe L PTS 6 Burnley
16.09.93 Shamus Casey W PTS 6 Hull
10.11.93 Roy Rowland W RSC 5 Watford
13.12.93 Chris Richards W PTS 6 Cleethorpes
17.03.94 Dave Johnson W PTS 6 Lincoln
15.04.94 Colin Pitters W PTS 8 Hull
16.05.94 Shamus Casey W PTS 6 Cleethorpes
25.10.94 Kevin Lueshing L RSC 2 Middlesbrough
24.11.94 Shamus Casey W PTS 6 Hull
16.02.95 Derek Wormald DREW 6 Bury
06.03.95 Paul Jones L PTS 6 Mayfair
22.09.95 Andrew Jervis W PTS 10 Hull
(Vacant Central Area L. Middleweight Title)
18.11.95 Willie Quinn L RTD 6 Glasgow
(WBO Inter-Continental Middleweight Title Challenge)
26.02.96 Earl Ling W PTS 6 Hull
09.05.96 Craig Winter W RSC 5 Hull
(Elim. British L. Middleweight Title)
Career: 19 contests, won 14, drew 1, lost 4.

Delroy Waul

Manchester. *Born* Manchester, 3 May, 1970
Former WBU Global L. Middleweight
Champion. Ht. 6'1"
Manager D. Powell

29.05.89 Calum Rattray W PTS 6 Dundee
12.06.89 Calum Rattray W PTS 6 Glasgow
25.09.89 Jimmy Reynolds W RSC 4 Birmingham
10.10.89 David Maw W PTS 4 Sunderland
05.12.89 Richard Adams W RSC 4 Dewsbury
11.01.90 Richard Adams W RSC 3 Dewsbury
22.10.90 Jim Talbot W RTD 3 Mayfair
15.11.90 Mike Russell W CO 1 Oldham
13.12.90 Kid Sylvester W RSC 6 Dewsbury
31.01.91 Kevin Hayde W RSC 6 Bredbury
13.02.91 Chris Richards W PTS 6 Wembley
14.03.91 Terry Morrill DREW 8 Middleton
02.05.91 Andrew Furlong W RSC 5 Northampton
16.05.91 Paul Wesley W RSC 7 Liverpool
20.06.91 Gordon Blair L CO 2 Liverpool
09.10.91 Paul King W RSC 6 Manchester
19.12.91 Jason Rowe W RSC 4 Oldham
31.01.92 Patrick Vungbo L DIS 8 Waregem, Belgium

02.07.92 Jimmy Thornton W RSC 6 Middleton
13.02.93 Wayne Shepherd W RSC 5 Manchester
25.06.93 Bruno Wuestenbergs L PTS 8 Brussels, Belgium
01.11.93 Lansana Diallo DREW 6 Izegem, Belgium
18.12.94 Patrick Vungbo L PTS 6 Vilvoorde, Belgium
18.01.95 Wayne Appleton W PTS 6 Solihull
27.05.95 Roberto Welin W PTS 12 Kiel, Germany
(Vacant WBU Global L. Middleweight Title)
04.11.95 Giovanni Pretorius L RTD 4 Sun City, South Africa
Career: 26 contests, won 19, drew 2, lost 5.

Jim Webb

Belfast. *Born* Belfast, 13 August, 1968
L. Middleweight. Ht. 5'6½"
Manager F. Warren

02.06.95 Rick North W PTS 6 Bethnal Green
09.09.95 J. P. Matthews W PTS 6 Cork
25.11.95 Rob Stevenson W PTS 6 Dublin
09.03.96 Phil Epton W PTS 4 Millstreet
11.05.96 Wayne Alexander L RSC 2 Bethnal Green
Career: 5 contests, won 4, lost 1.

Paul Webb

Nuneaton. *Born* Nuneaton, 5 July, 1970
Middleweight. Ht. 5'11"
Manager P. Byrne

08.03.95 Peter Mitchell L RSC 1 Bloomsbury
11.05.95 Robbie Bell L PTS 6 Sunderland
20.06.95 Steve Levene L PTS 6 Birmingham
24.01.96 Carlton Williams L PTS 6 Stoke
13.02.96 Andy Peach L PTS 6 Wolverhampton
29.02.96 Cam Raeside L PTS 6 Scunthorpe
27.03.96 Carlton Williams L PTS 6 Whitwick
22.04.96 Brian Dunn L PTS 6 Cleethorpes
29.04.96 Marty Duke L PTS 6 Mayfair
16.05.96 Marty Duke L PTS 6 Dunstable
04.06.96 Ron Hopley L PTS 6 York
Career: 11 contests, lost 11.

Ray Webb

Stepney. *Born* Hackney, 10 March, 1966
S. Middleweight. Ht. 5'11"
Manager Self

02.11.88 Doug Calderwood W RSC 6 Southwark
12.01.89 Robert Gomez W RSC 1 Southwark
30.11.89 Peter Vosper W PTS 6 Southwark
06.04.90 Carlo Colarusso W PTS 6 Telford
15.09.90 Ray Close L PTS 8 Belfast
06.11.90 Ahmet Canbakis W PTS 6 Mayfair
08.12.90 Franck Nicotra L PTS 8 Ferrara, Italy
10.01.91 Carlos Christie W PTS 6 Wandsworth
27.03.91 Silvio Branco L PTS 8 Mestre, Italy
30.05.91 Karl Barwise W PTS 8 Mayfair
11.12.91 Ian Strudwick L CO 8 Basildon
(Vacant Southern Area S. Middleweight Title)
06.03.92 Oleg Volkov L PTS 8 Berlin, Germany
28.11.93 Karl Barwise W PTS 6 Southwark
06.03.94 Trevor Ambrose W RSC 6 Southwark
27.04.94 Darron Griffiths L RSC 6 Bethnal Green
(Elim. British S. Middleweight Title)
20.02.95 Craig Joseph W PTS 6 Glasgow
29.11.95 Montell Griffin L RSC 6 Southwark
Career: 17 contests, won 9, lost 8.

153

Paul Webster

Barking. *Born* Doncaster, 26 December, 1974
S. Bantamweight. Ht. 5'6"
Manager Self

22.09.93 Kevin Simons W RSC 2 Bethnal Green
10.11.93 James Murray W PTS 4 Bethnal Green
17.02.94 Danny Ruegg W PTS 4 Dagenham
23.01.95 Marty Chestnut W RSC 3 Bethnal Green
27.04.95 Greg Upton W RSC 1 Bethnal Green
04.06.95 Barrie Kelley W RTD 1 Bethnal Green
16.06.95 Justin Murphy W PTS 6 Southwark
29.09.95 Elvis Parsley L RSC 5 Bethnal Green
Career: 8 contests, won 7, lost 1.

Paul Weir

Irvine. *Born* Glasgow, 16 September, 1967
Flyweight. Former WBO L. Flyweight Champion. Former Undefeated WBO M. Flyweight Champion. Ht. 5'3"
Manager T. Gilmour

27.04.92 Eduardo Vallejo W CO 2 Glasgow
09.07.92 Louis Veitch W PTS 6 Glasgow
21.09.92 Neil Parry W RSC 4 Glasgow
23.11.92 Shaun Norman W PTS 8 Glasgow
06.03.93 Kevin Jenkins W PTS 8 Glasgow
15.05.93 Fernando Martinez W RSC 7 Glasgow
 (Vacant WBO M. Flyweight Title)
25.10.93 Lindi Memani W PTS 12 Glasgow
 (WBO M. Flyweight Title Defence)
02.02.94 Josue Camacho L PTS 12 Glasgow
 (WBO L. Flyweight Title Challenge)
23.11.94 Paul Oulden W PTS 12 Irvine
 (Vacant WBO L. Flyweight Title)
05.04.95 Ric Magramo W PTS 12 Irvine
 (WBO L. Flyweight Title Defence)
29.07.95 Jose Luis Velarde W PTS 10 Whitley Bay
18.11.95 Jacob Matlala L TD 5 Glasgow
 (WBO L. Flyweight Title Defence)
13.04.96 Jacob Matlala L RSC 10 Liverpool
 (WBO L. Flyweight Title Challenge)
03.06.96 Louis Veitch W CO 1 Glasgow
Career: 14 contests, won 11, lost 3.

Tom Welsh   Les Clark

Tom Welsh

Holyhead. *Born* Bangor, 13 March, 1968
Welterweight. Ht. 5'8¾"
Manager D. Davies

12.04.95 Clive Sweetland W CO 2 Llanelli
17.05.95 Jason Spurling W PTS 4 Ipswich
12.06.95 Shaun Gledhill W RSC 4 Manchester
22.07.95 A. M. Milton W RSC 2 Millwall
05.10.95 Mike Watson W CO 3 Queensferry
28.10.95 Adrian Chase W RSC 2 Bristol
17.01.96 Anthony Maynard L RSC 8 Solihull
05.03.96 Paul Samuels L RSC 3 Bethnal Green
Career: 8 contests, won 6, lost 2.

Nigel Wenton

Liverpool. *Born* Liverpool, 5 April, 1969
Welterweight. Ht. 5'7"
Manager F. Warren

08.06.88 Steve Taggart W RSC 2 Sheffield
23.06.88 Rafael Saez W RSC 3 Panama City, Panama
19.10.88 Niel Leggett W RTD 2 Belfast
02.11.88 Kid Sumali W RTD 3 Southwark
15.11.88 Tony Graham W RSC 3 Piccadilly
07.12.88 John Bennie W RSC 5 Belfast
14.12.88 Young Joe Rafiu W RSC 1 Kirkby
18.01.89 Ian Honeywood W RSC 3 Kensington
25.01.89 Mark Perce W PTS 6 Belfast
08.03.89 Juan Torres W RTD 3 Belfast
12.04.89 Edwin Murillo W CO 2 Belfast
10.05.89 Nigel Senior W RSC 2 Kensington
07.06.89 Eamonn Payne W RSC 3 Wembley
28.07.89 Fabian Salazar L PTS 6 Isla Margarita, Venezuela
19.09.89 Sugar Gibiliru W PTS 8 Belfast
31.10.89 Tomas Arguelles W PTS 6 Belfast
13.12.89 Tony Dore W PTS 6 Kirkby
21.02.90 Luis Mendieta W RSC 3 Belfast
17.03.90 Scott de Pew W RSC 2 Belfast
29.04.90 Sharmba Mitchell L PTS 8 Atlantic City, USA
15.07.90 Bryant Paden DREW 10 Atlantic City, USA
07.09.91 Oliver Harrison W RTD 5 Belfast
13.11.91 Tony Richards W RSC 5 Belfast
11.12.91 Jeff Roberts W CO 2 Dublin
25.04.92 Ed Pollard W RTD 6 Belfast
10.12.92 Davy Robb W RSC 3 Bethnal Green
13.02.93 Charles Shepherd L PTS 8 Manchester
18.06.93 David Sample L PTS 10 Belfast
28.03.95 Kenny Louis W CO 2 Bay St Louis, USA
08.07.95 Walter Cowans W RSC 4 Laporte, USA
02.10.95 Howard Clarke W PTS 6 Mayfair
07.12.95 Scott Salaam W RSC 1 Hammond, USA
Career: 32 contests, won 27, drew 1, lost 4.

Paul Wesley

Birmingham. *Born* Birmingham, 2 May, 1962
Middleweight. Ht. 5'9"
Manager Self

20.02.87 B. K. Bennett L PTS 6 Maidenhead
18.03.87 Darryl Ritchie DREW 4 Stoke
08.04.87 Dean Murray W PTS 6 Evesham
29.04.87 John Wright W PTS 4 Loughborough
12.06.87 Leon Thomas W RSC 2 Leamington
16.11.87 Steve McCarthy L CO 8 Southampton

25.01.88 Paul Murray W PTS 8 Birmingham
29.02.88 Paul Murray DREW 8 Birmingham
15.03.88 Johnny Williamson W CO 2 Bournemouth
09.04.88 Joe McKenzie W RSC 6 Bristol
10.05.88 Tony Meszaros W PTS 8 Edgbaston
21.03.89 Carlton Warren L CO 2 Wandsworth
10.05.89 Rod Douglas L CO 1 Kensington
24.10.89 Nigel Rafferty L PTS 6 Wolverhampton
22.11.89 Nigel Rafferty L PTS 8 Stafford
28.11.89 Nigel Rafferty L PTS 6 Wolverhampton
05.12.89 Ian Strudwick L PTS 6 Catford
24.01.90 Rocky Feliciello W PTS 6 Solihull
19.02.90 Nigel Rafferty L PTS 8 Birmingham
22.03.90 John Ashton L PTS 10 Wolverhampton
 (Midlands Area Middleweight Title Challenge)
17.04.90 Winston May DREW 8 Millwall
09.05.90 Alan Richards W PTS 8 Solihull
04.06.90 Julian Eavis W PTS 8 Birmingham
18.09.90 Shaun Cummins L RSC 1 Wolverhampton
17.10.90 Julian Eavis W PTS 6 Stoke
23.01.91 Wally Swift Jnr L PTS 10 Solihull
 (Midlands Area L. Middleweight Title Challenge)
20.03.91 Horace Fleary L RSC 5 Solihull
16.05.91 Delroy Waul L RSC 7 Liverpool
04.07.91 Neville Brown W RSC 1 Alfreton
31.07.91 Francesco dell'Aquila L PTS 8 Casella, Italy
03.10.91 Neville Brown L PTS 8 Burton
29.10.91 Tony Collins DREW 8 Kensington
03.03.92 Antonio Fernandez L PTS 10 Cradley Heath
 (Vacant Midlands Area Middleweight Title)
10.04.92 Jean-Charles Meuret L PTS 8 Geneva, Switzerland
03.06.92 Sumbu Kalambay L PTS 10 Salice Terme, Italy
29.10.92 Ian Strudwick W RSC 1 Bayswater
14.11.92 Paul Busby L PTS 8 Cardiff
24.11.92 Paul Jones W RSC 2 Doncaster
16.03.93 Chris Pyatt L PTS 10 Mayfair
04.06.93 Jacques le Blanc L PTS 10 Moncton, Canada
28.07.93 Antonio Fernandez L RSC 3 Brixton
 (Midlands Area Middleweight Title Challenge)
09.10.93 Warren Stowe W PTS 10 Manchester
 (Elim. British L. Middleweight Title)
09.02.94 Steve Collins L PTS 8 Brentwood
10.02.95 Robert McCracken L PTS 12 Birmingham
 (British L. Middleweight Title Challenge)
24.02.95 Scott Doyle W PTS 8 Weston super Mare
18.03.95 Crisanto Espana L PTS 6 Millstreet
21.04.95 Gilbert Jackson L RSC 6 Dudley
 (Elim. British L. Middleweight Title)
31.01.96 Howard Eastman L RSC 1 Birmingham
21.03.96 Gary Logan L PTS 6 Southwark
13.04.96 Harry Simon L RTD 4 Wythenshawe
Career: 50 contests, won 16, drew 4, lost 30.

Darren Westover

Ilford. *Born* Plaistow, 3 September, 1968
Cruiserweight. Ht. 6'3"
Manager B. Hearn

04.10.89	Dave Furneaux W RSC 1 Kensington
25.10.89	David Haycock W RSC 2 Wembley
06.12.89	Kevin Roper W RSC 1 Wembley
03.03.90	Steve Osborne W RSC 6 Wembley
26.04.94	Newby Stevens W RSC 5 Bethnal Green
11.05.94	Art Stacey W PTS 6 Stevenage
09.05.95	Rob Albon W RSC 2 Basildon
13.06.95	Nicky Wadman W RSC 1 Basildon
17.07.95	Steve Osborne W RSC 5 Mayfair
20.09.95	Nigel Rafferty W PTS 6 Potters Bar
05.02.96	Chris Okoh L RSC 2 Bexleyheath

(Vacant WBO Inter-Continental Cruiserweight Title)

Career: 11 contests, won 10, lost 1.

Lee Whitehead
Manchester. *Born* Barton, 16 July, 1965
L. Heavyweight. Ht. 5'10¾"
Manager N. Basso

09.10.95	Roy Chipperfield W RSC 2 Manchester
04.12.95	Phil Ball W PTS 6 Manchester
13.01.96	Elwen Brooks W PTS 6 Manchester
26.02.96	Kevin Burton W PTS 6 Manchester
13.04.96	Mark Snipe L PTS 4 Wythenshawe
02.06.96	Andy Fletcher W RSC 2 Shaw

Career: 6 contests, won 5, lost 1.

Terry Whittaker
Barnsley. *Born* Barnsley, 15 July, 1971
Lightweight. Ht. 5'6½"
Manager K. Tate

17.11.94	Ram Singh W PTS 6 Sheffield
14.06.95	Ram Singh W PTS 6 Batley
18.10.95	Kid McAuley W PTS 6 Batley
29.11.95	Kid McAuley DREW 6 Solihull
21.02.96	Miguel Matthews W PTS 6 Batley
20.05.96	Arv Mittoo W CO 5 Cleethorpes
30.05.96	Kid McAuley W PTS 6 Lincoln

Career: 7 contests, won 6, drew 1.

Leigh Wicks
Brighton. *Born* Worthing, 29 July, 1965
Welterweight. Ht. 5'6¼"
Manager H. Holland

29.04.87	Fidel Castro W PTS 6 Hastings
26.09.87	Jason Rowe W PTS 6 Hastings
18.11.87	Lou Ayres W PTS 6 Holborn
26.01.88	Theo Marius L PTS 8 Hove
15.02.88	Shamus Casey W PTS 6 Copthorne
26.04.88	Franki Moro DREW 8 Hove
04.05.88	Tony Britton W PTS 8 Wembley
18.05.88	Mark Howell W RSC 8 Portsmouth
25.05.88	Newton Barnett DREW 8 Hastings
22.11.88	Roy Callaghan L PTS 8 Basildon
16.03.89	Tony Britland W PTS 8 Southwark
12.10.89	Tony Gibbs W CO 2 Southwark
08.02.90	Ernie Noble W PTS 8 Southwark
26.04.90	Julian Eavis DREW 8 Mayfair
06.11.90	Gordon Blair W PTS 8 Mayfair
10.01.91	Barry Messam W PTS 6 Wandsworth
14.02.91	Kevin Thompson W PTS 8 Southampton
21.10.91	Tony Britland W RSC 3 Mayfair
20.02.92	Mick Duncan L PTS 8 Glasgow
30.04.92	Darren Morris DREW 6 Mayfair
19.10.92	Bozon Haule W PTS 8 Mayfair
20.01.93	Robert McCracken L PTS 8 Wolverhampton

17.02.93	Kevin Lueshing L PTS 6 Bethnal Green
22.04.93	Warren Stowe L PTS 6 Bury
27.10.95	Danny Quacoe W RSC 4 Brighton
18.11.95	Gary Jacobs L RTD 3 Glasgow
26.01.96	Wayne Appleton L PTS 6 Brighton
05.03.96	Kevin Thompson L PTS 6 Bethnal Green

Career: 28 contests, won 15, drew 4, lost 9.

Leigh Wicks　　　　　Les Clark

Noel Wilders
Castleford. *Born* Castleford, 4 January, 1975
Bantamweight. Ht. 5'5"
Manager T. Callighan

16.03.96	Neil Parry W RTD 4 Sheffield
04.06.96	Graham McGrath W PTS 6 York

Career: 2 contests, won 2.

Carlton Williams
Leicester. *Born* Kingston, Jamaica, 2 August, 1969
Middleweight. Ht. 5'11½"
Manager J. Griffin

26.10.95	Barry Exton DREW 6 Birmingham
11.12.95	Brian Dunn L RSC 4 Cleethorpes
24.01.96	Paul Webb W PTS 6 Stoke
27.03.96	Paul Webb W PTS 6 Whitwick
09.05.96	Rob Stevenson W PTS 6 Hull
02.06.96	Jeff Finlayson W PTS 6 Shaw

Career: 6 contests, won 4, drew 1, lost 1.

Danny Williams
Brixton. *Born* London, 13 July, 1973
Heavyweight. Ht. 6'3"
Manager F. Warren

21.10.95	Vance Idiens W CO 2 Bethnal Green
09.12.95	Joey Paladino W RSC 1 Bethnal Green
13.02.96	Slick Miller W RSC 1 Bethnal Green
09.03.96	James Wilder W PTS 4 Millstreet

Career: 4 contests, won 4.

Gary Williams
Nottingham. *Born* Nottingham, 25 September, 1965
Heavyweight. Ht. 5'11½"
Manager Self

27.04.92	Damien Caesar L RSC 4 Mayfair
07.09.92	J. A. Bugner L PTS 4 Bethnal Green
06.10.92	Scott Welch L PTS 4 Antwerp, Belgium
01.12.92	Kenny Sandison W PTS 6 Liverpool
27.01.93	Kenny Sandison DREW 6 Stoke
13.02.93	Kevin McBride L PTS 4 Manchester
01.03.93	Ashley Naylor DREW 6 Bradford
29.03.93	Kevin Cullinane W RSC 2 Liverpool
26.04.93	Ashley Naylor W PTS 6 Bradford
10.08.93	Peter Smith L RSC 4 Marula, South Africa
08.12.93	Graham Arnold L PTS 6 Hull
02.02.94	Vincenzo Cantatore L CO 2 Ferrara, Italy
17.03.94	Neil Kirkwood L RSC 1 Lincoln
10.09.94	Clayton Brown L PTS 4 Birmingham
04.10.94	Mike Holden L RSC 4 Mayfair
13.12.94	Damien Caesar L RSC 2 Ilford
18.03.95	Darren Corbett DREW 4 Millstreet
06.05.95	Clayton Brown L PTS 4 Shepton Mallet
10.06.95	Joey Paladino L PTS 6 Manchester
15.09.95	Adrian Kneeshaw W RSC 6 Mansfield
11.10.95	Shane Woollas L PTS 6 Solihull
03.11.95	Tony Henry W PTS 6 Dudley
24.11.95	Pele Reid L RSC 1 Manchester
12.01.96	John Pettersson DREW 4 Copenhagen, Denmark
31.01.96	Robert Norton L RSC 2 Birmingham
21.03.96	Mika Kihlstrom L PTS 4 Southwark
02.04.96	Doug Liggion L PTS 4 Southwark
22.04.96	Shane Woollas L PTS 10 Cleethorpes

(Vacant Midlands Area Heavyweight Title)

27.05.96	Jukka Jarvinen L PTS 6 Helsinki, Finland

Career: 29 contests, won 5, drew 4, lost 20.

Gary Williams　　　　　Les Clark

(John) J. T. Williams

Cwmbran. *Born* Pontylottyn, 22 May, 1970
Welsh S. Featherweight Champion.
Ht. 5'6¾"
Manager D. Gardiner

21.01.91	Kelton McKenzie DREW 6 Crystal Palace
10.04.91	Dave Buxton W PTS 8 Newport
28.05.91	Frankie Ventura W PTS 6 Cardiff
18.07.91	Billy Barton W PTS 6 Cardiff
22.01.92	Derek Amory W PTS 6 Cardiff
30.03.92	Steve Pollard L PTS 6 Eltham
07.10.92	Kevin McKillan W PTS 6 Barry
14.11.92	Peter Judson DREW 6 Cardiff
19.05.93	Dominic McGuigan L PTS 6 Sunderland
01.10.93	Neil Haddock L PTS 10 Cardiff
10.11.93	Barrie Kelley W RTD 3 Ystrad *(Welsh S. Featherweight Title Challenge)*
03.03.94	Wayne Windle W RSC 3 Ebbw Vale
30.07.94	Tony Pep L RSC 1 Bethnal Green *(Commonwealth S. Featherweight Title Challenge)*
08.03.95	Edward Lloyd DREW 10 Cardiff *(Welsh S. Featherweight Title Defence)*
20.12.95	Norman Dhalie W CO 2 Usk

Career: 15 contests, won 8, drew 3, lost 4.

(Tony) Jetty Williams

Wolverhampton. *Born* Jamaica, 13 May, 1967
Middleweight. Ht. 5'9¼"
Manager Self

28.09.95	Robbie Bell L PTS 6 Sunderland
25.10.95	Mark Dawson L PTS 6 Telford
11.11.95	Darren Littlewood W PTS 6 Halifax
04.04.96	Simon Andrews L PTS 6 Plymouth

Career: 4 contests, won 1, lost 3.

Jetty Williams   Les Clark

(Lee) L. A. Williams

Blackwell. *Born* Caerphilly, 16 March, 1968
Heavyweight. Ht. 5'10"
Manager D. Gardiner

17.11.88	Ted Cofie L RSC 4 Ilkeston
15.09.89	Rob Albon DREW 6 High Wycombe
24.10.89	Herbie Hide L CO 2 Bethnal Green
16.12.93	Kent Davis L RSC 2 Newport
23.03.94	Darren Ashton L PTS 6 Stoke
07.04.94	John Foreman L RSC 7 Walsall
12.09.94	Monty Wright L RSC 1 Mayfair
30.11.94	Robert Norton L RSC 2 Wolverhampton
12.04.95	Darren Fearn L PTS 6 Llanelli
16.05.95	Martin Langtry L CO 2 Cleethorpes
10.11.95	Phill Day L PTS 6 Bristol
02.12.95	Gard Otnes L RSC 1 Belfast

Career: 12 contests, drew 1, lost 11.

Nigel Williams

Nottingham. *Born* Magherafelt, 28 August, 1964
Cruiserweight. Ht. 6'2"
Manager K. Richardson

18.10.95	Henry Brewer L RSC 2 Batley
06.12.95	Craig Jones W RSC 1 Stoke
26.01.96	Shane Woollas L RSC 2 Doncaster
26.02.96	Stuart Fleet L RSC 1 Hull
21.05.96	Stevie Pettit L RTD 3 Edgbaston

Career: 5 contests, won 1, lost 4.

Rowan Williams

Birmingham. *Born* Birmingham, 18 March, 1968
Midlands Area Bantamweight Champion.
Ht. 5'5½"
Manager Self

17.02.93	Nick Tooley W PTS 4 Bethnal Green
04.04.93	Des Gargano W PTS 4 Brockley
23.06.93	Graham McGrath W PTS 4 Edmonton
01.10.93	Neil Swain L PTS 6 Cardiff
10.02.94	Neil Armstrong L PTS 6 Glasgow
12.11.94	Jesper D. Jensen L PTS 6 Randers, Denmark
18.01.95	Graham McGrath W CO 6 Solihull *(Vacant Midlands Area Bantamweight Title)*
25.01.95	Neil Swain L PTS 6 Cardiff
02.03.95	Donnie Hood L PTS 8 Glasgow
20.04.95	Peter Culshaw L CO 6 Liverpool
01.06.95	Neil Parry W PTS 8 Musselburgh
19.01.96	Dharmendra Singh Yadav L PTS 4 Bracknell
21.03.96	Mark Reynolds DREW 6 Southwark
30.03.96	Vince Feeney L RSC 6 Dublin

Career: 14 contests, won 5, drew 1, lost 8.

Steve Williams

Nottingham. *Born* Worksop, 11 October, 1968
Bantamweight. Ht. 5'7"
Manager J. Ashton

06.03.95	Shaun Hall DREW 6 Bradford
06.04.95	Andy Roberts W PTS 6 Sheffield
20.10.95	Terry Gaskin W PTS 6 Mansfield
22.11.95	Neil Parry W PTS 6 Sheffield
22.03.96	Darren Noble W PTS 6 Mansfield

Career: 5 contests, won 4, drew 1.

George Wilson

Camberwell. *Born* London, 7 April, 1966
Welterweight. Ht. 5'10"
Manager Self

18.06.92	Sean Cave L PTS 6 Peterborough
07.07.92	Erwin Edwards L RSC 4 Bristol
08.09.92	Erwin Edwards L RSC 3 Southend
16.02.93	Derrick Daniel W PTS 6 Tooting
23.02.93	Sean Metherell W PTS 6 Kettering
29.03.93	Joel Ani L PTS 6 Mayfair
21.06.93	Jamie Davidson W RSC 4 Swindon
03.11.93	Sean Baker L RSC 2 Bristol
26.02.94	Michael Carruth L PTS 6 Earls Court
29.03.94	Mark Tibbs L RSC 6 Bethnal Green
27.10.94	Paul Dyer L PTS 4 Bayswater
04.02.95	Paul Ryan L RSC 4 Cardiff
26.04.95	Steve Tuckett L PTS 6 Solihull
12.05.95	Mohamed Boualleg L RSC 6 Rouen, France
28.07.95	Sean Baker L PTS 6 Bristol
26.08.95	Neil Sinclair L PTS 4 Belfast
15.09.95	James Donoghue L PTS 6 Darlington
27.09.95	Jason Beard L PTS 6 Bethnal Green
02.12.95	Frank Olsen L PTS 6 Belfast
26.03.96	George Richards L PTS 8 Wolverhampton
10.05.96	Geoff McCreesh L PTS 6 Wembley

Career: 21 contests, won 3, lost 18.

John Wilson

Edinburgh. *Born* Edinburgh, 4 January, 1972
L. Heavyweight. Ht. 6'1"
Manager A. Morrison/F. Warren

18.11.94	Steve Yorath W PTS 6 Glasgow
18.12.94	Craig Byrne W RSC 2 Glasgow
21.01.95	Tim Robinson W RSC 1 Glasgow
04.03.95	Darren Ashton NC 3 Livingston
08.06.95	Art Stacey W PTS 6 Glasgow
01.09.95	Marvin O'Brien W PTS 6 Wolverhampton
15.09.95	Marvin O'Brien W PTS 6 Glasgow
17.12.95	Barrie Bessant W RSC 1 Glasgow
12.02.96	Declan Faherty W PTS 6 Glasgow

Career: 9 contests, won 8, no contest 1.

Stephen Wilson

Wallyford. *Born* Edinburgh, 30 March, 1971
S. Middleweight. Ht. 6'0"
Manager Self

23.11.92	Lee Prudden W PTS 6 Glasgow
25.01.93	Paul Smith W RSC 1 Glasgow
06.03.93	Dave Owens W RSC 2 Glasgow
23.03.93	Nigel Rafferty L RSC 3 Wolverhampton
07.06.93	Shamus Casey W PTS 6 Glasgow
20.09.93	Stinger Mason W RSC 6 Glasgow
21.02.94	Carlos Christie W RSC 2 Glasgow
28.03.94	Dave Owens W CO 2 Musselburgh
25.04.94	John J. Cooke W PTS 6 Bury
19.09.94	Simon McDougall W RTD 3 Glasgow
24.10.94	Paul Wright W PTS 10 Glasgow *(Elim. British S. Middleweight Title)*
20.03.95	Glenn Campbell W PTS 10 Glasgow *(Final Elim. British S. Middleweight Title)*
28.10.95	Joe Calzaghe L RSC 8 Kensington *(Vacant British S. Middleweight Title)*
19.02.96	Neil Simpson W PTS 6 Glasgow

Career: 14 contests, won 12, lost 2.

Wayne Windle

Sheffield. *Born* Sheffield, 18 October, 1968
Former Central Area Lightweight
Champion. Ht. 5'8"
Manager Self

25.10.88	Mick Mulcahy L PTS 6 Cottingham
17.11.88	Dave Pratt L PTS 6 Ilkeston
02.02.89	Jeff Dobson L RSC 6 Croydon
04.04.89	John Ritchie DREW 4 Sheffield
05.10.89	Des Gargano L PTS 6 Middleton
16.10.89	Des Gargano W PTS 6 Manchester
16.11.89	Noel Carroll L PTS 6 Manchester
04.12.89	Brendan Ryan DREW 6 Manchester
29.01.90	Mike Close W PTS 6 Liverpool
05.02.90	Mike Close W PTS 6 Brierley Hill
12.03.90	Barry North W PTS 6 Hull
21.03.90	Neil Foran L PTS 6 Preston
29.05.90	Terry Collins L PTS 6 Bethnal Green
11.06.90	Muhammad Lovelock W PTS 6 Manchester
12.09.90	Brian Cullen W RSC 1 Stafford
22.09.90	Bernard McComiskey W PTS 6 Kensington
08.10.90	Johnny Walker DREW 6 Leicester
22.10.90	Mick Mulcahy W PTS 4 Cleethorpes
14.11.90	Andy Robins W PTS 6 Sheffield
26.11.90	Michael Driscoll L RSC 3 Bethnal Green
16.01.91	Karl Taylor L PTS 8 Stoke
06.02.91	Felix Kelly L PTS 6 Bethnal Green
12.03.91	Mark Antony W CO 1 Mansfield
24.04.91	Steve Foran L CO 3 Preston
13.06.91	Pete Roberts W RSC 7 Hull
	(Vacant Central Area Lightweight Title)
15.08.91	Suwanee Anukun L PTS 6 Marbella, Spain
21.09.91	George Scott L CO 2 Tottenham
10.12.91	Kevin Toomey W PTS 6 Sheffield
26.03.92	Kevin Toomey L DIS 8 Hull
	(Central Area Lightweight Title Defence)
03.09.92	Billy Schwer L CO 1 Dunstable
20.01.93	Mark Elliot L CO 3 Wolverhampton
01.06.93	Mick Mulcahy L PTS 6 Manchester
01.12.93	Gary Thornhill L PTS 6 Stoke
03.03.94	J. T. Williams L RSC 3 Ebbw Vale
01.10.94	Dave Anderson L RSC 2 Cardiff
14.04.95	Bernard McComiskey L RSC 5 Belfast
12.06.95	Ricky Sackfield L PTS 6 Manchester
11.11.95	Paul Samuels L RSC 2 Halifax

Career: 38 contests, won 12, drew 3, lost 23.

Carl Winstone

Newport. *Born* Pontypool, 21 December, 1967
Middleweight. Ht. 6'0"
Manager D. Gardiner

22.03.94	Nicky Thurbin L PTS 6 Bethnal Green
20.03.95	Darren Sweeney L PTS 6 Birmingham
12.04.95	Paul Matthews W PTS 6 Llanelli
08.07.95	David Larkin L RSC 2 York
13.11.95	Simon Andrews W PTS 6 Barnstaple
21.11.95	Darren Sweeney L PTS 6 Edgbaston
29.11.95	Paolo Roberto L PTS 4 Southwark
08.12.95	Jon Stocks L RSC 3 Liverpool
23.02.96	Ernie Loveridge L PTS 8 Weston super Mare
04.04.96	Peter Vosper L PTS 6 Plymouth
29.05.96	Paul Matthews L PTS 6 Ebbw Vale

Career: 11 contests, won 2, lost 9.

Craig Winter   Steve Parkin

Craig Winter

Warrington. *Born* Aylesbury, 10
September, 1971
L. Middleweight. Ht. 5'10"
Manager R. Jones/T. Gilmour

19.12.93	Allan Logan W PTS 6 Glasgow
28.02.94	Wayne Shepherd W PTS 6 Manchester
18.04.94	John Duckworth W RSC 5 Manchester
26.09.94	Dave Whittle W PTS 6 Liverpool
10.12.94	Hughie Davey W PTS 6 Manchester
25.03.95	David Maw W RSC 3 Rothwell
20.04.95	Paul King W RSC 4 Liverpool
16.06.95	Ernie Loveridge W PTS 6 Liverpool
08.09.95	Ernie Loveridge W PTS 6 Liverpool
14.02.96	Mark Cichocki W PTS 6 Sunderland
09.05.96	Peter Waudby L RSC 5 Hull
	(Elim. British L. Middleweight Title)

Career: 11 contests, won 10, lost 1.

Mark Winters

Antrim. *Born* Antrim, 29 December, 1971
L. Welterweight. Ht. 5'8"
Manager F. Warren

04.03.95	Trevor Smith W PTS 6 Livingston
10.06.95	Mark McGowan W PTS 6 Manchester
09.09.95	Anthony Campbell W PTS 4 Cork
25.11.95	John O. Johnson W RSC 2 Dublin
13.01.96	Rick North W PTS 4 Manchester
09.03.96	Danny Quacoe W RSC 2 Millstreet
08.06.96	Brian Coleman W PTS 4 Newcastle

Career: 7 contests, won 7.

Richie Woodhall

Telford. *Born* Birmingham, 17 April, 1968
Former Commonwealth Middleweight
Champion. Former Undefeated European
Middleweight Champion. Ht. 6'2"
Manager M. Duff

18.10.90	Kevin Hayde W RSC 3 Birmingham
30.11.90	Robbie Harron W RSC 2 Birmingham
16.01.91	Chris Haydon W RSC 3 Kensington
21.02.91	Shamus Casey W RSC 3 Walsall
30.05.91	Marty Duke W RSC 4 Birmingham
29.08.91	Nigel Moore W RSC 1 Oakengates
31.10.91	Colin Pitters W PTS 8 Oakengates
04.02.92	Graham Burton W RSC 2 Alfreton

Richie Woodhall   Les Clark

26.03.92	Vito Gaudiosi W CO 1 Telford *(Vacant Commonwealth Middleweight Title)*	
01.10.92	John Ashton W PTS 12 Telford *(Commonwealth Middleweight Defence)*	
04.12.92	Horace Fleary W PTS 8 Telford	
16.03.93	Carlo Colarusso W PTS 8 Wolverhampton	
24.04.93	Royan Hammond W PTS 10 Birmingham	
27.10.93	Garry Meekison W PTS 12 West Bromwich *(Commonwealth Middleweight Title Defence)*	
01.03.94	Heath Todd W RSC 7 Dudley	
16.03.94	Greg Lonon W RSC 6 Birmingham	

05.10.94	Jacques le Blanc W PTS 12 Wolverhampton *(Commonwealth Middleweight Title Defence)*
30.11.94	Art Serwano W RSC 11 Wolverhampton *(Commonwealth Middleweight Title Defence)*
22.02.95	Silvio Branco W RSC 9 Telford *(Vacant European Middleweight Title)*
25.10.95	Zdravko Kostic W PTS 12 Telford *(European Middleweight Title Defence)*
31.01.96	Derek Wormald W RSC 10 Birmingham *(European Middleweight Title Defence)*

Career: 21 contests, won 21.

Brandon Woodhouse
Coventry. *Born* Peterborough, 10 March, 1973
Welterweight. Ht. 5'9"
Manager J. Weaver

22.04.96	Wahid Fats L RSC 3 Manchester

Career: 1 contest, lost 1.

Clinton Woods
Sheffield. *Born* Sheffield, 1 May, 1972
S. Middleweight. Ht. 6'2"
Manager Self

17.11.94	Dave Proctor W PTS 6 Sheffield
12.12.94	Earl Ling W RSC 5 Cleethorpes
23.02.95	Paul Clarkson W RSC 1 Hull
06.04.95	Japhet Hans W RSC 3 Sheffield
16.05.95	Kevin Burton W PTS 6 Cleethorpes
14.06.95	Kevin Burton W RSC 6 Batley
21.09.95	Paul Murray W PTS 6 Sheffield
20.10.95	Phil Ball W RSC 4 Mansfield
22.11.95	Andy Ewen W RSC 3 Sheffield
05.02.96	Chris Walker W RSC 6 Bradford
16.03.96	John Duckworth W PTS 8 Sheffield
13.06.96	Ernie Loveridge W PTS 6 Sheffield

Career: 12 contests, won 12.

Harry Woods
Bargoed. *Born* Caerphilly, 13 February, 1975
Flyweight. Ht. 5'4"
Manager D. Gardiner

07.07.95	Henry Jones W PTS 4 Cardiff
29.09.95	Dave Martin DREW 4 Bloomsbury
25.10.95	Mark Hughes DREW 8 Cardiff
28.11.95	Chris Thomas W RSC 1 Cardiff
20.12.95	Dave Martin W CO 2 Usk
20.03.96	Anthony Hanna W PTS 6 Cardiff
29.05.96	Shaun Norman W RSC 5 Ebbw Vale

Career: 7 contests, won 5, drew 2.

Chris Woollas
Doncaster. *Born* Scunthorpe, 22 November, 1973
Cruiserweight. Ht. 5'11"
Manager J. Rushton

17.08.94	Darren Littlewood W RSC 4 Sheffield
05.10.94	Robert Norton DREW 6 Wolverhampton
05.12.94	Neil Simpson W PTS 6 Cleethorpes
10.02.95	Monty Wright L RSC 4 Birmingham
30.06.95	Kenny Nevers L RSC 2 Doncaster
25.09.95	Cliff Elden DREW 6 Cleethorpes
08.11.95	Stevie Pettit W PTS 6 Walsall
17.11.95	Markku Salminen L PTS 6 Helsinki, Finland
11.12.95	Cliff Elden DREW 6 Cleethorpes
15.02.96	Pele Lawrence W RSC 6 Sheffield
29.02.96	John Pierre DREW 6 Scunthorpe
16.03.96	David Jules W PTS 6 Sheffield
22.04.96	Jacklord Jacobs DREW 4 Crystal Palace
30.05.96	Martin Langtry L RSC 6 Lincoln *(Midlands Area Cruiserweight Title Challenge)*

Career: 14 contests, won 5, drew 5, lost 4.

Shane Woollas
Doncaster. *Born* Scunthorpe, 28 July, 1972
Heavyweight. Ht. 6'2"
Manager J. Rushton

26.08.94	Neil Kirkwood L RSC 6 Barnsley

28.07.95 Rob Albon W RTD 4 Epworth
11.10.95 Gary Williams W PTS 6 Solihull
08.11.95 David Jules W PTS 6 Scunthorpe
26.01.96 Nigel Williams W RSC 2 Doncaster
31.01.96 David Jules L PTS 6 Stoke
22.04.96 Gary Williams W PTS 10 Cleethorpes
(Vacant Midlands Area Heavyweight Title)
Career: 7 contests, won 5, lost 2.

Derek Wormald   Les Clark

Derek Wormald

Rochdale. *Born* Rochdale, 24 May, 1965
Middleweight. Ht. 5'10"
Manager J. Doughty/T. Gilmour

28.04.86 Dave Binsteed W RSC 2 Liverpool
20.05.86 Taffy Morris W PTS 6 Huddersfield
16.06.86 Claude Rossi W PTS 6 Manchester
23.09.86 Shamus Casey W PTS 8 Batley
16.10.86 Nigel Moore DREW 6 Merton
11.11.86 David Scere W RSC 3 Batley
25.11.86 Cliff Domville W RSC 4 Manchester
08.12.86 Martin McGough W RTD 4 Edgbaston
10.02.87 Manny Romain W CO 3 Batley
07.04.87 Tony Brown W RSC 6 Batley
28.04.87 Johnny Stone W RSC 1 Manchester
15.09.87 Sammy Sampson W PTS 10 Batley
09.02.88 Richard Wagstaff W RSC 6 Bradford
23.02.88 Judas Clottey W PTS 10 Oldham
12.04.88 John Ashton W RSC 4 Oldham
(Elim. British L. Middleweight Title)
11.10.89 Gary Stretch L RSC 1 Millwall
(British L. Middleweight Title Challenge)
24.09.92 Mark Jay W RSC 5 Stockport
27.05.93 Mark Dawson W RTD 5 Burnley
11.11.93 Paul Hitch W RSC 6 Burnley
25.04.94 Martin Jolley W RSC 4 Bury
20.10.94 Marvin O'Brien W PTS 6 Middleton
10.12.94 Dave Johnson DREW 8 Manchester
16.02.95 Peter Waudby DREW 6 Bury
30.06.95 Antonio Fernandez W PTS 10 Doncaster
(Final Elim. British Middleweight Title)

31.01.96 Richie Woodhall L RSC 10 Birmingham
(European Middleweight Title Challenge)
Career: 25 contests, won 20, drew 3, lost 2.

Dean Wray

Brigg. *Born* Scunthorpe, 5 April, 1973
Cruiserweight. Ht. 6'4"
Manager J. Rushton

08.11.95 Cliff Elden L RSC 3 Scunthorpe
Career: 1 contest, lost 1.

Carl Wright

Liverpool. *Born* Liverpoool, 19 February, 1969
L. Welterweight. Ht. 5'7"
Manager S. Vaughan

13.10.89 Mick Mulcahy W PTS 6 Preston
31.10.89 Mick Mulcahy W PTS 6 Manchester
24.01.90 Mike Morrison W PTS 6 Preston
19.12.90 Julian Eavis W PTS 6 Preston
31.03.92 Ricky Sackfield W RSC 1 Stockport
14.05.92 Brendan Ryan W PTS 4 Liverpool
12.06.92 Dean Bramhald W PTS 6 Liverpool
15.09.92 Wayne Panayiotiou W RSC 2 Liverpool
25.09.92 Mick Mulcahy W PTS 8 Liverpool
12.11.92 Jim Lawlor W RSC 3 Liverpool
29.04.93 Marcel Herbert W PTS 8 Mayfair
09.04.94 Paul Ryan L RSC 8 Mansfield
31.10.94 Richard Swallow W PTS 6 Liverpool
27.02.95 Hugh Forde W PTS 6 Barrow
20.04.95 John O. Johnson W PTS 6 Liverpool
04.11.95 Karl Taylor W PTS 6 Liverpool
10.05.96 Kevin McKillan W PTS 8 Liverpool
Career: 17 contests, won 16, lost 1.

Michael Wright

Chatham. *Born* Chatham, 2 April, 1974
S. Featherweight. Ht. 5'7"
Manager B. Hearn

30.09.95 Mark O'Callaghan L RSC 1 Basildon
25.11.95 Mark O'Callaghan W PTS 4 Dagenham
06.02.96 Wayne Jones W PTS 4 Basildon
Career: 3 contests, won 2, lost 1.

Michael Wright   Les Clark

Monty Wright

Biggleswade. *Born* Bedford, 1 November, 1969
L. Heavyweight. Ht. 5'9"
Manager M. Duff/T. Lawless

10.11.93 Steve Osborne W RSC 3 Watford
26.01.94 Nigel Rafferty W PTS 6 Birmingham
16.02.94 Bobby Mack W RSC 3 Stevenage
11.03.94 Greg Scott-Briggs W CO 1 Bethnal Green
05.04.94 Karl Barwise W PTS 6 Bethnal Green
11.05.94 Simon McDougall L PTS 6 Stevenage
12.09.94 L. A. Williams W RSC 1 Mayfair
11.10.94 Tim Robinson W CO 1 Bethnal Green
30.11.94 Greg Scott-Briggs W PTS 6 Wolverhampton
10.02.95 Chris Woollas W RSC 4 Birmingham
12.05.95 Nicky Wadman W CO 2 Bethnal Green
23.06.95 Art Stacey W RSC 2 Bethnal Green
27.09.95 Jerry Mortimer W RTD 3 Bethnal Green
03.11.95 John Keeton L RSC 4 Dudley
Career: 14 contests, won 12, lost 2.

Pat Wright

Cambridge. *Born* Bedford, 23 July, 1973
Welterweight. Ht. 5'10¾"
Managers M. Duff/T. Lawless

15.03.96 Peter Varnavas W PTS 6 Dunstable
25.06.96 Robbie Dunn W RSC 2 Stevenage
Career: 2 contests, won 2.

Paul Wright

Liverpool. *Born* Liverpool, 24 February, 1966
S. Middleweight. Ht. 5'9¾"
Manager S. Vaughan

13.10.89 Andy Balfe W RSC 1 Preston
31.10.89 John Tipping W RSC 1 Manchester
20.12.89 Nigel Rafferty DREW 6 Kirkby
13.04.92 Shaun McCrory W PTS 6 Manchester
14.05.92 Chris Walker W PTS 6 Liverpool
15.09.92 John Kaighin W DIS 5 Liverpool
23.10.92 Jason McNeill W RSC 1 Liverpool
28.11.92 Russell Washer W PTS 8 Manchester
05.02.93 Sean Smith W PTS 6 Manchester
22.04.93 Glenn Campbell L RSC 4 Bury
(Elim. British S. Middleweight Title & Central Area S. Middleweight Title Challenge)
06.09.93 Alan Baptiste W PTS 6 Liverpool
02.07.94 Shamus Casey W RSC 1 Liverpool
26.09.94 Carlos Christie W PTS 6 Liverpool
24.10.94 Stephen Wilson L PTS 10 Glasgow
(Elim. British S. Middleweight Title)
27.02.95 John Duckworth DREW 6 Barrow
20.04.95 Chris Richards W PTS 6 Liverpool
29.09.95 Paul Murray W RSC 5 Liverpool
08.12.95 Carl Smith W RSC 2 Liverpool
05.03.96 Ernie Loveridge W PTS 6 Barrow
13.04.96 Mark Dawson W PTS 6 Liverpool
Career: 20 contests, won 16, drew 2, lost 2.

Dharmendra Singh Yadav

London. *Born* New Delhi, India, 29 December, 1972
Flyweight. Ht. 5'3"
Manager F. Maloney

29.11.95 Shaun Norman W PTS 4 Southwark
19.01.96 Rowan Williams W PTS 4 Bracknell
02.04.96 Brendan Bryce W PTS 4 Southwark
14.05.96 Anthony Hanna W PTS 4 Dagenham
Career: 4 contests, won 4.

Lord Lonsdale Challenge Belts: Outright Winners

The original belts were donated to the National Sporting Club by Lord Lonsdale and did not bear his name, the inscription reading, "The National Sporting Club's Challenge Belt." It was not until the British Boxing Board of Control was formed that the emblems were reintroduced and the belts became known as the Lord Lonsdale Challenge Belts. The first contest involving the BBBoC belt was Benny Lynch versus Pat Palmer for the flyweight title on 16 September 1936. To win a belt outright, a champion must score three title match victories at the same weight, not necessarily consecutively.

Outright Winners of the National Sporting Club's Challenge Belt, 1909-1935 (20)

FLYWEIGHT	Jimmy Wilde; Jackie Brown
BANTAMWEIGHT	Digger Stanley; Joe Fox; Jim Higgins; Johnny Brown; Johnny King
FEATHERWEIGHT	Jim Driscoll; Tancy Lee; Johnny Cuthbert; Nel Tarleton
LIGHTWEIGHT	Freddie Welsh
WELTERWEIGHT	Johnny Basham; Jack Hood
MIDDLEWEIGHT	Pat O'Keefe; Len Harvey; Jock McAvoy
L. HEAVYWEIGHT	Dick Smith
HEAVYWEIGHT	Bombardier Billy Wells; Jack Petersen

Outright Winners of the BBBoC Lord Lonsdale Challenge Belt, 1936-1996 (94)

FLYWEIGHT	Jackie Paterson; Terry Allen; Walter McGowan; John McCluskey; Hugh Russell; Charlie Magri; Pat Clinton; Robbie Regan; Francis Ampofo
BANTAMWEIGHT	Johnny King; Peter Keenan (2); Freddie Gilroy; Alan Rudkin; Johnny Owen; Billy Hardy; Drew Docherty
S. BANTAMWEIGHT	Richie Wenton
FEATHERWEIGHT	Nel Tarleton; Ronnie Clayton (2); Charlie Hill; Howard Winstone (2); Evan Armstrong; Pat Cowdell; Robert Dickie; Paul Hodkinson; Colin McMillan; Sean Murphy
S. FEATHERWEIGHT	Jimmy Anderson; John Doherty; Floyd Havard
LIGHTWEIGHT	Eric Boon; Billy Thompson; Joe Lucy; Dave Charnley; Maurice Cullen; Ken Buchanan; Jim Watt; George Feeney; Tony Willis; Carl Crook; Billy Schwer; Michael Ayers
L. WELTERWEIGHT	Joey Singleton; Colin Power; Clinton McKenzie (2); Lloyd Christie; Andy Holligan; Ross Hale
WELTERWEIGHT	Ernie Roderick; Wally Thom; Brian Curvis (2); Ralph Charles; Colin Jones; Lloyd Honeyghan; Kirkland Laing; Del Bryan (2)
L. MIDDLEWEIGHT	Maurice Hope; Jimmy Batten; Pat Thomas; Prince Rodney; Andy Till; Robert McCracken
MIDDLEWEIGHT	Pat McAteer; Terry Downes; Johnny Pritchett; Bunny Sterling; Alan Minter; Kevin Finnegan; Roy Gumbs; Tony Sibson; Herol Graham; Neville Brown
S. MIDDLEWEIGHT	Sammy Storey
L. HEAVYWEIGHT	Randy Turpin; Chic Calderwood; Chris Finnegan; Bunny Johnson; Tom Collins; Dennis Andries; Tony Wilson; Crawford Ashley
CRUISERWEIGHT	Johnny Nelson; Terry Dunstan
HEAVYWEIGHT	Henry Cooper (3); Horace Notice; Lennox Lewis

NOTES: Jim Driscoll was the first champion to win an NSC belt outright, whilst Eric Boon later became the first champion to put three notches on a BBBoC belt.

Nel Tarleton and Johnny King are the only champions to have won both belts outright.

Freddie Welsh and Johnny King, each with just two notches on an NSC Lonsdale Belt, were allowed to keep their spoils after winning British Empire titles, while Walter McGowan and Charlie Magri, with one notch on a BBBoC Lonsdale Belt, kept their awards under the three years/no available challengers ruling.

Henry Cooper holds the record number of belts won by a single fighter, three in all.

Chris and Kevin Finnegan are the only brothers to have won belts outright.

Jim Higgins holds the record for winning an NSC belt outright in the shortest time, 279 days, whilst Michael Ayers won a BBBoC belt in just 95 days.

British Area Title Bouts During 1995-96

Central Area

Titleholders at 30 June 1996

Fly: *vacant.* **Bantam:** Marcus Duncan. **S. Bantam:** Paul Lloyd. **Feather:** Chris Jickells. **S. Feather:** Gary Thornhill. **Light:** Jimmy Phelan. **L. Welter:** Shea Neary. **Welter:** Trevor Meikle. **L. Middle:** Peter Waudby. **Middle:** *vacant.* **S. Middle:** *vacant.* **L. Heavy:** Michael Gale. **Cruiser:** Denzil Browne. **Heavy:** Neil Kirkwood.

8 September 1995	Shea Neary W RSC 2 Nigel Bradley, Liverpool (Vacant L. Welter)
22 September 1995	Tony Foster L PTS 10 Jimmy Phelan, Hull (Light)
22 September 1995	Peter Waudby W PTS 10 Andrew Jervis, Hull (Vacant L. Middle)
22 November 1995	Michael Gale W PTS 10 Simon McDougall, Sheffield (L. Heavy)
8 December 1995	Gary Thornhill W RTD 2 Des Gargano, Liverpool (Vacant S. Feather)
11 December 1995	Marcus Duncan W RSC 6 Lyndon Kershaw, Morecambe (Vacant Bantam)
29 February 1996	Trevor Meikle W PTS 10 Kevin Toomey, Scunthorpe (Vacant Welter)
5 March 1996	Louis Veitch L RSC 3 Peter Culshaw, Barrow (Fly)
3 May 1996	Chris Jickells W RSC 5 Trevor Sumner, Sheffield (Vacant Feather)
4 June 1996	Denzil Browne W PTS 10 Bobbi Joe Edwards, York (Vacant Cruiser)

During the above period, Peter Culshaw (Fly), Glenn Campbell (S. Middle) and Tony Booth (Cruiser) relinquished their titles.

Midlands Area

Titleholders at 30 June 1996

Fly: Anthony Hanna. **Bantam:** Rowan Williams. **S. Bantam:** Matthew Harris. **Feather:** Kelton McKenzie. **S. Feather:** *vacant.* **Light:** Karl Taylor. **L. Welter:** Malcolm Melvin. **Welter:** Richard O'Brien. **L. Middle:** Steve Goodwin. **Middle:** Antonio Fernandez. **S. Middle:** Carlos Christie. **L. Heavy:** Neil Simpson. **Cruiser:** Martin Langtry. **Heavy:** Shane Woollas.

25 October 1995	Pete Buckley L PTS 10 Matthew Harris, Telford (S. Bantam)
2 November 1995	Anthony Hanna DREW 10 Shaun Norman, London (Fly)
29 November 1995	Neil Simpson W DIS 7 Greg Scott-Briggs, Solihull (Vacant L. Heavy)
21 February 1996	Nigel Rafferty L CO 4 Martin Langtry, Batley (Cruiser)
22 April 1996	Shane Woollas W PTS 10 Gary Williams, Cleethorpes (Vacant Heavy)
20 May 1996	Richard O'Brien W PTS 10 Rick North, Cleethorpes (Vacant Welter)
21 May 1996	Malcolm Melvin W PTS 10 Karl Taylor, Edgbaston (L. Welter)
30 May 1996	Martin Langtry W RSC 6 Chris Woollas, Lincoln (Cruiser)

During the above period, John J. Cooke (L. Heavy) and Wayne Buck (Heavy) relinquished their titles, while Lindon Scarlett (Welter) forfeited his.

Northern Area

Titleholders at 30 June 1996

Fly: *vacant.* **Bantam:** *vacant.* **S. Bantam:** *vacant.* **Feather:** Colin Innes. **S. Feather:** Dominic McGuigan. **Light:** *vacant.* **L. Welter:** *vacant.* **Welter:** Paul King. **L. Middle:** Mark Cichocki. **Middle:** *vacant.* **S. Middle:** *vacant.* **L. Heavy:** Terry French. **Cruiser:** *vacant.* **Heavy:** *vacant.*

23 November 1995	Paul King L PTS 10 Kevin McKenzie, Marton (Welter)
2 March 1996	Kevin McKenzie L RSC 2 Paul King, Newcastle (Welter)
25 April 1996	Colin Innes W RSC 9 Chip O'Neill, Newcastle (Vacant Feather)

Northern Ireland Area

Titleholders at 30 June 1996 - None.

Bernard Paul (left) successfully defended his Southern Area light-welter title with a first round kayo of fancied Jason Rowland   Les Clark

161

Scottish Area

Titleholders at 30 June 1996

Fly: Keith Knox. **Bantam:** *vacant.* **S. Bantam:** *vacant.* **Feather:** Brian Carr. **S. Feather:** Mark Geraghty. **Light:** Kris McAdam. **L. Welter:** Steve McLevy. **Welter:** *vacant.* **L. Middle:** *vacant.* **Middle:** *vacant.* **S. Middle:** *vacant.* **L. Heavy:** *vacant.* **Cruiser:** *vacant.* **Heavy:** *vacant.*

23 October 1995   Steve McLevy W RSC 6 Alan Peacock, Glasgow (Vacant L. Welter)

20 November 1995 Keith Knox W RSC 6 Louis Veitch, Glasgow (Vacant Fly)

26 April 1996   Brian Carr W PTS 10 Mike Deveney, Glasgow (Vacant Feather)

During the above period, James Drummond (Fly) retired, while James Murray (Bantam) forfeited his title.

Southern Area

Titleholders at 30 June 1996

Fly: Mark Reynolds. **Bantam:** *vacant.* **S. Bantam:** *vacant.* **Feather:** *vacant.* **S. Feather:** *vacant.* **Light:** Colin Dunne. **L. Welter:** Bernard Paul. **Welter:** Harry Dhami. **L. Middle:** Nicky Thurbin. **Middle:** Mark Baker. **S. Middle:** *vacant.* **L. Heavy:** *vacant.* **Cruiser:** *vacant.* **Heavy:** Julius Francis.

1 July 1995   Julius Francis L RSC 10 Scott Welch, London (Heavy)

20 October 1995   Ricky Beard L PTS 10 Mark Reynolds, Ipswich (Fly)

8 November 1995   P. J. Gallagher W RSC 6 Justin Murphy, London (Vacant S. Feather)

29 November 1995 Bernard Paul W CO 1 Jason Rowland, London (L. Welter)

8 December 1995   Colin Dunne W RSC 5 Jonathan Thaxton, London (Vacant Light)

5 March 1996   Mark Baker W PTS 10 Sven Hamer, London (Vacant Middle)

9 April 1996   Julius Francis W CO 1 Damien Caesar, Stevenage (Vacant Heavy)

7 May 1996   Harry Dhami W RSC 5 Ojay Abrahams, London (Vacant Welter)

During the above period, P. J. Gallagher (S. Feather), Cham Joof (Light), Gary Logan (Welter), Garry Delaney (L. Heavy), Chris Okoh (Cruiser) and Scott Welch (Heavy) relinquished their titles.

Welsh Area

Titleholders at 30 June 1996

Fly: *vacant.* **Bantam:** *vacant.* **S. Bantam:** *vacant.* **Feather:** Peter Harris. **S. Feather:** J. T. Williams. **Light:** *vacant.* **L. Welter:** *vacant.* **Welter:** *vacant.* **L. Middle:** Carlo Colarusso. **Middle:** Barry Thorogood. **S. Middle:** Darron Griffiths. **L. Heavy:** *vacant.* **Cruiser:** *vacant.* **Heavy:** *vacant.*

25 October 1995   Mervyn Bennett W PTS 10 Gareth Jordan, Cardiff (Light)

During the above period, Mervyn Bennett (Light) and Chris Jacobs (Heavy) both retired

Western Area

Titleholders at 30 June 1996

Fly: *vacant.* **Bantam:** *vacant.* **S. Bantam:** Tony Falcone. **Feather:** *vacant.* **S. Feather:** Greg Upton. **Light:** *vacant.* **L. Welter:** *vacant.* **Welter:** *vacant.* **L. Middle:** *vacant.* **Middle:** *vacant.* **S. Middle:** Darren Dorrington. **L. Heavy:** *vacant.* **Cruiser:** *vacant.* **Heavy:** *vacant.*

During the above period, Dean Cooper (L. Middle) forfeited his title.

Mark Baker (right) won the vacant Southern Area middleweight title when outscoring Sven Hamer last March   Les Clark

British Title Bouts During 1995-96

All of last season's title bouts are shown in date order, and give the boxers' respective weights, along with the referee's scorecard, if going to a decision. Every bout is summarised briefly and all referees are named.

15 September 1995   Del Bryan 10.4½ (England) L PTS 12 Chris Saunders 10.7 (England), Leisure Centre, Mansfield (Welterweight Title). Referee: Roy Francis 116½-118. Unbeaten in his last six fights, but with more losses than wins in a 32 fight career, journeyman Saunders caused quite a shock when lifting the title. Although outboxed for long periods and cut over both eyes, the challenger swung it with four knockdowns.

20 September 1995   Mike Deveney 8.13 (Scotland) L PTS 12 Jonjo Irwin 8.13 (England), Furzefield Leisure Centre, Potters Bar (Featherweight Title). Making his first defence, Deveney was well beaten by a challenger who was prepared to throw aside his exemplary boxing skills to go on the offensive and make sure of victory. Referee: Richie Davies 114½-120.

30 September 1995   Michael Ayers 9.8¾ (England) W RTD 7 Dave Anderson 9.8 (Scotland), Festival Hall, Basildon (Lightweight Title). Anderson damaged his right hand in the first and saved referee, John Coyle, the job of calling a halt to the proceedings when not fighting back.

13 October 1995   Drew Docherty 8.4¼ (Scotland) W RSC 12 James Murray 8.5¾ (Scotland), Hospitality Inn, Glasgow (Bantamweight Title). Having floored the champion twice, the unfortunate Murray was put down in the final round and stopped by John Keane at 2.26, before lapsing into unconciousness, while mindless hooligans brought the sport into disrepute amid disgraceful scenes. Tragically, James died two days later.

27 October 1995   James Oyebola 16.10 (England) L RSC 10 Scott Welch 16.5 (England), Metropole Hotel, Brighton (Heavyweight Title). Reversing a previous inside the distance defeat, Welch brought his rival down with good old fashioned body punches, Dave Parris calling a halt at 2.36 of the tenth. Oyebola was decked earlier on and again prior to the stoppage. Also on the line was the vacant Commonwealth belt.

28 October 1995   Joe Calzaghe 11.13 (Wales) W RSC 8 Stephen Wilson 11.13 (Scotland), Albert Hall, London (Vacant S. Middleweight Title). The title became vacant when Sammy Storey relinquished his belt in September when taking on Henry Wharton for the European crown. Although there were no knockdowns, John Coyle stopped the fight at 2.18 of the eighth, with Wilson out on his feet.

28 October 1995   Ross Hale 10.0 (England) W CO 2 Charlie Kane 9.13¾ (Scotland), Whitchurch Leisure Centre, Bristol (L. Welterweight Title). With the Commonwealth belt also at stake, Richie Davies' count was completed at 1.35 of the second round. There were no other knockdowns.

10 November 1995   Neville Brown 11.5 (England) W CO 5 Shaun Cummins 11.4¾ (England), Moorways Leisure Centre, Derby (Middleweight Title). Cummins was counted out by Dave Parris at 2.40 of the fifth, after being put down by a jab/hook, having initially been drained by body punches.

9 December 1995   Ross Hale 10.0 (England) L CO 1 Paul Ryan 9.13½ (England), York Hall, London (L. Welterweight Title). In a huge upset, Hale was counted out by John Coyle at 2.12 of the opening round, having already been down once. The WBO Inter-Continental and Commonwealth crowns were also at stake.

18 December 1995   Jonjo Irwin 8.13¾ (England) W RSC 8 Elvis Parsley 8.13½ (England), Grosvenor House, London (Featherweight Title). There were no knockdowns, but Larry O'Connell called a halt after 2.10 of the eighth round, with Parsley unable to defend himself.

13 January 1996   Ensley Bingham 11.0 (England) W RSC 3 Gilbert Jackson 10.12¾ (England), Bowlers' Club, Manchester (Vacant L. Middleweight Title). The title initially became vacant last October when Robert McCracken moved up to middleweight. Referee Paul Thomas rescued Jackson, who was under a lot of pressure, at 1.09 of the round, despite him not being floored.

6 February 1996   Richie Wenton 8.9¾ (England) W PTS 12 Wilson Docherty 8.8¼ (Scotland), Festival Hall, Basildon (S. Bantamweight Title). Wenton, the first champion at the weight, also became the owner of a Lonsdale Belt following Richie Davies' 118½-116½ decision in his favour.

13 February 1996   Chris Saunders 10.6¾ (England) L RSC 3 Kevin Lueshing 10.7 (England), York Hall, London (Welterweight Title). In an up-and-downer, Lueshing visited the canvas twice to Saunders' five times, before referee Mickey Vann rescued the champion at 1.07 of round three.

13 February 1996   Terry Dunstan 13.7½ (England) W PTS 12 Dennis Andries 13.7¼ (England), York Hall, London (Cruiserweight Title). Larry O'Connell scored it 119-115½ for the champion, who was good value for his win and emphasised that he had Andries' measure this time around.

163

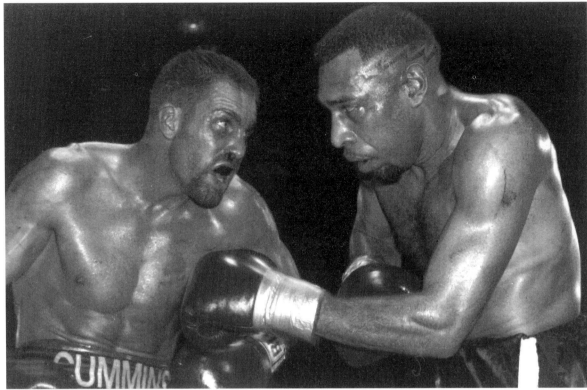

Neville Brown well beat Shaun Cummins (left) in defence of his British middles title   Les Clark

21 March 1996   Mickey Cantwell 7.11 (England) W PTS 12 Keith Knox 7.12¾ (Scotland), Elephant & Castle Leisure Centre, London (Vacant Flyweight Title). Mickey Vann's 117½-117 decision in favour of Cantwell certainly baffled Knox's supporters, and many neutrals, who thought the Scot had won clearly. With Francis Ampofo out of the ring since March 1995, the title had been vacated early in 1996.

13 April 1996   Ensley Bingham 10.13½ (England) W RSC 6 Gary Logan 10.13½ (England), The Forum, Wythenshawe (L. Middleweight Title). Down in the second, referee John Keane called a halt at 1.12 of the sixth after Logan struggled to his feet following another eight count.

20 April 1996   Joe Calzaghe 11.13¾ (Wales) W RSC 5 Mark Delaney 11.13½ (England), International Centre, Brentwood (S. Middleweight Title). Delaney lost his unbeaten record when he was rescued by John Coyle at 2.23 of the fifth, having been down four times, twice in the first and twice immediately prior to the stoppage.

22 April 1996   P. J. Gallagher 9.3 (England) W RSC 10 Dave McHale 9.3¾ (Scotland), National Sports Centre, Crystal Palace (Vacant S. Featherweight Title). One of Britain's most exciting title fights was brought to a close at 2.59 of the tenth, when McHale was rescued by Dave Parris, having hauled himself up from a count of nine. Fought to decide a successor to Floyd Havard, who relinquished the title in October in order to campaign at feather, there had been no previous knockdowns.

11 May 1996   Terry Dunstan 13.6½ (England) W RSC 1 John Keeton 13.7¾ (England), York Hall, London (Cruiserweight Title). In winning inside 44 seconds, the second fastest British title win of all-time, Dunstan won a Lonsdale Belt outright. The challenger was rescued by referee Roy Francis after the second knockdown.

14 May 1996   Jonjo Irwin 8.13¾ (England) L PTS 12 Colin McMillan 8.13¾ (England), Goresbrook Leisure Centre, Dagenham (Featherweight Title). In a fight full of skill and technique, McMillan regained the title following Paul Thomas' 117½-117 verdict in his favour. Irwin, however, is bound to be back.

29 June 1996   P. J. Gallagher 9.3¾ (England) W PTS 12 Charles Shepherd 9.3½ (England), Leisure Centre, Erith (S. Featherweight Title). Despite being floored for eight in the final round, Gallagher was deemed to be the 117-116½ winner on John Coyle's scorecard, following another all-action contest.

Note: Crawford Ashley did not defend the light-heavyweight belt during 1995-96.

British Champions Since Gloves, 1878-1996

The listings below show the tenure of all British champions at each weight since gloves (two ounces or more) were introduced to British rings under Queensberry Rules. Although Charley Davis (147 lbs) had beaten Charlie Napper (140 lbs) with gloves in 1873, we start with Denny Harrington, who defeated George Rooke for both the English and world middleweight titles in London on 12 March 1878. We also make a point of ignoring competition winners, apart from Anthony Diamond who beat Dido Plumb for the middles title over 12 rounds, basically because full championship conditions or finish fights of three minute rounds were not applied. Another point worth bearing in mind, is that prior to the 1880s there were only three weights – heavy, middle and light. Anything above 154 lbs, the middleweight limit, was classified a heavyweight contest, whereas below, say 133 lbs, was considered to be a lightweight bout. Therefore, to put things into current perspective, in many cases, we have had to ascertain the actual poundage of fighters concerned and relate them to the modern weight classes. Another point worth remembering is that men born outside Britain, who won open titles in this country, are not recorded for fear of added confusion, and, although many of the champions or claimants listed before 1909, were no more than English titleholders, having fought for the "championship of England", for our purposes they carry the "British" label.

Prior to 1909, the year that the Lord Lonsdale Challenge Belt was introduced and weight classes subsequently standardised, poundages within divisions could vary quite substantially, thus enabling men fighting at different weights to claim the same "title" at the same time. A brief history of the weight fluctuations between 1891 and 1909, shows:

Bantamweight   With the coming of gloves, the division did not really take off until Nunc Wallace established himself at 112 lbs on beating (small) Bill Goode after nine rounds in London on 12 March 1889. Later, with Wallace fighting above the weight, Billy Plimmer was generally recognised as the country's leading eight stoner, following victories over Charles Mansford and Jem Stevens, and became accepted as world champion when George Dixon, the number one in America's eyes, gradually increased his weight. In 1895 Pedlar Palmer took the British title at 112 lbs, but by 1900 he had developed into a 114 pounder. Between 1902 and 1904, Joe Bowker defended regularly at 116 lbs and in 1909 the NSC standardised the weight at 118 lbs, even though the USA continued for a short while to accept only 116 lbs.

Featherweight   Between 1886 and 1895, one of the most prestigious championship belts in this country was fought for at 126 lbs and, although George Dixon was recognised in the USA as world featherweight champion, gradually moving from 114 to 122 lbs, no major international contests took place in Britain during the above period at his weight. It was only in 1895, when Fred Johnson took the British title at 120 lbs, losing it to Ben Jordan two years later, that we came into line with the USA. Ben Jordan became an outstanding champion, who, between 1898 and 1899, was seen by the NSC as world champion at 120 lbs. However, first Harry Greenfield, then Jabez White and Will Curley, continued to claim the 126 lbs version of the British title and it was only in 1900, when Jack Roberts beat Curley, that the weight limit was finally standardised at nine stone.

Lightweight   Outstanding champions often carried their weights as they grew in size. A perfect example of this was Dick Burge, the British lightweight champion from 1891-1901, who gradually increased from 134 to 144 lbs, while still maintaining his right to the title. It was not until 1902 that Jabez White brought the division into line with the USA. Later, both White, and then Goldswain, carried their weight up to 140 lbs and it was left to Johnny Summers to set the current limit of 135 lbs.

Welterweight   The presence of Dick Burge fighting from 134 to 144 lbs plus up until 1900, explains quite adequately why the welterweight division, although very popular in the USA, did not take off in this country until 1902. The championship was contested between 142 and 146 lbs in those days and was not really supported by the NSC, but by 1909 with their backing it finally became established at 147 lbs.

Note that the Lonsdale Belt notches (title bout wins) relate to NSC, 1909-1935, and BBBoC, 1936-1996.

Champions in **bold** are accorded national recognition.

*Undefeated champions (Does not include men who forfeited titles).

Title Holder	Lonsdale Belt Notches	Tenure	Title Holder	Lonsdale Belt Notches	Tenure	Title Holder	Lonsdale Belt Notches	Tenure
Flyweight (112 lbs)			Jimmy Wilde		1914-1915	**Jackie Brown**	3	1931-1935
Sid Smith		1911	**Joe Symonds**	1	1915-1916	**Benny Lynch***	2	1935-1938
Sid Smith	1	1911-1913	**Jimmy Wilde***	3	1916-1923	**Jackie Paterson**	4	1939-1948
Bill Ladbury		1913-1914	**Elky Clark***	2	1924-1927	**Rinty Monaghan***	1	1948-1950
Percy Jones	1	1914	**Johnny Hill***	1	1927-1929	**Terry Allen**	1	1951-1952
Joe Symonds		1914	**Jackie Brown**		1929-1930	**Teddy Gardner***	1	1952
Tancy Lee	1	1914-1915	**Bert Kirby**	1	1930-1931	**Terry Allen***	2	1952-1954

Title Holder	Lonsdale Belt Notches	Tenure
Dai Dower*	1	1955-1957
Frankie Jones	2	1957-1960
Johnny Caldwell*	1	1960-1961
Jackie Brown	1	1962-1963
Walter McGowan*	1	1963-1966
John McCluskey*	3	1967-1977
Charlie Magri*	1	1977-1981
Kelvin Smart	1	1982-1984
Hugh Russell*	3	1984-1985
Duke McKenzie*	2	1985-1986
Dave Boy McAuley*	1	1986-1988
Pat Clinton*	3	1988-1991
Robbie Regan	1	1991
Francis Ampofo	1	1991
Robbie Regan*	2	1991-1992
Francis Ampofo	3	1992-1996
Mickey Cantwell	1	1996-

Bantamweight (118 lbs)

Title Holder	Lonsdale Belt Notches	Tenure
Nunc Wallace*		1889-1891
Billy Plimmer		1891-1895
Tom Gardner		1892
Willie Smith		1892-1896
Nunc Wallace		1893-1895
George Corfield		1893-1896
Pedlar Palmer		1895-1900
Billy Plimmer		1896-1898
Harry Ware		1899-1900
Harry Ware		1900-1902
Andrew Tokell		1901-1902
Jim Williams		1902

Title Holder	Lonsdale Belt Notches	Tenure
Andrew Tokell		1902
Harry Ware		1902
Joe Bowker		1902-1910
Owen Moran		1905-1907
Digger Stanley		1906-1910
Digger Stanley	2	1910-1913
Bill Beynon	1	1913
Digger Stanley	1	1913-1914
Curley Walker*	1	1914-1915
Joe Fox*	3	1915-1917
Tommy Noble	1	1918-1919
Walter Ross*	1	1919-1920
Jim Higgins	3	1920-1922
Tommy Harrison		1922-1923
Bugler Harry Lake	1	1923
Johnny Brown	3	1923-1928
Alf Pattenden	2	1928-1929
Johnny Brown		1928
Teddy Baldock		1928-1929
Teddy Baldock*	1	1929-1931
Dick Corbett	1	1931-1932
Johnny King	1	1932-1934
Dick Corbett*	1	1934
Johnny King	1+2	1935-1947
Jackie Paterson	2	1947-1949
Stan Rowan*	1	1949
Danny O'Sullivan	1	1949-1951
Peter Keenan	3	1951-1953
John Kelly	1	1953-1954
Peter Keenan	3	1954-1959
Freddie Gilroy*	4	1959-1963

Title Holder	Lonsdale Belt Notches	Tenure
Johnny Caldwell	1	1964-1965
Alan Rudkin	1	1965-1966
Walter McGowan	1	1966-1968
Alan Rudkin*	4	1968-1972
Johnny Clark*	1	1973-1974
Dave Needham	1	1974-1975
Paddy Maguire	1	1975-1977
Johnny Owen*	4	1977-1980
John Feeney	1	1981-1983
Hugh Russell	1	1983
Davy Larmour	1	1983
John Feeney	1	1983-1985
Ray Gilbody	2	1985-1987
Billy Hardy*	5	1987-1991
Joe Kelly	1	1992
Drew Docherty	4	1992-

S. Bantamweight (122 lbs)

Title Holder	Lonsdale Belt Notches	Tenure
Richie Wenton	3	1994-

Featherweight (126 lbs)

Title Holder	Lonsdale Belt Notches	Tenure
Bill Baxter		1884-1891
Harry Overton		1890-1891
Billy Reader		1891-1892
Fred Johnson		1891-1895
Harry Spurden		1892-1895
Jack Fitzpatrick		1895-1897
Fred Johnson		1895-1897
Harry Greenfield		1896-1899
Ben Jordan*		1897-1900
Jabez White		1899-1900

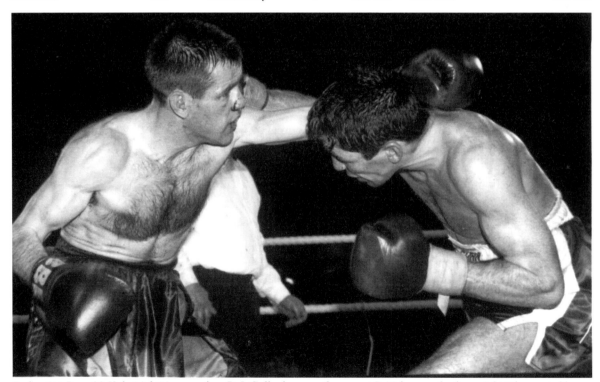

By beating Dave McHale (right) in a cracker, P. J. Gallagher won the vacant British super-featherweight title vacated by Floyd Havard

Les Clark

Title Holder	Lonsdale Belt Notches	Tenure
Will Curley		1900-1901
Jack Roberts		1901-1902
Will Curley		1902-1903
Ben Jordan*		1902-1905
Joe Bowker		1905
Johnny Summers		1906
Joe Bowker		1905-1906
Jim Driscoll		1906-1907
Spike Robson		1906-1907
Jim Driscoll*	3	1907-1913
Spike Robson		1907-1910
Ted Kid Lewis*	1	1913-1914
Llew Edwards*	1	1915-1917
Charlie Hardcastle	1	1917
Tancy Lee*	3	1917-1919
Mike Honeyman	2	1920-1921
Joe Fox*	1	1921-1922
George McKenzie	2	1924-1925
Johnny Curley	2	1925-1927
Johnny Cuthbert	1	1927-1928
Harry Corbett	1	1928-1929
Johnny Cuthbert	2	1929-1931
Nel Tarleton	1	1931-1932
Seaman Tommy Watson	2	1932-1934
Nel Tarleton	2	1934-1936
Johnny McGrory	1	1936-1938
Jim Spider Kelly	1	1938-1939
Johnny Cusick	1	1939-1940
Nel Tarleton*	3	1940-1947
Ronnie Clayton	6	1947-1954
Sammy McCarthy	1	1954-1955
Billy Spider Kelly	1	1955-1956
Charlie Hill	3	1956-1959
Bobby Neill	1	1959-1960
Terry Spinks	2	1960-1961
Howard Winstone*	7	1961-1969
Jimmy Revie	2	1969-1971
Evan Armstrong	2	1971-1972
Tommy Glencross	1	1972-1973
Evan Armstrong*	2	1973-1975
Vernon Sollas	1	1975-1977
Alan Richardson	2	1977-1978
Dave Needham	2	1978-1979
Pat Cowdell*	3	1979-1982
Steve Sims*	1	1982-1983
Barry McGuigan*	2	1983-1986
Robert Dickie	3	1986-1988
Peter Harris	1	1988
Paul Hodkinson*	3	1988-1990
Sean Murphy	2	1990-1991
Gary de Roux	1	1991
Colin McMillan*	3	1991-1992
John Davison*	1	1992-1993
Sean Murphy	1	1993
Duke McKenzie*	1	1993-1994
Billy Hardy*	1	1994
Michael Deveney	1	1995
Jonjo Irwin	2	1995-1996
Colin McMillan	1	1996-

S. Featherweight (130 lbs)

Title Holder	Lonsdale Belt Notches	Tenure
Jimmy Anderson*	3	1968-1970
John Doherty	1	1986
Pat Cowdell	1	1986
Najib Daho	1	1986-1987
Pat Cowdell	1	1987-1988
Floyd Havard	1	1988-1989
John Doherty	1	1989-1990
Joey Jacobs	1	1990
Hugh Forde	1	1990
Kevin Pritchard	1	1990-1991
Robert Dickie	1	1991
Sugar Gibiliru	1	1991
John Doherty	1	1991-1992
Michael Armstrong	1	1992
Neil Haddock	2	1992-1994
Floyd Havard*	3	1994-1995
P. J. Gallagher	2	1996-

Lightweight (135 lbs)

Title Holder	Lonsdale Belt Notches	Tenure
Dick Burge		1891-1897
Harry Nickless		1891-1894
Tom Causer		1894-1897
Tom Causer		1897
Dick Burge*		1897-1901
Jabez White		1902-1906
Jack Goldswain		1906-1908
Johnny Summers		1908-1909
Freddie Welsh	1	1909-1911
Matt Wells	1	1911-1912
Freddie Welsh*	1	1912-1919
Bob Marriott*	1	1919-1920
Ernie Rice	1	1921-1922
Seaman Nobby Hall		1922-1923
Harry Mason		1923-1924
Ernie Izzard	2	1924-1925
Harry Mason		1924-1925
Harry Mason*	1	1925-1928
Sam Steward		1928-1929
Fred Webster		1929-1930
Al Foreman*	1	1930-1932
Johnny Cuthbert		1932-1934
Harry Mizler		1934
Jackie Kid Berg		1934-1936
Jimmy Walsh	1	1936-1938
Dave Crowley	1	1938
Eric Boon	3	1938-1944
Ronnie James*	1	1944-1947
Billy Thompson	3	1947-1951
Tommy McGovern	1	1951-1952
Frank Johnson	1	1952-1953
Joe Lucy	1	1953-1955
Frank Johnson	1	1955-1956
Joe Lucy	2	1956-1957
Dave Charnley*	3	1957-1965
Maurice Cullen	4	1965-1968
Ken Buchanan*	2	1968-1971
Willie Reilly*	1	1972
Jim Watt	1	1972-1973
Ken Buchanan*	1	1973-1974
Jim Watt*	2	1975-1977
Charlie Nash*	1	1978-1979
Ray Cattouse	2	1980-1982
George Feeney*	3	1982-1985
Tony Willis	3	1985-1987
Alex Dickson	1	1987-1988
Steve Boyle	2	1988-1990
Carl Crook	5	1990-1992
Billy Schwer	1	1992-1993
Paul Burke	1	1993
Billy Schwer*	2	1993-1995
Michael Ayers	4	1995-

L. Welterweight (140 lbs)

Title Holder	Lonsdale Belt Notches	Tenure
Des Rea	1	1968-1969
Vic Andreetti*	2	1969-1970
Des Morrison	1	1973-1974
Pat McCormack	1	1974
Joey Singleton	3	1974-1976
Dave Boy Green*	1	1976-1977
Colin Power*	2	1977-1978
Clinton McKenzie	1	1978-1979
Colin Power	1	1979
Clinton McKenzie	5	1979-1984
Terry Marsh*	1	1984-1986
Tony Laing*	1	1986
Tony McKenzie	2	1986-1987
Lloyd Christie	3	1987-1989
Clinton McKenzie*	1	1989
Pat Barrett*	2	1989-1990
Tony Ekubia	1	1990-1991
Andy Holligan	3	1991-1994
Ross Hale	4	1994-1995
Paul Ryan	1	1995-

Welterweight (147 lbs)

Title Holder	Lonsdale Belt Notches	Tenure
Charlie Allum		1903-1904
Charlie Knock		1904-1906
Curly Watson		1906-1910
Young Joseph		1908-1910
Young Joseph	1	1910-1911
Arthur Evernden		1911-1912
Johnny Summers		1912
Johnny Summers	2	1912-1914
Tom McCormick		1914
Matt Wells		1914
Johnny Basham	3	1914-1920
Matt Wells		1914-1919
Ted Kid Lewis		1920-1924
Tommy Milligan*		1924-1925
Hamilton Johnny Brown		1925
Harry Mason		1925-1926
Jack Hood*	3	1926-1934
Harry Mason		1934
Pat Butler*		1934-1936
Dave McCleave		1936
Jake Kilrain	1	1936-1939
Ernie Roderick	5	1939-1948
Henry Hall	1	1948-1949
Eddie Thomas	2	1949-1951
Wally Thom	1	1951-1952
Cliff Curvis*	1	1952-1953
Wally Thom	2	1953-1956
Peter Waterman*	2	1956-1958
Tommy Molloy	2	1958-1960
Wally Swift	1	1960
Brian Curvis*	7	1960-1966
Johnny Cooke	2	1967-1968
Ralph Charles*	3	1968-1972
Bobby Arthur	1	1972-1973
John H. Stracey*	1	1973-1975
Pat Thomas	2	1975-1976
Henry Rhiney	2	1976-1979
Kirkland Laing	1	1979-1980
Colin Jones*	3	1980-1982
Lloyd Honeyghan*	2	1983-1985
Kostas Petrou	1	1985
Sylvester Mittee	1	1985
Lloyd Honeyghan*	1	1985-1986
Kirkland Laing	4	1987-1991
Del Bryan	2	1991-1992
Gary Jacobs*	2	1992-1993
Del Bryan	4	1993-1995
Chris Saunders	1	1995-1996
Kevin Lueshing	1	1996-

L. Middleweight (154 lbs)

Title Holder	Lonsdale Belt Notches	Tenure
Larry Paul	2	1973-1974
Maurice Hope*	3	1974-1977
Jimmy Batten	3	1977-1979
Pat Thomas	3	1979-1981
Herol Graham*	2	1981-1983
Prince Rodney*	1	1983-1984
Jimmy Cable	2	1984-1985
Prince Rodney	2	1985-1986
Chris Pyatt*	1	1986
Lloyd Hibbert*	1	1987
Gary Cooper	1	1988
Gary Stretch	2	1988-1990
Wally Swift Jnr	2	1991-1992
Andy Till	3	1992-1994
Robert McCracken*	3	1994-1995
Ensley Bingham	2	1996-

Middleweight (160 lbs)

Title Holder	Lonsdale Belt Notches	Tenure
Denny Harrington		1876-1880
William Sheriff*		1880-1883
Bill Goode		1887-1890
Toff Wall*		1890
Ted Pritchard		1890-1895
Ted White		1893-1895
Ted White*		1895-1896
Anthony Diamond*		1898
Dick Burge*		1898-1900
Jack Palmer		1902-1903
Charlie Allum		1905-1906
Pat O'Keefe		1906
Tom Thomas	1	1906-1910
Jim Sullivan*	1	1910-1912
Jack Harrison*	1	1912-1913
Pat O'Keefe	2	1914-1916
Bandsman Jack Blake	1	1916-1918
Pat O'Keefe*	1	1918-1919
Ted Kid Lewis		1920-1921
Tom Gummer	1	1920-1921
Gus Platts		1921
Johnny Basham		1921
Ted Kid Lewis	2	1921-1923
Johnny Basham		1921
Roland Todd		1923-1925
Roland Todd		1925-1927
Tommy Milligan	1	1926-1928
Frank Moody		1927-1928
Alex Ireland		1928-1929
Len Harvey	5	1929-1933
Jock McAvoy	3+2	1933-1944
Ernie Roderick	1	1945-1946
Vince Hawkins	1	1946-1948
Dick Turpin	2	1948-1950
Albert Finch	1	1950
Randy Turpin*	1	1950-1954
Johnny Sullivan	1	1954-1955
Pat McAteer*	3	1955-1958
Terry Downes	1	1958-1959
John Cowboy McCormack	1	1959
Terry Downes	2	1959-1962
George Aldridge	1	1962-1963
Mick Leahy	1	1963-1964
Wally Swift	1	1964-1965
Johnny Pritchett*	4	1965-1969
Les McAteer	1	1969-1970
Mark Rowe	1	1970
Bunny Sterling	4	1970-1974
Kevin Finnegan*	1	1974
Bunny Sterling*	1	1975
Alan Minter	3	1975-1977
Kevin Finnegan	1	1977
Alan Minter*	1	1977-1978
Tony Sibson	1	1979
Kevin Finnegan*	1	1979-1980
Roy Gumbs	3	1981-1983
Mark Kaylor	1	1983-1984
Tony Sibson	1	1984
Herol Graham*	1	1985-1986
Brian Anderson	1	1986-1987
Tony Sibson*	1	1987-1988
Herol Graham	4	1988-1992
Frank Grant	2	1992-1993
Neville Brown	5	1993-

S. Middleweight (168 lbs)

Title Holder	Lonsdale Belt Notches	Tenure
Sammy Storey	2	1989-1990
James Cook*	1	1990-1991
Fidel Castro	2	1991-1992
Henry Wharton*	1	1992-1993
James Cook	1	1993-1994
Cornelius Carr*	1	1994
Ali Forbes	1	1995
Sammy Storey*	1	1995
Joe Calzaghe	2	1995-

L. Heavyweight (175lbs)

Title Holder	Lonsdale Belt Notches	Tenure
Dennis Haugh		1913-1914
Dick Smith	2	1914-1916
Harry Reeve*	1	1916-1917
Dick Smith*	1	1918-1919
Boy McCormick*	1	1919-1921
Jack Bloomfield*	1	1922-1924
Tom Berry	1	1925-1927
Gipsy Daniels*	1	1927
Frank Moody	1	1927-1929
Harry Crossley	1	1929-1932
Jack Petersen*	1	1932
Len Harvey*	1	1933-1934
Eddie Phillips		1935-1937
Jock McAvoy	1	1937-1938
Len Harvey	2	1938-1942
Freddie Mills*	1	1942-1950
Don Cockell	2	1950-1952
Randy Turpin*	1	1952
Dennis Powell	1	1953
Alex Buxton	2	1953-1955
Randy Turpin*	1	1955
Ron Barton*	1	1956
Randy Turpin*	2	1956-1958
Chic Calderwood	3	1960-1963
Chic Calderwood*	1	1964-1966
Young John McCormack	2	1967-1969
Eddie Avoth	2	1969-1971
Chris Finnegan	2	1971-1973
John Conteh*	2	1973-1974
Johnny Frankham	1	1975
Chris Finnegan*	1	1975-1976
Tim Wood	1	1976-1977
Bunny Johnson	3	1977-1981
Tom Collins	3	1982-1984
Dennis Andries*	5	1984-1986
Tom Collins*	1	1987
Tony Wilson	3	1987-1989
Tom Collins*	1	1989-1990
Steve McCarthy	1	1990-1991
Crawford Ashley*	3	1991-1992
Maurice Core*	2	1992-1994
Crawford Ashley	1	1994-

Cruiserweight (190 lbs)

Title Holder	Lonsdale Belt Notches	Tenure
Sam Reeson*	1	1985-1986
Andy Straughn	1	1986-1987
Roy Smith	1	1987
Tee Jay	1	1987-1988
Glenn McCrory*	2	1988
Andy Straughn	1	1988-1989
Johnny Nelson*	3	1989-1991
Derek Angol*	2	1991-1992
Carl Thompson*	1	1992-1994
Dennis Andries	1	1995
Terry Dunstan	3	1995-

Heavyweight (190 lbs +)

Title Holder	Lonsdale Belt Notches	Tenure
Tom Allen*		1878-1882
Charlie Mitchell*		1882-1894
Jem Smith		1889-1891
Ted Pritchard		1891-1895
Jem Smith		1895-1896
George Chrisp		1901
Jack Scales		1901-1902
Jack Palmer		1903-1906
Gunner Moir		1906-1909
Iron Hague		1909-1910
P.O. Curran		1910-1911
Iron Hague		1910-1911
Bombardier Billy Wells	3	1911-1919
Joe Beckett		1919
Frank Goddard	1	1919
Joe Beckett*	1	1919-1923
Frank Goddard		1923-1926
Phil Scott*	1	1926-1931
Reggie Meen		1931-1932
Jack Petersen	3	1932-1933
Len Harvey		1933-1934
Jack Petersen		1934-1936
Ben Foord		1936-1937
Tommy Farr*	1	1937-1938
Len Harvey*	1	1938-1942
Jack London	1	1944-1945
Bruce Woodcock	1	1945-1950
Jack Gardner	1	1950-1952
Johnny Williams	1	1952-1953
Don Cockell*	1	1953-1956
Joe Erskine	2	1956-1958
Brian London	1	1958-1959
Henry Cooper*	9	1959-1969
Jack Bodell	1	1969-1970
Henry Cooper	1	1970-1971
Joe Bugner	1	1971
Jack Bodell	1	1971-1972
Danny McAlinden	1	1972-1975
Bunny Johnson	1	1975
Richard Dunn	2	1975-1976
Joe Bugner*	1	1976-1977
John L. Gardner*	2	1978 1980
Gordon Ferris	1	1981
Neville Meade	1	1981-1983
David Pearce*	1	1983-1985
Hughroy Currie	1	1985-1986
Horace Notice*	4	1986-1988
Gary Mason	2	1989-1991
Lennox Lewis*	3	1991-1993
Herbie Hide*	1	1993-1994
James Oyebola	1	1994-1995
Scott Welch	1	1995-

Retired British Champions: Career Summary

Includes all British champions, and claimants, or British boxers who have won international titles since the introduction of gloves, and who had retired by July, 1996. It does not include champions still active (for their records see under Current British-Based Champions or Active British-Based Boxers). Please make allowances for some of the early British champion's records possibly being incomplete. Undefeated champions are those who relinquished their titles, not forfeited them.

George Aldridge British Middleweight Champion, 1962-1963. *Born* 01.02.36. *From* Market Harborough. *Pro Career* 1956-1963 (52 contests, won 36, drew 2, lost 14).

Terry Allen British Flyweight Champion, 1951-1952, and Undefeated British Flyweight Champion, 1952-1954. European and World Flyweight Champion, 1950. *Born* 18.06.24. *From* Islington. Birthname - Edward Govier. *Deceased* 1987. *Pro Career* 1942-1954 (74 contests, won 60, drew 1, lost 13).

Charlie Allum British Welterweight Champion, 1903-1904. British Middleweight Championship Claimant, 1905-1906. *Born* 23.04.1876. *From* Notting Hill. *Deceased* 1918. *Pro Career* 1903-1910 (44 contests, won 21, drew 5, lost 18).

Francis Ampofo Undefeated British Flyweight Champion, 1992-1996. Commonwealth Flyweight Champion, 1993-1995. *Born* Ghana, 05.06.67. *From* Bethnal Green. *Pro Career* 1990-1995 (17 contests, won 13, lost 4).

Brian Anderson British Middleweight Champion, 1986-1987. *Born* 09.07.61. *From* Sheffield. *Pro Career* 1980-1987 (39 contests, won 27, drew 3, lost 9).

Jimmy Anderson Undefeated British S. Featherweight Champion, 1968-1970. *Born* 01.10.42. *From* Waltham Cross. *Pro Career* 1964-1971 (37 contests, won 27, drew 1, lost 9).

Vic Andreetti Undefeated British L. Welterweight Champion, 1969-1970. *Born* 29.01.42. *From* Hoxton. *Pro Career* 1961-1969 (67 contests, won 51, drew 3, lost 13).

Derek Angol Undefeated British Cruiserweight Champion, 1991-1992. Undefeated Commonwealth Cruiserweight Champion, 1989-1993. *Born* 28.11.64. *From* Camberwell. *Pro Career* 1986-1996 (31 contests, won 28, lost 3).

Evan Armstrong British Featherweight Champion, 1971-1972, and Undefeated British Featherweight Champion, 1973-1975. Commonwealth Featherweight Champion, 1974. *Born* 15.02.43. *From* Ayr. *Pro Career* 1963-1974 (54 contests, won 39, drew 1, lost 14).

Bobby Arthur British Welterweight Champion, 1972-1973. *Born* 25.07.47. *From* Coventry. *Pro Career* 1967-1976 (41 contests, won 26, lost 15).

Eddie Avoth British L. Heavyweight Champion, 1969-1971. Commonwealth L. Heavyweight Champion, 1970-1971. *Born* 02.05.45. *From* Cardiff. *Pro Career* 1963-1972 (53 contests, won 44, lost 9).

Teddy Baldock British Bantamweight Championship Claimant, 1928-1929. Undefeated British Bantamweight Champion, 1929-1931. British Empire Bantamweight Championship Claimant, 1928-1930. European Bantamweight Championship Claimant, 1928-1931. World Bantamweight Championship Claimant, 1927. *Born* 23.05.07. *From* Poplar. *Deceased* 1971. *Pro Career* 1921-1931 (80 contests, won 72, drew 3, lost 5).

Ron Barton Undefeated British L. Heavyweight Champion, 1956. *Born* 25.02.33. *From* West Ham. *Pro Career* 1954-1961 (31 contests, won 26, lost 5).

Johnny Basham British Welterweight Champion, 1914-1920. British Empire Welterweight Championship Claimant, 1919-1920. European Welterweight Championship Claimant, 1919-1920. British Middleweight Champion, 1921. British and European Middleweight Championship Claimant, 1921. *Born* 13.09.1890. *From* Newport. *Died* 1947. *Pro Career* 1910-1929 (87 contests, won 65, drew 7, lost 15).

Jimmy Batten British L. Middleweight Champion, 1977-1979. *Born* 07.11.55. *From* Millwall. *Pro Career* 1974-1983 (49 contests, won 40, lost 9).

Joe Beckett British Heavyweight Championship Claimant, 1919. Undefeated British Heavyweight Champion, 1919-1923. British Empire Heavyweight Championship Claimant, 1919-1923. Born 04.04.1892. *From* Southampton. *Deceased* 1965. *Pro Career* 1912-1923 (61 contests, won 49, drew 1, lost 11).

Jackie Kid Berg British Lightweight Champion, 1934-1936. World L. Welterweight Champion, 1930-1931 (NBA version). *Born* 28.06.09. *From* Stepney. Birthname - Judah Bergman. *Deceased* 1991. *Pro Career* 1924-1945 (192 contests, won 157, drew 9, lost 26).

Tom Berry British L. Heavyweight Champion, 1925-1927. British Empire L. Heavyweight Championship Claimant, 1927. *Born* 14.02.1890. *From* Custom House. *Deceased* 1943. *Pro Career* 1909-1931 (114 contests, won 67, drew 5, lost 41, no contest 1).

Bill Beynon British Bantamweight Champion, 1913. European Bantamweight Championship Claimant, 1913. *Born* 08.04.1891. *From* Taibach. *Deceased* 1932. *Pro Career* 1909-1931 (192 contests, won 70, drew 30, lost 91, no decision 1).

Bandsman Jack Blake British Middleweight Champion, 1916-1918. *Born* 1893. *From* Great Yarmouth. *Deceased* 1961. *Pro Career* 1910-1922 (64 contests, won 49, lost 14, no contest 1).

Jack Bloomfield Undefeated British L. Heavyweight Champion, 1922-1924. British Empire L. Heavyweight Championship Claimant, 1923-1924. *Born* 20.11.1899. *From* Islington. Birthname - Jack Blumenfeld. *Deceased* 1961. *Pro Career* 1918-1924 (38 contests, won 28, drew 1, lost 5, no decision 3, no contest 1).

Jack Bodell British Heavyweight Champion, 1969-1970 and 1971-1972. Commonwealth Heavyweight Champion, 1971-1972. European Heavyweight Champion, 1971. *Born* 11.08.40. *From* Swadlincote. *Pro Career* 1962-1972 (71 contests, won 58, lost 13).

Eric Boon British Lightweight Champion, 1938-1944. *Born* 28.12.19. *From* Chatteris. *Deceased* 1981. *Pro Career* 1935-1952 (122 contests, won 93, drew 5, lost 23. no contest 1).

Joe Bowker British Bantamweight Champion, 1902-1910. European Bantamweight Championship Claimant, 1910. World Bantamweight Champion, 1902-1904 (GB version). Undefeated World Bantamweight Champion, 1904-1905. British Featherweight Champion, 1905. British Featherweight Champion, 1905-1907. World Featherweight Champion, 1905-1907 (GB version). *Born* 20.07.1883. *From* Salford. Birthname - Tommy Mahon. *Deceased* 1955. *Pro Career* 1900-1919 (50 contests, won 39, drew 1, lost 8, no decision 2).

Steve Boyle British Lightweight Champion, 1988-1990. *Born* 28.11.62. *From* Glasgow. *Pro Career* 1983-1993 (33 contests, won 25, drew 2, lost 6).

Cornelius Boza-Edwards Undefeated European S. Featherweight Champion, 1982. World S. Featherweight Champion, 1981 (WBC version). *Born* Uganda, 27.05.56. *From* London. *Pro Career* 1976-1987 (53 contests, won 45, drew 1, lost 7).

Jim Brady British Empire Bantamweight Championship Claimant, 1941-1945. *From* Dundee. *Deceased* 1980. *Pro Career* 1932-1947 (169 contests, won 104, drew 15, lost 50).

Jackie Brown British and British Empire Flyweight Champion, 1962-1963. *Born* 02.03.35. *From* Edinburgh. *Pro Career* 1958-1966 (44 contests, won 32, drew 1, lost 10, no contest 1).

Jackie Brown British Flyweight Champion, 1929-1930 and 1931-1935. European Flyweight Championship Claimant, 1931-1935. World Flyweight Champion, 1932-1935 (NBA/IBU version). *Born* 29.11.09. *From* Manchester. *Deceased* 1971. *Pro Career* 1926-1939 (135 contests, won 103, drew 8, lost 24).

Hamilton Johnny Brown British Welterweight Champion, 1925. *Born* 1901. *From* Hamilton. Birthname - John Fleming. *Deceased* 1983. *Pro Career* 1920-1931 (55 contests, won 38, drew 2, lost 15).

Johnny Brown British Bantamweight Champion, 1923-1928. British Empire Bantamweight Championship Claimant, 1923-1928. British Bantamweight Championship Claimant, 1928. European Bantamweight Championship Claimant, 1923-1928. *Born* 18.07.02. *From* Stepney. Birthname - Phil Hackman. *Deceased* 1975. *Pro Career* 1919-1928 (99 contests, won 54, drew 5, lost 25, no decision 15).

Ken Buchanan Undefeated British Lightweight Champion, 1968-1971, and 1973-1974. Undefeated European Lightweight Champion, 1974-1975. World Lightweight Champion, 1970-1971. World Lightweight Champion, 1971-1972 (WBA version). *Born* 28.06.45. *From* Edinburgh. *Pro Career* 1965-1982 (69 contests, won 61, lost 8).

Joe Bugner British, Commonwealth and European Heavyweight Champion, 1971. Undefeated European Heavyweight Champion, 1972-1975. European Heavyweight Champion, 1976-1977. Undefeated British and Commonwealth Heavyweight Champion, 1976-1977. *Born* Hungary, 13.03.50. *From* Bedford. *Pro Career* 1967-1996 (77 contests, won 63, drew 1, lost 13).

Dick Burge British Lightweight Champion, 1891-1897. Undefeated British Lightweight Champion, 1897-1901. World Lightweight Champion, 1891-1896 (GB version). Undefeated British Middleweight Champion, 1898-1900. *Born* 19.02.1865. *From* Cheltenham. *Deceased* 1918. *Pro Career* 1882-1900 (25 contests, won 14, drew 2, lost 8, no decision 1).

Pat Butler Undefeated British Welterweight Champion, 1934-1936. *Born* 16.03.13. *From* Mountsorrel. *Pro Career* 1931-1936 (114 contests, won 65, drew 4, lost 44, no contest 1).

Alex Buxton British L. Heavyweight Champion, 1953-1955. *Born* 10.05.25. *From* Watford. *Pro Career* 1942-1963 (125 contests, won 78, drew 4, lost 43).

Jimmy Cable British L. Middleweight Champion, 1984-1985. European L. Middleweight Champion, 1984. *Born* 07.09.57. *From* Crawley. *Pro Career* 1980-1988 (41 contests, won 30, drew 2, lost 9).

Chic Calderwood British and British Empire L. Heavyweight Champion, 1960-1963. Undefeated British L. Heavyweight Champion, 1964-1966. *Born* 09.01.37. *From* Craigneuk. Birthname - Charles Calderwood. *Deceased* 1966. *Pro Career* 1957-1966 (55 contests, won 44, drew 1, lost 9, no contest 1).

Johnny Caldwell Undefeated British Flyweight Champion, 1960-1961. British and British Empire Bantamweight Champion, 1964-1965. World Bantamweight Champion, 1961-1962 (EBU version). *Born* 07.05.38. *From* Belfast. *Pro Career* 1958-1965 (35 contests, won 29, drew 1, lost 5).

Ray Cattouse British Lightweight Champion, 1980-1982. *Born* 24.07.52. *From* Balham. *Pro Career* 1975-1983 (31 contests, won 26, drew 3, lost 2).

Tom Causer British Lightweight Championship Claimant, 1894-1897. British Lightweight Champion, 1897. *Born* 15.01.1872. *From* Bermondsey. *Deceased* 1918. *Pro Career* 1891-1898 (36 contests, won 31, drew 2, lost 3).

Ralph Charles Undefeated British and British Empire/Commonwealth Welterweight Champion, 1968-1972. European Welterweight Champion, 1970-1971. *Born* 05.02.43. *From* West Ham. *Pro Career* 1963-1972 (43 contests, won 39, lost 4).

Dave Charnley Undefeated British Lightweight Champion, 1957-1965. British Empire Lightweight Champion, 1959-1962. European Lightweight Champion, 1960-1963. *Born* 10.10.35. *From* Dartford. *Pro Career* 1954-1964 (61 contests, won 48, drew 1, lost 12).

George Chrisp British Heavyweight Championship Claimant, 1901. *Born* 23.02.1872. *From* Newcastle. *Deceased*. *Pro Career* 1889-1906 (23 contests, won 15, lost 8).

Lloyd Christie British L. Welterweight Champion, 1987-1989. *Born* 28.02.62. *From* Wolverhampton. *Pro Career* 1981-1989 (46 contests, won 24, drew 1, lost 21).

Elky Clark Undefeated British Flyweight Champion, 1924-1927. British Empire Bantamweight Championship Claimant, 1924-1927. Undefeated European Flyweight Champion, 1925-1927. *Born* 04.01.1898. *From* Glasgow. Birthname - William Clark. *Deceased* 1956. *Pro Career* 1921-1927 (45 contests, won 29, drew 4, lost 12).

Johnny Clark Undefeated British and European Bantamweight Champion, 1973-1974. *Born* 10.09.47. *From* Walworth. *Pro Career* 1966-1974 (43 contests, won 39, drew 1, lost 3).

Ronnie Clayton British Featherweight Champion, 1947-1954. British Empire Featherweight Championship Claimant, 1947-1951. European Featherweight Champion, 1947-1948. *Born* 09.02.23. *From* Blackpool. *Pro Career* 1941-1954 (113 contests, won 79, drew 8, lost 26).

Pat Clinton Undefeated British Flyweight Champion, 1988-1991. Undefeated European Flyweight Champion, 1990-1991. World Flyweight Champion, 1992-1993 (WBO version). *Born* 04.04.64. *From* Croy. *Pro Career* 1985-1991 (23 contests, won 20, lost 3).

Ray Close Undefeated European S. Middleweight Champion, 1993. *Born* 20.01.69. *From* Belfast. *Pro Career* 1988-1995 (25 contests, won 21, drew 1, lost 3).

Don Cockell British L. Heavyweight Champion, 1950-1952. Undefeated European L. Heavyweight Champion, 1951-1952. Undefeated British Heavyweight Champion, 1953-1956. British Empire Heavyweight Championship Claimant, 1953-1954. Undefeated British Empire Heavyweight Champion, 1954-1956. *Born* 22.09.28. *From* Battersea. *Deceased* 1983. *Pro Career* 1946-1956 (80 contests, won 65, drew 1, lost 14).

Tom Collins British L. Heavyweight Champion, 1982-1984. Undefeated British L. Heavyweight Champion, 1987 and 1989-1990. European L. Heavyweight Champion, 1987-1988 and 1990-1991. *Born* Curacao, 01.07.55. *From* Leeds. *Pro Career* 1977-1993 (50 contests, won 26, drew 2, lost 22).

John Conteh Undefeated British, Commonwealth and European L. Heavyweight Champion, 1973-1974. World L. Heavyweight Champion, 1974-1977 (WBC version). *Born* 27.05.51. *From* Liverpool. *Pro Career* 1971-1980 (39 contests, won 34, drew 1, lost 4).

James Cook Undefeated British S. Middleweight Champion, 1990-1991. British S. Middleweight Champion, 1993-1994. European S. Middleweight Champion, 1991-1992. *Born* Jamaica, 17.05.59. *From* Peckham. *Pro Career* 1982-1994 (35 contests, won 25, lost 10).

Johnny Cooke British and British Empire Welterweight Champion, 1967-1968. *Born* 17.12.34. *From* Bootle. *Pro Career* 1960-1971 (93 contests, won 52, drew 7, lost 34).

Gary Cooper British L. Middleweight Champion, 1988. *Born* 31.05.57. *From* Lymington. *Pro Career* 1978-1989 (27 contests, won 16, drew 2, lost 9).

Henry Cooper Undefeated British Heavyweight Champion, 1959-1969. British Heavyweight Champion, 1970-1971. British Empire/Commonwealth Heavyweight Champion, 1959-1971. Undefeated European Heavyweight Champion, 1964 and 1968-1969 and European Heavyweight Champion, 1970-1971. *Born* 03.05.34. *From* Bellingham. *Pro Career* 1954-1971 (55 contests, won 40, drew 1, lost 14).

Dick Corbett British Bantamweight Champion, 1931-1932 and Undefeated British Bantamweight Champion, 1934. British Empire Bantamweight Championship Claimant, 1930-1932 and 1934. *Born* 28.09.08. *From* Bethnal Green. Birthname - Dick Coleman. *Deceased* 1943. *Pro Career* 1926-1943 (183 contests, won 130, drew 17, lost 36).

Harry Corbett British Featherweight Champion, 1928-1929. European Lightweight Championship Claimant, 1930-1931. *Born* 14.02.04. *From* Bethnal Green. Birthname - Henry Coleman. *Deceased* 1957. *Pro Career* 1921-1936 (219 contests, won 141, drew 25, lost 50, no contest 3).

George Corfield British Bantamweight Championship Claimant, 1893-1896. *Born* 1874. *From* Sheffield. *Deceased*. *Pro Career* 1890-1902 (32 contests, won 18, drew 4, lost 10).

Pat Cowdell Undefeated British Featherweight Champion, 1979-1982. Undefeated European Featherweight Champion, 1982-1983. British S. Featherweight Champion, 1986 and 1987-1988. European S. Featherweight Champion, 1984-1985. *Born* 18.08.53. *From* Warley. *Pro Career* 1977-1988 (42 contests, won 36, lost 6).

Carl Crook British & Commonwealth Lightweight Champion, 1990-1992. *Born* 10.11.63. *From* Chorley. *Pro Career* 1985-1993 (31 contests, won 26, drew 1, lost 4).

Harry Crossley British L. Heavyweight Champion, 1929-1932. *Born* 04.05.01. *From* Mexborough. *Deceased* 1948. *Pro Career* 1924-1934 (87 contests, won 58, drew 8, lost 20, no decision 1).

Dave Crowley British Lightweight Champion, 1938. *Born* 04.05.10. *From* Clerkenwell. *Deceased* 1974. *Pro Career* 1928-1946 (183 contests, won 129, drew 11, lost 42, no decision 1).

Maurice Cullen British Lightweight Champion, 1965-1968. *Born* 30.12.37. *From* Shotton. *Pro Career* 1959-1970 (55 contests, won 45, drew 2, lost 8).

Johnny Curley British Featherweight Champion, 1925-1927. *Born* 09.11.1897. *From* Lambeth. *Deceased* 1982. *Pro Career* 1912-1931 (181 contests, won 129, drew 18, lost 33, no decision 1).

Will Curley British Featherweight Championship Claimant, 1900-1901 and 1902-1903. *Born* 16.08.1877. *From* Newcastle. *Deceased* 1973. *Pro Career* 1892-1903 (33 contests, won 26, drew 3, lost 4).

P. O. Curran British Heavyweight Championship Claimant, 1910-1911. British Empire Heavyweight Championship Claimant, 1911. *Born* 1882. *From* Clarefield Lideen. Birthname - Matthew Curran. *Deceased* 1938. *Pro Career* 1908-1920 (86 contests, won 45, drew 3, lost 33, no contest 5).

Hughroy Currie British Heavyweight Champion, 1985-1986. *Born* Jamaica, 09.02.59. *From* Catford. *Pro Career* 1981-1989 (29 contests, won 17, drew 1, lost 11).

Brian Curvis Undefeated British and British Empire Welterweight Champion, 1960-1966. *Born* 14.08.37. *From* Swansea. Birthname - Brian Nancurvis. *Pro Career* 1959-1966 (41 contests, won 37, lost 4).

Cliff Curvis Undefeated British Welterweight Champion, 1952-1953. British Empire Welterweight Championship Claimant, 1952. *Born* 02.11.27. *From* Swansea. Birthname - Cliff Nancurvis. *Pro Career* 1944-1953 (55 contests, won 42, drew 1, lost 12).

Johnny Cusick British Featherweight Champion, 1939-1940. British Empire Featherweight Championship Claimant, 1939-1940. *Born* 27.01.16. *From* Manchester. *Deceased* 1990. *Pro Career* 1932-1949 (79 contests, won 64, drew 3, lost 12).

Johnny Cuthbert British Featherweight Champion, 1927-1928 and 1929-1931. British Lightweight Champion, 1932-1934. *Born* 09.07.05. *From* Sheffield. *Deceased* 1987. *Pro Career* 1921-1934 (153 contests, won 110, drew 14, lost 29).

Najib Daho British S. Featherweight Champion, 1986-1987. Commonwealth Lightweight Champion, 1989-1990. *Born* Morocco, 13.01.59. *From* Manchester. *Deceased* 1993. *Pro Career* 1977-1991 (60 contests, won 34, drew 1, lost 25).

Gipsy Daniels Undefeated British L. Heavyweight Champion, 1927. British Empire L. Heavyweight Championship Claimant, 1927. *Born* 1902. *From* Newport. Birthname - Danny Thomas. *Deceased* 1967. *Pro Career* 1920-1938 (139 contests, won 87, drew 11, lost 41).

John Davison Undefeated British Featherweight Champion, 1992-1993. *Born* 30.09.58. *From* Newcastle. *Pro Career* 1988-1993 (20 contests, won 15, lost 5).

Gary DeRoux British Featherweight Champion, 1991. *Born* 04.11.62. *From* Peterborough. *Pro Career* 1986-1993 (22 contests, won 13, drew 1, lost 8).

Anthony Diamond Undefeated British Middleweight Champion, 1898. *Born* 13.11.1861. *From* Birmingham. *Deceased* 1930. *Pro Career* 1887-1898 (12 contests, won 10, lost 2).

Robert Dickie British Featherweight Champion, 1986-1988. British S. Featherweight Champion, 1991. *Born* 23.06.64. *From* Swansea. *Pro Career* 1983-1993 (28 contests, won 22, drew 2, lost 4).

Alex Dickson British Lightweight Champion, 1987-1988. *Born* 01.10.62. *From* Larkhall. *Pro Career* 1985-1989 (22 contests, won 18, drew 1, lost 3).

John Doherty British S. Featherweight Champion, 1986, 1989-1990 and 1991-1992. *Born* 17.07.62. *From* Bradford. *Pro Career* 1982-1992 (39 contests, won 28, drew 3, lost 8).

Pat Doherty Commonwealth Lightweight Champion, 1989. *Born* 12.04.62. *From* Croydon. *Pro Career* 1981-1989 (32 contests, won 18, drew 3, lost 11).

Dai Dower Undefeated British Flyweight Champion, 1955-1957. Undefeated British Empire Flyweight Champion, 1954-1957. European Flyweight Champion, 1955. *Born* 26.06.33. *From* Abercynon. *Pro Career* 1953-1958 (37 contests, won 34, lost 3).

Terry Downes British Middleweight Champion, 1958-1959 and 1959-1962. World Middleweight Champion, 1961-1962 (NY/EBU version). *Born* 09.05.36. *From* Paddington. *Pro Career* 1957-1964 (44 contests, won 35, lost 9).

Jim Driscoll British Featherweight Championship Claimant, 1906-1907. Undefeated British Featherweight Champion, 1907-1913. Undefeated European Featherweight Champion, 1912-1913. British Empire Featherweight Championship Claimant, 1908-1913. Undefeated World Featherweight Champion, 1907-1913 (GB version). *Born* 15.12.1880. *From* Cardiff. *Deceased* 1925. *Pro Career* 1901-1919 (71 contests, won 52, drew 6, lost 3, no decision 10).

Richard Dunn British and Commonwealth Heavyweight Champion, 1975-1976. European Heavyweight Champion, 1976. *Born* 19.01.45. *From* Bradford. *Pro Career* 1969-1977 (45 contests, won 33, lost 12).

Llew Edwards Undefeated British Featherweight Champion, 1915-1917. British Empire Featherweight Championship Claimant, 1915-1917. *Born* 1894. *From* Porth. *Deceased* 1965. *Pro Career* 1913-1922 (106 contests, won 85, drew 5, lost 13, no decision 3).

Tony Ekubia British L. Welterweight Champion, 1990-1991. Commonwealth L. Welterweight Champion, 1989-1991. *Born* Nigeria, 06.03.60. *From* Manchester. *Pro Career* 1986-1993 (25 contests, won 21, lost 4).

Joe Erskine British Heavyweight Champion, 1956-1958. British Empire Heavyweight Champion, 1957-1958. *Born* 26.01.34. *From* Cardiff. *Deceased* 1990. *Pro Career* 1954-1964 (54 contests, won 45, drew 1, lost 8).

Arthur Evernden British Welterweight Champion, 1911-1912. *Born* 19.01.1886. *From* Chatham. *Deceased*. *Pro Career* 1908-1917 (74 contests, won 45, drew 5, lost 22, no decision 2).

Tommy Farr Undefeated British Heavyweight Champion, 1937-1938. British Empire Heavyweight Championship Claimant, 1937-1938. *Born* 12.03.14. *From* Tonypandy. *Deceased* 1986. Pro Career (125 contests, won 80, drew 13, lost 30, no decision 2).

George Feeney Undefeated British Lightweight Champion, 1982-1985. *Born* 09.02.57. *From* West Hartlepool. *Pro Career* 1977-1984 (29 contests, won 19, lost 10).

John Feeney British Bantamweight Champion, 1981-1983 and 1983-1985. *Born* 15.05.58. *From* West Hartlepool. *Pro Career* 1977-1987 (48 contests, won 35, lost 13).

Gordon Ferris British Heavyweight Champion, 1981. *Born* 21.11.52. *From* Enniskillen. *Pro Career* 1977-1982 (26 contests, won 20, lost 6).

Albert Finch British Middleweight Champion, 1950. *Born* 16.05.26. *From* Croydon. *Pro Career* 1945-1958 (103 contests, won 72, drew 9, lost 21, no contest 1).

Chris Finnegan British L. Heavyweight Champion, 1971-1973 and Undefeated British L. Heavyweight Champion, 1975-1976. Commonwealth L. Heavyweight Champion, 1971-1973. European L. Heavyweight Champion, 1972. *Born* 05.06.44. *From* Iver. *Pro Career* 1968-1975 (37 contests, won 29, drew 1, lost 7).

Kevin Finnegan British Middleweight Champion, 1977. Undefeated British Middleweight Champion, 1974 and 1979-1980. European Middleweight Champion, 1974-1975 and 1980. *Born* 18.04.48. *From* Iver. *Pro Career* 1970-1980 (47 contests, won 35, drew 1, lost 11).

Ben Foord British Heavyweight Champion, 1936-1937. British Empire Heavyweight Championship Claimant, 1936-1937. *Born* Vrede, South Africa, 21.01.13. *From* Leicester. *Deceased* 1942. *Pro Career* 1932-1940 (59 contests, won 40, drew 4, lost 15).

Al Foreman Undefeated British Lightweight Champion, 1930-1932. British Empire Lightweight Championship Claimant, 1930-1933 and 1933-1934. *Born* 03.11.04. *From* Bow. Birthname - Albert Harris. *Deceased* 1954. *Pro Career* 1920-1934 (164 contests, won 133, drew 11, lost 20).

Joe Fox Undefeated British Bantamweight Champion, 1915-1917. Undefeated British Featherweight Champion, 1921-1922. *Born* 08.02.1892. *From* Leeds. *Deceased* 1965. *Pro Career* 1910-1925 (117 contests, won 62, drew 11, lost 17, no contest 2, no decision 25).

Johnny Frankham British L. Heavyweight Champion, 1975. *Born* 06.06.48. *From* Reading. *Pro Career* 1970-1976 (40 contests, won 28, drew 1, lost 11).

Jack Gardner British Heavyweight Champion, 1950-1952. British Empire Heavyweight Championship Claimant, 1950-1952. European Heavyweight Champion, 1951. *Born* 06.11.26. *From* Market Harborough. *Deceased* 1978. *Pro Career* 1948-1956 (34 contests, won 28, lost 6).

John L. Gardner Undefeated British Heavyweight Champion, 1978-1980. Undefeated Commonwealth Heavyweight Champion, 1978-1981. Undefeated European Heavyweight Champion, 1980-1981. *Born* 19.03.53. *From* Hackney. *Pro Career* 1973-1983 (39 contests, won 35, lost 4).

171

Teddy Gardner Undefeated British and European Flyweight Champion, 1952. British Empire Flyweight Championship Claimant, 1952. *Born* 27.01.22. *From* West Hartlepool. *Deceased* 1977. *Pro Career* 1938-1952 (66 contests, won 55, drew 3, lost 8).

Tom Gardner British Bantamweight Championship Claimant, 1892. *Born* 27.06.1869. *From* Stepney. *Deceased* 1946. *Pro Career* 1886-1892 (27 contests, won 20, drew 1, lost 6).

Ray Gilbody British Bantamweight Champion, 1985-1987. *Born* 21.03.60. *From* Warrington. *Pro Career* 1983-1987 (16 contests, won 11, drew 1, lost 4).

Freddie Gilroy Undefeated British and British Empire Bantamweight Champion, 1959-1963. European Bantamweight Champion, 1959-1960. *Born* 07.03.36. *From* Belfast. *Pro Career* 1957-1962 (31 contests, won 28, lost 3).

Tommy Glencross British Featherweight Champion, 1972-1973. *Born* 31.07.47. *From* Glasgow. *Pro Career* 1967-1978 (48 contests, won 31, drew 1, lost 16).

Frank Goddard British Heavyweight Champion, 1919 and 1923-1926. *Born* 27.11.1891. *From* Clapham. *Deceased* 1957. *Pro Career* 1912-1926 (55 contests, won 40, lost 15).

Jack Goldswain British Lightweight Champion, 1906-1908. *Born* 22.07.1878. *From* Bermondsey. *Deceased* 1954. *Pro Career* 1896-1919 (144 contests, won 79, drew 12, lost 52, no contest 1).

Herol Graham Undefeated British L. Middleweight Champion, 1981-1983. Undefeated Commonwealth L. Middleweight Champion, 1981-1984. Undefeated European L. Middleweight Champion, 1983-1984. Undefeated British Middleweight Champion, 1985-1986. British Middleweight Champion, 1988-1992. European Middleweight Champion, 1986-1987. *Born* 13.09.59. *From* Sheffield. *Pro Career* 1978-1992 (49 contests, won 44, lost 5).

Frank Grant British Middleweight Champion, 1992-1993. *Born* 22.05.65. *From* Bradford. *Pro Career* 1986-1993 (26 contests, won 22, lost 4).

Dave Boy Green Undefeated British and European L. Welterweight Champion, 1976-1977. European Welterweight Champion, 1979. *Born* 02.06.53. *From* Chatteris. *Pro Career* 1974-1981 (41 contests, won 37, lost 4).

Harry Greenfield British Featherweight Championship Claimant, 1896-1899. *Born* 1873. *From* Camden Town. *Deceased* 1946. *Pro Career* 1889-1902 (50 contests, won 20, drew 5, lost 24, no decision 1).

Roy Gumbs British Middleweight Champion, 1981-1983. Commonwealth Middleweight Champion, 1983. *Born* St Kitts, 05.09.54. *From* Tottenham. *Pro Career* 1976-1985 (40 contests, won 26, drew 3, lost 11).

Tom Gummer British Middleweight Champion, 1920-1921. *Born* 04.12.1894. *From* Rotherham. *Deceased* 1982. *Pro Career* 1914-1922 (53 contests, won 39, drew 2, lost 12).

Neil Haddock British S. Featherweight Champion, 1992-1994. *Born* 22.06.64. *From* Llanelli. *Pro Career* 1987-1994 (26 contests, won 14, drew 1, lost 11).

Iron Hague British Heavyweight Champion, 1909-1910. British Heavyweight Championship Claimant, 1910-1911. *Born* 06.11.1885. *From* Mexborough. Birthname - William Hague. *Deceased* 1951. *Pro Career* 1904-1915 (37 contests, won 25, drew 1, lost 11).

Henry Hall British Welterweight Champion, 1948-1949. *Born* 06.09.22. *From* Sheffield. *Deceased* 1979. *Pro Career* 1945-1952 (66 contests, won 43, drew 3, lost 20).

Seaman Nobby Hall British Lightweight Champion, 1922-1923. European Lightweight Championship Claimant, 1922-1923. *Born* 15.10.1892. *From* Peebles. Birthname - James Hall. *Deceased* 1953. *Pro Career* 1909-1935 (165 contests, won 112, drew 12, lost 41).

Charlie Hardcastle British Featherweight Champion, 1917. *Born* 14.02.1894. *From* Barnsley, *Deceased* 1960. *Pro Career* 1911-1923 (66 contests, won 38, drew 5, lost 20, no decision 3).

Jack Harrison Undefeated British Middleweight Champion, 1912-1913. *Born* 15.10.1888. *From* Rushden. *Deceased* 1971. *Pro Career* 1905-1924 (32 contests, won 14, drew 3, lost 12, no decision 3).

Tommy Harrison British Bantamweight Champion, 1922-1923. British Empire Bantamweight Championship Claimant, 1922-1923. European

Bantamweight Championship Claimant, 1921-1922. *Born* 17.08.1892. *From* Stoke. *Deceased* 1931. *Pro Career* 1909-1923 (83 contests, won 50, drew 7, lost 25, no decision 1).

Len Harvey British Middleweight Champion, 1929-1933. British Empire Middleweight Championship Claimant, 1929-1933. Undefeated British L. Heavyweight Champion, 1933-1934 and British L. Heavyweight Champion, 1938-1942. British Empire L. Heavyweight Championship Claimant, 1939-1942. World L. Heavyweight Champion, 1939-1942 (GB version). British Heavyweight Championship Claimant, 1933-1934 and Undefeated British Heavyweight Champion, 1938-1942. British Empire Heavyweight Championship Claimant, 1934 and 1939-1942. *Born* 11.07.07. *From* Callington. *Deceased* 1976. *Pro Career* 1920-1942 (134 contests, won 112, drew 9, lost 13).

Paul Harvey Commonwealth S. Featherweight Champion, 1991-1992. *Born* 10.11.64. *From* Ilford. *Pro Career* 1989-1994 (22 contests, won 16, drew 1, lost 5).

Dennis Haugh British L. Heavyweight Championship Claimant, 1913-1914. *From* Tipperary. *Deceased*. *Pro Career* 1909-1916 (50 contests, won 26, drew 4, lost 18, no contest 2).

Vince Hawkins British Middleweight Champion, 1946-1948. *Born* 15.04.23. *From* Eastleigh. *Pro Career* 1940-1950 (86 contests, won 75, drew 1, lost 10).

Lloyd Hibbert Undefeated British L. Middleweight Champion, 1987. Commonwealth L. Middleweight Champion, 1987. *Born* 29.06.59. *From* Birmingham. *Pro Career* 1979-1987 (23 contests, won 19, lost 4).

Jim Higgins British Bantamweight Champion, 1920-1922. British Empire Bantamweight Championship Claimant, 1920-1922. *Born* 25.10.1897. *From* Hamilton. *Deceased* 1964. *Pro Career* 1919-1930 (34 contests, won 18, drew 3, lost 13).

Charlie Hill British Featherweight Champion, 1956-1959. *Born* 20.06.30. *From* Cambuslang. *Pro Career* 1953-1959 (36 contests, won 31, lost 5).

Johnny Hill Undefeated British Flyweight Champion, 1927-1929. European Flyweight Championship Claimant, 1928-1929. World Flyweight Champion, 1928-1929 (GB version). *Born* 14.12.05. *From* Edinburgh. *Deceased* 1929. Pro Career 1926-1929 (23 contests, won 18, drew 3, lost 1, no contest 1).

Paul Hodkinson Undefeated British Featherweight Champion, 1988-1990. Undefeated European Featherweight Champion, 1989-1991. World Featherweight Champion, 1991-1993 (WBC version). *Born* 14.09.65. *From* Liverpool. *Pro Career* 1986-1994 (26 contests, won 22, drew 1, lost 3).

Mike Honeyman British Featherweight Champion, 1920-1921. *Born* 11.11.1896. *From* Woolwich. *Deceased* 1944. *Pro Career* 1913-1926 (167 contests, won 109, drew 18, lost 40).

Jack Hood Undefeated British Welterweight Champion, 1926-1934. Undefeated European Welterweight Champion, 1933. *Born* 17.12.02. *From* Birmingham. *Deceased* 1992. *Pro Career* 1921-1935 (81 contests, won 66, drew 7, lost 6, no contest 1, no decision 1).

Maurice Hope Undefeated British L. Middleweight Champion, 1974-1977. Undefeated Commonwealth L. Middleweight Champion, 1976-1979. Undefeated European L. Middleweight Champion, 1976-1978. World L. Middleweight Champion, 1979-1981 (WBC version). *Born* Antigua, 06.12.51. *From* Hackney. *Pro Career* 1973-1982 (35 contests, won 30, drew 1, lost 4).

Alf Howard European Lightweight Champion, 1930. *Born* 1907. *From* Liverpool. *Deceased* 1959. *Pro Career* 1923-1937 (87 contests, won 62, drew 3, lost 22).

Mickey Hughes Commonwealth L. Middleweight Champion, 1992-1993. *Born* 13.06.62. *From* St Pancras. *Pro Career* 1985-1993 (31 contests, won 24, lost 7).

Mo Hussein Commonwealth Lightweight Champion, 1987-1989. *Born* 17.11.62. *From* West Ham. *Pro Career* 1982-1989 (27 contests, won 23, lost 4).

Alex Ireland British Middleweight Champion, 1928-1929. British Empire and European Middleweight Championship Claimant, 1928-1929. *Born* 11.02.01. *From* Leith. *Deceased* 1966. *Pro Career* 1922-1930 (47 contests, won 34, drew 3, lost 10).

Ernie Izzard British Lightweight Champion, 1924-1925. *Born* 25.02.05. *From* Herne Hill. *Deceased* 1970. *Pro Career* 1920-1935 (120 contests, won 90, drew 9, lost 19, no decision 2).

Joey Jacobs British S. Featherweight Champion, 1990. *Born* 01.10.60. *From* Manchester. *Pro Career* 1986-1991 (15 contests, won 10, lost 5).

Ronnie James Undefeated British Lightweight Champion, 1944-1947. *Born* 08.10.17. *From* Swansea. *Deceased* 1977. *Pro Career* 1933-1947 (119 contests, won 98, drew 5, lost 16).

Tee Jay British Cruiserweight Champion, 1987-1988. *Born* Ghana, 21.01.62. Birthname - Taju Akay. *From* Notting Hill. *Pro Career* 1985-1991 (19 contests, won 14, drew 1, lost 4).

Bunny Johnson British and Commonwealth Heavyweight Champion, 1975. British L. Heavyweight Champion, 1977-1981. *Born* Jamaica, 10.05.47. *From* Birmingham. Birthname - Frank Johnson. *Pro Career* 1968-1981 (73 contests, won 55, drew 1, lost 17).

Frank Johnson British Lightweight Champion, 1952-1953 and 1955-1956. British Empire Lightweight Championship Claimant, 1953. *Born* 27.11.28. *From* Manchester. Birthname - Frank Williamson. *Deceased* 1970. *Pro Career* 1946-1957 (58 contests, won 47, lost 11).

Fred Johnson British Featherweight Championship Claimant, 1891-1895. British Featherweight Champion, 1895-1897. *Born* 03.10.1865. *From* Hackney. *Deceased*. *Pro Career* 1884-1901 (38 contests, won 27, drew 1, lost 10).

Len Johnson British Empire Middleweight Championship Claimant, 1926. European Middleweight Championship Claimant, 1928-1929. *Born* 16.10.02. *From* Manchester. *Deceased* 1974. *Pro Career* 1921-1933 (100 contests, won 70, drew 3, lost 27).

Colin Jones Undefeated British Welterweight Champion, 1980-1982. Undefeated Commonwealth Welterweight Champion, 1981-1984. Undefeated European Welterweight Champion, 1982-1983. *Born* 21.03.59. *From* Gorseinon. *Pro Career* 1977-1985 (30 contests, won 26, drew 1, lost 3).

Frankie Jones British Flyweight Champion, 1957-1960. British Empire Flyweight Champion, 1957. *Born* 12.02.33. *From* Plean. *Deceased* 1991. *Pro Career* 1955-1960 (25 contests, won 17, lost 8).

Percy Jones British and European Flyweight Champion, 1914. World Flyweight Champion, 1914 (GB/IBU version). *Born* 26.12.1892. *From* Porth. *Deceased* 1922. *Pro Career* 1910-1915 (51 contests, won 45, drew 3, lost 3).

Ben Jordan Undefeated British Featherweight Champion, 1897-1900 and 1902-1905. World Featherweight Champion, 1898-1905 (GB version). *Born* 01.04.1873. *From* Bermondsey. *Deceased* 1945. *Pro Career* 1892-1905 (42 contests, won 35, drew 1, lost 3, no contests 3).

Young Joseph British Welterweight Championship Claimant, 1908-1910. British Welterweight Champion, 1910-1911. European Welterweight Championship Claimant, 1910-1911. *Born* 12.02.1885. *From* Aldgate. Birthname - Aschel Joseph. *Deceased* 1952. *Pro Career* 1903-1914 (129 contests, won 83, drew 21, lost 25).

Peter Kane Undefeated World Flyweight Champion, 1938-1939. European Bantamweight Champion, 1947-1948. *Born* 28.04.18. *From* Golborne. Birthname - Peter Cain. *Deceased* 1991. *Pro Career* 1934-1948 (102 contests, won 92, drew 2, lost 7, no contest 1).

Mark Kaylor British and Commonwealth Middleweight Champion, 1983-1984. *Born* 11.05.61. *From* West Ham. *Pro Career* 1980-1991 (48 contests, won 40, drew 1, lost 7).

Peter Keenan British Bantamweight Champion, 1951-1953 and 1954-1959. British Empire Bantamweight Champion, 1955-1959. European Bantamweight Champion, 1951-1952 and 1953. *Born* 08.08.28. *From* Glasgow. *Pro Career* 1948-1959 (66 contests, won 54, drew 1, lost 11).

Billy Spider Kelly British Featherweight Champion, 1955-1956. British Empire Featherweight Championship Claimant, 1954. British Empire Featherweight Champion, 1954-1955. *Born* 21.04.32. *From* Londonderry. *Pro Career* 1950-1962 (83 contests, won 56, drew 4, lost 23).

Jim Spider Kelly British Featherweight Champion, 1938-1939. British Empire Featherweight Championship Claimant, 1938-1939. *Born* 25.02.12. *From* Londonderry. *Deceased* 1988. *Pro Career* 1928-1948 (150 contests, won 105, drew 12, lost 33).

Joe Kelly British Bantamweight Champion, 1992. *Born* 18.05.64. *From* Glasgow. *Pro Career* 1985-1992 (27 contests, won 18, drew 2, lost 7).

John Kelly British and European Bantamweight Champion, 1953-1954. *Born* 17.01.32. *From* Belfast. *Pro Career* 1951-1957 (28 contests, won 24, lost 4).

Jake Kilrain British Welterweight Champion, 1936-1939. *Born* 29.05.14. *From* Bellshill. Birthname - Harry Owens. *Deceased* 1984. *Pro Career* 1931-1949 (133 contests, won 103, drew 4, lost 26).

Johnny King British Bantamweight Champion, 1932-1934 and 1935-1947. British Empire Bantamweight Championship Claimant, 1932-1934. *Born* 08.01.12. *From* Manchester. *Deceased* 1963. *Pro Career* 1926-1947 (222 contests, won 158, drew 15, lost 48, no contest 1).

Bert Kirby British Flyweight Champion, 1930-1931. *Born* 02.12.08. *From* Birmingham. *Deceased* 1975. *Pro Career* 1926-1938 (187 contests, won 111, drew 14, lost 61, no contest 1).

Charlie Knock British Welterweight Champion, 1904-1906. *Born* 18.08.1880. *From* Stratford. *Deceased* 1939. *Pro Career* 1899-1910 (92 contests, won 59, drew 7, lost 25, no contest 1).

Bill Ladbury British and European Flyweight Champion, 1913-1914. World Flyweight Champion, 1913-1914 (GB/IBU version). *Born* 14.10.1891. *From* Deptford. *Deceased* 1917. *Pro Career* 1908-1917 (53 contests, won 31, drew 5, lost 17).

Tony Laing Undefeated British L. Welterweight Champion, 1986. Commonwealth L. Welterweight Champion, 1987-1988. *Born* 22.09.57. *From* Nottingham. *Pro Career* 1977-1988 (18 contests, won 13, drew 1, lost 4).

Bugler Harry Lake British and European Bantamweight Championship Claimant, 1923. British Empire Bantamweight Championship Claimant, 1923. *Born* 17.10.02. *From* Devonport. *Deceased* 1970. *Pro Career* 1917-1933 (172 contests, won 108, drew 16, lost 48).

Davy Larmour British Bantamweight Champion, 1983. *Born* 02.04.52. *From* Belfast. *Pro Career* 1977-1983 (18 contests, won 11, lost 7).

Mick Leahy British Middleweight Champion, 1963-1964. *Born* Cork, 12.03.35. *From* Coventry. *Pro Career* 1956-1965 (72 contests, won 46, drew 7, lost 19).

Tancy Lee British Flyweight Champion, 1914-1915. European Flyweight Champion, 1914-1916. World Flyweight Champion, 1915 (GB/IBU version). Undefeated British Featherweight Champion, 1917-1919. *Born* 31.01.1882. *From* Paisley. Birthname - James Lee. *Deceased* 1941. *Pro Career* 1910-1926 (60 contests, won 48, drew 2, lost 10).

Ted Kid Lewis Undefeated British Featherweight Champion, 1913-1914. Undefeated European Featherweight Champion, 1913-1914. British Welterweight Champion, 1920-1924. British Empire Welterweight Championship Claimant, 1920-1924. European Welterweight Championship Claimant, 1920-1924. World Welterweight Champion, 1915-1916 and 1917-1919. British Middleweight Championship Claimant, 1920-1921. British Middleweight Champion, 1921-1923. British Empire Middleweight Championship Claimant, 1922-1923. European Middleweight Championship Claimant, 1921-1923 and 1924-1925. *Born* 24.10.1894. *From* Aldgate. Birthname - Gershon Mendelhoff. *Deceased* 1970. *Pro Career* 1909-1929 (281 contests, won 170, drew 13, lost 30, no decision 68).

Stewart Lithgo Commonwealth Cruiserweight Champion, 1984. *Born* 02.06.57. *From* West Hartlepool. *Pro Career* 1977-1987 (30 contests, won 16, drew 2, lost 12).

Brian London British and British Empire Heavyweight Champion, 1958-1959. *Born* 19.06.34. *From* Blackpool. Birthname - Brian Harper. *Pro Career* 1955-1970 (58 contests, won 37, drew 1, lost 20).

Jack London British Heavyweight Champion, 1944-1945. British Empire Heavyweight Championship Claimant, 1944-1945. *Born* 23.06.13. *From* West Hartlepool. Birthname - Jack Harper. *Deceased* 1964. *Pro Career* 1931-1949 (141 contests, won 95, drew 5, lost 39, no contests 2).

Joe Lucy British Lightweight Champion, 1953-1955 and 1956-1957. *Born* 09.02.30. *From* Mile End. *Deceased* 1991. *Pro Career* 1950-1957 (37 contests, won 27, lost 10).

Benny Lynch Undefeated British Flyweight Champion, 1935-1938. European Flyweight Championship Claimant, 1935-1938. World Flyweight Champion, 1935-1937 (NBA version). *Born* 02.04.13. *From* Glasgow. *Deceased* 1946. *Pro Career* 1931-1938 (110 contests, won 82, drew 15, lost 13).

Danny McAlinden British and Commonwealth Heavyweight Champion, 1972-1975. *Born* Newry, 01.06.47. *From* Coventry. *Pro Career* 1969-1981 (45 contests, won 31, drew 2, lost 12).

Barry McGuigan (left) in action against Steve Cruz

Les McAteer British and British Empire Middleweight Champion, 1969-1970. *Born* 19.08.45. *From* Birkenhead. *Pro Career* 1965-1979 (39 contests, won 27, drew 2, lost 10).

Pat McAteer Undefeated British Middleweight Champion, 1955-1958. British Empire Middleweight Champion, 1955-1958. *Born* 17.03.32. *From* Birkenhead. *Pro Career* 1952-1958 (57 contests, won 49, drew 2, lost 6).

Dave McAuley Undefeated British Flyweight Champion, 1986-1988. World Flyweight Champion, 1989-1992 (IBF version). *Born* 15.06.61. *From* Larne. *Pro Career* 1983-1992 (23 contests, won 18, drew 2, lost 3).

Jock McAvoy British Middleweight Champion, 1933-1944. British Empire Middleweight Championship Claimant, 1933-1939. British L. Heavyweight Champion, 1937-1938. *Born* 20.11.07. *From* Rochdale. Birthname - Joe Bamford. *Deceased* 1971. *Pro Career* 1927-1945 (148 contests, won 134, lost 14).

Sammy McCarthy British Featherweight Champion, 1954-1955. *Born* 05.11.31. *From* Stepney. *Pro Career* 1951-1957 (53 contests, won 44, drew 1, lost 8).

Steve McCarthy British L. Heavyweight Champion, 1990-1991. *Born* 30.07.62. *From* Southampton. *Pro Career* 1987-1994 (17 contests, won 12, drew 1, lost 4).

Dave McCleave British Welterweight Champion, 1936. *Born* 25.12.11. *From* Smithfield. *Deceased* 1988. *Pro Career* 1934-1945 (115 contests, won 84, drew 3, lost 28).

John McCluskey Undefeated British Flyweight Champion, 1967-1977. Commonwealth Flyweight Champion, 1970-1971. *Born* 23.01.44. *From* Hamilton. *Pro Career* 1965-1975 (38 contests, won 23, lost 15).

John Cowboy McCormack British Middleweight Champion, 1959. European Middleweight Champion, 1961-1962. *Born* 09.01.35. *From* Maryhill. *Pro Career* 1957-1966 (45 contests, won 38, lost 7).

Young John McCormack British L. Heavyweight Champion, 1967-1969.

Born Dublin, 11.12.44. *From* Brixton. *Pro Career* 1963-1970 (42 contests, won 33, drew 1, lost 8).

Pat McCormack British L. Welterweight Champion, 1974. *Born* Dublin, 28.04.46. *From* Brixton. *Pro Career* 1968-1975 (49 contests, won 30, drew 1, lost 18).

Boy McCormick Undefeated British L. Heavyweight Champion, 1919-1921. *Born* 25.12.1899. *From* Dublin. Birthname - Noel McCormick. *Deceased* 1939. *Pro Career* 1916-1926 (39 contests, won 22, drew 1, lost 10, no decision 6).

Tom McCormick British Welterweight Champion, 1914. British Empire Welterweight Championship Claimant, 1914. *Born* 08.08.1890. *From* Dundalk. *Deceased* 1916. *Pro Career* 1911-1915 (46 contests, won 35, drew 2, lost 9).

Glenn McCrory Undefeated British Cruiserweight Champion, 1988. Undefeated Commonwealth Cruiserweight Champion, 1987-1989. World Cruiserweight Champion, 1989-1990 (IBF version). *Born* 23.09.64. *From* Annfield Plain. *Pro Career* 1984-1993 (39 contests, won 30, drew 1, lost 8).

Jim McDonnell Undefeated European Featherweight Champion, 1985-1987. *Born* 12.09.60. *From* Camden Town. *Pro Career* 1983-1990 (29 contests, won 26, lost 3).

Tommy McGovern British Lightweight Champion, 1951-1952. *Born* 05.02.24. *From* Bermondsey. *Deceased* 1989. *Pro Career* 1947-1953 (66 contests, won 45, drew 4, lost 17).

Walter McGowan Undefeated British Flyweight Champion, 1963-1966. Undefeated British Empire Flyweight Champion, 1963-1969. World Flyweight Champion, 1966 (WBC version). British and British Empire Bantamweight Champion, 1966-1968. *Born* 13.10.42. *From* Hamilton. *Pro Career* 1961-1969 (40 contests, won 32, drew 1, lost 7).

Johnny McGrory British Featherweight Champion, 1936-1938. British Empire Featherweight Championship Claimant, 1936-1938. *Born* 25.04.15. *From* Glasgow. *Pro Career* 1933-1943 (103 contests, won 72, drew 8, lost 23).

Barry McGuigan Undefeated British Featherweight Champion, 1983-1986. Undefeated European Featherweight Champion, 1983-1985. World Featherweight Champion, 1985-1986 (WBA version). *Born* 28.02.61. *From* Clones. *Pro Career* 1981-1989 (35 contests, won 32, lost 3).

Billy Mack European Welterweight Championship Claimant, 1923. *Born* 1900. *From* Liverpool. *Deceased* 1973. *Pro Career* 1919-1928 (72 contests, won 47, drew 6, lost 18, no contest 1).

Clinton McKenzie British L. Welterweight Champion, 1978-1979 and 1979-1984. Undefeated British L. Welterweight Champion, 1989. European L. Welterweight Champion, 1981-1982. *Born* 15.09.55. *From* Croydon. *Pro Career* 1976-1989 (50 contests, won 36, lost 14).

George McKenzie British Featherweight Champion, 1924-1925. *Born* 22.09.1900. *From* Leith. *Deceased* 1941. *Pro Career* 1920-1929 (45 contests, won 36, drew 2, lost 7).

Tony McKenzie British L. Welterweight Champion, 1986-1987. *Born* 04.03.63. *From* Leicester. *Pro Career* 1983-1993 (34 contests, won 26, drew 1, lost 7).

Charlie Magri Undefeated British Flyweight Champion, 1977-1981. Undefeated European Flyweight Champion, 1979-1983 and 1984-1985. European Flyweight Champion, 1985-1986. World Flyweight Champion, 1983 (WBC version). *Born* Tunisia, 20.07.56. *From* Stepney. *Pro Career* 1977-1986 (35 contests, won 30, lost 5).

Paddy Maguire British Bantamweight Champion, 1975-1977. *Born* 26.09.48. *From* Belfast. *Pro Career* 1969-1977 (35 contests, won 26, drew 1, lost 8).

Bob Marriott Undefeated British Lightweight Champion, 1919-1920. *Born* 21.12.1891. *From* Bermondsey. *Deceased* 1970. *Pro Career* 1915-1920 (10 contests, won 8, lost 2).

Terry Marsh Undefeated British L. Welterweight Champion, 1984-1986. European L. Welterweight Champion, 1985-1986. Undefeated World L. Welterweight Champion, 1987 (IBF version). *Born* 07.02.58. *From* Basildon. *Pro Career* 1981-1987 (27 contests, won 26, drew 1).

Gary Mason British Heavyweight Champion, 1989-1991. *Born* Jamaica, 15.12.62. *From* Wandsworth. *Pro Career* 1984-1991 (36 contests, won 35, lost 1).

Harry Mason British Lightweight Champion, 1923-1924. Undefeated British Lightweight Champion, 1925-1928. European Lightweight Championship Claimant, 1923-1926. British Lightweight Championship Claimant, 1924-1925. British Welterweight Champion, 1925-1926 and 1934. *Born* 27.03.03. *From* Leeds. *Deceased* 1977. *Pro Career* 1920-1937 (208 contests, won 140, drew 14, lost 52, no decision 2).

Billy Matthews European Featherweight Championship Claimant, 1922. *Born* 13.04.01. *From* London. *Deceased* 1967. *Pro Career* 1917-1926 (64 contests, won 39, drew 3, lost 22).

Neville Meade British Heavyweight Champion, 1981-1983. *Born* Jamaica, 12.09.48. *From* Swansea. *Pro Career* 1974-1983 (34 contests, won 20, drew 1, lost 13).

Reggie Meen British Heavyweight Champion, 1931-1932. *Born* 20.11.07. *From* Desborough. *Deceased* 1984. *Pro Career* 1927-1939 (104 contests, won 57, drew 3, lost 44).

Tommy Milligan Undefeated British Welterweight Champion, 1924-1925. European Welterweight Championship Claimant, 1924-1925. British Empire Welterweight Championship Claimant, 1924-1925. British Middleweight Champion, 1926-1928. British Empire Middleweight Championship Claimant, 1926-1928. European Middleweight Championship Claimant, 1925-1928. *Born* 02.03.04. *From* Wishaw. Birthname - Tommy Mulligan. *Deceased* 1970. *Pro Career* 1921-1928 (51 contests, won 42, lost 9).

Freddie Mills Undefeated British L. Heavyweight Champion, 1942-1950. British Empire L. Heavyweight Championship Claimant, 1942-1950. Undefeated European L. Heavyweight Champion, 1947-1950. World L. Heavyweight Champion, 1942-1946 (GB version). World L. Heavyweight Champion, 1948-1950. *Born* 26.06.19. *From* Bournemouth. *Deceased* 1965. *Pro Career* 1936-1950 (101 contests, won 77, drew 6, lost 18).

Alan Minter British Middleweight Champion, 1975-1977. Undefeated British Middleweight Champion, 1977-1978. European Middleweight Champion, 1977. Undefeated European Middleweight Champion, 1978-1979. World Middleweight Champion, 1980. *Born* 17.08.51. *From* Crawley. *Pro Career* 1972-1981 (49 contests, won 39, lost 9, no contest 1).

Charlie Mitchell Undefeated British Heavyweight Champion, 1882-1894. *Born* 24.11.1861. *From* Birmingham. *Deceased* 1918.

Sylvester Mittee British Welterweight Champion, 1985. Commonwealth Welterweight Champion, 1984-1985. *Born* St Lucia, 29.10.56. *From* Bethnal Green. *Pro Career* 1977-1988 (33 contests, won 28, lost 5).

Harry Mizler British Lightweight Champion, 1934. *Born* 22.01.13. *From* Stepney. *Deceased* 1990. *Pro Career* 1933-1943 (81 contests, won 63, drew 2, lost 16).

Gunner Moir British Heavyweight Champion, 1906-1909. *Born* 17.04.1879. *From* Lambeth. Birthname - James Moir. *Deceased* 1939. *Pro Career* 1903-1913 (25 contests, won 14, lost 11).

Tommy Molloy British Welterweight Champion, 1958-1960. *Born* 02.02.34. *From* Birkenhead. *Pro Career* 1955-1963 (43 contests, won 34, drew 2, lost 6, no contest 1).

Rinty Monaghan Undefeated British and World Flyweight Champion, 1948-1950. British Empire Flyweight Championship Claimant, 1948-1950. Undefeated European Flyweight Champion, 1949-1950. World Flyweight Champion, 1947-1948 (NBA version). *Born* 21.08.20. *From* Belfast. Birthname - John Monaghan. *Deceased* 1984. *Pro Career* 1934-1949 (66 contests, won 51, drew 6, lost 9).

Frank Moody British Middleweight Championship Claimant, 1927-1928. British L. Heavyweight Champion, 1927-1929. *Born* 27.08.1900. *From* Pontypridd. *Deceased* 1963. *Pro Career* 1914-1936 (204 contests, won 129, drew 15, lost 51, no decision 9).

Owen Moran British Bantamweight Championship Claimant, 1905-1907. Undefeated World Bantamweight Champion, 1907 (GB version). *Born* 04.12.1884. *From* Birmingham. *Deceased* 1949. *Pro Career* 1900-1916 (110 contests, won 66, drew 6, lost 17, no decision 21).

Des Morrison British L. Welterweight Champion, 1973-1974. *Born* Jamaica, 01.02.50. *From* Bedford. *Pro Career* 1970-1982 (50 contests, won 36, drew 2, lost 12).

Sean Murphy British Featherweight Champion, 1990-1991 and 1993. *Born* 01.12.64. *From* St Albans. *Pro Career* 1986-1994 (27 contests, won 22, lost 5).

Charlie Nash Undefeated British Lightweight Champion, 1978-1979.

175

Undefeated European Lightweight Champion, 1979-1980. European Lightweight Champion, 1980-1981. *Born* 10.05.51. *From* Derry. *Pro Career* 1975-1983 (30 contests, won 25, lost 5).

Dave Needham British Bantamweight Champion, 1974-1975. British Featherweight Champion, 1978-1979. *Born* 15.08.51. *From* Nottingham. *Pro Career* 1971-1980 (39 contests, won 30, drew 1, lost 8).

Bobby Neill British Featherweight Champion, 1959-1960. *Born* 10.10.33. *From* Edinburgh. *Pro Career* 1955-1960 (35 contests, won 28, lost 7).

Kid Nicholson European Bantamweight Championship Claimant, 1928. *Born* 1904. *From* Leeds. Birthname - George Nicholson. *Deceased* 1968. *Pro Career* 1919-1934 (105 contests, won 57, drew 7, lost 40, no contest 1).

Harry Nickless British Lightweight Championship Claimant, 1891-1894. *Born* 1866. *From* Kew. *Deceased* 1899. *Pro Career* 1888-1894 (14 contests, won 11, drew 1, lost 2).

Tommy Noble British Bantamweight Champion, 1918-1919. *Born* 04.03.1897. *From* Bermondsey. *Deceased* 1966. *Pro Career* 1915-1926 (179 contests, won 84, drew 19, lost 67, no decision 8, no contest 1).

Horace Notice Undefeated British and Commonwealth Heavyweight Champion, 1986-1988. *Born* 07.08.57. *From* Birmingham. *Pro Career* 1983-1988 (16 contests, won 16).

John O'Brien British Empire Featherweight Champion, 1967. *Born* 20.02.37. *From* Glasgow. *Deceased* 1979. *Pro Career* 1956-1971 (47 contests, won 30, lost 17).

Pat O'Keefe British Middleweight Championship Claimant, 1906. British Middleweight Champion, 1906 and 1914-1916. Undefeated British Middleweight Champion, 1918-1919. *Born* 17.03.1883. *From* Bromley by Bow. *Deceased* 1960. *Pro Career* 1901-1918 (99 contests, won 70, drew 4, lost 22, no decision 3).

Danny O'Sullivan British Bantamweight Champion, 1949-1951. *Born* 06.01.23. *From* Finsbury Park. *Deceased* 1990. *Pro Career* 1947-1951 (43 contests, won 33, drew 1, lost 9).

Johnny Owen Undefeated British Bantamweight Champion, 1977-1980. Undefeated Commonwealth Bantamweight Champion, 1978-1980. Undefeated European Bantamweight Champion, 1980. *Born* 07.01.56. *From* Merthyr. *Deceased* 1980. *Pro Career* 1976-1980 (28 contests, won 25, drew 1, lost 2).

Jack Palmer British Middleweight Champion, 1902-1903. British Heavyweight Champion, 1903-1906. *Born* 31.03.1878. *From* Newcastle. Birthname - Jack Liddell. *Deceased* 1928. *Pro Career* 1896-1916 (40 contests, won 26, drew 2, lost 12).

Pedlar Palmer British Bantamweight Champion, 1895-1900. World Bantamweight Champion, 1895-1899. World Bantamweight Championship Claimant, 1900. *Born* 19.01.1876. *From* Canning Town. Birthname - Tom Palmer. *Deceased* 1949. *Pro Career* 1891-1919 (64 contests, won 45, drew 4, lost 15).

Jackie Paterson British Flyweight Champion, 1939-1948. British Empire Flyweight Championship Claimant, 1940-1948. World Flyweight Champion, 1943-1947. World Flyweight Champion, 1947-1948 (GB/NY version). British Bantamweight Champion, 1947-1949. British Empire Bantamweight Championship Claimant, 1945-1949. European Bantamweight Champion, 1946. *Born* 05.09.20. *From* Springfield. *Deceased* 1966. *Pro Career* 1938-1950 (92 contests, won 64, drew 3, lost 25).

Alf Kid Pattenden British Bantamweight Champion, 1928-1929. *Born* 24.09.03. *From* Mile End. *Deceased* 1982. *Pro Career* 1926-1931 (66 contests, won 38, drew 4, lost 24).

Larry Paul British L. Middleweight Champion, 1973-1974. *Born* 19.04.52. *From* Wolverhampton. *Pro Career* 1973-1978 (40 contests, won 30, lost 9).

David Pearce Undefeated British Heavyweight Champion, 1983-1985. *Born* 08.05.59. *From* Newport. *Pro Career* 1978-1984 (21 contests, won 17, drew 1, lost 3).

Jack Petersen Undefeated British L. Heavyweight Champion, 1932. British Heavyweight Champion, 1932-1933 and 1934-1936. British Empire Heavyweight Championship Claimant, 1934-1936. *Born* 02.09.11. *From* Cardiff. *Deceased* 1990. *Pro Career* 1931-1937 (38 contests, won 33, lost 5).

Kostas Petrou British Welterweight Champion, 1985. *Born* 17.04.59. *From* Birmingham. *Pro Career* 1981-1988 (37 contests, won 30, lost 7).

Tiger Al Phillips European Featherweight Champion, 1947. British Empire Featherweight Championship Claimant, 1947. *Born* 25.01.20. *From* Aldgate. *Pro Career* 1938-1951 (89 contests, won 72, drew 3, lost 14).

Eddie Phillips British L. Heavyweight Champion, 1935-1937. *Born* 1909. *From* Bow. *Deceased* 1995. *Pro Career* 1928-1945 (57 contests, won 47, drew 4, lost 6).

Gus Platts British Middleweight Champion, 1921. European Middleweight Championship Claimant, 1921. *Born* 24.10.1891. *From* Sheffield. *Deceased* 1943. *Pro Career* 1910-1927 (132 contests, won 87, drew 8, lost 30, no decision 7).

Billy Plimmer British Bantamweight Champion, 1891-1895. World Bantamweight Champion, 1892-1895. British Bantamweight Championship Claimant, 1896-1898. *Born* 06.02.1869. *From* Birmingham. *Deceased* 1929. *Pro Career* 1888-1900 (46 contests, won 33, drew 5, lost 5, no decision 3).

Dennis Powell British L. Heavyweight Champion, 1953. *Born* 12.12.24. *From* Four Crosses. *Deceased* 1993. *Pro Career* 1947-1954 (68 contests, won 42, drew 4, lost 22).

Colin Power Undefeated British L. Welterweight Champion, 1977-1978. British L. Welterweight Champion, 1979. European L. Welterweight Champion, 1978. *Born* 02.02.56. *From* Paddington. *Pro Career* 1975-1983 (34 contests, won 28, drew 1, lost 5).

Kevin Pritchard British S. Featherweight Champion, 1990-1991. *Born* 26.09.61. *From* Liverpool. *Pro Career* 1981-1991 (48 contests, won 23, drew 3, lost 22).

Ted Pritchard British Middleweight Champion, 1890-1895. British Heavyweight Championship Claimant, 1891-1895. *Born* 1866. *From* Lambeth. *Deceased* 1903. *Pro Career* 1887-1895 (16 contests, won 11, drew 1, lost 3, no decision 1).

Johnny Pritchett Undefeated British Middleweight Champion, 1965-1969. Undefeated British Empire Middleweight Champion, 1967-1969. *Born* 15.02.43. *From* Bingham. *Pro Career* 1963-1969 (34 contests, won 32, drew 1, lost 1).

Des Rea British L. Welterweight Champion, 1968-1969. *Born* 09.01.44. *From* Belfast. *Pro Career* 1964-1974 (69 contests, won 28, drew 5, lost 36).

Billy Reader British Featherweight Champion, 1891-1892. *From* Fulham. *Deceased*. *Pro Career* 1887-1892 (12 contests, won 8, lost 4).

Mark Reefer Undefeated Commonwealth S. Featherweight Champion, 1989-1990. *Born* 16.03.64. Birthname - Mark Thompson. *From* Dagenham. *Pro Career* 1983-1992 (32 contests, won 23, drew 1, lost 8).

Sam Reeson Undefeated British Cruiserweight Champion, 1985-1986. Undefeated European Cruiserweight Champion, 1987-1988. *Born* 05.01.63. *From* Battersea. *Pro Career* 1983-1989 (26 contests, won 24, lost 2).

Harry Reeve Undefeated British L. Heavyweight Champion, 1916-1917. *Born* 07.01.1893. *From* Stepney. *Deceased* 1958. *Pro Career* 1910-1934 (154 contests, won 83, drew 20, lost 49, no decision 2).

Willie Reilly Undefeated British Lightweight Champion, 1972. *Born* 25.03.47. *From* Glasgow. *Pro Career* 1968-1972 (23 contests, won 13, drew 3, lost 7).

Jimmy Revie British Featherweight Champion, 1969-1971. *Born* 08.07.47. *From* Stockwell. *Pro Career* 1966-1976 (48 contests, won 38, drew 1, lost 9).

Henry Rhiney British Welterweight Champion, 1976-1979. European Welterweight Champion, 1978-1979. *Born* Jamaica, 28.11.51. *From* Luton. *Pro Career* 1973-1980 (57 contests, won 32, drew 6, lost 19).

Ernie Rice British and European Lightweight Champion, 1921-1922. *Born* 17.11.1896. *From* Hounslow. *Deceased* 1979. *Pro Career* 1912-1930 (78 contests, won 51, drew 2, lost 24, no decision 1).

Alan Richardson British Featherweight Champion, 1977-1978. *Born* 04.11.48. *From* Fitzwilliam. *Pro Career* 1971-1978 (27 contests, won 17, drew 1, lost 9).

Dick Richardson European Heavyweight Champion, 1960-1962. *Born* 01.06.34. *From* Newport. *Pro Career* 1954-1963 (47 contests, won 31, drew 2, lost 14).

Jack Roberts British Featherweight Champion, 1901-1902. *Born* 11.11.1873. *From* Covent Garden. *Deceased*. *Pro Career* 1891-1910 (90 contests, won 51, drew 3, lost 36).

Spike Robson British Featherweight Champion, 1906-1907. British Featherweight Championship Claimant, 1907-1910. *Born* 05.11.1877. *From*

South Shields. Birthname - Frank Robson. *Deceased* 1957. *Pro Career* 1896-1915 (77 contests, won 45, drew 3, lost 11, no decision 17, no contest 1).

Ernie Roderick British Welterweight Champion, 1939-1948. European Welterweight Champion, 1946-1947. British Middleweight Champion, 1945-1946. *Born* 25.01.14. *From* Liverpool. *Deceased* 1986. *Pro Career* 1931-1950 (142 contests, won 114, drew 4, lost 24).

Prince Rodney Undefeated British L. Middleweight Champion, 1983-1984. British L. Middleweight Champion, 1985-1986. *Born* 31.10.58. *From* Huddersfield. *Pro Career* 1977-1990 (41 contests, won 31, drew 1, lost 9).

Walter Ross Undefeated British Bantamweight Champion, 1919-1920. *Born* 03.07.1898. *From* Glasgow. *Deceased*. *Pro Career* 1915-1926 (62 contests, won 35, drew 6, lost 19, no decision 2).

Stan Rowan Undefeated British Bantamweight Champion, 1949. British Empire Bantamweight Championship Claimant, 1949. *Born* 06.09.24. *From* Liverpool. *Pro Career* 1942-1953 (67 contests, won 46, drew 5, lost 16).

Mark Rowe British and Commonwealth Middleweight Champion, 1970. *Born* 12.07.47. *Born* 12.07.47. *From* Camberwell. *Pro Career* 1966-1973 (47 contests, won 38, drew 1, lost 8).

Alan Rudkin British Bantamweight Champion, 1965-1966 and Undefeated British Bantamweight Champion, 1968-1972. British Empire Bantamweight Champion, 1965-1966 and 1968-1969. European Bantamweight Champion, 1971. Undefeated Commonwealth Bantamweight Champion, 1970-1972. *Born* 18.11.41. *From* Liverpool. *Pro Career* 1962-1972 (50 contests, won 42, lost 8).

Hugh Russell Undefeated British Flyweight Champion, 1984-1985. British Bantamweight Champion, 1983. *Born* 15.12.59. *From* Belfast. *Pro Career* 1981-1985 (19 contests, won 17, lost 2).

Jack Scales British Heavyweight Championship Claimant, 1901-1902. *Born* 20.09.1874. *From* Bethnal Green. *Deceased*. *Pro Career* 1898-1911 (77 contests, won 41, drew 5, lost 30, no decision 1).

Phil Scott Undefeated British Heavyweight Champion, 1926-1931. British Empire Heavyweight Championship Claimant, 1926-1931. *Born* 03.01.1900. *From* Marylebone. Birthname - Phil Suffling. *Deceased* 1983. *Pro Career* 1919-1931 (85 contests, won 65, drew 4, lost 14, no contest 2).

Tony Sibson British Middleweight Champion, 1979. Undefeated British Middleweight Champion, 1984 and 1987-1988. Undefeated Commonwealth Middleweight Champion, 1980-1983 and 1984-1988. Undefeated European Middleweight Champion, 1980-1982. European Middleweight Champion, 1984-1985. *Born* 09.04.58. *From* Leicester. *Pro Career* 1976-1988 (63 contests, won 55, drew 1, lost 7).

Steve Sims Undefeated British Featherweight Champion, 1982-1983. *Born* 10.10.58. *From* Newport. *Pro Career* 1977-1987 (29 contests, won 14, drew 1, lost 14).

Joey Singleton British L. Welterweight Champion, 1974-1976. *Born* 06.06.51. *From* Kirkby. *Pro Career* 1973-1982 (40 contests, won 27, drew 2, lost 11).

Kelvin Smart British Flyweight Champion, 1982-1984. *Born* 18.12.60. *From* Caerphilly. *Pro Career* 1979-1987 (29 contests, won 17, drew 2, lost 10).

Dick Smith British L. Heavyweight Champion, 1914-1916. Undefeated British L. Heavyweight Champion, 1918-1919. *Born* 10.02.1886. *From* Woolwich. *Deceased* 1950. *Pro Career* 1913-1924 (21 contests, won 7, drew 1, lost 13).

Jem Smith British Heavyweight Champion, 1895-1896. British Heavyweight Championship Claimant, 1889-1891. *Born* 21.01.1863. *From* Cripplegate. *Deceased* 1931. *Pro Career* 1885-1897 (11 contests, won 4, drew 3, lost 4).

Roy Smith British Cruiserweight Champion, 1987. *Born* 31.08.61. *From* Nottingham. *Pro Career* 1985-1991 (26 contests, won 18, lost 8).

Sid Smith British Flyweight Championship Claimant, 1911. British Flyweight Champion, 1911-1913. World Flyweight Champion, 1913 (GB/IBU version). European Flyweight Champion, 1913. *Born* 25.02.1889. *From* Bermondsey. *Deceased* 1948. *Pro Career* 1907-1919 (106 contests, won 82, drew 5, lost 18, no decision 1).

Willie Smith British Bantamweight Championship Claimant, 1892-1896. *Born* 1871. *From* Shoreditch. *Deceased*. *Pro Career* 1890-1901 (18 contests, won 10, lost 7, no decision 1).

Young Joey Smith European Featherweight Championship Claimant, 1911. *Born* 1894. *From* Mile End. *Deceased*. *Pro Career* 1909-1914 (24 contests, won 18, drew 3, lost 3).

Vernon Sollas British Featherweight Champion, 1975-1977. *Born* 14.08.54. *From* Edinburgh. *Pro Career* 1973-1977 (33 contests, won 25, drew 1, lost 7).

Terry Spinks British Featherweight Champion, 1960-1961. *Born* 28.02.38. *From* Canning Town. *Pro Career* 1957-1962 (49 contests, won 41, drew 1, lost 7).

Harry Spurden British Featherweight Champion, 1892-1895. *Born* 06.02.1869. *From* Cambridge. *Deceased*. *Pro Career* 1888-1901 (27 contests, won 19, drew 1, lost 7).

Digger Stanley British Bantamweight Championship Claimant, 1906-1910. British Bantamweight Champion, 1910-1913 and 1913-1914. European Bantamweight Championship Claimant, 1910-1912. World Bantamweight Champion, 1909-1912 (GB version). *Born* 28.02.1883. *From* Norwich. Birthname - George Stanley. *Deceased* 1919. *Pro Career* 1899-1918 (86 contests, won 56, drew 7, lost 21, no decision 2).

Bunny Sterling British Middleweight Champion, 1970-1974 and Undefeated British Middleweight Champion, 1975. Commonwealth Middleweight Champion, 1970-1972. European Middleweight Champion, 1976. *Born* Jamaica, 04.04.48. *From* Finsbury Park. *Pro Career* 1966-1977 (57 contests, won 35, drew 4, lost 18).

Sam Steward British Lightweight Champion, 1928-1929. *Born* 1905. *From* Lewisham. *Deceased*. *Pro Career* 1923-1936 (118 contests, won 80, drew 20, lost 18).

John H. Stracey Undefeated British Welterweight Champion, 1973-1975. Undefeated European Welterweight Champion, 1974-1975. World Welterweight Champion, 1975-1976 (WBC version). *Born* 22.09.50. *From* Bethnal Green. *Pro Career* 1969-1978 (51 contests, won 45, drew 1, lost 5).

Andy Straughn British Cruiserweight Champion, 1986-1987 and 1988-1989. *Born* Barbados, 25.12.59. *From* Hitchin. *Pro Career* 1982-1990 (27 contests, won 18, drew 2, lost 7).

Gary Stretch British L. Middleweight Champion, 1988-1990. *Born* 04.11.65. *From* St Helens. *Pro Career* 1985-1993 (25 contests, won 23, lost 2).

Jim Sullivan Undefeated British Middleweight Champion, 1910-1912. *Born* 07.06.1886. *From* Bermondsey. *Deceased* 1949. *Pro Career* 1904-1920 (83 contests, won 56, drew 5, lost 22).

Johnny Sullivan British Empire Middleweight Championship Claimant, 1954. British and British Empire Middleweight Champion, 1954-1955. *Born* 19.12.32. *From* Preston. Birthname - John Hallmark. *Pro Career* 1948-1960 (97 contests, won 68, drew 3, lost 26).

Johnny Summers British Featherweight Champion, 1906. British Lightweight Champion, 1908-1909. British Welterweight Championship Claimant, 1912. British Welterweight Champion, 1912-1914. British Empire Welterweight Championship Claimant, 1912-1914. *Born* 21.01.1883. *From* Middlesbrough. Birthname - Johnny Somers. *Deceased* 1946. *Pro Career* 1900-1920 (179 contests, won 104, drew 29, lost 32, no contest 1, no decision 13).

Wally Swift British Welterweight Champion, 1960. British Middleweight Champion, 1964-1965. *Born* 10.08.36. *From* Nottingham. *Pro Career* 1957-1969 (88 contests, won 68, drew 3, lost 17).

Wally Swift Jnr British L. Middleweight Champion, 1991-1992. *Born* 17.02.66. *From* Birmingham. *Pro Career* 1985-1994 (38 contests, won 26, drew 1, lost 11).

Joe Symonds British and European Flyweight Championship Claimant, 1914. British Flyweight Champion, 1915-1916. World Flyweight Champion, 1915-1916 (GB/IBU version). *Born* 28.12.1894. *From* Plymouth. Birthname - Hubert Toms. *Deceased* 1953. *Pro Career* 1911-1924 (136 contests, won 97, drew 11, lost 27, no decision 1).

Nel Tarleton British Featherweight Champion, 1931-1932 and 1934-1936. Undefeated British Featherweight Champion, 1940-1947. Undefeated British Empire Featherweight Championship Claimant, 1940-1947. *Born* 14.01.06. *From* Liverpool. *Deceased* 1956. *Pro Career* 1926-1945 (144 contests, won 116, drew 8, lost 20).

Wally Thom British Welterweight Champion, 1951-1952 and 1953-1956. British Empire Welterweight Championship Claimant, 1951-1952. European

Welterweight Champion, 1954-1955. *Born* 14.06.26. *From* Birkenhead. *Deceased* 1980. *Pro Career* 1949-1956 (54 contests, won 42, drew 1, lost 11).

Eddie Thomas British Welterweight Champion, 1949-1951. European Welterweight Champion, 1951. British Empire Welterweight Championship Claimant, 1951. *Born* 27.07.26. *From* Merthyr. *Pro Career* 1946-1954 (48 contests, won 40, drew 2, lost 6).

Pat Thomas British Welterweight Champion, 1975-1976. British L. Middleweight Champion, 1979-1981. *Born* St Kitts, 05.05.50. *From* Cardiff. *Pro Career* 1970-1984 (57 contests, won 35, drew 3, lost 18, no contest 1).

Tom Thomas British Middleweight Champion, 1906-1910. *Born* 19.04.1880. *From* Penygraig. *Deceased* 1911. *Pro Career* 1899-1911 (44 contests, won 41, lost 3).

Billy Thompson British Lightweight Champion, 1947-1951. European Lightweight Champion, 1948-1949. *Born* 20.12.25. *From* Hickleton Main. *Pro Career* 1945-1953 (63 contests, won 46, drew 4, lost 13).

Andrew Tokell British Bantamweight Championship Claimant, 1901-1902. British Bantamweight Champion, 1902. World Bantamweight Champion, 1902 (GB version). *Born* 01.03.1878. *From* Jarrow. *Deceased* 1915. *Pro Career* 1897-1908 (36 contests, won 27, lost 8, no contest 1).

Roland Todd British Middleweight Champion, 1923-1925. British Empire Middleweight Championship Claimant, 1923-1925. British Middleweight Championship Claimant, 1925-1927. European Middleweight Championship Claimant, 1923-1924. *Born* 09.01.1900. *From* Doncaster. *Deceased* 1969. *Pro Career* 1917-1929 (116 contests, won 81, drew 6, lost 27, no decision 2).

Dick Turpin British Middleweight Champion, 1948-1950. British Empire Middleweight Championship Claimant, 1948-1949. *Born* 26.11.20. *From* Leamington Spa. *Deceased* 1990. *Pro Career* 1937-1950 (103 contests, won 76, drew 6, lost 20, no contest 1).

Randy Turpin Undefeated British Middleweight Champion, 1950-1954. British Empire Middleweight Championship Claimant, 1952-1954. European Middleweight Champion, 1951-1954. World Middleweight Champion, 1951. World Middleweight Champion, 1953 (EBU version). Undefeated British L. Heavyweight Champion, 1952, 1955 and 1956-1958. British Empire L. Heavyweight Championship Claimant, 1952-1954. Undefeated British Empire L. Heavyweight Champion, 1954-1955. *Born* 07.06.28. *From* Leamington Spa. *Deceased* 1966. *Pro Career* 1946-1958 (73 contests, won 64, drew 1, lost 8).

Curley Walker Undefeated British Bantamweight Champion, 1914-1915. *Born* 04.02.1894. *From* Lambeth. Birthname - Con Walker. *Deceased* 1973. *Pro Career* 1909-1923 (117 contests, won 64, drew 11, lost 42).

Keith Wallace Undefeated Commonwealth Flyweight Champion, 1983-1984. *Born* 29.03.61. *From* Liverpool. *Pro Career* 1982-1990 (25 contests, won 20, lost 5).

Nunc Wallace Undefeated British Bantamweight Champion, 1889-1891. British Bantamweight Championship Claimant, 1893-1895. *From* Birmingham. Birthname - Edward Wallace. *Deceased*. *Pro Career* 1886-1895 (27 contests, won 18, lost 9).

Jimmy Walsh British Lightweight Champion, 1936-1938. *Born* 1913. *From* Chester. *Deceased* 1964. *Pro Career* 1931-1940 (89 contests, won 67, drew 2, lost 19, no contest 1).

Harry Ware British Bantamweight Championship Claimant, 1899-1900. British Bantamweight Champion, 1900-1902 and 1902. World Bantamweight Champion, 1900-1902 (GB version). *Born* 1875. *From* Mile End. *Deceased*. *Pro Career* 1895-1911 (59 contests, won 33, drew 8, lost 18).

Peter Waterman Undefeated British Welterweight Champion, 1956-1958. Undefeated European Welterweight Champion, 1958. *Born* 08.12.34. *From* Clapham. *Deceased* 1986. *Pro Career* 1952-1958 (46 contests, won 41, drew 2, lost 3).

Curly Watson British Welterweight Champion, 1906-1910. *Born* 05.10.1884. *From* Barrow. Birthname - Robert Watson. *Deceased* 1910. *Pro Career* 1902-1910 (78 contests, won 41, drew 6, lost 30, no contest 1).

Michael Watson Undefeated Commonwealth Middleweight Champion, 1989-1991. *Born* 15.03.65. *From* Islington. *Pro Career* 1984-1991 (30 contests, won 25, drew 1, lost 4).

Seaman Tommy Watson British Featherweight Champion, 1932-1934. *Born* 02.06.08. *From* Newcastle. *Deceased* 1971. *Pro Career* 1927-1935 (116 contests, won 106, drew 1, lost 9).

Jim Watt British Lightweight Champion, 1972-1973 and Undefeated British Lightweight Champion, 1975-1977. Undefeated European Lightweight Champion, 1977-1979. World Lightweight Champion, 1979-1981 (WBC version). *Born* 18.07.48. *From* Glasgow. *Pro Career* 1968-1981 (46 contests, won 38, lost 8).

Fred Webster British Lightweight Champion, 1929-1930. *Born* 18.06.08. *From* Kentish Town. *Deceased* 1971. *Pro Career* 1928-1934 (65 contests, won 46, drew 5, lost 14).

Bombardier Billy Wells British Heavyweight Champion, 1911-1919. British Empire Heavyweight Championship Claimant, 1911-1919. *Born* 31.08.1889. *From* Mile End. *Deceased* 1967. *Pro Career* 1909-1925 (59 contests, won 48, lost 11).

Matt Wells British Lightweight Champion, 1911-1912. European Lightweight Championship Claimant, 1911-1912. British Welterweight Champion, 1914. British Welterweight Championship Claimant, 1914-1919. British Empire Welterweight Championship Claimant, 1914-1919. World Welterweight Champion, 1914-1915 (Australian version). *Born* 14.12.1886. *From* Walworth. *Deceased* 1953. *Pro Career* 1909-1922 (86 contests, won 34, drew 3, lost 19, no decision 30).

Freddie Welsh British Lightweight Champion, 1909-1911. Undefeated British Lightweight Champion, 1912-1919. European Lightweight Championship Claimant, 1909-1911. Undefeated European Lightweight Champion, 1912-1914. British Empire Lightweight Championship Claimant, 1912-1914. World Lightweight Champion, 1912-1914 (GB version). World Lightweight Champion, 1914-1917. *Born* 05.03.1886. *From* Pontypridd. Birthname - Frederick Thomas. *Deceased* 1927. *Pro Career* 1905-1922 (168 contests, won 76, drew 7, lost 4, no decision 81).

Jabez White British Featherweight Championship Claimant, 1899-1900. British Lightweight Champion, 1902-1906. World Lightweight Championship Claimant, 1902-1905 (GB version). *Born* 20.10.1873. *From* Birmingham. *Deceased* 1966. *Pro Career* 1895-1913 (40 contests, won 31, drew 1, lost 7, no decision 1).

Ted White British Middleweight Championship Claimant, 1893-1895. Undefeated British Middleweight Champion, 1895-1896. *Born* 18.05.1867. *From* Charing Cross. *Deceased*. *Pro Career* 1888-1896 (28 contests, won 22, lost 6).

Jimmy Wilde British and European Flyweight Championship Claimant, 1914-1915. Undefeated British and European Flyweight Champion, 1916-1923. World Flyweight Champion, 1916 (GB/IBU version). World Flyweight Champion, 1916-1923. *Born* 15.05.1892. *From* Tylorstown. *Deceased* 1969. *Pro Career* 1910-1923 (153 contests, won 132, drew 2, lost 6, no decision 13).

Jim Williams British Bantamweight Championship Claimant, 1902. *Born* 01.08.1876. *From* Marylebone. *Deceased*. *Pro Career* 1892-1903 (45 contests, won 36, drew 1, lost 8).

Johnny Williams British Heavyweight Champion, 1952-1953. British Empire Heavyweight Championship Claimant, 1952-1953. *Born* 25.12.26. *From* Rugby. *Pro Career* 1946-1956 (75 contests, won 60, drew 4, lost 11).

Tony Willis British Lightweight Champion, 1985-1987. *Born* 17.06.60. *From* Liverpool. *Pro Career* 1981-1989 (29 contests, won 25, lost 4).

Nick Wilshire Commonwealth L. Middleweight Champion, 1985-1987. *Born* 03.11.61. *From* Bristol. *Pro Career* 1981-1987 (40 contests, won 36, lost 4).

Tony Wilson British L. Heavyweight Champion, 1987-1989. *Born* 25.04.64. *From* Wolverhampton. *Pro Career* 1985-1993 (29 contests, won 20, drew 1, lost 8).

Howard Winstone Undefeated British Featherweight Champion, 1961-1969. European Featherweight Champion, 1963-1967. World Featherweight Champion, 1968 (WBC version). *Born* 15.04.39. *From* Merthyr. *Pro Career* 1959-1968 (67 contests, won 61, lost 6).

Tim Wood British L. Heavyweight Champion, 1976-1977. *Born* 10.08.51. *From* Leicester. *Pro Career* 1972-1979 (31 contests, won 19, drew 1, lost 11).

Bruce Woodcock British Heavyweight Champion, 1945-1950. British Empire Heavyweight Championship Claimant, 1945-1950. European Heavyweight Champion, 1946-1949. *Born* 18.01.21. *From* Doncaster. *Pro Career* 1942-1950 (39 contests, won 35, lost 4).

Commonwealth Title Bouts During 1995-96

All of last season's title bouts are shown in date order and give the boxers' respective weights, along with the scorecard, if going to a decision. There is also a short summary of any bout that involved a British contestant and British officials, where applicable, are listed.

28 July 1995   Neil Swain 8.8¼ (Wales) W RSC 5 Tony Falcone 8.9¼ (England), Whitchurch Leisure Centre, Bristol (S. Bantamweight Title). Falcone, who was down for three counts, was finally rescued by John Coyle at 1.01 of the fifth. He had fought with great courage, but had lacked firepower and technique to turn things round.

10 September 1995   Leo Young 10.13 (Australia) L PTS 12 Kevin Kelly 11.0 (Australia), Adelaide, Australia (L. Middleweight Title). Scorecard: 111-119, 111-118, 114-114.

29 September 1995   Francis Wanyama 13.12¾ (Uganda) L RSC 8 Chris Okoh 13.6½ (England), York Hall, London (Cruiserweight Title). Having only his eighth contest, Okoh showed great maturity, dominating much of the action, and ultimately forcing referee Mickey Vann to stop the fight at 1.53 of the eighth, with Wanyama reeling defenceless against the ropes.

30 September 1995   Noel Magee 12.7 (Ireland) L CO 9 Nicky Piper 12.7 (Wales), The Rugby Ground, Cardiff (L. Heavyweight Title). After making a slow start, Piper began to find the range and a series of combination punches, culminating in a right hander, dropped Magee for Mickey Vann's full count at 1.29 of the ninth.

30 September 1995   Tony Pep 9.3¾ (Canada) L PTS 12 Justin Juuko 9.3¼ (Uganda), The Rugby Ground, Cardiff (S. Featherweight Title). Juuko proved what a good many people knew already – that he was world class. Certainly, he came of age in this one, his ability to dictate from the centre of the ring and added power well worth referee John Keane's 116½-118½ verdict.

27 October 1995   Scott Welch 16.5 (England) W RSC 10 James Oyebola 16.5 (England), Metropole Hotel, Brighton (Vacant Heavyweight Title). For a summary, see under British Title Bouts during 1995-96.

28 October 1995   Billy Schwer 9.8¼ (England) W CO 8 Ditau Molefyane 9.8¼ (South Africa), Albert Hall, London (Lightweight Title). Although the challenger was elusive, he lacked the power to embarrass Schwer, who bided his time and was especially effective with the jab and his work downstairs. It was a body punch that brought the contest to an end when Molefyane toppled through the ropes to be counted out by Larry O'Connell at 1.58 of the eighth.

28 October 1995   Ross Hale 10.0 (England) W CO 2 Charlie Kane 9.13¾ (Scotland), Whitchurch Leisure Centre, Bristol (L. Welterweight Title). For a summary, see under British Title bouts during 1995-96.

3 November 1995   Robert McCracken 11.5½ (England) W PTS 12 Fitzgerald Bruney 11.2½ (Canada), Town Hall, Dudley (Vacant Middleweight Title). Having moved up from light-middle, McCracken failed to impress against the clever Canadian and seemed less than good value for Roy Francis' 118½-116 decision in his favour. The title had been vacant since July, following Richie Woodhall being stripped for not defending within the prescribed period.

8 November 1995   Chris Okoh 13.6½ (England) W RSC 1 Paul Lawson 13.7 (England), York Hall, London (Cruiserweight Title). Paul Thomas called the fight off at 2.22 of the first, following four knockdowns. Okoh just had too much power for his rival, a man he had already beaten inside the distance, and the writing was on the wall within seconds of the start.

11 November 1995   Henry Wharton 12.0 (England) W CO 4 Sammy Storey 11.13¾ (Ireland), North Bridge Sports Centre, Halifax (S. Middleweight Title). Paul Thomas counted Storey out at 0.27 of the fourth, a left hook doing the damage. Leading up to the finish, the Irishman had boxed rather well, despite being badly hampered by a cut eye, but once Wharton had got to him there was no way back.

David Tetteh, the new Commonwealth lightweight champion   Les Clark

25 November 1995 Billy Schwer 9.8½ (England) L RSC 12 David Tetteh 9.8¾ (Ghana), Goresbrook Leisure Centre, Dagenham (Lightweight Title). Richie Davies stopped the fight at 1.04 of the final round with Schwer badly cut and under pressure, although trying to fight back. Most judges had the contest close, but Tetteh's power, despite an occasional lack of accuracy, made it difficult for the champion to find any real rhythm to his work.

9 December 1995 Ross Hale 10.0 (England) L CO 1 Paul Ryan 9.13½ (England), York Hall, London (L. Welterweight Title). For a summary, see under British Title Bouts during 1995-96.

16 December 1995 Kevin Kelly 10.13 (Australia) L PTS 12 Chris Pyatt 10.13½ (England), Welsh Institute of Sport, Cardiff (L. Middleweight Title). Viewed by many as being a bad decision, Kelly finished unmarked, while the challenger, who was quite marked up, appeared to have been outscored. However, the man whose opinion counted most, Dave Parris, scored it 118-116½ in Pyatt's favour.

26 January 1996 Justin Juuko 9.3 (Uganda) W RSC 7 Jackie Gunguluza 9.3¼ (South Africa), Metropole Hotel, Brighton (S. Featherweight Title). Dave Parris waved it off at 2.07 of the seventh, with Gunguluza having fallen through the ropes and appearing to have nothing left to offer. Competitive earlier on, ultimately Juuko's good jab, allied to power, settled it.

13 February 1996 Neil Swain 8.9½ (Wales) W PTS 12 Nathan Sting 8.8 (Australia), Welsh Institute of Sport, Cardiff (Vacant S. Bantamweight Title). Having lost to South African, Anton Gilmore, in a non-title contest on 4 November, with both men inside the championship weight, Swain forfeited his crown 20 days later. However, given the chance of reclaiming it in this one, referee John Coyle scored it 119½-115½ in his favour. The fight seemed a step up in class for Sting, who was dominated by both volume and quality, although not disgraced.

3 April 1996 Robert McCracken 11.6 (England) W RTD 7 Paul Busby 11.6 (England), York Hall, London (Middleweight Title). Under pressure and running out of steam fast in the seventh, Busby was pulled out by his corner at the completion of the round. It was no surprise as the challenger had been out-jabbed and out-thought from the start and had never been able to get into the fight.

25 June 1996 Danny Ward 7.12¾ (South Africa) L RSC 3 Peter Culshaw 7.12½ (England), Leisure Centre, Stevenage (Flyweight Title). One punch, a long right hand which put Ward down for six, did the damage, and when the South African got to his feet Culshaw was all over him, forcing Richie Davies to call a halt at 0.55 of the round.

Note: John Armour relinquished his bantamweight title in April, due to being indisposed, while Billy Hardy (feather) and Andrew Murray (welter) did not defend in 1995-96.

Robert McCracken (left) successfully defended his Commonwealth middleweight title against Paul Busby   Les Clark

Commonwealth Champions, 1908-1996

Over the years, record books, including this one, have continued to show Jim Driscoll's 15 round points win over the Australian, Charlie Griffin, at the NSC on 24 February 1908 for the featherweight title, as being the first recorded Empire title fight. I assume that was because for the first time a belt was authorised to be presented to the winner. However, there were many earlier fighters, such as the great Peter Jackson (Australia), who knocked out Frank Slavin in the tenth round at the NSC on 30 May 1892 in a contest billed for the British, Australian, Imperial (Empire) and world titles, along with men such as Jim Hall (Australia) and Dan Creedon (New Zealand), who should also be accorded similar status. Harold Alderman, the well-known boxing historian, and a specialist in the field of research covering the early period of gloved fighting onwards, is currently putting together a list of fights previously not seen in record books that carried Imperial title billing. Initially, it was expected to be ready in time for this edition, but work was held up and the deadline was missed. For the record, it was not until July 1954 that an exploratory meeting, held in London, led to a body being set up and named as the British Commonwealth and Empire Board, which was duly formed during its inaugural meeting at the BBBoC on 12 October 1954. At that meeting, Great Britain, South Africa, Trinidad, British Guyana, Canada, Nigeria, New Zealand and Australia, were all represented and a Championship Committee issued their list of champions, recognising Don Cockell (heavy), Randy Turpin (l. heavy), Johnny Sullivan (middle), Barry Brown (welter), Billy Spider Kelly (feather) and Jake Tuli (fly), with the light and bantamweight divisions seen as vacant. Earlier, pressure had been mounting because countries outside of Britain often felt that their best fighters were not getting a fair crack of the whip. Matters were finally brought to a head when Stadiums Ltd (Melbourne), who ran the sport in Australia, decided to support two of their own, Al Bourke (from 12 December 1952) and Pat Ford (from 28 August 1953 to 9 April 1954 and 2 July 1954). The situations were finally resolved when Bourke retired in December 1954 and Ford in June 1955. Known then as the British Empire title, it became the Commonwealth title in 1970.

COMMONWEALTH COUNTRY CODE

A = Australia; BAH = Bahamas; BAR = Barbados; BER = Bermuda; C = Canada; E = England; F = Fiji; GH = Ghana; GU = Guyana; I = Ireland; J = Jamaica; K = Kenya; N = Nigeria; NZ = New Zealand; NI = Northern Ireland; PNG = Papua New Guinea; SA = South Africa; SAM = Samoa; S = Scotland; T = Tonga; TR = Trinidad; U = Uganda; W = Wales; ZA = Zambia; ZI = Zimbabwe.

Champions in **bold** denote those recognised by the British Commonwealth and Empire Board (1954)

*Undefeated champions (Does not include men who forfeited titles)

Title Holder	Country	Tenure	Title Holder	Country	Tenure	Title Holder	Country	Tenure
Flyweight (112 lbs)			Johnny Brown	E	1923-1928	Johnny McGrory	S	1936-1938
Elky Clark	S	1924-1927	Teddy Baldock	E	1928-1930	Jim Spider Kelly	NI	1938-1939
Jackie Paterson	S	1940-1948	Dick Corbett	E	1930-1932	Johnny Cusick	E	1939-1940
Rinty Monaghan	NI	1948-1950	Johnny King	E	1932-1934	Nel Tarleton	E	1940-1947
Teddy Gardner	E	1952	Dick Corbett	E	1934	Tiger Al Phillips	E	1947
Jake Tuli	SA	1952-1954	Jim Brady	S	1941-1945	Ronnie Clayton	E	1947-1951
Jake Tuli	SA	1954	Jackie Paterson	S	1945-1949	Roy Ankrah	GH	1951-1954
Dai Dower*	W	1954-1957	Stan Rowan	E	1949	Billy Spider Kelly	NI	1954
Frankie Jones	S	1957	Vic Toweel	SA	1949-1952	**Billy Spider Kelly**	NI	1954-1955
Dennis Adams*	SA	1957-1962	Jimmy Carruthers	A	1952-1954	**Hogan Kid Bassey***	N	1955-1957
Jackie Brown	S	1962-1963	**Peter Keenan**	S	1955-1959	**Percy Lewis**	TR	1957-1960
Walter McGowan*	S	1963-1969	**Freddie Gilroy***	NI	1959-1963	**Floyd Robertson**	GH	1960-1967
John McCluskey	S	1970-1971	**Johnny Caldwell**	NI	1964-1965	**John O'Brien**	S	1967
Henry Nissen	A	1971-1974	**Alan Rudkin**	E	1965-1966	**Johnny Famechon***	A	1967-1969
Big Jim West*	A	1974-1975	**Walter McGowan**	S	1966-1968	**Toro George**	NZ	1970-1972
Patrick Mambwe	ZA	1976-1979	**Alan Rudkin**	E	1968-1969	**Bobby Dunne**	A	1972-1974
Ray Amoo	N	1980	**Lionel Rose***	A	1969	**Evan Armstrong**	S	1974
Steve Muchoki	K	1980-1983	**Alan Rudkin***	E	1970-1972	**David Kotey***	GH	1974-1975
Keith Wallace*	E	1983-1984	**Paul Ferreri**	A	1972-1977	**Eddie Ndukwu**	N	1977-1980
Richard Clarke	J	1986-1987	**Sulley Shittu**	GH	1977-1978	**Pat Ford***	GU	1980-1981
Nana Yaw Konadu*	GH	1987-1989	**Johnny Owen***	W	1978-1980	**Azumah Nelson***	GH	1981-1985
Alfred Kotey*	GH	1989-1993	**Paul Ferreri**	A	1981-1986	**Tyrone Downes**	BAR	1986-1988
Francis Ampofo*	E	1993	**Ray Minus***	BAH	1986-1991	**Thunder Aryeh**	GH	1988-1989
Daren Fifield	E	1993-1994	**John Armour***	E	1992-1996	**Oblitey Commey**	GH	1989-1990
Francis Ampofo	E	1994-1995				**Modest Napunyi**	K	1990-1991
Danny Ward	SA	1995-1996	**S. Bantamweight (122 lbs)**			**Barrington Francis***	C	1991
Peter Culshaw	E	1996-	**Neil Swain**	W	1995	**Colin McMillan***	E	1992
			Neil Swain	W	1996-	**Billy Hardy**	E	1992-
Bantamweight (118 lbs)								
Jim Higgins	S	1920-1922	**Featherweight (126 lbs)**			**S. Featherweight (130 lbs)**		
Tommy Harrison	E	1922-1923	Jim Driscoll	W	1908-1913	**Billy Moeller**	A	1975-1977
Bugler Harry Lake	E	1923	Llew Edwards	W	1915-1917	**Johnny Aba***	PNG	1977-1982

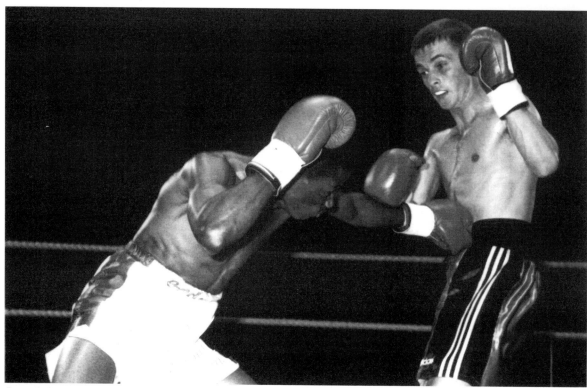

Peter Culshaw (right) surprised many by the manner of his shock Commonwealth flyweight title win over Danny Ward

Les Clark

Title Holder	Country	Tenure
Langton Tinago	ZI	1983-1984
John Sichula	ZA	1984
Lester Ellis*	A	1984-1985
John Sichula	ZA	1985-1986
Sam Akromah	GH	1986-1987
John Sichula	ZA	1987-1989
Mark Reefer*	E	1989-1990
Thunder Aryeh	GH	1990-1991
Hugh Forde	E	1991
Paul Harvey	E	1991-1992
Tony Pep	C	1992-1995
Justin Juuko	U	1995-

Lightweight (135 lbs)

Title Holder	Country	Tenure
Freddie Welsh	W	1912-1914
Al Foreman	E	1930-1933
Jimmy Kelso	A	1933
Al Foreman	E	1933-1934
Laurie Stevens	SA	1936
Arthur King	C	1948-1951
Frank Johnson	E	1953
Pat Ford	A	1953-1954
Ivor Germain	BAR	1954
Pat Ford	A	1954-1955
Johnny van Rensburg	SA	1955-1956
Willie Toweel	SA	1956-1959
Dave Charnley	E	1959-1962
Bunny Grant	J	1962-1967
Manny Santos*	NZ	1967
Love Allotey	GH	1967-1968
Percy Hayles	J	1968-1975
Jonathan Dele	N	1975-1977

Title Holder	Country	Tenure
Lennox Blackmore	GU	1977-1978
Hogan Jimoh	N	1978-1980
Langton Tinago	ZI	1980-1981
Barry Michael	A	1981-1982
Claude Noel	T	1982-1984
Graeme Brooke	A	1984-1985
Barry Michael*	A	1985-1986
Langton Tinago	ZI	1986-1987
Mo Hussein	E	1987-1989
Pat Doherty	E	1989
Najib Daho	E	1989-1990
Carl Crook	E	1990-1992
Billy Schwer	E	1992-1993
Paul Burke	E	1993
Billy Schwer	E	1993-1995
David Tetteh	GH	1995-

L. Welterweight (140 lbs)

Title Holder	Country	Tenure
Joe Tetteh	GH	1972-1973
Hector Thompson	A	1973-1977
Baby Cassius Austin	A	1977-1978
Jeff Malcolm	A	1978-1979
Obisia Nwankpa	N	1979-1983
Billy Famous	N	1983-1986
Tony Laing	E	1987-1988
Lester Ellis	A	1988-1989
Steve Larrimore	BAH	1989
Tony Ekubia	E	1989-1991
Andy Holligan	E	1991-1994
Ross Hale	E	1994-1995
Paul Ryan	E	1995-

Welterweight (147 lbs)

Title Holder	Country	Tenure
Johnny Summers	E	1912-1914
Tom McCormick	I	1914
Matt Wells	E	1914-1919
Johnny Basham	W	1919-1920
Ted Kid Lewis	E	1920-1924
Tommy Milligan	S	1924-1925
Eddie Thomas	W	1951
Wally Thom	E	1951-1952
Cliff Curvis	W	1952
Gerald Dreyer	SA	1952-1954
Barry Brown	NZ	1954
Barry Brown	NZ	1954
George Barnes	A	1954-1956
Darby Brown	A	1956
George Barnes	A	1956-1958
Johnny van Rensburg	SA	1958
George Barnes	A	1958-1960
Brian Curvis*	W	1960-1966
Johnny Cooke	E	1967-1968
Ralph Charles*	E	1968-1972
Clyde Gray	C	1973-1979
Chris Clarke	C	1979
Clyde Gray*	C	1979-1980
Colin Jones*	W	1981-1984
Sylvester Mittee	E	1984-1985
Lloyd Honeyghan*	E	1985-1986
Brian Janssen	A	1987
Wilf Gentzen	A	1987-1988
Gary Jacobs	S	1988-1989
Donovan Boucher	C	1989-1992
Eamonn Loughran*	NI	1992-1993
Andrew Murray	GU	1993-

L. Middleweight (154 lbs)

Charkey Ramon*	A	1972-1975
Maurice Hope*	E	1976-1979
Kenny Bristol	GU	1979-1981
Herol Graham*	E	1981-1984
Ken Salisbury	A	1984-1985
Nick Wilshire	E	1985-1987
Lloyd Hibbert	E	1987
Troy Waters*	A	1987-1991
Chris Pyatt*	E	1991-1992
Mickey Hughes	E	1992-1993
Lloyd Honeyghan	E	1993-1994
Leo Young	A	1994-1995
Kevin Kelly	A	1995
Chris Pyatt	E	1995-

Middleweight (160 lbs)

Ted Kid Lewis	E	1922-1923
Roland Todd	E	1923-1925
Len Johnson	E	1926
Tommy Milligan	S	1926-1928
Alex Ireland	S	1928-1929
Len Harvey	E	1929-1933
Jock McAvoy	E	1933-1939
Ron Richards	A	1940-1941
Bos Murphy	NZ	1948
Dick Turpin	E	1948-1949
Dave Sands	A	1949-1952
Randy Turpin	E	1952-1954
Al Bourke	A	1952-1954
Johnny Sullivan	E	1954
Johnny Sullivan	E	1954-1955
Pat McAteer	E	1955-1958
Dick Tiger	N	1958-1960
Wilf Greaves	C	1960
Dick Tiger*	N	1960-1962
Gomeo Brennan	BAH	1963-1964
Tuna Scanlon*	NZ	1964
Gomeo Brennan	BAH	1964-1966
Blair Richardson*	C	1966-1967
Milo Calhoun	J	1967
Johnny Pritchett*	E	1967-1969
Les McAteer	E	1969-1970
Mark Rowe	E	1970
Bunny Sterling	E	1970-1972
Tony Mundine*	A	1972-1975
Monty Betham	NZ	1975-1978
Al Korovou	A	1978
Ayub Kalule	U	1978-1980
Tony Sibson*	E	1980-1983
Roy Gumbs	E	1983
Mark Kaylor	E	1983-1984
Tony Sibson*	E	1984-1988
Nigel Benn	E	1988-1989
Michael Watson*	E	1989-1991
Richie Woodhall	E	1992-1995
Robert McCracken	E	1995-

S. Middleweight (168 lbs)

Rod Carr	A	1989-1990
Lou Cafaro	A	1990-1991
Henry Wharton	E	1991-

L. Heavyweight (175 lbs)

Jack Bloomfield	E	1923-1924
Tom Berry	E	1927
Gipsy Daniels	W	1927
Len Harvey	E	1939-1942
Freddie Mills	E	1942-1950
Randy Turpin	E	1952-1954
Randy Turpin*	E	1952-1955

Gordon Wallace	C	1956-1957
Yvon Durelle*	C	1957-1959
Chic Calderwood	S	1960-1963
Bob Dunlop*	A	1968-1970
Eddie Avoth	W	1970-1971
Chris Finnegan	E	1971-1973
John Conteh*	E	1973-1974
Steve Aczel	A	1975
Tony Mundine	A	1975-1978
Gary Summerhays	C	1978-1979
Lottie Mwale	ZA	1979-1985
Leslie Stewart*	TR	1985-1987
Willie Featherstone	C	1987-1989
Guy Waters*	A	1989-1993
Brent Kosolofski	C	1993-1994
Garry Delaney	E	1994-1995
Noel Magee	I	1995
Nicky Piper	W	1995-

Cruiserweight (190 lbs)

Stewart Lithgo	E	1984
Chisanda Mutti	ZA	1984-1987
Glenn McCrory*	E	1987-1989
Apollo Sweet	A	1989
Derek Angol*	E	1989-1993
Francis Wanyama	U	1994-1995
Chris Okoh	E	1995-

Heavyweight (190 lbs +)

Tommy Burns	C	1910
P.O. Curran	I	1911
Dan Flynn	I	1911

Bombardier Billy Wells	E	1911-1919
Joe Beckett	E	1919-1923
Phil Scott	E	1926-1931
Larry Gains	C	1931-1934
Len Harvey	E	1934
Jack Petersen	W	1934-1936
Ben Foord	SA	1936-1937
Tommy Farr	W	1937-1938
Len Harvey	E	1939-1942
Jack London	E	1944-1945
Bruce Woodcock	E	1945-1950
Jack Gardner	E	1950-1952
Johnny Williams	W	1952-1953
Don Cockell	E	1953-1954
Don Cockell*	E	1954-1956
Joe Bygraves	J	1956-1957
Joe Erskine	W	1957-1958
Brian London	E	1958-1959
Henry Cooper	E	1959-1971
Joe Bugner	E	1971
Jack Bodell	E	1971-1972
Danny McAlinden	NI	1972-1975
Bunny Johnson	E	1975
Richard Dunn	E	1975-1976
Joe Bugner*	E	1976-1977
John L. Gardner*	E	1978-1981
Trevor Berbick	C	1981-1986
Horace Notice*	E	1986-1988
Derek Williams	E	1988-1992
Lennox Lewis*	E	1992-1993
Henry Akinwande	E	1993-1995
Scott Welch	E	1995-

Scott Welch won the vacant Commonwealth heavyweight title when stopping James Oyebola in the tenth round

Les Clark

BRITANNIA BOXING EQUIPMENT (PRESTON) LTD

UNIT 4, THORN BUILDING, KENT STREET, PRESTON, LANCASHIRE, PR1 1PJ

SUPPLIERS OF TOP QUALITY BOXING EQUIPMENT THROUGHOUT THE WORLD

DISTRIBUTORS OF REYES BOXING EQUIPMENT

APPROVED BY THE INTERNATIONAL AMATEUR BOXING ASSOCIATION

OFFICIAL SUPPLIERS TO THE BRITISH BOXING BOARD OF CONTROL

FOR A FULL RANGE OF BOXING EQUIPMENT PLEASE CONTACT
TELESALES:- 01772 201711
or FAX: 01772 201770

European Title Bouts During 1995-96

All of last season's title bouts are shown in date order and give the boxers' respective weights, along with the scorecard, if going to a decision. There is also a short summary of any bout that involved a British contestant and British officials, where applicable, are listed.

4 July 1995   Jacobin Yoma 9.2½ (France) L PTS 12 Anatoly Alexandrov 9.3½ (Kazakhstan), Thiais, France (S. Featherweight Title). Scorecards: 114-117, 113-117, 111-118.

8 July 1995   Henry Wharton 12.0 (England) W CO 4 Mauro Galvano 11.12¾ (Italy), Barbican Centre, York (Vacant S. Middleweight Title). Wharton made a fine start in his attempt to land the title that had been vacated by Frederic Seillier the previous April, and soon found the range. Although the Italian boxed competently, it counted for nothing once Wharton had landed his pet left hook, Galvano being counted out amidst a deafening din.

18 July 1995   Valery Kayumba 10.5½ (France) L PTS 12 Patrick Charpentier 10.5¾ (France), Val Thorens, France (Welterweight Title). Scorecards: 113-115, 112-117, 115-115.

18 July 1995   Angel Mona 9.8¾ (France) W RSC 5 Andrej Sinepupov 9.8¼ (Ukraine), Val Thorens, France (Vacant Lightweight Title). Jean-Baptiste Mendy had vacated the title on 31 May 1995 to prepare for a world title fight.

18 July 1995   Khalid Rahilou 9.13½ (France) W PTS 12 Pasquale Perna 9.13 (Italy), Val Thorens, France (L. Welterweight Title). Scorecards: Dave Parris (referee) 119-109, 118-111, 118-111.

18 July 1995   Patrice Aouissi 13.6 (France) W PTS 12 Valery Vikhor 13.0 (Ukraine), Val Thorens, France (Cruiserweight Title). Scorecards: 115-114, 115-112, Dave Parris 113-114.

19 July 1995   Vincenzo Belcastro 8.10 (Italy) W PTS 12 Bagdad Touama 8.9¾ (France), San Remo, Italy (S. Bantamweight Title). Scorecards: 119-107, Paul Thomas 118-108, 118-108.

8 September 1995   Khalid Rahilou 9.13 (France) W RTD 9 Soren Sondergaard 9.13¼ (Denmark), Aalborg, Denmark (L. Welterweight Title). John Keane was one of the judges. Rahilou relinquished title the following January to concentrate on a world title challenge.

15 September 1995   Luigi Camputaro 7.13½ (Italy) W PTS 12 Salvatore Fanni 7.13¼ (Italy), Naples, Italy (Vacant Flyweight Title). Scorecards: 115-113, 115-114, 115-115. This was the couples second attempt to sort the title out after Robbie Regan relinquished the belt in May. Camputaro himself vacated in March with a world title challenge in mind.

2 October 1995   Eddy Smulders 12.4¾ (Holland) W RSC 4 Jan Lefeber 12.4¾ (Holland), Rotterdam, Holland (L. Heavyweight Title).

9 October 1995   Vincenzo Belcastro 8.9¾ (Italy) W PTS 12 Richie Wenton 8.9½ (England), San Benedetto del Tronto, Italy (S. Bantamweight Title). Scorecards: 115-114, 116-111, 116-112. It was never going to be easy for Wenton, especially as he lacked the power at this level to do real damage, but to his credit he was always in the fight, despite being docked a point and continually niggled by an over-officious referee. That, plus Belcastro's aggression and workrate, ultimately proved too much.

24 October 1995   Patrice Aouissi 13.5 (France) L RTD 5 Alexander Gurov 13.5 (Ukraine), Levallois-Perret, France (Cruiserweight Title). Roy Francis acted as referee, while Larry O'Connell was one of the judges. Gurov relinquished the title in February with a world title fight in prospect.

25 October 1995   Richie Woodhall 11.5½ (England) W PTS 12 Zdravko Kostic 11.4 (Slovenia), the Ice Rink, Telford (Middleweight Title). Scorecards: 119-110, 119-111, 117-112. Although scoring a comprehensive points victory, Woodhall could not halt the teak-tough challenger, who took everything thrown at him to come back for more. Kostic finished badly marked up but still looking to get his punches in.

28 October 1995   Mehdi Labdouni 8.13½ (France) L PTS 12 Billy Hardy 8.13½ (England), Fontenay sous Bois, France (Featherweight Title). Scorecards: 113-117, 113-117, 112-116. In what was probably Hardy's finest hour, he outboxed and outpunched a champion who had an unbeaten run of 18 and was fighting on home territory. Labdouni hit the deck four times, and although up without a count on each occasion, he lacked the armoury to change the course of the fight.

28 October 1995   Angel Mona 9.9 (France) W PTS 12 Oscar Palomino 9.9 (Spain), Perpignon, France (Lightweight Title). Scorecards: 119-111, 116-112, 115-114.

11 November 1995   Henry Wharton 12.0 (England) W CO 4 Sammy Storey 11.13¾ (Ireland), North Bridge Sports Centre, Halifax (S. Middleweight Title). The officials were Paul Thomas (referee) and Mickey Vann, Richie Davies and John Coyle (judges). For a summary, see under Commonwealth Title Bouts during 1995-96.

25 November 1995   Patrick Charpentier 10.7 (France) W RSC 1 Javier Martinez 10.5½ (Spain), Orleans, France (Welterweight Title).

29 November 1995 John Armour 8.6 (England) W CO 5 Redha Jean Abbas 8.5½ (France), York Hall, London (Bantamweight Title). What on paper seemed to be an easy defence became hard work as the champion plodded after his rival, often unable to avoid the oncoming punches. However, it all came right in the end, Abbas being counted out at 2.58 of the fifth, a solid left to the chest doing the trick. Armour relinquished the title the following April.

9 December 1995 Zeljko Mavrovic 15.8¾ (Croatia) W CO 1 Przemyslaw Saleta 16.4½ (Poland), Stuttgart, Germany (Heavyweight Title). John Keane was one of the judges.

6 January 1996 Laurent Boudouani 10.12¾ (France) W PTS 12 Javier Castillejos 10.13½ (Spain), Levallois-Perret, France (L. Middleweight Title). Scorecards: John Keane 120-107, 120-107, 120-105.

13 January 1996 Henry Wharton 12.0 (England) W RSC 6 Vincenzo Nardiello 11.12¾ (Italy), North Bridge Leisure Centre, Halifax (S. Middleweight Title). Knocked down for the first time in his career, Wharton fought back to force a stoppage at 0.52 of the sixth, due to Nardiello being badly cut. Until Wharton found the range for his punches, he had fallen incredibly short of championship class, but once again his power cancelled out his limitations. Wharton relinquished title in March to concentrate on a world title challenge.

20 January 1996 Eddy Smulders 12.7 (Holland) W RTD 2 Andrea Magi 12.6½ (Italy), Marsala, Italy (L. Heavyweight Title). Mickey Vann refereed.

31 January 1996 Richie Woodhall 11.3¾ (England) W RSC 10 Derek Wormald 11.5¾ (England), Aston Villa Leisure Centre, Birmingham (Middleweight Title). Decked for the fifth time, with all resistence evaporated, Larry O'Connell rescued the brave Wormald at 2.10 of the tenth. Prior to the finish, the gutsy challenger had made it difficult for the first seven rounds, but once Woodhall had imposed his authority the end was always in sight. Roy Francis, Mickey Vann and John Coyle acted as judges. Woodhall relinquished the crown in March to concentrate on a world title shot.

3 February 1996 Anatoly Alexandrov 9.3¼ (Kazakhstan) W PTS 12 Djamel Lifa 9.3 (France), Levallois-Perret, France (S. Featherweight Title). Scorecards: 117-112, 117-113, 115-114.

14 February 1996 Billy Hardy 8.13¾ (England) W PTS 12 Michael Alldis 8.13½ (England), Crowtree Leisure Centre, Sunderland (Featherweight Title). Referee: John Keane. Scorecards: Dave Parris 120-108, Paul Thomas 117-113, Richie Davies 117-113. Keeping Hardy at distance was the challenger's game plan and that he did well. However, winning championships are all about imposing a presence and although Alldis boxed well from the perimeter he was never close enough to Hardy to do any real damage, hence the scorelines.

16 March 1996 Vincenzo Belcastro 8.9¾ (Italy) DREW 12 Serge Poilblan 8.9 (France), Cagliari, Italy (S. Bantamweight Title). Scorecards: 116-114, 114-115, 115-115.

23 March 1996 Anatoly Alexandrov 9.3½ (Kazakhstan) W PTS 12 Didier Scheaffer 9.2½ (France), Grande Synthe, France (S. Featherweight Title). Scorecards: 120-106, 119-110, 118-107. Paul Thomas refereed.

20 April 1996 Zeljko Mavrovic 15.10½ (Croatia) W PTS 12 Christophe Bizot 17.0 (France), Dusseldorf, Germany (Heavyweight Title). Scorecards: Dave Parris 120-107, 120-107, 118-110.

26 April 1996 Soren Sondergaard 9.13¼ (Denmark) W PTS 12 Michele Piccirillo 9.13¾ (Italy), Aalborg, Denmark (Vacant L. Welterweight Title). Scorecards: 118-110, 119-112, 119-110. Paul Thomas refereed.

27 April 1996 Angel Mona 9.8¾ (France) W RSC 6 Oscar Palomino 9.9 (Spain), Antibes, France (Lightweight Title).

25 May 1996 Akim Tafer 13.6½ (France) W RSC 4 Alexei Illin 13.7 (Russia), St Petersburg, Russia (Vacant Cruiserweight Title).

31 May 1996 Johnny Bredahl 8.6 (Denmark) W PTS 12 Alexander Yagupov 8.3 (Russia), Copenhagen, Denmark (Vacant Bantamweight Title). Scorecards: 118-111, 118-110, 119-111. John Keane refereed.

31 May 1996 Jesper Jensen 8.0 (Denmark) W PTS 12 Salvatore Fanni 7.11 (Italy), Copenhagen, Denmark (Vacant Flyweight Title). Scorecards: John Keane 118-112, 118-112, 118-111.

3 June 1996 Eddy Smulders 12.6¾ (Holland) W RSC 2 Dirk Wallyn 12.3 (Belgium), Eindhoven, Holland (L. Heavyweight Title).

14 June 1996 Patrick Charpentier 10.6¼ (France) W RSC 7 Gary Jacobs 10.6 (Scotland), Gravelines, France (Welterweight Title). Cut, and well on the way to defeat, Charpentier pulled the fight round in the seventh when flooring the challenger for three counts before the referee called a halt to the proceedings. Once hurt, Jacobs appeared to freeze and following the fight he admitted that his welterweight days were over, although he might continue in a higher division.

20 June 1996 Billy Hardy 8.13 (England) W PTS 12 Stefano Zoff 8.11½ (Italy), San Remo, Italy (Featherweight Title). Scorecards: 116-113, 117-112, 116-112. Having made a good start, Hardy was only occasionally called upon to dig in deep in order to retain his title, his body punching giving him a commanding position. From a challenger's perspective, the light-punching Zoff was unable to exert any real influence to change the tide, despite a strong finish.

29 June 1996 Alexandre Zaitsev 11.4½ (Russia) W CO 10 Agostino Cardamone 11.5½ (Italy), Sassari, Italy (Vacant Middleweight Title).

European Champions, 1909-1996

Prior to 1946, the championship was contested under the auspices of the International Boxing Union, re-named that year as the European Boxing Union (EBU). The IBU had come into being when Victor Breyer, a Paris-based journalist and boxing referee who later edited the Annuaire du Ring (first edition in 1910), warmed to the idea of an organisation that controlled boxing right across Europe, regarding rules and championship fights between the champions of the respective countries. He first came to London at the end of 1909 to discuss the subject with the NSC, but went away disappointed. However, at a meeting between officials from Switzerland and France in March 1912, the IBU was initially formed and, by June of that year, had published their first ratings. By April 1914, Belgium had also joined the organisation, although it would not be until the war was over that the IBU really took off. Many of the early champions shown on the listings were the result of promoters, especially the NSC, billing their own championship fights. Although the (French dominated) IBU recognised certain champions, prior to being re-formed in May 1920, they did not find their administrative "feet" fully until other countries such as Italy (1922), Holland (1923), and Spain (1924), produced challengers for titles. Later in the 1920s, Germany (1926), Denmark (1928), Portugal (1929) and Romania (1929) also joined the fold. Unfortunately, for Britain, its representatives (Although the BBBoC, as we know it today, was formed in 1929, an earlier attempt to form a Board of Control had been initiated in April 1918 by the NSC and it was that body who were involved here) failed to reach agreement on the three judges' ruling, following several meetings with the IBU early in 1920 and, apart from Elky Clark (fly), Ernie Rice and Alf Howard (light), and Jack Hood (welter), who conformed to that stipulation, fighters from these shores would not be officially recognised as champions until the EBU was formed in 1946. This led to British fighters claiming the title after beating IBU titleholders, or their successors, under championship conditions in this country. The only men who did not come into this category were Kid Nicholson (bantam), and Ted Kid Lewis and Tommy Milligan (welter), who defeated men not recognised by the IBU. For the record, the first men recognised and authorised, respectively, as being champions of their weight classes by the IBU were: Sid Smith and Michel Montreuil (fly), Charles Ledoux (bantam), Jim Driscoll and Louis de Ponthieu (feather), Freddie Welsh and Georges Papin (light), Georges Carpentier and Albert Badoud (welter), Georges Carpentier and Ercole Balzac (middle), Georges Carpentier and Battling Siki (light-heavy and heavy).

EUROPEAN COUNTRY CODE
AU = Austria; BEL = Belgium; CRO = Croatia; CZ = Czechoslovakia; DEN = Denmark; E = England; FIN = Finland; FR = France; GER = Germany; GRE = Greece; HOL = Holland; HUN = Hungary; ITA = Italy; KAZ = Kazakhstan; LUX = Luxembourg; NI = Northern Ireland; NOR = Norway; POR = Portugal; ROM = Romania; RUS = Russia; S = Scotland; SP = Spain; SWE = Sweden; SWI = Switzerland; TU = Turkey; UK = Ukraine; W = Wales; YUG = Yugoslavia.

Champions in **bold** denote those recognised by the IBU/EBU

*Undefeated champions (Does not include men who may have forfeited titles)

Title Holder	Country	Tenure	Title Holder	Country	Tenure	Title Holder	Country	Tenure
Flyweight (112 lbs)			Teddy Gardner*	E	1952	Digger Stanley	E	1910-1912
Sid Smith	E	1913	Louis Skena*	FR	1953-1954	**Charles Ledoux**	FR	1912-1921
Bill Ladbury	E	1913-1914	Nazzareno Giannelli	ITA	1954-1955	Bill Beynon	W	1913
Percy Jones	W	1914	**Dai Dower**	W	1955	Tommy Harrison	E	1921-1922
Joe Symonds	E	1914	**Young Martin**	SP	1955-1959	**Charles Ledoux**	FR	1922-1923
Tancy Lee	S	1914-1916	Risto Luukkonen	FIN	1959-1961	Bugler Harry Lake	E	1923
Jimmy Wilde	W	1914-1915	Salvatore Burruni*	ITA	1961-1965	Johnny Brown	E	1923-1928
Jimmy Wilde*	W	1916-1923	**Rene Libeer**	FR	1965-1966	**Henry Scillie***	BEL	1925-1928
Michel Montreuil	BEL	1923-1925	Fernando Atzori	ITA	1967-1972	Kid Nicholson	E	1928
Elky Clark	S	1925-1927	Fritz Chervet	SWI	1972-1973	Teddy Baldock	E	1928-1931
Victor Ferrand	SP	1927	Fernando Atzori	ITA	1973	**Domenico Bernasconi**	ITA	1929
Emile Pladner	FR	1928-1929	Fritz Chervet*	SWI	1973-1974	**Carlos Flix**	SP	1929-1931
Johnny Hill	S	1928-1929	Franco Udella	ITA	1974-1979	**Lucien Popescu**	ROM	1931-1932
Eugene Huat	FR	1929	Charlie Magri*	E	1979-1983	**Domenico Bernasconi**	ITA	1932
Emile Degand	BEL	1929-1930	Antoine Montero	FR	1983-1984	**Nicholas Biquet**	BEL	1932-1935
Kid Oliva	FR	1930	Charlie Magri*	E	1984-1985	**Maurice Dubois**	SWI	1935-1936
Lucien Popescu	ROM	1930-1931	Franco Cherchi	ITA	1985	**Joseph Decico**	FR	1936
Jackie Brown	E	1931-1935	Charlie Magri	E	1985-1986	**Aurel Toma**	ROM	1936-1937
Praxile Gyde	FR	1932-1935	Duke McKenzie*	E	1986-1988	**Nicholas Biquet**	BEL	1937-1938
Benny Lynch	S	1935-1938	Eyup Can*	TU	1989-1990	**Aurel Toma**	ROM	1938-1939
Kid David*	BEL	1935-1936	Pat Clinton*	S	1990-1991	**Ernst Weiss**	AU	1939
Ernst Weiss	AU	1936	Salvatore Fanni	ITA	1991-1992	**Gino Cattaneo**	ITA	1939-1941
Valentin Angelmann*	FR	1936-1938	Robbie Regan*	W	1992-1993	**Gino Bondavilli***	ITA	1941-1943
Enrico Urbinati*	ITA	1938-1943	Luigi Camputaro	ITA	1993-1994	Jackie Paterson	S	1946
Raoul Degryse	BEL	1946-1947	Robbie Regan*	W	1994-1995	Theo Medina	FR	1946-1947
Maurice Sandeyron	FR	1947-1949	Luigi Camputaro*	ITA	1995-1996	Peter Kane	E	1947-1948
Rinty Monaghan*	NI	1949-1950	Jesper Jensen	DEN	1996-	Guido Ferracin	ITA	1948-1949
Terry Allen	E	1950				Luis Romero	SP	1949-1951
Jean Sneyers*	BEL	1950-1951	**Bantamweight (118 lbs)**			Peter Keenan	S	1951-1952
			Joe Bowker	E	1910			

187

Title Holder	Country	Tenure
Jean Sneyers*	BEL	1952-1953
Peter Keenan	S	1953
John Kelly	NI	1953-1954
Robert Cohen*	FR	1954-1955
Mario D'Agata	ITA	1955-1958
Piero Rollo	ITA	1958-1959
Freddie Gilroy	NI	1959-1960
Pierre Cossemyns	BEL	1961-1962
Piero Rollo	ITA	1962
Alphonse Halimi	FR	1962
Piero Rollo	ITA	1962-1963
Mimoun Ben Ali	SP	1963
Risto Luukkonen	FIN	1963-1964
Mimoun Ben Ali	SP	1965
Tommaso Galli	ITA	1965-1966
Mimoun Ben Ali	SP	1966-1968
Salvatore Burruni*	ITA	1968-1969
Franco Zurlo	ITA	1969-1971
Alan Rudkin	E	1971
Agustin Senin*	SP	1971-1973
Johnny Clark*	E	1973-1974
Bob Allotey	SP	1974-1975
Daniel Trioulaire	FR	1975-1976
Salvatore Fabrizio	ITA	1976-1977
Franco Zurlo	ITA	1977-1978
Juan Francisco Rodriguez	SP	1978-1980
Johnny Owen*	W	1980
Valerio Nati	ITA	1980-1982
Giuseppe Fossati	ITA	1982-1983
Walter Giorgetti	ITA	1983-1984
Ciro de Leva*	ITA	1984-1986
Antoine Montero	FR	1986-1987
Louis Gomis*	FR	1987-1988
Fabrice Benichou	FR	1988
Vincenzo Belcastro*	ITA	1988-1990
Thierry Jacob*	FR	1990-1992
Johnny Bredahl*	DEN	1992
Vincenzo Belcastro	ITA	1993-1994
Prince Nassem Hamed*	E	1994-1995
John Armour*	E	1995-1996
Johnny Bredahl	DEN	1996-

S. Bantamweight (122 lbs)

Title Holder	Country	Tenure
Vincenzo Belcastro	ITA	1995-

Featherweight (126 lbs)

Title Holder	Country	Tenure
Young Joey Smith	E	1911
Jean Poesy	FR	1911-1912
Jim Driscoll*	W	1912-1913
Ted Kid Lewis*	E	1913-1914
Louis de Ponthieu*	FR	1919-1920
Arthur Wyns	BEL	1920-1922
Billy Matthews	E	1922
Eugene Criqui*	FR	1922-1923
Edouard Mascart	FR	1923-1924
Charles Ledoux	FR	1924
Henri Hebrans	BEL	1924-1925
Antonio Ruiz	SP	1925-1928
Luigi Quadrini	ITA	1928-1929
Knud Larsen	DEN	1929
Jose Girones	SP	1929-1934
Maurice Holtzer*	FR	1935-1938
Phil Dolhem	BEL	1938-1939
Lucien Popescu	ROM	1939-1941
Ernst Weiss	AU	1941
Gino Bondavilli	ITA	1941-1945
Ermanno Bonetti*	ITA	1945-1946
Tiger Al Phillips	E	1947

Title Holder	Country	Tenure
Ronnie Clayton	E	1947-1948
Ray Famechon	FR	1948-1953
Jean Sneyers	BEL	1953-1954
Ray Famechon	FR	1954-1955
Fred Galiana*	SP	1955-1956
Cherif Hamia	FR	1957-1958
Sergio Caprari	ITA	1958-1959
Gracieux Lamperti	FR	1959-1962
Alberto Serti	ITA	1962-1963
Howard Winstone	W	1963-1967
Jose Legra*	SP	1967-1968
Manuel Calvo	SP	1968-1969
Tommaso Galli	ITA	1969-1970
Jose Legra*	SP	1970-1972
Gitano Jiminez	SP	1973-1975
Elio Cotena	ITA	1975-1976
Nino Jimenez	SP	1976-1977
Manuel Masso	SP	1977
Roberto Castanon*	SP	1977-1981
Salvatore Melluzzo	ITA	1981-1982
Pat Cowdell*	E	1982-1983
Loris Stecca*	ITA	1983
Barry McGuigan*	NI	1983-1985
Jim McDonnell*	E	1985-1987
Valerio Nati*	ITA	1987
Jean-Marc Renard*	BEL	1988-1989
Paul Hodkinson*	E	1989-1991
Fabrice Benichou	FR	1991-1992
Maurizio Stecca	ITA	1992-1993
Herve Jacob	FR	1993
Maurizio Stecca	ITA	1993
Stephane Haccoun	FR	1993-1994
Stefano Zoff	ITA	1994
Medhi Labdouni	FR	1994-1995
Billy Hardy	E	1995-

S. Featherweight (130 lbs)

Title Holder	Country	Tenure
Tommaso Galli	ITA	1971-1972
Domenico Chiloiro	ITA	1972
Lothar Abend	GER	1972-1974
Sven-Erik Paulsen*	NOR	1974-1976
Roland Cazeaux	FR	1976
Natale Vezzoli	ITA	1976-1979
Carlos Hernandez	SP	1979
Rodolfo Sanchez	SP	1979
Carlos Hernandez	SP	1979-1982
Cornelius Boza-Edwards*	E	1982
Roberto Castanon	SP	1982-1983
Alfredo Raininger	ITA	1983-1984
Jean-Marc Renard	BEL	1984
Pat Cowdell	E	1984-1985
Jean-Marc Renard*	BEL	1986-1987
Salvatore Curcetti	ITA	1987-1988
Piero Morello	ITA	1988
Lars Lund Jensen	DEN	1988
Racheed Lawal	DEN	1988-1989
Daniel Londas*	FR	1989-1991
Jimmy Bredahl*	DEN	1992
Regilio Tuur	HOL	1992-1993
Jacobin Yoma	FR	1993-1995
Anatoly Alexandrov	KAZ	1995-

Lightweight (135 lbs)

Title Holder	Country	Tenure
Freddie Welsh	W	1909-1911
Matt Wells	E	1911-1912
Freddie Welsh*	W	1912-1914
Georges Papin	FR	1920-1921
Ernie Rice	E	1921-1922

Title Holder	Country	Tenure
Seaman Nobby Hall	E	1922-1923
Harry Mason	E	1923-1926
Fred Bretonnel	FR	1924
Lucien Vinez	FR	1924-1927
Luis Rayo*	SP	1927-1928
Aime Raphael	FR	1928-1929
Francois Sybille	BEL	1929-1930
Alf Howard	E	1930
Harry Corbett	E	1930-1931
Francois Sybille	BEL	1930-1931
Bep van Klaveren	HOL	1931-1932
Cleto Locatelli	ITA	1932
Francois Sybille	BEL	1932-1933
Cleto Locatelli*	ITA	1933
Francois Sybille	BEL	1934
Carlo Orlandi*	ITA	1934-1935
Enrico Venturi*	ITA	1935-1936
Vittorio Tamagnini	ITA	1936-1937
Maurice Arnault	FR	1937
Gustave Humery	FR	1937-1938
Aldo Spoldi*	ITA	1938-1939
Karl Blaho	AU	1940-1941
Bruno Bisterzo	ITA	1941
Ascenzo Botta	ITA	1941
Bruno Bisterzo	ITA	1941-1942
Ascenzo Botta	ITA	1942
Roberto Proietti	ITA	1942-1943
Bruno Bisterzo	ITA	1943-1946
Roberto Proietti*	ITA	1946
Emile Dicristo	FR	1946-1947
Kid Dussart	BEL	1947
Roberto Proietti	ITA	1947-1948
Billy Thompson	E	1948-1949
Kid Dussart	BEL	1949
Roberto Proietti*	ITA	1949-1950
Pierre Montane	FR	1951
Elis Ask	FIN	1951-1952
Jorgen Johansen	DEN	1952-1954
Duilio Loi*	ITA	1954-1959
Mario Vecchiatto	ITA	1959-1960
Dave Charnley	E	1960-1963
Conny Rudhof*	GER	1963-1964
Willi Quatuor*	GER	1964-1965
Franco Brondi	ITA	1965
Maurice Tavant	FR	1965-1966
Borge Krogh	DEN	1966-1967
Pedro Carrasco*	SP	1967-1969
Miguel Velazquez	SP	1970-1971
Antonio Puddu	ITA	1971-1974
Ken Buchanan*	S	1974-1975
Fernand Roelandts	BEL	1976
Perico Fernandez*	SP	1976-1977
Jim Watt*	S	1977-1979
Charlie Nash*	NI	1979-1980
Francisco Leon	SP	1980
Charlie Nash	NI	1980-1981
Joey Gibilisco	ITA	1981-1983
Lucio Cusma	ITA	1983-1984
Rene Weller	GER	1984-1986
Gert Bo Jacobsen	DEN	1986-1988
Rene Weller*	GER	1988
Policarpo Diaz*	SP	1988-1990
Antonio Renzo	ITA	1991-1992
Jean-Baptiste Mendy*	FR	1992-1994
Racheed Lawal	DEN	1994
Jean-Baptiste Mendy*	FR	1994-1995
Angel Mona	FR	1995-

L. Welterweight (140 lbs)

Title Holder	Country	Tenure
Olli Maki	FIN	1964-1965

Title Holder	Country	Tenure
Juan Sombrita-Albornoz	SP	1965
Willi Quatuor*	GER	1965-1966
Conny Rudhof	GER	1967
Johann Orsolics	AU	1967-1968
Bruno Arcari*	ITA	1968-1970
Rene Roque	FR	1970-1971
Pedro Carrasco*	SP	1971-1972
Roger Zami	FR	1972
Cemal Kamaci	TU	1972-1973
Toni Ortiz	SP	1973-1974
Perico Fernandez*	SP	1974
Jose Ramon Gomez-Fouz	SP	1975
Cemal Kamaci	TU	1975-1976
Dave Boy Green*	E	1976-1977
Primo Bandini	ITA	1977
Jean-Baptiste Piedvache	FR	1977-1978
Colin Power	E	1978
Fernando Sanchez	SP	1978-1979
Jose Luis Heredia	SP	1979
Jo Kimpuani	FR	1979-1980
Giuseppe Martinese	ITA	1980
Antonio Guinaldo	SP	1980-1981
Clinton McKenzie	E	1981-1982
Robert Gambini	FR	1982-1983
Patrizio Oliva*	ITA	1983-1985
Terry Marsh	E	1985-1986
Tusikoleta Nkalankete	FR	1987-1989
Efren Calamati	ITA	1989-1990
Pat Barrett	E	1990-1992
Valery Kayumba	ITA	1992-1993
Christian Merle	FR	1993-1994
Valery Kayumba	FR	1994
Khalid Rahilou*	FR	1994-1996
Soren Sondergaard	DEN	1996-

Welterweight (147 lbs)

Title Holder	Country	Tenure
Young Joseph	E	1910-1911
Georges Carpentier*	FR	1911-1912
Albert Badoud*	SWI	1915-1921
Johnny Basham	W	1919-1920
Ted Kid Lewis	E	1920-1924
Piet Hobin	BEL	1921-1925
Billy Mack	E	1923
Tommy Milligan	S	1924-1925
Mario Bosisio*	ITA	1925-1928
Leo Darton	BEL	1928
Alf Genon	BEL	1928-1929
Gustave Roth	BEL	1929-1932
Adrien Aneet	BEL	1932-1933
Jack Hood*	E	1933
Gustav Eder	GER	1934-1936
Felix Wouters	BEL	1936-1938
Saverio Turiello	ITA	1938-1939
Marcel Cerdan*	FR	1939-1942
Ernie Roderick	E	1946-1947
Robert Villemain*	FR	1947-1948
Livio Minelli	ITA	1949-1950
Michele Palermo	ITA	1950-1951
Eddie Thomas	W	1951
Charles Humez*	FR	1951-1952
Gilbert Lavoine	FR	1953-1954
Wally Thom	E	1954-1955
Idrissa Dione	FR	1955-1956
Emilio Marconi	ITA	1956-1958
Peter Waterman*	E	1958
Emilio Marconi	ITA	1958-1959
Duilio Loi*	ITA	1959-1963
Fortunato Manca*	ITA	1964-1965
Jean Josselin	FR	1966-1967
Carmelo Bossi	ITA	1967-1968

Title Holder	Country	Tenure
Fighting Mack	HOL	1968-1969
Silvano Bertini	ITA	1969
Jean Josselin	FR	1969
Johann Orsolics	AU	1969-1970
Ralph Charles	E	1970-1971
Roger Menetrey	FR	1971-1974
John H. Stracey*	E	1974-1975
Marco Scano	ITA	1976-1977
Jorgen Hansen	DEN	1977
Jorg Eipel	GER	1977
Alain Marion	FR	1977-1978
Jorgen Hansen	DEN	1978
Josef Pachler	AU	1978
Henry Rhiney	E	1978-1979
Dave Boy Green	E	1979
Jorgen Hansen*	DEN	1979-1981
Hans-Henrik Palm	DEN	1982
Colin Jones*	W	1982-1983
Gilles Elbilia	FR	1983-1984
Gianfranco Rosi	ITA	1984-1985
Lloyd Honeyghan*	E	1985-1986
Jose Varela	GER	1986-1987
Alfonso Redondo	SP	1987
Mauro Martelli*	SWI	1987-1988
Nino la Rocca	ITA	1989
Antoine Fernandez	FR	1989-1990
Kirkland Laing	E	1990
Patrizio Oliva*	ITA	1990-1992
Ludovic Proto	FR	1992-1993
Gary Jacobs*	S	1993-1994
Jose Luis Navarro	SP	1994-1995
Valery Kayumba	FR	1995
Patrick Charpentier	FR	1995-

L. Middleweight (154 lbs)

Title Holder	Country	Tenure
Bruno Visintin	ITA	1964-1966
Bo Hogberg	SWE	1966
Yolande Leveque	FR	1966
Sandro Mazzinghi*	ITA	1966-1968
Remo Golfarini	ITA	1968-1969
Gerhard Piaskowy	GER	1969-1970
Jose Hernandez	SP	1970-1972
Juan Carlos Duran	ITA	1972-1973
Jacques Kechichian	FR	1973-1974
Jose Duran	SP	1974-1975
Eckhard Dagge	GER	1975-1976
Vito Antuofermo	ITA	1976
Maurice Hope*	E	1976-1978
Gilbert Cohen	FR	1978-1979
Marijan Benes	YUG	1979-1981
Louis Acaries	FR	1981
Luigi Minchillo*	ITA	1981-1983
Herol Graham*	E	1983-1984
Jimmy Cable	E	1984
Georg Steinherr	GER	1984-1985
Said Skouma*	FR	1985-1986
Chris Pyatt	E	1986-1987
Gianfranco Rosi*	ITA	1987
Rene Jacquot*	FR	1988-1989
Edip Secovic	AU	1989
Giuseppe Leto	ITA	1989
Gilbert Dele*	FR	1989-1990
Said Skouma	FR	1991
Mourad Louati	HOL	1991
Jean-Claude Fontana	FR	1991-1992
Laurent Boudouani	FR	1992-1993
Bernard Razzano	FR	1993-1994
Javier Castillejos	SP	1994-1995
Laurent Boudouani	FR	1995-

Middleweight (160 lbs)

Title Holder	Country	Tenure
Georges Carpentier*	FR	1912-1918
Ercole Balzac	FR	1920-1921
Gus Platts	E	1921
Johnny Basham	W	1921
Ted Kid Lewis	E	1921-1923
Roland Todd	E	1923-1924
Ted Kid Lewis	E	1924-1925
Bruno Frattini	ITA	1924-1925
Tommy Milligan	S	1925-1928
Rene Devos	BEL	1926-1927
Barthelemy Molina	FR	1928
Alex Ireland	S	1928-1929
Mario Bosisio	ITA	1928
Leone Jacovacci	ITA	1928-1929
Len Johnson	E	1928-1929
Marcel Thil	FR	1929-1930
Mario Bosisio	ITA	1930-1931
Poldi Steinbach	AU	1931
Hein Domgoergen	GER	1931-1932
Ignacio Ara	SP	1932-1933
Gustave Roth	BEL	1933-1934
Marcel Thil*	FR	1934-1938
Edouard Tenet	FR	1938
Bep van Klaveren	HOL	1938
Anton Christoforidis	GRE	1938-1939
Edouard Tenet	FR	1939
Josef Besselmann*	GER	1942-1943
Marcel Cerdan	FR	1947-1948
Cyrille Delannoit	BEL	1948
Marcel Cerdan*	FR	1948
Cyrille Delannoit	BEL	1948-1949
Tiberio Mitri*	ITA	1949-1950
Randy Turpin	E	1951-1954
Tiberio Mitri	ITA	1954
Charles Humez	FR	1954-1958
Gustav Scholz*	GER	1958-1961
John Cowboy McCormack	S	1961-1962
Chris Christensen	DEN	1962
Laszlo Papp*	HUN	1962-1965
Nino Benvenuti*	ITA	1965-1967
Juan Carlos Duran	ITA	1967-1969
Tom Bogs	DEN	1969-1970
Juan Carlos Duran	ITA	1970-1971
Jean-Claude Bouttier	FR	1971-1972
Tom Bogs*	DEN	1973
Elio Calcabrini	ITA	1973-1974
Jean-Claude Bouttier	FR	1974
Kevin Finnegan	E	1974-1975
Gratien Tonna*	FR	1975
Bunny Sterling	E	1976
Angelo Jacopucci	ITA	1976
Germano Valsecchi	ITA	1976-1977
Alan Minter	E	1977
Gratien Tonna	FR	1977-1978
Alan Minter*	E	1978-1979
Kevin Finnegan	E	1980
Matteo Salvemini	ITA	1980
Tony Sibson*	E	1980-1982
Louis Acaries	FR	1982-1984
Tony Sibson	E	1984-1985
Ayub Kalule	DEN	1985-1986
Herol Graham	E	1986-1987
Sumbu Kalambay*	ITA	1987
Pierre Joly	FR	1987-1988
Christophe Tiozzo*	FR	1988-1989
Francesco dell' Aquila	ITA	1989-1990
Sumbu Kalambay*	ITA	1990-1993

189

Title Holder	Country	Tenure
Agostino Cardamone*	ITA	1993-1994
Richie Woodhall*	E	1995-1996
Alexandre Zaitsoz	RUS	1996-

S. Middleweight (168 lbs)

Title Holder	Country	Tenure
Mauro Galvano*	ITA	1990-1991
James Cook	E	1991-1992
Franck Nicotra*	FR	1992
Vincenzo Nardiello	ITA	1992-1993
Ray Close*	NI	1993
Vinzenzo Nardiello	ITA	1993-1994
Frederic Seillier*	FR	1994-1995
Henry Wharton*	E	1995-1996

L. Heavyweight (175 lbs)

Title Holder	Country	Tenure
Georges Carpentier	FR	1913-1922
Battling Siki	FR	1922-1923
Emile Morelle	FR	1923
Raymond Bonnel	FR	1923-1924
Louis Clement	SWI	1924-1926
Herman van T'Hof	HOL	1926
Fernand Delarge	BEL	1926-1927
Max Schmeling*	GER	1927-1928
Michele Bonaglia*	ITA	1929-1930
Ernst Pistulla*	GER	1931-1932
Adolf Heuser	GER	1932
John Andersson	SWE	1933
Martinez de Alfara	SP	1934
Marcel Thil	FR	1934-1935
Merlo Preciso	ITA	1935
Hein Lazek	AU	1935-1936
Gustave Roth	BEL	1936-1938
Adolf Heuser*	GER	1938-1939
Luigi Musina*	ITA	1942-1943
Freddie Mills*	E	1947-1950
Albert Yvel	FR	1950-1951
Don Cockell*	E	1951-1952

Title Holder	Country	Tenure
Conny Rux*	GER	1952
Jacques Hairabedian	FR	1953-1954
Gerhard Hecht	GER	1954-1955
Willi Hoepner	GER	1955
Gerhard Hecht	GER	1955-1957
Artemio Calzavara	ITA	1957-1958
Willi Hoepner	GER	1958
Erich Schoeppner	GER	1958-1962
Giulio Rinaldi	ITA	1962-1964
Gustav Scholz*	GER	1964-1965
Giulio Rinaldi	ITA	1965-1966
Piero del Papa	ITA	1966-1967
Lothar Stengel	GER	1967-1968
Tom Bogs*	DEN	1968-1969
Yvan Prebeg	YUG	1969-1970
Piero del Papa	ITA	1970-1971
Conny Velensek	GER	1971-1972
Chris Finnegan	E	1972
Rudiger Schmidtke	GER	1972-1973
John Conteh*	E	1973-1974
Domenico Adinolfi	ITA	1974-1976
Mate Parlov*	YUG	1976-1977
Aldo Traversaro	ITA	1977-1979
Rudi Koopmans	HOL	1979-1984
Richard Caramonolis	FR	1984
Alex Blanchard	HOL	1984-1987
Tom Collins	E	1987-1988
Pedro van Raamsdonk	HOL	1988
Jan Lefeber	HOL	1988-1989
Eric Nicoletta	FR	1989-1990
Tom Collins	E	1990-1991
Graciano Rocchigiani*	GER	1991-1992
Eddie Smulders	HOL	1993-1994
Fabrice Tiozzo*	FR	1994-1995
Eddy Smulders	HOL	1995-

Cruiserweight (190 lbs)

Title Holder	Country	Tenure
Sam Reeson*	E	1987-1988

Title Holder	Country	Tenure
Angelo Rottoli	ITA	1989
Anaclet Wamba*	FR	1989-1990
Johnny Nelson*	E	1990-1992
Akim Tafer*	FR	1992-1993
Massimiliano Duran	ITA	1993-1994
Carl Thompson	E	1994
Alexander Gurov	UK	1995
Patrice Aouissi	FR	1995
Alexander Gurov*	UK	1995-1996
Akim Tafer	FR	1996-

Heavyweight (190 lbs +)

Title Holder	Country	Tenure
Georges Carpentier	FR	1913-1922
Battling Siki	FR	1922-1923
Erminio Spalla	ITA	1923-1926
Paolino Uzcudun	SP	1926-1928
Pierre Charles	BEL	1929-1931
Hein Muller	GER	1931-1932
Pierre Charles	BEL	1932-1933
Paolino Uzcudun	SP	1933
Primo Carnera	ITA	1933-1935
Pierre Charles	BEL	1935-1937
Arno Kolblin	GER	1937-1938
Hein Lazek	AU	1938-1939
Adolf Heuser	GER	1939
Max Schmeling*	GER	1939-1941
Olle Tandberg	SWE	1943
Karel Sys*	BEL	1943-1946
Bruce Woodcock	E	1946-1949
Joe Weidin	AU	1950-1951
Jack Gardner	E	1951
Hein Ten Hoff	GER	1951-1952
Karel Sys	BEL	1952
Heinz Neuhaus	GER	1952-1955
Franco Cavicchi	ITA	1955-1956
Ingemar Johansson*	SWE	1956-1959
Dick Richardson	W	1960-1962
Ingemar Johansson*	SWE	1962-1963
Henry Cooper*	E	1964
Karl Mildenberger	GER	1964-1968
Henry Cooper*	E	1968-1969
Peter Weiland	GER	1969-1970
Jose Urtain	SP	1970
Henry Cooper	E	1970-1971
Joe Bugner	E	1971
Jack Bodell	E	1971
Jose Urtain	SP	1971-1972
Jurgen Blin	GER	1972
Joe Bugner*	E	1972-1975
Richard Dunn	E	1976
Joe Bugner	E	1976-1977
Jean-Pierre Coopman	BEL	1977
Lucien Rodriguez	FR	1977
Alfredo Evangelista	SP	1977-1979
Lorenzo Zanon*	SP	1979-1980
John L. Gardner*	E	1980-1981
Lucien Rodriguez	FR	1981-1984
Steffen Tangstad	NOR	1984-1985
Anders Eklund	SWE	1985
Frank Bruno*	E	1985-1986
Steffen Tangstad	NOR	1986
Alfredo Evangelista	SP	1987
Anders Eklund	SWE	1987
Francesco Damiani	ITA	1987-1989
Derek Williams	E	1989-1990
Jean Chanet	FR	1990
Lennox Lewis*	E	1990-1992
Henry Akinwande*	E	1993-1995
Zeljko Mavrovic	CRO	1995-

Prior to abdicating his EBU super-middles title, Henry Wharton (left) pounded fellow Brit, Sammy Storey, to a four round defeat in defence of his belt

Les Clark

A-Z of Current World Champions

by Eric Armit

Shows the record since 1 July 1995, plus career summary and pen-portrait, of all men holding IBF, WBA, WBC and WBO titles as at 30 June 1996. The author has also produced similar data for those who first won titles between 1 July 1995 and 30 June 1996, but were no longer champions at the end of the period in question. Incidentally, the place name given is the respective boxer's domicile and may not necessarily be his birthplace, while all nicknames are shown where applicable. Not included are British fighters, Henry Akinwande (WBO heavyweight champion), Frank Bruno (Former WBC heavyweight champion), Steve Collins (WBO s. middleweight champion), Prince Nassem Hamed (WBO featherweight champion), Paul Jones (Former WBO l. middleweight champion) and Robbie Regan (WBO bantamweight champion). Their full records can be found in either the Current British-Based Champions or Active British-Based Boxers: Career Records' sections.

Rosendo Alvarez

Managua, Nicaragua. *Born* 6 May, 1970
WBA M. Flyweight Champion.
Former Undefeated Latin American M. Flyweight Champion

One of only three world champions produced by Nicaragua, along with Alexis Arguello and Eddie Gazo, Rosendo turned professional in December 1992 after winning 55 of his 67 amateur fights. Defeated experienced Rudy Crawford in two rounds in August 1993 and won the Latin American title in September 1994 by stopping Venezuelan, Jose Bonilla, in 11 rounds. Scored a tremendous upset when he tackled unbeaten Chana Porpaoin in Thailand and almost knocked the WBA champion out in the eighth before winning a split decision. Showed the title victory was no fluke by knocking out Colombian, Kermin Guardia, in three rounds and outclassing former IBF champion, Eric Chavez. An upright, stylish fighter, he has 14 inside the distance wins.

15.07.95	Alfred Virgen W PTS 10 Managua	
02.09.95	Vidal Cerna W RSC 6 Managua	
02.12.95	Chana Porpaoin W PTS 12 Bangkok *(WBA M. Flyweight Title Challenge)*	
30.03.96	Kermin Guardia W CO 3 Managua *(WBA M. Flyweight Title Defence)*	
15.06.96	Eric Chavez W PTS 12 Sendai *(WBA M. Flyweight Title Defence)*	

Career: 22 contests, won 22.

Yuri (Ebihara) Arbachakov

Kemerova, Armenia. *Born* 22 October, 1966
WBC Flyweight Champion. Former Undefeated Japanese Flyweight Champion

The first fighter to win a world title whilst still a Russian citizen. A gold medal winner in both the World Championships and the European Games, Yuri turned professional in Japan in February 1990. Won the Japanese title in his eighth fight, knocked out Muangchai Kitikasem in June 1992 to become WBC champion, and has made eight successful defences. Is a cool, upright stylist with good defence, but not a heavy puncher. Has 15 quick wins.

25.09.95	Chartchai Elite-Gym W PTS 12 Tokyo *(WBC Flyweight Title Defence)*	
05.02.96	Raul Juarez W PTS 12 Osaka *(WBC Flyweight Title Defence)*	

Career: 22 contests, won 22.

Marco Antonio Barrera

Mexico City, Mexico. *Born* 17 January, 1974
WBO S. Bantamweight Champion.
Former Undefeated Mexican S. Flyweight Champion

Baby-faced assassin who has become the darling of Mexican fans in California. Turned professional in November 1989 at 15 and won the Mexican super-flyweight title in April 1992 by beating Josefino Suarez, prior to taking the NABF title in August 1993. Having failed to make the weight when outpointing Carlos Salazar in a final eliminator for the WBC title in April 1994, Marco moved up to super-bantamweight. Won the WBO title in March 1995, when beating Daniel Jimenez on points and has made six defences, stopping five of his challengers. A destructive puncher with either hand, he has 29 quick wins.

15.07.95	Maui Diaz W CO 1 Los Angeles *(WBO S. Bantamweight Title Defence)*	
22.08.95	Agapito Sanchez W PTS 12 South Padre Island *(WBO S. Bantamweight Title Defence)*	
04.11.95	Eddie Croft W RSC 7 Las Vegas *(WBO S. Bantamweight Title Defence)*	
03.02.96	Kennedy McKinney W RSC 12 Los Angeles *(WBO S. Bantamweight Title Defence)*	
04.05.96	Jesse Benavides W RSC 3 Anaheim *(WBO S. Bantamweight Title Defence)*	

Career: 41 contests, won 41.

Frans (The White Buffalo) Botha

Johannesburg, South Africa. *Born* 28 September, 1968
Former IBF Heavyweight Champion.

6'2" tall former South African amateur champion. Trained by Gerrie Coetzee, he turned professional in February 1990, and has had most of his fights in the USA. Defeated Ginger Tshabalala on a controversial decision in 1991 and outpointed Mike Hunter in September 1992 and, on one occasion, scored three first round knockouts on the same night. Guided to a fight for the vacant IBF title by Don King, Frans won the crown with a hotly disputed decision over Axel Schulz, but then failed a drugs test. Although the IBF confirmed him as a champion, a judge later forced them to overturn the decision and Botha was stripped of the title. Strong, with a fair defence and a good chin, but slow and methodical, he has 21 wins inside the distance.

09.12.95	Axel Schulz W PTS 12 Stuttgart
	(Vacant IBF Heavyweight Title)

Career: 36 contests, won 36.

Mbulelo Botile

East London, South Africa. *Born* 23 July, 1972

IBF Bantamweight Champion. Former Undefeated South African Bantamweight Champion

A stable-mate of IBF super-bantamweight champion, Vuyani Bungu, he turned professional at the age of 17, but found it very difficult to get work until he changed management. Won the South African title in his 12th fight, outpointing former IBF title challenger, Derrick Whiteboy, in May 1994, and collected the IBF title in April 1995 with a second round kayo of Harold Mestre. Has defended his crown three times and continues to show improvement with every fight. 5'5" tall, he is a good boxer and an excellent counter puncher, with 12 of his wins coming inside the distance.

04.07.95	Sammy Stewart W PTS 12 Hammanskraal
	(IBF Bantamweight Title Defence)
25.11.95	Reynaldo Hurtado W RSC 2 East London
	(IBF Bantamweight Title Defence)
02.04.96	Ancee Gedeon W CO 11 Providence
	(IBF Bantamweight Title Defence)
29.06.96	Marlon Arlos W RTD 8 East London
	(IBF Bantamweight Title Defence)

Career: 20 contests, won 20.

Lonnie Bradley

Lonnie Bradley

New York, USA. *Born* 16 September, 1968

WBO Middleweight Champion

5'11" tall. The first world champion to emerge from Harlem since Sugar Ray Robinson, Lonnie is a former National Golden Gloves champion and is trained by ex-boxer, Bobby Cassidy. A professional since November 1992, he was carefully protected and guided through a string of easy wins until May 1995 when he won the vacant WBO title by stopping David Mendez in 12 rounds. Having made three defences against moderate opposition, and proving to be a compact boxer with a

good jab, he has done everything asked of him, although he has yet to be really tested. Has 19 early finishes.

15.07.95	Dario Galindez W CO 1 Los Angeles
	(WBO Middleweight Title Defence)
06.02.96	Randy Smith W RSC 2 New York City
	(WBO Middleweight Title Defence)
07.05.96	Lonnie Beasley W PTS 12 Steubenville
	(WBO Middleweight Title Defence)

Career: 24 contests, won 24.

Vuyani (The Beast) Bungu

Mdantsane, South Africa. *Born* 26 February, 1967

IBF S. Bantamweight Champion. Former Undefeated South African S. Bantamweight Champion

Taking his nickname from John Mugabi, Vuyani, turned professional in April 1987. Floored three times and outpointed by Fransie Badenhorst in a challenge for the South African title in 1989, he gained revenge with a points win to become national champion in 1990. Lost on points to Freddie Norwood in 1992, but made five defences of his national title. In 1994, the South African scored an upset points victory over Kennedy McKinney to win the IBF title and has turned back six challenges since then, although all against only modest opposition. 5'5" tall, he is a good body puncher and has won 18 times inside the scheduled distance.

26.09.95	Laureano Ramirez W PTS 12 Hammanskraal
	(IBF S. Bantamweight Title Defence)
23.01.96	Johnny Lewus W PTS 12 Biloxi
	(IBF S. Bantamweight Title Defence)
15.04.96	Pablo Osuna W RSC 2 Hammanskraal
	(IBF S. Bantamweight Title Defence)

Career: 32 contests, won 30, lost 2.

Michael Carbajal

Phoenix, USA. *Born* 17 September, 1967

IBF L. Flyweight Champion. Former WBC L. Flyweight Champion. Former Undefeated WBO & NABF L. Flyweight Champion

Managed by his brother, Danny, the former truck driver turned professional in February 1989 after winning a silver medal in the 1988 Olympic Games.

Mbulelo Botile

Captured the NABF title when decisioning Tony de Luca in February 1990, before adding the IBF crown to his collection in July 1990, stopping Muangchai Kitikasem in seven rounds. Knocked out Humberto Gonzalez in March 1993 for the WBC title, but was outpointed in a return in February 1994. Came back to decision Josue Camacho for the WBO title in July 1994, but again lost on points to Gonzalez in a challenge for the IBF and WBC titles in November 1994. Has since regained the IBF title with a points victory over Melchor Cob Castro. 5'5" tall, Michael is an aggressive hard puncher, with 26 wins inside the distance.

12.08.95	Jose Quirino W CO 1 Las Vegas
16.09.95	Gregorio Garcia W CO 3 Las Vegas
16.11.95	Francisco Montiel W RSC 3 Phoenix
19.02.96	Mauro Diaz W RSC 7 Tempe
16.03.96	Melchor Cob Castro W PTS 12 Las Vegas
	(Vacant IBF L. Flyweight Title)
14.07.96	Manuel Serabia W CO 1 Denver

Career: 43 contests, won 41, lost 2.

Antonio (Goloso) Cermeno

Miranda, Venezuela. *Born* 6 March, 1969
WBA S. Bantamweight Champion. Former Undefeated Latin American S. Bantamweight Champion

5'10" tall, but deceptively strong, Antonio collected a gold medal at the Central American Games in 1989 and turned professional the following year as a super-featherweight. Moved down a couple of divisions to win the Latin American title in August 1993, halting Ramon Guzman, before losing on points in a title eliminator to Jae-Won Choi in Korea in December that year. Having upset the odds when outfighting Wilfredo Vasquez to collect the WBA crown on a disputed points verdict in May 1995, a broken right-hand put him out of action for a few months. His style is not pretty, although effective, and despite 15 stoppage wins he is not a big puncher.

26.11.95	Jesus Salud W PTS 12 Maracay
	(WBA S. Bantamweight Title Defence)
23.03.96	Yober Orgega W PTS 12 Miami
	(WBA S. Bantamweight Title Defence)

Career: 25 contests, won 24, lost 1.

Yong-Soo Choi

Yong-Soo Choi

South Korea. *Born* 20 August, 1972
WBA S. Featherweight Champion. Former Undefeated OPBF S. Featherweight Champion

Turned professional in November 1990, but did not look to be an outstanding prospect, especially when losing a couple of early bouts. Won the South Korean title in March 1993, outpointing Byung-Sae Ahn, and then sprang a major surprise in December 1993 by knocking out world-rated Eun-Sik Lee in three rounds to win the OPBF crown. Despite being a rank outsider, he floored Victor Hugo Paz twice and stopped him in ten rounds to win the vacant WBA title and came off the floor to kayo the tough Panamanian, Orlando Soto, in his most recent defence. A lanky boxer, and a good body puncher, he has 13 quick wins.

21.10.95	Victor Hugo Paz W RSC 10 Salta
	(Vacant WBA S. Featherweight Title)
27.01.96	Yamato Mitani W PTS 12 Tokyo
	(WBA S. Featherweight Title Defence)
11.05.96	Orlando Soto W CO 8 Chejudo
	(WBA S. Featherweight Title Defence)

Career: 22 contests, won 20, lost 2.

Juan M. (Latigo) Coggi

Santa Fe, Argentina. *Born* 19 December, 1961
WBA L. Welterweight Champion. Former Undefeated Argentinian L. Welterweight Champion

Hard-punching southpaw who is in his third reign as WBA champion. A professional since 1982, the Argentinian first won the WBA title in 1987 with a kayo of Italian star, Patrizio Oliva. Defended his title four times, scoring wins over Harold Brazier and Jose Luis Ramirez, before losing to Loreto Garza in 1990. Regained the title in 1993 by knocking out Morris East, and made six successful defences, before losing the crown on points in September 1994 to Frankie Randall. Became champion again on a controversial technical decision when he was unable to continue after a clash of heads in a return with Randall.

13.01.96	Frankie Randall W TD 5 Miami
	(WBA L. Welterweight Title Challenge)

Career: 75 contests, won 70, drew 2, lost 3.

Juan M. Coggi

Al (Ice) Cole

Suffern, USA. *Born* 21 April, 1964
IBF Cruiserweight Champion. Former Unbeaten USBA Cruiserweight Champion

193

6'4" tall. A good boxer, but lacking variety in his work, Al turned professional in March 1989 after just failing to make the US team for the 1988 Olympics. Won the vacant USBA cruiserweight title in March 1991 by decisioning Leon Taylor and took the IBF crown in July 1992 with a points win over James Warring. After beating Glenn McCrory on points in a defence in July 1993, he has almost put the title in cold storage, with only one defence in 1994 and one in 1995, outpointing Uriah Grant in June. It would appear that his ambitions lie at heavyweight.

12.01.96	Tim Witherspoon L PTS 10 New York City
Career: 29 contests, won 27, lost 2.	

Oscar de la Hoya

Montebello, USA. *Born* 4 February, 1973
WBC L. Welterweight Champion. Former Undefeated IBF & WBO Lightweight Champion. Former Undefeated WBO S. Featherweight Champion

The new star of American boxing. After winning the gold medal at the 1992 Olympic Games, Oscar was paid $1 million to turn professional, having his first fight in November 1992. Became WBO super-featherweight champion in his 12th fight, in April 1994, when stopping Jimmy Bredahl in ten rounds, and took the vacant WBO lightweight title in July 1994 by knocking out Jorge Paez in two rounds. Added the IBF crown to his growing collection in May 1995, when stopping Rafael Ruelas in two, and moved up to light-welterweight to halt Julio Cesar Chavez on a cut and collect his fourth world title at the age of 23. With fast hands and great combination punches, he has already beaten eight former world champions.

09.09.95	Genaro Hernandez W RTD 6 Las Vegas *(WBO Lightweight Title Defence)*
15.12.95	James Leija W RSC 2 New York City *(WBO Lightweight Title Defence)*
09.02.96	Darryl Tyson W CO 2 Las Vegas
06.06.96	Julio Cesar Chavez W RSC 4 Las Vegas *(WBC L. Welterweight Title Challenge)*
Career: 22 contests, won 22.	

Marcelo Dominguez

Buenos Aires, Argentina. *Born* 15 January, 1970
WBC Cruiserweight Champion. Former Undefeated Argentinian Cruiserweight Champion

Lost only three of 42 fights as an amateur before becoming a professional in October 1991. Held to a draw in his third fight by Raul Aguiar, he beat former WBO champion, Nestor Giovannini, on a disqualification in February 1993 to win the vacant Argentinian crown and went on to challenge Anaclet Wamba for the WBC title in December 1994, losing on a majority decision. Won the WBC interim title in July 1995, when coming from behind to knock out Akim Tafer, and defended by beating Reynaldo Gimenez, before overcoming a broken rib to defeat Russian, Sergei Kobozev on a split decision. Proclaimed champion when Anaclet Wamba failed to make the weight for a title defence against him, Marcello is tough, stocky and durable.

01.07.95	Luiz Alves W RSC 4 Buenos Aires
25.07.95	Akim Tafer W RSC 9 St Jean de Luz *(Vacant WBC Interim Cruiserweight Title)*
02.09.95	Reynaldo Gimenez W RSC 12 Gualeguaychu *(WBC Interim Cruiserweight Title Defence)*
24.10.95	Sergei Kobozev W PTS 12 Levallois-Perret *(WBC Interim Cruiserweight Title Defence)*
Career: 21 contests, won 19, drew 1, lost 1.	

Marcelo Dominguez

Luisito (Golden Boy) Espinosa

Manila, Philippines. *Born* 26 June, 1967
WBC Featherweight Champion. Former WBA Bantamweight Champion

Luisito is the nephew of former top fighter, Leo Espinosa. Turned professional in May 1984 and suffered some early set-backs, being stopped by Juan Jose Estrada in March 1988 for the WBC international bantamweight title. Not deterred, he lifted the WBA crown in October 1989 with a spectacular first round stoppage of Kaokor Galaxy and made two successful defences before being knocked out by Israel Contreras in October 1991. Looked to be finished as a top fighter when he was halted in three rounds by Alejandro Gonzalez, but revived his career with a first round kayo of former world champion, Raul Perez, and then upset Manuel Medina to win the WBC title. Gaining revenge over Gonzalez, when overpowering him in four rounds, he is a good aggressive boxer who has stopped or knocked out 20 opponents.

09.10.95	Raul Perez W CO 1 Tokyo
11.12.95	Manuel Medina W PTS 12 Tokyo *(WBC Featherweight Title Challenge)*
01.03.96	Alejandro Gonzalez W CO 4 Guadalajara *(WBC Featherweight Title Defence)*
Career: 45 contests, won 38, lost 7.	

Arturo Gatti

Arturo (Thunder) Gatti

New Jersey, USA. *Born* Canada, 15 April, 1972
IBF S. Featherweight Champion. Former Undefeated USBA S. Featherweight Champion

5'8" tall. Born in Montreal, his brother Joe is also a professional, Arturo had his first paid fight in June 1991, his only loss to date coming on points to King Solomon in November 1992. Won the USBA title in June 1994 by halting Pete Taliaferro in the first round and retained the title through three defences. Floored and outpointed Tracy Harris Patterson to take the IBF title on a unanimous decision, but had to climb off the floor in a dramatic war against Wilson Rodriguez before pulling the fight out of the fire with one punch. Is a fast starter and big hitter, with 21 stoppages or kayos.

13.07.95	Barrington Francis W RSC 6 Atlantic City
	(USBA S. Featherweight Title Defence)
07.10.95	Carlos Vergara W CO 1 Atlantic City
15.12.95	Tracy Harris Patterson W PTS 12 New York City
	(IBF S. Featherweight Title Challenge)
23.03.96	Wilson Rodriguez W CO 6 New York City
	(IBF S. Featherweight Title Defence)
Career: 26 contests, won 25, lost 1.	

Alimi Goitia

Puerto Cabello, Venezuela. *Born* 28 June, 1970
WBA S. Flyweight Champion. Former Undefeated Latin American S. Flyweight Champion

A former outstanding amateur who has made rapid progress, he had his first paid fight in March 1993 and won the Latin American title in September 1994, stopping Venezuelan, Ernesto Briceno, in only his ninth fight. Although showing his class with a first round win over Julio Gamboa in a title defence in November, Alimi was given little chance against Hyung-Chul Lee, but was ahead when a punch after the bell knocked the South Korean out. Halted former WBA flyweight champion, Aquiles Guzman, before settling any controversy by easily beating Lee in a return and halting the previously unbeaten, Satoshi Iida. Recognised as a stylish southpaw and

a good left hand puncher, only three opponents have heard the final bell.

22.07.95	Hyung-Chul Lee W CO 4 Seoul
	(WBA S. Flyweight Title Challenge)
25.11.95	Aquiles Guzman W RSC 5 Porlama
	(WBA S. Flyweight Title Defence)
24.02.96	Hyung-Chul Lee W RSC 12 Kwangyang
	(WBA S. Flyweight Title Defence)
29.04.96	Satoshi Iida W RSC 5 Nagoya
	(WBA S. Flyweight Title Defence)
Career: 15 contests, won 15.	

Harold Grey

Arjona Bolivar, Colombia. *Born* 20 December, 1971
IBF S. Flyweight Champion

A 5'7" tall, long armed, busy fighter, Harold joined the paid ranks in November 1990. After 16 fights without defeat, and never going beyond six rounds, he collected the IBF title with an upset victory over Julio Borboa in August 1994. Decisioned Vincenzo Belcastro, Orlando Tobon and Borboa (again) in defences, before losing to Carlos Salazar in Argentina. Regaining the title with a close verdict over Salazar in Colombia, his 15 quick wins have been against modest opposition.

06.10.95	Carlos Salazar L PTS 12 Mar del Plata
	(IBF S. Flyweight Title Defence)
27.04.96	Carlos Salazar W PTS 12 Cartagena
	(IBF S. Flyweight Title Challenge)
Career: 22 contests, won 21, lost 1.	

Virgil (Sugar) Hill

Bismark, USA. *Born* 18 January, 1964
WBA L. Heavyweight Champion. Former Undefeated WBC International & Con Am L. Heavyweight Champion

6'1" tall. Having won a silver medal in the 1984 Olympic Games, prior to turning professional that November, Virgil picked up the WBA title in September 1987 by halting Leslie Stewart in four rounds. Made ten successful defences, but was then easily outpointed by Tommy Hearns, before regaining the title in September 1992 when outpointing Frank Tate. Has since made another nine defences to set a record for the division, proving to be a strong, methodical fighter with a stiff jab who rarely excites,

although being a great local hero. Has 20 wins inside the distance, only six of those in title fights.

02.09.95	Drake Thadzi W PTS 12 Wembley
	(WBA L. Heavyweight Title Defence)
20.04.96	Louis Del Valle W PTS 12 Grand Forks
	(WBA L. Heavyweight Title Defence)
Career: 43 contests, won 42, lost 1.	

Phillip Holiday

Phillip Holiday

Benoni, South Africa. *Born* 23 May, 1970
IBF Lightweight Champion

A member of a fundamentalist Christian sect which frowns on boxing, Phillip is a former South African amateur champion. Turned professional in April 1991, and trained by Harold Volbrecht, he scored 24 consecutive wins, including victories over Sugar Baby Rojas and Danny Myburgh, but was still considered lucky to get a shot at the vacant IBF title. Took his chance in style by wearing down and stopping the dangerous Colombian, Miguel Julio. Has made three successful defences, but is still really untested as a slow starter who gets stronger as the fight goes on. Although not a particularly heavy puncher, his record shows 15 stoppages or knockouts.

19.08.95	Miguel Julio W RTD 10 Sun City	
	(Vacant IBF Lightweight Title)	
04.11.95	Ray Martinez W PTS 12 Sun City	
	(IBF Lightweight Title Defence)	
17.02.96	John Lark W RSC 10 Hammanskraal	
	(IBF Lightweight Title Defence)	
18.05.96	Jeff Fenech W RSC 2 Melbourne	
	(IBF Lightweight Title Defence)	
Career: 28 contests, won 28.		

Keith Holmes

Washington, USA. *Born* 30 March, 1969

WBC Middleweight Champion. Former Undefeated USBA L. Middleweight Champion

6'2" tall southpaw. Turned professional as a welterweight in October 1989 and suffered his only defeat so far when being outpointed by Ron Hammond in July 1990. Having come to prominence with third round stoppage of Kelcie Banks in May 1994, Keith won the vacant USBA light-middleweight title in September 1994 with a points victory over Andy Council. Later in the year, he was charged with being involved in a shooting, but was cleared and resumed his career in 1995 under the Don King banner, jumping up to middleweight and causing a minor upset by halting Quincy Taylor for the WBC title. A fair puncher, but a bit mechanical, there are 18 wins inside the distance on his record.

19.08.95	Tommy Small W RSC 4 Las Vegas
16.12.95	Kevin Tillman W PTS 6 Philadelphia
16.03.96	Quincy Taylor W RSC 9 Las Vegas
	(WBC Middleweight Title Challenge)
Career: 29 contests, won 28, lost 1.	

Bernard (The Executioner) Hopkins

Philadelphia, USA. *Born* 15 January, 1965

IBF Middleweight Champion. Former Undefeated USBA Middleweight Champion

Hailing from the tough north Philadelphia district, his uncle, Art McCloud, was also a professional. Spent some time in jail before turning professional in October 1988, losing his first fight, but was then unbeaten until Roy Jones outpointed him in a challenge for the IBF middleweight crown. Failed in another attempt to win the title when he was floored twice in a draw against Segundo Mercado in

Ecuador in December 1994, but made no mistake in the return in April 1995 when he halted Mercado in seven rounds. After easily disposing of poor Steve Frank, he was much more impressive in destroying the previously unbeaten, Joe Lipsey. A hard puncher, as his 22 quick wins attest, although sometimes lacking variety in his work.

27.01.96	Steve Frank W RSC 1 Phoenix
	(IBF Middleweight Title Defence)
16.03.96	Joe Lipsey W RSC 4 Las Vegas
	(IBF Middleweight Title Defence)
Career: 32 contests, won 29, drew 1, lost 2.	

Alberto (Raton) Jimenez

Mexico City, Mexico. *Born* 8 April, 1969

WBO Flyweight Champion. Former Undefeated Mexican Flyweight Champion

Although he did not take up boxing, until he was 16, and only fought for one year as an amateur, Alberto won the Mexican flyweight title in June 1991, halting Gonzalo Villalobos in four rounds. Challenged for the WBC title in October 1991 and almost knocked out Muangchai Kitikasem, but wound up losing on points. Following another points loss, this time to Mark Johnson in May 1993, he overcame that set-back to win the WBO title in February 1995 with an eighth round stoppage of Jacob Matlala. Also impressed in a defence against Robbie Regan, showing class in halting the Welshman in nine rounds in June 1995. An aggressive little fighter, who is a good body puncher, he has disposed of 27 opponents inside the distance.

09.10.95	Zolile Mbitiyi W RSC 2 Tijuana
	(WBO Flyweight Title Defence)
23.03.96	Mike Martinez W RSC 5 Las Vegas
	(WBO Flyweight Title Defence)
01.06.96	Jose Lopez W PTS 12 Lake Tahoe
	(WBO Flyweight Title Defence)
Career: 37 contests, won 32, drew 2, lost 3.	

Daniel Jimenez

Camuy, Puerto Rico. *Born* 21 November, 1969

Former WBO Bantamweight & S. Bantamweight Champion. Puerto Rican S. Bantamweight Champion

Turned professional in June 1988 and lost three of his first six fights. Scored an upset victory over Duke McKenzie in June 1993 to collect the WBO super-bantamweight title and made four successful defences, including a 19 second kayo of Harald Geier, before losing the title to Marco Barrera on points in March 1995. Moved down to bantamweight and won the WBO title in that division by coming off the floor to outpoint Alfred Kotey in October, retaining the title with a points victory over Drew Docherty, before losing it to Robbie Regan in April. A good, skilful boxer, but not really a hard puncher, he bounced back to win the Puerto Rican title in June.

21.10.95	Alfred Kotey W PTS 12 London
	(WBO Bantamweight Title Challenge)
20.01.96	Drew Docherty W PTS 12 Mansfield
	(WBO Bantamweight Title Defence)
26.04.96	Robbie Regan L PTS 12 Cardiff
	(WBO Bantamweight Title Defence)
23.03.96	Alejandro Sanabria W CO 5 Dorado
22.06.96	Pedro Rodriguez W PTS 12 Dorado
	(Vacant Puerto Rican S. Bantamweight Title)
Career: 29 contests, won 23, drew 1, lost 5.	

Mark (Too Sharp) Johnson

Washington, USA. *Born* 13 August, 1971

IBF Flyweight Champion

A strong, quick, aggressive southpaw, Mark won National Golden Gloves title at light-flyweight in 1988. Became a professional in February 1990 and, although losing on points to Richie Wenton in March of that year, beat Alberto Jimenez on points in August 1993. From that moment, his form frightened the various world champions and, despite a long run of wins, he had to wait until last May to get his title shot, crushing former champion, Francisco Tejedor, in one round to win the vacant IBF title. Now unbeaten in his last 28 fights, he has 21 wins inside the distance.

15.07.95	Josue Camacho W RSC 8 Los Angeles
11.09.95	Marcos Pacheco W RSC 4 Los Angeles
15.10.95	Ernest Sneed W RSC 1 Washington
11.12.95	Raul Rios W CO 3 Los Angeles
04.05.96	Francisco Tejedor W CO 1 Anaheim
	(Vacant IBF Flyweight Title)
Career: 30 contests, won 29, lost 1.	

196

Tom (Boom Boom) Johnson

Evansville, USA. *Born* 15 July, 1964
IBF Featherweight Champion. Former
Undefeated WBA Americas
Featherweight Champion

5'5" tall. Having turned professional in
October 1986, Tom challenged for the
NABF featherweight title in November
1990, being held to a draw by Troy
Dorsey, before facing Manuel Medina
for the IBF title in November 1991,
losing a technical decision when
Medina was badly cut whilst in front.
Won the return on points in February
1993 and has made ten defences of his
crown, including a second win over
Medina. A classy boxer, and an
excellent counter-puncher, although
sometimes lazy, he has 25 wins by
stoppage or kayo. Has been followed
by tragedy, with two members of his
team murdered.

09.12.95	Jose Badillo W PTS 12 Stuttgart
	(IBF Featherweight Title Defence)
02.03.96	Ever Beleno W RSC 12 Newcastle
	(IBF Featherweight Title Defence)
26.04.96	Claudio Martinet W CO 7 Antibes
	(IBF Featherweight Title Defence)
Career: 46 contests, won 43, drew 1, lost 2.	

Roy Jones Jnr

Pensacola, USA. *Born* 16 January,
1969
IBF S. Middleweight Champion.
Former Undefeated IBF & WBC Con
Am Middleweight Champion

5'11" tall. Beat Richie Woodhall in the
1988 Olympic Games, but was robbed
of the gold medal by a disgraceful
decision in favour of his South Korean
opponent in the final. Turned
professional with his father as his
manager in May 1989, eventually
parting from him, and won the vacant
IBF middleweight title in May 1993 by
outpointing Bernard Hopkins. Moved
up to super-middleweight to defeat
James Toney on points in November
1994 and win the IBF crown, he has
stopped all four of his challengers with
none lasting beyond the sixth round. A
brilliant boxer, who is too good for his
own good, Roy has never been
extended and may have to move up a
division to find a real test, only four of
his opponents ever taking him the
distance.

30.09.95	Tony Thornton W RSC 3 Pensacola
	(IBF S. Middleweight Title Defence)
12.01.96	Merqui Sosa W RSC 2 New York City
15.06.96	Eric Lucas W RSC 11 Jacksonville
	(IBF S. Middleweight Title Defence)
Career: 32 contests, won 32.	

William Joppy

Tacoma Park, USA. *Born* 11
September, 1970
WBA Middleweight Champion

Reached the semi-finals of both the
national championships and the
Olympic trials in 1992, turning
professional in February 1993, and
scoring wins over Carl Sullivan and
Joaquin Velasquez before drawing
with Rodney Toney for the vacant
NABF crown in September 1995. Won
the WBA title when challenging the
unbeaten Shinji Takehara, flooring and
stopped the tall champion in nine
rounds. 5'9" tall, William is a fast
boxer with a hard right-hand punch
that has given him 17 quick wins.

16.09.95	Rodney Toney DREW 12 Las Vegas
	(Vacant NABF Middleweight Title)
10.02.96	David Boone W RSC 2 Las Vegas
24.06.96	Shinji Takehara W RSC 9 Yokohama
	(WBA Middleweight Title Challenge)
Career: 23 contests, won 22, drew 1.	

Hiroshi Kawashima

Hiroshi (Untouchable) Kawashima

Tokushima, Japan. *Born* 27 March, 1970
WBC S. Flyweight Champion. Former
Undefeated Japanese S. Flyweight
Champion

Although an outstanding amateur
before turning professional in August
1988, a couple of early stoppage losses
put a question against his chin. However, he won the Japanese title in July
1992 by decisioning Hideki Koike and
defended the title four times to put
those setbacks behind him. An outsider
when he challenged Jose Luis Bueno
for the WBC crown in May 1994, he
overcame the Mexican to win on
points and went on to beat the future
IBF champion, Carlos Salazar, and
Bueno again, in defences.

08.11.95	Boy Arum W RSC 3 Tokyo
	(WBC S. Flyweight Title Defence)
27.04.96	Cecilio Espino W PTS 12 Tokyo
	(WBC S. Flyweight Title Defence)
Career: 22 contests, won 19, drew 1, lost 2.	

Nana Yaw Konadu

Sunyani, Ghana. *Born* 14 February,
1965
WBA Bantamweight Champion.
Former WBC S. Flyweight Champion.
Former Undefeated WBC International
S. Flyweight Champion. Former
Undefeated Commonwealth & ABC
Flyweight Champion. Former
Undefeated ABC Bantamweight
Champion.

Started boxing at the age of ten and
won 37 of 38 amateur fights, before
becoming a professional in May 1985.
Won the WBC international title in
March 1989, decisioning Cesar
Polanco, and the WBC crown in
November of the same year with a
points victory over the Mexican star,
Gilberto Roman, before losing it in his
first defence on a technical decision
against Sung-Kil Moon and then failing
in a return in March 1991. Came back
strongly to earn a shot at the WBA
bantamweight title by beating Victor
Rabanales and Habran Torres, and then
easily destroyed unbeaten Veeraphol
Sahaprom in two rounds to become
champion. Is a hard hitter who has 29
wins inside the distance.

27.01.96	Veerapol Sahaprom W RSC 2 Kanchunburi
	(WBA Bantamweight Title Challenge)
Career: 39 contests, won 36, drew 1, lost 2.	

Frank (Fabulous) Lilles

Syracuse, USA. *Born* 15 February, 1965
WBA S. Middleweight Champion.
Former Undefeated NABF S. Middleweight Champion

A 6'3" tall southpaw, and three times national amateur champion, Frank lost to Roy Jones for a spot in the team for the 1988 Olympic Games. Moved over to the professionals in August 1989, losing for the first and only time to Tim Littles for the USBA title in July 1992, but beat Merqui Sosa on a stoppage three months later to win the vacant NABF title. Progressed from there to take the WBA crown from Steve Little on points in August 1994 and then beat former world champion, Michael Nunn, on points in his first defence in December 1994. Has made three more defences, including a revenge win over Littles. Is a cagey fighter and solid puncher, who has 20 wins inside the distance.

09.12.95	Mauricio Amaral W PTS 12 Stuttgart
	(WBA S. Middleweight Title Defence)
08.06.96	Tim Littles W RSC 3 Newcastle
	(WBA S. Middleweight Title Defence)
Career: 31 contests, won 29, lost 1, no contest 1.	

Jose Luis (Maestrito) Lopez

Durango, Mexico. *Born* 28 May, 1973
WBO Welterweight Champion.
Former Undefeated Mexican Welterweight Champion

Southpaw. Having turned professional at the age of 15, and losing in only his third fight, he then scored 25 wins in a row. Challenged for the Mexican welterweight title in December 1993, losing on points to Rene Herrera, but went on to beat Herrera for the same title in March 1994, making a couple of defences before stopping Eamonn Loughran inside a round to win the WBO crown. With 28 quick wins, his fight against Loughran was the first time he has ventured out of the Mexican provinces.

04.08.95	Gabino Mendoza W RSC 4 Durango
	(Mexican Welterweight Title Defence)
20.10.95	Ulfiminio Segura W RSC 5 Durango
15.03.96	Oscar Burgos W RSC 4 Durango
13.04.96	Eamonn Loughran W RSC 1 Liverpool
	(WBO Welterweight Title Challenge)
Career: 40 contests, won 36, drew 1, lost 3.	

Jose Luis Lopez   Les Clark

Ricardo (Finito) Lopez

Cuernavaca, Mexico. *Born* 25 July, 1967
WBC M. Flyweight Champion.
Former Undefeated WBC Con Am M. Flyweight Champion

One of the best fighters pound for pound in the world today, and a man who has dominated his division for six years, Ricardo collected ten amateur titles before turning professional in January 1985. Won the WBC title in October 1990 by knocking out Hideyuki Ohashi in Japan and has since made 15 defences, only being taken the distance three times, and never being threatened, even though he has met the best in the division. Outclassed and halted the current WBC light-flyweight champion, Saman Sorjaturong, in two rounds in July 1993, he would probably win that title any time he chose to move up. A stylish boxer, with ability to finish with just one punch, he was sidelined for a while with a hand injury. Has 32 wins inside the distance.

16.03.96	Ala Villamor W CO 8 Las Vegas
	(WBC M. Flyweight Title Defence)
29.06.96	Kitichai Preecha W CO 3 Indio
	(WBC M. Flyweight Title Defence)
Career: 42 contests, won 42.	

Wayne McCullough

Belfast, Northern Ireland. *Born* 7 July, 1970
WBC Bantamweight Champion.
Former Undefeated NABF Bantamweight Champion

Having won gold at the Commonwealth Games, silver in the 1992 Olympic Games, and bronze in the European Championships, Wayne turned professional in February 1993, in the United States, winning the vacant NABF title in his 11th fight, halting Javier Medina in January 1994. Beat former WBC champion, Victor Rabanales, on points in a final eliminator in June 1994 and put up a great display to outbox Yasuei Yakushiji in Japan to take the WBC crown. Impressed again in overpowering Johnny Bredahl, but struggled badly against Jose Luis Bueno due to weight problems.

30.07.95	Yasuei Yakushiji W PTS 12 Nagoya
	(WBC Bantamweight Title Challenge)
02.12.95	Johnny Bredahl W RSC 8 Belfast
	(WBC Bantamweight Title Defence)
30.03.96	Jose Luis Bueno W PTS 12 Dublin
	(WBC Bantamweight Title Defence)
Career: 19 contests, won 19.	

Bronco McKart

Monroe, USA. *Born* March 20, 1971
Former WBO L. Middleweight Champion. Former Undefeated WBC International L. Middleweight Champion

A small town bible teacher, who is ruthless inside the ring, Bronco turned professional in July 1992 with the Galaxy gym following an undistinguished time as an amateur. After losing in February 1993 to Clayton Williams, but then beating Skipper Kelp and Brandon Croly, he took the WBC international title by halting Alain Bonnamie in July 1994, prior to stopping Engles Pedroza and Ian Garrett in defences. Having overcome a bad cut to win a split verdict against Aaron Davis in June 1995, Bronco won the vacant WBO title, after Paul Jones pulled out of a title defence, stopping Santos Cardona, only to lose it just over two months later to Ronald Wright. A 6'0" tall southpaw, he has 20 quick wins.

26.09.95	Wendall Hall W RSC 1 Auburn Hills
21.11.95	Francisco Mendez W RSC 2 Auburn Hills
01.03.96	Santos Cardona W RSC 9 Indio *(Vacant WBO L. Middleweight Title)*
17.05.96	Ronald Wright L PTS 12 Monroe *(WBO L. Middleweight Title Defence)*

Career: 30 contests, won 28, lost 2.

Thulani Malinga

Thulani (Sugarboy) Malinga

Ladysmith, South Africa. *Born* 11 December, 1959
WBC S. Middleweight Champion. Former Undefeated South African Middleweight, S. Middleweight and L. Heavyweight Champion. Former Undefeated African S. Middleweight Champion

Had over 200 amateur fights before following his brother, Maxwell, into the professional ring in August 1981. Scored good wins over Vince Boulware, Jim McDonald, and Gary Ballard, but failed in two shots at the IBF super-middleweight title, losing on points against Graciano Rocchigiani in January 1989, and Lindell Holmes in December 1990, and for the WBO title against Chris Eubank in February 1992. Looked to be finished when he was knocked out in six rounds by Roy Jones in August 1993, but reversed a May 1992 points loss when beating Nigel Benn to lift the WBC title on a split decision. Is a tough, stylish boxer who can be lazy at times.

22.07.95	Trevor Ambrose W PTS 8 London
02.03.96	Nigel Benn W PTS 12 Newcastle *(WBC S. Middleweight Title Challenge)*

Career: 50 contests, won 41, lost 9.

Henry Maske

Treunbrietzen, Germany. *Born* 6 January, 1964
IBF L. Heavyweight Champion

A 6'3" tall southpaw, he is a German sporting hero who draws vast crowds whenever he fights, having won gold medals at both the Olympic Games and the World Championships and being European champion three times, before turning professional in May 1990. True to form, he won the IBF crown in March 1993, decisioning Prince Charles Williams, and now has ten defences behind him. Although having a cool upright style, with a good jab and left cross, he is too mechanical and lacks real punching power, as his 11 stoppage wins show.

14.10.95	Graciano Rocchigiani W PTS 12 Munich *(IBF L. Heavyweight Title Defence)*
17.02.96	Duran Williams W PTS 12 Dortmund *(IBF L. Heavyweight Title Defence)*
25.05.96	John Scully W PTS 12 Leipzig *(IBF L. Heavyweight Title Defence)*

Career: 30 contests, won 30.

Jacob (Baby Jake) Matlala

Johannesburg, South Africa. *Born* 8 January, 1962
WBO Flyweight Champion. Former Undefeated South African L. Flyweight Champion.

Only 4'10" tall. For many years, Jacob was considered to be just a tough journeyman, but has proved he is so much more than that since turning professional in February 1980. Winning the South African light-flyweight title three years later, after losing it he was unsuccessful in six further title bouts and was lucky to receive a shot at Dave McAuley for the IBF flyweight title in 1991. Despite that, he put up a good fight before being knocked out in round ten. Came good when knocking out Pat Clinton in May 1993 to win the WBO crown, but after three defences he fought when in

poor health and was stopped by Alberto Jimenez in eight rounds in February 1995. Moving down to light-flyweight, and winning the WBO title with a technical verdict over Paul Weir in November 1995, he is a very strong little battler who has 21 stoppages or knockouts.

26.08.95	Francisco Mendoza W PTS 8 Durban
18.11.95	Paul Weir W TD 5 Glasgow *(WBO L. Flyweight Title Challenge)*
13.04.96	Paul Weir W RSC 10 Liverpool *(WBO L. Flyweight Title Defence)*

Career: 56 contests, won 44, drew 2, lost 10.

Manuel (Mantecas) Medina

Nayariet, Mexico. *Born* 30 March, 1967
Former WBC & IBF Featherweight Champion. Former Undefeated NABF & Fecarbox Featherweight Champion

5'8" tall with a 71 inch reach, Manuel turned professional in October 1985 at the age of 18 and lost two of his first four fights. Won the IBF title in August 1991 with a points victory over Troy Dorsey, and beat Tom Johnson on a technical decision in his first defence in November 1991, going on to make three further defences before losing on points to Johnson in February 1993 and dropping a decision to John John Molina in a challenge for the IBF super-featherweight title in June 1993. Regained the WBC featherweight crown with an upset decision over Alejandro Gonzalez in September 1995, but lost the title to Luisito Espinosa three months later. Has great stamina and a rock hard chin, although a light puncher with only 23 quick wins.

23.09.95	Alejandro Gonzalez W PTS 12 Sacramento *(WBC Featherweight Title Challenge)*
11.12.95	Luisito Espinosa L PTS 12 Tokyo *(WBC Featherweight Title Defence)*
12.04.96	Benito Rodriguez W PTS 10 Tijuana

Career: 59 contests, won 52, lost 7.

Jean-Baptiste Mendy

Paris, France. *Born* Senegal, 16 March, 1963
WBC Lightweight Champion. Former Undefeated European and French Lightweight Champion

A 5'9" tall southpaw and a professional since February 1983, early losses put a question over his chin. Despite that, he went on to win the French title in May 1991 with a first round stoppage of Angel Mona and collected the European crown in March 1992 by halting Antonio Renzo. Having relinquished the European title after six defences to challenge for the WBC title in March 1994, only to be stopped in five rounds by Miguel Gonzalez, Jean-Baptiste regained the EBU crown in December 1994 with a ninth round stoppage of Racheed Lawal. Finally won the WBC title last April with a points victory over Lamar Murphy

04.07.95	Rimvidas Bilius W RTD 6 Thaiais
20.04.96	Lamar Murphy W PTS 12 Levallois-Perret
	(Vacant WBC Lightweight Title)
Career: 56 contests, won 49, drew 2, lost 5.	

Dariusz Michalczewski

Hamburg, Germany. *Born* Danzig, Poland, 5 May, 1968
WBO L. Heavyweight Champion. Former Undefeated WBO Cruiserweight Champion. Former Undefeated IBF Inter-Continental & German International L. Heavyweight Champion

Won a European Junior Games' bronze medal for Poland and a gold medal in the Senior Championships for Germany before turning professional in September 1991. Collected the WBO title in September 1994, when scoring an upset points verdict over Leonzer Barber, in his next fight he added the WBO cruiserweight title by outpointing Nestor Giovannini, but quickly relinquished. Has made seven defences of his light-heavyweight title, mainly against moderate opposition, and has proved to be an aggressive, hard puncher with 24 victories inside the scheduled distance.

19.08.95	Everado Armenta W CO 5 Dusseldorf
	(WBO L. Heavyweight Title Defence)
07.10.95	Philippe Michel W PTS 12 Frankfurt
	(WBO L. Heavyweight Title Defence)
06.04.96	Asludin Umarov W CO 5 Hanover
	(WBO L. Heavyweight Title Defence)
08.06.96	Christophe Girard W PTS 12 Cologne
	(WBO L. Heavyweight Title Defence)
Career: 31 contests, won 31.	

Nate Miller

Philadelphia, USA. *Born* 3 August, 1963
WBA Cruiserweight Champion. Former NABF Cruiserweight Champion

A former American amateur international, the 6'2" tall cruiserweight is trained by Buster Drayton. Strong, durable, and a sharp puncher, Nate had his first professional fight in September 1986, going on to beat Bert Cooper for the NABF title in February 1989, and, despite a lay-off for a broken jaw, made three successful defences before losing to James Warring and Alfred Cole in successive fights. Bounced back with victories over Jade Scott and Dwight Muhammad Qawi, but lost to Cole again in a challenge for the IBF title in July 1994. Sprang a big surprise, however, when he knocked out Orlin Norris to win the WBA title and stoppages of Reynaldo Gimenez and Brian la Spada have taken his total of inside the distance victories to 24.

22.07.95	Orlin Norris W CO 8 London
	(WBA Cruiserweight Title Challenge)
13.01.96	Reynaldo Gimenez W RTD 4 Miami
	(WBA Cruiserweight Title Defence)
23.03.96	Brian la Spada W RSC 9 Miami
	(WBA Cruiserweight Title Defence)
Career: 32 contests, won 28, lost 4.	

Michael Moorer

New York, USA. *Born* 12 November, 1967
IBF Heavyweight Champion. Former IBF & WBA Heavyweight Champion. Former Undefeated WBO L. Heavyweight Champion

6'2" tall southpaw. Took gold in the 1986 USBA championships at light-middleweight and silver in 1985, before turning professional in March 1988. Won the vacant WBO light-heavyweight title by halting Victor Claudio in two rounds in January 1989 and made eight defences, without ever being taken the distance, before moving up to heavyweight in 1991 and collecting the vacant WBO title in May 1992 by stopping Bert Cooper in five rounds. Having relinquished the title in 1993 without defending, Michael won the WBA and IBF titles in April 1994 with a points victory

over Evander Holyfield, but was knocked out in ten rounds by George Foreman in his first defence. Went to court to obtain a promised shot at regaining the IBF title and decisioned Axel Schulz as a result. Has 30 wins inside the distance.

22.06.96	Axel Schulz W PTS 12 Dortmund
	(Vacant IBF Heavyweight Title)
Career: 38 contests, won 37, lost 1.	

Carlos (Little Duran) Murillo

Panama City, Panama. *Born* 10 December, 1970
Former WBA L. Flyweight Champion. Former Undefeated Latin American M. Flyweight and L. Flyweight Champion. Former Undefeated Panamanian and Fecarbox L. Flyweight Champion

Tigerish fighter with fast hands and good movement. Had his first professional contest in May 1990 and won the Latin American mini-flyweight title in his eighth fight, going on to make five successful defences of the title before losing a clear decision to Chana Porpaoin for the WBA title in May 1993. Having challenged Porpaoin again in March 1994, and looking unlucky to lose on a majority verdict, he moved up to light-flyweight later in the year and compiled a run of victories which led to his points win over Hi-Yong Choi for the WBA title. However, a poor performance in losing to Keiji Yamaguchi, saw him drop his crown after just four months in possession. Has 28 wins inside the distance.

15.07.95	Ignacio Aguilar W PTS 12 Managua
	(Latin American L. Flyweight Title Defence)
16.09.95	Rafael Orozco W CO 6 Las Vegas
	(Latin American L. Flyweight Title Defence)
13.01.96	Hi-Yong Choi W PTS 12 Miami
	(WBA L. Flyweight Title Challenge)
15.03.96	Jose Garcia Bernal W CO 10 Panama City
	(WBA L. Flyweight Title Defence)
21.05.96	Keiji Yamaguchi L PTS 12 Osaka
	(WBA L. Flyweight Title Defence)
Career: 37 contests, won 34, lost 3.	

Orzubek (Gussie) Nazarov

Kant, Kyrghyzstan. *Born* 30 August, 1966

WBA Lightweight Champion. Former Undefeated OPBF & Japanese Lightweight Champion

The tough, hard-punching southpaw, who collected a gold medal in the 1987 European Championships, moved to Japan to turn professional in February 1990 and won the Japanese title in April 1991 in only his sixth bout. Went on to add the OPBF title in May 1992, before travelling to South Africa in October 1993 and outpointing Dingaan Thobela for the WBA crown. Gussie has made four defences, including an impressive second round kayo of former WBA champion, Joey Gamache, and has 17 wins inside the distance.

| 14.11.95 | Dindo Canoy W PTS 12 Iwaki City *(WBA Lightweight Title Defence)* |
| 15.04.96 | Adrianus Taroreh W CO 4 Tokyo *(WBA Lightweight Title Defence)* |

Career: 23 contests, won 23.

Azumah Nelson

Accra, Ghana. *Born* 19 July, 1958
WBC S. Featherweight Champion. Former Undefeated WBC Featherweight Champion. Former Undefeated Ghanaian, ABU & Commonwealth Featherweight Champion

Probably the greatest boxer to come out of Africa, Azumah turned professional in December 1979 and in his first ten contests collected the Ghanaian, African, and Commonwealth featherweight titles. Really made his mark, however, when, after just 13 fights, he went the distance with Salvador Sanchez in a WBC title challenge. Became WBC champion in December 1984 when he stopped Wilfredo Gomez, making six defences, before moving up to super-featherweight to collect the vacant WBC crown with a points win over Mario Martinez in February 1988. Challenged unsuccessfully for the IBF and WBC lightweight titles in May 1990, losing on points to Pernell Whitaker, and then dropped his WBC title in May 1994 when outpointed by James Leija. Inactive until December 1995, he came back strongly to halt Gabriel Ruelas and to turn the tables on Leija.

| 01.12.95 | Gabriel Ruelas W RSC 5 Indio *(WBC S. Featherweight Title Challenge)* |
| 01.06.96 | James Leija W RSC 6 Las Vegas *(WBC S. Featherweight Title Defence)* |

Career: 44 contests, won 39, drew 2, lost 3.

Terry Norris

Lubbock, USA. *Born* 17 June, 1967
WBC and IBF L. Middleweight Champion. Former Undefeated NABF L. Middleweight Champion

5'8" tall. Fast and flashy and a brilliant hard puncher, but vulnerable and lacking discipline in the ring, his brother Orlin is a former WBC cruiserweight champion. A professional since August 1986, he knocked out Steve Little in December 1988 to win the NABF title and later challenged Julian Jackson for the WBA crown in July 1989, only to be halted in two rounds. After flattening John Mugabi in one round in March 1990 to win the WBC title, ten defences later he was knocked out by Simon Brown, but came back to decision the same man six months later to regain the title. Was disqualified against Luis Santana in November 1994, which cost him his title, and was then disqualified again five months later in a return, before finally knocking Santana out in August 1995. Added the IBF crown to his collection in December when decisioning Paul Vaden.

19.08.95	Luis Santana W RSC 2 Las Vegas *(WBC L. Middleweight Title Challenge)*
16.09.95	David Gonzales W RSC 9 Las Vegas *(WBC L. Middleweight Title Defence)*
16.12.95	Paul Vaden W PTS 12 Philadelphia *(WBC L. Middleweight Title Defence. IBF L. Middleweight Title Challenge)*
27.01.96	Jorge Luis Vado W CO 2 Phoenix *(IBF L. Middleweight Title Defence)*
24.02.96	Vince Pettway W RSC 8 Richmond *(WBC & IBF L. Middleweight Title Defence)*

Career: 49 contests, won 43, lost 6.

Giovanni Parisi

Vibo Valencia, Italy. *Born* 2 December, 1967
WBO L. Welterweight Champion. Former WBO Lightweight Champion. Former Undefeated Italian Lightweight Champion

An outstanding amateur who won the gold medal at featherweight in the 1988 Olympics, Giovanni turned professional in February 1989. However, after 12 wins, he overreached himself and was knocked out in three rounds by Antonio Rivera. Won the vacant WBO lightweight title in September 1992 by stopping Javier Altamirano in ten rounds, and beat Michael Ayers and Rivera in title defences, before moving up to light-welterweight. Although outpointed in a challenge for the WBC title by Julio Cesar Chavez, the Italian came back strongly to win the WBO crown by battering Sammy Fuentes to defeat in eight rounds. Is a slick boxer with fast hands and 24 quick wins on his record.

14.07.95	Angel Fernandez W CO 5 Rome
16.12.95	Hector Chong W RSC 7 Voghera
09.03.96	Sammy Fuentes W RSC 8 Milan *(WBO L. Welterweight Title Challenge)*
20.06.96	Carlos Gonzalez DREW 12 Milan *(WBO L. Welterweight Title Defence)*

Career: 35 contests, won 32, drew 1, lost 2.

Tracy Harris Patterson

Birmingham, USA. *Born* 26 December, 1964
Former IBF S. Featherweight Champion. Former WBC S. Bantamweight Champion. Former Undefeated NABF S. Bantamweight Champion

5'5" tall. The adopted son of former world heavyweight champion, Floyd Patterson, Tracy turned professional in June 1985 after winning the New York Golden Gloves title the previous year. Won the vacant NABF crown in February 1990 by knocking out George Garcia, he became WBC champion in June 1992, stopping Thierry Jacob in two rounds. Made four successful defences, before losing the title in August 1994 on a disputed decision against Hector Acero Sanchez. Following that, he moved up to super-featherweight and won the IBF title in July 1995, stopping Eddie Hopson in two rounds, before again becoming an ex-champion five months later when decisioned by Arturo Gatti. Is a strong fighter, with 39 wins inside the distance.

09.07.95	Eddie Hopson W RSC 2 Reno *(IBF S. Featherweight Title Challenge)*
26.10.95	Bruno Rabanales W RSC 6 Happaugue
15.12.95	Arturo Gatti L PTS 12 New York City *(IBF S. Featherweight Title Defence)*
14.04.96	Harold Warren W PTS 10 Ledyard
Career: 60 contests, won 55, drew 1, lost 4.	

Ike (Bazooka) Quartey

Accra, Ghana. *Born* 27 November, 1969
WBA Welterweight Champion.
Former Undefeated Ghanaian, ABC and WBC International Welterweight Champion

Competed in the 1988 Olympic Games before turning professional in November of that year. Based in France, Ike won the vacant WBC international title in March 1992, halting Dindo Canoy, and went on to take the WBA crown from Cristano Espana on an 11th round stoppage in June 1994. Has made four defences, with all of his challengers being finished inside five rounds, and in fact only four of his opponents have lasted the distance. Strong, with a hard punch in each hand, he grinds down and overpowers his victims.

23.08.95	Andrew Murray W RSC 4 Le Cannet- Rochville *(WBA Welterweight Title Defence)*
03.02.96	Jorge Ramirez Aquino W RTD 4 Levallois-Perret
12.04.96	Vince Phillips W RSC 3 St Maarten *(WBA Welterweight Title Defence)*
Career: 32 contests, won 32.	

Ralf Rocchigiani

Rheinhausen, Germany. *Born* 13 March, 1963
WBO Cruiserweight Champion.
Former German Cruiserweight Champion

Following his brother, Graciano, a former IBF champion, into professional boxing in 1983, Ralf failed in challenges for the European light-heavyweight title in 1986 and 1989, and was outpointed by Tyrone Booze when he tried for the WBO cruiserweight crown in 1992. Finally got lucky when he beat Carl Thompson on an injury stoppage for

the vacant WBO title in June 1995. 6'0" tall, and a good boxer, he lacks power at the highest level.

30.09.95	Mark Randazzo W PTS 12 Hanover *(WBO Cruiserweight Title Defence)*
25.11.95	Dan Ward W RSC 8 Hanover *(WBO Cruiserweight Title Defence)*
16.03.96	Jay Snyder W RSC 4 Berlin *(WBO Cruiserweight Title Defence)*
Career: 52 contests, won 37, drew 7, lost 8.	

Veerapol Sahaprom

Nakonrachasima, Thailand. *Born* 16 November, 1968
Former WBA Bantamweight Champion. Former Undefeated WBC International S. Flyweight Champion

Real name Veerapol Sumranklang. A former kick-boxer, in his first bout as an international style fighter, in December 1994, he won the vacant WBC international super-flyweight title with a third round stoppage of Joel Junio. Won the WBA bantamweight title in only his fourth bout, outpointing Daorung Chuwatana in September 1995, but lost it in his first defence four months later, being halted in two rounds by Nana Yaw Konadu.

17.09.95	Daorung Chuwatana W PTS 12 Bangkok *(WBA Bantamweight Title Challenge)*
27.01.96	Nana Yaw Konadu L RSC 2 Kanchunburi *(WBA Bantamweight Title Defence)*
06.04.96	Ledion Ceniza W RSC 9 Nontaburi
15.06.96	Willy Salazar W RSC 5 Nontaburi
Career: 7 contests, won 6, lost 1.	

Carlos Salazar

Buenos Aires, Argentina. *Born* 5 September, 1964
Former IBF S. Flyweight Champion. Former Undefeated South American Flyweight Champion. Former Argentinian Flyweight Champion

Selected to represent Argentina at the 1984 Olympic, but failed to make the weight and turned a professional in December 1985. Lost on points in a shot at Sot Chitalada for the WBC flyweight title in May 1990 and in WBC super-flyweight title challenges against Sung-Kil Moon (July 1993) and Hiroshi Kawashima (August 1994), before finally flooring and easily outpointing Harold Grey for the

IBF title in October 1995. Unfortunately, after just one defence, Carlos dropped the title to Grey in a return. Has 17 wins inside the distance.

02.09.95	Mario Romero W CO 3 Buenos Aires
06.10.95	Harold Grey W PTS 12 Mar del Plata *(IBF S. Flyweight Title Challenge)*
10.02.96	Antonio Melis W RTD 6 Rome *(IBF S. Flyweight Title Defence)*
27.04.96	Harold Grey L PTS 12 Cartagena *(IBF S. Flyweight Title Defence)*
Career: 49 contests, won 41, drew 1, lost 7.	

Carlos Salazar

Alex (Nene) Sanchez

Playa Ponce, Puerto Rico. *Born* 5 June, 1973
WBO M. Flyweight Champion

After turning professional at the age of 16 in 1991, Alex had a two year period of inactivity before winning the vacant WBO title in his eighth fight. Has since made five defences against very poor opposition, and is still untested at the highest level. Is speedy with a good punch.

29.07.95	Tomas Rivera W PTS 12 San Antonio *(WBO M. Flyweight Title Defence)*
27.10.95	Pablo Tiznado W RSC 1 San Juan
04.05.96	Jose Luis Velarde W RSC 6 Anaheim
Career: 24 contests, won 24.	

Bruce (The Atlantic City Express) Seldon

Atlantic City, USA. *Born* 30 January, 1967
WBA Heavyweight Champion.
Former Undefeated IBF Inter-Continental Heavyweight Champion

6' 3" tall. Sent to jail for ten years when just 15 years old, Bruce started boxing inside, winning the New Jersey Prison title. Had his first professional fight in October 1988 and won his first 18 bouts before being stopped in nine rounds by Oliver McCall, and then in one round by Riddick Bowe, in 1991. Having well and truly put his only other defeat, a points loss to Tony Tubbs in October 1992, behind him, he won the vacant WBA title by beating Tony Tucker in seven rounds in April 1995. A good boxer with a classy jab, but with questions over his chin, there are 29 wins inside the distance on his record.

19.08.95	Joe Hipp W RSC 10 Las Vegas
	(WBA Heavyweight Title Defence)

Career: 36 contests, won 33, lost 3.

Saman Sorjaturong

Kampangsaen, Thailand. *Born* 2 August, 1969
WBC L. Flyweight Champion. Former Undefeated IBF L. Flyweight Champion

Real name Saman Srirataet. As a former outstanding kick-boxer, in December 1989, Saman was inspired to take up boxing by watching videos of Joe Louis. Challenged Ricardo Lopez for the WBC mini-flyweight title in July 1993, but was outclassed and stopped in seven rounds, before taking on Humberto Gonzalez for the WBC and IBF light-flyweight titles and coming off the floor to win in round seven. Relinquished the IBF title, but has now made four defences of his WBC crown and has 25 wins by stoppage or knockout. Although a hard puncher with his right hand, his defence is poor.

15.07.95	Humberto Gonzalez W CO 7 Los Angeles
	(WBC & IBF L. Flyweight Title Challenge)
12.11.95	Yuichi Hosono W CO 4 Ratchaburi
	(WBC L. Flyweight Title Defence)
24.02.96	Antonio Perez W RSC 4 Chachoensao
	(WBC L. Flyweight Title Defence)
27.04.96	Joma Gamboa W RSC 7 Mahasarakam
	(WBC L. Flyweight Title Defence)
07.06.96	Terado Benfasio W PTS 6 Chiangrai

Career: 34 contests, won 31, drew 1, lost 2.

Saen Sowploenchit

Pratumthani, Thailand. *Born* 18 May, 1972
WBA Flyweight Champion

A 5'6" tall former kick-boxer, and an excellent stylist, Saen is not a great puncher, with only seven opponents finished inside the distance. Turned to international style boxing in 1990 and won the WBA title in February 1994 after only 17 bouts when decisioning David Griman. Has eight successful defences, five against former world champions.

17.10.95	Hiroki Ioka W RSC 10 Osaka
	(WBA Flyweight Title Defence)
14.01.96	Yong-Soon Chang W PTS 12 Nontaburi
	(WBA Flyweight Title Defence)
23.03.96	Silvio Gamez W PTS 12 Tathum Thani
	(WBA Flyweight Title Defence)

Career: 25 contests, won 25.

Ratanapol Sowvoraphin

Dankoonthod, Thailand. *Born* 6 June, 1973
IBF M. Flyweight Champion. Former Undefeated IBF Inter-Continental M. Flyweight Champion

The hard-punching southpaw, who now boxes under the name of Dutchboygym, turned professional in October 1990 and overcame a couple of early losses to win the IBF mini-flyweight title with a points victory over Manny Melchor in December 1992. Made 12 defences, before being stripped of the title when he failed to make the weight against Lee Castillo. However, he was immediately awarded a chance to regain the title and decisioned Jun Arlos to become champion again. In all, 21 opponents have failed to last the distance.

20.08.95	Dario Orate W RSC 2 Bangkok
29.10.95	Jack Russell W CO 2 Suphan Buri
	(IBF M. Flyweight Title Defence)
30.12.95	Osvaldo Guerrero W RSC 6 Chiang Mai
	(IBF M. Flyweight Title Defence)
16.03.96	Lee Castillo W RSC 11 Seesaket
18.05.96	Jun Arlos W PTS 12 Yala
	(Vacant IBF M. Flyweight Title)

Career: 30 contests, won 27, drew 1, lost 2.

Shinji Takehara

Hiroshima, Japan. *Born* 25 January, 1972
Former WBA Middleweight Champion. Former Undefeated Japanese & OPBF Middleweight Champion

6'2" tall. A hard puncher with both hands, Shinji picked up the Japanese novice title in his first year as a professional in 1989, before winning the national title in his 11th fight and making four defences. He next collected the vacant OPBF title in May 1993 with a 12th round kayo of Sung-Chun Lee and retained it through six defences, on his way to easily outpointing Jorge Castro to become the first ever Japanese world middleweight champion. Eighteen of his wins have come inside the distance.

12.09.95	Sung-Chun Lee W PTS 12 Tokyo
	(OPBF Middleweight Title Defence)
19.12.95	Jorge Castro W PTS 12 Tokyo
	(WBA Middleweight Title Challenge)
24.06.96	William Joppy L RSC 9 Yokohama
	(WBA Middleweight Title Defence)

Career: 25 contests, won 24, lost 1.

Johnny (Tap Tap) Tapia

Albuquerque, USA. *Born* 13 February, 1967
WBO S. Flyweight Champion. Former Undefeated USBA & NABF S. Flyweight Champion

A former double National Golden Gloves champion, Johnny disappeared from the scene for three years due to drugs problems. Finally turned professional in March 1988 and won the USBA title in May 1990, before being out for another four years, having failed numerous drugs tests. After returning in 1994, and winning the vacant WBO crown in October 1994, he has defended his title six times. In 38 contests, 22 of his opponents have either been stopped or kayoed.

203

02.07.95	Arthur Johnson W PTS 12 Albuquerque
	(WBO S. Flyweight Title Defence)
09.09.95	Jesse Miranda W PTS 10 Las Vegas
19.10.95	Raul Rios W PTS 10 Las Vegas
01.12.95	Willy Salazar W RTD 9 Indio
	(WBO S. Flyweight Title Defence)
03.02.96	Giovanni Andrade W RSC 2 Los Angeles
	(WBO S. Flyweight Title Defence)
30.04.96	Ramon Gonzalez W CO 2 San Antonio
07.06.96	Ivan Alvarez W RSC 8 Las Vegas
	(WBO S. Flyweight Title Defence)
Career: 38 contests, won 36, drew 2.	

Quincy (The Terminator) Taylor

Campo, USA. *Born* 18 July, 1963
Former WBC Middleweight
Champion. Former Undefeated NABF
Middleweight Champion

Southpaw. Once managed by Sugar
Ray Leonard, and now trained by
Curtis Cokes, Quincy is a hard puncher
who turned professional in 1986 but
retired from the sport in 1991 after
losing twice to Jorge Vaca. Came back
two years later and knocked out Otis
Grant in March 1994 to win the NABF
title, before getting his hands on the
WBC crown in August 1995 after
stopping Julian Jackson. Unfortunately, an upset defeat at the hands of
Keith Holmes means that he is
currently an ex-champion. Has 23
quick wins.

19.08.95	Julian Jackson W RSC 6 Las Vegas
	(WBC Middleweight Title Challenge)
16.03.96	Keith Holmes L RSC 9 Las Vegas
	(WBC Middleweight Title Defence)
Career: 30 contests, won 26, lost 4.	

Fabrice Tiozzo

St Denis, France. *Born* 8 May, 1969
WBC L. Heavyweight Champion.
Former Undefeated European &
French L. Heavyweight Champion

The elder brother of Christophe, a
former WBA super-middleweight
champion, Fabrice is a 6'1" upright
stylist. Turned professional in New
York in November 1988 and later won
the French title in 1991 by outpointing
Eric Nicoletta, before losing on points
in a challenge to Virgil Hill for the
WBA title in April 1993. Came back
strongly to relieve Eddy Smulders of
his European title in March 1994, prior
to taking the WBC crown from the
head of Mike McCallum (June 1995)

and defending against Eric Lucas last
January.

13.01.96	Eric Lucas W PTS 12 St Etienne
	(WBC L. Heavyweight Title Defence)
Career: 34 contests, won 33, lost 1.	

Fabrice Tiozzo

Felix (Tito) Trinidad

Cupoy Alto, Puerto Rico. *Born* 10
January, 1973
IBF Welterweight Champion

5'11" tall. Following his father, Felix
Snr, into the professional ring, he
started out in March 1990 at the age of
17. Knocked out Maurice Blocker in
two rounds in June 1993 to win the
IBF crown and has made nine
defences, with only Hector Camacho
in January 1994 managing to take him
the distance in a title fight and heavy
hitting accounting for 25 opponents
inside the distance. One of the most
exciting fighters around, Felix has fast
hands, but can be rocked himself.

18.11.95	Larry Barnes W RSC 4 Atlantic City
	(IBF Welterweight Title Defence)
10.02.96	Rodney Moore W RTD 4 Las Vegas
	(IBF Welterweight Title Defence)
18.05.96	Fred Pendleton W CO 5 Las Vegas
	(IBF Welterweight Title Defence)
Career: 29 contests, won 29.	

Konstantin (Kostya) Tszyu

Australia. *Born* Serov, Russia, 19
September, 1969
IBF L. Welterweight Champion

5'7" tall. As an amateur was twice
European champion and won the world
title in 1991, claiming only three losses
in 272 fights. Turned professional in
Australia in March 1992, beating
former world champion, Juan Laporte,
in only his fourth fight, before taking
the IBF title from Jake Rodriguez in
January 1995, flooring him five times
and halting him in round six. With
three successful defences behind him,
Kostya is a dangerous southpaw
stalker with power in both hands and
has stopped or knocked out 13 victims.

20.01.96	Hugo Pineda W RSC 11 Parramatta
	(IBF L. Welterweight Title Defence)
24.05.96	Corey Johnson W RSC 4 Sydney
	(IBF L. Welterweight Title Defence)
Career: 17 contests, won 17.	

Regilio (Turbo) Tuur

Paramaribo, Surinam. *Born* 12 August,
1967
WBO S. Featherweight Champion.
Former European S. Featherweight
Champion

Made his name in the 1988 Olympic
Games when he knocked out the
American, Kelcie Banks, in one round,
before turning professional in the
United States in July 1989 and boxing
both there and in Europe. His first title
came when he won the vacant
European crown in December 1992,
outpointing Jacobin Yoma, but he lost
it in a return six months later. Came
back well to collect the vacant WBO
title in September 1994, decisioning
Eugene Speed, and has defended his
title five times. 5'7" tall, he is an
aggressive fighter with a good left
hook and has 26 quick wins.

09.09.95	Luis Mendoza W RTD 10 Arnhem
	(WBO S. Featherweight Title Defence)
23.12.95	Giorgio Campanella W PTS 12 Amsterdam
	(WBO S. Featherweight Title Defence)
01.04.96	Narciso Valenzuela W PTS 12 Hertogenbosch
	(WBO S. Featherweight Title Defence)
Career: 46 contests, won 42, drew 1, lost 3.	

(Iron) Mike Tyson

New York, USA, *Born* 30 June, 1966
WBC Heavyweight Champion. Former
WBC, IBF & WBA Heavyweight
Champion

Discovered by Cus D'Amato, the
former National Golden Gloves
champion turned professional in
March 1985 and won the WBC title in
November 1986 by halting Trevor
Berbick in two rounds. In his next
fight, in March 1987, he decisioned
James "Bonecrusher" Smith to pick up
the WBA title and, after defending it
with a stoppage of Pinklon Thomas,
collected the IBF crown with a points
victory against Tony Tucker in August
1987 to gain general recognition as
world champion. Made six successful
title defences, including a first round
kayo of Michael Spinks, and a
stoppage of Frank Bruno, before being
knocked out by James Douglas in
Tokyo in February 1990 in a huge
upset. Scored four more wins and was
then jailed for rape. Returned in
August 1995 and, in March 1996,
stopped Frank Bruno again to regain
the WBC title. Has lost some of his
edge, but is still the hottest property in
boxing.

19.08.95	Peter McNeeley W RSC 1 Las Vegas
16.12.95	Buster Mathis W CO 3 Philadelphia
16.03.96	Frank Bruno W RSC 3 Las Vegas *(WBC Heavyweight Title Challenge)*
Career: 45 contests, won 44, lost 1.	

Paul (The Ultimate) Vaden

San Diego, USA. *Born* 29 December,
1967
Former IBF L. Middleweight
Champion

6'1" tall and a converted southpaw.
The United States amateur champion
in 1989 and 1990, prior to turning
professional in April 1991, Paul scored
good wins over Greg Lonon, John
Montes and Jason Papillion, before
coming from behind to halt Vince
Pettway in the last round of their fight
in August 1995 to win the IBF crown.
Lost the title four months later on a
wide decision to WBC champion,
Terry Norris. Although he has fast
hands with good chin, he is not a big
puncher, with only 13 wins coming
inside the distance.

12.08.95	Vince Pettway W RSC 12 Las Vegas *(IBF L. Middleweight Title Challenge)*
16.12.95	Terry Norris L PTS 12 Las Vegas *(IBF L. Middleweight Title Defence. WBC L. Middleweight Title Challenge)*
18.05.96	Clem Tucker W RSC 6 Las Vegas
Career: 26 contests, won 25, lost 1.	

Julio Cesar Vasquez

Santa Fe, Argentina. *Born* 13 July,
1966
WBA L. Middleweight Champion

Tough, crude and strong, with a hard
punch, but a poor defence, the 5'9"
southpaw turned professional in June
1986, winning his first 30 contests,
before losing on disqualification to
Verno Phillips in June 1991. Won the
vacant WBA light-middleweight title
in December 1992 with a first round
stoppage of Hitoshi Kamiyama and
was successful in ten defences, beating
Ronald Wright and Aaron Davis,
before losing on points to Pernell
Whitaker in March 1995. Regained the
title by knocking out Carl Daniels in
December and has 39 wins inside the
full route.

19.08.95	Carlos Leturia W CO 1 Buenos Aires
16.12.95	Carl Daniels W RSC 11 Philadelphia *(WBC L. Middleweight Title Challenge)*
Career: 58 contests, won 56, lost 2.	

Wilfredo Vasquez

Bayamon, Puerto Rico. *Born* 2 August,
1961
WBA Featherweight Champion.
Former WBA Bantamweight & S.
Bantamweight Champion. Former
Undefeated Puerto Rican
Bantamweight Champion. Former
Undefeated Latin American
Featherweight Champion

A former stablemate of Mike Tyson,
the 5'4" Puerto Rican lost his first
professional fight in 1981, but was
then unbeaten until February 1986,
when defeated on points by Miguel
Lora in a challenge for the WBC
bantamweight title. Won the WBA
crown in October 1987, halting Chan-
Yong Park, but lost it on points to
Kaokor Galaxy in May 1988, prior to
moving up to take the WBA super-
bantamweight title in March 1992,
following an upset kayo of Raul
Perez. Made nine defences, before
losing the title on points to Antonio
Cermeno in May 1995, but bounced
back to take the featherweight title
with an 11th round stoppage of Eloy
Rojas in May 1996. Is a sharp little
fighter with a hard punch in both
hands.

26.08.95	Pablo Valenzuela W PTS 10 Miami
26.10.95	Carlos Rocha W CO 1 Ponce
09.12.95	Jose Velasquez W RSC 3 San Juan *(Vacant Latin American Featherweight Title)*
18.05.96	Eloy Rojas W RSC 11 Las Vegas *(WBA Featherweight Title Challenge)*
Career: 56 contests, won 46, drew 3, lost 7.	

Wilfredo Vasquez

Pernell (Sweet Pea) Whitaker

Norfolk, USA. *Born* 2 January, 1964
WBC Welterweight Champion.
Former Undefeated WBA
L. Middleweight Champion. Former
Undefeated IBF L. Welterweight
Champion. Former Undefeated IBF,
WBA & WBC Lightweight Champion.
Former Undefeated NABF & USBA
Lightweight Champion

5'9" tall southpaw. Arguably the best boxer in the world, pound for pound, over the past five years, Pernell won a gold medal at the 1984 Olympic Games, before becoming a professional in November 1984. Lost a controversial decision to Jose Luis Ramirez in March 1988, in a challenge for the WBC lightweight title, but came back to win the IBF title in February 1989 with a points victory over Greg Haugen and to beat Ramirez on points four months later to add the vacant WBC title to his coming collection. Having knocked out Juan Nazario in one round in August, 1990, to take the WBA crown, he moved up to light-welterweight in July 1992, outpointing Rafael Pineda for the IBF title, and then up to welterweight in March 1993 to beat James McGirt on points and become WBC champion. Unlucky to only be given a draw against Julio Cesar Chavez in a title defence in September 1993, he has 16 wins inside the distance.

26.08.95	Gary Jacobs W PTS 12 Atlantic City
	(WBC Welterweight Title Defence)
18.11.95	Jake Rodriguez W CO 6 Atlantic City
	(WBC Welterweight Title Defence)
12.04.96	Wilfredo Rivera W PTS 12 St Maarten
	(WBC Welterweight Title Defence)
Career: 40 contests, won 38, drew 1, lost 1.	

Ronald (Winkie) Wright

St Petersburg, USA. *Born* 26 November, 1971
WBO L. Middleweight Champion. Former Undefeated NABF L. Middleweight Champion

A 5'10" tall southpaw, Ronald claimed numerous local titles before becoming a professional in October 1990. After winning his first 25 fights, he was floored six times and outpointed by Julio Cesar Vasquez in August 1994, in a challenge for the WBA title, but came back to win the NABF title when decisioning Tony Marshall in February 1995. Currently the WBO champion,

having outpointed Bronco McKart in May 1996, he is a stylish, intelligent boxer, with only 21 wins inside the distance.

25.07.95	Larry Lacoursiere W RSC 1 St Jean de Luz
23.08.95	Anthony Ivory W PTS 12 Le Cannet
	(NABF L. Middleweight Title Defence)
23.10.95	Young Dick Tiger W RSC 9 Los Angeles
	(NABF L. Middleweight Title Defence)
06.01.96	Jean Paul D'Alessandro W PTS 8 Levallois-Perret
05.03.96	Andrew Council W PTS 12 Norfolk
	(NABF L. Middleweight Title Defence)
17.05.96	Bronco McKart W PTS 12 Monroe
	(WBO L. Middleweight Title Challenge)
Career: 36 contests, won 35, lost 1.	

Ronald Wright

Keiji Yamaguchi

Osaka, Japan.
WBA L. Flyweight Champion. Former Undefeated Japanese L. Flyweight Champion

The fast, skinny, clever southpaw, who lacks a real punch, was three times Japanese High School champion, finishing with a 28-3 record. Turned professional in May 1992 and won the vacant Japanese title in September 1994 with a points victory over Katsunori Zagabi. Having challenged unsuccessfully for the WBA crown in

September 1995, losing on points to Hi-Yong Choi, Keiji sprang an upset when he decisioned dangerous Carlos Murillo in a second attempt at the title last May.

05.09.95	Hi-Yong Choi L PTS 12 Osaka
	(WBA L. Flyweight Title Challenge)
23.12.95	Joel Saguid W PTS 10 Gifu
21.05.96	Carlos Murillo W PTS 12 Osaka
	(WBA L. Flyweight Title Challenge)
Career: 20 contests, won 19, lost 1.	

Daniel Zaragoza

Mexico City, Mexico. *Born* 11 December, 1957
WBC S. Bantamweight Champion. Former WBC Bantamweight Champion. Former Undefeated Mexican Bantamweight Champion. Former Undefeated NABF S. Bantamweight Champion

A strong, courageous southpaw, who has overcome paper-thin eyebrows to take part in 18 world title bouts, Daniel signed off with a gold medal in the Pan American Games before turning professional in October 1980. Won the vacant WBC bantamweight title in May 1985, beating Fred Jackson on a disqualification, but lost it in his first defence three months later to Miguel Lora on points. Moved up to super-bantamweight and again won the vacant WBC title by stopping Carlos Zarate in February 1988, successfully defending five times until being stopped by Paul Banke in April 1990. After regaining the championship from Kiyoshi Hatanaka, there were two more defences, including a revenge win over Banke, before a points defeat at the hands of Thierry Jacob (March 1992), prior to an amazing comeback at the age of 37 to wrest title away from Hector Acero Sanchez last November.

06.11.95	Hector Acero Sanchez W PTS 12 Los Angeles
	(WBC S. Bantamweight Title Challenge)
03.03.96	Joichiro Tatsuyoshi W RSC 11 Yokohama
	(WBC S. Bantamweight Title Defence)
Career: 62 contests, won 52, drew 3, lost 7.	

World Title Bouts During 1995-96

by Bob Yalen

All of last season's title bouts for the IBF, WBA, WBC and WBO are recorded separately and are listed in date order, showing the boxers respective weights, along with the scorecard, if going to a decision. There is also a short summary of any bout that involved a British contestant, and British officials, where applicable, are listed. The reason for keeping the four leading world bodies segregated is due to the fact that politics govern and, once again, there was not one contest that involved the WORLD TITLE. Although giving many boxers the opportunity to fight for so-called world titles, the truth of the matter is that many do not deserve a top ten rating. Also, until other bodies can raise their standards, they will not be mentioned in this section.

International Boxing Federation

4 July 1995   Mbulelo Botile 117$^1/_2$ (South Africa) W PTS 12 Sammy Stewart 116$^1/_2$ (Liberia), Hammanskraal, South Africa (Bantam). Scorecards: 118-110, 118-110, 119-109.

9 July 1995   Eddie Hopson 129 (USA) L RSC 2 Tracy Harris Patterson 129 (USA), Reno, USA (J. Light).

15 July 1995   Humberto Gonzalez 107$^1/_2$ (Mexico) L CO 7 Saman Sorjaturong 107$^1/_2$ (Thailand), Los Angeles, USA (J. Fly). Although winning the IBF and WBC titles in the same fight, Sorjaturong made no move to defend the IBF version and relinquished the belt towards the end in order to concentrate on the WBC crown.

29 July 1995   Danny Romero 110$^3/_4$ (USA) W CO 6 Miguel Martinez 111 (Mexico), San Antonio, USA (Fly).

12 August 1995   Vince Pettway 153 (USA) L RSC 12 Paul Vaden 154 (USA), Las Vegas, USA (J. Middle).

19 August 1995   Phillip Holiday 133$^3/_4$ (South Africa) W RTD 10 Miguel Julio 134$^1/_4$ (Colombia), Sun City, South Africa (Vacant Light). Dave Parris was one of the judges. The title became vacant after Oscar de la Hoya relinquished his belt in July.

26 September 1995   Vuyani Bungu 122 (South Africa) W PTS 12 Laureano Ramirez 121 (Dominican Republic), Hammanskraal, South Africa (J. Feather). Scorecards: 117-111, 117-111, 118-112.

30 September 1995   Roy Jones 167$^1/_2$ (USA) W RSC 3 Tony Thornton 165$^3/_4$ (USA), Pensacola, USA (S. Middle).

6 October 1995   Harold Grey 115 (Colombia) L PTS 12 Carlos Salazar 113$^3/_4$ (Argentine), Mar del Plata, Argentina (J. Bantam). Scorecards: 110-116, 110-116, 114-112.

14 October 1995   Henry Maske 173$^3/_4$ (Germany) W PTS 12 Graciano Rocchigiani 173$^1/_4$ (Germany), Munich, Germany (L. Heavy). Scorecards: 117-111, 116-112, 115-113.

29 October 1995   Ratanapol Sowvoraphin 105 (Thailand) W CO 2 Jack Russell 104$^3/_4$ (Australia), Suphan Buri, Thailand (M. Fly).

4 November 1995   Phillip Holiday 134$^1/_4$ (South Africa) W PTS 12 Ray Martinez 134$^3/_4$ (USA), Sun City, South Africa (Light). Scorecards: 118-111, 120-108, 117-111.

18 November 1995   Felix Trinidad 147 (Puerto Rico) W RSC 4 Larry Barnes 146 (USA), Atlantic City, USA (Welter).

25 November 1995   Mbulelo Botile 117$^1/_2$ (South Africa) W RSC 2 Reynaldo Hurtado 117$^3/_4$ (Colombia), East London, South Africa (Bantam).

9 December 1995   Frans Botha 227 (South Africa) W PTS 12 Axel Schulz 222$^3/_4$ (Germany), Stuttgart, Germany (Vacant Heavy). Scorecards: 113-115, 116-112, 118-111. The title had been vacated by George Foreman the previous August after he refused a rematch against Schulz. Following the fight, and having failed a post-fight drugs test, Botha was stripped by the courts at the end of March.

9 December 1995   Tom Johnson 125$^3/_4$ (USA) W PTS 12 Jose Badillo 125$^1/_2$ (Puerto Rico), Stuttgart, Germany (Feather). Scorecards: 113-113, 114-112, 115-111.

15 December 1995   Tracy Harris Patterson 129$^3/_4$ (USA) L PTS 12 Arturo Gatti 130 (USA), New York City, USA (J. Light). Scorecards: 111-116, 112-115, 113-114.

16 December 1995   Paul Vaden 154 (USA) L PTS 12 Terry Norris 151$^1/_2$ (USA), Philadelphia, USA (J. Middle). Scorecards: 109-119, 108-120, 110-119.

16 December 1995   Robbie Regan 111$^3/_4$ (Wales) W RSC 2 Ferid Ben Jeddou 112 (Tunisia), Welsh Institute of Sport, Cardiff (Vacant Interim Fly). Roy Francis refereed and Dave Parris was one of the judges. The fight came about when Danny Romero was injured in a non-title loss to Willy Salazar. A month later, Romero relinquished the title, while Regan moved up to bantam to challenge Daniel Jimenez for the WBO crown.

30 December 1995   Ratanapol Sowvoraphin 104$^1/_2$ (Thailand) W RSC 6 Osvaldo Guerrero 104$^3/_4$ (Mexico), Chiang Mai, Thailand (M. Fly). Sowvoraphin was stripped in March after failing to make the weight for a title defence.

20 January 1996   Konstantin Tszyu 139$^3/_4$ (Russia) W RSC 11 Hugo Pineda 139$^1/_2$ (Colombia), Parramatta, Australia (J. Welter).

23 January 1996   Vuyani Bungu 122 (South Africa) W PTS 12 Johnny Lewus 122 (USA), Biloxi, USA (J. Feather). Scorecards: 118-111, 118-112, 120-110 (J. Feather).

27 January 1996   Terry Norris 152$^1/_2$ (USA) W CO 2 Jorge Luis Vado 153$^1/_2$ (Nicaragua), Phoenix, USA (J. Middle).

27 January 1996   Bernard Hopkins 159 (USA) W RSC 1 Steve Frank 160 (USA), Phoenix, USA (Middle).

10 February 1996   Carlos Salazar 114³/₄ (Argentine) W RTD 6 Antonio Melis 114¹/₂ (Italy), Rome, Italy (J. Bantam).

10 February 1996   Felix Trinidad 147 (Puerto Rico) W RTD 4 Rodney Moore 147 (USA), Las Vegas, USA (Welter).

17 February 1996   Henry Maske 174¹/₂ (Germany) W PTS 12 Duran Williams 174 (USA), Dortmund, Germany (L. Heavy). Scorecards: 117-111, 117-111, 118-110.

17 February 1996   Phillip Holiday 133¹/₂ (South Africa) W RSC 10 John Lark 134 (USA), Hammanskraal, South Africa (Light).

24 February 1996   Terry Norris 150³/₄ (USA) W RSC 8 Vince Pettway 151 (USA), Richmond, USA (J. Middle).

2 March 1996   Tom Johnson 126 (USA) W RSC 12 Ever Beleno 126 (Colombia), The Arena, Newcastle (Feather). Dave Parris was one of the judges.

16 March 1996   Michael Carbajal 107 (USA) W PTS 12 Melchor Cob Castro 107 (Mexico), Las Vegas, USA (Vacant L. Fly). Scorecards: 117-111, 116-112, 115-113.

16 March 1996   Bernard Hopkins 160 (USA) W RSC 4 Joe Lipsey 158 (USA), Las Vegas, USA (Middle).

23 March 1996   Arturo Gatti 130 (USA) W CO 6 Wilson Rodriguez 128 (Dominican Republic), New York City, USA (J. Light).

2 April 1996   Mbulelo Botile 118 (South Africa) W CO 11 Ancee Gedeon 117¹/₄ (Haiti), Providence, USA (Bantam).

15 April 1996   Vuyani Bungu 121¹/₂ (South Africa) W RSC 2 Pablo Osuna 121¹/₄ (Colombia), Hammanskraal, South Africa (J. Feather).

26 April 1996   Tom Johnson 126 (USA) W CO 7 Claudio Martinet 126 (Argentine), Antibes, France (Feather).

27 April 1996   Carlos Salazar 115 (Argentine) L PTS 12 Harold Grey 115 (Colombia), Cartagena, Colombia (J. Bantam). Scorecards: 113-115, 113-115, 113-115.

4 May 1996   Mark Johnson 111¹/₂ (USA) W CO 1 Francisco Tejedor 112 (Colombia), Anaheim, USA (Vacant Fly).

18 May 1996   Felix Trinidad 147 (Puerto Rico) W CO 5 Fred Pendleton 147 (USA), Las Vegas, USA (Welter).

18 May 1996   Ratanapol Sowvoraphin 104 (Thailand) W PTS 12 Jun Arlos 101³/₄ (Philippines), Yala, Thailand (Vacant M. Fly). Scorecards: 120-107, 118-109, 120-107.

18 May 1996   Phillip Holiday 133³/₄ (South Africa) W RSC 2 Jeff Fenech 134 (Australia), Melbourne, Australia (Light).

24 May 1996   Konstantin Tszyu 139³/₄ (Russia) W RSC 4 Corey Johnson 140 (USA), Sydney, Australia (J. Welter).

25 May 1996   Henry Maske 173³/₄ (Germany) W PTS 12 John Scully 174¹/₂ (USA), Leipzig, Germany (L. Heavy). Scorecards: 120-108, 120-108, 119-109.

15 June 1996   Roy Jones 166 (USA) W RSC 11 Eric Lucas 165³/₄ (Canada), Jacksonville, USA (S. Middle).

22 June 1996   Michael Moorer 222¹/₄ (USA) W PTS 12 Axel Schulz 222³/₄ (Germany), Dortmund, Germany (Vacant Heavy). Scorecards: Dave Parris 116-113, 116-113, 113-115.

29 June 1996   Mbulelo Botile 117¹/₂ (South Africa) W RTD 8 Marlon Arlos 115 (Philippines), East London, South Africa. (Bantam).

World Boxing Association

22 July 1995   Orlin Norris 188³/₄ (USA) L CO 8 Nate Miller 186³/₄ (USA), London Arena, London (Cruiser). John Coyle refereed.

22 July 1995   Hyung-Chul Lee 114¹/₂ (South Korea) L CO 4 Alimi Goitia 115 (Venezuela), Seoul, South Korea (J. Bantam).

6 August 1995   Chana Porpaoin 105 (Thailand) W CO 6 Ernesto Rubillar 105 (Philippines), Bangkok, Thailand (M. Fly).

13 August 1995   Eloy Rojas 125¹/₄ (Venezuela) W PTS 12 Nobutoshi Hiranaka 125³/₄ (Japan), Tagawa City, Japan (Feather). Scorecards: 116-112, 116-111, 116-112.

19 August 1995   Bruce Seldon 234 (USA) W RSC 10 Joe Hipp 233 (USA), Las Vegas, USA (Heavy).

23 August 1995   Ike Quartey 145¹/₄ (Ghana) W RSC 4 Andrew Murray 145¹/₂ (Guyana), Le Cannet-Rochville, France (Welter).

2 September 1995   Virgil Hill 174 ³/₄ (USA) W PTS 12 Drake Thadzi 172³/₄ (Malawi), The Stadium, Wembley (L. Heavy). Scorecards: 117-111, 119-110, 118-112.

5 September 1995   Hi-Yong Choi 107¹/₂ (South Korea) W PTS 12 Keiji Yamaguchi 108 (Japan), Osaka, Japan (J. Fly). Scorecards: 117-111, 115-116, 114-114.

17 September 1995   Daorung Chuwatana 118 (Thailand) L PTS 12 Veerapol Sahaprom 118 (Thailand), Bangkok, Thailand (Bantam). Scorecards: 113-118, 114-117, 115-114.

13 October 1995   Jorge Castro 160 (Argentine) W PTS 12 Reggie Johnson 157³/₄ (USA), Comodoro Rivadavia, Argentina (Middle). Scorecards: 118-113, 115-113, 112-115. John Coyle refereed.

17 October 1995   Saen Sowploenchit 111¹/₂ (Thailand) W RSC 10 Hiroki Ioka 112 (Japan), Osaka, Japan (Fly).

21 October 1995   Yong-Soo Choi 130 (South Korea) W RSC 10 Victor Hugo Paz 128¹/₂ (Argentine), Salta,

Argentina (Vacant J. Light). The title became vacant in August when the champion, Genaro Hernandez, turned down a mandatory defence against Paz in favour of a match with Oscar de la Hoya.

14 November 1995   Orzubek Nazarov 134$\frac{1}{2}$ (Russia) W PTS 12 Dindo Canoy 133$\frac{3}{4}$ (Philippines), Iwaki City, Japan (Light). Scorecards: 119-110, 120-113, 120-107,

25 November 1995   Alimi Goitia 114$\frac{3}{4}$ (Venezuela) W RSC 5 Aquiles Guzman 114$\frac{1}{4}$ (Venezuela). Porlama, Venezuela (J. Bantam). John Coyle refereed.

26 November 1995   Antonio Cermeno 120$\frac{1}{2}$ (Venezuela) W PTS 12 Jesus Salud 121$\frac{1}{4}$ (USA), Maracay, Venezuela (J. Feather). Scorecards: 118-111, 119-110, 120-110.

2 December 1995   Chana Porpaoin 105 (Thailand) L PTS 12 Rosendo Alvarez 105 (Nicaragua), Bangkok, Thailand (M. Fly). Scorecards: 114-116, 116-115, 113-115.

9 December 1995   Frank Lilles 168 (USA) W PTS 12 Mauricio Amaral 165$\frac{3}{4}$ (Brazil), Stuttgart, Germany (S. Middle). Scorecards: 119-108, 118-110, 118-111.

In a crash-bang affair at the Newcastle Arena, Frank Lilles (left) nearly came unstuck against fellow-American, Tim Littles   Les Clark

16 December 1995   Carl Daniels 153 (USA) L RSC 11 Julio Cesar Vasquez 154 (Argentine), Philadelphia, USA (J. Middle).

19 December 1995   Jorge Castro 160 (Argentine) L PTS 12 Shinji Takehara 160 (Japan), Tokyo, Japan (Middle). Scorecards: 114-116, 112-118, 111-117.

13 January 1996   Frankie Randall 140 (USA) L TD 5 Juan M. Coggi 140 (Argentine), Miami, USA (J. Welter). Scorecards: 38-39, 37-38, 37-38.

13 January 1996   Hi-Yong Choi 107$\frac{1}{2}$ (South Korea) L PTS 12 Carlos Murillo 107 (Panama), Miami, USA (J. Fly). Scorecards: 113-116, 112-116, 110-119.

13 January 1996   Nate Miller 188$\frac{1}{2}$ (USA) W RTD 4 Reynaldo Gimenez 189 (Argentine), Miami, USA (Cruiser).

14 January 1996   Saen Sowploenchit 112 (Thailand) W PTS 12 Yong-Soon Chang 112 (South Korea), Nontaburi, Thailand (Fly). Scorecards: 119-111, 117-113, 116-113.

27 January 1996   Veerapol Sahaprom 118 (Thailand) L RSC 2 Nana Yaw Konadu 117 (Ghana), Kanchunburi, Thailand (Bantam).

27 January 1996   Eloy Rojas 125$\frac{1}{2}$ (Venezuela) W PTS 12 Miguel Arrozal 124$\frac{1}{4}$ (Philippines), Phoenix, USA (Feather). Scorecards: 120-110, 118-110, 118-110.

27 January 1996   Yong-Soo Choi 130 (South Korea) W PTS 12 Yamato Mitani 129$\frac{1}{4}$ (Japan), Tokyo, Japan (J. Light). Scorecards: 115-113, 115-114, 115-114.

24 February 1996   Alimi Goitia 115 (Venezuela) W RSC 12 Hyung-Chul Lee 115 (South Korea), Kwangyang, South Korea (J. Bantam).

15 March 1996   Carlos Murillo 107$\frac{3}{4}$ (Panama) W CO 10 Jose Garcia Bernal 107$\frac{1}{2}$ (Colombia), Panama City, Panama (J. Fly).

23 March 1996   Nate Miller 188$\frac{1}{4}$ (USA) W RSC 9 Brian la Spada 187 (USA), Miami, USA (Cruiser).

23 March 1996   Antonio Cermeno 121 (Venezuela) W PTS 12 Yober Ortega 120$\frac{3}{4}$ (Venezuela), Miami, USA (J. Feather). Scorecards: 116-112, 116-115, 115-114.

23 March 1996   Saen Sowploenchit 112 (Thailand) W PTS 12 Silvio Gamez 114$\frac{1}{4}$ (Venezuela), Tathum Thani, Thailand (Fly). Scorecards: 116-113, 117-111, 113-115.

30 March 1996   Rosendo Alvarez 105 (Nicaragua) W CO 3 Kermin Guardia 105 (Colombia), Managua, Nicaragua (M. Fly).

12 April 1996   Ike Quartey 147 (Ghana) W RSC 3 Vince Phillips 147 (USA), St Maarten, Netherlands Antilles (Welter).

15 April 1996   Orzubek Nazarov 135 (Russia) W CO 4 Adrianus Taroreh 135 (Indonesia), Tokyo, Japan (Light).

20 April 1996   Virgil Hill 174^1/$_2$ (USA) W PTS 12 Louis del Valle 175 (Puerto Rico), Grand Forks, USA (L. Heavy). Scorecards: 114-113, 116-112, 116-114.

29 April 1996   Alimi Goitia 114^1/$_2$ (Venezuela) W RSC 5 Satoshi Iida 114^3/$_4$ (Japan), Nagoya, Japan (J. Bantam). John Coyle refereed.

11 May 1996   Yong-Soo Choi 130 (South Korea) W CO 8 Orlando Soto 129^3/$_4$ (Panama), Chechudo, South Korea (J. Light).

18 May 1996   Eloy Rojas 125^1/$_2$ (Venezuela) L RSC 11 Wilfredo Vasquez 126 (Puerto Rico), Las Vegas, USA (Feather).

21 May 1996   Carlos Murillo 107^1/$_2$ (Panama) L PTS 12 Keiji Yamaguchi 108 (Japan), Osaka, Japan (J. Fly). Scorecards: 116-112, 114-115, 113-116.

8 June 1996   Frank Lilles 167^1/$_4$ (USA) W RSC 3 Tim Littles 167 (USA), The Arena, Newcastle (S. Middle).

15 June 1996   Rosenda Alvarez 105 (Nicaragua) W PTS 12 Eric Chavez 104^1/$_4$ (Philippines), Sendai, Japan (M. Fly). Scorecards: 114-114, 119-111, 115-113.

24 June 1996   Shinji Takehara 160 (Japan) L RSC 9 William Joppy 160 (USA), Yokohama, Japan (Middle). John Coyle refereed.

World Boxing Council

15 July 1995   Humberto Gonzalez 107^1/$_2$ (Mexico) L CO 7 Saman Sorjaturong 107^1/$_2$ (Thailand), Los Angeles, USA (J. Fly).

27 July 1995   Nigel Benn 168 (England) W RTD 8 Vincenzo Nardiello 167 (Italy), London Arena, London (S. Middle). The Italian corner threw the towel in at 1.43 of the eighth after Nardiello had been down five times, twice officially. Refereed by Larry O'Connell, the three judges had Benn 68-64, 68-63, 67-66 ahead at the time of the finish.

25 July 1995   Marcelo Dominguez 186^1/$_2$ (Argentine) W RSC 9 Akim Tafer 185^3/$_4$ (France), St Jean de Luz, France (Vacant Interim Cruiser). Following an injury that forced the champion, Anaclet Wamba, out of his defence against Tafer, the above match was hurriedly arranged on the proviso that the winner would get first crack at the title.

30 July 1995   Yasuei Yakushiji 118 (Japan) L PTS 12 Wayne McCullough 117^3/$_4$ (Ireland), Nagoya, Japan (Bantam). Scorecards: 110-118, 116-115, 113-116.

19 August 1995   Miguel Gonzalez 135 (Mexico) W PTS 12 Lamar Murphy 135 (USA), Las Vegas, USA (Light). Scorecards: 117-109, 114-114, 114-112.

19 August 1995   Luis Santana 154 (Dominican Republic) L RSC 2 Terry Norris 152 (USA), Las Vegas, USA (S. Welter).

19 August 1995   Julian Jackson 160 (Virgin Islands) L RSC 6 Quincy Taylor 159^1/$_2$ (USA), Las Vegas, USA (Middle).

26 August 1995   Pernell Whitaker 147 (USA) W PTS 12 Gary Jacobs 147 (Scotland), Atlantic City, USA (Welter). Scorecards: 118-108, 118-109, 117-109. Despite a disastrous last round when he was floored twice and saved by the bell, Jacobs often made Whitaker appear ordinary, his performance ridiculing the scorecards. The Scot also proved stronger on the inside, with the champion hell-bent on keeping the fight at distance, using speed and slippery tactics to his advantage.

2 September 1995   Marcelo Dominguez 188^1/$_2$ (Argentine) W RSC 12 Reynaldo Gimenez 189^1/$_2$ (Argentine), Gualeguaychu, Argentina (Interim Cruiser).

2 September 1995   Nigel Benn 166^1/$_4$ (England) W CO 7 Danny Perez 167 (USA), The Stadium, Wembley (S. Middle). Counted out at 2.23 of the seventh by referee, Mickey Vann, Perez had been decked two rounds earlier and the finishing blow, a clubbing right hander, was hardly a surprise. However, he had fought bravely against a man who had too much power for him, with the end always in sight.

2 September 1995   Oliver McCall 234^1/$_4$ (USA) L PTS 12 Frank Bruno 247^3/$_4$ (England), The Stadium, Wembley (Heavy). Scorecards: 111-117, 111-117, 113-115. This was the night that "Big Frank" and the British public had been waiting for, the night where their favourite son put all his set-backs behind him to win the title. To be fair to all concerned, McCall hardly looked inspired, while Bruno laboured badly towards the end, but at the final bell it was the latter who well won the day.

16 September 1995   Julio Cesar Chavez 140 (Mexico) W PTS 12 David Kamau 140 (Kenya), Las Vegas, USA (S. Light). Scorecards: 117-110, 116-112, Larry O'Connell 116-114.

16 September 1995   Terry Norris 151 (USA) W RSC 9 David Gonzalez 153 (USA), Las Vegas, USA (S. Welter).

23 September 1995   Alejandro Gonzalez 126 (Mexico) L PTS 12 Manuel Medina 126 (Mexico), Sacramento, USA (Feather). Scorecards: 112-116, 113-115, 115-113.

25 September 1995   Yuri Arbachakov 112 (Russia) W PTS 12 Chartchai Elite-Gym 112 (Thailand), Tokyo, Japan (Fly). Scorecards: 116-112, 116-114, 117-113.

24 October 1995   Marcelo Dominguez 186 (Argentine) W PTS 12 Sergei Kobozev 187 (Russia), Levallois-Perret, France (Interim Cruiser). Scorecards: 116-113, 115-113, 115-116. Booked to meet Dominguez on 20 April, the champion, Anaclet Wamba, failed to make the weight and was stripped, the former being proclaimed the new titleholder in his place.

6 November 1995   Hector Acero Sanchez 122 (Dominican Republic) L PTS 12 Daniel Zaragoza 122 (Mexico), Los Angeles, USA (S. Bantam). Scorecards: 112-115, 112-116, 114-113.

8 November 1995   Hiroshi Kawashima 115 (Japan) W RSC 3 Boy Arum 114$\frac{1}{2}$ (Indonesia), Tokyo, Japan (S. Fly).

12 November 1995   Saman Sorjaturong 106$\frac{1}{2}$ (Thailand) W CO 4 Yuichi Hosono 107$\frac{1}{4}$ (Japan), Ratchaburi, Thailand (L. Fly)

18 November 1995   Pernell Whitaker 147 (USA) W CO 6 Jake Rodriguez 146$\frac{1}{4}$ (USA), Atlantic City, USA (Welter).

1 December 1995   Gabriel Ruelas 130 (USA) L RSC 5 Azumah Nelson 130 (Ghana), Indio, USA (S. Feather).

2 December 1995   Wayne McCullough 117$\frac{1}{2}$ (Ireland) W RSC 8 Johnny Bredahl 117$\frac{1}{2}$ (Denmark), King's Hall, Belfast (Bantam).

11 December 1995   Manuel Medina 126 (Mexico) L PTS 12 Luisito Espinosa 125 (Philippines), Tokyo, Japan (Feather). Scorecards: 113-115, 112-116, 113-115.

16 December 1995   Terry Norris 151$\frac{1}{2}$ (USA) W PTS 12 Paul Vaden 154 (USA), Philadelphia, USA (S. Welter). Scorecards: 119-109, 120-108, 118-110.

13 January 1996   Fabrice Tiozzo 174$\frac{1}{4}$ (France) W PTS 12 Eric Lucas 173$\frac{1}{2}$ (Canada), St Etienne, France (L. Heavy). Scorecards: 119-108, 118-109, 117-110.

5 February 1996   Yuri Arbachakov 112 (Russia) W PTS 12 Raul Juarez 111$\frac{1}{2}$ (Mexico), Osaka, Japan (Fly). Scorecards: 117-110, 117-111, 114-112.

24 February 1996   Terry Norris 150$\frac{3}{4}$ (USA) W RSC 8 Vince Pettway 151 (USA), Richmond, USA (S. Welter).

24 February 1996   Saman Sorjaturong 107 (Thailand) W RSC 4 Antonio Perez 108 (Mexico), Chachoensao, Thailand (L. Fly).

1 March 1996   Luisito Espinosa 126 (Philippines) W CO 4 Alejandro Gonzalez 126 (Mexico), Guadalajara, Mexico (Feather).

2 March 1996   Nigel Benn 166$\frac{1}{2}$ (England) L PTS 12 Thulani Malinga 165$\frac{3}{4}$ (South Africa), The Arena, Newcastle (S. Middle). Scorecards: 109-118, 114-112, 111-115. Unlucky to lose to Benn in their first fight, Malinga made no mistake in the return match, his better boxing giving him a healthy points margin. Benn seemed to have nothing left in the tank and when he announced his retirement from the ring, the crowd rose to a man who, more than anyone else, brought respect to British boxing.

3 March 1996   Daniel Zaragoza 122 (Mexico) W RSC 11 Joichiro Tatsuyoshi 122 (Japan), Yokohama, Japan (S. Bantam).

16 March 1996   Frank Bruno 247 (England) L RSC 3 Mike Tyson 220 (USA), Las Vegas, USA (Heavy). Sadly, all the hype amounted to nothing as Bruno was battered without a struggle by the still highly dangerous Tyson, the end coming at 0.50 of round three. Bruno had not been floored, but was badly cut, disorientated, and not fighting

back when rescued by Mills Lane. Larry O'Connell was one of the judges.

16 March 1996   Quincy Taylor 160 (USA) L RSC 9 Keith Holmes 159 (USA), Las Vegas, USA (Middle).

16 March 1996   Ricardo Lopez 104$\frac{1}{2}$ (Mexico) W CO 8 Ala Villamor 105 (Philippines), Las Vegas, USA (M. Fly).

30 March 1996   Wayne McCullough 117$\frac{1}{2}$ (Ireland) W PTS 12 Jose Luis Bueno 117$\frac{1}{4}$ (Mexico), Dublin, Ireland (Bantam). Scorecards: 118-114, 116-112, 113-116.

12 April 1996   Pernell Whitaker 147 (USA) W PTS 12 Wifredo Rivera 147 (Puerto Rico), St Maarten, Netherlands Antilles (Welter). Scorecards: 117-112, 115-113, 113-116. Larry O'Connell refereed.

20 April 1996   Jean-Baptiste Mendy 132 (France) W PTS 12 Lamar Murphy 134$\frac{1}{4}$ (USA), Levallois-Perret, France (Vacant Light). Scorecards: John Keane 117-112, 117-112, 116-112. Mickey Vann refereed. Gonzalez relinquished the title in February due to weight-making problems.

27 April 1996   Saman Sorjaturong 108 (Thailand) W RSC 7 Joma Gamboa 108 (Philippines), Mahasarakam, Thailand (L. Fly).

27 April 1996   Hiroshi Kawashima 115 (Japan) W PTS 12 Cecilio Espino 115 (Mexico), Tokyo, Japan (S. Fly). Scorecards: 120-107, 119-110, 118-109.

1 June 1996   Azumah Nelson 130 (Ghana) W RSC 6 James Leija 130 (USA), Las Vegas, USA (S. Feather), Richie Davies was one of the judges.

6 June 1996   Julio Cesar Chavez 139 (Mexico) L RSC 4 Oscar de la Hoya 139 (USA), Las Vegas, USA (S. Light). Larry O'Connell was one of the judges.

29 June 1996   Ricardo Lopez 105 (Mexico) W CO 3 Kitichai Preecha 104 (Thailand), Indio, USA (M. Fly).

World Boxing Organisation

2 July 1995   Johnny Tapia 114$\frac{1}{4}$ (USA) W PTS 12 Arthur Johnson 114$\frac{3}{4}$ (USA), Albuquerque, USA (J. Bantam). Scorecards: 116-112, 114-114, 115-113.

7 July 1995   Steve Robinson 125$\frac{1}{2}$ (Wales) W RSC 9 Pedro Ferradas 125$\frac{1}{2}$ (Spain), Ice Rink, Cardiff (Feather). An unspectacular fight saw Robinson wear down his limited challenger for a stoppage win at 0.45 of the ninth, the end coming after Ferradas had been floored in the previous round, was badly cut, and was slumped against the ropes, not firing back.

15 July 1995   Lonnie Bradley 160 (USA) W CO 1 Dario Galindez 159$\frac{1}{2}$ (Argentine), Los Angeles, USA (Middle).

15 July 1995   Marco Antonio Barrera 121$\frac{1}{2}$ (Mexico) W CO 1 Maui Diaz 122 (USA), Los Angeles, USA (J. Feather).

29 July 1995 Alex Sanchez 104 (Puerto Rico) W PTS 12 Tomas Rivera 104 (Mexico), San Antonio, USA (M. Fly). Scorecards: 115-112, 119-108, 116-111.

19 August 1995 Dariusz Michalczewski 175 (Germany) W CO 5 Everardo Armenta 174^1/$_2$ (Mexico), Dusseldorf, Germany (L. Heavy).

22 August 1995 Marco Antonio Barrera 121^1/$_2$ (Mexico) W PTS 12 Agapito Sanchez 122 (Dominican Republic, South Padre Island, USA (J. Feather). Scorecards: 118-107, 119-106, 118-109.

26 August 1995 Eamonn Loughran 147 (Ireland) W RSC 6 Tony Ganarelli 146 (USA), Ulster Hall, Ireland (Welter). Taking the fight at three weeks notice, and on his honeymoon, was not the ideal preparation for the American. However, he acquitted himself well before being rescued by referee, Roy Francis, at 1.52 of round six, having been decked seconds earlier after falling somewhat short of the required class. Paul Thomas was one of the judges.

9 September 1995 Steve Collins 167 (Ireland) W PTS 12 Chris Eubank 167^1/$_2$ (England), Cork, Ireland (S. Middle). Scorecards: 115-113, 115-113, 114-115. For the second time, Collins hustled and bustled an opponent who was unable to move up a gear, this, despite being badly cut in the seventh and tiring. Once again, Eubank disappointed, especially with his workrate, and shortly after announced his retirement.

9 September 1995 Oscar de la Hoya 135 (USA) W RTD 6 Genaro Hernandez 133 (USA), Las Vegas, USA (Light).

9 September 1995 Regilio Tuur 130 (Holland) W RTD 10 Luis Mendoza 129^1/$_2$ (Colombia), Arnhem, Holland (J. Light). Dave Parris refereed.

30 September 1995 Ralf Rocchigiani 186^1/$_2$ (Germany) W PTS 12 Mark Randazzo 186 (USA), Hanover, Germany (Cruiser). Scorecards: 117-111, 118-110, Roy Francis 116-113.

30 September 1995 Steve Robinson 125^1/$_2$ (Wales) L RSC 8 Prince Nassem Hamed 125^1/$_4$ (England), The Rugby Ground, Cardiff (Feather). Blasted to the floor in the fifth, and outclassed throughout, Robinson finally lost his crown to the new kid on the block, when the referee rescued him at 1.40 of the eighth, after he had risen from another count. While the brave Robinson went out like a champion, his successor looks to be on course to become one of Britain's greatest ever fighters. Paul Thomas was one of the judges.

7 October 1995 Dariusz Michalczewski 174 (Germany) W PTS 12 Philippe Michel 173 (France), Frankfurt, Germany (L. Heavy). Scorecards: 117-109, 120-107, Dave Parris 120-107.

7 October 1995 Eamonn Loughran 146^1/$_4$ (Ireland) W PTS 12 Angel Beltre 145^1/$_2$ (Dominican Republic), Ulster Hall, Belfast (Welter). Scorecards: 120-109, 119-109, 119-110. Despite winning handily, Loughran was unable to translate his advantage into a stoppage victory, Beltre being quite content to box on the outside. While Beltre may have lacked ambition, the champion lacked the guile to catch up with him, leaving one to wonder what might have happened had there been a tougher opponent in front of him.

9 October 1995 Alberto Jimenez 111^1/$_2$ (Mexico) W RSC 2 Zolile Mbitye 111^3/$_4$ (South Africa), Tijuana, Mexico (Fly).

21 October 1995 Alfred Kotey 117^1/$_2$ (Ghana) L PTS 12 Daniel Jimenez 117^3/$_4$ (Puerto Rico), York Hall, London (Bantam). Scorecards: 111-116, 113-115, 113-114. Dave Parris refereed.

4 November 1995 Marco Antonio Barrera 122 (Mexico) W RSC 7 Eddie Croft 121^1/$_2$ (USA), Las Vegas, USA (J. Feather).

18 November 1995 Paul Weir 107^3/$_4$ (Scotland) L TD 5 Jacob Matlala 105^1/$_4$ (South Africa), Kelvin Hall, Glasgow (J. Fly). Scorecards: 37-38, 37-38, Roy Francis 37-38. With Weir under pressure from the hands of the diminutive challenger, a head clash deemed accidental by the referee, left him badly cut over the right-eye. Amid some confusion, the referee misinterpreting the doctor's advice, the fight was called off and went to the scorecards, leaving the Scot shorn of his title at 2.36 of the fifth.

22 November 1995 Verno Phillips 154 (USA) L PTS 12 Paul Jones 153^1/$_2$ (England), Hillsborough Leisure Centre, Sheffield (J. Middle). Scorecards: 113-114, 113-113, Roy Francis 111-116. Having lost his title to Gianfranco Rosi the previous May, Phillips was reinstated as champion a couple of weeks later after the former tested positive for amphetamines. Despite having a point deducted for butting and being dumped in the first, Jones looked a comfortable winner, leading the bemused Phillips on a wild goose chase, round after round. In a fight that was too defensive to be exciting, even when in range, Phillips failed to take advantage, often punching with the open glove and rarely looking championship material.

25 November 1995 Steve Collins 167^3/$_4$ (Ireland) W PTS 12 Cornelius Carr 167^1/$_2$ (England), Dublin, Ireland (S. Middle). Scorecards: 116-112, 116-112, 117-111. After all the excitement of his earlier defences, this one was a bit of a damp squib for Collins. Had Carr showed more aggression there might have been a different result, but he did not and the champion plodded to victory on what for him was an off night.

25 November 1995 Ralf Rocchigiani 186^1/$_4$ (Germany) W RSC 8 Dan Ward 187 (USA), Hanover, Germany (Cruiser).

1 December 1995 Johnny Tapia 115 (USA) W RTD 9 Willy Salazar 114 (Mexico), Indio, USA (J. Bantam).

15 December 1995 Oscar de la Hoya 135 (USA) W RTD 2 James Lejia 134^3/$_4$ (USA), New York City, USA (Light).

23 December 1995   Regilio Tuur 128³/₄ (Holland) W PTS 12 Giorgio Campanella 129¹/₂ (Italy), Amsterdam, Holland (J. Light). Scorecards: 118-110, Dave Parris 119-109, 119-111. Paul Thomas refereed.

20 January 1996   Daniel Jimenez 118 (Puerto Rico) W PTS 12 Drew Docherty 117¹/₂ (Scotland), The Leisure Centre, Mansfield (Bantam). Scorecards: 118-112, 118-112, 115-114. Although the result went against him, Docherty made an excellent showing, firmly putting the trauma of the James Murray fight behind him and impressing those who gave him no chance against the champion. Certainly, it seemed closer than the scorelines suggested and had Docherty possessed a heavy wallop, the result could well have been different.

3 February 1996   Marco Antonio Barrera 121 (Mexico) W RSC 12 Kennedy McKinney 122 (USA), Los Angeles, USA (J. Feather).

3 February 1996   Johnny Tapia 115 (USA) W RSC 2 Giovanni Andrade 115 (Brazil), Los Angeles, USA (J. Bantam).

6 February 1996   Lonnie Bradley 159¹/₂ (USA) W RSC 2 Randy Smith 158¹/₂ (USA), New York City, USA (Middle).

1 March 1996   Bronco McKart 153¹/₂ (USA) W RSC 9 Santos Cardona 154 (Puerto Rico), Indio, USA (Vacant J. Middle). Cardona came in as a last minute replacement for the champion, Paul Jones, who pulled out with a damaged hand and was subsequently stripped.

9 March 1996   Steve Collins 167³/₄ (Ireland) W RSC 11 Neville Brown 167¹/₂ (England), Millstreet, Ireland (S. Middle). In moving up a weight to challenge Collins, while lacking the power to put the Irishman away, Brown did well to get through to the penultimate round, having been in trouble in the tenth. However, after a cracking right-hand had deposited him on the canvas, he was rescued by the referee with 0.54 on the clock.

9 March 1996   Sammy Fuentes 139³/₄ (Puerto Rico) L RSC 8 Giovanni Parisi 138¹/₄ (Italy), Milan, Italy (J. Welter). Roy Francis was one of the judges.

16 March 1996   Prince Nassem Hamed 125³/₄ (England) W RSC 1 Said Lawal 125 (Nigeria), Scottish Exhibition Centre, Glasgow (Feather). Three punches, all right-handers, spelt the end of Lawal's title challenge in one of the quickest ever world title finishes – 35 seconds. Flattened with the first punch of the fight, the Austrian-

Paul Weir (left) seen losing his WBO light-flyweight title to the teak-tough, Jacob Matlala   Les Clark

based challenger was up at 15 seconds, only to be clinically destroyed two punches later.

16 March 1996   Ralf Rocchigiani 186½ (Germany) W RSC 4 Jay Snyder 184½ (USA), Berlin, Germany (Cruiser).

23 March 1996   Alberto Jimenez 111 (Mexico) W RSC 5 Mike Martinez 112 (Mexico), Las Vegas, USA (Fly).

1 April 1996   Regilio Tuur 129½ (Holland) W PTS 12 Narciso Valenzuela 129¾ (Mexico), Hertogenbosch, Holland (J. Light). Scorecards: Dave Parris 120-108, 120-108, 120-109. Paul Thomas refereed.

6 April 1996   Dariusz Michalczewski 174¾ (Germany) W CO 5 Asludin Umarov 174¼ (Kazakhstan), Hanover, Germany (L. Heavy).

13 April 1996   Artur Grigorjan 135 (Uzbekistan) W RSC 12 Antonio Rivera 135 (Dominican Republic), Hamburg, Germany (Vacant Interim Light). Following his victory, Grigorjan was expected to be crowned champion if Oscar de la Hoya went ahead with a proposed welterweight title fight.

13 April 1996   Eamonn Loughran 146¾ (Ireland) L RSC 1 Jose Luis Lopez 146¼ (Mexico), Everton Park Sports Centre, Liverpool (Welter). Battered to defeat inside 51 seconds, Loughran became yesterday's man as the unheralded Mexican stunned the fans when downing the champion three times to curtail the action under WBO regulations. Roy Francis refereed, while Paul Thomas was one of the judges.

13 April 1996   Jacob Matlala 106¾ (South Africa) W RSC 10 Paul Weir 107¼ (Scotland), Everton Park Sports Centre, Liverpool (J. Fly). Having campaigned vociferously for a return match, Weir was mauled relentlessly before twice slumping to the canvas in the tenth, more from exhaustion than anything else. Up at nine the first time round, referee Paul Thomas called a halt to proceedings immediately following the second knockdown. Roy Francis was one of the judges.

26 April 1996   Daniel Jimenez 117½ (Puerto Rico) L PTS 12 Robbie Regan 117¾ (Wales), National Institute of Sport, Cardiff (Bantam). Scorecards: 112-115, 111-116, 113-116. Moving up a weight normally has the reverse effect, but in this case Regan was a revelation, pounding Jimenez to a clear points defeat after having him in trouble during the eighth. The determined Welshman was never prepared to let Jimenez dictate the fight and, although finishing marked up, was great value for his shock win, being specially effective on the inside with heavy hooks.

4 May 1996   Marco Antonio Barrera 122 (Mexico) W RSC 3 Jesse Benavides 122 (USA), Anaheim, USA (J. Feather).

7 May 1996   Lonnie Bradley 160 (USA) W PTS 12 Lonnie Beasley 159 (USA), Steubenville, USA (Middle). Scorecards: 118-110, 120-106, 119-109.

Robbie Regan puts Daniel Jimenez down on his way to the WBO bantam title   Les Clark

17 May 1996   Bronco McCart 154 (USA) L PTS 12 Ronald Wright 152 (USA), Monroe, USA (J. Middle). Scorecards: 116-113, 113-115, 113-115.

1 June 1996   Alberto Jimenez 112 (Mexico) W PTS 12 Jose Lopez 111½ (Puerto Rico), Lake Tahoe, USA (Fly). Scorecards: 118-110, 118-110, 120-108.

7 June 1996 Johnny Tapia 115 (USA) W RSC 8 Ivan Alvarez 114 (Colombia), Las Vegas, USA (J. Bantam).

8 June 1996   Dariusz Michalczewski 175 (Germany) W PTS 12 Christophe Girard 175 (France), Cologne, Germany (L. Heavy). Scorecards: Dave Parris 117-112, 117-112, 117-111.

8 June 1996   Prince Nassem Hamed 125¾ (England) W RSC 2 Daniel Alicea 125¾ (Puerto Rico), The Arena, Newcastle (Feather). Put down for the first time in his career, in the opener, Hamed rose immediately to go to work in the second, quickly blasting his rival to the canvas. Up and seemingly recovered, Alicea was then poleaxed by a tremendous right-left that stretched him out and brought the referee to his rescue after 2.46.

20 June 1996   Giovanni Parisi 137¼ (Italy) DREW 12 Carlos Gonzalez 138¾ (Mexico), Milan, Italy (J. Welter). Scorecards: 114-112, 112-114, 114-114.

29 June 1996   Henry Akinwande 232 (England) W CO 3 Jeremy Williams 216½ (USA), Indio, USA (Vacant Heavy). Having relinquished his title in July 1995, but reclaiming it towards the end of the year, Bowe finally gave up his belt in May. However, with Akinwande matched to fight Alex Zolkin for the vacant crown, Williams was drafted in when the latter was injured in training and was quickly despatched by a man who has grown in confidence and stature in recent months. The finish came after Akinwande, using the jab to open his man up, got in a short right to send Williams down to be counted out at 0.43 of the third.

One of Our Champions is Missing

by Robert Soderman

The title of this short essay on boxing was suggested by a World War II British movie – *"One of our Aircraft is Missing"*. And, just like that single British plane that wound up missing, one of our world boxing champions has been truly "missing" for the last 73 years – since 19 October, 1923!

How could this be – you ask? A world boxing champion lost to recorded boxing history and for over seven decades. Impossible! Just who was this unheralded world champion! How could he have escaped being acclaimed as such by the two boxing record books that were extant in the 1920 years, especially in their editions for the year, 1924 – Everlast and T S Andrews.

This "missing" world champion was one of the top-rated bantamweights in the world during 1923 and had been one of the finest 118 pounders since before World War I. His name, which you will not find listed among the roster of world bantamweight champions in any of the Ring Record Books, not even the final one ever published, the 1986-1987 edition – JOE BURMAN!

On Friday 19 October, 1923, the then recognised world bantamweight champion, Joe Lynch, was scheduled to defend his title against a persistent challenger from Chicago in Joe Burman. These two had met five times previously, with their respective score a dead heat – two decision wins apiece, and one draw. Their last set-to had seen Burman outpoint Lynch in ten no-decision rounds in Chicago's Dexter Park Arena on 19 March, 1923. Ten thousand fans had been on hand, attracting a $48,000 gate. Although Lynch scored a first round knockdown, Burman came back to hand the champion a decisive lacing.

The New York Times of Thursday 18 October, 1923, reported that Joe Lynch would enter the Madison Square Garden ring on Friday night a favourite to defeat Joe Burman and thus retain his world bantamweight title. Lynch's friends were reported to be wagering heavily on him, and he was supposedly in superb form after intensive training.

Thus, New York boxing fans were thunderstruck the next morning, when their morning newspapers announced that, "LYNCH IS INJURED, TITLE BATTLE OFF"! It seems that on Thursday afternoon, about four o'clock, Lynch alighted from his automobile, tripped over his pet collie dog, and fell heavily to the sidewalk on his left side. On being helped to his feet, the champion found he could not lift his left arm. His manager, Eddie Mead, hurriedly took his world champion to a closeby doctor's office, where the diagnosis was that Lynch had suffered a dislocation of his left shoulder, and had also suffered torn ligaments in the arm. Manager Mead then informed the promoter, Tex Rickard, that Lynch had called off the bout. A second medical examination was performed, an hour or so later, by the Garden's physician and the New York State Athletic Commission's doctor. Both of these men said they could find no evidence to show that Lynch's shoulder was dislocated.

On being told that the bout with Lynch was off, Tom Walsh, Joe Burman's manager, said he would go immediately to the boxing commission on Friday and lay claim to Lynch's title. "Burman will weigh in Friday afternoon under the bantamweight limit of 118 pounds, before the State Athletic Commission, as originally scheduled, and we will then file a formal claim to Lynch's title at the same time."

After the second medical examination on Thursday, at which Tex Rickard's matchmaker, Frank Flournoy, was in attendance, promoter Rickard quickly sought out a substitute to replace Joe Lynch. Tex and his matchmaker came up with Abe Goldstein, out of Harlem, to face Joe Burman as a replacement for champion, Joe Lynch. Goldstein had already fought three times in the month of October 1923, the most recent occasion having been in New York the past Monday, scoring a two round knockout win over Johnny Naselli.

Joe Burman

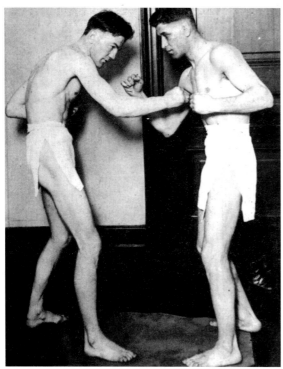

Joe Lynch (left) shapes up to heir apparent, Abe Goldstein, immediately prior to their fight

At Friday's morning meeting at the New York Commission office, with Joe Lynch himself in attendance to exhibit his injured shoulder, and with the doctor who had first examined Lynch on Thursday testifying that he had immediately re-set Lynch's dislocated shoulder after his initial diagnosis, the Commission declared Lynch's world bantamweight title forfeited to Joe Burman. The championship distinction was assigned to that night's bout at the Garden and Abe Goldstein was approved as the opponent for Burman; in what would be world champion Joe Burman's first, and official, defense of his newly gained title.

The championship bout that night, trimmed down to 12 rounds duration from the original 15 rounds, was fought before a slim paid attendance crowd of 4,105, who contributed to a gate of $11,793. The result was as unexpected as all the events that preceded it – the last-minute substitute, Abe Goldstein, handed out a 12 round shellacking to world bantamweight champion Joe Burman! Abe "showed himself clearly the master of Burman in every department of boxing," the *New York Times* reported the next morning. "Displaying a brand of boxing ability, which at times made Burman appear like a novice," as the *Times* also reported, "Goldstein easily boxed his way to the decision of judges' Harold Barnes and Al Commanchio, and referee, Jack O'Sullivan. "The Harlem youngster earned eight of the 12 rounds," the Times concluded. The *Chicago Tribune* had their own representative at ringside, Harry Newman, and his story summed it up best when the headline of his report read: "CHAMP FOR FEW HOURS,

BURMAN LOSES HIS CROWN". Newman's first two paragraphs told it in succinct fashion: "Abe Goldstein is now the bantamweight champion of the world, if the ruling of the New York State Athletic Commission counts for anything west of the Hudson River." The second of Newman's opening paragraphs gave the "why" of how this came about: "The boxing bosses had decreed that Joe Burman was champion when Joe Lynch refused to mingle with the westerner but Joe (Burman) didn't retain his crown long." Newman had a good final paragraph in his story, opining: "There have been many queer twists in that bantamweight crew and we will have to accept Abe Goldstein as the new champion until all the returns are in."

On Tuesday 23 October, 1923, Joe Lynch got his hearing before the New York Commission. Joe had petitioned the board to revoke the suspension given to him when he had called off his last Friday night title bout versus Joe Burman. The very first line of the story on the hearing, as reported in the *New York Times,* was a classic of unconscious, and unintended humor: "Joe Lynch, who is unrecognised as world's bantamweight champion in this State, was conditionally restored to good standing by the State Athletic Commission." The Commission's ruling went on to say that Lynch would remain "unrecognised" as bantamweight champion in this State, but that he will receive recognition as first challenger for the class title when he convinces the Commission that he is in condition to box. Then followed more of the Commission's ruling, again with more words of unintended humor: "Lynch will not necessarily be compelled to box Burman before he boxes for the title, unless Burman is recognised as champion at the time Lynch is declared qualified, from a physical standpoint, to box for the championship."

The usually authoritative 1986-1987 Ring Record Book is silent on this long ago, and historic bantamweight bout. On page 449, in their chronological listing of world bantamweight championship bouts, there is a gap between their 22 December 1922 contest between then champion Joe Lynch's successful defense of his title against Midget Smith, and the next listing – shown as 21 March 1924 and Abe Goldstein defeating (and ostensibly capturing the title) Joe Lynch. In that same Ring Record Book, in Abe Goldstein's record on page 470 – where it shows Abe's 19 October, 1923 bout with Joe Burman, it just says – W12 – and makes no additional mention that this was a New York State recognised world championship contest. And the book does not include Joe Burman, among its listing of world champions on page 448, nor does it include Joe Burman's record among the records of the world bantamweight champions. In all of the Ring Record Books, Joe Burman's record appears in just one of them – in the 1942 All-Time Ring Record Book.

On Friday 27 October, 1923, the New York State Athletic Commission proposed an amendment to the Walker Law governing boxing in New York State. More than likely this amendment was prompted by criticism of their recent action in taking Joe Lynch's world bantam title from him, and then bestowing that title on Joe Burman. The amendment simply stated, in essence, "that world champions (as recognised as such by New York State) must defend... within a period of six months after winning or defending the title in a bona fide bout to a decision." The amendment went on to state that any champion not defending his title following the six month period, after being challenged by another fighter, would be suspended by the Commission until such time as he agreed to defend his title. In the past, and especially in Joe Lynch's case, the Commission summarily stepped in and removed championship recognition and championship approval. In the instance of Joe Lynch, the Commission did not just take Lynch's title away from him, it awarded Joe Lynch's championship to the opponent he was supposed to meet – Joe Burman. Commission chairman, William Muldoon, said it was not the intention to make champions by proclamation and, "The Commission realised that championships are won and lost in the ring and there only." Certainly, this belated Commission action was of no consolation to deposed world champion, Joe Lynch.

Of the three principals in this somewhat strange event – deposed champion Joe Lynch's next bout would not be until 23 November, 1923, in Peoria, Illinois, when he scored a five round knockout over Frankie Murray (his shoulder injury must have healed satisfactorily). New champion, Abe Goldstein, did not appear in the ring again until 8 January, 1924, winning a ten round decision over Wilbur Cohen, at New York's Pioneer AC, while the champion for a few hours, Joe Burman's next bout was a ten round decision loss to Johnny Curtin in St Louis on 27 November, 1923. Indeed, after his world championship title was gone, Burman appears to have fought just four times, his last bout being on 25 March, 1924.

This somewhat unusual story of these three world bantamweight champions had its climax on 21 March, 1924, in New York's Madison Square Garden, where it all began on Friday 19 October, 1923. On this night, Joe Lynch was to meet Abe Goldstein for the world bantamweight championship. Which fighter was defending the title, and which was the challenger? It seems that the *New York Times*, in their report on the day of the fight, was more than somewhat confused as to which was which and who was who. Their lead paragraph said: "Joe Lynch, bantamweight champion of the world, defends his title against Abe Goldstein in a 15 round battle to a decision." An exclamation point really should be at the end of that sentence, but follow what else the *New York Times* day-of-the-fight report said: "Lynch and Goldstein were matched to meet in the Garden on 19 October (this is unbelievable reporting!), but the day prior to the contest, Lynch reported that he had dislocated his shoulder and cancelled the match. (They got that fact right, but read on) Joe Burman was chosen to substitute for Lynch against Goldstein (what boxing fan reading the *Times* report on this day would be able to believe this) with the understanding that the Goldstein v Burman fight would be recognised by the Commission for the world's bantamweight championship. Goldstein won the decision, but the attempt to have him regarded as the champion was not accepted by the fans.

In the *New York Times'* Eye (yes, their newspaper only had "one eye") was, or was not, Abe Goldstein a recognised world champion? From 20 October, 1923, the *New York Times* invariably referred to Abe Goldstein as being the New York State version of the world bantamweight champion. On 19 February, 1924, the *Times* wrote of Goldstein's bout that night, at New York's Pioneer AC. The report said: "Abe Goldstein, who holds the title of world's bantamweight champion in New York State, will meet Danny Edwards in the feature ten round bout at the Pioneer AC tonight."

On 20 February, 1924, the *Times* had a report of Goldstein's win of the previous night. One line in the lead paragraph of that report has to be considered astounding, in light of previous events reported in the *Times*, and in this essay! Here is what the *Times* said: "Abe Goldstein, East Side bantam, showed that he is deserving of a title bout with Joe Lynch when he outpointed Danny Edwards...last night. Goldstein, who, until yesterday, was recognised as the world's champion in his class in New York State...."

In one day, Abe Goldstein becomes an ex-champion! The New York Commission giveth, and the New York Commission taketh away! What happened? How could Abe Goldstein suddenly become a non-champion, and how could the previously deposed champion, Joe Lynch, be restored to world championship status? It seems that "the recently re-organised State Athletic Commission yesterday (19 February, 1924) determined to start all over again in the matter of conducting boxing in this state... it voted to wipe the slate clean of all suspensions and penalties imposed prior to 13 February. The most important result of this decision will be to restore Joe Lynch, world's bantamweight champion, to good standing at once..."

On 21 March, 1924, this bantamweight contretemps came to its conclusion. And here is what the *New York Times* told the world – at least to the readers of the Times – "Abe Goldstein, young Harlem boxer, is the new world's bantamweight champion. He won this title last night (on 21 March) in Madison Square Garden, where, before another capacity crowd, he outboxed Joe Lynch of the West Side, the defending champion." The decision was unanimous, and met with the approval of the 12,482, who paid $48,477 to see the contest. So, this time it was official; New York State Athletic Commission official – but was it not supposed to be official on 19 October, 1923? New champion Goldstein collected a purse of $5,708 as his end, representing $12^1/_2\%$ of the receipts. Former champion, Lynch, supposedly collected the lion's share, with his purse being $15,000. Goldstein also cashed in on the usual winning warrior's "spoils" – a three day vaudeville engagement at a Brooklyn theatre, followed by a week's showing at a mid-town showhouse.

Joe Lynch was apparently just about at the end of his fistic road. He only fought nine more times – dropping four decisions, fighting four draws, and scoring a knockout win in his last ever recorded bout, on 22 September, 1926. Abe Goldstein won two title defenses, both in 1924, but lost his title on 19 December, 1924, to "Cannonball" Eddie Martin, in the Garden, on a very close 15 round decision. Goldstein fought for three more years, calling it quits on 24 June, 1927, after being stopped by Ignacio Fernandez in seven rounds at Chicago.

So endeth this essay, of a forgotten episode of boxing history – a forgotten episode of bantamweight boxing history.

World Title Bouts Since Gloves: Addendum and Appendages

This section is the follow-up to the last two Yearbooks, which set out to provide a history of world championship boxing, fight by fight, in the most comprehensive form ever published. Where new information has come to hand, the title entry has been re-written, while an (+) following the date determines a fight never previously recorded as involving the championship. There is still much work to do, especially after it was discovered that champions in America during the no-decision era, more often than not, defended their title claims in bouts of that nature. Six men, Georges Carpentier (light-heavy), George Chip, Al McCoy, Mike O'Dowd (middles), Jack Britton (welter) and Benny Leonard (light), actually won their so-called championships in no-decision bouts, while the first million dollar gate, Dempsey v Carpentier in Jersey City, was articled as a fight where the referee would not be called upon to render a points verdict if it went the full distance. The most persistent abuser of the system appears to be former featherweight champion, Johnny Kilbane, who consistently asked his opponents to make the championship weight of 122 lbs, thus allowing the promoter to bill accordingly, while he would invariably come to the ring at around 130 lbs with his own referee in tow. However, conversely, Benny Leonard seemed quite happy to fight two ten rounders a week in different towns against men inside the limit as long as he was able to make as near to 135 lbs as he could manage without having to boil down. Although the opposition had to win inside the distance to stand any chance of being accorded championship status, both men continuously risked their title claims in these affairs, as did all the other leading men at the time. While no-decision boxing was a euphemism for exhibitions, and a way round the State laws during the early part of the century, without it the noble art in America would have died. That is why it must be considered of the utmost importance.

Country Code (Codes relate to place of domicile, not necessarily birthplace)
A-Australia; ARG-Argentina; ARM-Armenia; AU-Austria; BAH-Bahamas; BAR-Barbados; BEL-Belgium; BR-Brazil; C-Canada; CH-Chile; COL-Colombia; CR-Costa Rica; CUB-Cuba; CZ-Czechoslovakia; DEN-Denmark; DOM-Dominican Republic; EC-Ecuador; FIN-Finland; FR-France; GB-Great Britain; GER-Germany; GH-Ghana; GRE-Greece; GU-Guyana; HA-Hawaii; HOL-Holland; I-Ireland; IC-Ivory Coast; INDON-Indonesia; ITA-Italy; J-Jamaica; JAP-Japan; K-Kenya; MEX-Mexico; MOR-Morocco; N-Nigeria; NIC-Nicaragua; NOR-Norway; NZ-New Zealand; PAN-Panama; PAR-Paraguay; PE-Peru; PH-Philippines; PNG-Papua New Guinea; PR-Puerto Rico; SA-South Africa; SK-South Korea; SP-Spain; SWE-Sweden; SWI-Switzerland; TH-Thailand; TO-Togo; TR-Trinidad; TUN-Tunisia; U-Uganda; UR-Uruguay; USA-United States of America; VEN-Venezuela; YUG-Yugoslavia; ZA-Zambia.

Flyweight (112 lbs)

03.03.20+ **Jimmy Wilde** (GB) ND-W PTS 6 Patsy Wallace (USA), Philadelphia. *Although articles called for a 3.0 pm weigh-in at 112 lbs, Wilde failed to arrive in time. That aside, the fight went ahead with both men inside the required weight.*

12.03.20+ **Jimmy Wilde** (GB) ND-W PTS 12 Frankie Mason (USA), Toledo. *Billed as a title fight, Articles of Agreement called for both men to be inside 108 lbs. For the record, Wilde scaled 106¼ lbs to Mason's 106½.*

12.04.20+ **Jimmy Wilde** (GB) ND-W PTS 10 Young Zulu Kid (USA), Windsor. *According to the Chicago Tribune (newspaper), Wilde was never in any danger of losing his title.*

21.04.20+ **Jimmy Wilde** (GB) ND-W CO 8 Battling Murray (USA), Camden. *Although the New York Times (newspaper) reported Murray as challenging for Wilde's title, the Trenton State Gazette (newspaper) reported the match being made at 116 lbs in order to protect the Welshman's laurels.*

13.05.20+ **Jimmy Wilde** (GB) ND-W CO 2 Battling Murray (USA), Philadelphia. *According to the New York World (newspaper), Wilde's title was put at risk after Murray weighed in at 110 lbs. Wilde scaled 107 lbs.*

24.05.20+ **Jimmy Wilde** (GB) W PTS 10 Patsy Wallace (USA), Toronto. *Billed as a title fight although it was announced that the contest had been made at 116 lbs. However, according to the Toronto Daily Mail (newspaper), Wilde and Wallace weighed 105 and 110 lbs, respectively.*

22.10.27 Pinky Silverberg (USA) W DIS 7 Ruby Bradley (USA), Bridgeport. *While the Ring Magazine (December 1927) reported that Silverberg became champion of the world in the eyes of 24 States and four countries, the Boston Post (newspaper) merely said it was supposed to be sanctioned by the NBA as a title bout. In truth, at their convention four days earlier, the NBA had stated that a series of eliminators, involving men such as Frenchy Belanger, Newsboy Brown and Frankie Genaro were being set up to find an opponent to meet England's Ernie Jarvis for the title. Regardless of billing, one can be sure that this was just another eliminator and, following a poor performance against Bradley, Silverberg dropped out of the reckoning.*

24.04.28+ Newsboy Brown (USA) W CO 6 Speedy Dado (PH), Los Angeles - CALIFORNIA. *With both men inside 112 lbs, this was a defence of Brown's Californian version of the world title.*

23.07.28+ Frankie Genaro (USA) DREW 10 Steve Rocco (C), Toronto - NBA. *Never recorded as a title fight by the Ring Record Book, the Toronto Daily Mail (newspaper) tells us that it was billed for the NBA version of the championship and that both men were inside 112 lbs.*

31.08.28+ Izzy Schwartz (USA) W CO 8 Frisco Grande (PH), Long Branch. *The passing of the Altman Bill, permitting 15 round fights to a decision in New Jersey, saw Schwartz and Grande benefitting from that piece of legislation, but while the New York Times (newspaper) reported it to be a title fight (Schwartz held the New York version of the championship), it was fought outside the jurisdiction of the NYSAC. However, with both men inside 112 lbs, had Schwartz lost he would have undoubtedly been stripped of his title.*

14.12.28+ Frankie Genaro (USA) W DIS 2 Steve Rocco (C), Detroit - NBA. *Although the New York Times (newspaper) failed to mention the fighters' weights, it reported this scheduled ten rounder as being for Genaro's NBA title.*

18.06.34 Jackie Brown (GB) DREW 15 Valentin Angelmann (FR), Belle Vue, Manchester - NBA/IBU. *Brown forfeited IBU recognition at their annual conference on 6 June 1935, for failing to give Angelmann a return. The fact that Brown had already signed for a defence against Benny Lynch was given no due consideration.*

09.09.35 Benny Lynch (GB) W RTD 2 Jackie Brown (GB), Belle Vue, Manchester - GB/NBA. *Immediately following his victory, the IBU, who had not recognised Brown v Lynch as a title fight, gave Lynch until 25 September to sign for a contest against Valentin Angelmann. When he failed to do so they announced that the Frenchman would box the current European champion, Kid David, for their version of the title, instead.*

12.12.36 Valentin Angelmann (FR) W PTS 15 Ernst Weiss (AU), Paris - IBU. *During an international boxing convention held in Rome during the third week of April 1938, the IBU agreed to refuse to recognise all individually made world champions, including their own Valentin Angelmann, in an effort to stand by one universally recognised titleholder.*

22.09.38 **Peter Kane** (GB) W PTS 15 Jackie Jurich (USA), Anfield

Football Ground, Liverpool. *Having won the title, Kane also found he was struggling to make the weight and in May 1939 he announced that he was relinquishing the title in order to campaign as a bantam.*

21.02.41 Little Dado (PH) W PTS 10 Jackie Jurich (USA), Honolulu - NBA. *Inactive for almost all of 1942, Dado came back towards the end of that year as a fully-fledged bantam, but reigned on as champion until 14 October 1943, the day the NBA formally decided he could no longer make the weight.*

19.06.43 Jackie Paterson (GB) W CO 1 Peter Kane (GB), Hampden Park, Glasgow - GB/NY. *With Kane still able to make eight stone, and despite having earlier relinquished the title, he was allowed to "defend" against Paterson, in a fight seen by Britain and the NYSAC as being for the championship. Paterson was eventually recognised by the NBA following their decision to strip Dado four months later.*

13.04.55 **Pascual Perez** (ARG) W CO 3 Albert Barenghi (ARG), Buenos Aires. *Initially, the Ring Record Book stated that the title was at stake, with Barenghi coming in under the limit. However, it has now come to light that the so-called challenger weighed 112½ lbs.*

22.10.55 **Pascual Perez** (ARG) W PTS 10 Danny Kid (PH), Buenos Aires. *Billed a non-title fight, Perez unnecessarily risked his crown when allowing Kid to weigh inside 112 lbs. The Le Nacion (newspaper) tells us that Perez scaled 49.1 kilos (108¼ lbs) to Kid's 50.5 (111¼).*

11.02.56 **Pascual Perez** (ARG) W PTS 10 Antonio Gomez (ARG), Mar del Plata. *Reported to involve the title in the 1995 Yearbook, it did not, with Gomez coming in at 51.15 kilos (112¾ lbs), according to the Le Nacion (newspaper).*

31.03.56 **Pascual Perez** (ARG) W PTS 10 Marcelo Quiroga (ARG), Buenos Aires. *Another non-title fight where the champion risked his crown against an opponent who, at 50.75 kilos (111¾ lbs), was inside the class weight limit. The Le Nacion (newspaper) reported Perez to be 105 lbs.*

03.08.56 **Pascual Perez** (ARG) W RSC 5 Ricardo Valdez (ARG), Buenos Aires. *A ten round non-title bout, Perez yet again risked his crown by allowing Valdez to scale 50.2 kilos (110¾ lbs) to his 49.3 (108¾). Again, the author used the Le Nacion (newspaper) to uncover weights.*

25.08.56 **Pascual Perez** (ARG) W CO 3 Hector Almaraz (ARG), Rosario. *Perez's crown was again put at risk in a non-title bout, when Almaraz scaled 50.1 kilos (110½ lbs). The champion's weight was given as 48.3 kilos (106½ lbs) in the Le Nacion (newspaper).*

12.07.57 **Pascual Perez** (ARG) W CO 3 Luis Angel Jimenez (ARG), Buenos Aires. *Although reported in the 1995 Yearbook as a non-title fight that saw Perez's crown at stake, it was not. The Le Nacion (newspaper) gave Jimenez's weight as 50.9 kilos (112¼ lbs).*

02.08.57+ **Pascual Perez** (ARG) W CO 3 Urbieta Sosa (ARG), Buenos Aires. *According to the Le Nacion (newspaper), this was yet another non-title bout for Perez where his opponent, at 50.800 kilos (112 lbs), came to the ring inside the championship limit.*

16.08.57 **Pascual Perez** (ARG) W CO 3 Pablo Sosa (ARG), Buenos Aires. *Confirmation that this non-title bout involved Perez's championship status came in the shape of the Le Nacion (newspaper), which reported Sosa weighing 50.5 kilos (111¼ lbs) to Perez's 48.9 (107¾).*

Super-Flyweight (115 lbs)

31.01.83 Rafael Orono (VEN) W CO 4 Pedro Romero (PAN), Caracas - WBC. *This was the first championship contest of 12 rounds duration after many years of the distance being set at 15. Innaugurated by the WBC on 1 January 1983, within a short period of time all other world bodies had fallen into line.*

Bantamweight (118 lbs)

Named after the bantam cock, a ferocious bird from the illegal sport of cock-fighting, the weight class goes back to the days of the London Prize Ring. However, the earliest recorded information uncovered is in 1856, when an American bare-fist fighter, Charley Lynch, weighing around 112 lbs, arrived in England to fight Simon Finighty. After 95 rounds, Finighty was declared the winner, but then lost the title after 43 rounds of a return engagement in November 1859. Next came three Britons, Billy Shaw (1860), George Holden (1861) and Peter Morris (1862). Later, after running out of opposition on this side of the Atlantic, Morris went to America, but, unable to raise a challenge there either, retired undefeated in 1870, one of the few bare-knuckle fighters to do so. Interest in the division then lapsed until an American, Tommy Kelly, claimed the title in 1887. With bare-fist fights now beginning to give way to those of the skin-tight glove variety, he was knocked out in eight rounds on 24 December 1887 in New York City by Hughey Boyle, who later decided to retire and go back to painting and decorating for a living. Kelly then took on a young Canadian, George Dixon, at 105 lbs, but, after the pair had fought a nine round draw in Boston on 10 May 1888, and with the position still unresolved, they went their separate ways. In another bout billed for the title, Kelly drew over eight rounds with Cal McCarthy in New York City on 24 December 1888. Meanwhile, an Englishman called Chappie Moran stopped Frank Donovan inside 14 rounds of a billed title fight in New York City on 22 May 1889 and successfully defended against Kelly (a ten round points win in Brooklyn on 5 June 1889), before being knocked out in ten rounds by the latter on 31 January 1890 in New York City. The British, who saw 105 lbs as being the poundage for the weight class, refused to recognise Kelly as champion after he came to the ring at 106½ lbs, and continued to support Moran. Following this fight, Moran went back to England, leaving Kelly to successfully defend his claim against Benny Murphy (a third round kayo in New York City on 5 March 1890), while Dixon, who had put on weight, was defending his version of the title at 115 lbs. His fights, which fell into this category, against Cal McCarthy, Nunc Wallace and Johnny Murphy, in 1890, are shown in more detail within the featherweight listings. We now arrive at the division's first recognised title fight with gloves. With Dixon considered too heavy, and accepting Moran's ten round draw at 105 lbs with Eddie Avery in Brooklyn on 2 April 1892, the NSC agreed to the weight class limit being 110 lbs in order to suit a match between the new British champion, Billy Plimmer, and Kelly. Their criteria was that during Moran's continued absence, the British bantam limit, which had already been hiked up to 108 lbs, would still be in line with the featherweight division, then standing between 122 and 124 lbs.

09.05.92 **Billy Plimmer** (GB) W CO 10 Tommy Kelly (USA), Coney Island. *Made at 110 lbs, Plimmer scaled 108 to Kelly's 108½. The New York Herald (newspaper) reported on the four ounce gloves looking to be no more than two ounce.*

28.12.92 **Billy Plimmer** (GB) W RSC 8 Joe McGrath (USA), Coney Island (110 lbs). *Plimmer continued to campaign in America without defending the title and, following a lengthy period of inactivity, his right to be called champion was challenged by Jimmy Barry.*

15.09.94 Jimmy Barry (USA) W CO 28 Casper Leon (USA), Lamont - USA. *Billed for the 105 lbs bantamweight championship of the world, according to the Chicago Tribune (newspaper), Barry weighed 104½ lbs to Leon's 104¾. Barry, previously the 100 lbs titleholder, thus picked up and re-established the title at the old weight.*

30.03.95 Jimmy Barry (USA) DREW 14 Casper Leon (USA), Chicago. *According to the Chicago Tribune (newspaper), this was not a 105 lbs title fight. The paper reported that both men were inside 110 lbs and Leon, having got up at seven, was on the verge of being knocked out before being rescued by a police stoppage.*

21.10.95 Jimmy Barry (USA) W CO 4 Jack Madden (USA), Long Island - USA. *Billed for the 105 lbs title, with both men inside the weight, the New York Herald (newspaper) reported Barry as being an easy winner.*

30.01.97 Jimmy Barry (USA) DREW 20 Sammy Kelly (USA), New York City. *Not for the 105 lbs title as previously shown, the New York Herald (newspaper) tells us that it was made at 115 lbs, with Kelly coming in at 122 lbs.*

01.03.97+ Jimmy Barry (USA) W PTS 20 Jack Ward (USA), New York City. *According to the New York Herald (newspaper), both men weighed inside the stipulated 110 lbs. Although there was no title billing, with Pedlar Palmer defending at 116 lbs in England, Barry was now claiming the 110 lbs version.*

18.10.97 Pedlar Palmer (GB) W PTS 20 Dave Sullivan (USA), NSC, London - GB. *Articled at 116 lbs (plus or minus two pounds), and billed for the title, Palmer scaled 115½, while Sullivan came in at 118 lbs. Prior to the contest, Palmer had been informed by the NSC that unless he weighed below 116 lbs, they would insist on matching him against Ben Jordan, who they recognised as champion between 118 and 122 lbs.*

06.12.97 Jimmy Barry (USA) W CO 20 Walter Croot (GB), NSC, London - USA. *Billed at 110 lbs, Barry won international recognition at the weight by his victory and was seen in America as the* *bantamweight champion. Unfortunately, though, there was a tragic aftermath when Croot failed to regain consciousness and died.*

19.02.98+ Steve Flanagan (USA) DREW 20 Dan Dougherty (USA), Toronto. *With Jimmy Barry now fighting at 110 lbs, Flanagan had claimed the American 105 lbs title. The Toronto Daily Mail (newspaper) reported that the fight was billed and announced as such and that both men were inside the weight at the ringside weigh-in.*

30.05.98 Jimmy Barry (USA) DREW 20 Casper Leon (USA), New York City - USA. *According to the New York Herald (newspaper), both men were inside the stipulated 110 lbs.*

30.09.98+ Steve Flanagan (USA) DREW 25 Casper Leon (USA), New York City. *Although Prof. L. V. Davis' record of Leon states that this fight was billed for the world 105 lbs title, the New York Herald (newspaper) report failed to confirm whether it was or not.*

29.12.98 Jimmy Barry (USA) DREW 20 Casper Leon (USA), Davenport - USA. *Billed for the 110 lbs title, the Chicago Tribune (newspaper) reported both men to be inside the weight. This successful defence proved to be Barry's penultimate fight and he retired undefeated in September 1899.*

30.01.99+ Terry McGovern (USA) W CO 12 Casper Leon (USA), Brooklyn. *Occasionally shown in title fight listings, according to the New York Herald (newspaper, Leon weighed 110 lbs to McGovern's 115. While there was no mention of title involvement, McGovern was certainly recognised by many to be the American 115 lbs champion at this time.*

03.06.99+ Patsy Donovan (USA) W PTS 20 Casper Leon (USA), Brooklyn. *According to the St Louis Post-Dispatch (newspaper), Donovan defeated Leon for the 110 lbs championship in this one. Not even reported in the New York Herald (newspaper), Donovan's claim appears to go nowhere.*

09.06.99+ Clarence Forbes (USA) W PTS 12 Casper Leon (USA), St Louis. *The St Louis Post-Dispatch (newspaper) reported the fight as being for the 112 lbs bantamweight championship of America, with both inside the weight. Incidentally, Forbes was the 17-year-old brother of another title front-runner, Harry.*

23.06.99+ Clarence Forbes (USA) DREW 12 Casper Leon (USA), St Louis. *A return fight, this time it was billed as a world bantamweight championship battle according to the St Louis Post-Dispatch (newspaper). However, there was no mention of weights.*

01.07.99+ Terry McGovern (USA) W CO 3 Johnny Ritchie (USA), Tuckahoe. *Scheduled for 25 rounds, the New York Herald (newspaper) reported this as being billed for the 118 lbs bantamweight championship of America. Following this, McGovern went forward to fight Britain's Pedlar Palmer to decide the world 116 lbs title.*

29.08.99+ Clarence Forbes (USA) W CO 11 Con Suffield (USA), Dubuque. *Involving Forbes' 115 lbs title claim, the Dubuque Daily Times (newspaper) reported this as being for the championship of the West with Suffield coming in at 114 lbs.*

12.09.99 **Terry McGovern** (USA) W CO 1 Pedlar Palmer (GB), Tuckahoe. *Following the retirement of Jimmy Barry, the American and British class limit finally came together at 116 lbs in this one, with Palmer weighing 113¹/₂ lbs to McGovern's 115¹/₂.*

04.10.99+ Steve Flanagan (USA) DREW 20 Casper Leon (USA), St Louis. *Although reported in the New Orleans Daily Picayune (newspaper) as a title fight, with both men weighing 112 lbs and Leon having earlier lost to Clarence Forbes at that weight, it settled nothing.*

09.10.99 **Terry McGovern** (USA) W CO 1 Billy Rotchford (USA), Chicago. *Further research of this fight saw it reported in the New York Herald (newspaper) as being at catchweights and not involving McGovern's title.*

27.10.99+ Steve Flanagan (USA) W PTS 25 Casper Leon (USA), St Louis. *While the New Orleans Daily Picayune (newspaper) reported that Flanagan won the bantam title in this one without mention of weights, the St Louis Post-Dispatch (newspaper) showed it to be at 110 lbs.*

22.12.99 **Terry McGovern** (USA) W CO 2 Harry Forbes (USA), New York City. *While billed as a title bout, it was contested at 118 lbs, two pounds above the recognised limit. This was merely symptomatic of the fact that McGovern was growing fast and in January 1900 he became world featherweight champion. Early in April of that year, he announced that he was handing his bantam crown to stablemate and sparring partner, Dan Dougherty, but, regardless of that action, it was only towards the end of 1900 that he was generally no longer seen as the champion of the division.*

21.04.00+ Clarence Forbes (USA) W CO 2 Jimmy Smith (C), Toronto.

Scheduled for 20 rounds and billed for the Canadian version of the 115 lbs title, the Toronto Daily Mail (newspaper) tells us that both men made the weight.

24.07.00+ Johnny Reagan (USA) W PTS 20 Clarence Forbes (USA), Brooklyn. *Following the result in a match made at 115 lbs, and despite the absence of the championship billing. Reagan took over Forbes' title claim at the weight.*

14.08.00+ Johnny Reagan (USA) W PTS 20 Casper Leon (USA), Brooklyn. *Although the New York Herald (newspaper) reported this as being contested at 110 lbs, Reagan's 115 lbs title claim would have been at stake in this one.*

12.11.00+ Harry Ware (GB) W PTS 20 Pedlar Palmer (GB), NSC, London - GB. *Earlier, when it was clear that Terry McGovern would not be fighting again in this weight class, Palmer had reclaimed his old title. Made at 114 lbs and carrying "English" (British) title billing only, it must be remembered that when a world title became vacant at that time, until the British and American champions of the day had met, both countries recognised their own. Following his victory, Ware challenged all at 114 lbs without response.*

18.03.01 Harry Harris (USA) W PTS 15 Pedlar Palmer (GB), NSC, London. *Unable to agree terms with the British champion, Harry Ware, Harris took on Palmer in a match made at 116 lbs, instead. Bearing in mind that over the past few years there has been much confusion whether this fight involved the British version of the world title, the author went back to the Sporting Life (newspaper) of the day. There it was reported as being for the world (International) title, with both men weighing 115 lbs. As it was, Harris had great difficulty making the weight and declared afterwards that he would not enter into any future engagement under 118 lbs.*

02.04.01 Harry Forbes (USA) W RSC 15 Casper Leon (USA), Memphis. *Reported by the Memphis Daily Appeal (newspaper) as a match made at 116 lbs with no mention of title status, this appears to be the start of Forbes' title claim.*

04.11.01+ Harry Forbes (USA) W PTS 15 Abe Attell (USA), St Louis. *Made at 116 lbs, with both men inside, Forbes extended his title claim at that weight.*

30.04.01+ Kid McFadden (USA) W DIS 10 Dan Dougherty (USA), San Francisco. *Made at 115 lbs ringside and surprisingly scheduled for ten rounds, with the result, the San Francisco Chronicle (newspaper) reported that McFadden gained the unearned title of bantamweight champion.*

29.05.01 Dan Dougherty (USA) W PTS 10 Kid McFadden (USA), San Francisco. *Advertised for the 115 lbs title, this, a return fight between the pair, was merely a support to Terry McGovern v Aurelio Herrera.*

13.02.02+ Andrew Tokell (GB) W PTS 20 Harry Ware (GB), New Adelphi, London - GB. *On becoming the new British champion at 114 lbs, Tokell challenged the world at 114/116 lbs.*

13.03.02+ Johnny Reagan (USA) DREW 15 Tommy Feltz (USA), St Louis. *Made at 115 lbs, Reagan held on to his title claim at the weight.*

31.03.02+ Johnny Reagan (USA) W PTS 20 Tommy Feltz (USA), St Louis. *Again, Reagan put his 115 lbs title claim at risk against Feltz.*

12.05.02+ Andrew Tokell (GB) W DIS 10 Jim Williams (GB), NSC, London - GB *(114 lbs).*

08.09.02+ Harry Ware (GB) W DIS 8 Andrew Tokell (GB), National Athletic Club, London - GB. *Billed for the title at 116 lbs, but only scheduled for ten rounds, although Tokell disputed the verdict, Ware was generally accepted as the new British champion.*

09.10.02+ Tommy Feltz (USA) W PTS 20 Johnny Reagan (USA), St Louis. *Although Reagan's 115 lbs title claim came to an end at the hands of Feltz, the latter had already been beaten at the weight by Harry Forbes, who thus tightened his hold on the American title.*

16.10.02+ Harry Forbes (USA) W CO 1 Chick Sullivan (USA), Dubuque - USA. *Without mention of weights, George Siler of the Chicago Tribune (newspaper) reported that Sullivan was bidding for the title.*

15.12.02+ Joe Bowker (GB) W PTS 15 Harry Ware (GB), NSC, London - GB *(116 lbs).*

25.05.03+ Joe Bowker (GB) W PTS 15 Andrew Tokell (GB), NSC, London - GB *(116 lbs).*

03.10.03+ Joe Bowker (GB) W PTS 15 Bill King (GB), NSC, London - GB *(116 lbs).*

16.10.03 Frankie Neil (USA) DREW 20 Johnny Reagan (USA), Los Angeles - USA. *Although no weights were given in the Los Angeles Times (newspaper), the previous day the paper had quoted Reagan as saying that he expected to be well within the articled 116 lbs at the weigh-in.*

27.05.04 Frankie Neil (USA) W CO 1 Tommy Moore (USA), Chicago - USA. *Although shown in some early record books as being a title defence, it was not, with Chicago unable to stage anything more than six rounders and with the match made at 120 lbs. Incidentally, the Chicago Tribune (newspaper) made no mention of Moore's weight.*

30.05.04 Joe Bowker (GB) W PTS 20 Owen Moran (GB), NSC, London - GB *(116 lbs)*.

17.06.04 Frankie Neil (USA) W CO 3 Harry Forbes (USA), Chicago - USA. *This fight should be deleted from the title listings, with the contest made at 120 lbs and, according to the Chicago Tribune (newspaper), not involving any risk to Neil's championship.*

17.10.04 **Joe Bowker** (GB) W PTS 20 Frankie Neil (USA), NSC, London. *Although weighing 116½ to Bowker's 116 lbs, on arriving back in America, Neil continued to claim the title at 115 lbs (ringside). However, while Bowker was recognised as the International title-holder, Neil was generally perceived to be the American champion and successfully defended that title on points over 25 rounds at 116 lbs against Harry Tenny in San Francisco on 28 July 1905, before moving up to feather.*

29.03.05 Jimmy Walsh (USA) ND-W RSC 6 Monte Attell (USA), Philadelphia. *Although recorded in the Boxing News Annual as a title fight it was merely a no-decision affair. Add the fact that Joe Bowker was still recognised on both sides of the Atlantic as champion, even though he had recently won the British featherweight crown, and that Frankie Neil continued, in the main, to be seen as the American titleholder, it was hardly surprising that Walsh, who laid claim to the title following this victory, could only find support in New England.*

23.05.05 Jimmy Walsh (USA) W PTS 15 Willie Gibbs (USA), Chelsea, Mass. *Another Walsh fight recorded by the Boxing News Annual as a title bout, yet, according to the Boston Herald and Post (newspapers), there was no mention of weights or that a championship was involved. However, prior to the fight, the Post stated that the New England boxing community was claiming the 116 lbs championship for Walsh, despite the fact that Frankie Neil was accepted as the American champion throughout the rest of the country.*

20.10.05 Jimmy Walsh (USA) W PTS 15 Digger Stanley (GB), Chelsea, Mass. *Recorded as a title fight in the Ring Record Book, with both men inside 116 lbs, according to the Boston Post (newspaper) report, the bantamweight crown was not at stake as Frankie Neil was still recognised as the American champion. However, that hardly deterred Walsh.*

15.03.07+ Kid Murphy (USA) W PTS 10 Eddie Grunwald (USA), Milwaukee. *While the Milwaukee Sentinel (newspaper) reported this as being a championship opportunity for Grunwald, the match was set for 112 lbs.*

03.07.07+ Kid Murphy (USA) DREW 15 Young Britt (USA), Baltimore *(105 lbs)*.

31.03.08+ Jimmy Walsh (USA) DREW 12 Al Delmont (USA), Boston. *The Boston Post (newspaper), in calling Walsh the world champion, went on to say that although the match has been made above 116 lbs, the winner would have every prospect of claiming the title as both can make the weight with ease. The Post had earlier announced that this fight would settle the championship.*

26.06.08 Jimmy Walsh (USA) W CO 11 Jimmy Carroll (USA), San Francisco. *Articled at 116 lbs, neither the Philadelphia Item or San Francisco Chronicle (newspapers) mentioned it as a title fight, but that did not stop Walsh from continuing to claim the title.*

09.10.08 Jimmy Walsh (USA) W PTS 15 Young Britt (USA), Baltimore. *Although there was no mention of weights, championship billing was given in the Baltimore Sun (newspaper), while the Chicago Tribune (newspaper) reported Walsh to be claiming the 116 lbs title. Early Boxing News Annuals had listed this fight as involving Walsh's claim to the championship and one can only assume that the men weighed in below that poundage.*

21.12.08 Jimmy Walsh (USA) DREW 15 Monte Attell (USA), San Francisco. *While there was no mention in the San Francisco Chronicle (newspaper) of this being a title fight, the match was made at 116 lbs, a poundage that Walsh was claiming to be champion of. With the result, Attell laid claim to the title after Walsh, who refused to make 116 lbs at the last moment and then renegotiated an extra two pounds instead, was unable to make that weight either.*

22.02.09 Monte Attell (USA) W PTS 20 Jimmy Reagan (USA), San Francisco. *Reported in the San Francisco Chronicle (newspaper) as an eliminator for the championship held by Johnny Coulon, with both men announced as being inside 116 lbs, it was the heavy bantam crown that Attell was claiming, not the latter's 105 lbs title.*

24.05.09 Jimmy Walsh (USA) DREW 15 Digger Stanley (GB), NSC,

London. *Following the result, Stanley continued to be supported in Britain, while Walsh and Monte Attell carried sway in America.*

20.08.09+ Monte Attell (USA) W RSC 10 Percy Cove (USA), San Francisco. *The San Francisco Chronicle (newspaper) pre-fight report claimed that both men were already down to weight (116 lbs) for this scheduled 20 rounder.*

12.10.09 Monte Attell (USA) ND-L PTS 10 Danny Webster (USA), Los Angeles. *Following the fight, which was made at 116 lbs, Webster was presented with a championship belt after being awarded the "press" decision.*

23.11.09 Monte Attell (USA) ND-DREW 10 Danny Webster (USA), Los Angeles. *Billed for the world title, according to the Los Angeles Evening Herald Express (newspaper), the paper went on to say that both men were inside the required 116 lbs.*

15.01.10+ Johnny Coulon (USA) W PTS 10 George Kitson (USA), New Orleans. *Earlier, Coulon was claiming the bantamweight title at 105 lbs, but, due to increasing weight, the match was made at 112 lbs. While not billed as involving his title claim, had he lost it would have been a severe dent to his championship ambitions. Immediately following the fight, Coulon staked his claim at 112 lbs.*

29.01.10 Johnny Coulon (C) W CO 9 Earl Denning (USA), New Orleans. *Billed as a title bout at 112 lbs.*

11.04.10+ Johnny Coulon (C) ND-DREW 10 Young O'Leary (USA), New York City. *The New York Times (newspaper) stated that both men were within the required 115 lbs.*

25.04.10+ Johnny Coulon (C) ND-L PTS 10 Frankie Burns (USA), Brooklyn *(115 lbs)*.

12.05.10+ Johnny Coulon (C) ND-W PTS 10 Phil McGovern (USA), New York City *(115 lbs)*.

08.06.10+ Johnny Coulon (C) ND-W PTS 10 Frankie Burns (USA), New York City *(115 lbs)*.

03.12.10+ Johnny Coulon (C) W PTS 10 Charlie Harvey (USA), New Orleans *(115 lbs)*.

19.01.11+ Johnny Coulon (C) W CO 2 Terry Moran (USA), Memphis *(115 lbs)*.

22.03.11+ Johnny Coulon (C) ND-W CO 5 George Kitson (USA), Akron - USA. *Made at 114 lbs (6.00 pm weigh-in), this fight automatically involved Coulon's 116 lbs title.*

28.03.11 Johnny Coulon (C) ND-W PTS 10 Harry Forbes (USA), Kenosha - USA. *Both men were inside 116 lbs.*

20.04.11+ Johnny Coulon (C) ND-W PTS 10 Phil McGovern (USA), Kenosha - USA *(116 lbs)*.

16.05.11+ Jimmy Walsh (USA) DREW 12 Al Delmont (USA), Boston. *With Walsh still claiming the 116 lbs title, the Boston Post (newspaper) reported that the result would decide who was the best bantam on the American East Coast. From hereon, however, Walsh boxed at featherweight.*

25.05.11+ Johnny Coulon (C) ND-W PTS 10 Johnny Daly (USA), Fort Wayne - USA. *Recorded in various published title listings as involving the championship, heavy research to date has failed to uncover weight or billing. The same conditions apply where asterisked (*).*

11.01.12+ Johnny Coulon (C) ND-W CO 3 George Kitson (USA), South Bend - USA. *Although no individual weights were reported, the Chicago Tribune (newspaper) gave this as a bout where the title was involved at 116 lbs.*

22.01.12 Johnny Coulon (C) ND-W CO 3 Harry Forbes (USA), Kenosha - USA. *With Forbes weighing 115 lbs, both men were inside 116 lbs.*

08.05.12+ Johnny Coulon (C) ND-W PTS 10 Young Solsberg (USA), Brooklyn - USA. *The New York newspapers reported that Solsberg, weighing 112½ lbs, was a very inexperienced challenger. Coulon came in a pound heavier at 113½.*

12.06.12+ Johnny Coulon (C) ND-W CO 4 Frankie Hayes (USA), New Haven - USA. *According to the Chicago Tribune (newspaper), both men made 116 lbs ringside.*

02.07.12 Johnny Coulon (C) ND-W PTS 10 Young Wagner (USA), New York City - USA. *Coulon weighed 114¼ lbs to Wagner's 114.*

18.10.12 Johnny Coulon (C) ND-L PTS 10 Kid Williams (USA), New York City - USA. *Both men were inside 116 lbs at the ringside weigh-in.*

20.11.12+ Johnny Coulon (C) ND-W PTS 10 Charley Goldman (USA), Brooklyn - USA. *Coulon, at 113½ lbs, had a slight pull in the weights over Goldman who scaled 113.*

12.05.13+ Johnny Coulon (C) ND-W PTS 6 Frankie Bradley (USA), Philadelphia - USA. *Articled at 116 lbs ringside, this was yet another occasion that Coulon risked his title in a no-decision fight.*

23.06.13 Johnny Coulon (C) ND-W PTS 10 Frankie Burns (USA),

Kenosha - USA. *Made at 116 lbs, the Chicago Tribune (newspaper) reported that neither man had difficulty in making the weight.*

21.01.14+ Johnny Coulon (C) ND-W PTS 10 Young Sinnett (USA), Racine - USA. *The Chicago Tribune (newspaper) reported that both men were articled to scale under 116 lbs at the 3.0 pm weigh-in.*

14.09.14+ **Kid Williams** (USA) ND-W PTS 6 Louisiana (USA), Philadelphia. *While only a six round no-decision contest, both men agreed to come to the ring inside 116 lbs. Incidentally, Louisiana's real name was Joe Lavigne.*

28.09.14 **Kid Williams** (USA) ND-W CO 4 Kid Herman (USA), Philadelphia*

25.12.14 **Kid Williams** (USA) ND-W PTS 10 Johnny Daly (USA), New York City. *Daly weighed 112¾ lbs.*

23.03.15+ **Kid Williams** (USA) ND-W PTS 10 Freddie Diggins (USA), Baltimore*

24.07.15 **Kid Williams** (USA) ND-W PTS 10 Jimmy Taylor (USA), Baltimore. *Both men were inside the required 116 lbs.*

10.09.15 **Kid Williams** (USA) ND-L DIS 5 Johnny Ertle (USA), St Paul. *Following the fight, Williams' right to the title was disputed by Ertle (112 lbs) after the champion had been disqualified for persistently landing low blows. Although Williams (117 lbs) argued that the fight had taken place in a State where decisions were prohibited and therefore he could not legally have been disqualified, Ertle continued to claim the championship.*

05.10.15+ Kid Williams (USA) ND-W PTS 10 Dutch Brandt (USA), Baltimore. *According to the Baltimore Sun (newspaper), both men were inside 118 lbs.*

28.10.15 Kid Williams (USA) ND-L PTS 8 Pal Moore (USA), Memphis (118 lbs).

04.12.15+ Johnny Ertle (USA) ND-W RSC 3 Young O'Leary (USA), Brooklyn. *With O'Leary scaling 116 lbs, it was another defence of his claim for Ertle (115 lbs).*

06.12.15+ Johnny Ertle (USA) ND-W CO 1 Freddie Diggins (USA), Philadelphia. *The Philadelphia Ledger (newspaper) tells us that Ertle weighed in at 114½ lbs, while Diggins scaled 115 for this six rounder.*

21.01.16+ Johnny Ertle (USA) ND-W PTS 10 Jack Sayles (USA), New York City. *Again Ertle (115 lbs) risked his claim, this time against Sayles (113¾ lbs).*

09.02.16+ Johnny Ertle (USA) ND-W PTS 10 Teddy Martin (USA), Brooklyn. *If you accept the New York Times' (newspaper) assertion that Ertle (115 lbs) had earned the right to be called champion, then his claim was automatically on the line against Martin (115¼ lbs) in this one.*

12.03.16+ Johnny Ertle (USA) ND-W PTS 10 Young Zulu Kid (USA), Brooklyn. *Ertle (117½ lbs), who was reported as the champion by the New York Times (newspaper), by definition, defended his title claim against the 110 lbs Kid.*

12.02.17+ Pete Herman (USA) ND-W PTS 10 Sammy Sandow (USA), Cincinnati. *According to the Toronto Daily Mail (newspaper), the title was on the line with both men inside 118 lbs.*

15.03.17+ Pete Herman (USA) ND-W PTS 10 Dutch Brandt (USA), Brooklyn. *Articled to meet at 118 lbs, both men scaled 117½ exactly.*

14.05.17+ Pete Herman (USA) ND-W RSC 3 Johnny Coulon (C), Racine. *Coulon weighed 109¼ lbs.*

13.06.17 Pete Herman (USA) ND-L PTS 6 Kid Williams (USA), Philadelphia. *The New Orleans Daily Picayune (newspaper) reported that both men were inside 118 lbs at ringside.*

21.08.17+ Pete Herman (USA) ND-W PTS 10 Jack Douglas (USA), New Orleans. *The New Orleans Daily Picayune (newspaper) pre-fight report claimed that, with both men contracted to make the championship weight, the title would change hands if Douglas won.*

03.09.17+ Pete Herman (USA) ND-W PTS 10 Nate Jackson (USA), Tulsa. *The Tulsa World (newspaper) reported that Herman had no trouble at all in defending his title. Jackson was well within the required 118 lbs.*

10.09.17+ Pete Herman (USA) ND-W PTS 10 Earl Puryear (USA), Tulsa. *The Tulsa World (newspaper) reported this as a billed title fight, inferring that Puryear, a small bantam, was easily inside 118 lbs.*

17.09.17+ Pete Herman (USA) ND-W PTS 6 Johnny Eggers (USA), Philadelphia. *Articled to make 118 lbs, according to the New York Times (newspaper) report, Eggers was inside, while Herman, a fraction over, was forced to pay forfeit.*

21.11.17+ Johnny Ertle (USA) ND-W PTS 10 Joe Burman (USA), Milwaukee. *Both men were inside 118 lbs, with Ertle scaling 115¾ lbs to Burman's 117.*

14.12.17+ Pete Herman (USA) ND-W RSC 3 Frankie Mason (USA), Fort Wayne. *Mason weighed 107¾ lbs.*

10.04.18 Pal Moore (USA) W PTS 15 Johnny Ertle (USA), Baltimore. *Although Pete Herman was generally recognised, with both men inside 116 lbs, it did not stop Moore self-styling himself as champion following his victory over Ertle. However, his claim evaporated when he was outpointed by Jimmy Wilde over 20 rounds of a 116 lbs non-title fight at the NSC in London on 17 July 1919. Wilde, the world flyweight champion, who found it difficult to make 112 lbs let alone the bantam limit of 118, declined to make an assault on the heavier division.*

03.07.18 Pete Herman (USA) ND-L PTS 10 Frankie Burns (USA), Jersey City. *Although shown in last year's Yearbook as involving the title, the New York Times (newspaper) reported it being at catchweights, with Herman scaling 120 lbs to Burns' 119.*

06.09.18+ Pete Herman (USA) ND-W PTS 8 Young Zulu Kid (USA), Jersey City*

24.03.19 Pete Herman (USA) ND-L PTS 8 Pal Moore (USA), Memphis. *Articled at 120 lbs ringside, neither Moore or Herman's title claims were at risk as previously thought.*

08.04.19+ Pete Herman (USA) ND-W PTS 10 Al Shubert (USA), Baltimore. *The Pittsburgh Gazette (newspaper) reported that, in the final analysis, the title did not change hands as Herman fought the kind of fight that made Al McCoy famous. That is to say, with the challenger inside 118 lbs, Herman took all that Shubert had to offer without ever looking likely to "bite the dust".*

21.04.19+ Pete Herman (USA) ND-W PTS 8 Patsy Johnson (USA), Trenton. *Johnson weighed 117 lbs.*

03.05.19+ Pete Herman (USA) ND-W CO 6 Patsy Wallace (USA), Philadelphia. *Wallace weighed 114 lbs.*

23.05.19+ Pete Herman (USA) ND-W CO 5 Johnny Ertle (USA), Minneapolis. *According to the St Paul Pioneer (newspaper), it was a billed title fight over ten rounds which saw Ertle weigh 116½ lbs to Herman's 118.*

01.09.19+ **Pete Herman** (USA) ND-L PTS 10 Joe Lynch (USA), Waterbury. *Boxing, the trade paper, reported that although billed as a title bout, both fighters were over the 118 lbs limit.*

27.11.19+ **Pete Herman** (USA) ND-W PTS 8 Mickey Russell (USA), Jersey City. *Russell weighed 118 lbs.*

01.03.20 **Pete Herman** (USA) ND-DREW 8 Earl Puryear (USA), Trenton. *Billed as a title fight at 118 lbs, Puryear was easily inside according to the Trenton State Gazette (newspaper).*

10.05.20+ **Pete Herman** (USA) ND-W PTS 8 Jabez White (USA), Philadelphia. *White weighed 118 lbs.*

11.09.20+ **Pete Herman** (USA) ND-L PTS 10 Jackie Sharkey (USA), Chicago. *Strangely, the Chicago Tribune (newspaper) reported this as a title fight even though Sharkey was forced to weigh in at 119 lbs.*

22.02.21+ **Joe Lynch** (USA) ND-W PTS 8 Jabez White (USA), Philadelphia. *White weighed 118 lbs.*

28.02.21+ **Joe Lynch** (USA) ND-W PTS 10 Young Montreal (USA), Detroit. *The Detroit Free Press (newspaper) reported Montreal (118 lbs) as challenging for the title in this one.*

10.03.21+ **Joe Lynch** (USA) ND-W PTS 10 Joe Burman (USA), Cleveland. *The Cleveland Press (newspaper) reported that Burman, inside 118 lbs, tried in earnest to take the title in this one.*

08.04.21+ **Joe Lynch** (USA) ND-L PTS 10 Young Montreal (USA), Cleveland. *Montreal weighed 118 lbs.*

06.05.21+ **Joe Lynch** (USA) ND-L PTS 10 Pal Moore (USA), Louisville. *With both men down to weight (118 lbs), the Vancouver Daily Province (newspaper) reported Moore as challenging for the title. The Chicago Tribune (newspaper) thought Lynch would come in at 119 lbs to Moore's 118.*

15.12.21+ **Johnny Buff** (USA) ND-L PTS 10 Pal Moore (USA), Milwaukee. *Both men were inside the weight at the 3.0 pm weigh-in, with Buff scaling 113½ lbs to Moore's 116½.*

21.08.22+ **Joe Lynch** (USA) W CO 2 Frankie Murray (USA), Shreveport. *Scheduled for 15 rounds, the Chicago Tribune's newspaper reporter, in summing up, stated that Lynch easily defended his title against Murray.*

04.09.22+ **Joe Lynch** (USA) ND-W PTS 10 Pal Moore (USA), Michigan City. *According to the New York Times (newspaper) report, Lynch's title was at risk in this one.*

30.11.22+ **Joe Lynch** (USA) ND-W PTS 10 Frankie Dailey (USA), Indianapolis. *The Indianapolis Star (newspaper) report gave this as a title defence for Lynch at 118 lbs.*

19.03.23+ **Joe Lynch** (USA) ND-L PTS 10 Joe Burman (USA), Chicago. *Advertised as a title fight, the Chicago Tribune (newspaper) reported that the Articles of Agreement called for Burman to be inside 119 lbs, one pound over the recognised limit. That being the case, regardless of the billing, Lynch appeared not to risk his title this time round.*

04.04.23 **Joe Lynch** (USA) ND-W PTS 10 Midget Smith (USA), Chicago.

223

Not a title fight as previously implied, although Lynch came in at 118 lbs, Smith scaled 120.

19.10.23 Abe Goldstein (USA) W PTS 12 Joe Burman (USA), New York City. *Booked to defend his title against Burman, Joe Lynch withdrew after being supposedly injured just two days before the contest was due to take place. Goldstein substituted and, after finally making 118 lbs at the weigh-in, Burman was proclaimed champion by the NYSAC under clause VII of their rule book. Burman's reign, however, was brief to say the least, while, eight days later, it was unclear as to the true extent of Goldstein's title status also after the NYSAC stated that they had re-drafted clause VII to read: Ring champions who decline to defend their titles in a decision bout within the six month period specified by the revised "Walker Law" governing boxing in New York, will be suspended until such time they agree to defend. This parlous state of affairs came to a head, according to research carried out by a leading boxing historian, Bob Soderman, when the recently re-organised Commission, determined to start all over again, voted to wipe the slate clean of all suspensions and penalties imposed prior to 13 February 1924. The news obviously did not travel well as far as the New York Times (newspaper) was concerned, for they reported Goldstein as world champion on 19 February, the day of his ten rounder against Danny Edwards in New York City. The following day, though, the Times reported that Goldstein (115½ lbs) was fully deserving of a crack at Joe Lynch after outpointing Edwards (118 lbs).*

24.02.25 **Eddie Martin** (USA) ND-L PTS 12 Carl Tremaine (USA), Cleveland. *Another fight reported in the 1995 Yearbook where it has since been discovered that the title was not involved. The New York Times (newspaper) reported tht both men weighed 121¼ lbs.*

02.03.26 **Charlie Rosenberg** (USA) W PTS 10 George Butch (USA), St Louis. *Since the 1995 edition of the Yearbook, research of the San Francisco Chronicle and New York Times (newspapers) found this to have been reported as a title fight. However, with Butch scaling 121 lbs to Rosenberg's 120, it could not have been. Following the failure to post his forfeit for a forthcoming title defence against Bud Taylor, the NBA stripped Rosenberg on 18 October 1926 and pronounced the latter as their champion.*

04.02.27 Charlie Rosenberg (USA) W PTS 15 Bushy Graham (USA), New York City - NY. *Somewhat surprisingly, Rosenberg had his suspension lifted for this fight, but then forfeited his title on the scales when weighing at 122½ lbs. The fight went ahead as planned and had Graham won he would have been proclaimed champion. However, not only did Graham not win, but both men were suspended in New York for a year, following the discovery of a secret agreement regarding purse money.*

24.02.27 Bud Taylor (USA) W PTS 10 Eddie Shea (USA), Chicago. *Although recorded in the 1995 Yearbook as an Illinois sanctioned title fight, closer inspection uncovered the fact that this was an over the weight contest made at 123 lbs.*

05.05.27 Teddy Baldock (GB) W PTS 15 Archie Bell (USA), Albert Hall, London. *While billed for the world 118 lbs title by the International Syndicate, with Baldock not even the recognised British champion, it was not given backing by the country's ruling body. Add to that the fact Bell was not that highly regarded in America, having been stopped by Willie LaMorte (1925) and Tony Canzoneri (1926), then one can see why support was not forthcoming.*

06.10.27 Willie Smith (SA) W PTS 15 Teddy Baldock (GB), Albert Hall, London. *Previously listed as a title fight, it should not have been. Made at 120 lbs, with no championship billing, Smith only took over Baldock's claim to the title after coming in below 118 lbs. However, he passed up the opportunity of entering an elimination series when deciding to move into the featherweight division in January 1928. Shortly after this, Bushy Graham, who had finally served his 12 month suspension, was matched with Izzy Schwartz for the New York version of the title.*

29.07.31+ Pete Sanstol (NOR) W PTS 10 Eugene Huat, Montreal - CANADA

26.09.32+ **Al Brown** (PAN) W PTS 10 Mose Butch (USA), Pittsburgh. *The December edition of the 1932 Ring Magazine reported that Brown upheld his laurels in the bantam class in winning. However, with both men weighing 121½ lbs, it was not a title clash. Earlier, on 14 December 1931, Butch had stopped Willie Davies in the first round of a fight billed as the "local championship", with the winner guaranteed a shot at Brown.*

12.10.32 Speedy Dado (PH) W PTS 10 Young Tommy (PH), Oakland. *We mentioned in the 1995 Yearbook that Dado was recognised as world champion by the California State Boxing Commission following his victory, a statement that was supported by the Everlast Record Book. However, after much research of both the Los Angeles Times and San Francisco Chronicle (newspapers), the writer can find no proof of that ever being the case.*

19.05.33 Young Tommy (PH) W PTS 10 Speedy Dado (PH), San Francisco. *Another fight listed in the 1995 Yearbook that needs to be deleted, it was billed for the Californian State bantamweight title only.*

24.10.33 Speedy Dado (PH) W PTS 10 Young Tommy (PH), Los Angeles - CALIFORNIA. *Prior to the fight, the California State Boxing Commission said they would recognise the winner as being the world champion, a statement they confirmed on 27 October 1933.*

29.06.36 Tony Marino (USA) W CO 14 Baltasar Sangchili (SP), New York City. *Sangchili, the IBU titleholder, finally came to America to press his claim after the NYSAC persisted in not recognising him as champion. Although the Ring Magazine saw the Spaniard as the lineal champion, by dint of his victory over Al Brown, this fight was not given "official" title billing as New York already supported Sixto Escobar as champion. Despite the result, and despite it being held under championship conditions, the IBU, at their annual congress on 8 August 1936, maintained that Sangchili should still be recognised as their champion.*

20.02.38 Sixto Escobar (PR) W PTS 15 Harry Jeffra (USA), San Juan - NBA/NY

27.08.38 Star Frisco (PH) W DIS 6 Mickey Miller (A), Newcastle. *Outside of Newcastle, Frisco (116 lbs) was accorded no recognition whatsoever and following just two wins in his next eight contests he retired. In a match made for 15 rounds, Miller scaled 117½ lbs.*

14.12.39 Tony Olivera (USA) W PTS 10 Lou Salica (USA), San Francisco - CALIFORNIA. *Although Nat Fleischer, when writing in Ring Magazine, insisted that the official records of the Californian Boxing Commission showed Olivera to weigh 118¼ lbs, the San Francisco Chronicle (newspaper) reported that the local man took one and a quarter pounds off to qualify for his title shot. Regardless of anything written here, Olivera was recognised in California as holding a version of the world championship after his points win.*

24.04.40 Little Dado (PH) W PTS 10 Tony Olivera (USA), Oakland - CALIFORNIA. *Made at 118 lbs, Dado (116) took over the Californian version of the world title following his defeat of Olivera (117). Both the New York Times and San Francisco Chronicle (newspapers) pre-fight reports confirmed that the fight had been sanctioned by the Californian Boxing Commision as a world title fight.*

30.07.40+ Little Dado (PH) ND-W PTS 12 Jackie Jurich (USA), San Jose. *Not billed for the Californian version of the title, being a no-decision contest, but, with Jurich weighing 113¾ lbs to Dado's 116, there was an element of risk to the latter's claim. By the beginning of 1941, however, Dado had moved his base to Honolula, Hawaii, and it was there he took in two billed world title eliminators over ten rounds, outpointing Tony Olivera on 24 January, before outscored himself by David Kui Kong Young on 4 April.*

15.04.41 Kenny Lindsay (C) W PTS 10 Tony Olivera (USA), Vancouver - CANADA. *Advertised as a title fight in Canada, with neither man considered the outstanding challenger at the time, Lindsay (121 lbs) forfeited the support of the Montreal Boxing Commission after being outscored by Olivera (116 lbs) over ten rounds of a non-title fight held in Oakland on 19 June 1941.*

02.01.42 Manuel Ortiz (USA) W PTS 10 Tony Olivera (USA), Los Angeles. *Recorded in some annuals as being for the Californian version of the world title, it was only the State championship that was at stake in this one.*

07.08.42 Manuel Ortiz (USA) W PTS 12 Lou Salica (USA), Los Angeles - NBA. *Because it was not contested over 15 rounds, the NYSAC refused to accept it as a title fight and continued to recognise Salica as champion. However, having failed to defend for six months, the latter was stripped by New York on 15 December 1942, the body eventually recognising Ortiz as their titleholder the following February.*

14.11.44 Manuel Ortiz (USA) W RSC 9 Luis Castillo (MEX), Los Angeles - NY/NBA. *With Ortiz inducted into the US Army early in 1945, in order to keep the division active, Castillo was matched against Tony Olivera for the "duration" title. Having outpointed the Mexican over 15 rounds in Minneapolis on 15 June 1945, Olivera twice retained his newly won spoils against the same opponent, drawing over the same distance in San Francisco on 9 July and 27 August 1945, before Ortiz picked up his career in November. However, it was Castillo, not Olivera, who was selected for the champion's next defence, having outscored the latter over ten rounds in San Francisco on 10 December 1945.*

30.10.60+ Piero Rollo (ITA) W PTS 15 Billy Rafferty (GB), Cagliari. *Originally billed as being for the title, the Italian authorities, in failing to get the backing of the EBU, withdrew their support. As the winner, Rollo got first crack at the NBA champion, Eder Jofre.*

Super-Bantamweight (122 lbs)

On 21 September 1922, in a fight billed by the promoter as being for the vacant 122 lbs junior-featherweight title, Jack Kid Wolfe outpointed Joe Lynch over 15 rounds in New York City. The contest was not given official backing in New York, however, as the commission simply did not recognise the weight class at that time. Taking his unofficial title to Toronto on 26 December 1922, Wolfe lost on points over ten rounds to the Russian-Canadian, Benny Gould. While the fight was billed for the title it is difficult to ascertain whether it had official backing, but regardless of that, Gould does not appear to fight at the weight again and no more is heard of the 122 lbs title until a little known body calling themselves the American Federation of Boxing started the ball rolling again with a series of eight rounders in New York City. After appointing Lou Barbetta as their champion, he was outpointed by Davey Crawford (22 July 1941), before Crawford befell a similar fate himself at the hands of Aaron Seltzer (2 September 1941). His successor was Joey Iannotti, who, after outscoring Seltzer (6 October 1941), held on to his laurels next time out with a draw against Johnny Compo (29 January 1942), before going down on points to Seltzer (17 February 1942) in a rematch that turned out to be the last contest held under the auspices of the ABF. Resurrected as the super-bantamweight division by the World Boxing Council in 1976, the weight class is currently recognised as the junior featherweight division by the World Boxing Association, the International Boxing Federation, and the World Boxing Organisation.

Featherweight (126 lbs)

The division started life in the early 1860s, when Nobby Clark was recognised as being the best man at the weight. However, the first man to claim the championship appears to have been Dick Hollywood, with wins over Johnny Keating in 1867 and 1868, followed by England's George Seddons, also in 1868. When Seddons found he could no longer make the weight, the title was later claimed, to no great effect, by a succession of fighters including Tommy Kelly, Johnny Keating, Long Tom Ryan, Jack Keenan, Tommy Warren, Young Mitchell, Jack Farrell and Harry Gilmore. The latter made his claim in 1887 at 122 lbs, and it is around this time that the division became popularised. Although 1889 opened with the British regarding 116 to 118 lbs as the limit, the Americans by now generally recognised somewhere between 118 and 122 to be the requisite poundage and it was on that basis the Frank Murphy v Ike Weir (both British) fight at 122 lbs in Kouts, Indiana, on 31 March 1889, was designated as being for the vacant title. Fought in skin-tight gloves, Weir was getting the better of things before the police broke it up after 80 rounds, leaving both men with a share of the spoils. From hereon, the division's biggest fights would be contested with two ounce gloves, minimum. A so-called title bout, according to early Ring Record Books, in San Francisco, between Dal Hawkins and Fred Bogan in June 1889, was not even reported by the San Francisco Chronicle (newspaper). The fight, which started on 4 June before being halted at five a.m. after 75 rounds had been completed and announced as a draw, continued the following day and ended with a 15th round kayo win for the former. Years later, former fighter, Packy O'Gatty, claimed to have discovered it involved the local championship, only. On 30 July in San Francisco, in another contest stopped by the police, Frank Murphy fought his namesake, Billy, from New Zealand. Halted in the 27th round, both men weighed 119½ lbs and wore regulation gloves. We now come to the first recognised gloved title fight for the division between Ike Weir and Billy Murphy.

13.01.90 Billy Murphy (NZ) W CO 14 Ike Weir (GB), San Francisco. *In a match made at 120 lbs, with the fighters appearing to use smaller gloves than the regulation size, Murphy entered the ring at 118½ lbs compared to Weir's overweight 124½. Strangely, in the light of the fight's importance, there was no mention of title billing in the San Francisco Chronicle (newspaper), even though the "Police Gazette" featherweight championship belt was at stake. Years later, certain American scribes insisted that only the British version of the title had been involved, a view, however, that was not supported unilaterally at the time.*

07.02.90 George Dixon (C) DREW 70 Cal McCarthy (USA), Boston. *The San Francisco Chronicle (newspaper) reported that both men entered the ring at 114½ lbs, hands encased in regulation gloves, to do battle for the American 115 lbs title. Although billed as a bantam title bout, with the Pelican Club (London) and America recognising 106 and 105 lbs, respectively, as being the bantam limit, this was really a light-featherweight contest. However, from hereon, Dixon is really the champion of whatever weight he comes in at.*

14.03.90+ Billy Murphy (NZ) W CO 4 Tommy Warren (USA), San Francisco. *Billed for the 118 lbs world featherweight title, Murphy scaled 116½ lbs to Warren's 118. The San Francisco Chronicle (newspaper) went on to say it was to be fought to a finish using four ounce gloves.*

27.06.90 George Dixon (C) W CO 18 Nunc Wallace (GB), Pelican Club, London. *Although billed for the bantam title, by his victory, Dixon won the British version of the 115 lbs championship, a weight not far short of the featherweight class. Using four ounce gloves, Dixon (112) and Wallace (113) were recognised as feathers by the San Francisco Chronicle (newspaper).*

02.09.90 Young Griffo (A) W RSC 16 Billy Murphy (NZ), Sydney. *Although billed for the featherweight title, it was not Murphy's 118-120 lbs version that Griffo won, with the winner scaling 123 lbs to the New Zealander's 116. The Newcastle Morning Herald (newspaper) tells us that Murphy threw the gloves off in the 16th round saying they were rigged, a claim that was found to be false.*

23.10.90 George Dixon (C) W CO 40 Johnny Murphy (USA), Providence. *Again billed for the (heavy) bantam title at 115 lbs, following his victory over Murphy (114), Dixon (113) was recognised as a featherweight. The gloves used were of the two ounce variety.*

14.11.90 Young Griffo (A) W CO 13 Paddy Moran (A), Sydney. *Billed for the 126 lbs featherweight title, according to the Newcastle Morning Herald (newspaper), Griffo scaled 123 lbs to Moran's 125¼. Conversely, weights supplied by John Hogg show Griffo weighing 118½ lbs to Moran's 123.*

12.03.91 Young Griffo (A) W DIS 20 George Powell (A), Sydney. *The Newcastle Morning Herald (newspaper) reported this as a world title fight, with Griffo weighing 120 lbs to Powell's 119½.*

31.03.91 George Dixon (C) W CO 22 Cal McCarthy (USA), Troy. *With the weight set at 115 lbs, and wearing two ounce gloves, Dixon (111½) beat McCarthy (114½) in a fight billed for the American version of the title. While he might not have been recognised throughout America, Dixon was acclaimed throughout the eastern side of the country.*

25.04.91 Ike Weir (GB) DREW 4 Johnny Griffin (USA), Nantasket. *Both prior to and following the fight, Griffin (121) laid claim to the 122 lbs title after Murphy returned to Australia. The New York Herald (newspaper) report claimed that Weir (122), who was trying to quit from the second round, was all in when the police came to his rescue.*

22.07.91 Young Griffo (A) W DIS 24 Billy Murphy (NZ), Sydney. *Billed as a fight to decide the featherweight title, The Newcastle Morning Herald (newspaper) gave Murphy's weight as 119 lbs, while recognising Griffo to be around four pounds heavier. However, weights supplied by the Australian historian, John Hogg, show Murphy scaling 116 lbs to Griffo's 123.*

28.07.91 George Dixon (C) W CO 5 Abe Willis (A), San Francisco. *In a billed 115 lbs title fight, using regulation gloves, Dixon (114½) beat Willis (115).*

22.03.92 Young Griffo (A) W CO 4 Mick McCarthy (A), Sydney. *Recognised in Britain as a title fight at 126 lbs, Griffo weighed 125¼ lbs to McCarthy's 125¼.*

31.05.92+ Johnny Murphy (USA) DREW 40 Billy Murphy (NZ), San Francisco. *This fight marked the return of Murphy to America. Now it has come to light that the New Zealander did not lose his 120 lbs title to Young Griffo, along with both men inside 122 lbs, the above, even if not billed as a championship contest, would have carried similar status. However, Billy did himself no favours when he refused to go through with the rematch on 8 June, claiming that his injuries had not responded in time.*

27.06.92 George Dixon (C) W CO 14 Fred Johnson (GB), Coney Island. *Billed for the 117 lbs featherweight title, and recognised in Britain as a championship fight, Dixon weighed 115½ lbs to Johnson's 116.*

06.09.92 George Dixon (C) W CO 8 Jack Skelly (USA), New Orleans. *Made at 118 lbs and billed for the feathers title, Dixon scaled 115 lbs to Skelly's 116½. A gallant failure, Skelly will remain in the record books as the first man to challenge for a world title on his professional debut.*

26.09.92+ Johnny Griffin (USA) W CO 5 Jimmy Lynch (USA), Coney Island. *Billed for the 122 lbs featherweight title, the New York*

Herald (newspaper) reported that both men were inside the weight and that Griffin should now be recognised as the champion of that weight class.

09.11.92 Young Griffo (A) DREW 25 Martin Denny (A), Sydney. *Griffo defended his version of the feathers title in this one at 130 lbs, a weight four pounds heavier than his previous defence and one that effectively took him into the lightweight class.*

20.12.92 Young Griffo (A) W PTS 12 Jerry Marshall (A), Sydney. *Another defence for Griffo at 130 lbs.*

06.02.93+ Johnny Griffin (USA) W CO 7 Billy Murphy (NZ), Coney Island. *Billed for the 122 lbs featherweight championship of the world, the New York Herald (newspaper) reported the weights for Griffin and Murphy as being 121 and 120½ lbs, respectively. With the result, Murphy lost any vestage of claim he might still have harboured.*

28.02.93 Young Griffo (A) W DIS 4 Jerry Marshall (A), Sydney. *Following this defence at 130 lbs, Griffo moved his base to America to fight as a lightweight.*

10.07.93+ Solly Smith (USA) W CO 4 Johnny Griffin (USA), Roby. *Billed for the world 122 lbs title, according to the San Francisco Chronicle, the newspaper went on to confirm that both men were inside the weight at 3.0 pm on the day of the fight.*

07.09.93 George Dixon (C) W CO 3 Eddie Pierce (USA), Coney Island. *Although Dixon weighed 116 lbs to Pierce's 120, he effectively moved the class limit to the latter. On winning, he was awarded the Police Gazette featherweight championship belt.*

25.09.93 **George Dixon** (C) W CO 7 Solly Smith (USA), Coney Island. *Made at 120 lbs, by his victory, Dixon would be regarded as champion at 118, 120 and 122 lbs from this moment in time.*

27.11.96 Frank Erne (USA) W PTS 20 George Dixon (C), New York City. *The New York Herald (newspaper) reported that with both men inside the articled 122 lbs, the world title changed hands. While Erne was recognised as the champion in most quarters, Tom O'Rourke, Dixon's manager, was telling all who would listen that his man still held the 118 and 120 lb versions of the title.*

22.01.97 George Dixon (C) W CO 6 Billy Murphy (NZ), New York City. *Having lost the 122 lbs version of the title, Dixon "defended" at 120 lbs in this one, scaling 118¾ to Murphy's 120. The New York Herald (newspaper) still referrred to Dixon as world featherweight champion.*

15.02.97 George Dixon (C) DREW 20 Jack Downey (USA), New York City. *Incorrectly reported as a world title fight in the Yearbook, it was made at 126 lbs, with Downey coming in at 129½.*

24.03.97 **George Dixon** (C) W PTS 25 Frank Erne (USA), New York City. *Advertised for the 122 lbs title, Dixon, who comfortably made the weight, while, having struggled with an injury, Erne came in at a whopping 130¼ lbs.*

04.10.97 **Solly Smith** (USA) W PTS 20 George Dixon (C), San Francisco. *Made at 120 lbs, with both men inside, the San Francisco Chronicle (newspaper) reported that the title changed hands. That was the general view among boxing circles, regardless of what Nat Fleischer, who was obviously influenced by Tom O'Rourke, wrote some 30 years later in Black Dynamite (volume 111).*

21.02.98 Spike Sullivan (USA) W CO 15 Harry Greenfield (GB), NSC, London. *Not a defence of Greenfield's 126 lbs title claim as suggested in the 1995 Yearbok, it was merely an international match made at 131 lbs.*

07.07.98 **Solly Smith** (USA) W DIS 7 Billy O'Donnell (USA), Buffalo - USA. *The Toronto Daily Mail (newspaper) gave it as a world title bout with both men inside 122 lbs.*

10.10.99 Eddie Santry (USA) W CO 10 Ben Jordan (GB), New York City. *Again, not an advertised title fight as implied in the Ring Record Book, by his victory, Santry merely took over Jordan's claim. For the record, Jordan weighed 124 lbs.*

01.02.00 **Terry McGovern** (USA) W CO 5 Eddie Santry (USA), Chicago. *Although recorded in the Ring Record Book as a championship fight, it was not, with Chicago only able to stage contests of six rounds duration at the time and Santry scaling 124 lbs to McGovern's 122. However, by his defeat, Santry lost any claim he had to the title.*

28.05.00 Ben Jordan (GB) W CO 4 Tommy Hogan (USA), NSC, London. *Although Jordan v Hogan was billed for the "English" version of the title at 124 lbs, McGovern, even though he had refused to meet Jordan in Britain, was generally perceived to be world featherweight champion at this moment in time.*

02.11.00 **Terry McGovern** (USA) W CO 7 Joe Bernstein (USA), Louisville. *By now it was obvious that McGovern could not make 122 lbs any more, but, because he was recognised as an outstanding champion, the boxing fraternity, including the majority of the press, accepted him hiking the weight class limit to suit his growing frame. The New Orleans Daily Picayune*

(newspaper) reported this fight as being at 126 lbs for the featherweight title. They went on to say both men were announced as making the weight, with Bernstein claiming to be 125 lbs.

30.04.01 **Terry McGovern** (USA) W CO 4 Oscar Gardner (USA), San Francisco. *Billed for the title at 124 lbs, the San Francisco Chronicle (newspaper) reported that Gardner scaled 123½ lbs to the champion's 123.*

29.05.01 **Terry McGovern** (USA) W CO 5 Aurelio Herrera (USA), San Francisco. *Scheduled for 20 rounds and accepted as a title fight at 126 lbs, the San Francisco Chronicle (newspaper) claimed that McGovern carried the challenger throughout. Although no weights were announced, the Chicago Tribune (newspaper), reporting the day before, stated that neither man had any problem in getting down to the weight, with McGovern probably the lighter of the two.*

28.11.01 **Young Corbett II** (USA) W CO 2 Terry McGovern (USA), Hartford. *Made at 126 lbs, with Corbett right on the limit, the winner was generally accepted as the featherweight champion even though the weight class had increased by four pounds during the previous 18 months.*

20.10.01 Abe Attell (USA) DREW 20 George Dixon (C), Cripple Creek. *Early Ring Record Books tell us that this was billed as a fight where the winner would claim the 122 lbs featherweight title. In truth, however, it was a fight made at 116 lbs, one pound above the recognised featherweight limit.*

28.10.01 Abe Attell (USA) W PTS 15 George Dixon (C), St Louis. *Made at 116 lbs, the St Louis Post-Dispatch (newspaper) reported nothing about featherweight title involvement whatsoever. In his very next fight seven days later, in the same town, Attell lost on points to Harry Forbes (see under bantamweight listings).*

23.05.02 **Young Corbett II** (USA) W PTS 10 Kid Broad (USA), Denver. *Recent research, using the Chicago Tribune (newspaper), found that the fight was billed for the featherweight championship, with both men inside 126 lbs at the 3.0 pm weigh-in.*

23.06.02 Ben Jordan (GB) W CO 15 Kid McFadden (USA), NSC, London. *Billed for the British version of the 120 lbs championship, it should not be seen as involving the "popular" title.*

16.10.02 Young Corbett II (USA) W RTD 7 Joe Bernstein (USA), Baltimore. *Billed for the featherweight title, Corbett, now unable to make 126 lbs, was surprisingly still recognised in America by the majority as champion. Had Bernstein (124½ lbs) got lucky and won, he would undoubtedly have claimed the title, but, unfortunately for him, that was not to be and Corbett continued to "defend" at 130 lbs.*

20.10.02+ Ben Jordan (GB) W CO 5 Jack Roberts (GB), NSC, London - GB *(124 lbs). Although billed for the British title only, it is fair to say that with Young Corbett having recently moved up to 130 lbs, Jordan was recognised on our side of the Atlantic as the featherweight champion. This view was supported by the Sporting Life (newspaper) pre-fight reports and, from hereon, neither Corbett, or his successors, Abe Attell and Johnny Kilbane, would be accepted universally in Britain.*

14.01.03 Young Corbett II (USA) W RSC 18 Austin Rice (USA), Hot Springs. *According to the Chicago Tribune (newspaper), it was billed for the featherweight title, but no weights were mentioned in the report.*

26.02.03 Young Corbett II (USA) DREW 20 Eddie Hanlon (USA), San Francisco. *The San Francisco Chronicle (newspaper) reported title billing at 130 lbs, with neither man raising the bar.*

31.03.03 Young Corbett II (USA) W CO 11 Terry McGovern (USA), San Francisco. *Made at 127 lbs and billed for the featherweight title, the San Francisco Chronicle (newspaper) reported that both men were safely inside, while the Chicago Tribune (newspaper) claimed it to be more of a lightweight fight.*

30.06.03+ Eddie Hanlon (USA) DREW 20 Benny Yanger (USA), San Francisco. *Following Hanlon's 20 round draw against Young Corbett on 26 February 1903, the San Francisco Chronicle (newspaper) reported this as being advertised for the "legitimate" 130 lbs featherweight title.*

03.09.03 Abe Attell (USA) W PTS 20 Johnny Reagan (USA), St Louis. *Although this was advertised as being for the 122 lbs title, and with Young Corbett II continuing to defend his so-called featherweight crown at up to 130 lbs, one would have thought that Attell would have been generally recognised in America following his victory. However, writing in the Chicago Tribune (newspaper) shortly afterwards, George Siler, a noted referee of the day, made the point that while Corbett was still regarded as the champion in many parts of the country, he, for one, would give his blessing to a bout between Attell and Harry Forbes as being for the legitimate 122 lbs title.*

29.09.03+ Eddie Hanlon (USA) W PTS 20 Benny Yanger (USA), San Francisco. *A return match for the strangely advertised "legitimate" 130 lbs featherweight title saw Hanlon set himself up for another go at Young Corbett.*

27.10.03 Young Corbett II (USA) W CO 11 Hugh Murphy (USA), Boston. *At one time listed in the Ring Record Book as a title defence for Corbett, the Boston Post (newspaper) reported that it did not involve the title, without mention of weights.*

29.12.03 Young Corbett II (USA) W RSC 16 Eddie Hanlon (USA), San Francisco. *Billed for the title at 129 lbs, Hanlon scaled 128 to Corbett's 129.*

04.01.04+ Abe Attell (USA) DREW 10 Harry Forbes (USA), Indianapolis. *Articled at 122 lbs, with both men inside, this should be seen as a defence of Attell's title claim at that weight.*

01.02.04 Abe Attell (USA) W CO 5 Harry Forbes (USA), St Louis - USA. *With both men inside the stipulated 120 lbs, the Chicago Tribune (newspaper) reported that Attell won the featherweight title following his victory. From hereon, he was generally recognised in America as the division's kingpin.*

29.02.04 Young Corbett II (USA) W CO 11 Dave Sullivan (USA), San Francisco. *At this moment in time, Corbett was generally recognised throughout America as a lightweight, even though this fight was billed for the 130 lbs featherweight title.*

25.03.04 Jimmy Britt (USA) W PTS 20 Young Corbett II (USA), San Francisco. *Although billed for the 130 lbs feathers title, the San Francisco Chronicle (newspaper) claimed that the winner would move into the lightweight division, while the Chicago Tribune (newspaper) reported the fight as a battle between featherweights, as the 130 pounders had recently been termed. The Chronicle went on to say that the billing was a surprise to most followers of the game, who presumed it to be Britt's "white" lightweight crown that would have been at stake (see under lightweights, also). By his victory, Britt finally took the 130 lbs title up a weight class.*

23.06.04 Abe Attell (USA) W PTS 15 Johnny Reagan (USA), St Louis. *Mistakenly shown as a 20 rounder in the Ring Record Book, the St Louis Post-Dispatch (newspaper) confirmed that Attell's title was at stake in a match made at 122 lbs.*

13.10.04 Tommy Sullivan (USA) W CO 5 Abe Attell (USA), St Louis. *Recent Ring Record Books have shown this fight to be a title defence for Attell, something that was corroborated by the San Francisco Chronicle (newspaper). The fight ended when Attell went down claiming a foul, only to be counted out by the referee. However, according to the Philadelphia Item (newspaper) report, the match was made at 124 lbs and there was no mention of the championship being at stake. Afterwards, Attell continued to claim the 122 lbs title, while Sullivan remained inactive for almost two years.*

12.12.04+ Ben Jordan (GB) W CO 12 Pedlar Palmer (GB), NSC, London - GB *(124 lbs). Jordan vacated the British version of the title when retiring early in 1905.*

20.03.05+ Joe Bowker (GB) W RSC 12 Pedlar Palmer (GB), NSC, London - GB *(124 lbs).*

23.10.05+ Joe Bowker (GB) W PTS 20 Spike Robson (GB), NSC, London - GB *(122 lbs). In the Mirror of Life (newspaper) in March 1906, it was stated that Abe Attell, who called himself the champion, had signed articles to fight Bowker at 122 lbs at the NSC. Unfortunately, when Attell lost his home in the San Francisco earthquake a few weeks later, the match fell through.*

22.02.06 Abe Attell (USA) W PTS 15 Jimmy Walsh (USA), Chelsea - USA. *In a fight that was practically for the championship of all the States, as written in the Mirror of Life (newspaper), Attell (120 lbs) met the American bantamweight champion, Jimmy Walsh (120 lbs), who had eliminated Johnny Reagan from the title chase in the same town, via a fifth round kayo on 12 February 1906.*

15.03.06 Abe Attell (USA) W DIS 3 Tony Moran (USA), Baltimore. *Once reported in the Ring Record Book as a title bout, research of the Baltimore Sun (newspaper) showed the fight to have been made at 126 lbs, four pounds above the limit.*

11.05.06 Abe Attell (USA) DREW 20 Kid Herman (USA), Los Angeles - USA. *Although no weights were given in the Los Angeles Times, the paper was quick to point out that on top of his purse, Attell was fighting for a championship belt. However, the Los Angeles Evening Express threw up the fact that Herman, at 129 lbs, was seven pounds over the class limit.*

04.07.06 Abe Attell (USA) W PTS 20 Frankie Neil (USA), Los Angeles - USA. *Weights (lbs): Attell (120), Neil (118).*

30.10.06 Abe Attell (USA) W PTS 20 Harry Baker (USA), Los Angeles - USA. *Billed as a title defence for Attell, according to the Los Angeles Times (newspaper) report, the Articles of Agreement had explicitly stated that Baker should make 122 lbs in ring gear. The*

fight went ahead under championship conditions even though Baker was unable to improve on 121½ lbs in ring attire, whereas Attell scaled a comfortable 120½.

16.11.06 Abe Attell (USA) W PTS 15 Billy de Coursey (USA), San Diego - USA. *Although weights were not given, the San Francisco Chronicle (newspaper) report of the fight confirmed that Attell retained the 122 lbs title on his victory.*

07.12.06 Abe Attell (USA) W CO 8 Jimmy Walsh (USA), Los Angeles - USA. *The Mirror of Life (newspaper) reported that both men were inside 122 lbs ringside.*

18.01.07 Abe Attell (USA) W CO 8 Harry Baker (USA), Los Angeles - USA. *Weighing in at ringside, the Los Angeles Times (newspaper) reported that Attell was comfortable at 121¾ lbs, while Baker only made 122 lbs after several attempts.*

24.05.07 Abe Attell (USA) W PTS 20 Kid Solomon (USA), Los Angeles - USA. *Solomon was forced to make 122 lbs just 30 minutes before the fight, a concession that considerably weakened him. In another twist, having kept the audience waiting and threatening to depart, Attell only stepped into the ring after $1,500 had been advanced.*

03.06.07+ Jim Driscoll (GB) W CO 17 Joe Bowker (GB) NSC, London - GB *(122 lbs).*

29.10.07 Abe Attell (USA) W CO 4 Freddie Weeks (USA), Los Angeles - USA. *Scheduled for 20 rounds, Attell failed to tip the beam at 122 lbs, while Weeks, after several attempts, only made it at the expense of everything bar his trunks.*

01.01.08 Abe Attell (USA) DREW 25 Owen Moran (GB), San Francisco - USA. *Moran weighed 120¼ lbs, with Attell also inside the 122 lbs mark. Confirmation that Attell was only recognised as the champion in America came in the Mirror of Life (newspaper) fight report.*

31.01.08 Abe Attell (USA) W RTD 13 Frankie Neil (USA), San Francisco - USA. *With the weights not shown in the Ring Record Book, the Philadelphia Item (newspaper) reported that with both men inside 122 lbs, the title was undoubtedly on the line.*

24.02.08+ Jim Driscoll (GB) W DIS 15 Charlie Griffin (NZ), NSC, London - GB. *Billed for the "English" (British) version of the 126 lbs title, according to the Sporting Life (newspaper), Griffin's manager was in no doubt that it was the world title that was really on the line.*

28.02.08 Abe Attell (USA) W RSC 7 Eddie Kelly (USA), San Francisco - USA. *According to the San Francisco Chronicle (newspaper) report, it was a championship bout with both men thought to be inside 122 lbs (no weights were announced). The fight came to an end when the police called a halt after the third knockdown.*

20.04.08+ Abe Attell (USA) ND-W RSC 8 Eddie Kelly (USA), Seattle - USA. *With both men inside 122 lbs, the Seattle Daily Times (newspaper) reported that Attell easily retained his title against the game Kelly.*

30.04.08 Abe Attell (USA) W RSC 4 Tommy Sullivan (USA), San Francisco. *Original articles were signed for a match at 123 lbs, but when Sullivan found that he could not make the weight a few days before the fight was due to take place, it was agreed that he could come in at 126 lbs. Although billed as a championship fight it should not be considered as such and, following his defeat, Sullivan lost any remaining claim he may have had to the title.*

07.09.08 Abe Attell (USA) DREW 23 Owen Moran (GB), San Francisco - USA. *Both men were inside 122 lbs and, for the second time, Attell was unable to score a victory in an international match.*

29.12.08 Abe Attell (USA) W CO 8 Biz Mackey (USA), New Orleans - USA. *Not included in post-war record books as a title fight, according to the New Orleans Daily Picayune (newspaper) report, Attell successfully defended the championship with both men inside 122 lbs.*

14.01.09 Abe Attell (USA) W CO 10 Freddie Weeks (USA), Goldfield - USA *(122 lbs).*

04.02.09 Abe Attell (USA) W RTD 7 Eddie Kelly (USA), New Orleans - USA. *While not openly called a title match, in the New Orleans Daily Picayune (newspaper) pre-fight report, Attell was quoted as saying that he anticipated scoring a comprehensive victory over his challenger. The New Orleans Times Democrat (newspaper), however, reported it to be a ten round title fight at 122 lbs.*

19.02.09 Abe Attell (USA) ND-L PTS 10 Jim Driscoll (GB), New York City. *Following his "press" win in a match made at 125 lbs, Driscoll, who was recognised in Britain at 126 lbs, tried to force a championship fight with the American titleholder without success.*

01.03.09+ Abe Attell (USA) ND-W PTS 6 Young Pierce (USA), Philadelphia - USA. *According to the Philadelphia Inquirer (newspaper), both men were inside the articled 122 lbs ringside.*

10.03.09+ Abe Attell (USA) ND-W CO 6 Young Pierce (USA), Philadelphia - USA. *Just nine days after their first contest, the pair were again matched at 122 lbs, only this time over 15 rounds.*

14.09.09+ Abe Attell (USA) W PTS 12 Tommy O'Toole (USA), Boston - USA. *Although no weights were printed, the Boston Post (newspaper) reported that Attell's title was on the line. However, history shows us that Boston's pressmen at the time were thin on the ground when it came to substantiating their headlines and we should tread carefully on this one until more facts emerge.*

14.02.10+ Jim Driscoll (GB) W RSC 6 Seaman Hayes (GB), NSC, London - GB *(126 lbs).*

28.02.10 Abe Attell (USA) ND-W CO 7 Harry Forbes (USA), Troy - USA. *According to the Chicago Tribune (newspaper), both men were inside the 122 lbs limit.*

18.03.10+ Abe Attell (USA) ND-W PTS 10 Johnny Marto (USA), New York City. *While Attell scaled 128 lbs fully clothed, Marto came in at 121, one pound inside the championship limit.*

18.04.10+ Jim Driscoll (GB) W CO 15 Spike Robson (GB), NSC, London - GB *(126 lbs).*

10.10.10+ Abe Attell (USA) ND-W PTS 15 Jack White (USA), Winnipeg - USA. *Although advertised as a championship go, the Winnipeg Telegraph (newspaper) failed to record weights.*

09.01.11+ Abe Attell (USA) ND-L PTS 10 Joe Coster (USA), Brooklyn - USA. *With Coster inside 122 lbs, the New York Times (newspaper) reported that the crafty champion was never in real danger of losing his title.*

13.01.11+ Abe Attell (USA) ND-W PTS 10 Patsy Kline (USA), New York City - USA. *According to the New York Times (newspaper), Kline was again trying to relieve Attell of the 122 lbs title. Although the paper said both men looked to be of even poundage, no weights were given.*

30.01.11+ Jim Driscoll (GB) W RSC 7 Spike Robson (GB), NSC, London - GB *(126 lbs).*

31.03.11+ Abe Attell (USA) ND-L PTS 10 Frankie Burns (USA), New York - USA. *Attell's title was on the line in a match made at 118 lbs. Surprisingly, the champion did not appear to weaken himself in coming to the ring at a weight four pounds below the class limit.*

28.05.11 Joe Coster (USA) W PTS 20 Frankie Conley (USA), New Orleans. *With both men having difficulty inducing the champion, Abe Attell, back into the ring with them, the promoter announced that he was billing this as a world title fight. Made at 122 lbs, Coster laid claim to the championship following his victory.*

04.07.11+ Joe Rivers (MEX) W CO 13 Joe Coster (USA), Los Angeles. *Scheduled for 20 rounds at 122 lbs and the semi-final leg of a competition to find an opponent for the champion, Abe Attell, Conley's title claim passed to Rivers.*

04.09.11+ Johnny Kilbane (USA) W CO 16 Joe Rivers (MEX), Los Angeles. *The final leg of the 122 lbs competition held at Vernon, Kilbane inherited Rivers' title claim on the result.*

30.09.11+ Johnny Kilbane (USA) W PTS 20 Frankie Conley (USA), Los Angeles. *Kilbane, who had already won promoter Jim Coffroth's 122 lbs featherweight competition, defended his title claim in this one before going forward to meet Abe Attell.*

15.11.11+ Abe Attell (USA) ND-W PTS 10 Young Cohen (GB), New York City - USA. *The New York Times (newspaper) reported that both men were inside 122 lbs.*

20.11.11+ Abe Attell (USA) ND-W PTS 10 Willie Jones (USA), New York City - USA. *Although no weights were given, the New York Tribune (newspaper) stated that this was one of two fights that week where Attell was happy to risk his title in a no-decision affair.*

23.11.11+ Abe Attell (USA) ND-W RSC 5 Leo Johnson (USA), New York City - USA. *Prior to the fight, Attell said he would retain his title no matter what Johnson did. The New York Times (newspaper) went on to say that both men were inside 122 lbs ringside.*

01.12.11+ Abe Attell (USA) ND-W PTS 10 Patsy Kline (USA), New York City - USA. *According to the New York Tribune (newspaper) report, both men were inside 122 lbs at the 6.0 pm weigh-in.*

14.05.12+ Johnny Kilbane (USA) ND-W PTS 10 Frankie Burns (USA), New York City - USA. *Burns weighed 122 lbs.*

04.07.12 Johnny Kilbane (USA) ND-W PTS 12 Tommy Dixon (USA), Cleveland - USA. *Although no weights were provided, the Chicago Tribune (newspaper) stated that Kilbane ably retained his title.*

04.09.12+ Johnny Kilbane (USA) ND-DREW 10 Johnny Dundee (USA), New York City - USA. *According to the New York Times (newspaper), both men were inside 122 lbs at 2.0 pm.*

19.09.12 Johnny Kilbane (USA) ND-W PTS 10 Eddie O'Keefe (USA), New York City - USA. *O'Keefe weighed 121½ lbs.*

14.10.12 Johnny Kilbane (USA) ND-W PTS 12 Eddie O'Keefe (USA), Cleveland - USA. *Although no weights were given, the Cleveland Plain Dealer reported that O'Keefe was out to win the title via an inside the distance victory.*

03.12.12 Johnny Kilbane (USA) ND-W RSC 9 Monte Attell (USA), Cleveland - USA. *Recorded in various published title listings as involving the title, heavy research to date has failed to uncover either weights or billing. The same conditions apply where asterisked(*).*

12.12.12+ Johnny Kilbane (USA) ND-W PTS 8 Tommy Dixon (USA), St Louis - USA. *Dixon weighed inside 122 lbs.*

19.02.13+ Johnny Kilbane (USA) ND-W CO 6 George Kirkwood (USA), New York City - USA. *Kirkwood weighed 122 lbs.*

29.04.13 Johnny Kilbane (USA) DREW 20 Johnny Dundee (USA), Los Angeles - USA *(122 lbs).* *With the rest of the world happy to accept 126 lbs as being the featherweight limit, Kilbane, who continued to defend his title at 122 lbs, would never receive universal recognition.*

10.06.13 Johnny Kilbane (USA) W RSC 6 Jimmy Fox (USA), Oakland. *Although recorded in the Ring Record Book as a title fight, Gary Phillips, who specialises in researching Californian boxing, reports that the match was made at 124 lbs and did not involve the championship. After two no-decision affairs in New York City against Benny Leonard, a fourth round kayo win on 3 May 1912 and a ten round "press" victory on 18 August 1913, and following repeated challenges to Kilbane to no avail, Canadian, Frankie Fleming, laid claim to the title. Other men to do likewise around this time were Willie Jackson, K.O. Chaney and Johnny Dundee. While Dundee was unable to entice Kilbane into the ring again, the other three men would be dismissed by the champion in no-decision bouts.*

16.09.13 Johnny Kilbane (USA) W PTS 12 Jimmy Walsh (USA), Boston. *While initial information gathered from the Boston Post showed nothing to suggest that Kilbane's American title was on the line, further research of the newspaper discovered that although there was no championship billing as such, and despite the fact that Kilbane weighed 130 lbs and had his own referee, Walsh, who was inside 122 lbs, would have certainly claimed the crown had he won.*

30.10.13+ Johnny Kilbane (USA) ND-W CO 7 K.O. Mars (USA), Cincinnati - USA. *The Pittsburgh Gazette (newspaper) condemned Kilbane, who weighed in at 132 lbs, for coming into the ring as a fully-fledged lightweight when taking on Mars, a recognised featherweight. Mars scaled 122 lbs.*

10.11.13 Johnny Kilbane (USA) ND-W CO 1 Eddie O'Keefe (USA), Philadelphia - USA*

29.05.14+ Johnny Kilbane (USA) ND-W CO 2 Benny Chavez (USA), Denver - USA. *The Chicago Tribune (newspaper) reported that Kilbane easily retained his title in a scheduled 15 rounder.*

01.01.15+ Johnny Kilbane (USA) ND-L PTS 6 Patsy Brannigan (USA), Pittsburgh - USA. *The Pittsburgh Daily Gazette (newspaper) reported that with the Articles of Agreement calling for both men to be inside 122 lbs, Kilbane's title was most certainly at risk.*

17.03.15+ Johnny Kilbane (USA) ND-W PTS 6 Kid Williams (USA), Philadelphia - USA. *Both men were inside 122 lbs.*

30.03.15+ Johnny Kilbane (USA) ND-DREW 10 Eddie Wallace (USA), Brooklyn. *Although the New York Times (newspaper) said that Kilbane's title was at risk that evening, with the championship weight standing at 122 lbs, Kilbane scaled 130¼ lbs to Wallace's 126.*

06.09.15 Johnny Kilbane (USA) ND-W PTS 12 Alvie Miller (USA), Cedar Point - USA*. *Although the class limit had been recommended as 125 lbs (3.0 pm weigh-in) by the American Boxing Association in Cleveland on 21 August 1915, Kilbane refused to accede to that ruling, stating that he would continue to defend the title at 122 lbs.*

11.10.15 Johnny Kilbane (USA) ND-W PTS 12 Cal Delaney (USA), Akron - USA*

02.12.15+ Johnny Kilbane (USA) ND-W PTS 10 Patsy Brannigan (USA), Scranton - USA*

24.05.16+ Johnny Kilbane (USA) ND-DREW 10 Eddie Wallace (USA), Montreal. *The Montreal Herald (newspaper) pre-fight report qualified it as a battle for titular honours at 122 lbs. However, no weights were given and the fact that Wallace weighed 126 lbs for their previous meeting and would be fighting Freddie Welsh at 133 lbs just six months later makes it unlikely that he made the required limit.*

11.12.16+ Johnny Kilbane (USA) ND-W PTS 12 Alvie Miller (USA), Youngstown - USA*

26.03.17 Johnny Kilbane (USA) DREW 12 Eddie Wallace (USA), Bridgeport. *Recorded in the Ring Record Book as a title bout, there was nothing in the Boston Daily Globe (newspaper) report* *to indicate that it was. Incidentally, Wallace's true fighting weight at this time was around 130 lbs, and was another good reason to believe that this fight did not involve the 122 lbs title.*

24.05.17+ Johnny Kilbane (USA) ND-W PTS 10 Frankie Fleming (C), Montreal. *After perusing the Montreal Herald (newspaper) for details of the fight there appeared to be no title billing accorded but, with both men inside 126 lbs, had the Canadian feathers champion won, he would surely have claimed the title at that weight.*

28.07.19+ Johnny Kilbane (USA) ND-W PTS 6 Joe Fox (GB), Philadelphia - USA. *In order to get the fight, the former British bantamweight champion agreed to meet Kilbane at catchweights. The Pittsburgh Gazette (newspaper) claimed that while Kilbane came to the ring at 126 lbs, Fox, aiming to claim the title with a stoppage win or at the very least force the champion into a contest under full championship conditions, was careful to be inside 122 lbs on the night.*

16.09.19+ Johnny Kilbane (USA) ND-W RSC 5 Frankie Burns (USA), Jersey City - USA. *The title was on the line in this fight, with both men inside the New Jersey 125 lbs limit for the weight class, Kilbane scaling 125 to Burns' 124.*

29.12.19+ Johnny Kilbane (USA) ND-L PTS 8 Andy Chaney (USA), Jersey City - USA. *For the second time in little more than three months, Kilbane risked his title in New Jersey. In accordance with State regulations, the title was on the line when both men came in under the 125 lbs limit, with Kilbane scaling 125 to Chaney's 122.*

25.02.20+ Johnny Kilbane (USA) ND-L PTS 8 Benny Valgar (USA), Newark - USA. *Again fighting in New Jersey at 125 lbs, Kilbane scaled 125$\frac{1}{4}$ lbs to Valgar's 124$\frac{3}{4}$. The New Orleans Daily Picayune (newspaper) quoted Valgar as predicting that he would stop Kilbane inside the distance to win the title.*

21.04.20 Johnny Kilbane (USA) ND-W CO 7 Alvie Miller (USA), Lorain - USA*

02.06.20+ Johnny Kilbane (USA) ND-L PTS 8 Andy Chaney (USA), Philadelphia - USA. *Although Kilbane came in at 125$\frac{1}{4}$ lbs, with Chaney weighing 124 lbs, the title was technically at stake.*

25.05.21 Johnny Kilbane (USA) ND-W PTS 10 Freddie Jacks (GB), Cleveland - USA. *Jacks came in spot on the now universally recognised class limit of 126 lbs, while Kilbane was thought to be in the region of 130 lbs.*

17.09.21 Johnny Kilbane (USA) ND-W CO 7 Danny Frush (GB), Cleveland - USA. *While the champion refused to weigh in, Frush was forced to make 126 lbs. Following this, Kilbane was inactive for nearly 18 months and had all but retired. It therefore came as no surprise when the NYSAC "officially" stripped him of the title for his inability to defend against the long-term number one challenger, Johnny Dundee.*

23.03.25+ Red Chapman (USA) W PTS 10 Johnny Dundee (USA), Boston. *Following the fight, Chapman (127 lbs) claimed the title after defeating former champion, Dundee (131 lbs). Even though this fight was above the championship limit and that the NYSAC recognised Kid Kaplan as champion, Chapman found some support for his claim, especially in Massachussets. Another man to lay claim to the 126 lbs title was Eddie Mack, who did just that after boxing a four round draw with Chapman in Denver on 15 October 1926.*

28.06.26 **Kid Kaplan** (USA) W RSC 10 Bobby Garcia (USA), Hartford. *With Kaplan having difficulty making the weight, this would be his last defence. According to the New York Times (newspaper), Kaplan scaled 125$\frac{1}{2}$ lbs to Garcia's 124$\frac{1}{2}$ before relinquishing his title just seven days later. In the moves to find a new champion, Massachusetts, who had a vested interest, pipped both New York and the NBA when matching Honeyboy Finnegan against Chic Suggs for their version of the title. The match was made after Suggs had outpointed Babe Herman over ten rounds in Boston on 9 June 1926 and Finnegan had achieved a similar result against Red Chapman at the same venue on 16 September 1926.*

16.09.32 Baby Arizmendi (MEX) W PTS 10 Tommy Paul (USA), Mexico City. *Although this was an overweight match and Paul continued to be recognised by the NBA as the holder of the 126 lbs title, in view of his victory, Arizmendi was proclaimed champion by the Californian State Boxing Commission on 14 October 1932. Incidentally, Arizmendi scaled 124$\frac{1}{2}$ lbs to Paul's 127$\frac{3}{4}$ and it was because the former was inside the featherweight limit that his claim was upheld.*

18.10.32+ Baby Arizmendi (MEX) W PTS 10 Newsboy Brown (USA), Los Angeles - CALIFORNIA. *Made at 122 lbs and billed for the State version of the world title, Arizmendi weighed 122 and Brown, 121.*

22.11.32+ Baby Arizmendi (MEX) DREW 10 Varias Milling (PH), Los Angeles - CALIFORNIA. *According to the Los Angeles Times (newspaper), both men were inside 122 lbs, with Arizmendi's title claim on the line.*

02.12.32+ Baby Arizmendi (MEX) W PTS 10 Archie Bell (USA), Los Angeles - CALIFORNIA. *There was no mention of the Californian version of the title being at stake, but the fact that both men were inside 122 lbs automatically involved Arizmendi's claim.*

06.01.33+ Baby Arizmendi (MEX) W PTS 10 Archie Bell (USA), San Francisco - CALIFORNIA. *Made at 122 lbs, with the San Francisco Chronicle (newspaper) not reporting it as a title fight, nevertheless, Arizmendi's claim was still at risk.*

24.01.33+ Baby Arizmendi (MEX) W PTS 10 Speedy Dado (PH), Los Angeles - CALIFORNIA. *According to the Los Angeles Times (newspaper), this was advertised as a world title fight at 122 lbs, with Arizmendi and Dado coming to the ring at 122 and 119, respectively.*

04.05.34+ Freddie Miller (USA) W CO 6 Paul Dazzo (USA), Louisville - NBA. *To my knowledge, this one has never been recorded in the record books as a title fight. However, according to the San Francisco Chronicle (newspaper), it was, with Miller weighing in at 124$\frac{1}{4}$ lbs and Dazzo scaling 124$\frac{3}{4}$.*

30.08.34 Baby Arizmendi (MEX) W PTS 10 Mike Belloise (USA), New York City. *With the NYSAC still not recognising Miller as champion, they had planned to set up an extensive elimination tournament in order to produce a successor, but, unfortunately, too many good men were unavailable. After much debate, a fight between Arizmendi and Belloise went ahead to decide the New York State title, not the NYSAC version of the world championship as recorded in some boxing annuals. In the semi-final legs, held on 11 May, Arizmendi and Belloise had gained ten round points decisions over Al Roth and Petey Hayes, respectively. That was what Nat Fleischer said in Ring Magazine at the time, however, according to the Everlast Boxing Record Book and supported by the Californian papers of the day, Arizmendi definitely held the New York version of the world title following his victory.*

01.01.35 Baby Arizmendi (MEX) W PTS 12 Henry Armstrong (USA), Mexico City - MEXICO. *On 5 May 1936, with Arizmendi still recognised by Mexico, as well as the NYSAC, as world champion, and Armstrong, by now, the Californian State titleholder, the former (128 lbs) outpointed the Filipino, Pablo Dano, in Los Angeles over ten rounds. Although a catchweight affair, Dano (124$\frac{1}{2}$ lbs) was inside the featherweight limit and, had he won, it is possible that Arizmendi could have been stripped.*

03.04.36 Mike Belloise (USA) W CO 14 Everette Rightmire (USA), Chicago. *Another Belloise fight recorded in the Boxing News Annual as a title bout, although later corrected, this was a final eliminator, with the winner to take on Baby Arizmendi for the NYSAC, Illinois and Californian versions of the title. That was the general idea, but somehow the match was never made and on 19 May 1936, according to the Los Angeles Times (newspaper), Arizmendi was stripped as titleholder by the NYSAC who then proclaimed Belloise as champion.*

23.06.36+ Petey Sarron (USA) W PTS 10 Lloyd Pine (USA), Akron - NBA. *Never listed as a title fight in the Ring Record Book, even though the fight was reported as one in Ring Magazine. To quote from the September 1936 issue: "Pine, Ohio's bantam titleholder, made his debut as a feather when taking on the NBA 126 lbs champion, Sarron, in a ten round title match."*

01.01.37+ Henry Armstrong (USA) W CO 3 Baby Casanova (MEX), Mexico City - MEXICO/CALIFORNIA. *As reported in the Mexican Excelsior (newspaper), it was a ten round title bout with Armstrong weighing 125$\frac{1}{2}$ lbs to Casanova's 125.*

29.10.37 Henry Armstrong (USA) W CO 6 Petey Sarron (USA), New York City - NY/NBA. *Henry Armstrong relinquished the NY/NBA version of the title on 12 September 1938, having become world champion at welterweight and lightweight in his two previous fights.*

17.06.38 Leo Rodak (USA) W PTS 15 Jackie Wilson (USA), Baltimore - MARYLAND. *Recognised in Maryland as the champion, following his defeat of Wilson, Rodak later outscored Richie Fontaine over ten rounds in New Orleans on 10 October 1938. Made at 126 lbs, the NBA saw it as a semi-final leg of a competition to find a worthy opponent for the winner of the New York version of the title between Joey Archibald and Mike Belloise.*

24.10.38 Leo Rodak (USA) W PTS 15 Freddie Miller (USA), Washington - MARYLAND. *Rodak was appointed the NBA champion on 10 November 1938 after Joey Archibald, the New York titleholder, had refused to give the body an affirmative regarding a unification fight.*

04.11.38 Claude Varner (USA) W CO 9 Mickey Miller (A), Melbourne. *Billed as the first title bout in Australia for many years, and conveniently forgetting Star Frisco v Miller in Newcastle on 27 August 1938, it was contested over 15 rounds with Miller scaling 123½ lbs to Varner's 126. Following his win, Varner was accorded no recognition whatsoever. Even when he was outpointed over 12 rounds by fellow-American, Jackie Wilson, with both men inside 126 lbs, at the same venue on 11 March 1939 there was no title billing and no mention of a claim.*

29.12.38 Leo Rodak (USA) W PTS 10 Leone Efrati (USA), Chicago. *Although shown in early Boxing News Annuals as a title fight, it was, in fact, decided at catchweights, with Rodak weighing 129 lbs to Efrati's 130½.*

28.09.39 **Joey Archibald** (USA) W PTS 15 Harry Jeffra (USA), Washington. *Archibald forfeited NBA recognition on 29 March 1940 for failing to defend within the sixth month ruling and Petey Scalzo was selected to meet Jimmy Perrin for the vacant title. However, on 1 May, after Perrin pulled out when the fight was designated for Washington, Scalzo was proclaimed NBA champion. Within days of that, Louisiana announced that they recognised Perrin as world champion and he would make his first defence against Bobby Ruffin.*

13.09.68+ Johnny Famechon (A) W RSC 12 Billy McGrandle (C), Melbourne. *Billed as a defence of his British Empire title, with both men inside the weight, Famechon's Australian version of the world championship was automatically at stake.*

Super-Featherweight (130 lbs)

19.01.23+ Johnny Dundee (USA) W PTS 10 Pepper Martin (USA), Boston - NY. *According to the Boston Post (newspaper) headlines, with Martin making the weight, Dundee's title was technically on the line. Martin was quoted as saying that he was sure to be the champion at the final bell.*

25.06.23 Jack Bernstein (USA) ND-W CO 5 Freddie Jacks (GB), Philadelphia - NBA/NY. *Although there was to be no decision given if going the full course, effectively, it involved the title, with Jacks scaling 130 lbs to Bernstein's 129.*

15.12.24+ Steve Sullivan (USA) ND-L PTS 10 Mike Ballerino (USA), Milwaukee - NY/NBA. *Ballerino weighed 129½ lbs.*

14.08.25+ Mike Ballerino (USA) ND-W PTS 10 Billy Henry (USA), Bayonne - NY/NBA. *The New York Times (newspaper) gave this one as a successful defence for Ballerino, when, in reality, the so-called challenger weighed in at 131 lbs, one pound over the limit.*

26.02.26+ Tod Morgan (USA) ND-W PTS 10 Don Davis (USA), Chicago - NY/NBA. *The Chicago Tribune (newspaper) reported that the title was on the line with both men inside 130 lbs.*

01.01.29 Tod Morgan (USA) ND-L PTS 10 Joey Sangor (USA), Milwaukee - NBA/NY. *Both men were inside 130 lbs, with Morgan weighing 128½ and Sangor 128.*

03.02.30 Benny Bass (USA) ND-W RSC 4 Davey Abad (PAN), St Louis - NBA. *Reported in the St Louis Post-Dispatch (newspaper) as a ten round no-decision title fight at 130 lbs, Abad scaled 129 lbs to Bass' 129½.*

28.03.30 Benny Bass (USA) ND-L PTS 10 Eddie Shea (USA), St Louis - NBA. *Bass weighed in at 128 lbs, while Shea scaled 126½.*

01.10.31+ Kid Chocolate (CUB) W RSC 1 Joey Scalfaro (USA), Long Island. *Although contested in New York, a State which ignored junior titles, and only scheduled for ten rounds, Chocolate's newly won junior crown was certainly at risk with both men inside 130 lbs. For the record, Scalfaro weighed 126 lbs to Chocolate's 128½.*

06.03.32+ Kid Chocolate (CUB) W PTS 10 Dom Petrone (USA), Havana - NBA. *Research of the Havana Post (newspaper) found this to be a billed title fight, with Chocolate scaling 126½ lbs to Petrone's 130.*

06.12.49 Sandy Saddler (USA) W PTS 10 Orlando Zulueta (CUB), Cleveland - NBA. *Supported by the Cleveland Boxing Commission, the title was re-introduced by the NBA. While waiting for a crack at his old 126 lbs title, Saddler beat Chuck Burton (first round kayo in Holyoke on 6 February 1950) and Reuben Davis (seventh round stoppage in Newark on 10 April 1950), both men being inside 130 lbs. These were seen as featherweight non-title ten rounders and were not authorised super-featherweight defences.*

18.04.50 Sandy Saddler (USA) W RSC 9 Lauro Salas (MEX), Cleveland - NBA. *Scheduled for 15 rounds, Saddler made a successful defence of the 130 lbs title. However, after regaining his old featherweight crown on 8 September 1950, the NBA ceased to recognise Saddler as the super-featherweight king under their only one title at a time ruling. Prior to that, on 25 May 1950, in Minneapolis, Saddler stopped the Cuban, Miguel Acevedo (130 lbs), in another non-title featherweight contest over ten rounds.*

28.02.51 Sandy Saddler (USA) W CO 2 Diego Sosa (CUB), Havana. *Originally intended to be a ten round non-title bout, the day before the contest it was announced that Saddler would be defending the Cleveland Boxing Commission's version of the 130 lbs championship over 12 rounds. I have no idea as to whether Cleveland had been consulted or not, but, as far as Saddler was concerned, he had yet to lose the title in the ring. Other contests he took part in after winning back his featherweight crown where the opponent weighed less than 130 lbs and where there was apparently no official backing, came against Harry LaSane (ten round points win in St Louis on 12 October 1950), Charley Riley (ten round points win in St Louis on 1 November 1950) and Lauro Salas (sixth round stoppage win in Los Angeles on 27 March 1951).*

Lightweight (135 lbs)

The lightweight division can be traced back to Caleb Baldwin at the end of the 18th century and involved many memorable contests, none more so than the one on 6 October 1872, when two Englishmen fought for the American title and a purse of $2,000. The bare-fist champion, Arthur Chambers, beat his great rival, Billy Edwards, on a 35th round disqualification at Squirrel Island, Canada, but, after he retired in 1879, there was no recognised champion until 1883. It was then that Jack "The Nonpareil" Dempsey forged to the top, but he quickly outgrew the weight class and another Irish-American, Jack McAuliffe, was next to claim the title. There is no way that McAuliffe, who knocked out Billy Frazier (21 rounds at Boston on 29 October 1886) and Harry Gilmore, only a featherweight (28 rounds in Lawrence on 14 January 1887), in skin-tight glove fights, should be seen as being any more than the American champion when matched against Englishman, Jem Carney, in Revere on 16 November 1887. If he was, our American brothers certainly overlooked Carney, who was recognised in England as champion after kayoing another American title claimant, Jimmy Mitchell, inside 11 rounds at Long Island the previous June. To the fight itself. Contested in skin-tight gloves, McAuliffe was put down twice and rescued by the referee, who called it a draw in the 74th round, with Carney well in front. Further skin-tight glove fights saw McAuliffe successfully defend the American version of the title against Billy Dacey (11th round kayo on 10 October 1888 in Dover, New Jersey) and Billy Myer (64 round draw on 23 February 1889 in Judson, Indiana), immediately prior to the arrival of regulated glove fights. Challenged at 133 lbs by Jimmy Carroll, an English-born fighter who had been in America since 1877, McAuliffe would never again make that poundage and, although credited with further defences, he effectively carried the weight.

19.03.89+ Jimmy Carroll (GB) W CO 16 Samuel Blakelock (GB), San Francisco. *Made at 133 lbs with small gloves, Carroll weighed 131¾, while Blakelock came in at 132½ lbs. According to the New York Herald (newspaper), it was a finish fight for the world lightweight title.*

21.03.90 Jack McAuliffe (USA) W CO 47 Jimmy Carroll (GB), San Francisco. *With McAuliffe unable to make the articled 133 lbs, a few days before the fight it was announced that he had surrendered it to Carroll. According to the San Francisco Chronicle (newspaper), both men eventually agreed to come to the ring under 137 lbs and McAuliffe made 134½ to Carroll's 135½ lbs. Five ounce gloves were used.*

16.09.90+ Jimmy Carroll (GB) W CO 21 Andy Bowen (USA), New Orleans. *Billed for the American 135 lbs lightweight title, the New Orleans Daily Picayune (newspaper) reported Carroll to weigh 133½ lbs to Bowen's 130½. Following a 43rd round kayo defeat at the hands of Billy Myer in New Orleans on 22 December 1891, Carroll's claim appears to expire, even though the match was made at 140 lbs.*

25.05.91 Dick Burge (GB) W DIS 11 Jem Carney, Hop & Malt Exchange, London. *Billed for Carney's version of the 133 lbs title, both men were announced as being inside the weight. Two ounce gloves were used.*

11.09.91 Jack McAuliffe (USA) W RSC 6 Austin Gibbons (USA), Hoboken. *The San Francisco Chronicle (newspaper) reported the fight as being for the championship of the weight class with four ounce gloves. Made at 135 lbs, McAuliffe was spot on, while Gibbons came in at 130½.*

27.06.92+ Dick Burge (GB) W CO 2 Lachie Thompson (GB), Kennington Social Club, London. *Supposedly defending his British version of the lightweight title, Burge, at 138 lbs, gave away six pounds and a beating to his rival.*

05.09.92 Jack McAuliffe (USA) W CO 15 Billy Myer (USA), New Orleans. *Shown in the Ring Record Book as a title fight, it was made at 138 (133 was the recognised limit) lbs, with McAuliffe scaling 137¾ to Myer's 137½ lbs and four ounce gloves in use.*

04.05.94 Dick Burge (GB) W CO 28 Harry Nickless (GB), Bolingbroke Club, London. *Billed for the British version of the lightweight title at 140 lbs. With no active welter division operating in Britain, Burge merely carried his title up the weight scale.*

27.08.94 Jack McAuliffe (USA) W PTS 10 Young Griffo (A), Coney Island. *The New Orleans Daily Picayune (newspaper) reported that the crowd thought Griffo had won the title. However, in a match made at 140 lbs, with McAuliffe weighing 139½ to Griffo's 133½, it was not the "popular" lightweight title that was at stake.*

19.11.94+ Jack McAuliffe (USA) NC 3 Owen Ziegler (USA), Coney Island. *Following this match made at 138 lbs, with McAuliffe still recognised as the lightweight champion according to the New York Herald (newspaper), he announced his retirement, leaving the way clear for George Lavigne to pick up where he left off.*

14.12.94 George Lavigne (USA) W CO 18 Andy Bowen (USA), New Orleans. *Billed for the championship of America, Lavigne weighed 135 to Bowen's 133 lbs. Unfortunately, Bowen never regained consciousness and was pronounced dead during the early hours of the following morning.*

21.01.95+ Dick Burge (GB) W CO 4 Tom Williams (A), NSC, London. *Although made at 142 lbs, it was, in effect, a defence of Burge's British or "English" (as it was known as then) version of the lightweight title. Both men were well inside the weight, with Burge scaling 138 lbs to William's 139½.*

30.05.95+ George Lavigne (USA) W PTS 20 Jack Everhardt (USA), Coney Island. *Shown as a title fight in Jack Solomons' International Boxing Annual, in fact it was made at 138 lbs.*

26.08.95 George Lavigne (USA) W CO 5 Jimmy Handler (USA), Maspeth. *Made at 133 lbs, and over 20 rounds, the New York Herald (newspaper) reported that Handler's title aspirations were settled there and then. Strangely, the paper went on to say that the winner would have first call on Jack McAuliffe (retired and unable to make 133 lbs anyway) for the championship.*

12.10.95 George Lavigne (USA) DREW 20 Young Griffo (A), Maspeth. *Although there was no mention of the title in the New York Herald (newspaper) report, with both men inside 133 lbs it had to be at stake.*

02.12.95 George Lavigne (USA) W PTS 15 Joe Walcott (USA), Maspeth. *The New York Herald (newspaper) reported it to be for the 133 lbs lightweight championship of America, with both men weighing in at 130½ lbs. Incidentally, according to the Articles of Agreement, Walcott had to kayo Lavigne to win the title.*

01.06.96 **George Lavigne** (USA) W CO 17 Dick Burge (GB), NSC, London. *Although the match was made at 138 lbs (five pounds above the recognised weight scale in America), a weight stipulated by the American, the winner would be seen on both sides of the Atlantic as the lightweight champion. Unfortunately, Burge's natural weight at this time was 144 lbs and getting down to 138 weakened him considerably. For the record, Burge made 136 lbs to the American's 134.*

27.10.96 **George Lavigne** (USA) W CO 24 Jack Everhardt (USA), New York City. *Recorded in the Ring Record Book as a title bout, neither the New York Herald and Philadelphia Item (newspapers) gave any indication that it was, with the match being made at 138 lbs and the American limit standing at 133. However, it must be remembered that Lavigne had been recognised as champion after beating Burge at that weight.*

08.02.97 **George Lavigne** (USA) W PTS 25 Kid McPartland (USA), New York City. *The Elmira Daily Advertiser (newspaper) reported that Lavigne scaled 131½ lbs to McPartland's 133.*

29.10.97 **George Lavigne** (USA) W RTD 12 Joe Walcott (USA), San Francisco. *Another title defence credited to Lavigne by the Ring Record Book, the San Francisco Chronicle (newspaper) claimed that Walcott, who was recognised in California as the welter champion, lost his claim to Lavigne. Made at 135 lbs, Lavigne scaled 134 and reckoned his opponent would have weighed in the region of 140 lbs on coming to the ring.*

17.03.98 **George Lavigne** (USA) DREW 20 Jack Daly (USA), Cleveland. *Although in the Ring Record Book as a title bout, and, according to the San Francisco Chronicle (newspaper), billed as one, the Philadelphia Item (newspaper) merely stated it to be a match made at 137 lbs, four pounds over the limit.*

03.07.99 **Frank Erne** (USA) W PTS 20 George Lavigne (USA), Buffalo. *While the New York Herald and Chicago Tribune (newspapers) reported it to be a match made at 133 lbs, the Buffalo Courier (newspaper) reported that the scales were set at 135 lbs, with Erne tipping the bar and Lavigne not moving it. To further*

complicate the issue, according to the Herald, Billy Lavigne (George's brother) claimed that Erne weighed 135 lbs. However, that aside, Erne was recognised as the new champion.

12.05.02 Joe Gans (USA) W CO 1 Frank Erne (USA), Fort Erie. *Billed for the world title, with both men agreeing to scale 135 lbs, the title changed hands. For the record, Gans tipped the beam at 133¼ lbs and Erne at 132½.*

27.06.02 Joe Gans (USA) W RTD 3 George McFadden (USA), San Francisco. *Although no weights were given in the San Francisco Chronicle, the paper reported it to be a title bout at 133 lbs. According to Gary Phillips, the Californian boxing historian, McFadden weighed 131 lbs the day before the fight, while Gans made 135.*

24.07.02 Joe Gans (USA) W CO 15 Rufe Turner (USA), Oakland. *Although the class limit was seen to be 133 lbs in America, the Ring Record Book listed this as a title fight, even though Turner scaled 135½ lbs to Gans' 135.*

17.09.02 Joe Gans (USA) W CO 5 Gus Gardner (USA), Baltimore. *Recorded by the Ring Record Book as involving the lightweight championship, the Baltimore Sun (newspaper) informed us that, although billed for the title over 20 rounds, it was made at 138 lbs, some five pounds over the popular limit.*

13.10.02 Joe Gans (USA) W CO 5 Kid McPartland (USA), Fort Erie. *The Buffalo Courier (newspaper) reported this one as a title bout with the scales set at 135 lbs and neither man tipping the beam.*

26.11.02 Jimmy Britt (USA) W CO 7 Frank Erne (USA), San Francisco. *Made at 135 lbs ringside, Britt claimed the "white" title on the grounds that he would not be challenging Joe Gans, preferring to draw the colour bar instead. Having knocked out the former champion, George Lavigne, inside eight rounds on 25 May 1902 at the same venue, this was Britt's fourth professional start.*

09.03.03 Jack O'Keefe (USA) W DIS 6 Jimmy Britt (USA), Portland. *Billed for the "white" American 133 lbs title, with both at weight, Britt was mysteriously disqualified after having O'Keefe down several times and all but done for. Justice was served, when, following the fight, it was discovered that the referee was part of a syndicate that had bet heavily against Britt. On that basis, Britt retained public support.*

11.03.03 Joe Gans (USA) W CO 11 Steve Crosby (USA), Hot Springs. *Another fight for Gans above 133 lbs, the Philadelphia Item (newspaper) reported that the champion made a successful defence of his title at 134 lbs.*

28.04.03 Jimmy Britt (USA) W PTS 20 Willie Fitzgerald (USA), San Francisco. *Billed for the "white" lightweight title at 133 lbs, with both men making the weight.*

29.05.03 Joe Gans (USA) W CO 10 Willie Fitzgerald (USA), San Francisco. *According to the San Francisco Chronicle (newspaper), Gans continued his hold on the title following a successful defence at 135 lbs.*

13.06.03 Jimmy Britt (USA) DREW 20 Jack O'Keefe (USA), Butte. *Advertised for the 133 lbs "white" title, following the fight, Britt demanded that Joe Gans prove his ability to make the same weight.*

04.07.03 Joe Gans (USA) W CO 5 Buddy King (USA), Butte. *The New Orleans Daily Picayune (newspaper) reported this go as a "coloured" title defence for Gans, but, while the Philadelphia Inquirer (newspaper) also showed it as a championship fight, they went on to say it was a match made at 138 lbs (five pounds above the recognised class limit).*

10.11.03 Jimmy Britt (USA) W PTS 20 Charley Sieger (USA), San Francisco. *Made at 133 lbs for the "white" title, Britt weighed little more than 130 lbs.*

20.11.03 Jimmy Britt (USA) W PTS 25 Martin Canole (USA), Colma. *The San Francisco Chronicle (newspaper) called Britt the undisputed "white" lightweight champion following his victory at 133 lbs.*

21.01.04 Joe Gans (USA) W PTS 10 Willie Fitzgerald (USA), Detroit. *The Chicago Tribune (newspaper) reported this as a billed title defence for Gans at 135 lbs. Recorded in the last Ring Record Book's championship listings, it was not shown within Gans' record as such.*

25.03.04+ Jimmy Britt (USA) W PTS 20 Young Corbett (USA), San Francisco. *Billed for the world 130 lbs featherweight title, with both men inside, the San Francisco Chronicle (newspaper) went on to say that the billing came as a surprise to most followers of the game, who would have presumed it to be a battle for Britt's "white" lightweight claim.*

31.10.04 Joe Gans (USA) W DIS 5 Jimmy Britt (USA), San Francisco. *For over two years, Britt had disputed the title, firstly drawing the colour bar and later claiming that Gans was incapable of making 133 lbs. However, while Gans proved he could make the weight for this one, it obviously left him weakened, something that was painfully exploited by Britt. The only thing that saved Gans was Britt's impetuosity. Having downed Gans twice in the* *fourth round, Britt was excused hitting him after the bell because of the din, but there was to be no let off in the fifth when he was finally disqualified after hitting his rival who was in the act of rising from another knockdown. Despite the result, Britt continued to claim the title on the grounds that the action of the referee was unwarranted and that in the eyes of Californians he was still champion.*

20.12.04 Jimmy Britt (USA) W PTS 20 Battling Nelson (USA), San Francisco. *Although George Siler, the famous referee, writing in the Chicago Tribune (newspaper), reported that Joe Gans should still be considered the champion, this was billed for the title, and accepted as such by many, at 133 lbs.*

05.05.05 Jimmy Britt (USA) W CO 20 Jabez White (GB), San Francisco. *Billed for the championship of the world at 133 lbs, with both men inside, Britt strengthened his right to the title following his win over the British champion. Although Gans was currently fighting at a higher poundage, his challenge to the winner at 133 lbs fell on deaf ears.*

21.07.05 Jimmy Britt (USA) W PTS 20 Kid Sullivan (USA), San Francisco. *The San Francisco Chronicle (newspaper) reported that in their eyes, Britt was still the world lightweight champion. In a match made at 133 lbs, neither tipped the beam.*

09.09.05 Battling Nelson (USA) W CO 18 Jimmy Britt (USA), San Francisco. *Although scheduled for 45 rounds and billed for the championship at 133 lbs, with both men inside, George Siler, writing in the Chicago Tribune (newspaper), was not slow to extol the virtues of Joe Gans as the real champion. However, it would be almost another year before Gans surprised everyone by making 133 lbs yet again.*

14.03.06+ Battling Nelson (USA) ND-W PTS 6 Terry McGovern (USA), Philadelphia. *Both men were inside the articled 133 lbs at the ringside weigh-in, according to the Philadelphia Inquirer (newspaper).*

23.07.06+ Joe Gans (USA) W PTS 20 Dave Holly (USA), Seattle. *Not listed as a title fight previously, the Seattle Daily Times (newspaper) reported it to have been made at 135 lbs, with Gans scaling 133½ and Holly also inside the required weight.*

03.09.06 **Joe Gans** (USA) W DIS 42 Battling Nelson (USA), Goldfield. *In a "finish" fight that introduced Tex Rickard as a boxing promoter, Gans once again achieved general recognition as champion. However, it was a "hell of a price to pay". Forced to make 133 lbs ringside, he made it but ruined his health beyond repair as the tuberculosis that would ultimately ravage his body and kill him (Gans died on 10 August 1910), set in.*

03.03.08+ Jimmy Britt (USA) ND-DREW 10 Battling Nelson (USA), Los Angeles. *Made at 133 lbs, it would have been Britt's "white" title that would have been at stake in this one. The day before the fight, the Los Angeles Times (newspaper) reported that Nelson was already down to 131½ lbs, while Britt, at 134, would easily be inside the limit on the night.*

01.04.08 Joe Gans (USA) ND-W CO 3 Spike Robson (GB), Philadelphia. *Recorded in various published title listings as involving the title, heavy research to date has failed to uncover either weight or billing. The same conditions apply where (*).*

22.02.09 Johnny Summers (USA) W PTS 20 Jimmy Britt (USA), NSC, London. *Shown in the 1995 Yearbook as being an advertised title fight, according to the Sporting Life (newspaper), it was contested at catchweights. However, it spelt the end of Britt's "white" title claim.*

22.06.09 **Battling Nelson** (USA) W CO 5 Jack Clifford (USA), Oklahoma City. *According to the Daily Oklahoman (newspaper), it was billed for the title and both men were asked to make 133 lbs or less. There was nothing in the paper's fight report to suggest either failed to make the weight.*

13.07.09+ **Battling Nelson** (USA) ND-L PTS 10 Ad Wolgast (USA), Los Angeles. *Made at 133 lbs, the Los Angeles Times (newspaper) reported that both men made the weight, with Wolgast purportedly in the region of 128 lbs.*

21.01.10 **Battling Nelson** (USA) W CO 8 Eddie Lang (USA), Memphis. *Although only an eight rounder, confirmation of Nelson's title status being at risk comes in the Memphis Daily Appeal (newspaper) fight report with the notification that both fighters made 133 lbs.*

30.05.10 Freddie Welsh (GB) DREW 20 Packey McFarland (USA), NSC, London - GB. *Surprisingly billed as a title fight, especially as Ad Wolgast was generally recognised as the division's champion, the match was made at 133 lbs (the American limit), and not 135 lbs as stipulated for British championship matches.*

10.06.10+ Ad Wolgast (USA) ND-L PTS 10 Jack Redmond (USA), Milwaukee. *With both men inside 130 lbs, the Los Angeles Times (newspaper) reported that the champion snapped a bone in his left forearm early on, but carried on in order to safeguard the title.*

08.02.11 **Ad Wolgast** (USA) ND-L PTS 6 Knockout Brown (USA), Philadelphia. *According to the Los Angeles Times (newspaper), both men were inside 133 lbs.*

03.03.11+ Ad Wolgast (USA) ND-L PTS 10 Knockout Brown (USA), New York City. *A return match at 133 lbs, less than a month after their first go, saw Brown yet again have the better of things.*

26.04.11 **Ad Wolgast** (USA) ND-W RSC 2 One Round Hogan (USA), Philadelphia. *Although only a six rounder, both men were inside the championship weight, Hogan scaling 132½ lbs to the champion's 131.*

04.11.12+ Ad Wolgast (USA) ND-DREW 10 Joe Mandot (USA), New Orleans. *According to the New Orleans Daily Picayune (newspaper), with both men inside 133 lbs, Mandot was bidding to win the title. On the day, the challenger scaled 130 lbs.*

10.11.13 Willie Ritchie (USA) ND-W PTS 10 Leach Cross (USA), New York City - USA. *Again, in quick succession, Ritchie raised the American version of the weight class by one pound to 135 lbs, which then fell into line with Britain, where it has remained to this day. The exact weights were 134½ lbs for Ritchie and 133¼ for Cross.*

12.03.14 Willie Ritchie (USA) ND-W PTS 10 Ad Wolgast (USA), Milwaukee - USA. *The two men were articled to make 135 lbs at 3.0 pm on the day of the fight.*

26.05.14 Willie Ritchie (USA) ND-L PTS 10 Charley White (USA), Milwaukee - USA. *The New York Times (newspaper) reported that both Ritchie and White were inside 135 lbs at the afternoon weigh-in.*

27.10.14+ Freddie Welsh (GB) W PTS 12 Matty Baldwin (USA), Boston. *Although not making mention of the fighters' weights, the Boston Post (newspaper) reported this as a title fight, claiming that Baldwin was down to his best fighting weight and would give it his best shot. Afterwards, the paper's headlines highlighted that Welsh was still champion. However, the Mirror of Life (newspaper) claimed that Welsh v Baldwin, one of three fights in 13 days for the Welshman, had no bearing on the championship whatsoever.*

02.11.14 Freddie Welsh (GB) ND-W RSC 8 Ad Wolgast (USA), New York City. *Shown in last year's Yearbook as involving the title, it could not have been. Although the New York Times (newspaper) stated that the championship was at stake, with both men agreeing to be inside 135 lbs, ultimately, Wolgast scaled 135½ to Welsh's 136.*

09.11.14+ Freddie Welsh (GB) ND-L PTS 10 Charley White (USA), Milwaukee. *According to the Chicago Tribune (newspaper), this was a billed title fight held at catchweights. That is to say White made sure he was inside 135 lbs, although there was no mention of Welsh's weight.*

24.11.14+ Freddie Welsh (GB) W PTS 12 Fred Yelle (USA), Boston. *According to the Boston Post (newspaper), with Yelle making the weight the champion's title was at risk. The paper went on to say that Welsh had a pull in the weights which was a sure indication that he was not inside 135 lbs for this one.*

02.12.14 Freddie Welsh (GB) ND-L PTS 10 Joe Shugrue (USA), New York City. *Billed for the title and with Articles of Agreement calling for 135 lbs at the 2.0 pm weigh-in, both Welsh and Shugrue scaled 133½ lbs.*

09.02.15+ Freddie Welsh (GB) ND-DREW 10 Joe Shugrue (USA), New York City. *The Articles of Agreement called for a 2.0 pm weigh-in at 135 lbs.*

25.02.15+ Freddie Welsh (GB) ND-W PTS 10 Charley White (USA), Milwaukee. *With both men inside the championship limit, Welsh weighed 135 lbs to White's 134.*

11.03.15 Freddie Welsh (GB) ND-L PTS 10 Willie Ritchie (USA), New York City. *Both men were inside 135 lbs.*

17.03.15 Freddie Welsh (GB) ND-W PTS 10 Hal Stewart (USA), Fort Wayne*.

24.03.15+ Freddie Welsh (GB) ND-W PTS 8 Patsy Drouillard (C), Windsor. *The Windsor Evening Record (newspaper), while recognising the fight for what it was, reported that the only way Drouillard, who was down to weight, could win the title, was to knock Welsh out.*

27.03.15+ Freddie Welsh (GB) ND-DREW 10 Johnny Lustig (USA), Montreal. *Although articled at 135 lbs and billed as a title defence for Welsh, the fighters' weights were not reported in the Montreal Gazette (newspaper).*

09.04.15+ Freddie Welsh (GB) ND-W PTS 10 Billy Wagner (USA), Toledo. *This was effectively a title fight with Welsh weighing 134½ lbs to Wagner's 133.*

24.05.15+ Freddie Welsh (GB) ND-DREW 10 Frankie Fleming (C), Montreal. *Billed for the world title, the Montreal Herald (newspaper) had Fleming scaling a fraction over 126 lbs, with*

Welsh close on 140, having been articled to make 133 lbs at the 3.0 pm weigh-in.

18.06.15+ Freddie Welsh (GB) ND-W PTS 10 Johnny Lustig (USA), Brooklyn*

03.07.15+ Freddie Welsh (GB) ND-L PTS 10 Charley White (USA), Brooklyn. *White weighed 133½ lbs.*

15.11.15+ Freddie Welsh (GB) ND-W PTS 12 Johnny O'Leary (USA), Winnipeg. *O'Leary weighed 130 lbs.*

06.03.16+ Freddie Welsh (GB) ND-W PTS 10 Ad Wolgast (USA), Milwaukee. *Wolgast weighed 126¾ lbs.*

21.03.16+ Freddie Welsh (GB) ND-W PTS 10 Phil Bloom (USA), Brooklyn. *Bloom weighed 133½ lbs.*

31.03.16 Freddie Welsh (GB) ND-L PTS 10 Benny Leonard (USA), New York City. *Leonard weighed 132 lbs.*

07.04.16+ Freddie Welsh (GB) ND-W PTS 10 Richie Mitchell (USA), Milwaukee. *Mitchell weighed 131¼ lbs.*

08.06.16+ Freddie Welsh (GB) W PTS 10 Tommy Lowe (USA), Washington. *Although no weights were given, the Washington Post (newspaper) advertised this as a title fight.*

04.07.16 Freddie Welsh (GB) ND-W DIS 11 Ad Wolgast (USA), Denver. *Billed for the title, although Welsh probably came in over the weight, Wolgast was certainly inside the required 135 lbs.*

24.11.16+ Freddie Welsh (GB) ND-L PTS 10 Eddie Wallace (USA), Montreal. *A billed title fight, according to the Montreal Herald (newspaper), Wallace was inside the 135 lbs mark with Welsh a pound or two over.*

16.01.17 Freddie Welsh (GB) ND-L PTS 10 Ritchie Mitchell (USA), Milwaukee. *While the Chicago Tribune (newspaper) pre-fight report stated that Welsh's title was on the line with the match made at 135 lbs, it was later confirmed that neither man was inside the championship weight on the night after Welsh scaled 140 lbs to Mitchell's 135½.*

17.04.17+ Freddie Welsh (GB) ND-W PTS 12 Battling Nelson (USA), St Louis. *The Chicago Tribune (newspaper) reported that Welsh (135 lbs) retained his title with a clear cut win over the former champion, Nelson (132 lbs).*

20.04.17+ Freddie Welsh (GB) ND-L PTS 10 Rocky Kansas (USA), Buffalo. *Kansas weighed 131 lbs.*

01.05.17+ Freddie Welsh (GB) ND-L PTS 10 Johnny Kilbane (USA), New York City. *Welsh, at 135, risked his title against the featherweight champion who came to the ring inside 129 lbs.*

04.06.17 Benny Leonard (USA) ND-W PTS 6 Joe Welsh (USA), Philadelphia. *Although shown in the 1995 Yearbook as a fight where Leonard risked his title, it should not have been, with the match made at 140 lbs and both men in excess of 135 lbs.*

25.07.17 Benny Leonard (USA) ND-W CO 3 Johnny Kilbane (USA), Philadelphia. *The Chicago Tribune (newspaper) stated that both men were safely inside 133 lbs at the 8.0 pm weigh-in.*

21.09.17 Benny Leonard (USA) ND-W RSC 1 Leo Johnson (USA), New York City. *We can add that Johnson weighed 130 lbs to Leonard's 133.*

05.10.17+ Benny Leonard (USA) ND-W CO 2 Vic Moran (USA), New York City. *Signed articles called for both men to come to the ring inside 133 lbs.*

23.10.17+ Benny Leonard (USA) ND-W PTS 10 Young Erne (USA), Buffalo. *Both men were inside the championship limit, with Leonard tipping the beam at 134 lbs to Erne's 135.*

20.01.19+ Benny Leonard (USA) ND-W PTS 8 Johnny Dundee (USA), Newark. *Dundee weighed 130 lbs.*

28.04.19 Benny Leonard (USA) ND-W RSC 8 Willie Ritchie (USA), Newark. *This was a catchweight contest, with Leonard weighing 136 lbs to Ritchie's 138½, and should not have been included in last year's listings.*

16.06.19+ Benny Leonard (USA) ND-W PTS 6 Johnny Dundee (USA), Philadelphia. *Both men were inside 135 lbs at the 6.0 pm weigh-in.*

11.08.19 Benny Leonard (USA) ND-W PTS 6 Irish Patsy Cline (USA), Philadelphia. *The Philadelphia Inquirer (newspaper) reported this match being made at 138 lbs, three pounds above the limit.*

17.09.19+ Benny Leonard (USA) ND-W PTS 8 Johnny Dundee (USA), Newark. *Dundee weighed 130½ lbs.*

10.12.19+ Benny Leonard (USA) ND-W CO 2 Mel Coogan (USA), Jersey City. *Coogan weighed 134 lbs.*

25.09.20 Benny Leonard (USA) ND-W PTS 10 Pal Moran (USA), Chicago. *Both men were inside the championship limit, with Moran, at 130 lbs, giving away five pounds to the champion.*

25.02.22 Benny Leonard (USA) ND-W PTS 10 Pal Moran (USA), New Orleans. *Moran weighed 134½ lbs.*

20.03.22+ Benny Leonard (USA) ND-W PTS 10 Johnny Clinton (USA), Boston. *The Boston Post (newspaper) reported that Leonard's title was never in danger. However, with Clinton making the*

weight there had always been the chance that he could have got lucky.

04.07.22 Benny Leonard (USA) ND-W RSC 8 Rocky Kansas (USA), Michigan City. *Billed as a title fight, Kansas was listed as the challenger by the Chicago Tribune (newspaper), who then went on to say that both men were expected to weigh in the region of 136 lbs. However, the Toronto Daily Mail (newspaper) declared that Kansas would weigh 133 lbs, with the champion coming to the ring four pounds heavier.*

27.07.22 Benny Leonard (USA) ND-W PTS 12 Lew Tendler (USA), Jersey City. *Billed as a title fight, Leonard scaled 135 lbs to Tendler's 134¼.*

05.08.22 Benny Leonard (USA) ND-W PTS 10 Ever Hammer (USA), Michigan City. *Although billed as a title battle, the Chicago Tribune (newspaper) reported it as being at catchweights. The paper went on to explain that the only way Leonard, who weighed in the region of 138 lbs, could lose his title was if he was knocked out. Hammer was already inside 135 lbs on the morning of the fight.*

29.05.23 Benny Leonard (USA) ND-W RSC 10 Pinkey Mitchell (USA), Chicago. *With both men inside 140 lbs, this did not involve the lightweight title as suggested in last year's Yearbook. The Chicago Tribune (newspaper) went on to say that because there was no mention of weights within the Articles of Agreement, Leonard would have no right to claim Mitchell's junior title either.*

09.07.23 Benny Leonard (USA) ND-W PTS 8 Alex Hart (USA), Philadelphia. *Hart weighed 134 lbs.*

07.09.23 Benny Leonard (USA) ND-W PTS 8 Johnny Mendelsohn (USA), Philadelphia. *Mendelsohn weighed 135 lbs.*

01.08.24 Benny Leonard (USA) ND-W PTS 10 Pal Moran (USA), Cleveland. *Billed as a title fight, the New York Times (newspaper) reported Moran's weight to be 133¾ lbs, with Leonard coming to the ring at around the 140 mark. In January 1925, Leonard relinquished his title on announcing his retirement and, with the division thrown into disarray, the NYSAC sponsored an elimination tournament to determine his successor. Over 50 men were involved and it took more than six months to reach a conclusion. However, after beating Eddie Wagner, Clyde Jeakle, Sammy Mandell and Benny Valgar, the surprise package, Jimmy Goodrich, fought his way through to the final to face Stanislaus Loayza, a man who had defeated Cirilin Orlano, Tommy White, Lou Paluso, Pete Hartley, Aramis del Pino and Alf Simmons, on his way to a title shot. The pre-tournament favourites had been Mandell and Sid Terris, who dropped out following a points defeat at the hands of the former.*

01.06.27+ Sammy Mandell (USA) W CO 2 Steve Adams (USA), Kansas City. *Researching the New York Times (newspaper), I discovered that both men were inside 135 lbs. Not only that, but Adams collapsed and died in round two of a bout scheduled for ten. No blow was struck as Adams slumped to the floor and the attending doctor expressed the opinion that the unfortunate challenger had suffered a heart attack.*

16.07.27+ Sammy Mandell (USA) W PTS 10 Phil McGraw, Detroit. *Another title fight discovery made while perusing back copies of the New York Times (newspaper). The report stated, prior to Mandell's successful defence at 135 lbs: "this was the first time a title fight had come to Detroit since the days of Harry Forbes."*

26.01.31+ Tony Canzoneri (USA) ND-W PTS 10 Johnny Farr (USA), New Orleans. *Although reported in the Ring magazine as a title fight, the Ring Record Book never acknowledged the fact. For the record, Canzoneri weighed 132 lbs to Farr's 132¼.*

04.01.43 Slugger White (USA) W PTS 15 Willie Joyce (USA), Baltimore - MARYLAND. *On 20 April 1943, having already won Maryland recognition by his defeat of Joyce, White (133 lbs) took on something of a risk in Los Angeles when allowing Johnny Thomas to make 135 lbs. However, all ended well after a ten round points win. Meantime, Sammy Angott announced that he was returning to the ring and was looking to regain his old crown. With the New York title already under challenge from Bob Montgomery, who had earlier, on 8 January, stopped Chester Rico in the eighth round of an eliminator, the NBA eventually matched the former champion against White for their version of the title.*

L. Welterweight (140 lbs)

22.10.26 Mushy Callahan (USA) W CO 2 Charlie Pitts (A), Los Angeles. *Reported in the 1996 Yearbook as a title defence for Callahan, Gary Phillips, the Californian boxing historian, advised the author that Pitts came in at 141 lbs.*

05.07.39 Maxie Berger (C) W PTS 10 Wesley Ramey (USA), Montreal - CANADA. *Billed as a world title fight and recognised as such* *by the Montreal Boxing Commission, who recommended that the NBA revive the weight class, Berger weighed 139¾ lbs to Ramey's 132¾.*

06.09.39+ Maxie Berger (C) W CO 3 Felix Garcia (PR), Montreal - CANADA. *Billed for the Montreal Boxing Commission's version of the title, both men weighed 140 lbs. However, Berger failed to capitalise on his newly won title and moved his operating base to New York in search of welterweight honours.*

28.10.40 Harry Weekly (USA) W PTS 15 Jerome Conforto (USA), New Orleans. *Shown in the 1996 Yearbook as being for the Louisianan version of the light-welterweight title, in truth, it involved the Southern welter crown only, with Weekly weighing 141 lbs to Conforto's 143½.*

27.06.41 Harry Weekly (USA) W PTS 10 Carmelo Fenoy (USA), Birmingham. *The New Orleans Daily Picayune (newspaper) called this an ordinary ten rounder for Weekly and failed to list weights. Not having that information available, it is difficult to assess the importance of the contest, but Weekly's claim could have stemmed from it.*

28.07.41 Harry Weekly (USA) W PTS 15 Baby Breese (USA), New Orleans - LOUISIANA. *The New Orleans Daily Picayune (newspaper), in summing up, stated that this would be the first time Weekly would defend the Louisianan version of the title which had been bequeathed on him. The paper gave Weekly as 139¾ lbs, with Breese a pound lighter, and went on to say that the winner would be presented with a gold belt. There was no doubting Weekly had great difficulty in making 140 lbs and that was to be his only defence before he was inducted into the US Army in May 1942.*

20.10.41 Harry Weekly (USA) W CO 5 Ervin Berlier (USA), New Orleans. *Another contest inadvertantly shown as a title fight in the 1996 Yearbook, the New Orleans Daily Picayune (newspaper) reported that Weekly came in at 143 lbs to Berlier's 142.*

13.09.46 Tippy Larkin (USA) W PTS 12 Willie Joyce (USA), New York City - NBA/NY. *Following a non-title defeat by Ike Williams (136¼ lbs), the Boxing News stated that the latter could now consider himself as champion of the pseudo class. Needless to say he did not and the 140 lbs division again fell into disuse.*

Welterweight (147 lbs)

26.07.94 Tommy Ryan (USA) W PTS 20 Mysterious Billy Smith (USA), Minneapolis - USA. *Billed for the championship at 142 lbs, with the weight division unrecognised elsewhere in the world of boxing, it was the American title only that was at stake.*

28.01.97+ Dick Burge (GB) DREW 10 Eddie Connolly (C), Olympic Club, Birmingham. *Advertised for the world 144 lbs title, Burge made 143 lbs compared to Connolly's 137. Burge was far more comfortable at this poundage than he had been at the lightweight limit and with the welterweight division not recognised in Britain, this fight should be seen as its equivalent.*

26.05.97+ George Green (USA) W CO 15 Charley McKeever (USA), San Francisco. *With Green claiming the title, the San Francisco Chronicle (newspaper) reported this as being a great welterweight contest scheduled for 20 rounds. Despite the ommission of weights and the fact that Green looked to be several pounds heavier than McKeever, who was a natural welter at the time, the billing suggests that Green's claim was on the line in this one.*

31.05.97+ Tom Causer (GB) W DIS 7 Dick Burge (GB), NSC, London. *Billed as a defence of Burge's 144 lbs title claim over 20 rounds, Burge, at 142 lbs, considerably outweighed Causer (133 lbs), who was still considered a lightweight.*

08.10.97+ Dick Burge (GB) W CO 1 Tom Causer (GB), Bolingbroke Club, London. *In a match made for the 144 lbs title, both men were announced as having made the weight.*

29.10.97+ George Lavigne (USA) W RTD 12 Joe Walcott (USA), San Francisco. *Reported as a lightweight title defence (see under that weight class, also) for Lavigne, with Walcott recognised as the welter champion in California at the time, and both men inside 142 lbs, the latter's claim would have passed to the winner.*

27.08.98 Mysterious Billy Smith (USA) W PTS 25 Matty Matthews (USA), New York City - USA. *The New York Herald (newspaper) reported that both men were inside the agreed 142 lbs, and, on the result, Smith was generally recognised in America as the new leader of the weight class. Meanwhile, Ryan was still claiming the championship at 150 lbs and continued to defend as such.*

05.09.98 Mysterious Billy Smith (USA) DREW 25 Andy Walsh (USA), Brooklyn. *Shown in the Ring Record Book as involving the championship, it was billed as a title match at 145 lbs, three pounds above the "popular" weight.*

06.12.98 Mysterious Billy Smith (USA) W PTS 20 Joe Walcott (USA), New York City. *According to the New York Times (newspaper), the fight was billed for the title at 145 lbs.*

12.03.00+ Mysterious Billy Smith (USA) DREW 25 Young Mahoney (USA), Brooklyn. *The New York Herald (newspaper) reported this to be a title defence for Smith at 145 lbs.*

13.08.00 Rube Ferns (USA) W RTD 15 Eddie Connolly (C), Buffalo - USA. *The Buffalo Courier (newspaper) reported that the American title changed hands on the result, with both men weighing under 140 lbs.*

29.11.00+ Owen Ziegler (USA) W CO 2 Eddie Connolly (C), Hartford. *Although recorded in early Ring Record Books as an American title fight, the Hartford Courant (newspaper) reported Ziegler, a last minute substitute, to weigh 150 lbs, well outside the acceptable weight limit.*

28.11.01 Rube Ferns (USA) W PTS 15 Charley Thurston (USA), Detroit. *Reported in the Chicago Tribune (newspaper) as a title fight, the Detroit Free Press (newspaper) confirmed that it was a defence of Ferns' 145 lbs title claim, with both men making the weight.*

18.12.01 Joe Walcott (USA) W RSC 5 Rube Ferns (USA), Fort Erie - USA. *Scheduled for 20 rounds, with both men inside the stipulated 142 lbs, the title changed hands. At this moment in time, however, the weight class was still only generally recognised in America, with Britain seeing the poundage as belonging to the "heavy" lightweight division.*

29.05.02 Rube Ferns (USA) W CO 3 Owen Ziegler (USA), Joplin. *Shown in last year's Yearbook as a title fight, I have yet to find evidence to support that notion and it should be deleted from the title listings until something more tangible is uncovered.*

20.11.02 Jim Maloney (GB) W PTS 20 Bobby Dobbs (USA), National Athletic Club, London. *Given world championship billing at 138 lbs, a weight four pounds below the American welterweight limit, it received no support whatsoever.*

26.01.03 Eddie Connolly (C) W PTS 15 Tom Woodley (GB), NSC, London. *Having just one more contest after beating Woodley for the British version of the world 146 lbs title, a weight four pounds heavier than the American welterweight limit, Connolly went home.*

23.02.03+ Matty Matthews (USA) W PTS 10 Tom Couhig (USA), Pittsburgh. *Matthews, who was introduced as the "white" welter champion, defended his 145 lbs title claim in this one, according to the Pittsburgh Gazette (newspaper).*

27.04.03 Rube Ferns (USA) W RSC 19 Matty Matthews (USA), Fort Erie. *In a match made at 145 lbs, the Chicago Tribune (newspaper) reported that the "white" welter title changed hands.*

18.06.03+ Joe Walcott (USA) DREW 20 Young Peter Jackson (USA), Portland. *Research of the Morning Oregonian (newspaper) showed this as being billed for the 150 lbs welter title, some eight pounds above the recognised limit.*

03.07.03+ Joe Walcott (USA) W CO 3 Mose la Fontise (USA), Butte. *Made at 142 lbs, the Anaconda Standard (newspaper) reported that La Fontise safely made the weight.*

13.01.04+ Honey Mellody (USA) W PTS 12 Matty Matthews (USA), Boston. *After beating the former champion in a match articled at 142 lbs, Mellody claimed the "white" version of the championship at that weight.*

22.04.04 Honey Mellody (USA) W CO 4 Martin Duffy (USA), Chicago. *Although only a six rounder, the Boston Post (newspaper) reported that, with Mellody inside 142 lbs, the "white" welter title changed hands following the result. Articled for 142 lbs, Duffy, at 147½, looked ill-trained and out of condition.*

29.04.04 Dixie Kid (USA) W DIS 20 Joe Walcott (USA), San Francisco. *Weighing in at 144½ lbs, Walcott, winning easily, was disqualified for no discernable reason. Later, the contest was generally disregarded when it was discovered that the referee had placed a bet on the Dixie Kid (138 lbs), and Walcott continued to claim the title.*

13.06.04+ Honey Mellody (USA) DREW 20 Jack O'Keefe (USA), Butte. *According to the Boston Post (newspaper), it was a defence of Mellody's "white" welterweight claim.*

12.09.04 Jack Clancy (USA) DREW 20 Bobby Dobbs (USA), Ginnett's Circus, Newcastle. *After retaining the English version of the world 144/146 lbs title, Clancy set sail for America.*

30.09.04 Joe Walcott (USA) DREW 20 Joe Gans (USA), San Francisco. *Billed for the title, despite the Dixie Kid's continuing claim, Walcott weighed 141 lbs to Gans' 137. In October 1904, Walcott accidentally shot himself through the right hand (his friend and fellow boxer, Nelson Hall, was killed by the same bullet) and later, in November 1905, announced his retirement.*

24.10.04+ Honey Mellody (USA) W PTS 10 Jack O'Keefe (USA), Chicago. *With both men inside 142 lbs, the Chicago Tribune (newspaper) reported it as being advertised for the title, assuming that Joe Walcott had retired.*

14.11.04 Buddy Ryan (USA) W CO 1 Honey Mellody (USA), Chicago. *Scheduled for ten rounds and billed for the 142 lbs title, the*

Chicago Tribune (newspaper) reported that while Mellody was at weight, Ryan came in at 148 lbs (Ryan's camp said he came in one pound overweight, but worked it off). Whatever the truth, the paper went on to say that Mellody was quite prepared to enter the ring knowing full well his title claim hinged on the result. The author of that statement, George Siler, also claimed that by his victory, Ryan became the acknowledge American champion.

17.06.05+ George Petersen (USA) W PTS 20 Jack Clancy (USA), San Francisco. *Made at 145 lbs, with both comfortably inside, Petersen claimed Clancy's English 144/146 lbs title.*

04.07.05 Buddy Ryan (USA) W CO 11 George Herberts (USA), Butte. *Reported in the Chicago Tribune and San Francisco Chronicle (newspapers) as a defence of Ryan's 142 lbs title claim.*

19.07.05 Buddy Ryan (USA) W RTD 20 George Petersen (USA), San Francisco. *Billed for the world title at 145 lbs, on account of Petersen's win over Jack Clancy, the San Francisco Chronicle (newspaper) reported that both men were down to weight for their scheduled 25 rounder. Ryan was described as the holder of a much neglected title.*

10.07.06 Joe Walcott (USA) W CO 8 Jack Dougherty (USA), Chelsea - USA. *With the Dixie Kid in prison for offences committed outside the ring and Joe Gans back among the lightweights, Walcott reclaimed the American title. The Boston Post (newspaper) reported this as a billed championship fight, with both men inside the prescribed 142 lbs.*

23.04.08 Mike Twin Sullivan (USA) W PTS 25 Jimmy Gardner (USA), Los Angeles. *Reported as a so-called championship fight by the Los Angeles Times (newspaper), both men made the 142 lbs required of them, with Gardner down to 141½ the day before. Following the fight, although unable to make that poundage again, Sullivan continued to claim the title at 145 lbs.*

23.06.08+ Harry Lewis (USA) W PTS 12 Larry Temple (USA), Boston. *Articled at 145 lbs, Lewis' title claim at that poundage would have been at stake if Temple made the weight. Unfortunately, the Boston Post (newspaper) failed to report whether both fighters were inside or not.*

26.11.08 Jimmy Gardner (USA) DREW 20 Jimmy Clabby (USA), New Orleans. *This was a defence of Gardner's 142 lbs title claim, according to the New Orleans Daily Picayune (newspaper).*

25.05.09+ Mike Twin Sullivan (USA) DREW 20 Kyle Whitney (USA), San Francisco. *With both men inside 145 lbs, Sullivan successfully defended his claim at that weight. Although the TS Andrews' Annual showed Sullivan continuing to claim the title into early 1911, the author can find no more fights at that weight for him.*

09.06.09+ Jimmy Gardner (USA) DREW 12 Tommy Quill (USA), Boston. *The Boston Post (newspaper) reported this as a defence of Gardner's 142 lbs title claim, with both men inside the weight. The paper went on to say that if the title was really on the line then Quill seemed to win it. The following November, Harry Lewis demanded that Gardner make 142 lbs in order to decide the championship, but as neither could make that weight anymore it came to nothing.*

15.09.09+ Jimmy Gardner (USA) ND-W PTS 10 Clarence English (USA), Omaha. *Although no weights were reported in the Omaha World Herald, the paper called Gardner the world champion and went on to say that English expected to land the title. However, from hereon, the former was recognised in the main as a middle, despite the TS Andrews Annual continuing to show him claiming the welterweight title.*

23.05.12+ Ray Bronson (USA) ND-L PTS 10 Harry Brewer (USA), St Louis. *Reported as a billed title fight in the Chicago Tribune (newspaper), the St Louis Post-Dispatch (newspaper) stated that both men were inside 142 lbs.*

29.05.12+ Ray Bronson (USA) ND-L PTS 10 Packey McFarland (USA), Indianapolis. *With both men inside 138 lbs, this was effectively a defence of Bronson's title claim.*

09.09.12+ Ray Bronson (USA) ND-L PTS 12 Hilliard Lang (C), Winnipeg. *With both men inside 142 lbs, the Winnipeg Telegram (newspaper) reported this as a battle between the American champion, and world title claimant, and the best Canada had to offer in Lang.*

11.10.12+ Clarence Ferns (USA) ND-W CO 2 Art Magirl (USA), St Louis. *Carded for eight rounds, with both men inside 145 lbs, Ferns claimed the American title on the result.*

13.01.13+ Spike Kelly (USA) W PTS 8 Ray Bronson (USA), Memphis. *A substitute match for Kelly v Clarence Ferns, the Memphis Daily Appeal (newspaper) reported it to be a welter title debate at 142 lbs.*

07.02.13+ Spike Kelly (USA) DREW 10 Tommy Howell (USA), Kansas City. *Without notification of actual weights, the Chicago Tribune (newspaper) reported this as a billed title fight at 145 lbs.*

10.03.13+ Clarence Ferns (USA) W PTS 10 Spike Kelly (USA), Kansas

City. *Ferns strengthened his claim to the title following this victory.*

18.03.13+ Clarence Ferns (USA) DREW 10 Jimmy Perry, Atlanta. *Billed as one of a series of eliminators to decide the welter title, Ferns put his title claim on the line.*

05.04.13+ Clarence Ferns (USA) W PTS 10 Jimmy Perry (USA), Kansas City. *By his victory, Ferns effectively eliminated Perry from the title chase.*

11.04.13+ Spike Kelly (USA) ND-W PTS 10 Billy Walters (USA), Kenosha. *In a match made at 145 lbs, with both men inside, the Chicago Tribune (newspaper) reported that the winner would claim the title, despite Kelly's recent defeat at the weight by Clarence Ferns.*

12.05.13+ Ray Bronson (USA) ND-L PTS 10 Young Denny (USA), New Orleans. *Having successfully risked his claim to the American title in a fight articled for 142 lbs, the following December, Bronson sailed for Australia to meet another world title claimant in Waldemar Holberg.*

04.07.13+ Clarence Ferns (USA) ND-W PTS 10 Young Denny (USA), New Orleans. *The New Orleans Daily Picayune (newspaper) reported this as being a billed championship match at 142 lbs.*

16.07.13 Mike Glover (USA) ND-W PTS 10 Young Hickey (USA), New York City. *Incorrectly shown in last year's Yearbook as supporting Glover's right to the title, it was his win over Marcel Thomas, six days later, where the claim really emanated from.*

22.07.13 Mike Glover (USA) W RSC 4 Marcel Thomas (FR), Boston. *Although Thomas held the European version of the title at 147 lbs, the Boston Post (newspaper) failed to report weights and billing. However, they did state: "this was as near a title fight you will get" and, following the result, Glover laid claim to the 142 lbs championship.*

26.09.13+ Clarence Ferns (USA) ND-W PTS 10 Billy Walters (USA), Kenosha. *The Chicago Tribune (newspaper) gave both men as being inside 145 lbs in what was a successful defence of Ferns' title claim.*

09.10.13+ Spike Kelly (USA) ND-L PTS 10 Mike Gibbons (USA), Kenosha. *The Chicago Tribune (newspaper) reported this as being articled for the 145 lbs version of the title.*

24.11.13+ Spike Kelly (USA) DREW 10 Lee Barrett (USA), Milwaukee. *In a match made at 145 lbs (3.0 pm weigh-in), Kelly's title claim would have been at stake.*

27.11.13+ Mike Glover (USA) ND-W PTS 10 Jack Britton (USA), Brooklyn. *Britton, really considered to be a lightweight at this stage of his career, weighed 134¼ lbs to Glover's 137¼.*

10.12.13 Mike Gibbons (USA) ND-W CO 2 Clarence Ferns (USA), New Orleans. *Although a ten round no-decision fight, it was billed for the title. However, with Gibbons weighing 147 lbs to Ferns' 146, and with the popular limit in America standing at 142 lbs ringside, it received scant recognition. From hereon, Gibbons would be recognised as a middleweight.*

16.12.13+ Spike Kelly (USA) W PTS 15 Billy Walters (USA), St Joseph. *Made at 145 lbs, Kelly's title claim at the weight was at stake in this one, but, with scant recognition forthcoming, it was all but forgotten.*

19.01.14+ Mike Glover (USA) ND-W PTS 10 Jack Britton (USA), New York City. *A defence of Glover's title claim saw him scale 137¼ lbs as opposed to Britton at 134½.*

09.06.15+ Kid Graves (USA) ND-L PTS 10 Ted Kid Lewis (GB), New York City. *Graves (145 lbs) held on to his claim with Lewis still standing at the finish against the future champion, Lewis (140 lbs).*

29.06.15+ Kid Graves (USA) ND-W PTS 10 Walter Mohr (USA), Brooklyn. *Graves weighed 143½ lbs and Mohr 139.*

21.02.16+ Ted Kid Lewis (GB) ND-L PTS 10 Jimmy Duffy (USA), Buffalo. *Lewis scaled 141 lbs to Duffy's 142.*

21.02.16 Eddie Moha (USA) W DIS 7 Kid Graves (USA), Dayton. *Although Graves had dropped press decisions to both Ted Kid Lewis and Jack Britton, he was still claiming the title. Following the result of this match, although no weights are at hand, Moha claimed the championship with very little backing, while Graves, not satisfied with being disqualified, continued to be recognised in some quarters as the best man at the weight (refer to TS Andrews' annuals). Enter Ted Kid Lewis. In Moha's next fight, on 24 May 1916 (Dayton), he was kayoed inside 13 rounds by the Englishman, who went on to despatch Graves in the ninth on 6 February 1917 (New York City). Although Lewis was inside 145 lbs for both contests, he considered Britton to be the rightful champion and neither Moha's and Graves weak claims were pursued.*

06.06.16 Jack Britton (USA) W PTS 12 Mike O'Dowd (USA), Boston. *According to the Boston Post (newspaper) report, this was a battle for titular honours, while the Boston Daily Globe*

(newspaper) failed to indicate whether the title was at stake. With O'Dowd fighting as a middleweight, and in the absence of any weights, in all probability it was merely an overweight clash.

14.11.16 Jack Britton (USA) DREW 12 Ted Kid Lewis (GB), Boston. *The Boston Herald (newspaper) reported that Lewis made the required 142 lbs.*

01.01.17 Jack Britton (USA) ND-W PTS 10 Jimmy Duffy (USA), Buffalo. *According to the Buffalo Morning Express (newspaper), Duffy's attack on the championship was ably warded off. Both men weighed 144¹/₂ lbs.*

05.03.17+ Jack Britton (USA) ND-L PTS 12 Bryan Downey (USA), Columbus. *The Columbus Ohio State Journal (newspaper) reported that Downey was one pound inside the required weight when scaling 144 lbs.*

26.03.17 Jack Britton (USA) ND-L PTS 10 Ted Kid Lewis (GB), Cleveland. *With Lewis weighing in at 144 lbs, the title was at stake. Britton came in at 145 lbs.*

06.06.17 Jack Britton (USA) ND-DREW 10 Ted Kid Lewis (GB), St Louis. *The St Louis Globe Democrat (newspaper) gave this as a match at 145 lbs, a weight Lewis was perfectly comfortable at.*

25.06.17 **Ted Kid Lewis** (GB) W PTS 20 Jack Britton (USA), Dayton. *With both men inside the agreed 142 lbs at 3.0 pm, and with all the leading challengers disposed of, this fight should be recognised as the one that finally cleared up the long-standing title mess.*

04.07.17 **Ted Kid Lewis** (GB) ND-L PTS 15 Johnny Griffiths (USA), Akron. *Recorded in various published title listings as involving the title, heavy research to date has failed to uncover either weights or billing. The same conditions apply where asterisked (*).*

06.03.18+ **Ted Kid Lewis** (GB) ND-DREW 10 Jack Britton (USA), Atlanta. *Billed as a title match at 145 lbs.*

02.05.18+ **Ted Kid Lewis** (GB) ND-DREW 10 Jack Britton (USA), Scranton*

07.08.19 **Jack Britton** (USA) ND-DREW 12 Johnny Griffiths (USA), Denver. *Reported in the Rocky Mountain News (newspaper) as title defence for Britton at 145 lbs.*

05.11.19 **Jack Britton** (USA) ND-DREW 10 Johnny Tillman (USA), Detroit. *Britton's title was at risk in a match made at 145 lbs.*

03.09.20 **Jack Britton** (USA) ND-W PTS 10 Johnny Tillman (USA), Cleveland. *According to the Cleveland Plain Dealer (newspaper), Tillman, who was outweighed by some six pounds, easily made the required 145 lbs.*

17.05.21 **Jack Britton** (USA) ND-W PTS 10 Johnny Tillman (USA), Des Moines. *Reported as Des Moines' first ever title fight in the Des Moines Register (newspaper), we can be sure that Tillman made the articled 145 lbs.*

27.07.23 Jimmy Jones (USA) W PTS 10 Dave Shade (USA), Boston. *Recognised in Massachusetts as a world title fight, on 31 July 1923, after reports of the bout had satisfied the New York Commissioner that the decision in favour of Jones (145¹/₂ lbs) over Shade (143 lbs) was fully justified, the former was acclaimed champion by the NYSAC. Later, outside the jurisdiction of Massachussets and New York, Jones tangled with Johnny Tillman (winning the press decision over 10 rounds in Newark on 30 August 1923) and Bermondsey Billy Wells (both men fell out of the ring in the sixth round and the bout was called off). Both fights were of the no-decision variety and were both made at 147 lbs.*

08.10.23 Mickey Walker (USA) ND-NC 9 Jimmy Jones (USA), Newark. *With Walker (148 lbs) carrying an injured hand, both he and Jones (145¹/₄ lbs) were thrown out before the start of the tenth round of a scheduled 12, for not trying. And, just to add insult to injury, it was New Jersey's Chief Inspector, Platt Adams, who ordered the referee to end the contest. It did not stop there, however. On 10 October, Walker was suspended for a year by the New Jersey Commission and, the following day, the NYSAC rescinded Jones' title claim. Earlier, Jones had been warned by the NYSAC that he risked indefinite suspension if he went ahead with the fight against a man already serving out a suspension, a decision which would undoubtedly be upheld by Massachussets, who had a close working relationship with the New York authority. Walker was eventually reinstated as champion, even though he would remain suspended until April 1924, after the NYSAC held a special meeting on 27 October 1923. The upshot of the meeting was that, in future, the Commission decided it would no longer make champions by proclamation when existing champions failed to make defences within the stipulated period, but would merely place them under suspension until such time they co-operated.*

17.08.38 **Henry Armstrong** (USA) W PTS 15 Lou Ambers (USA), New York City. *Although billed for the lightweight title, with both men naturally inside 135 lbs, the NBA stated that it recognised the fight as involving the welter crown also.*

14.04.41 Izzy Jannazzo (USA) W PTS 15 Jimmy Leto (USA), Baltimore - MARYLAND. *Jannazzo forfeited Maryland's recognition after two consecutive defeats at the hands of Sugar Ray Robinson. In their first fight, on 19 October 1942, Robinson (143¹/₂ lbs) won on points over ten rounds in Philadelphia, while their return in Cleveland, on 1 December 1942, saw the "Sugar Man", weighing 145 lbs, achieving the "double" after Jannazzo was rescued in the eighth round.*

29.07.41 Red Cochrane (USA) W PTS 15 Fritizie Zivic (USA), Newark - NY/NBA. *Following a ten round non-title points loss to Zivic on 10 September 1942, Cochrane enlisted in the US Navy and the title was frozen. Unlike other weight divisions, with Sugar Ray Robinson the outstanding challenger, no moves to find a "duration" titleholder were deemed to be necessary.*

25.11.67+ Willie Ludick (SA) W PTS 15 Carmelo Bossi (ITA), Johannesburg - SOUTH AFRICA

Middleweight (160 lbs)

02.03.96 Kid McCoy (USA) W CO 15 Tommy Ryan (USA), Long Island. *A fight made famous by the fact that McCoy, Ryan's old sparring partner, tricked the welterweight (see under that weight class, also) champion into taking him on at 154 lbs by claiming he was out of condition. To add insult to injury, the Brooklyn Eagle (newspaper) tells us that McCoy was a pound over the articled weight at 155 lbs to Ryan's 148. Following the fight, the famous slogan "The real McCoy" was coined, but, with Fitzsimmons still considered the champion in many quarters, the winner was not generally recognised, despite the fact that contest had title billing, as reported in the Philadelphia Item (newspaper), and that Fitzsimmons was no longer fighting at the weight. Regardless of how Ryan viewed himself, McCoy took over his middleweight claim on the result.*

23.10.96+ Dan Creedon (NZ) W PTS 20 Harry Baker (USA), Maspeth. *Having his first fight in America since arriving from Britain, Creedon, who held the British version of the title, was claiming to be world champion at 160 lbs. Although there was no mention of a title in the New York Herald (newspaper) report, both men were inside the articled 160 lbs for this one.*

12.01.97+ Dan Creedon (NZ) W RSC 4 Jim Williams (USA), Albany. *The Buffalo Courier (newspaper) reported the fight as a 20 rounder for the 160 lbs world title between the champion, Creedon, who claimed to weigh 159 lbs, and Williams (158).*

24.10.98 Tommy Ryan (USA) W PTS 20 Jack Bonner (USA), Brooklyn. *According to the New York Herald (newspaper) report of the fight, Ryan (149 lbs) v Bonner (158 lbs), involved the 158 lbs title. The Ring Record Book lists this contest as being for the vacant crown, but, in reality, it was only the American version which was at stake and even that was not conclusive, with Bob Fitzsimmons continuing to class himself the champion.*

31.08.99 Tommy Ryan (USA) W PTS 20 Jack Moffatt (USA), Dubuque. *Billed as a welterweight title defence for Ryan (see under that weight class, also), with both men weighing 152 lbs, according to the Chicago Tribune (newspaper), it was effectively Ryan's middleweight claim that was at stake here.*

18.09.99 Tommy Ryan (USA) W RSC 10 Frank Craig (USA), Brooklyn. *The New York Herald (newspaper) reported that these two candidates for middleweight honours had agreed to meet over 20 rounds at 158 lbs. Unfortunately, Craig failed to make the weight. Following the fight, Ryan challenged Kid McCoy at 154 lbs, knowing full well his rival would have difficulty in getting down to that mark. McCoy declined the offer, stating that 158 lbs was the true class limit and, apart from that, he recognised Bob Fitzsimmons, not Ryan, as the champion.*

15.10.00 Charley McKeever (USA) W PTS 15 Dido Plumb (GB), NSC, London. *Billed for the world title at 152 lbs, the result carried no weight on the other side of the Atlantic.*

27.11.00 Tommy Ryan (USA) W PTS 6 Kid Carter (USA), Chicago. *The Chicago Tribune (newspaper) reported that while this could hardly be classified as a championship match, both men were inside 158 lbs at the 6.0 pm weigh-in.*

04.03.01 Tommy Ryan (USA) W RTD 17 Tommy West (USA), Louisville. *Billed as a title match at 158 lbs, the Chicago Tribune (newspaper) reported afterwards that Ryan had strengthened his claim to the world title.*

04.07.01 George Gardner (USA) W RSC 3 Jack Moffatt (USA), San Francisco. *Advertised for the middleweight title at 158 lbs, according to the San Francisco Chronicle (newspaper), Gardner (158) and Moffatt (156) failed to conform to the Articles of Agreement when they weighed in only four hours before the fight. Despite that, with Ryan now generally recognised in America as the champion, there would have been little support for Gardner outside California.*

30.01.02 Tommy Ryan (USA) W CO 7 George Green (USA), Kansas City. *Sometimes referred to as a title fight, it was not even reported in either the Philadelphia Item or Boston Daily Globe, while the Chicago Tribune (newspaper) made no mention of any championship involvement.*

31.01.02 Jack Root (USA) W DIS 7 George Gardner (USA), San Francisco. *According to the Chicago Tribune (newspaper), this was advertised as a title fight, even though the Articles of Agreement called for catchweights. Regardless of that, neither man was inside 158 lbs and they would eventually meet to decide the championship of the newly created light-heavyweight class.*

24.06.02 Tommy Ryan (USA) W CO 3 Johnny Gorman (USA), London. *Billed as a world title bout, despite the fact that a rival promoter had earlier matched another two Americans, Jack O'Brien and Charley McKeever, for the open title. Prior to the above contest, Ryan, who scaled 151 lbs to Gorman's 158, was referred to in the press as the American champion, presumably because he had yet to beat an international representative.*

15.09.02 Tommy Ryan (USA) W CO 6 Kid Carter (USA), Fort Erie. *Billed for the championship at 158 lbs, with both men inside, George Siler, writing in the Chicago Tribune (newspaper), made the point that it was the American, not world, title that Ryan successfully defended.*

24.11.02+ Jack Palmer (GB) W PTS 15 Eddie Connolly (C), NSC, London. *Following two contests between the pair in Newcastle, they were matched at 158 lbs for the "English" open title.*

25.05.03+ Jack Palmer (GB) DREW 15 Jack Twin Sullivan (USA), NSC, London. *Billed for the "English" open title at 158 lbs, Palmer came in at 156 lbs to Sullivan's 153, according to the Mirror of Life (newspaper) report. While Sullivan eventually went on to claim the world title, Palmer quickly outgrew the division and moved up to heavyweight.*

22.12.03+ Jack O'Brien (USA) W PTS 15 Jack Twin Sullivan (USA), Boston. *The Boston Post (newspaper) reported that this fight should be seen as involving the world title. Confirmation of the fighters' weights came in the Boston Herald (newspaper), showing O'Brien to be 158 lbs to Sullivan's 153.*

27.01.04+ Tommy Ryan (USA) ND-L PTS 6 Jack O'Brien (USA), Philadelphia. *Although only a six round no-decision fight, having been made at 158 lbs (neither man moved the bar), the Chicago Tribune (newspaper) reported that Ryan's right to the championship was clearly at stake. Afterwards, Ryan was challenged to a fight at the weight by Bob Fitzsimmons, who claimed never to have resigned the title and that the former had been "ducking" his challenge for years. Several years later, O'Brien was quoted as saying that Ryan had tricked him by threatening to pull out of the above fight at the last moment unless he deposited £1,000 to be forfeited in case the champion was knocked out. According to O'Brien, rather than having the match called off he complied with Ryan's wishes.*

14.04.04+ Jack O'Brien (USA) W CO 3 Jack Twin Sullivan (USA), St Louis. *With O'Brien's 158 lbs middleweight claim on the line, the St Louis Post-Dispatch (newspaper) reported that the winner should meet Tommy Ryan in an effort to sort out the championship position as far as America was concerned.*

07.04.05+ Jack O'Brien (USA) W PTS 10 Young Peter Jackson (USA), Baltimore. *The Baltimore Sun (newspaper) reported that O'Brien weighed 158 lbs to Jackson's 154. With Jackson inside 158 lbs, O'Brien's title claim was therefore automatically at stake.*

25.04.05+ Hugo Kelly (USA) W PTS 10 Jack O'Brien (USA), Indianapolis. *Ignoring all challenges, more than a year passed by before it was rumoured that Tommy Ryan would defend the championship in a distance fight against O'Brien, but that fell through when he insisted on 154 lbs. Instead, O'Brien took on Ryan's protege, Hugo Kelly. Made at 158 lbs, with O'Brien reckoned to be heavier, Kelly effectively took over the former's title claim. Of this fight, and coupled with his earlier comments, O'Brien argued that both he and Kelly had agreed in advance not to try for a kayo and that the referee should declare a draw. Having felt he had clearly outpointed Kelly, he went on to say his surprise turned to anger when the referee awarded the fight to his opponent. Early in 1906, it was reported that Ryan had posted a forfeit to meet O'Brien at 158 lbs. However, with O'Brien now looking to win the heavyweight crown and not interested in having further dealings with Ryan, it came to nothing and at the age of 36, and having been inactive for over a year, Ryan handed his crown to Kelly.*

07.06.05+ Hugo Kelly (USA) DREW 10 Tommy Burns (C), Detroit. *In a match made at 158 lbs, the Detroit News (newspaper) stated that although limited to ten rounds the fight had more to do with the championship than any other recently held in Detroit.*

17.10.05+ Jack Twin Sullivan (USA) W PTS 20 Tommy Burns (C), Los Angeles. *Taking into account his three round kayo win over*

Hugo Kelly in Kansas City on 14 April 1904, Sullivan (153 lbs) claimed the title on the strength of this victory over Burns (163 lbs).

11.12.05+ Hugo Kelly (USA) DREW 10 Young Mahoney (USA), Indianapolis. *Kelly's title claim was at stake in a match made at 158 lbs.*

25.06.06+ Hugo Kelly (USA) W CO 3 Young Mahoney (USA), Indianapolis. *In a successful defence of his 158 lbs title claim, Kelly eliminated Mahoney from the championship running.*

24.08.06+ Hugo Kelly (USA) W CO 6 Tony Caponi (USA), Leavenworth. *Scheduled for 20 rounds, the Leavenworth Times (newspaper) reported both men to be inside the required 158 lbs.*

10.06.10 **Stanley Ketchel** (USA) ND-W CO 5 Jim Smith (USA), New York City. *For some reason or other a latter edition of the Ring Record Book decided to show this as involving the title, although it was eventually rectified. According to the Los Angeles Times (newspaper), it was contested at catchweights with Smith the heavier man by some eight pounds. Later, on 15 October 1910, Ketchel was murdered and Billy Papke reclaimed the title. The T.S. Andrews Annual for 1912 tells us that other men who served notice of intent at that time included Hugo Kelly, Sam Langford and Jack Twin Sullivan, although the last two never followed up their claims.*

20.12.10+ Hugo Kelly (USA) W PTS 12 Frank Klaus (USA), Boston. *The Boston Post (newspaper) reported that by his defeat of Klaus, presumably at 158 lbs, Kelly fully justified his title claim.*

21.03.11+ Hugo Kelly (USA) W PTS 12 Bill McKinnon (USA), Boston. *With Kelly and McKinnon articled to make 158 lbs ringside, the Boston Post (newspaper) confirmed this was a defence of the former's title claim.*

28.04.11+ Cyclone Johnny Thompson (USA) ND-L PTS 10 Hugo Kelly (USA), Racine. *With both men claiming the title, this contest was made at 158 lbs. The Chicago Tribune (newspaper) went on to report that while Kelly safely make the weight, Thompson came in at 159½ lbs.*

17.08.11 Cyclone Johnny Thompson (USA) ND-L PTS 10 Frank Klaus (USA), New York City. *The New York Times (newspaper) reported that Thompson was still claiming the title and that both men were inside 158 lbs.*

01.01.12+ Jack Dillon (USA) ND-W RSC 6 Leo Houck (USA), Indianapolis. *With both men inside 158 lbs, Dillon took over Houck's title claim on the result.*

23.03.12 Frank Klaus (USA) W PTS 20 Jack Dillon (USA), San Francisco. *Billed as a middleweight elimination fight at 158 lbs, on his victory, Klaus took over Dillon's title claim.*

28.05.12+ Jack Dillon (USA) ND-W CO 3 Hugo Kelly (USA), Indianapolis. *Often reported flimsily as the start of Dillon's light-heavyweight claim, what is certain is that Kelly was no longer regarded as a middleweight championship claimant following the result of this, a match made at 158 lbs. Although recently losing to Frank Klaus, Dillon continued to claim the title.*

16.09.12+ Cyclone Johnny Thompson (USA) ND-DREW 10 Eddie McGoorty (USA), Cincinnati. *Made at 160 lbs, Thompson, who looked to be over the weight, failed to weigh in, while McGoorty scaled 159 lbs. The New York Times (newspaper) reported that Thompson's championship aspirations appeared to be over.*

23.09.12+ Eddie McGoorty (USA) W CO 1 Jack Harrison (GB), New York City. *Although McGoorty (158 lbs) had long been recognised as a legitimate contender, his title claim only gained credence following his victory over the British champion, who also weighed in at 158 lbs. Prior to this fight, on 2 September 1912, McGoorty had scored a first round kayo over leading Australian, Dave Smith (162 lbs), also in New York City.*

07.10.12+ Eddie McGoorty (USA) W RTD 5 Jack Denning (USA), New York City. *With both men weighing 157¼ lbs, this should be seen as a defence of McGoorty's title claim.*

04.12.12+ Eddie McGoorty (USA) ND-W PTS 10 Mike Gibbons (USA), New York City. *Billed for the middleweight title, the New York Times (newspaper) gave Gibbons as 148¾ lbs to McGoorty's 155.*

09.01.13 Jack Dillon (USA) W PTS 15 Frank Mantell (USA), Providence. *Made at 160 lbs, with both men inside, Dillon strengthened his championship aspirations, while Mantell was effectively eliminated. The winner would continue to claim the title into early 1915 until increasing weight saw him finally concentrating on the light-heavyweight front.*

14.04.13 Pat O'Keefe (GB) W PTS 20 Frank Mantell (USA), The Ring, London. *Announced as a title fight at 160 lbs, with both men reported as being inside, the billing was meaningless in the light of Mantell's defeat at the hands of Dillon.*

02.05.13+ Eddie McGoorty (USA) DREW 10 Jimmy Clabby (USA), Denver. *Billed for the title at 158 lbs, both were inside with Clabby making 154 lbs.*

13.06.13+ Jimmy Clabby (USA) W PTS 12 Eddie McGoorty (USA), Butte. *According to the TS Andrews' Annuals, Clabby (151 lbs) had been claiming the middleweight title since 1912, but it was only after defeating McGoorty (158 lbs) in this billed title battle that his claim was taken seriously.*

20.04.14 Joe Borrell (USA) NC 4 Bandsman Blake (GB), The Ring, London. *Although billed as a title bout at 160 lbs, with both men inside, it was not even recognised as such in Britain and Borrell's already weak claim appears to be groundless following the result.*

17.11.14+ Al McCoy (USA) ND-W PTS 10 Jack McCarron (USA), Pottsville*

04.12.14+ Al McCoy (USA) ND-W PTS 10 Kid Wagner (USA), Wilkes Barre*

01.01.15+ Jack Dillon (USA) ND-DREW 6 Young Ahearn (GB), Philadelphia. *With Dillon weighing 164 lbs to Ahearn's 156½, and obviously unable to make 158/160 lbs anymore, his already weakened title claim petered out.*

13.02.15+ Young Ahearn (GB) W CO 2 Willie Lewis (USA), Havana. *Billed as Cuba's first world title fight, and set for 20 rounds at 160 lbs, Ahearn came in at 155 to Lewis' 159. The publicity surrounding the fight incorrectly claimed that the Englishman was the champion of continental Europe, while, to be fair, Lewis was well past his best.*

17.03.15+ Young Ahearn (GB) ND-W PTS 6 Jimmy Clabby (USA), Philadelphia. *Just a no-decision six rounder, but, at 158 lbs, Ahearn's title claim was undoubtedly at stake.*

09.09.15 Al McCoy (USA) ND-L PTS 10 Young Ahearn (GB), Brooklyn - USA. *With Ahearn (154 lbs) having a valid claim to the title, his fight with McCoy (157½ lbs), regardless it being of the no-decision variety, was given championship billing.*

11.09.15 Mike Gibbons (USA) ND-W PTS 10 Packey McFarland (USA), Brooklyn. *Reported in the New York Times (newspaper) as a title fight, it was certainly not recognised as one. Initially made at 147 lbs ringside, McFarland, who had been out of the ring for almost two years, scaled 152 lbs to Gibbons' 153 and the fight went ahead at 154 lbs (3.0 pm weigh-in). While there is no doubt that Gibbons was recognised by many as the best around at the time, and over 30,000 fans saw the fight, it was a "stinker" which damaged boxing and is best forgotten.*

01.11.15+ Les Darcy (A) W CO 6 Billy Murray (USA), Melbourne. *Not billed as a title fight, the Melbourne Daily Telegraph (newspaper) recorded the weights as being 162 lbs for Darcy and 160 for Murray, which, if correct, would have placed the Australian version of the championship at risk.*

25.11.15+ Young Ahearn (GB) ND-W PTS 10 Kid Wagner (USA), Brooklyn. *Ahearn (156½) risked his title claim when allowing Wagner to weigh in at 160 lbs.*

25.11.15 Al McCoy (USA) ND-L PTS 15 Silent Martin (USA), Waterbury - USA. *Although no weights were reported in the Hartford Courant (newspaper), the paper claimed that Martin let the title slip through his fingers.*

27.12.15+ Les Darcy (A) W CO 8 Eddie McGoorty (USA), Sydney - AUSTRALIA. *For some reason missed out of the record books as involving Darcy's middleweight title claim, according to the Sydney Daily Telegraph (newspaper), it was a billed championship fight with Darcy scaling 159¼ lbs to McGoorty's 159¾.*

01.01.16 Al McCoy (USA) ND-L PTS 10 Young Ahearn (GB), Brooklyn - USA. *In a return meeting between the pair, Ahearn (156 lbs) again came close to taking over from McCoy (162 lbs).*

18.01.16+ Mike Gibbons (USA) ND-W CO 1 Young Ahearn (GB), St Paul. *Billed to decide the championships of England and America over ten rounds, following his victory, Gibbons had more support in the States than Al McCoy. Both men were well inside the limit, with Gibbons weighing 155½ lbs to Ahearn's 154¾.*

20.01.16 Al McCoy (USA) ND-L PTS 10 George Chip (USA), Brooklyn. *Chip weighed 157¼ lbs.*

17.03.16 Mike Gibbons (USA) ND-W PTS 10 Jeff Smith (USA), St Paul. *A defence of Gibbons' title claim saw him weighing in at 156½ lbs as opposed to Smith's 156¾.*

21.03.16 Al McCoy (USA) ND-W PTS 10 Lou Benz (USA), Brooklyn. *Benz weighed 156 lbs.*

17.04.16 Al McCoy (USA) ND-L PTS 10 Al Thiel (USA), New York City*

18.05.16+ Mike Gibbons (USA) ND-W PTS 10 Ted Kid Lewis (GB), New York City. *Considered at this stage to be the best middleweight in America, Gibbons (152½ lbs) risked his title claim against the former welter champion, Lewis, who scaled 143 lbs at ringside.*

28.09.16+ Al McCoy (USA) ND-L PTS 10 Jackie Clark (USA), Scranton*

28.11.16+ Al McCoy (USA) ND-W PTS 10 Jack McCarron (USA), Allentown*

30.04.17 Al McCoy (USA) ND-L PTS 10 Harry Greb (USA), Pittsburgh. *According to the Pittsburgh Gazette (newspaper), Greb was expected to be inside 160 lbs. However, with the American limit still standing at 158 lbs, it remains doubtful as to whether McCoy's title claim was on the line.*

04.07.17+ Mike Gibbons (USA) ND-W PTS 12 George Chip (USA), Youngstown. *According to the Chicago Tribune (newspaper), Gibbons successfully defended his title claim in this one. Earlier, in February 1917, Gibbons had signed articles to meet Les Darcy at 160 lbs in Milwaukee on 10 April 1917 to decide who was the best man at the weight in the world. Unfortunately, Darcy was taken ill and the fight never took place.*

04.07.17+ Al McCoy (USA) ND-L PTS 10 Jackie Clark (USA), Lonaconing. *Despite the absence of weights, the Baltimore Sun (newspaper) reported that McCoy easily retained his title.*

12.10.17+ Mike Gibbons (USA) ND-W RSC 3 Frank Mantell (USA), St Paul. *Following this, a successful defence of his 158 lbs title claim, Gibbons summarily retired from the ring to concentrate on his post of boxing instructor at Camp Dodge, Iowa.*

25.02.18 **Mike O'Dowd** (USA) ND-W PTS 10 Harry Greb (USA), St Paul. *Now confirmed by George D. Blair as being a billed championship fight of the no-decision variety, O'Dowd weighed 157 lbs as opposed to the challenger's 156¾.*

01.09.19 **Mike O'Dowd** (USA) ND-W PTS 10 Ted Kid Lewis (GB), Syracuse. *Made at 158 lbs, Lewis weighed 145 lbs to O'Dowd's 154.*

19.09.19 **Mike O'Dowd** (USA) ND-W PTS 10 Soldier Bartfield (USA), St Paul. *Made at 158 lbs, the St Paul Pioneer (newspaper) reported that at no time during the contest were O'Dowd's titular laurels at risk.*

10.11.19 **Mike O'Dowd** (USA) ND-W CO 2 Jimmy O'Hagen (USA), Detroit. *Although the Chicago Tribune (newspaper) acknowledged O'Hagen as the challenger, both the Detroit News and Free Press (newspapers) reported it to be at catchweights, with the latter weighing in the region of 160 lbs plus.*

14.01.20+ **Mike O'Dowd** (USA) ND-W PTS 10 Frank Carbone (USA), Detroit. *Reported as a 158 lbs title fight by the Detroit Free Press (newspaper).*

17.03.20+ **Mike O'Dowd** (USA) ND-W PTS 10 Augie Ratner (USA), St Paul. *While attaching no apparent title billing to the fight, the St Paul Pioneer (newspaper) reported that Ratner (155½ lbs) threw many punches in the hope one might just give him the championship. With O'Dowd weighing 157½ lbs, both men were inside the weight class limit.*

10.02.21 **Johnny Wilson** (USA) ND-W CO 2 Navy Rostan (USA), Kenosha. *Articled at 158 lbs, Rostan scaled 154¼ lbs, while Wilson at 160½ was forced to pay forfeit.*

27.07.21 **Johnny Wilson** (USA) ND-W DIS 7 Bryan Downey (USA), Cleveland. *After the contest came to an end when the referee disqualified Downey (154 lbs), the Cleveland Boxing Commission refused to accept the decision and declared Downey the winner by kayo, a decision that was eventually supported by the Ohio Boxing Commission. The referee, who had been brought in to protect Wilson (165 lbs), claimed he disqualified Downey for attempting to hit the champion while he was down, but Wilson had already been decked three times and appeared well beaten at the finish.*

05.09.21 Johnny Wilson (USA) ND-DREW 12 Bryan Downey (USA), Jersey City. *Following the fight, Wilson (159 lbs) had his purse suspended for "spoiling" and not being interested in making a fight of it, while Downey (154½ lbs) was exhonerated.*

31.10.21+ Mike Gibbons (USA) W PTS 15 Happy Littleton (USA), New Orleans. *Billed by the promoter as a world title fight after Johnny Wilson had positively refused to box either man, no champion was forthcoming as, according to the New Orleans Daily Picayune (newspaper), the winner scaled 160½ lbs to Littleton's 160. The fight had been made at 160 lbs, the championship weight limit.*

12.12.21+ Bryan Downey (USA) W RSC 5 Happy Littleton (USA), New Orleans. *Billed as a world title fight after the local authority was granted permission by the Cleveland Boxing Commission. Strangely, Littleton fluffed his opportunity by coming in at 160½ lbs to Downey's 157¾. In his next fight, Downey drew over 15 rounds against Young Fisher in Syracuse on 10 February 1922, with both men inside 158 lbs. Although there would have been some risk to his claim, it was outside the jurisdiction of both the Cleveland and Ohio Boxing Commissions.*

22.02.22 Bryan Downey (USA) W PTS 12 Frank Carbone (USA), Canton - OHIO. *Although outside the jurisdiction of the Ohio Boxing Commission, Downey risked his title claim when taking on Carbone again at 160 lbs in a ten round no-decision affair in Indianapolis on 13 March 1922. It was "all right on the night", however, as Downey did enough to gain the "press" verdict.*

15.05.22 Bryan Downey (USA) W PTS 12 Mike O'Dowd (USA), Columbus - OHIO. *Another fight outside the offices of the Ohio Boxing Commission, saw Downey (154½ lbs) lose a ten round "press" verdict to Jock Malone (153 lbs) in Aurora on 13 June 1922.*

04.07.22 Johnny Wilson (USA) ND-W CO 4 Al de Maris (USA), Rutland. *The Chicago Tribune (newspaper) reported, despite no mention of weights, that Wilson could only draw some 500 people to Vermont's first ever world title fight. Earlier, Wilson had contracted to defend the title against Harry Greb in Madison Square Garden, but had decided not to go ahead on the grounds that he had been forced to sign in order to recover his due purse monies from the Bryan Downey fight, a decision that led to him being stripped by the NYSAC in July 1922, following the de Maris affair.*

14.08.22 Dave Rosenberg (USA) W PTS 15 Phil Krug (USA), New York City - NY. *Krug was a replacement for Harry Greb, who had pulled out after being matched against Rosenberg, following New York's decision to strip Johnny Wilson.*

16.03.23 Jock Malone (USA) ND-W CO 1 Mike O'Dowd (USA), St Paul. *There was no mention of world title billing in the Chicago Tribune (newspaper), although Malone (152½ lbs), who was announced as the holder of the Ohio version, and O'Dowd (158½ lbs), as the New York champion, were both within the required 160 lbs. To confuse matters further, the Boston Post (newspaper) would later report Malone as having won the world title as a result of his win. While it is unclear at this moment in time whether Malone was even recognised in Ohio, O'Dowd certainly forfeited his New York crown in this fight and announced his retirement. Following that, in early May 1923, the NYSAC reinstated Johnny Wilson as champion after he had agreed to defend the title against Harry Greb at the Polo Grounds in New York City during August.*

09.01.25+ Harry Greb (USA) W PTS 10 Bob Sage (USA), Detroit. *Although the Ring Record Book gives this one as a no-decision non-title bout, the New York Times (newspaper) reported that verdict was given by a referee of Greb's own preference. This concession allowed Sage to weigh less than that earlier agreed (inside 160 lbs) and gave the promoter the right to attach championship billing.*

05.06.28 Mickey Walker (USA) ND-W PTS 10 Jock Malone (USA), St Paul. *Billed for the title, at the 3.0 pm weigh-in, Walker scaled 160 lbs to Malone's 157.*

21.08.33 Teddy Yarosz (USA) W PTS 10 Vince Dundee (USA), Pittsburgh - PENNSYLVANIA. *Recognised as being for the Pennsylvanian version of the title, Yarosz next took on three opponents, who weighed inside the limit, in fights outside the State, prior to making his first defence in Pittsburgh. The men who gave way, following ten round points defeats, were Vince Dundee (Newark on 18 September 1933), Paul Pirrone (Cleveland on 4 December 1933) and Tony Alessandro (Holyoke on 11 December 1933).*

09.05.41 Billy Soose (USA) W PTS 15 Ken Overlin (USA), New York City - NY. *Having won the NYSAC version of the championship, Soose never defended it, mainly due to increasing weight problems and, following an eight round technical draw against Ceferino Garcia in Los Angeles on 15 September 1941, in which he weighed 169½ lbs, he relinquished the title on 31 October.*

28.11.41 Tony Zale (USA) W PTS 15 Georgie Abrams (USA), New York City. *When Zale was called up to serve in the US Navy, following an over the weight 12 round points defeat at the hands of Billy Conn on 13 February 1942, the title was frozen. Later that year, two of his leading challengers, Charley Burley and Holman Williams, were matched for the unofficial "black" title in New Orleans. On 14 August 1942, the former scored a ninth round stoppage win, while, in a return on 16 October, Williams outpointed his rival over 15 rounds. Apart from several Californian State title fights, which saw a succession of champions during the wartime period, from Eddie Booker, Jack Chase, Archie Moore, Jack Chase (again), to Charley Burley, no moves were made to hold a "duration" tournament.*

Light-Heavyweight (175 lbs)

08.05.07 Tommy Burns (C) W PTS 20 Jack O'Brien (USA), Los Angeles. *Billed for the world heavyweight title (see under those listings, also), some record books saw this fight as deciding the light-heavyweight issue as well. However, with Burns scaling 180 lbs, and the weight limit recognised as being no more than 175 lbs, the Canadian should not be seen as the divisional champion, even though the T.S. Andrews Annual strangely listed him as such until early 1913.*

15.08.11 Sam Langford (USA) ND-W RSC 5 Jack O'Brien (USA), New York City. *On the basis of this victory, Langford, who weighed 173 lbs when beating O'Brien (166 lbs), was recognised by the IBU as world light-heavyweight champion when they first published ratings in June 1912. However, there is no record of him being the least bit interested. Also around this time, the newly formed New York State Athletic Commission announced that they would recognise the weight class at 165 lbs, and Fireman Jim Flynn laid claim to their version of the title without ever bothering to make the weight.*

28.05.12 Jack Dillon (USA) ND-W CO 3 Hugo Kelly (USA), Indianapolis. *Shown in the 1996 Yearbook as a fight that involved the light-heavyweight title, recent research has discovered that with both men inside 158 lbs, Dillon took over Kelly's middleweight claim (see in that weight class, also).*

12.02.13+ Georges Carpentier (FR) W CO 2 Bandsman Rice (GB), Paris - IBU. *Accorded recognition as world champion in the 1914 T.S. Andrews Annual, Carpentier carried off the IBU version of the title following his win over Rice.*

14.04.14 Jack Dillon (USA) W PTS 12 Battling Levinsky (USA), Butte. *According to the Anaconda Standard (newspaper), this was billed for the vacant 175 lbs title, with Levinsky scaling 170½ lbs to Dillon's 164½. Although receiving scant support at the time, it was recognised as such in the TS Andrews Annuals.*

28.04.14 Jack Dillon (USA) W PTS 10 Al Norton (USA), Kansas City. *Recorded in various published title listings as involving a claim to the title, heavy research to date has failed to uncover either weight or billing. The same conditions apply where (*).*

29.05.14+ Jack Dillon (USA) ND-W PTS 10 Battling Levinsky (USA), Indianapolis. *Made at 175 lbs, the Indianapolis Star (newspaper) reported both men made the weight, with Dillon (162 lbs) and Levinsky (170 lbs) well inside the day before.*

15.06.14 Jack Dillon (USA) W PTS 12 Bob Moha (USA), Butte. *Moha scaled 163½ lbs to Dillon's 163, according to the Anaconda Standard (newspaper) report.*

03.07.14 Jack Dillon (USA) W PTS 10 Sailor Petroskey (USA), Kansas City*

15.09.14+ Jack Dillon (USA) ND-DREW 10 George K.O. Brown (USA), Vincennes*

28.09.14+ Jack Dillon (USA) ND-W PTS 12 Frank Mantell (USA), Columbus. *Mantell weighed 172 lbs.*

09.11.14+ Jack Dillon (USA) ND-W CO 2 Charley Weinert (USA), Philadelphia. *In a six round no-decision fight, Weinert scaled 173½ lbs to Dillon's 174.*

20.02.15+ Jack Dillon (USA) ND-W PTS 10 Frank Mantell (USA), New York City*

23.02.15+ Jack Dillon (USA) ND-W PTS 10 Johnny Howard (USA), Brooklyn. *Howard weighed 162½ lbs.*

06.04.15+ Jack Dillon (USA) ND-W PTS 10 Billy Murray (USA), Hudson*

11.06.15+ Jack Dillon (USA) ND-W PTS 10 Frank Mantell (USA), Cincinnati. *Mantell scaled 168½ lbs to Dillon's 169.*

05.07.15+ Jack Dillon (USA) DREW 10 George Chip (USA), Kansas City*

12.07.15+ Jack Dillon (USA) ND-W PTS 10 Johnny Howard (USA), Rockaway*

16.07.15+ Jack Dillon (USA) ND-W PTS 10 Zulu Kid (USA), Rockaway*

28.01.16+ Jack Dillon (USA) ND-L PTS 10 Billy Miske (USA), Superior*

08.02.16+ Jack Dillon (USA) ND-DREW 10 Battling Levinsky (USA), Brooklyn. *Occasionally shown in title listings as a fight that involved Dillon's claim, the New York Times (newspaper) reported Levinsky to be over the class limit at 175½ lbs.*

14.04.16+ Jack Dillon (USA) ND-W PTS 10 Billy Miske (USA), St Paul*

25.04.16 Jack Dillon (USA) W PTS 15 Battling Levinsky (USA), Kansas City. *Listed as a title fight in the Ring Record Book, without mention of weights, the Chicago Tribune (newspaper) reported that if there was any question as to where the light-heavyweight title should be, it was settled tonight.*

12.09.16+ Jack Dillon (USA) ND-DREW 8 Battling Levinsky (USA), Memphis. *Both men were inside 175 lbs according to the Memphis Daily Appeal (newspaper).*

17.10.16+ Jack Dillon (USA) ND-W PTS 10 Tim O'Neill (USA), Brooklyn. *O'Neill weighed 172 lbs to Dillon's 173.*

30.10.16+ Battling Levinsky (USA) ND-L PTS 10 Billy Miske (USA), Brooklyn. *Miske weighed 170½ lbs.*

08.12.16+ Battling Levinsky (USA) ND-W PTS 10 Gus Christie (USA), Dayton*

17.01.17+ Battling Levinsky (USA) ND-W PTS 12 Bob Moha (USA), Youngstown*

27.02.17+ Battling Levinsky (USA) ND-W PTS 10 Billy Miske (USA), St Paul*

23.03.17+ Battling Levinsky (USA) ND-L PTS 10 Tommy Gibbons (USA), St Paul. *Following research in local papers, George D. Blair* *tells us that this was a billed title fight at 175 lbs that saw Gibbons win eight of the ten rounds.*

09.05.17+ Battling Levinsky (USA) ND-DREW 10 Bob McAllister (USA), New York City. *McAllister weighed 175 lbs.*

20.06.17+ Battling Levinsky (USA) W PTS 12 Johnny Howard (USA), Providence. *Billed as a world title defence at 175 lbs for Levinsky, the Providence Journal (newspaper) reported that Howard was handicapped in height, weight and reach.*

06.09.17+ Battling Levinsky (USA) ND-L PTS 10 Harry Greb (USA), Pittsburgh. *Although a catchweight contest, The Pittsburgh Gazette (newspaper) reported Greb to be 162 lbs with Levinsky a good ten pounds heavier.*

31.10.17+ Battling Levinsky (USA) ND-W PTS 10 Zulu Kid (USA), Montreal. *While making no mention of weights, the Montreal Herald (newspaper) poured cold water on Levinsky's title claim by recognising the Kid as a middleweight and stating that if only the former could punch he would surely be a champion.*

17.02.19+ Battling Levinsky (USA) ND-L PTS 10 Harry Greb (USA), Buffalo. *The Toronto Daily Star (newspaper) reported Greb as weighing 160½ lbs to Levinsky's 175.*

28.04.19+ Battling Levinsky (USA) ND-L PTS 12 Harry Greb (USA), Canton*

19.07.19+ Georges Carpentier (FR) W CO 8 Dick Smith (GB), Paris - IBU

25.07.19+ Battling Levinsky (USA) ND-W PTS 8 Ed Kinley (USA), Long Branch. *Kinley weighed 175 lbs.*

03.09.19+ Battling Levinsky (USA) ND-L PTS 10 Harry Greb (USA), Wheeling. *The Wheeling Register (newspaper) reported that with Greb well inside 175 lbs, the title would change hands if he could land a kayo wallop.*

24.11.19+ Battling Levinsky (USA) ND-W PTS 10 Clay Turner (USA), Detroit. *According to the Detroit News (newspaper), the fight could justifiably be billed for the title and the reporter felt that there was every chance that a new champion would be crowned. Unfortunately, there was no mention of weights.*

23.01.20+ Battling Levinsky (USA) ND-W PTS 8 Johnny Howard (USA), Perth Amboy*

16.02.20+ Battling Levinsky (USA) ND-W PTS 10 Clay Turner (USA), Detroit*

26.03.20+ Battling Levinsky (USA) ND-W PTS 10 Clay Turner (USA), Hartford*

03.05.20+ Battling Levinsky (USA) ND-W PTS 12 Clay Turner (USA), Portland*

21.05.20+ Battling Levinsky (USA) DREW 12 Chuck Wiggins (USA), Dayton*

15.05.31 **Maxie Rosenbloom** (USA) W PTS 10 Don Petrin (USA), Los Angeles. *Announced as a non-title fight, even though the Los Angeles Times (newspaper) stated that both men weighed 170 lbs (this was five pounds inside the limit and had to be a printing error). On 6 June 1931, the NBA withdrew recognition from Rosenbloom and decided to set up an elimination tournament to find a worthier champion. The move, apparently a political one, came about after Rosenbloom, a ten round points non-title victim of Billy Jones in Pittsburgh on 6 April 1931, had failed to make a defence within the stipulated sixth month regulation period. With wins over Petrin, Charley Belanger, Lou Scozza and George Nichols, George Nichols was matched against Dave Maier, a man who had already beaten him, along with Rosenbloom, Abe Bain and Mike Mandell, during the same period.*

31.05.32 Lou Scozza (USA) W PTS 10 George Nichols (USA), Buffalo. *Incorrectly recorded as an NBA title fight in the Boxing News Annual (it was an overweight match), Scozza went on to challenge the New York champion, Maxie Rosenbloom, in a contest many thought would have unified the title. In truth, Scozza did not represent the NBA and Nichols remained their champion. However, after losing three of his next four contests (all at catchweights), and ducking out of a defence against Ad Heuser that was booked for Boston on 17 November 1932, the NBA declared the title vacant in December.*

16.11.34 **Bob Olin** (USA) W PTS 15 Maxie Rosenbloom (USA), New York City. *Olin forfeited Canadian recognition in August 1935, having ignored the claims of Al McCoy, who had recently outpointed leading contenders, Al Gainer and Billy Jones.*

05.09.35 Al McCoy (C) W PTS 15 Joe Knight (USA), Montreal - CANADA. *Just 15 days later, on 20 September, McCoy met fellow Canadian, Lou Brouillard, in a fight the Boston Post (newspaper) viewed as a final eliminator for the world title. Although he won on points over ten rounds, with both men inside 175 lbs, there was obviously some risk attached to his Canadian recognition.*

17.09.35 Hein Lazek (AU) W DIS 13 Merlo Preciso (ITA), Vienna. *Shown in the 1985 Ring Record Book as being for the IBU*

version of the world title, it involved the IBU championship only and should be removed from the listings.

23.10.35+ Al McCoy (C) W CO 2 Abe Bain (USA), Montreal - CANADA. *Billed as a world title fight under the auspices of the Montreal Boxing Commission, McCoy weighed 174¼ lbs to Bain's 172¾. After being outpointed over ten rounds by England's Jock McAvoy in a match made at 171 lbs on 29 November 1935 (New York City), the French-Canadian moved up to heavyweight, while McAvoy went on to challenge the new world light-heavy champion, John Henry Lewis.*

25.02.36 Hein Lazek (AU) W RTD 5 Reinus de Boer (HOL), Vienna. *This fight should also be removed from the title listings as it involved the IBU championship only.*

13.03.36 **John Henry Lewis** (USA) W PTS 15 Jock McAvoy (GB), New York City. *For some reason, known only to themselves, the IBU announced at their congress on 8 August 1936 that they would recognise the winner of the forthcoming European title fight between Hein Lazek and Gustav Roth, as world champion.*

03.08.36 Hein Lazek (AU) W CO 9 Emil Olive (FR), Vienna. *As in Lazek's fights with Preciso and de Boer, it should be removed from the title listings.*

13.01.41 Anton Christoforidis (GRE) W PTS 15 Melio Bettina (USA), Cleveland - NBA. *Following Christoforidis' win and the likelihood that Billy Conn would move up to fight Joe Louis for the heavyweight crown, the NYSAC set up an eliminating series, in which Jimmy Webb stopped Tommy Tucker in the ninth of their 15 rounder in New York City on 21 February 1941.*

22.05.41 Gus Lesnevich (USA) W PTS 15 Anton Christoforidis (GRE), New York City - NBA. *Billed as a semi-final leg of the NYSAC elimination series and for the NBA title, Lesnevich won the right to meet Jimmy Webb for the championship that was officially vacated by Billy Conn on 3 June 1941. However, Webb got himself beaten in a mundane fight and Tami Mauriello was substituted.*

29.10.63 Eddie Cotton (USA) W PTS 15 Henry Hank (USA), Flint - MICHIGAN. *Prior to a non-title fight in New York City against Johnny Persol on 21 February 1964, the New York Times (newspaper) reported that Cotton could claim to hold the dubious Michigan version of the world title. However, his ten round points defeat, with both men inside 175 lbs, spelt an end to that.*

Heavyweight (190 lbs+)

21.02.96 Bob Fitzsimmons (A) W CO 1 Peter Maher (USA), Couhuahua. *Although most people still considered Corbett as being the champion, even though he had been inactive for over two years, this fight was billed for the heavyweight title and took Fitzsimmons just 91 seconds to win at least a share of the spoils.*

02.12.96+ Tom Sharkey (USA) W DIS 8 Bob Fitzsimmons (A), San Francisco. *Although Fitzsimmons was announced in the ring as the world champion, earlier, in August, the Police Gazette (newspaper) decided that he had forfeited his claim to the title by reason of his refusal for six months to cover an existing forfeit and accept a bona-fide challenge. A few weeks later, however, he signed articles to meet James J. Corbett, but nothing was organised until after the meeting with Sharkey. Following the above fight, Fitzsimmons, who could justifiably claim to have been a victim at the hands of referee, Wyatt Earp, the famous gunslinger, put his case to the courts, only for the referee's decision to be upheld. Meanwhile, Sharkey took in a tour of Britain before eventually getting a shot at James J. Jeffries for the title.*

06.04.00 **Jim Jeffries** (USA) W CO 1 Jack Finnegan (USA), Detroit. *Articled for ten rounds, Jeffries did not even know who his opponent was until three days before the fight, with little or no media coverage whatsoever, but it was not an exhibition bout either. As a warm-up for his forthcoming defence against Corbett, the champion wasted little time in scoring a 55 second kayo.*

Further corrections to information in previous BBBoC Yearbooks
Results
Bantamweight

02.11.05 Owen Moran (GB) W CO 3 Al Fellows (USA), The Gymnastic Club, Liverpool

Welterweight

27.05.95 Tommy Ryan (USA) DREW 18 Mysterious Billy Smith (USA), Brooklyn

22.02.99 Bobby Dobbs (USA) DREW 1 Joe McDonald (GB), Wellington Palace, Glasgow

Middleweight

17.12.80 William Sherriff (GB) W RTD 11 Denny Harrington (GB), Lapworth

17.12.97 Kid McCoy (USA) W RTD 15 Dan Creedon (NZ), Long Island

L. Heavyweight

13.05.03 George Gardner (USA) W RTD 12 Marvin Hart (USA), Louisville

Heavyweight

26.08.04 James J. Jeffries (USA) W RSC 2 Jack Munroe (USA), San Francisco

03.07.05 Marvin Hart (USA) W CO 12 Jack Root (USA), Reno

Recognition

Flyweight

16.09.36 Benny Lynch (GB) W CO 8 Pat Palmer (GB), Shawfield Park, Glasgow - GB/NBA

19.01.37 Benny Lynch (GB) W PTS 15 Small Montana (PH), The Arena, Wembley - GB/USA

13.10.37 Benny Lynch (GB) W CO 13 Peter Kane (GB), Shawfield Park, Glasgow - GB/USA

Bantamweight

28.05.95 Billy Plimmer (GB) W CO 7 George Corfield (GB), NSC, London - GB

25.11.95 Pedlar Palmer (GB) W DIS 14 Billy Plimmer (GB), NSC, London - GB

12.10.96 Pedlar Palmer (GB) W PTS 20 Johnny Murphy (USA), NSC, London - GB

25.01.97 Pedlar Palmer (GB) W RSC 14 Ernie Stanton (USA), NSC, London - GB

12.12.98 Pedlar Palmer (GB) W RSC 17 Billy Plimmer (GB), NSC, London - GB

17.04.99 Pedlar Palmer (GB) W RSC 3 Billy Rotchford (USA), NSC, London - GB

19.06.09 Monte Attell (USA) W RSC 18 Frankie Neil (USA), San Francisco

17.12.09 Monte Attell (USA) DREW 20 Danny Webster (USA), San Francisco

22.02.10 Frankie Conley (USA) W RTD 42 Monte Attell (USA), Los Angeles

06.12.15 Kid Williams (USA) DREW 20 Frankie Burns (USA), New Orleans

07.02.16 Kid Williams (USA) DREW 20 Pete Herman (USA), New Orleans

09.01.17 Pete Herman (USA) W PTS 20 Kid Williams (USA), New Orleans

05.11.17 Pete Herman (USA) W PTS 20 Frankie Burns (USA), New Orleans

18.03.33 **Al Brown** (PAN) W PTS 12 Dom Bernasconi (ITA), Milan

03.07.33 **Al Brown** (PAN) W PTS 15 Johnny King (GB), Belle Vue, Manchester

31.08.36 Sixto Escobar (PR) W RSC 13 Tony Marino (USA), New York City - NBA/NY

13.10.36 Sixto Escobar (PR) W CO 1 Carlos Quintana (PAN), New York City - NBA/NY

21.02.37 Sixto Escobar (PR) W PTS 15 Lou Salica (USA), San Juan - NBA/NY

23.09.37 Harry Jeffra (USA) W PTS 15 Sixto Escobar (PR), New York City - NBA/NY

Featherweight

04.09.16 Johnny Kilbane (USA) W CO 3 K. O. Chaney (USA), Cedar Point - USA

L. Welterweight

29.04.46 Tippy Larkin (USA) W PTS 12 Willie Joyce (USA), Boston - NY/NBA

Welterweight

18.01.95 Tommy Ryan (USA) W RSC 3 Nonpareil Jack Dempsey (USA), Brooklyn - USA

27.05.95 Tommy Ryan (USA) DREW 18 Mysterious Billy Smith (USA), Brooklyn - USA

07.10.98 Mysterious Billy Smith (USA) W PTS 25 Charley McKeever (USA), New York City - USA

10.03.99 Mysterious Billy Smith (USA) W RSC 14 George Lavigne (USA), San Francisco - USA

30.08.00 Rube Ferns (USA) W PTS 15 Matty Matthews (USA), Detroit - USA

16.10.00 Matty Matthews (USA) W PTS 15 Rube Ferns (USA), Detroit - USA

29.04.01 Matty Matthews (USA) W PTS 20 Tom Couhig (USA), Detroit - USA

24.05.01 Rube Ferns (USA) W CO 10 Matty Matthews (USA), Toronto - USA

23.09.01 Rube Ferns (USA) W CO 9 Frank Erne (USA), Fort Erie - USA

29.09.06 Joe Walcott (USA) DREW 20 Billy Rhodes (USA), Kansas City - USA

29.11.06 Honey Mellody (USA) W RSC 12 Joe Walcott (USA), Chelsea - USA

28.12.15 Ted Kid Lewis (GB) ND-W PTS 10 Willie Ritchie (USA), New York City

17.01.16 Ted Kid Lewis (GB) ND-W PTS 10 Kid Graves (USA), Milwaukee

20.01.16 Ted Kid Lewis (GB) ND-L PTS 10 Jack Britton (USA), Buffalo

15.02.16 Ted Kid Lewis (GB) ND-L PTS 10 Jack Britton (USA), Brooklyn

01.03.16 Ted Kid Lewis (GB) W PTS 20 Harry Stone (USA), New Orleans

24.04.16 Jack Britton (USA) W PTS 20 Ted Kid Lewis (GB), New Orleans

05.09.16 Jack Britton (USA) ND-W PTS 10 Joe Welling (USA), Buffalo

17.10.16 Jack Britton (USA) W PTS 12 Ted Kid Lewis (GB), Boston

21.11.16 Jack Britton (USA) W PTS 12 Charley White (USA), Boston

19.05.17 Jack Britton (USA) ND-L PTS 10 Ted Kid Lewis (GB), Toronto

14.06.17 Jack Britton (USA) ND-DREW 10 Ted Kid Lewis (GB), New York City

17.01.41 Fritzie Zivic (USA) W RSC 12 Henry Armstrong (USA), New York City - NY/NBA

Country Codes

Welterweight

09.08.91 Tommy Ryan (USA) W CO 3 Billy McMillan (GB), Richardson

Winners not to be shown in bold (bold = internationally recognised champions)

Flyweight

24.03.38 Benny Lynch (GB) DREW 12 Peter Kane (GB), The Stadium, Liverpool

Lightweight

01.01.03 Joe Gans (USA) W DIS 11 Gus Gardner (USA), New Britain

25.03.04 Joe Gans (USA) W PTS 15 Jack Blackburn (USA), Baltimore

28.03.04 Joe Gans (USA) W PTS 10 Gus Gardner (USA), Saginaw

21.04.04 Joe Gans (USA) W PTS 15 Sam Bolen (USA), Baltimore

Welterweight

03.10.98 Mysterious Billy Smith (USA) W CO 20 Jim Judge (USA), Scranton

07.10.98 Mysterious Billy Smith (USA) W PTS 25 Charley McKeever (USA), New York City

24.01.99 Mysterious Billy Smith (USA) W CO 14 Billy Edwards (A), New York City

30.06.99 Mysterious Billy Smith (USA) DREW 20 Charley McKeever (USA), New York City

04.08.99 Mysterious Billy Smith (USA) DREW 25 Andy Walsh (USA), Brooklyn

08.11.99 Mysterious Billy Smith (USA) W PTS 20 Charley McKeever (USA), New York City

23.06.02 Joe Walcott (USA) W PTS 15 Tommy West (USA), NSC, London

01.04.03 Joe Walcott (USA) DREW 20 Billy Woods (USA), Los Angeles

08.01.07 Honey Mellody (USA) W PTS 15 Terry Martin (USA), Augusta

11.02.07 Honey Mellody (USA) W RSC 4 Willie Lewis (USA), Valley Falls

Also, please note that IBU champions, Valentin Angelmann (fly), Al Brown (bantam), Maurice Holtzer (feather), Felix Wouters (welter), Edouard Tenet (middle), and Ad Heuser (light-heavy), lost their world title recognition at the international boxing convention during the third week of April (not May) 1938. Also, Bat Battalino (feather) forfeited NYSAC recognition on 8 January 1932, while Lou Ambers (light) was stripped by the NBA on 25 March 1940.

Unofficial Black Heavyweight Champions: From Gloves to Joe Louis

The whole purpose of this presentation is that during the above period just one black man, Jack Johnson, not forgetting Jim Johnson who challenged him in a so-called title bout, was allowed to fight for the richest prize in sport – the heavyweight title. Prior to the ascent of Joe Louis, the top black heavyweights of the day were to be avoided at all costs and Jack Johnson, the only man to be given an opportunity of winning the world title, and a belated one at that, had to chase Tommy Burns halfway around the world before being crowned champion. Even if Johnson was forced to wait six or seven years, he was luckier than men like George Godfrey and Peter Jackson, who were blocked completely. The trouble, which has been well documented over the years, was the now much maligned "colour bar", which firstly John L. Sullivan, and then James J. Jeffries, put up. Or looked at in another way, it was a ploy that enabled white heavyweight champions to "duck" the leading challenger if he was coloured on the grounds that the two races did not mix. Unfortunately, Johnson, who could have helped other black heavyweights considerably, became the most unpopular champion of all time. His general behaviour so incensed the public, especially his associations with white women (illegal at the time) and his taunting of opponents, that when he fled to Europe in late 1912 to escape arrest, the most powerful promoters in America spent the next year or two trying to find a white fighter good enough to win the title back for the white population. This became known as the era of the "Great White Hope", which ended with Johnson being defeated by Jess Willard in 1915. The damage Johnson did to his race, not only in boxing terms, was so great that it would be 22 years before another black man, Joe Louis, would get a fair crack of the whip. Other notables who suffered because of Johnson were men such as Joe Jeannette, Sam McVey, the legendary Sam Langford, Harry Wills and George Godfrey, number two. All of these would have been favoured at one time or another to wear the world heavyweight crown if given the opportunity. However, the nearest any of them got to the elusive title was Harry Wills, who, supported by the New York State Athletic Commission, tried to force a match with Jack Dempsey after a Wills v Dempsey fight booked for 6 September 1924 had fallen through. Later, the promoter, Tex Rickard, told the press that he had decided against a "mixed" bout in New York on the grounds that the Governor had declared such a contest would not be desired, a statement that was refuted most vociferously. Action was immediate and involved Dempsey being banned in New York until he was prepared to meet Wills under championship conditions. Following that, Rickard matched Dempsey against Gene Tunney in Philadelphia and the rest is history. This then is the unofficial black heavyweight line of succession.

The first black heavyweight of any real note appears to have been Bill Richmond, who was born into slavery in New York and was brought to England by the Duke of Northumberland. He was followed by Tom Molineux, another former slave, and well-known for his two famous fights with Tom Cribb in 1810 and '11. Neither made it as a London Prize Ring champion, but were an inspiration to all those who took to the ring in later years. The next top-class black heavyweight from America to appear in England was John Perry, but, before he could really make a name for himself, he was transported to Australia in 1847 when convicted of passing counterfeit money. In 1870, and again a few years later, with boxing on the increase in America, Charles A. Smith, the "Michigan Thunderbolt", challenged all and sundry without acceptance, but he never really made his mark. The first time a "black" title of any kind was contested was in 1878, when the Police Gazette organised a "black" heavyweight competition in New York City. Won by Morris Grant that year and again in 1881, before the competition ended in 1883 after Harry Woodson took the honours by default, Charles Hadley had been awarded a championship medal outright for three victories in four years (1879, 1880 and 1882). In 1882, George Godfrey, considered to be the outstanding coloured heavyweight of the day, claimed the "black" American title after more than holding his own in sparring with Frank Slavin and having being denied a crack at John L. Sullivan by the police. With Woodson not disputing Godfrey's claim, the latter went forward to meet Hadley, who had a 1880 six round points victory over his rival.

22.02.83 George Godfrey W CO 6 Charles Hadley, Boston. *Billed as a battle for the coloured heavyweight title to a finish using 2oz gloves, the purse was $300, plus $50 aside, winner take all.*

10.05.84 George Godfrey DREW 4 McHenry Johnson, Boston. *Police stopped the fight after McHenry "Black Star" Johnson was floored, with Godfrey well on top. In 1887, Godfrey was challenged by Samuel Grant, "The Indiana Darky", for the title with $1,000 aside. However, despite a club in New Orleans offering a $3,000 purse, the fight never came off.*

25.01.88 George Godfrey W CO 4 McHenry Johnson, Boston. *After Johnson was knocked down by a right to the jaw, his seconds claimed a foul. To much surprise, the referee went along with it. Later, however, the committee overruled the decision saying that Godfrey was the rightful winner. On 14 May, Godfrey challenged John L. Sullivan, who refused point blank. Following that, the Boston Police News (paper) stated that Godfrey had every right to claim the coloured title.*

24.08.88 Peter Jackson W RTD 19 George Godfrey, San Francisco. *Billed*

for the coloured heavyweight title, by 1896, both men had dropped out of the heavyweight reckoning. Jackson, who drew with James J. Corbett over 61 rounds in San Francisco on 21 May 1891 and kayoed Frank Slavin in the tenth round at the NSC (London) on 30 May 1892, took almost six years away from boxing and was demolished by Jim Jeffries on his return to the ring in 1898. His final contest on 2 December 1899 was a 25 round draw against Peter Felix in Melbourne, although the Ring Record Book showed the opponent to be Billy Warren.

21.12.96 Bob Armstrong W CO 19 Charley Strong, New York City. *With Armstrong and Strong seemingly the two top black heavyweights at the time, this was billed for the vacant title.*

06.03.97 Bob Armstrong ND-W RSC 6 Joe Butler, Philadelphia

29.01.98 Frank Childs W CO 2 Bob Armstrong, Chicago

26.02.98 Frank Childs W DIS 3 Klondike Haines, Chicago

04.06.98 Frank Childs DREW 6 Charley Strong, Chicago

14.09.98 George Byers W PTS 20 Frank Childs, New York City

06.05.99 Klondike Haines W RSC 5 Jack Johnson, Chicago. *Although*

Haines claimed the "black" title after his victory, he was not generally recognised.

24.07.99 George Byers W CO 9 Charley Strong, Brooklyn

11.08.99 Frank Childs W PTS 6 Klondike Haines, Chicago. *By his victory, Childs took over Haines' claim.*

28.10.99 Frank Childs W RSC 3 Klondike Haines, Chicago

16.03.00 George Byers DREW 6 Frank Childs, Chicago

15.12.00 Frank Childs W CO 4 Joe Butler, Chicago

16.03.01 Frank Childs W CO 17 George Byers, Hot Springs

18.01.01 Frank Childs W PTS 6 Walter Johnson, Chicago

24.02.02 Denver Ed Martin W PTS 6 Frank Childs, Chicago. *Martin claimed the title following this six rounder.*

25.07.02 Denver Ed Martin W PTS 15 Bob Armstrong, The Crystal Palace Grounds, London

16.08.02 Denver Ed Martin W RTD 3 Frank Craig, Ginnett's Circus, Newcastle.

30.08.02 Denver Ed Martin W CO 4 Frank Craig, Ginnett's Circus, Newcastle

04.10.02 Frank Childs W RSC 3 Joe Walcott, Chicago. *Childs was still generally recognised as the champion.*

21.10.02 Jack Johnson W CO 12 Frank Childs, Los Angeles

11.12.02 Denver Ed Martin ND-W PTS 6 Bob Armstrong, Philadelphia

03.02.03 Jack Johnson W PTS 20 Denver Ed Martin, Los Angeles

27.02.03 Jack Johnson W PTS 20 Sam McVey, Los Angeles

11.05.03 Jack Johnson ND-W CO 3 Joe Butler, Philadelphia

27.10.03 Jack Johnson W PTS 20 Sam McVey, Los Angeles

16.02.04 Jack Johnson ND-W PTS 6 Black Bill, Philadelphia

22.04.04 Jack Johnson W CO 20 Sam McVey, San Francisco

02.06.04 Jack Johnson W PTS 6 Frank Childs, Chicago

18.10.04 Jack Johnson W CO 2 Denver Ed Martin, Los Angeles

03.05.05 Jack Johnson ND-W CO 4 Black Bill, Philadelphia

09.05.05 Jack Johnson ND-W CO 3 Walter Johnson, Philadelphia

19.05.05 Jack Johnson ND-W PTS 6 Joe Jeannette, Philadelphia

13.07.05 Jack Johnson ND-W CO 3 Morris Harris, Philadelphia

13.07.05 Jack Johnson ND-W PTS 6 Black Bill, Philadelphia

25.11.05 Jack Johnson ND-L DIS 2 Joe Jeannette, Philadelphia. *Although Johnson was disqualified, he remained the leading black heavyweight.*

01.12.05 Jack Johnson W PTS 12 Young Peter Jackson, Baltimore

02.12.05 Jack Johnson ND-W PTS 6 Joe Jeannette, Philadelphia

16.01.06 Jack Johnson ND-W PTS 3 Joe Jeannette, New York City

14.03.06 Jack Johnson W PTS 15 Joe Jeannette, Baltimore

19.04.06 Jack Johnson ND-W CO 7 Black Bill, Wilkes Barre

26.04.06 Jack Johnson W PTS 15 Sam Langford, Chelsea

20.09.06 Jack Johnson ND-W PTS 6 Joe Jeannette, Philadelphia

26.11.06 Jack Johnson DREW 10 Joe Jeannette, Portland

09.12.06 Jack Johnson ND-W PTS 3 Joe Jeannette, New York City

19.02.07 Jack Johnson W CO 1 Peter Felix, Sydney

03.01.08 Jack Johnson ND-DREW 3 Joe Jeannette, New York City. *On Johnson becoming world champion on 26 December 1908, and losing interest in the coloured title, the leading French promoters matched McVey against Jeannette at the Cirque de Paris for what many considered to be a "black" title fight.*

20.02.09 Sam McVey W PTS 20 Joe Jeannette, Paris

09.04.09 Sam McVey W CO 2 Billy Warren, Paris

17.04.09 Joe Jeannette W RTD 49 Sam McVey, Paris

13.07.09 Sam Langford ND-W PTS 6 Klondike Haines, Pittsburgh. *Langford was now claiming the title after Johnson had refused to meet him under the auspices of the NSC.*

28.09.09 Sam Langford W RSC 5 Dixie Kid, Boston

02.11.09 Sam Langford W CO 2 Klondike Haines, Boston

11.12.09 Joe Jeannette DREW 30 Sam McVey, Paris

10.01.10 Sam Langford W CO 3 Dixie Kid, Memphis

14.05.10 Sam Langford ND-W PTS 6 Battling Jim Johnson, Philadelphia

24.05.10 Joe Jeannette W RSC 3 Andrew Morris, Boston

01.07.10 Joe Jeannette ND-W PTS 10 Morris Harris, New York City

The legendary Jack Johnson

06.09.10 Sam Langford W PTS 15 Joe Jeannette, Boston. *Following his victory, Langford was generally recognised as the "black" champion.*

10.11.10 Sam Langford W CO 2 Jeff Clarke, Joplin

06.12.10 Sam Langford W CO 2 Morris Harris, Boston

10.01.11 Sam Langford W PTS 12 Joe Jeannette, Boston

01.04.11 Sam Langford DREW 20 Sam McVey, Paris

05.09.11 Sam Langford ND-DREW 10 Joe Jeannette, New York City

26.12.11 Sam McVey W PTS 20 Sam Langford, Sydney

08.04.12 Sam Langford W PTS 20 Sam McVey, Sydney

03.08.12 Sam Langford W PTS 20 Sam McVey, Sydney

09.10.12 Sam Langford W RSC 11 Sam McVey, Perth

26.12.12 Sam Langford W CO 13 Sam McVey, Sydney

24.03.13 Sam Langford DREW 20 Sam McVey, Brisbane

09.09.13 Sam Langford ND-W CO 1 John Lester Johnson, New York City

03.10.13 Sam Langford ND-L PTS 10 Joe Jeannette, New York City

20.12.13   Sam Langford W PTS 20 Joe Jeannette, Paris

27.03.14   Sam Langford ND-W PTS 10 Battling Jim Johnson, New York City

15.04.14   Sam Langford W PTS 8 George Cotton, Chattanooga

01.05.14   Harry Wills W PTS 10 Sam Langford, New York

09.06.14   Harry Wills ND-DREW 10 Joe Jeannette, New Orleans

26.11.14   Sam Langford W CO 14 Harry Wills, Los Angeles

06.04.15   Sam Langford ND-W PTS 10 Battling Jim Johnson, New York City

13.04.15   Joe Jeannette W PTS 12 Sam Langford, Boston

27.04.15   Joe Jeannette DREW 12 Sam McVey, Boston

29.06.15   Sam McVey W PTS 12 Sam Langford, Boston. *With Johnson deposed as world champion, the Boston Post said that the winner would be proclaimed as the black champion. This was after Joe Jeannette had recently beaten Langford and drawn with McVey in the same town.*

07.09.15   Harry Wills W PTS 12 Sam McVey, Boston

03.12.15   Harry Wills ND-W PTS 10 Sam Langford, New York City

03.01.16   Harry Wills W PTS 20 Sam Langford, New Orleans

11.02.16   Sam Langford W CO 19 Harry Wills, New Orleans

17.02.16   Sam Langford ND-DREW 10 Sam McVey, New York City

26.02.16   Joe Jeannette ND-W CO 6 Silas Green, Montreal

28.02.16   Sam Langford ND-W PTS 10 Cleve Hawkins, New York City

07.03.16   Sam Langford ND-L PTS 10 Harry Wills, Brooklyn

23.03.16   Sam Langford ND-W RSC 2 Dave Mills, Syracuse

31.03.16   Sam Langford ND-W CO 5 Jeff Clarke, St Louis

07.04.16   Sam Langford ND-L PTS 10 Sam McVey, Syracuse

25.04.16   Sam Langford ND-L PTS 8 Harry Wills, St Louis

02.05.16   Sam Langford ND-DREW 12 Sam McVey, Akron

12.05.16   Sam Langford ND-W CO 7 Joe Jeannette, Syracuse. *This win brought Langford overall leadership of the black heavyweights, although technically Johnson had yet to be beaten for the title.*

12.08.16   Sam Langford DREW 20 Sam McVey, Buenos Aires

30.11.16   Sam Langford ND-L PTS 10 Bill Tate, Syracuse

12.12.16   Sam Langford ND-W CO 12 Battling Jim Johnson, St Louis

01.11.17   Sam Langford W PTS 12 Battling Jim Johnson, Kansas City

25.01.17   Bill Tate W PTS 12 Sam Langford, Kansas City

02.05.17   Sam Langford ND-W CO 6 Bill Tate, St Louis

11.05.17   Sam Langford ND-L PTS 6 Harry Wills, Philadelphia

14.09.17   Sam Langford ND-W PTS 12 Joe Jeannette, Toledo

20.09.17   Sam Langford ND-L PTS 10 Harry Wills, Brooklyn

12.11.17   Sam Langford ND-L PTS 10 Harry Wills, Toledo

17.12.17   Sam Langford ND-W CO 2 Kid Norfolk, Denver

14.04.18   Harry Wills W CO 6 Sam Langford, Panama City

19.05.18   Harry Wills W RSC 7 Sam Langford, Panama City

19.08.18   Harry Wills ND-W RSC 5 Jeff Clarke, Atlantic City

14.09.18   Harry Wills ND-W PTS 6 Jack Thompson, Philadelphia

10.06.19   Harry Wills ND-W PTS 8 John Lester Johnson, Jersey City

04.07.19   Harry Wills ND-W PTS 8 Sam Langford, St Louis

18.08.19   Harry Wills ND-W RSC 4 Jeff Clarke, Syracuse

30.09.19   Harry Wills ND-W PTS 10 Sam Langford, Syracuse

20.10.19   Harry Wills ND-W PTS 8 Joe Jeannette, Jersey City

05.11.19   Harry Wills W PTS 15 Sam Langford, Tulsa

01.01.20   Harry Wills ND-NC 3 Jack Thompson, San Francisco

12.01.20   Harry Wills W PTS 15 Jack Thompson, Tulsa

15.03.20   Harry Wills ND-W CO 3 Andy Johnson, Newark

19.04.20   Harry Wills W PTS 15 Sam Langford, Denver

08.09.20   Harry Wills ND-NC 6 Sam McVey, Philadelphia

17.01.21   Harry Wills W CO 2 Bill Tate, Buffalo

27.01.21   Harry Wills ND-W PTS 10 Sam Langford, Portland

15.02.21   Harry Wills W CO 2 Jeff Clarke, Baltimore

27.05.21   Harry Wills W CO 1 Andy Johnson, Brooklyn

02.07.21   Harry Wills W CO 6 Bill Tate, Long Island

18.11.21   Harry Wills W CO 1 Denver Ed Martin, Portland

25.11.21   Harry Wills NC 5 Jack Thompson, Denver

07.12.21   Harry Wills W PTS 12 Bill Tate, Denver

02.01.22   Harry Wills NC 1 Bill Tate, Portland. *Wills lost his coloured title by disqualification here, according to the Ring Record Book, having flattened Tate after the referee had called for the two men to break, in a fight that was also considered to be a final eliminator for the world title. However, after much discussion, the local Commissioner refused to accept the result because it left a bad taste in the mouth, withheld both mens' pay, and demanded the fight be re-started in four days time.*

06.01.22   Harry Wills DREW 10 Bill Tate, Portland

17.01.22   Harry Wills W PTS 10 Sam Langford, Portland

02.03.22   Harry Wills W CO 2 Kid Norfolk, New York City

29.06.22   Harry Wills ND-W CO 2 Jeff Clarke, Trenton

17.07.22   Harry Wills W CO 3 Jeff Clarke, Winnipeg

21.08.22   Harry Wills ND-W CO 2 Buddy Jackson, Newark

29.08.22   Harry Wills W CO 3 Tut Jackson, Brooklyn

29.09.22   Harry Wills W RSC 12 Clem Johnson, New York City

05.11.23   Harry Wills ND-W CO 4 Jack Thompson, Newark. *After suffering a 13 round disqualification loss at the hands of future world champion, Jack Sharkey, on 12 October 1926, Wills was a spent force among the heavyweights.*

08.11.26   George Godfrey W CO 6 Larry Gains, Buffalo

22.11.26   George Godfrey DNC 10 Bearcat Wright, Portland

05.07.27   George Godfrey W CO 7 Neil Clisby, Los Angeles

21.11.27   George Godfrey ND-W CO 1 Clem Johnson, Atlantic City

15.08.28   Larry Gains W DIS 3 George Godfrey, Toronto

20.12.28   Larry Gains ND-L PTS 10 Cecil Harris, Indianapolis. *Gains moved his base to Europe where the "black" title was of no significance and it would be more than five years before he was involved in a fight of that kind again.*

19.12.30   George Godfrey DREW 10 Bearcat Wright, Atlantic City. *Billed for the "black" American title.*

24.08.31   George Godfrey W CO 2 Cecil Harris, Toronto

05.09.32   George Godfrey W CO 5 Ace Clark, Laredo

31.01.33   George Godfrey W PTS 10 Tiger Jack Fox, Indianapolis

10.03.33   George Godfrey NC 6 Bearcat Wright, Kansas City

09.10.33   Obie Walker W PTS 10 George Godfrey, Philadelphia

20.07.35   Larry Gains W PTS 15 Obie Walker, Leicester. *With Joe Louis making good progress in the pro ranks, and less than two years away from winning the world title, this would be the last "black" title fight of record.*

Harry Wills (seated right) and Jack Dempsey (left) sign to do battle at Benton Harbor, Michigan. Needless to say, the fight never came off

World Champions Since Gloves, 1889-1996

Since I began to carry out extensive research into world championship boxing from the very beginnings of gloved action, I discovered much that needed to be amended regarding the historical listings as we know them, especially prior to the 1920s. However, because I have yet to finalise my researches, although making considerable changes, rest assured that the 1998 Yearbook will, hopefully, introduce even more advanced lists than have ever been published previously. Bearing all that in mind, and using a wide range of American newspapers, the aim has been to discover just who had claims, valid or otherwise. Studying the records of all the recognised champions, supplied by Professor Luckett Davis and his team, fights against all opposition has been analysed to produce the ultimate data. Because there were no boxing commissions as such in America prior to the 1920s, the yardstick used to determine valid claims were victories over the leading fighters of the day and recognition given within the newspapers. Only where that criteria has been met have I adjusted previous information.

Championship Status Code:

AU = Austria; AUST = Australia; CALIF = California; CAN = Canada; CLE = Cleveland Boxing Commission; EBU = European Boxing Union; FR = France; GB = Great Britain; IBF = International Boxing Federation; IBU = International Boxing Union; ILL = Illinois; LOUIS = Louisiana; MARY = Maryland; MASS = Massachusetts; NBA = National Boxing Association; NY = New York; PEN = Pennsylvania; SA = South Africa; TBC = Territorial Boxing Commission; USA = United States; WBA = World Boxing Association; WBC = World Boxing Council; WBO = World Boxing Organisation.

Champions in **bold** are accorded universal recognition.

* Undefeated champions (Does not include men who forfeited titles).

Title Holder	Birthplace	Tenure	Status
M. Flyweight (105 lbs)			
Kyung-Yung Lee*	S Korea	1987-1988	IBF
Hiroki Ioka	Japan	1987-1988	WBC
Silvio Gamez*	Venezuela	1988-1989	WBA
Samuth Sithnaruepol	Thailand	1988-1989	IBF
Napa Kiatwanchai	Thailand	1988-1989	WBC
Bong-Jun Kim	S Korea	1989-1991	WBA
Nico Thomas	Indonesia	1989	IBF
Rafael Torres	Dom Republic	1989-1992	WBO
Eric Chavez	Philippines	1989-1990	IBF
Jum-Hwan Choi	S Korea	1989-1990	WBC
Hideyuki Ohashi	Japan	1990	WBC
Fahlan Lukmingkwan	Thailand	1990-1992	IBF
Ricardo Lopez	Mexico	1990-	WBC
Hi-Yon Choi	S Korea	1991-1992	WBA
Manny Melchor	Philippines	1992	IBF
Hideyuki Ohashi	Japan	1992-1993	WBA
Ratanapol Sowvoraphin	Thailand	1992-1996	IBF
Chana Porpaoin	Thailand	1993-1995	WBA
Paul Weir*	Scotland	1993-1994	WBO
Alex Sanchez	Puerto Rico	1993-	WBO
Rosendo Alvarez	Nicaragua	1995-	WBA
Ratanapol Sowvoraphin	Thailand	1996-	IBF
L. Flyweight (108 lbs)			
Franco Udella	Italy	1975	WBC
Jaime Rios	Panama	1975-1976	WBA
Luis Estaba	Venezuela	1975-1978	WBC
Juan Guzman	Dom Republic	1976	WBA
Yoko Gushiken	Japan	1976-1981	WBA
Freddie Castillo	Mexico	1978	WBC
Sor Vorasingh	Thailand	1978	WBC
Sun-Jun Kim	S Korea	1978-1980	WBC
Shigeo Nakajima	Japan	1980	WBC
Hilario Zapata	Panama	1980-1982	WBC
Pedro Flores	Mexico	1981	WBA
Hwan-Jin Kim	S Korea	1981	WBA
Katsuo Tokashiki	Japan	1981-1983	WBA
Amado Ursua	Mexico	1982	WBC
Tadashi Tomori	Japan	1982	WBC
Hilario Zapata	Panama	1982-1983	WBC
Jung-Koo Chang*	S Korea	1983-1988	WBC

Title Holder	Birthplace	Tenure	Status
Lupe Madera	Mexico	1983-1984	WBA
Dodie Penalosa	Philippines	1983-1986	IBF
Francisco Quiroz	Dom Republic	1984-1985	WBA
Joey Olivo	USA	1985	WBA
Myung-Woo Yuh	S Korea	1985-1991	WBA
Juan-Hwan Choi	S Korea	1987-1988	IBF
Tacy Macalos	Philippines	1988-1989	IBF
German Torres	Mexico	1988-1989	WBC
Yul-Woo Lee	S Korea	1989	WBC
Muangchai Kitikasem	Thailand	1989-1990	IBF
Jose de Jesus	Puerto Rico	1989-1992	WBO
Humberto Gonzalez	Mexico	1989-1990	WBC
Michael Carbajal	USA	1990-1993	IBF
Rolando Pascua	Philippines	1990-1991	WBC
Melchor Cob Castro	Mexico	1991	WBC
Humberto Gonzalez	Mexico	1991-1993	WBC
Hiroki Ioka	Japan	1991-1992	WBA
Josue Camacho	Puerto Rico	1992-1994	WBO
Myung-Woo Yuh*	S Korea	1992-1993	WBA
Michael Carbajal	USA	1993-1994	IBF/WBC
Silvio Gamez	Venezuela	1993-1995	WBA
Humberto Gonzalez	Mexico	1994-1995	WBC/IBF
Michael Carbajal*	USA	1994	WBO
Paul Weir	Scotland	1994-1995	WBO
Hi-Yong Choi	S Korea	1995-1996	WBA
Saman Sorjaturong	Thailand	1995	WBC/IBF
Jacob Matlala	South Africa	1995-	WBO
Saman Sorjaturong	Thailand	1995-	WBC
Carlos Murillo	Panama	1996	WBA
Michael Carbajal	USA	1996-	IBF
Keiji Yamaguchi	Japan	1996-	WBA
Flyweight (112 lbs)			
Sid Smith	England	1913	GB/IBU
Bill Ladbury	England	1913-1914	GB/IBU
Percy Jones	Wales	1914	GB/IBU
Tancy Lee	Scotland	1915	GB/IBU
Joe Symonds	England	1915-1916	GB/IBU
Jimmy Wilde	Wales	1916	GB/IBU
Jimmy Wilde	Wales	1916-1923	
Pancho Villa*	Philippines	1923-1925	
Fidel la Barba*	USA	1925-1927	

WORLD CHAMPIONS SINCE GLOVES, 1889-1996

Title Holder	Birthplace	Tenure	Status
Johnny McCoy	USA	1927-1928	CALIF
Izzy Schwartz	USA	1927-1929	NY
Frenchy Belanger	Canada	1927-1928	NBA
Newsboy Brown	Russia	1928	CALIF
Frankie Genaro	USA	1928-1929	NBA
Johnny Hill	Scotland	1928-1929	GB/CALIF
Emile Pladner	France	1929	NBA/IBU
Frankie Genaro	USA	1929-1931	NBA/IBU
Midget Wolgast	USA	1930-1935	NY
Young Perez	Tunisia	1931-1932	NBA/IBU
Jackie Brown	England	1932-1935	NBA/IBU
Benny Lynch	Scotland	1935-1937	GB/NBA
Small Montana	Philippines	1935-1937	NY/CALIF
Valentin Angelmann	France	1936-1938	IBU
Peter Kane*	England	1938-1939	
Little Dado	Philippines	1938-1939	CALIF
Little Dado	Philippines	1939-1943	NBA/CALIF
Jackie Paterson	Scotland	1943-1947	
Jackie Paterson	Scotland	1947-1948	GB/NY
Rinty Monaghan	Ireland	1947-1948	NBA
Rinty Monaghan*	Ireland	1948-1950	
Terry Allen	England	1950	
Dado Marino	Hawaii	1950-1952	
Yoshio Shirai	Japan	1952-1954	
Pascual Perez	Argentine	1954-1960	
Pone Kingpetch	Thailand	1960-1962	
Fighting Harada	Japan	1962-1963	
Pone Kingpetch	Thailand	1963	
Hiroyuki Ebihara	Japan	1963-1964	
Pone Kingpetch	Thailand	1964-1965	
Salvatore Burruni	Italy	1965	
Salvatore Burruni	Italy	1965-1966	WBC
Horacio Accavallo*	Argentine	1966-1968	WBA
Walter McGowan	Scotland	1966	WBC
Chartchai Chionoi	Thailand	1966-1969	WBC
Efren Torres	Mexico	1969-1970	WBC
Hiroyuki Ebihara	Japan	1969	WBA
Bernabe Villacampo	Philippines	1969-1970	WBA
Chartchai Chionoi	Thailand	1970	WBC
Berkerk Chartvanchai	Thailand	1970	WBA
Masso Ohba*	Japan	1970-1973	WBA
Erbito Salavarria	Philippines	1970-1971	WBC
Betulio Gonzalez	Venezuela	1972	WBC
Venice Borkorsor*	Thailand	1972-1973	WBC
Chartchai Chionoi	Thailand	1973-1974	WBA
Betulio Gonzalez	Venezuela	1973-1974	WBC
Shoki Oguma	Japan	1974-1975	WBC
Susumu Hanagata	Japan	1974-1975	WBA
Miguel Canto	Mexico	1975-1979	WBC
Erbito Salavarria	Philippines	1975-1976	WBA
Alfonso Lopez	Panama	1976	WBA
Guty Espadas	Mexico	1976-1978	WBA
Betulio Gonzalez	Venezuela	1978-1979	WBA
Chan-Hee Park	S Korea	1979-1980	WBC
Luis Ibarra	Panama	1979-1980	WBA
Tae-Shik Kim	S Korea	1980	WBA
Shoji Oguma	Japan	1980-1981	WBC
Peter Mathebula	S Africa	1980-1981	WBA
Santos Lacial	Argentine	1981	WBA
Antonio Avelar	Mexico	1981-1982	WBC
Luis Ibarra	Panama	1981	WBA
Juan Herrera	Mexico	1981-1982	WBA
Prudencio Cardona	Colombia	1982	WBC
Santos Laciar*	Argentine	1982-1985	WBA
Freddie Castillo	Mexico	1982	WBC
Eleonicio Mercedes	Dom Republic	1982-1983	WBC
Charlie Magri	Tunisia	1983	WBC
Frank Cedeno	Philippines	1983-1984	WBC
Soon-Chun Kwon	S Korea	1983-1985	IBF
Koji Kobayashi	Japan	1984	WBC
Gabriel Bernal	Mexico	1984	WBC

Title Holder	Birthplace	Tenure	Status
Sot Chitalada	Thailand	1984-1988	WBC
Hilario Zapata	Panama	1985-1987	WBA
Chong-Kwan Chung	S Korea	1985-1986	IBF
Bi-Won Chung	S Korea	1986	IBF
Hi-Sup Shin	S Korea	1986-1987	IBF
Fidel Bassa	Colombia	1987-1989	WBA
Dodie Penalosa	Philippines	1987	IBF
Chang-Ho Choi	S Korea	1987-1988	IBF
Rolando Bohol	Philippines	1988	IBF
Yong-Kang Kim	S Korea	1988-1989	WBC
Elvis Alvarez*	Colombia	1989	WBO
Duke McKenzie	England	1988-1989	IBF
Sot Chitalada	Thailand	1989-1991	WBC
Dave McAuley	Ireland	1989-1992	IBF
Jesus Rojas	Venezuela	1989-1990	WBA
Yul-Woo Lee	S Korea	1990	WBA
Isidro Perez	Mexico	1990-1992	WBO
Yukihito Tamakuma	Japan	1990	WBA
Muangchai Kitikasem	Thailand	1991-1992	WBC
Elvis Alvarez	Colombia	1991	WBA
Yong-Kang Kim	S Korea	1991-1992	WBA
Pat Clinton	Scotland	1992-1993	WBO
Rodolfo Blanco	Colombia	1992	IBF
Yuri Arbachakov	Russia	1992-	WBC
Aquiles Guzman	Venezuela	1992	WBA
Pichit Sitbangprachan*	Thailand	1992-1994	IBF
David Griman	Venezuela	1992-1994	WBA
Jacob Matlala	S Africa	1993-1995	WBO
Saen Sowploenchit	Thailand	1994-	WBA
Alberto Jimenez	Mexico	1995-	WBO
Francisco Tejedor	Colombia	1995	IBF
Danny Romero*	USA	1995-1996	IBF
Mark Johnson	USA	1996-	IBF

S. Flyweight (115 lbs)

Title Holder	Birthplace	Tenure	Status
Rafael Orono	Venezuela	1980-1981	WBC
Chul-Ho Kim	S Korea	1981-1982	WBC
Gustavo Ballas	Argentine	1981	WBA
Rafael Pedroza	Panama	1981-1982	WBA
Jiro Watanabe	Japan	1982-1984	WBA
Rafael Orono	Venezuela	1982-1983	WBC
Payao Poontarat	Thailand	1983-1984	WBC
Joo-Do Chun	S Korea	1983-1985	IBF
Jiro Watanabe	Japan	1984-1986	WBA
Elly Pical	Indonesia	1985-1986	IBF
Kaosai Galaxy*	Thailand	1984-1991	WBA
Cesar Polanco	Dom Republic	1986	IBF
Gilberto Roman	Mexico	1986-1987	WBC
Elly Pical	Indonesia	1986-1987	IBF
Santos Laciar	Argentine	1987	WBC
Tae-Il Chang	S Korea	1987	IBF
Jesus Rojas	Colombia	1987-1988	WBC
Elly Pical	Indonesia	1987-1989	IBF
Gilberto Roman	Mexico	1988-1989	WBC
Jose Ruiz	Puerto Rico	1989-1992	WBO
Juan Polo Perez	Colombia	1989-1990	IBF
Nana Yaw Konadu	Ghana	1989-1990	WBC
Sung-Il Moon	S Korea	1990-1993	WBC
Robert Quiroga	USA	1990-1993	IBF
Jose Quirino	Mexico	1992	WBO
Katsuya Onizuka	Japan	1992-1994	WBA
Johnny Bredahl*	Denmark	1992-1994	WBO
Julio Cesar Borboa	Mexico	1993-1994	IBF
Jose Luis Bueno	Mexico	1993-1994	WBC
Hiroshi Kawashima	Japan	1994-	WBC
Harold Grey	Colombia	1994-1995	IBF
Hyung-Chul Lee	S Korea	1994-1995	WBA
Johnny Tapia	USA	1994-	WBO
Alimi Goitia	Venezuela	1995-	WBA
Carlos Salazar	Argentine	1995-1996	IBF
Harold Grey	Colombia	1996-	IBF

Title Holder	Birthplace	Tenure	Status	Title Holder	Birthplace	Tenure	Status
Bantamweight (118 lbs)				Lou Salica	USA	1942	NY
Billy Plimmer	England	1892-1895		Manuel Ortiz	USA	1942	NY/NBA
Pedlar Palmer	England	1895-1899		Kui Kong Young	Hawaai	1943	TBC
Terry McGovern*	USA	1899-1900		Rush Dalma	Philippines	1943-1945	TBC
Pedlar Palmer	England	1900		**Manuel Ortiz**	USA	1945-1947	
Danny Dougherty	USA	1900-1901		**Harold Dade**	USA	1947	
Harry Ware	England	1900-1902	GB	**Manuel Ortiz**	USA	1947-1950	
Harry Harris	USA	1901		**Vic Toweel**	S Africa	1950-1952	
Kid McFadden	USA	1901		**Jimmy Carruthers***	Australia	1952-1954	
Danny Dougherty	USA	1901		**Robert Cohen**	Algeria	1954	
Harry Forbes	USA	1901-1903	USA	Robert Cohen	Algeria	1954-1956	NY/EBU
Andrew Tokell	England	1902	GB	Raton Macias	Mexico	1955-1957	NBA
Harry Ware	England	1902	GB	Mario D'Agata	Italy	1956-1957	NY/ EBU
Joe Bowker	England	1902-1904	GB	Alphonse Halimi	Algeria	1957	NY/EBU
Frankie Neil	USA	1903-1904	USA	**Alphonse Halimi**	Algeria	1957-1959	
Joe Bowker*	England	1904-1905		**Joe Becerra***	Mexico	1959-1960	
Jimmy Walsh	USA	1905-1911		Alphonse Halimi	Algeria	1960-1961	EBU
Owen Moran	England	1907	GB	Eder Jofre	Brazil	1960-1962	NBA
Digger Stanley	England	1909-1912	GB	Johnny Caldwell	Ireland	1961-1962	EBU
Monte Attell	USA	1909-1910		**Eder Jofre**	Brazil	1962-1965	
Frankie Conley	Italy	1910-1911	USA	**Fighting Harada**	Japan	1965-1968	
Johnny Coulon	Canada	1911-1914	USA	**Lionel Rose**	Australia	1968-1969	
Charles Ledoux	France	1912-1913	GB/IBU	**Ruben Olivares**	Mexico	1969-1970	
Eddie Campi	USA	1913-1914	IBU	**Chuchu Castillo**	Mexico	1970-1971	
Kid Williams	Denmark	1914	IBU	**Ruben Olivares**	Mexico	1971-1972	
Kid Williams	Denmark	1914-1915		**Rafael Herrera**	Mexico	1972	
Kid Williams	Denmark	1915-1917		**Enrique Pinder**	Panama	1972	
Johnny Ertle	USA	1915-1918		Enrique Pinder	Panama	1972-1973	WBC
Pete Herman	USA	1917-1919		Romeo Anaya	Mexico	1973	WBA
Pal Moore	USA	1918-1919		Rafael Herrera	Mexico	1973-1974	WBC
Pete Herman	USA	1919-1920		Arnold Taylor	S Africa	1973-1974	WBA
Joe Lynch	USA	1920-1921		Soo-Hwan Hong	S Korea	1974-1975	WBA
Pete Herman	USA	1921		Rodolfo Martinez	Mexico	1974-1976	WBC
Johnny Buff	USA	1921-1922		Alfonso Zamora	Mexico	1975-1977	WBA
Joe Lynch	USA	1922-1923		Carlos Zarate	Mexico	1976-1979	WBC
Joe Lynch	USA	1923-1924	NBA	Jorge Lujan	Panama	1977-1980	WBA
Joe Burman	England	1923	NY	Lupe Pintor*	Mexico	1979-1983	WBC
Abe Goldstein	USA	1923-1924	NY	Julian Solis	Puerto Rico	1980	WBA
Joe Lynch	USA	1924		Jeff Chandler	USA	1980-1984	WBA
Abe Goldstein	USA	1924		Albert Davila	USA	1983-1985	WBC
Eddie Martin	USA	1924-1925		Richard Sandoval	USA	1984-1986	WBA
Charlie Rosenberg	USA	1925-1927		Satoshi Shingaki	Japan	1984-1985	IBF
Bud Taylor*	USA	1927-1928	NBA	Jeff Fenech*	Australia	1985-1987	IBF
Teddy Baldock	England	1927		Daniel Zaragoza	Mexico	1985	WBC
Willie Smith	S Africa	1927-1928		Miguel Lora	Colombia	1985-1988	WBC
Bushy Graham*	Italy	1928-1929	NY	Gaby Canizales	USA	1986	WBA
Al Brown	Panama	1929-1931	NY/IBU	Bernardo Pinango*	Venezuela	1986-1987	WBA
Pete Sanstol	Norway	1931	CAN	Takuya Muguruma	Japan	1987	WBA
Al Brown	Panama	1931-1932		Kelvin Seabrooks	USA	1987-1988	IBF
Al Brown	Panama	1932-1934	NY/NBA/IBU	Chan-Yung Park	S Korea	1987	WBA
Speedy Dado	Philippines	1933	CALIF	Wilfredo Vasquez	Puerto Rico	1987-1988	WBA
Baby Casanova	Mexico	1933-1934	CALIF	Kaokor Galaxy	Thailand	1988	WBA
Al Brown	Panama	1934-1935	NY/IBU	Orlando Canizales*	USA	1988-1994	IBF
Sixto Escobar	Puerto Rico	1934	CAN	Sung-Il Moon	S Korea	1988-1989	WBA
Sixto Escobar	Puerto Rico	1934-1935	NBA	Raul Perez	Mexico	1988-1991	WBC
Lou Salica	USA	1935	CALIF	Israel Contrerras*	Venezuela	1989-1991	WBO
Baltazar Sangchilli	Spain	1935-1938	IBU	Kaokor Galaxy	Thailand	1989	WBA
Lou Salica	USA	1935	NBA/NY	Luisito Espinosa	Philippines	1989-1991	WBA
Sixto Escobar	Puerto Rico	1935-1937	NBA/NY	Greg Richardson	USA	1991	WBC
Tony Marino	USA	1936		Gaby Canizales	USA	1991	WBO
Harry Jeffra	USA	1937-1938	NY/NBA	Duke McKenzie	England	1991-1992	WBO
Sixto Escobar	Puerto Rico	1938	NY/NBA	Joichiro Tatsuyoshi*	Japan	1991-1992	WBC
Al Brown	Panama	1938	IBU	Israel Contrerras	Venezuela	1991-1992	WBA
Sixto Escobar	Puerto Rico	1938-1939		Eddie Cook	USA	1992	WBA
Georgie Pace	USA	1939-1940	NBA	Victor Rabanales	Mexico	1992-1993	WBC
Lou Salica	USA	1939	CALIF	Rafael del Valle	Puerto Rico	1992-1994	WBO
Tony Olivera	USA	1939-1940	CALIF	Jorge Eliecer Julio	Colombia	1992-1993	WBA
Little Dado	Philippines	1940	CALIF	Il-Jung Byun	S Korea	1993	WBC
Lou Salica	USA	1940-1942	NY/NBA	Junior Jones	USA	1993-1994	WBA
Kenny Lindsay	Canada	1941-1943	CAN	Yasuei Yakushiji	Japan	1993-1995	WBC
Manuel Ortiz	USA	1942-1945	NBA	John Michael Johnson	USA	1994	WBA

Title Holder	Birthplace	Tenure	Status
Daorung Chuwatana	Thailand	1994-1995	WBA
Alfred Kotey	Ghana	1994-1995	WBO
Harold Mestre	Colombia	1995	IBF
Mbulelo Botile	S Africa	1995-	IBF
Wayne McCullough	Ireland	1995-	WBC
Veeraphol Sahaprom	Thailand	1995-1996	WBA
Daniel Jimenez	Puerto Rico	1995-1996	WBO
Nana Yaw Konadu	Ghana	1996-	WBA
Robbie Regan	Wales	1996-	WBO

S. Bantamweight (122 lbs)

Title Holder	Birthplace	Tenure	Status
Rigoberto Riasco	Panama	1976	WBC
Royal Kobayashi	Japan	1976	WBC
Doug-Kyun Yum	S Korea	1976-1977	WBC
Wilfredo Gomez*	Puerto Rico	1977-1983	WBC
Soo-Hwan Hong	S Korea	1977-1978	WBA
Ricardo Cardona	Colombia	1978-1980	WBA
Leo Randolph	USA	1980	WBA
Sergio Palma	Argentine	1980-1982	WBA
Leonardo Cruz	Dom Republic	1982-1984	WBA
Jaime Garza	USA	1983-1984	WBC
Bobby Berna	Philippines	1983-1984	IBF
Loris Stecca	Italy	1984	WBA
Seung-In Suh	S Korea	1984-1985	IBF
Victor Callejas	Puerto Rico	1984-1986	WBA
Juan Meza	Mexico	1984-1985	WBC
Ji-Won Kim*	S Korea	1985-1986	IBF
Lupe Pintor	Mexico	1985-1986	WBC
Samart Payakarun	Thailand	1986-1987	WBC
Louie Espinosa	USA	1987	WBA
Seung-Hoon Lee*	S Korea	1987-1988	IBF
Jeff Fenech*	Australia	1987-1988	WBC
Julio Gervacio	Dom Republic	1987-1988	WBA
Bernardo Pinango	Venezuela	1988	WBA
Daniel Zaragoza	Mexico	1988-1990	WBC
Jose Sanabria	Venezuela	1988-1989	IBF
Juan J. Estrada	Mexico	1988-1989	WBA
Fabrice Benichou	Spain	1989-1990	IBF
Kenny Mitchell	USA	1989	WBO
Valerio Nati	Italy	1989-1990	WBO
Jesus Salud	USA	1989-1990	WBA
Welcome Ncita	S Africa	1990-1992	IBF
Paul Banke	USA	1990	WBC
Orlando Fernandez	Puerto Rico	1990-1991	WBO
Luis Mendoza	Colombia	1990-1991	WBA
Pedro Decima	Argentine	1990-1991	WBC
Kiyoshi Hatanaka	Japan	1991	WBC
Jesse Benavides	USA	1991-1992	WBO
Daniel Zaragoza	Mexico	1991-1992	WBC
Raul Perez	Mexico	1991-1992	WBA
Thierry Jacob	France	1992	WBC
Wilfredo Vasquez	Puerto Rico	1992-1995	WBA
Tracy Harris Patterson	USA	1992-1994	WBC
Duke McKenzie	England	1992-1993	WBO
Kennedy McKinney	USA	1992-1994	IBF
Daniel Jimenez	Puerto Rico	1993-1995	WBO
Vuyani Bungu	S Africa	1994-	IBF
Hector Acero-Sanchez	Dom Republic	1994-1995	WBC
Marco Antonio Barrera	Mexico	1995-	WBO
Antonio Cermeno	Venezuela	1995-	WBA
Daniel Zaragoza	Mexico	1995-	WBC

Featherweight (126 lbs)

Title Holder	Birthplace	Tenure	Status
Billy Murphy	New Zealand	1890-1893	
George Dixon	Canada	1890-1893	
Young Griffo	Australia	1890-1893	
Johnny Griffin	USA	1892-1893	
Solly Smith	USA	1892-1893	
George Dixon	Canada	1893-1896	
Frank Erne	USA	1896-1897	
George Dixon	Canada	1896-1897	

Title Holder	Birthplace	Tenure	Status
George Dixon	Canada	1987	
Solly Smith	USA	1897-1898	
Solly Smith	USA	1898	USA
Ben Jordan	England	1898-1905	GB
Dave Sullivan	Ireland	1898	USA
George Dixon	Canada	1899-1900	USA
Eddie Santry	USA	1899-1900	
Terry McGovern	USA	1900-1901	
Young Corbett II	USA	1901-1904	
Abe Attell	USA	1903-1912	USA
Joe Bowker	England	1905-1907	GB
Jim Driscoll	Wales	1907-1912	GB
Joe Coster	USA	1911	
Joe Rivers	Mexico	1911	
Johnny Kilbane	USA	1911-1913	
Jim Driscoll*	Wales	1912-1913	GB/IBU
Johnny Kilbane	USA	1913-1922	
Johnny Kilbane	USA	1922-1923	NBA
Johnny Dundee	Italy	1922-1923	NY
Eugene Criqui	France	1923	
Johnny Dundee*	Italy	1923-1924	
Kid Kaplan*	Russia	1925-1926	
Honeyboy Finnegan	USA	1926-1927	MASS
Benny Bass	Russia	1927-1928	NBA
Tony Canzoneri	USA	1927-1928	NY
Tony Canzoneri	USA	1928	
Andre Routis	France	1928-1929	
Bat Battalino	USA	1929-1932	
Tommy Paul	USA	1932-1933	NBA
Kid Chocolate*	Cuba	1932-1933	NY
Baby Arizmendi	Mexico	1932-1933	CALIF
Freddie Miller	USA	1933-1936	NBA
Baby Arizmendi	Mexico	1934-1936	NY
Baby Arizmendi	Mexico	1935-1936	NY/MEX
Petey Sarron	USA	1936-1937	NBA
Henry Armstrong	USA	1936-1937	CALIF
Mike Belloise	USA	1936	NY
Maurice Holtzer	France	1937-1938	IBU
Henry Armstrong*	USA	1937-1938	NBA/NY/CALIF
Leo Rodak	USA	1938	MARY
Leo Rodak	USA	1938-1939	NBA
Joey Archibald	USA	1938-1939	NY
Joey Archibald	USA	1939-1940	
Joey Archibald	USA	1940	NY
Jimmy Perrin	USA	1940	LOUIS
Harry Jeffra	USA	1940-1941	NY/MARY
Petey Scalzo	USA	1940-1941	NBA
Joey Archibald	USA	1941	NY/MARY
Richie Lemos	USA	1941	NBA
Chalky Wright	Mexico	1941-1942	NY/MARY
Jackie Wilson	USA	1941-1943	NBA
Willie Pep	USA	1942-1946	NY
Jackie Callura	Canada	1943	NBA
Phil Terranova	USA	1943-1944	NBA
Sal Bartolo	USA	1944-1946	NBA
Willie Pep	USA	1946-1948	
Sandy Saddler	USA	1948-1949	
Willie Pep	USA	1949-1950	
Sandy Saddler*	USA	1950-1957	
Hogan Kid Bassey	Nigeria	1957-1959	
Davey Moore	USA	1959-1963	
Sugar Ramos	Cuba	1963-1964	
Vicente Saldivar*	Mexico	1964-1967	
Raul Rojas	USA	1967-1968	WBA
Howard Winstone	Wales	1968	WBC
Johnny Famechon	France	1968-1969	AUST
Jose Legra	Cuba	1968-1969	WBC
Shozo Saijyo	Japan	1968-1971	WBA
Johnny Famechon	France	1969-1970	WBC
Vicente Saldivar	Mexico	1970	WBC
Kuniaki Shibata	Japan	1970-1972	WBC

Title Holder	Birthplace	Tenure	Status
Antonio Gomez	Venezuela	1971-1972	WBA
Clemente Sanchez	Mexico	1972	WBC
Ernesto Marcel*	Panama	1972-1974	WBA
Jose Legra	Cuba	1972-1973	WBC
Eder Jofre	Brazil	1973-1974	WBC
Ruben Olivares	Mexico	1974	WBA
Bobby Chacon	USA	1974-1975	WBC
Alexis Arguello*	Nicaragua	1974-1977	WBA
Ruben Olivares	Mexico	1975	WBC
David Kotey	Ghana	1975-1976	WBC
Danny Lopez	USA	1976-1980	WBC
Rafael Ortega	Panama	1977	WBA
Cecilio Lastra	Spain	1977-1978	WBA
Eusebio Pedroza	Panama	1978-1985	WBA
Salvador Sanchez*	Mexico	1980-1982	WBC
Juan Laporte	Puerto Rico	1982-1984	WBC
Min-Keun Chung	S Korea	1984-1985	IBF
Wilfredo Gomez	Puerto Rico	1984	WBC
Azumah Nelson*	Ghana	1984-1987	WBC
Barry McGuigan	Ireland	1985-1986	WBA
Ki-Yung Chung	S Korea	1985-1986	IBF
Steve Cruz	USA	1986-1987	WBA
Antonio Rivera	Puerto Rico	1986-1987	IBF
Antonio Esparragoza	Venezuela	1987-1991	WBF
Calvin Grove	USA	1988	IBF
Jeff Fenech*	Australia	1988-1989	WBC
Jorge Paez	Mexico	1988-1990	IBF
Maurizio Stecca	Italy	1989-1992	WBO
Louie Espinosa	USA	1989-1990	WBO
Jorge Paez*	Mexico	1990-1991	IBF/WBO
Marcos Villasana	Mexico	1990-1991	WBC
Kyun-Yung Park	S Korea	1991-1993	WBA
Troy Dorsey	USA	1991	IBF
Maurizio Stecca	Italy	1991-1992	WBO
Manuel Medina	Mexico	1991-1993	IBF
Paul Hodkinson	England	1991-1993	WBC
Colin McMillan	England	1992	WBO
Ruben Palacio	Colombia	1992-1993	WBO
Tom Johnson	USA	1993-	IBF
Steve Robinson	Wales	1993-1995	WBO
Gregorio Vargas	Mexico	1993	WBC
Kevin Kelley	USA	1993-1995	WBC
Eloy Rojas	Venezuela	1993-1996	WBA
Alejandro Gonzalez	Mexico	1995	WBC
Manuel Medina	Mexico	1995	WBC
Prince Nassem Hamed	England	1995-	WBO
Luisito Espinosa	Philippines	1995-	WBC
Wilfredo Vasquez	Puerto Rico	1996-	WBA

S. Featherweight (130 lbs)

Title Holder	Birthplace	Tenure	Status
Johnny Dundee	Italy	1921-1923	NY
Jack Bernstein	USA	1923	NBA/NY
Johnny Dundee	Italy	1923-1924	NBA/NY
Kid Sullivan	USA	1924-1925	NBA/NY
Mike Ballerino	USA	1925	NBA/NY
Tod Morgan	USA	1925-1929	NBA/NY
Benny Bass	Russia	1929	NBA/NY
Benny Bass	Russia	1929-1931	NBA
Kid Chocolate	Cuba	1931-1933	NBA
Frankie Klick*	USA	1933-1934	NBA
Sandy Saddler*	USA	1949-1950	NBA
Sandy Saddler*	USA	1950-1951	CLE
Harold Gomes	USA	1959-1960	NBA
Flash Elorde	Philippines	1960-1967	NBA
Yoshiaki Numata	Japan	1967	WBA
Hiroshi Kobayashi	Japan	1967-1971	WBA
Rene Barrientos	Philippines	1969-1970	WBC
Yoshiaki Numata	Japan	1970-1971	WBC
Alfredo Arredondo	Mexico	1971-1974	WBC
Ricardo Arredondo	Mexico	1971-1974	WBC
Ben Villaflor	Philippines	1972-1973	WBA

Title Holder	Birthplace	Tenure	Status
Kuniaki Shibata	Japan	1973	WBA
Ben Villaflor	Philippines	1973-1976	WBA
Kuniaki Shibata	Japan	1974-1975	WBC
Alfredo Escalera	Puerto Rico	1975-1978	WBC
Sam Serrano	Puerto Rico	1976-1980	WBA
Alexis Arguello*	Nicaragua	1978-1980	WBC
Yasutsune Uehara	Japan	1980-1981	WBA
Rafael Limon	Mexico	1980-1981	WBC
Cornelius Boza-Edwards	Uganda	1981	WBC
Sam Serrano	Puerto Rico	1981-1983	WBA
Roland Navarrete	Philippines	1981-1982	WBC
Rafael Limon	Mexico	1982	WBC
Bobby Chacon	USA	1982-1983	WBC
Roger Mayweather	USA	1983-1984	WBA
Hector Camacho*	Puerto Rico	1983-1984	WBC
Rocky Lockridge	USA	1984-1985	WBA
Hwan-Kil Yuh	S Korea	1984-1985	IBF
Julio Cesar Chavez*	Mexico	1984-1987	WBC
Lester Ellis	England	1985	IBF
Wilfredo Gomez	Puerto Rico	1985-1986	WBA
Barry Michael	England	1985-1987	IBF
Alfredo Layne	Panama	1986	WBA
Brian Mitchell*	S Africa	1986-1991	WBA
Rocky Lockridge	USA	1987-1988	IBF
Azumah Nelson	Ghana	1988-1994	WBC
Tony Lopez	USA	1988-1989	IBF
Juan Molina*	Puerto Rico	1989	WBO
Juan Molina	Puerto Rico	1989-1990	IBF
Kamel Bou Ali	Tunisia	1989-1992	WBO
Tony Lopez	USA	1990-1991	IBF
Joey Gamache*	USA	1991	WBA
Brian Mitchell*	S Africa	1991-1992	IBF
Genaro Hernandez	USA	1991-1995	WBA
Juan Molina*	Puerto Rico	1992-1995	IBF
Daniel Londas	France	1992	WBO
Jimmy Bredahl	Denmark	1992-1994	WBO
Oscar de la Hoya*	USA	1994	WBO
James Leija	USA	1994	WBC
Gabriel Ruelas	USA	1994-1995	WBC
Regilio Tuur	Holland	1994-	WBO
Eddie Hopson	USA	1995	IBF
Tracy Harris Patterson	USA	1995	IBF
Yong-Soo Choi	South Korea	1995-	WBA
Arturo Gatti	USA	1995-	IBF
Azumah Nelson	Ghana	1996-	WBC

Lightweight (135 lbs)

Title Holder	Birthplace	Tenure	Status
Jack McAuliffe	Ireland	1890-1894	USA
Dick Burge	England	1891-1896	GB
George Lavigne	USA	1894-1896	USA
George Lavigne	USA	1896-1899	
Frank Erne	Switzerland	1899-1902	
Joe Gans	USA	1902-1908	
Jabez White	England	1902-1905	GB
Jimmy Britt	USA	1902-1905	
Battling Nelson	Denmark	1905-1906	
Battling Nelson	Denmark	1906-1907	
Jimmy Britt	USA	1907-1909	
Battling Nelson	Denmark	1908-1909	
Battling Nelson	Denmark	1909-1910	
Ad Wolgast	USA	1910-1912	
Willie Ritchie	USA	1912	
Freddie Welsh	Wales	1912-1914	GB
Willie Ritchie	USA	1912-1914	USA
Freddie Welsh	Wales	1914-1917	
Benny Leonard*	USA	1917-1925	
Jimmy Goodrich	USA	1925	NY
Rocky Kansas	USA	1925-1926	
Sammy Mandell	USA	1926-1930	
Al Singer	USA	1930	
Tony Canzoneri	USA	1930-1933	

249

Title Holder	Birthplace	Tenure	Status
Barney Ross*	USA	1933-1935	
Tony Canzeroni	USA	1935-1936	
Lou Ambers	USA	1936-1938	
Henry Armstrong	USA	1938-1939	
Lou Ambers	USA	1939-1940	
Sammy Angott	USA	1940-1941	NBA
Lew Jenkins	USA	1940-1941	NY
Sammy Angott*	USA	1941-1942	
Beau Jack	USA	1942-1943	NY
Slugger White	USA	1943	MARY
Bob Montgomery	USA	1943	NY
Sammy Angott	USA	1943-1944	NBA
Beau Jack	USA	1943-1944	NY
Bob Montgomery	USA	1944-1947	NY
Juan Zurita	Mexico	1944-1945	NBA
Ike Williams	USA	1945-1947	NBA
Ike Williams	USA	1947-1951	
Jimmy Carter	USA	1951-1952	
Lauro Salas	Mexico	1952	
Jimmy Carter	USA	1952-1954	
Paddy de Marco	USA	1954	
Jimmy Carter	USA	1954-1955	
Wallace Bud Smith	USA	1955-1956	
Joe Brown	USA	1956-1962	
Carlos Ortiz	Puerto Rico	1962-1965	
Ismael Laguna	Panama	1965	
Carlos Ortiz	Puerto Rico	1965-1968	
Carlos Teo Cruz	Dom Republic	1968-1969	
Mando Ramos	USA	1969-1970	
Ismael Laguna	Panama	1970	
Ken Buchanan	Scotland	1970-1971	
Ken Buchanan	Scotland	1971-1972	WBA
Pedro Carrasco	Spain	1971-1972	WBC
Mando Ramos	USA	1972	WBC
Roberto Duran	Panama	1972-1978	WBA
Chango Carmona	Mexico	1972	WBC
Rodolfo Gonzalez	Mexico	1972-1974	WBC
Guts Ishimatsu	Japan	1974-1976	WBC
Esteban de Jesus	Puerto Rico	1976-1978	WBC
Roberto Duran*	Panama	1978-1979	
Jim Watt	Scotland	1979-1981	WBC
Ernesto Espana	Venezuela	1979-1980	WBA
Hilmer Kenty	USA	1980-1981	WBA
Sean O'Grady	USA	1981	WBA
Alexis Arguello*	Nicaragua	1981-1983	WBC
Claude Noel	Trinidad	1981	WBA
Arturo Frias	USA	1981-1982	WBA
Ray Mancini	USA	1982-1984	WBA
Edwin Rosario	Puerto Rico	1983-1984	WBC
Charlie Brown	USA	1984	IBF
Harry Arroyo	USA	1984-1985	IBF
Livingstone Bramble	USA	1984-1986	WBA
Jose Luis Ramirez	Mexico	1984-1985	WBC
Jimmy Paul	USA	1985-1986	IBF
Hector Camacho*	Puerto Rico	1985-1987	WBC
Edwin Rosario	Puerto Rico	1986-1987	WBA
Greg Haugen	USA	1986-1987	IBF
Vinnie Pazienza	USA	1987-1988	IBF
Jose Luis Ramirez	Mexico	1987-1988	WBC
Julio Cesar Chavez	Mexico	1987-1988	WBA
Greg Haugen	USA	1988-1989	IBF
Julio Cesar Chavez*	Mexico	1988-1989	WBA/WBC
Maurizio Aceves	Mexico	1989-1990	WBO
Pernell Whitaker	USA	1989	IBF
Edwin Rosario	Puerto Rico	1989-1990	WBA
Pernell Whitaker	USA	1989-1990	IBF/WBC
Juan Nazario	Puerto Rico	1990	WBA
Pernell Whitaker*	USA	1990-1992	IBF/WBC/WBA
Dingaan Thobela*	S Africa	1990-1992	WBO
Joey Gamache	USA	1992	WBA
Giovanni Parisi*	Italy	1992-1994	WBO
Tony Lopez	USA	1992-1993	WBA
Miguel Gonzalez*	Mexico	1992-1996	WBC
Fred Pendleton	USA	1993-1994	IBF
Dingaan Thobela	S Africa	1993	WBA
Orzubek Nazarov	Russia	1993-	WBA
Rafael Ruelas	USA	1994-1995	IBF
Oscar de la Hoya	USA	1994-1995	WBO
Oscar de la Hoya*	USA	1995	WBO/IBF
Oscar de la Hoya*	USA	1995-1996	WBO
Phillip Holiday	South Africa	1995-	IBF
Jean-Baptiste Mendy	France	1996-	WBC

L. Welterweight (140 lbs)

Title Holder	Birthplace	Tenure	Status
Pinky Mitchell	USA	1922-1926	
Mushy Callahan	USA	1926-1929	NBA/NY
Mushy Callahan	USA	1929-1930	NBA
Jackie Kid Berg	England	1930-1931	NBA
Jackie Kid Berg	England	1931-1932	
Tony Canzoneri	USA	1931-1932	NBA
Sammy Fuller	USA	1932-1933	
Johnny Jadick	USA	1932	NBA
Johnny Jadick	USA	1932-1933	PEN
Battling Shaw	Mexico	1933	LOUIS
Tony Canzoneri	USA	1933	LOUIS
Barney Ross*	USA	1933-1935	ILL
Maxie Berger	Canada	1939	CAN
Harry Weekly	USA	1941-1942	LOUIS
Tippy Larkin*	USA	1946-1947	NY/NBA
Carlos Oritz	Puerto Rico	1959-1960	NBA
Duilio Loi	Italy	1960-1962	NBA
Eddie Perkins	USA	1962	NBA
Duilio Loi*	Italy	1962-1963	NBA
Roberto Cruz	Philippines	1963	WBA
Eddie Perkins	USA	1963-1965	WBA
Carlos Hernandez	Venezuela	1965-1966	WBA
Sandro Lopopolo	Italy	1966-1967	WBA
Paul Fujii	Hawaii	1967-1968	WBA
Nicolino Loche	Argentine	1968-1972	WBA
Pedro Adigue	Philippines	1968-1970	WBC
Bruno Arcari*	Italy	1970-1974	WBC
Alfonso Frazer	Panama	1972	WBA
Antonio Cervantes	Colombia	1972-1976	WBA
Perico Fernandez	Spain	1974-1975	WBC
Saensak Muangsurin	Thailand	1975-1976	WBC
Wilfred Benitez	USA	1976	WBA
Miguel Velasquez	Spain	1976	WBC
Saensak Muangsurin	Thailand	1976-1978	WBC
Antonio Cervantes	Colombia	1977-1980	WBA
Wilfred Benitez*	USA	1977	NY
Sang-Hyun Kim	S Korea	1978-1980	WBC
Saoul Mamby	USA	1980-1982	WBC
Aaron Pryor*	USA	1980-1983	WBA
Leroy Haley	USA	1982-1983	WBC
Bruce Curry	USA	1983-1984	WBC
Johnny Bumphus	USA	1984	WBA
Bill Costello	USA	1984-1985	WBC
Gene Hatcher	USA	1984-1985	IBF
Aaron Pryor	USA	1984-1985	IBF
Ubaldo Sacco	Argentine	1985-1986	WBA
Lonnie Smith	USA	1985-1986	WBC
Patrizio Oliva	Italy	1986-1987	WBA
Gary Hinton	USA	1986	IBF
Rene Arredondo	Mexico	1986	WBC
Tsuyoshi Hamada	Japan	1986-1987	WBC
Joe Manley	USA	1986-1987	IBF
Terry Marsh*	England	1987	IBF
Juan M. Coggi	Argentine	1987-1990	WBA
Rene Arredondo	Mexico	1987	WBC
Roger Mayweather	USA	1987-1989	WBC
James McGirt	USA	1988	IBF
Meldrick Taylor	USA	1988-1990	IBF

Title Holder	Birthplace	Tenure	Status		Title Holder	Birthplace	Tenure	Status
Hector Camacho	Puerto Rico	1989-1991	WBO		Mickey Walker	USA	1923-1925	NBA
Julio Cesar Chavez	Mexico	1989-1990	WBC		Dave Shade	USA	1923	NY
Julio Cesar Chavez	Mexico	1990-1991	IBF/WBC		Jimmy Jones	USA	1923	NY/MASS
Loreto Garza	USA	1990-1991	WBA		**Mickey Walker**	USA	1925-1926	
Greg Haugen	USA	1991	WBO		**Pete Latzo**	USA	1926-1927	
Hector Camacho*	Puerto Rico	1991-1992	WBO		**Joe Dundee**	Italy	1927-1929	
Edwin Rosario	Puerto Rico	1991-1992	WBA		Joe Dundee	Italy	1929	NY
Julio Cesar Chavez	Mexico	1991-1992	WBC		Jackie Fields	USA	1929	NBA
Rafael Pineda	Colombia	1991-1992	IBF		**Jackie Fields**	USA	1929-1930	
Akinobu Hiranaka	Japan	1992	WBA		**Young Jack Thompson**	USA	1930	
Carlos Gonzalez	Mexico	1992-1993	WBO		**Tommy Freeman**	USA	1930-1931	
Pernell Whitaker*	USA	1992-1993	IBF		**Young Jack Thompson**	USA	1931	
Morris East	Philippines	1992-1993	WBA		**Lou Brouillard**	Canada	1931-1932	
Juan M. Coggi	Argentine	1993-1994	WBA		**Jackie Fields**	USA	1932-1933	
Charles Murray	USA	1993-1994	IBF		**Young Corbett III**	Italy	1933	
Zack Padilla*	USA	1993-1994	WBO		**Jimmy McLarnin**	Ireland	1933-1934	
Jake Rodriguez	USA	1994-1995	IBF		**Barney Ross**	USA	1934	
Frankie Randall	USA	1994	WBC		**Jimmy McLarnin**	Ireland	1934-1935	
Julio Cesar Chavez	Mexico	1994-1996	WBC		**Barney Ross**	USA	1935-1938	
Frankie Randall	USA	1994-1996	WBA		Barney Ross	USA	1938	NY/NBA
Konstantin Tszyu	Russia	1995-	IBF		Felix Wouters	Belgium	1938	IBU
Sammy Fuentes	Puerto Rico	1995-1996	WBO		**Henry Armstrong**	USA	1938-1940	
Juan M. Coggi	Argentine	1996-	WBA		**Fritzie Zivic**	USA	1940-1941	
Giovanni Parisi	Italy	1996-	WBO		Fritzie Zivic	USA	1940-1941	NY/NBA
Oscar de la Hoya	USA	1996-	WBC		Izzy Jannazzo	USA	1940-1942	MARY
					Red Cochrane	USA	1941-1942	NY/NBA
Welterweight (147 lbs)					**Red Cochrane**	USA	1942-1946	
Paddy Duffy	USA	1889-1890			**Marty Servo**	USA	1946	
Tommy Ryan	USA	1891-1894			**Sugar Ray Robinson***	USA	1946-1951	
Mysterious Billy Smith	USA	1892-1894			Johnny Bratton	USA	1951	NBA
Tommy Ryan	USA	1894-1899			Kid Gavilan	Cuba	1951-1952	NBA/NY
Joe Walcott	USA	1897			**Kid Gavilan**	Cuba	1952-1954	
George Lavigne	USA	1897-1899			**Johnny Saxton**	USA	1954-1955	
Mysterious Billy Smith	USA	1898-1900			**Tony de Marco**	USA	1955	
Rube Ferns	USA	1900			**Carmen Basilio**	USA	1955-1956	
Matty Matthews	USA	1900			**Johnny Saxton**	USA	1956	
Eddie Connolly	USA	1900			**Carmen Basilio***	USA	1956-1957	
Matty Matthews	USA	1900-1901			Virgil Akins	USA	1957-1958	MASS
Rube Ferns	USA	1901			**Virgil Akins**	USA	1958	
Joe Walcott	USA	1901-1906			**Don Jordan**	Dom Republic	1958-1960	
Matty Matthews	USA	1902-1903			**Benny Kid Paret**	Cuba	1960-1961	
Rube Ferns	USA	1903			**Emile Griffith**	Virgin Islands	1961	
Martin Duffy	USA	1903-1904			Benny Kid Paret	Cuba	1961-1962	
Jack Clancy	USA	1904-1905	GB		**Emile Griffith**	Virgin Islands	1962-1963	
Honey Mellody	USA	1904			**Luis Rodriguez**	Cuba	1963	
Dixie Kid	USA	1904-1905			**Emile Griffith***	Virgin Islands	1963-1966	
Buddy Ryan	USA	1904-1905			Willie Ludick	S Africa	1966-1968	SA
George Petersen	USA	1905			Curtis Cokes	USA	1966-1968	WBA/WBC
Honey Mellody	USA	1906-1907			Curtis Cokes	USA	1966-1967	WBA
Joe Thomas	USA	1906-1907			Charley Shipes	USA	1966-1967	CALIF
Mike Twin Sullivan	USA	1907-1911			**Curtis Cokes**	USA	1968-1969	
Jimmy Gardner	USA	1907-1908			**Jose Napoles**	Cuba	1969-1970	
Frank Mantell	USA	1907-1908			**Billy Backus**	USA	1970-1971	
Harry Lewis	USA	1908-1910			**Jose Napoles**	Cuba	1971-1975	
Jimmy Gardner	USA	1908-1909			Jose Napoles	Cuba	1972-1974	WBA/WBC
Harry Lewis	USA	1910-1912	GB/FR		Hedgemon Lewis	USA	1972-1974	NY
Jimmy Clabby	USA	1910-1912			**Jose Napoles**	Cuba	1974-1975	
Dixie Kid	USA	1911-1912	GB/FR		Jose Napoles	Cuba	1975	WBC
Ray Bronson	USA	1912-1914			Angel Espada	Puerto Rico	1975-1976	WBA
Marcel Thomas	France	1912-1913	FR		John H. Stracey	England	1975-1976	WBC
Clarence Ferns	USA	1912-1913			Carlos Palomino	Mexico	1976-1979	WBC
Spike Kelly	USA	1913-1914			Pipino Cuevas	Mexico	1976-1980	WBA
Mike Glover	USA	1913-1915			Wilfred Benitez	USA	1979	WBC
Mike Gibbons	USA	1913-1914			Sugar Ray Leonard	USA	1979-1980	WBC
Matt Wells	England	1914-1915	AUSTR		Roberto Duran	Panama	1980	WBC
Kid Graves	USA	1914-1917			Thomas Hearns	USA	1980-1981	WBA
Ted Kid Lewis	England	1915-1916			Sugar Ray Leonard	USA	1980-1981	WBC
Jack Britton	USA	1916-1917			**Sugar Ray Leonard***	USA	1981-1982	
Ted Kid Lewis	England	1917-1919			Don Curry	USA	1983-1984	WBA
Jack Britton	USA	1919-1922			Milton McCrory	USA	1983-1985	WBC
Mickey Walker	USA	1922-1923			Don Curry	USA	1984-1985	WBA/IBF

251

Title Holder	Birthplace	Tenure	Status
Don Curry	USA	1985-1986	
Lloyd Honeyghan	Jamaica	1986	
Lloyd Honeyghan	Jamaica	1986-1987	WBC/IBF
Mark Breland	USA	1987	WBA
Marlon Starling	USA	1987-1988	WBA
Jorge Vaca	Mexico	1987-1988	WBC
Lloyd Honeyghan	Jamaica	1988-1989	WBC
Simon Brown	Jamaica	1988-1991	IBF
Tomas Molinares	Colombia	1988	WBA
Mark Breland	USA	1989-1990	WBA
Marlon Starling	USA	1989-1990	WBC
Genaro Leon*	Mexico	1989	WBO
Manning Galloway	USA	1989-1993	WBO
Aaron Davis	USA	1990-1991	WBA
Maurice Blocker	USA	1990	WBC
Meldrick Taylor	USA	1991-1992	WBA
Simon Brown	Jamaica	1991	WBC/IBF
Simon Brown	Jamaica	1991	WBC
Maurice Blocker	USA	1991-1993	IBF
James McGirt	USA	1991-1993	WBC
Crisanto Espana	Venezuela	1992-1994	WBA
Gert Bo Jacobsen*	Denmark	1993	WBO
Pernell Whitaker	USA	1993-	WBC
Felix Trinidad	Puerto Rico	1993-	IBF
Eamonn Loughran	Ireland	1993-1996	WBO
Ike Quartey	Ghana	1994-	WBA
Jose Luis Lopez	Mexico	1996-	WBO

L. Middleweight (154 lbs)

Title Holder	Birthplace	Tenure	Status
Emile Griffith*	USA	1962-1963	AU
Denny Moyer	USA	1962-1963	WBA
Ralph Dupas	USA	1963	WBA
Sandro Mazzinghi	Italy	1963-1965	WBA
Nino Benvenuti	Italy	1965-1966	WBA
Ki-Soo Kim	S Korea	1966-1968	WBA
Sandro Mazzinghi	Italy	1968-1969	WBA
Freddie Little	USA	1969-1970	WBA
Carmelo Bossi	Italy	1970-1971	WBA
Koichi Wajima	Japan	1971-1974	WBA
Oscar Albarado	USA	1974-1975	WBA
Koichi Wajima	Japan	1975	WBA
Miguel de Oliveira	Brazil	1975	WBC
Jae-Do Yuh	S Korea	1975-1976	WBA
Elisha Obed	Bahamas	1975-1976	WBC
Koichi Wajima	Japan	1976	WBA
Jose Duran	Spain	1976	WBA
Eckhard Dagge	Germany	1976-1977	WBC
Miguel Castellini	Argentine	1976-1977	WBA
Eddie Gazo	Nicaragua	1977-1978	WBA
Rocky Mattioli	Italy	1977-1979	WBC
Masashi Kudo	Japan	1978-1979	WBA
Maurice Hope	Antigua	1979-1981	WBC
Ayub Kalule	Uganda	1979-1981	WBA
Wilfred Benitez	USA	1981-1982	WBC
Sugar Ray Leonard*	USA	1981	WBA
Tadashi Mihara	Japan	1981-1982	WBA
Davey Moore	USA	1982-1983	WBA
Thomas Hearns*	USA	1982-1986	WBC
Roberto Duran*	Panama	1983-1984	WBA
Mark Medal	USA	1984	IBF
Mike McCallum*	Jamaica	1984-1987	WBA
Carlos Santos	Puerto Rico	1984-1986	IBF
Buster Drayton	USA	1986-1987	IBF
Duane Thomas	USA	1986-1987	WBC
Matthew Hilton	Canada	1987-1988	IBF
Lupe Aquino	Mexico	1987	WBC
Gianfranco Rosi	Italy	1987-1988	WBC
Julian Jackson*	Virgin Islands	1987-1990	WBA
Don Curry	USA	1988-1989	WBC
Robert Hines	USA	1988-1989	IBF
John David Jackson*	USA	1988-1993	WBO

Title Holder	Birthplace	Tenure	Status
Darrin van Horn	USA	1989	IBF
Rene Jacqot	France	1989	WBC
John Mugabi	Uganda	1989-1990	WBC
Gianfranco Rosi	Italy	1989-1994	IBF
Terry Norris	USA	1990-1993	WBC
Gilbert Dele	France	1991	WBA
Vinnie Pazienza*	USA	1991-1992	WBA
Julio Cesar Vasquez	Argentine	1992-1995	WBA
Verno Phillips	USA	1993-1995	WBO
Simon Brown	USA	1993-1994	WBC
Terry Norris	USA	1994	WBC
Vince Pettway	USA	1994-1995	IBF
Luis Santana	Dom Republic	1994-1995	WBC
Pernell Whitaker*	USA	1995	WBA
Gianfranco Rosi	Italy	1995	WBO
Carl Daniels	USA	1995	WBA
Verno Phillips	USA	1995	WBO
Paul Vaden	USA	1995	IBF
Terry Norris	USA	1995	WBC
Paul Jones	England	1995-1996	WBO
Terry Norris	USA	1995-	IBF/WBC
Julio Cesar Vasquez	Argentine	1995-	WBA
Bronco McKart	USA	1996	WBO
Ronald Wright	USA	1996-	WBO

Middleweight (160 lbs)

Title Holder	Birthplace	Tenure	Status
Bob Fitzsimmons	England	1891-1894	
Kid McCoy*	USA	1896-1898	
Tommy Ryan*	USA	1898-1907	
Charley McKeever	USA	1900-1902	GB
Jack O'Brien	USA	1901-1905	GB
Hugo Kelly	USA	1905-1908	
Jack Twin Sullivan	USA	1905-1908	
Stanley Ketchel	USA	1907-1908	
Billy Papke	USA	1908	
Stanley Ketchel	USA	1908	
Billy Papke	USA	1908	
Stanley Ketchel	USA	1908-1910	
Billy Papke	USA	1910-1913	
Stanley Ketchel*	USA	1910	
Hugo Kelly	USA	1910-1912	
Cyclone Johnny Thompson	USA	1911-1912	
Harry Lewis	USA	1911	
Leo Houck	USA	1911-1912	
Jack Dillon	USA	1912	
Frank Mantell	USA	1912-1913	
Frank Klaus	USA	1912-1913	
Georges Carpentier	France	1912	IBU
Jack Dillon	USA	1912-1915	
Eddie McGoorty	USA	1912-1913	
Frank Klaus	USA	1913	IBU
Jimmy Clabby	USA	1913-1914	
George Chip	USA	1913-1914	
Eddie McGoorty	USA	1914	AUSTR
Jeff Smith	USA	1914	AUSTR
Al McCoy	USA	1914-1917	
Jimmy Clabby	USA	1914-1915	
Mick King	Australia	1914	AUSTR
Jeff Smith	USA	1914-1915	AUSTR
Young Ahearn	England	1915-1916	
Les Darcy*	Australia	1915-1917	AUSTR
Mike Gibbons	USA	1916-1917	
Mike O'Dowd	USA	1917-1920	
Johnny Wilson	USA	1920-1922	
Johnny Wilson	USA	1922-1923	NBA
Bryan Downey	USA	1922	OHIO
Dave Rosenberg	USA	1922	NY
Jock Malone	USA	1922-1923	
Mike O'Dowd	USA	1922-1923	NY
Harry Greb	USA	1923-1926	
Tiger Flowers	USA	1926	

Title Holder	Birthplace	Tenure	Status	Title Holder	Birthplace	Tenure	Status
Mickey Walker*	USA	1926-1931		**Jake la Motta**	USA	1949-1950	
Gorilla Jones	USA	1932	NBA	Jake la Motta	USA	1950-1951	NY/NBA
Marcel Thil	France	1932-1937	IBU	Sugar Ray Robinson	USA	1950-1951	PEN
Ben Jeby	USA	1933	NY	**Sugar Ray Robinson**	USA	1951	
Lou Brouillard	Canada	1933	NY/NBA	**Randy Turpin**	England	1951	
Teddy Yarosz	USA	1933-1934	PENN	**Sugar Ray Robinson***	USA	1951-1952	
Vince Dundee	USA	1933-1934	NY/NBA	Randy Turpin	England	1953	EBU
Teddy Yarosz	USA	1934-1935	NY/NBA	**Carl Bobo Olson**	Hawaii	1953-1955	
Babe Risko	USA	1935-1936	NY/NBA	**Sugar Ray Robinson**	USA	1955-1957	
Freddie Steele	USA	1936-1938	NY/NBA	**Gene Fullmer**	USA	1957	
Fred Apostoli	USA	1937-1938		**Sugar Ray Robinson**	USA	1957	
Edouard Tenet	France	1938	IBU	**Carmen Basilio**	USA	1957-1958	
Freddie Steele	USA	1938	NBA	**Sugar Ray Robinson**	USA	1958-1959	
Al Hostak	USA	1938	NBA	Sugar Ray Robinson	USA	1959-1960	NY/EBU
Solly Krieger	USA	1938-1939	NBA	Gene Fullmer	USA	1959-1962	NBA
Fred Apostoli	USA	1938-1939	NY	Paul Pender	USA	1960-1961	NY/EBU
Al Hostak	USA	1939-1940	NBA	Terry Downes	England	1961-1962	NY/EBU
Ceferino Garcia	Philippines	1939-1940	NY	Paul Pender	USA	1962-1963	NY/EBU
Ken Overlin	USA	1940-1941	NY	Dick Tiger	Nigeria	1962-1963	NBA
Tony Zale	USA	1940-1941	NBA	**Dick Tiger**	Nigeria	1963	
Billy Soose	USA	1941	NY	**Joey Giardello**	USA	1963-1965	
Tony Zale	USA	1941-1947		**Dick Tiger**	Nigeria	1965-1966	
Rocky Graziano	USA	1947-1948		**Emile Griffith**	Virgin Islands	1966-1967	
Tony Zale	USA	1948		**Nino Benvenuti**	Italy	1967	
Marcel Cerdan	Algeria	1948-1949		**Emile Griffith**	Virgin Islands	1967-1968	

Terry Downes (left), seen here beating Phil Edwards for the British middleweight title, went on to win the world crown from Paul Pender in 1961

Title Holder	Birthplace	Tenure	Status
Nino Benvenuti	Italy	1968-1970	
Carlos Monzon	Argentine	1970-1974	
Carlos Monzon	Argentine	1974-1976	WBA
Rodrigo Valdez	Colombia	1974-1976	WBC
Carlos Monzon	Argentine	1976-1977	
Carlos Monzon*	Argentine	1977	WBA
Rodrigo Valdez	Colombia	1977-1978	
Hugo Corro	Argentine	1978-1979	
Vito Antuofermo	Italy	1979-1980	
Alan Minter	England	1980	
Marvin Hagler	USA	1980-1987	
Marvin Hagler	USA	1987	WBC/IBF
Sugar Ray Leonard	USA	1987	WBC
Frank Tate	USA	1987-1988	IBF
Sumbu Kalambay	Zaire	1987-1989	WBA
Thomas Hearns	USA	1987-1988	WBC
Iran Barkley	USA	1988-1989	WBC
Michael Nunn	USA	1988-1991	IBF
Roberto Duran	Panama	1989-1990	WBC
Doug de Witt	USA	1989-1990	WBO
Mike McCallum	Jamaica	1989-1991	WBA
Nigel Benn	England	1990	WBO
Chris Eubank*	England	1990-1991	WBO
Julian Jackson	Virgin Islands	1990-1993	WBC
James Toney*	USA	1991-1993	IBF
Gerald McClellan*	USA	1991-1993	WBO
Reggie Johnson	USA	1992-1993	WBA
Gerald McClellan*	USA	1993-1995	WBC
Chris Pyatt	England	1993-1994	WBO
Roy Jones*	USA	1993-1994	IBF
John David Jackson	USA	1993-1994	WBA
Steve Collins*	Ireland	1994-1995	WBO
Jorge Castro	Argentine	1994	WBA
Julian Jackson	Virgin Islands	1995	WBC
Bernard Hopkins	USA	1995-	IBF
Lonnie Bradley	USA	1995-	WBO
Quincy Taylor	USA	1995-1996	WBC
Shinji Takehara	Japan	1995-1996	WBA
Keith Holmes	USA	1996-	WBC
William Joppy	USA	1996-	WBA

S. Middleweight (168 lbs)

Title Holder	Birthplace	Tenure	Status
Murray Sutherland	Scotland	1984	IBF
Chong-Pal Park*	S Korea	1984-1987	IBF
Chong-Pal Park	S Korea	1987-1988	WBA
Graciano Rocchigiani*	Germany	1988-1989	IBF
Fully Obelmejias	Venezuela	1988-1989	WBA
Sugar Ray Leonard*	USA	1988-1990	WBC
Thomas Hearns*	USA	1988-1991	WBO
In-Chul Baek	S Korea	1989-1990	WBA
Lindell Holmes	USA	1990-1991	IBF
Christophe Tiozzo	France	1990-1991	WBA
Mauro Galvano	Italy	1990-1992	WBC
Victor Cordoba	Panama	1991-1992	WBA
Darrin van Horn	USA	1991-1992	IBF
Chris Eubank	England	1991-1995	WBO
Iran Barkley	USA	1992-1993	IBF
Michael Nunn	USA	1992-1994	WBA
Nigel Benn	England	1992-1996	WBC
James Toney	USA	1993-1994	IBF
Steve Little	USA	1994	WBA
Frank Lilles	USA	1994-	WBA
Roy Jones	USA	1994-	IBF
Steve Collins	Ireland	1995-	WBO
Thulani Malinga	South Africa	1996-	WBC

L. Heavyweight (175 lbs)

Title Holder	Birthplace	Tenure	Status
Jack Root	Austria	1903	USA
George Gardner	Ireland	1903	USA
Bob Fitzsimmons	England	1903-1905	USA
Jack Dillon	USA	1914-1916	USA
Battling Levinsky	USA	1916-1920	USA
Georges Carpentier	France	1920-1922	
Battling Siki	Senegal	1922-1923	
Mike McTigue	Ireland	1923-1925	
Paul Berlenbach	USA	1925-1926	
Jack Delaney*	Canada	1926-1927	
Jimmy Slattery	USA	1927	NBA
Tommy Loughran	USA	1927	NY
Tommy Loughran*	USA	1927-1929	
Jimmy Slattery	USA	1930	NY
Maxie Rosenbloom	USA	1930-1931	
Maxie Rosenbloom	USA	1931-1933	NY
George Nichols	USA	1932	NBA
Bob Godwin	USA	1933	NBA
Maxie Rosenbloom	USA	1933-1934	
Bob Olin	USA	1934-1935	
Al McCoy	Canada	1935	CAN
Bob Olin	USA	1935	NY/NBA
John Henry Lewis	USA	1935-1938	NY/NBA
Gustav Roth	Belgium	1936-1938	IBU
Ad Heuser	Germany	1938	IBU
John Henry Lewis*	USA	1938	
Melio Bettina	USA	1939	NY
Len Harvey	England	1939-1942	GB
Billy Conn	USA	1939-1940	NY/NBA
Anton Christoforidis	Greece	1941	NBA
Gus Lesnevich	USA	1941	NBA
Gus Lesnevich	USA	1941-1946	NY/NBA
Freddie Mills	England	1942-1946	GB
Gus Lesnevich	USA	1946-1948	
Freddie Mills	England	1948-1950	
Joey Maxim	USA	1950-1952	
Archie Moore	USA	1952-1960	
Archie Moore	USA	1960-1962	NY/EBU
Harold Johnson	USA	1961-1962	NBA
Harold Johnson	USA	1962-1963	
Willie Pastrano	USA	1963-1965	
Jose Torres	Puerto Rico	1965-1966	
Dick Tiger	Nigeria	1966-1968	
Bob Foster	USA	1968-1971	
Bob Foster	USA	1971-1972	WBC
Vicente Rondon	Venezuela	1971-1972	WBA
Bob Foster*	USA	1972-1974	
John Conteh	England	1974-1977	WBC
Victor Galindez	Argentine	1974-1978	WBA
Miguel Cuello	Argentine	1977-1978	WBC
Mate Parlov	Yugoslavia	1978	WBC
Mike Rossman	USA	1978-1979	WBA
Marvin Johnson	USA	1978-1979	WBC
Victor Galindez	Argentine	1979	WBA
Matt Saad Muhammad	USA	1979-1981	WBC
Marvin Johnson	USA	1979-1980	WBA
Mustafa Muhammad	USA	1980-1981	WBA
Michael Spinks	USA	1981-1983	WBA
Dwight Muhammad Qawi	USA	1981-1983	WBC
Michael Spinks*	USA	1983-1985	
J. B. Williamson	USA	1985-1986	WBC
Slobodan Kacar	Yugoslavia	1985-1986	IBF
Marvin Johnson	USA	1986-1987	WBA
Dennis Andries	Guyana	1986-1987	WBC
Bobby Czyz	USA	1986-1987	IBF
Thomas Hearns*	USA	1987	WBC
Leslie Stewart	Trinidad	1987	WBA
Virgil Hill	USA	1987-1991	WBA
Charles Williams	USA	1987-1993	IBF
Don Lalonde	Canada	1987-1988	WBC
Sugar Ray Leonard*	USA	1988	WBC
Michael Moorer*	USA	1988-1991	WBO
Dennis Andries	Guyana	1989	WBC
Jeff Harding	Australia	1989-1990	WBC
Dennis Andries	England	1990-1991	WBC

254

Title Holder	Birthplace	Tenure	Status
Thomas Hearns	USA	1991-1992	WBA
Leonzer Barber	USA	1991-1994	WBO
Jeff Harding	Australia	1991-1994	WBC
Iran Barkley*	USA	1992	WBA
Virgil Hill	USA	1992-	WBA
Henry Maske	Germany	1993-	IBF
Mike McCallum	Jamaica	1994-1995	WBC
Dariusz Michalczewski	Germany	1994-	WBO
Fabrice Tiozzo	France	1995-	WBC

Cruiserweight (190 lbs)

Title Holder	Birthplace	Tenure	Status
Marvin Camel	USA	1979-1980	WBC
Carlos de Leon	Puerto Rico	1980-1982	WBC
Ossie Ocasio	Puerto Rico	1982-1984	WBA
S. T. Gordon	USA	1982-1983	WBC
Marvin Camel	USA	1983-1984	IBF
Carlos de Leon	Puerto Rico	1983-1985	WBC
Lee Roy Murphy	USA	1984-1986	IBF
Piet Crous	S Africa	1984-1985	WBA
Alfonso Ratliff	USA	1985	WBC
Dwight Muhammad Qawi	USA	1985-1986	WBA
Bernard Benton	USA	1985-1986	WBC
Carlos de Leon	Puerto Rico	1986-1988	WBC
Rickey Parkey	USA	1986-1987	IBF
Evander Holyfield	USA	1986-1987	WBA
Evander Holyfield	USA	1987-1988	WBA/IBF
Evander Holyfield*	USA	1988	
Taoufik Belbouli*	France	1989	WBA
Carlos de Leon	Puerto Rico	1989-1990	WBC
Glenn McCrory	England	1989-1990	IBF
Robert Daniels	USA	1989-1991	WBA
Boone Pultz	USA	1989-1990	WBO
Jeff Lampkin*	USA	1990-1991	IBF
Magne Havnaa*	Norway	1990-1992	WBO
Masimilliano Duran	Italy	1990-1991	WBC
Bobby Czyz	USA	1991-1993	WBA
Anaclet Wamba	France	1991-1995	WBC
James Warring	USA	1991-1992	IBF
Tyrone Booze	USA	1992-1993	WBO
Al Cole	USA	1992-	IBF
Markus Bott	Germany	1993	WBO
Nestor Giovannini	Argentine	1993-1994	WBO
Orlin Norris	USA	1993-1995	WBA
Dariusz Michalczewski*	Germany	1994-1995	WBO
Ralf Rocchigiani	Germany	1995-	WBO
Nate Miller	USA	1995-	WBA
Marcelo Dominguez	Argentine	1995-	WBC

Heavyweight (190 lbs +)

Title Holder	Birthplace	Tenure	Status
Frank Slavin	Australia	1890-1892	GB/AUST
Peter Jackson	Australia	1892	GB/AUST
James J. Corbett	USA	1892-1895	
James J. Corbett	USA	1895-1897	
Peter Maher	USA	1895-1896	
Bob Fitzsimmons	England	1896	
Bob Fitzsimmons	England	1897-1899	
James J. Jeffries*	USA	1899-1905	
Marvin Hart	USA	1905-1906	
Jack O'Brien	USA	1905-1906	
Tommy Burns	Canada	1906-1908	
Jack Johnson	USA	1908-1912	
Jack Johnson	USA	1912-1915	
Luther McCarty	USA	1913	
Arthur Pelkey	Canada	1913-1914	
Gunboat Smith	USA	1914	
Georges Carpentier	France	1914	
Jess Willard	USA	1915-1919	
Jack Dempsey	USA	1919-1926	
Gene Tunney*	USA	1926-1928	
Max Schmeling	Germany	1930-1932	
Jack Sharkey	USA	1932-1933	

Title Holder	Birthplace	Tenure	Status
Primo Carnera	Italy	1933-1934	
Max Baer	USA	1934-1935	
James J. Braddock	USA	1935	
James J. Braddock	USA	1935-1936	NY/NBA
George Godfrey	USA	1935-1936	IBU
James J. Braddock	USA	1936-1937	
Joe Louis*	USA	1937-1949	
Ezzard Charles	USA	1949-1951	NBA
Lee Savold	USA	1950-1951	GB/EBU
Ezzard Charles	USA	1951	
Jersey Joe Walcott	USA	1951-1952	
Rocky Marciano*	USA	1952-1956	
Floyd Patterson	USA	1956-1959	
Ingemar Johansson	Sweden	1959-1960	
Floyd Patterson	USA	1960-1962	
Sonny Liston	USA	1962-1964	
Muhammad Ali	USA	1964-1965	
Muhammad Ali	USA	1965-1967	WBC
Ernie Terrell	USA	1965-1967	WBA
Muhammad Ali	USA	1967	
Joe Frazier	USA	1968-1970	WBC
Jimmy Ellis	USA	1968-1970	WBA
Joe Frazier	USA	1970-1973	
George Foreman	USA	1973-1974	
Muhammad Ali	USA	1974-1978	
Leon Spinks	USA	1978	
Leon Spinks	USA	1978	WBA
Larry Holmes*	USA	1978-1983	WBC
Muhammad Ali*	USA	1978-1979	WBA
John Tate	USA	1979-1980	WBA
Mike Weaver	USA	1980-1982	WBA
Michael Dokes	USA	1982-1983	WBA
Gerrie Coetzee	S Africa	1983-1984	WBA
Tim Witherspoon	USA	1984	WBC
Pinklon Thomas	USA	1984-1986	WBC
Larry Holmes	USA	1984-1985	IBF
Greg Page	USA	1984-1985	WBA
Tony Tubbs	USA	1985-1986	WBA
Michael Spinks	USA	1985-1987	IBF
Tim Witherspoon	USA	1986	WBA
Trevor Berbick	Jamaica	1986	WBC
Mike Tyson	USA	1986-1987	WBC
James Smith	USA	1986-1987	WBA
Mike Tyson	USA	1987	WBA/WBC
Tony Tucker	USA	1987	IBF
Mike Tyson	USA	1987-1989	
Mike Tyson	USA	1989-1990	IBF/WBA/WBC
Francesco Damiani	Italy	1989-1991	WBO
James Douglas	USA	1990	IBF/WBA/WBC
Evander Holyfield	USA	1990-1992	IBF/WBA/WBC
Ray Mercer	USA	1991-1992	WBO
Michael Moorer*	USA	1992-1993	WBO
Riddick Bowe	USA	1992	IBF/WBA/WBC
Riddick Bowe	USA	1992-1993	IBF/WBA
Lennox Lewis	England	1992-1994	WBC
Tommy Morrison	USA	1993	WBO
Michael Bentt	USA	1993-1994	WBO
Evander Holyfield	USA	1993-1994	WBA/IBF
Herbie Hide	England	1994-1995	WBO
Michael Moorer	USA	1994	WBA/IBF
Oliver McCall	USA	1994-1995	WBC
George Foreman	USA	1994-1995	WBA/IBF
Riddick Bowe*	USA	1995-1996	WBO
George Foreman*	USA	1995	IBF
Bruce Seldon	USA	1995-	WBA
Frank Bruno	England	1995-1996	WBC
Frans Botha	South Africa	1995-1996	IBF
Mike Tyson	USA	1996-	WBC
Michael Moorer	USA	1996-	IBF
Henry Akinwande	England	1996-	WBO

Welcome to the International Boxing Hall of Fame

by Neil Blackburn

On Wednesday, 5 June 1996, I finally made it to the Boxing Hall of Fame in Canastota, New York State. Arriving at the front door with my wife, Kathy, and finding it shut, but hearing voices inside, I knocked heavily until a young lady answered that the building was closed to the public. "But we have come all the way from England", I replied. Then a voice said: "Let them in, I come from Wales". Thus we walked into a boxing mecca.

All around the walls were plaques of the boxers who have been inducted, posters, tickets, and every kind of memorabilia you could possibly think of, including Carlos Ortiz's boxing robe, Flash Elorde's golden boots, Vito Antuofermo's boots and robe, plus an association to a great many more legends. All members who were alive at the time of their inauguration, have had their fists put in plaster casts and made into bronzes, Primo Carnera's being the biggest. Also on display were Willie Pep and Carmen Basilio's "Ring" world championship belts and a Buck belt, which looks a real treasure. The Hall of Fame, apart from selling all the usual T-shirts, baseball hats, etc, has also made available the first edition of the "Boxing Register", which has recently been published. With a short story on each inductee, plus their boxing record, it was certainly appealing.

Back outside and close to the Hall of Fame, alongside the Day Inn, we found a small building called the Carmen Basilio and Billy Backus' Show Case. Here you are surrounded by memorabilia and subject matter on the two former champions, who, incidentally, are close relatives.

On Thursday evening, Kathy and I, along with two other English couples we had met up with, Maureen and Derek Grunhill from Boston (Lincs), and Debbie and Brian Watkins, who run the Gate Hotel, Portobello Road in London, went to the Bar-B-Q at the American Legion. There we met Archie Moore, Carlos Ortiz, Ruben Olivares, Willie Pep, Joe Brown, Ken Norton, and many more "names" – it was great. Aaron Pryor was selling his new book, "Flight of the Hawk", which gives an extraordinary insight into the troubled life of a great fighter, and among the guests, Gene Fullmer and Carmen Basilio were deep in conversation, no doubt discussing their common foe, Sugar Ray Robinson. Having satisfied our hunger well and truly, we retired to Graziano's Bar for a few well earned "Buds". It was there we came across Bob Foster, Norton, Pryor and Moore, who were all so friendly, talking and remembering their fights and careers. This really was a boxing fan's heaven.

The next day started with Gerry Cooney doing a question and answer routine, which was extremely interesting. One of the points he made was that he never regretted "passing up" on Don King (who could blame him), was glad he stayed independent, and really enjoyed his boxing career.

In the evening, we went to Turning State Casino on the Indian Reservation. An amateur boxing show was held in a tent in the car park and, with the rain pouring down outside, every winner was presented with a trophy from one of the legends in attendance. Also on the show, was a bout between two girls aged between 14-15. This was the first time I had ever seen females boxing and I found it tasteless. The girls really went at each other and the loser was extremely upset at the decision, far more so than any defeated male I have come across.

After the boxing, we returned to the Casino to watch the De La Hoya v Chavez fight on a bank of TV screens in the bar. This was the first TV fight I had seen in ten days of travelling through Canada and America, and it was apparent that we in Britain have a lot more boxing available through satellite and cable than our friends on the other side of the Atlantic. Every hotel, or motel, we stayed in, I accessed the TV and went through the channels, but could find no boxing. Talking to several Americans on the subject, the general consensus was that it depended where you lived in the States, but it was not brilliant.

On Saturday morning, we headed for a boxing memorabilia sale at Canastota High School. There, the whole of the main hall was filled to overflow with boxing books, photos, posters, autographs and much more. John, a fan from Rochester, New York, who had a bedroom next to us in our Canastota motel, even bought an IBF world championship belt for $1,200, but, in the main, Americans

The author of this article, Neil Blackburn, meets the lightweight legend, Carlos Ortiz, and his grandchildren

seemed to go more for photos and autographs. Anything from John L. Sullivan to Carlos Zarate was on display, although you had to wonder how genuine they were. Elsewhere, the sale of books varied greatly from one stall to another and it really did pay to shop around, especially when *The Champ Nobody Knew"*, a Sonny Liston book, was selling at $90 in hardback on one stall, while next door it was priced at $250. The best purchase I found was the *"Boxing Record Book, 1996"* published by Fight Fax Inc, selling for $40 against £56 in the UK. My main memories of that morning, however, will be of Jake LaMotta, Gerry Cooney, Wilfred Benitez and Aaron Pryor busy signing autographs, it was certainly a great sight to behold.

That night, Kathy and I were driven by Chuck Emmi to the Banquet of Champions at the Rusty Rail Party House, just outside Canastota. Chuck, one of the nicest people you would wish to meet, helps to run the Graziano Bar and Motel. He also promotes boxing in the area under the name of Title Town Promotions and if you ever get to go to these parts look him up as he loves talking about boxing and is a real gent.

Having entered the banqueting rooms, we were given free drinks of our choice and, although not being seated in the main area, we were made extremely comfortable in the Video Room, where a big screen showed all that was of interest. Although some of our friends sat in the main area, they could not always see what was going on, while we, seated next to Jose Torres' wife, brother and mother, had an excellent view. Among those at the top table were Archie Moore, Jake LaMotta, Floyd Patterson, Joey Maxim, "Bonecrusher" Smith, Bob Foster, Wilfred Benitez, Billy Backus, Carmen Basilio, Gene Fullmer, Carlos Ortiz, Arthur Mercante jnr, Emanuel Steward, Jose Torres, Livingston Bramble, Tony DeMarco, Ken Norton, Christy Martin, Gerry Cooney, Willie Pep, Ruben Olivares, Joe Brown, Buster Mathis jnr, Aaron Pryor, and Dick Diveronica. Many made speeches, but the one by LaMotta was hilarious, his references to his six wives bringing the house down. For us, it was a great thrill to be introduced to Jose Torres by his wife after the meal.

Sunday started at the Fire Station, where we breakfasted with the champs, all of us tucking into pancakes, bacon, egg, sausages and trimmings. Then it was on to the 1.00pm parade. Lasting about an hour, bands, majorettes, fire engines, and floats were followed by the champions in open-topped cars, before we were back at the Hall of Fame for the Induction Ceremony.

After Herb Goldman had introduced the deceased inductees – Kid Williams, William Muldoon, Tommy Burns, Manuel Ortiz, Jack Delaney, Fidel LaBarba, Young Stribling, John Morrissey and Don Parker, it was the turn of more recent big guns. Wilfred Benitez made a speech, aided by Jose Torres; Joe Brown explained what an honour it was for him and how great it was to have taken his boxing career all over the world; an emotional Aaron Pryor, who had lost his mother a few days earlier, praised his manager, Buddy LaRosa, and his friend Ken Hawk;

while Emanuel Steward explained how he would have paid to come to Canastota as he is firstly a boxing fan. And, in what were surely the most sensible words I heard throughout our stay, he went on to say that with so many world champions around these days, future generations will judge boxers not by whether they were world champions, but if they are in the Hall of Fame.

Following the induction we went back to Graziano's, where I unfortunately missed out on a video master piece when Archie Moore started to spar between the tables. The batteries were so flat that I missed the best bit of action of our stay.

Then it was all over. Those few days had provided one of the greatest experiences of my life, something I would not have missed for anything, especially in being able to meet so many great boxers and being able to have a drink and a chat with them. It was wonderful and I can wholeheartedly recommend that every boxing fan should try and get there at least once in their lives.

Former middleweight champion, Jake LaMotta, arrives at the Hall of Fame

Note: The Boxing Hall of Fame was founded in 1984 with a mission to honour and preserve boxing's rich heritage, chronicle the achievements of those who excelled, provide an educational experience for the many visitors and operate the facility in a manner that enhances the image of the sport. If you want details on the subject, write to Hall of Fame Drive, Canastota, New York, USA 13032.

Highlights From the 1995-96 Amateur Season

by David Prior

The message from the Olympics in Atlanta was unmistakably clear. . . the Cubans are still the top amateur boxing nation, with the rest of the world (21 other countries won medals) falling into line behind them. This, despite the last minute defections to the paid ranks in America of their 1992 Olympic bantamweight titleholder, Joel Casamayor, and light-heavyweight, Ramon Garbey.

The Caribbean island collected four gold medals and three silver. Not as good as their seven gold and two silver in Barcelona or the American's record busting nine champions in the 1984 Games boycotted by Cuba and most of the East European boxing nations, but still an impressive performance. It remains to be seen whether they can continue producing this never-ending stream of talent, the average age of their seven finalists in Atlanta being 26, particularly if more of their boxers move over to the pro side.

The European continent, from the Eastern sector, won four gold, via Bulgaria, Hungary, Russia and Ukraine, while there was one each for Africa (Algeria), the Far East (Thailand), the host country (USA) and for Asia (Kazakhstan).

Three of Cuba's gold medal winners had won in Barcelona, with Ariel Hernandez doubling up at middleweight, winning over Turkey's Malik Beyleroglu in the final and the incredible Felix Savon again taking the heavyweight title, beating David Defiagbon (Canada). Defiagbon had previously won welterweight gold in the 1990 Commonwealth Games for Nigeria. Their third 1992 champion, light-welter Hector Vinent, won his second Olympic title, following a win against Oktay Urkal (Germany), with the fourth Atlanta success for Cuba coming from flyweight, Maikvo Romero, who defeated Bolat Dzumadilov (Kazakhstan).

A potential nightmare (no American gold) was avoided with the delivery of one single right-hand punch thrown by light-middleweight David Reid, who was trailing on points in the third round to another Cuban finalist, Alfredo Duvergel. A seemingly points loss for Reid was thus turned into a stoppage win and the whole American nation breathed a sigh of relief!

Cuban welterweight Juan Hernandez's bid for gold in Barcelona was thwarted by Ireland's Michael Carruth and this time it was Oleg Saitov from Russia, who took the decision and gold, leaving Hernandez once again with silver. Strictly speaking, it was Russia's first Olympic boxing title win.

Only two of the 1996 European champions proceeded to the higher level of Olympic gold – light-fly Daniel Petrov (Bulgaria) and Istvan Kovacs (Hungary) at bantamweight – against Mansueto Velasco (Philippines) and Arnaldo Mesa (Cuba), respectively.

Featherweight Somluck Kamsing became Thailand's first ever Olympic champion (winning against Serafim Todorov of Bulgaria) and there was another first-time country win for Algeria when Hocine Soltani bested Tontcho Tontchev, also from Bulgarian, at lightweight.

There was a title winning debut for Kazakhstan (and Vassili Jirov) in the light-heavyweight category, with Seung-Bae Lee (South Korea) in the opposite and losing corner. Jirov was later awarded the Val Barker trophy as "best stylist". Ukraine also made the Olympic record books for the first time when Vladimir Klitchko, at 20, the youngest champion, took the super-heavyweight title. His win in the final against the popular Paea Wolfgram, ended a Tongan dream of Olympic glory.

The two-man squad from Great Britain failed to win a medal, as happened twice before in post-war years, the last time being in Tokyo in 1964. It was the smallest GB entry since 1932 (three boxers in Los Angeles), with David Burke (featherweight) and Fola Okesola (heavyweight) losing in their first bouts to Germany's Falk Huste and Nate Jones, one of America's five bronze medallists, respectively.

It was a similar story for the four boxers from Ireland, with no medals for the eighth time since 1948. It was also their lowest entry since 1932 (when they sent four to Los Angeles, with no entries at all in the 1936 Games).

Heavyweight Cathal O'Grady lost in his first outing to Garth de Silva (New Zealand); flyweight Damaen Kelly won twice before losing to eventual bronze medalist, Bulat Dzumadilov from Kazaghstan in the quarter-finals; Brian Magee (middleweight) also scored two wins, before he lost to Mohamed Bahari (Algeria), another bronze medalist, at the quarter-final stage; and light-welterweight Francis Barrett lost in his second bout to third-place medalist, Fethi Missaoui (Tunisia).

Before Atlanta, the European Senior Championships in Vejle, Denmark (March/April 1996) was the highly competitive arena, not only for medals, but also a chance to qualify for the Olympic Games. After a record breaking 305 bouts, the 33 boxers from England (nine), Ireland (12), Scotland and Wales (six each) won three bronze medals – David Burke (England), Scott Harrison (Scotland) and Damaen Kelly (Ireland). In the end, two boxers from Great Britain and four from Ireland qualified for the Olympics. The Eastern European countries again dominated the championships with three gold for Russia, two for Romania and one each for Bulgaria and Hungary. Germany (three) equalled the Russian tally, with Italy, and the host country, Denmark, completing the gold medals list with one each. A trio of multi-titled champions, Daniel Petrov (Bulgaria) at light-fly, Istvan Kovacs (Hungary) at bantamweight, and light-middle Fransisc Vastag (Romania), added to their already "well-filled" trophy cabinets.

England opened the season with a team event against Holland in Rotterdam in September. Ahead in the senior bouts 4-2, following three draws and two losing U17 bouts, the match finished all square, as did the international against America (4-4) in London in November. There was a 6-5 win over Ireland in Dublin (December) and finally, in February, a comprehensive 7-1 defeat of South Africa in London. In the one outing for the U19s, Germany were beaten 5-4 in Blackpool (January). Ireland travelled to Denmark in October 1995 to lose 8-3 and to Italy for a 6-4 defeat in April, while Scotland lost 5-3 to Norway away from home in November, and it was a similar story in Glasgow in April, when they were again defeated on a similar 5-3 scoreline.

It was a somewhat "slow" scene for international team events with much of the programme focused on the European Championships and Olympic qualificazion, but, in Wales, a squabble between the Welsh ABA and the Welsh Trainers Association led to the cancellation of their entire international fixture list.

The third Liverpool International Festival of Amateur Boxing (June 1996) once again provided a high quality world-class entry, including several Olympic qualifiers, with a record breaking 119 boxers from 20 countries and 101 contests. Australia and Russia (three gold medals each) were the leading nations in Liverpool, followed by Ukraine (two), with England achieving top status at middleweight (Steven Bendall). Canada, the Philippines and Sweden were also on the winner's rostrum. There were silver medals for Carl Wall and John Pearce and bronze for Darrell Easton, David Walker, and Michael Jones, all from England. Scotland's Russell Laing won a silver medal and there was bronze for his countryman, Alex Arthur, and for Grant Briggs from Wales.

In October 1995, England were back in the Tammer tournament in Tampere, Finland – they were last there in 1992 – and David Burke won gold. There were silver medals for Steven Bendall and Matthew Ellis, and bronze for Chris Bessey, Michael Gibbons, Tommy Peacock and Harry Senior.

Before that, in April 1995, Jason Cook from Wales won a bronze medal in a multi-national tournament in Vienna and followed that with a gold medal in the Acropolis Cup in May. There were also medals for Ireland at the same event in Greece – silver for Jim Prior and Willie Valentine, and bronze for Martin Reneghan and Stephen Kirk.

Ireland were also amongst the medals in the Alghero U19 fixture in May 1995 – gold for Cathal O'Grady and bronze for Francis Barrett, Darren Hyland and Eugene Lecumber. And then it was silver for William Egan in the World Military Championships in Italy in September. There were more medals for Ireland in the Wiener Neustadt multi-national in Vienna (October), gold from Neil Gough and Declan Higgins, and silver for Glenn Stephens.

In the June 1995 AIBA ratings, Jason Cook from Wales made the number nine spot at lightweight, while David Burke attained the same ranking (at featherweight) in October.

Two amateur boxing legends, Hungarian Laszlo Papp and Teofilo Stevenson from Cuba, both Olympic triple gold medallists, were among the many notables at the AIBA Congress in Dublin in January 1996, which included celebrations for the half century of the AIBA and the 25th anniversary of the EABA.

All four domestic championship finals were staged in the month of March 1996, starting with England at the National Indoor Arena, Birmingham, when the Liverpool based Gemini club crashed into the senior title stakes in style with first-time ABA champions in Lee Eedle (bantamweight), Tony Mulholland (featherweight) and light-welter Carl Wall. There were seven other debut champions in Birmingham. At light-fly, it was Ronnie Mercer of St Helen Glass, Kelvin Wing (Repton Boys) achieved title status at lightweight, Jawaid Khaliq (Meadows & Ruddington) at welterweight and Scott Dann (Mayflower) in the light-middleweight division. The Wellington middleweight, John Pearce, was another new champion, as was Courtney Fry from Islington Boys, who came top in the light-heavyweight class, and heavyweight, Tony Oakey (Leigh Park). Danny Costello (Hollington), the only 1995 defending champion in the finals, won the flyweight for the third consecutive year and another Londoner, boxing for the Army, Danny Watts, won for the

Lee Eedle (left), from the Gemini club, took the 1996 ABA bantam title after outpointing Londoner, Darrell Easton

Les Clark

The 1996 ABA lightweight title was won by Repton's Kelvin Wing (left), courtesy of a points win over Andy Walsh, one of two Portsmouth University brothers to reach the finals   Les Clark

second time at super-heavyweight, something he had done in 1994. Michael and Andy Walsh, from Portsmouth University, failed to match the 1979 and 1980 brotherly title double of Ray and George Gilbody; Michael losing to Tony Mulholland, while Andy was beaten by Kelvin Wing.

There were six new names for the Welsh ABA record books at the Welsh Institute of Sport, with Darren Fox (light-fly), Jason Kerrigan (bantam), Anthony Fletcher (feather), Michael Spragg (light), Darren Williams (light-middle), and finally, Steven Donaldson (light-heavy). Defending super-heavyweight supremo, Kevin McCormack, won again – a recording breaking ten titles – as did Grant Briggs, with his third in a row at middleweight. The 1995 lightweight title holder, Jason Cook, won for the fourth time, this time at light-welterweight, while last year's light-heavyweight champion, Scott Gammer, moved up to win at heavyweight and the 1992 light-welter titleholder, Jason Williams, completed a 1996 family double by taking the welterweight honours.

It was more of the same as previous years at the National Stadium in Dublin when seven of the 12 Irish champions added to past championships wins, with Damaen Kelly and Neil Gough winning for the fourth time at fly and welterweight, respectively. Defending champions, Jim Prior (light-fly), Adrian Patterson (feather), Declan Higgins (light-middle), Brian Magee (middle), and Stephen Kirk (light-heavy), all won for the second time. And, finally, there were a number of boxers winning a

national title for the first time – Damien McKenna (bantam), Martin Reneghan (light), Francis Barrett (light-welter), Cathal O'Grady (heavy) and Sean Murphy in the super-heavyweight category.

At the Monklands Time Capsule in Coatbridge, Scotland maintained the season's trend of first-time champions; their tally of eight putting them in second place behind England (ten), but ahead of Wales (six) and Ireland (five). Moving up the weight scale from light-fly to bantamweight it was James Smith, Russell Laing and Alex Arthur who were successful debut titleholders. Then came David Stewart (light), Graham McLevy (light-welter), Colin McNeill (welter), James Daley (middle) and Willie Cane (heavy), all first-time champions. The 1989 super-heavyweight champion, John Cowie, took that division for the second time, but two titleholders from 1994, Ronnie McPhee and Alan Wolecki, moved up one weight to succeed at feather and light-middleweight, respectively. From that same year, but moving down a weight, Alex Kelly won at light-heavyweight.

The finals of the inaugural national Senior Novice Championships, Class "A" and "B" – in England – were held at Brent Town Hall in April and although London did not take part, their own title event at York Hall the following month included a new cruiserweight category (81-86 kg) won by Kevin Barrett (St Monicas).

Ricky Mann and Lee Bryan were the "Best Winners" in their respective Class 5 and 6 divisions in the Youth Championship finals, in England, held at the Fox Hollies

The Fisher's David Walker (left) fends off a long left from Carl Wall, the winner and new champion of the 1996 ABA light-welter class
Les Clark

Leisure Centre in Birmingham. The "Best Loser" was Graham Earl (Luton Hightown) who was beaten by Lee Bryan. James Hegney, James Rooney, Craig Skelton and Richard Hatton won Class 6 titles; they had all won Class 5 in 1995. Hegney (silver) and Hatton (bronze) went on to win medals in the 1996 Alghero U19 multi-national tournament in June.

Moving further down the age scale, Irish youngsters continued to do well at international level. In June 1996 they again dominated the Gaelic Games by winning six gold medals in Nova Scotia, Canada; they had also won in 1995 with a remarkable ten golds. In between these two events, Paul Stephens was a gold medallist in the European Youth Championships in Turkey (October 1995), his CIE clubmate, Bernard Dunne, winning a bronze medal. Stephens had also won gold in the lower age group in 1994.

Finishing off the previous season with a win (5-3) and a loss (7-5) to Russia in April 1995 and then a loss (7-6) to Wales in Cardiff in May, England's schoolboys at long last broke a 19 match unbeaten run by Wales by defeating them 11-3 in London in June 1996. The Welsh Schoolboy finals were held in Swansea in February 1996, but for the first time they did not go on to the 49th SABA finals at the Aston Villa Leisure Centre in Birmingham, in March. There, the Dale Youth Club had an excellent day out from London with five champions out of six finalists, Lee Beavis, John Doherty, Martin O'Donnell, Martin Ward and Mark Weatherhead all winning titles, as did Tony Dodson from the Gemini club in Liverpool, who won the senior age group, his fourth schoolboy title. The Schools ABA decided to become a national association within the Amateur Boxing Association of England Limited.

In January 1996, the Boys' Club finals were staged, the first, (Class "A"), being at the Mansfield Leisure Centre where Sean Power achieved "Best Winner" status, with his opponent, Kieran McKeown, from Northern Ireland, selected as the "Best Runner-Up". The "Best Stylist" was Londoner, Tony Chapman. The Class "B" finals, at the Cutler's Hall, Sheffield, saw Scott Miller recognised as the "Best Winner", Terry Rowley the "Best Runner-Up" and Nicky Cook, who lost to Scott Miller, the "Best Stylist". Finally, at the Grosvenor House Hotel, London, Luke Daws was chosen as the "Best Winner" and his opponent, Craig Skelton, the "Best Runner-Up" in the Class "C" finals. The "Best Stylist" was Mark Thompson, while the "Most Courageous" trophy went to Martin Lacey.

Already, the first training camp at Crystal Palace has been held on the first step of the 1996-97 international programme and, further ahead, the Commonwealth Games in 1998 are the mid-point to the next Olympic Games in Sydney, Australia in the year 2000. I wonder how many of our leading boxers during 1995-96 will still be in the amateur ranks and whether the Government and all those involved in all sports, and not just boxing, will finally realise that although money is not everything, regular and sufficient payments for living and training expenses must be part of any package to halt our downward spiral in the international sporting arena.

(David Prior writes on amateur boxing in Boxing News/Amateur Boxing Scene, is the author of *Ringside with the Amateurs* and is the ABAE Press Liaison Officer)

ABA National Championships, 1995-96

Southern Counties v North-East Counties

Southern Counties

Hampshire, Kent, Surrey & Sussex Divisions   Hayling School & the Lakeside Holiday Camp, Hayling Island - 27 January & 3 February

L. Fly: no entries. **Fly:** *final:* N. Bell (Brighton) w pts T. Craig (Basingstoke). **Bantam:** *final:* D. Western (Leigh Park) wo. **Feather:** *semi-finals:* P. Halpin (Brighton) wo, M. Walsh (Portsmouth University) w pts J. Matthews (Onslow): *final:* M. Walsh w pts P. Halpin. **Light:** *quarter-finals:* D. Lavender (Foley) wo, T. Elcock (Camberley) wo, B. Urquhart (Westree) w pts P. Bedford (Basingstoke), A. Walsh (Portsmouth University) w dis 3 R. Cox (Brighton); *semi-finals:* B. Urquhart w pts D. Lavender, A. Walsh w pts T. Elcock; *final:* A. Walsh w pts B. Urquhart. **L. Welter:** *semi-finals:* N. Philpott (Leigh Park) wo, J. Ball (Onslow) w rsc 2 J. Newton (Crawley); *final:* N. Philpott w pts J. Newton - replaced J. Ball. **Welter:** *quarter-finals:* A. Wilkes (Broadstairs) wo, J. Honey (Basingstoke) w pts S. Cullen (Faversham), P. Larner (Bognor) w rsc 1 W. Rothwell (Westree), D. Brazil (Aldershot & Farnham) w rtd 1 D. Beech (Woking); *semi-finals:* P. Larner w pts A. Wilkes, D. Brazil wo J. Honey; *final:* D. Brazil w pts A. Wilkes - replaced P. Larner. **L. Middle:** *quarter-finals:* M. Takalobigashi (Ramsgate) wo, S. Laight (Southampton) wo, D. Blair (Gosport) wo, A. Coppard (Crawley) w rsc 2 M. Hobday (Hayling Island); *semi-finals:* M. Takalobigashi w pts S. Laight, D. Blair w pts A. Coppard; *final:* M. Takalobigashi w rsc 1 D. Blair. **Middle:** *quarter-finals:* J. Fletcher (Woking) wo, S. James (Broadstairs) wo, Y. Bello (Parade) wo, D. Guilfoyle (Crawley) w rsc 2 K. Breen (Shepway); *semi-finals:* J. Fletcher w pts S. James, Y. Bello w pts D. Guilfoyle; *final:* Y. Bello w pts J. Fletcher. **L. Heavy:** *semi-finals:* J. McCreaney (Hove) wo, L. Morris (Basingstoke) w pts M. Michael (Ramsgate); *final:* L. Morris w rsc 2 J. McCreaney. **Heavy:** *quarter-finals:* M. Alexander (Southampton) wo, G. Russell (Shepway) wo, D. Whitman (Woking) w rsc 2 F. Booker (Crawley), T. Oakey (Leigh Park) w rsc 2 J. McCormack (Birchington); *semi-finals:* D. Whitman w rtd 2 M. Alexander, T. Oakey w pts G. Russell; *final:* T. Oakey w pts D. Whitman. **S. Heavy:** *semi-finals:* J. Flisher (Shepway) wo, D. French (Gosport) w pts M. Brown (Ryde); *final:* J. Flisher w pts D. French.

North East Counties

North-East Division   The Leisure Centre, Spennymoor - 12 & 19 January

L. Fly: no entries. **Fly:** *final:* no entries. **Bantam:** *final:* M. Thompson (Phil Thomas SoB) wo. **Feather:** no entries. **Light:** *semi-finals:* M. Catterick (Old Vic) wo, A. McLean (Birtley) w pts G. Williams (Hartlepool BW); *final:* A. McLean w pts M. Catterick. **L. Welter:** *final:* I. Walker (Blyth) w co 1 A. Welsh (Peterlee). **Welter:** *semi-finals:* M. McLean (Birtley) w pts B. Booth (Horsley Hill), J. Green (Phil Thomas (SoB) w pts N. Patterson (Shildon); *final:* J. Green w pts M. McLean. **L. Middle:** *semi-finals:* I. Cooper (Hartlepool BW) wo, S. McCready (Birtley) w pts M. Smillie (Hylton Castle); *final:* I. Cooper w pts S. McCready. **Middle:** *quarter-finals:* G. Smith (Hartlepool Catholic) wo, G. Corbyn (Phil Thomas SoB) w pts C. Wake (Shildon), J. Pearce (Wellington) w rsc 1 A. Exley (Grainger Park), B. Bell (Aycliffe) w pts D. Toward (Birtley); *semi-finals:* G. Corbyn w pts G. Smith, J. Pearce wo B. Bell; *final:* J. Pearce wo G. Corbyn. **L. Heavy:** *final:* M. Thompson (Spennymoor) wo. **Heavy:** *semi-finals:* D. Wilson (Wellington) wo, M. Chandler (Darlington) w pts L. Blackman (Grainger Park); *final:* M. Chandler w rtd 3 D. Wilson. **S. Heavy:** *final:* G. McGhin (Sunderland) wo.

Humberside Divisions   St Paul's Gym, Hull - 16 January

L. Fly: no entries. **Fly:** *final:* M. Cairns (St Paul's) wo. **Bantam:** no entries. **Feather:** *final:* J. Betts (St Paul's) wo. **Light:** no entries. **L. Welter:** *final:* L. Crosby (St Paul's) wo. **Welter:** *final:* G. Matsell (Hull Fish Trades) wo. **L. Middle:** *final:* S. Pollard (Humberside Police) wo. **Middle:** *final:* C. Harman (Withernsea) wo. **L. Heavy:** *final:* G. Dunbar (St Paul's) wo. **Heavy:** no entries. **S. Heavy:** no entries.

Yorkshire Division   Painthorpe Country Club, Wakefield - 5 January

L. Fly: no entries. **Fly:** *final:* S. Green (Tom Hill) wo. **Bantam:** no entries. **Feather:** *final:* B. Turner (Bradford Police) w pts L. Pattison (Hunslet). **Light:** *semi-finals:* G. Williams (Sedbergh) w co 2 L. Clegg (Keighley), J. Whittaker (Halifax) w rsc 2 C. Grosvenor (Market District); *final:* G. Williams w pts J. Whittaker. **L. Welter:** *final:* no entries. **Welter:** *semi-finals:* B. Grandage (White Rose) wo, J. Witter (Bradford Police) w co 2 S. Razaq (Sedbergh); *final:* J. Witter w rsc 2 B. Grandage. **L. Middle:** *semi-finals:* D. Smillie (Sedbergh) wo, D. Galloway (Parsons Cross) w pts M. Owens (White Rose); *final:* D. Galloway w pts D. Smillie. **Middle:** *final:* D. Rhodes (Hunslet) w pts D. Reece (Sedbergh). **L. Heavy:** *final:* M. Hobson (Sedbergh) wo. **Heavy:** *final:* M. Asfar (Sedbergh) w rsc 3 P. Callaghan (Market District). **S. Heavy:** no entries.

North-East Counties Semi-Finals & Finals   The Dale WMC, Worsborough & The Civic Theatre, Barnsley - 26 January & 2 February

L. Fly: no entries. **Fly:** *final:* M. Cairns (St Paul's) w rsc 2 S. Green (Tom Hill). **Bantam:** *final:* M. Thompson (Phil Thomas (SoB) wo. **Feather:** *final:* J. Betts (St Paul's) w pts B. Turner (Bradford Police). **Light:** *final:* A. McLean (Birtley) w pts G. Williams (Sedbergh). **L. Welter:** *final:* I. Walker (Blyth) w rtd 1 L. Crosby (St Paul's). **Welter:** *semi-finals:* J. Witter (Bradford Police) wo, J. Green (Phil Thomas SoB) w pts G. Matsell (Hull Fish Trades); *final:* J. Green w pts J. Witter. **L. Middle:** *semi-finals:* I. Cooper (Hartlepool BW) wo, D. Galloway (Parsons Cross) w rsc 2 S. Pollard (Humberside Police); *final:* I. Cooper w pts D. Galloway. **Middle:** *semi-finals:* C. Harman (Withernsea) wo, J. Pearce (Wellington) w pts D. Rhodes (Hunslet); *final:* J. Pearce w co 1 C. Harman. **L. Heavy:** *semi-finals:* G. Dunbar (St Paul's) wo, M. Thompson (Spennymoor) w pts M. Hobson (Sedbergh); *final:* M. Thompson w co 1 G. Dunbar (St Paul's). **Heavy:** *final:* M. Chandler (Darlington) w co 1 M. Asfar (Sedbergh). **S. Heavy:** *final:* G. McGhin (Sunderland) wo.

Southern Counties v North-East Counties

The Guildhall, Portsmouth - 10 February

L. Fly: no entries. **Fly:** N. Bell (Brighton) w pts M. Cairns (St Paul's). **Bantam:** M. Thompson (Phil Thomas SoB) w pts D.

Western (Leigh Park). **Feather:** M. Walsh (Portsmouth University) w pts J. Betts (St Paul's). **Light:** A. Walsh (Portsmouth University) w pts A. McLean (Birtley). **L. Welter:** N. Philpott (Leigh Park) w co 3 I. Walker (Blyth). **Welter:** J. Green (Phil Thomas SoB) w pts D. Brazil (Aldershot & Farnham). **L. Middle:** I. Cooper (Hartlepool BW) w pts M. Takalobigashi (Ramsgate). **Middle:** J. Pearce (Wellington) w pts Y. Bello (Parade). **L. Heavy:** M. Thompson (Spennymoor) w pts L. Morris (Basingstoke). **Heavy:** T. Oakey (Leigh Park) w pts M. Chandler (Darlington). **S. Heavy:** G. McGhin (Sunderland) w rsc 2 J. Flisher (Shepway).

Western Counties v North-West Counties

Western Counties

Northern Division   The Leisure Centre, Yate - 20 & 24 January
L. Fly: no entries. **Fly:** no entries. **Bantam:** *final:* M. Braden (Walcot) wo. **Feather:** no entries. **Light:** *final:* R. Scutt (Sydenham) wo. **L. Welter:** *final:* J. Hudson (Bronx) w pts A. Christian (Watchet). **Welter:** *semi-finals:* C. Johnson (Empire) wo, N. Thomas (Kingswood) w pts D. Nardiello (Reckleford); *final:* N. Thomas w pts C. Johnson. **L. Middle:** *final:* J. Turley (Penhill) w pts A. Derrick (Taunton). **Middle:** *final:* D. Holder (Gloucester) wo. **L. Heavy:** P. Rogers (Penhill) wo. **Heavy:** *quarter-finals:* S. Gray (Penhill) wo, G. Lee (Synwell) wo, H. Scott (Walcot) wo, P. Lewis (Taunton) w pts D. Beatty (Frome); *semi-finals:* P. Lewis w pts S. Gray, G. Lee w pts H. Scott; *final:* P. Lewis w rsc 2 G. Lee. **S. Heavy:** *final:* H. Williams (Bronx) w pts B. Harding (Penhill).

Southern Division   The Pavilion, Exmouth - 13 January
L. Fly: no entries. **Fly:** *final:* D. Barriball (Launceston) wo. **Bantam:** *final:* G. Nicette (Torbay) wo. **Feather:** *final:* S. Gawron (Devonport) w pts D. Jeffrey (Poole). **Light:** *final:* D. Maton (Poole) wo. **L. Welter:** *semi-finals:* V. Saunders (Dawlish) wo, P. Hardcastle (Devonport) w co 2 C. McBurnie (Pisces); *final:* P. Hardcastle w co 2 V. Saunders. **Welter:** *final:* J. Batten (Launceston) wo. **L. Middle:** S. Dann (Mayflower) w rtd 1 S. Buckingham (Launceston). **Middle:** *final:* G. Wharton (Bournemouth) w rsc 2 M. Dunlop (Leonis). **L. Heavy:** *final:* R. Mann (Torbay) w co 2 A. Stables (Devonport). **Heavy:** *final:* N. Hosking (Devonport) wo. **S. Heavy:** *final:* N. Kendall (Apollo) w pts J. Smith (Poole).

Western Counties Finals   The City Hall, Salisbury - 27 January
L. Fly: no entries. **Fly:** D. Barriball (Launceston) wo. **Bantam:** G. Nicette (Torbay) w pts M. Braden (Walcot). **Feather:** S. Gawron (Devonport) wo. **Light:** R. Scutt (Sydenham) w pts D. Maton (Poole). **L. Welter:** J. Hudson (Bronx) w pts P. Hardcastle (Devonport). **Welter:** N. Thomas (Kingswood) w rsc 3 J. Batten (Launceston). **L. Middle:** S. Dann (Mayflower) w pts J. Turley (Penhill). **Middle:** G. Wharton (Bournemouth) w pts D. Holder (Gloucester). **L. Heavy:** P. Rogers (Penhill) wo R. Mann (Torbay). **Heavy:** P. Lewis (Taunton) w rtd 2 N. Hosking (Devonport). **S. Heavy:** N. Kendall (Apollo) w co 1 H. Williams (Bronx).

North-West Counties

East Lancashire & Cheshire Division   The Willows, Salford - 11 & 18 January
L. Fly: *final:* no entries. **Fly:** no entries. **Bantam:** *final:* M. Stewart (Our Lady & St John) wo. **Feather:** *final:* S. Bell (Louvolite) wo. **Light:** *semi-finals:* G. Hibbert (Gallagher) wo, E. Nevins (Benchill) w pts R. Francis (Preston & Fulwood); *final:* G. Hibbert w rsc 3 E. Nevins. **L. Welter:** *quarter-finals:* G. Kirby (Horizon) wo, C. Smith (Louvolite) wo, M. Sewell (Workington) wo, J. Spence (Ardwick) w co 3 J. McGirl (Benchill); *semi-finals:* J. Spence w co 2 G. Kirby, C. Smith w pts M. Sewell; *final:* C. Smith w pts J. Spence. **Welter:** *final:* J. Barrow (Sandygate) w pts A. Golding (Bolton). **L. Middle:** *semi-finals:* A. Page (Louvolite) wo, D. Bateman (Benchill) w rsc 3 M. Porter (Northside); *final:* A. Page w co 3 D. Bateman. **Middle:** *final:* J. Whiteside (Preston Red Rose) wo. **L. Heavy:** *quarter-finals:* C. Crook (Lancashire Constabulary) wo, R. Jones (Horizon) wo, N. Harrison (Bolton) wo, R. Finlay (Burn Naze) w pts G. Dixon (Carlisle); *semi-finals:* R. Finlay w rsc 2 C. Crook, L. Valentine w rsc 2 N. Harrison; *final:* R. Finlay w co 1 L. Valentine. **Heavy:** *final:* V. Docherty (Lancashire Constabulary) wo. **S. Heavy:** *final:* C. Bowen-Price (Burn Naze) w rsc 2 G. Wilson (Bury).

West Lancashire & Cheshire Division   Everton Park Sports Centre, Liverpool - 16, 19 & 26 January
L. Fly: *final:* R. Mercer (St Helens) w pts G. Jones (Sefton). **Fly:** *final:* C. Toohey (Gemini) wo. **Bantam:** *semi-finals:* L. Eedle (Gemini) wo, D. Vlasman (Salisbury) w pts T. Blundell (Stockbridge); *final:* L. Eedle w pts D. Vlasman. **Feather:** *quarter-finals:* C. Ainscough (Transport) wo, M. Parker (Kirkby) wo, L. Holmes (Vauxhall Motors) wo, T. Mulholland w pts W. Grant (Tower Hill); *semi-finals:* T. Mulholland w pts C. Ainscough, M. Parker w pts L. Holmes; *final:* T. Mulholland w pts T. Parker. **Light:** *final:* J. Farrell (Marsh Lane) w co 1 K. Roberts (Gemini). **L. Welter:** *semi-finals:* J. Mellor (Transport) wo, C. Wall (Gemini) w pts J. Vlasman (Roseheath); *final:* C. Wall w pts J. Mellor. **Welter:** R. Murray (Gemini) w co 3 S. Garrett (Waterloo). **L. Middle:** *final:* L. Burns (Gemini) w pts R. Turner (Warrington). **Middle:** *quarter-finals:* S. Miller (Runcorn) wo, M. Brookes (Transport) wo, L. Malloy (Tuebrook) w pts C. Black (Golden Star), A. Roberts (St Helens) w pts M. Donoghue (Salisbury); *semi-finals:* A. Roberts w pts L. Malloy, S. Miller w co 1 M. Brookes; *final:* S. Miller w co 2 A. Roberts. **L. Heavy:** *final:* T. Smith (Long Lane) wo. **Heavy:** D. Keough (Roseheath) wo. **S. Heavy:** no entries.

North-West Counties Finals   Everton Park Sports Centre, Liverpool - 2 February
L. Fly: R. Mercer (St Helens) wo. **Fly:** C. Toohey (Gemini) wo. **Bantam:** L. Eedle (Gemini) wo M. Stewart (Our Lady & St John). **Feather:** T. Mulholland (Gemini) w pts S. Bell (Louvolite). **Light:** J. Farrell (Marsh Lane) w co 2 G. Hibbert (Gallagher). **L. Welter:** C. Wall (Gemini) w pts C. Smith (Louvolite). **Welter:** R. Murray (Gemini) w rsc 3 J. Barrow (Sandygate). **L. Middle:** L. Burns (Gemini) w rsc 3 A. Page (Louvolite). **Middle:** S. Miller (Runcorn) w co 1 J. Whiteside (Preston Red Rose). **L. Heavy:** T. Smith (Long Lane) w pts R. Finlay (Burn Naze). **Heavy:** D. Keough (Roseheath) w co 1 V. Docherty (Lancashire Constabulary). **S. Heavy:** C. Bowen-Price (Burn Naze) wo.

Western Counties v North-West Counties

Everton Park Sports Centre, Liverpool - 9 February
L. Fly: R. Mercer (St Helens) wo. **Fly:** D. Barriball (Launceston) wo C. Toohey (Gemini). **Bantam:** L. Eedle (Gemini) w pts G. Nicette (Torbay). **Feather:** T. Mulholland (Gemini) w rsc 2 S.

Gawron (Devonport). **Light:** J. Farrell (Marsh Lane) w rsc 1 R. Scutt (Sydenham). **L. Welter:** C. Wall (Gemini) w pts J. Hudson (Bronx). **Welter:** R. Murray (Gemini) w co 1 N. Thomas (Kingswood). **L. Middle:** S. Dann (Mayflower) w rsc 2 L. Burns (Gemini). **Middle:** G. Wharton (Bourneouth) w pts S. Miller (Runcorn). **L. Heavy:** P. Rogers (Penhill) w rsc 3 T. Smith (Long Lane). **Heavy:** P. Lewis (Taunton) w pts D. Keough (Roseheath). **S. Heavy:** C. Bowen-Price (Burn Naze) w rsc 1 N. Kendall (Apollo).

Midland Counties v Eastern Counties / Home Counties

Midland Counties

Derbyshire Division   The Pennine Hotel, Derby - 9 January

L. Fly: no entries. **Fly:** no entries. **Bantam:** no entries. **Feather:** no entries. **Light:** *final:* C. Spacie (St Michael's) w pts C. Rowland (Merlin). **L. Welter:** *final:* D. Ashley (Merlin) wo. **Welter:** *final:* K. Barry (Homewood) wo. **L. Middle:** *final:* K. Gibbons (Derby) w pts A. Palmer (Trinity). **Middle:** D. Grafton (Bolsover) wo. **L. Heavy:** *final:* M. Krence (St Michael's) wo. **Heavy:** *final:* A. Aziz (Derby) wo. **S. Heavy:** no entries.

Leicester, Rutland & Northamptonshire Division   The Moat House Hotel, Northampton - 4 December

L. Fly: no entries. **Fly:** no entries. **Bantam:** *final:* P. Neale (Alexton) wo. **Feather:** no entries. **Light:** no entries. **L. Welter:** *final:* S. Bradshaw (Wellingborough) wo. **Welter:** S. Mabbett (Belgrave) w pts P. Bench (Wellingborough). **L. Middle:** *final:* A. Foster (Kingsthorpe) w pts L. Walsh (Braunstone). **Middle:** no entries. **L. Heavy:** no entries. **Heavy:** no entries. **S. Heavy:** *final:* D. McCafferty (Wellingborough) wo.

Nottinghamshire & Lincolnshire Division   The Clifton Entertainment Centre, Nottingham - 11 January

L. Fly: No entries. **Fly:** *final:* J. Booth (Radford) wo. **Bantam:** E. Pickering (RHP) wo. **Feather:** no entries. **Light:** C. Greaves (RHP) w pts K. Gerowski (Cotgrave). **L. Welter:** *final:* D. Kirk (Huthwaite) w pts A. Psaltis (Grantham). **Welter:** *semi-finals:* J. Khaliq (Meadows & Ruddington) wo, I. Brown (Highbury Vale) w rsc 2 I. Bradford (Harworth Colliery); *final:* J. Khaliq w rsc 3 I. Brown. **L. Middle:** *quarter-finals:* R. Watson (Grantham) wo, N. Ellis (Boston) wo, S. Jenkinson (Lincoln) wo, M. Wheat (Nottingham) w rsc 2 R. Inquetti (Eastwood); *semi-finals:* R. Watson w pts N. Ellis, S. Jenkinson w pts M. Wheat; *final:* R. Watson wo S. Jenkinson. **Middle:** *semi-finals:* A. Lovelace (Boston) wo, M. Monaghan (Radford) w co 2 J. Andrews (Bracebridge); *final:* A. Lovelace w pts M. Monaghan. **L. Heavy:** *final:* A. Kerr (Grantham) wo. **Heavy:** *final:* T. Dowling (Bracebridge) wo. **S. Heavy:** *final:* N. Moore (Good Intentions) w rsc 2 D. Castle (Radford).

Warwickshire Division   The Sporting Triumph Sporting Club, Coventry - 11 January

L. Fly: no entries. **Fly:** *final:* G. Payne (Bell Green) wo. **Bantam:** no entries. **Feather:** *final:* M. Payne (Bell Green) wo. **Light:** *final:* R. Rutherford (Bell Green) wo. **L. Welter:** *final:* I. Carroll (Triumph) wo. **Welter:** no entries. **L. Middle:** no entries. **Middle:** *final:* G. Behan (Warwick) w pts P. Haughney (Triumph). **L. Heavy:** *final:* E. Cleary (Warwick) w rsc 2 J. Twite (Triumph). **Heavy:** *final:* D. Bendall (Triumph) wo. **S. Heavy:** no entries.

Midland Counties (North Zone) Semi-Finals & Finals   The Pennine Hotel, Derby - 16 January, The Coventry Colliery Club, Keresley - 19 January & The Commodore International Hotel, Nottingham - 25 January

L. Fly: no entries. **Fly:** *final:* J. Booth (Radford) w pts G. Payne (Bell Green). **Bantam:** *final:* E. Pickering (RHP) w pts P. Neale (Alexton). **Feather:** *final:* M. Payne (Bell Green) wo. **Light:** *semi-finals:* R. Rutherford (Bell Green) wo, C. Spacie (St Michael's) w pts C. Greaves (RHP); *final:* R. Rutherford w pts C. Spacie. **L. Welter:** *semi-finals:* D. Kirk (Huthwaite) w pts D. Ashley (Merlin), I. Carroll (Triumph) w rsc 1 S. Bradshaw (Wellingborough); *final:* D. Kirk w pts I. Carroll. **Welter:** *semi-finals:* S. Mabbett (Belgrave) wo, J. Khaliq (Meadows & Ruddington) w pts K. Barry (Homewood); *final:* J. Khaliq w pts S. Mabbett. **L. Middle:** *semi-finals:* A. Foster (Kingsthorpe) wo, K. Gibbons (Derby) w rsc 1 R. Watson (Grantham); *final:* A. Foster w pts K. Gibbons. **Middle:** *semi-finals:* G. Behan (Warwick) wo, D. Grafton (Bolsover) w rsc 2 A. Lovelace (Boston); *final:* G. Behan w pts D. Grafton. **L. Heavy:** *semi-finals:* E. Cleary (Warwick) wo, M. Krence (St Michael's) w rsc 2 A. Kerr (Grantham); *final:* M. Krence w pts E. Cleary. **Heavy:** *semi-finals:* D. Bendall (Triumph) wo, T. Dowling (Bracebridge) w pts A. Aziz (Derby); *final:* A. Aziz - replaced T. Dowling - w pts D. Bendall. **S. Heavy:** *final:* D. McCafferty (Keystone) w rsc 3 N. Moore (Good Intentions).

Birmingham Division   The Irish Centre, Digbeth - 7 January & The Kingsbury Club, Kingsbury - 12 January

L. Fly: no entries. **Fly:** no entries. **Bantam:** no entries. **Feather:** no entries. **Light:** no entries. **L. Welter:** *final:* I. Smith (Birmingham City) wo. **Welter:** *final:* J. Scanlon (Birmingham City) wo. **L. Middle:** *semi-finals:* G. Harris (Rover) w pts S. Baumant (Birmingham Irish), S. Sherrington (Birmingham City) w pts D. Burridge (Coleshill); *final:* S. Sherrington w pts G. Harris. **Middle:** *final:* W. Elcock (Erdington) wo. **L. Heavy:** no entries. **Heavy:** no entries. **S. Heavy:** D. Redmond (Rover) wo.

North Staffordshire Division   The Longton Country & Western Club, Stoke - 12 January

L. Fly: no entries. **Fly:** no entries. **Bantam:** no entries. **Feather:** no entries. **Light:** *final:* S. Lawton (Queensberry) wo. **L. Welter:** no entries. **Welter:** no entries. **L. Middle:** *final:* M. Gaylor (Burton) wo. **Middle:** no entries. **L. Heavy:** *final:* P. Scope (Burton) w pts I. Thomas (Queensberry). **Heavy:** *final:* T. Lowe (The George) wo. **S. Heavy:** no entries.

South Staffordshire Division   The Labour Club, Brierley Hill - 11 January & The Pleck WMC, Walsall - 17 January

L. Fly: no entries. **Fly:** *final:* D. Spencer (Pleck) wo. **Bantam:** no entries. **Feather:** no entries. **Light:** *final:* G. Reid (Wolverhampton) wo. **L. Welter:** *final:* M. Richards (Wednesbury) wo. **Welter:** *final:* P. Nightingale (Wednesbury) wo. **L. Middle:** *semi-finals:* P. Garrett (Wednesbury) wo, M. Bamford (Silver Street) w pts M. Hough (Pleck); *final:* P. Garrett w pts M. Bamford. **Middle:** *final:* S. Martin (Wolverhampton) w pts J. Collins (Pleck). **L. Heavy:** *final:* M. O'Connell (Wolverhampton) wo. **Heavy:** no entries. **S. Heavy:** *final:* B. Turner (Wolverhampton) w co 2 S. Murray (Pleck).

West Mercia Division   The Heath Hotel, Bewdley - 9 January

L. Fly: no entries. **Fly:** no entries. **Bantam:** no entries. **Feather:** *final:* N. Marston (Shrewsbury) wo. **Light:** no entries. **L. Welter:** *final:* S. Cartwright (Tudorville) wo. **Welter:** no entries. **L. Middle:** *final:* D. Woodley (Tudorville) wo. **Middle:** *final:* B. Carr (Tudorville) wo. **L. Heavy:** *final:* D. Norton (Stourbridge) wo. **Heavy:** *final:* F. Woodrow (Hereford) wo. **S. Heavy:** no entries.

Midland Counties (South Zone) Semi-Finals & Finals   The Heath Hotel, Bewdley - 9 January, The Gala Baths, West Bromwich - 19 January & Garrington Sports & Social Club, Bromsgrove - 27 January

L. Fly: no entries. **Fly:** *final:* D. Spencer (Pleck) wo. **Bantam:** no entries. **Feather:** *final:* N. Marston (Shrewsbury) wo. **Light:** *final:* S. Lawton (Queensberry) w pts G. Reid (Wolverhampton). **L. Welter:** *semi-finals:* I. Smith (Birmingham City) wo, M. Richards (Wednesbury) w pts S. Cartwright (Tudorville); *final:* M. Richards w pts I. Smith. **Welter:** *final:* P. Nightingale (Wednesbury) w pts J. Scanlon (Birmingham City). **L. Middle:** *semi-finals:* P. Garrett (Wednesbury) w pts D. Woodley (Tudorville), S. Sherrington (Birmingham City) w pts M. Gaylor (Burton); *final:* S. Sherrington w pts D. Woodley. **Middle:** *semi-finals:* W. Elcock (Erdington) wo, B. Carr (Tudorville) w rsc 1 S. Martin (Wolverhampton); *final:* W. Elcock w rsc 2 B. Carr. **L. Heavy:** *semi-finals:* P. Scope (Burton) wo, D. Norton (Stourbridge) w rsc 1 M. O'Connell (Wolverhampton); *final:* D. Norton w rsc 3 P. Scope. **Heavy:** *final:* F. Woodrow (Hereford) w pts T. Lowe (The George). **S. Heavy:** *final:* B. Turner (Wolverhampton) w pts D. Redmond (Rover).

Midland Counties Finals   The Lea Hall Colliery Club, Rugeley - 3 February

L. Fly: no entries. **Fly:** D. Spencer (Pleck) w pts J. Booth (Radford). **Bantam:** E. Pickering (RHP) wo. **Feather:** M. Payne (Bell Green) w rsc 1 N. Marston (Shrewsbury). **Light:** R. Rutherford (Bell Green) w pts S. Lawton (Queensberry). **L. Welter:** M. Richards (Wednesbury) w pts D. Kirk (Huthwaite). **Welter:** J. Khaliq (Meadows & Ruddington) w pts P. Nightingale (Wednesbury). **L. Middle:** S. Sherrington (Birmingham City) w pts A. Foster (Kingsthorpe). **Middle:** W. Elcock (Erdington) w dis 3 G. Behan (Warwick). **L. Heavy:** M. Krence (St Michael's) w pts D. Norton (Stourbridge). **Heavy:** A. Aziz (Derby) w dis 2 F. Woodrow (Hereford). **S. Heavy:** D. McCafferty (Keystone) w pts D. Redmond (Rover) - replaced B. Turner (Wolverhampton).

Eastern Counties v Home Counties

Eastern Counties

Essex Division   The Civic Hall, Grays - 12 January

L. Fly: no entries. **Fly:** no entries. **Bantam:** *final:* J. Martin (Canvey) wo. **Feather:** *final:* D. Dainty (Canvey) wo. **Light:** *final:* D. Goodrum (Rayleigh Mill) wo. **L. Welter:** *semi-finals:* G. Ling (Lee Chapel) wo, J. Deadman (Rayleigh Mill) w dis 3 M. Saliu (Colchester); *final:* J. Deadman w rtd 2 G. Ling. **Welter:** *final:* D. Bruce (Belhus Park) w rsc 2 P. Reynolds (Belhus Park). **L. Middle:** *final:* A. Sims (Canvey) w pts R. Hadley (Canvey). **Middle:** *final:* M. Woodcraft (Canvey) wo. **L. Heavy:** *final:* M. Quirey (Berry) w pts J. Warren (Canvey). **Heavy:** *final:* R. Skeels (Clacton) wo. **S. Heavy:** no entries.

Mid -Anglia Division   The Lucky Break Leisure Centre, Bury St Edmunds - 12 January

L. Fly: no entries. **Fly:** no entries. **Bantam:** no entries. **Feather:** no entries. **Light:** no entries. **L. Welter:** no entries. **Welter:** no entries. **L. Middle:** no entries. **Middle:** *final:* A. Beaumont (Howard Mallet) wo. **L. Heavy:** no entries. **Heavy:** no entries. **S. Heavy:** no entries.

Norfolk Division   The High School, Aylesham - 13 January

L. Fly: no entries. **Fly:** no entries. **Bantam:** *final:* S. Williams (Norwich City) wo. **Feather:** no entries. **Light:** no entries. **L. Welter:** *final:* S. Garner (Dereham) wo. **Welter:** *final:* J. Fitzgerald (Norwich City) w pts S. Johnston (Norwich Lads). **L. Middle:** no entries. **Middle:** *final:* M. Rodgers (Norwich Lads) w pts G. Smith (Kingfishers). **L. Heavy:** *final:* S. Wilton (Aylesham) wo. **Heavy:** *final:* J. Bevis (Norwich Lads) wo. **S. Heavy:** no entries.

Suffolk Division   The Lucky Break Leisure Centre, Bury St Edmunds - 12 January

L. Fly: no entries. **Fly:** no entries. **Bantam:** no entries. **Feather:** *final:* N. Drury (New Astley) wo. **Light:** *final:* M. Hawthorne (Lowestoft) wo. **L. Welter:** *final:* D. James (Bury) wo. **Welter:** no entries. **L. Middle:** *final:* A. Carey (Bury) w rsc 3 R. Smith (Ipswich). **L. Heavy:** *final:* S. Mann (Sudbury) wo. **Heavy:** *final:* S. Smith (Hurstleigh & Kerridge) w pts K. Potter (Ipswich). **S. Heavy:** no entries.

Eastern Counties Semi-Finals & Finals   The Civic Hall, Grays - 27 January

L. Fly: no entries. **Fly:** no entries. **Bantam:** *final:* J. Martin (Canvey) w pts S. Williams (Norwich City). **Feather:** *final:* D. Dainty (Canvey) w pts N. Drury (New Astley). **Light:** *final:* M. Hawthorne (Lowestoft) w rsc 2 D. Goodrum (Rayleigh Mill). **L. Welter:** J. Deadman (Rayleigh Mill) withdrew. *final:* S. Garner (Dereham) w pts D. James (Bury). **Welter:** *final:* D. Bruce (Belhus Park) w pts J. Fitzgerald (Norwich City). **L. Middle:** *final:* A. Sims (Canvey) w rtd 1 A. Carey (Bury). **Middle:** M. Rodgers (Norwich Lads) withdrew. *final:* M. Woodcraft (Canvey) w co 1 A. Beaumont (Howard Mallet). **L. Heavy:** *semi-finals:* S. Wilton (Aylesham) wo, M. Quirey (Bury) w rsc 1 S. Mann (Sudbury); *final:* M. Quirey w pts S. Wilton. **Heavy:** *semi-finals:* S. Smith (Hurstleigh & Kerridge) wo, R. Skeels (Clacton) w pts J. Bevis (Norwich Lads); *final:* S. Smith w rsc 1 R. Skeels. **S. Heavy:** no entries.

Home Counties

Bedfordshire, Hertfordshire & North Buckinghamshire & Oxfordshire, Berkshire & South Buckinghamshire Divisions Molin's Recreation Club, Saunderton - 13 January

L. Fly: no entries. **Fly:** *final:* M. Sen (Stevenage) wo. **Bantam:** *final:* M. Bell (Mo's) wo. **Feather:** *final:* D. Maher (Marlow) wo. **Light:** *final:* D. Curran (Luton Irish) w pts A. McBean (Hitchin). **L. Welter:** *semi-finals:* M. Leonard (South Oxhey) w pts D. Holt (Farley), K. Herbert (Mo's) w rtd 2 S. McBeal (Hitchin); *final:* M. Leonard w pts K. Herbert. **Welter:** *final:* K. McCarthy (Bedford) w rsc 3 M. Calvert (Stevenage). **L. Middle:** *semi-finals:* W. Shotbolt (Bedford) wo, S. Wright (Sandy) w pts E. Randall (Bushey); *final:* W. Shotbolt w pts S. Wright. **Middle:** *final:* C. Marshall (Stevenage) wo. **L. Heavy:** *final:* P. Corkery (Pinewood Starr) w pts S. Lawlor (Luton High Town). **Heavy:** *semi-finals:* S. Power (Watford) wo, P. Reading (Hitchin) w pts T. Wright (Bedford); *final:* P. Reading w pts S. Power. **S. Heavy:** *final:* M. Sprott (Bulmershe) wo.

Eastern Counties v Home Counties

The Festival Hall, Basildon - 3 February

L. Fly: no entries. **Fly:** M. Sen (Stevenage) wo. **Bantam:** J. Martin (Canvey) w pts M. Bell (Mo's). **Feather:** D. Dainty (Canvey) w pts D. Maher (Marlow). **Light:** M. Hawthorne

(Lowestoft) w rsc 1 D. Curran (Luton Irish). **L. Welter:** S. Garner (Dereham) w pts M. Leonard (South Oxhey). **Welter:** K. McCarthy (Bedford) w pts D. Bruce (Belhus Park). **L. Middle:** A. Sims (Canvey) w pts W. Shotbolt (Bedford). **Middle:** C. Marshall (Stevenage) wo M. Woodcraft (Canvey). **L. Heavy:** M. Quirey (Berry) w pts P. Corkery (Pinewood Starr). **Heavy:** S. Smith (Hurstleigh & Kerridge) w rsc 1 P. Reading (Hitchin). **S. Heavy:** M. Sprott (Bulmershe) wo.

Midland Counties v Eastern Counties / Home Counties

Molin's Recreation Centre, Saunderton - 10 February

L. Fly: no entries. **Fly:** D. Spencer (Pleck) w pts M. Sen (Stevenage). **Bantam:** E. Pickering (RHP) w pts J. Martin (Canvey). **Feather:** D. Dainty (Canvey) w pts M. Payne (Bell Green). **Light:** M. Hawthorne (Lowestoft) w pts R. Rutherford (Bell Green). **L. Welter:** M. Richards (Wednesbury) w pts S. Garner (Dereham). **Welter:** J. Khaliq (Meadows & Ruddington) w rsc 1 K. McCarthy (Bedford). **L. Middle:** A. Sims (Canvey) w rsc 3 S. Sherrington (Birmingham City). **Middle:** W. Elcock (Erdington) w pts C. Marshall (Stevenage). **L. Heavy:** M. Quirey (Berry) w pts M. Krence (St Michael's). **Heavy:** A. Aziz (Derby) w pts S. Smith (Hurstleigh & Kerridge). **S. Heavy:** M. Sprott (Bulmershe) wo.

London v Combined Services

London

North-East Division   York Hall, Bethnal Green - 11 January

L. Fly no entries. **Fly:** no entries. **Bantam:** *final:* M. Bush (Newham) w pts S. Oates (Repton). **Feather:** *final:* D. Adams (Repton) w pts A. Spelling (St George's). **Light:** *final:* K. Wing (Repton) w pts S. Turner (Repton). **L. Welter:** *semi-finals:* K. Asare (Lion) w pts R. Bruce (St Monica's); D. Happe (Repton) w pts P. Swinney (Repton); *final:* D. Happe w pts K. Asare. **Welter:** *semi-finals:* C. Houliston (Alma) wo, T. Cesay (Repton) w pts M. Riviere (Newham); *final:* T. Cesay w pts C. Houliston. **L. Middle:** *semi-finals:* L. Omar (Repton) w pts E. Monteith (Gator), R. Maguire (Hornchurch & Elm Park) w rsc 2 M. Marriott (Lion); *final:* R. Maguire w rsc 2 M. Marriott. **Middle:** *final:* J. Ratcliffe (Alma) w pts A. Lowe (Repton). **L. Heavy:** *final:* P. Maskell (Newham) wo. **Heavy:** *final:* M. Lee (Newham) w pts D. Negus (Five Star). **S. Heavy:** *final:* T. Cherubin (Repton) w co 1 J. Beecroft (Gator).

North-West Division   The Irish Centre, Camden Town - 18 January

L. Fly: no entries. **Fly:** *final:* R. Ramzan (St Patrick's) wo. **Bantam:** *final:* P. Black (Dale Youth) w pts M. Alexander (Islington). **Feather:** *final:* J. Waters (St Patrick's) wo. **Light:** *final:* S. Bardoville (Trojan Police) w rsc 2 D. Browne (St Patrick's). **L. Welter:** *semi-finals:* J. Hall (St Patrick's) w pts P. Temple (Angel). **Welter:** *final:* A. Neunie (Islington) w pts A. Lazarus (St Patrick's). **L. Middle:** *final:* G. Ubiro (Trojan Police) w pts C. Ifekoya (Ruislip). **Middle:** *final:* O. Newman (Hanwell) w dis 2 G. Reyniers (St Patrick's). **L. Heavy:** *semi-finals:* C. Fry (Islington) wo, R. Ogodo (Trojan Police) w co 2 M. Fallon (Trojan Police); *final:* C. Fry w rsc 2 R. Ogodo. **Heavy:** *semi-finals:* I. Ajose (Trojan Police) wo, W. Barima (Northolt) w rsc 1 N. Siggs (Trojan Police); *final:* I. Ajose w dis 2 W. Barima. **S. Heavy:** *final:* S. Miller (Angel) wo.

South-East Division   The Crook Log Sports Centre, Bexleyheath - 16 December

L.Fly: no entries. **Fly:** *final:* D. Costello (Hollington) wo. **Bantam:** *final:* D. Easton (New Addington) wo. **Feather:** *semi-finals:* N. Gormley (Danson Youth) wo, I. Sebaduka (Lynn) w pts E. Lam (Fitzroy Lodge); *final:* I. Sebaduka w pts N. Gormley. **Light:** *final:* J. Alldis (Lynn) w pts P. McCabe (Fitzroy Lodge). **L. Welter:** *semi-finals:* D. Walker (Fisher) wo, C. Stanley (Fitzroy Lodge) w pts T. Rossiter (St Joseph's); *final:* D. Walker w rsc 1 C. Stanley. **Welter:** *quarter-finals:* M. Reigate (Fitzroy Lodge) wo, M. Clarke (Lynn) wo, F. Sarfo (Lynn) wo, D. Morgan (Fitzroy Lodge) w pts A. Martin (Fitzroy Lodge); *semi-finals:* M. Reigate w pts M. Clarke, F. Sarfo w rsc 3 D. Morgan; *final:* M. Reigate w pts F. Sarfo. **L. Middle:** *semi-finals:* S. Fearon (Lynn) wo, N. Travis (Fitzroy Lodge) w co 1 T. Thirlwell (Fisher); *final:* N. Travis w pts S. Fearon. **Middle:** *semi-finals:* J. Banjo (Honour Oak) wo, S. Johnson (Lynn) w pts D. Powell (Eltham); *final:* S. Johnson w pts J. Banjo. **L. Heavy:** *final:* M. Thomas (Hollington) wo. **Heavy:** *final:* D. Blake (Fitzroy Lodge) wo. **S. Heavy:** *semi-finals:* H. Senior (Lynn) wo, S. Cranston (Fisher) w rsc 1 S. Dumez (New Peckham); *final:* H. Senior w co 1 S. Cranston.

South-West Division   The Town Hall, Battersea - 17 January

L. Fly: *final:* L. Harris (Balham) wo. **Fly:** S. Mallon (Kingston) wo. **Bantam:** no entries. **Feather:** no entries. **Light:** no entries. **L. Welter:** no entries. **Welter:** *final:* D. Baptiste (Balham) w rsc 1 J. Hunt (Kingston). **L. Middle:** *final:* R. Williams (Earlsfield) w rsc 1 M. Barr (Kingston). **Middle:** *final:* C. Campbell (Earlsfield) w rsc 1 M. Lodge (Kingston). **L. Heavy:** *final:* F. Annan (Battersea) wo. **Heavy:** *final:* J. Quayson (Earlsfield) wo. **S. Heavy:** *final:* P. Thompson (Balham) wo.

London Semi-Finals & Finals   York Hall, Bethnal Green - 25 January & 1 February

L. Fly: *final:* L. Harris (Balham) wo. **Fly:** *semi-finals:* R. Ramzan (St Patrick's) wo, D. Costello (Hollington) w rsc 1 S. Mallon (Kingston); *final:* D. Costello w co 1 R. Ramzan. **Bantam:** *semi-finals:* P. Black (Dale Youth) wo, D. Easton (New Addington) w pts M. Bush (Newham); *final:* D. Easton w pts P. Black. **Feather:** *semi-finals:* J. Waters (St Patrick's) wo, D. Adams (Repton) w pts I. Sebaduka (Lynn); *final:* D. Adams w pts J. Waters. **Light:** *semi-finals:* S. Bardoville (Trojan Police) wo, K. Wing (Repton) w pts J. Alldis (Lynn); *final:* K. Wing w pts S. Bardoville. **L. Welter:** *semi-finals:* J. Hall (St Patrick's) wo, D. Walker (Fisher) w pts D. Happe (Repton); *final:* D. Walker w pts J. Hall. **Welter:** *semi-finals:* A. Neunie (Islington) w pts M. Reigate (Fitzroy Lodge), T. Cesay (Repton) w pts D. Baptiste (Balham); *final:* T. Cesay w rsc 2 A. Neunie. **L. Middle:** *semi-finals:* N. Travis (Fitzroy Lodge) w rsc 2 R. Maguire (Hornchurch & Elm Park), R. Williams (Earlsfield) w rsc 3 G. Ubiro (Trojan Police); *final:* N. Travis w pts G. Ubiro - replaced R. Williams. **Middle:** *semi-finals:* S. Johnson (Lynn) w pts O. Newman (Hanwell), J. Ratcliffe (Alma) w pts C. Campbell (Earlsfield); *final:* J. Ratcliffe w pts S. Johnson. **L. Heavy:** *semi-finals:* F. Annan (Battersea) w pts M. Thomas (Hollington), C. Fry (Islington) w rsc 1 P. Maskell (Newham); *final:* C. Fry w rtd 2 F. Annan. **Heavy:** *semi-finals:* M. Lee (Newham) w pts D. Blake (Fitzroy Lodge), I. Ajose (Trojan Police) w rsc 3 J. Quayson (Earlsfield); *final:* I. Ajose w rsc 3 M. Lee. **S. Heavy:** *semi-finals:* T. Cherubin (Repton) w rsc 2 S. Miller (Angel), H. Senior (Lynn) w dis 3 P. Thompson (Balham); *final:* H. Senior w pts T. Cherubin.

Combined Services

RAF, RN & Army Championships   HMS Nelson, Portsmouth - 5 & 6 December

L. Fly: *final:* P. Charlton (Army) w rsc 1 T. Lyons (RAF). **Fly:** *final:* D. Fox (RAF) wo. **Bantam:** *final:* O. Spensley (RAF) w pts A. Jessiman (Army). **Feather:** *final:* J. Turner (RN) w rsc 2 P. Williams (Army). **Light:** *final:* K. Bennett (Army) w rtd 1 J. Twycross (RN). **L. Welter:** *final:* V. Powell (Army) w pts T. Henderson (RAF). **Welter:** *semi-finals:* A. Davies (RAF) wo, J. Gardner (Army) w pts D. Maher (RN); *final:* J. Gardner w rsc 2 A. Davies. **L. Middle:** *final:* S. Pepperall (RAF) w pts S. Whyte (RN). **Middle:** *final:* D. Edwards (RN) w pts J. Ollerhead (Army). **L. Heavy:** *final:* V. Jones (Army) wo. **Heavy:** *final:* A. Walton (Army) w pts B. Bessey (Army). **S. Heavy:** *final:* D. Watts (Army) wo.

London v Combined Services

York Hall, Bethnal Green - 9 February

L. Fly: P. Charlton (Army) w pts L. Harris (Balham). **Fly:** D. Costello (Hollington) w pts D. Fox (RAF). **Bantam:** D. Easton (New Addington) w pts O. Spensley (RAF). **Feather:** J. Turner (RN) w pts D. Adams (Repton). **Light:** K. Wing (Repton) w pts K. Bennett (Army). **L. Welter:** D. Walker (Fisher) w rsc 2 D. Duggan (Army) - replaced V. Powell (Army). **Welter:** J. Gardner (Army) w rsc 2 T. Cesay (Repton). **L. Middle:** S. Whyte (RN) - replaced S. Pepperall (RAF) - w pts N. Travis (Fitzroy Lodge). **Middle:** J. Ratcliffe (Alma) w pts D. Edwards (RN). **L. Heavy:** C. Fry (Islington) w pts V. Jones (Army). **Heavy:** I. Ajose (Trojan Police) w pts A. Walton (Army). **S. Heavy:** D. Watts (Army) w pts H. Senior (Lynn).

English ABA Semi-Final & Finals

HMS Nelson, Portsmouth - 20 February, The Cocksmoor Woods Leisure Centre, Birmingham - 21 February & The National Indoor Arena, Birmingham - 6 March

L. Fly: *final:* R. Mercer (St Helens) w rsc 1 P. Charlton (Army). **Fly:** *semi-finals:* D. Costello (Hollington) w pts N. Bell (Brighton); D. Spencer (Pleck) w pts D. Barriball (Launceston); *final:* D. Costello w rsc 3 D. Spencer. **Bantam:** *semi-finals:* D. Easton (New Addington) w pts E. Pickering (RHP), L. Eedle (Gemini) w pts M. Thompson (Phil Thomas SoB); *final:* L. Eedle w pts D. Easton. **Feather:** *semi-finals:* M. Walsh (Portsmouth University) w pts J. Turner (RN), T. Mulholland (Gemini) w dis 3 D. Dainty (Canvey); *final:* T. Mulholland w rsc 2 M. Walsh. **Light:** *semi-finals:* A. Walsh (Portsmouth University) w pts M. Hawthorne (Lowestoft), K. Wing (Repton) w pts J. Farrell (Marsh Lane); *final:* K. Wing w pts A. Walsh. **L. Welter:** *semi-finals:* D. Walker (Fisher) w rsc 1 J. Newton (Crawley) - replaced N. Philpott (Leigh Park), C. Wall (Gemini) w dis 3 M. Richards (Wednesbury); *final:* C. Wall w pts D. Walker. **Welter:** *semi-finals:* J. Gardner (Army) w dis 3 R. Murray (Gemini), J. Khaliq (Meadows & Ruddington) w pts J. Green (Phil Thomas SoB); *final:* J. Khaliq w pts J. Gardner. **L. Middle:** *semi-finals:* S. Dann (Mayflower) w pts S. Whyte (RN), I. Cooper (Hartlepool BW) w rsc 2 A. Sims (Canvey); *final:* S. Dann w co 2 I. Cooper. **Middle:** *semi-finals:* W. Elcock (Erdington) w pts J. Ratcliffe (Alma), J. Pearce (Wellington) w co 1 G. Wharton (Bournemouth); *final:* J. Pearce w rsc 1 W. Elcock. **L. Heavy:** *semi-finals:* C. Fry (Islington) w pts M. Quirey (Berry), P. Rogers (Penhill) w pts M. Thompson (Spennymoor); *final:* C. Fry w pts P. Rogers. **Heavy:** *semi-finals:* T. Oakey (Leigh Park) w pts I. Ajose (Trojan Police), P. Lewis (Taunton) w pts A. Aziz (Derby); *final:* T. Oakey w rsc 2 P. Lewis. **S. Heavy:** *semi-finals:* M. Sprott (Bulmershe) w pts C. Bowen-Price (Burn Naze), D. Watts (Army) w rsc 1 G. McGhin (Sunderland); *final:* D. Watts w rsc 3 M. Sprott.

Tony Mulholland, now a professional with the Stephen Vaughan stable, won the 1996 ABA featherweight title following a comprehensive second round stoppage win over university boy, Michael Walsh (left)

Les Clark

Irish Championships, 1995-96

Senior Tournament

The National Stadium, Dublin - 23 & 24 February & 1 & 8 March
L. Fly: *final:* J. Prior (Darndale, Dublin) w pts C. Moffat (Holy Family, Belfast). **Fly:** *final:* D. Kelly (Holy Trinity, Belfast) w pts D. Sweetman (Golden Cobra, Dublin). **Bantam:** *quarter-finals:* W. Valentine (St Saviour's, Dublin) w rsc 1 P. Hennessey (St Colman's, Cork), O. Duddy (Coleraine, Derry) w pts T. Hamilton (St Saviour's, Dublin), T. Waite (Cairn Lodge, Belfast) w pts E. Brannigan (Docker's, Belfast), D. McKenna (Holy Family, Drogheda) w pts D. Hosford (Greenmount, Cork); *semi-finals:* O. Duddy w pts W. Valentine, D. McKenna w pts T. Waite; *final:* D. McKenna w pts O. Duddy.. **Feather:** *quarter-finals:* A. Patterson (St Patrick's, Newry) wo, D. Hyland (Golden Cobra, Dublin) wo, T. Carlyle (Sacred Heart, Dublin) wo, J. Conlon (Holy Trinity, Belfast) w pts P. Whelan (Neilstown, Dublin); *semi-finals:* A. Patterson w pts D. Hyland, T. Carlyle w pts J. Conlon; *final:* A. Patterson w pts T. Carlyle. **Light:** *prelims:* E. McEneaney (Dealgan, Dundalk) wo, G. Stephens (Crumlin, Dublin) wo, O. Montague (Antrim) wo, E. Bolger (Wexford CBS) wo, S. Cowman (St Paul's, Waterford) wo, D. Lowry (Albert Foundry, Belfast) wo, M. Reneghan (Keady, Armagh) wo, D. Barrett (Rylane, Cork) w co 2 M. O'Kane (Holy Trinity, Belfast); *quarter-finals:* E. McEneaney w pts G. Stephens, O. Montague w pts E. Bolger, S. Cowman w pts D. Lowry, M. Reneghan w pts D. Barrett; *semi-finals:* O. Montague w pts E. McEneaney, M. Reneghan w pts S. Cowman; *final:* M. Reneghan w pts O. Montague. **L. Welter:** *prelims:* J. Morrissey (Sunnyside, Cork) wo, G. McClarnon (Clann Eireann, Lurgan) wo, F. Carruth (Drimnagh, Dublin) wo, R. Murray (St Matthew's, Dublin) wo, W. Walsh (St Colman's, Cork) wo, F. Barrett (Olympic, Galway) w rsc 3 A. Magee (St Saviour's, Dublin), J. Fox (Carrickmore, Tyrone) w pts M. McCartan (St Patrick's, Newry), M. Dillon (Golden Cobra, Dublin) w rsc 1 J. McCombe (Antrim); *quarter-finals:* J. Morrissey w pts G. McClarnon, F. Carruth w pts R. Murray, F. Barrett w pts W. Walsh, M. Dillon w pts J. Fox; *semi-finals:* J. Morrissey w pts F. Carruth, F. Barrett w rsc 3 M. Dillon; *final:* F. Barrett w pts J. Morrissey. **Welter:** *prelims:* N. Gough (St Paul's, Waterford) wo, D. Devers (St Mary's, Ballina) wo, T. Crosby (Crumlin, Dublin) wo, C. McFarland (Bishop Kelly's, Tyrone) wo, S. Barrett (Rylane, Cork) wo, W. Egan (Neilstown, Dublin) wo, M. Blaney (Holy Trinity, Belfast) w pts J. Mitchell (Cavan), M. Riggs (Finglas, Dublin) w pts G. Ormonde (Quarryvale, Dublin); *quarter-finals:* N. Gough w pts D. Devers, T. Crosby w pts C. McFarland, S. Barrett w pts W. Egan, M. Riggs w pts M. Blaney; *semi-finals:* N. Gough w pts T. Crosby, S. Barrett w pts M. Riggs; *final:* N. Gough w pts S. Barrett. **L. Middle:** *prelims:* D. Higgins (Fermoy, Cork) wo, R. Forde (Galway) wo, K. Walsh (St Colman's, Cork) w co 2 T. Roche (St Luke's, Dublin), F. Webb (Holy Trinity, Belfast) w pts D. Taite (Glasnevin, Dublin), J. Payne (Tramore, Waterford) w pts S. Keeler (St Saviour's, Dublin), S. Gibson (Immaculata, Belfast) w pts P. Doherty (Buncrana, Donegal), J. Kelly (Manorhamilton, Leitrim) w rsc 2 F. McQuaid (Trim, Meath), M. Roche (Sunnyside, Cork) w pts W. Walsh (St Ibar's, Wexford); *quarter-finals:* D. Higgins w rsc 2 R. Forde, F. Webb w pts K. Walsh, S. Gibson w pts J. Payne, J. Kelly w pts M. Roche; *semi-finals:* D. Higgins w pts F. Webb, J. Kelly w pts S. Gibson; *final:* D. Higgins w pts J. Kelly. **Middle:** *quarter-finals:* B. Magee (Holy Trinity, Belfast) wo, R. Fox (Phibsboro, Dublin) wo, D. Galvin (St Saviour's, Dublin) wo, B. Crowley (Ennis, Clare) w pts A. Kelly (Brosna, Offaly); *semi-finals:* B. Magee w pts R. Fox, B. Crowley w pts D. Galvin; *final:* B. Magee

w pts B. Crowley (bout stopped in 2nd due to cuts, Magee ahead on pts). **L. Heavy:** *prelims:* S. Kirk (Cairn Lodge, Belfast) wo, T. Donnelly (Mark Heagney's, Tyrone) wo, A. Sheerin (Swinford, Mayo) wo, S. Lawlor (Grangecon, Kildare) wo, M. Fallon (Trojan, London) wo, P. Taylor (Enniskerry, Wicklow) wo, G. Joyce (Sunnyside, Cork) wo, S. Collier (Loch Gorman, Wexford) w co 1 J. O'Leary (Rylane, Cork); *quarter-finals:* S. Kirk w pts T. Donnelly, A. Sheerin w rsc 1 S. Lawlor, M. Fallon w pts P. Taylor, G. Joyce w pts S. Collier; *semi-finals:* S. Kirk w rsc 3 A. Sheerin, G. Joyce w pts M. Fallon; *final:* S. Kirk w pts G. Joyce. **Heavy:** *quarter-finals:* P. Douglas (Holy Family, Belfast) w pts D. Griffin (Castleisland, Kerry), J. Kiely (Limerick) w rsc 1 M. Sutton (St Saviour's, Dublin), C. O'Grady (St Saviour's, Dublin) w rsc 1 P. Deane (Ballina, Mayo), B. McGarrigle (Omagh, Tyrone) w pts A. Brady (Galway); *semi-finals:* P. Douglas w pts J. Kiely, C. O'Grady wo B. McGarrigle; *final:* C. O'Grady w pts P. Douglas. **S. Heavy:** *quarter-finals:* S. Murphy (St Michael's, New Ross) w pts G. Douglas (South Meath, Meath), D. Greene (Trim, Meath) w pts D. Horan (Dunboyne, Meath), T. O'Connor (Knocknagashel, Kerry, and Trinity College, Dublin) w pts T. Clarke (Buncrana, Donegal), T. Clifford (Rylane, Cork) w pts D. Ward (Ballymun, Dublin); *semi-finals:* S. Murphy w pts D. Greene, T. O'Connor w pts T. Clifford; *final:* S. Murphy w rsc 1 T. O'Connor.

Intermediate Finals

The National Stadium, Dublin - 1 December
L. Fly: J. Muldoon (St Mary's, Ballina) w pts B. Mathers (St Patrick's, Newry). **Fly:** D. Sweetman (Golden Cobra, Dublin) w pts K. Moore (St Francis, Limerick). **Bantam:** R. Lyons (St Brigid's, Dublin) w pts J. Simpson (St Saviour's, Dublin, and Crystal, Waterford). **Feather:** D. Hyland (Golden Cobra, Dublin) w pts M. Kelleher (Ballyvolane, Cork). **Light:** D. Barrett (Rylane, Cork) w pts M. O'Kane (Holy Trinity, Belfast). **L. Welter:** F. Barrett (Olympic, Galway) w pts T. Ennis (Mount Tallant, Dublin). **Welter:** M. Riggs (West Finglas, Dublin) w pts M. Blaney (Holy Trinity, Belfast). **L. Middle:** D. Devers (St Mary's, Ballina) w rsc 3 T. Kelly (Moate, Westmeath). **Middle:** A. Kelly (Brosna, Westmeath) w pts J. McKay (HML, Down). **L. Heavy:** D. Cuttriss (Crumlin, Dublin) w pts S. O'Grady (St Saviour's, Dublin). **Heavy:** D. Ward (Galway) w pts S. McKay (HML, Down). **S. Heavy:** T. O'Connor (Knocknagashel, Kerry, and Trinity College, Dublin) w rsc 3 B. Devine (Holy Family, Belfast).

Junior Finals

The National Stadium, Dublin - 3 May
L. Fly: no entries. **Fly:** C. Nash (Ring, Derry) w pts J. P. Campbell (South Meath, Meath). **Bantam:** T. O'Shaughnessy (Golden Cobra, Dublin) w pts J. Philips (St Michael's, Wexford). **Feather:** A. Carlyle (Sacred Heart, Belfast) w pts D. O'Sullivan (Blarney, Cork). **Light:** R. Hore (CBS Wexford) w pts L. Duncliffe (Ballyvolane, Cork). **L. Welter:** D. Conlon (Lochglinn, Roscommon). **Welter:** P. Walsh (St Colman's, Cork) w pts I. Timms (Quarryvale, Dublin). **L. Middle:** D. Conlon (Lochglinn, Roscommon) w pts S. Crudden (Cooneen, Tyrone). **Middle:** A. Kelly (Brosna, Westmeath) w rsc 3 J. McDonagh (St Ann's, Westport). **L. Heavy:** T. Crampton (St Broughan's, Offaly) w pts J. O'Brien (Matt Talbot, Dublin). **Heavy:** P. Byrne (Swinford, Mayo) wo. **S. Heavy:** D. Desmond (Bandon, Cork) w rsc 1 D. Mullen (St Ann's, Westport).

Scottish and Welsh Senior Championships, 1995-96

Scottish

The Monklands Time Capsule, Coatbridge - 2 & 29 March, The Fairfield Social Club, Glasgow - 18 March & The Hydro Hotel, Dunblane - 22 March

L. Fly: *final:* J. Smith (Barn) wo. **Fly:** *final:* R. Laing (Haddington) w pts S. Hay (Barn). **Bantam:** *semi-finals:* A. Arthur (Leith Victoria) wo, W. Logue (Phoenix) w pts M. Keen (Condorrat); *final:* A. Arthur w pts W. Logue. **Feather:** *semi-finals:* R. McPhee (Glenboig) wo, R. Silverstein (Selkirk) w rsc 1 T. McDonald (Perth Railway); *final:* R. McPhee w pts R. Silverstein. **Light:** *quarter-finals:* M. Gowans (Selkirk) wo, D. Clair (Springhill) wo, D. Stewart (St Francis) w pts G. Fernie (Bonnyrigg), K. Stuart (Elgin) w pts J. Leys (Aberdeen); *semi-finals:* M. Gowans w pts D. Clair, D. Stewart w pts K. Stuart; *final:* M. Gowans w pts D. Stewart. **L. Welter:** *quarter-finals:* G. McLevy (Clydeview) wo, L. Sharp (Leith Victoria) wo, J. Howitt (Lochee) wo, W. Leckie (Haddington) w pts A. McDonald (Bannockburn); *semi-finals:* G. McLevy w pts L. Sharp, J. Howitt w pts W. Leckie; *final:* G. McLevy w pts J. Howitt. **Welter:** *quarter-finals:* J. Miller (Stirling) wo, L. McBride (Elgin) w rsc 1 J. Boyd (Perth Railway), S. Kelly (Dennistoun) w pts A. Gordon (Hayton), C. McNeill (Springhill) w pts P. Munro (Lochee); *semi-finals:* L. McBride w rsc 2 J. Miller, C. McNeill wo S. Kelly; *final:* C. McNeill w pts L. McBride. **L. Middle:** *prelims:* F. Clews (Barn) wo, A. Howitt (Lochee) wo, A. Wolecki (St Francis) wo, K. Jack (Haddington) wo, M. Flynn (Blantyre Miners) w pts P. Court (Springhill), C. Edmond (Sparta) w pts J. Gilhaney (Cleland Miners), A. Craig (Aberdeen) w pts J. Heaney (Croy Miners), B. Laidlaw (Cardenden) w pts M. Black (Chirnside); *quarter-finals:* A. Howitt w rsc 1 F. Clews, A. Wolecki w rsc 2 K. Jack, M. Flynn w pts C. Edmond, A. Craig w pts B. Laidlaw; *semi-finals:* A. Wolecki w rsc 3 A. Howitt, A. Craig w pts M. Flynn; *final:* A. Wolecki w pts A. Craig. **Middle:** *quarter-finals:* J. Daley (Bannockburn) wo, S. McFarlane (Cleland Miners) w pts D. Evans (Arbroath), M. Fleming (Kingdom) w pts J. Day (Aberdeen University), P. Grainger (Sparta) w pts D. Hamilton (Sparta); *semi-finals:* J. Daley w pts S. McFarlane, M. Fleming w pts P Grainger; *final:* J. Daley w pts M. Fleming. **L. Heavy:** *quarter-finals:* L. Ramsay (Kingdom) wo, D. Sharkey (Lanarkshire Welfare) wo, L. Hutcheon (Aberdeen) wo, A. Kelly (Meadowbank) w rsc 1 R. Keisler (Sparta); *semi-finals:* L. Ramsay wo D. Sharkey, A. Kelly w rsc 2 L. Hutcheon; *final:* A. Kelly w pts L. Ramsay. **Heavy:** *quarter-finals:* P. Geddes (Elgin) wo, W. Cane (Four Isles) w rsc 1 I. Burgess (Bathgate), J. Williams (North West) w rsc 1 S. Wilson (Cleland Miners), I. McCabe (Penicuik) w pts D. Sipple (Meadowbank); *semi-finals:* W. Cane w pts P. Geddes, J. Williams w pts I. McCabe; *final:* W. Cane w rsc 2 J. Williams. **S. Heavy:** *final:* J. Cowie (Bannockburn) w pts D. Buchan (St Francis).

Welsh

The Afan Lido, Port Talbot - 10 February, The Workmens' Club, Mountain Ash - 24 February & The Institute of Sport, Cardiff - 7 March

L. Fly: no entries. **Fly:** *final:* D. Fox (RAF/Vale) w rsc 3 K. Ali (Splott Adventure). **Bantam:** *final:* J. Kerrigan (Llansamlet) wo. **Feather:** *final:* A. Fletcher (Newtown) wo. **Light:** *semi-finals:* M. Spragg (Splott Adventure) wo, A. Dummer (Kyber Colts) w pts P. Dennis (Aberkenfig); *final:* M. Spragg w pts A. Dummer. **L. Welter:** *semi-finals:* V. Powell (Army) wo, J. Cook (Cwmavon Hornets) w pts L. Winney (Telfi Valley); *final:* J. Cook w pts V. Powell. **Welter:** *quarter-finals:* K. Shuker (Newtown) wo, R. Weston (Highfields) w pts K. Thomas (Pontypridd), J. Cheal (Whitlands) w rsc 2 D. Pugh (Newtown), J. Williams (Gwent) w rsc 1 A. Davies (Vale); *semi-finals:* R. Weston w rsc 1 K. Shuker, J. Williams w rtd 1 J. Cheal; *final:* J. Williams w pts R. Weston. **L. Middle:** *quarter-finals:* J. Samuels (Prince of Wales) wo, K. Short (Aberkenfig) wo, M. Gammer (Pembroke Dock) w pts M. Phillips (Carmarthen), D. Williams (Gwent) w rsc 3 A. Potterton (Cwmavon Hornets); *semi-finals:* D. Williams wo M. Gammer, J. Samuels w pts K. Short; *final:* D. Williams w pts J. Samuels. **Middle:** *final:* G. Briggs (Pontypridd) w pts S. Stradling (Vale). **L. Heavy:** *quarter-final:* S. Thomas (Shotton) wo, H. Hughes-Williams (Newtown) wo, M. Tolton (Montana) wo, S. Donaldson (Highfields) w pts M. McCauley (Pontypridd); *semi-finals:* S. Thomas w rsc 2 H. Hughes-Williams, S. Donaldson w rsc 3 M. Tolton; *final:* S. Donaldson w pts S. Thomas. **Heavy:** *final:* S. Gammer (Pembroke Dock) w rsc 1 J. Smith (Highfields). **S. Heavy:** *final:* K. McCormack (RN) wo.

Former English ABA champion, Kevin Short, failed in his attempt to land a Welsh title, losing at the light-middleweight semi-final stage to Jason Samuels

Les Clark

British and Irish International Matches and Championships, 1995-96

Internationals

England (4) v Holland (2)   Rotterdam, Holland - 25 September
(English names first): **Feather:** D. Burrows w pts W. Thompson. **Light:** A. McLean l pts A. Santana. **L. Welter:** L. Crosby drew A. Medina, J. Mellor drew N. Armine. **Welter:** M. Hall l pts H. Janssen, M. Jones w pts T. Bakker. **Middle:** A. Lowe drew F. Lopes. **L. Heavy:** J. Branch w pts W. Sterkenburg. **S. Heavy:** H. Senior w pts H. de Keizer. There were three draws.

Ireland (3) v Denmark (8)   Grenaa, Denmark - 27 October
(Irish names first): **Bantam:** W. Valentine l pts M. Mollenberg. **Feather:** T. Carlyle l pts R. Idrissi. **Light:** G. Stephens w pts E. Jensen, M. Dillon l pts S. Jorgenson. **L. Welter:** G. McLarnon l pts T. Damgaard, W. Walsh w pts M. Erslan. **Welter:** F. Carruth l pts H. Al. **Middle:** D. Higgins w pts P. Andersen. **Middle:** B. Magee l pts O. Nielsen. **L. Heavy:** S. Kirk l pts B. Lentz. **Heavy:** J. Clancy l pts O. Nielsen.

Scotland (2) v Norway (5)   Gol, Norway - 11 November
(Scottish names first): **Bantam:** M. Crossan l rsc 3 R. Walstad. **Light:** K. McIntyre l pts P. Risan. **L. Welter:** D. Evans l pts S. Aagaard, G. McLevy w pts S. Elmari. **Welter:** C. McNeil l pts A. Styve. **L. Heavy:** R. Campbell w pts F. Steinsvik. **Heavy:** S. Hardie w pts P. Magne Tronvold.

England (4) v USA (4)   Hilton Hotel, London - 20 November
(English names first): **Bantam:** D. Adams l pts Z. Raheem. **Feather:** D. Burke w co 1 A. Ramos. **L. Welter:** A. Vaughan l rsc 2 D. Corley. **Welter:** M. Jones w pts D. Palac. **Middle:** A. Lowe w pts S. Swartz. **L. Heavy:** J. Branch w pts O. Anderson. **Heavy:** M. Sprott l pts J. Cruz. **S. Heavy:** H. Senior l rtd 1 J. Mesi.

Ireland (5) v England (6)   National Stadium, Dublin - 8 December
(Irish names first): **Bantam:** W. Valentine l pts M. Gibbons, D. McKenna w pts D. Burrows. **Light:** G. Stephens w pts T. Peacock. **L. Welter:** G. McLarnon w pts L. Crosby. **Welter:** N. Gough w pts M. Jones, F. Carruth l pts M. Hall. **L. Middle:** D. Higgins l pts C. Bessey. **Middle:** B. Magee l pts S. Bendall, B. Crowley w pts A. Lowe. **Heavy:** J. Clancy l pts F. Okesola. **S. Heavy:** G. Douglas l pts G. McGinn.

Young England (5) v Young Germany (4)   Winter Gardens, Blackpool - 26 January
(English names first): **Fly:** J. Hegney l pts G. Ringmann. **Bantam:** J. Rooney w rsc 1 P. Miermeister. **Feather:** D. Tokeley l pts R. Hensel. **Light:** B. Beck w pts A. Phillip, A. Kelly w pts C. Rummell. **L. Welter:** N. Lee w pts J. Thieme. **Welter:** R. Hatton l rtd 1 J. Brahmer. **L. Middle:** R. Rooney w pts A. Golombeck. **Middle:** S. Lee l co 1 S. Muller.

England (6) v South Africa (1)   Royal Lancaster Hotel, London - 5 February
(English names first): **Fly:** D. Costello w pts K. Buhalao. **Bantam:** M. Gibbons l pts S. Mabuza. **Light:** T. Peacock w co 2 E. Makama. **L. Welter:** A. Vaughan w pts S. Carr. **Welter:** M. Hall w pts A. Segopa. **L. Middle:** C. Bessey w pts V. Kunene. **L. Heavy:** J. Branch w rsc 1 S. Botes.

Scotland (2) v Norway (5)   Fairfield Social Club, Glasgow - 25 April
(Scottish names first): **Feather:** R. McGrath l pts R. Walstad.

Light: D. Clair l rsc 2 P. R. Haagensen. **L. Welter:** G. McLevy w pts S. Elmari, F. Kerr w pts G. Jorgensen. **Welter:** L. McBride l rsc 3 F. R.Walstad. **L. Heavy:** A. Kelly l pts F. Steinsvik. **Heavy:** W. Cane l pts R. Lillebuen.

Ireland (4) v Italy (6)   Marcianese, Italy - 27 April
(Irish names first): **Feather:** D. Hyland l pts Letizia. **Light:** M. Dillon l pts G. Lauri. **L. Welter:** J. Morrissey w pts M. Delli Paoli. **Welter:** S. Barrett w pts Maietta. **L. Middle:** S. Keeler l pts C. D'Alessandro, J. Payne l pts F. Dellicurti, M. Roche l pts C. Perugino. **Middle:** B. Crowley w pts Pasqualetti. **L. Heavy:** A. Sheerin l rsc 2 M. Giovannini. **Heavy:** J. Kieley l co 2 G. Fragomeni.

Championships

European Seniors   Velje, Denmark - 30 March to 7 April
L. Fly: J. Prior (Ireland) l dis 2 S. Stroem (Sweden). **Fly:** D. Costello (England) l pts J. Turunen (Finland); D. Fox (Wales) l pts C. Molaro (Italy); M. Crossan (Scotland) l pts V. Christoforidis (Greece); D. Kelly (Ireland) w pts D. Olsson (Sweden), w pts M. Musamedin (Yugoslavia), w pts C. Molaro (Italy), l pts A. Pakeev (Russia). **Bantam:** L. Eedle (England) l rsc 3 G. Krizan (Slovakia); D. McKenna (Ireland) w pts T. Janevski (Macedonia), l rsc 1 R. Bouaita (France). **Feather:** T. Carlyle (Ireland) l pts S. Todorov (Bulgaria); S. Harrison (Scotland) w rsc 3 T. Naskovski (Macedonia), w pts J. Nagy (Hungary), w pts E. Shestakov (Ukraine), l pts R. Paliani (Russia); D. Burke (England) w pts S. Vagasky (Slovakia), w pts A. Sachbazjan (Czechoslovakia), w rsc 1 S. Yagli (Turkey), l pts S. Todorov (Bulgaria). **Light:** J. Coyle (Scotland) l rsc 1 T. Tontchev (Bulgaria); M. Reneghan (Ireland) l co 1 K. Gogoladze (Georgia); T. Peacock (England) l pts M. Varga (Hungary); J. Cook (Wales) w pts P. Gvasalia (Russia), l pts J. Konecny (Czechoslovakia). **L. Welter:** J. Pender (Scotland) l pts J. Bielski (Poland); V. Powell (Wales) l rsc 1 R. Suslekov (Bulgaria); F. Barrett (Ireland) w pts V. Groushak (Moldova), l pts E. Zakharov (Russia). **Welter:** G. Murphy (Scotland) l pts V. Mezga (Belarus); M. Jones (England) l pts H. Al (Denmark); J. Williams (Wales) l pts P. Dostal (Czechoslovakia); N. Gough (Ireland) l pts S. Dzinzirouk (Ukraine). **L. Middle:** D. Higgins (Ireland) l pts R. Pettersson (Sweden); C. Bessey (England) l pts M. Beyer (Germany); J. Murphy (Scotland) w pts S. Kokkinos (Cyprus), l rsc 1 M. Beyer (Germany). **Middle:** G. Briggs (Wales) l pts A. Kakauridze (Georgia); S. Bendall (England) l pts V. Kushmintzev (Bulgaria); B. Magee (Ireland) w pts G. Oprea (Romania), w pts P. Maennikoe (Finland), l rsc 1 J-P Mendy (France). **L. Heavy:** S. Kirk (Ireland) l pts V. Davidov (Bulgaria); J. Branch (England) l pts Y. Oztuerk (Turkey). **Heavy:** F. Okesola (England) w rsc 1 D. Karanovic (Yugoslavia), w rsc 1 K. Turkson (Sweden); C. O'Grady (Ireland) w co 1 R. Marnota (Slovakia), l pts C. Mendy (France). **S. Heavy:** S. Murphy (Ireland) l dis 2 V. Klitchko (Ukraine); K. McCormack (Wales) l rsc 3 A. Lezin (Russia).

Olympic Games   Atlanta, USA - 20 July to 4 August
Fly: D. Kelly (Ireland) w pts J. Strogov (Bulgaria), w pts H. Hussein (Australia), l pts B. Dzumadilov (Kazakhstan). **Feather:** D. Burke (England) l pts F. Huste (Germany). **L. Welter:** F. Barrett (Ireland) w pts Z. Ferreira (Brazil), l pts F. Missaoui (Tunisia). **Middle:** B. Magee (Ireland) w pts R. Thompson (Canada), w pts B. Tietsia (Camaroon), l pts M. Bahari (Algeria). **Heavy:** C. O'Grady (Ireland) l rsc 1 G. da Silva (New Zealand); F. Okesola (England) l rsc 3 N. Jones (USA).

British Junior Championship Finals, 1995-96

National Association of Boy's Clubs

Civic Centre, Mansfield - 5 January
Class A: 42 kg: S. Symes (West Hill) w pts J. O'Sullivan (Bracebridge). 45 kg: B. Tokeley (West Ham) w pts H. Cunningham (Saints). 48 kg: T. Chapman (Newham) w pts C. Solway (West Hull). 51 kg: M. Power (St Pancras) w pts K. McKeown (Halls Mill). 54 kg: D. Price (West Ham) w pts T. Khan (Sedbergh). 57 kg: A. Buchanan (Teams) w pts G. Smith (Foley). 60 kg: L. Hallett (Pleck) w rsc 2 J. Kiely (Repton). 63.5 kg: K. Concepcion (Belgrave) w pts D. Cadman (Repton). 67 kg: T. Henson (Radford) w rsc 1 S. Mullins (Didcot). 71 kg: P. Ayres (St Thomas') wo.

Cutler's Hall, Sheffield - 12 January
Class B: 45 kg: J. Kerrin (Tilbury Dockers) w pts K. Brierley (Market District). 48 kg: W. Johnson (Desborough) w pts J. Brazil (Foley). 51 kg: S. Miller (Foley) w pts N. Cook (Hornchurch & Elm Park). 54 kg: J. Chambers (Highfield) w pts T. Rowley (Hartlepool Boys Welfare). 57 kg: S. Smith (St Joseph's) w pts J. Beech (Pleck). 60 kg: C. Carmichael (Emerald) w pts V. Lynes (Hornchurch & Elm Park). 63.5 kg: G. Wake (Hunslet) w pts T. James (Eltham). 67 kg: S. Swales (Phil Thomas SOB) w pts B. Hierons (Rayleigh Mill). 71 kg: W. Curwood (St Paul's) w pts A. Larkins (Bracknell). 74 kg: S. Lee (West Ham) w co 1 S. McLean (Atherstone). 77 kg: P. Souter (Newham) w pts D. Dolan (Plains Farm).

Grosvenor House, London - 15 January
Class C: 48 kg: I. Napa (Crown & Manor) w pts S. Groves (Tower Hill). 51 kg: C. Johanneson (Burmantofts) w pts T. Joyett (Alma). 54 kg: D. Tokeley (West Ham) w pts D. Coyle (Benchill). 57 kg: M. Thompson (Phil Thomas SOB) w pts S. Morgan (Farley). 60 kg: L. Daws (Rosehill) w rsc 3 C. Skelton (South Bank). 63.5 kg: N. Lee (Repton) w pts G. Down (Chesterfield). 67 kg: M. Jennings (Preston Red Rose) w pts L. Clayfield (Broad Plain). 71 kg: C. Lynes (Hornchurch & Elm Park) w rsc 1 M. Jennings (Salisbury). 75 kg: D. Doyle (Belhus Park) w pts J. Dolan (Plains Farm). 81 kg: S. Hellon (South Bank) w pts G. Turner (Warrington). 91 kg: S. St John (Berry) w pts M. Lacey (Louth).

Schools

Aston Villa Leisure Centre, Birmingham - 16 March
Junior A: 32 kg: D. Lanigan (Mottram & Hattersley) w pts B. Dodds (Hornchurch & Elm Park). 34 kg: J. Evans (Foley) w rsc 2 C. Elliott (Golden Gloves). 36 kg: R. Notman (West Ham) w pts N. Kell (Spennymoor). 39 kg: G. Brotherton (Newbiggin Dolphin) w pts S. Bishop (Walcot). 42 kg: W. Killick (Marvel Lane) w pts C. Orman (Bury). 45 kg: S. Power (St Pancras) w pts G. Nicholls (Burn Naze). 48 kg: C. Pratt (Bracknell) w rsc 1 M. Grosvenor (Vehicle Body Care). 51 kg: M. Ward (Dale) w pts D. Teasdale (Unity). 54 kg: S. Coughlan (Northolt) w rsc 1 P. Moore (Trinity). 57 kg: S. Coyle (Lynn) w pts J. Horne (Lancaster).

Junior B: 36 kg: S. McDonald (St Joseph's) w pts D. Lambert (Karmand Centre). 39 kg: C. Lyon (St Helens) w pts M. Corcoran (Trojan). 42 kg: D. Byrnes (Lynn) w pts F. Fehintola (Karmand Centre). 45 kg: J. Doherty (Dale) w rsc 1 G. Howe (Shildon). 48 kg: M. O'Donnell (Dale) w rsc 3 G. Smith (Karmand Centre). 51 kg: L. Beavis (Dale) w pts M. Macklin (Small Heath). 54 kg: R. Murray (Newbiggin Dolphin) w co 1 N. Wray (Southwick). 57 kg: C. Masterton (Coventry Colliery) w pts D. Cooper (Faversham). 60 kg: D. Spensley (Aycliffe) w pts C. Wilkinson (Focus). 63 kg: P. Buchanan (Teams) wo. 66 kg: B. Slate (Five Star) w rsc 1 N. McGarry (Doncaster Plant).

Intermediate: 39 kg: R. Wyatt (Stourbridge) w pts K. Smith (West Ham). 42 kg: D. Robson (Hartlepool Catholic) w rsc 3 D. Lorentson (St Mary's). 45 kg: W. Corcoran (Stowe) w pts J. Mulhearn (Triumph) - replaced A. Turnbull (Old Vic). 48 kg: B. Tokeley (West Ham) w pts L. Byrne (Fox). 51 kg: H. Rahman (Bushey) w pts B. Scholte (St Paul's). 54 kg: M. Weatherhead (Dale) wo C. Johnson (Chesterfield). 57 kg: D. Holland (Tower Hill) w dis 2 T. Shaw (Sporting Ring). 60 kg: G. Patient (Woodham & Wickford) w rsc 3 R. Wood (Pleck). 63 kg: D. Smith (Partington) w rsc 3 A. Barratt (Newham). 66 kg: J. Poulson (Tuebrook) w pts L. King (Shepway). 69 kg: P. Price (Pinewood Starr) w dis 2 R. Singh (Belgrave).

Senior: 42 kg: S. Symes (West Hill) w pts J. O'Sullivan (Bracebridge). 45 kg: R. Nelson (Batley & Dewsbury) w pts L. Burmingham (Eltham). 48 kg: N. Cook (Hornchurch & Elm Park) w rsc 1 D. Parkinson (Bradford Police). 51 kg: D. Mulholland (Transport) w pts M. Power (St Pancras). 54 kg: M. Gallagher (Finchley) wo T. Khan (Sedbergh). 57 kg: N. Smith (Birmingham Irish) w pts S. Wood (Westree). 60 kg: L. Hallett (Pleck) w rsc 2 L. Delaney (Dale). 63.5 kg: S. Yates (Dawlish) w rsc 1 A. Palmer (Chorley). 67 kg: G. Stevens (Mo's) w pts T. Henson (Radford). 71 kg: T. Dodson (Gemini) w pts L. Coates (Medway Golden Gloves). 75 kg: W. Fleming (West Wirral) w co 1 H. Vincent (Eltham).

ABA Youth

Fox Hollies Leisure Centre, Birmingham - 11 May
Class 5 (born 1979): 48 kg: N. Cook (Hornchurch & Elm Park) w co 1 K. Brierley (Vehicle Body Care). 51 kg: S. Miller (St Paul's) w pts D. Mulholland (Transport). 54 kg: J. De St Aubin (Dale) w pts J. Vassallo (Belhus Park). 57 kg: V. Lynes (Hornchurch & Elm Park) w pts T. Rowley (Hartlepool Boys Welfare). 60 kg: R. Mann (Newham) w pts L. Maltby (Focus). 63.5 kg: G. McAnaney (Lambton Street) w pts S. Yates (Dawlish). 67 kg: J. Weatherhead (Dale) w pts R. Yunis (Small Heath). 71 kg: A. Larkins (Bracknell) w pts L. Coates (Medway Golden Gloves). 75 kg: S. Lee (West Ham) w pts J. Callaghan (Vehicle Body Care). 81 kg: T. Eastwood (Foley) w pts P. Souter (Newham).

Class 6 (born 1978): 51 kg: J. Hegney (Castle Vale) w pts M. Hunter (Hartlepool Boys Welfare). 54 kg: J. Rooney (Hartlepool Catholic) w pts A. Gribbin (Ardwick). 57 kg: C. Skelton (South Bank) w pts G. Algar (Eltham). 60 kg: L. Bryan (Penhill RBL) w pts G. Earl (Luton Hightown). 63.5 kg: A. Farnell (Collyhurst) w pts M. Lomax (West Ham). 67 kg: R. Hatton (Sale West) w rsc 1 K. Khan (Earlsfield). 71 kg: D. Thornton (Meanwood) w pts W. Pinder (Northside). 75 kg: R. Rooney (Croxteth) w pts G. Ashraf (Slough). 81 kg: P. Haymer (St Pancras) w rsc 2 M. Fenton (Belgrave).

ABA Champions, 1881-1996

L. Flyweight
1971 M. Abrams
1972 M. Abrams
1973 M. Abrams
1974 C. Magri
1975 M. Lawless
1976 P. Fletcher
1977 P. Fletcher
1978 J. Dawson
1979 J. Dawson
1980 T. Barker
1981 J. Lyon
1982 J. Lyon
1983 J. Lyon
1984 J. Lyon
1985 M. Epton
1986 M. Epton
1987 M. Epton
1988 M. Cantwell
1989 M. Cantwell
1990 N. Tooley
1991 P. Culshaw
1992 D. Fifield
1993 M. Hughes
1994 G. Jones
1995 D. Fox
1996 R. Mercer

Flyweight
1920 H. Groves
1921 W. Cuthbertson
1922 E. Warwick
1923 L. Tarrant
1924 E. Warwick
1925 E. Warwick
1926 J. Hill
1927 J. Roland
1928 C. Taylor
1929 T. Pardoe
1930 T. Pardoe
1931 T. Pardoe
1932 T. Pardoe
1933 T. Pardoe
1934 P. Palmer
1935 G. Fayaud
1936 G. Fayaud
1937 P. O'Donaghue
1938 A. Russell
1939 D. McKay
1944 J. Clinton
1945 J. Bryce
1946 R. Gallacher
1947 J. Clinton
1948 H. Carpenter
1949 H. Riley
1950 A. Jones
1951 G. John
1952 D. Dower
1953 R. Currie
1954 R. Currie
1955 D. Lloyd
1956 T. Spinks
1957 R. Davies
1958 J. Brown
1959 M. Gushlow
1960 D. Lee
1961 W. McGowan
1962 M. Pye
1963 M. Laud
1964 J. McCluskey
1965 J. McCluskey
1966 P. Maguire
1967 S. Curtis
1968 J. McGonigle
1969 D. Needham
1970 D. Needham
1971 P. Wakefield
1972 M. O'Sullivan
1973 R. Hilton
1974 M. O'Sullivan
1975 C. Magri
1976 C. Magri
1977 C. Magri
1978 G. Nickels
1979 R. Gilbody
1980 K. Wallace
1981 K. Wallace
1982 J. Kelly
1983 S. Nolan
1984 P. Clinton
1985 P. Clinton
1986 J. Lyon
1987 J. Lyon
1988 J. Lyon
1989 J. Lyon
1990 J. Armour
1991 P. Ingle
1992 K. Knox
1993 P. Ingle
1994 D. Costello
1995 D. Costello
1996 D. Costello

Bantamweight
1884 A. Woodward
1885 A. Woodward
1886 T. Isley
1887 T. Isley
1888 H. Oakman
1889 H. Brown
1890 J. Rowe
1891 E. Moore
1892 F. Godbold
1893 E. Watson
1894 P. Jones
1895 P. Jones
1896 P. Jones
1897 C. Lamb
1898 F. Herring
1899 A. Avent
1900 J. Freeman
1901 W. Morgan
1902 A. Miner
1903 H. Perry
1904 H. Perry
1905 W. Webb
1906 T. Ringer
1907 E. Adams
1908 H. Thomas
1909 J. Condon
1910 W. Webb
1911 W. Allen
1912 W. Allen
1913 A. Wye
1914 W. Allen
1919 W. Allen
1920 G. McKenzie
1921 L. Tarrant
1922 W. Boulding
1923 A. Smith
1924 L. Tarrant
1925 A. Goom
1926 F. Webster
1927 E. Warwick
1928 J. Garland
1929 F. Bennett
1930 H. Mizler
1931 F. Bennett
1932 J. Treadaway
1933 G. Johnston
1934 A. Barnes
1935 L. Case
1936 A. Barnes
1937 A. Barnes
1938 J. Pottinger
1939 R. Watson
1944 R. Bissell
1945 P. Brander
1946 C. Squire
1947 D. O'Sullivan
1948 T. Profitt
1949 T. Miller
1950 K. Lawrence
1951 T. Nicholls
1952 T. Nicholls
1953 J. Smillie
1954 J. Smillie
1955 G. Dormer
1956 O. Reilly
1957 J. Morrissey
1958 H. Winstone
1959 D. Weller
1960 F. Taylor
1961 P. Benneyworth
1962 P. Benneyworth
1963 B. Packer
1964 B. Packer
1965 R. Mallon
1966 J. Clark
1967 M. Carter
1968 M. Carter
1969 M. Piner
1970 A. Oxley
1971 G. Turpin
1972 G. Turpin
1973 P. Cowdell
1974 S. Ogilvie
1975 S. Ogilvie
1976 J. Bambrick
1977 J. Turner
1978 J. Turner
1979 R. Ashton
1980 R. Gilbody
1981 P. Jones
1982 R. Gilbody
1983 J. Hyland
1984 J. Hyland
1985 S. Murphy
1986 S. Murphy
1987 J. Sillitoe
1988 K. Howlett
1989 K. Howlett
1990 P. Lloyd
1991 D. Hardie
1992 P. Mullings
1993 R. Evatt
1994 S. Oliver
1995 N. Wilders
1996 L. Eedle

Featherweight
1881 T. Hill
1882 T. Hill
1883 T. Hill
1884 E. Hutchings
1885 J. Pennell
1886 T. McNeil
1887 J. Pennell
1888 J. Taylor
1889 G. Belsey
1890 G. Belsey
1891 F. Curtis
1892 F. Curtis
1893 T. Davidson
1894 R. Gunn
1895 R. Gunn
1896 R. Gunn
1897 N. Smith
1898 P. Lunn
1899 J. Scholes
1900 R. Lee
1901 C. Clarke
1902 C. Clarke
1903 J. Godfrey
1904 C. Morris
1905 H. Holmes
1906 A. Miner
1907 C. Morris
1908 T. Ringer
1909 A. Lambert
1910 C. Houghton
1911 H. Bowers
1912 G. Baker
1913 G. Baker
1914 G. Baker
1919 G. Baker
1920 J. Fleming
1921 G. Baker
1922 E. Swash
1923 E. Swash
1924 A. Beavis
1925 A. Beavis
1926 R. Minshull
1927 F. Webster
1928 F. Meachem
1929 F. Meachem
1930 J. Duffield
1931 B. Caplan
1932 H. Mizler
1933 J. Walters
1934 J. Treadaway
1935 E. Ryan
1936 J. Treadaway
1937 A. Harper
1938 C. Gallie
1939 C. Gallie
1944 D. Sullivan
1945 J. Carter
1946 P. Brander
1947 S. Evans
1948 P. Brander
1949 H. Gilliland
1950 P. Brander
1951 J. Travers
1952 P. Lewis
1953 P. Lewis
1954 D. Charnley
1955 T. Nicholls
1956 T. Nicholls
1957 M. Collins
1958 M. Collins
1959 G. Judge
1960 P. Lundgren
1961 P. Cheevers
1962 B. Wilson
1963 A. Riley
1964 R. Smith
1965 K. Buchanan
1966 H. Baxter
1967 K. Cooper
1968 J. Cheshire
1969 A. Richardson
1970 D. Polak
1971 T. Wright
1972 K. Laing
1973 J. Lynch
1974 G. Gilbody
1975 R. Beaumont
1976 P. Cowdell
1977 P. Cowdell
1978 M. O'Brien
1979 P. Hanlon
1980 M. Hanif
1981 P. Hanlon
1982 H. Henry
1983 P. Bradley
1984 K. Taylor
1985 F. Havard
1986 P. Hodkinson
1987 P. English
1988 D. Anderson
1989 P. Richardson
1990 B. Carr
1991 J. Irwin
1992 A. Temple
1993 J. Cook
1994 D. Pithie
1995 D. Burrows
1996 T. Mulholland

Lightweight
1881 F. Hobday
1882 A. Bettinson
1883 A. Diamond
1884 A. Diamond
1885 A. Diamond
1886 G. Roberts
1887 J. Hair
1888 A. Newton
1889 W. Neale
1890 A. Newton
1891 E. Dettmer
1892 E. Dettmer
1893 W. Campbell
1894 W. Campbell
1895 A. Randall
1896 A. Vanderhout
1897 A. Vanderhout
1898 H. Marks
1899 H. Brewer

1900 G. Humphries	1979 G. Gilbody
1901 A. Warner	1980 G. Gilbody
1902 A. Warner	1981 G. Gilbody
1903 H. Fergus	1982 J. McDonnell
1904 M. Wells	1983 K. Willis
1905 M. Wells	1984 A. Dickson
1906 M. Wells	1985 E. McAuley
1907 M. Wells	1986 J. Jacobs
1908 H. Holmes	1987 M. Ayers
1909 F. Grace	1988 C. Kane
1910 T. Tees	1989 M. Ramsey
1911 A. Spenceley	1990 P. Gallagher
1912 R. Marriott	1991 P. Ramsey
1913 R. Grace	1992 D. Amory
1914 R. Marriott	1993 B. Welsh
1919 F. Grace	1995 R. Rutherford
1920 F. Grace	1996 K. Wing
1921 G. Shorter	
1922 G. Renouf	**L. Welterweight**
1923 G. Shorter	1951 W. Connor
1924 W. White	1952 P. Waterman
1925 E. Viney	1953 D. Hughes
1926 T. Slater	1954 G. Martin
1927 W. Hunt	1955 F. McQuillan
1928 F. Webster	1956 D. Stone
1929 W. Hunt	1957 D. Stone
1930 J. Waples	1958 R. Kane
1931 D. McCleave	1959 R. Kane
1932 F. Meachem	1960 R. Day
1933 H. Mizler	1961 B. Brazier
1934 J. Rolland	1962 B. Brazier
1935 F. Frost	1963 R. McTaggart
1936 F. Simpson	1964 R. Taylor
1937 A. Danahar	1965 R. McTaggart
1938 T. McGrath	1966 W. Hiatt
1939 H. Groves	1967 B. Hudspeth
1944 W. Thompson	1968 E. Cole
1945 J. Williamson	1969 J. Stracey
1946 E. Thomas	1970 D. Davies
1947 C. Morrissey	1971 M. Kingwell
1948 R. Cooper	1972 T. Waller
1949 A. Smith	1973 N. Cole
1950 R. Latham	1974 P. Kelly
1951 R. Hinson	1975 J. Zeraschi
1952 F. Reardon	1976 C. McKenzie
1953 D. Hinson	1977 J. Douglas
1954 G. Whelan	1978 D. Williams
1955 S. Coffey	1979 E. Copeland
1956 R. McTaggart	1980 A. Willis
1957 J. Kidd	1981 A. Willis
1958 R. McTaggart	1982 A. Adams
1959 P. Warwick	1983 D. Dent
1960 R. McTaggart	1984 D. Griffiths
1961 P. Warwick	1985 I. Mustafa
1962 B. Whelan	1986 J. Alsop
1963 B. O'Sullivan	1987 A. Holligan
1964 J. Dunne	1988 A. Hall
1965 A. White	1989 A. Hall
1966 J. Head	1990 J. Pender
1967 T. Waller	1991 J. Matthews
1968 J. Watt	1992 D. McCarrick
1969 H. Hayes	1993 P. Richardson
1970 N. Cole	1994 A. Temple
1971 J. Singleton	1995 A. Vaughan
1972 N. Cole	1996 C. Wall
1973 T. Dunn	
1974 J. Lynch	**Welterweight**
1975 P. Cowdell	1920 F. Whitbread
1976 S. Mittee	1921 A. Ireland
1977 G. Gilbody	1922 E. White
1978 T. Marsh	1923 P. Green

Jawaid Khaliq (standing) of Meadows & Ruddington won the 1996 ABA welter title by outpointing the Army's Jason Gardner   Les Clark

1924 P. O'Hanrahan	1946 J. Ryan	1964 M. Varley
1925 P. O'Hanrahan	1947 J. Ryan	1965 P. Henderson
1926 B. Marshall	1948 M. Shacklady	1966 P. Cragg
1927 H. Dunn	1949 A. Buxton	1967 D. Cranswick
1928 H. Bone	1950 T. Ratcliffe	1968 A. Tottoh
1929 T. Wigmore	1951 J. Maloney	1969 T. Henderson
1930 F. Brooman	1952 J. Maloney	1970 T. Waller
1931 J. Barry	1953 L. Morgan	1971 D. Davies
1932 D. McCleave	1954 N. Gargano	1972 T. Francis
1933 P. Peters	1955 N. Gargano	1973 T. Waller
1934 D. McCleave	1956 N. Gargano	1974 T. Waller
1935 D. Lynch	1957 R. Warnes	1975 W. Bennett
1936 W. Pack	1958 B. Nancurvis	1976 C. Jones
1937 D. Lynch	1959 J. McGrail	1977 C. Jones
1938 C. Webster	1960 C. Humphries	1978 E. Byrne
1939 R. Thomas	1961 A. Lewis	1979 J. Frost
1944 H. Hall	1962 J. Pritchett	1980 T. Marsh
1945 R. Turpin	1963 J. Pritchett	1981 T. Marsh

1982 C. Pyatt
1983 R. McKenley
1984 M. Hughes
1985 E. McDonald
1986 D. Dyer
1987 M. Elliot
1988 M. McCreath
1989 M. Elliot
1990 A. Carew
1991 J. Calzaghe
1992 M. Santini
1993 C. Bessey
1994 K. Short
1995 M. Hall
1996 J. Khaliq

L. Middleweight
1951 A. Lay
1952 B. Foster
1953 B. Wells
1954 B. Wells
1955 B. Foster
1956 J. McCormack
1957 J. Cunningham
1958 S. Pearson
1959 S. Pearson
1960 W. Fisher
1961 J. Gamble
1962 J. Lloyd
1963 A. Wyper
1964 W. Robinson
1965 P. Dwyer
1966 T. Imrie
1967 A. Edwards
1968 E. Blake
1969 T. Imrie
1970 D. Simmonds
1971 A. Edwards
1972 L. Paul
1973 R. Maxwell
1974 R. Maxwell
1975 A. Harrison

1976 W. Lauder
1977 C. Malarkey
1978 E. Henderson
1979 D. Brewster
1980 J. Price
1981 E. Christie
1982 D. Milligan
1983 R. Douglas
1984 R. Douglas
1985 R. Douglas
1986 T. Velinor
1987 N. Brown
1988 W. Ellis
1989 N. Brown
1990 T. Taylor
1991 T. Taylor
1992 J. Calzaghe
1993 D. Starie
1994 W. Alexander
1995 C. Bessey
1996 S. Dann

Middleweight
1881 T. Bellhouse
1882 A. H. Curnick
1883 A. J. Curnick
1884 W. Brown
1885 M. Salmon
1886 W. King
1887 R. Hair
1888 R. Hair
1889 G. Sykes
1890 J. Hoare
1891 J. Steers
1892 J. Steers
1893 J. Steers
1894 W. Sykes
1895 G. Townsend
1896 W. Ross
1897 W. Dees
1898 G. Townsend
1899 R. Warnes

1900 E. Mann
1901 R. Warnes
1902 E. Mann
1903 R. Warnes
1904 E. Mann
1905 J. Douglas
1906 A. Murdock
1907 R. Warnes
1908 W. Child
1909 W. Child
1910 R. Warnes
1911 W. Child
1912 E. Chandler
1913 W. Bradley
1914 H. Brown
1919 H. Mallin
1920 H. Mallin
1921 H. Mallin
1922 H. Mallin
1923 H. Mallin
1924 J. Elliot
1925 J. Elliot
1926 F. P. Crawley
1927 F. P. Crawley
1928 F. Mallin
1929 F. Mallin
1930 F. Mallin
1931 F. Mallin
1932 F. Mallin
1933 A. Shawyer
1934 J. Magill
1935 J. Magill
1936 A. Harrington
1937 M. Dennis
1938 H. Tiller
1939 H. Davies
1944 J. Hockley
1945 R. Parker
1946 R. Turpin
1947 R. Agland
1948 J. Wright
1949 S. Lewis

1950 P. Longo
1951 E. Ludlam
1952 T. Gooding
1953 R. Barton
1954 K. Phillips
1955 F. Hope
1956 R. Redrup
1957 P. Burke
1958 P. Hill
1959 F. Elderfield
1960 R. Addison
1961 J. Caiger
1962 A. Matthews
1963 A. Matthews
1964 W. Stack
1965 W. Robinson
1966 C. Finnegan
1967 A. Ball
1968 P. McCann
1969 D. Wallington
1970 J. Conteh
1971 A. Minter
1972 F. Lucas
1973 F. Lucas
1974 D. Odwell
1975 D. Odwell
1976 E. Burke
1977 R. Davies
1978 H. Graham
1979 N. Wilshire
1980 M. Kaylor
1981 B. Schumacher
1982 J. Price
1983 T. Forbes
1984 B. Schumacher
1985 D. Cronin
1986 N. Benn
1987 R. Douglas
1988 M. Edwards
1989 S. Johnson
1990 S. Wilson
1991 M. Edwards

1992 L. Woolcock
1993 J. Calzaghe
1994 D. Starie
1995 J. Matthews
1996 J. Pearce

L. Heavyweight
1920 H. Franks
1921 L. Collett
1922 H. Mitchell
1923 H. Mitchell
1924 H. Mitchell
1925 H. Mitchell
1926 D. McCorkindale
1927 A. Jackson
1928 A. Jackson
1929 J. Goyder
1930 J. Murphy
1931 J. Petersen
1932 J. Goyder
1933 G. Brennan
1934 G. Brennan
1935 R. Hearns
1936 J. Magill
1937 J. Wilby
1938 A. S. Brown
1939 B. Woodcock
1944 E. Shackleton
1945 A. Watson
1946 J. Taylor
1947 A. Watson
1948 D. Scott
1949 *Declared no contest*
1950 P. Messervy
1951 G. Walker
1952 H. Cooper
1953 H. Cooper
1954 A. Madigan
1955 D. Rent
1956 D. Mooney
1957 T. Green
1958 J. Leeming
1959 J. Ould
1960 J. Ould
1961 J. Bodell
1962 J. Hendrickson
1963 P. Murphy
1964 J. Fisher
1965 E. Whistler
1966 R. Tighe
1967 M. Smith
1968 R. Brittle
1969 J. Frankham
1970 J. Rafferty
1971 J. Conteh
1972 W. Knight
1973 W. Knight
1974 W. Knight
1975 M. Heath
1976 G. Evans
1977 C. Lawson
1978 V. Smith
1979 A. Straughn
1980 A. Straughn
1981 A. Straughn
1982 G. Crawford
1983 A. Wilson
1984 A. Wilson
1985 J. Beckles
1986 J. Moran
1987 J. Beckles
1988 H. Lawson
1989 N. Piper

John Pearce, the 1996 middleweight titleholder from Wellington   Les Clark

275

To win the 1996 ABA light-heavyweight title, Londoner, Courtney Fry (right), thwarted the hopes of the consistent runner-up, Paul Rogers

Les Clark

1952 E. Hearn	1983 H. Notice	
1953 J. Erskine	1984 D. Young	
1954 B. Harper	1985 H. Hylton	
1955 D. Rowe	1986 E. Cardouza	
1956 D. Rent	1987 J. Moran	
1957 D. Thomas	1988 H. Akinwande	
1958 D. Thomas	1989 H. Akinwande	
1959 D. Thomas	1990 K. Inglis	
1960 L. Hobbs	1991 P. Lawson	
1961 W. Walker	1992 S. Welch	
1962 R. Dryden	1993 P. Lawson	
1963 R. Sanders	1994 S. Burford	
1964 C. Woodhouse	1995 M. Ellis	
1965 W. Wells	1996 T. Oakey	
1966 A. Brogan		
1967 P. Boddington	**S. Heavyweight**	
1968 W. Wells	1982 A. Elliott	
1969 A. Burton	1983 K. Ferdinand	
1970 J. Gilmour	1984 R. Wells	
1971 L. Stevens	1985 G. Williamson	
1972 T. Wood	1986 J. Oyebola	
1973 G. McEwan	1987 J. Oyebola	
1974 N. Meade	1988 K. McCormack	
1975 G. McEwan	1989 P. Passley	
1976 J. Rafferty	1990 K. McCormack	
1977 G. Adair	1991 K. McCormack	
1978 J. Awome	1992 M. Hopper	
1979 A. Palmer	1993 M. McKenzie	
1980 F. Bruno	1994 D. Watts	
1981 A. Elliott	1995 R. Allen	
1982 H. Hylton	1996 D. Watts	

1990 J. McCluskey	1896 W. E. Johnstone	1924 A. Clifton
1991 A. Todd	1897 G. Townsend	1925 D. Lister
1992 K. Oliver	1898 G. Townsend	1926 T. Petersen
1993 K. Oliver	1899 F. Parks	1927 C. Capper
1994 K. Oliver	1900 W. Dees	1928 J. L. Driscoll
1995 K. Oliver	1901 F. Parks	1929 P. Floyd
1996 C. Fry	1902 F. Parks	1930 V. Stuart
	1903 F. Dickson	1931 M. Flanagan
Heavyweight	1904 A. Horner	1932 V. Stuart
1881 R. Frost-Smith	1905 F. Parks	1933 C. O'Grady
1882 H. Dearsley	1906 F. Parks	1934 P. Floyd
1883 H. Dearsley	1907 H. Brewer	1935 P. Floyd
1884 H. Dearsley	1908 S. Evans	1936 V. Stuart
1885 W. West	1909 C. Brown	1937 V. Stuart
1886 A. Diamond	1910 F. Storbeck	1938 G. Preston
1887 E. White	1911 W. Hazell	1939 A. Porter
1888 W. King	1912 R. Smith	1944 M. Hart
1889 A. Bowman	1913 R. Smith	1945 D. Scott
1890 J. Steers	1914 E. Chandler	1946 P. Floyd
1891 V. Barker	1919 H. Brown	1947 G. Scriven
1892 J. Steers	1920 R. Rawson	1948 J. Gardner
1893 J. Steers	1921 R. Rawson	1949 A. Worrall
1894 H. King	1922 T. Evans	1950 P. Toch
1895 W. E. Johnstone	1923 E. Eagan	1951 A. Halsey

Bernard Hart, the Managing Director of Lonsdale Sports Equipment Ltd, presents the 1996 heavyweight trophy to the new champion, Tony Oakey

Les Clark

276

International Amateur Champions, 1904-1996

Shows all Olympic, World, European & Commonwealth champions since 1904. British silver and bronze medal winners are shown throughout, where applicable.

Country Code

ALG = Algeria; ARG = Argentine; ARM = Armenia; AUS = Australia; AUT = Austria; AZE = Azerbaijan; BEL = Belgium; BUL = Bulgaria; CAN = Canada; CEY = Ceylon (now Sri Lanka); CI = Channel Islands; CUB = Cuba; DEN = Denmark; DOM = Dominican Republic; ENG = England; ESP = Spain; EST = Estonia; FIJ = Fiji Islands; FIN = Finland; FRA = France; GBR = United Kingdom; GDR = German Democratic Republic; GEO = Georgia; GER = Germany (but West Germany only from 1968-1990); GHA = Ghana; GUY = Guyana; HOL = Netherlands; HUN = Hungary; IRL = Ireland; ITA = Italy; JAM = Jamaica; JPN = Japan; KAZ = Kazakhstan; KEN = Kenya; LIT = Lithuania; MEX = Mexico; NKO = North Korea; NIG = Nigeria; NIR = Northern Ireland; NOR = Norway; NZL = New Zealand; POL = Poland; PUR = Puerto Rico; ROM = Romania; RUS = Russia; SAF = South Africa; SCO = Scotland; SKO = South Korea; SR = Southern Rhodesia; STV = St Vincent; SWE = Sweden; TCH = Czechoslovakia; THA = Thailand; TUR = Turkey; UGA = Uganda; UKR = Ukraine; URS = USSR; USA = United States of America; VEN = Venezuela; WAL = Wales; YUG = Yugoslavia; ZAM =

Olympic Champions, 1904-1996

St Louis, USA - 1904
Fly: G. Finnegan (USA). **Bantam:** O. Kirk (USA). **Feather:** O. Kirk (USA). **Light:** H. Spangler (USA). **Welter:** A. Young (USA). **Middle:** C. May (USA). **Heavy:** S. Berger (USA).

London, England - 1908
Bantam: H. Thomas (GBR). **Feather:** R. Gunn (GBR). **Light:** F. Grace (GBR). **Middle:** J.W.H.T. Douglas (GBR). **Heavy:** A. Oldman (GBR).
Silver medals: J. Condon (GBR), C. Morris (GBR), F. Spiller (GBR), S. Evans (GBR).
Bronze medals: W. Webb (GBR), H. Rodding (GBR), T. Ringer (GBR), H. Johnson (GBR), R. Warnes (GBR), W. Philo (GBR), F. Parks (GBR).

Antwerp, Belgium - 1920
Fly: F. Genaro (USA). **Bantam:** C. Walker (SAF). **Feather:** R. Fritsch (FRA). **Light:** S. Mossberg (USA). **Welter:** T. Schneider (CAN). **Middle:** H. Mallin (GBR). **L. Heavy:** E. Eagan (USA). **Heavy:** R. Rawson (GBR).
Silver medal: A. Ireland (GBR).
Bronze medals: W. Cuthbertson (GBR), G. McKenzie (GBR), H. Franks (GBR).

Paris, France - 1924
Fly: F. la Barba (USA). **Bantam:** W. Smith (SAF). **Feather:** J. Fields (USA). **Light:** H. Nielson (DEN). **Welter:** J. Delarge (BEL). **Middle:** H. Mallin (GBR). **L. Heavy:** H. Mitchell (GBR). **Heavy:** O. von Porat (NOR).
Silver medals: J. McKenzie (GBR), J. Elliot (GBR).

Amsterdam, Holland - 1928
Fly: A. Kocsis (HUN). **Bantam:** V. Tamagnini (ITA). **Feather:** B. van Klaveren (HOL). **Light:** C. Orlando (ITA). **Welter:** E. Morgan (NZL). **Middle:** P. Toscani (ITA). **L. Heavy:** V. Avendano (ARG). **Heavy:** A. Rodriguez Jurado (ARG).

Los Angeles, USA - 1932
Fly: I. Enekes (HUN). **Bantam:** H. Gwynne (CAN). **Feather:** C. Robledo (ARG). **Light:** L. Stevens (SAF). **Welter:** E. Flynn (USA). **Middle:** C. Barth (USA). **L. Heavy:** D. Carstens (SAF). **Heavy:** A. Lovell (ARG).

Berlin, West Germany - 1936
Fly: W. Kaiser (GER). **Bantam:** U. Sergo (ITA). **Feather:** O. Casanova (ARG). **Light:** I. Harangi (HUN). **Welter:** S. Suvio (FIN). **Middle:** J. Despeaux (FRA). **L. Heavy:** R. Michelot (FRA). **Heavy:** H. Runge (GER).

London, England - 1948
Fly: P. Perez (ARG). **Bantam:** T. Csik (HUN). **Feather:** E. Formenti (ITA). **Light:** G. Dreyer (SAF). **Welter:** J. Torma (TCH). **Middle:** L. Papp (HUN). **L. Heavy:** G. Hunter (SAF). **Heavy:** R. Iglesas (ARG).
Silver medals: J. Wright (GBR), D. Scott (GBR).

Helsinki, Finland - 1952
Fly: N. Brooks (USA). **Bantam:** P. Hamalainen (FIN). **Feather:** J. Zachara (TCH). **Light:** A. Bolognesi (ITA). **L. Welter:** C. Adkins (USA). **Welter:** Z. Chychla (POL). **L. Middle:** L. Papp (HUN). **Middle:** F. Patterson (USA). **L. Heavy:** N. Lee (USA). **Heavy:** E. Sanders (USA).
Silver medal: J. McNally (IRL).

Melbourne, Australia - 1956
Fly: T. Spinks (GBR). **Bantam:** W. Behrendt (GER). **Feather:** V. Safronov (URS). **Light:** R. McTaggart (GBR). **L. Welter:** V. Jengibarian (URS). **Welter:** N. Linca (ROM). **L. Middle:** L. Papp (HUN). **Middle:** G. Schatkov (URS). **L. Heavy:** J. Boyd (USA). **Heavy:** P. Rademacher (USA).
Silver medals: T. Nicholls (GBR), F. Tiedt (IRL).
Bronze medals: J. Caldwell (IRL), F. Gilroy (IRL), A. Bryne (IRL), N. Gargano (GBR), J. McCormack (GBR).

George Foreman, the 1968 Olympic heavyweight champion

277

Rome, Italy - 1960
Fly: G. Torok (HUN). **Bantam:** O. Grigoryev (URS). **Feather:** F. Musso (ITA). **Light:** K. Pazdzior (POL). **L. Welter:** B. Nemecek (TCH). **Welter:** N. Benvenuti (ITA). **L. Middle:** W. McClure (USA). **Middle:** E. Crook (USA). **L. Heavy:** C. Clay (USA). **Heavy:** F. de Piccoli (ITA).
Bronze medals: R. McTaggart (GBR), J. Lloyd (GBR), W. Fisher (GBR).

Tokyo, Japan - 1964
Fly: F. Atzori (ITA). **Bantam:** T. Sakurai (JPN). **Feather:** S. Stepashkin (URS). **Light:** J. Grudzien (POL). **L. Welter:** J. Kulej (POL). **Welter:** M. Kasprzyk (POL). **L. Middle:** B. Lagutin (URS). **Middle:** V. Popenchenko (URS). **L. Heavy:** C. Pinto (ITA). **Heavy:** J. Frazier (USA).
Bronze medal: J. McCourt (IRL).

Mexico City, Mexico - 1968
L. Fly: F. Rodriguez (VEN). **Fly:** R. Delgado (MEX). **Bantam:** V. Sokolov (URS). **Feather:** A. Roldan (MEX). **Light:** R. Harris (USA). **L. Welter:** J. Kulej (POL). **Welter:** M. Wolke (GDR). **L. Middle:** B. Lagutin (URS). **Middle:** C. Finnegan (GBR). **L. Heavy:** D. Poznyak (URS). **Heavy:** G. Foreman (USA).

Munich, West Germany - 1972
L. Fly: G. Gedo (HUN). **Fly:** G. Kostadinov (BUL). **Bantam:** O. Martinez (CUB). **Feather:** B. Kusnetsov (BUL). **Light:** J. Szczepanski (POL). **L. Welter:** R. Seales (USA). **Welter:** E. Correa (CUB). **L. Middle:** D. Kottysch (GER). **Middle:** V. Lemeschev (URS). **L. Heavy:** M. Parlov (YUG). **Heavy:** T. Stevenson (CUB).
Bronze medals: R. Evans (GBR), G. Turpin (GBR), A. Minter (GBR).

Montreal, Canada - 1976
L. Fly: J. Hernandez (CUB). **Fly:** L. Randolph (USA). **Bantam:** Y-J. Gu (NKO). **Feather:** A. Herrera (CUB). **Light:** H. Davis (USA). **L. Welter:** R. Leonard (USA). **Welter:** J. Bachfield (GDR). **L. Middle:** J. Rybicki (POL). **Middle:** M. Spinks (USA). **L. Heavy:** L. Spinks (USA). **Heavy:** T. Stevenson (CUB).
Bronze medal: P. Cowdell (GBR).

Moscow, USSR - 1980
L. Fly: S. Sabirov (URS). **Fly:** P. Lessov (BUL). **Bantam:** J. Hernandez (CUB). **Feather:** R. Fink (GDR). **Light:** A. Herrera (CUB). **L. Welter:** P. Oliva (ITA). **Welter:** A. Aldama (CUB). **L. Middle:** A. Martinez (CUB). **Middle:** J. Gomez (CUB). **L. Heavy:** S. Kacar (YUG). **Heavy:** T. Stevenson (CUB).
Bronze medals: H. Russell (IRL), A. Willis (GBR).

Los Angeles, USA - 1984
L. Fly: P. Gonzalez (USA). **Fly:** S. McCrory (USA). **Bantam:** M. Stecca (ITA). **Feather:** M. Taylor (USA). **Light:** P. Whitaker (USA). **L. Welter:** J. Page (USA). **Welter:** M. Breland (USA). **L. Middle:** F. Tate (USA). **Middle:** J-S. Shin (SKO). **L. Heavy:** A. Josipovic (YUG). **Heavy:** H. Tillman (USA). **S. Heavy:** T. Biggs (USA).
Bronze medal: B. Wells (GBR).

Seoul, South Korea - 1988
L. Fly: I. Mustafov (BUL). **Fly:** H-S. Kim (SKO). **Bantam:** K. McKinney (USA). **Feather:** G. Parisi (ITA). **Light:** A. Zuelow (GDR). **L. Welter:** V. Yanovsky (URS). **Welter:** R. Wangila (KEN). **L. Middle:** S-H. Park (SKO). **Middle:** H. Maske (GDR). **L. Heavy:** A. Maynard (USA). **Heavy:** R. Mercer (USA). **S. Heavy:** L. Lewis (CAN).
Bronze medal: R. Woodhall (GBR).

Barcelona, Spain - 1992
L. Fly: R. Marcelo (CUB). **Fly:** C-C. Su (NKO). **Bantam:** J. Casamayor (CUB). **Feather:** A. Tews (GER). **Light:** O. de la Hoya (USA). **L. Welter:** H. Vinent (CUB). **Welter:** M. Carruth (IRL). **L. Middle:** J. Lemus (CUB). **Middle:** A. Hernandez (CUB). **L. Heavy:** T. May (GER). **Heavy:** F. Savon (CUB). **S. Heavy:** R. Balado (CUB).
Silver medal: W. McCullough (IRL).
Bronze medal: R. Reid (GBR).

Atlanta, USA - 1996
L. Fly: D. Petrov (BUL). **Fly:** M. Romero (CUB). **Bantam:** I. Kovaks (HUN). **Feather:** S. Kamsing (THA). **Light:** H. Soltani (ALG). **L. Welter:** H. Vinent (CUB). **Welter:** O. Saitov (RUS). **L. Middle:** D. Reid (USA). **Middle:** A. Hernandez (CUB). **L. Heavy:** V. Jirov (KAZ). **Heavy:** F. Savon (CUB). **S. Heavy:** V. Klitchko (UKR).

World Champions, 1974-1995

Havana, Cuba - 1974
L. Fly: J. Hernandez (CUB). **Fly:** D. Rodriguez (CUB). **Bantam:** W. Gomez (PUR). **Feather:** H. Davis (USA). **Light:** V. Solomin (URS). **L. Welter:** A. Kalule (UGA). **Welter:** E. Correa (CUB). **L. Middle:** R. Garbey (CUB). **Middle:** R. Riskiev (URS). **L. Heavy:** M. Parlov (YUG). **Heavy:** T. Stevenson (CUB).

Belgrade, Yugoslavia - 1978
L. Fly: S. Muchoki (KEN). **Fly:** H. Strednicki (POL). **Bantam:** A. Horta (CUB). **Feather:** A. Herrera (CUB). **Light:** D. Andeh (NIG). **L. Welter:** V. Lvov (URS). **Welter:** V. Rachkov (URS). **L. Middle:** V. Savchenko (URS). **Middle:** J. Gomez (CUB). **L. Heavy:** S. Soria (CUB). **Heavy:** T. Stevenson (CUB).

Munich, West Germany - 1982
L. Fly: I. Mustafov (BUL). **Fly:** Y. Alexandrov (URS). **Bantam:** F. Favors (USA). **Feather:** A. Horta (CUB). **Light:** A. Herrera (CUB). **L. Welter:** C. Garcia (CUB). **Welter:** M. Breland (USA). **L. Middle:** A. Koshkin (URS). **Middle:** B. Comas (CUB). **L. Heavy:** P. Romero (CUB). **Heavy:** A. Jagubkin (URS). **S. Heavy:** T. Biggs (USA).
Bronze medal: T. Corr (IRL).

Reno, USA - 1986
L. Fly: J. Odelin (CUB). **Fly:** P. Reyes (CUB). **Bantam:** S-I. Moon (SKO). **Feather:** K. Banks (USA). **Light:** A. Horta (CUB). **L. Welter:** V. Shishov (URS). **Welter:** K. Gould (USA). **L. Middle:** A. Espinosa (CUB). **Middle:** D. Allen (USA). **L. Heavy:** P. Romero (CUB). **Heavy:** F. Savon (CUB). **S. Heavy:** T. Stevenson (CUB).

Moscow, USSR - 1989
L. Fly: E. Griffin (USA). **Fly:** Y. Arbachakov (URS). **Bantam:** E. Carrion (CUB). **Feather:** A. Khamatov (URS). **Light:** J. Gonzalez (CUB). **L. Welter:** I. Ruzinkov (URS). **Welter:** F. Vastag. **L. Middle:** I. Akopokhian (URS). **Middle:** A. Kurniavka (URS). **L. Heavy:** H. Maske (GDR). **Heavy:** F. Savon (CUB). **S. Heavy:** R. Balado (CUB).
Bronze medal: M. Carruth (IRL).

Sydney, Australia - 1991
L. Fly: E. Griffin (USA). **Fly:** I. Kovacs (HUN). **Bantam:** S. Todorov (BUL). **Feather:** K. Kirkorov (BUL). **Light:** M. Rudolph (GER). **L. Welter:** K. Tsziu (URS). **Welter:** J. Hernandez (CUB). **L. Middle:** J. Lemus (CUB). **Middle:** T. Russo (ITA). **L. Heavy:** T. May (GER). **Heavy:** F. Savon (CUB). **S. Heavy:** R. Balado (CUB).

Tampere, Finland - 1993
L. Fly: N. Munchian (ARM). **Fly:** W. Font (CUB). **Bantam:** A. Christov (BUL). **Feather:** S. Todorov (BUL). **Light:** D. Austin (USA). **L. Welter:** H. Vinent (CUB). **Welter:** J. Hernandez (CUB). **L. Middle:** F. Vastag (ROM). **Middle:** A. Hernandez (CUB). **L. Heavy:** R. Garbey (CUB). **Heavy:** F. Savon (CUB). **S. Heavy:** R. Balado (CUB).
Bronze medal: D. Kelly (IRL).

Berlin, Germany - 1995
L. Fly: D. Petrov (BUL). **Fly:** Z. Lunka (GER). **Bantam:** R. Malachbekov (RUS). **Feather:** S. Todorov (BUL). **Light:** L. Doroftei (ROM). **L. Welter:** H. Vinent (CUB). **Welter:** J. Hernandez (CUB). **L. Middle:** F. Vastag (ROM). **Middle:** A. Hernandez (CUB). **L. Heavy:** A. Tarver (USA). **Heavy:** F. Savon (CUB). **S. Heavy:** A. Lezin (RUS).

World Junior Champions, 1979-1994

Yokohama, Japan - 1979
L. Fly: R. Shannon (USA). **Fly:** P. Lessov (BUL). **Bantam:** P-K. Choi (SKO). **Feather:** Y. Gladychev (URS). **Light:** R. Blake (USA). **L. Welter:** I. Akopokhian (URS). **Welter:** M. McCrory (USA). **L. Middle:** A. Mayes (USA). **Middle:** A. Milov (URS). **L. Heavy:** A. Lebedev (URS). **Heavy:** M. Frazier (USA).
Silver medals: N. Wilshire (ENG), D. Cross (ENG).
Bronze medal: I. Scott (SCO).

Santa Domingo, Dominican Republic - 1983
L. Fly: M. Herrera (DOM). **Fly:** J. Gonzalez (CUB). **Bantam:** J. Molina (PUR). **Feather:** A. Miesses (DOM). **Light:** A. Beltre (DOM). **L. Welter:** A. Espinoza (CUB). **Welter:** M. Watkins (USA). **L. Middle:** U. Castillo (CUB). **Middle:** R. Batista (CUB). **L. Heavy:** O. Pought (USA). **Heavy:** A. Williams (USA). **S. Heavy:** L. Lewis (CAN).

Bucharest, Romania - 1985
L. Fly: R-S. Hwang (SKO). **Fly:** T. Marcelica (ROM). **Bantam:** R. Diaz (CUB). **Feather:** D. Maeran (ROM). **Light:** J. Teiche (GDR). **L. Welter:** W. Saeger (GDR). **Welter:** A. Stoianov (BUL). **L. Middle:** M. Franek (TCH). **Middle:** O. Zahalotskih (URS). **L. Heavy:** B. Riddick (USA). **Heavy:** F. Savon (CUB). **S. Heavy:** A. Prianichnikov (URS).

Havana, Cuba - 1987
L. Fly: E. Paisan (CUB). **Fly:** C. Daniels (USA). **Bantam:** A. Moya (CUB). **Feather:** G. Iliyasov (URS). **Light:** J. Hernandez (CUB). **L. Welter:** L. Mihai (ROM). **Welter:** F. Vastag (ROM). **L. Middle:** A. Lobsyak (URS). **Middle:** W. Martinez (CUB). **L. Heavy:** D. Yeliseyev (URS). **Heavy:** R. Balado (CUB). **S. Heavy:** L. Martinez (CUB).
Silver medal: E. Loughran (IRL).
Bronze medal: D. Galvin (IRL).

San Juan, Puerto Rico - 1989
L. Fly: D. Petrov (BUL). **Fly:** N. Monchai (FRA). **Bantam:** J. Casamayor (CUB). **Feather:** C. Febres (PUR). **Light:** A. Acevedo (PUR). **L. Welter:** E. Berger (GDR). **Welter:** A. Hernandez (CUB). **L. Middle:** L. Bedey (CUB). **Middle:** R. Garbey (CUB). **L. Heavy:** R. Alvarez (CUB). **Heavy:** K. Johnson (CAN). **S. Heavy:** A. Burdiantz (URS).
Silver medals: E. Magee (IRL), R. Reid (ENG), S. Wilson (SCO).

Lima, Peru - 1990
L. Fly: D. Alicea (PUR). **Fly:** K. Pielert (GDR). **Bantam:** K. Baravi (URS). **Feather:** A. Vaughan (ENG). **Light:** J. Mendez (CUB). **L. Welter:** H. Vinent (CUB). **Welter:** A. Hernandez (CUB). **L. Middle:** A. Kakauridze (URS). **Middle:** J. Gomez (CUB). **L. Heavy:** B. Torsten (GDR). **Heavy:** I. Andreev (URS). **S. Heavy:** J. Quesada (CUB).
Bronze medal: P. Ingle (ENG).

Montreal, Canada - 1992
L. Fly: W. Font (CUB). **Fly:** J. Oragon (CUB). **Bantam:** N. Machado (CUB). **Feather:** M. Stewart (CAN). **Light:** D. Austin (CUB). **L. Welter:** O. Saitov (RUS). **Welter:** L. Brors (GER). **L. Middle:** J. Acosta (CUB). **Middle:** I. Arsangaliev (RUS). **L. Heavy:** S. Samilsan (TUR). **Heavy:** G. Kandeliaki (GEO). **S. Heavy:** M. Porchnev (RUS).
Bronze medal: N. Sinclair (IRL).

Istanbul, Turkey - 1994
L. Fly: J. Turunen (FIN). **Fly:** A. Jimenez (CUB). **Bantam:** J. Despaigne (CUB). **Feather:** D. Simion (ROM). **Light:** L. Diogenes (CUB). **L. Welter:** V. Romero (CUB). **Welter:** E. Aslan (TUR). **L. Middle:** G. Ledsvanys (CUB). **Middle:** M. Genc (TUR). **L. Heavy:** P. Aurino (ITA). **Heavy:** M. Lopez (CUB). **S. Heavy:** P. Carrion (CUB).

European Champions, 1924-1996

Paris, France - 1924
Fly: J. McKenzie (GBR). **Bantam:** J. Ces (FRA). **Feather:** R. de Vergnie (BEL). **Light:** N. Nielsen (DEN). **Welter:** J. Delarge (BEL). **Middle:** H. Mallin (GBR). **L. Heavy:** H. Mitchell (GBR). **Heavy:** O. von Porat (NOR).

Stockholm, Sweden - 1925
Fly: E. Pladner (FRA). **Bantam:** A. Rule (GBR). **Feather:** P. Andren (SWE). **Light:** S. Johanssen (SWE). **Welter:** H. Nielsen (DEN). **Middle:** F. Crawley (GBR). **L. Heavy:** T. Petersen (DEN). **Heavy:** B. Persson (SWE).
Silver medals: J. James (GBR), E. Viney (GBR), D. Lister (GBR).

Berlin, Germany - 1927
Fly: L. Boman (SWE). **Bantam:** K. Dalchow (GER). **Feather:** F. Dubbers (GER). **Light:** H. Domgoergen (GER). **Welter:** R. Caneva (ITA). **Middle:** J. Christensen (NOR). **L. Heavy:** H. Muller (GER). **Heavy:** N. Ramm (SWE).

Amsterdam, Holland - 1928
Fly: A. Kocsis (HUN). **Bantam:** V. Tamagnini (ITA). **Feather:** B. van Klaveren (HOL). **Light:** C. Orlandi (ITA). **Welter:** R. Galataud (FRA).

Middle: P. Toscani (ITA). **L. Heavy:** E. Pistulla (GER). **Heavy:** N. Ramm (SWE).

Budapest, Hungary - 1930
Fly: I. Enekes (HUN). **Bantam:** J. Szeles (HUN). **Feather:** G. Szabo (HUN). **Light:** M. Bianchini (ITA). **Welter:** J. Besselmann (GER). **Middle:** C. Meroni (ITA). **L. Heavy:** T. Petersen (DEN). **Heavy:** J. Michaelson (DEN).

Los Angeles, USA - 1932
Fly: I. Enekes (HUN). **Bantam:** H. Ziglarski (GER). **Feather:** J. Schleinkofer (GER). **Light:** T. Ahlqvist (SWE). **Welter:** E. Campe (GER). **Middle:** R. Michelot (FRA). **L. Heavy:** G. Rossi (ITA). **Heavy:** L. Rovati (ITA).

Budapest, Hungary - 1934
Fly: P. Palmer (GBR). **Bantam:** I. Enekes (HUN). **Feather:** O. Kaestner GER). **Light:** E. Facchini (ITA). **Welter:** D. McCleave (GBR). **Middle:** S. Szigetti (HUN). **L. Heavy:** P. Zehetmayer (AUT). **Heavy:** G. Baerlund (FIN).
Bronze medal: P. Floyd (GBR).

Milan, Italy - 1937
Fly: I. Enekes (HUN). **Bantam:** U. Sergo (ITA). **Feather:** A. Polus (POL). **Light:** H. Nuremberg (GER). **Welter:** M. Murach (GER). **Middle:** H. Chmielewski (POL). **L. Heavy:** S. Szigetti (HUN). **Heavy:** O. Tandberg (SWE).

Dublin, Eire - 1939
Fly: J. Ingle (IRL). **Bantam:** U. Sergo (ITA). **Feather:** P. Dowdall (IRL). **Light:** H. Nuremberg (GER). **Welter:** A. Kolczyski (POL). **Middle:** A. Raedek (EST). **L. Heavy:** L. Musina (ITA). **Heavy:** O. Tandberg (SWE).
Bronze medal: C. Evenden (IRL).

Dublin, Eire - 1947
Fly: L. Martinez (ESP). **Bantam:** L. Bogacs (HUN). **Feather:** K. Kreuger (SWE). **Light:** J. Vissers (BEL). **Welter:** J. Ryan (ENG). **Middle:** A. Escudie (FRA). **L. Heavy:** H. Quentemeyer (HOL). **Heavy:** G. O'Colmain (IRL).
Silver medals: J. Clinton (SCO), P. Maguire (IRL), W. Thom (ENG), G. Scriven (ENG).
Bronze medals: J. Dwyer (SCO), A. Sanderson (ENG), W. Frith (SCO), E. Cantwell (IRL), K. Wyatt (ENG).

Oslo, Norway - 1949
Fly: J. Kasperczak (POL). **Bantam:** G. Zuddas (ITA). **Feather:** J. Bataille (FRA). **Light:** M. McCullagh (IRL). **Welter:** J. Torma (TCH). **Middle:** L. Papp (HUN). **L. Heavy:** G. di Segni (ITA). **Heavy:** L. Bene (HUN).
Bronze medal: D. Connell (IRL).

Milan, Italy - 1951
Fly: A. Pozzali (ITA). **Bantam:** V. Dall'Osso (ITA). **Feather:** J. Ventaja (FRA). **Light:** B. Visintin (ITA). **L. Welter:** H. Schelling (GER). **Welter:** Z. Chychla (POL). **L. Middle:** L. Papp (HUN). **Middle:** S. Sjolin (SWE). **L. Heavy:** M. Limage (BEL). **Heavy:** G. di Segni (ITA).
Silver medal: J. Kelly (IRL).
Bronze medals: D. Connell (IRL), T. Milligan (IRL), A. Lay (ENG).

Warsaw, Poland - 1953
Fly: H. Kukier (POL). **Bantam:** Z. Stefaniuk (POL). **Feather:** J. Kruza (POL). **Light:** V. Jengibarian (URS). **L. Welter:** L. Drogosz (POL). **Welter:** Z. Chychla (POL). **L. Middle:** B. Wells (ENG). **Middle:** D. Wemhoner (GER). **L. Heavy:** U. Nietchke (GER). **Heavy:** A. Schotzikas (URS).
Silver medal: T. Milligan (IRL).
Bronze medals: J. McNally (IRL), R. Barton (ENG).

Berlin, West Germany - 1955
Fly: E. Basel (GER). **Bantam:** Z. Stefaniuk (POL). **Feather:** T. Nicholls (ENG). **Light:** H. Kurschat (GER). **L. Welter:** L. Drogosz (POL). **Welter:** N. Gargano (ENG). **L. Middle:** Z. Pietrzykowski (POL). **Middle:** G. Schatkov (URS). **L. Heavy:** E. Schoeppner (GER). **Heavy:** A. Schotzikas (URS).

Prague, Czechoslovakia - 1957

Fly: M. Homberg (GER). **Bantam:** O. Grigoryev (URS). **Feather:** D. Venilov (BUL). **Light:** K. Pazdzior (POL). **L. Welter:** V. Jengibarian (URS). **Welter:** M. Graus (GER). **L. Middle:** N. Benvenuti (ITA). **Middle:** Z. Pietrzykowski (POL). **L. Heavy:** G. Negrea (ROM). **Heavy:** A. Abramov (URS).
Bronze medals: R. Davies (WAL), J. Morrissey (SCO), J. Kidd (SCO), F. Teidt (IRL).

Lucerne, Switzerland - 1959

Fly: M. Homberg (GER). **Bantam:** H. Rascher (GER). **Feather:** J. Adamski (POL). **Light:** O. Maki (FIN). **L. Welter:** V. Jengibarian (URS). **Welter:** L. Drogosz (POL). **L. Middle:** N. Benvenuti (ITA). **Middle:** G. Schatkov (URS). **L. Heavy:** Z. Pietrzykowski (POL). **Heavy:** A. Abramov (URS).
Silver medal: D. Thomas (ENG).
Bronze medals: A. McClean (IRL), H. Perry (IRL), C. McCoy (IRL), H. Scott (ENG).

Belgrade, Yugoslavia - 1961

Fly: P. Vacca (ITA). **Bantam:** S. Sivko (URS). **Feather:** F. Taylor (ENG). **Light:** R. McTaggart (SCO). **L. Welter:** A. Tamulis (URS). **Welter:** R. Tamulis (URS). **L. Middle:** B. Lagutin (URS). **Middle:** T. Walasek (POL). **L. Heavy:** G. Saraudi (ITA). **Heavy:** A. Abramov (URS).
Bronze medals: P. Warwick (ENG), I. McKenzie (SCO), J. Bodell (ENG).

Moscow, USSR - 1963

Fly: V. Bystrov (URS). **Bantam:** O. Grigoryev (URS). **Feather:** S. Stepashkin (URS). **Light:** J. Kajdi (HUN). **L. Welter:** J. Kulej (POL). **Welter:** R. Tamulis (URS). **L. Middle:** B. Lagutin (URS). **Middle:** V. Popenchenko (URS). **L. Heavy:** Z. Pietrzykowski (POL). **Heavy:** J. Nemec (TCH).
Silver medal: A. Wyper (SCO).

Berlin, East Germany - 1965

Fly: H. Freisdadt (GER). **Bantam:** O. Grigoryev (URS). **Feather:** S. Stepashkin (URS). **Light:** V. Barranikov (URS). **L. Welter:** J. Kulej (POL). **Welter:** R. Tamulis (URS). **L. Middle:** V. Ageyev (URS). **Middle:** V. Popenchenko (URS). **L. Heavy:** D. Poznyak (URS). **Heavy:** A. Isosimov (URS).
Silver medal: B. Robinson (ENG).
Bronze medals: J. McCluskey (SCO), K. Buchanan (SCO), J. McCourt (IRL).

Rome, Italy - 1967

Fly: H. Skrzyczak (POL). **Bantam:** N. Giju (ROM). **Feather:** R. Petek (POL). **Light:** J. Grudzien (POL). **L. Welter:** V. Frolov (URS). **Welter:** B. Nemecek (TCH). **L. Middle:** V. Ageyev (URS). **Middle:** M. Casati (ITA). **L. Heavy:** D. Poznyak (URS). **Heavy:** M. Baruzzi (ITA).
Silver medal: P. Boddington (ENG).

Bucharest, Romania - 1969

L. Fly: G. Gedo (HUN). **Fly:** C. Ciuca (ROM). **Bantam:** A. Dumitrescu (ROM). **Feather:** L. Orban (HUN). **Light:** S. Cutov (ROM). **L. Welter:** V. Frolov (URS). **Welter:** G. Meier (GER). **L. Middle:** V. Tregubov (URS). **Middle:** V. Tarasenkov (URS). **L. Heavy:** D. Poznyak (URS). **Heavy:** I. Alexe (ROM).
Bronze medals: M. Dowling (IRL), M. Piner (ENG), A. Richardson (ENG), T. Imrie (SCO).

Madrid, Spain - 1971

L. Fly: G. Gedo (HUN). **Fly:** J. Rodriguez (ESP). **Bantam:** T. Badar (HUN). **Feather:** R. Tomczyk (POL). **Light:** J. Szczepanski (POL). **L. Welter:** U. Beyer (GER). **Welter:** J. Kajdi (HUN). **L. Middle:** V. Tregubov (URS). **Middle:** J. Juotsiavitchus (URS). **L. Heavy:** M. Parlov (YUG). **Heavy:** V. Tchernishev (URS).
Bronze medals: N. McLaughlin (IRL), M. Dowling (IRL), B. McCarthy (IRL), M. Kingwell (ENG), L. Stevens (ENG).

Belgrade, Yugoslavia - 1973

L. Fly: V. Zasypko (URS). **Fly:** C. Gruescu (ROM). **Bantam:** A. Cosentino (FRA). **Feather:** S. Forster (GDR). **Light:** S. Cutov (ROM). **L. Welter:** M. Benes (YUG). **Welter:** S. Csjef (HUN). **L. Middle:** A. Klimanov (URS). **Middle:** V. Lemechev (URS). **L. Heavy:** M. Parlov (YUG). **Heavy:** V. Ulyanich (URS).
Bronze medal: J. Bambrick (SCO).

Katowice, Poland - 1975

L. Fly: A. Tkachenko (URS). **Fly:** V. Zasypko (URS). **Bantam:** V. Rybakov (URS). **Feather:** T. Badari (HUN). **Light:** S. Cutov (ROM). **L. Welter:** V. Limasov (URS). **Welter:** K. Marjaama (FIN). **L. Middle:** W. Rudnowski (POL). **Middle:** V. Lemechev (URS). **L. Heavy:** A. Klimanov (URS). **Heavy:** A. Biegalski (POL).
Bronze medals: C. Magri (ENG), P. Cowdell (ENG), G. McEwan (ENG).

Halle, East Germany - 1977

L. Fly: H. Srednicki (POL). **Fly:** L. Blazynski (POL). **Bantam:** S. Forster (GDR). **Feather:** R. Nowakowski (GDR). **Light:** A. Rusevski (YUG). **L. Welter:** B. Gajda (POL). **Welter:** V. Limasov (URS). **L. Middle:** V. Saychenko (URS). **Middle:** I. Shaposhnikov (URS). **L. Heavy:** D. Kvachadze (URS). **Heavy:** E. Gorstkov (URS).
Bronze medal: P. Sutcliffe (IRL).

Cologne, West Germany - 1979

L. Fly: S. Sabirov (URS). **Fly:** H. Strednicki (POL). **Bantam:** N. Khrapzov (URS). **Feather:** V. Rybakov (URS). **Light.** V. Demianenko (URS). **L. Welter:** S. Konakbaev (URS). **Welter:** E. Muller (GER). **L. Middle:** M. Perunovic (YUG). **Middle:** T. Uusiverta (FIN). **L. Heavy:** A. Nikolyan (URS). **Heavy:** E. Gorstkov (URS). **S. Heavy:** P. Hussing (GER).
Bronze medal: P. Sutcliffe (IRL).

Tampere, Finland - 1981

L. Fly: I. Mustafov (BUL). **Fly:** P. Lessov (BUL). **Bantam:** V. Miroschnichenko (URS). **Feather:** R. Nowakowski (GDR). **Light:** V. Rybakov (URS). **L. Welter:** V. Shisov (URS). **Welter:** S. Konakvbaev (URS). **L. Middle:** A. Koshkin (URS). **Middle:** J. Torbek (URS). **L. Heavy:** A Krupin (URS). **Heavy:** A. Jagupkin (URS). **S. Heavy:** F. Damiani (ITA).
Bronze medal: G. Hawkins (IRL).

Varna, Bulgaria - 1983

L. Fly: I. Mustafov (BUL). **Fly:** P. Lessov (BUL). **Bantam:** Y. Alexandrov (URS). **Feather:** S. Nurkazov (URS). **Light:** E. Chuprenski (BUL). **L. Welter:** V. Shishov (URS). **Welter:** P. Galkin (URS). **L. Middle:** V. Laptev (URS). **Middle:** V. Melnik (URS). **L. Heavy:** V. Kokhanovski (URS). **Heavy:** A. Jagubkin (URS). **S. Heavy:** F. Damiani (ITA).
Bronze medal: K. Joyce (IRL).

Budapest, Hungary - 1985

L. Fly: R. Breitbarth (GDR). **Fly:** D. Berg (GDR). **Bantam:** L. Simic (YUG). **Feather:** S. Khachatrian (URS). **Light:** E. Chuprenski (BUL) **L. Welter:** S. Mehnert (GDR). **Welter:** I. Akopokhian (URS). **L. Middle:** M. Timm (GDR). **Middle:** H. Maske (GDR). **L. Heavy:** N. Shanavasov (URS). **Heavy:** A. Jagubkin (URS). **S. Heavy:** F. Somodi (HUN).
Bronze medals: S. Casey (IRL), J. Beckles (ENG).

Turin, Italy - 1987

L. Fly: N. Munchyan (URS). **Fly:** A. Tews (GDR). **Bantam:** A. Hristov (BUL). **Feather:** M. Kazaryan (URS). **Light:** O. Nazarov (URS). **L. Welter:** B. Abadjier (BUL). **Welter:** V. Shishov (URS). **L. Middle:** E. Richter (GDR). **Middle:** H. Maske (GDR). **L. Heavy:** Y. Vaulin (URS). **Heavy:** A. Vanderlijde (HOL). **S. Heavy:** U. Kaden (GDR).
Bronze medal: N. Brown (ENG).

Athens, Greece - 1989

L. Fly: I.Mustafov (BUL). **Fly:** Y. Arbachakov (URS). **Bantam:** S. Todorov (BUL). **Feather:** K. Kirkorov (BUL). **Light:** K. Tsziu (URS). **L. Welter:** I. Ruznikov (URS). **Welter:** S. Mehnert (GDR). **L. Middle:** I. Akopokhian (URS). **Middle:** H. Maske (GDR). **L. Heavy:** S. Lange (GDR). **Heavy:** A. Vanderlijde (HOL). **S. Heavy:** U. Kaden (GDR).
Bronze Medal: D. Anderson (SCO).

Gothenburg, Sweden - 1991

L. Fly: I. Marinov (BUL). **Fly:** I. Kovacs (HUN). **Bantam:** S. Todorov (BUL). **Feather:** P. Griffin (IRL). **Light:** V. Nistor (ROM). **L. Welter:** K. Tsziu (URS). **Welter:** R. Welin (SWE). **L. Middle:** I. Akopokhian (URS). **Middle:** S. Otke (GER). **L. Heavy:** D. Michalczewski (GER). **Heavy:** A. Vanderlijde (HOL). **S. Heavy:** E. Beloussov (URS).
Bronze medals: P. Weir (SCO), A. Vaughan (ENG).

Bursa, Turkey - 1993

L. Fly: D. Petrov (BUL). **Fly:** R. Husseinov (AZE). **Bantam:** R. Malakhbetov (RUS). **Feather:** S. Todorov (BUL). **Light:** J. Bielski (POL). **L. Welter:** N. Suleymanogiu (TUR). **Welter:** V. Karpaclauskas (LIT). **L. Middle:** F. Vastag (ROM). **Middle:** D. Eigenbrodt (GER). **L. Heavy:** I. Kshinin (RUS). **Heavy:** G. Kandelaki (GEO). **S. Heavy:** S. Rusinov (BUL). **Bronze medals:** P. Griffin (IRL), D. Williams (ENG), K. McCormack (WAL).

Vejle, Denmark - 1996

L. Fly: D. Petrov (BUL). **Fly:** A. Pakeev (RUS). **Bantam:** I. Kovacs (HUN). **Feather:** R. Paliani (RUS). **Light:** L. Doroftei (ROM). **L. Welter:** O. Urkal (GER). **Welter:** H. Al (DEN). **L. Middle:** F. Vastag (ROM). **Middle:** S. Ottke (GER). **L. Heavy:** P. Aurino (ITA). **Heavy:** L. Krasniqi (GER). **S. Heavy:** A. Lezin (RUS). **Bronze medals:** S. Harrison (SCO), D. Burke (ENG), D. Kelly (IRL).

Note: Gold medals were awarded to the Europeans who went the furthest in the Olympic Games of 1924, 1928 & 1932.

European Junior Champions, 1970-1995

Miskolc, Hungary - 1970

L. Fly: Gluck (HUN). **Fly:** Z. Kismeneth (HUN). **Bantam:** A. Levitschev (URS). **Feather:** Andrianov (URS). **Light:** L. Juhasz (HUN). **L. Welter:** K. Nemec (HUN). **Welter:** Davidov (URS). **L. Middle:** A. Lemeschev (URS). **Middle:** N. Anfimov (URS). **L. Heavy:** O. Sasche (GDR). **Heavy:** J. Reder (HUN). **Bronze medals:** D. Needham (ENG), R. Barlow (ENG), L. Stevens (ENG).

Bucharest, Romania - 1972

L. Fly: A. Turei (ROM). **Fly:** Condurat (ROM). **Bantam:** V. Solomin (URS). **Feather:** V. Lvov (URS). **Light:** S. Cutov (ROM). **L. Welter:** K. Pierwieniecki (POL). **Welter:** Zorov (URS). **L. Middle:** Babescu (ROM). **Middle:** V. Lemeschev (URS). **L. Heavy:** Mirounik (URS). **Heavy:** Subutin (URS). **Bronze medals:** J. Gale (ENG), R. Maxwell (ENG), D. Odwell (ENG).

Kiev, Russia - 1974

L. Fly: A. Tkachenko (URS). **Fly:** V. Rybakov (URS). **Bantam:** C. Andreikovski (BUL). **Feather:** V. Sorokin (URS). **Light:** V. Limasov (URS). **L. Welter:** N. Sigov (URS). **Welter:** M. Bychkov (URS). **L. Middle:** V. Danshin (URS). **Middle:** D. Jende (GDR). **L. Heavy:** K. Dafinoiu (ROM). **Heavy:** K. Mashev (BUL). **Silver medal:** C. Magri (ENG). **Bronze medals:** G. Gilbody (ENG), K. Laing (ENG).

Izmir, Turkey - 1976

L. Fly: C. Seican (ROM). **Fly:** G. Khratsov (URS). **Bantam:** M. Navros (URS). **Feather:** V. Demoianeko (URS). **Light:** M. Puzovic (YUG). **L. Welter:** V. Zverev (URS). **Welter:** K. Ozoglouz (TUR). **L. Middle:** W. Lauder (SCO). **Middle:** H. Lenhart (GER). **L. Heavy:** I. Yantchauskas (URS). **Heavy:** B. Enjenyan (URS). **Silver medal:** J. Decker (ENG). **Bronze medals:** I. McLeod (SCO), N. Croombes (ENG).

Dublin, Ireland - 1978

L. Fly: R. Marx (GDR). **Fly:** D. Radu (ROM). **Bantam:** S. Khatchatrian (URS). **Feather:** H. Loukmanov (URS). **Light:** P. Oliva (ITA). **L. Welter:** V. Laptiev (URS). **Welter:** R. Filimanov (URS). **L. Middle:** A. Beliave (URS). **Middle:** G. Zinkovitch (URS). **L. Heavy:** I. Jolta (ROM). **Heavy:** P. Stoimenov (BUL). **Silver medals:** M. Holmes (IRL), P. Hanlon (ENG), M. Courtney (ENG). **Bronze medals:** T. Thompson (IRL), J. Turner (ENG), M. Bennett (WAL), J. McAllister (SCO), C. Devine (ENG).

Rimini, Italy - 1980

L. Fly: A. Mikoulin (URS). **Fly:** J. Varadi (HUN). **Bantam:** F. Rauschning (GDR). **Feather:** J. Gladychev (URS). **Light:** V. Shishov (URS). **L. Welter:** R. Lomski (BUL). **Welter:** T. Holonics (GDR). **L. Middle:** N. Wilshire (ENG). **Middle:** S. Laptiev (URS). **L. Heavy:** V. Dolgoun (URS). **Heavy:** V. Tioumentsev (URS). **S. Heavy:** S. Kormihtsine (URS).

Bronze medals: N. Potter (ENG), B. McGuigan (IRL), M. Brereton (IRL), D. Cross (ENG).

Schwerin, East Germany - 1982

L. Fly: R. Kabirov (URS). **Fly:** I. Filchev (BUL). **Bantam:** M. Stecca (ITA). **Feather:** B. Blagoev (BUL). **Light:** E. Chakimov (URS). **L. Welter:** S. Mehnert (GDR). **Welter:** T. Schmitz (GDR). **L. Middle:** B. Shararov (URS). **Middle:** E. Christie (ENG). **L. Heavy:** Y. Waulin (URS). **Heavy:** A. Popov (URS). **S. Heavy:** V. Aldoshin (URS). **Silver medal:** D. Kenny (ENG). **Bronze medal:** O. Jones (ENG).

Tampere, Finland - 1984

L. Fly: R. Breitbart (GDR). **Fly:** D. Berg (GDR). **Bantam:** K. Khdrian (URS). **Feather:** O. Nazarov (URS). **Light:** C. Furnikov (BUL). **L. Welter:** W. Schmidt (GDR). **Welter:** K. Doinov (BUL). **L. Middle:** O. Volkov (URS). **Middle:** R. Ryll (GDR). **L. Heavy:** G. Peskov (URS). **Heavy:** R. Draskovic (YUG). **S. Heavy:** L. Kamenov (BUL). **Bronze medals:** J. Lowey (IRL), F. Harding (ENG), N. Moore (ENG).

Copenhagen, Denmark - 1986

L. Fly: S. Todorov (BUL). **Fly:** S. Galotian (URS). **Bantam:** D. Drumm (GDR). **Feather:** K. Tsziu (URS). **Light:** G. Akopkhian (URS). **L. Welter:** F. Vastag (ROM). **Welter:** S. Karavaya (URS). **L. Middle:** E. Elibaev (URS). **Middle:** A. Kurnabka (URS). **L. Heavy:** A. Schultz (GDR). **Heavy:** A. Golota (POL). **S. Heavy:** A. Prianichnikov (URS).

Gdansk, Poland - 1988

L. Fly: I. Kovacs (HUN). **Fly:** M. Beyer (GDR). **Bantam:** M. Aitzanov (URS). **Feather:** M. Rudolph (GDR). **Light:** M. Shaburov (URS). **L. Welter:** G. Campanella (ITA). **Welter:** D. Konsun (URS). **L. Middle:** K. Kiselev (URS). **Middle:** A. Rudenko (URS). **L. Heavy:** O. Velikanov (URS). **Heavy:** A. Ter-Okopian (URS). **S. Heavy:** E. Belusov (URS). **Bronze medals:** P. Ramsey (ENG), M. Smyth (WAL).

Usti Nad Labem, Czechoslovakia - 1990

L. Fly: Z. Paliani (URS). **Fly:** K. Pielert (GDR). **Bantam:** K. Baravi (URS). **Feather:** P. Gvasalia (URS). **Light:** J. Hildenbrandt (GDR). **L. Welter:** N. Smanov (URS). **Welter:** A. Preda (ROM). **L. Middle:** A. Kakauridze (URS). **Middle:** J. Schwank (GDR). **L. Heavy:** Iljin (URS). **Heavy:** I. Andrejev (URS). **S. Heavy:** W. Fischer (GDR). **Silver medal:** A. Todd (ENG). **Bronze medal:** P. Craig (ENG).

Edinburgh, Scotland - 1992

L. Fly: M. Ismailov (URS). **Fly:** F. Brennfuhrer (GER). **Bantam:** S. Kuchler (GER). **Feather:** M. Silantiev (URS). **Light:** S. Shcherbakov (URS). **L. Welter:** O. Saitov (URS). **Welter:** H. Kurlumaz (TUR). **L. Middle:** Z. Erdie (HUN). **Middle:** V. Zhirov (URS). **L. Heavy:** D. Gorbachev (URS). **Heavy:** L. Achkasov (URS). **S. Heavy:** A. Mamedov (URS). **Silver medals:** M. Hall (ENG), B. Jones (WAL). **Bronze medals:** F. Slane (IRL), G. Stephens (IRL), C. Davies (WAL).

Salonika, Greece - 1993

L. Fly: O. Kiroukhine (UKR). **Fly:** R. Husseinov (AZE). **Bantam:** M. Kulbe (GER). **Feather:** E. Zakharov (RUS). **Light:** O. Sergeev (RUS). **L. Welter:** A. Selihanov (RUS). **Welter:** O. Kudinov (UKR). **L. Middle:** E. Makarenko (RUS). **Middle:** D. Droukovski (RUS). **L. Heavy:** A. Voida (RUS). **Heavy:** V. Klitchko (UKR). **S. Heavy:** A. Moiseev (RUS). **Bronze medal:** D. Costello (ENG).

Sifok, Hungary - 1995

L. Fly: D. Gaissine (RUS). **Fly:** A. Kotelnik (UKR). **Bantam:** A. Loutsenko (UKR). **Feather:** S. Harrison (SCO). **Light:** D. Simon (ROM). **L. Welter:** B. Ulusoy (TUR). **Welter:** O. Bouts (UKR). **L. Middle:** O. Bukalo (UKR). **Middle:** V. Plettnev (RUS). **L. Heavy:** A. Derevtsov (RUS). **Heavy:** C. O'Grady (IRL). **S. Heavy:** D. Savvine (RUS). **Silver medal:** G. Murphy (SCO). **Bronze medal:** N. Linford (ENG).

Note: The age limit for the championships were reduced from 21 to 19 in 1976.

Commonwealth Champions, 1930-1994

Hamilton, Canada - 1930
Fly: W. Smith (SAF). **Bantam:** H. Mizler (ENG). **Feather:** F. Meacham (ENG). **Light:** J. Rolland (SCO). **Welter:** L. Hall (SAF). **Middle:** F. Mallin (ENG). **L. Heavy:** J. Goyder (ENG). **Heavy:** V. Stuart (ENG).
Silver medals: T. Pardoe (ENG), T. Holt (SCO).
Bronze medals: A. Lyons (SCO), A. Love (ENG), F. Breeman (ENG).

Wembley, England - 1934
Fly: P. Palmer (ENG). **Bantam:** F. Ryan (ENG). **Feather:** C. Cattarall (SAF). **Light:** L. Cook (AUS). **Welter:** D. McCleave (ENG). **Middle:** A. Shawyer (ENG). **L. Heavy:** G. Brennan (ENG). **Heavy:** P. Floyd (ENG).
Silver medals: A. Barnes (WAL), J. Jones (WAL), F. Taylor (WAL), J. Holton (SCO).
Bronze medals: J. Pottinger (WAL), T. Wells (SCO), H. Moy (ENG), W. Duncan (NIR), J. Magill (NIR), Lord D. Douglas-Hamilton (SCO).

Melbourne, Australia - 1938
Fly: J. Joubert (SAF). **Bantam:** W. Butler (ENG). **Feather:** A. Henricus (CEY). **Light:** H. Groves (ENG). **Welter:** W. Smith (AUS). **Middle:** D. Reardon (WAL). **L. Heavy:** N. Wolmarans (SAF). **Heavy:** T. Osborne (CAN).
Silver medals: J. Watson (SCO), M. Dennis (ENG).
Bronze medals: H. Cameron (SCO), J. Wilby (ENG).

Auckland, New Zealand - 1950
Fly: H. Riley (SCO). **Bantam:** J. van Rensburg (SAF). **Feather:** H. Gilliland (SCO). **Light:** R. Latham (ENG). **Welter:** T. Ratcliffe (ENG). **Middle:** T. van Schalkwyk (SAF). **L. Heavy:** D. Scott (ENG). **Heavy:** F. Creagh (NZL).
Bronze medal: P. Brander (ENG).

Vancouver, Canada - 1954
Fly: R. Currie (SCO). **Bantam:** J. Smillie (SCO). **Feather:** L. Leisching (SAF). **Light:** P. van Staden (SR). **L. Welter:** M. Bergin (CAN). **Welter:** N. Gargano (ENG). **L. Middle:** W. Greaves (CAN). **Middle:** J. van de Kolff (SAF). **L. Heavy:** P. van Vuuren (SAF). **Heavy:** B. Harper (ENG).
Silver medals: M. Collins (WAL), F. McQuillan (SCO).
Bronze medals: D. Charnley (ENG), B. Wells (ENG).

Cardiff, Wales - 1958
Fly: J. Brown (SCO). **Bantam:** H. Winstone (WAL). **Feather:** W. Taylor (AUS). **Light:** R. McTaggart (SCO). **L. Welter:** H. Loubscher (SAF). **Welter:** J. Greyling (SAF). **L. Middle:** G. Webster (SAF). **Middle:** T. Milligan (NIR). **L. Heavy:** A. Madigan (AUS). **Heavy:** D. Bekker (SAF).
Silver medals: T. Bache (ENG), M. Collins (WAL), J. Jordan (NIR), R. Kane (SCO), S. Pearson (ENG), A. Higgins (WAL), D. Thomas (ENG).
Bronze medals: P. Lavery (NIR), D. Braithwaite (WAL), R. Hanna (NIR), A. Owen (SCO), J. McClory (NIR), J. Cooke (ENG), J. Jacobs (ENG), B. Nancurvis (ENG), R. Scott (SCO), W. Brown (WAL), J. Caiger (ENG), W. Bannon (SCO), R. Pleace (WAL).

Perth, Australia - 1962
Fly: R. Mallon (SCO). **Bantam:** J. Dynevor (AUS). **Feather:** J. McDermott (SCO). **Light:** E. Blay (GHA). **L. Welter:** C. Quartey (GHA). **Welter:** W. Coe (NZL). **L. Middle:** H. Mann (CAN). **Middle:** M. Calhoun (JAM). **L. Heavy:** A. Madigan (AUS). **Heavy:** G. Oywello (UGA).
Silver medals: R. McTaggart (SCO), J. Pritchett (ENG).
Bronze medals: M. Pye (ENG), P. Benneyworth (ENG), B. Whelan (ENG), B. Brazier (ENG), C. Rice (NIR), T. Menzies (SCO), H. Christie (NIR), A. Turmel (CI).

Kingston, Jamaica - 1966
Fly: S. Shittu (GHA). **Bantam:** E. Ndukwu (NIG). **Feather:** P. Waruinge (KEN). **Light:** A. Andeh (NIG). **L. Welter:** J. McCourt (NIR). **Welter:** E. Blay (GHA). **L. Middle:** M. Rowe (ENG). **Middle:** J. Darkey (GHA). **L. Heavy:** R. Tighe (ENG). **Heavy:** W. Kini (NZL).
Silver medals: P. Maguire (NIR), R. Thurston (ENG), R. Arthur (ENG), T. Imrie (SCO).
Bronze medals: S. Lockhart (NIR), A. Peace (SCO), F. Young (NIR), J. Turpin (ENG), D. McAlinden (NIR).

Edinburgh, Scotland - 1970
L. Fly: J. Odwori (UGA). **Fly:** D. Needham (ENG). **Bantam:** S. Shittu (GHA). **Feather:** P. Waruinge (KEN). **Light:** A. Adeyemi (NIG). **L. Welter:** M. Muruli (UGA). **Welter:** E. Ankudey (GHA). **L. Middle:** T. Imrie (SCO). **Middle:** J. Conteh (ENG). **L. Heavy:** F. Ayinla (NIG). **Heavy:** B. Masanda (UGA).
Silver medals: T. Davies (WAL), J. Gillan (SCO), D. Davies (WAL), J. McKinty (NIR).
Bronze medals: M. Abrams (ENG), A. McHugh (SCO), D. Larmour (NIR), S. Oglivie (SCO), A. Richardson (ENG), T. Joyce (SCO), P. Doherty (NIR), J. Rafferty (SCO), L. Stevens (ENG).

Christchurch, New Zealand - 1974
L. Fly: S. Muchoki (KEN). **Fly:** D. Larmour (NIR). **Bantam:** P. Cowdell (ENG). **Feather:** E. Ndukwu (NIG). **Light:** A. Kalule (UGA). **L. Welter:** O. Nwankpa (NIG). **Welter:** M. Muruli (UGA). **L. Middle:** L. Mwale (ZAM). **Middle:** F. Lucas (STV). **L. Heavy:** W. Knight (ENG). **Heavy:** N. Meade (ENG).
Silver medals: E. McKenzie (WAL), A. Harrison (SCO).
Bronze medals: J. Bambrick (SCO), J. Douglas (SCO), J. Rodgers (NIR), S. Cooney (SCO), R. Davies (ENG), C. Speare (ENG), G. Ferris (NIR).

Edmonton, Canada - 1978
L. Fly: S. Muchoki (KEN). **Fly:** M. Irungu (KEN). **Bantam:** B. McGuigan (NIR). **Feather:** A. Nelson (GHA). **Light:** G. Hamill (NIR). **L. Welter:** W. Braithwaite (GUY). **Welter:** M. McCallum (JAM). **L. Middle:** K. Perlette (CAN). **Middle:** P. McElwaine (AUS). **L. Heavy:** R. Fortin (CAN). **Heavy:** J. Awome (ENG).
Silver medals: J. Douglas (SCO), K. Beattie (NIR), D. Parkes (ENG), V. Smith (ENG).
Bronze medals: H. Russell (NIR), M. O'Brien (ENG), J. McAllister (SCO), T. Feal (WAL).

Brisbane, Australia - 1982
L. Fly: A. Wachire (KEN). **Fly:** M. Mutua (KEN). **Bantam:** J. Orewa (NIG). **Feather:** P. Konyegwachie (NIG). **Light:** H. Khalili (KEN). **L. Welter:** C. Ossai (NIG). **Welter:** C. Pyatt (ENG). **L. Middle:** S. O'Sullivan (CAN). **Middle:** J. Price (ENG). **L. Heavy:** F. Sani (FIJ). **Heavy:** W. de Wit (CAN).
Silver medals: J. Lyon (ENG), J. Kelly (SCO), R. Webb (NIR), P. Hanlon (ENG), J. McDonnell (ENG), N. Croombes (ENG), H. Hylton (ENG).
Bronze medals: R. Gilbody (ENG), C. McIntosh (ENG), R. Corr (NIR).

Edinburgh, Scotland - 1986
L. Fly: S. Olson (CAN). **Fly:** J. Lyon (ENG). **Bantam:** S. Murphy (ENG). **Feather:** B. Downey (CAN). **Light:** A. Dar (CAN). **L. Welter:** H. Grant (CAN). **Welter:** D. Dyer (ENG). **L. Middle:** D. Sherry (CAN). **Middle:** R. Douglas (ENG). **L. Heavy:** J. Moran (ENG). **Heavy:** J. Peau (NZL). **S. Heavy:** L. Lewis (CAN).
Silver medals: M. Epton (ENG), R. Nash (NIR), P. English (ENG), N. Haddock (WAL), J. McAlister (SCO), H. Lawson (SCO), D. Young (SCO), A. Evans (WAL).
Bronze medals: W. Docherty (SCO), J. Todd (NIR), K. Webber (WAL), G. Brooks (SCO), J. Wallace (SCO), C. Carleton (NIR), J. Jacobs (ENG), B. Lowe (NIR), D. Denny (NIR), G. Thomas (WAL), A. Mullen (SCO), G. Ferrie (SCO), P. Tinney (NIR), B. Pullen (WAL), E. Cardouza (ENG), J. Oyebola (ENG), J. Sillitoe (CI).

Auckland, New Zealand - 1990
L. Fly: J. Juuko (UGA). **Fly:** W. McCullough (NIR). **Bantam:** S. Mohammed (NIG). **Feather:** J. Irwin (ENG). **Light:** G. Nyakana (UGA). **L. Welter:** C. Kane (SCO). **Welter:** D. Defiagbon (NIG). **L. Middle:** R. Woodhall (ENG). **Middle:** C. Johnson (CAN). **L. Heavy:** J. Akhasamba (KEN). **Heavy:** G. Onyango (KEN). **S. Heavy:** M. Kenny (NZL).
Bronze medals: D. Anderson (SCO), M. Edwards (ENG), P. Douglas (NIR).

Victoria, Canada - 1994
L. Fly: H. Ramadhani (KEN). **Fly:** P. Shepherd (SCO). **Bantam:** R. Peden (AUS). **Feather:** C. Patton (CAN). **Light:** M. Strange (CAN). **L. Welter:** P. Richardson (ENG). **Welter:** N. Sinclair (NIR). **L. Middle:** J. Webb (NIR). **Middle:** R. Donaldson (CAN). **L. Heavy:** D. Brown (CAN). **Heavy:** O. Ahmed (KEN). **S. Heavy:** D. Dokiwari (NIG).
Silver medals: S. Oliver (ENG), J. Cook (WAL), M. Reneghan (NIR), M. Winters (NIR), J. Wilson (SCO).
Bronze medals: D. Costello (ENG), J. Townsley (SCO), D. Williams (ENG).

The Triple Hitters' Boxing Quiz

by Ralph Oates

QUESTIONS

1. Bob Fitzsimmons won the world heavyweight title when he knocked out defending champion, James J. Corbett, in round 14. In which year did this contest take place?
   A. 1896.   B. 1897.   C. 1898.

2. In defence of his world heavyweight crown on 14 September 1923, Jack Dempsey knocked out his challenger, Luis Angel Firpo, in round two. How many times did Dempsey floor Firpo in round one?
   A. Five.   B. Six.   C. Seven.

3. In which year was world light-heavyweight champion, John Henry Lewis, forced to retire due to failing eyesight?
   A. 1939.   B. 1940.   C. 1941.

4. To win the WBC version of the world light-heavyweight title, John Conteh outpointed Jorge Ahumada over 15 rounds for the vacant crown on 1 October 1974. In which country did this contest take place?
   A. Argentina.   B. England.   C. France.

5. Who was the first holder of the IBF super-middleweight title?
   A. Chong-Pal Park.   B. Murray Sutherland.
   C. Graciano Rocchigiani.

6. Which version of the world super-middleweight title did Sugar Ray Leonard hold?
   A. WBA.   C. WBC.   D. IBF.

7. Randolph Turpin won the world middleweight championship when he outpointed defending

champion, Sugar Ray Robinson, over 15 rounds on 10 July 1951. Who was the referee for this contest?
   A. Eugene Henderson.   B. Ruby Goldstein.
   C. Jack Downey.

8. Which version of the world middleweight crown did Nigel Benn hold?
   A. WBA.   B. WBO.   C. WBC.

9. Ralph Charles challenged Jose Napoles for the world welterweight title on 28 March 1972, but failed in his bid when he was knocked out. In which round?
   A. Five.   B. Six.   C. Seven.

10. Who did Lloyd Honeyghan outpoint over 12 rounds on 5 April 1983 to win the vacant British welterweight title?
   A. Cliff Gilpin.   B. Peter Neal.   C. Kirkland Laing.

11. To retain his WBA light-welterweight crown, Antonio Cervantes outpointed Esteban de Jesus on 17 May 1975. In which country did this contest take place?
   A. Spain.   B. Panama.   C. Argentina.

12. Which light-welterweight crown did Clinton McKenzie not hold during his career?
   A. British.   B. European.   C. Commonwealth.

13. Did Maurice Cullen ever challenge for the world lightweight championship during his career?
   Yes or No.

14. Billy Schwer won the British and Commonwealth lightweight titles on 28 October 1992, when defending champion, Carl Crook, retired. In which round?
   A. Nine.   B. Ten.   C. Eleven.

15. On 11 December 1982, Bobby Chacon won the WBC version of the world super-featherweight title by defeating champion, Rafael Limon. By which method?
   A. Fifth round knockout.   B. Eighth round retirement.
   C. Fifteen round points decision.

16. Floyd Havard failed in his bid on 22 January 1994 to win the IBF version of the world super-featherweight title against defending champion, Juan Molina, when he retired in round six. In which part of Wales did this contest take place?
   A. Cardiff.   B. Aberavon.   C. Llanelli.

17. Did former British, European and WBC world featherweight champion, Howard Winstone, ever box in America during his pro career?
   Yes or No.

18. Who did Johnny Famechon outpoint over 15 rounds on 21 January 1969 to win the WBC version of the world featherweight title?
   A. Jose Legra.   B. Mitsunori Seki.   C. Raul Rojas.

19. In which year was Frank Bruno born?
   A. 1960.   B. 1961.   C. 1962.

20. Who became the first holder of the British super-bantamweight title?
   A. Richie Wenton.   B. Neil Swain.   C. Paul Lloyd.

21. Who became the first holder of the Commonwealth super-bantamweight title?
A. Mike Parris.   B. Richie Wenton.   C. Neil Swain.

22. In which year did Chris Finnegan win a gold medal in the Olympic Games at middleweight?
A. 1967.   B. 1968.   C. 1969.

23. Which heavyweight was nicknamed the Pottawatomie Giant?
A. Jack Dempsey.   B. Jess Willard.   C. Gene Tunney.

24. On 30 November 1965, Alan Rudkin challenged Masahiko Harada for the world bantamweight title, but failed in his bid when outpointed over 15 rounds. In which country did this contest take place?
A. England.   B. America.   C. Japan.

25. To win the vacant Commonwealth bantamweight title, John Armour stopped his opponent, Ndabe Dube. Name the round?
A. Ten.   B. Eleven.   C. Twelve.

26. How tall is Henry Akinwande?
A. 6'7".   B. 6'8".   C. 6'9".

27. Which former world lightweight champion was

nicknamed Old Bones?
A. Carlos Ortiz.   B. Joe Brown.   C. Ike Williams.

28. Which version of the world light-middleweight title did Maurice Hope hold?
A. WBA.   B. IBF.   C. WBC.

29. Who did Walter McGowan outpoint over 15 rounds on 14 June 1966 to win the WBC version of the world flyweight title?
A. Pone Kingpetch.   B. Salvatore Burruni.
C. Horacio Accavallo.

30. Did Charlie Magri ever box in France during his pro career?
Yes or No.

31. Which boxer did Terry Lawless not manage during the course of their careers?
A. Ralph Charles.   B. Maurice Hope.   C. Ken Buchanan.

32. On 24 January 1981, Chul-Ho Kim won the WBC version of the world super-flyweight crown when he knocked out defending champion, Rafael Orono. Name the round?
A. Seven.   B. Eight.   C. Nine.

33. On 21 November 1984, Kaosai Galaxy won the vacant WBA verson of the world super-flyweight crown when he knocked out opponent, Eusebio Espinal. In which round?
A. Six.   B. Seven.   C. Eight.

34. Gerardo Gonzalez, seen here (left) with Peter

Waterman, was the real name of which former world welterweight champion?
A. Johnny Bratton.   B. Virgil Akins.   C. Kid Gavilan.

35. In which year was the mini-flyweight poundage instigated by the IBF?
A. 1986.   B. 1987.   C. 1988.

36. On 15 May 1993, Paul Weir stopped Fernando Martinez in round seven to win the vacant WBO version of the world mini-flyweight crown. Prior to this contest, how many bouts had Weir taken part in during his pro career?
A. Three.   B. Four.   C. Five.

37. During his pro career, did Charlie Magri ever challenge for the British bantamweight title?
Yes or No.

38. In which year did Katherine Morrison receive her promoters' license from the BBBoC?
A. 1992. B. 1993. C. 1994.

39. In which country did Chris Eubank have his first five pro contests?
A. Canada. B. America. C. France.

40. In 1987, Nigel Benn had 12 bouts. How many did he win in the first round?
A. Six. B. Seven. C. Eight.

41. Prior to defeating Frank Bruno in defence of his world heavyweight title, by a stoppage in round seven on 1 October 1993. Who did Lennox Lewis outpoint over 12 rounds on 8 May 1993 to retain his crown?
A. Tony Tucker. B. Tony Tubbs. C. Phil Jackson.

42. Who did Prince Nassem Hamed outpoint over 12 rounds on 11 May 1994 to win the European bantamweight title?
A. Vincenzo Belcastro. B. Antonio Picardi.
C. Johnny Bredahl.

43. Which boxers real name was Walker Smith Jnr?
A. Terry Downes. B. Sugar Ray Robinson.
C. Gene Fullmer.

44. Which manager guided Lennox Lewis to the world heavyweight title?
A. Terry Lawless. B. Frank Maloney. C. Frank Warren.

45. During 1994, Henry Wharton challenged twice for versions of the world super-middleweight crown. On each occasion he failed in his bid when outpointed over 12 rounds. Which champion did he not meet?
A. Nigel Benn. B. Chris Eubank. C. James Toney.

46. In which weight division was Bunny Johnson not a British champion?
A. Middleweight. B. Light-Heavyweight.
C. Heavyweight.

47. To retain his British super-middleweight crown, Joe Calzaghe stopped Mark Delaney on 20 April 1996. In which round?
A. Three. B. Four. C. Five.

48. On 26 April 1996, Robbie Regan outpointed defending champion, Daniel Jimenez, over 12 rounds to win the WBO version of the world bantamweight title. Who was the referee of this contest?
A. Lou Filippo. B. Tony Perez. C. Gino Rodriguez.

49. Which role does Tania Follett play in boxing?
A. Manager. B. Second. C. MC.

50. To win the WBO version of the world featherweight crown on 17 April 1993, Steve Robinson outpointed John Davison over 12 rounds. Was the said title vacant at the time?
Yes or No.

MUNRO & HYLAND BROS.

INTERNATIONAL BOXING PROMOTERS AND MANAGERS

TEAM FOR 1996/97

Richie Elder
GENERAL MANAGER

Martin Cain
PROMOTIONAL MANAGER

John Gaynor
MATCHMAKER

BOXERS

Mathew Ellis
HEAVYWEIGHT

Gary Lockett
LIGHT-MIDDLEWEIGHT

Paul Burns
WELTERWEIGHT

Shea Neary
LIGHT-WELTERWEIGHT

Gary Ryder
LIGHT-WELTERWEIGHT

Danny 'Boy' Peters
SUPER-MIDDLEWEIGHT

Alex Moon
FEATHERWEIGHT

TRAINERS

Kenny Willis, George Schofield (JNR), George Schofield (SNR)

THE MORTON SUITE • THE MOAT HOUSE HOTEL • 1 PARADISE STREET • LIVERPOOL • ENGLAND L1 8JD
TELEPHONE: 0151-708 8331 • FAX: 0151-708 6701

Licensed by The British Boxing Board of Control

Directory of Ex-Boxers' Associations

by Ron Olver

BIRMINGHAM Founded 1985. Disbanded. Re-formed 1995. HQ: Emerald Club, Green Lane, Birmingham. Ernie Cashmore (P); Paddy Maguire (C), 265 Mackadown Lane, Tilecross, Birmingham. Bobby Sexton (T); Tom Byrne(S).

BOURNEMOUTH Founded 1980. HQ: Mallard Road Bus Services Social Club, Bournemouth. Dai Dower (P); Peter Fay (C); Percy Singer (T); Ken Wells (VC); Les Smith (S), Flat L, 592 Charminster Road, Bournemouth BH8 9SL.

CORK Founded 1973. HQ: Acra House, Maylor Street, Cork. Johnny Fitzgerald (P & C); John Cronin (VC); Eamer Coughlan (T); Tim O'Sullivan (S & PRO), Acra House, Maylor Street, Dublin.

CORNWALL Founded 1989. HQ: St Austell British Legion and Royal Hotel, Camborne in alternate months. Roy Coote (P); Len Magee (C), Fred Edwards (VC); Jimmy Miller (T); John Soloman (S), 115 Albany Road, Redruth.

CROYDON Founded 1982. HQ: The Prince Of Wales, Thornton Heath. Tom Powell, BEM (P); Martin Olney (C), Chris Wood (VC); Morton Lewis (T); Gilbert Allnutt (S), 37 Braemar Avenue, Thornton Heath, Croydon CR9 7RJ.

EASTERN AREA Founded 1973. HQ: Norfolk Dumpling, Cattle Market, Hall Road, Norwich. Brian Fitzmaurice (P); Alfred Smith (C); Clive Campling (VC); Eric Middleton (T & S), 48 City Road, Norwich NR1 3AU.

IPSWICH Founded 1970. HQ: Flying Horse, Waterford Road, Ipswich. Alby Kingham (P); Frank Webb (C); Vic Thurlow (T); Nigel Wheeler (PRO & S); 20 Stratford Road, Ipswich 1PL 6OF.

IRISH Founded 1973. HQ: National Boxing Stadium, South Circular Road, Dublin. Maxie McCullagh (P); Jack O'Rourke (C); Willie Duggan (VC); Tommy Butler (T); Denis Morrison (S), 55 Philipsburgh Terrace, Marino, Dublin.

KENT Founded 1967. HQ: Chatham WMC, New Road, Chatham. Teddy Bryant (P); Bill Warner (C); Mick Smith (VC); Fred Atkins (T); Ray Lambert (PRO); Paul Nihill MBE, (S), 59 Balfour Road, Rochester, Kent.

LEEDS Founded 1952. HQ: North Leeds WMC, Burmantofts, Lincoln Green, Leeds 9. Johnny Durkin (P); Frankie Brown (VC); Alan Alster (T); Steve Butler (PRO); Malcolm Bean (S), 11 Crawshaw Gardens, Pudsey, Leeds LS28 7 BW

LEFT-HOOK CLUB Betty Faux (S), 144 Longmoor Lane, Aintree, Liverpool. No regular meetings. Formed specifically with the aim of holding functions to raise money in order to help former boxers in need.

LEICESTER Founded 1972. HQ: Belgrave WMC, Checketts Road, Leicester. Pat Butler (P); Mick Greaves (C); Mrs Rita Jones (T); Norman Jones (S), 60 Dumbleton Avenue, Leicester LE3 2EG.

LONDON Founded 1971. HQ; St Pancras Conservative Club, Argyle Street, London. Stephen Powell (P); Micky O'Sullivan (C); Andy Williamson (VC); Ron Olver (PRO); Ray Caulfield (T); Mrs Mary Powell (S), 36 St Peters Street, Islington, London N1 8JT.

MANCHESTER Founded 1968. HQ: British Rail Social Club, Store Street, Manchester. Jackie Braddock (Life P); Jack Jamieson (P); Tommy Proffitt (C); Jack Edwards (VC); Eddie Lillis (T); John Fleming (S).

MERSEYSIDE (Liverpool) Founded 1973. HQ: Queens Hotel, Derby Square, Liverpool. Johnny Cooke (P); Terry Riley (C); Jim Boyd (VC); Jim Jenkinson (T); Johnny Holmes (S), 41 Higher End Park, Bootle 20.

NORTHAMPTONSHIRE Founded 1981. HQ: Exclusive Club, Gold Street, Northampton. Tony Perrett (P); Pat Boyle (C); Keith Hall (S), 29 Sydney Street, Kettering, Northants NN16 0HZ.

NORTHERN FEDERATION Founded 1974. Several member EBAs. Annual Gala. Eddie Monahan (S), 16 Braemar Avenue, Marshside, Southport.

NORTHERN IRELAND Founded 1970. HQ: Ulster Sports Club, Belfast. Derek Wade (P); Benny Vaughan (C); Sammy Cosgrove (VC & PRO); Sammy Thompson (T); Al Gibson (S), 900 Crumlin Road, Belfast.

NORTH STAFFS & SOUTH CHESHIRE Founded 1969. HQ: The Saggar Makers Bottom Knocker, Market Place, Burslem, Stoke on Trent. Tut Whalley (P); Roy Simms (VC); Les Dean (S); John Greatbach (T); Billy Tudor (C & PRO), 133 Sprinkbank Road, Chell Heath, Stoke on Trent, Staffs ST6 6HW.

NORWICH HQ: West End Retreat, Brown Street, Norwich. Les King (P); John Pipe (C); Jack Wakefield (T); Dick Sadd (S), 76 Orchard Street, Norwich.

NOTTINGHAM Founded 1979. HQ: The Lion Hotel, Clumber Street, Nottingham. Frank Parkes (P); Frank Hayes (C); John Kinsella (S).

NOTTS & DERBY Founded 1973. Dick Johnson (S & PRO), 15 Church Street, Pinxton, Nottingham.

PLYMOUTH Founded 1982. HQ: Exmouth Road Social Club, Stoke, Plymouth. George Borg (P); Tom Pryce-Davies (C); Doug Halliday (VC); Arthur Willis (T); Buck Taylor (S), 15 Greenbank Avenue, St Judes, Plymouth PL4 9BT.

PRESTON Founded 1973. HQ: County Arms Hotel, Deepdale Road, Preston. Albert Bradley (P); Brian Petherwick (C); Frank Brown (T); Ted Sumner (S), 7 Kew Gardens, Penwortham, Preston PR1 0DR.

READING Founded 1977. HQ: Salisbury Club, Kings Road, Reading. Roland Dakin (P); Bob Pitman (C); Arnold Whatmore (T); Bob Sturgess (S).

ST HELENS Founded 1983. HQ: Travellers Rest Hotel, Crab Street, St Helens. George Thomas (C); Jimmy O'Keefe (VC); Tommy McNamara (T); Paul Britch (S), 40 Ashtons Green Drive, Parr, St Helens.

SEFTON Founded 1975. HQ: St Benet's Parochial Club, Netherton, Bootle. Alf Lunt (T); Johnny Holmes (S); 41 Higher End Park, Sefton, Bootle.

SLOUGH Founded 1973. HQ: Luton Arndale Centre Social Club. Max Quartermain (P); Jack Bridge (C); Charlie Knight (T); Ernie Watkins (S), 5 Sunbury Road, Eton, Windsor.

SQUARE RING Founded 1978. HQ: Torquay Social Club. George Pook (P); Maxie Beech (VC); Johnny Mudge (S); Jim Banks (T); Paul King (C), 10 Pine Court Apartments, Middle Warberry Road, Torquay.

SUNDERLAND Founded 1959. HQ: Hendon Gardens, Sunderland. Bert Ingram (P); Terry Lynn (C); Joe Riley (PRO); Les Simm (S), 21 Orchard Street, Pallion, Sunderland SR4 6QL.

SUSSEX Founded 1974. HQ: Brighton & Hove Sports & Social Club, Conway Street, Hove. Geoff Williams (P & T); Bert Hollows (C); John Ford (S), 69 Moyne Close, Hove, Sussex.

SWANSEA & SOUTH WEST WALES Founded 1983. HQ: Villiers Arms, Neath Road, Hafod, Swansea. Cliff Curvis (P); Gordon Pape (C); Ernie Wallis (T); Len Smith (S), Cockett Inn, Cockett, Swansea SA2 0GB.

TRAMORE Founded 1981. HQ: Robinson Bar, Main Street, Tramore, Co Waterford. T. Flynn (P); J. Dunne (C); C. O'Reilly (VC); W. Hutchinson (T); N. Graham (PRO); Pete Graham (S), 3 Riverstown, Tramore.

TYNESIDE Founded 1970. HQ: The Swan Public House, Heworth. Billy Charlton (P); Maxie Walsh (C); Gordon Smith (VC); Malcolm Dinning (T); Bill Wilkie (S & PRO), 60 Calderdale Avenue, Walker, Newcastle NE6 4HN.

WELSH Founded 1976. HQ: Rhydyfelin Rugby Club, Pontypridd, Mid-Glamorgan. Terry Pudge (C); Howard Winstone (VC); Llew Miles (T & PRO), 7 Edward Street, Miskin, Mountain Ash, Mid-Glamorgan; Johnny Jones (S).

The above information is set at the time of going to press and no responsibility can be taken for any changes in officers or addresses of HQs that may happen between then and publication and/or have not been notified to me.

ABBREVIATIONS

P - President. C - Chairman. VC - Vice Chairman. T - Treasurer. S - Secretary. PRO - Public Relations and/or Press Officer.

Enjoying a chat at an annual dinner of the London Ex-Boxers' Association, are Ron Olver (left), former world flyweight champion, Walter McGowan (centre), and Morton Lewis, the son of the late, great Ted Kid Lewis, who, besides being a LEBA member, is also treasurer of the Croydon EBA

Obituaries

by Ron Olver

It is impossible to list everyone, but I have again done my best to include final tributes for as many of the well-known boxers and other familiar names within the sport, who have passed away since the 1996 Yearbook was published. We honour them and will remember them.

ALDRIDGE Al *From* London. *Died* 27 November 1995. In the Army, and evacuated from Dunkirk, Al also served in the Western Desert. A prominent member of several EBAs, including LEBA, Kent, Croydon and Sussex, he was a great supporter of the Royal Star & Garter Home and was a leading light in arranging tribute nights for ex-boxers. Al was a great organiser and worked hard for several charities. One of his last efforts was to raise £1,120 for the Croydon, Sussex and District Spastics Society, which was attended by Mark Rowe, Johnny Clark, and many other notables from the fight fraternity.

ALEXANDER Derek *From* Willenhall. *Born* 9 November 1928. *Died* 31 January 1996. Pro 1946-1953. Although defeated by Allan Cooke for the vacant North Midlands light-heavyweight title (1950), Derek beat Gene Fowler, Johnny Barton, and Dennis Powell. The eldest of ten (five boys and five girls), his father was a former Army champion and his grandfather boxed in the bareknuckle days. Did his National Service from the age of 18, then joined George Gill's stable at Yeovil, starting with five straight wins, having an unbeaten run of nine between 1947 (November) and 1948 (November). After retiring, he went into the licensing trade, looking after several local pubs, but following his wife's death (1992), his health deteriorated. One of his proudest moments was to be engaged as a sparring-partner to American heavyweight, Joe Baksi, who was due to meet Bruce Woodcock.

ARNOLD Billy *From* Philadelphia, USA. *Died* June 1995. Pro 1943-1948. Noted for his power of punch, Billy won his first 29 bouts, all but two inside the distance. His first two fights in 1945 were against world champions, Fritzie Zivic and Rocky Graziano, going the full eight rounds with the former, but being stopped in round three by Rocky. Beat Manny Morales, Milo Theodorescu, Sandy Mack, Cat Robinson, Johnny Jones and Joey Falco, and twice outpointed Ralph Zanelli. Also met Steve Belloise.

AUSTIN George *From* Nottingham. *Died* June 1996. Most of his boxing was in the Army with the Kings Own Regiment in India. A tireless worker and a great organiser, he later became a member of Nottingham EBA, then treasurer, temporary secretary, and editor of the Newsletter.

BAINES Billy *From* Norwich. *Died* 1996. Started boxing as a schoolboy in Wales. Joined the Army in World War II and was involved in the Dunkirk evacuation, later being posted to London, where he continued to box, and then Africa, the Sudan and Italy, prior to his discharge in 1946. Returned to Norwich and retired from boxing in 1951.

BAKER Stan *From* London. *Died* 26 November 1995. Was just six years old when his uncle Teddy Baker met Ernie Izzard for the British lightweight title at the National Sporting Club in 1925. After listening to Teddy's stories on the sport, Stan was hooked and started to box as soon as he was old enough, becoming a finalist in the National Schoolboy Championships. Turned pro in 1938 under the management of Ernie Izzard's father and drew with Jack Watkins on his debut. After 25 bouts came World War II. In 1939 he joined the Army, becoming the Boxing Instructor to a Battalion of the Queens Regiment, and was posted to France, where he was lucky to be one of the Dunkirk survivors. In 1940, he was a victim of the bombing at Kings Cross, where he received leg injuries, necessitating six months in hospital. His boxing career being at an end, in 1949 he got a chance to promote an open-air show at Bromley. It was a lovely August afternoon, but after the first three bouts and an exhibition by Freddie Mills, down came the rain and the rest of the bill had to be cancelled. However, no one asked for their money back. Stan then moved on to higher things, promoting at Streatham Ice Rink with Jim Wicks as his matchmaker. As Britain's youngest promoter, he ran 40 shows at Streatham from 1950 to the early '60s, also a dozen at the Royal Albert Hall, and a similar number at Manor Place Baths, plus several at other venues. In later years, as a regular member of the London Ex-Boxers' Association, he enjoyed attending shows and being introduced from the ring. The receptions he got were tributes to his popularity.

BARNARD Ron *From* Carlisle. *Born* 22 January 1932. *Died* June 1996. Born in London, where he boxed for St Pancras BC, Ron did his National Service in Carlisle, married a local lady and settled there. Turned pro with manager, Jim Turner, whose stable included Tex Williams and Stan Barnett, and had around 60 bouts. After retiring he coached Carrock House BC, helping Gary Sanderson to win two national titles.

BENNETT George *From* Gosport. *Died* 6 February 1996, aged 82. Boxed in the Army and turned pro 1935, meeting George Merritt, Freddie Simpson, Angus McGregor, Seaman Jim Lawlor, Arnold Kid Shepherd and Vince Hawkins. After his pro career, George worked in the Albert Docks (1947-1974), then on the Thames Barrier until retiring at 67. Born at Greenwich, he lived at Charlton for the last 47 years.

BINT Charlie *From* Croydon. *Died* 16 April 1996. Pro 1933-1937. A regular at the Acacias Hall, Pitlake, and Streatham Baths, he met Les Ridge, former Croydon EBA chairman, three times, his last opponent being Tommy Williams, another Croydon EBA member. Originally managed by Albert Jeal, but for most of his career handled by Alf Bliss, they operated from a gym in Surrey Street. During World War II, Charlie rose to the rank of petty officer in the Royal Navy.

BRADY Chic *From* Scotland. *Died* January 1996 in Philadelphia. Managed by Tommy Gilmour Senior, and a pro between 1951 and 1953, Chic beat George Lamont in eliminator for Scottish lightweight title (1952). In a short career of ten bouts, winning seven and losing three, he was beaten by Roy Edwards and Al Hunter, both in New York.

BYARS Walter *From* Boston, USA. *Born* 6 December 1931. *Died* March 1996. Turned pro 1954, losing only two of his first 20 bouts, winning the New England welterweight title by beating Bob Murphy (February 1956) and outpointing former world champion, Kid Gavilan (December 1956), before losing a return with Gavilan (1957). Defeated Garnett Sugar Hart (1957) and went the distance with Tony DeMarco, Virgil Akins, Isaac Logart and Del Flanagan, all big name fighters.

CARLOS Max *From* Victoria, Australia. *Died* May 1996. Having represented Australia in the 1956 Olympic Games, where he was outpointed by the American, Joe Shaw, in the first series, Max turned pro in 1957, beating men such as Sammy Bonnici, George Bracken, Bobby Sinn (twice), Hocine Khalfi and Germano Cavalieri, before outpointing Bracken for the national lightweight title over 15 rounds in July 1958. Never defended, and faded from the scene following defeats by Johnny van Rensburg and Bracken.

CARTIER Walter *From* Mount Vernon, New York, USA. *Born* 29 March 1924. *Died* 17 August 1995. Turned pro in 1946, beating Gene Boland, Pete Mead, Gene Hairston, Otis Graham, Billy Kilgore, and Garth Panter. Also met world champions, Carl Bobo Olson, Joey Giardello, Kid Gavilan, and Randolph Turpin, when coming to Britain in 1953, being disqualified in round two. After retiring he became an actor, and was a regular performer in the popular TV series *Sergeant Bilko* with Phil Silvers.

COLLINS Tommy *From* Boston, USA. *Born* 1929. *Died* 3 June 1996. Turned pro 1946, and the following year had 26 contests, losing only one, and winning all but seven inside the distance. Won the New England featherweight title by stopping Joey Cam in one round (1951) and apart from a defeat by Sandy Saddler, 1952 was a great year, in which he stopped Joey Cam (again), Fabela Chavez, and Willie Pep, outpointed Glen Flanagan, stopped Britisher, Ronnie Clayton, and outpointed Lauro Sales. Lost in four rounds to Jimmy Carter for the world lightweight title in 1933, but could no longer be considered a contender after

being kayoed by Lulu Perez inside two rounds in December 1955.

Tommy Collins pictured here halting the former world featherweight champion, Willie Pep

COPP Alan *From* Swansea. *Born* 3 July 1953. *Died* January 1996 from liver failure. Having been the Welsh amateur lightweight champion (1972 and 1974) and light-welter champion (1976), Alan turned pro in 1976, going unbeaten in five contests (four wins and a draw) before retiring in 1978. A worker at the Swansea Docks for the past 20 years, his younger brother, Michael, the pro manager/trainer, was also a pro fighter (1976-1980).

D'ARCY Mick *From* Royston. *Born* 16 August 1936. *Died* May 1996. As a keen youngster, he boxed in the stable lads competition, while in training under the legendary, Willie Stevenson, doing well enough to consider a career in the ring, turning pro with Joe Jones in 1958. Ten fights later, however, on 17 December 1959, Mick called it a day following a first round stoppage at the hands of the more than useful Al McCarthy.

DORAN Eddie "Bunty" *From* Belfast. *Born* 16 December 1921. *Died* 6 January 1996. Pro 1938-1953. Won the Northern Ireland flyweight title in 1942, losing it to Rinty Monaghan (1945), before moving up to take the Northern Ireland bantamweight title (1947), and successfully defended against Jackie Briers (1951). Beat world champion, Jackie Paterson, and European champion, Theo Medina, in successive fights (1946), but was outpointed by Peter Kane, a former world champion (1947), and coming in as a substitute was again beaten by Kane (1948). Twice beat Jimmy Warnock, who did the double over world champion Benny Lynch, Bunty floored Stan Rowan nine times, before stopping him in six rounds (1949), prior to being beaten by world bantam champion, Vic Toweel, in South Africa (1950). Had a sensational fight with British bantam champion, Danny O'Sullivan, opinions varying as to who was ahead when Bunty was kayoed in the final round. However, in spite of his fine record, he never even got a shot at the British title.

EKASSI Norbert *From* Paris, France, via Cameroon. *Died* 24 December 1995, aged 29. Trained by the former world heavyweight champion, Joe Frazier, in Philadelphia, Norbert was the WBC's top-rated cruiserweight prior to his contest with Alexander Gurov for the EBU title in January 1995. A heavy favourite, and a fighter who had victories over Brits, Cordwell Hylton, R. F. McKenzie and Johnny Nelson, to his credit, he was crushed in just 90 seconds. Tragically, his demise came during a domestic argument after putting his hand through a window and bleeding to death.

FULTON Matt *From* Coatbridge. *Born* 23 October 1934. *Died* April 1996. Pro 1954-1957. Although beaten by Bobby Neill for the Scottish featherweight title (1956), his next fight saw him outpoint Frenchman, Francis Bonnardel, having earlier scored good wins over Sammy Odell, Alby Tissong and Jim Shackleton. However, 1957 was to be his "Swan Song", bowing out following a first round kayo over Jim Loughans, after being outscored by Ayree Jackson (twice) and Spike McCormack.

GODDARD Bill *From* Croydon. *Died* 8 April 1996. In the 1930s, Bill played soccer and cricket, but after visiting a boxing gym at the Earl Russell in Croydon under Tom Fisher's guidance it became the first game for him. Following a hard contest with George Stanbridge at the Acacias Hall, Bill soon became Tom Fisher's right-hand man. In World War II he served in the Burma Campaign, during which he still managed to find time for boxing, his special pal being Nick Johnson of Islington. After the end of the war he came back to help train Tom Fisher's stable, whose gym was now at "The Gun" in Croydon. This was a golden era for Croydon boxing and, when it ended, Bill took out a whip's licence at Epsom, Wembley Town Hall and the National Sporting Club. A founder-member of Croydon EBA, serving on the committee, and later as chairman, he ran the bookstall to help raise funds, among the donors being the Gleeson Group, for whom he used to work and go back to for regular visits. It was at the 25th Anniversary of th Tyneside EBA that Bill suffered a severe stroke in June 1995. It seemed that he was making good progress and actually attended a Croydon EBA meeting, before sadly passing away in his mid-70s.

GRIVER Harry *From* London. *Born* 14 March 1934. *Died* 2 February 1996. Started boxing when he was ten years old, and two years later became an amateur. Turned pro in 1954, beating Jimmy Barker, Harold Clarke and Fred Angell, and drew with Ken Jones. Also met Peter East and Dave Robins. Retired to become a trainer, and top boxers like Michael Watson, Darren Dyer, and Dennis Andries, all benefited from his tutorage. He gave most of his spare time to the Colvestone BC until exception was taken in some official circles to his professional involvement, and reluctantly he had to leave. In 1974 he became a taxi-driver, and all went well until 1986, when he was diagnosed as having a malignant brain tumour. Treatment appeared to be successful, and prompted him to devote much of his time to Cancer Charities. As a member of the London Ex-Boxers' Association, Harry was very proud of being presented with the Joe Bromley Memorial Award by the Boxing Writers' Club for Special Services to Boxing.

GUNN Dickie *From* Hayes. *Died* April 1996, aged 69. As a youngster, Dickie joined Lynn ABC, winning the Middle East middleweight title just after World War II, and when discharged from the Army he turned pro. Unfortunately, a broken nose caused him to cut short a promising career. Following that, he helped form Hayes BC and became head trainer, his first successful protege being Leo Maloney, who went on to win the Southern Area welter title as a pro. Although he trained several champions, his two most famous were the Finnegan brothers, Chris and Kevin. A self-employed carpenter, he decided to train professionals in the 1980s, and among his boxers were Steve Watt, who died tragically, and Gypsy Carman.

GUY George *From* London. *Died* April 1996, aged 59. Boxed for Fairbairn House and Dagenham, representing the London Federation of Boys' Clubs against the New York Boys' Clubs on two occasions, being outpointed at London's Empress Hall (1953) by Carlos Ortiz, who went on to win the world professional lightweight title, and outscoring Joseph Santarpia the following year in New York. Never really made his mark as a senior and never boxed as a pro.

HACK Derek *From* Hemel Hempstead. *Died* January 1996. Was the secretary of Markyate BC for many years, being associated with the successful promotion of amateur tournaments at the Hemel Hempstead Pavilion. Although never turning pro, Derek was a top class amateur, representing England against Poland (twice) in 1956, despite never winning a major title.

HAYCOX Les *Born* Stanton Hill, near Mansfield. *Died* September 1995. Pro 1931-1947. Trained by Johnny Kid Moffatt, Les beat Colin McDonald, Tiger Bert Ison, Morrie Goldstein, Jock Ewart, Dixie Kid, and drew with Eric Jones and Johnny Softly in a career that saw him win 67 and draw 32 out of 164 bouts. Later became a prominent member of the London Ex-Boxers' Association, attending meetings on a regular basis with his wife, Peggy.

HENDRIE Tommy *From* Glasgow. *Born* 2 June 1919. *Died* September 1995. Pro 1937-1950. Beat Joe Riley, Johnny Dale, Sandy McEwan, Paul Jones, and Peter Gardner, and in 1948 defeated Johnny Smith, who was on an unbeaten run of nearly 20. This win should have brought him a Scottish title fight with Harry Hughes, but it was Smith who was selected instead. He also boxed a lot on the booths, for Woods, Mapelbeck, Stewart and Paterson. When war broke out, Tommy set sail for Australia as a Merchant Seaman, returning in 1940, and joining a troopship called the Monarch, bound for Egypt and Norway. He also served on other ships, was blown out of the water by an Italian plane and was interned by the Vichy French. All the time he continued to box, giving exhibitions on board and on land, including places such as Canada and America, drawing with Bert Hornby (1944) and losing a close one to Jimmy Molloy (1945). He then worked on whalers, in the Falklands, before becoming a cabbie. In 1958 he was granted a referee's licence, and became chairman of the Scottish Area Council. Also ran youth clubs and boxing clubs until he was 60.

HOBLYN Reg *From* Fulham, London. *Born* 3 October 1918. *Died* April 1996. From a family of eight (six boys), Reg joined Twickenham BC at the age of ten, and was also a member of Battersea BC. One of the family's proudest moments was when brothers Reg, Harry and Leslie all won their bouts for Twickenham BC against Lyons BC at Hammersmith. Reg joined the Royal Navy in World War II, serving on destroyers, and while docked in Freetown, West Africa, won the South Atlantic Fleet light-heavyweight title, weighing 11 stones. On returning to Britain, he continued his amateur career, knocking out the ABA middleweight champion, Bob Parker, at the Boomerang Club, Australia House. Turned pro 1942, too light for a middleweight and too heavy for a welterweight, something that was to prove a handicap throughout his career. Among his victims were Bert Sanders, Gordon Woodhouse, Dusty Wellard, Jimmy Hockley, Jack Lewis, Battling Charlie Parkin, Jimmy Stewart, Dick Shields, and Ivor Thomas, flooring Bernard Murphy nine times before the latter retired. Reg's best performance was in knocking out Scottish welterweight champion, Willie Whyte, who was a contender for the British crown, but, alas, Reg never got that coveted title shot. His career ended in 1949 when he was giving weight to some of the best middles, such as Jimmy Davis, Les Allen (twice), and Alex Buxton, to whom he conceded nine pounds, a well-nigh impossible task. After the war Reg became PTI at Eton College and among those he instructed was Lord Snowdon. Became a regular member of the London Ex-Boxers' Association, and only stopped attending meetings when his doctor advised him to avoid smoky atmospheres.

HUNTER Alex *Died* January 1996, aged 59. Known as "Spangles" and a former Scottish international, as a member of the famed Woodside ABC under the tuition of Peter Guichan, Alex reached three Scottish finals at flyweight and bantamweight between 1959 and 1961. Died while refereeing an Eastern District title fight in Edinburgh.

JAMES Peter *Died* 17 March 1996, aged 65. First came to light in 1951, when, as the Navy heavyweight champion, he was beaten by Arthur Worrall in the Imperial Services semi-finals. Eventually surfacing again in 1955 to win the Imperial Services title, something he repeated in 1958 and 1961, Peter reached the ABA final only to lose to Welshman, Dennis Rowe. An amateur through and through, he represented England three times, losing only to the Russian, Algirdas Shotsikas.

Peter James

LAMBERT Andy *From* Manchester. *Born* 17 March 1937. *Died* January 1996. Pro 1953-1955. Beat Les Radcliffe, Don Martin, John Skelly, Tex Williams and Jim Cottrell in a career that took in 34 contests, two in 1953, 17 in 1954, and 15 in 1955. Beaten by Billy Anderson in his first two fights, Andy came back to stop Billy in the fourth round of their third meeting, before defeats at the hands of Trevor Sykes (twice) and Bobby Gill saw him leave the ring with 19 wins to his name.

LAUSSE Eduardo *From* Buenos Aires, Argentina. *Born* 8 November 1927. *Died* July 1995. Turned pro in 1948, in which year he lost only the last of 18 contests, with one draw and only one of his victories going the distance. Outpointed by Kid Gavilan in Buenos Aires (1952), he turned the tables in 1955, when he won on points. Also in 1955, he beat Ralph Jones, Gene Fullmer, and Britain's

Johnny Sullivan. Won the South American middleweight title by beating Humberto Loayza (June 1956), before losing it against Andres Selpa (October 1956), just two months later. In 15 fights on mainland America between 1953 and 1956, only five men went the distance with him, Bobby Boyd being the only winner.

LIVERSIDGE Derek *From* Retford. *Born* 14 January 1936. *Died* October 1995. Pro 1956-1960. Although beaten by George Aldridge for the Midlands Area middleweight title (1959), Derek beat Tex Woodward, Billy Wooding, Joe Rufus, Orlando Paso, and Tony French. Also met Terry Downes, Boswell St Louis, Fred Elderfield, Freddie Cross and Malcolm Worthington.

McELHINNEY Peter *Died* 31 January 1996, collapsing due to a heart attack at the Aston Villa Leisure Centre, Birmingham, where he was acting as chief second to Derek Wormald, who was meeting Richie Woodhall for the European middleweight title. Peter had been with Derek for five years, and helped promote and advertise shows in the North West, while training Jack Doughty's stable at the Tara Gym.

McKENZIE Dudley *From* Bromley. *Born* 3 December 1961. *Died* 15 November 1995. The brother of Duke, Winston and Clinton, Dudley boxed southpaw and was a successful amateur, winning six national junior titles, including a victory over Nick Wilshire in the 1977 junior ABAs. Turned pro 1981 at the age of 19 and won his first eight bouts until suffering a defeat in Paris at the hands of Paul Tchoue, who was unbeaten. Boxed only once more, being outpointed by James Cook, a man who went on to become British and European super-middleweight champion. Beat Billy Bryce, Neville Wilson, Willie Wright and Winston Davies, before retiring.

McKINLAY Peter *From* Edinburgh. *Died* September 1995. Pro 1929-1939. Was the "House" fighter in Edinburgh for Leeds promoter, Harold Bo'ness, going the distance with Jim Cowie for the Scottish featherweight title (1934). Also went the full course with former world champion, Kid Berg (1935).

McSHANE Laurie *From* Glasgow. *Born* 7 June 1930. *Died* 30 December 1995. Before joining the RAF and boxing for the Grove ABC while on leave, Laurie won a West Midlands' youth title (1946) when with Evesham ABC. An RAF championship finalist (1949), he turned pro in 1950 and, having been awarded a *Boxing News' Certificate of Merit* for beating Ron Johnson (1951), was also voted the paper's outstanding bantam prospect prior to beating Peter Fay and moving up to featherweight. Defeated Rolly Blyce (three times), Teddy Peckham, Stan Skinkiss and Malcolm Ames, and also met Ken Lawrence, Charlie Tucker, Freddie Reardon, Sammy McCarthy and John Kelly, the last two named being future and former British champions. Managed by Wally Lesley, Laurie retired from boxing in 1956 and later worked as a steel

erector, also having a spell as a stand-up comedian under the name of "Larry Mack".

MAHONEY Danny *From* Bermondsey, London. *Died* November 1995. The only son of a pro, Danny was a good boxer at schoolboy level, before joining the SS Cid as a cabin-boy and serving in many parts of Europe. Back home, and aiming to resume boxing, World War II intervened and he joined the Indian Army, seeing action in Burma, and the Western Desert, and ended his military career with the Special Branch, escorting many top statesmen. Following that, he decided to settle for being a trainer and a coach, learning his trade at various gyms before taking over his own and being engaged in training stars like Dave Charnley and Ron Barton. In later life he moved to Bournemouth.

MARTIN Leotis *From* Toledo, Ohio, USA. *Died* 20 November 1995. The national AAU 165 lb champion (1961), Leotis turned pro in 1962. In 1968 he came to London to stop fellow-American, Thad Spencer, which turned out to be a great fight between two worthy opponents. Among his victims were Von Clay, Amos Johnson, Sonny Banks, Roberto Davila, Mariano Echevarria and Billy Daniels. Beaten by Jimmy Ellis in 1947, only the second defeat of his career, most of his bouts were at Philadelphia.

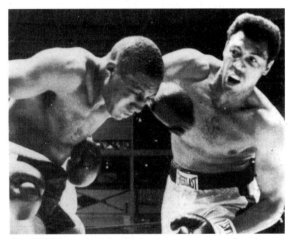

In a WBA heavyweight elimination tournament, Leotis Martin (left) was stopped inside nine rounds by Jimmy Ellis at Houston in 1967

MATHIS Buster *Born* 5 June 1944, Sledge, Mississippi, but billed out of Grand Rapids, Michigan, USA. *Died* September 1995. The US AAU heavyweight champion in 1964, Buster twice beat Joe Frazier in the Olympic trials that year, but broke a hand and Frazier substituted to win the title. A pro between 1965 and 1972, being stopped by Frazier for the NYSAC version of the world heavyweight title (1968) and travelling the full 12 rounds to lose on points to Muhammad Ali (1971), in a career total of 34 contests, he lost just four. Managed by Cus D'Amato, prior to the Frazier defeat, he had won his first 23 bouts, 17 inside the distance and the only other men to beat him were Jerry Quarry and Ron Lyle. From 18 stone, his weight rose to 36 stone through over-eating and he was judged unfit for work, eventually suffering two strokes, a heart attack, and kidney failure. Although severely handicapped by a lack of mobility, it did not stop him training his son, Buster jnr, who recently fought Mike Tyson.

MORTIMER Mike *Died* January 1996. The chairman of the National Board of South Africa, his diplomatic skills kept boxing alive in his country. Not long before his death Mike had attended a meeting of the Commonwealth Boxing Council in London.

MURRAY James *From* Lanark, Scotland. *Born* 7 December 1969. *Died* 15 October 1995, following a fight with Drew Docherty for the British bantamweight title in Glasgow on 13 October. Murray, floored in the 12th and final round, was stretchered from the ring and taken to the Southern General Hospital, where he underwent a three-hour emergency operation to remove a blood clot on the brain. Having been pronounced clinically dead, his parents were told it was their choice to decide whether the respiratory machine should be switched off. Having turned pro in 1993, James had never before been floored and this was only his second defeat in 17 bouts. Had won the Scottish bantam title in 1994 by outpointing Shaun Anderson for the vacant crown, prior to successfully defending it against Louis Veitch (1995).

MYERS David (Captain) *From* West Ham, London. *Died* September 1995, aged 93. A Justice of the Peace, and later awarded the OBE, Captain Myers was secretary to Sir Isaac Wolfson, while retaining his Army rank. Worked hard for the poor youngsters in his area and was a tower of strength with West Ham BC, the club he founded in 1922, producing members who went on to win professional titles, including Ron Barton, Ralph Charles and Jimmy Batten, also other prominent pros like Ron and Dennis Hinson, Brian Bissmire, Mark Kaylor, Roy Enifer, Ron Redrup, Terry Gill and Billy Walker. One of his favourite boxers was Terry Spinks, who won Olympic and British professional titles. When he retired as chairman of West Ham, he was succeeded by Terry's father, Titch Spinks.

NORKUS Charley *From* Bellrose, Long Island, New York. *Born* 15 July 1928. *Died* March 1996. Turned pro in 1948, beating Danny Nardico (twice), Cesar Brion, Charley Powell and Roland LaStarza, and in 1953, defeated Britain's up-and-coming Ray Wilding. Outpointed by world champions, Ezzard Charles, Willie Pastrano and Archie Moore, past, future and present, respectively, Charley was less fortunate against James J. Parker and Tommy "Hurricane" Jackson, who stopped him. Retired in 1959.

ODD Gilbert *From* Sutton, Surrey. *Died* 12 May 1996, aged 93. Worked as a clerk in the offices of the London, Brighton and South Coast Railways, later being associated with Link House Publications and the Health and Strength magazine. During the war he worked with the Ministry of Aircraft Productions, before joining the staff of *Boxing (Boxing News)* and becoming editor in 1941, when John Murray retired through ill-health. After the Fetter Lane offices were bombed and the whole building destroyed, the paper was re-launched with Bert Callis as editor, and when he retired, Gilbert again became editor, holding this position until 1957, when he left to write books and syndicated articles, having started the *Boxing News Annual* in 1944. Married to Stella in 1937, they lived in a cottage in Northiam, Sussex, his father and grandfather made cricket bats, and Gilbert was a member of Surrey Cricket Club for many years. As a member of the British Boxing Board of Control, a founder-member of the Boxing Writers' Club, chairman of the Board's Benevolent Fund Grants Committee, and the only journalist to be made a member of the National Sporting Club, he was an historian of note, who made a major contribution to the sport he loved.

PAOLOZZI Alf *From* Bill Pit, Long Benton, Newcastle. *Died* London, February 1996, aged 90. From a family who came from Italy in 1897, Alf worked in the mines for three years, then surfaced to work in his father's ice-cream business. However, when brother Joseph brought home a set of boxing gloves, Alf was hooked. Jim Falcus taught him the basics and Alf turned pro in 1925, becoming one of the busiest boxers in Britain. For instance, in 1931 he had 36 recorded fights, seven in the month of October. Having married Edie, and moving to London, when war broke out Alf joined the ARP and was in the Heavy Rescue Crew. Although continuing to box, in 1944 he fell off a building in Camden Town and broke his shoulder. It was the end of his long career, which had included boxing on the booths from the age of 17, during which he could have qualified for the Guinness Book of Records, as his surname was spelt 17 different ways on fight bills. Became a matchmaker and later staged wrestling, before founding the London Ex-Boxers' Association in 1971 and becoming their first chairman. Later, he was appointed a vice-president and was also a prominent member of Tyneside EBA. In 1976 he attended a meeting of Sunderland EBA, only to find he was the subject of a *This Is Your Life* tribute, arranged by the EBA. A sad loss, Alf was always thinking up ideas of fund-raising for the LEBA cause.

PARKER Bob *From* Basildon. *Died* 13 October 1995, on his 74th birthday, while visiting his daughter Patricia and mowing the lawn. Having won Imperial Services and ABA titles (1945), the following year he again won an Army title, but was outpointed by Randolph Turpin in the ISBA championships. Unfortunately, that fight brought Bob's career to an end after he had suffered a detached retina in the second round. A true-blue amateur, earlier in his career, he had turned down big money professional offers.

PASTOR Bob *From* New York, USA. *Born* 26 January 1914. *Died* 26 January 1996. Turning pro in 1935, and managed by James J. Johnston, Bob did not box more than eight rounds in his first 18 bouts, his first ten-rounder being in August 1936, when he outpointed the experienced, Unknown Winston. The following December he stopped Ray Impellitiere, which led to his next fight being against Joe Louis, who outpointed him. Two fights later, Louis was world champion. Bob continued to beat good opposition in Bob Nestell, Al Ettore, Lee Ramage, Tony Shucco, Maurice Strickland, Roscoe Toles and Freddie Fiducia, his good form leading to a world title fight with Louis in September 1939. Stopped in round 11, he was also stopped in round 13 by Billy Conn (1940), but then had an unbeaten streak of 14 before being outpointed by Jimmy Bivins, whom he had beaten six months earlier. His victims in 1942, included Claudio Villar, Gus Lesnevich, Lem Franklin and Buddy Scott. During World War II, Bob was in the US Army.

PEACOCK Alan *From* Hull. *Born* 29 March 1936. *Died* 7 January 1996. Boxed for Hull Boys Club and won Army and ISBA titles. In the ABA final (1957), Alan met Tommy Green, also from Hull BC, and it was reported that this was the first ABA final to be contested by members of the same club. Green won on points, and Alan turned pro in 1958, retiring in 1961 after 15 contests and wins over Billy Smith, Vernon Goodman, Johnny Hunt, Joe Walcott (Trinidad), Laci Tomazi, Gordon Corbett and Don Sainsbury. In 1960, he was beaten by Ted Williams for the vacant Northern Area light-heavyweight title, sustaining an eye injury that required plastic surgery and ended his career. Later became the landlord of several pubs, moving to Reading and then back to Hull.

POTTS Jackie *From* Crewe. *Died* May 1996, aged 79. Turned pro at the age of 15 at the Crewe Corn Exchange, retiring in 1945, but not before meeting men of the calibre of Mark Hart, Ernie Roderick. Lefty Flynn and Harry Mizler. A blacksmith at the Crewe Railway Works, in 1938 he won the "unofficial" Cheshire title by beating Les Lloyd. Before passing away, Jackie had been the landlord of the Leopard Hotel in Nantwich and was a regular member of the North Staffs Sporting Club.

POWELL Jack *From* Sheffield. *Born* 3 October 1915, at Barnsley. *Died* 18 January 1996. Pro 1934-1941. Awarded a *Boxing News Certificate of Merit* for defeating Buster Osborne (1936), other men Jack beat included the Canadian, Paul Schaefer, Australian Cyril Pluto, South African Johnny Rust, former champion Harry Mason, George Bunter, Tommy Ireland, Seaman Jim Lawlor, Jack McKnight, Len Phillips, George Davis, Pat Haley, Lefty Flynn and Pat Mulcahy. Also met the welterweight champion, Ernie Roderick, and in 1939 was rated the number three middleweight in the Southern Area, behind Nat Franks and Elfryn Morris. When World War II broke out, Jack joined the Royal Air Force and, in 1941, was beaten by Freddie Mills, to whom he conceded a stone. "I

got £32 and needed the money" he said. It was his last official bout, although in 1946 he was a sparring partner to world light-heavyweight champion, Gus Lesnevich. After the war he worked as a van driver and as a cabbie, and in 1947 he married Maria Napolitano, settling at 36 St Peters Street, Islington, London, which they opened as a general stores in 1957. In 1971, Alf Paolozzi founded the London Ex-Boxers' Association, calling on Jack for help, Alf becoming the first chairman and Jack the first secretary. The HQ was, and still is, the shop. As LEBA flourished, Maria (now Mary) became treasurer and later secretary (still is), and on the death of Jack Kid Berg, his successor as president was Jack Powell, who held that position up until his death. For the past two years, Jack had been a resident at St Anne's Home For The Elderly.

PUGH Bernard *From* Liverpool. *Born* 13 August 1925. *Died* 8 May 1996. Was a good amateur before turning pro in 1945, becoming a busy fighter, with 18 bouts in 1948 and 24 in 1949. His best victory being in 1951, when he outpointed featherweight champion, Ronnie Clayton. Among his other victims were Kid Tanner, Micky Forrester, Tony Lombard, Jackie Turpin and Freddie Hicks, and he went the distance with champions, Ray Famechon, Roy Ankrah and Al Phillips. During the 1940s, the American *Ring Magazine* rated him in their World Top Ten featherweights. Bernard retired from boxing in 1952 and later became an active member of the Merseyside EBA.

ROBINSON Alf *From* Manchester. *Died* February 1996, aged 83. Started working life as a meat porter, turning pro in 1930. Retiring in 1939 after 81 bouts, during his career, Alf beat Jack Doyle (disqualification), Bert Ikin, Bernard Cook, Harry Briers, Charlie Bundy, Frank Borrington, Norman Baines, Alf Buxton, George Dower, Max Hodgetts, Bob Carvill and Dick Allen. Heavyweight competitions were popular in the 1930s, normally with eight entrants and qualifying rounds, semi-finals and final. Alf competed in them all, at Crystal Palace in 1931, 1932 and 1933 (reaching the semi-finals), winning the competition at Manchester in 1934 and also winning at Wembley later the same year. Beaten by George Slack for the Northern Area title, during World War II he was a PTI in the Scots Guards. After the war he turned to wrestling and was a popular performer at Belle Vue, later running a chain of greengrocers' shops with wife, Eileen. Only two boxers beat Alf inside the distance – Johnny Rice (twice) and Chris Cole.

RODRIGUEZ Luis *From* Camaguey, Cuba. *Born* 17 June 1937. *Died* 8 July 1996. Turning pro in 1956, his first 22 fights were in Havana, winning all but one, which was a no contest, and annexing the Cuban welterweight title by beating Kid Fighicue (1958). Had his first fight in America on his 22nd birthday, outpointing Virgil Akins (1959), and during a career of 16 years never boxed in Havana again. In the United States, he was looked after by Angelo Dundee and, was in fact, Angelo's first world champion, when he defeated Emile Griffith (March 1963). Had four memorable fights with Griffith. Griffith won a ten-rounder (1960), then came the world title fight (1963), with Griffith winning the title back (June 1963) and successfully retaining it (1964). Later, Luis lost what was described as a "WBA welterweight eliminator" to Curtis Cokes (1966), before turning his attention to the middleweight division, losing to Nino Benvenuti in a title fight (1969). He continued fighting with success until 1972, but was never the same force again, although he did beat Tony Mundine in round one at Melbourne (April 1971). His following fight was against Bunny Sterling in London just over a month later, with Sterling winning on points, and Luis looking just a shadow of when he was in his prime. A total of 121 contests, with just 13 defeats, speaks for itself, and, apart from the title fights, he defeated top men like Gomeo Brennan, Charley Scott, Joe Miceli, Yama Bahama, Johnny Gonsalves, Curtis Cokes, Joey Giambra, Denny Moyer, Wilbert McClure, Holly Mims, Ruben Carter and Bennie Briscoe. Luis was one of the busiest and most popular fighters of all-time.

Luis Rodriguez (left) seen losing the welterweight title back to Emile Griffith in June 1963

SCOTT Wally *From* West Ham, London. *Born* 4 February 1932. *Died* October 1995. Boxed for West Ham BC, before turning pro in 1956, Wally was noted for his power of punch, stopping Ken Lancaster, Dudley Cox, Fred Britton, Ron Duncombe, Tony Ratcliffe and Peter Goldie. Also met Dick Tiger and John "Cowboy" McCormack, prior to retiring in 1958 following a win over Ron Vale. Worked for many years in the East India Docks.

SHIELDS Dick *From* Liverpool. *Died* February 1995, aged 74. Pro 1941-1949. Beat Tommy Granton, Johnny Ward, Harry "Kid" Silver, Jack Carrick, Jimmy Brunt, Jim Wellard and Ginger Roberts. Also met Eddie Thomas, Henry Hall, George Odwell and Cyril Gallie, making around 50 appearances at the Liverpool Stadium where he was a great favourite. After retiring, he coached the youngsters at Southern BC. A few years ago, Merseyside EBA members paid tribute to Dick, when the Left Hook Club organised a special night for him.

STERN George *From* Glasgow. *Born* 27 February 1927. *Died* March 1996. Won the Scottish heavyweight title by beating Hugh McDonald (1951). After turning pro in 1949, George beat Matt Hardy, Frank Ronan, Bill Brennan, Johnny Pilkington, Frank Bell, Jim Moran, Reg Andrews, George Nuttall and Lou Strydom, before retiring in 1952 following a stoppage defeat at the hands of Strydom. In a career of 28 contests, 18 were won.

STRICKLAND Maurice *Died* 1995, aged 81. A former New Zealand heavyweight champion, Maurice paid two or three visits to Britain, where he had around 15 contests, stopping Ben Foord, Salah El Din, Eddie Steele, Jack Pettifer, Dave Carstens and Gustav Limousin and also outpointing Larry Gains, Obie Walker and Al Delaney. Among those who outpointed him were world lightheavyweight champion, Tommy Loughran, Jim Wilde, and Walter Neusel. His early bouts were in New Zealand and Australia, but most of his later contests were in America, where he continued boxing until the early 1940s. In March 1939, he met the American, Bob Pastor, the plan being that the winner would tackle world heavyweight champion, Joe Louis. Maurice lost on points, and Pastor duly met Joe the following September.

SUTTON George *From* Roath, Wales. *Born* 15 September 1922. *Died* December 1995. Won the Welsh flyweight championship by beating Billy Davies (1948), but lost it to Norman Lewis (1949) and was beaten by Glyn David for the vacant crown before beating Davies again to regain the title (1951). One of four boxing brothers, the others being Albert, Jimmy and Jackie, George was a cornerman for his two sons, Gary and George Junior, who boxed as a pro with some success between 1975 and 1981.

THOMAS Tudor *From* Twynyrodyn, Merthyr. *Died* 1996, aged 80. Crushed in a pit fall, and spending six months in hospital with spinal tuberculosis, Tudor became known as "The Miracle Man" when he eventually returned to the ring. Beaten by Len Beynon in a final eliminator for the Welsh featherweight title (1936), he had suffered from Alzheimer's Disease for the past 15 years.

TOCH Peter *From* Tooting, London. *Born* 22 October 1931. *Died* August 1995. Boxed for the Gainsford BC and the Army, making eight international appearances for England between 1950 and 1952, winning six, and becoming ABA heavyweight champion (1950). Had a short professional career, beating Ben Bowden, Eddie Hearn, Dinny Ball, Mick Cowan and Dennis Fewkes, before being beaten by Joe Bygraves, all in 1953. In beating Ball and Cowan, Peter won a Jack Solomons' heavyweight competition on the Randy Turpin v Charles Humez world middleweight title bill at the White City.

TOWEEL Alan *From* Benoni, South Africa. *Died* December 1995. One of the famous family of six boxing brothers, Alan had an amateur career of 126 wins in 134 bouts, 104 inside the distance, before going undefeated in eight pro fights and retiring because of a chest complaint.

Becoming a successful trainer, his stable included brother Willie, the British Empire lightweight champion. Among other champions he handled were Kosie Smith, Gerrie Coetzee, Pierre Fourie, Pierre Coetzer, Kokkie Oliver and Sydney Bensch. At the time of his death he was managing unbeaten heavyweight, Peter Smith. Came to Britain in 1957 with Willie, brother Maurice (manager) and South African welterweight champion, Evie Vorster.

TOWEEL Maurice *From* Benoni, South Africa. *Born* 1930. *Died* 20 May 1996. One of the famous family of six boxing brothers, Maurice was stricken by polio at an early age, and was the only brother never to have boxed in serious competition. Although crippled, he often propped himself up between two beds and sparred with his brothers and as a result of his hobbling about with crutches, he had very powerful arms. He became Willie's manager from the start of the latter's professional career, making light of his handicap, and although having to operate from a wheelchair, travelled all over the world with his brothers.

TSHABALALA Ginger *From* Ladysmith, South Africa. *Died* 29 October 1995, the victim of a shooting by a "carjacking" gang. Started his amateur career at Soweto at the age of 20, and won 99 of his 100 bouts, turning pro in 1990. Won the Transvaal light-heavyweight title in only his fifth contest, before being outpointed by Transvaal heavyweight champion, Frans Botha, in his next bout, when unlucky to lose a split decision. Ginger boxed in America, in Germany, and three times in Britain, where he stopped Gil Lewis in four, Tony Wilson in three, and Bobbi Joe Edwards in five. Won the South African light-heavyweight title vacated by his friend and stablemate, "Sugarboy" Malinga, and with a career record of 18 wins, one draw and one defeat, he was rated number three contender for the WBC light-heavyweight title. At the time of his death, he had been short-listed for a bout with champion, Fabrice Tiozzo.

TURNER Gil *From* Philadelphia, USA. *Born* 9 October 1930. *Died* 13 May 1996. Turning pro in 1950, Gil won his first 15 fights inside the distance and remained undefeated until July 1952, when he was stopped by Kid Gavilan for the world welterweight title. At that stage, he had beaten former world champions, Beau Jack and Ike Williams. After the Gavilan defeat he continued to beat world champions in Johnny Saxton and Gene Fullmer (1953 and 1955), although subsequently beaten in return bouts. Also defeated top contenders, Charley Fusari, Charley Scott and Joe Miceli.

WEBB Billy *From* Chatham, Kent. *Died* 26 September 1995, aged 83. A pro between 1930 and 1936, Billy had 91 bouts and was known as "King Of The Casinos", having boxed at Rochester Casino on 64 occasions. Later became a life member of the Kent EBA.

WORGAN Syd *From* Llanharan, Wales. *Born* 1 January 1917. *Died* 1996. Turning pro at 18, before World War II,

Gil Turner

Syd beat Kid Simmons, Pancho Ford, Jean Locatelli, Douglas Coleman and Jack Gubbins, drawing with Cuthbert Taylor, and twice being outpointed by Len Beynon. Although a miner at Llanharan Colliery, throughout the war, he continued boxing, with 30 bouts during the six years, also giving exhibitions in Army and RAF camps. After beating Kid Tanner and Warren Kendall, he was unofficially rated number eight contender for Nel Tarleton's British featherweight title. In 1942, he lost three in a row to Al Phillips, Nel Tarleton and Bert Jackson, before coming back to beat Bobby Watson and Kid Tanner. Outpointed Dave Crowley in 1944 and also won the Welsh title by outscoring Tommy Davies. With the war coming to an end, Syd continued to win some and lose some, beating Willie Grey, Kid Tanner and Hal Cartwright, and being defeated by Bert Jackson, Billy Thompson and Stan Hawthorne. In his last fight in Wales, he was beaten by his lifelong friend, Vernon Ball, and in his final bout he lost to Hal Bagwell on an eye injury. A collier for 35 years, and a publican at the Bear Inn for $2^{1}/_2$ years, he was the founder-member of the Welsh EBA, being the secretary until last December, and was president at the time of his death.

STEPHEN VAUGHAN PROMOTIONS LTD
Lombard Chambers, Ormond Street, Liverpool, L3 9NA
Tel: 0151 286 3092   Fax: 0151 286 3093

STEPHEN VAUGHAN
INTERNATIONAL PROMOTER / MANAGER
(Licensed by the British Boxing Board of Control)

HEAD TRAINER
GEORGE VAUGHAN

TRAINER
TONY CARROLL

TRAINER
DANNY VAUGHAN

THE LIVERPOOL BOXING TEAM 1996/97

Flyweight
Peter "The Choirboy" Culshaw
The Commonwealth Champion. Unbeaten

Super-Bantamweight
Tony Mulholland
1996 ABA Featherweight Champion
and International Representative

Featherweight
John Sillo
Former Commonwealth Games bronze medalist
8 wins, 2 losses

Chris Ainscough
Former Junior ABA Champion
and International Representative

Super-Featherweight
Gary "Tornado" Thornhill
Central Area Champion
12 wins, 1 draw, 0 losses

Light-Welterweight
Carl "Wildcat" Wright
Former International, 16 wins, 1 loss

Andy Holligan
The British and Commonwealth Champion

Welterweight
Tony Mock
Former International Representative, 7 wins, 1 loss

John Jones
ABA Finalist and Former International, 3 wins, 0 losses

Light-Middleweight
Jon "No Nonsense" Stocks
Former International, 8 wins, 1 loss

Middleweight
Paul "Do It" Wright
Central Area Champion, 17 wins, 2 draws, 2 losses

Cruiserweight
Steve Bristow
Former NW Counties Super-Heavy Champion, 1 win, 0 losses

Kenley Price
Former International, 5 wins, 1 draw, 0 losses

Matchmaker
John Gaynor

General Manager
Lee Maloney

Ring Whip
Colin Gallagher

A Boxing Quiz With a Few Below the Belt

Compiled by Les Clark

QUESTIONS

1. Can you name the boxer who won a world title by a first round knockout and lost it in his first defence, also by first round kayo?

2. Can you name the British boxer who twice fought a draw in world title fights against the same opponent?

3. Can you name the boxer who fought Dennis Andries on no less than five occasions professionally?

4. When did Las Vegas stage its first world championship bout, and what was the title at stake, and who contested it?

5. Where and when was the world flyweight championship last contested by two British boxers and who were they?

6. Name the heavyweight who won the world title in the least amount of professional bouts?

7. Can you name a former Nigel Benn trainer who fought Sugar Ray Leonard?

8. Can you name a heavyweight who contested the world title on eight occasions, losing to three champions and winning only twice?

9. It is well known that Henry Armstrong was the only man to hold three titles simultaneously – feather, light and welter. From whom did he take his third title to achieve this feat and to whom did he lose the last of his titles?

10. Shortly after boxing a draw in defence of his title against Joe Gans in September 1904, welterweight Joe

Walcott was forced out of the ring for almost two years. Do you know why?

11. Can you name a former heavyweight champion who kayoed a father and son, both in the third round?

12. What did world welterweight champions, Ray Robinson, Carmen Basilio, and Emile Griffith have in common?

13. Can you name a boxer who successfully defended his world title five times within a month?

14. What did Casper Leon, Abe Attell, and Gene Fullmer have in common?

15. Can you name the boxers who beat Muhammad Ali during his pro career?

16. Can you name the British boxers who have fought Roberto Duran?

17. Welshman Pat Thomas was British champion at two weights. Who did he beat for the titles?

18. How many boxers, who won an ABA middleweight title between 1945 and 1995, went on to win a world middleweight title and who were they?

19. In April 1979, Tommy Hearns decisioned Alfonso Hayman over ten rounds in Philadelphia. What was significant about this fight?

20. When Kelvin Smart won the British flyweight title, which fellow countryman did he kayo to win the title?

21. What have Carl Crook and Colin McMillan in common?

22. Can you name the first world heavyweight champion to lose his title in his first defence?

23. Can you name brothers who have each won five consecutive ABA middleweight titles?

24. When did a Gorilla beat a Tiger to qualify for a world title shot?

25. Can you name former ABA champions from 1990 until present (end of June 1996), who have gone on to win a British title?

26. Emile Griffith took part in 21 world title fights, winning four inside the distance. How many title fights did he lose inside the distance?

27. Who said, "I just got caught by a good shot that I didn't see coming. My head was clear, but my legs said stay down." Was it Archie Moore, Frank Warren, or Mike Weaver?

28. What did John Conteh and Bob Fitzsimmons have in common?

29. Can you name the first boxer to successfully defend his Olympic title?

30. Who refereed the world flyweight title bout between Benny Lynch and Peter Kane?

31. Can you name the referee who controlled the second Ali v Liston fight?

32. Who took the welterweight title from Carlos Palomino?

33. Can you name the first two Welshmen to contest a British championship?

34. Who was the first man to take Muhammad Ali the full 15 rounds in a title fight?

35. How many times did Randy Turpin contest the world middleweight title?

36. Who was the first boxer to win a Lonsdale Belt outright?

37. How many British boxers contested European titles during July '94 and July '95?

38. How many European boxers challenged Muhammad Ali for the world heavyweight title and who were they?

39. Can you name the first two southpaws to contest a British title?

40. At which weight have the most boxers won Lonsdale Belts outright?

41. Cassius Clay had his very first bout aged 12 (which was in fact televised on Joe Martin's TV show). Who was his opponent?

42. How many ABA titles did Olympic gold medallist, Dick McTaggart, win?

43. How many times was Carlos Monzon stopped during his career?

44. Willie Pastrano defeated Terry Downes for the world light-heavyweight title. Where was the venue that this took place?

45. Who was Ali's last opponent before he was stripped and refused the right to box by the authorities?

46. The Lonsdale Belt was preceded by the National Sporting Club Challenge Belt, which extended from 1909 to 1935. How many of these belts were won outright?

47. How many 1988 Olympic gold medallists went on to win world titles and can you name them?

48. Can you name a former boxer who wrote PENNY A PUNCH and A FEW PUNCHES MORE?

49. During the 1980s, Roy ------ stopped Joe ------ in defence of his IBF title. Can you fill in the names?

50. Can you name the country of birth for the following: Arturo Frias, Battling Nelson, Newsboy Brown, Fidel la Barba, Chalky Wright, and Don Jordon?

ANSWERS

1: Al Singer (Singer beat Sammy Mandell and lost four months later to Tony Canzoneri). 2: Owen Moran (Moran twice fought a draw with champion, Abe Attell of the USA, for the featherweight title, first in January 1908, and again in September 1908). 3: Tom Collins. 4: Benny Paret took the welterweight title from Don Jordon on 27 May 1960. 5: Pat Clinton v Danny Porter at the Exhibition Centre Glasgow on 19 September 1992. 6: Leon Spinks won the title in his eighth bout. 7: Graham Moughton fought Sugar Ray as an amateur. 8: Jersey Joe Walcott (Walcott lost twice to each of the following; Rocky Marciano, Joe Louis, and Ezzard Charles. He then went on to beat Ezzard Charles twice. 9: He beat Lou Ambers to take his third title and lost it to Fritzie Zivic on 4 October 1940. 10: Walcott accidentally shot himself in the hand (this friend and fellow boxer was killed by the same bullet) and was out of the ring until July 1906. 11: Jersey Joe Walcott kayoed Phil Johnson and son, Harold Johnson, both contests ending in the third round. 12: All relinquished the welterweight title on winning the middleweight belt. 13: Henry Armstrong in October 1939. 14: All three fought three drawn world title fights. 15: Joe Frazier, Kenny Norton, Leon Spinks, Larry Holmes, and Trevor Berbick. 16: Ken Buchanan, Kirkland Laing, and Jimmy Batten. 17: He kayoed Pat McCormack in the 13th round of the welterweight title in December 1975 for the welterweight title and stopped Jimmy Batten in the ninth round in October 1979 for the light-middleweight crown. 18: Randy Turpin, Alan Minter, and Nigel Benn. 19: It was the first time in 18 professional fights that he had failed to win inside the distance. 20: Dave George. 21: Both won Lonsdale Belts outright in 1991. 22: Bob Fitzsimmons. 23: Harry and Fred Mallin. 24: On 25 August 1931, Gorilla Jones beat Tiger Thomas, before going on to successfully challenge Oddone Piazza for the vacant world middleweight title. 25: Scott Welch, Joe Calzaghe, and Jonjo Irwin. 26: Only once (in 14 rounds to Carlos Monzon). 27: Mike Weaver (on being kayoed by Pinklon Thomas). 28: Both contested seven world championships. Conteh won four and lost three, and Fitzsimmons also won four and lost three. 29: Harry Mallin in 1920 and 1924. 30: Barrington Dalby, a well known BBC commentator at the time. 31: Jersey Joe Walcott. 32: Wilfred Benitez. 33: Eddie Thomas v Cliff Curvis. 34: George Chuvalo. 35: Four times. Ray Robinson twice, Bobo Olson, and Charles Humez (the Humez fight was recognised in Europe as for the world title). 36: Eric Boon. 37: Twelve. 38: Six. Henry Cooper, Brian London, Karl Mildenberger, Jurgen Blin, Joe Bugner, and Rudi Lubbers. 39: Cliff Curvis v Wally Thom in 1952. 40: Lightweight. 41: Ronnie O'Keefe. Clay won on a split decision. 42: He won five ABA titles. 43: He was never stopped. 44: Manchester. 45: Zora Folley in Ali's ninth defence of his title in March 1967. 46: There were 20 belts won outright. 47: Five. Lennox Lewis, Ray Mercer, Henry Maske, Giovanni Parisi, and Kennedy McKinney. 48: Harry Legge. 49: Lee Roy Murphy stopped Young Joe Louis. 50: USA, Denmark, Russia, USA, Mexico, and the Dominion Republic.

Leading BBBoC License Holders: Names and Addresses

Licensed Promoters

Sam Adair
Ashfield House
Ashford
Barnstable
Devon

Michael Andrew
38 Kennedy Avenue
Laindon West
Basildon
Essex

John Ashton
1 Charters Close
Kirkby in Ashfield
Nottinghamshire
NG17 8PF

Lance Billany
32 Beaconsfield Carrs
  Meadow
Withernsea
HU19 2EP

Pat Brogan
112 Crewe Road
Haslington
Crewe
Cheshire

Harry Burgess
25 Calthorpe Street
London
WC1X 0JX

Roy Cameron
5 Birbeck Road
Acton
London W3 6BG

Carlton Carew
18 Mordaunt Street
Stockwell
London SW9 9RB

Eva Christian
80 Alma Road
Plymouth
Devon PL3 4HU

John Cox
11 Fulford Drive
Links View
Northampton

Michael Dalton
16 Edward Street
Grimsby
South Humberside

John Robert Davies
5 Welsh Road
Garden City
Deeside
Clwyd

Shaun Doyle
15 Jermyn Croft
Dodworth
Barnsley
South Yorkshire

Eastwood Promotions
Bernard Eastwood
Eastwood House
2-4 Chapel Lane
Belfast 1
Northern Ireland

James Evans
88 Windsor Road
Bray
Berkshire SL6 2DJ

**Evesham Sporting
Club**
Mike Goodall
Schiller
Gibbs Lane
Offenham
Evesham
WR11 5RR

Norman Fawcett
4 Wydsail Place
Gosforth
Newcastle upon Tyne
NE3 4QP

John Forbes
5 Durham Road
Sedgefield
Stockton on Tees
Cleveland
TS21 3DW

Joe Frater
The Cottage
Main Road
Grainthorpe
Louth
Lincolnshire

Dai Gardiner
13 Hengoed Hall Drive
Cefn Hengoed
Hengoed
Mid Glamorgan
CF8 7JW

Harold Gorton
Gorton House
4 Hollius Road
Oldham
Lancashire

Ron Gray
Ingrams Oak
19 Hatherton Road
Cannock
Staffordshire

Johnny Griffin
26 Christow Street
Leicester
Leicestershire
LE1 2GN

Clive Hall
23 Linnett Drive
Barton Seagrave
Kettering
Northamptonshire

Jess Harding
70 Hatfield Road
Potters Bar
Hertfordshire

Dennis Hobson
The Lodge
Stone Lane
Woodhouse
Sheffield
Yorkshire S13 7BR

Steve Holdsworth
85 Sussex Road
Watford
Hertfordshire
WD2 5HR

**Hull & District
Sporting Club**
Mick Toomey
25 Purton Grove
Bransholme
Hull HU7 4QD

John Hyland
The Morton Suite
The Moat House Hotel
1 Paradise Street
Liverpool L1 8JD

Alma Ingle
26 Newman Road
Wincobank
Sheffield S9 1LP

Owen McMahon
3 Atlantic Avenue
Belfast BT15 2HN

M & M Promotions
Unit 5
Fieldway
Northfield Industrial
  Estate
Rotherham
South Yorkshire
S60 1QD

Matchroom
Barry Hearn
10 Western Road
Romford
Essex RM1 3JT

**Alan Matthews
(Special Licence)**
256 Lodge Avenue
Dagenham
Essex RM8 2HF

**Midland Sporting
Club**
D. L. Read
Ernest & Young
Windsor House
3 Temple Row
Birmingham
B2 5LA

Katherine Morrison
85 Sydney Street
Glasgow
G31 2ND

National Promotions
National House
60-66 Wardour Street
London
W1V 3HP

Noble Art Promotions
Greg Steene/Bruce
  Baker
150 Brick Lane
London
E1 6RU

**North Staffs Sporting
Club**
J Baddeley
29 Redwood Avenue
Stone
Staffordshire
ST15 0DB

Panix Promotions
Frank Maloney
99 Middlesex Street
London
E1 7DA

Peacock Promotions
Anthony Bowers
Peacock Gym
Caxton Street North
Canning Town
London
E16 1JR

Steve Pollard
35 Gorthorte
Orchard Park Estate
Hull
HU9 EY

**Queensberry Yeo Ltd
(Special Licence)**
1 Concorde Drive
5(c) Business Centre
Clevedon
Avon
BS21 6UH

Gus Robinson
Stranton House
Westview Road
Hartlepool
TS24 0BB

**Round One Boxing
Promotions**
Dave Furneaux
251 Embankment Road
Prince Rock
Plymouth
Cornwall
PL4 9JH

Christine Rushton
20 Alverley Lane
Balby
Doncaster
Yorkshire
DN4 9AS

**St Andrews Sporting
Club**
Tommy Gilmour
Anderson Suite
Forte Crest Hotel
Bothwell Street
Glasgow
G2 7EN

Chris Sanigar
147 Two Mile Hill Road
Kingswood
Bristol
Avon BS15 1BH

John Spensley
The Black Swan Hotel
Tremholme Bar
Near Stokesley
North Yorkshire
DL6 3JY

Sporting Club of Wales
Paul Boyce
79 Church Street
Britton Ferry
Neath SA11 2TU

Sportsman Promotions
Frank Quinlan
Hollinthorpe Low Farm
Swillington Lane
Leeds
Yorkshire LS26 8BZ

Tara Promotions
Jack Doughty
Grains Road
Shaw, Oldham
Lancashire OL2 8JB

Team Promotions
David Gregory
Contract House
Split Crow Road
Gateshead
Tyne and Wear
NE10 9JX

Jack Trickett
Acton Court Hotel
187 Buxton Road
Stockport
Cheshire

UK Pro Box Promotions
David Matthews
22 Copt Royd Grove
Yeadon
Leeds
Yorkshire LS19 7HQ

Michael Edward Ulyatt
28 Blackthorn Lane
Willerby
Hull

Stephen Vaughan
Lombard Chambers
Ormond Street
Liverpool L3 9NA

Frank Warren
Centurion House
Bircherley Green
Hertford
Hertfordshire
SG14 1AP

Winning Combination
Annette Conroy
144 High Street East
Sunderland
Tyne and Wear
SR1 2BL

Wolverhampton Sporting Club
J R Mills
24 Perton Road
Wightwick
Wolverhampton
Staffordshire
WV6 8DN

Stephen Mark Wood
29 Falconwood Chase
Worsley
Manchester

Note: At the time of going to press, Anthony Gee, Harry Holland and the Yorkshire Executive Sporting Club, who all promoted shows during 1995-96, were no longer licensed.

Licensed Managers

Isola Akay
129 Portnall Road
Paddington
London W9 3BN

John Ashton
1 Charters Close
Kirkby in Ashfield
Nottinghamshire
NG17 8PF

Chris Aston
23 Juniper Grove Mews
Netherton
Huddersfield
West Yorkshire
HD4 7WG

Mike Atkinson
9 Tudor Road
Ainsdale
Southport
Lancashire PR8 2RY

Don Austin
14 Whinchat Road
Broadwaters
Thamesmead
London SE28 0DZ

Albert Barrow
236 Frenchfield Road
Brighton
BN2 2YG

Nat Basso
38 Windsor Road
Prestwich
Lancashire
M25 8FF

John Baxter
6 Havencrest Drive
Leicester LE5 2AG

Lance Billany
32 Beaconsfield
Carrs Meadow
Withernsea
North Humberside
HU19 2EP

Jack Bishop
76 Gordon Road
Fareham
Hampshire PO16 7SS

Gerald Bousted
4 Firlands Road
Barton
Torquay
Devon TQ2 8EW

Paul Boyce
Brynamlwg
2 Pant Howell Ddu
Ynysmerdy
Briton Ferry
Neath SA11 2TU

David Bradley
Dallicote Cottage
Worfield
Shropshire
WV15 5PL

Mike Brennan
2 Canon Avenue
Chadwell Heath
Romford
Essex

Fred Britton
71 Henrietta Street
Leigh
Lancashire
WN7 1LH

Michael Brooks
114 Gildane
Orchard Park Estate
Hull HU6 9AY

Winston Burnett
6 Faber Way
City Gardens
Sloper Road
Grangetown
Cardiff
CF1 8DN

Paddy Byrne
70 Benfield Way
Portslade by Sea
Sussex BN4 2DL

Pat Byrne
16 Barbridge Close
Bulkington
Warwickshire
CV12 9PW

Trevor Callighan
40 Prescott Street
Halifax
West Yorkshire
HX1 2QW

Carlton Carew
18 Mordaunt Street
Brixton
London SW9 9RB

Ernie Cashmore
18 North Drive
Handsworth
Birmingham
B20 8SX

John Cheshire
38 Achilles Close
St James Place
Rolls Road
London SE1

Nigel Christian
80 Alma Road
Plymouth
Devon
PL3 4HU

Peter Coleman
29 The Ring Road
Leeds
Yorkshire
LS14 1NH

William Connelly
72 Clincart Road
Mount Florida
Glasgow G42

Tommy Conroy
144 High Street East
Sunderland
Tyne and Wear

Chris Coughlan
27 Maes Yr Haf
Llansamlet
Swansea
Wales
SA7 9ST

Pat Cowdell
129a Moat Road
Oldbury
Warley
West Midlands
B68 8EE

John Cox
11 Fulford Drive
Links View
Northampton NN2 7NX

Bingo Crooks
37 Helming Drive
Danehust Estate
Wolverhampton
West Midlands
WV1 2AF

Dave Currivan
15 Northolt Avenue
South Ruislip
Middlesex

David Davies
10 Bryngelli
Carmel
Llanelli
Dyfed SA14 7EL

Glyn Davies
63 Parc Brynmawr
Felinfoel
Llanelli
Dyfed SA15 4PG

John Davies
5 Kent Road
Connah's Quay
Deeside
Clywd
Wales

Ronnie Davies
3 Vallensdean Cottages
Hangleton Lane
Portslade
Sussex

Brian Dawson
30 Presdales Drive
Ware
Hertfordshire
SG12 9NN

Peter Defreitas
13 Electric Parade
Seven Kings
Essex IG3 8BY

Brendan Devine
12 Birkdale Close
Clubmoor
Liverpool L6 0DL

Jack Doughty
Tara Sports & Leisure
Ltd
Grains Road
Shaw
Near Oldham
Lancashire OL2 8JB

Shaun Doyle
15 Jermyn Croft
Dodworth
Barnsley
South Yorkshire
S75 3LR

Phil Duckworth
The Hampton Hotel
Longclose Lane
Richmond Hill
Leeds LS9 8NP

Mickey Duff
National House
60-66 Wardour Street
London W1V 3HP

Pat Dwyer
93 Keir Hardie Avenue
Bootle
Liverpool 20
Merseyside L20 0DN

Bernard Eastwood
Eastwood House
2-4 Chapel Lane
Belfast 1
Northern Ireland

Greg Evans
21 Portman Road
Liverpool
Merseyside
L15 2HH

Jim Evans
88 Windsor Road
Maidenhead
Berkshire
SL6 2DJ

Norman Fawcett
4 Wydsail Place
Gosforth
Newcastle upon Tyne
NE3 4QP

Colin Flute
84 Summerhill Road
Coseley
West Midlands
WV14 8RE

Steve Foster
The Priory Arms
29 Gardner Street
Pendleton
Salford M6 6PP

George Francis
11 Hillway
Holly Lodge Estate
London N6

Dai Gardiner
13 Hengoed Hall Drive
Cefn Hengoed
Mid Glamorgan

John Gaynor
7 Westhorne Fold
Counthill Drive
Brooklands Road
Crumpsall
Manchester
M8 4JN

Jimmy Gill
21 Hartwood Drive
Stapleford
Nottingham
NG9 8HF

Tommy Gilmour
Forte Crest Hotel
Bothwell Street
Glasgow
G2 7EN

Ron Gray
Ingrams Oak
19 Hatherton Road
Cannock
Staffordshire

Dave Gregory
10 Mill Farm Road
Hamsterley Mill
'Nr Rowlands Gill
Tyne & Wear

Johnny Griffin
26 Christow Street
Leicester
LE1 2GN

Jess Harding
70 Hatfield Road
Potters Bar
Hertfordshire

Billy Hardy
24 Dene Park
Castletown
Sunderland
SR5 3AG

Frank Harrington
178 Kingsway
Heysham
Lancashire
LA3 2EG

Kevin Hayde
93 St Mary Street
Cardiff
CF1 1DW

Howard Hayes
16 Hyland Crescent
Warmsworth
Doncaster
South Yorkshire
DN9 9JS

Patrick Healy
1 Cranley Buildings
Brookes Market
Holborn
London EC1

Barry Hearn
Matchroom
10 Western Road
Romford
Essex
RM1 3JT

George Hill
52 Hathaway
Marton
Blackpool
Lancashire
FY4 4AB

Steve Holdsworth
85 Sussex Road
Watford
Hertfordshire
WD2 5HR

Lloyd Honeyghan
22 Risborough
Deacon Way
Walworth Road
London SE17

John Hyland
The Morton Suite
The Moat House Hotel
1 Paradise Street
Liverpool L1 8JD

Brendan Ingle
26 Newman Road
Wincobank
Sheffield S9 1LP

Derek Isaamen
179 Liverpool Road
South
Maghill
Liverpool
L31 8AA

Richard Jones
1 Churchfields
Croft
Warrington
Cheshire WA3 7JR

Duncan Jowett
Cedarhouse
Caplethill Road
Paisley
Strathclyde
Scotland

Billy Kane
17 Bamburn Terrace
Byker
Newcastle upon Tyne
NE6 2GH

Freddie King
7 St Charles Road
Brentwood
Essex CM14 4TS

Johnny Kramer
115 Crofton Road
Plaistow
London E13

Terry Lawless
National House
60-66 Wardour Street
London
W1V 3HP

Buddy Lee
The Walnuts
Roman Bank
Leverington
Wisbech
Cambridgeshire
PE13 5AR

Paul Lister
7 Murrayfield
Seghill
Northumberland

Graham Lockwood
106 Burnside Avenue
Skipton
Yorkshire
BB23 2DB

Brian Lynch
53 Hall Lane
Upminster
Essex

Pat Lynch
Gotherinton
68 Kelsey Lane
Balsall Common
Near Coventry
West Midlands

Burt McCarthy
Danecourt
Copt Hill
Danbury
Essex
CM3 4NW

John McIntyre
941 Aikenhead Road
Glasgow
G44 4QE

Jim McMillan
21 Langcliffe Road
Preston
Lancashire
PR2 6UE

Charlie Magri
48 Tavistock Gardens
Seven Kings
Ilford
Essex
IG3 1BE

Frank Maloney
Panix Promotions
99 Middlesex Street
London
E1 7DA

Dennie Mancini
16 Rosedew Road
Off Fulham Palace
 Road
London
W6 9ET

Terry Marsh
141 Great Gregorie
Basildon
Essex

Arthur Melrose
33 Easterhill Street
Glasgow
G32 8LN

Tommy Miller
128 Clapton Mount
King Cross Road
Halifax
West Yorkshire

Glyn Mitchell
28 Furneaux Road
Milehouse
Plymouth
Devon

Alex Morrison
39 Armour Street
Glasgow
G31 2ND

Graham Moughton
1 Hedgemans Way
Dagenham
Essex
RM9 6DB

James Murray
87 Spean Street
Glasgow
G44 4DS

Herbert Myers
The Lodge
Lower House Lane
Burnley
Lancashire

David Nelson
29 Linley Drive
Stirchley Park
Telford
Shropshire
TF3 1RQ

Paul Newman
8 Teg Close
Downs Park Estate
Portslade
Sussex
BN41 2GZ

Norman Nobbs
364 Kings Road
Kingstanding
Birmingham
B44 0UG

Terry O'Neill
48 Kirkfield View
Colton Village
Leeds
LS15 9DX

Bob Paget
8 Masterman House
New Church Road
London
SE5 7HU

George Patrick
84 Wooler Road
Edmonton
London N18 2JS

Billy Pearce
Flat D
36 Courtfield Gardens
South Kensington
London SW5 0PJ

Terry Petersen
54 Green Leafe Avenue
Wheatley Hills
Doncaster
South Yorkshire
DN2 5RF

Des Piercy
190 Harrington Road
South Norwood
London SE25 4NE

Steve Pollard
35 Gorthorpe
Orchard Park Estate
Hull HU6 9EY

Dean Powell
10 Cuddington
Deacon Way
Heygate Estate
Walworth
London SE17 1SP

Howard Rainey
55 Colwyn House
Hercules Road
London SE1

Glyn Rhodes
8 Valentine Crescent
Shine Green
Sheffield
S5 0NW

Ken Richardson
15 East Walk
North Road Estate
Retford
Nottinghamshire
DN22 7YF

Gus Robinson
Stranton House
Westview Road
Hartlepool
TS24 0BB

Ronnie Rush
4 Marcross Road
Ely
Cardiff
South Glamorgan
CF5 4RP

John Rushton
20 Alverley Lane
Balby
Doncaster
DN4 9AS

Joe Ryan
22B Adeyfield House
Cranwood Street
City Road
London EC1V 9NX

Chris Sanigar
147 Two Mile Hill Road
Kingswood
Bristol
BS15 1BH

Mike Shinfield
126 Birchwood Lane
Somercotes
Derbyshire
DE55 4NE

Steve Sims
132 Chepstow Road
Newport
Gwent

Len Slater
78 Sutcliffe Avenue
Nunsthorpe
Grimsby
Lincolnshire

Andy Smith
Valandra
19 St Audreys Lane
St Ives
Cambridgeshire

Darkie Smith
21 Northumberland
House
Gaisford Street
London NW5

Brian Snagg
The Heath Hotel
Green Hill Road
Allerton
Liverpool

Les Southey
Oakhouse
Park Way
Hillingdon
Middlesex

John Spensley
The Black Swan Hotel
Tremholme Bar
Near Stokesley
North Yorkshire
DL6 3JY

Ken Squires
27 University Close
Syston
Leicestershire
LE7 2AY

Greg Steene
22 Welbeck Street
London
W1M 7PG

Danny Sullivan
29 Mount Gould
Avenue
Mount Gould
Plymouth
Devon
PL4 9HA

Norrie Sweeney
3 Saucehill Terrace
Paisley
Scotland
PA2 6SY

Wally Swift
Grove House
54 Grove Road
Knowle
Solihull
West Midlands
B93 0PJ

Amos Talbot
70 Edenfield Road
Rochdale
OL11 5AE

Keith Tate
214 Dick Lane
Tyersal
Bradford
BD4 8JH

Glenroy Taylor
95 Devon Close
Perivale
Middlesex

Jimmy Tibbs
44 Gylingdune Gardens
Seven Kings
Essex

Mick Toomey
25 Purton Grove
Bransholme
Hull
HU7 4QD

Jack Trickett
Acton Court Hotel
187 Buxton Road
Stockport
Cheshire

Frankie Turner
67 Camden High
Street
London NW1

Bill Tyler
Northcroft House
Chorley
Lichfield
Staffordshire
WS13 8DL

Danny Urry
26 Nella Road
Hammersmith
London W6

Stephen Vaughan
Lombard Chambers
Ormond Street
Liverpool
L3 9NA

Frank Warren
Centurion House
Bircherley Green
Hertford
Hertfordshire
SG14 1AP

Robert Watt
32 Dowanhill Street
Glasgow G11

Gerry Watts
20 Taunton Crescent
Llanrumney
Cardiff
South Glamorgan

Jack Weaver
301 Coventry Road
Hinckley
Leicestershire
LE10 0NE

Ken Whitney
38 Shakespeare Way
Corby
Northamptonshire
NN17 2ND

William Wigley
4 Renfrew Drive
Wollaton
Nottinghamshire
NG8 2FX

Mick Williamson
34a St Marys Grove
Cannonbury
London N1

Licensed Matchmakers

Nat Basso
38 Windsor Road
Prestwich
Lancashire
M25 8FF

David Davis
179 West Heath Road
Hampstead
London NW3

Ernie Fossey
26 Bell Lane
Brookmans Park
Hertfordshire

John Gaynor
7 Westhorne Fold
Counthill Drive
Brooklands Road
Crumpsall
Manchester
M8 4JN

Tommy Gilmour
Fort Crest Hotel
Bothwell Street
Glasgow
G2 7EN

Ron Gray
Ingrams Oak
19 Hatherton Road
Cannock
Staffordshire

Bobby Holder
17 Merredene Street
Brixton
London
SW9 6LR

Steve Holdsworth
85 Sussex Road
Watford
Herts
WD2 5HR

Jason King
7 St Charles Road
Brentwood
EssexCM14 4TS

Terry Lawless
National Promotions
National House
60-66 Wardour Street
London W1V 3HP

Graham Lockwood
106 Burnside Avenue
Skipton
N. Yorkshire
BD23 2DB

Dennie Mancini
16 Rosedew Road
Off Fulham Palace Road
Hammersmith
London
W6 9ET

Tommy Miller
128 Clapton Mount
King Cross Road
Halifax
West Yorkshire

Alex Morrison
39 Armour Street
Glasgow
G31 2ND

Norman Nobbs
364 Kings Road
Kingstanding
Birmingham
B44 0UG

Dean Powell
10 Cuddington
Deacon Way
Heygate Estate
Walworth
London SE17 1SP

Len Slater
78 Sutcliffe Avenue
Nunsthorpe
Grimsby
Lincolnshire

Darkie Smith
21 Northumberland
 House
Gaisford Street
London NW5

Terry Toole
14c Warren Road
North Chingford
London
E4 6QS

Frank Turner
67 Camden High
 Street
London NW1

Licensed Referees

Class 'B'

Kenneth Curtis	Southern Area
Keith Garner	Central Area
Mark Green	Southern Area
Jeffrey Hinds	Southern Area
Al Hutcheon	Scottish Area
David Irving	Northern Ireland
Ian John-Lewis	Southern Area
Philip Moyse	Midlands Area
Roy Snipe	Central Area
Grant Wallis	Western Area

Class 'A'

Ivor Bassett	Welsh Area
Arnold Bryson	Northern Area
Phil Cowsill	Central Area
Roddy Evans	Welsh Area
Anthony Green	Central Area
Michael Heatherwick	Welsh Area
Wynford Jones	Welsh Area
Denzil Lewis	Western Area
Marcus McDonnell	Southern Area
Len Mullen	Scottish Area
Terry O'Connor	Midlands Area
James Pridding	Midlands Area
Lawrence Thompson	Northern Area
Anthony Walker	Southern Area
Gerald Watson	Northern Area
Barney Wilson	Northern Ireland

Class 'A' Star

John Coyle	Midlands Area
Richard Davies	Southern Area
Roy Francis	Southern Area
John Keane	Midlands Area
Larry O'Connell	Southern Area
Dave Parris	Southern Area
Paul Thomas	Midlands Area
Mickey Vann	Central Area

Barry Pinder	Central Area
Raymond Rice	Southern Area
Tommy Rice	Southern Area
Colin Roberts	Central Area
Russell Routledge	Northern Area
James Russell	Scottish Area
Nick White	Southern Area

Licensed Ringwhips

Bob Ainsley-Matthews	Southern Area
George Andrews	Central Area
Robert Brazier	Southern Area
Albert Brewer	Southern Area
Steve Butler	Central Area
Alan Caffell	Southern Area
John Davis	Southern Area
Ernie Draper	Southern Area
Danny Gill	Midlands Area
Chris Gilmore	Scottish Area
Mike Goodall	Midlands Area
Simon Goodall	Midlands Area
Peter Gray	Midlands Area
Arran Lee Grinnell	Midlands Area
David Hall	Central Area
John Hardwick	Southern Area
Frank Hutchinson	Northern Area
Keith Jackson	Midlands Area
Fred Little	Western Area
James McGinnis	Scottish Area
Tommy Miller (Jnr)	Central Area
Dennis Pinching	Southern Area
Sandy Risley	Southern Area
Neil Sinclair	Southern Area
John Vary	Southern Area
Paul Wainwright	Northern Area
James Wallace	Scottish Area

David Hughes	Welsh Area
Freddie King	Southern Area
Bob Lonkhurst	Southern Area
Ken Lyas	Southern Area
Sam McAughtry	Northern Ireland
William McCrory	Northern Ireland
Pat Magee	Northern Ireland
Stuart Meiklejohn	Central Area
David Ogilvie	Northern Area
Charlie Payne	Southern Area
Fred Potter	Northern Area
Les Potts	Midlands Area
David Renicke	Western Area
Bob Rice	Midlands Area
Bert Smith	Central Area
David Stone	Southern Area
Reg Thompson	Southern Area
Charlie Thurley	Southern Area
John Toner	Northern Ireland
Nigel Underwood	Midlands Area
Ernie Wallis	Welsh Area
Robert Warner	Central Area
Clive Williams	Western Area
Geoff Williams	Midlands Area
David Wilson	Southern Area
Harry Woods	Scottish Area
Paul Woollard	Scottish Area

Licensed Timekeepers

Alan Archbold	Northern Area
Roy Bicknell	Midlands Area
Roger Bowden	Western Area
Neil Burder	Welsh Area
Ivor Campbell	Welsh Area
Frank Capewell	Central Area
Robert Edgeworth	Southern Area
Dale Elliott	Northern Ireland
Harry Foxall	Midlands Area
Eric Gilmour	Scottish Area
Brian Heath	Midlands Area
Ken Honiball	Western Area
Winston Hughes	Midlands Area
Albert Kelleher	Northern Area
Michael McCann	Southern Area
Norman Maddox	Midlands Area
Gordon Pape	Welsh Area
Daniel Peacock	Southern Area

Inspectors

Alan Alster	Central Area
Michael Barnett	Central Area
Don Bartlett	Midlands Area
Fred Breyer	Southern Area
David Brown	Western Area
Ray Chichester	Welsh Area
Geoff Collier	Midlands Area
Jaswinder Dhaliwal	Midlands Area
Les Dean	Midlands Area
Phil Edwards	Central Area
Stephen Ellison	Scottish Area
Kevin Fulthorpe	Welsh Area
Bob Galloway	Southern Area
Paul Gooding	Northern Area
John Hall	Central Area
Eric Higgins	Scottish Area
Terry Hutcheon	Scottish Area

ST. ANDREW'S SPORTING CLUB

EXCLUSIVE GENTLEMEN'S CLUB
AND
THE HOME OF SCOTTISH BOXING

Team 1996-97

Flyweight

PAUL WEIR, *former W.B.O. Mini-Flyweight &*
Light-Flyweight Champion of the World
KEITH KNOX

Bantamweight

DREW DOCHERTY, *British Champion*

Super-Bantamweight — WILSON DOCHERTY

Featherweight

BILLY HARDY, *European & Commonwealth Champion*
IAN McLEOD, *Undefeated*   GARRY BURRELL
RICHARD VOWLES

Super-Featherweight

DAVE McHALE   HUGH COLLINS

Lightweight — MARK BRESLIN, *Undefeated*

Light-Welterweight

CHARLIE KANE   ALAN PEACOCK
JOHN DOCHERTY

Welterweight — JOE TOWNSLEY

Light Middleweight — BILLY COLLINS

Light-Heavyweight — STEVIE WILSON

Cruiserweight — COLIN BROWN, *Undefeated*

Co-Manager of the following:

DEREK WORMALD   GLENN CAMPBELL
WARREN STOWE   CRAIG WINTER
ADEY LEWIS   MICHAEL GALE

1996-97 Fixture List

Monday 23rd September 1996

Monday 28th October 1996

Monday 18th November 1996

Monday 9th December 1996
(Ladies Night Dinner & Dance)

Monday 27th January 1997

Monday 24th February 1997

Monday 17th March 1997

Monday 28th April 1997

Monday 2nd June 1997

ADMINISTRATIVE OFFICES:
FORTE POSTHOUSE, BOTHWELL STREET, GLASGOW G2 7EN, SCOTLAND
Telephone: + 44 141 248 5461 and + 44 141 248 2656   Fax: + 44 141 221 8986   Telex: 77440

DIRECTOR: TOMMY GILMOUR JNR.

DAI GARDINER BOXING STABLE

sponsored by

Empress Car Sales

Prince of Wales Industrial Estate, Cwmcarn, Gwent.
Tel: 01495 248882

ROBBIE REGAN	Bantamweight – World WBC Champion
STEVE ROBINSON	Featherweight
NEIL SWAIN	Super Bantamweight – Commonwealth Champion
MICHAEL SMYTH	Welterweight
GARETH LAWRENCE	Super Featherweight
BARRY THOROGOOD	Middleweight – Welsh Champion
J. T. WILLIAMS	Super Featherweight – Welsh Champion
L. A. WILLIAMS	Heavyweight
EDDIE LLOYD	Super Featherweight
JOHN JANES	Welterweight
HARRY WOODS	Flyweight
JASON PAUL MATTHEWS	Welterweight
ANDREW BLOOMER	Super Bantamweight
TOMMY JANES	Lightweight
CARL WINSTONE	Light Middleweight
DAVID JAY	Super Featherweight
CHRIS DAVIES	Super Middleweight
GRANT BRIGGS	Super Middleweight
IAN TURNER	Bantamweight

LICENCED MANAGER - DAI GARDINER

- TRAINERS -

RONNIE RUSH ▪ ROY AGLAND ▪ PAT CHIDGEY

EDDIE GREEN ▪ GARY THOMAS ▪ BOB AVOTH

Boxers' Record Index

Alito Color Group of Companies

Wish Barry Hugman
every success in producing
THE BRITISH BOXING YEARBOOK 1997.
Once again you can count on our supporting
this valuable publication for the Boxing
fraternity.

Terry Brady
Chairman